D1759083

Informix® Guide to SQL

Reference and Syntax

Second Edition

ISBN 0-13-016166-7

9 780130 161666

90000

Inform*i*x® Press

For a complete list of Informix Press titles, please visit
www.phptr.com or www.informix.com/ipress

Informix® Guide to SQL

Reference and Syntax

Second Edition

 **Informix®** Press

Informix Enterprise Decision Server, Version 8.3
Informix Dynamic Server.2000, Version 9.2

 **Prentice Hall PTR**
Upper Saddle River, NJ 07458
www.phptr.com

Editorial/Production Supervision: *Nicholas Radhuber*
Acquisitions Editor: *Miles Williams*
Marketing Manager: *Kate Hargett*
Manufacturing Manager: *Alexis Heydt*
Cover Design: *Talar Agasyan*
Cover Design Direction: *Jerry Votta*
Series Design: *Gail Cocker-Bogusz*
Manager, Informix Press: *Judy Bowman*

© 2000 Informix Corporation. All rights reserved.
Informix Corporation
4100 Bohannon Drive
Menlo Park, CA 94025-1032

Published by Prentice Hall PTR
Prentice-Hall, Inc.
Upper Saddle River, NJ 07458

The following are trademarks of Informix Corporation or its affiliates, one or more of which may be registered in the United States or other jurisdictions:

Answers OnLine™; C-ISAM®; Client SDK™; DataBlade®; Data Director™; Decision Frontier™; Dynamic Scalable Architecture™; Dynamic Server™; Dynamic Server™, Developer Edition™; Dynamic Server™ with Advanced Decision Support Option™; Dynamic Server™ with Extended Parallel Option™; Dynamic Server™ with MetaCube®; Dynamic Server™ with Universal Data Option™; Dynamic Server™ with Web Integration Option™; Dynamic Server™, Workgroup Edition™; Dynamic Virtual Machine™; Enterprise Decision Server™; Formation™; Formation Architect™; Formation Flow Engine™; Gold Mine Data Access®; IIF.2000™; i.Reach™; i.Sell™; Illustra®; Informix®; Informix® 4GL; Informix® Inquire℠; Informix® Internet Foundation.2000™; InformixLink®; Informix® Red Brick® Decision Server™; Informix Session Proxy™; Informix® Vista™; InfoShelf™; Interforum™; I-Spy™; Mediazation™; MetaCube®; NewEra™; ON-Bar™; OnLine Dynamic Server™; OnLine/Secure Dynamic Server™; OpenCase®; Orca™; PaVER™; Red Brick® and Design; Red Brick® Data Mine™; Red Brick® Mine Builder™; Red Brick® Decisionscape™; Red Brick® Ready™; Red Brick Systems®; Regency Support®; Rely on Red Brick℠; RISQL®; Solution Design℠; STARindex™; STARjoin™; SuperView®; TARGETindex™; TARGETjoin™; The Data Warehouse Company®; The one with the smartest data wins.™; The world is being digitized. We're indexing it.℠; Universal Data Warehouse Blueprint™; Universal Database Components™; Universal Web Connect™; ViewPoint®; Visionary™; Web Integration Suite™. The Informix logo is registered with the United States Patent and Trademark Office. The DataBlade logo is registered with the United States Patent and Trademark Office.

Documentation Team: *Linda Briscoe, Brian Deutscher, Evelyn Eldridge, Kathy Schaefer Francis, Mary Kraemer, Jennifer Leland, Barbara Nomiyama, Tom Noronha, Elaina Von Haas, Richelle White*

GOVERNMENT LICENSE RIGHTS

Software and documentation acquired by or for the US Government are provided with rights as follows:
(1) if for civilian agency use, with rights as restricted by vendor's standard license, as prescribed in FAR 12.212; (2) if for Dept. of Defense use, with rights as restricted by vendor's standard license, unless superseded by a negotiated vendor license, as prescribed in DFARS 227.7202. Any whole or partial reproduction of software or documentation marked with this legend must reproduce this legend.

Prentice Hall books are widely used by corporations and government agencies for training, marketing, and resale.

The publisher offers discounts on this book when ordered in bulk quantities. For more information, contact Corporate Sales Department, Phone: 800-382-3419; fax: 201-236-7141; email: corpsales@prenhall.com or write Corporate Sales Department, Prentice Hall PTR, One Lake Street, Upper Saddle River, NJ 07458.

All rights reserved. No part of this book may be reproduced, in any form or by any means, without permission in writing from the publisher.

Printed in the United States of America

10 9 8 7 6 5 4 3 2 1

ISBN 0-13-016166-7

Prentice-Hall International (UK) Limited, *London*
Prentice-Hall of Australia Pty. Limited, *Sydney*
Prentice-Hall Canada Inc., *Toronto*
Prentice-Hall Hispanoamericana, S.A., *Mexico*
Prentice-Hall of India Private Limited, *New Delhi*
Prentice-Hall of Japan, Inc., *Tokyo*
Prentice-Hall (Singapore) Pte. Ltd., *Singapore*
Editora Prentice-Hall do Brasil, Ltda., *Rio de Janeiro*

Table of Contents

Section I Reference

Chapter 2   **Data Types**

Chapter 3　　**Environment Variables**

Section II Syntax

Introduction

Chapter 3   **SPL Statements**

Reference

Introduction

In This Introduction

This Introduction provides an overview of the information in this book and describes the conventions it uses.

About This book

This book includes information about system catalog tables, data types, and environment variables that Informix products use. It also includes a glossary that contains definitions of common terms found in Informix documentation and a description of the demonstration databases that Version 9.2 of Informix Dynamic Server 2000 and Version 8.3 of Informix Enterprise Decision Server provide.

This book is one of a series of books that discusses the Informix implementation of SQL. Section Two of this book, *Syntax*, contains all the syntax descriptions for SQL and stored procedure language (SPL). The *Informix Guide to SQL: Tutorial, Second Edition* shows how to use basic and advanced SQL and SPL routines to access and manipulate the data in your databases. The *Informix Guide to Designing Databases and Data Warehouses* shows how to use SQL to implement and manage your databases.

Types of Users

This book is written for the following users:

- Database users
- Database administrators
- Database server administrators

- Database-application programmers
- Performance engineers

This book assumes that you have the following background:

- A working knowledge of your computer, your operating system, and the utilities that your operating system provides
- Some experience working with relational databases or exposure to database concepts
- Some experience with computer programming
- Some experience with database server administration, operating-system administration, or network administration

If you have limited experience with relational databases, SQL, or your operating system, refer to the *Getting Started* manual for your database server for a list of supplementary titles.

Software Dependencies

This book assumes that you are using one of the following database servers:

- Informix Enterprise Decision Server, Version 8.3
- Informix Dynamic Server 2000, Version 9.2

Assumptions About Your Locale

Informix products can support many languages, cultures, and code sets. All culture-specific information is brought together in a single environment, called a Global Language Support (GLS) locale.

This book assumes that you use the U.S. 8859-1 English locale as the default locale. The default is **en_us.8859-1** (ISO 8859-1) on UNIX platforms or **en_us.1252** (Microsoft 1252) for Windows NT environments. This locale supports U.S. English format conventions for dates, times, and currency, and also supports the ISO 8859-1 or Microsoft 1252 code set, which includes the ASCII code set plus many 8-bit characters such as é, è, and ñ.

If you plan to use nondefault characters in your data or your SQL identifiers, or if you want to conform to the nondefault collation rules of character data, you need to specify the appropriate nondefault locale.

For instructions on how to specify a nondefault locale, additional syntax, and other considerations related to GLS locales, see the *Informix Guide to GLS Functionality*.

Demonstration Databases

The DB-Access utility, which is provided with your Informix database server products, includes one or more of the following demonstration databases:

- The **stores_demo** database illustrates a relational schema with information about a fictitious wholesale sporting-goods distributor. Many examples in Informix manuals are based on the **stores_demo** database.

EDS

- The **sales_demo** database illustrates a dimensional schema for data-warehousing applications. For conceptual information about dimensional data modeling, see the *Informix Guide to Database Design and Implementation*. ♦

IDS

- The **superstores_demo** database illustrates an object-relational schema. The **superstores_demo** database includes examples of extended data types, type and table inheritance, and user-defined routines. ♦

For information about how to create and populate the demonstration databases, see the *DB-Access User's Manual*. For descriptions of the databases and their contents, see this manual.

The scripts that you use to install the demonstration databases reside in the **$INFORMIXDIR/bin** directory on UNIX platforms and in the **%INFORMIXDIR%\bin** directory in Windows environments.

New Features

For a comprehensive list of new database server features, see the release notes. This section lists new features relevant to this book.

New Features in Version 8.3

This book describes the DBCENTURY environment variable, which is a Year 2000 compliance feature in Version 8.3 of Enterprise Decision Server.

New Features in Version 9.2

This book describes new features in Version 9.2 of Dynamic Server. The features fall into the following areas:

- Year 2000 Compliance
- Version 9.2 features from Version 7.30 of Dynamic Server

Year 2000 Compliance

This book describes the DBCENTURY environment variable in Version 9.2 of Dynamic Server:

Version 9.2 Features from Dynamic Server 7.30

This book also describes the **IFX_UPDDESC** environment variable, which was first released in Version 7.30.

Documentation Conventions

This section describes the conventions that this book uses. These conventions make it easier to gather information from this and other volumes in the documentation set.

The following conventions are discussed:

- Typographical conventions
- Icon conventions
- Command-line conventions
- Sample-code conventions

Typographical Conventions

This book uses the following conventions to introduce new terms, illustrate screen displays, describe command syntax, and so forth.

Convention	Meaning
KEYWORD	All primary elements in a programming language statement (keywords) appear in uppercase letters in a serif font.
italics **italics** *italics*	Within text, new terms and emphasized words appear in italics. Within syntax and code examples, variable values that you are to specify appear in italics.
boldface *boldface*	Names of program entities (such as classes, events, and tables), environment variables, file and pathnames, and interface elements (such as icons, menu items, and buttons) appear in boldface.
`monospace` `monospace`	Information that the product displays and information that you enter appear in a monospace typeface.
KEYSTROKE	Keys that you are to press appear in uppercase letters in a sans serif font.
◆	This symbol indicates the end of one or more product- or platform-specific paragraphs.
→	This symbol indicates a menu item. For example, "Choose **Tools→Options**" means choose the **Options** item from the **Tools** menu.

Tip: *When you are instructed to "enter" characters or to "execute" a command, immediately press* RETURN *after the entry. When you are instructed to "type" the text or to "press" other keys, no* RETURN *is required.*

Icon Conventions

Throughout the documentation, you will find text that is identified by several different types of icons. This section describes these icons.

Comment Icons

Comment icons identify three types of information, as the following table describes. This information always appears in italics.

Icon	Label	Description
	Warning:	Identifies paragraphs that contain vital instructions, cautions, or critical information
	Important:	Identifies paragraphs that contain significant information about the feature or operation that is being described
	Tip:	Identifies paragraphs that offer additional details or shortcuts for the functionality that is being described

Feature, Product, and Platform Icons

Feature, product, and platform icons identify paragraphs that contain feature-specific, product-specific, or platform-specific information.

Icon	Description
EDS	Identifies information or syntax that is specific to Informix Enterprise Decision Server
GLS	Identifies information that relates to the Informix Global Language Support (GLS) feature

(1 of 2)

Icon	Description
IDS	Identifies information that is specific to Informix Dynamic Server 2000
UNIX	Identifies information that is specific to UNIX platforms
WIN NT	Identifies information that is specific to the Windows NT environment

(2 of 2)

These icons can apply to an entire section or to one or more paragraphs within a section. If an icon appears next to a section heading, the information that applies to the indicated feature, product, or platform ends at the next heading at the same or higher level. A ♦ symbol indicates the end of feature-, product-, or platform-specific information that appears within one or more paragraphs within a section.

Command-Line Conventions

This section defines and illustrates the format of commands that are available in Informix products. These commands have their own conventions, which might include alternative forms of a command, required and optional parts of the command, and so forth.

Each diagram displays the sequences of required and optional elements that are valid in a command. A diagram begins at the upper-left corner with a command. It ends at the upper-right corner with a vertical line. Between these points, you can trace any path that does not stop or back up. Each path describes a valid form of the command. You must supply a value for words that are in italics.

You might encounter one or more of the following elements on a command-line path.

Element	Description
command	This required element is usually the product name or other short word that invokes the product or calls the compiler or preprocessor script for a compiled Informix product. It might appear alone or precede one or more options. You must spell a command exactly as shown and use lowercase letters.
variable	A word in italics represents a value that you must supply, such as a database, file, or program name. A table following the diagram explains the value.
-flag	A flag is usually an abbreviation for a function, menu, or option name, or for a compiler or preprocessor argument. You must enter a flag exactly as shown, including the preceding hyphen.
.ext	A filename extension, such as **.sql** or **.cob**, might follow a variable that represents a filename. Type this extension exactly as shown, immediately after the name of the file. The extension might be optional in certain products.
(. , ; + * - /)	Punctuation and mathematical notations are literal symbols that you must enter exactly as shown.
' '	Single quotes are literal symbols that you must enter as shown.
Privileges p. 5-17 Privileges	A reference in a box represents a subdiagram. Imagine that the subdiagram is spliced into the main diagram at this point. When a page number is not specified, the subdiagram appears on the same page.
— ALL —	A shaded option is the default action.
──▶	Syntax within a pair of arrows indicates a subdiagram.
─┤	The vertical line terminates the command.

(1 of 2)

Element	Description
-f —— OFF —— / ON	A branch below the main path indicates an optional path. (Any term on the main path is required, unless a branch can circumvent it.)
, variable	A loop indicates a path that you can repeat. Punctuation along the top of the loop indicates the separator symbol for list items.
, /3\ size	A gate (/3\ ) on a path indicates that you can only use that path the indicated number of times, even if it is part of a larger loop. You can specify *size* no more than three times within this statement segment.

(2 of 2)

How to Read a Command-Line Diagram

Figure 1 shows a command-line diagram that uses some of the elements that are listed in the previous table.

Figure 1
Example of a Command-Line Diagram

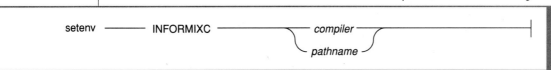

To construct a command correctly, start at the top left with the command. Follow the diagram to the right, including the elements that you want. The elements in the diagram are case sensitive.

Figure 1 illustrates the following steps:

1. Type `setenv`.
2. Type `INFORMIXC`.
3. Supply either a compiler name or a pathname.

   After you choose *compiler* or *pathname*, you come to the terminator. Your command is complete.
4. Press RETURN to execute the command.

Sample-Code Conventions

Examples of SQL code occur throughout this book. Except where noted, the code is not specific to any single Informix application development tool. If only SQL statements are listed in the example, they are not delimited by semicolons. For instance, you might see the code in the following example:

```
CONNECT TO stores_demo
...

DELETE FROM customer
    WHERE customer_num = 121
...

COMMIT WORK
DISCONNECT CURRENT
```

To use this SQL code for a specific product, you must apply the syntax rules for that product. For example, if you are using DB-Access, you must delimit multiple statements with semicolons. If you are using an SQL API, you must use EXEC SQL at the start of each statement and a semicolon (or other appropriate delimiter) at the end of the statement.

Tip: *Ellipsis points in a code example indicate that more code would be added in a full application, but it is not necessary to show it to describe the concept being discussed.*

For detailed directions on using SQL statements for a particular application development tool or SQL API, see the book for your product.

Additional Documentation

For additional information, you might want to refer to the following types of documentation:

- On-line manuals
- Printed manuals
- Error message documentation
- Documentation notes, release notes, and machine notes
- Related reading

On-Line Manuals

An Answers OnLine CD that contains Informix manuals in electronic format is provided with your Informix products. You can install the documentation or access it directly from the CD. For information about how to install, read, and print on-line manuals, see the installation insert that accompanies Answers OnLine.

Informix on-line manuals are also available on the following Web site:

```
www.informix.com/answers
```

Printed Manuals

To order printed manuals, call 1-800-331-1763 or send email to moreinfo@informix.com. Please provide the following information when you place your order:

- The documentation that you need
- The quantity that you need
- Your name, address, and telephone number

Error Message Documentation

Informix software products provide ASCII files that contain all of the Informix error messages and their corrective actions.

UNIX

To read error messages and corrective actions on UNIX, use one of the following utilities.

Utility	Description
finderr	Displays error messages on line
rofferr	Formats error messages for printing

♦

WIN NT

To read error messages and corrective actions in Windows environments, use the **Informix Find Error** utility. To display this utility, choose **Start→Programs→Informix** from the Task Bar. ♦

Instructions for using the preceding utilities are available in Answers OnLine. Answers OnLine also provides a listing of error messages and corrective actions in HTML format.

Documentation Notes, Release Notes, Machine Notes

In addition to printed documentation, the following sections describe the on-line files that supplement the information in this book. Please examine these files before you begin using your database server. They contain vital information about application and performance issues.

UNIX

On UNIX platforms, the following on-line files appear in the **$INFORMIXDIR/release/en_us/0333** directory. Replace *x.y* in the filenames with the version number of your database server.

On-Line File	Purpose
SQLRDOC_*x.y*	The documentation notes file for your version of this book describes topics that are not covered in the book or that were modified since publication.
SERVERS_*x.y*	The release notes file describes feature differences from earlier versions of Informix products and how these differences might affect current products. This file also contains information about any known problems and their workarounds.
IDS_*x.y* or IDS_EDS_*x.y*	The machine notes file describes any special actions that you must take to configure and use Informix products on your computer. Machine notes are named for the product described.

◆

WIN NT

The following items appear in the **Informix** folder. To display this folder, choose **Start→Programs→Informix** from the Task Bar.

Program Group Item	Description
Documentation Notes	This item includes additions or corrections to manuals and information about features that might not be covered in the manuals or that have been modified since publication.
Release Notes	This item describes feature differences from earlier versions of Informix products and how these differences might affect current products. This file also contains information about any known problems and their workarounds.

The machine notes do not apply to Windows environments. ♦

Related Reading

For a list of publications that provide an introduction to database servers and operating-system platforms, refer to your *Getting Started* manual.

Compliance with Industry Standards

The American National Standards Institute (ANSI) has established a set of industry standards for SQL. Informix SQL-based products are fully compliant with SQL-92 Entry Level (published as ANSI X3.135-1992), which is identical to ISO 9075:1992. In addition, many features of Informix database servers comply with the SQL-92 Intermediate and Full Level and X/Open SQL CAE (common applications environment) standards.

Informix Welcomes Your Comments

Let us know what you like or dislike about our books. To help us with future versions of our books, we want to know about any corrections or clarifications that you would find useful. Include the following information:

- The name and version of the book that you are using
- Any comments that you have about the book
- Your name, address, and phone number

Send electronic mail to us at the following address:

doc@informix.com

The **doc** alias is reserved exclusively for reporting errors and omissions in our documentation.

We appreciate your suggestions.

System Catalog

In This Chapter

The system catalog consists of tables that describe the structure of the database. Each system catalog table contains specific information about an element in the database.

This chapter details the following material:

- Objects that the system catalog tables track
- Using the system catalog (page 1-6)
- Structure of the system catalog (page 1-14)
- Information Schema (page 1-86)

Objects That the System Catalog Tables Track

The system catalog tables track the following objects:

- Tables and constraints
- Views
- Triggers
- Authorized users and privileges associated with every table that you create
- User-defined routines
- Data types
- Casts

- Access methods and operator classes
- Error, warning, and informational messages associated with user-defined routines
- Inheritance relationships ◆

IDS

Using the System Catalog

Informix database servers automatically generate the system catalog tables when you create a database. You can query them as you would query any other table in the database. For a newly created database, the system catalog tables for the database reside in a common area of the disk called a dbspace.

Every database has its own system catalog tables. All tables in the system catalog have the prefix **sys** (for example, the **systables** system catalog table).

Not all tables that have the prefix *sys* are true system catalog tables. For example, a common DataBlade builds a table called **sysbuiltintypes** that looks like a system table and contains similar information. However, it has an id > 99. System catalog tables all have an id < 99.

Tip: *Do not confuse the system catalog tables of a database with the tables in the* **sysmaster** *database. The* **sysmaster** *tables also have the* **sys** *prefix, but they contain information about an entire database server, which might manage many databases. The information in the* **sysmaster** *tables is primarily useful for database administrators (DBAs). For more information about the* **sysmaster** *tables, see the "Administrator's Guide."*

The database server accesses the system catalog constantly. Each time an SQL statement is processed, the database server accesses the system catalog to determine system privileges, add or verify table names or column names, and so on. For example, the following CREATE SCHEMA block adds the **customer** table, with its respective indexes and privileges, to the **stores_demo** database. This block also adds a view, **california**, that restricts the *view* in the **customer** table to only the first and last names of the customer, the company name, and the phone number for all customers who reside in California.

```
CREATE SCHEMA AUTHORIZATION maryl
CREATE TABLE customer
    (customer_num SERIAL(101), fname CHAR(15), lname CHAR(15), company CHAR(20),
    address1 CHAR(20), address2 CHAR(20), city CHAR(15), state CHAR(2),
    zipcode CHAR(5), phone CHAR(18))
GRANT ALTER, ALL ON customer TO cathl WITH GRANT OPTION AS maryl
GRANT SELECT ON CUSTOMER TO public
GRANT UPDATE (fname, lname, phone) ON customer TO nhowe
CREATE VIEW california AS
    SELECT fname, lname, company, phone FROM customer WHERE state = 'CA'
CREATE UNIQUE INDEX c_num_ix ON customer (customer_num)
CREATE INDEX state_ix ON customer (state)
```

To process this CREATE SCHEMA block, the database server first accesses the system catalog to verify the following information:

- The new table and view names do not already exist in the database. (If the database is ANSI compliant, the database server verifies that the table and view names do not already exist for the specified owners.)

- The user has permission to create the tables and grant user privileges.

- The column names in the CREATE VIEW and CREATE INDEX statements exist in the **customer** table.

In addition to verifying this information and creating two new tables, the database server adds new rows to the following system catalog tables:

- **systables**
- **syscolumns**
- **sysviews**
- **systabauth**

- **syscolauth**
- **sysindexes** ♦
- **sysindices** ♦

The following two new rows of information are added to the **systables** system catalog table after the CREATE SCHEMA block is run, as page 1-7 shows.

```
tabname      customer
owner        maryl
partnum      16778361
tabid        101
rowsize      134
ncols        10
nindexes     2
nrows        0
created      01/26/1999
version      1
tabtype      T
locklevel    P
npused       0
fextsize     16
nextsize     16
flags        0
site
dbname

tabname      california
owner        maryl
partnum      0
tabid        102
rowsize      134
ncols        4
nindexes     0
nrows        0
created      01/26/1999
version      0
tabtype      V
locklevel    B
npused       0
fextsize     0
nextsize     0
flags        0
site
dbname
```

Each table recorded in the **systables** system catalog table is assigned a **tabid**, a system-assigned sequential ID number that uniquely identifies each table in the database. The system catalog tables receive **tabid** numbers 1 through 24, and the user-created tables receive **tabid** numbers that begin with 100.

The CREATE SCHEMA block adds 14 rows to the **syscolumns** system catalog table. These rows correspond to the columns in the table **customer** and the view **california**, as the following example shows.

colname	tabid	colno	coltype	collength	colmin	colmax
customer_num	101	1	262	4		
fname	101	2	0	15		
lname	101	3	0	15		
company	101	4	0	20		
address1	101	5	0	20		
address2	101	6	0	20		
city	101	7	0	15		
state	101	8	0	2		
zipcode	101	9	0	5		
phone	101	10	0	18		
fname	102	1	0	15		
lname	102	2	0	15		
company	102	3	0	20		
phone	102	4	0	18		

In the **syscolumns** system catalog table, each column within a table is assigned a sequential column number, **colno**, that uniquely identifies the column within its table. In the **colno** column, the **fname** column of the **customer** table is assigned the value 2 and the **fname** column of the view **california** is assigned the value 1. The **colmin** and **colmax** columns contain no entries. These two columns contain values when a column is the first key in a composite index or is the only key in the index, has no null or duplicate values, and the UPDATE STATISTICS statement has been run.

The rows that the following example shows are added to the **sysviews** system catalog table. These rows correspond to the CREATE VIEW portion of the CREATE SCHEMA block.

tabid	seqview	text
102	1	,address1, address2, city, state, zipcode, phone) a s select x0.custom
102	2	er_num, x0.fname, x0.lname, x0.company, x0.address1, x0.address2
102	3	,x0.city, x0.state, x0.zipcode, x0.phone from 'maryl'.customer
102	4	x0 where (x0.state = 'CA');

The **sysviews** system catalog table contains the CREATE VIEW statement that creates the view. Each line of the CREATE VIEW statement in the current schema is stored in this table. In the **viewtext** column, the **x0** that precedes the column names in the statement (for example, **x0.fname**) operates as an alias name that distinguishes among the same columns that are used in a self-join.

The CREATE SCHEMA block also adds rows to the **systabauth** system catalog table. These rows correspond to the user privileges granted on **customer** and **california** tables, as the following example shows.

grantor	grantee	tabid	tabauth
maryl	public	101	su-idx--
maryl	cathl	1 01	SU-IDXAR
maryl	nhowe	101	--*-----
maryl	maryl	102	SU-ID---

The **tabauth** column of this table specifies the table-level privileges granted to users on the **customer** and **california** tables. This column uses an 8-byte pattern, such as s (select), u (update), * (column-level privilege), i (insert), d (delete), x (index), a (alter), and r (references), to identify the type of privilege. In this example, the user **nhowe** has column-level privileges on the **customer** table.

If the **tabauth** privilege code is uppercase (for example, S for select), the user who is granted this privilege can also grant it to others. If the **tabauth** privilege code is lowercase (for example, s for select), the user who has this privilege cannot grant it to others.

In addition, three rows are added to the **syscolauth** system catalog table. These rows correspond to the user privileges that are granted on specific columns in the **customer** table, as the following example shows.

grantor	grantee	tabid	colno	colauth
maryl	nhowe	101	2	-u-
maryl	nhowe	101	3	-u-
maryl	nhowe	101	10	-u-

The **colauth** column specifies the column-level privileges that are granted on the **customer** table. This column uses a 3-byte pattern, such as s (select), u (update), and r (references), to identify the type of privilege. For example, the user **nhowe** has update privileges on the second column (because the **colno** value is 2) of the **customer** table (indicated by **tabid** value of 101).

The CREATE SCHEMA block adds two rows to the **sysindexes** system catalog table (the **sysindices** system catalog table for Informix Dynamic Server 2000.) These rows correspond to the indexes created on the **customer** table, as the following example shows.

idxname	c_num_ix	state_ix
owner	maryl	maryl
tabid	101	101
idxtype	U	D
clustered		
part1	1	8
part2	0	0
part3	0	0
part4	0	0
part5	0	0
part6	0	0
part7	0	0
part8	0	0
part9	0	0
part10	0	0
part11	0	0
part12	0	0
part13	0	0
part14	0	0
part15	0	0
part16	0	0
levels		
leaves		
nunique		
clust		

In this table, the **idxtype** column identifies whether the created index is unique or a duplicate. For example, the index **c_num_ix** that is placed on the **customer_num** column of the **customer** table is unique.

Accessing the System Catalog

Normal user access to the system catalog is read only. Users with Connect or Resource privileges cannot alter the system catalog. They can, however, access data in the system catalog tables on a read-only basis using standard SELECT statements. For example, the following SELECT statement displays all the table names and corresponding table ID numbers of user-created tables in the database:

```
SELECT tabname, tabid FROM systables WHERE tabid > 99
```

When you use DB-Access, only the tables that you created are displayed. To display the system catalog tables, enter the following statement:

```
SELECT tabname, tabid FROM systables WHERE tabid < 100
```

You can use SUBSTR or SUBSTRING function to select only part of a source string. To display the list of database tables in columns, enter the following statement:

```
SELECT SUBSTR(tabname, 1, 18), tabid FROM systables
```

Warning: *Although user **informix** and DBAs can modify most system catalog tables (only user **informix** can modify **systables**), Informix strongly recommends that you do not update, delete, or insert any rows in them. Modifying the system catalog tables can destroy the integrity of the database. Informix supports the use of the ALTER TABLE statement to modify the size of the next extent of system catalog tables.*

IDS

*However, in certain cases with Dynamic Server, it is valid to add entries to the system catalog tables. For instance, in the case of the **syserrors** system catalog table and the **systracemsgs** system catalog table, a developer of DataBlade modules can add message entries that appear in these system catalog tables.* ♦

Updating System Catalog Data

The optimizer in Informix database servers determines the most efficient strategy for executing SQL queries. The optimizer allows you to query the database without having to fully consider which tables to search first in a join or which indexes to use. The optimizer uses information from the system catalog to determine the best query strategy.

If you use the UPDATE STATISTICS statement to update the system catalog, you can ensure that the information provided to the optimizer is current. When you delete or modify a table, the database server does not automatically update the related statistical data in the system catalog. For example, if you delete rows in a table with the DELETE statement, the **nrows** column in the **systables** system catalog table, which holds the number of rows for that table, is not updated.

The UPDATE STATISTICS statement causes the database server to recalculate data in the **systables, sysdistrib, syscolumns**, and **sysindexes** (**sysindices** for Dynamic Server) system catalog tables. After you run UPDATE STATISTICS, the **systables** system catalog table holds the correct value in the **nrows** column. If you use the medium or high mode with the UPDATE STATISTICS statement, the **sysdistrib** system catalog table holds the updated data-distribution data after you run UPDATE STATISTICS.

Whenever you modify a table extensively, use the UPDATE STATISTICS statement to update data in the system catalog. For more information on the UPDATE STATISTICS statement, see the *Informix Guide to SQL: Syntax.*

Structure of the System Catalog

The following system catalog tables describe the structure of an Informix database.

System Catalog Table	EDS	IDS	Page
sysaggregates		✔	1-16
sysams		✔	1-17
sysattrtypes		✔	1-23
sysblobs	✔	✔	1-24
syscasts		✔	1-25
syschecks	✔	✔	1-26
syscolattribs		✔	1-27
syscolauth	✔	✔	1-28
syscoldepend	✔	✔	1-29
syscolumns	✔	✔	1-30
sysconstraints	✔	✔	1-36
sysdefaults	✔	✔	1-37
sysdepend	✔	✔	1-38
sysdistrib	✔	✔	1-39
syserrors		✔	1-41
sysextcols	✔		1-42
sysextdfiles	✔		1-43
sysexternal	✔		1-44
sysfragauth		✔	1-45
sysfragments	✔	✔	1-46

(1 of 3)

System Catalog Table	EDS	IDS	Page
sysindexes	✔		1-49
sysindices		✔	1-51
sysinherits		✔	1-53
syslangauth		✔	1-53
syslogmap			1-54
sysnewdepend	✔		1-54
sysobjstate	✔	✔	1-55
sysopclasses		✔	1-56
sysopclstr		✔	1-57
sysprocauth	✔	✔	1-59
sysprocbody	✔	✔	1-60
sysprocedures	✔	✔	1-61
sysprocplan	✔	✔	1-65
sysreferences	✔	✔	1-66
sysrepository	✔		1-67
sysroleauth		✔	1-68
sysroutinelangs		✔	1-68
syssynonyms			1-69
syssyntable	✔	✔	1-70
systabamdata		✔	1-71
systabauth	✔	✔	1-72
systables	✔	✔	1-73
systraceclasses		✔	1-75
systracemsgs		✔	1-76

(2 of 3)

System Catalog Table	EDS	IDS	Page
systrigbody		✔	1-77
systriggers		✔	1-78
sysusers	✔	✔	1-79
sysviews	✔	✔	1-80
sysviolations	✔	✔	1-81
sysxtddesc		✔	1-82
systdtypeauth		✔	1-83
sysxtdtypes		✔	1-84

(3 of 3)

GLS

In a database whose collation order is locale dependent, all character information in the system catalog tables is stored in NCHAR rather than CHAR columns. However, for those databases where the collation order is code-set dependent, all character information in the system catalog tables is stored in CHAR columns. For more information on collation orders and NCHAR and NVARCHAR data types, see the *Informix Guide to GLS Functionality*. For information about data types, see Chapter 2 of this manual. ♦

IDS

SYSAGGREGATES

The **sysaggregates** system catalog table records user-defined aggregates (UDAs). The **sysaggregates** system catalog table has the following columns.

Column Name	Type	Explanation
name	NVARCHAR(128)	Aggregate name
owner	NCHAR(32)	Aggregate owner
aggid	SERIAL	Aggregate identifier
init_func	NVARCHAR(128)	Name of initialization UDR
iter_func	NVARCHAR(128)	Name of iterator UDR

(1 of 2)

Column Name	Type	Explanation
combine_func	NVARCHAR(128)	Name of combine UDR
final_func	NVARCHAR(128)	Name of finalization UDR
handlesnulls	BOOLEAN	Whether nulls should be considered

(2 of 2)

Each UDA has one entry in **sysaggregates** that is uniquely identified by its aggregate identifier (the **aggid** column). Only new aggregates (aggregates that are not built in) have entries in **sysaggregates**.

IDS

SYSAMS

The **sysams** system catalog table contains information that is needed to use built-in access methods as well as those created by the CREATE ACCESS METHOD SQL statement that is described in the *Virtual-Table Interface Programmer's Manual*. The **sysams** table has the following columns.

Column Name	Type	Explanation
am_name	NVARCHAR(128)	Name of the access method
am_owner	NCHAR(32)	Owner of the access method
am_id	INTEGER	Unique identifier for the access method. This value corresponds to the *am_id* in the **systables** system catalog table and to the *am_id* in the **sysindices** and **sysopclasses** system catalog tables.
am_type	NCHAR(1)	Type of access method: P = Primary S = Secondary

(1 of 6)

Column Name	Type	Explanation
am_sptype	NCHAR(3)	Type(s) of space(s) in which the access method can live:
		D or d = dbspaces only
		X or x = extspaces only
		S or s = sbspaces only (smart-large-object space)
		A or a = all types: extspaces, dbspaces, or sbspaces. If the access method is not user defined (that is, if it is built-in or registered during database creation by the server), it supports dbspaces.
am_defopclass	INTEGER	Default-operator class identifier. The *opclassid* from the entry for this operator class in the **sysopclasses** system catalog table.
am_keyscan	INTEGER	Whether a secondary access method supports a key scan
		An access method supports a key scan if it can return a key as well as a rowid from a call to the **am_getnext** function
		Non-Zero = access method supports key scan
		Zero = access method does not support key scan
am_unique	INTEGER	Whether a secondary access method can support unique keys
		Non-Zero = access method supports unique keys
		Zero = access method does not support unique keys

(2 of 6)

Column Name	Type	Explanation
am_cluster	INTEGER	Whether a primary access method supports clustering
		Non-Zero = access method supports clustering
		Zero = access method does not support clustering
am_rowids	INTEGER	Whether a primary access method supports rowids
		Non-Zero = access method supports rowids
		Zero = access method does not support rowids
am_readwrite	INTEGER	Whether a primary access method is read/write
		Non-Zero = access method is read/write
		Zero = access method is read only
am_parallel	INTEGER	Whether an access method supports parallel execution
		Non-Zero = access method supports parallel execution
		Zero = access method does not support parallel execution
am_costfactor	SMALLFLOAT	The value to be multiplied by the cost of a scan in order to normalize it to costing done for built-in access methods. The scan cost is the output of the *am_scancost* function
am_create	INTEGER	The routine specified for the AM_CREATE purpose for this access method
		The value of **am_create** is the *procid* for the routine in the **sysprocedures** system catalog table

(3 of 6)

Column Name	Type	Explanation
am_drop	INTEGER	The routine specified for the AM_DROP purpose for this access method
		The value of **am_drop** is the *procid* listed for the routine in the **sysprocedures** system catalog table
am_open	INTEGER	The routine specified for the AM_OPEN purpose for this access method
		The value of **am_open** is the *procid* listed for the routine in the **sysprocedures** system catalog table
am_close	INTEGER	The routine specified for the AM_CLOSE purpose for this access method
		The value of **am_close** is the *procid* listed for the routine in the **sysprocedures** system catalog table
am_insert	INTEGER	The routine specified for the AM_INSERT purpose for this access method
		The value of **am_insert** is the *procid* listed for the routine in the **sysprocedures** system catalog table
am_delete	INTEGER	The routine specified for the AM_DELETE purpose for this access method
		The value of **am_delete** is the *procid* listed for the routine in the **sysprocedures** system catalog table
am_update	INTEGER	The routine specified for the AM_UPDATE purpose for this access method
		The value of **am_update** is the *procid* listed for the routine in the **sysprocedures** system catalog table
am_stats	INTEGER	The routine specified for the AM_STATS purpose for this access method
		The value of **am_stats** is the *procid* listed for the routine in the **sysprocedures** system catalog table

(4 of 6)

Column Name	Type	Explanation
am_scancost	INTEGER	The routine specified for the AM_SCANCOST purpose for this access method
		The value of **am_scancost** is the *procid* listed for the routine in the **sysprocedures** system catalog table
am_check	INTEGER	The routine specified for the AM_CHECK purpose for this access method
		The value of **am_check** is the *procid* listed for the routine in the **sysprocedures** system catalog table
am_beginscan	INTEGER	The routine specified for the AM_BEGINSCAN purpose for this access method
		The value of **am_beginscan** is the *procid* listed for the routine in the **sysprocedures** system catalog table
am_endscan	INTEGER	The routine specified for the AM_ENDSCAN purpose for this access method
		The value of **am_endscan** is the *procid* listed for the routine in the **sysprocedures** system catalog table
am_rescan	INTEGER	The routine specified for the AM_RESCAN purpose for this access method
		The value of **am_rescan** is the *procid* listed for the routine in the **sysprocedures** system catalog table
am_getnext	INTEGER	The routine specified for the AMGETNEXT purpose for this access method
		The value of **am_getnext** is the *procid* listed for the routine in the **sysprocedures** system catalog table

(5 of 6)

Column Name	Type	Explanation
am_getbyid	INTEGER	The routine specified for the AM_GETBYID purpose for this access method
		The value of **am_getbyid** is the *procid* listed for the routine in the **sysprocedures** system catalog tables
am_build	Reserved for future use	
am_init	INTEGER	For internal use

(6 of 6)

The composite index for the **am_name** and **am_owner** columns in this table allows only unique values. The **am_id** column is indexed and must contain unique values.

The **am_sptype** column can have multiple entries. For example:

- A means the access method supports extspaces and sbspaces. If the access method is built-in, such as a b-tree, it also supports dbspaces.
- DS means the access method supports dbspaces and sbspaces.
- SX means the access method supports sbspaces and extspaces.

For information about access method functions, refer to the documentation for your custom access method.

IDS

SYSATTRTYPES

The **sysattrtypes** system catalog table contains information about members of a complex data type. Each row of **sysattrtypes** contains information about elements of a collection data type or fields of a row data type. The **sysattrtypes** system catalog table has the following columns.

Column Name	Type	Explanation
extended_id	INTEGER	Identifier for extended data types, same as in sysxtdtypes
seqno	SMALLINT	Value to order and identify entries for specific values of **extended_id**
levelno	SMALLINT	Position of member in collection hierarchy
parent_no	SMALLINT	Value in the **seqno** column of the complex type that contains this member
fieldname	NVARCHAR(128)	Name of the field in a row type. Null for other complex types
fieldno	SMALLINT	Field number sequentially assigned by the system (from left to right within each row type)
type	SMALLINT	Identifier of the data type. For a complete list of values associated with different data types, see the **coltype** column entries in the **syscolumns** system catalog table.
length	SMALLINT	Length of the data type
xtd_type_id	INTEGER	The identifier used for this data type in the *extended_id* column of the **sysxtdtypes** system catalog table

The two indexes on the **extended_id** column and the **xtd_type_id** column, respectively, allow duplicate values. The composite index on **extended_id** and **seqno** columns allows only unique values.

SYSBLOBS

The title **sysblobs** is a legacy name based on a term that was used to refer to BYTE and TEXT columns (also known as simple large objects).

The **sysblobs** system catalog table specifies the storage location of a BYTE or TEXT column. It contains one row for each BYTE or TEXT column in a table. The **sysblobs** system catalog table has the following columns.

Column Name	Type	Explanation
spacename	NVARCHAR(128)	Partition BYTE or TEXT data, dbspace, or family name
type	NCHAR(1)	Media type:
		M = Magnetic
		O = Optical. Only available for Dynamic Server
tabid	INTEGER	Table identifier
colno	SMALLINT	Column number

A composite index for the **tabid** and **colno** columns allows only unique values.

For information about the location and size of chunks of blobspaces, dbspaces, and sbspaces for TEXT, BYTE, BLOB, and CLOB columns, see your *Administrator's Guide* and the *Administrator's Reference*.

IDS

SYSCASTS

The **syscasts** system catalog table describes the casts in the database. It contains one row for each built-in cast and one row for each implicit or explicit cast that a user defines. The **syscasts** system catalog table has the following columns.

Column Name	Type	Explanation
owner	NCHAR(32)	Owner of cast (user **informix** for built-in casts and user name for implicit and explicit casts)
argument_type	SMALLINT	Source data type on which the cast operates
argument_xid	INTEGER	Data type identifier of the source data type named in the **argument_type** column
result_type	SMALLINT	Data type returned by the cast
result_xid	INTEGER	Data type identifier of the data type named in the **result_type** column
routine_name	NVARCHAR(128)	Function or procedure used to implement the cast (might be null if the data types named in the **argument_type** and **result_type** columns have the same length and alignment and are both passed either by reference or by value)
routine_owner	NCHAR(32)	User name of the owner of the function or procedure named in the **routine_name** column
class	NCHAR	Type of cast: E = Explicit cast I = Implicit cast S = Built-in cast

If **routine_name** and **routine_owner** have null values, it indicates that the cast is defined without a routine.

The index on columns **argument_type, argument_xid, result_type**, and **result_xid** allows only unique values. The index on columns **argument_type** and **argument_xid** allows duplicate values.

SYSCHECKS

The **syschecks** system catalog table describes each check constraint defined in the database. Because the **syschecks** system catalog table stores both the ASCII text and a binary encoded form of the check constraint, it contains multiple rows for each check constraint. The **syschecks** system catalog table has the following columns.

Column Name	Type	Explanation
constrid	INTEGER	Constraint identifier
type	NCHAR(1)	Form in which the check constraint is stored:
		B = Binary encoded
		T = ASCII text
seqno	SMALLINT	Line number of the check constraint
checktext	NCHAR(32)	Text of the check constraint

A composite index for the **constrid, type,** and **seqno** columns allows only unique values.

The text in the **checktext** column associated with B type in the **type** column is in computer-readable format. To view the text associated with a particular check constraint, use the following query with the appropriate constraint ID:

```
SELECT * FROM syschecks WHERE constrid=10 AND type='T'
```

Each check constraint described in the **syschecks** system catalog table also has its own row in the **sysconstraints** system catalog table.

IDS

SYSCOLATTRIBS

The **syscolattribs** system catalog table describes the characteristics of smart large objects, namely CLOB and BLOB data types. It contains one row for each characteristic. The **syscolattribs** system catalog table has the following columns.

Column Name	Type	Explanation	
tabid	INTEGER	Table identifier	
colno	SMALLINT	Column number	
extentsize	INTEGER	Pages in smart-large-object extent, expressed in kilobytes	
flags	INTEGER	An integer representation of the combination (addition) of hexadecimal values of the following parameters:	
		LO_NOLOG	The smart large object is not logged.
		LO_LOG	Logging of smart-large-object data is done in accordance with the current database log mode.
		LO_KEEP_LASTACCESS_TIME	A record is kept of the most recent access of this smart-large-object column by a user.
		LO_NOKEEP_LASTACCESS_TIME	No record is kept of the most recent access of this smart-large-object column by a user.

(1 of 2)

Column Name	Type	Explanation	
		HI_INTEG	Data pages have headers and footers to detect incomplete writes and data corruption.
		MODERATE_INTEG (Not available at this time)	Data pages do not have headers and footers.
flags1	INTEGER	Reserved for future use	
sbspace	NVARCHAR(128)	Name of sbspace	

(2 of 2)

SYSCOLAUTH

The **syscolauth** system catalog table describes each set of privileges granted on a column. It contains one row for each set of column privileges granted in the database. The **syscolauth** system catalog table has the following columns.

Column Name	Type	Explanation
grantor	NCHAR(32)	Grantor of privilege
grantee	NCHAR(32)	Grantee of privilege
tabid	INTEGER	Table identifier
colno	SMALLINT	Column number
colauth	NCHAR(3)	3-byte pattern that specifies column privileges: s = Select u = Update r = References

If the **colauth** privilege code is uppercase (for example, S for select), a user who has this privilege can also grant it to others. If the **colauth** privilege code is lowercase (for example, s for select), the user who has this privilege cannot grant it to others.

A composite index for the **tabid, grantor, grantee**, and **colno** columns allows only unique values. A composite index for the **tabid** and **grantee** columns allows duplicate values.

SYSCOLDEPEND

The **syscoldepend** system catalog table tracks the table columns specified in check and not null constraints. Because a check constraint can involve more than one column in a table, the **syscoldepend** table can contain multiple rows for each check constraint. One row is created in the **syscoldepend** table for each column involved in the constraint. The **syscoldepend** system catalog table has the following columns.

Column Name	Type	Explanation
constrid	INTEGER	Constraint identifier
tabid	INTEGER	Table identifier
colno	SMALLINT	Column number

A composite index for the **constrid, tabid**, and **colno** columns allows only unique values. A composite index for the **tabid** and **colno** columns allows duplicate values.

SYSCOLUMNS

The **syscolumns** system catalog table describes each column in the database. One row exists for each column that is defined in a table or view.

Column Name	Type	Explanation
colname	NVARCHAR(128)	Column name
tabid	INTEGER	Table identifier
colno	SMALLINT	Column number that the system sequentially assigns (from left to right within each table)
coltype	SMALLINT	Code for column data type:

0 = CHAR	14 = INTERVAL
1 = SMALLINT	15 = NCHAR
2 = INTEGER	16 = NVARCHAR
3 = FLOAT	17 = INT8
4 = SMALLFLOAT	18 = SERIAL8 *
5 = DECIMAL	19 = SET
6 = SERIAL *	20 = MULTISET
7 = DATE	21 = LIST
8 = MONEY	22 = rOW (unnamed)
9 = NULL	23 = COLLECTION
10 = DATETIME	24 = ROWREF
11 = BYTE	40 = Variable-length opaque type
12 = TEXT	41 = Fixed-length opaque type
13 = VARCHAR	4118 = Named row type

(1 of 2)

Column Name	Type	Explanation
collength	SMALLINT	Column length (in bytes)
colmin	INTEGER	Second minimum value
colmax	INTEGER	Second maximum value
minlen	INTEGER	Minimum column length (in bytes)
maxlen	INTEGER	Maximum column length (in bytes)
extended_id	INTEGER	Type identifier, from the **sysxtdtypes** system catalog table, of the data type named in the **coltype** column

* An offset value of 256 is added to these columns to indicate that they do not allow null values.

(2 of 2)

A composite index for the **tabid** and **colno** columns allows only unique values.

The **coltype** 4118 for named row types is the decimal representation of the hexadecimal value 0x1016, which is the same as the hexadecimal **coltype** value for an unnamed row type (0 x 016), with the named-row type bit set.

Null-Valued Columns

If the **coltype** column contains a value greater than 256, it does not allow null values. To determine the data type for a **coltype** column that contains a value greater than 256, subtract 256 from the value and evaluate the remainder, based on the possible **coltype** values. For example, if a column has a **coltype** value of 262, subtracting 256 from 262 leaves a remainder of 6, which indicates that this column uses a SERIAL data type.

The next sections provide the following additional information about information in the **syscolumns** system catalog table:

- How the **coltype** and **collength** columns encode the type and length values, respectively, for certain data types.
- How the **colmin** and **colmax** columns store column values.

Storing Column Data Type

The database server stores the column data type as an integer value. For a list of the column data type values, see the description of the **coltype** column in the preceding table. The following sections provide additional information on data type values.

IDS

The following data types are implemented by the database server as *built-in opaque* types:

- BLOB
- CLOB
- BOOLEAN
- LVARCHAR

A built-in opaque data type is one for which the database server provides the type definition. Because these data types are built-in opaque types, they do not have a unique **coltype** value. Instead, they have one of the **coltype** values for opaque types: 41 (fixed-length opaque type), or 40 (varying-length opaque type). The different fixed-length opaque types are distinguished by the **extended_id** column in the **sysxtdtypes** system catalog table.

The following table summarizes the **coltype** values for the predefined data types.

Predefined Data Type	Value for coltype Column
BLOB	41
CLOB	41
BOOLEAN	41
LVARCHAR	40

♦

Storing Column Length

The value that the **collength** column holds depends on the data type of the column.

Length of Integer-Based Columns

A **collength** value for a SMALLINT, INTEGER, or INT8 column is *not* machine-dependent. The database server uses the following lengths for SQL integer-based data types.

Integer-Based Data Type	Length (in bytes)
SMALLINT	2
INTEGER	4
INT8	8

The database server stores a SERIAL data type as an INTEGER value and a SERIAL8 data type as an INT8 value. Therefore, SERIAL has the same length as INTEGER (4 bytes) and SERIAL8 has the same length as INT8 (8 bytes).

Length of Fixed-Point Columns

A **collength** value for a MONEY or DECIMAL column is determined using the following formula:

```
(precision * 256) + scale
```

Length of Varying-Length Character Columns

For columns of type VARCHAR, the *max_size* and *min_space* values are encoded in the **collength** column using one of the following formulas:

- If the **collength** value is positive:
    ```
    collength = (min_space * 256) + max_size
    ```
- If the **collength** value is negative:
    ```
    collength + 65536 = (min_space * 256) + max_size
    ```

GLS

The database server uses the preceding formulas to encode the **collength** column for an NVARCHAR data type. For more information about the NVARCHAR data type, see the *Informix Guide to GLS Functionality*. ♦

Length for Time Data Types

For columns of type DATETIME or INTERVAL, **collength** is determined using the following formula:

```
(length * 256) + (largest_qualifier_value * 16) + smallest_qualifier_value
```

The length is the physical length of the DATETIME or INTERVAL field, and *largest_qualifier* and *smallest_qualifier* have the values that the following table shows.

Field Qualifier	Value
YEAR	0
MONTH	2
DAY	4
HOUR	6
MINUTE	8
SECOND	10
FRACTION(1)	11
FRACTION(2)	12
FRACTION(3)	13
FRACTION(4)	14
FRACTION(5)	15

For example, if a DATETIME YEAR TO MINUTE column has a length of 12 (such as *YYYY:DD:MM:HH:MM*), a *largest_qualifier value* of 0 (for YEAR), and a *smallest_qualifier value* of 8 (for MINUTE), the **collength** value is 3080 or `(256 * 12) + (0 * 16) + 8`.

Length of Simple-Large-Object Columns

If the data type of the column is BYTE or TEXT, **collength** holds the length of the descriptor.

Storing Maximum and Minimum Values

The **colmin** and **colmax** column values hold the second-smallest and second-largest data values in the column, respectively. For example, if the values in an indexed column are 1, 2, 3, 4, and 5, the **colmin** value is 2 and the **colmax** value is 4. Storing the second-smallest and second-largest data values lets the database server make assumptions about the range of values in a given column and, in turn, further optimize searching strategies.

The **colmin** and **colmax** columns contain values only if the column is indexed and you have run the UPDATE STATISTICS statement. If you store BYTE or TEXT data in the tblspace, the **colmin** value is -1. The values for all other noninteger column types are the initial 4 bytes of the maximum or minimum value, which are treated as an integer.

IDS

The database server does not calculate **colmin** and **colmax** values for user-defined data types. However, these columns have values for user-defined data types if a user-defined secondary access method supplies them.
♦

SYSCONSTRAINTS

The **sysconstraints** system catalog table lists the constraints placed on the columns in each database table. An entry is also placed in the **sysindexes** (**sysindices** for Dynamic Server) system catalog table for each unique, primary key, or referential constraint that you create, if the constraint does not already have a corresponding entry in the **sysindexes** or **sysindices** system catalog table. Because indexes can be shared, more than one constraint can be associated with an index. The **sysconstraints** system catalog table has the following columns.

Column Name	Type	Explanation
constrid	SERIAL	System-assigned sequential identifier
constrname	NVARCHAR(128)	Constraint name
owner	NCHAR(32)	User name of owner
tabid	INTEGER	Table identifier
constrtype	NCHAR(1)	Constraint type:
		C = Check constraint
		P = Primary key
		R = Referential
		U = Unique
		N = Not null
idxname	NVARCHAR(128)	Index name

A composite index for the **constrname** and **owner** columns allows only unique values. The index for the **tabid** column allows duplicate values, and the index for the **constrid** column allows only unique values.

For check constraints (where **constrtype** = C), the **idxname** is always null. Additional information about each check constraint is contained in the **syschecks** system catalog table.

SYSDEFAULTS

The **sysdefaults** system catalog table lists the user-defined defaults that are placed on each column in the database. One row exists for each user-defined default value. If a default is not explicitly specified in the CREATE TABLE statement, no entry exists in this table. The **sysdefaults** system catalog table has the following columns.

Column Name	Type	Explanation
tabid	INTEGER	Table identifier
colno	SMALLINT	Column identifier
type	NCHAR(1)	Default type:
		L = Literal default
		U = User
		C = Current
		N = Null
		T = Today
		S = Dbservername
default	NCHAR(256)	If default type = L, the literal default value
class	CHAR(1)	Type of column:
		T = table
		t = row type

If you specify a literal for the default value, it is stored in the **default** column as ASCII text. If the literal value is not of type NCHAR, the **default** column consists of two parts. The first part is the 6-bit representation of the binary value of the default value structure. The second part is the default value in English text. A space separates the two parts.

If the data type of the column is not NCHAR or NVARCHAR, a binary representation is encoded in the **default** column. A composite index for the **tabid**, **colno**, and **class** columns allows only unique values.

SYSDEPEND

The **sysdepend** system catalog table describes how each view or table depends on other views or tables. One row exists in this table for each dependency, so a view based on three tables has three rows. The **sysdepend** system catalog table has the following columns.

Column Name	Type	Explanation
btabid	INTEGER	Table identifier of base table or view
btype	NCHAR(1)	Base object type: T = Table V = View
dtabid	INTEGER	Table identifier of dependent table
dtype	NCHAR(1)	Dependent object type (V = View); currently, only view is implemented

The **btabid** and **dtabid** columns are indexed and allow duplicate values.

SYSDISTRIB

The **sysdistrib** system catalog table stores data-distribution information for the database server to use. Data distributions provide detailed table-column information to the optimizer to improve the choice of execution paths of SQL SELECT statements.

Information is stored in the **sysdistrib** system catalog table when an UPDATE STATISTICS statement with mode MEDIUM or HIGH is run for a table. (UPDATE STATISTICS LOW does not insert a value in the mode column of **sysdistrib**.)

The **sysdistrib** system catalog table has the following columns.

Column Name	Type	Explanation
tabid	INTEGER	Table identifier of the table where data was gathered
colno	SMALLINT	Column number in the source table
seqno	INTEGER	Sequence number for multiple entries
constructed	DATE	Date when the data distribution was created
mode	NCHAR(1)	Optimization level:
		M = Medium
		H = High
resolution	FLOAT	Specified in the UPDATE STATISTICS statement
confidence	FLOAT	Specified in the UPDATE STATISTICS statement
encdat	STAT	Statistics information
type	NCHAR(1)	Type of statistics:
		A = **encdat** has ASCII-encoded histogram in fixed-length character field
		S = **encdat** has-user defined statistics
udtstat	STAT	UDT statistics information

You can select any column from **sysdistrib** except **encdat** and **udtstat**. Only user **informix** can select the **encdat** and **udtstat** columns.

Each row in the **sysdistrib** system catalog table is keyed by the **tabid** and **colno** for which the statistics are collected.

For built-in data type columns, the **type** field is set to A. The **encdat** column stores an ASCII-encoded histogram that is broken down into multiple rows, each of which contains 256 bytes.

For UDT columns, the **type** field is set to S. The **encdat** column stores the statistics collected by the statcollect UDR in multirepresentational form. Only one row is stored for each **tabid** and **colno** pair.

IDS

The **sysdistrib** system catalog table supports extensions for user-defined statistics in Dynamic Server only. ♦

IDS

SYSERRORS

The **syserrors** system catalog table stores information about error, warning, and informational messages returned by DataBlade modules and user-defined routines using the **mi_db_error_raise()** DataBlade API function.

To create a new message, insert a row directly into the **syserrors** system catalog table. By default, all users can view this table, but only users with the DBA privilege can modify it. The **syserrors** system catalog table has the following columns.

Column Name	Type	Explanation
sqlstate	NCHAR(5)	SQLSTATE value associated with the error. For more information about SQLSTATE values and their meanings, see the GET DIAGNOSTICS statement in the *Informix Guide to SQL: Syntax*.
locale	NCHAR(36)	The locale with which this version of the message is associated (for example, 'en_us.8859-1')
level	Reserved for future use	
seqno	Reserved for future use	
message	NVARCHAR(255)	Message text

The composite index on columns **sqlstate**, **locale**, **level** and **seqno** allows only unique values.

EDS

SYSEXTCOLS

The **sysextcols** system catalog table contains a row that describes each of the internal columns in external table tabid of format type (fmttype) FIXED. No entries are stored in **sysextcols** for DELIMITED or Informix-format external files.

Column	Type	Description
tabid	INTEGER	Table identifier
colno	SMALLINT	Column identifier
exttype	SMALLINT	External column type
extstart	SMALLINT	Starting position of column in the external data file
extlength	SMALLINT	External column length in bytes
nullstr	NCHAR(256)	Represents null in external data
picture	NCHAR(256)	Reserved for future use
decimal	SMALLINT	Precision for external decimals
extstype	NCHAR(18)	The external type name

You can use DBSCHEMA to write out the description of the external tables. To query these catalogs about an external table, use the tabid as stored in **systables** with tabtype = 'E'.

SYSEXTDFILES

For each external table, at least one row exists in the **sysextdfiles** system catalog table.

Column	Type	Description
tabid	INTEGER	Table identifier
dfentry	NCHAR(152)	Data file entry

You can use DBSCHEMA to write out the description of the external tables. To query these system catalogs about an external table, use the tabid as stored in **systables** with tabtype = 'E'.

EDS

SYSEXTERNAL

For each external table, a single row exists in the **sysexternal** system catalog table. The **tabid** column associates the external table in this system catalog table with an entry in **systables**.

Column	Type	Description
tabid	INTEGER	Table identifier
fmttype	NCHAR(1)	'D' (delimiter), 'F' (fixed), 'I' (Informix)
recdelim	NCHAR(4)	The record delimiter
flddelim	NCHAR(4)	The field delimiter
codeset	NCHAR(18)	ASCII, EBCDIC
datefmt	NCHAR(8)	Reserved for future use
moneyfmt	NCHAR(20)	Reserved for future use
maxerrors	INTEGER	Number of errors to allow per coserver
relectfile	NCHAR(128)	Name of reject file
flags	INTEGER	Optional load flags
ndfiles	INTEGER	Number of data files in **sysextdfiles**

You can use DBSCHEMA to write out the description of the external tables. To query these catalogs about an external table, use the tabid as stored in **systables** with tabtype = 'E'.

IDS

SYSFRAGAUTH

The **sysfragauth** system catalog table stores information about the privileges that are granted on table fragments.

The **sysfragauth** system catalog table has the following columns.

Column Name	Type	Explanation
grantor	NCHAR(32)	Grantor of privilege
grantee	NCHAR(32)	Grantee of privilege
tabid	INTEGER	Table identifier of the table that contains the fragment named in the **fragment** column.
fragment	NVARCHAR (128)	Name of dbspace where fragment is stored. Identifies the fragment on which privileges are granted.
fragauth	NCHAR(6)	A 6-byte pattern that specifies fragment-level privileges (including 3 bytes reserved for future use). This pattern contains one or more of the following codes:

> u = Update
>
> i = Insert
>
> d = Delete

If a code in the **fragauth** column is lowercase (such as u for Update), the grantee cannot grant the privilege to other users. If a code in the **fragauth** column is uppercase (such as U for Update), the grantee can grant the privilege to other users.

A composite index for the **tabid, grantor, grantee**, and **fragment** columns allows only unique values. A composite index on the **tabid** and **grantee** columns allows duplicate values.

The following example displays the fragment-level privileges for one base table, as they appear in the **sysfragauth** system catalog table. The grantee **ted** can grant the UPDATE, DELETE, and INSERT privileges to other users.

grantor	grantee	tabid	fragment	fragauth
dba	dick	101	dbsp1	-ui---
dba	jane	101	dbsp3	--i---
dba	mary	101	dbsp4	--id--
dba	ted	101	dbsp2	-UID--

SYSFRAGMENTS

The **sysfragments** system catalog table stores fragmentation information for tables and indexes. One row exists for each table or index fragment.

The **sysfragments** table has the following columns.

Column Name	Type	Explanation
fragtype	NCHAR(1)	Fragment type:
		I = Index
		T = Table
		B = TEXT or BYTE data (Enterprise Decision Server)
		i = Index fragments of a duplicated table (Enterprise Decision Server)
		d = data fragments of a duplicated table (Enterprise Decision Server)
tabid	INTEGER	Table identifier
indexname	NVARCHAR(128)	Index identifier

(1 of 3)

Column Name	Type	Explanation
colno	INTEGER	TEXT or BYTE column identifier
		Replica identifier (Enterprise Decision Server)
partn	INTEGER	Physical location identifier
strategy	NCHAR(1)	Distribution scheme type:
		R = Round-robin strategy was used to distribute the fragments
		E = Expression-based strategy was used to distribute the fragments
		T = Table-based strategy was used to distribute the fragments
		I = IN DBSPACE clause specified a specific location as part of the fragmentation strategy
		H = hash-based strategy was used to distribute the fragments (Enterprise Decision Server)
location	NCHAR(1)	Reserved for future use; shows L for local
servername	NVARCHAR(128)	Reserved for future use
evalpos	INTEGER	Position of fragment in the fragmentation list
exprtext	TEXT	Expression that was entered for fragmentation strategy
		For Enterprise Decision Server, contains the names of the columns that are hashed. Contains composite information for hybrid fragmentation strategies; shows hashed columns followed by the fragmentation expression of the dbslice.
exprbin	BYTE	Binary version of expression
exprarr	BYTE	Range-partitioning data used to optimize expression in range-expression fragmentation strategy

(2 of 3)

Column Name	Type	Explanation
flags	INTEGER	Used internally
		For Enterprise Decision Server, a bit value indicates the existence of a hybrid fragmentation strategy (value = 0x10). Also, an additional flag (value = 0x20) will be set on the first fragment of a globally detached index.
dbspace	NVARCHAR(128)	Dbspacename for fragment
levels	SMALLINT	Number of B+ tree index levels
npused	INTEGER	For table-fragmentation strategy, npused represents the number of data pages; for index-fragmentation strategy, npused represents the number of leaf pages.
nrows	INTEGER	For tables, nrows represents the number of rows in the fragment; for indexes, nrows represents the number of unique keys.
clust	INTEGER	Degree of index clustering; smaller numbers correspond to greater clustering
hybdpos	INTEGER	Contains the relative position of the hybrid fragment within a dbslice or list of dbspaces associated with a particular expression. The hybrid fragmentation strategy and the set of fragments against which the hybrid strategy is applied determines the relative position. The first fragment has a **hybdpos** value of zero (0). (Enterprise Decision Server)

(3 of 3)

The **strategy** type T is used for attached indexes (where index fragmentation is the same as the table fragmentation).

The composite index on the **fragtype, tabid, indexname**, and **evalpos** columns allows duplicate values.

EDS

The **hybdpos** field is the last field of the composite key in the fraginfo index on the **SYSFRAGMENTS** table.

EDS

SYSINDEXES

The **sysindexes** system catalog table describes the indexes in the database. It contains one row for each index that is defined in the database. The **sysindexes** system catalog table has the following columns.

Column Name	Type	Explanation
idxname	NVARCHAR(18)	Index name
owner	NCHAR(32)	Owner of index (user **informix** for system catalog tables and user name for database tables)
tabid	INTEGER	Table identifier
idxtype	NCHAR(1)	Index type:
		U = Unique
		G = Nonbitmap generalized-key index (Enterprise Decision Server only)
		D = Duplicates
		g = Bitmap generalized-key index (Enterprise Decision Server only)
		u = unique, bitmap (Enterprise Decision Server only)
		d = nonunique, bitmap (Enterprise Decision Server only)
clustered	NCHAR(1)	Clustered or nonclustered index (C = Clustered)
part1	SMALLINT	Column number (**colno**) of a single index or the 1st component of a composite index
part2	SMALLINT	2nd component of a composite index
part3	SMALLINT	3rd component of a composite index
part4	SMALLINT	4th component of a composite index
part5	SMALLINT	5th component of a composite index
part6	SMALLINT	6th component of a composite index

(1 of 2)

Column Name	Type	Explanation
part7	SMALLINT	7th component of a composite index
part8	SMALLINT	8th component of a composite index
part9	SMALLINT	9th component of a composite index
part10	SMALLINT	10th component of a composite index
part11	SMALLINT	11th component of a composite index
part12	SMALLINT	12th component of a composite index
part13	SMALLINT	13th component of a composite index
part14	SMALLINT	14th component of a composite index
part15	SMALLINT	15th component of a composite index
part16	SMALLINT	16th component of a composite index
levels	SMALLINT	Number of B+ tree levels
leaves	INTEGER	Number of leaves
nunique	INTEGER	Number of unique keys in the first column
clust	INTEGER	Degree of clustering: smaller numbers correspond to greater clustering
idxflags	INTEGER	Stores the current locking mode of the index: Normal = 0x01 Coarse = 0x02

(2 of 2)

Changes that affect existing indexes are reflected in this table only after you run the UPDATE STATISTICS statement.

Each **part***nth* column component of a composite index (the **part1** through **part16** columns in this table) holds the column number (**colno**) of each part of the 16 possible parts of a composite index. If the component is ordered in descending order, the **colno** is entered as a negative value.

The **clust** column is blank until the UPDATE STATISTICS statement is run on the table. The maximum value is the number of rows in the table, and the minimum value is the number of data pages in the table.

The **tabid** column is indexed and allows duplicate values. A composite index for the **idxname, owner,** and **tabid** columns allows only unique values.

SYSINDICES

IDS

The **sysindices** system catalog table describes the indexes in the database. It contains one row for each index that is defined in the database. The **sysindices** system catalog table has the following columns.

Column Name	Type	Explanation
idxname	NVARCHAR(128)	Index name
owner	NCHAR(32)	Owner of index (user **informix** for system catalog tables and user name for database tables)
tabid	INTEGER	Table identifier
idxtype	NCHAR(1)	Index type:
		U = Unique
		D = Duplicates
clustered	NCHAR(1)	Clustered or nonclustered index (C = Clustered)
levels	SMALLINT	Number of tree levels
leaves	INTEGER	Number of leaves
nunique	INTEGER	Number of unique keys in the first column
clust	INTEGER	Degree of clustering: smaller numbers correspond to greater clustering. The maximum value is the number of rows in the table, and the minimum value is the number of data pages in the table.
		This column is blank until the UPDATE STATISTICS statement is run on the table.
nrows	INTEGER	Estimated number of rows in the table (zero until UPDATE STATISTICS is run on the table).

(1 of 2)

Column Name	Type	Explanation
indexkeys	INDEXKEYARRAY	This column has a maximum of three fields, displayed in the following form: <function id>(col1, ..., coln) [operator class id] The function id shows only if the index is on return values of a function defined over the columns of the table; that is, if it is a functional index. The function id is the same as the **procid** of the function showing in the **sysprocedures** system catalog table. The list of the columns (col1,..., coln) in the second field gives columns over which the index is defined. The operator class id signifies the particular secondary access method used to build and search the index.
amid	INTEGER	Identifier of the access method used to implement this index. It is the value of the *am_id* for that access method in the **sysams** system catalog table.
amparam	LVARCHAR	List of parameters used to customize the behavior of this access method.

(2 of 2)

Tip: *This system catalog table is changed from the system catalog table in the 7.2 version of the Informix database server. The previous version of this system catalog table is still available as a view and can be accessed under its original name:* **sysindexes.** *The columns* **part1** *through* **part16** *in* **sysindexes** *are filled in for B-tree indexes that do not use user-defined types or functional indexes. For generic B-trees and all other access methods, the* **part1** *to* **part16** *columns contain zeros.*

Changes that affect existing indexes are reflected in this system catalog table only after you run the UPDATE STATISTICS statement.

The **tabid** column is indexed and allows duplicate values. A composite index for the **idxname, owner,** and **tabid** columns allows only unique values.

The system indexes **tabid** and **idxname** are used to index **sysindices.**

IDS

SYSINHERITS

The **sysinherits** system catalog table stores information about table and type inheritance. Every supertype, subtype, supertable, and subtable in the database has a corresponding row in the **sysinherits** table. The **sysinherits** system catalog table has the following columns.

Column Name	Type	Explanation
child	INTEGER	Identifier of the subtable or subtype in an inheritance relationship
parent	INTEGER	Identifier of the supertable or supertype in an inheritance relationship
class	NCHAR(1)	Inheritance class: t = named row type T = table

IDS

SYSLANGAUTH

The **syslangauth** system catalog table contains the authorization information on computer languages that are used to write user-defined routines (UDRs).

Column Name	Type	Explanation
grantor	NCHAR(32)	The grantor of the language authorization
grantee	NCHAR(32)	The grantee of the language authorization
langid	INTEGER	The language id reference to the **sysroutinelangs** system catalog table
langauth	NCHAR(1)	The language authorization u = Usage permission granted U = Usage permission granted WITH GRANT OPTION

A nonunique index on the **langid** and **grantee** columns is created for faster access to the **syslangauth** table.

SYSLOGMAP

The **syslogmap** system catalog table is not implemented in this version.

Column Name	Type	Explanation
tabloc		Reserved for future use
tabid		Reserved for future use
fragid		Reserved for future use
flags		Reserved for future use

EDS

SYSNEWDEPEND

The **sysnewdepend** system catalog table contains information about generalized-key indexes that is not available in the **sysindexes** system catalog table. The dependencies between a generalized-key index and the tables in the FROM clause of the CREATE INDEX statement are stored in the **sysnewdepend** system catalog table. The **sysnewdepend** system catalog table has the following columns.

Column Name	Type	Explanation
scrid1	CHAR	The name of the generalized-key index
scrid2	INTEGER	The tableid of the indexed table
type	INTEGER	The type of generalized-key index
destid1	INTEGER	The tableid of the table that the generalized-key index depends
destid2	INTEGER	The column name in the table that the generalized-key index depends

SYSOBJSTATE

The **sysobjstate** system catalog table stores information about the state (object mode) of database objects. The types of database objects listed in this table are indexes, triggers, and constraints.

Every index, trigger, and constraint in the database has a corresponding row in the **sysobjstate** table if a user creates the object. Indexes that the database server creates on the system catalog tables are not listed in the **sysobjstate** table because their object mode cannot be changed.

The **sysobjstate** system catalog table has the following columns.

Column Name	Type	Explanation
objtype	NCHAR(1)	The type of database object. This column has one of the following codes: C = Constraint I = Index T = Trigger
owner	NCHAR(32)	The owner of the database object
name	NVARCHAR(128)	The name of the database object
tabid	INTEGER	Table identifier of the table on which the database object is defined
state	NCHAR(1)	The current state (object mode) of the database object. This column has one of the following codes: D = Disabled E = Enabled F = Filtering with no integrity-violation errors G = Filtering with integrity-violation errors

A composite index for the **objtype**, **name**, **owner**, and **tabid** columns allows only unique values.

IDS

SYSOPCLASSES

The **sysopclasses** system catalog table contains information about operator classes associated with secondary access methods. It contains one row for each operator class that has been defined. The **sysopclasses** system catalog table has the following columns.

Column Name	Type	Explanation
opclassname	NVARCHAR(128)	Name of the operator class
owner	NCHAR(32)	Owner of the operator class
amid	INTEGER	Identifier of the secondary access method associated with this operator class
opclassid	SERIAL	Identifier of the operator class. This identifier is used in the **sysams** system catalog table to specify the default operator class (**am_defopclass**) for the access method.
ops	LVARCHAR	List of names of the operators that belong to this operator class
support	LVARCHAR	List of names of support functions defined for this operator class

The **sysopclasses** system catalog table has two indexes. There is a composite index on **opclassname** and **owner** columns and an index on **opclassid** column. Both indexes allow only unique values.

IDS

SYSOPCLSTR

The **sysopclstr** system catalog table defines each optical cluster in the database. It contains one row for each optical cluster.

The **sysopclstr** system catalog table has the following columns.

Column Name	Type	Explanation
owner	NCHAR(32)	Owner of the cluster
clstrname	NVARCHAR(128)	Name of the cluster
clstrsize	INTEGER	Size of the cluster
tabid	INTEGER	Table identifier
blobcol1	SMALLINT	BYTE or TEXT column number 1
blobcol2	SMALLINT	BYTE or TEXT column number 2
blobcol3	SMALLINT	BYTE or TEXT column number 3
blobcol4	SMALLINT	BYTE or TEXT column number 4
blobcol5	SMALLINT	BYTE or TEXT column number 5
blobcol6	SMALLINT	BYTE or TEXT column number 6
blobcol7	SMALLINT	BYTE or TEXT column number 7
blobcol8	SMALLINT	BYTE or TEXT column number 8
blobcol9	SMALLINT	BYTE or TEXT column number 9
blobcol10	SMALLINT	BYTE or TEXT column number 10
blobcol11	SMALLINT	BYTE or TEXT column number 11
blobcol12	SMALLINT	BYTE or TEXT column number 12
blobcol13	SMALLINT	BYTE or TEXT column number 13
blobcol14	SMALLINT	BYTE or TEXT column number 14
blobcol15	SMALLINT	BYTE or TEXT column number 15
blobcol16	SMALLINT	BYTE or TEXT column number 16

(1 of 2)

Column Name	Type	Explanation
clstrkey1	SMALLINT	Cluster key number 1
clstrkey2	SMALLINT	Cluster key number 2
clstrkey3	SMALLINT	Cluster key number 3
clstrkey4	SMALLINT	Cluster key number 4
clstrkey5	SMALLINT	Cluster key number 5
clstrkey6	SMALLINT	Cluster key number 6
clstrkey7	SMALLINT	Cluster key number 7
clstrkey8	SMALLINT	Cluster key number 8
clstrkey9	SMALLINT	Cluster key number 9
clstrkey10	SMALLINT	Cluster key number 10
clstrkey11	SMALLINT	Cluster key number 11
clstrkey12	SMALLINT	Cluster key number 12
clstrkey13	SMALLINT	Cluster key number 13
clstrkey14	SMALLINT	Cluster key number 14
clstrkey15	SMALLINT	Cluster key number 15
clstrkey16	SMALLINT	Cluster key number 16

(2 of 2)

A composite index for both the **clstrname** and **owner** columns allows only unique values. The **tabid** column allows duplicate values.

SYSPROCAUTH

The **sysprocauth** system catalog table describes the privileges granted on a procedure or function. It contains one row for each set of privileges that are granted. The **sysprocauth** system catalog table has the following columns.

Column Name	Type	Explanation
grantor	NCHAR(32)	Grantor of routine
grantee	NCHAR(32)	Grantee of routine
procid	INTEGER	Routine identifier
procauth	NCHAR(1)	Type of routine permission granted: e = Execute permission on routine E = Execute permission and the ability to grant it to others

A composite index for the **procid, grantor,** and **grantee** columns allows only unique values. The composite index for the **procid** and **grantee** columns allows duplicate values.

SYSPROCBODY

The **sysprocbody** system catalog table describes the compiled version of each procedure or function in the database. Because the **sysprocbody** system catalog table stores the text of the routine, each routine can have multiple rows. The **sysprocbody** system catalog table has the following columns.

Column Name	Type	Explanation
procid	INTEGER	Routine identifier
datakey	NCHAR(1)	Data-descriptor type:
		D = User document text
		T = Actual routine source
		R = Return value type list
		S = Routine symbol table
		L = Constant routine data string (that is, literal numbers or quoted strings)
		P = Interpreter instruction code
seqno	INTEGER	Line number of the routine
data	NCHAR(256)	Actual text of the routine

Although the **datakey** column indicates the type of data that is stored, the **data** column contains the actual data, which can be one of the following types:

- Encoded return values list
- Encoded symbol table
- Constant data
- Compiled code for the routine
- Text of the routine and its documentation

A composite index for the **procid**, **datakey**, and **seqno** columns allows only unique values.

SYSPROCEDURES

The **sysprocedures** system catalog table lists the characteristics for each function and procedure in the database. It contains one row for each routine.

EDS

For Enterprise Decision Server, the **sysprocedures** system catalog table has the following columns.

Column Name	Type	Explanation
procname	NVARCHAR(128)	Routine name
owner	NCHAR(32)	Owner name
procid	SERIAL	Routine identifier
mode	NCHAR(1)	Mode type:
		D, d = DBA
		O, o = Owner
		P, p = Protected
		R, r = Restricted
retsize	INTEGER	Compiled size (in bytes) of values
symsize	INTEGER	Compiled size (in bytes) of symbol table
datasize	INTEGER	Compiled size (in bytes) constant data
codesize	INTEGER	Compiled size (in bytes) of routine instruction code
numargs	INTEGER	Number of routine arguments

IDS

For Dynamic Server, the **sysprocedures** system catalog table has the following columns.

Column Name	Type	Explanation
procname	NVARCHAR(128)	Routine name
owner	NCHAR(32)	Owner name
procid	SERIAL	Routine identifier
mode	NCHAR(1)	Mode type:
		D, d = DBA
		O, o = Owner
		P, p = Protected
		R, r = Restricted
retsize	INTEGER	Compiled size (in bytes) of values
symsize	INTEGER	Compiled size (in bytes) of symbol table
datasize	INTEGER	Compiled size (in bytes) constant data
codesize	INTEGER	Compiled size (in bytes) of routine instruction code
numargs	INTEGER	Number of routine arguments
isproc	NCHAR(1)	Whether the routine is a procedure or a function
		t = procedure
		f = function
specificname	NVARCHAR(128)	The specific name for the routine
externalname	NVARCHAR(255)	Location of the external routine. This item is language-specific in content and format.
paramstyle	NCHAR(1)	Parameter style
		I = Informix

(1 of 3)

Column Name	Type	Explanation
langid	INTEGER	Language identifier (from the **sysroutinelangs** system catalog table)
paramtypes	rtnparamtypes	Data types of the parameters; *rtnparamtypes* indicates a built-in data type
variant	BOOLEAN	Indicates whether the routine is VARIANT or not
		t = is variant
		f = is not variant
handlesnulls	BOOLEAN	Null handling indicator:
		t = handles nulls
		f = does not handle nulls
percallcost	INTEGER	Amount of CPU per call; integer cost to execute UDR: cost/call - 0 -(2^31-1)
commutator	NVARCHAR(128)	Field commutator
negator	NVARCHAR(128)	Negator function name
selfunc	NVARCHAR(128)	Function used to estimate function selectivity
iterator	BOOLEAN	Iterator routine
internal	BOOLEAN	Whether the routine can be called from SQL
		t = routine is internal, not callable from SQL
		f = routine is external, can be called from SQL
class	NCHAR(18)	CPU class in which the routine should be executed
stack	INTEGER	Stack size in bytes required per invocation
costfunc	NVARCHAR(128)	Name of cost function for UDR
selconst	INTEGER	Selectivity constant for UDR

(2 of 3)

Column Name	Type	Explanation
parallelizable	BOOLEAN	Parallelization indicator for UDR: t = Parallelizable f = Not parallelizable

(3 of 3)

♦

A unique index on the **procid** column indexes the routine id. A composite index on the **procname, isproc, numargs,** and **owner** columns maintains the uniqueness of the routines in the database. This index allows duplicate values. The index on the **specificname** and **owner** columns maintains the uniqueness of the routines with specific names. It allows duplicate values.

For the **sysprocedures** system catalog table, the R mode is a special case of the O mode. A routine is in restricted (R) mode if it was created with a specified owner that is different from the routine creator. If routine statements involving a remote database are executed, the database server uses the permissions of the user that executes the routine instead of the permissions of the routine owner. In all other scenarios, R mode routines behave the same as O mode routines.

Starting with Version 9.x, protected routines (which cannot be deleted) are indicated differently in the mode column. In earlier versions, protected routines were simply indicated by a P. Currently, protected routines are treated as DBA routines and cannot be Owner routines. Thus D and O indicate DBA and Owner routines, and d and o indicate protected DBA and protected Owner routines.

Important: *After a SET SESSION AUTHORIZATION is done, all owner routines created while using the new identity are given a restricted mode.*

A database server can create protected routines for internal use. The **sysprocedures** table identifies these protected routines with the letter P or p in the mode column. You cannot modify or drop protected routines or display them through **dbschema**.

SYSPROCPLAN

The **sysprocplan** system catalog table describes the query-execution plans and dependency lists for data-manipulation statements within each routine. If new plans are generated during the execution of a routine, the new plans are also recorded in **sysprocplan**. Because different parts of a routine plan can be created on different dates, the table can contain multiple rows for each routine.

It is possible to delete all the plans for a particular routine with the DELETE statement on **sysprocplan**. When the routine is executed, new plans are automatically generated and recorded in **sysprocplan**.

Only Dynamic Server stores plans in **sysprocplan**. ♦

The **sysprocplan** system catalog table has the following columns.

Column Name	Type	Explanation
procid	INTEGER	Routine identifier
planid	INTEGER	Plan identifier
datakey	NCHAR(1)	Identifier routine plan part:
		D = Dependency list
		Q = Execution plan
seqno	INTEGER	Line number of plan
created	DATE	Date plan created
datasize	INTEGER	Size (in bytes) of the list or plan
data	NCHAR(256)	Encoded (compiled) list or plan

A composite index for the **procid, planid, datakey**, and **seqno** columns allows only unique values.

SYSREFERENCES

The **sysreferences** system catalog table lists the referential constraints that are placed on columns in the database. It contains a row for each referential constraint in the database. The **sysreferences** system catalog table has the following columns.

Column Name	Type	Explanation
constrid	INTEGER	Constraint identifier
primary	INTEGER	Constraint identifier of the corresponding primary key
ptabid	INTEGER	Table identifier of the primary key
updrule	NCHAR(1)	Reserved for future use; displays an R
delrule	NCHAR(1)	Displays cascading delete or restrict rule: C = Cascading delete R = Restrict (default)
matchtype	NCHAR(1)	Reserved for future use; displays an N
pendant	NCHAR(1)	Reserved for future use; displays an N

The **constrid** column is indexed and allows only unique values. The **primary** column is indexed and allows duplicate values.

EDS

SYSREPOSITORY

The **sysrepository** system catalog table contains information about generalized-key indexes that is not available in the **sysindexes** system catalog table. The **sysrepository** system catalog table contains the CREATE statement for each generalized-key index in the database in its **desc** column. The contents of the **sysrepository** system catalog table are useful when a generalized-key index has to be rebuilt during a recovery or if a user wants to see the CREATE statement for a specific generalized-key index.

Column Name	Type	Explanation
id1	NCHAR	Index from the generalized-key index
id2	INTEGER	Tabid of table with the generalized-key index
type	INTEGER	Integer representing object type
		In this release, the only integer that shows is 1, indicating generalized-key index type.
seqid	INTEGER	For future use
desc	TEXT	The CREATE statement used for each generalized-key index in the database
bin	BYTE	Internal representation of the generalized-key index

IDS

SYSROLEAUTH

The **sysroleauth** system catalog table describes the roles that are granted to users. It contains one row for each role that is granted to a user in the database. The **sysroleauth** system catalog table has the following columns.

Column Name	Type	Explanation
rolename	NCHAR(32)	Name of the role
grantee	NCHAR(32)	Grantee of role
is_grantable	NCHAR(1)	Specifies whether the role is grantable: Y = Grantable N = Not grantable

The **rolename** and **grantee** columns are indexed and allow only unique values. The **is_grantable** column indicates whether the role was granted with the WITH GRANT OPTION on the GRANT statement.

IDS

SYSROUTINELANGS

The **sysroutinelangs** system catalog table contains the supported languages for writing user-defined routines (UDRs).

Column Name	Type	Explanation
langid	SERIAL	Identifies the supported language
langname	NCHAR(30)	The name of the language, such as C or SPL
langinitfunc	NVARCHAR(128)	The name of the initialization function for the language
langpath	NCHAR(255)	The path for the UDR language
langclass	NCHAR(18)	The class of the UDR language

SYSSYNONYMS

Important: *Version 4.0 or later Informix products no longer use this table; however, any* **syssynonyms** *entries made before Version 4.0 remain in this table. See the discussion of* **syssyntable***.*

The **syssynonyms** system catalog table lists the synonyms for each table or view. It contains a row for every synonym defined in the database. The **syssynonyms** system catalog table has the following columns.

Column Name	Type	Explanation
owner	NCHAR(32)	User name of owner
synname	NVARCHAR(128)	Synonym identifier
created	DATE	Date synonym created
tabid	INTEGER	Table identifier

A composite index for the **owner** and **synonym** columns allows only unique values. The **tabid** column is indexed and allows duplicate values.

SYSSYNTABLE

The **syssyntable** system catalog table outlines the mapping between each synonym and the object that it represents. It contains one row for each entry in the **systables** table that has a **tabtype** of S. The **syssyntable** system catalog table has the following columns.

Column Name	Type	Explanation
tabid	INTEGER	Table identifier
servername	NVARCHAR(128)	Server name
dbname	NVARCHAR(128)	Database name
owner	NCHAR(32)	User name of owner
tabname	NVARCHAR(128)	Name of table
btabid	INTEGER	Table identifier of base table or view

If you define a synonym for a table that is in your current database, only the **tabid** and **btabid** columns are used. If you define a synonym for a table that is external to your current database, the **btabid** column is not used, but the **tabid**, **servername**, **dbname**, **owner**, and **tabname** columns are used.

The **tabid** column maps to the **tabid** column in **systables**. With the **tabid** information, you can determine additional facts about the synonym from **systables**.

An index for the **tabid** column allows only unique values. The **btabid** column is indexed to allow duplicate values.

IDS

SYSTABAMDATA

The **systabamdata** system catalog table stores the parameterization option choices (table-specific hashing parameters) that you make when you create a table using a primary access method. It stores configuration parameters that determine how a primary access method accesses a particular table. The table might reside in a cooked file, a different database, or an sbspace within the database server.

The **systabamdata** system catalog table has the following columns.

Column Name	Type	Explanation
tabid	INTEGER	Table identifier
am_param	NCHAR(256)	Access method parameterization option choices
am_space	NVARCHAR(128)	The name of the space where the table data is stored

The **tabid** column, the key to the **systables** system catalog table, is indexed and must contain unique values. Each configuration parameter in the **am_param** list has the format *keyword=value* or *keyword*.

SYSTABAUTH

The **systabauth** system catalog table describes each set of privileges that are granted in a table. It contains one row for each set of table privileges that are granted in the database. The **systabauth** system catalog table has the following columns.

Column Name	Type	Explanation
grantor	NCHAR(32)	Grantor of privilege
grantee	NCHAR(32)	Grantee of privilege
tabid	INTEGER	Table identifier
tabauth	NCHAR(9)	9-byte pattern that specifies table privileges:
		s = Select
		u = Update
		* = Column-level privilege
		i = Insert
		d = Delete
		x = Index
		a = Alter
		r = References
		n = Under privilege
		N = Under privilege with grant option

If the **tabauth** privilege code is uppercase (for example, S for select), a user who has this privilege can grant it to others. If the **tabauth** privilege code is lowercase (for example, s for select), the user who has this privilege cannot grant it to others.

A composite index for the **tabid**, **grantor**, and **grantee** columns allows only unique values. The composite index for the **tabid** and **grantee** columns allows duplicate values.

SYSTABLES

The **systables** system catalog table describes each table in the database. It contains one row for each table, view, or synonym that is defined in the database. The information in the **systables** system catalog table includes all database tables and the system catalog tables. The **systables** system catalog table has the following columns

Column Name	Type	Explanation
tabname	NVARCHAR(128)	Name of table, view, or synonym
owner	NCHAR(32)	Owner of table (user **informix** for system catalog tables and user name for database tables)
partnum	INTEGER	Physical location identifier
tabid	SERIAL	System-assigned sequential ID number (system tables: 1-24, user tables: 100-nnn)
rowsize	SMALLINT	Row size
ncols	SMALLINT	Number of columns
nindexes	SMALLINT	Number of indexes
nrows	INTEGER	Number of rows
created	DATE	Date created
version	INTEGER	Number that changes when table is altered
tabtype	NCHAR(1)	Table type: T = Table V = View P = Private synonym S = Public synonym (not available in an ANSI-compliant database)

(1 of 2)

Column Name	Type	Explanation
locklevel	NCHAR(1)	Lock mode for a table:
		B = Page
		P = Page
		R = Row
		T = Table (Enterprise Decision Server only)
npused	INTEGER	Number of data pages in use
fextsize	INTEGER	Size of initial extent (in kilobytes)
nextsize	INTEGER	Size of all subsequent extents (in kilobytes)
flags	SMALLINT	Has a unique value for the following types of permanent tables:
		ST_RAW represents a raw (nonlogging permanent) table in a logging database
		RAW 0x00000002 (Enterprise Decision Server only)
		STATIC 0x00000004 (Enterprise Decision Server only)
		OPERATIONAL 0x00000010 (Enterprise Decision Server only)
		STANDARD 0x00000020 (Enterprise Decision Server only)
		EXTERNAL 0x00000020 (Enterprise Decision Server only)
site	NVARCHAR(128)	Reserved for future use (used to store database collation and C-type information)
dbname	NVARCHAR(128)	Reserved for future use
am_id	INTEGER	Access method ID (key to **sysams** table); null value or 0 indicates built-in storage manager used

(2 of 2)

Each table recorded in the **systables** system catalog table is assigned a **tabid**, which is a system-assigned sequential number that uniquely identifies each table in the database. The first **tabid** numbers up to 99 are reserved for system catalog tables. The user-created **tabid** numbers begin with 100.

The **tabid** column is indexed and must contain unique values. A composite index for the **tabname** and **owner** columns allows only unique values. The **version** column contains an encoded number that is put in the **systables** system catalog table when the table is created. Portions of the encoded value are incremented when data-definition statements, such as ALTER INDEX, ALTER TABLE, DROP INDEX, and CREATE INDEX, are performed.

When a prepared statement is executed, the **version** number is checked to make sure that nothing has changed since the statement was prepared. If the **version** number has changed, your statement does not execute, and you must prepare your statement again.

The **npused** column does not reflect BYTE or TEXT data used.

GLS

The **systables** system catalog table has two additional rows to store the database locale: GL_COLLATE with a **tabid** of 90 and GL_CTYPE with a **tabid** of 91. To view these rows, enter the following SELECT statement:

```
SELECT tabname, tabid FROM systables
```

IDS

SYSTRACECLASSES

The **systraceclasses** system catalog table contains the names and identifiers of trace classes. A trace class is a category of trace messages that you can use in the development and testing of new DataBlade modules and user-defined routines. Developers use the tracing facility by calling the appropriate DataBlade API routines within their code.

To create a new trace class, insert a row directly into the **systraceclasses** system catalog table. By default, all users can view this table, but only users with the DBA privilege can modify it.

A unique index on the **name** column ensures that each trace class has a unique name. The database server also assigns each class a sequential identifier. Therefore, the index on the **classid** column also allows only unique values.

The **systraceclasses** system catalog table has the following columns.

Column Name	Type	Explanation
name	NCHAR(18)	Name of the class of trace messages
classid	SERIAL	Trace class identifier

IDS

SYSTRACEMSGS

The **systracemsgs** system catalog table stores internationalized trace messages that you can use in debugging user-defined routines. DataBlade module developers create a trace message by inserting a row directly into the **systracemsgs** system catalog table. Once a message is created, the development team can specify it either by name or by ID, using trace statements that the DataBlade API provides.

To create a trace message, you must specify its name, locale, and text. By default, all users can view the **systracemsgs** table, but only users with the DBA privilege can modify it.

The **systracemsgs** system catalog table has the following columns.

Column Name	Type	Explanation
name	NVARCHAR(128)	The name of the message
msgid	SERIAL	The message template identifier
locale	NCHAR(36)	The locale with which this version of the message is associated (for example, en_us.8859-1)
seqno	Reserved for future use	
message	NVARCHAR(255)	The message text

A unique index defined on columns **name** and **locale**. A unique index is also on the **msgid** column.

IDS

SYSTRIGBODY

The **systrigbody** system catalog table contains the English text of the trigger definition and the linearized code for the trigger. Linearized code is binary data and code that is represented in ASCII format.

Warning: *The database server uses the linearized code that is stored in* **systrigbody**. *You must not alter the content of rows that contain linearized code.*

The **systrigbody** system catalog table has the following columns.

Column Name	Type	Explanation
trigid	INT	Trigger identifier
datakey	NCHAR	Type of data:
		D = English text for the header, trigger definition
		A = English text for the body, triggered actions
		H = Linearized code for the header
		S = Linearized code for the symbol table
		B = Linearized code for the body
seqno	INT	Sequence number
data	NCHAR(256)	English text or linearized code

A composite index for the **trigid**, **datakey**, and **seqno** columns allows only unique values.

SYSTRIGGERS

`IDS`

The **systriggers** system catalog table contains miscellaneous information about the SQL triggers in the database. This information includes the trigger event and the correlated reference specification for the trigger. The **systriggers** system catalog table has the following columns.

Column Name	Type	Explanation
trigid	SERIAL	Trigger identifier
trigname	NVARCHAR(128)	Trigger name
owner	NCHAR(32)	Owner of trigger
tabid	INT	ID of triggering table
event	NCHAR	Triggering event:
		I = Insert trigger
		U = Update trigger
		D = Delete trigger
		S = Select trigger
old	NVARCHAR(128)	Name of value before update
new	NVARCHAR(128)	Name of value after update
mode	NCHAR	Reserved for future use

A composite index for the **trigname** and **owner** columns allows only unique values. The **trigid** column is indexed and must contain unique values. An index for the **tabid** column allows duplicate values.

SYSUSERS

The **sysusers** system catalog table describes each set of privileges that are granted in the database. It contains one row for each user who has privileges in the database. The **sysusers** system catalog table has the following columns.

Column Name	Type	Explanation
username	NCHAR(32)	Name of the database user or role
usertype	NCHAR(1)	Specifies database-level privileges:
		D = DBA (all privileges)
		R = Resource (create permanent tables, user-defined data types, and indexes)
		G = Role
		C = Connect (work within existing tables)
priority	SMALLINT	Reserved for future use
password	NCHAR(16	Reserved for future use

The **username** column is indexed and allows only unique values. The **username** can be the name of a role.

SYSVIEWS

The **sysviews** system catalog table describes each view that is defined in the database. Because the **sysviews** system catalog table stores the SELECT statement that you use to create the view, it can contain multiple rows for each view in the database. The **sysviews** system catalog table has the following columns.

Column Name	Type	Explanation
tabid	INTEGER	Table identifier
seqno	SMALLINT	Line number of the SELECT statement
viewtext	NCHAR(64)	Actual SELECT statement used to create the view

A composite index for the **tabid** and **seqno** columns allows only unique values.

SYSVIOLATIONS

The **sysviolations** system catalog table stores information about the constraint violations for base tables. Every table in the database that has a violations table and a diagnostics table associated with it has a corresponding row in the **sysviolations** table. The **sysviolations** system catalog table has the following columns.

Column Name	Type	Explanation
targettid	INTEGER	Table identifier of the target table. The target table is the base table on which the violations table and the diagnostic table are defined.
viotid	INTEGER	Table identifier of the violations table
diatid	INTEGER	Table identifier of the diagnostics table
maxrows	INTEGER	Maximum number of rows that can be inserted in the diagnostics table during a single insert, update, or delete operation on a target table that has a filtering mode object defined on it.
		Also signifies the maximum number of rows that can be inserted in the diagnostics table during a single operation that enables a disabled object or sets a disabled object to filtering mode (provided that a diagnostics table exists for the target table).
		For Enterprise Decision Server, indicates the maximum number of rows that are allowed in the violations table for each coserver.
		If no maximum is specified for the diagnostics or violations table, this column contains a null value.

The primary key of the **sysviolations** table is the **targettid** column. Unique indexes are also defined on the **viotid** and **diatid** columns.

EDS

Enterprise Decision Server does not use the diagnostic table when a constraint violation occurs. Rather, the database server stores additional information in the violations table. The violations table contains the data that the transaction refused and an indication of the cause. ◆

IDS

SYSXTDDESC

The **sysxtddesc** system catalog table provides a text description of each user-defined data type (opaque, distinct, and complex (named row types, unnamed row types, and collection types)) that you define in the database. The **sysxtddesc** system catalog table has the following columns.

Column Name	Type	Explanation
extended_id	SERIAL	Unique identifier for extended data types
seqno	SMALLINT	Value to order and identify one line of description for specific values of **extended_id**. A new sequence is created only if the text string is larger than the 255 limit of the text string.
description	NCHAR(256)	Textual description of the extended data type

IDS

SYSXTDTYPEAUTH

The **sysxtdtypeauth** system catalog table provides privileges for each user-defined data type (opaque and distinct) and for each named row type that you define in the database. The table contains one row for each set of privileges granted.

The **sysxtdtypeauth** system catalog table has the following columns.

Column Name	Type	Explanation
grantor	NCHAR(32)	Grantor of privilege
grantee	NCHAR(32)	Grantee of privilege
type	INTEGER	Identifier of the user-defined type
auth	NCHAR(2)	Privileges on the user-defined data type:
		n = Under privilege
		N = Under privilege with grant option
		u = Usage privilege
		U = Usage privilege with grant option

If the **sysxtdtypeauth** privilege code is uppercase (for example, 'U' for usage), a user who has this privilege can also grant it to others. If the **sysxtdtypeauth** privilege code is lowercase (for example, 'u' for usage), the user who has this privilege cannot grant it to others.

A composite index for the **type**, **grantor**, and **grantee** columns allows only unique values. The composite index for the **type** and **grantee** columns allows duplicate values.

IDS

SYSXTDTYPES

The **sysxtdtype** system catalog table has an entry for each user-defined data type (opaque and distinct data types) and complex data type (named row type, unnamed row type, and collection type) that is defined in the database. Each extended data type has a unique id, called an extended id (**extended_id**), a data type identifier (**type**), and the length and description of the data type.

The **sysxtdtypes** system catalog table has the following columns.

Column Name	Type	Explanation
extended_id	SERIAL	Unique identifier for extended data types
mode	NCHAR(1)	Detailed description of the user-defined type. One of the following values: B = Base (opaque) C = Collection type as well as unnamed row type D = Distinct R = Named row type ' ' (blank) = Built-in type
owner	NCHAR(32)	Owner of the data type
name	NVARCHAR(128)	Name of the data type
type	SMALLINT	The identifier of the data type. See the coltype column values of the syscolumns system catalog table for a complete list of identifiers associated with different data types. For distinct types created from built-in data types, the value in this column corresponds with the value of the **coltype** column (indicating the source type) in the **syscolumns** system catalog table. A value of 40 indicates a distinct data type created from a variable-length opaque type. A value of 41 indicates a distinct type created from a fixed-length opaque type.

(1 of 2)

Column Name	Type	Explanation
source	INTEGER	The sysxtdtypes reference for this type, if it is a distinct type. A value of 0 indicates that the distinct type was created from a built-in data type.
maxlen	INTEGER	The maximum length for variable-length data types. A value of 0 indicates a fixed-length data type.
length	INTEGER	The length in bytes for fixed-length data types. A value of 0 indicates a variable-length data type.
byvalue	NCHAR(1)	If the data type is passed by value 'T' = type is passed by value 'F' = type is not passed by value
cannothash	NCHAR(1)	Is data type hashable using the default bit-hashing function? 'T' = type is hashable 'F' = type is not hashable
align	SMALLINT	Alignment for this data type. One of the following values: 1, 2, 4, 8.
locator	INTEGER	Locator (key) for unnamed row types.

(2 of 2)

The index on the **extended_id** column allows only unique values. Similarly the index on columns **name** and **type** columns also allows only unique values. The index on the **source** and **maxlen** columns allow duplicate values.

IDS

Information Schema

The Information Schema consists of read-only views that provide information about all the tables, views, and columns on the current database server to which you have access. In addition, Information Schema views provide information about SQL dialects (such as Informix, Oracle, or Sybase) and SQL standards.

This version of the Information Schema views are X/Open CAE standards. Informix provides them so that applications developed on other database systems can obtain Informix system catalog information without having to use the Informix system catalogs directly.

Important: *Because the X/Open CAE standards Information Schema views differ from ANSI-compliant Information Schema views, Informix recommends that you do not install the X/Open CAE Information Schema views on ANSI-compliant databases.*

The following Information Schema views are available:

- **tables**
- **columns**
- **sql_languages**
- **server_info**

The following sections contain information about how to generate and access Information Schema views as well as information about their structure.

Generating the Information Schema Views

The Information Schema views are generated automatically when you, as DBA, run the following DB-Access command:

```
dbaccess database-name $INFORMIXDIR/etc/xpg4_is.sql
```

Data in the Informix system catalog tables populates the views. If tables, views, or routines exist with any of the same names as the Information Schema views, you need to either rename the database objects or rename the views in the script before you can install the views. You can drop the views with the DROP VIEW statement on each view. To re-create the views, rerun the script.

Important: *In addition to the columns specified for each Information Schema view, individual vendors might include additional columns or change the order of the columns. Informix recommends that applications not use the forms SELECT * or SELECT table-name* to access an Information Schema view.*

Accessing the Information Schema Views

All Information Schema views have the Select privilege granted to PUBLIC WITH GRANT OPTION so that all users can query the views. Because no other privileges are granted on the Information Schema views, they cannot be updated.

You can query the Information Schema views as you would query any other table or view in the database.

Structure of the Information Schema Views

The following views are described in this section:

- **tables**
- **columns**
- **sql_languages**
- **server_info**

Most of the columns in the views are defined as VARCHAR data types with large maximums to accept large names and in anticipation of long identifier names in future standards.

The tables Information Schema View

The **tables** Information Schema view contains one row for each table to which you have access. It contains the following columns.

Column Name	Data Type	Explanation
table_schema	VARCHAR(128)	Owner of table
table_name	VARCHAR(128)	Name of table or view
table_type	VARCHAR(128)	BASE TABLE for table or VIEW for view
remarks	VARCHAR(255)	Reserved

The visible rows in the **tables** view depend on your privileges. For example, if you have one or more privileges on a table (such as Insert, Delete, Select, References, Alter, Index, or Update on one or more columns), or if these privileges are granted to PUBLIC, you see one row that describes that table.

The columns Information Schema View

The **columns** Information Schema view contains one row for each accessible column. It contains the following columns.

Column Name	Data Type	Explanation
table_schema	VARCHAR(128)	Owner of table
table_name	VARCHAR(128)	Name of table or view
column_name	VARCHAR(128)	Name of the column of the table or view
ordinal_position	INTEGER	Ordinal position of the column. The ordinal_position of a column in a table is a sequential number that starts at 1 for the first column.This column is an Informix extension to XPG4.
data_type	VARCHAR(254)	Data type of the column, such as CHARACTER or DECIMAL

(1 of 2)

Column Name	Data Type	Explanation
char_max_length	INTEGER	Maximum length for character data types; null otherwise
numeric_precision	INTEGER	Total number of digits allowed for exact numeric data types (DECIMAL, INTEGER, MONEY, and SMALLINT), and the number of digits of mantissa precision for approximate data types (FLOAT and SMALLFLOAT), and null for all other data types. The value is machine dependent for FLOAT and SMALLFLOAT.
numeric_prec_radix	INTEGER	Uses one of the following values: 2 = approximate data types (FLOAT and SMALLFLOAT) 10 = exact numeric data types (DECIMAL, INTEGER, MONEY, and SMALLINT) Null for all other data types
numeric_scale	INTEGER	Number of significant digits to the right of the decimal point for DECIMAL and MONEY data types: 0 for INTEGER and SMALLINT data types Null for all other data types
datetime_precision	INTEGER	Number of digits in the fractional part of the seconds for DATE and DATETIME columns; null otherwise. This column is an Informix extension to XPG4.
is_nullable	VARCHAR(3)	Indicates whether a column allows nulls; either YES or NO
remarks	VARCHAR(254)	Reserved

(2 of 2)

The sql_languages Information Schema View

The **sql_languages** Information Schema view contains a row for each instance of conformance to standards that the current database server supports. The **sql_languages** Information Schema view contains the following columns.

Column Name	Data Type	Explanation
source	VARCHAR(254)	Organization that defines this SQL version
source_year	VARCHAR(254)	Year the source document was approved
conformance	VARCHAR(254)	Which conformance is supported
integrity	VARCHAR(254)	Indicates whether this is an integrity enhancement feature; either YES or NO
implementation	VARCHAR(254)	Identifies the SQL product of the vendor
binding_style	VARCHAR(254)	Direct, module, or other bind style
programming_lang	VARCHAR(254)	Host language for which the binding style is adopted

The **sql_languages** Information Schema view is completely visible to all users.

The server_info Information Schema View

The **server_info** Information Schema view describes the database server to which the application is currently connected. It contains the following columns.

Column Name	Data Type	Explanation
server_attribute	VARCHAR(254)	An attribute of the database server
attribute_value	VARCHAR(254)	Value of the **server_attribute** as it applies to the current database server

Each row in this view provides information about one attribute. X/Open-compliant databases must provide applications with certain required information about the database server. The **server_info** view includes the following information.

server_attribute	Description
identifier_length	Maximum number of characters for a user-defined name
row_length	Maximum length of a row
userid_length	Maximum number of characters of a user name (or "authorization identifier")
txn_isolation	Initial transaction isolation level that the database server assumes:
	Read Committed Default isolation level for databases created without logging
	Read Uncommitted Default isolation level for databases created with logging but not ANSI compliant
	Serializable Default isolation level for ANSI-compliant databases
collation_seq	Assumed ordering of the character set for the database server. The following values are possible:
	ISO 8859-1
	EBCDIC
	The Informix representation shows ISO 8859-1.

The **server_info** Information Schema view is completely visible to all users.

Data Types

In This Chapter

Every column in a table in a database is assigned a data type. The data type precisely defines the kinds of values that you can store in that column.

This chapter covers the following topics:

IDS

- Built-in data types
- Extended data types ♦
- Casting or converting between two data types
- Operator precedence

Summary of Data Types

Figure 2-1 charts the categories of data types that Informix database servers support.

Figure 2-1 *Overview of Supported Data Types*

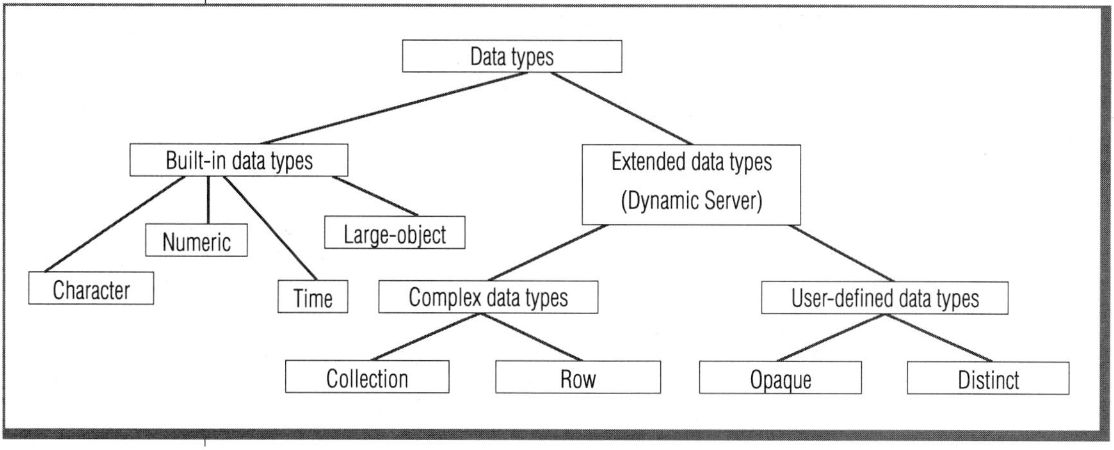

Built-in data types and extended data types share the following characteristics. You can:

- use them to create columns of tables.
- use them as arguments and as return types of functions.
- use them to create distinct types.
- cast them to other data types.
- declare and access them with SPL and ESQL/C.

Specific exceptions are mentioned in the description of each data type. For an overview, see "Built-In Data Types" on page 2-48 and "Extended Data Types" on page 2-58.

You assign data types to columns with the CREATE TABLE statement and change them with the ALTER TABLE statement. When you change an existing column data type, all data is converted to the new data type, if possible.

For information on the ALTER TABLE and CREATE TABLE statements, SQL statements that create specific data types and create and drop casts, and other data type syntax conventions, refer to the *Informix Guide to SQL: Syntax*.

IDS

For information about how to create and use complex data types, see the *Informix Guide to Database Design and Implementation*.

For information about how to create user-defined data types, see *Extending Informix Dynamic Server 2000*. ♦

All Informix database servers support the data types that Figure 2-2 lists. This chapter describes each of these data types.

Figure 2-2
Data Types That All Informix Database Servers Support

Data Type	Explanation	Page
BYTE	Stores any kind of binary data	2-12
CHAR(*n*)	Stores single-byte or multibyte sequences of characters, including letters, numbers, and symbols; collation is code-set dependent	2-13
CHARACTER(*n*)	Is a synonym for CHAR	2-14

(1 of 3)

Data Type	Explanation	Page
CHARACTER VARYING(*m,r*)	Stores single-byte and multibyte sequences of characters, including letters, numbers, and symbols of varying length (ANSI compliant); collation is code-set dependent	2-15
DATE	Stores calendar date	2-16
DATETIME	Stores calendar date combined with time of day	2-17
DEC	Is a synonym for DECIMAL	2-21
DECIMAL	Stores numbers with definable scale and precision	2-21
DOUBLE PRECISION	Behaves the same way as FLOAT	2-24
FLOAT(*n*)	Stores double-precision floating-point numbers corresponding to the **double** data type in C	2-24
INT	Is a synonym for INTEGER	2-25
INTEGER	Stores whole numbers from −2,147,483,647 to +2,147,483,647	2-26
INTERVAL	Stores a span of time	2-26
MONEY(*p,s*)	Stores currency amount	2-32
MULTISET(*e*)	Stores a collection (all elements of same element type, *e*) of values; allows duplicate values.	2-33
NCHAR(*n*)	Stores single-byte and multibyte sequences of characters, including letters, numbers, and symbols; collation is locale dependent	2-34
NUMERIC(*p,s*)	Is a synonym for DECIMAL	2-34
NVARCHAR(*m,r*)	Stores single-byte and multibyte sequences of characters, including letters, numbers, and symbols of varying length; collation is locale dependent	2-34
REAL	Is a synonym for SMALLFLOAT	2-35
Row, Named	Stores a named row type	2-36
SERIAL	Stores sequential integers	2-39

(2 of 3)

Data Type	Explanation	Page
SERIAL8	Stores large sequential integers; has same range as INT8	2-40
SMALLFLOAT	Stores single-precision floating-point numbers corresponding to the **float** data type in C	2-43
SMALLINT	Stores whole numbers from −32,767 to +32,767	2-44
TEXT	Stores any kind of text data.	2-44
VARCHAR(*m,r*)	Stores single-byte and multibyte strings of letters, numbers, and symbols of varying length; collation is code-set dependent.	2-46

(3 of 3)

IDS

Dynamic Server also supports the data types that Figure 2-3 lists. This chapter describes each of these data types.

Figure 2-3
Additional Data Types that Dynamic Server Supports

Data Type	Explanation	Page
BLOB	Stores binary data in random-access chunks	2-9
BOOLEAN	Stores Boolean values `true` and `false`	2-11
CLOB	Stores text data in random-access chunks	2-15
Distinct	Is a user-defined data type that is stored in the same way as the source data type on which it is based but has different casts and functions defined over it than those on the source type	2-23
INT8	Stores an 8-byte integer value. These whole numbers can be in the range $-(2^{63}-1)$ to $2^{63}-1$.	2-25
LIST(*e*)	Stores a collection of elements of the same element type, *e*; elements have an implicit order (first, second, and so on); allows duplicate values	2-30
LVARCHAR	Stores variable-length data that can be larger than 255 bytes	2-31

(1 of 2)

Data Type	Explanation	Page
MULTISET(*e*)	Stores a collection of elements of the same element type, *e*; allows duplicate values.	2-33
Opaque	Stores a user-defined data type whose internal structure is inaccessible to the database server	2-35
Row, Named	Stores a named row type	2-36
Row, Unnamed	Stores an unnamed row type	2-37
SERIAL8	Stores large sequential integers; has same range as INT8	2-40
SET(*e*)	Stores a collection of elements of the same element type, *e*; does not allow duplicate values	2-42

(2 of 2)

♦

For information about Informix internal data types that SQL statements support (IMPEX, IMPEXBIN, and SENDRECV), see *Extending Informix Dynamic Server 2000*.

Description of Data Types

This section describes the data types that Informix database servers support.

IDS

BLOB

The BLOB data type stores any kind of binary data in random-access chunks, called sbspaces. Binary data typically consists of saved spreadsheets, program-load modules, digitized voice patterns, and so on. The database server performs no interpretation on the contents of a BLOB column. A BLOB column can be up to 4 terabytes in length.

The term *smart large object* refers to BLOB and CLOB data types. Use the CLOB data type (see page 2-15) for random access to text data. For general information about BLOB and CLOB data types, see "Smart Large Objects" on page 2-50.

You can use the following SQL functions to perform some operations on a BLOB column:

- **FILETOBLOB** copies a file into a BLOB column.
- **LOTOFILE** copies a BLOB (or CLOB) value into an operating-system file.
- **LOCOPY** copies an existing smart large object to a new smart large object.

For more information on these SQL functions, see the *Informix Guide to SQL: Syntax*.

No casts exist for BLOB data. Therefore, the database server cannot convert data of type BLOB to any other data type. Within SQL, you are limited to the equality (=) comparison operation for BLOB data. To perform additional operations, you must use one of the application programming interfaces (APIs) from within your client application.

You can insert data into BLOB columns in the following ways:

- With the **dbload** or **onload** utilities
- With the LOAD statement (DB-Access)
- With the **FILETOBLOB** function
- From BLOB (**ifx_lo_t**) host variables (Informix ESQL/C)

If you select a BLOB column using DB-Access, only the phrase *SBlob value* is returned; no actual value is displayed.

IDS

BOOLEAN

The BOOLEAN data type stores single-byte true/false type data. The following table gives internal and literal representations of the BOOLEAN data type.

BOOLEAN Value	Internal Representation	Literal Representation
TRUE	\0	't'
FALSE	\1	'f'
NULL	Internal Use Only	NULL

You can compare two BOOLEAN values to determine whether they are equal or not equal. You can also compare a BOOLEAN value to the Boolean literals 't' and 'f'. BOOLEAN values are case insensitive; 't' is equivalent to 'T' and 'f' to 'F'.

You can use a BOOLEAN column to capture the results of an expression. In the following example, the value of **boolean_column** is 't' if **column1** is less than **column2**, 'f' if **column1** is greater than or equal to **column2**, and null if the value of either **column1** or **column2** is unknown:

```
UPDATE my_table SET boolean_column = (column1 < column2)
```

BYTE

The BYTE data type stores any kind of binary data in an undifferentiated byte stream. Binary data typically consists of saved spreadsheets, program load modules, digitized voice patterns, and so on.

The term *simple large object* is used to refer to BYTE and TEXT data types.

The BYTE data type has no maximum size. A BYTE column has a theoretical limit of 2^{31} bytes and a practical limit that your disk capacity determines.

You can store, retrieve, update, or delete the contents of a BYTE column. However, you cannot use BYTE data items in arithmetic or string operations or assign literals to BYTE items with the SET clause of the UPDATE statement. You also cannot use BYTE items in any of the following ways:

- With aggregate functions
- With the IN clause
- With the MATCHES or LIKE clauses
- With the GROUP BY clause
- With the ORDER BY clause

You can use BYTE objects in a Boolean expression only if you are testing for null values.

You can insert data into BYTE columns in the following ways:

- With the **dbload** or **onload** utilities
- With the LOAD statement (DB-Access)
- From BYTE host variables (Informix ESQL/C)

You cannot use a quoted text string, number, or any other actual value to insert or update BYTE columns.

When you select a BYTE column, you can choose to receive all or part of it. To retrieve it all, use the regular syntax for selecting a column. You can also select any part of a BYTE column by using subscripts, as the following example shows:

```
SELECT cat_picture [1,75] FROM catalog WHERE catalog_num = 10001
```

This statement reads the first 75 bytes of the **cat_picture** column associated with the catalog number 10001.

The database server provides a cast to convert BYTE values to BLOB values. For more information, see the *Informix Guide to Database Design and Implementation*.

If you select a BYTE column using the DB-Access Interactive Schema Editor, only the phrase "BYTE value" is returned; no actual value is displayed.

Important: *If you try to return a BYTE column from a subquery, you get an error message even when the BYTE column is not used in a comparison condition or with the IN predicate.*

CHAR(*n*)

The CHAR data type stores any sequence of letters, numbers, and symbols. It can store single-byte and multibyte characters, based on what the chosen locale supports. For more information on multibyte CHARS, see "Multibyte Characters with CHAR" on page 2-14.

A character column has a maximum length n bytes, where $1 \le n \le 32,767$. If you do not specify n, CHAR(1) is assumed. Character columns typically store names, addresses, phone numbers, and so on.

Because the length of this column is fixed, when a character value is retrieved or stored, exactly n bytes of data are transferred. If the character string is shorter than n bytes, the string is extended with spaces to make up the length. If the string value is longer than n bytes, the string is truncated, without the database server raising an exception.

Treating CHAR Values as Numeric Values

If you plan to perform calculations on numbers stored in a column, you should assign a number data type to that column. Although you can store numbers in CHAR columns, you might not be able to use them in some arithmetic operations. For example, if you insert the sum of values into a character column, you might experience overflow problems if the character column is too small to hold the value. In this case, the insert fails. However, numbers that have leading zeros (such as some zip codes) have the zeros stripped if they are stored as number types INTEGER or SMALLINT. Instead, store these numbers in CHAR columns.

CHAR values are compared to other CHAR values by taking the shorter value and padding it on the right with spaces until the values have equal length. Then the two values are compared for the full length. Comparisons use the code-set collation order.

Nonprintable Characters with CHAR

A CHAR value can include tabs, spaces, and other nonprintable characters. However, you must use an application to insert the nonprintable characters into host variables and to insert the host variables into your database. After passing nonprintable characters to the database server, you can store or retrieve the characters. When you select nonprintable characters, fetch them into host variables and display them with your own display mechanism.

The only nonprintable character that you can enter and display with DB-Access is a tab. If you try to display other nonprintable characters with DB-Access, your screen returns inconsistent results.

GLS

Collating CHAR Data

The collation order of the CHAR data type depends on the code set. That is, this data is sorted by the order of characters as they appear in the code set. For more information, see the *Informix Guide to GLS Functionality*.

GLS

Multibyte Characters with CHAR

The database locale must support the multibyte characters that a database uses. If you are storing multibyte characters, make sure to calculate the number of bytes needed. For more information on multibyte characters and locales, see the *Informix Guide to GLS Functionality*.

CHARACTER(*n*)

The CHARACTER data type is a synonym for CHAR.

CHARACTER VARYING(*m,r*)

The CHARACTER VARYING data type stores any multibyte string of letters, numbers, and symbols of varying length, where *m* is the maximum size of the column and *r* is the minimum amount of space reserved for that column.

The CHARACTER VARYING data type complies with ANSI standards; the non-ANSI Informix VARCHAR data type supports the same functionality. See the description of the VARCHAR data type on page 2-46.

IDS

CLOB

The CLOB data type stores any kind of text data in random-access chunks, called sbspaces. Text data can include text-formatting information as long as this information is also textual, such as PostScript, Hypertext Markup Language (HTML), or Standard Graphic Markup Language (SGML) data.

The term *smart large object* refers to CLOB and BLOB data types. The CLOB data type includes special operations for character strings that are inappropriate for BLOB values. A CLOB column can be up to 4 terabytes in length.

Use the BLOB data type (see page 2-9) for random access to binary data. For general information about the CLOB and BLOB data types, see "Smart Large Objects" on page 2-50.

You can use the following SQL functions to perform some operations on a CLOB column:

- **FILETOCLOB** copies a file into a CLOB column.
- **LOTOFILE** copies a CLOB (or BLOB) value into an operating-system file.
- **LOCOPY** copies an existing smart large object to a new smart large object.

For more information on these SQL functions, see the *Informix Guide to SQL: Syntax*.

No casts exist for CLOB data. Therefore, the database server cannot convert data of the CLOB type to any other data type. Within SQL, you are limited to the equality (=) comparison operation for CLOB data. To perform additional operations, you must use one of the application programming interfaces from within your client application.

Multibyte Characters with CLOB

You can insert data into CLOB columns in the following ways:

- With the **dbload** or **onload** utilities
- With the LOAD statement (DB-Access)
- From CLOB (**ifx_lo_t**) host variables (Informix ESQL/C)

For more information and examples for using the CLOB data type, see the *Informix Guide to SQL: Tutorial* and the *Informix Guide to Database Design and Implementation*.

GLS

With GLS, the following rules apply:

- Multibyte CLOB characters must be supported by the database locale.
- The CLOB data type is collated in code-set order.
- For CLOB columns, the database server handles any required code-set conversions for the data.

For more information on database locales, collation order, and codeset conversion, see the *Informix Guide to GLS Functionality*. ◆

DATE

The DATE data type stores the calendar date. DATE data types require 4 bytes. A calendar date is stored internally as an integer value equal to the number of days since December 31, 1899.

Because DATE values are stored as integers, you can use them in arithmetic expressions. For example, you can subtract a DATE value from another DATE value. The result, a positive or negative INTEGER value, indicates the number of days that elapsed between the two dates.

The following example shows the default display format of a DATE column:

mm/dd/yyyy

In this example, *mm* is the month (1-12), *dd* is the day of the month (1-31), and *yyyy* is the year (0001-9999). For the month, Informix products accept a number value 1 or 01 for January, and so on. For the day, Informix products accept a value 1 or 01 that corresponds to the first day of the month, and so on.

If you enter only a two-digit value for the year, how Informix products fill in the century digits depends on how you set the **DBCENTURY** environment variable. For example, if you enter the year value as 99, whether that year value is interpreted as 1999 or 2099 depends on the setting of your **DBCENTURY** environment variable. If you do not set the **DBCENTURY** environment variable, then your Informix products consider the present century as the default. For information on how to set the **DBCENTURY** environment variable, refer to page 3-32.

GLS

If you specify a locale other than the default locale, you can display culture-specific formats for dates. The locales and the **GL_DATE** and **DBDATE** environment variables affect the display formatting of DATE values. They do not affect the internal format used in a DATE column of a database. To change the default DATE format, set the **DBDATE** or **GL_DATE** environment variable. GLS functionality permits the display of international DATE formats. For more information, see the *Informix Guide to GLS Functionality.* ♦

DATETIME

The DATETIME data type stores an instant in time expressed as a calendar date and time of day. You choose how precisely a DATETIME value is stored; its precision can range from a year to a fraction of a second.

The DATETIME data type is composed of a contiguous sequence of fields that represents each component of time that you want to record and uses the following syntax:

```
DATETIME largest_qualifier TO smallest_qualifier
```

The *largest_qualifier* and *smallest_qualifier* can be any one of the fields that Figure 2-4 on page 2-18 lists.

Figure 2-4
DATETIME Field Qualifiers

Qualifier Field	Valid Entries
YEAR	A year numbered from 1 to 9,999 (A.D.)
MONTH	A month numbered from 1 to 12
DAY	A day numbered from 1 to 31, as appropriate to the month
HOUR	An hour numbered from 0 (midnight) to 23
MINUTE	A minute numbered from 0 to 59
SECOND	A second numbered from 0 to 59
FRACTION	A decimal fraction of a second with up to 5 digits of precision. The default precision is 3 digits (a thousandth of a second). To indicate explicitly other precisions, write FRACTION(n), where n is the desired number of digits from 1 to 5.

A DATETIME column does not need to include all fields from YEAR to FRACTION; it can include a subset of fields or even a single field. For example, you can enter a value of MONTH TO HOUR in a column that is defined as YEAR TO MINUTE, as long as each entered value contains information for a contiguous sequence of fields. You cannot, however, define a column for just MONTH and HOUR; this entry must also include a value for DAY.

If you use the DB-Access TABLE menu, and you do not specify the DATETIME qualifiers, the default DATETIME qualifier, YEAR TO YEAR, is assigned.

A valid DATETIME literal must include the DATETIME keyword, the values to be entered, and the field qualifiers. You must include these qualifiers because, as noted earlier, the value you enter can contain fewer fields than defined for that column. Acceptable qualifiers for the first and last fields are identical to the list of valid DATETIME fields that Figure 2-4 lists.

Write values for the field qualifiers as integers and separate them with delimiters. Figure 2-5 lists the delimiters that are used with DATETIME values in the U.S. ASCII English locale.

Figure 2-5
Delimiters Used with DATETIME

Delimiter	Placement in DATETIME Expression
Hyphen	Between the YEAR, MONTH, and DAY portions of the value
Space	Between the DAY and HOUR portions of the value
Colon	Between the HOUR and MINUTE and the MINUTE and SECOND portions of the value
Decimal point	Between the SECOND and FRACTION portions of the value

Figure 2-6 shows a DATETIME YEAR TO FRACTION(3) value with delimiters.

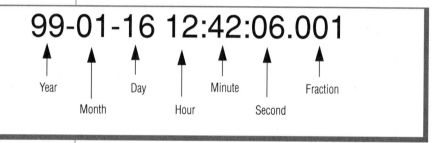

Figure 2-6
*Example DATETIME
Value with
Delimiters*

When you enter a value with fewer fields than the defined column, the value that you enter is expanded automatically to fill all the defined fields. If you leave out any more significant fields, that is, fields of larger magnitude than any value that you supply, those fields are filled automatically with the current date. If you leave out any less-significant fields, those fields are filled with zeros (or a 1 for MONTH and DAY) in your entry.

You can also enter DATETIME values as character strings. However, the character string must include information for each field defined in the DATETIME column. The INSERT statement in the following example shows a DATETIME value entered as a character string:

```
INSERT into cust_calls (customer_num, call_dtime, user_id,
    call_code, call_descr)
  VALUES (101, '1999-01-14 08:45', 'maryj', 'D',
    'Order late - placed 6/1/98')
```

In this example, the **call_dtime** column is defined as DATETIME YEAR TO MINUTE. This character string must include values for the year, month, day, hour, and minute fields. If the character string does not contain information for all defined fields (or adds additional fields), the database server returns an error.

All fields of a DATETIME column are two-digit numbers except for the year and fraction fields. The year field is stored as four digits. When you enter a two-digit value in the year field, how the century digits are filled in and interpreted depends on the value that you assign to the **DBCENTURY** environment variable.

For example, if you enter 99 as the year value, whether the year is interpreted as 1999 or 2099 depends on the setting of the **DBCENTURY** environment variable. If you do not set the **DBCENTURY** environment variable, then your Informix products consider the present century to be the default. For information on how to set and use the **DBCENTURY** environment variable, see page 3-32.

The fraction field requires n digits where $1 \leq n \leq 5$, rounded up to an even number. You can use the following formula (rounded up to a whole number of bytes) to calculate the number of bytes that a DATETIME value requires:

```
total number of digits for all fields/2 + 1
```

For example, a YEAR TO DAY qualifier requires a total of eight digits (four for year, two for month, and two for day). This data value requires 5, or (8/2) + 1, bytes of storage.

For information on how to use DATETIME data in arithmetic and relational expressions, see "Manipulating DATE with DATETIME and INTERVAL Values" on page 2-55. For more information on the DATETIME data type, see the *Informix Guide to SQL: Syntax* and the *Informix Guide to GLS Functionality*.

GLS

If you specify a locale other than U.S. ASCII English, the locale defines the culture-specific display formats for DATETIME values. To change the default display format, change the setting of the **GL_DATETIME** environment variable.

With an ESQL API, the **DBTIME** environment variable also affects DATETIME formatting. Locales and the **GL_DATE** and **DBDATE** environment variables affect the display of datetime data. They do not affect the internal format used in a DATETIME column.

For information on how the USEOSTIME configuration parameter can affect the subsecond granularity when the database server obtains the current time from the operating system for SQL statements, see the *Administrator's Reference*.

For more information on **DBTIME**, see page 3-53. For more information on locales and GLS environment variables, see the *Informix Guide to GLS Functionality*. ♦

DEC

The DEC data type is a synonym for DECIMAL.

DECIMAL

The DECIMAL data type can take two forms: DECIMAL(p) floating point and DECIMAL(p,s) fixed point. In an ANSI-compliant database, all DECIMAL numbers are fixed point.

DECIMAL Floating Point

The DECIMAL data type stores decimal floating-point numbers up to a maximum of 32 significant digits, where p is the total number of significant digits (the *precision*). Specifying precision is optional. If you do not specify the precision (p), DECIMAL is treated as DECIMAL(16), a floating decimal with a precision of 16 places. DECIMAL(p) has an absolute exponent range between 10^{-130} and 10^{124}.

If you use an ANSI-compliant database and specify DECIMAL(p), the value defaults to DECIMAL(p, 0). For more information about fixed-point decimal values, see the following discussion.

DECIMAL Fixed Point

In fixed-point numbers, DECIMAL(p,s), the decimal point is fixed at a specific place, regardless of the value of the number. When you specify a column of this type, you write its precision (p) as the total number of digits that it can store, from 1 to 32. You write its *scale* (s) as the total number of digits that fall to the right of the decimal point.

All numbers with an absolute value less than $0.5 * 10^{-s}$ have the value zero. The largest absolute value of a variable of this type that you can store without an error is $10^{p-s} - 10^{-s}$. A DECIMAL data type column typically stores numbers with fractional parts that must be stored and displayed exactly (for example, rates or percentages). In an ANSI-compliant database, all DECIMAL numbers must be in the range 10^{-32} to 10^{+31}.

DECIMAL Storage

The database server uses 1 byte of disk storage to store two digits of a decimal number. The database server uses an additional byte to store the exponent and sign. The significant digits to the left of the decimal and the significant digits to the right of the decimal are stored on separate groups of bytes. The way the database server stores decimal numbers is best illustrated with an example.

If you specify DECIMAL(6,3), the data type consists of three significant digits to the left of the decimal and three significant digits to the right of the decimal (for instance, 123.456). The three digits to the left of the decimal are stored on 2 bytes (where one of the bytes only holds a single digit) and the three digits to the right of the decimal are stored on another 2 bytes, as Figure 2-7 illustrates. (The exponent byte is not shown.) With the additional byte required for the exponent and sign, this data type requires a total of 5 bytes of storage.

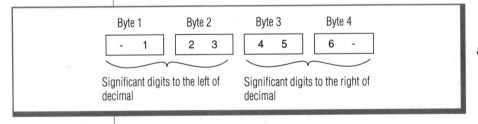

Byte 1   Byte 2   Byte 3   Byte 4

| - | 1 | | 2 | 3 | | 4 | 5 | | 6 | - |

Significant digits to the left of decimal

Significant digits to the right of decimal

Figure 2-7
Schematic That Illustrates the Storage of Digits in a Decimal Value

You can use the following formulas (rounded down to a whole number of bytes) to calculate the byte storage (N) for a decimal data type (N includes the byte required to store the exponent and sign):

```
If the scale is odd:  N = (precision + 4) / 2
If the scale is even: N = (precision + 3) / 2
```

For example, the data type DECIMAL(5,3) requires 4 bytes of storage (9/2 rounded down equals 4).

One caveat to these formulas exists. The maximum number of bytes the database server uses to store a decimal value is 17. One byte is used to store the exponent and sign leaving 16 bytes to store up to 32 digits of precision. If you specify a precision of 32 and an *odd* scale, however, you lose 1 digit of precision. Consider, for example, the data type DECIMAL(32,31). This decimal is defined as 1 digit to the left of the decimal and 31 digits to the right. The 1 digit to the left of the decimal requires 1 byte of storage. This leaves only 15 bytes of storage for the digits to the right of the decimal. The 15 bytes can accommodate only 30 digits, so 1 digit of precision is lost.

IDS

Distinct

A distinct type is a data type that is based on one of the following source types:

- A built-in type
- An existing distinct type
- An existing named row type
- An existing opaque type

A distinct type inherits the casts and functions of its source types as well as the length and alignment on the disk. A distinct type thus makes efficient use of the pre-existing functionality of the database server.

When you create a distinct data type, the database server automatically creates two explicit casts: one cast from the distinct type to its source type and one cast from the source type to the distinct type. A distinct type of a built-in type does not inherit the built-in casts that are provided for the built-in type. However, a distinct type does inherit any user-defined casts that have been defined on the source type.

A distinct type and a source type cannot be compared directly. To compare a distinct type and its source type, you must explicitly cast one type to the other.

You must define a distinct type in the database. Definitions for distinct types are stored in the **sysxtdtypes** system catalog table.

The following SQL statements maintain the definitions of distinct types in the database:

- The CREATE DISTINCT TYPE statement adds a distinct type to the database.
- The DROP TYPE statement removes a previously defined distinct type from the database.

For more information on the SQL statements mentioned above, see the *Informix Guide to SQL: Syntax*. For information about casting distinct data types, see "Casts for Distinct Types" on page 2-69. For examples that show how to create and register cast functions for a distinct type, see the *Informix Guide to Database Design and Implementation*.

DOUBLE PRECISION

Columns defined as DOUBLE PRECISION behave the same as those defined as FLOAT.

FLOAT(*n*)

The FLOAT data type stores double-precision floating-point numbers with up to 16 significant digits. FLOAT corresponds to the **double** data type in C. The range of values for the FLOAT data type is the same as the range of values for the C **double** data type on your computer.

You can use *n* to specify the precision of a FLOAT data type, but SQL ignores the precision. The value *n* must be a whole number between 1 and 14.

A column with the FLOAT data type typically stores scientific numbers that can be calculated only approximately. Because floating-point numbers retain only their most significant digits, the number that you enter in this type of column and the number the database server displays can differ slightly.

The difference between the two values depends on how your computer stores floating-point numbers internally. For example, you might enter a value of 1.1000001 into a FLOAT field and, after processing the SQL statement, the database server might display this value as 1.1. This situation occurs when a value has more digits than the floating-point number can store. In this case, the value is stored in its approximate form with the least significant digits treated as zeros.

FLOAT data types usually require 8 bytes per value.

Conversion of a FLOAT value to a DECIMAL value results in 17 digits of precision.

INT

The INT data type is a synonym for INTEGER.

INT8

IDS

The INT8 data type stores whole numbers that range from -9,223,372,036,854,775,807 to 9,223,372,036,854,775,807 [or $-(2^{63}-1)$ to $2^{63}-1$]. The maximum negative number (-9,223,372,036,854,775,808) is a reserved value and cannot be used. The INT8 data type is typically used to store large counts, quantities, and so on.

The way that the database server stores the INT8 data is platform dependent. On 64-bit platforms, INT8 is stored as a signed binary integer; the data type requires 8 bytes per value. On 32-bit platforms, the database server uses an internal format that consists of several integer values; the data type can require 10 bytes.

Arithmetic operations and sort comparisons are performed more efficiently on integer data than on float or decimal data. However, INT8 columns can store only a limited range of values. If the data value exceeds the numeric range, the database server does not store the value.

INTEGER

The INTEGER data type stores whole numbers that range from –2,147,483,647 to 2,147,483,647. The maximum negative number, –2,147,483,648, is a reserved value and cannot be used. The INTEGER data type is stored as a signed binary integer and is typically used to store counts, quantities, and so on.

Arithmetic operations and sort comparisons are performed more efficiently on integer data than on float or decimal data. However, INTEGER columns can store only a limited range of values. If the data value exceeds the numeric range, the database server does not store the value.

INTEGER data types require 4 bytes per value.

INTERVAL

The INTERVAL data type stores a value that represents a span of time. INTERVAL types are divided into two classes: *year-month intervals* and *day-time intervals*. A year-month interval can represent a span of years and months, and a day-time interval can represent a span of days, hours, minutes, seconds, and fractions of a second.

An INTERVAL value is always composed of one value, or a contiguous sequence of values, that represents a component of time. The following example defines an INTERVAL data type:

```
INTERVAL largest_qualifier(n) TO smallest_qualifier(n)
```

In this example, the *largest_qualifier* and *smallest_qualifier* fields are taken from one of the two INTERVAL classes, as Figure 2-8 shows, and *n* optionally specifies the precision of the largest field (and smallest field if it is a FRACTION).

Figure 2-8
Interval Classes

Interval Class	Qualifier Field	Valid Entry
YEAR-MONTH INTERVAL	YEAR	A number of years
	MONTH	A number of months
DAY-TIME INTERVAL	DAY	A number of days
	HOUR	A number of hours
	MINUTE	A number of minutes
	SECOND	A number of seconds
	FRACTION	A decimal fraction of a second, with up to 5 digits of precision. The default precision is 3 digits (thousandth of a second). To indicate explicitly other precisions, write FRACTION(n), where n is the desired number of digits from 1 to 5.

As with a DATETIME column, you can define an INTERVAL column to include a subset of the fields that you need; however, because the INTERVAL data type represents a span of time that is independent of an actual date, you cannot combine the two INTERVAL classes. For example, because the number of days in a month depends on which month it is, a single INTERVAL data value cannot combine months and days.

A value entered into an INTERVAL column need not include all fields contained in the column. For example, you can enter a value of HOUR TO SECOND into a column defined as DAY TO SECOND. However, a value must always consist of a contiguous sequence of fields. In the previous example, you cannot enter just HOUR and SECOND values; you must also include MINUTE values.

A valid INTERVAL literal contains the INTERVAL keyword, the values to be entered, and the field qualifiers. (See the discussion of the Literal Interval in the *Informix Guide to SQL: Syntax*.) When a value contains only one field, the largest and smallest fields are the same.

When you enter a value in an INTERVAL column, you must specify the largest and smallest fields in the value, just as you do for DATETIME values. In addition, you can use *n* optionally to specify the precision of the first field (and the last field if it is a FRACTION). If the largest and smallest field qualifiers are both FRACTIONS, you can specify only the precision in the last field. Acceptable qualifiers for the largest and smallest fields are identical to the list of INTERVAL fields that Figure 2-8 displays.

If you use the DB-Access TABLE menu, and you do not specify the INTERVAL field qualifiers, the default INTERVAL qualifier, YEAR TO YEAR, is assigned.

The *largest_qualifier* in an INTERVAL value can be up to nine digits (except for FRACTION, which cannot be more than five digits), but if the value that you want to enter is greater than the default number of digits allowed for that field, you must explicitly identify the number of significant digits in the value that you enter. For example, to define an INTERVAL of DAY TO HOUR that can store up to 999 days, you could specify it the following way:

```
INTERVAL DAY(3) TO HOUR
```

INTERVAL values use the same delimiters as DATETIME values. Figure 2-9 shows the delimiters.

Figure 2-9
INTERVAL Delimiters

Delimiter	Placement in DATETIME Expression
Hyphen	Between the YEAR and MONTH portions of the value
Space	Between the DAY and HOUR portions of the value
Colon	Between the HOUR and MINUTE and the MINUTE and SECOND portions of the value
Decimal point	Between the SECOND and FRACTION portions of the value

You can also enter INTERVAL values as character strings. However, the character string must include information for the identical sequence of fields defined for that column. The INSERT statement in the following example shows an INTERVAL value entered as a character string:

```
INSERT INTO manufact (manu_code, manu_name, lead_time)
      VALUES ('BRO', 'Ball-Racquet Originals', '160')
```

Because the **lead_time** column is defined as INTERVAL DAY(3) TO DAY, this INTERVAL value requires only one field, the span of days required for lead time. If the character string does not contain information for all fields (or adds additional fields), the database server returns an error. For more information on entering INTERVAL values as character strings, see the *Informix Guide to SQL: Syntax*.

By default, all fields of an INTERVAL column are two-digit numbers except for the year and fraction fields. The year field is stored as four digits. The fraction field requires n digits where $1 \le n \le 5$, rounded up to an even number. You can use the following formula (rounded up to a whole number of bytes) to calculate the number of bytes required for an INTERVAL value:

```
total number of digits for all fields/2 + 1
```

For example, a YEAR TO MONTH qualifier requires a total of six digits (four for year and two for month). This data value requires 4, or (6/2) + 1, bytes of storage.

For information on using INTERVAL data in arithmetic and relational operations, see "Manipulating DATE with DATETIME and INTERVAL Values" on page 2-55. For information on using INTERVAL as a constant expression, see the description of the INTERVAL Field Qualifier in the *Informix Guide to SQL: Syntax.*

IDS

LIST(*e*)

The LIST data type is a collection type that stores ordered, nonunique elements; that is it allows duplicate element values. The elements of a LIST have ordinal positions; with a first, second, and third element in a LIST. (For a collection type with no ordinal positions, see the MULTISET data type on page 2-33 and the SET data type on page 2-42.)

By default, the database server inserts LIST elements at the end of the list. To support the ordinal position of a LIST, the INSERT statement provides the AT clause. This clause allows you to specify the position at which you want to insert a list-element value. For more information, see the INSERT statement in the *Informix Guide to SQL: Syntax.*

All elements in a LIST have the same element type. To specify the element type, use the following syntax:

```
LIST(element_type NOT NULL)
```

The *element_type* of a collection can be any of the following types:

- A built-in type, except SERIAL, SERIAL8, BYTE, and TEXT
- A distinct type
- An unnamed or named row type
- Another collection type
- An opaque type

You must specify the NOT NULL constraint for LIST elements. No other constraints are valid for LIST columns. For more information on the syntax of the LIST collection type, see the *Informix Guide to SQL: Syntax.*

You can use LIST anywhere that you would use any other data type, for example:

- After the IN predicate in the WHERE clause of a SELECT statement to search for matching LIST values
- As an argument to the SQL CARDINALITY function to determine the number of elements in a LIST column

You *cannot* use LIST with an aggregate function such as AVG, MAX, MIN, or SUM.

Two lists are equal if they have the same elements in the same order. The following examples are lists but are not equal:

```
LIST{"blue", "green", "yellow"}
LIST{"yellow", "blue", "green"}
```

The above statements are not equal because the values are not in the same order. To be equal, the second statement would have to be:

```
LIST{"blue", "green", "yellow"}
```

LVARCHAR

The LVARCHAR data type is an SQL data type that you can use to create a column of variable-length character data types that are potentially larger than 255 bytes.

The LVARCHAR data type is also used for input and output casts for opaque data types. The LVARCHAR data type stores opaque data types in the string (external) format. Each opaque type has an input support function and cast, which convert it from LVARCHAR to a form that database servers can manipulate. Each opaque type also has an output support function and cast, which convert it from its internal representation to LVARCHAR. ♦

Important: *When LVARCHAR data is stored in a table column, the value is limited to 2 kilobytes (2Kb). When LVARCHAR is used in I/O operations on an opaque type, it has the theoretical size limit of 4 gigabytes (4Gb).*

The LVARCHAR data type supports only a subset of the string operations that you can perform on CHAR and VARCHAR data types.

For more information about LVARCHAR, see *Extending Informix Dynamic Server 2000.*

MONEY(*p,s*)

The MONEY data type stores currency amounts. As with the DECIMAL data type, the MONEY data type stores fixed-point numbers up to a maximum of 32 significant digits, where *p* is the total number of significant digits (the precision) and *s* is the number of digits to the right of the decimal point (the scale).

Unlike the DECIMAL data type, the MONEY data type is always treated as a fixed-point decimal number. The database server defines the data type MONEY(*p*) as DECIMAL(*p*,2). If the precision and scale are not specified, the database server defines a MONEY column as DECIMAL(16,2).

You can use the following formula (rounded down to a whole number of bytes) to calculate the byte storage for a MONEY data type:

```
If the scale is odd:  N = (precision + 4) / 2
If the scale is even: N = (precision + 3) / 2
```

For example, a MONEY data type with a precision of 16 and a scale of 2 (MONEY(16,2)) requires 10 or (16 + 3)/2, bytes of storage.

Client applications format values in MONEY columns with the following currency notation:

- A currency symbol: a dollar sign ($) at the front of the value
- A thousands separator: a comma (,) that separates every three digits of the value
- A decimal point: a period (.)

To change the format for MONEY values, change the **DBMONEY** environment variable. For information on how to set the **DBMONEY** environment variable, see page 3-44.

GLS

The default value that the database server uses for scale is locale-dependent. The default locale specifies a default scale of two. For nondefault locales, if the scale is omitted from the declaration, the database server creates MONEY values with a locale-specific scale.

The currency notation that client applications use is locale-dependent. If you specify a nondefault locale, the client uses a culture-specific format for MONEY values.

For more information on locale dependency, see the *Informix Guide to GLS Functionality.* ♦

MULTISET(*e*)

IDS

The MULTISET data type is a collection type that stores nonunique elements: it allows duplicate element values. The elements in a MULTISET have no ordinal position. That is, there is no concept of a first, second, or third element in a MULTISET. (For a collection type with ordinal positions for elements, see the LIST data type on page 2-30.)

All elements in a MULTISET have the same element type. To specify the element type, use the following syntax:

```
MULTISET(element_type NOT NULL)
```

The *element_type* of a collection can be any of the following types:

- A built-in type, except SERIAL, SERIAL8, BYTE, and TEXT
- An unnamed or a named row type
- Another collection type
- An opaque type

You must specify the NOT NULL constraint for MULTISET elements. No other constraints are valid for MULTISET columns. For more information on the syntax of the MULTISET collection type, see the *Informix Guide to SQL: Syntax.*

You can use MULTISET anywhere that you use any other data type, unless otherwise indicated. For example:

- After the IN predicate in the WHERE clause of a SELECT statement to search for matching MULTISET values
- As an argument to the SQL **CARDINALITY** function to determine the number of elements in a MULTISET column

You *cannot* use MULTISET with an aggregate function such as AVG, MAX, MIN, or SUM.

Two multisets are equal if they have the same elements, even if the elements are in different positions in the set. The following examples are multisets but are not equal:

```
MULTISET {"blue", "green", "yellow"}
MULTISET {"blue", "green", "yellow", "blue"}
```

The following multisets are equal:

```
MULTISET {"blue", "green", "blue", "yellow"}
MULTISET {"blue", "green", "yellow", "blue"}
```

Named Row

See "Row, Named" on page 2-36.

GLS

NCHAR(*n*)

The NCHAR data type stores fixed-length character data. This data can be a sequence of single-byte or multibyte letters, numbers, and symbols. The main difference between CHAR and NCHAR data types is the collation order. While the collation order of the CHAR data type is defined by the code-set order, the collation order of the NCHAR data type depends on the locale-specific localized order. For more information about the NCHAR data type, see the *Informix Guide to GLS Functionality*.

NUMERIC(*p*,*s*)

The NUMERIC data type is a synonym for fixed-point DECIMAL.

GLS

NVARCHAR(*m*,*r*)

The NVARCHAR data type stores character data of varying lengths. This data can be a sequence of single-byte or multibyte letters, numbers, and symbols. The main difference between VARCHAR and NVARCHAR data types is the collation order. While the collation order of the VARCHAR data type is defined by the code-set order, the collation order of the NVARCHAR data type depends on the locale-specific localized order. For more information about the NVARCHAR data type, see the *Informix Guide to GLS Functionality*.

IDS

Opaque

An opaque type is a data type for which you provide the following information to the database server:

- A data structure for how the data is stored on disk
- Support functions to determine how to convert between the disk format and the user format
- Secondary access methods that determine how the index on this data type is built, used, and manipulated
- User functions that use the data type
- A row in a system catalog table to register the opaque type in the database

The internal structure of an opaque type is not visible to the database server. The internal structure can only be accessed through user-defined routines. Definitions for opaque types are stored in the **sysxtdtypes** system catalog table. The following SQL statements maintain the definitions of opaque types in the database:

- The CREATE OPAQUE TYPE statement adds an opaque type to the database.
- The DROP TYPE statement removes a previously defined opaque type from the database.

For more information on the above-mentioned SQL statements, see the *Informix Guide to SQL: Syntax*. For information on how to create opaque types and an example of an opaque type, see *Extending Informix Dynamic Server 2000*.

REAL

The REAL data type is a synonym for SMALLFLOAT.

IDS

Row, Named

A named row type is defined by its name. That name must be unique within the schema. An unnamed row type is a row type that contains fields but has no user-defined name. Use a named row type if you want to use type inheritance. For more information, see "Row Data Types" on page 2-61.

Defining Named Row Types

You must define a named row type in the database. Definitions for named row types are stored in the **sysxtdtypes** system catalog table.

The fields of a row type can be any data type. The fields of a row type that are TEXT or BYTE type can be used in typed tables only. If you want to assign a row type to a column, then the elements of the row cannot be of TEXT and BYTE data types.

In general, the data type of the field of a row type can be any of the following types:

- A built-in type, except for the restriction against TEXT and BYTE mentioned above
- A collection type
- A distinct type
- A row type
- An opaque type

The following SQL statements maintain the definitions of named row types in the database:

- The CREATE ROW TYPE statement adds a named row type to the database.
- The DROP ROW TYPE statement removes a previously defined named row type from the database.

For details about the preceding SQL syntax statements, see the *Informix Guide to SQL: Syntax*. For examples of how to create and used named row types, see the *Informix Guide to Database Design and Implementation*.

Equivalence and Named Row Types

No two named row types can be equal, even if they have identical structures, because they have different names. For example, the following named row types have the same structure but are not equal:

```
name_t (lname CHAR(15), initial CHAR(1) fname CHAR(15))
emp_t (lname CHAR(15), initial CHAR(1) fname CHAR(15))
```

Named Row Types and Inheritance

Named row types can be part of a type-inheritance hierarchy. That is, one named row type can be the parent (supertype) of another named row type. A subtype in a hierarchy inherits all the properties of its supertype. Type inheritance is discussed in the CREATE ROW TYPE statement in the *Informix Guide to SQL: Syntax* and in the *Informix Guide to Database Design and Implementation*.

Typed Tables

Tables that are part of an inheritance hierarchy must be typed tables. Typed tables are tables that have been assigned a named row type. For the syntax you use to create typed tables, see the CREATE TABLE statement in the *Informix Guide to SQL: Syntax*. Table inheritance and how it relates to type inheritance is also discussed in that section. For information about how to create and use typed tables, see the *Informix Guide to Database Design and Implementation*.

IDS

Row, Unnamed

An unnamed row type contains fields but has no user-defined name. An unnamed row type is defined by its structure. Two unnamed row types are equal if they have the same structure. If two unnamed row types have the same number of fields, and if the data type of each field in one row type matches the data type of the corresponding field in the other row type, the two unnamed row types are equal.

For example, the following unnamed row types are equal:

```
ROW (lname char(15), initial char(1) fname char(15))
ROW (dept char(15), rating char(1) name char(15))
```

The following row types are not equivalent, even though they have the same number of fields and the same data types, because the fields are not in the same order:

```
ROW (x integer, y varchar(20), z real)
ROW (x integer, z real, y varchar(20))
```

The data type of the field of an unnamed row type can be any of the following types:

- A built-in type
- A collection type
- A distinct type
- A row type
- An opaque type

Unnamed row types cannot be used in type tables or in type inheritance hierarchies.

For more information on unnamed row types, see the *Informix Guide to SQL: Syntax* and the *Informix Guide to Database Design and Implementation*.

Creating Unnamed Row Types

You can create an unnamed row type in several ways:

- You can declare an unnamed row type using the ROW keyword. Each field in a ROW can have a different field type. To specify the field type, use the following syntax:

  ```
  ROW(field_name field_type, ...)
  ```

  The *field_name* must conform to the rules for SQL identifiers. For more information, see the Identifier segment in the *Informix Guide to SQL: Syntax*.

- You can generate an unnamed row type using ROW as a constructor and a series of values. A corresponding unnamed row type is created, using the default data types of the specified values.

  For example, a declaration of the following row value:

  ```
  ROW(1, 'abc', 5.30)
  ```

  defines this row type:

  ```
  ROW (x INTEGER, y VARCHAR, z DECIMAL)
  ```

- You can create an unnamed row type by an implicit or explicit cast from a named row type or from another unnamed row type.

- The rows of any table (except a table defined on a named row type) are unnamed row types.

Inserting Values into Unnamed Row Type Columns

When you specify field values for an unnamed row type, list the field values after the constructor and between parentheses. For example, suppose you have an unnamed row-type column. The following INSERT statement adds one group of field values to this ROW column:

```
INSERT INTO table1 VALUES (ROW(4, 'abc'))
```

You can specify a ROW column in the IN predicate in the WHERE clause of a SELECT statement to search for matching ROW values. For more information, see the Condition segment in the *Informix Guide to SQL: Syntax*.

SERIAL(*n*)

The SERIAL data type stores a sequential integer assigned automatically by the database server when a row is inserted. You can define only one SERIAL column in a table. For information on inserting values in SERIAL columns, see the *Informix Guide to SQL: Syntax*.

The SERIAL data type is not automatically a unique column. You must apply a unique index or primary key constraint to this column to prevent duplicate serial numbers. If you use the interactive schema editor in DB-Access to define the table, a unique index is applied automatically to a SERIAL column.

Also, serial numbers might not be contiguous due to such factors as multiuser systems and rollbacks.

The default serial starting number is 1, but you can assign an initial value, *n*, when you create or alter the table. You can assign any number greater than 0 as your starting number. The highest serial number that you can assign is 2,147,483,647. If you assign a number greater than 2,147,483,647, you receive a syntax error.

Once a nonzero number is assigned, it cannot be changed. You can, however, insert a value in a SERIAL column (using the INSERT statement) or reset the serial value *n* (using the ALTER TABLE statement), as long as that value does not duplicate any existing values in the table. When you insert a number in a SERIAL column or reset the next value of a SERIAL column, your database server assigns the next number in sequence to the number entered. However, if you reset the next value of a SERIAL column to a value that is less than the values already in that column, the next value is computed with the following formula:

```
maximum existing value in SERIAL column + 1
```

For example, if you reset the serial value of the **customer_num** column in the **customer** table to 50 and the highest-assigned customer number is 128, the next customer number assigned is 129.

A SERIAL data column is commonly used to store unique numeric codes (for example, order, invoice, or customer numbers). SERIAL data values require 4 bytes of storage.

SERIAL8

IDS

The SERIAL8 data type stores a sequential integer assigned automatically by the database server when a row is inserted. (For more information on how to insert values into SERIAL8 columns, see the *Informix Guide to SQL: Syntax*.)

A SERIAL8 data column is commonly used to store large, unique numeric codes (for example, order, invoice, or customer numbers). SERIAL8 data values require 8 bytes of storage. The following restrictions apply to SERIAL8 columns:

- You can define only one SERIAL8 column in a table.

  However, a table can have one SERIAL8 and one SERIAL column.

- The SERIAL8 data type is not automatically a unique column.

  You must apply a unique index to this column to prevent duplicate SERIAL8 numbers.

- The SERIAL8 data type does not allow a null value.

If you are using the interactive schema editor in DB-Access to define the table, a unique index is applied automatically to a SERIAL8 column.

Assigning a Starting Value for SERIAL8

The default serial starting number is 1, but you can assign an initial value, *n*, when you create or alter the table. To start the values at 1 in a serial column of a table, give the value 0 for the SERIAL8 column when you insert rows into that table. The database server will assign the value 1 to the serial column of the first row of the table. The highest serial number you can assign is 2^{63}-1 (9,223,372,036,854,775,807). If you assign a number greater than this value, you receive a syntax error. When the database server generates a SERIAL8 value of this maximum number, it wraps around and starts generating values beginning at 1.

Once a nonzero number is assigned, it cannot be changed. You can, however, insert a value into a SERIAL8 column (using the INSERT statement) or reset the serial value *n* (using the ALTER TABLE statement), as long as that value does not duplicate any existing values in the table.

When you insert a number into a SERIAL8 column or reset the next value of a SERIAL8 column, your database server assigns the next number in sequence to the number entered. However, if you reset the next value of a SERIAL8 column to a value that is less than the values already in that column, the next value is computed using the following formula:

```
maximum existing value in SERIAL8 column + 1
```

For example, if you reset the serial value of the **customer_num** column in the **customer** table to 50 and the highest-assigned customer number is 128, the next customer number assigned is 129.

Using SERIAL8 with INT8

The database server treats the SERIAL8 data type as a special case of the INT8 data type. Therefore, all the arithmetic operators that are legal for INT8 (such as +, −, *, and /) and all the SQL functions that are legal for INT8 (such as ABS, MOD, POW, and so on) are also legal for SERIAL8 values. All data conversion rules that apply to INT8 also apply to SERIAL8.

The value of a SERIAL8 column of a table can be stored in the columns of another table. However, when the values of the SERIAL8 column are put into the second table, their values lose the constraints imposed by their original SERIAL8 column and they are stored as INT8 values.

IDS

SET(*e*)

The SET data type is a collection type that stores unique elements; it does not allow duplicate element values. (For a collection type that does allow duplicate values, see the description of MULTISET on page 2-33.)

The elements in a SET have no ordinal position. That is, no concept of a first, second, or third element in a SET exists. (For a collection type with ordinal positions for elements, see the LIST data type on page 2-30.)

All elements in a SET have the same element type. To specify the element type, use the following syntax:

```
SET(element_type NOT NULL)
```

The *element_type* of a collection can be any of the following types:

- A built-in type, except SERIAL, SERIAL8, BYTE, and TEXT
- A named or unnamed row type
- Another collection type
- An opaque type

You must specify the NOT NULL constraint for SET elements. No other constraints are valid for SET columns. For more information on the syntax of the SET collection type, see the *Informix Guide to SQL: Syntax*.

You can use SET anywhere that you use any other data type, unless otherwise indicated. For example:

- After the IN predicate in the WHERE clause of a SELECT statement to search for matching SET values
- As an argument to the SQL CARDINALITY function to determine the number of elements in a SET column

For more information, see the Condition and Expression segments in the *Informix Guide to SQL: Syntax*.

You *cannot* use the SET column with an aggregate function such as AVG, MAX, MIN, or SUM.

The following examples declare two sets. The first example declares a set of integers and the second declares a set of character elements.

```
SET(INTEGER NOT NULL)
SET(CHAR(20) NOT NULL)
```

The following examples construct the same sets from value lists:

```
SET{1, 5, 13}
SET{"Oakland", "Menlo Park", "Portland", "Lenexa"}
```

In the following example, a SET constructor is part of a CREATE TABLE statement:

```
CREATE TABLE tab
(
    c CHAR(5),
    s SET(INTEGER NOT NULL)
);
```

The following sets are equal:

```
SET{"blue", "green", "yellow"}
SET{"yellow", "blue", "green"}
```

SMALLFLOAT

The SMALLFLOAT data type stores single-precision floating-point numbers with approximately eight significant digits. SMALLFLOAT corresponds to the **float** data type in C. The range of values for a SMALLFLOAT data type is the same as the range of values for the C **float** data type on your computer.

A SMALLFLOAT data type column typically stores scientific numbers that can be calculated only approximately. Because floating-point numbers retain only their most significant digits, the number that you enter in this type of column and the number the database displays might differ slightly depending on how your computer stores floating-point numbers internally.

For example, you might enter a value of 1.1000001 in a SMALLFLOAT field and, after processing the SQL statement, the application development tool might display this value as 1.1. This difference occurs when a value has more digits than the floating-point number can store. In this case, the value is stored in its approximate form with the least significant digits treated as zeros.

SMALLFLOAT data types usually require 4 bytes per value.

Conversion of a SMALLFLOAT value to a DECIMAL value results in 9 digits of precision.

SMALLINT

The SMALLINT data type stores small whole numbers that range from −32,767 to 32,767. The maximum negative number, −32,768, is a reserved value and cannot be used. The SMALLINT value is stored as a signed binary integer.

Integer columns typically store counts, quantities, and so on. Because the SMALLINT data type takes up only 2 bytes per value, arithmetic operations are performed efficiently. However, this data type stores a limited range of values. If the values exceed the range between the minimum and maximum numbers, the database server does not store the value and provides you with an error message.

TEXT

The TEXT data type stores any kind of text data. It can contain both single and multibyte characters.

The TEXT data type has no maximum size. A TEXT column has a theoretical limit of 2^{31} bytes and a practical limit that your available disk storage determines.

The term *simple large object* is used to refer to TEXT and BYTE data types.

TEXT columns typically store memos, manual chapters, business documents, program source files, and so on. In the default locale U.S. ASCII English, data object of type TEXT can contain a combination of printable ASCII characters and the following control characters:

- Tabs (CTRL-I)
- New lines (CTRL-J)
- New pages (CTRL-L)

You can store, retrieve, update, or delete the contents of a TEXT column. However, you cannot use TEXT data items in arithmetic or string operations or assign literals to TEXT items with the SET clause of the UPDATE statement. You also cannot use TEXT items in the following ways:

- With aggregate functions
- With the IN clause
- With the MATCHES or LIKE clauses
- With the GROUP BY clause
- With the ORDER BY clause

You can use TEXT objects in Boolean expressions only if you are testing for null values.

You can insert data in TEXT columns in the following ways:

- With the **dbload** or **onload** utilities
- With the LOAD statement (DB-Access)
- From TEXT host variables (Informix ESQL/C)

You cannot use a quoted text string, number, or any other actual value to insert or update TEXT columns.

When you select a TEXT column, you can choose to receive all or part of it. To see all of a column, use the regular syntax for selecting a column into a variable. You can also select any part of a TEXT column with subscripts, as the following example shows:

```
SELECT cat_descr [1,75] FROM catalog WHERE catalog_num = 10001
```

This statement reads the first 75 bytes of the **cat_descr** column associated with catalog number 10001.

The database server provides a cast to convert TEXT objects to CLOB objects. For more information, see the *Informix Guide to Database Design and Implementation*.

 Important: *If you try to return a TEXT column from a subquery, you get an error message even when the TEXT column is not used in a comparison condition or with the IN predicate.*

Nonprintable Characters with TEXT

Both printable and nonprintable characters can be inserted in text columns. Informix products do not do any checking of the data that is inserted in a column with the TEXT data type. For detailed information on entering and displaying nonprintable characters, refer to "Nonprintable Characters with CHAR" on page 2-14.

Collating TEXT Data

The TEXT data type is collated in code-set order. For more information on collation orders, see the *Informix Guide to GLS Functionality*.

GLS

Multibyte Characters with TEXT

The database locale must support multibyte TEXT characters. For more information, see the *Informix Guide to GLS Functionality*.

Unnamed Row

See "Row, Unnamed" on page 2-37.

VARCHAR(*m,r*)

The VARCHAR data type stores character sequences that contain single-byte and multibyte character sequences of varying length, where *m* is the maximum byte size of the column and *r* is the minimum amount of byte space reserved for that column.

The VARCHAR data type is the Informix implementation of a character varying data type. The ANSI standard data type for varying character strings is CHARACTER VARYING and is described on page 2-15.

You must specify the maximum size (*m*) of the VARCHAR column. The size of this parameter can range from 1 to 255 bytes. If you are placing an index on a VARCHAR column, the maximum size is 254 bytes. You can store shorter, but not longer, character strings than the value that you specify.

Specifying the minimum reserved space (*r*) parameter is optional. This value can range from 0 to 255 bytes but must be less than the maximum size (*m*) of the VARCHAR column. If you do not specify a minimum space value, it defaults to 0. You should specify this parameter when you initially intend to insert rows with short or null data in this column, but later expect the data to be updated with longer values.

Although the use of VARCHAR economizes on space used in a table, it has no effect on the size of an index. In an index based on a VARCHAR column, each index key has length *m*, the maximum size of the column.

When you store a VARCHAR value in the database, only its defined characters are stored. The database server does not strip a VARCHAR object of any user-entered trailing blanks, nor does the database server pad the VARCHAR to the full length of the column. However, if you specify a minimum reserved space (*r*) and some data values are shorter than that amount, some space reserved for rows goes unused.

VARCHAR values are compared to other VARCHAR values and to character values in the same way that character values are compared. The shorter value is padded on the right with spaces until the values have equal lengths; then they are compared for the full length.

Nonprintable Characters with VARCHAR

Nonprintable VARCHAR characters are entered, displayed, and treated in the same way as nonprintable CHAR characters are. For detailed information on entering and displaying nonprintable characters, refer to "Nonprintable Characters with CHAR" on page 2-14.

Storing Numeric Values in a VARCHAR Column

When you insert a numeric value in a VARCHAR column, the stored value does not get padded with trailing blanks to the maximum length of the column. The number of digits in a numeric VARCHAR value is the number of characters that you need to store that value. For example, given the following statement, the value that gets stored in table **mytab** is 1.

```
create table mytab (col1 varchar(10));
insert into mytab values (1);
```

Tip: VARCHAR treats C null (binary 0) and string terminators as termination characters for nonprintable characters.

GLS

Multibyte Characters with VARCHAR

The database locale must support multibyte VARCHAR characters. If you store multibyte characters, make sure to calculate the number of bytes needed. For more information, see the *Informix Guide to GLS Functionality*.

Collating VARCHAR

The main difference between the NVARCHAR and the VARCHAR data types is the difference in collation sequencing. Collation order of NVARCHAR characters depends on the GLS locale chosen, while collation of VARCHAR characters depends on the code set. For more information, see the *Informix Guide to GLS Functionality*.

Built-In Data Types

Informix database servers support the following built-in data types.

Category	Data Types
Character	CHAR, CHARACTER VARYING, LVARCHAR, NCHAR, NVARCHAR, VARCHAR
Numeric	DECIMAL, FLOAT, INT8, INTEGER, MONEY, SERIAL, SERIAL8, SMALLFLOAT, SMALLINT
Large-object	Simple-large-object types: BYTE, TEXT
	Smart-large-object types: BLOB, CLOB
Time	DATE, DATETIME, INTERVAL
Miscellaneous	BOOLEAN

For a description of character, numeric, and miscellaneous data types, refer to the appropriate entry in "Description of Data Types" on page 2-9. Page references are in the alphabetical list in Figure 2-2 on page 2-6.

The following sections provide additional information on large-object and time data types.

Large-Object Data Types

A large object is a data object that is logically stored in a table column but physically stored independently of the column. Large objects are stored separately from the table because they typically store a large amount of data. Separation of this data from the table can increase performance.

Figure 2-10 shows the large-object data types.

Figure 2-10
Large-Object Data Types

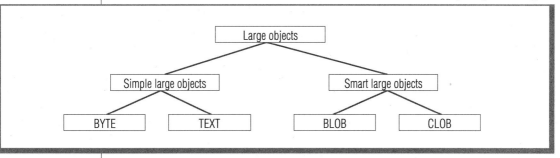

Only Dynamic Server supports BLOB and CLOB data types. ◆

For the relative advantages and disadvantages of simple and smart large objects, see the *Informix Guide to Database Design and Implementation*.

Simple Large Objects

Simple large objects are a category of large objects that have a theoretical limit of 2^{31} bytes and a practical limit that your disk capacity determines. Informix database servers support the following simple-large-object data types:

BYTE   Stores binary data. For more detailed information about this data type, see the description on page 2-12.

TEXT   Stores text data. For more detailed information about this data type, see the description on page 2-44.

Unlike smart large objects, simple large objects do not support random access to the data. When you transfer a simple large object between a client application and the database server, you must transfer the entire BYTE or TEXT value. If the data does not fit into memory, you must store it in an operating-system file and then retrieve it from that file.

The database server stores simple large objects in *blobspaces*. A *blobspace* is a logical storage area that contains one or more chunks that only store BYTE and TEXT data. For information on how to define blobspaces, see your *Administrator's Guide*.

IDS

Smart Large Objects

Smart large objects are a category of large objects that support random access to the data and are generally recoverable. The random access feature allows you to seek and read through the smart large object as if it were an operating-system file.

Smart large objects are also useful for opaque data types with large storage requirements. (See the description of opaque data types on page 2-62.) ♦

Dynamic Server supports the following smart-large-object data types:

BLOB   Stores binary data. For more information about this data type, see the description on page 2-9.

CLOB   Stores text data. For more information about this data type, see the description on page 2-15.

Dynamic Server stores smart large objects in *sbspaces*. An *sbspace* is a logical storage area that contains one or more chunks that store only BLOB and CLOB data. For information on how to define sbspaces, see your *Performance Guide*.

When you define a BLOB or CLOB column, you can determine the following large-object characteristics:

- LOG and NOLOG: whether the database server should log the smart large object in accordance with the current database log mode.

- KEEP ACCESS TIME and NO KEEP ACCESS TIME: whether the database server should keep track of the last time the smart large object was accessed.

- HIGH INTEG and MODERATE INTEG: whether the database server should use page headers to detect data corruption.

Use of these characteristics can affect performance. For information, see your *Performance Guide*.

When you access a smart-large-object column with an SQL statement, the database server does not send the actual BLOB or CLOB data. Instead, it establishes a pointer to the data and returns this pointer. The client application can then use this pointer to perform the open, read, or write operations on the smart large object.

To access a BLOB or CLOB column from within a client application, use one of the following application programming interfaces (APIs):

- From within an Informix ESQL/C program, use the smart-large-object API.

  For more information, see the *Informix ESQL/C Programmer's Manual*.

- From within a DataBlade module, use the Client and Server API.

  For more information, see the *DataBlade API Programmer's Manual*.

For information on smart large objects, see the *Informix Guide to SQL: Syntax* and *Informix Guide to Database Design and Implementation*.

Time Data Types

You can use DATE, DATETIME, and INTERVAL data in a variety of arithmetic and relational expressions. You can manipulate a DATETIME value with another DATETIME value, an INTERVAL value, the current time (identified by the keyword CURRENT), or a specified unit of time (identified by the keyword UNITS).

In most situations, you can use a DATE value wherever it is appropriate to use a DATETIME value and vice versa. You also can manipulate an INTERVAL value with the same choices as a DATETIME value. In addition, you can multiply or divide an INTERVAL value by a number.

An INTERVAL column can hold a value that represents the difference between two DATETIME values or the difference between (or sum of) two INTERVAL values. In either case, the result is a span of time, which is an INTERVAL value. On the other hand, if you add or subtract an INTERVAL value from a DATETIME value, another DATETIME value is produced because the result is a specific time.

Figure 2-11 indicates the range of expressions that you can use with DATE, DATETIME, and INTERVAL data and the data type that results from each expression.

Figure 2-11
Range of Expressions for DATE, DATETIME, and INTERVAL

Data Type of Operand 1	Operator	Data Type of Operand 2	Result
DATE	−	DATETIME	INTERVAL
DATETIME	−	DATE	INTERVAL
DATE	+ or −	INTERVAL	DATETIME
DATETIME	−	DATETIME	INTERVAL
DATETIME	+ or −	INTERVAL	DATETIME
INTERVAL	+	DATETIME	DATETIME
INTERVAL	+ or −	INTERVAL	INTERVAL
DATETIME	−	CURRENT	INTERVAL

(1 of 2)

Data Type of Operand 1	Operator	Data Type of Operand 2	Result
CURRENT	−	DATETIME	INTERVAL
INTERVAL	+	CURRENT	DATETIME
CURRENT	+ or −	INTERVAL	DATETIME
DATETIME	+ or −	UNITS	DATETIME
INTERVAL	+ or −	UNITS	INTERVAL
INTERVAL	* or /	NUMBER	INTERVAL

(2 of 2)

No other combinations are allowed. You cannot add two DATETIME values because this operation does not produce either a specific time or a span of time. For example, you cannot add December 25 and January 1, but you can subtract one from the other to find the time span between them.

Manipulating DATETIME Values

You can subtract most DATETIME values from each other. Dates can be in any order and the result is either a positive or a negative INTERVAL value. The first DATETIME value determines the field precision of the result.

If the second DATETIME value has fewer fields than the first, the shorter value is extended automatically to match the longer one. (See the discussion of the EXTEND function in the Expression segment in the *Informix Guide to SQL: Syntax*.)

In the following example, subtracting the DATETIME YEAR TO HOUR value from the DATETIME YEAR TO MINUTE value results in a positive interval value of 60 days, 1 hour, and 30 minutes. Because minutes were not included in the second value, the database server sets the minutes for the result to 0.

```
DATETIME (1999-9-30 12:30) YEAR TO MINUTE
    - DATETIME (1999-8-1 11) YEAR TO HOUR

Result: INTERVAL (60 01:30) DAY TO MINUTE
```

If the second DATETIME value has more fields than the first (regardless of whether the precision of the extra fields is larger or smaller than those in the first value), the additional fields in the second value are ignored in the calculation.

In the following expression (and result), the year is not included for the second value. Therefore, the year is set automatically to the current year, in this case 1999, and the resulting INTERVAL is negative, which indicates that the second date is later than the first.

```
DATETIME (1999-9-30) YEAR TO DAY
   - DATETIME (10-1) MONTH TO DAY

Result: INTERVAL (1) DAY TO DAY [assuming current year
is 1999]
```

Manipulating DATETIME with INTERVAL Values

INTERVAL values can be added to or subtracted from DATETIME values. In either case, the result is a DATETIME value. If you are adding an INTERVAL value to a DATETIME value, the order of values is unimportant; however, if you are subtracting, the DATETIME value must come first. Adding or subtracting an INTERVAL value simply moves the DATETIME value forward or backward in time. The expression shown in the following example moves the date ahead three years and five months:

```
DATETIME (1994-8-1) YEAR TO DAY
   + INTERVAL (3-5) YEAR TO MONTH

Result: DATETIME (1998-01-01) YEAR TO DAY
```

 Important: *Evaluate the logic of your addition or subtraction. Remember that months can be 28, 29, 30, or 31 days and that years can be 365 or 366 days.*

In most situations, the database server automatically adjusts the calculation when the initial values do not have the same precision. However, in certain situations, you must explicitly adjust the precision of one value to perform the calculation. If the INTERVAL value you are adding or subtracting has fields that are not included in the DATETIME value, you must use the EXTEND function to explicitly extend the field qualifier of the DATETIME value. (For more information on the EXTEND function, see the Expression segment in the *Informix Guide to SQL: Syntax*.)

For example, you cannot subtract a minute INTERVAL value from the DATETIME value in the previous example that has a YEAR TO DAY field qualifier. You can, however, use the EXTEND function to perform this calculation, as the following example shows:

```
EXTEND (DATETIME (1998-8-1) YEAR TO DAY, YEAR TO MINUTE)
    - INTERVAL (720) MINUTE(3) TO MINUTE

Result: DATETIME (1998-07-31 12:00) YEAR TO MINUTE
```

The EXTEND function allows you to explicitly increase the DATETIME precision from YEAR TO DAY to YEAR TO MINUTE. This allows the database server to perform the calculation, with the resulting extended precision of YEAR TO MINUTE.

Manipulating DATE with DATETIME and INTERVAL Values

You can use DATE values in arithmetic expressions with DATETIME or INTERVAL values by writing expressions that allow the manipulations that Figure 2-12 shows.

Figure 2-12
Results of Expressions That Manipulate DATE with DATETIME or INTERVAL Values

Expression	Result
DATE – DATETIME	INTERVAL
DATETIME – DATE	INTERVAL
DATE + or – INTERVAL	DATETIME

In the cases that Figure 2-12 shows, DATE values are first converted to their corresponding DATETIME equivalents, and then the expression is computed normally.

Although you can interchange DATE and DATETIME values in many situations, you must indicate whether a value is a DATE or a DATETIME data type. A DATE value can come from the following sources:

- A column or program variable of type DATE
- The TODAY keyword
- The DATE() function
- The MDY function
- A DATE literal

A DATETIME value can come from the following sources:

- A column or program variable of type DATETIME
- The CURRENT keyword
- The EXTEND function
- A DATETIME literal

The database locale defines the default DATE and DATETIME formats. For the default locale, U.S. English, these formats are '*mm/dd/yy*' for DATE values and '*yyyy-mm-dd hh:MM:ss*' for DATETIME values.

When you represent DATE and DATETIME values as quoted character strings, the fields in the strings must be in proper order. In other words, when a DATE value is expected, the string must be in DATE format and when a DATETIME value is expected, the string must be in DATETIME format. For example, you can use the string '10/30/1999' as a DATE string but not as a DATETIME string. Instead, you must use '1999-10-30' or '99-10-30' as the DATETIME string.

GLS

If you use a nondefault locale, the DATE and DATETIME strings must match the formats that your locale defines. For more information, see the *Informix Guide to GLS Functionality*.

You can customize the DATE format that the database server expects with the **DBDATE** and **GL_DATE** environment variables. You can customize the DATETIME format that the database server expects with the **DBTIME** and **GL_DATETIME** environment variables. For more information, see "DBDATE" on page 3-36 and "DBTIME" on page 3-53. For more information on all these environment variables, see the *Informix Guide to GLS Functionality*. ◆

You can also subtract one DATE value from another DATE value, but the result is a positive or negative INTEGER value rather than an INTERVAL value. If an INTERVAL value is required, you can either convert the INTEGER value into an INTERVAL value or one of the DATE values into a DATETIME value before subtracting.

For example, the following expression uses the DATE() function to convert character string constants to DATE values, calculates their difference, and then uses the UNITS DAY keywords to convert the INTEGER result into an INTERVAL value:

```
(DATE ('5/2/1994') - DATE ('4/6/1955')) UNITS DAY

Result: INTERVAL (12810) DAY(5) TO DAY
```

If you need YEAR TO MONTH precision, you can use the EXTEND function on the first DATE operand, as the following example shows:

```
EXTEND (DATE ('5/2/1994'), YEAR TO MONTH) - DATE ('4/6/1955')

Result: INTERVAL (39-01) YEAR TO MONTH
```

The resulting INTERVAL precision is YEAR TO MONTH because the DATETIME value came first. If the DATE value had come first, the resulting INTERVAL precision would have been DAY(5) TO DAY.

Manipulating INTERVAL Values

You can add or subtract INTERVAL values as long as both values are from the same class; that is, both are year-month or both are day-time. In the following example, a SECOND TO FRACTION value is subtracted from a MINUTE TO FRACTION value:

```
INTERVAL (100:30.0005) MINUTE(3) TO FRACTION(4)
   - INTERVAL (120.01) SECOND(3) TO FRACTION

Result: INTERVAL (98:29.9905) MINUTE TO FRACTION(4)
```

The use of numeric qualifiers alerts the database server that the MINUTE and FRACTION in the first value and the SECOND in the second value exceed the default number of digits.

When you add or subtract INTERVAL values, the second value cannot have a field with greater precision than the first. The second INTERVAL, however, can have a field of smaller precision than the first. For example, the second INTERVAL can be HOUR TO SECOND when the first is DAY TO HOUR. The additional fields (in this case MINUTE and SECOND) in the second INTERVAL value are ignored in the calculation.

Multiplying or Dividing INTERVAL Values

You can multiply or divide INTERVAL values by a number that can be an integer or a fraction. However, any remainder from the calculation is ignored and the result is truncated. The following expression multiplies an INTERVAL by a fraction:

```
INTERVAL (15:30.0002) MINUTE TO FRACTION(4) * 2.5

Result: INTERVAL (38:45.0005) MINUTE TO FRACTION(4)
```

In this example, 15 * 2.5 = 37.5 minutes, 30 * 2.5 = 75 seconds, and 2 * 2.5 = 5 fraction(4). The 0.5 minute is converted into 30 seconds and 60 seconds are converted into 1 minute, which produces the final result of 38 minutes, 45 seconds, and 0.0005 of a second. The results of any calculation include the same amount of precision as the original INTERVAL value.

IDS

Extended Data Types

Dynamic Server lets you create the following kinds of extended data types to characterize data that cannot be easily represented with the built-in data types:

- Complex data types
- Distinct data types
- Opaque data types

The following sections provide an overview of each of these data types.

For more information about extended data types, see the *Informix Guide to Database Design and Implementation* and *Extending Informix Dynamic Server 2000*.

Complex Data Types

A *complex data type* is a data type that you build from other data types (built-in and extended). Figure 2-13 shows the complex types that Dynamic Server supports. The table that follows briefly describes the structure of these data types.

Figure 2-13
Supported Complex Data Types

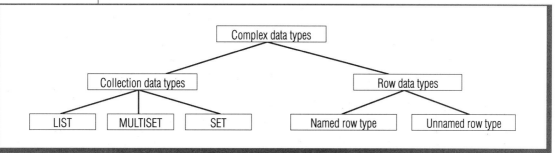

Data Type		Description
Collection types		Complex data types that are made up of elements, each of which is the same data type.
	LIST	A group of ordered elements, each of which need not be unique.
	MULTISET	A group of elements, each of which need not be unique. The order of the elements is ignored.
	SET	A group of elements, each of which is unique. The order of the elements is ignored.
Row types		Complex data types that are made up of fields.
	Named row type	Row types that are identified by their name.
	Unnamed row type	Row types that are identified by their structure.

Complex data types can be nested. For example, you can construct a row type whose fields include one or more sets, multisets, row types, and/or lists. Likewise, a collection type can have elements whose data type is a row type or a collection type.

All complex types inherit the following support functions:

input	assign
output	destroy
send	LO handles
recv	hash
import	lessthan
export	equal
import binary	lessthan (ROW only)
export binary	

The following sections summarize the complex types. For more information on complex types, see the *Informix Guide to Database Design and Implementation*.

Collection Data Types

A collection data type is a complex type that is made up of one or more elements. Every element in a collection has the same data type. A collection element can have any data type (including other complex types) except BYTE, TEXT, SERIAL, or SERIAL8.

Important: *An element cannot have a null value. You must specify the not null constraint for collection elements. No other constraints are valid for collections.*

Dynamic Server supports three kinds of collection types: LIST, SET, and MULTISET. The keywords used to construct these collections are called *type constructors* or just *constructors*. For a description of each of these collection data types, see its entry in this chapter. For the syntax of collection types, see the *Informix Guide to SQL: Syntax*.

Using Complex Data Types in Table Columns

When you specify element values for a collection, list the element values after the constructor and between curly brackets. For example, suppose you have a collection column with the following type:

```
CREATE TABLE table1
(
    mset_col MULTISET(INTEGER NOT NULL)
)
```

The following INSERT statement adds one group of element values to this MULTISET column. The word MULTISET in the two examples is the MULTISET constructor.

```
INSERT INTO table1 VALUES (MULTISET{5, 9, 7, 5})
```

Leave the brackets empty to indicate an empty set:

```
INSERT INTO table1 VALUE (MULTISET{})
```

An empty collection is not equivalent to a null value for the column.

Accessing Collection Data

To access the elements of a collection column, you must fetch the collection into a collection variable and modify the contents of the collection variable. Collection variables can be either of the following types:

- Variables in an SPL routine

  For more information, see the *Informix Guide to SQL: Tutorial.*
- Host variables in an Informix ESQL/C program

  For more information, see the *Informix ESQL/C Programmer's Manual.*

You can also use nested dot notation to access collection data. To learn more about accessing the elements of a collection, see the *Informix Guide to SQL: Tutorial.*

Row Data Types

A row type is a sequence of one or more elements called fields. Each field has a name and a data type. The fields of a row are comparable to the columns of a table, but with important differences: a field has no default clause, you cannot define constraints on a field, and you cannot use fields with tables, only with row types.

Two kinds of row types exist:

- Named row types are identified by their names.
- Unnamed row types are identified by their structure.

The structure of an unnamed row type consists of the number and data types of its fields. For more information about row types, see "Row, Named" on page 2-36 and "Row, Unnamed" on page 2-37.

You can cast between named and unnamed row types. For information about casting between row types, see the *Informix Guide to Database Design and Implementation*.

Distinct Data Types

A distinct data type has the same internal structure as some other source data type in the database. The source data type can be either a built-in type or an extended type. What distinguishes a distinct type from the source type are the functions defined on this type. For more information, see the description on page 2-23.

Opaque Data Types

An opaque data type is a user-defined data type that is fully encapsulated, that is, whose internal structure is unknown to the database server. For more information, see the description on page 2-35.

Data Type Casting and Conversion

Occasionally, the data type that was assigned to a column with the CREATE TABLE statement is inappropriate. You might want to change the data type of a column when you need to store larger values than the current data type can accommodate. The database server allows you to change the data type of the column or to cast its values to a different data type with either of the following methods:

- Use the ALTER TABLE statement to modify the data type of a column.

  For example, if you create a SMALLINT column and later find that you need to store integers larger than 32,767, you must change the data type of that column to store the larger value. You can use ALTER TABLE to change the data type to INTEGER. The conversion changes the data type of all values that currently exist in the column as well as any new values that might be added.

- Use the CAST AS keywords or the double colon (::) cast operator to cast a value to a different data type.

  Casting does not permanently alter the data type of a value; it expresses the value in a more convenient form. Casting user-defined data types into built-in types allows client programs to manipulate data types without knowledge of their internal structure.

If you change data types, the new data type must be able to store all the old values. For example, if you try to convert a column from the INTEGER data type to the SMALLINT data type and the following values exist in the INTEGER column, the database server does not change the data type because SMALLINT columns cannot accommodate numbers greater than 32,768:

```
100 400 700 50000700
```

The same situation might occur if you attempt to transfer data from FLOAT or SMALLFLOAT columns to INTEGER, SMALLINT, or DECIMAL columns.

Both data type conversion and casting depend on casts defined in the **syscasts** system catalog table. For information about syscasts, see "SYSCASTS" on page 1-25.

A cast is either built-in or user-defined. Guidelines exist for casting distinct and extended data types.

For more information about casting opaque types, see *Extending Informix Dynamic Server 2000*. For information about casting other extended types, see the *Informix Guide to Database Design and Implementation*.

Using Built-in Casts

User **informix** owns built-in casts. They govern conversions from one built-in data type to another. Built-in casts allow the database server to convert:

- A character type to any other character type
- A character type to or from any other built-in type
- A numeric type to any other numeric type
- A time data type to or from a datetime type

The database server automatically invokes the appropriate built-in casts when required. An infinite number of built-in casts might be invoked to evaluate and compare expressions or to change a column from one built-in data type to another.

When you convert a column from one built-in data type to another, the database server applies the appropriate built-in casts to each value already in the column. If the new data type cannot store any of the resulting values, the ALTER TABLE statement fails.

For example, if you try to convert a column from the INTEGER data type to the SMALLINT data type and the following values exist in the INTEGER column, the database server does not change the data type because SMALLINT columns cannot accommodate numbers greater than 32,767:

```
100 400 700 50000700
```

The same situation might occur if you attempt to transfer data from FLOAT or SMALLFLOAT columns to INTEGER, SMALLINT, or DECIMAL columns.

The following sections describe database server behavior during certain types of casts and conversions.

Converting from Number to Number

When you convert data from one number data type to another, you occasionally find rounding errors. Figure 2-14 on page 2-65 indicates which numeric data type conversions are acceptable and what kinds of errors you can encounter when you convert between certain numeric data types.

Figure 2-14
Numeric Data Type Conversion Chart

FROM	TO SMALLINT	INTEGER	INT8	SMALLFLOAT	FLOAT	DECIMAL
SMALLINT	OK	OK	OK	OK	OK	OK
INTEGER	E	OK	OK	E	OK	P
INT8	E	E	OK	D	E	P
SMALLFLOAT	E	E	E	OK	OK	P
FLOAT	E	E	E	D	OK	P
DECIMAL	E	E	E	D	D	P

Legend:
OK = No error
P = An error can occur depending on the precision of the decimal
E = An error can occur depending on data
D = No error, but less significant digits might be lost

For example, if you convert a FLOAT value to DECIMAL(4,2), your database server rounds off the floating-point numbers before storing them as decimal numbers. This conversion can result in an error depending on the precision assigned to the DECIMAL column.

Converting Between Number and CHAR

You can convert a CHAR (or NCHAR) column to a numeric column. However, if the CHAR or NCHAR column contains any characters that are not valid in a number column (for example, the letter *l* instead of the number *1*), your database server returns an error.

You can also convert a numeric column to a character column. However, if the character column is not large enough to receive the number, the database server generates an error.

If the database server generates an error, it cannot complete the ALTER TABLE statement or cast and leaves the column values as characters. You receive an error message and the statement is rolled back (whether you are in a transaction or not).

Converting Between INTEGER and DATE or DATETIME

You can convert an integer column (SMALLINT, INTEGER, or INT8) to a DATE or DATETIME value. The database server interprets the integer as a value in the internal format of the DATE or DATETIME column. You can also convert a DATE or DATETIME column to an integer column. The database server stores the internal format of the DATE or DATETIME column as an integer.

For a DATE column, the internal format is a Julian date. For a DATETIME column, the internal format stores the date and time in a condensed integer format.

Converting Between DATE and DATETIME

You can convert DATE columns to DATETIME columns. However, if the DATETIME column contains more fields than the DATE column, the database server either ignores the fields or fills them with zeros. The illustrations in the following list show how these two data types are converted (assuming that the default date format is *mm/dd/yyyy*):

- If you convert DATE to DATETIME YEAR TO DAY, the database server converts the existing DATE values to DATETIME values. For example, the value 08/15/1999 becomes 1999-08-15.

- If you convert DATETIME YEAR TO DAY to the DATE format, the value 1999-08-15 becomes 08/15/1999.

- If you convert DATE to DATETIME YEAR TO SECOND, the database server converts existing DATE values to DATETIME values and fills in the additional DATETIME fields with zeros. For example, 08/15/1999 becomes 1999-08-15 00:00:00.

- If you convert DATETIME YEAR TO SECOND to DATE, the database server converts existing DATETIME to DATE values but drops fields more precise than DAY. For example, 1999-08-15 12:15:37 becomes 08/15/1999.

Using User-Defined Casts

Implicit and explicit casts are owned by the users who create them. They govern casts and conversions between user-defined data types and other data types.

Developers of user-defined data types must create certain implicit and explicit casts and the functions that are used to implement them. The casts allow user-defined types to be expressed in a form that clients can manipulate.

For information on how to create and use implicit and explicit casts, see the CREATE CAST statement in the *Informix Guide to SQL: Syntax* and the *Informix Guide to Database Design and Implementation*.

Implicit Casts

The database server automatically invokes a single implicit cast when needed to evaluate and compare expressions or pass arguments. Operations that require more than one implicit cast fail.

Implicit casts allow you to convert a user-defined data type to a built-in type or vice versa.

Users can explicitly invoke an implicit cast using the CAST AS keywords or the double colon (::) cast operator.

Explicit Casts

Explicit casts, unlike implicit casts or built-in casts, are *never* invoked automatically by the database server. Users must invoke them explicitly with the CAST AS keywords or the double colon (::) cast operator.

Explicit casts do not allow you to convert a user-defined data type to a built-in data type or vice versa.

Determining Which Cast to Apply

The database server uses the following rules to determine which cast to apply in a particular situation:

- To compare two built-in types, the database server automatically invokes the appropriate built-in casts.

- The database server applies only one implicit cast per operand. If two or more casts are needed to convert the operand to the desired type, the user must explicitly invoke the additional casts.

- To compare a distinct type to its source type, the user must explicitly cast one type to the other.

- To compare a distinct type to a type other than its source, the database server looks for an implicit cast between the source type and the desired type

   If neither cast is registered, the user must invoke an explicit cast between the distinct type and the desired type. If this cast is not registered, the database server automatically invokes a cast from the source type to the desired type.

   If none of these casts is defined, the comparison fails.

- To compare an opaque type to a built-in type, the user must explicitly cast the opaque type to a form that the database server understands (LVARCHAR, SENDRECV, IMPEX, or IMPEXBIN). The database server then invokes built-in casts to convert the results to the desired built-in type.

- To compare two opaque types, the user must explicitly cast one opaque type to a form that the database server understands (LVARCHAR, SENDRECV, IMPEX, or IMPEXBIN), then explicitly cast this type to the second opaque type.

For information about casting and the IMPEX, IMPEXBIN, LVARCHAR, and SENDRECV data types, see *Extending Informix Dynamic Server 2000.*

Casts for Distinct Types

You define a distinct type based on a built-in type or an existing opaque type or row type. Although data of the distinct type has the same length and alignment and is passed in the same way as data of the source type, the two cannot be compared directly. To compare a distinct type and its source type, you must explicitly cast one type to the other.

When you create a new distinct type, the database server automatically registers two explicit casts:

- A cast from the distinct type to its source type
- A cast from the source type to the distinct type

You can create an implicit cast between a distinct type and its source type. However, to create an implicit cast, you must first drop the default explicit cast between the distinct type and its source type.

You also can use all casts that have been registered for the source type without modification on the distinct type. You can also define new casts and support functions that apply *only* to the distinct type.

For examples that show how to create a cast function for a distinct type and register the function as cast, see the *Informix Guide to Database Design and Implementation.*

What Extended Data Types Can Be Cast?

The following table shows the data type combinations that you can cast. The table shows only whether or not a cast between a source type and a target type are possible. In some cases, you must first create a user-defined cast before you can perform a conversion between two data types. In other cases, the database server automatically provides a cast that is implicitly invoked or that you must explicitly invoke.

Target Type --->	Opaque Type	Distinct Type	Named Row Type	Unnamed Row Type	Collection Type	Built-in Type
Opaque Type	explicit or implicit	explicit	explicit[3]	Not Allowed	Not Allowed	explicit or implicit[3]
Distinct Type	explicit	explicit	explicit	Not Allowed	Not Allowed	explicit or implicit
Named Row Type	explicit[3]	explicit	explicit3	explicit1	Not Allowed	Not Allowed
Unnamed Row Type	Not Allowed	Not Allowed	explicit[1]	implicit1	Not Allowed	Not Allowed
Collection Type	Not Allowed	Not Allowed	Not Allowed	Not Allowed	explicit[2]	Not Allowed
Built-in Type	explicit or implicit[3]	explicit or implicit	Not Allowed	Not Allowed	Not Allowed	system defined (implicit)

[1] Applies when two row types are structurally equivalent or casts exist to handle data conversions where corresponding field types are not the same.

[2] Applies when a cast exists to convert between the element types of the respective collection types.

[3] Applies when a user-defined cast exists to convert between the two data types.

Operator Precedence

An operator is a symbol or keyword that is used for operations on data types. Some operators only support built in data types; other operators support both built-in and extended data types.

The following table shows the precedence of the operators that Informix database servers support, in descending order of precedence. Operators with the same precedence are listed in the same row.

Operator Precedence
UNITS
+ (unary)   -(unary)
::
*   /
+   -
||
ANY   ALL   SOME
NOT
<   <=   =   >   >=   !=   <>   IN   BETWEEN   LIKE   MATCHES
AND
OR

Environment Variables

In This Chapter

Various *environment variables* affect the functionality of your Informix products. You can set environment variables that identify your terminal, specify the location of your software, and define other parameters.

Some environment variables are required; others are optional. For example, you must either set or accept the default setting for certain UNIX environment variables.

This chapter describes how to use the environment variables that apply to one or more Informix products and shows how to set them. For specific information, see the following pages:

- The environment variables that this chapter discusses are listed alphabetically beginning on page 3-19.
- The environment variables are described beginning on page 3-24.
- A topical index of environment variables is included at the end of this chapter beginning on page 3-99.

Types of Environment Variables

The following types of environment variables are discussed in this chapter:

- Informix-specific environment variables

  Set Informix environment variables when you want to work with Informix products. Each Informix product manual specifies the environment variables that you must set to use that product.

- Operating-system-specific environment variables

  Informix products rely on the correct setting of certain standard operating-system environment variables. For example, you must always set the **PATH** environment variable.

  In a UNIX environment, you might also have to set the **TERMCAP** or **TERMINFO** environment variable to use some products effectively.

GLS

The GLS environment variables that let you work in a nondefault locale are described in the *Informix Guide to GLS Functionality*. These GLS variables are included in the list of environment variables in Figure 3-1 on page 3-19 and in the topic index in Figure 3-2 on page 3-99 but are not discussed in this manual. ♦

Tip: *Additional environment variables that are specific to your client application or SQL API might be discussed in the manual for that product.*

UNIX

Where to Set Environment Variables in UNIX

You can set environment variables in UNIX in the following places:

- At the system prompt on the command line

  When you set an environment variable at the system prompt, you must reassign it the next time you log into the system. For more information, see "Using Environment Variables in UNIX" on page 3-8.

- In an environment-configuration file

  An environment-configuration file is a common or private file where you can define all the environment variables that Informix products use. Use of an environment-configuration file reduces the number of environment variables that you must set at the command line or in a shell file.

- In a login file

  When you set an environment variable in your **.login**, **.cshrc**, or **.profile** file, it is assigned automatically every time you log into the system.

E/C

In Informix ESQL/C, you can set supported environment variables within an application with the **putenv()** system call and retrieve values with the **getenv()** system call, if your UNIX system supports these functions. For more information on **putenv()** and **getenv()**, see the *Informix ESQL/C Programmer's Manual* and your C documentation. ♦

WIN NT

Where to Set Environment Variables in Windows NT

You might be able to set environment variables in several places in a Windows environment, depending on which Informix application you use.

For native Windows Informix applications, such as the database server, environment variables can be set only in the Windows registry. Environment variables set in the registry cannot be modified elsewhere.

For utilities that run in a command-prompt session, such as **dbaccess**, environment variables can be set in several ways, as described in "Setting Environment Variables for Command-Prompt Utilities" on page 3-15.

To use client applications such as ESQL/C or the Relational Object Manager in a Windows environment, use the Setnet32 utility to set environment variables. For information about the Setnet32 utility, see the *Informix Client Products Installation Guide* for your operating system.

E/C

In Informix ESQL/C, you can set supported environment variables within an application with the **ifx_putenv()** function and retrieve values with the **ifx_getenv()** function, if your Windows NT system supports them. For more information on **ifx_putenv()** and **ifx_getenv()**, see the *Informix ESQL/C Programmer's Manual.* ♦

UNIX

Using Environment Variables in UNIX

The following sections discuss setting, unsetting, modifying, and viewing environment variables. If you already use an Informix product, some or all of the appropriate environment variables might be set.

Setting Environment Variables in an Environment-Configuration File

The common (shared) environment-configuration file that is provided with Informix products resides in **$INFORMIXDIR/etc/informix.rc**. The permission for this shared file must be set to 644.

A user can override the system or shared environment variables by setting variables in a private environment-configuration file. This file must have the following characteristics:

- Stored in the user's home directory
- Named **.informix**
- Permissions set to readable by the user

An environment-configuration file can contain comment lines (preceded by #) and variable lines and their values (separated by blanks and tabs), as the following example shows:

```
# This is an example of an environment-configuration file
#
DBDATE DMY4-
#
# These are ESQL/C environment variable settings
#
INFORMIXC gcc
CPFIRST TRUE
```

You can use the **ENVIGNORE** environment variable, described on page 3-58, to override one or more entries in an environment-configuration file. Use the Informix **chkenv** utility, described on page 3-12, to perform a sanity check on the contents of an environment-configuration file. The **chkenv** utility returns an error message if the file contains a bad environment variable or if the file is too large.

The first time you set an environment variable in a shell file or environment-configuration file, you must tell the shell process to read your entry before you work with your Informix product. If you use a C shell, *source* the file; if you use a Bourne or Korn shell, use a period (.) to execute the file.

Setting Environment Variables at Login Time

Add the commands that set your environment variables to the following login file:

For the C shell	**.login** or **.cshrc**
For the Bourne shell or Korn shell	**.profile**

Syntax for Setting Environment Variables

Use standard UNIX commands to set environment variables. The examples in the following table show how to set the **ABCD** environment variable to *value* for the C shell, Bourne shell, and Korn shell. The Korn shell supports a shortcut, as the fourth item indicates. The environment variables are case sensitive.

Shell	Command
C	`setenv ABCD value`
Bourne	`ABCD=value` `export ABCD`
Korn	`ABCD=value` `export ABCD`
Korn	`export ABCD=value`

The following diagram shows how the syntax for setting an environment variable is represented throughout this chapter. These diagrams indicate the setting for the C shell; for the Bourne or Korn shells, use the syntax illustrated in the preceding table.

```
setenv ——————— ABCD ——————— value ————————————————————————————
```

For more information on how to read syntax diagrams, see "Command-Line Conventions" in the Introduction.

Unsetting Environment Variables

To unset an environment variable, enter the following command.

Shell	Command
C	`unsetenv ABCD`
Bourne or Korn	`unset ABCD`

Modifying an Environment-Variable Setting

Sometimes you must add information to an environment variable that is already set. For example, the **PATH** environment variable is always set in UNIX environments. When you use an Informix product, you must add to the **PATH** the name of the directory where the executable files for the Informix products are stored.

In the following example, the **INFORMIXDIR** is **/usr/informix**. (That is, during installation, the Informix products were installed in the **/usr/informix** directory.) The executable files are in the **bin** subdirectory, **/usr/informix/bin**. To add this directory to the front of the C shell **PATH** environment variable, use the following command:

```
setenv PATH /usr/informix/bin:$PATH
```

Rather than entering an explicit pathname, you can use the value of the **INFORMIXDIR** environment variable (represented as **$INFORMIXDIR**), as the following example shows:

```
setenv INFORMIXDIR /usr/informix
setenv PATH $INFORMIXDIR/bin:$PATH
```

You might prefer to use this version to ensure that your **PATH** entry does not contradict the path that was set in **INFORMIXDIR**, and so that you do not have to reset **PATH** whenever you change **INFORMIXDIR**.

If you set the **PATH** environment variable on the C shell command line, you might need to include curly braces with the existing **INFORMIXDIR** and **PATH**, as the following command shows:

```
setenv PATH ${INFORMIXDIR}/bin:${PATH}
```

For more information about setting and modifying environment variables, refer to the manuals for your operating system.

Viewing Your Environment-Variable Settings

After you have installed one or more Informix products, enter the following command at the system prompt to view your current environment settings.

UNIX Version	Command
BSD UNIX	env
UNIX System V	printenv

Checking Environment Variables with the chkenv Utility

The **chkenv** utility checks the validity of shared or private environment-configuration files. It validates the names of the environment variables in the file but not their values. Use **chkenv** to provide debugging information when you define, in an environment-configuration file, all the environment variables that your Informix products use.

```
chkenv ─────── filename ─────────────────────────────┤
```

Element	Purpose	Key Considerations
filename	Specifies the name of the environment-configuration file that you want to debug.	None

The shared environment-configuration file is stored in **$INFORMIXDIR/etc/informix.rc**. A private environment-configuration file is stored in the user's home directory as **.informix**.

If you do not provide the filename for **chkenv**, the utility checks both the shared and private environment configuration files. If you provide a file path, **chkenv** checks only that file.

Issue the following command to check the contents of the shared environment-configuration file:

```
chkenv informix.rc
```

The **chkenv** utility returns an error message if it finds a bad environment-variable name in the file or if the file is too large. You can modify the file and rerun the utility to check the modified environment-variable names.

Informix products ignore all lines in the environment-configuration file, starting at the point of the error, if the **chkenv** utility returns the following message:

```
-33523  filename: Bad environment variable on line number.
```

If you want the product to ignore specified environment-variables in the file, you can also set the **ENVIGNORE** environment variable. For a discussion of the use and format of environment-configuration files and the **ENVIGNORE** environment variable, see page 3-58.

Rules of Precedence

When an Informix product accesses an environment variable, normally the following rules of precedence apply:

1. The highest precedence goes to the value that is defined in the environment (shell) by explicitly setting the value at the shell prompt.

2. The second highest precedence goes to the value that is defined in the private environment-configuration file in the user's home directory (**~/.informix**).

3. The next highest precedence goes to the value that is defined in the common environment-configuration file (**$INFORMIXDIR/etc/informix.rc**).

4. The lowest precedence goes to the default value.

For precedence information about GLS environment variables, see the *Informix Guide to GLS Functionality*.

Important: *If you set one or more environment variables before you start the database server, and you do not explicitly set the same environment variables for your client products, the clients will adopt the original settings.*

WIN NT

Using Environment Variables in Windows NT

The following sections discuss setting, viewing, unsetting, and modifying environment variables for native Windows applications and command-line utilities.

Setting Environment Variables for Native Windows Applications

Native Windows Informix applications, such as the database server itself, store their configuration information in the Windows registry. To modify this information, you must use the Registry Editor, **regedt32.exe**.

Manipulating environment variables with the Registry Editor

1. Launch the Registry Editor, **regedt32.exe**, and choose the window titled **HKEY_LOCAL_MACHINE**.

2. In the left pane, double-click the SOFTWARE registry key (shown as a small, yellow file folder icon). The SOFTWARE registry key expands to show several subkeys, one of which is Informix. Continue down the tree in the following sequence:

        OnLine, *dbservername*, Environment.

    Substitute the name of your database server in place of *dbservername*.

3. With the Environment registry key selected in the left pane, you should see a list of environment variables and their defined values in the right pane (for example,
    CLIENT_LOCALE:REG_SZ:EN_US.CP1252).

4. Change existing environment variables if needed.

    a. Double-click the environment variable.

    b. Type the new value in the String Editor dialog box.

    c. Click **OK** to accept the value.

5. Add new environment variables if needed.

   a. Choose **Edit→Add Value** in the Registry Editor.

   b. Enter the name of the environment variable in the Value Name edit box and choose **REG_SZ** as the data type.

   c. Click **OK** and type a value for the environment variable in the String Editor dialog box.

6. Delete an environment variable, if needed.

   a. Select the variable name.

   b. Choose **Edit→Delete** in the Registry Editor.

For more information on using the Registry Editor, see your operating-system documentation.

Important: *In order to use the Registry Editor to change database server environment variables, you must belong to either the Administrators' or Informix-Admin groups. For information on assigning users to groups, see your operating-system documentation.*

Setting Environment Variables for Command-Prompt Utilities

You can set environment variables for command-prompt utilities in the following ways:

- With the System applet in the Control Panel
- In a command-prompt session

Using the System Applet to Work with Environment Variables

The System applet provides a graphical interface to create, modify, and delete system-wide and user-specific variables. Environment variables that are set with the System applet are visible to all command-prompt sessions.

To change environment variables with the System applet in the control panel

1. Double-click the System applet icon from the Control Panel window.

   Click the Environment tab near the top of the window. Two list boxes display System Environment Variables and User Environment Variables. System Environment Variables apply to an entire system, and User Environment Variables apply only to the sessions of the individual user.

2. To change the value of an existing variable, select that variable.

   The name of the variable and its current value appear in the boxes at the bottom of the window.

3. Highlight the existing value and type the new value.

4. To add a new variable, highlight an existing variable and type the new variable name in the box at the bottom of the window.

5. Next, enter the value for the new variable at the bottom of the window and click the **Set** button.

6. To delete a variable, select the variable and click the **Delete** button.

Important: *In order to use the System applet to change System environment variables, you must belong to the Administrators' group. For information on assigning users to groups, see your operating-system documentation.*

Using the Command Prompt to Work with Environment Variables

The following diagram shows the syntax for setting an environment variable at a command prompt in Windows NT.

set ——————— ABCD ——————— = ——————— *value* ———————————————|

For more information on how to read syntax diagrams, see "Command-Line Conventions" in the introduction.

To view your current settings after one or more Informix products are installed, enter the following command at a command prompt.

```
set ──────── ABCD ──────── = ──────────────────────────────┤
```

Sometimes you must add information to an environment variable that is already set. For example, the **PATH** environment variable is always set in Windows NT environments. When you use an Informix product, you must add the name of the directory where the executable files for the Informix products are stored to the **PATH**.

In the following example, **INFORMIXDIR** is **d:\informix**, (that is, during installation, Informix products were installed in the **d: \informix** directory). The executable files are in the **bin** subdirectory, **d:\informix\bin**. To add this directory at the beginning of the **PATH** environment-variable value, use the following command:

```
set PATH=d:\informix\bin;%PATH%
```

Rather than entering an explicit pathname, you can use the value of the **INFORMIXDIR** environment variable (represented as **%INFORMIXDIR%**), as the following example shows:

```
set INFORMIXDIR=d:\informix
set PATH=%INFORMIXDIR%\bin;%PATH%
```

You might prefer to use this version to ensure that your **PATH** entry does not contradict the path that was set in **INFORMIXDIR** and to avoid resetting **PATH** whenever you change **INFORMIXDIR**.

For more information about setting and modifying environment variables, refer to your operating-system manuals.

Using dbservername.cmd to Initialize a Command-Prompt Environment

Each time that you open a Windows NT command prompt, it acts as an independent environment. Therefore, environment variables that you set within it are valid only for that particular command-prompt instance. For example, if you open one command prompt and set the variable, **INFORMIXDIR**, and then open another command prompt and type set to check your environment, you will find that **INFORMIXDIR** is not set in the new command-prompt session.

The database server installation program creates a *batch file* that you can use to configure command-prompt utilities, ensuring that your command-prompt environment is initialized correctly each time that you run a command-prompt session. The batch file, *dbservername*.**cmd**, is located in **%INFORMIXDIR%**, and is a plain text file that you can modify with any text editor. If you have more than one database server installed in **%INFORMIXDIR%**, there will be more than one batch file with the **.cmd** extension, each bearing the name of the database server with which it is associated.

To run *dbservername*.**cmd** from a command prompt, type *dbservername* or configure a command prompt so that it runs *dbservername*.**cmd** automatically at start up.

Rules of Precedence

When an Informix product accesses an environment variable, normally the following rules of precedence apply:

1. The highest precedence goes to the value that is defined in the environment by explicitly setting the value at the command prompt.

2. The second highest precedence goes to the value that is defined in the System control panel as a User Environment Variable.

3. The third highest precedence goes to the value that is defined in the System control panel as a System Environment Variable.

4. The lowest precedence goes to the default value.

Important: *Because Windows NT services access only environment variables that are set in the registry, the preceding rules of precedence do not apply for Informix native Windows applications. For native Windows applications, the highest precedence goes to variables that are explicitly defined in the registry, and the lowest precedence goes to the default value. In addition, if you set one or more environment variables before you start the database server, and you do not explicitly set the same environment variables for your client products, the clients will adopt the original settings.*

List of Environment Variables

Figure 3-1 contains an alphabetical list of the environment variables that you can set for an Informix database server and SQL API products. Most of these environment variables are described in this chapter on the pages listed in the last column.

GLS

Although the GLS environment variables that let you work in a nondefault locale are listed in Figure 3-1, they are described in the *Informix Guide to GLS Functionality.* ♦

Figure 3-1
Alphabetical List Of Environment Variables

Environment Variable	EDS	IDS	Restrictions	Page
AC_CONFIG	✔	✔	None	3-24
ARC_CONFIG		✔	UNIX only	3-25
ARC_DEFAULT		✔	UNIX only	3-25
ARC_KEYPAD		✔	UNIX only	3-25
CC8BITLEVEL			ESQL/C only	GLS guide
CLIENT_LOCALE	✔	✔	None	GLS guide
COCKPITSERVICE	✔	✔	DB/Cockpit only	3-27

(1 of 5)

Environment Variable	EDS	IDS	Restrictions	Page
CPFIRST	✔	✔	None	3-28
DBACCNOIGN	✔	✔	DB-Access only	3-29
DBANSIWARN	✔	✔	None	3-30
DBBLOBBUF	✔	✔	None	3-31
DBCENTURY			SQL APIs only	3-32
DBDATE	✔	✔	None	3-36; GLS guide
DBDELIMITER	✔	✔	None	3-39
DBEDIT	✔	✔	None	3-40
DBFLTMASK	✔	✔	DB-Access only	3-41
DBLANG	✔	✔	None	3-42; GLS guide
DBMONEY	✔	✔	None	3-44; GLS guide
DBONPLOAD		✔	HPL only	3-45
DBPATH	✔	✔	None	3-46
DBPRINT	✔	✔	UNIX only	3-48
DBREMOTECMD	✔	✔	UNIX only	3-49
DBSPACETEMP	✔	✔	None	3-50
DBTEMP			Gateways only	3-52
DBTIME			SQL APIs only	3-53; GLS guide
DBUPSPACE	✔	✔	None	3-56

(2 of 5)

Environment Variable	EDS	IDS	Restrictions	Page
DB_LOCALE	✔	✔	None	GLS guide
DELIMIDENT	✔	✔	None	3-57
ENVIGNORE	✔	✔	UNIX only	3-58
ESQLMF	✔	✔	ESQL/C only	GLS guide
FET_BUF_SIZE	✔	✔	SQL APIs, DB-Access only	3-59
GLS8BITSYS	✔	✔	None	GLS guide
GL_DATE	✔	✔	None	GLS guide
GL_DATETIME	✔	✔	None	GLS guide
IFMX_SMLTBL_BROADCAST_SIZE	✔		None	3-60
IFX_DIRECTIVES	✔	✔	None	3-61
IFX_LONGID		✔	None	3-62
IFX_NETBUF_PVTPOOL_SIZE	✔	✔	UNIX only	3-63
IFX_NETBUF_SIZE	✔	✔	None	3-63
IFX_UPDDESC		✔	None	3-64
INFORMIXC			ESQL/C, UNIX only	3-64
INFORMIXCONCSMCFG		✔	None	3-65
INFORMIXCONRETRY	✔	✔	None	3-66
INFORMIXCONTIME	✔	✔	None	3-66
INFORMIXCPPMAP		✔	None	3-68

(3 of 5)

Environment Variable	EDS	IDS	Restrictions	Page
INFORMIXDIR	✔	✔	None	3-68
INFORMIXKEYTAB	✔	✔	UNIX only	3-69
INFORMIXOPCACHE		✔	Optical Sub-system only	3-70
INFORMIXSERVER	✔	✔	None	3-70
INFORMIXSHMBASE	✔	✔	UNIX only	3-72
INFORMIXSQLHOSTS	✔	✔	None	3-73
INFORMIXSTACKSIZE	✔	✔	None	3-74
INFORMIXTERM	✔	✔	DB-Access, UNIX only	3-75
INF_ROLE_SEP		✔	None	3-76
ISM_COMPRESSION	✔	✔	ISM, ON-Bar only	3-77
ISM_DEBUG_FILE	✔	✔	ISM only	3-77
ISM_DEBUG_LEVEL	✔	✔	ISM, ON-Bar only	3-78
ISM_ENCRYPTION	✔	✔	ISM, ON-Bar only	3-79
ISM_MAXLOGSIZE	✔	✔	ISM only	3-79
ISM_MAXLOGVERS	✔	✔	ISM only	3-80
LD_LIBRARY_PATH			SQL APIs, UNIX only	3-80
LIBPATH			SQL APIs, UNIX only	3-81
NODEFDAC	✔	✔	None	3-81
ONCONFIG	✔	✔	None	3-82
OPTCOMPIND	✔	✔	None	3-83

(4 of 5)

Environment Variable	EDS	IDS	Restrictions	Page
OPTMSG			ESQL/C only	3-84
OPTOFC			ESQL/C only	3-85
OPT_GOAL	✔	✔	UNIX only	3-86
PATH	✔	✔	None	3-87
PDQPRIORITY	✔	✔	None	3-88
PLCONFIG		✔	HPL only	3-90
PLOAD_LO_PATH		✔	HPL only	3-91
PLOAD_SHMBASE		✔	HPL only	3-91
PSORT_DBTEMP	✔	✔	None	3-92
PSORT_NPROCS	✔	✔	None	3-93
SERVER_LOCALE	✔	✔	None	GLS guide
SHLIB_PATH	✔	✔	UNIX only	3-94
STMT_CACHE		✔	None	3-95
TERM	✔	✔	UNIX only	3-96
TERMCAP	✔	✔	UNIX only	3-96
TERMINFO	✔	✔	UNIX only	3-97
THREADLIB			ESQL/C, UNIX only	3-98
XFER_CONFIG	✔		None	3-98

(5 of 5)

Tip: *You might encounter references to environment variables that are not listed in Figure 3-1. Most likely, these environment variables are not supported in Version 8.3, Version 9.2, or are used to maintain backward compatibility with certain earlier product versions. For information, refer to an earlier version of your Informix documentation.*

Environment Variables

The following sections discuss the environment variables that Informix products use.

Important: *The descriptions of the following environment variables include the syntax for setting the environment variable in the UNIX environment. For a general description of how to set these environment variables in Windows NT environments, see "Setting Environment Variables for Native Windows Applications" on page 3-14 and "Setting Environment Variables for Command-Prompt Utilities" on page 3-15.*

AC_CONFIG

You can set the **AC_CONFIG** environment variable to specify the path for the **ac_config.std** configuration file for the **archecker** utility. The **archecker** utility checks the validity and completeness of an ON-Bar storage-space backup. The **ac_config.std** file contains default **archecker** configuration parameters.

```
setenv ──────────────── AC_CONFIG ──────── pathname ──────────┤
```

pathname   is the location of the **ac_config.std** configuration file in **$INFORMIXDIR/etc** or **%INFORMIXDIR%\etc**.

For information on **archecker,** see your *Backup and Restore Guide*.

ARC_CONFIG

If you use the ON-Archive archive and tape-management system for your database server, you can set the **ARC_CONFIG** environment variable to specify the name of a nondefault configuration file.

```
setenv ─────────────────── ARC_CONFIG ──────── filename ───────────────┤
```

filename	is the name of the configuration file in **$INFORMIXDIR/etc**.

The default configuration file for ON-Archive is **config.arc**, located in the **$INFORMIXDIR/etc** directory. When you want to create and use a different configuration file for ON-Archive, set **ARC_CONFIG** to the name of the file. Dynamic Server looks for the specified file in the directory **$INFORMIXDIR/etc**.

The **ARC_CONFIG** environment variable lets you change configuration parameters while preserving the default **config.arc** file. It lets you create multiple configuration files and select the one you want.

For more information on archiving, see your *Archive and Backup Guide*.

ARC_DEFAULT

If you use the ON-Archive archive and tape-management system for your database server, you can set the **ARC_DEFAULT** environment variable to indicate where a personal default qualifier file is located.

```
setenv ─────────────────── ARC_DEFAULT ──────── pathname ───────────────┤
```

pathname	is the full pathname of the personal default qualifier file.

For example, to set the **ARC_DEFAULT** environment variable to specify the file **/usr/jane/arcdefault.janeroe**, enter the following command:

```
setenv ARC_DEFAULT /usr/jane/arcdefault.janeroe
```

For more information on archiving, see your *Archive and Backup Guide*.

ARC_KEYPAD

If you use the ON-Archive archive and tape-management system for your database server, you can set your **ARC_KEYPAD** environment variable to point to a **tctermcap** file that is different from the default **tctermcap** file. The default is the **$INFORMIXDIR/etc/tctermcap** file, and it contains instructions on how to modify the **tctermcap** file.

The **tctermcap** file serves the following purposes for the ON-Archive menu interface:

- It defines the terminal control attributes that allow ON-Archive to manipulate the screen and cursor.
- It defines the mappings between commands and key presses.
- It defines the characters used in drawing menus and borders for an API.

```
setenv ───────────── ARC_KEYPAD ─────── pathname ───────────┤
```

pathname   is the pathname for a **tctermcap** file.

For example, to set the **ARC_KEYPAD** environment variable to specify the file **/usr/jane/tctermcap.janeroe**, enter the following command:

```
setenv ARC_KEYPAD /usr/jane/tctermcap.janeroe
```

For more information on archiving, see your *Archive and Backup Guide*.

COCKPITSERVICE

Set the **COCKPITSERVICE** environment variable to specify a nondefault TCP service for DB/Cockpit.

setenv ——————— COCKPITSERVICE ——————— *servicename* ———————|

servicename   is the name of the TCP service for client/server communication.

The **onprobe** server and **oncockpit** client components of DB/Cockpit communicate with each other through a TCP *service*. Before you can launch DB/Cockpit, **onprobe**, or **oncockpit**, you should define the TCP service and assign it a unique service number. For example:

```
setenv COCKPITSERVICE cockpit2
```

If you do not specify the service name either with the *-service* command-line option or in the **COCKPITSERVICE** environment variable, the default is **cockpit**.

CPFIRST

Set the **CPFIRST** environment variable to determine the nondefault compilation order for all ESQL/C source files in your programming environment.

When compiling an ESQL/C program, the default order is to run the ESQL/C preprocessor on the program source file and pass the resulting file to the C language preprocessor and compiler. However, you can compile an ESQL/C program source file in the following order:

1. Run the C preprocessor
2. Run the ESQL/C preprocessor
3. Run the C compiler and linker

To determine the nondefault compilation order for a specific program, you can either give the program source file a **.ecp** extension, run the **-cp** option with the **esql** command on a program source file with a **.ec** extension, or set **CPFIRST**.

Set the **CPFIRST** environment variable to TRUE (uppercase only) to run the C preprocessor on all ESQL/C source files. The C preprocessor will run before the ESQL/C preprocessor on all ESQL/C source files in your environment, irrespective of whether the **-cp** option is passed to the **esql** command or the source files have the **.ec** or the **.ecp** extension.

```
setenv ─────────────── CPFIRST ─────── TRUE ───────────┤
```

DBACCNOIGN

The **DBACCNOIGN** environment variable affects the behavior of the DB-Access utility if an error occurs under one of the following circumstances:

IDS

- You run DB-Access in nonmenu mode.
- You execute the LOAD command with DB-Access in menu mode. ◆

Set the **DBACCNOIGN** environment variable to 1 to roll back an incomplete transaction if an error occurs while you run the DB-Access utility under either of the preceding conditions.

```
setenv ——————————— DBACCNOIGN ——————— 1 ——————————|
```

Nonmenu Mode Example

For example, assume DB-Access runs the following SQL commands:

```
DATABASE mystore
BEGIN WORK

INSERT INTO receipts VALUES (cust1, 10)
INSERT INTO receipt VALUES (cust1, 20)
INSERT INTO receipts VALUES (cust1, 30)

UPDATE customer
    SET balance =
        (SELECT (balance-60)
        FROM customer WHERE custid = 'cust1')
    WHERE custid = 'cust1

COMMIT WORK
```

In this example, one statement has a misspelled table name. The **receipt** table does not exist.

If your environment does not have **DBACCNOIGN** set, DB-Access inserts two records into the **receipts** table and updates the **customer** table. The decrease in the **customer** balance exceeds the sum of the inserted receipts.

If **DBACCNOIGN** is set to 1, messages display to indicate that DB-Access rolled back all the INSERT and UPDATE statements. The messages also identify the cause of the error so that you can resolve the problem.

IDS

Load Statement Example

You can set **DBACCNOIGN** to protect data integrity during a LOAD statement, even if DB-Access runs the LOAD statement in menu mode.

Assume you execute the LOAD statement from the DB-Access SQL menu page. Forty-nine rows of data load correctly, but the fiftieth row contains an invalid value that causes an error.

If you set **DBACCNOIGN** to 1, the database server does not insert the forty-nine previous rows into the database. If **DBACCNOIGN** is not set, the database server inserts the first forty-nine rows.

DBANSIWARN

Setting the **DBANSIWARN** environment variable indicates that you want to check for Informix extensions to ANSI standard syntax. Unlike most environment variables, you do not need to set **DBANSIWARN** to a value. You can set it to any value or to no value.

```
setenv ──────────────── DBANSIWARN ────────────────┤
```

If you set the **DBANSIWARN** environment variable for DB-Access, it is functionally equivalent to including the **-ansi** flag when you invoke the utility from the command line. If you set **DBANSIWARN** before you run DB-Access, warnings are displayed on the screen within the SQL menu.

Set the **DBANSIWARN** environment variable before you compile an Informix ESQL/C program to check for Informix extensions to ANSI standard syntax. When Informix extensions to ANSI standard syntax are encountered in your program at compile time, warning messages are written to the screen.

At run time, the **DBANSIWARN** environment variable causes the sixth character of the **sqlwarn** array in the SQL Communication Area (SQLCA) to be set to W when a statement is executed that includes any Informix extension to the ANSI standard for SQL syntax. (For more information on SQLCA, see the *Informix ESQL/C Programmer's Manual.*

After you set **DBANSIWARN**, Informix extension checking is automatic until you log out or unset **DBANSIWARN**. To turn off Informix extension checking, unset the **DBANSIWARN** environment variable by entering the following command:

```
unsetenv DBANSIWARN
```

DBBLOBBUF

The **DBBLOBBUF** environment variable controls whether TEXT or BYTE data is stored temporarily in memory or in a file while being unloaded with the UNLOAD statement.

setenv ──────── DBBLOBBUF ──────────── *n* ──────────────┤

n   represents the maximum size of TEXT or BYTE data in kilobytes.

If TEXT or BYTE (simple large object) data is smaller than the default of 10 kilobytes or the setting of the **DBBLOBBUF** environment variable, it is temporarily stored in memory. If the TEXT or BYTE data is larger than the default or the setting of the environment variable, it is written to a temporary file. This environment variable applies to the UNLOAD command only.

For instance, to set a buffer size of 15 kilobytes, set the **DBBLOBBUF** environment variable as the following example shows:

```
setenv DBBLOBBUF 15
```

In the example, any TEXT or BYTE data that is smaller than 15 kilobytes is stored temporarily in memory. TEXT or BYTE data larger than 15 kilobytes is stored temporarily in a file.

DBCENTURY

The **DBCENTURY** environment variable lets you choose the appropriate expansion for DATE and DATETIME values that have only a one- or two-digit year, such as 4/15/3 or 04/15/99.

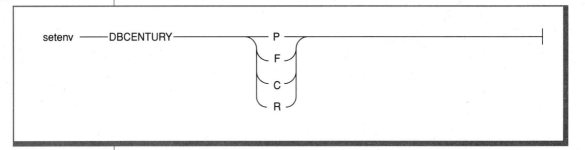

By default, if only the decade is provided for a literal DATE or DATETIME value in a table column, the current century is used to expand the year. For example, if today's date is 09/30/1999, the date 12/31/99 expands to 12/31/1999, and 12/31/00 expands to 12/31/1900. **DBCENTURY** algorithms let you determine the century value of a year (the desired expansion of a two-digit year).

Algorithm	Explanation
P = Past	The previous and current centuries are used to expand the year value. These two dates are compared against the current date, and the date that is prior to the current date is chosen. If both dates are prior to the current date, the date that is closest to the current date is chosen.
F = Future	The previous and the next centuries are used to expand the year value. These two dates are compared against the current date, and the date that is after the current date is chosen. If both the expansions are after the current date, the date that is closest to the current date is chosen.
C = Closest	The previous, current, and next centuries are used to expand the year value, and the date that is closest to the current date is used.
R = Present	The two high-order digits of the current year are used to expand the year value.

When the **DBCENTURY** environment variable is not set or is set to R, the two high-order digits of the current year in its four-digit form are used to expand the year value. To override the default, specify all four digits.

Tip: *Setting **DBCENTURY** does not affect Informix products when the locale specifies a non-Gregorian calendar such as Hebrew or Islamic. A default century is used for alternate calendar systems when the century is not specified.*

Examples of How the DBCENTURY Environment Variable Expands Date Values

The following examples illustrate how the **DBCENTURY** environment variable expands DATE and DATETIME year formats.

Behavior of DBCENTURY = P

```
Example data type: DATE
Current date: 4/6/1999
User enters: 1/1/1
DBCENTURY = P, Past century algorithm
Previous century expansion : 1/1/1801
Present century expansion: 1/1/1901
Analysis: Both results are prior to the current date, but 1/1/1901 is closer to
the current date. 1/1/1901 is chosen.
```

Behavior of DBCENTURY = F

```
Example data type: DATETIME year to month
Current date: 5/7/2005
User enters: 1-1
DBCENTURY = F, Future century algorithm
Present century expansion: 2001-1
Next century expansion: 2101-1
Analysis: Only date 2101-1 is after the current date, so it is chosen as the
expansion of the year value.
```

Behavior of DBCENTURY = C

```
Example data type: DATE
Current date: 4/6/1999
User enters: 1/1/1
DBCENTURY = C, Closest century algorithm
Previous century expansion : 1/1/1801
Present century expansion: 1/1/1901
Next century expansion: 1/1/2001
Analysis: Because the next century expansion is the closest to the current date
1/1/2001 is chosen.
```

Behavior of DBCENTURY = R or DBCENTURY Not Set

```
Example data type: DATETIME year to month
Current date: 4/6/1999
User enters: 1-1
DBCENTURY = R, Present century algorithm
Present century expansion: 1901-1

Example data type: DATE
Current date: 4/6/2003
User enters: 0/1/1
DBCENTURY = not set
Present century expansion: 2000/1
Analysis: In both examples, the Present algorithm is used.
```

Important: *The interpretation of the variables P, F, and C will always vary with the current date. In the first example, 1/1/1 will be expanded as 1/1/2001 if the current date is 4/6/2001 and DBCENTURY = P. In the second example, 1/1 will be expanded as 2001/1 if the current date is 5/7/1995 and DBCENTURY = F.*

Behavior of DBCENTURY with Expressions that Contain Date Values

This section describes how the database server uses the **DBCENTURY** environment variable to interpret dates in fragmentation expressions, triggers, check constraints, and UDRs.

When an expression (check constraint, fragmentation expression, trigger, or UDR) contains a date value in which the year has 1 or 2 digits, the database server uses the setting of **DBCENTURY** at the time the database object (table, trigger, or UDR) is created. The setting of **DBCENTURY** at creation time is used to expand date values during execution of UDRs and triggers and during evaluation of date values within check constraints and fragment expressions.

For example, suppose a user creates a table and defines the following check constraint on a column named **birthdate**:

```
birthdate < '01/25/50'
```

The preceding expression is interpreted according to the value of **DBCENTURY** when the constraint is defined. If the table that contains the **birthdate** column is created on 06/29/98 and `DBCENTURY=C`, the check constraint expression is consistently interpreted as `birthdate < '01/25/1950'` regardless of the value of **DBCENTURY** when inserts or updates are performed on the **birthdate** column. In other words, even if different values of **DBCENTURY** are set when users perform inserts or updates on the **birthdate** column, the check constraint expression is interpreted according to the **DBCENTURY** setting at the time the check constraint is defined.

The value of **DBCENTURY** and the current date are not the only factors that determine how the database server interprets a date expression. The **DBDATE, DBTIME, GL_DATE,** and **GL_DATETIME** environment variables also influence how dates are interpreted. For information about **GL_DATE** and **GL_DATETIME**, see the *Informix Guide to GLS Functionality*.

Important: *The behavior of **DBCENTURY** for Dynamic Server and Enterprise Decision Server is not backwards compatible.*

DBDATE

The **DBDATE** environment variable specifies the end-user formats of DATE values. End-user formats affect the following situations:

- When you input DATE values, Informix products use the **DBDATE** environment variable to interpret the input.

  For example, if you specify a literal DATE value in an INSERT statement, Informix database servers expect this literal value to be compatible with the format that **DBDATE** specifies. Similarly, the database server interprets the date that you specify as input to the DATE() function in the format that the **DBDATE** environment variable specifies.

- When you display DATE values, Informix products use the **DBDATE** environment variable to format the output.

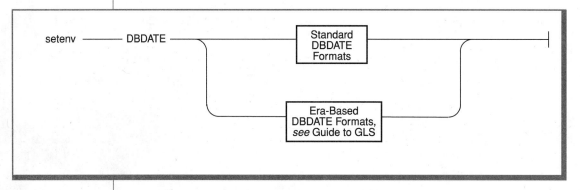

Standard Formats for DBDATE

This section describes standard **DBDATE** formats.

GLS

For a description of era-based formats, see the *Informix Guide to GLS Functionality.* ♦

With standard formats, you can specify the following attributes:

- The order of the month, day, and year in a date
- Whether the year should be printed with two digits (Y2) or four digits (Y4)
- The separator between the month, day, and year

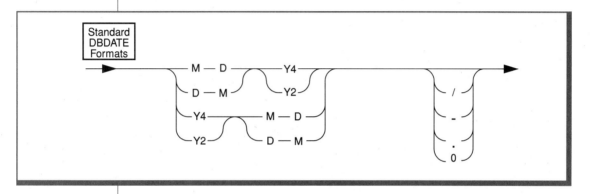

- . /	are characters that can be used as separators in a date format.
0	indicates that no separator is displayed.
D, M	are characters that represent the day and the month.
Y2, Y4	are characters that represent the year and the number of digits in the year.

For the U.S. ASCII English locale, the default setting for **DBDATE** is MDY4/, where M represents the month, D represents the day, Y4 represents a four-digit year, and slash (/) is a separator (for example, 01/08/1999).

Other acceptable characters for the separator are a hyphen (-), a period (.), or a zero (0). To indicate no separator, use the zero.

The slash (/) appears if you attempt to use a character other than a hyphen, period, or zero as a separator, or if you do not include a separator character in the **DBDATE** definition.

The following table shows some variations for setting the **DBDATE** environment variable.

Variation	January 8, 1999, appears as:
MDY4/	01/08/1999
DMY2-	08-01-99
MDY4	01/08/1999
Y2DM.	99.08.01
MDY20	010899
Y4MD*	1999/01/08

The formats Y4MD* (the asterisk is an unacceptable separator) and MDY4 (no separator is defined) both display the default (slash) as a separator.

Important: *If you use the Y2 format, the setting of the **DBCENTURY** environment variable affects how the DATE values are expanded.*

*Also, certain routines that Informix ESQL/C calls can use the **DBTIME** variable, rather than **DBDATE**, to set DATETIME formats to international specifications. For more information, see the discussion of the **DBTIME** environment variable on page 3-53 and the "Informix ESQL/C Programmer's Manual."*

GLS

The setting of the **DBDATE** variable takes precedence over that of the **GL_DATE** environment variable, as well as over the default DATE formats that **CLIENT_LOCALE** specifies. For information about the **GL_DATE** and **CLIENT_LOCALE** environment variables, see the *Informix Guide to GLS Functionality*. ♦

Behavior of DBDATE with Expressions that Contain Date Values

This section describes how the database server uses the **DBDATE** environment variable to interpret date values in UDRs, triggers, fragmentation expressions, and check constraints.

When an expression (UDR, trigger, check constraint, or fragmentation expression) contains a date value, the database server uses the setting of **DBDATE** at the time the database object (UDR, trigger, or table) is created. The value of **DBDATE** at creation time determines the format for date values during execution of UDRs and triggers and during evaluation of date values within check constraints and fragment expressions.

Suppose **DBDATE** is set to `MDY2/` and a user creates a table with the following check constraint on the column **orderdate**:

```
orderdate < '06/25/98'
```

The date of the preceding expression is formatted according to the value of **DBDATE** when the constraint is defined. The check constraint expression is interpreted as `orderdate < '06/25/98'` regardless of the value of **DBDATE** during inserts or updates on the **orderdate** column. Suppose **DBDATE** is set to `DMY2/` when a user inserts the value `'30/01/98'` into the **orderdate** column. The date value inserted uses the date format `DMY2/`, whereas the check constraint expression uses the date format `MDY2/`.

Important: *The behavior of **DBDATE** for Dynamic Server and Enterprise Decision Server is not backwards compatible.*

DBDELIMITER

The **DBDELIMITER** environment variable specifies the field delimiter used by the **dbexport** utility and with the LOAD and UNLOAD statements.

```
setenv ──────── DBDELIMITER ──────────── 'delimiter' ──────────────────┤
```

delimiter   is the field delimiter for unloaded data files.

The delimiter can be any single character, except the characters in the following list:

- Hexadecimal numbers (0 through 9, a through f, A through F)
- Newline or CTRL-J
- The backslash symbol (\)

The vertical bar (|=ASCII 124) is the default. To change the field delimiter to a plus (+), set the **DBDELIMITER** environment variable, as the following example shows:

```
setenv DBDELIMITER '+'
```

DBEDIT

The **DBEDIT** environment variable lets you name the text editor that you want to use to work with SQL statements and command files in DB-Access. If **DBEDIT** is set, the specified text editor is called directly. If **DBEDIT** is not set, you are prompted to specify a text editor as the default for the rest of the session.

```
setenv ──────── DBEDIT ──────────── editor ──────────────┤
```

editor   is the name of the text editor you want to use.

For most systems, the default text editor is **vi**. If you use another text editor, be sure that it creates flat ASCII files. Some word processors in *document mode* introduce printer control characters that can interfere with the operation of your Informix product.

To specify the EMACS text editor, set the **DBEDIT** environment variable by entering the following command:

```
setenv DBEDIT emacs
```

DBFLTMASK

The DB-Access utility displays the floating-point values of data types FLOAT, SMALLFLOAT, and DECIMAL within a 14-character buffer. By default, DB-Access displays as many digits to the right of the decimal point as will fit into this character buffer. Therefore, the actual number of decimal digits that DB-Access displays depends on the size of the floating-point value.

To reduce the number of digits that display to the right of the decimal point for floating-point values, you can set the **DBFLTMASK** environment variable to the number of digits desired.

```
setenv ———————— DBFLTMASK ———————— n ————————————————————┤
```

n   is the number of decimal digits that you want the Informix client application to display in the floating-point values. n must be smaller than 16, the default number of digits displayed.

If the floating-point value contains more digits to the right of the decimal than **DBFLTMASK** specifies, DB-Access rounds the value to the specified number of digits. If the floating-point value contains fewer digits to the right of the decimal, DB-Access pads the value with zeros. However, if you set **DBFLTMASK** to a value greater than can fit into the 14-character buffer, DB-Access rounds the value to the number of digits that can fit.

DBLANG

The **DBLANG** environment variable specifies the subdirectory of **$INFORMIXDIR** or the full pathname of the directory that contains the compiled message files that an Informix product uses.

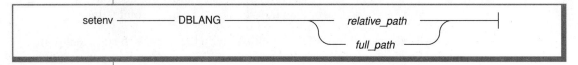

relative_path   is the subdirectory of **$INFORMIXDIR**.
full_path   is the full pathname of the directory that contains the
                 compiled message files.

By default, Informix products put compiled messages in a locale-specific subdirectory of the **$INFORMIXDIR/msg** directory. These compiled message files have the suffix **.iem**. If you want to use a message directory other than **$INFORMIXDIR/msg**, where, for example, you can store message files that you create, perform the following steps:

1. Use the **mkdir** command to create the appropriate directory for the message files.

    You can make this directory under the directory **$INFORMIXDIR** or **$INFORMIXDIR/msg**, or you can make it under any other directory.

2. Set the owner and group of the new directory to **informix** and the access permission for this directory to 755.

3. Set the **DBLANG** environment variable to the new directory.

    If this directory is a subdirectory of **$INFORMIXDIR** or **$INFORMIXDIR/msg**, you need only list the relative path to the new directory. Otherwise, you must specify the full pathname of the directory.

4. Copy the **.iem** files or the message files that you created to the new message directory that **$DBLANG** specifies.

    All the files in the message directory should have the owner and group **informix** and access permission 644.

Informix products that use the default U.S. ASCII English search for message files in the following order:

1. In **$DBLANG**, if **DBLANG** is set to a full pathname
2. In **$INFORMIXDIR/msg/$DBLANG**, if **DBLANG** is set to a relative pathname
3. In **$INFORMIXDIR/$DBLANG**, if **DBLANG** is set to a relative pathname
4. In **$INFORMIXDIR/msg/en_us/0333**
5. In **$INFORMIXDIR/msg/en_us.8859-1**
6. In **$INFORMIXDIR/msg**
7. In **$INFORMIXDIR/msg/english**

GLS

For more information on access paths for messages, see the description of **DBLANG** in the *Informix Guide to GLS Functionality*. ♦

DBMONEY

The **DBMONEY** environment variable specifies the display format of monetary values with FLOAT, DECIMAL, or MONEY data types.

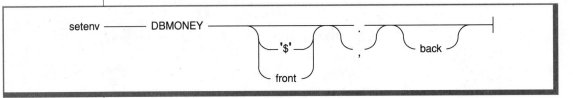

$	is the default symbol that precedes the MONEY value.
,	is an optional symbol (comma) that separates the integral from the fractional part of the MONEY value.
.	is the default symbol that separates the integral from the fractional part of the MONEY value.
back	is the optional symbol that follows the MONEY value. The *back* symbol can be up to seven characters and can contain any character except an integer, a comma, or a period. If *back* contains a dollar sign ($), you must enclose the whole string in single quotes (').
front	is the optional symbol that precedes the MONEY value. The *front* symbol can be up to seven characters and can contain any character except an integer, a comma, or a period. If *front* contains a dollar sign ($), you must enclose the whole string in single quotes (').

If you use any character except an alphabetic character for *front* or *back*, you must enclose the character in quotes.

When you display MONEY values, Informix products use the **DBMONEY** environment variable to format the output.

Tip: *The setting of* **DBMONEY** *does not affect the internal format of the MONEY column in the database.*

If you do not set **DBMONEY**, then MONEY values for the default locale, U.S. ASCII English, are formatted with a dollar sign ($) that precedes the MONEY value, a period (.) that separates the integral from the fractional part of the MONEY value, and no *back* symbol. For example, `10050` is formatted as `$100.50`.

Suppose you want to represent MONEY values in DM (Deutsche Mark), which uses the currency symbol DM and a comma. Enter the following command to set the **DBMONEY** environment variable:

```
setenv DBMONEY DM,
```

Here, DM is the currency symbol that precedes the MONEY value, and a comma separates the integral from the fractional part of the MONEY value. As a result, the amount 10050 is displayed as DM100,50.

GLS

For more information about how the **DBMONEY** environment variable handles MONEY formats for nondefault locales, see the *Informix Guide to GLS Functionality*. ◆

IDS

DBONPLOAD

The **DBONPLOAD** environment variable specifies the name of the database that the **onpload** utility of the High-Performance Loader (HPL) uses. If the **DBONPLOAD** environment variable is set, the specified name is the name of the database. If the **DBONPLOAD** environment variable is not set, the default name of the database is **onpload**.

```
setenv ──────── DBONPLOAD ──────────── dbname ─────────────┤
```

dbname   specifies the name of the database that the **onpload** utility uses.

For example, to specify the name **load_db** as the name of the database, enter the following command:

```
setenv DBONPLOAD load_db
```

For more information, see the *Guide to the High-Performance Loader*.

DBPATH

Use **DBPATH** to identify the database servers that contain databases. The **DBPATH** environment variable also specifies a list of directories (in addition to the current directory) in which DB-Access looks for command scripts (**.sql** files).

The CONNECT, DATABASE, START DATABASE, and DROP DATABASE statements use **DBPATH** to locate the database under two conditions:

- If the location of a database is not explicitly stated
- If the database cannot be located in the default server

The CREATE DATABASE statement does not use **DBPATH**.

To add a new **DBPATH** entry to existing entries, see "Modifying an Environment-Variable Setting" on page 3-11.

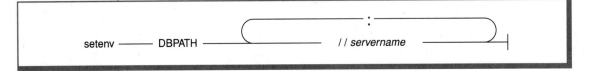

setenv ──── DBPATH ────── *// servername* ──────

servername   is the name of an Informix database server on which databases are stored. You cannot reference database files with a servername.

DBPATH can contain up to 16 entries. Each entry (*full_pathname, servername,* or *servername* and *full_pathname*) must be less than 128 characters. In addition, the maximum length of **DBPATH** depends on the hardware platform on which you set **DBPATH**.

When you access a database with the CONNECT, DATABASE, START DATABASE, or DROP DATABASE statement, the search for the database is done first in the directory and/or database server specified in the statement. If no database server is specified, the default database server as set in the **INFORMIXSERVER** environment variable is used.

If the database is not located during the initial search, and if **DBPATH** is set, the database servers and/or directories in **DBPATH** are searched for in the indicated database. The entries to **DBPATH** are considered in order.

Using DBPATH with DB-Access

If you use DB-Access and select the **Choose** option from the SQL menu without having already selected a database, you see a list of all the **.sql** files in the directories listed in your **DBPATH**. Once you select a database, the **DBPATH** is not used to find the **.sql** files. Only the **.sql** files in the current working directory are displayed.

Searching Local Directories

Use a pathname without a database server name to have the database server search for **.sql** scripts on your local computer.

In the following example, the **DBPATH** setting causes DB-Access to search for the database files in your current directory and then in Joachim's and Sonja's directories on the local computer:

```
setenv DBPATH /usr/joachim:/usr/sonja
```

As the previous example shows, if the pathname specifies a directory name but not a database server name, the directory is sought on the computer that runs the default database server that the **INFORMIXSERVER** environment variable specifies (see page 3-70). For instance, with the previous example, if **INFORMIXSERVER** is set to **quality**, the **DBPATH** value is *interpreted,* as the following example shows, where the double slash precedes the database server name:

```
setenv DBPATH //quality/usr/joachim://quality/usr/sonja
```

Searching Networked Computers for Databases

If you use more than one database server, you can set **DBPATH** to explicitly contain the database server and/or directory names that you want to search for databases. For example, if **INFORMIXSERVER** is set to **quality** but you also want to search the **marketing** database server for **/usr/joachim**, set **DBPATH** as the following example shows:

```
setenv DBPATH //marketing/usr/joachim:/usr/sonja
```

Specifying a Servername

You can set **DBPATH** to contain only database server names. This setting allows you to locate only databases and not locate command files.

The database administrator must include each database server mentioned by **DBPATH** in the **$INFORMIXDIR/etc/sqlhosts** file. For information on communication-configuration files and dbservernames, see your *Administrator's Guide* and the *Administrator's Reference*.

For example, if **INFORMIXSERVER** is set to **quality**, you can search for a database first on the **quality** database server and then on the **marketing** database server by setting **DBPATH** as the following example shows:

```
setenv DBPATH //marketing
```

If you use DB-Access in this example, the names of all the databases on the **quality** and **marketing** database servers are displayed with the **Select** option of the DATABASE menu.

UNIX

DBPRINT

The **DBPRINT** environment variable specifies the printing program that you want to use.

```
setenv ──────── DBPRINT ──────── program ───────────────────────┤
```

| program | names any command, shell script, or UNIX utility that handles standard ASCII input. |

The default program is found in one of two places:

- For most BSD UNIX systems, the default program is **lpr**.
- For UNIX System V, the default program is usually **lp**.

Enter the following command to set the **DBPRINT** environment variable to specify the **myprint** print program:

```
setenv DBPRINT myprint
```

UNIX

DBREMOTECMD

You can set the **DBREMOTECMD** environment variable to override the default remote shell used when you perform remote tape operations with the database server.

You can set the **DBREMOTECMD** environment variable with either a simple command or the full pathname. If you use the full pathname, the database server searches your **PATH** for the specified command.

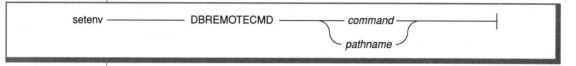

| *command* | is the command to override the default remote shell. |
| *pathname* | is the pathname to override the default remote shell. |

Informix highly recommends the use of the full pathname syntax on the interactive UNIX platform to avoid problems with similarly named programs in other directories and possible confusion with the *restricted shell* (**/usr/bin/rsh**).

Enter the following command to set the **DBREMOTECMD** environment variable for a simple command name:

```
setenv DBREMOTECMD rcmd
```

Enter the following command to set the **DBREMOTECMD** environment variable to specify the full pathname:

```
setenv DBREMOTECMD /usr/bin/remsh
```

For more information on **DBREMOTECMD**, see the discussion in your *Archive and Backup Guide* about how to use remote tape devices with your database server for archives, restores, and logical-log backups.

DBSPACETEMP

You can set your **DBSPACETEMP** environment variable to specify the dbspaces in which temporary tables are to be built. You can specify multiple dbspaces to spread temporary space across any number of disks.

punct   can be either colons or commas.

temp_dbspace   is a valid existing temporary dbspace.

The **DBSPACETEMP** environment variable overrides the default dbspaces that the DBSPACETEMP configuration parameter specifies in the configuration file for your database server.

Important: *The dbspaces that you list in **DBSPACETEMP** must be composed of chunks that are allocated as raw UNIX devices.*

For example, you might set the **DBSPACETEMP** environment variable with the following command:

```
setenv DBSPACETEMP sorttmp1:sorttmp2:sorttmp3
```

Separate the dbspace entries with either colons or commas. The number of dbspaces is limited by the maximum size of the environment variable, as defined by your operating system. Your database server does not create a dbspace specified by the environment variable if the dbspace does not exist.

The two classes of temporary tables are explicit temporary tables that the user creates and implicit temporary tables that the database server creates. Use the **DBSPACETEMP** environment variable to specify the dbspaces for both types of temporary tables.

If you create an explicit temporary table with the CREATE TEMP TABLE statement and do not specify a dbspace for the table either in the IN *dbspace* clause or in the FRAGMENT BY clause, the database server uses the settings in the **DBSPACETEMP** environment variable to determine where to create the table.

If you create an explicit temporary table with the SELECT INTO TEMP statement, the database server uses the settings in the **DBSPACETEMP** environment variable to determine where to create the table. If the **DBSPACETEMP** environment variable is not set, the database server uses the ONCONFIG parameter DBSPACETEMP. If this parameter is not set, the database server creates the explicit temporary table in the same dbspace where the database resides.

The database server creates implicit temporary tables for its own use while executing join operations, SELECT statements with the GROUP BY clause, SELECT statements with the ORDER BY clause, and index builds. When it creates these implicit temporary tables, the database server uses disk space for writing the temporary data, in the following order:

UNIX

1. The operating-system directory or directories that the environment variable **PSORT_DBTEMP** specifies, if it is set. ♦

2. The dbspace or dbspaces that the environment variable **DBSPACETEMP** specifies, if it is set.

3. The dbspace or dbspaces that the ONCONFIG parameter DBSPACETEMP specifies.

4. The operating-system file space in **/tmp** (UNIX) or **%temp%** (Windows NT).

If the **DBSPACETEMP** environment variable is set to a nonexistent dbspace, the database server defaults to the root dbspace for explicit temporary tables and to **/tmp** for implicit temporary tables, not to the DBSPACETEMP configuration parameter.

Important: *If the **DBSPACETEMP** environment variable is set to an invalid value, the database server might fill **/tmp** to the limit and eventually bring down the system or kill the file system.*

DBTEMP

Set the **DBTEMP** environment variable to specify the full pathname of the directory into which you want Informix Enterprise Gateway products to place their temporary files and temporary tables.

```
setenv ──────────── DBTEMP ─────────── pathname ──────────────┤
```

pathname   is the full pathname of the directory for temporary files and temporary tables.

Set the **DBTEMP** environment variable to specify the pathname **usr/magda/mytemp** by entering the following command:

```
setenv DBTEMP usr/magda/mytemp
```

Important: *DBTEMP must not point to an NFS directory.*

If you do not set **DBTEMP**, temporary files are created in **/tmp**. If **DBTEMP** is not set, temporary tables are created in the directory of the database (that is, the **.dbs** directory). For more information, see your *INFORMIX-Enterprise Gateway User Manual*.

DBTIME

The **DBTIME** environment variable specifies the end-user formats of DATETIME values for a set of SQL API library functions.

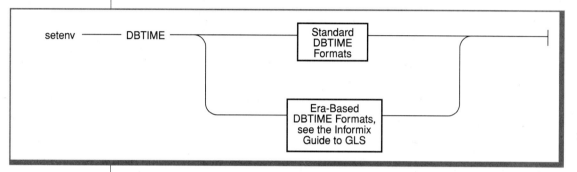

You can set the **DBTIME** environment variable to manipulate DATETIME formats so that the formats conform more closely to various international or local TIME conventions. **DBTIME** takes effect only when you call certain Informix ESQL/C DATETIME routines; otherwise, use the **DBDATE** environment variable. (For details, see the *Informix ESQL/C Programmer's Manual*.)

You can set **DBTIME** to specify the exact format of an input/output (I/O) DATETIME string field with the formatting directives described in the following list. Otherwise, the behavior of the DATETIME formatting routine is undefined.

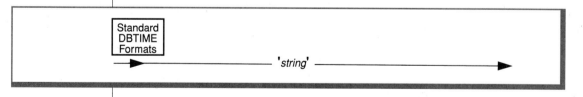

string   the formatting directives that you can use, as the following list describes:

    %b   is replaced by the abbreviated month name.

    %B   is replaced by the full month name.

%d	is replaced by the day of the month as a decimal number [01,31].
%Fn	is replaced by the value of the fraction with precision that the integer n specifies. The default value of n is 2; the range of n is $0 \le n \le 5$.
%H	is replaced by the hour (24-hour clock).
%I	is replaced by the hour (12-hour clock).
%M	is replaced by the minute as a decimal number [00,59].
%m	is replaced by the month as a decimal number [01,12].
%p	is replaced by A.M. or P.M. (or the equivalent in the local standards).
%S	is replaced by the second as a decimal number [00,59].
%y	is replaced by the year as a four-digit decimal number. If the user enters a two-digit value, the format of this value is affected by the setting of the **DBCENTURY** environment variable. If **DBCENTURY** is not set, then the current century is used for the century digits.
%Y	is replaced by the year as a four-digit decimal number. User must enter a four-digit value.
%%	is replaced by % (to allow % in the format string).

For example, consider how to convert a DATETIME YEAR TO SECOND to the following ASCII string format:

```
Mar 21, 1999 at 16 h 30 m 28 s
```

Set **DBTIME** as the following list shows:

```
setenv DBTIME '%b %d, %Y at %H h %M m %S s'
```

The default **DBTIME** produces the conventional ANSI SQL string format that the following line shows:

```
1999-03-21 16:30:28
```

Set the default **DBTIME** as the following example shows:

```
setenv DBTIME '%Y-%m-%d %H:%M:%S'
```

An optional field width and precision specification can immediately follow the percent (%) character; it is interpreted as the following list describes:

[-|0]w where w is a decimal digit string specifying the minimum field width. By default, the value is right justified with spaces on the left.
If - is specified, it is left justified with spaces on the right.
If 0 is specified, it is right justified and padded with zeros on the left.

.p where p is a decimal digit string specifying the number of digits to appear for d, H, I, m, M, S, y, and Y conversions, and the maximum number of characters to be used for b and B conversions. A precision specification is significant only when converting a DATETIME value to an ASCII string and not vice versa.

When you use field width and precision specifications, the following limitations apply:

- If a conversion specification supplies fewer digits than a precision specifies, it is padded with leading zeros.

- If a conversion specification supplies more characters than a precision specifies, excess characters are truncated on the right.

- If no field width or precision is specified for d, H, I, m, M, S, or y conversions, a default of 0.2 is used. A default of 0.4 is used for Y conversions.

The F conversion does not follow the field width and precision format conversions that are described earlier.

For related information, see the discussion of **DBDATE** on page 3-36.

GLS

For more information about how the **DBTIME** environment variable handles time formats for nondefault locales, see the *Informix Guide to GLS Functionality.* ◆

DBUPSPACE

The **DBUPSPACE** environment variable lets you specify and constrain the amount of system disk space that the UPDATE STATISTICS statement can use when trying to simultaneously construct multiple column distributions.

```
setenv ─────────── DBUPSPACE ─────────── value ───────────────────────
```

value   represents a disk space amount in kilobytes.

For example, to set **DBUPSPACE** to 2,500 kilobytes, enter the following command:

```
setenv DBUPSPACE 2500
```

Once you set this value, the database server can use no more than 2,500 kilobytes of disk space during the execution of an UPDATE STATISTICS statement. If a table requires 5 megabytes of disk space for sorting, then UPDATE STATISTICS accomplishes the task in two passes; the distributions for one half of the columns are constructed with each pass.

If you try to set **DBUPSPACE** to any value less than 1,024 kilobytes, it is automatically set to 1,024 kilobytes, but no error message is returned. If this value is not large enough to allow more than one distribution to be constructed at a time, at least one distribution is done, even if the amount of disk space required for the one is greater than specified in **DBUPSPACE**.

DELIMIDENT

The **DELIMIDENT** environment variable specifies that strings set off by double quotes are delimited identifiers.

```
setenv ——————— DELIMIDENT ——————— value ——————————————————┤
```

You can use delimited identifiers to specify identifiers that are identical to reserved keywords, such as TABLE or USAGE. You can also use them to specify database identifiers that contain nonalpha characters, but you cannot use them to specify storage identifiers that contain nonalpha characters. Database identifiers are names for database objects such as tables and columns, and storage identifiers are names for storage objects such as dbspaces and partition simple large objects.

Delimited identifiers are case sensitive.

To use delimited identifiers, applications in ESQL/C must set the **DELIMIDENT** environment variable at compile time and execute time.

UNIX

ENVIGNORE

Use the **ENVIGNORE** environment variable to deactivate specified environment variable entries in the common (shared) and private environment-configuration files, **informix.rc** and **.informix** respectively.

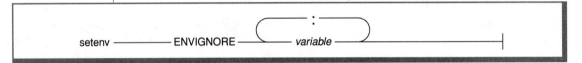

variable   is the list of environment variables that you want to deactivate.

For example, to ignore the **DBPATH** and **DBMONEY** entries in the environment-configuration files, enter the following command:

```
setenv ENVIGNORE DBPATH:DBMONEY
```

The common environment-configuration file is stored in **$INFORMIXDIR/etc/informix.rc**. The private environment-configuration file is stored in the user's home directory as **.informix**. For information on creating or modifying an environment-configuration file, see "Setting Environment Variables in an Environment-Configuration File" on page 3-8.

ENVIGNORE cannot be set in an environment-configuration file.

FET_BUF_SIZE

The **FET_BUF_SIZE** environment variable lets you override the default setting for the size of the fetch buffer for all data except simple large objects. When set, **FET_BUF_SIZE** is effective for the entire environment.

```
setenv ─────── FET_BUF_SIZE ───────    n   ────────────────┤
```

n   represents the size of the buffer in bytes.

When set to a valid value, the environment variable overrides the previously set value. The default setting for the fetch buffer is dependent on row size.

If the buffer size is set to less than the default size or is out of the range of the small integer value, no error is raised. The new buffer size is ignored.

For example, to set a buffer size to 5,000 bytes, set the **FET_BUF_SIZE** environment variable by entering the following command:

```
setenv FET_BUF_SIZE 5000
```

EDS

IFMX_SMLTBL_BROADCAST_SIZE

The **IFMX_SMLTBL_BROADCAST_SIZE** environment variable setting determines the threshold size of tables that are used in Small Table Broadcast when the table size exceeds 128 kilobytes. The **IFMX_SMLTBL_BROADCAST_SIZE** environment variable is set on the database server.

setenv ——— IFMX_SMLTBL_BROADCAST ——————— n ———————|

n represents the size of the table in kilobytes.

Important: *Query performance can suffer if the **IFMX_SMLTBL_BROADCAST** environment variable is set beyond a certain table size. The recommended upper limit on table size depends on your computer and the configuration of your database server.*

For more information about the **IFMX_SMLTBL_BROADCAST** environment variable, see your documentation notes or release notes.

IFX_DIRECTIVES

The **IFX_DIRECTIVES** environment variable setting determines whether the optimizer allows query optimization directives from within a query. The **IFX_DIRECTIVES** environment variable is set on the client.

You can use either ON and OFF or 1 and 0 to set the environment variable.

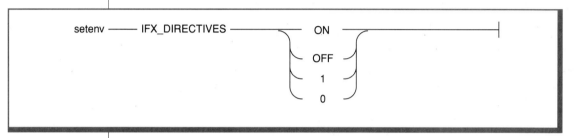

ON	Optimizer directives accepted
OFF	Optimizer directives not accepted
1	Optimizer directives accepted
0	Optimizer directives not accepted

The setting of the **IFX_DIRECTIVES** environment variable overrides the value of the DIRECTIVES configuration parameter that is set for the database server. If the **IFX_DIRECTIVES** environment variable is not set, however, then all client sessions will inherit the database server configuration for directives that the ONCONFIG parameter DIRECTIVES determines. The default setting for the DIRECTIVES parameter is ON.

For more information about the DIRECTIVES parameter, see the *Administrator's Reference*. For more information on the performance impact of directives, see your *Performance Guide*.

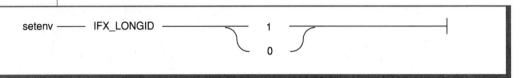

IFX_LONGID

Use the **IFX_LONGID** environment variable setting and the version number of the client application to determine whether a particular client application is capable of handling long identifiers. Valid **IFX_LONGID** values are 1 and 0.

setenv ─── IFX_LONGID ─────────┬─── 1 ──┬───────────┤
                                └─── 0 ──┘

| 1 | Client can handle long identifiers |
| 0 | Client cannot handle long identifiers |

If **IFX_LONGID** is unset or is set to a value other than 1 or 0, the determination is based on the internal version of the client application. If the version is >= 9.0304, the client is considered *new* and thus capable of handling long identifiers. Otherwise, the client application is considered incapable.

The **IFX_LONGID** setting overrides the internal version of the client application. If the client cannot handle long identifiers despite a newer version number, set **IFX_LONGID** to 0. If the client version can handle long identifiers despite an older version number, set **IFX_LONGID** to 1.

If you set the **IFX_LONGID** environment variable at the client, the setting affects only that client. If you bring up the database server with **IFX_LONGID** set, all client applications will adhere to that setting. If **IFX_LONGID** is set at both the client and the database server, the client setting takes precedence.

Important: *ESQL executables that have been built with the **-static** option using the **libos.a** library version that does not support long identifiers cannot use the IFX_LONGID environment variable. You must recompile such applications with the new **libos.a** library that includes support for long identifiers. Executables that use shared libraries (no **-static** option) can use **IFX_LONGID** without recompilation provided that they use the new **libifos.so** that provides support for long identifiers. For details, see your ESQL product manual.*

UNIX

IFX_NETBUF_PVTPOOL_SIZE

The **IFX_NETBUF_PVTPOOL_SIZE** environment variable specifies the maximum size of the free (unused) private network buffer pool for each database server session.

setenv —— IFX_NETBUF_PVTPOOL_SIZE —— *n* ——————————|

n   represents the number of units (buffers) in the pool.

The default size is 1 buffer. If **IFX_NETBUF_PVTPOOL_SIZE** is set to 0, each session obtains buffers from the free global network buffer pool. You must specify the value in decimal form.

IFX_NETBUF_SIZE

The **IFX_NETBUF_SIZE** environment variable lets you configure the network buffers to the optimum size. It specifies the size of all network buffers in the free (unused) global pool and the private network buffer pool for each database server session.

setenv —— IFX_NETBUF_SIZE —— *n* ——————————|

n   represents the size (in bytes) for one network buffer.

The default size is 4 kilobytes (4,096 bytes). The maximum size is 64 kilobytes (65,536 bytes) and the minimum size is 512 bytes. You can specify the value in hexadecimal or decimal form.

Tip: *You cannot set a different size for each session.*

IDS

IFX_UPDDESC

The **IFX_UPDDESC** environment variable controls the use of the describe-for-updates functionality. You must set **IFX_UPDDESC** at execution time before you do a DESCRIBE of an UPDATE statement.

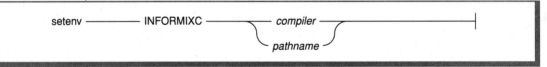

setenv ─────────────── IFX_UPDDESC ───────── *value* ─────────────┤

You can set **IFX_UPDDESC** to any value. A null value (the environment variable is not set) indicates that the feature is not being used. Any nonnull value indicates that the feature is enabled.

UNIX

INFORMIXC

The **INFORMIXC** environment variable specifies the name or pathname of the C compiler to be used to compile files that Informix ESQL/C generates.

If **INFORMIXC** is not set, the default compiler is cc.

Tip: *On Windows NT, you pass either **-mcc** or **-bcc** options to the **esql** preprocessor to use either the Microsoft or Borland C compilers.*

setenv ─────── INFORMIXC ───────┬─ *compiler* ─┬──────────────┤
                                 └─ *pathname* ─┘

compiler   is the name of the C compiler.
pathname   is the full pathname of the C compiler.

For example, to specify the GNU C compiler, enter the following command:

```
setenv INFORMIXC gcc
```

The setting is required only during the C compilation stage.

IDS

INFORMIXCONCSMCFG

The **INFORMIXCONCSMCFG** environment variable specifies the location of the **concsm.cfg** file that describes communications support modules.

setenv ──────── INFORMIXCONCSMCFG ──────── *pathname* ──────────┤

pathname   specifies the full pathname of the **concsm.cfg** file.

The following sample command specifies that the **concsm.cfg** file is in **/usr/myfiles**:

```
setenv INFORMIXCONCSMCFG /usr/myfiles
```

You can also specify a different name for the file. The following example specifies a filename of **csmconfig**:

```
setenv INFORMIXCONCSMCFG /usr/myfiles/csmconfig
```

The default location of the **concsm.cfg** file is in **$INFORMIXDIR/etc**. For more information about communications support modules and the contents of the **concsm.cfg** file, refer to the *Administrator's Reference*.

INFORMIXCONRETRY

The **INFORMIXCONRETRY** environment variable specifies the maximum number of additional connection attempts that should be made to each server by the client during the time limit that the **INFORMIXCONTIME** environment variable specifies.

```
setenv ————————INFORMIXCONRETRY———————— value ————————————————
```

value　　　　represents the number of connection attempts to each server.

For example, enter the following command to set **INFORMIXCONRETRY** to three additional connection attempts (after the initial attempt):

```
setenv INFORMIXCONRETRY 3
```

The default value for **INFORMIXCONRETRY** is one retry after the initial connection attempt. The **INFORMIXCONTIME** setting, described in the following section, takes precedence over the **INFORMIXCONRETRY** setting.

INFORMIXCONTIME

The **INFORMIXCONTIME** environment variable lets you specify that an SQL CONNECT statement should keep trying for at least the given number of seconds before returning an error.

You might encounter connection difficulties related to system or network load problems. For instance, if the database server is busy establishing new SQL client threads, some clients might fail because the database server cannot issue a network function call fast enough. The **INFORMIXCONTIME** and **INFORMIXCONRETRY** environment variables let you configure your client-side connection capability to retry the connection instead of returning an error.

```
setenv ———————— INFORMIXCONTIME ———————— value ————————————————
```

value　　　　represents the minimum number of seconds spent in attempts to establish a connection to a database server.

For example, enter the following command to set **INFORMIXCONTIME** to 60 seconds:

```
setenv INFORMIXCONTIME 60
```

If **INFORMIXCONTIME** is set to 60 and **INFORMIXCONRETRY** is set to 3, attempts to connect to the database server (after the initial attempt at 0 seconds) are made at 20, 40, and 60 seconds, if necessary, before aborting. This 20-second interval is the result of **INFORMIXCONTIME** divided by **INFORMIXCONRETRY**.

If execution of the CONNECT statement involves searching **DBPATH**, the following rules apply:

- All appropriate servers in the **DBPATH** setting are accessed at least once, even though the **INFORMIXCONTIME** value might be exceeded. Thus, the CONNECT statement might take longer than the **INFORMIXCONTIME** time limit to return an error that indicates connection failure or that the database was not found.

- The **INFORMIXCONRETRY** value specifies the number of additional connections that should be attempted for each server entry in **DBPATH**.

- The **INFORMIXCONTIME** value is divided among the number of server entries specified in **DBPATH**. Thus, if **DBPATH** contains numerous servers, you should increase the **INFORMIXCONTIME** value accordingly. For example, if **DBPATH** contains three entries, to spend at least 30 seconds attempting each connection, set **INFORMIXCONTIME** to 90.

The default value for **INFORMIXCONTIME** is 15 seconds. The setting for **INFORMIXCONTIME** takes precedence over the **INFORMIXCONRETRY** setting. Retry efforts could end after the **INFORMIXCONTIME** value is exceeded but before the **INFORMIXCONRETRY** value is reached.

INFORMIXCPPMAP

IDS

Set the **INFORMIXCPPMAP** environment variable to specify the fully qualified pathname of the map file for C++ programs. Information in the map file includes the database server type, the name of the shared library that supports the database object or value object type, the library entry point for the object, and the C++ library for which an object was built.

```
setenv ———— INFORMIXCPPMAP ———— pathname ————|
```

pathname   is the directory path where the C++ map file is stored.

The map file is a text file that can have any file name. The **INFORMIXCPPMAP** setting can include several map files separated by colons (:) on UNIX or semicolons (;) on Windows NT. On UNIX, the default map file is **$INFORMIXDIR/etc/c++map**. On Windows NT, the default map file is **%INFORMIXDIR%\etc\c++map**.

INFORMIXDIR

The **INFORMIXDIR** environment variable specifies the directory that contains the subdirectories in which your product files are installed. You must always set the **INFORMIXDIR** environment variable. Verify that the **INFORMIXDIR** environment variable is set to the full pathname of the directory in which you installed your database server. If you have multiple versions of a database server, set **INFORMIXDIR** to the appropriate directory name for the version that you want to access. For information about when to set the **INFORMIXDIR** environment variable, see your *Installation Guide*.

```
setenv ———— INFORMIXDIR ———— pathname ————|
```

pathname   is the directory path where the product files are installed.

To set the **INFORMIXDIR** environment variable to the desired installation directory, enter the following command:

```
setenv INFORMIXDIR /usr/informix
```

UNIX

INFORMIXKEYTAB

The **INFORMIXKEYTAB** environment variable specifies the location of the **keytab** file. The **keytab** file contains authentication information that database servers and clients access at connection time, if they use the DCE-GSS communications support module (CSM). It contains key tables that store keys, each of which contains a principal name (database server or user name), type, version, and value.

The database server uses the **keytab** file to find the key to register the server and to acquire a credential for it. A client application uses the key if the user did not do **dce_login** with the current operating-system user name (which is the same as the DCE principle name) or did not explicitly provide a credential.

```
setenv ——————————— INFORMIXKEYTAB ——————————— pathname
```

pathname   specifies the full path of the **keytab** file.

For example, the following command specifies that the name and location of the **keytab** file is **/usr/myfiles/mykeytab**:

```
setenv INFORMIXKEYTAB /usr/myfiles/mykeytab
```

For more information about the DCE-GSS communications support module, see the *Administrator's Guide*.

IDS

INFORMIXOPCACHE

The **INFORMIXOPCACHE** environment variable lets you specify the size of the memory cache for the staging-area blobspace of the client application.

```
setenv ──────────────────── INFORMIXOPCACHE ─────────────── kilobytes
```

kilobytes   specifies the value you set for the optical memory cache.

Set the **INFORMIXOPCACHE** environment variable by specifying the size of the memory cache in kilobytes. The specified size must be equal to or smaller than the size of the system-wide configuration parameter, OPCACHEMAX.

If you do not set the **INFORMIXOPCACHE** environment variable, the default cache size is 128 kilobytes or the size specified in the configuration parameter OPCACHEMAX. The default for OPCACHEMAX is 128 kilobytes. If you set **INFORMIXOPCACHE** to a value of 0, Optical Subsystem does not use the cache.

INFORMIXSERVER

The **INFORMIXSERVER** environment variable specifies the default database server to which an explicit or implicit connection is made by an SQL API client or the DB-Access utility.

The database server can be either local or remote. You must always set **INFORMIXSERVER** before you use an Informix product.

```
setenv ───────── INFORMIXSERVER ──────── dbservername ──────────────┤
```

dbservername   is the name of the default database server.

The value of **INFORMIXSERVER** must correspond to a valid *dbservername* entry in the **$INFORMIXDIR/etc/sqlhosts** file on the computer running the application. The *dbservername* must be specified using lowercase characters and cannot exceed 128 characters. For example, to specify the **coral** database server as the default for connection, enter the following command:

```
setenv INFORMIXSERVER coral
```

INFORMIXSERVER specifies the database server to which an application connects if the CONNECT DEFAULT statement is executed. It also defines the database server to which an initial implicit connection is established if the first statement in an application is not a CONNECT statement.

Important: *You must set **INFORMIXSERVER** even if the application or DB-Access does not use implicit or explicit default connections.*

EDS

For Enterprise Decision Server, the **INFORMIXSERVER** environment variable specifies the name of a dbserver group. To specify a coserver name, use the following format:

```
dbservername.coserver_number
```

In the coserver name, dbservername is the value that you assigned to the DBSERVERNAME configuration parameter when you prepared the ONCONFIG configuration file, and *coserver_number* is the value that you assigned to the COSERVER configuration parameter for the connection coserver.

Strictly speaking, **INFORMIXSERVER** is not required for initialization. However, if **INFORMIXSERVER** is not set, Enterprise Decision Server does not build the **sysmaster** tables. ♦

UNIX

INFORMIXSHMBASE

The **INFORMIXSHMBASE** environment variable affects only client applications connected to Informix databases that use the interprocess communications (IPC) shared-memory (**ipcshm**) protocol.

 Important: *Resetting **INFORMIXSHMBASE** requires a thorough understanding of how the application uses memory. Normally you do not reset **INFORMIXSHMBASE**.*

Use **INFORMIXSHMBASE** to specify where shared-memory communication segments are attached to the client process so that client applications can avoid collisions with other memory segments that the application uses. If you do not set **INFORMIXSHMBASE**, the memory address of the communication segments defaults to an implementation-specific value such as 0x800000.

```
setenv ──────── INFORMIXSHMBASE ──────── value ────────┤
```

value   is used to calculate the memory address.

The database server calculates the memory address where segments are attached by multiplying the value of **INFORMIXSHMBASE** by 1,024. For example, to set the memory address to the value 0x800000, set the **INFORMIXSHMBASE** environment variable by entering the following command:

```
setenv INFORMIXSHMBASE 8192
```

For more information, see your *Administrator's Guide* and the *Administrator's Reference*.

INFORMIXSQLHOSTS

The **INFORMIXSQLHOSTS** environment variable specifies the full pathname
to the place where client-database server connectivity information is
stored. On UNIX, by default, this environment variable points to the
$INFORMIXDIR/etc/sqlhosts file. For example, to specify that the client or
database server will look for connectivity information in the **mysqlhosts**
file in the **/work/envt** directory, enter the following command:

```
setenv INFORMIXSQLHOSTS /work/envt/mysqlhosts
```

When the **INFORMIXSQLHOSTS** environment variable is set, the client or
database server looks in the specified file for connectivity information.
When the **INFORMIXSQLHOSTS** environment variable is not set, the client
or database server looks in the **$INFORMIXDIR/etc/sqlhosts** file.

```
setenv ──────────────── INFORMIXSQLHOSTS ──────────── pathname ──────┤
```

pathname	specifies the full pathname and filename of the file that contains connectivity information.

On Windows NT, by default, this environment variable points to the
computer whose registry contains the SQLHOSTS subkey. To specify that the
client or database server look for connectivity information on a computer
named **arizona**, enter the following command:

```
set INFORMIXSQLHOSTS = \\arizona
```

For a description of the SqlHosts information, see your *Administrator's Guide*.

INFORMIXSTACKSIZE

INFORMIXSTACKSIZE specifies the stack size (in kilobytes) that the database server uses for a particular client session.

Use **INFORMIXSTACKSIZE** to override the value of the ONCONFIG parameter STACKSIZE for a particular application or user.

setenv ─────────── INFORMIXSTACKSIZE ──────── *value* ───────────┤

value   is the stack size for SQL client threads in kilobytes.

For example, to decrease the **INFORMIXSTACKSIZE** to 20 kilobytes, enter the following command:

```
setenv INFORMIXSTACKSIZE 20
```

If **INFORMIXSTACKSIZE** is not set, the stack size is taken from the database server configuration parameter STACKSIZE, or it defaults to a platform-specific value. The default stack size value for the primary thread for an SQL client is 32 kilobytes for nonrecursive database activity.

Warning: *For specific instructions on setting this value, see the "Administrator's Reference." If you incorrectly set the value of* **INFORMIXSTACKSIZE**, *it can cause the database server to fail.*

UNIX

INFORMIXTERM

The **INFORMIXTERM** environment variable specifies whether DB-Access should use the information in the **termcap** file or the **terminfo** directory.

The **termcap** file and **terminfo** directory determine terminal-dependent keyboard and screen capabilities, such as the operation of function keys, color and intensity attributes in screen displays, and the definition of window borders and graphic characters.

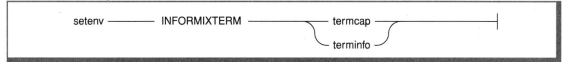

If **INFORMIXTERM** is not set, the default setting is **termcap**. When DB-Access is installed on your system, a **termcap** file is placed in the **etc** subdirectory of **$INFORMIXDIR**. This file is a superset of an operating-system **termcap** file.

You can use the **termcap** file that Informix supplies, the system **termcap** file, or a **termcap** file that you create. You must set the **TERMCAP** environment variable if you do not use the default **termcap** file. For information on setting the **TERMCAP** environment variable, see page 3-96.

The **terminfo** directory contains a file for each terminal name that has been defined. The **terminfo** setting for **INFORMIXTERM** is supported only on computers that provide full support for the UNIX System V **terminfo** library. For details, see the machine notes file for your product.

IDS

INF_ROLE_SEP

The **INF_ROLE_SEP** environment variable configures the security feature of role separation when the database server is installed. Role separation enforces separating administrative tasks that different people who are involved in running and auditing the database server perform.

Tip: *To enable role separation for database servers on Windows NT, choose the role-separation option during installation.*

If **INF_ROLE_SEP** is set, role separation is implemented and a separate group is specified to serve each of the following responsibilities: the database system security officer (DBSSO), the audit analysis officer (AAO), and the standard user. If **INF_ROLE_SEP** is not set, user **informix** (the default) can perform all administrative tasks.

setenv ──────────────── INF_ROLE_SEP ──────────────── *n* ──────┤

n   is any positive integer.

For more information about the security feature of role separation, see the *Trusted Facility Manual*. To learn how to configure role separation when you install your database server, see your *Installation Guide*.

ISM_COMPRESSION

Set the **ISM_COMPRESSION** environment variable in the ON-Bar environment to specify whether the Informix Storage Manager (ISM) should use data compression.

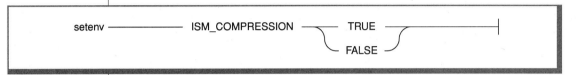

If **ISM_COMPRESSION** is set to TRUE in the environment of the ON-Bar process that makes a request, the ISM server uses a data-compression algorithm to store or retrieve the data specified in that request.

If **ISM_COMPRESSION** is set to FALSE or is not set, the ISM server does not use compression.

ISM_DEBUG_FILE

Set the **ISM_DEBUG_FILE** environment variable in the Informix Storage Manager server environment to specify where the XBSA messages should be written.

```
setenv ——————— ISM_DEBUG_FILE ——————— pathname ———————|
```

pathname   specifies the location of the XBSA message log file.

If you do not set **ISM_DEBUG_FILE**, the XBSA message log is located in **$INFORMIXDIR/ism/applogs/xbsa.messages** on UNIX or **c:\nsr\applogs\xbsa.messages** on Windows NT.

ISM_DEBUG_LEVEL

Set the **ISM_DEBUG_LEVEL** environment variable in the ON-Bar
environment to control the level of reporting detail recorded in the XBSA
messages log. The XBSA shared library writes to this log.

setenv ──────────── ISM_DEBUG_LEVEL ──────── *value* ──────────────────┤

value   specifies the level of reporting detail.

You can specify a value between 0 and 9. If **ISM_DEBUG_LEVEL** is not set, has
a null value, or has a value outside this range, the default detail level is 1.

A detail level of 0 suppresses all XBSA debugging records. A detail level of 1
reports only XBSA failures.

ISM_ENCRYPTION

Set the **ISM_ENCRYPTION** environment variable in the ON-Bar environment to specify whether the Informix Storage Manager (ISM) should use data encryption.

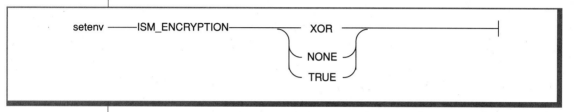

XOR	uses encryption.
NONE	does not use encryption.
TRUE	uses encryption.

If the **ISM_ENCRYPTION** environment variable is set to TRUE or XOR in the environment of the ON-Bar process that makes a request, the ISM server uses encryption to store or retrieve the data specified in that request.

If **ISM_ENCRYPTION** is set to NONE or is not set, the ISM server does not use encryption.

ISM_MAXLOGSIZE

Set the **ISM_MAXLOGSIZE** environment variable in the Informix Storage Manager (ISM) server environment to specify the size threshold of the ISM activity log.

setenv ——————— ISM_MAXLOGSIZE ——— *value* ———————	

value specifies the size threshold of the activity log.

If **ISM_MAXLOGSIZE** is not set, the default size limit is 1 megabyte. If **ISM_MAXLOGSIZE** is set to a null value, the threshold is 0 bytes.

ISM_MAXLOGVERS

Set the **ISM_MAXLOGSVERS** environment variable in the Informix Storage Manager (ISM) server environment to specify the maximum number of activity-log files to be preserved by the ISM server.

```
setenv ─────────── ISM_MAXLOGVERS ─────── value ───────────────┤
```

value   specifies the number of files to be preserved.

If **ISM_MAXLOGSVERS** is not set, the default number of files to be preserved is four. If **ISM_MAXLOGSVERS** is set to a null value, the ISM server preserves no activity log files.

UNIX

LD_LIBRARY_PATH

The **LD_LIBRARY_PATH** environment variable tells the shell on Solaris systems which directories to search for client or shared Informix general libraries. You must specify the directory that contains your client libraries before you can use the product.

```
                                      ┌──── : ────┐
setenv ──── LD_LIBRARY_PATH ──── $PATH: ─┴── pathname ─┴─────────┤
```

pathname   specifies the search path for the library.

The following example sets the **LD_LIBRARY_PATH** environment variable to the desired directory:

```
setenv LD_LIBRARY_PATH
${INFORMIXDIR}/lib:${INFORMIXDIR}/lib/esql:$LD_LIBRARY_PATH
```

For INTERSOLV DataDirect ODBC Driver on AIX, set **LIBPATH**. For INTERSOLV DataDirect ODBC Driver on HP-UX, set **SHLIB_PATH**.

UNIX

LIBPATH

The **LIBPATH** environment variable tells the shell on AIX systems which directories to search for dynamic-link libraries for the INTERSOLV DataDirect ODBC Driver. You must specify the full pathname for the directory where you installed the product.

```
setenv ———————— LIBPATH ——————⟨ : ⟩———————|
                                  pathname
```

pathname　　　　　specifies the search path for the libraries.

On Solaris, set **LD_LIBRARY_PATH**. On HP-UX, set **SHLIB_PATH**.

NODEFDAC

When the **NODEFDAC** environment variable is set to yes, it prevents default table privileges (Select, Insert, Update, and Delete) from being granted to PUBLIC when a new table is created in a database that is not ANSI compliant. If you do not set the **NODEFDAC** variable, it is, by default, set to no.

```
setenv ————————————— NODEFDAC ————⟨ yes ⟩————|
                                      no
```

yes　　　　prevents default table privileges from being granted to PUBLIC on new tables in a database that is not ANSI compliant. This setting also prevents the Execute privilege for a new user-defined routine from being granted to PUBLIC when the routine is created in owner mode.

no　　　　allows default table privileges to be granted to PUBLIC. Also allows the Execute privilege on a new user-defined routine to be granted to PUBLIC when the user-defined routine is created in owner mode.

ONCONFIG

The **ONCONFIG** environment variable specifies the name of the active file that holds configuration parameters for the database server. This file is read as input during the initialization procedure. After you prepare the ONCONFIG configuration file, set the **ONCONFIG** environment variable to the name of the file.

If the **ONCONFIG** environment variable is not set, the database server uses configuration values from either the **$ONCONFIG** file or the **$INFORMIXDIR/etc/onconfig** file.

setenv ────────── ONCONFIG ────────── *filename* ────────────────────┤

filename   is the name of a file in **$INFORMIXDIR/etc** that contains the configuration parameters for your database.

To prepare the ONCONFIG file, make a copy of the **onconfig.std** file and modify the copy. Informix recommends that you name the ONCONFIG file so that it can easily be related to a specific database server. If you have multiple instances of a database server, each instance *must* have its own uniquely named ONCONFIG file.

EDS

To prepare the ONCONFIG file for Enterprise Decision Server, make a copy of the **onconfig.std** file if you are using a single coserver configuration or make a copy of the **onconfig.xps** file if you are using a multiple coserver configuration. You can use the **onconfig.std** file for a multiple coserver configuration, but you would have to add additional keywords and configuration parameters such as END, NODE, and COSERVER, which are already provided for you in the **onconfig.xps** file. ♦

For more information on configuration parameters and the ONCONFIG file, see the *Administrator's Reference*.

OPTCOMPIND

You can set the **OPTCOMPIND** environment variable so that the optimizer can select the appropriate join method.

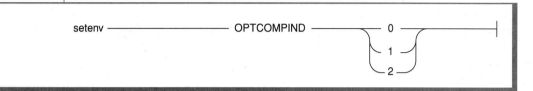

0   A nested-loop join is preferred, where possible, over a sort-merge join or a hash join.

1   When the transaction isolation mode is *not* Repeatable Read, the optimizer behaves as in setting 2; otherwise, the optimizer behaves as in setting 0.

2   Nested-loop joins are not necessarily preferred. The optimizer bases its decision purely on costs, regardless of transaction isolation mode.

When the **OPTCOMPIND** environment variable is not set, the database server uses the value specified for the ONCONFIG configuration parameter OPTCOMPIND. When neither the environment variable nor the configuration parameter is set, the default value is 2.

For more information on the ONCONFIG configuration parameter OPTCOMPIND, see the *Administrator's Reference*. For more information on the different join methods for your database server that the optimizer uses, see your *Performance Guide*.

OPTMSG

Set the **OPTMSG** environment variable at runtime before you start an Informix ESQL/C application to enable optimized message transfers (message chaining) for all SQL statements in an application. You also can disable optimized message transfers for statements that require immediate replies, for debugging, or to ensure that the database server processes all messages before the application exits.

0   disables optimized message transfers.
1   enables optimized message transfers and implements the feature for any subsequent connection.

The default value is 0 (zero), which explicitly disables message chaining.

When you set **OPTMSG** within an application, you can activate or deactivate optimized message transfers for each connection or within each thread. To enable optimized message transfers, you must set **OPTMSG** before you establish a connection.

For more information about setting **OPTMSG** and defining related global variables, see the *Informix ESQL/C Programmer's Manual*.

OPTOFC

Set the **OPTOFC** environment variable to enable optimize-OPEN-FETCH-CLOSE functionality in an Informix ESQL/C application that uses DECLARE and OPEN statements to execute a cursor. The **OPTOFC** environment variable reduces the number of message requests between the application and the database server.

0   disables **OPTOFC** for all threads of the application.

1   enables **OPTOFC** for every cursor in every thread of the application.

The default value is 0 (zero).

If you set **OPTOFC** from the shell, you must set it before you start the ESQL/C application.

For more information about enabling **OPTOFC** and related features, see the *Informix ESQL/C Programmer's Manual*.

UNIX

OPT_GOAL

Set the **OPT_GOAL** environment variable in the user environment, before you start an application, to specify the query performance goal for the optimizer.

0   specifies user-response-time optimization.

-1   specifies total-query-time optimization.

The default behavior is for the optimizer to choose query plans that optimize the total query time.

You can also specify the optimization goal for individual queries with optimizer directives or for a session with the SET OPTIMIZATION statement. Both methods take precedence over the **OPT_GOAL** environment variable setting. You can also set the OPT_GOAL configuration parameter for the Dynamic Server system; this method has the lowest level of precedence.

For more information about optimizing queries for your database server, see your *Performance Guide*. For information on the SET OPTIMIZATION statement, see the *Informix Guide to SQL: Syntax*.

PATH

The **PATH** environment variable tells the operating system where to search for executable programs. You must include the directory that contains your Informix product to your **PATH** environment variable before you can use the product. This directory should appear before **$INFORMIXDIR/bin**, which you must also include.

The UNIX **PATH** environment variable tells the shell which directories to search for executable programs. You must add the directory that contains your Informix product to your **PATH** environment variable before you can use the product.

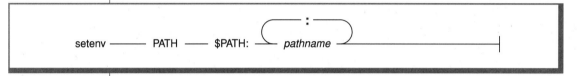

pathname specifies the search path for the executables.

You can specify the correct search path in various ways. Be sure to include a colon between the directory names.

For additional information about how to modify your path, see "Modifying an Environment-Variable Setting" on page 3-11.

PDQPRIORITY

The **PDQPRIORITY** environment variable determines the degree of parallelism that the database server uses and affects how the database server allocates resources, including memory, processors, and disk reads.

EDS

For Enterprise Decision Server, the **PDQPRIORITY** environment variable determines only the allocation of memory resources. ♦

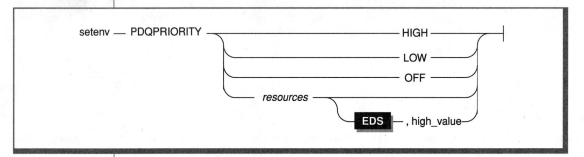

HIGH When the database server allocates resources among all users, it gives as many resources as possible to the query.

LOW Data is fetched from fragmented tables in parallel.

For supported database servers other than Enterprise Decision Server, when you specify LOW, the database server uses no forms of parallelism.

For Enterprise Decision Server, other parallel operations can occur when the setting is LOW.

OFF   PDQ processing is turned off (for supported database servers other than Enterprise Decision Server).

resources   Integer value in the range 0 to 100.

Value 0 is the same as OFF (for supported database servers other than Enterprise Decision Server only).

Value 1 is the same as LOW.

For supported database servers other than Enterprise Decision Server, the *resources* value specifies the query priority level and the amount of resources that the database server uses to process the query.

For Enterprise Decision Server, the *resources* value establishes the minimum percentage of memory when you also specify *high_value* to request a range of memory allocation.

high_value   Optional integer value that requests the maximum percentage of memory (for Enterprise Decision Server only). When you specify this value after the resources value, you request a range of memory percentage.

IDS

When the **PDQPRIORITY** environment variable is:

- not set, the default value is OFF.
- set to HIGH, the database server determines an appropriate value to use for **PDQPRIORITY** based on several criteria. These include the number of available processors, the fragmentation of tables queried, the complexity of the query, and so on. ♦

EDS

When the **PDQPRIORITY** environment variable is:

- not set, the default value is the value of the PDQPRIORITY configuration parameter.
- set to 0, the database server can execute a query in parallel, depending on the number of available processors, the fragmentation of tables queried, the complexity of the query, and so on. PDQPRIORITY does not affect the degree of parallelism in Enterprise Decision Server. ♦

Usually, the more resources a database server uses, the better its performance for a given query. However, if the database server uses too many resources, contention among the resources can result and take resources away from other queries, which results in degraded performance. For more information on performance considerations for **PDQPRIORITY**, refer to your *Performance Guide*.

An application can override the setting of the environment variable when it issues the SQL statement SET PDQPRIORITY, which the *Informix Guide to SQL: Syntax* describes.

IDS

PLCONFIG

The **PLCONFIG** environment variable specifies the name of the configuration file that the High-Performance Loader (HPL) uses. This configuration file must reside in the **$INFORMIXDIR/etc** directory. If the **PLCONFIG** environment variable is not set, **$INFORMIXDIR/etc/plconfig** is the default configuration file.

```
setenv ─────────── PLCONFIG ──────────── filename ─────────────────┤
```

filename   specifies the simple filename of the configuration file that the High-Performance Loader uses.

For example, to specify the **$INFORMIXDIR/etc/custom.cfg** file as the configuration file for the High-Performance Loader, enter the following command:

```
setenv PLCONFIG custom.cfg
```

For more information, see the *Guide to the High-Performance Loader*.

IDS

PLOAD_LO_PATH

The **PLOAD_LO_PATH** environment variable lets you specify the pathname for smart-large-object handles (which identify the location of smart large objects such as BLOB, CLOB, and BOOLEAN data types).

```
setenv ──────PLOAD_LO_PATH──────── pathname ──────────────────┤
```

pathname   specifies the directory for the smart-large-object handles.

If **PLOAD_LO_PATH** is not set, the default directory is **/tmp**.

For more information, see the *Guide to the High-Performance Loader*.

IDS

PLOAD_SHMBASE

The **PLOAD_SHMBASE** environment variable lets you specify the shared-memory address at which the High-Performance Loader (HPL) **onpload** processes will attach. If **PLOAD_SHMBASE** is not set, the HPL determines which shared-memory address to use.

```
setenv ────────── PLOAD_SHMBASE ─────────── value ──────────┤
```

value   is used to calculate the shared-memory address.

If the **onpload** utility cannot attach, an error appears and you must specify a new value.

The **onpload** utility tries to determine at which address to attach, as follows:

1.   Attach at the same address (SHMBASE) as the database server.
2.   Attach beyond the database server segments.
3.   Attach at the address specified in **PLOAD_SHMBASE**.

Tip: *Informix recommends that you let the HPL decide where to attach and that you set **PLOAD_SHMBASE** only if necessary to avoid shared-memory collisions between **onpload** and the database server.*

For more information, see the *Guide to the High-Performance Loader.*

PSORT_DBTEMP

The **PSORT_DBTEMP** environment variable specifies a directory or directories where the database server writes the temporary files it uses when it performs a sort.

The database server uses the directory that **PSORT_DBTEMP** specifies even if the environment variable **PSORT_NPROCS** is not set.

```
setenv ──── PSORT_DBTEMP ──── pathname ────
                          ⤷─── ; ───⤴
```

pathname   is the name of the UNIX directory used for intermediate writes during a sort.

To set the **PSORT_DBTEMP** environment variable to specify the directory (for example, **/usr/leif/tempsort**), enter the following command:

```
setenv PSORT_DBTEMP /usr/leif/tempsort
```

For maximum performance, specify directories that reside in file systems on different disks.

You might also want to consider setting the environment variable **DBSPACETEMP** to place temporary files used in sorting in dbspaces rather than operating-system files. See the discussion of the **DBSPACETEMP** environment variable on page 3-50.

For additional information about the **PSORT_DBTEMP** environment variable, see your *Administrator's Guide* and your *Performance Guide.*

PSORT_NPROCS

The **PSORT_NPROCS** environment variable enables the database server to improve the performance of the parallel-process sorting package by allocating more threads for sorting.

EDS

PSORT_NPROCS does not necessarily improve sorting speed for Enterprise Decision Server because the database server sorts in parallel whether this environment variable is set or not. ♦

Before the sorting package performs a parallel sort, make sure that the database server has enough memory for the sort.

```
setenv ─────── PSORT_NPROCS ─────── threads ─────────────────┤
```

threads　　　　specifies the maximum number of threads to be used to sort a query. The maximum value of threads is 10.

The following command sets the **PSORT_NPROCS** environment variable to 4:

```
setenv PSORT_NPROCS 4
```

To disable parallel sorting, enter the following command:

```
unsetenv PSORT_NPROCS
```

Informix recommends that you initially set **PSORT_NPROCS** to 2 when your computer has multiple CPUs. If subsequent CPU activity is lower than I/O activity, you can increase the value of **PSORT_NPROCS**.

Tip: *If the PDQPRIORITY environment variable is not set, the database server allocates the minimum amount of memory to sorting. This minimum memory is insufficient to start even two sort threads. If you have not set the PDQPRIORITY environment variable, check the available memory before you perform a large-scale sort (such as an index build) and make sure that you have enough memory.*

Default Values for Ordinary Sorts

If the **PSORT_NPROCS** environment variable is set, the database server uses the specified number of sort threads as an upper limit for ordinary sorts. If **PSORT_NPROCS** is not set, parallel sorting does not take place. The database server uses one thread for the sort. If **PSORT_NPROCS** is set to 0, the database server uses three threads for the sort.

Default Values for Attached Indexes

The default number of threads is different for attached indexes.

If the **PSORT_NPROCS** environment variable is set, you get the specified number of sort threads for each fragment of the index that is being built.

If the **PSORT_NPROCS** environment variable is not set, or if it is set to 0, you get two sort threads for each fragment of the index unless you have a single-CPU virtual processor. If you have a single-CPU virtual processor, you get one sort thread for each fragment of the index.

For additional information about the **PSORT_NPROCS** environment variable, see your *Administrator's Guide* and your *Performance Guide*.

| UNIX |

SHLIB_PATH

The **SHLIB_PATH** environment variable tells the shell on HP-UX systems which directories to search for dynamic-link libraries for the INTERSOLV DataDirect ODBC Driver. You must specify the full pathname for the directory where you installed the product.

```
                                            :
setenv ──── SHLIB_PATH ──────── $PATH: ──( pathname )──────────
```

pathname   specifies the search path for the libraries.

On Solaris, set **LD_LIBRARY_PATH**. On AIX, set **LIBPATH**.

STMT_CACHE

IDS

Use the **STMT_CACHE** environment variable to control the use of the shared-statement cache on a session. This feature can reduce memory consumption and speed query processing among different user sessions. Valid **STMT_CACHE** values are 1 and 0.

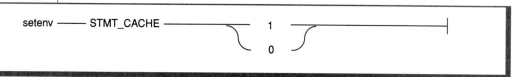

1	enables the SQL statement cache.
0	disables the SQL statement cache.

Set the **STMT_CACHE** environment variable for applications that do not use the SET STMT_CACHE statement to control the use of the SQL statement cache.

This environment variable has no effect if the SQL statement cache is disabled through the configuration setting. The SET STMT_CACHE statement in the application overrides the **STMT_CACHE** environment variable setting.

UNIX

TERM

The **TERM** environment variable is used for terminal handling. It lets DB-Access recognize and communicate with the terminal that you are using.

```
setenv ─────────── TERM ─────────── type ─────────────────────┤
```

type   specifies the terminal type.

The terminal type specified in the **TERM** setting must correspond to an entry in the **termcap** file or **terminfo** directory. Before you can set the **TERM** environment variable, you must obtain the code for your terminal from the database administrator.

For example, to specify the vt100 terminal, set the **TERM** environment variable by entering the following command:

```
setenv TERM vt100
```

UNIX

TERMCAP

The **TERMCAP** environment variable is used for terminal handling. It tells DB-Access to communicate with the **termcap** file instead of the **terminfo** directory.

```
setenv ─────────── TERMCAP ─────────── pathname ─────────────────┤
```

pathname   specifies the location of the **termcap** file.

The **termcap** file contains a list of various types of terminals and their characteristics. For example, to provide DB-Access terminal-handling information, which is specified in the **/usr/informix/etc/termcap** file, enter the following command:

```
setenv TERMCAP /usr/informix/etc/termcap
```

You can use any of the following settings for **TERMCAP**. Use them in the following order:

1. The **termcap** file that you create
2. The **termcap** file that Informix supplies (that is, **$INFORMIXDIR/etc/termcap**)
3. The operating-system **termcap** file (that is, **/etc/termcap**)

If you set the **TERMCAP** environment variable, be sure that the **INFORMIXTERM** environment variable is set to the default, **termcap**.

If you do not set the **TERMCAP** environment variable, the system file (that is, **/etc/termcap**) is used by default.

UNIX

TERMINFO

The **TERMINFO** environment variable is used for terminal handling.

The environment variable is supported only on platforms that provide full support for the **terminfo** libraries that System V and Solaris UNIX systems provide.

setenv ──────── TERMINFO ──────── /usr/lib/terminfo ──────────┤

TERMINFO tells DB-Access to communicate with the **terminfo** directory instead of the **termcap** file. The **terminfo** directory has subdirectories that contain files that pertain to terminals and their characteristics.

To set **TERMINFO**, enter the following command:

```
setenv TERMINFO /usr/lib/terminfo
```

If you set the **TERMINFO** environment variable, you must also set the **INFORMIXTERM** environment variable to **terminfo**.

UNIX

THREADLIB

Use the **THREADLIB** environment variable to compile multithreaded ESQL/C applications. A multithreaded ESQL/C application lets you establish as many connections to one or more databases as there are threads. These connections can remain active while the application program executes.

The **THREADLIB** environment variable indicates which thread package to use when you compile an application. Currently only the Distributed Computing Environment (DCE) is supported.

```
setenv ──────── THREADLIB ──────────── DCE ───────────────┤
```

The **THREADLIB** environment variable is checked when the **-thread** option is passed to the ESQL/C script when you compile a multithreaded ESQL/C application. When you use the **-thread** option while compiling, the ESQL/C script generates an error if the **THREADLIB** environment variable is not set or if the variable is set to an unsupported thread package.

EDS

XFER_CONFIG

The **XFER_CONFIG** environment variable specifies the location of the **xfer_config** configuration file.

```
setenv ──────── XFER_CONFIG ──────────── pathname ───────────────┤
```

pathname   specifies the location of the **xfer_config** file.

The **xfer_config** file works with the **onxfer** utility to help users migrate from Version 7.x to Version 8.x. It contains various configuration parameter settings that users can modify and a list of tables that users can select to be transferred.

The default **xfer_config** file is located in the **$INFORMIXDIR/etc** directory on UNIX systems or in the **%INFORMIXDIR%\etc** directory on Windows NT.

Index of Environment Variables

Figure 3-2 provides an overview of the uses for the various Informix and UNIX environment variables that Version 8.3 and Version 9.2 support. It serves as an index to general topics and lists the related environment variables and the pages where the environment variables are introduced.

GLS

The term *GLS guide* in the Page column in Figure 3-2 indicates that the GLS environment variables are described in the *Informix Guide to GLS Functionality*. ♦

Figure 3-2
Uses for Environment Variables

Topic	Environment Variable	Page
ANSI compliance	**DBANSIWARN**	3-30
archecker utility	**AC_CONFIG**	3-24
Buffer: fetch size	**FET_BUF_SIZE**	3-59
Buffer: network size	**IFX_NETBUF_SIZE**	3-63
Buffer: network pool size	**IFX_NETBUF_PVTPOOL_SIZE**	3-63
BYTE or TEXT data buffer	**DBBLOBBUF**	3-31
C compiler	**INFORMIXC**	3-64
C compiler: processing of multibyte characters	**CC8BITLEVEL**	GLS guide
C++	**INFORMIXCPPMAP**	3-68
Cache: enabling	**STMT_CACHE**	3-95
Cache: size for Optical Subsystem	**INFORMIXOPCACHE**	3-70
Client locale	**CLIENT_LOCALE**	GLS guide
Client/server	**INFORMIXSERVER**	3-70
	INFORMIXSHMBASE	3-72

(1 of 12)

Topic	Environment Variable	Page
	INFORMIXSTACKSIZE	3-74
Client/server: GLS	CLIENT_LOCALE	GLS guide
	DB_LOCALE	GLS guide
	SERVER_LOCALE	GLS guide
Code-set conversion	CLIENT_LOCALE	GLS guide
	DB_LOCALE	GLS guide
Communication Support Module: DCE-GSS	INFORMIXKEYTAB	3-69
Communications Support Module: location of **concsm.cfg** file	INFORMIXCONCSMCFG	3-65
Compilation: ESQL/C	THREADLIB	3-98
Compiler	CC8BITLEVEL	GLS guide
	INFORMIXC	3-64
Configuration file: database server	ONCONFIG	3-82
Configuration file: ignore variables	ENVIGNORE	3-58
Configuration file: ON-Archive	ARC_CONFIG	3-25
	ARC_DEFAULT	3-25
Configuration file: **tctermcap**	ARC_KEYPAD	3-25
Configuration file: **xfer_config**	XFER_CONFIG	3-98
Configuration parameter: COSERVER	INFORMIXSERVER	3-70
Configuration parameter: DBSERVERNAME	INFORMIXSERVER	3-70
Configuration parameter: DBSPACETEMP	DBSPACETEMP	3-50
Configuration parameter: DIRECTIVES	IFX_DIRECTIVES	3-61

(2 of 12)

Topic	Environment Variable	Page
Database server: shared memory	INFORMIXSHMBASE	3-72
Database server: stacksize	INFORMIXSTACKSIZE	3-74
Database server: tape management	ARC_CONFIG	3-25
	ARC_DEFAULT	3-25
	ARC_KEYPAD	3-26
	DBREMOTECMD	3-49
Database server: temporary tables, sort files	DBSPACETEMP	3-50
Date and time values	DBCENTURY	3-32
	DBDATE	3-36; GLS guide
	DBTIME	3-53; GLS guide
	GL_DATE	GLS guide
	GL_DATETIME	GLS guide
DB-Access utility	DBACCNOIGN	3-29
	DBANSIWARN	3-30
	DBDELIMITER	3-39
	DBEDIT	3-40
	DBFLTMASK	3-41
	DBPATH	3-46
	FET_BUF_SIZE	3-59
	INFORMIXSERVER	3-70
	INFORMIXTERM	3-75
	TERM	3-96

(5 of 12)

Index of Environment Variables

Topic	Environment Variable	Page
Files: map for C++	INFORMIXCPPMAP	3-68
Files: message	DBLANG	3-42
Files: temporary	DBSPACETEMP	3-50
Files: temporary, for Gateways	DBTEMP	3-52
Files: temporary sorting	PSORT_DBTEMP	3-92
Files: **termcap, terminfo**	INFORMIXTERM	3-75
	TERM	3-96
	TERMCAP	3-96
	TERMINFO	3-97
Gateways	DBTEMP	3-52
High-Performance Loader	DBONPLOAD	3-45
	PLCONFIG	3-90
	PLOAD_LO_PATH	3-91
	PLOAD_SHMBASE	3-91
Identifiers: delimited	DELIMIDENT	3-57
Identifiers: long	IFX_LONGID	3-62
Identifiers: multibyte characters	CLIENT_LOCALE	GLS guide
	ESQLMF	GLS guide
Informix Storage Manager	ISM_COMPRESSION	3-77
	ISM_DEBUG_FILE	3-77
	ISM_DEBUG_LEVEL	3-78
	ISM_ENCRYPTION	3-79
	ISM_MAXLOGSIZE	3-79
	ISM_MAXLOGVERS	3-80

Topic	Environment Variable	Page
Installation	INFORMIXDIR	3-68
	PATH	3-87
Language environment	DBLANG	3-42; GLS guide
Libraries	LD_LIBRARY_PATH	3-80
	LIBPATH	3-81
	SHLIB_PATH	3-94
Locale	CLIENT_LOCALE	GLS guide
	DB_LOCALE	GLS guide
	SERVER_LOCALE	GLS guide
Long Identifiers	IFX_LONGID	3-62
Map file for C++	INFORMIXCPPMAP	3-68
Message chaining	OPTMSG	3-84
Message files	DBLANG	3-42; GLS guide
Money values	DBMONEY	3-44; GLS guide
Multibyte characters	CLIENT_LOCALE	GLS guide
	DB_LOCALE	GLS guide
	SERVER_LOCALE	GLS guide
Multibyte filter	ESQLMF	GLS guide
Multithreaded applications	THREADLIB	3-98
Network	DBPATH	3-46

(7 of 12)

Topic	Environment Variable	Page
Nondefault locale	**CLIENT_LOCALE**	GLS guide
	DB_LOCALE	GLS guide
	SERVER_LOCALE	GLS guide
ON-Archive utility	**ARC_DEFAULT**	3-25
	ARC_KEYPAD	3-26
	DBREMOTECMD	3-49
ON-Bar utility	**ISM_COMPRESSION**	3-77
	ISM_DEBUG_LEVEL	3-78
	ISM_ENCRYPTION	3-79
ONCONFIG parameters	See the "Configuration parameter" entries	
onprobe and **oncockpit** programs	**COCKPITSERVICE**	3-27
Optical Subsystem	**INFORMIXOPCACHE**	3-70
Optimization: directives, setting in the query	**IFX_DIRECTIVES**	3-61
Optimization: message transfers	**OPTMSG**	3-84
Optimization: selecting join method	**OPTCOMPIND**	3-83
Optimization: specifying query performance goal	**OPT_GOAL**	3-86
OPTOFC feature	**OPTOFC**	3-85
Parameters	See the "Configuration parameter" entries	
Pathname: for **archecker** configuration file	**AC_CONFIG**	3-24
Pathname: for C COMPILER	**INFORMIXC**	3-64
Pathname: for database files	**DBPATH**	3-46

(8 of 12)

Topic	Environment Variable	Page
Server locale	**SERVER_LOCALE**	GLS guide
Shared memory	**INFORMIXSHMBASE**	3-72
	PLOAD_SHMBASE	3-91
Shell: remote	**DBREMOTECMD**	3-49
Shell: search path	**PATH**	3-87
Sorting	**PSORT_DBTEMP**	3-92
	PSORT_NPROCS	3-93
	DBSPACETEMP	3-50
SQL statement: caching	**STMT_CACHE**	3-95
SQL statement: CONNECT	**INFORMIXCONTIME**	3-66
	INFORMIXSERVER	3-70
SQL statement: CREATE TEMP TABLE	**DBSPACETEMP**	3-50
SQL statement: DESCRIBE FOR UPDATE	**IFX_UPDDESC**	3-64
SQL statement: editing	**DBEDIT**	3-40
SQL statement: LOAD, UNLOAD	**DBDELIMITER**	3-39
SQL statement: SELECT INTO TEMP	**DBSPACETEMP**	3-50
SQL statement: SET PDQPRIORITY	**PDQPRIORITY**	3-88
SQL statement: SET STMT_CACHE	**STMT_CACHE**	3-95
SQL statement: UNLOAD	**DBBLOBBUF**	3-31
SQL statement: UPDATE STATISTICS	**DBUPSPACE**	3-56
Stacksize	**INFORMIXSTACKSIZE**	3-74
Tables: temporary	**DBSPACETEMP**	3-50
	PSORT_DBTEMP	3-92

(10 of 12)

Topic	Environment Variable	Page
Tables: temporary, for Gateways	DBTEMP	3-52
Temporary tables	DBSPACETEMP	3-50
	DBTEMP	3-52
	PSORT_DBTEMP	3-92
Terminal handling	INFORMIXTERM	3-75
	TERM	3-96
	TERMCAP	3-96
	TERMINFO	3-97
Utilities: **archecker**	AC_CONFIG	3-24
Utilities: DB-Access	DBANSIWARN	3-30
	DBDELIMITER	3-39
	DBEDIT	3-40
	DBFLTMASK	3-41
	DBPATH	3-46
	FET_BUF_SIZE	3-59
	INFORMIXSERVER	3-70
	INFORMIXTERM	3-75
	TERM	3-96
	TERMCAP	3-96
	TERMINFO	3-97
Utilities: **dbexport**	DBDELIMITER	3-39
Utilities: ON-Archive	ARC_DEFAULT	3-25
	ARC_KEYPAD	3-26
	DBREMOTECMD	3-49

Topic	Environment Variable	Page
Utilities: ON-Bar	ISM_COMPRESSION	3-77
	ISM_DEBUG_LEVEL	3-78
	ISM_ENCRYPTION	3-79
Values: date and time	DBDATE	3-36; GLS guide
	DBTIME	3-53; GLS guide
Values: money	DBMONEY	3-44; GLS guide
Variables: overriding	ENVIGNORE	3-58
Year 2000	DBCENTURY	3-32

(12 of 12)

The stores_demo Database

The **stores_demo** database contains a set of tables that describe an imaginary business. The examples in the *Informix Guide to SQL: Syntax*, the *Informix Guide to SQL: Tutorial*, and other Informix manuals are based on this demonstration database. The **stores_demo** database is not ANSI compliant.

This appendix contains the following sections:

- The first section describes the structure of the tables in the **stores_demo** database. It identifies the primary key of each table, lists the name and data type of each column, and indicates whether the column has a default value or check constraint. Indexes on columns are also identified and classified as unique or if they allow duplicate values.

- The second section (page A-10) shows a graphic map of the tables in the **stores_demo** database and indicates the relationships among columns.

- The third section (page A-12) describes the primary-foreign key relationships among columns in tables.

- The final section (page A-19) shows the data contained in each table of the **stores_demo** database.

For information on how to create and populate the **stores_demo** database, see the *DB-Access User's Manual*. For information on how to design and implement a relational database, see the *Informix Guide to Database Design and Implementation*.

Structure of the Tables

The **stores_demo** database contains information about a fictitious sporting-goods distributor that services stores in the Western United States. This database includes the following tables:

- **customer** (page A-3)
- **orders** (page A-4)
- **items** (page A-5)
- **stock** (page A-6)
- **catalog** (page A-7)
- **cust_calls** (page A-8)
- **call_type** (page A-9)
- **manufact** (page A-9)
- **state** (page A-10)

The following sections describe each table. The unique identifier for each table (primary key) is shaded and indicated by a key symbol.

The customer Table

The **customer** table contains information about the retail stores that place orders from the distributor. Figure A-1 shows the columns of the **customer** table.

The **zipcode** column in Figure A-1 is indexed and allows duplicate values.

Column Name	Data Type	Description
customer_num	SERIAL(101)	system-generated customer number
fname	CHAR(15)	first name of store representative
lname	CHAR(15)	last name of store representative
company	CHAR(20)	name of store
address1	CHAR(20)	first line of store address
address2	CHAR(20)	second line of store address
city	CHAR(15)	city
state	CHAR(2)	state (foreign key to **state** table)
zipcode	CHAR(5)	zipcode
phone	CHAR(18)	telephone number

The orders Table

The **orders** table contains information about orders placed by the customers of the distributor. Figure A-2 shows the columns of the **orders** table.

Figure A-2
The orders Table

Column Name	Data Type	Description
order_num	SERIAL(1001)	system-generated order number
order_date	DATE	date order entered
customer_num	INTEGER	customer number (foreign key to **customer** table)
ship_instruct	CHAR(40)	special shipping instructions
backlog	CHAR(1)	indicates order cannot be filled because the item is backlogged: ■ y = yes ■ n = no
po_num	CHAR(10)	customer purchase order number
ship_date	DATE	shipping date
ship_weight	DECIMAL(8,2)	shipping weight
ship_charge	MONEY(6)	shipping charge
paid_date	DATE	date order paid

The items Table

An order can include one or more items. One row exists in the **items** table for each item in an order. Figure A-3 shows the columns of the **items** table.

Column Name	Data Type	Description
item_num	SMALLINT	sequentially assigned item number for an order
order_num	INTEGER	order number (foreign key to **orders** table)
stock_num	SMALLINT	stock number for item (foreign key to **stock** table)
manu_code	CHAR(3)	manufacturer code for item ordered (foreign key to **manufact** table)
quantity	SMALLINT	quantity ordered (value must be > 1)
total_price	MONEY(8)	quantity ordered * unit price = total price of item

The stock Table

The distributor carries 41 types of sporting goods from various manufacturers. More than one manufacturer can supply an item. For example, the distributor offers racing goggles from two manufacturers and running shoes from six manufacturers.

The **stock** table is a catalog of the items sold by the distributor. Figure A-4 shows the columns of the **stock** table.

Figure A-4
The stock Table

Column Name	Data Type	Description
stock_num	SMALLINT	stock number that identifies type of item
manu_code	CHAR(3)	manufacturer code (foreign key to **manufact** table)
description	CHAR(15)	description of item
unit_price	MONEY(6,2)	unit price
unit	CHAR(4)	unit by which item is ordered: ■ each ■ pair ■ case ■ box
unit_descr	CHAR(15)	description of unit

The catalog Table

The **catalog** table describes each item in stock. Retail stores use this table when placing orders with the distributor. Figure A-5 shows the columns of the **catalog** table.

Column Name	Data Type	Description
catalog_num	SERIAL(10001)	system-generated catalog number
stock_num	SMALLINT	distributor stock number (foreign key to **stock** table)
manu_code	CHAR(3)	manufacturer code (foreign key to **manufact** table)
cat_descr	TEXT	description of item
cat_picture	BYTE	picture of item (binary data)
cat_advert	VARCHAR(255, 65)	tag line underneath picture

The cust_calls Table

All customer calls for information on orders, shipments, or complaints are logged. The **cust_calls** table contains information about these types of customer calls. Figure A-6 shows the columns of the **cust_calls** table.

Column Name	Data Type	Description
customer_num	INTEGER	customer number (foreign key to **customer** table)
call_dtime	DATETIME YEAR TO MINUTE	date and time call received
user_id	CHAR(18)	name of person logging call (default is user login name)
call_code	CHAR(1)	type of call (foreign key to **call_type** table)
call_descr	CHAR(240)	description of call
res_dtime	DATETIME YEAR TO MINUTE	date and time call resolved
res_descr	CHAR(240)	description of how call was resolved

The call_type Table

The call codes associated with customer calls are stored in the **call_type** table. Figure A-7 shows the columns of the **call_type** table.

Figure A-7
The call_type Table

Column Name	Data Type	Description
call_code	CHAR(1)	call code
code_descr	CHAR (30)	description of call type

The manufact Table

Information about the nine manufacturers whose sporting goods are handled by the distributor is stored in the **manufact** table. Figure A-8 shows the columns of the **manufact** table.

Figure A-8
The manufact Table

Column Name	Data Type	Description
manu_code	CHAR(3)	manufacturer code
manu_name	CHAR(15)	name of manufacturer
lead_time	INTERVAL DAY(3) TO DAY	lead time for shipment of orders

The state Table

The **state** table contains the names and postal abbreviations for the 50 states of the United States. Figure A-9 shows the columns of the **state** table.

Figure A-9
The state Table

Column Name	Data Type	Description
code	CHAR(2)	state code
sname	CHAR(15)	state name

The stores_demo Database Map

Figure A-10 displays the joins in the **stores_demo** database. The grey shading that connects a column in one table to the same column in another table indicates the relationships, or *joins*, between tables.

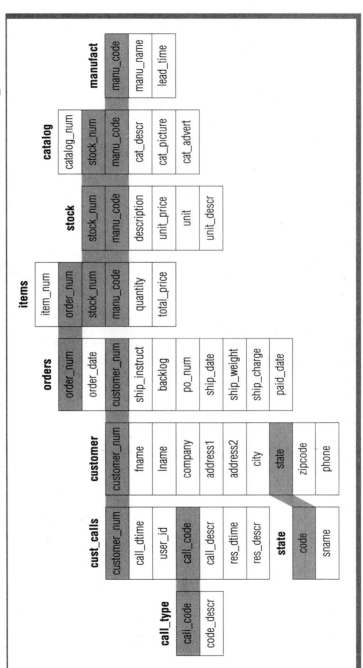

Figure A-10
Joins in the stores_demo Database

Primary-Foreign Key Relationships

The tables of the **stores_demo** database are linked by the primary-foreign key relationships that Figure A-10 on page A-11 shows and are identified in this section. This type of relationship is called a *referential constraint* because a foreign key in one table *references* the primary key in another table. Figure A-11 through Figure A-18 show the relationships among tables and how information stored in one table supplements information stored in others.

The customer and orders Tables

The **customer** table contains a **customer_num** column that holds a number that identifies a customer and columns for the customer name, company, address, and telephone number. For example, the row with information about Anthony Higgins contains the number 104 in the **customer_num** column. The **orders** table also contains a **customer_num** column that stores the number of the customer who placed a particular order. In the **orders** table, the **customer_num** column is a foreign key that references the **customer_num** column in the **customer** table. Figure A-11 shows this relationship.

customer Table (detail)

customer_num	fname	lname
101	Ludwig	Pauli
102	Carole	Sadler
103	Philip	Currie
104	Anthony	Higgins

orders Table (detail)

order_num	order_date	customer_num
1001	05/20/1998	104
1002	05/21/1998	101
1003	05/22/1998	104
1004	05/22/1998	106

Figure A-11
Tables That the customer_num Column Joins

According to Figure A-11, customer 104 (Anthony Higgins) has placed two orders, as his customer number appears in two rows of the **orders** table. Because the customer number is a foreign key in the **orders** table, you can retrieve Anthony Higgins' name, address, and information about his orders at the same time.

The orders and items Tables

The **orders** and **items** tables are linked by an **order_num** column that contains an identification number for each order. If an order includes several items, the same order number appears in several rows of the **items** table. In the **items** table, the **order_num** column is a foreign key that references the **order_num** column in the **orders** table. Figure A-12 shows this relationship.

orders Table (detail)

order_num	order_date	customer_num
1001	05/20/1998	104
1002	05/21/1998	101
1003	05/22/1998	104

items Table (detail)

item_num	order_num	stock_num	manu_code
1	1001	1	HRO
4	1002	4	HSK
3	1002	3	HSK
9	1003	9	ANZ
8	1003	8	ANZ
5	1003	5	ANZ

Figure A-12
Tables That the order_num Column Joins

The items and stock Tables

The **items** table and the **stock** table are joined by two columns: the **stock_num** column, which stores a stock number for an item, and the **manu_code** column, which stores a code that identifies the manufacturer. You need both the stock number and the manufacturer code to uniquely identify an item. For example, the item with the stock number 1 and the manufacturer code HRO is a Hero baseball glove; the item with the stock number 1 and the manufacturer code HSK is a Husky baseball glove. The same stock number and manufacturer code can appear in more than one row of the **items** table, if the same item belongs to separate orders. In the **items** table, the **stock_num** and **manu_code** columns are foreign keys that reference the **stock_num** and **manu_code** columns in the **stock** table. Figure A-13 shows this relationship.

items Table (detail)

item_num	order_num	stock_num	manu_code
1	1001	1	HRO
1	1002	4	HSK
2	1002	3	HSK
1	1003	9	ANZ
2	1003	8	ANZ
3	1003	5	ANZ
1	1004	1	HRO

stock Table (detail)

stock_num	manu_code	description
1	HRO	baseball gloves
1	HSK	baseball gloves
1	SMT	baseball gloves

Figure A-13
Tables That the stock_num and manu_code Columns Join

The stock and catalog Tables

The **stock** table and **catalog** table are joined by two columns: the **stock_num** column, which stores a stock number for an item, and the **manu_code** column, which stores a code that identifies the manufacturer. You need both columns to uniquely identify an item. In the **catalog** table, the **stock_num** and **manu_code** columns are foreign keys that reference the **stock_num** and **manu_code** columns in the **stock** table. Figure A-14 shows this relationship.

Figure A-14
Tables That the stock_num and manu_code Columns Join

stock Table (detail)

stock_num	manu_code	description
1	HRO	baseball gloves
1	HSK	baseball gloves
1	SMT	baseball gloves

catalog Table (detail)

catalog_num	stock_num	manu_code
10001	1	HRO
10002	1	HSK
10003	1	SMT
10004	2	HRO

The stock and manufact Tables

The **stock** table and the **manufact** table are joined by the **manu_code** column. The same manufacturer code can appear in more than one row of the **stock** table if the manufacturer produces more than one piece of equipment. In the **stock** table, the **manu_code** column is a foreign key that references the **manu_code** column in the **manufact** table. Figure A-15 shows this relationship.

stock Table (detail)

stock_num	manu_code	description
1	HRO	baseball gloves
1	HSK	baseball gloves
1	SMT	baseball gloves

manufact Table (detail)

manu_code	manu_name
NRG	Norge
HSK	Husky
HRO	Hero

Figure A-15
Tables That the
manu_code Column
Joins

The cust_calls and customer Tables

The **cust_calls** table and the **customer** table are joined by the **customer_num** column. The same customer number can appear in more than one row of the **cust_calls** table if the customer calls the distributor more than once with a problem or question. In the **cust_calls** table, the **customer_num** column is a foreign key that references the **customer_num** column in the **customer** table. Figure A-16 shows this relationship.

Figure A-16
Tables That the customer_num Column Joins

customer Table (detail)

customer_num	fname	lname
101	Ludwig	Pauli
102	Carole	Sadler
103	Philip	Currie
104	Anthony	Higgins
105	Raymond	Vector
106	George	Watson

cust_calls Table (detail)

customer_num	call_dtime	user_id
106	1998-06-12 08:20	maryj
127	1998-07-31 14:30	maryj
116	1997-11-28 13:34	mannyh
116	1997-12-21 11:24	mannyh

The call_type and cust_calls Tables

The **call_type** and **cust_calls** tables are joined by the **call_code** column. The same call code can appear in more than one row of the **cust_calls** table because many customers can have the same *type* of problem. In the **cust_calls** table, the **call_code** column is a foreign key that references the **call_code** column in the **call_type** table. Figure A-17 shows this relationship.

call_type Table (detail)	
call_code	**code_descr**
B	billing error
D	damaged goods
I	incorrect merchandise sent
L	late shipment
O	other

cust_calls Table (detail)		
customer_num	**call_dtime**	**call_code**
106	1998-06-12 08:20	D
127	1998-07-31 14:30	I
116	1997-11-28 13:34	I
116	1997-12-21 11:24	I

Figure A-17
Tables That the call_code Column Joins

The state and customer Tables

The **state** table and the **customer** table are joined by a column that contains the state code. This column is called **code** in the **state** table and **state** in the **customer** table. If several customers live in the same state, the same state code appears in several rows of the table. In the **customer** table, the **state** column is a foreign key that references the **code** column in the **state** table. Figure A-18 shows this relationship.

customer Table (detail)

customer_num	fname	lname	---	state
101	Ludwig	Pauli	---	CA
102	Carole	Sadler	---	CA
103	Philip	Currie	---	CA

state Table (detail)

code	sname
AK	Alaska
AL	Alabama
AR	Arkansas
AZ	Arizona
CA	California

Figure A-18
Tables That the state/code Column Joins

Data in the stores_demo Database

The following tables display the data in the **stores_demo** database.

Data in the stores_demo Database

customer Table

customer_num	fname	lname	company	address1	address2	city	state	zipcode	phone
101	Ludwig	Pauli	All Sports Supplies	213 Erstwild Court		Sunnyvale	CA	94086	408-789-8075
102	Carole	Sadler	Sports Spot	785 Geary Street		San Francisco	CA	94117	415-822-1289
103	Philip	Currie	Phil's Sports	654 Poplar	P. O. Box 3498	Palo Alto	CA	94303	650-328-4543
104	Anthony	Higgins	Play Ball!	East Shopping Center	422 Bay Road	Redwood City	CA	94026	650-368-1100
105	Raymond	Vector	Los Altos Sports	1899 La Loma Drive		Los Altos	CA	94022	650-776-3249
106	George	Watson	Watson & Son	1143 Carver Place		Mountain View	CA	94063	650-389-8789
107	Charles	Ream	Athletic Supplies	41 Jordan Avenue		Palo Alto	CA	94304	650-356-9876
108	Donald	Quinn	Quinn's Sports	587 Alvarado		Redwood City	CA	94063	650-544-8729
109	Jane	Miller	Sport Stuff	Mayfair Mart	7345 Ross Blvd.	Sunnyvale	CA	94086	408-723-8789
110	Roy	Jaeger	AA Athletics	520 Topaz Way		Redwood City	CA	94062	650-743-3611
111	Frances	Keyes	Sports Center	3199 Sterling Court		Sunnyvale	CA	94085	408-277-7245

customer_num	fname	lname	company	address1	address2	city	state	zipcode	phone
112	Margaret	Lawson	Runners & Others	234 Wyandotte Way		Los Altos	CA	94022	650-887-7235
113	Lana	Beatty	Sportstown	654 Oak Grove		Menlo Park	CA	94025	650-356-9982
114	Frank	Albertson	Sporting Place	947 Waverly Place		Redwood City	CA	94062	650-886-6677
115	Alfred	Grant	Gold Medal Sports	776 Gary Avenue		Menlo Park	CA	94025	650-356-1123
116	Jean	Parmelee	Olympic City	1104 Spinosa Drive		Mountain View	CA	94040	650-534-8822
117	Arnold	Sipes	Kids Korner	850 Lytton Court		Redwood City	CA	94063	650-245-4578
118	Dick	Baxter	Blue Ribbon Sports	5427 College		Oakland	CA	94609	650-655-0011
119	Bob	Shorter	The Triathletes Club	2405 Kings Highway		Cherry Hill	NJ	08002	609-663-6079
120	Fred	Jewell	Century Pro Shop	6627 N. 17th Way		Phoenix	AZ	85016	602-265-8754
121	Jason	Wallack	City Sports	Lake Biltmore Mall	350 W. 23rd Street	Wilmington	DE	19898	302-366-7511
122	Cathy	O'Brian	The Sporting Life	543 Nassau Street		Princeton	NJ	08540	609-342-0054
123	Marvin	Hanlon	Bay Sports	10100 Bay Meadows Road	Suite 1020	Jacksonville	FL	32256	904-823-4239

(2 of 3)

Data in the stores_demo Database

customer_num	fname	lname	company	address1	address2	city	state	zipcode	phone
124	Chris	Putnum	Putnum's Putters	4715 S.E. Adams Blvd	Suite 909C	Bartlesville	OK	74006	918-355-2074
125	James	Henry	Total Fitness Sports	1450 Commonwealth Avenue		Brighton	MA	02135	617-232-4159
126	Eileen	Neelie	Neelie's Discount Sports	2539 South Utica Street		Denver	CO	80219	303-936-7731
127	Kim	Satifer	Big Blue Bike Shop	Blue Island Square	12222 Gregory Street	Blue Island	NY	60406	312-944-5691
128	Frank	Lessor	Phoenix University	Athletic Department	1817 N. Thomas Road	Phoenix	AZ	85008	602-533-1817

(3 of 3)

items Table

item_num	order_num	stock_num	manu_code	quantity	total_price
1	1001	1	HRO	1	250.00
1	1002	4	HSK	1	960.00
2	1002	3	HSK	1	240.00
1	1003	9	ANZ	1	20.00
2	1003	8	ANZ	1	840.00
3	1003	5	ANZ	5	99.00
1	1004	1	HRO	1	250.00
2	1004	2	HRO	1	126.00
3	1004	3	HSK	1	240.00
4	1004	1	HSK	1	800.00
1	1005	5	NRG	10	280.00
2	1005	5	ANZ	10	198.00
3	1005	6	SMT	1	36.00
4	1005	6	ANZ	1	48.00
1	1006	5	SMT	5	125.00
2	1006	5	NRG	5	140.00
3	1006	5	ANZ	5	99.00
4	1006	6	SMT	1	36.00
5	1006	6	ANZ	1	48.00
1	1007	1	HRO	1	250.00
2	1007	2	HRO	1	126.00
3	1007	3	HSK	1	240.00
4	1007	4	HRO	1	480.00

(1 of 3)

Data in the stores_demo Database

item_num	order_num	stock_num	manu_code	quantity	total_price
5	1007	7	HRO	1	600.00
1	1008	8	ANZ	1	840.00
2	1008	9	ANZ	5	100.00
1	1009	1	SMT	1	450.00
1	1010	6	SMT	1	36.00
2	1010	6	ANZ	1	48.00
1	1011	5	ANZ	5	99.00
1	1012	8	ANZ	1	840.00
2	1012	9	ANZ	10	200.00
1	1013	5	ANZ	1	19.80
2	1013	6	SMT	1	36.00
3	1013	6	ANZ	1	48.00
4	1013	9	ANZ	2	40.00
1	1014	4	HSK	1	960.00
2	1014	4	HRO	1	480.00
1	1015	1	SMT	1	450.00
1	1016	101	SHM	2	136.00
2	1016	109	PRC	3	90.00
3	1016	110	HSK	1	308.00
4	1016	114	PRC	1	120.00
1	1017	201	NKL	4	150.00
2	1017	202	KAR	1	230.00
3	1017	301	SHM	2	204.00
1	1018	307	PRC	2	500.00

(2 of 3)

item_num	order_num	stock_num	manu_code	quantity	total_price
2	1018	302	KAR	3	15.00
3	1018	110	PRC	1	236.00
4	1018	5	SMT	4	100.00
5	1018	304	HRO	1	280.00
1	1019	111	SHM	3	1499.97
1	1020	204	KAR	2	90.00
2	1020	301	KAR	4	348.00
1	1021	201	NKL	2	75.00
2	1021	201	ANZ	3	225.00
3	1021	202	KAR	3	690.00
4	1021	205	ANZ	2	624.00
1	1022	309	HRO	1	40.00
2	1022	303	PRC	2	96.00
3	1022	6	ANZ	2	96.00
1	1023	103	PRC	2	40.00
2	1023	104	PRC	2	116.00
3	1023	105	SHM	1	80.00
4	1023	110	SHM	1	228.00
5	1023	304	ANZ	1	170.00
6	1023	306	SHM	1	190.00

(3 of 3)

Data in the stores_demo Database

call_type Table

call_code	code_descr
B	billing error
D	damaged goods
I	incorrect merchandise sent
L	late shipment
O	other

orders Table

order_num	order_date	customer_num	ship_instruct	backlog	po_num	ship_date	ship_weight	ship_charge	paid_date
1001	05/20/1998	104	express	n	B77836	06/01/1998	20.40	10.00	07/22/1998
1002	05/21/1998	101	PO on box; deliver back door only	n	9270	05/26/1998	50.60	15.30	06/03/1998
1003	05/22/1998	104	express	n	B77890	05/23/1998	35.60	10.80	06/14/1998
1004	05/22/1998	106	ring bell twice	y	8006	05/30/1998	95.80	19.20	
1005	05/24/1998	116	call before delivery	n	2865	06/09/1998	80.80	16.20	06/21/1998
1006	05/30/1998	112	after 10AM	y	Q13557		70.80	14.20	
1007	05/31/1998	117		n	278693	06/05/1998	125.90	25.20	
1008	06/07/1998	110	closed Monday	y	LZ230	07/06/1998	45.60	13.80	07/21/1998
1009	06/14/1998	111	door next to grocery	n	4745	06/21/1998	20.40	10.00	08/21/1998
1010	06/17/1998	115	deliver 776 King St. if no answer	n	429Q	06/29/1998	40.60	12.30	08/22/1998
1011	06/18/1998	104	express	n	B77897	07/03/1998	10.40	5.00	08/29/1998
1012	06/18/1998	117		n	278701	06/29/1998	70.80	14.20	
1013	06/22/1998	104	express	n	B77930	07/10/1998	60.80	12.20	07/31/1998
1014	06/25/1998	106	ring bell, kick door loudly	n	8052	07/03/1998	40.60	12.30	07/10/1998

(1 of 2)

Data in the stores_demo Database

order_num	order_date	customer_num	ship_instruct	backlog	po_num	ship_date	ship_weight	ship_charge	paid_date
1015	06/27/1998	110	closed Mondays	n	MA003	07/16/1998	20.60	6.30	08/31/1998
1016	06/29/1998	119	delivery entrance off Camp St.	n	PC6782	07/12/1998	35.00	11.80	
1017	07/09/1998	120	North side of clubhouse	n	DM354331	07/13/1998	60.00	18.00	
1018	07/10/1998	121	SW corner of Biltmore Mall	n	S22942	07/13/1998	70.50	20.00	08/06/1998
1019	07/11/1998	122	closed til noon Mondays	n	Z55709	07/16/1998	90.00	23.00	08/06/1998
1020	07/11/1998	123	express	n	W2286	07/16/1998	14.00	8.50	09/20/1998
1021	07/23/1998	124	ask for Elaine	n	C3288	07/25/1998	40.00	12.00	08/22/1998
1022	07/24/1998	126	express	n	W9925	07/30/1998	15.00	13.00	09/02/1998
1023	07/24/1998	127	no deliveries after 3 p.m.	n	KF2961	07/30/1998	60.00	18.00	08/22/1998

(2 of 2)

stock Table

stock_num	manu_code	description	unit_price	unit	unit_descr
1	HRO	baseball gloves	250.00	case	10 gloves/case
1	HSK	baseball gloves	800.00	case	10 gloves/case
1	SMT	baseball gloves	450.00	case	10 gloves/case
2	HRO	baseball	126.00	case	24/case
3	HSK	baseball bat	240.00	case	12/case
3	SHM	baseball bat	280.00	case	12/case
4	HSK	football	960.00	case	24/case
4	HRO	football	480.00	case	24/case
5	NRG	tennis racquet	28.00	each	each
5	SMT	tennis racquet	25.00	each	each
5	ANZ	tennis racquet	19.80	each	each
6	SMT	tennis ball	36.00	case	24 cans/case
6	ANZ	tennis ball	48.00	case	24 cans/case
7	HRO	basketball	600.00	case	24/case
8	ANZ	volleyball	840.00	case	24/case
9	ANZ	volleyball net	20.00	each	each
101	PRC	bicycle tires	88.00	box	4/box
101	SHM	bicycle tires	68.00	box	4/box
102	SHM	bicycle brakes	220.00	case	4 sets/case
102	PRC	bicycle brakes	480.00	case	4 sets/case
103	PRC	front derailleur	20.00	each	each
104	PRC	rear derailleur	58.00	each	each
105	PRC	bicycle wheels	53.00	pair	pair

(1 of 4)

stock_num	manu_code	description	unit_price	unit	unit_descr
105	SHM	bicycle wheels	80.00	pair	pair
106	PRC	bicycle stem	23.00	each	each
107	PRC	bicycle saddle	70.00	pair	pair
108	SHM	crankset	45.00	each	each
109	PRC	pedal binding	30.00	case	6 pairs/case
109	SHM	pedal binding	200.00	case	4 pairs/case
110	PRC	helmet	236.00	case	4/case
110	ANZ	helmet	244.00	case	4/case
110	SHM	helmet	228.00	case	4/case
110	HRO	helmet	260.00	case	4/case
110	HSK	helmet	308.00	case	4/case
111	SHM	10-spd, assmbld	499.99	each	each
112	SHM	12-spd, assmbld	549.00	each	each
113	SHM	18-spd, assmbld	685.90	each	each
114	PRC	bicycle gloves	120.00	case	10 pairs/case
201	NKL	golf shoes	37.50	each	each
201	ANZ	golf shoes	75.00	each	each
201	KAR	golf shoes	90.00	each	each
202	NKL	metal woods	174.00	case	2 sets/case
202	KAR	std woods	230.00	case	2 sets/case
203	NKL	irons/wedges	670.00	case	2 sets/case
204	KAR	putter	45.00	each	each
205	NKL	3 golf balls	312.00	case	24/case
205	ANZ	3 golf balls	312.00	case	24/case

stock_num	manu_code	description	unit_price	unit	unit_descr
205	HRO	3 golf balls	312.00	case	24/case
301	NKL	running shoes	97.00	each	each
301	HRO	running shoes	42.50	each	each
301	SHM	running shoes	102.00	each	each
301	PRC	running shoes	75.00	each	each
301	KAR	running shoes	87.00	each	each
301	ANZ	running shoes	95.00	each	each
302	HRO	ice pack	4.50	each	each
302	KAR	ice pack	5.00	each	each
303	PRC	socks	48.00	box	24 pairs/box
303	KAR	socks	36.00	box	24 pair/box
304	ANZ	watch	170.00	box	10/box
304	HRO	watch	280.00	box	10/box
305	HRO	first-aid kit	48.00	case	4/case
306	PRC	tandem adapter	160.00	each	each
306	SHM	tandem adapter	190.00	each	each
307	PRC	infant jogger	250.00	each	each
308	PRC	twin jogger	280.00	each	each
309	HRO	ear drops	40.00	case	20/case
309	SHM	ear drops	40.00	case	20/case
310	SHM	kick board	80.00	case	10/case
310	ANZ	kick board	89.00	case	12/case
311	SHM	water gloves	48.00	box	4 pairs/box
312	SHM	racer goggles	96.00	box	12/box

(3 of 4)

Data in the stores_demo Database

stock_num	manu_code	description	unit_price	unit	unit_descr
312	HRO	racer goggles	72.00	box	12/box
313	SHM	swim cap	72.00	box	12/box
313	ANZ	swim cap	60.00	box	12/box

(4 of 4)

catalog Table

catalog_num	stock_num	manu_code	cat_descr	cat_picture	cat_advert
10001	1	HRO	Brown leather. Specify first baseman's or infield/outfield style. Specify right- or left-handed.	\<BYTE value\>	Your First Season's Baseball Glove
10002	1	HSK	Babe Ruth signature glove. Black leather. Infield/outfield style. Specify right- or left-handed.	\<BYTE value\>	All-Leather, Hand-Stitched, Deep-Pockets, Sturdy Webbing that Won't Let Go
10003	1	SMT	Catcher's mitt. Brown leather. Specify right- or left-handed.	\<BYTE value\>	A Sturdy Catcher's Mitt With the Perfect Pocket
10004	2	HRO	Jackie Robinson signature glove. Highest Professional quality, used by National League.	\<BYTE value\>	Highest Quality Ball Available, from the Hand-Stitching to the Robinson Signature
10005	3	HSK	Pro-style wood. Available in sizes: 31, 32, 33, 34, 35.	\<BYTE value\>	High-Technology Design Expands the Sweet Spot
10006	3	SHM	Aluminum. Blue with black tape. 31", 20 oz or 22 oz; 32", 21 oz or 23 oz; 33", 22 oz or 24 oz.	\<BYTE value\>	Durable Aluminum for High School and Collegiate Athletes
10007	4	HSK	Norm Van Brocklin signature style.	\<BYTE value\>	Quality Pigskin with Norm Van Brocklin Signature
10008	4	HRO	NFL-Style pigskin.	\<BYTE value\>	Highest Quality Football for High School and Collegiate Competitions
10009	5	NRG	Graphite frame. Synthetic strings.	\<BYTE value\>	Wide Body Amplifies Your Natural Abilities by Providing More Power Through Aerodynamic Design

(1 of 10)

catalog_num	stock_num	manu_code	cat_descr	cat_picture	cat_advert
10010	5	SMT	Aluminum frame. Synthetic strings.	\<BYTE value>	Mid-Sized Racquet for the Improving Player
10011	5	ANZ	Wood frame, cat-gut strings.	\<BYTE value>	Antique Replica of Classic Wooden Racquet Built with Cat-Gut Strings
10012	6	SMT	Soft yellow color for easy visibility in sunlight or artificial light.	\<BYTE value>	High-Visibility Tennis, Day or Night
10013	6	ANZ	Pro-core. Available in neon yellow, green, and pink.	\<BYTE value>	Durable Construction Coupled with the Brightest Colors Available
10014	7	HRO	Indoor. Classic NBA style. Brown leather.	\<BYTE value>	Long-Life Basketballs for Indoor Gymnasiums
10015	8	ANZ	Indoor. Finest leather. Professional quality.	\<BYTE value>	Professional Volleyballs for Indoor Competitions
10016	9	ANZ	Steel eyelets. Nylon cording. Double-stitched. Sanctioned by the National Athletic Congress.	\<BYTE value>	Sanctioned Volleyball Netting for Indoor Professional and Collegiate Competition
10017	101	PRC	Reinforced, hand-finished tubular. Polyurethane belted. Effective against punctures. Mixed tread for super wear and road grip.	\<BYTE value>	Ultimate in Puncture Protection, Tires Designed for In-City Riding
10018	101	SHM	Durable nylon casing with butyl tube for superior air retention. Center-ribbed tread with herringbone side. Coated sidewalls resist abrasion.	\<BYTE value>	The Perfect Tire for Club Rides or Training

(2 of 10)

catalog_num	stock_num	manu_code	cat_descr	cat_picture	cat_advert
10019	102	SHM	Thrust bearing and coated pivot washer/spring sleeve for smooth action. Slotted levers with soft gum hoods. Two-tone paint treatment. Set includes calipers, levers, and cables.	\<BYTE value>	Thrust-Bearing and Spring-Sleeve Brake Set Guarantees Smooth Action
10020	102	PRC	Computer-aided design with low-profile pads. Cold-forged alloy calipers and beefy caliper bushing. Aero levers. Set includes calipers, levers, and cables.	\<BYTE value>	Computer Design Delivers Rigid Yet Vibration-Free Brakes
10021	103	PRC	Compact leading-action design enhances shifting. Deep cage for super-small granny gears. Extra strong construction to resist off-road abuse.	\<BYTE value>	Climb Any Mountain: ProCycle's Front Derailleur Adds Finesse to Your ATB
10022	104	PRC	Floating trapezoid geometry with extra thick parallelogram arms. 100-tooth capacity. Optimum alignment with any freewheel.	\<BYTE value>	Computer-Aided Design Engineers 100-Tooth Capacity Into ProCycle's Rear Derailleur
10023	105	PRC	Front wheels laced with 15g spokes in a 3-cross pattern. Rear wheels laced with 14g spikes in a 3-cross pattern.	\<BYTE value>	Durable Training Wheels That Hold True Under Toughest Conditions
10024	105	SHM	Polished alloy. Sealed-bearing, quick-release hubs. Double-butted. Front wheels are laced 15g/2-cross. Rear wheels are laced 15g/3-cross.	\<BYTE value>	Extra Lightweight Wheels for Training or High-Performance Touring
10025	106	PRC	Hard anodized alloy with pearl finish. 6mm hex bolt hardware. Available in lengths of 90-140mm in 10mm increments.	\<BYTE value>	ProCycle Stem with Pearl Finish

(3 of 10)

catalog_num	stock_num	manu_code	cat_descr	cat_picture	cat_advert
10026	107	PRC	Available in three styles: Men's racing; Men's touring; and Women's. Anatomical gel construction with lycra cover. Black or black/hot pink.	\<BYTE value\>	The Ultimate In Riding Comfort, Lightweight With Anatomical Support
10027	108	SHM	Double or triple crankset with choice of chainrings. For double crankset, chainrings from 38-54 teeth. For triple crankset, chainrings from 24-48 teeth.	\<BYTE value\>	Customize Your Mountain Bike With Extra-Durable Crankset
10028	109	PRC	Steel toe clips with nylon strap. Extra wide at buckle to reduce pressure.	\<BYTE value\>	Classic Toeclip Improved To Prevent Soreness At Clip Buckle
10029	109	SHM	Ingenious new design combines button on sole of shoe with slot on a pedal plate to give riders new options in riding efficiency. Choose full or partial locking. Four plates mean both top and bottom of pedals are slotted—no fishing around when you want to engage full power. Fast unlocking ensures safety when maneuverability is paramount.	\<BYTE value\>	Ingenious Pedal/Clip Design Delivers Maximum Power And Fast Unlocking
10030	110	PRC	Super-lightweight. Meets both ANSI and Snell standards for impact protection. 7.5 oz. Quick-release shadow buckle.	\<BYTE value\>	Feather-Light, Quick-Release, Maximum Protection Helmet
10031	110	ANZ	No buckle so no plastic touches your chin. Meets both ANSI and Snell standards for impact protection. 7.5 oz. Lycra cover.	\<BYTE value\>	Minimum Chin Contact, Feather-Light, Maximum Protection Helmet

(4 of 10)

catalog_num	stock_num	manu_code	cat_descr	cat_picture	cat_advert
10032	110	SHM	Dense outer layer combines with softer inner layer to eliminate the mesh cover, no snagging on brush. Meets both ANSI and Snell standards for impact protection. 8.0 oz.	<BYTE value>	Mountain Bike Helmet: Smooth Cover Eliminates the Worry of Brush Snags But Delivers Maximum Protection
10033	110	HRO	Newest ultralight helmet uses plastic shell. Largest ventilation channels of any helmet on the market. 8.5 oz.	<BYTE value>	Lightweight Plastic with Vents Assures Cool Comfort Without Sacrificing Protection
10034	110	HSK	Aerodynamic (teardrop) helmet covered with anti-drag fabric. Credited with shaving 2 seconds / mile from winner's time in Tour de France time-trial. 7.5 oz.	<BYTE value>	Teardrop Design Used by Yellow Jerseys, You Can Time the Difference
10035	111	SHM	Light-action shifting 10 speed. Designed for the city commuter with shock-absorbing front fork and drilled eyelets for carry-all racks or bicycle trailers. Internal wiring for generator lights. 33 lbs.	<BYTE value>	Fully Equipped Bicycle Designed for the Serious Commuter Who Mixes Business With Pleasure
10036	112	SHM	Created for the beginner enthusiast. Ideal for club rides and light touring. Sophisticated triple-butted frame construction. Precise index shifting. 28 lbs.	<BYTE value>	We Selected the Ideal Combination of Touring Bike Equipment, then Turned It Into This Package Deal: High-Performance on the Roads, Maximum Pleasure Everywhere
10037	113	SHM	Ultra-lightweight. Racing frame geometry built for aerodynamic handlebars. Cantilever brakes. Index shifting. High-performance gearing. Quick-release hubs. Disk wheels. Bladed spokes.	<BYTE value>	Designed for the Serious Competitor, The Complete Racing Machine

(5 of 10)

catalog_num	stock_num	manu_code	cat_descr	cat_picture	cat_advert
10038	114	PRC	Padded leather palm and stretch mesh merged with terry back; Available in tan, black, and cream. Sizes S, M, L, XL.	\<BYTE value>	Riding Gloves for Comfort and Protection
10039	201	NKL	Designed for comfort and stability. Available in white & blue or white & brown. Specify size.	\<BYTE value>	Full-Comfort, Long-Wearing Golf Shoes for Men and Women
10040	201	ANZ	Guaranteed waterproof. Full leather upper. Available in white, bone, brown, green, and blue. Specify size.	\<BYTE value>	Waterproof Protection Ensures Maximum Comfort and Durability In All Climates
10041	201	KAR	Leather and leather mesh for maximum ventilation. Waterproof lining to keep feet dry. Available in white & gray or white & ivory. Specify size.	\<BYTE value>	Karsten's Top Quality Shoe Combines Leather and Leather Mesh
10042	202	NKL	Complete starter set utilizes gold shafts. Balanced for power.	\<BYTE value>	Starter Set of Woods, Ideal for High School and Collegiate Classes
10043	202	KAR	Full set of woods designed for precision control and power performance.	\<BYTE value>	High-Quality Woods Appropriate for High School Competitions or Serious Amateurs
10044	203	NKL	Set of eight irons includes 3 through 9 irons and pitching wedge. Originally priced at $489.00.	\<BYTE value>	Set of Irons Available From Factory at Tremendous Savings: Discontinued Line
10045	204	KAR	Ideally balanced for optimum control. Nylon-covered shaft.	\<BYTE value>	High-Quality Beginning Set of Irons Appropriate for High School Competitions

(6 of 10)

catalog_num	stock_num	manu_code	cat_descr	cat_picture	cat_advert
10046	205	NKL	Fluorescent yellow.	\<BYTE value\>	Long Drive Golf Balls: Fluorescent Yellow
10047	205	ANZ	White only.	\<BYTE value\>	Long Drive Golf Balls: White
10048	205	HRO	Combination fluorescent yellow and standard white.	\<BYTE value\>	HiFlier Golf Balls: Case Includes Fluorescent Yellow and Standard White
10049	301	NKL	Super shock-absorbing gel pads disperse vertical energy into a horizontal plane for extraordinary cushioned comfort. Great motion control. Men's only. Specify size.	\<BYTE value\>	Maximum Protection For High-Mileage Runners
10050	301	HRO	Engineered for serious training with exceptional stability. Fabulous shock absorption. Great durability. Specify men's/women's, size.	\<BYTE value\>	Pronators and Supinators Take Heart: A Serious Training Shoe For Runners Who Need Motion Control
10051	301	SHM	For runners who log heavy miles and need a durable, supportive, stable platform. Mesh/synthetic upper gives excellent moisture dissipation. Stability system uses rear antipronation platform and forefoot control plate for extended protection during high-intensity training. Specify men's/women's size.	\<BYTE value\>	The Training Shoe Engineered for Marathoners and Ultra-Distance Runners
10052	301	PRC	Supportive, stable racing flat. Plenty of forefoot cushioning with added motion control. Women's only. D widths available. Specify size.	\<BYTE value\>	A Woman's Racing Flat That Combines Extra Forefoot Protection With a Slender Heel

(7 of 10)

catalog_num	stock_num	manu_code	cat_descr	cat_picture	cat_advert
10053	301	KAR	Anatomical last holds your foot firmly in place. Feather-weight cushioning delivers the responsiveness of a racing flat. Specify men's/women's size.	\<BYTE value\>	Durable Training Flat That Can Carry You Through Marathon Miles
10054	301	ANZ	Cantilever sole provides shock absorption and energy rebound. Positive traction shoe with ample toe box. Ideal for runners who need a wide shoe. Available in men's and women's. Specify size.	\<BYTE value\>	Motion Control, Protection, and Extra Toebox Room
10055	302	KAR	Reusable ice pack with velcro strap. For general use. Velcro strap allows easy application to arms or legs.	\<BYTE value\>	Finally, an Ice Pack for Achilles Injuries and Shin Splints that You Can Take to the Office
10056	303	PRC	Neon nylon. Perfect for running or aerobics. Indicate color: Fluorescent pink, yellow, green, and orange.	\<BYTE value\>	Knock Their Socks Off With YOUR Socks
10057	303	KAR	100% nylon blend for optimal wicking and comfort. We've taken out the cotton to eliminate the risk of blisters and reduce the opportunity for infection. Specify men's or women's.	\<BYTE value\>	100% Nylon Blend Socks - No Cotton
10058	304	ANZ	Provides time, date, dual display of lap/cumulative splits, 4-lap memory, 10 hr count-down timer, event timer, alarm, hour chime, waterproof to 50m, velcro band.	\<BYTE value\>	Athletic Watch w/4-Lap Memory
10059	304	HRO	Split timer, waterproof to 50m. Indicate color: Hot pink, mint green, space black.	\<BYTE value\>	Waterproof Triathlete Watch In Competition Colors

(8 of 10)

catalog_num	stock_num	manu_code	cat_descr	cat_picture	cat_advert
10060	305	HRO	Contains ace bandage, anti-bacterial cream, alcohol cleansing pads, adhesive bandages of assorted sizes, and instant-cold pack.	<BYTE value>	Comprehensive First-Aid Kit Essential for Team Practices, Team Traveling
10061	306	PRC	Converts a standard tandem bike into an adult/child bike. User-tested assembly instructions	<BYTE value>	Enjoy Bicycling With Your Child on a Tandem; Make Your Family Outing Safer
10062	306	SHM	Converts a standard tandem bike into an adult/child bike. Lightweight model.	<BYTE value>	Consider a Touring Vacation for the Entire Family: A Lightweight, Touring Tandem for Parent and Child
10063	307	PRC	Allows mom or dad to take the baby out too. Fits children up to 21 pounds. Navy blue with black trim.	<BYTE value>	Infant Jogger Keeps A Running Family Together
10064	308	PRC	Allows mom or dad to take both children! Rated for children up to 18 pounds.	<BYTE value>	As Your Family Grows, Infant Jogger Grows With You
10065	309	HRO	Prevents swimmer's ear.	<BYTE value>	Swimmers Can Prevent Ear Infection All Season Long
10066	309	SHM	Extra-gentle formula. Can be used every day for prevention or treatment of swimmer's ear.	<BYTE value>	Swimmer's Ear Drops Specially Formulated for Children
10067	310	SHM	Blue heavy-duty foam board with Shimara or team logo.	<BYTE value>	Exceptionally Durable, Compact Kickboard for Team Practice
10068	310	ANZ	White. Standard size.	<BYTE value>	High-Quality Kickboard
10069	311	SHM	Swim gloves. Webbing between fingers promotes strenghening of arms. Cannot be used in competition.	<BYTE value>	Hot Training Tool - Webbed Swim Gloves Build Arm Strength and Endurance

Data in the stores_demo Database

catalog_num	stock_num	manu_code	cat_descr	cat_picture	cat_advert
10070	312	SHM	Hydrodynamic egg-shaped lens. Ground-in anti-fog elements; Available in blue or smoke.	<BYTE value>	Anti-Fog Swimmer's Goggles: Quantity Discount
10071	312	HRO	Durable competition-style goggles. Available in blue, grey, or white.	<BYTE value>	Swim Goggles: Traditional Rounded Lens For Greater Comfort
10072	313	SHM	Silicone swim cap. One size. Available in white, silver, or navy. Team Logo Imprinting Available.	<BYTE value>	Team Logo Silicone Swim Cap
10073	314	ANZ	Silicone swim cap. Squared-off top. One size. White	<BYTE value>	Durable Squared-off Silicone Swim Cap
10074	315	HRO	Re-usable ice pack. Store in the freezer for instant first-aid. Extra capacity to accommodate water and ice.	<BYTE value>	Water Compartment Combines With Ice to Provide Optimal Orthopedic Treatment

(10 of 10)

cust_calls Table

customer_num	call_dtime	user_id	call_code	call_descr	res_dtime	res_descr
106	1998-06-12 8:20	maryj	D	Order was received, but two of the cans of ANZ tennis balls within the case were empty.	1998-06-12 8:25	Authorized credit for two cans to customer, issued apology. Called ANZ buyer to report the QA problem.
110	1998-07-07 10:24	richc	L	Order placed one month ago (6/7) not received.	1998-07-07 10:30	Checked with shipping (Ed Smith). Order sent yesterday- we were waiting for goods from ANZ. Next time will call with delay if necessary.
119	1998-07-01 15:00	richc	B	Bill does not reflect credit from previous order.	1998-07-02 8:21	Spoke with Jane Akant in Finance. She found the error and is sending new bill to customer.
121	1998-07-10 14:05	maryj	O	Customer likes our merchandise. Requests that we stock more types of infant joggers. Will call back to place order.	1998-07-10 14:06	Sent note to marketing group of interest in infant joggers.

(1 of 2)

customer_num	call_dtime	user_id	call_code	call_descr	res_dtime	res_descr
127	1998-07-31 14:30	maryj	I	Received Hero watches (item # 304) instead of ANZ watches.		Sent memo to shipping to send ANZ item 304 to customer and pickup HRO watches. Should be done tomorrow, 8/1.
116	1997-11-28 13:34	mannyn	I	Received plain white swim caps (313 ANZ) instead of navy with team logo (313 SHM).	1997-11-28 16:47	Shipping found correct case in warehouse and express mailed it in time for swim meet.
116	1997-12-21 11:24	mannyn	I	Second complaint from this customer! Received two cases right-handed outfielder gloves (1 HRO) instead of one case lefties.	1997-12-27 08:19	Memo to shipping (Ava Brown) to send case of left-handed gloves, pick up wrong case; memo to billing requesting 5% discount to placate customer due to second offense and lateness of resolution because of holiday.

(2 of 2)

manufact Table

manu_code	manu_name	lead_time
ANZ	Anza	5
HSK	Husky	5
HRO	Hero	4
NRG	Norge	7
SMT	Smith	3
SHM	Shimara	30
KAR	Karsten	21
NKL	Nikolus	8
PRC	ProCycle	9

state Table

code	sname	code	sname
AK	Alaska	MT	Montana
AL	Alabama	NE	Nebraska
AR	Arkansas	NC	North Carolina
AZ	Arizona	ND	North Dakota
CA	California	NH	New Hampshire
CT	Connecticut	NJ	New Jersey
CO	Colorado	NM	New Mexico
DC	D.C.	NV	Nevada
DE	Delaware	NY	New York
FL	Florida	OH	Ohio

(1 of 2)

Data in the stores_demo Database

code	sname	code	sname
GA	Georgia	OK	Oklahoma
HI	Hawaii	OR	Oregon
IA	Iowa	PA	Pennsylvania
ID	Idaho	PR	Puerto Rico
IL	Illinois	RI	Rhode Island
IN	Indiana	SC	South Carolina
KY	Kentucky	TN	Tennessee
LA	Louisiana	TX	Texas
MA	Massachusetts	UT	Utah
MD	Maryland	VA	Virginia
ME	Maine	VT	Vermont
MI	Michigan	WA	Washington
MN	Minnesota	WI	Wisconsin
MO	Missouri	WV	West Virginia
MS	Mississippi	WY	Wyoming

(2 of 2)

The sales_demo and superstores_demo Databases

In addition to the **stores_demo** database that is described in detail in Appendix A, Informix products include the following demonstration databases:

EDS

IDS

- The **sales_demo** database illustrates a dimensional schema for data-warehousing applications. ◆
- The **superstores_demo** database illustrates an object-relational schema. ◆

This appendix discusses the contents of these two demonstration databases.

For information on how to create and populate the demonstration databases, including relevant SQL files, see the *DB-Access User's Manual*. For conceptual information about demonstration databases, see the *Informix Guide to Database Design and Implementation*.

EDS

The sales_demo Database

Your database server product contains SQL scripts for the **sales_demo** dimensional database. The **sales_demo** database provides an example of a simple data-warehousing environment and works in conjunction with the **stores_demo** database. The scripts for the **sales_demo** database create new tables and add extra rows to the **items** and **orders** tables of **stores_demo**.

To create the **sales_demo** database, you must first create the **stores_demo** database with the logging option. Once you create the **stores_demo** database, you can execute the scripts that create and load the **sales_demo** database from DB-Access. The files are named **createdw.sql** and **loaddw.sql**.

Dimensional Model of the sales_demo Database

Figure B-1 gives an overview of the tables in the **sales_demo** database.

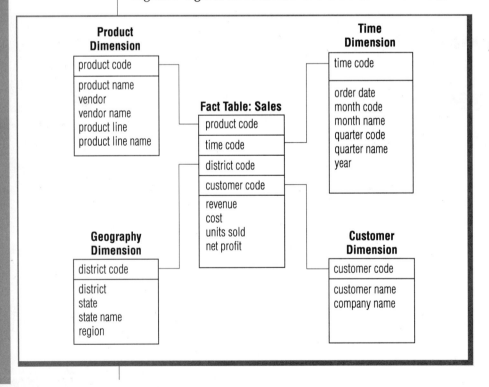

Figure B-1
The sales_demo Dimensional Data Model

For information on how to create and populate the **sales_demo** database, see the *DB-Access User's Manual*. For information on how to design and implement dimensional databases, see the *Informix Guide to Database Design and Implementation*. For information on the **stores_demo** database, see Appendix A.

Structure of the sales_demo Tables

The **sales_demo** database includes the following tables:

- **customer**
- **geography**
- **product**
- **sales**
- **time**

The tables are listed alphabetically, not in the order in which they are created. The customer, geography, **product**, and **time** tables are the dimensions for the **sales** fact table.

The **sales_demo** database is not ANSI compliant.

The following sections describe the column names, data types, and column descriptions for each table. A SERIAL field serves as the primary key for the **district_code** column of the **geography** table. However, the primary and foreign key relationships that exist between the fact (**sales**) table and its dimension tables are not defined because data-loading performance improves dramatically when the database server does not enforce constraint checking.

The customer Table

The **customer** table contains information about sales customers. Figure B-2 shows the columns of the **customer** table.

Figure B-2
The customer Table

Name	Type	Description
customer_code	INTEGER	customer code
customer_name	CHAR(31)	customer name
company_name	CHAR(20)	company name

The geography Table

The **geography** table contains information about the sales district and region. Figure B-3 shows the columns of the **geography** table.

Figure B-3
The geography Table

Name	Type	Description
district_code	SERIAL	district code
district_name	CHAR(15)	district name
state_code	CHAR(2)	state code
state_name	CHAR(18)	state name
region	SMALLINT	region name

The product Table

The **product** table contains information about the products sold through the data warehouse. Figure B-4 shows the columns of the **product** table.

Name	Type	Description
product_code	INTEGER	product code
product_name	CHAR(31)	product name
vendor_code	CHAR(3)	vendor code
vendor_name	CHAR(15)	vendor name
product_line_code	SMALLINT	product line code
product_line_name	CHAR(15)	name of product line

The sales Table

The **sales** fact table contains information about product sales and has a pointer to each dimension table. For example, the **customer_code** column references the **customer** table, the **district_code** column references the **geography** table, and so on. The **sales** table also contains the measures for the units sold, revenue, cost, and net profit. Figure B-5 shows the columns of the **sales** table.

Figure B-5
The sales Table

Name	Type	Description
customer_code	INTEGER	customer code (references **customer**)
district_code	SMALLINT	district code (references **geography**)
time_code	INTEGER	time code (references **time**)
product_code	INTEGER	product code (references **product**)
units_sold	SMALLINT	number of units sold
revenue	MONEY(8,2)	amount of sales revenue
cost	MONEY(8,2)	cost of sale
net_profit	MONEY(8,2)	net profit of sale

The time Table

The **time** table contains time information about the sale. Figure B-6 shows the columns of the **time** table.

Name	Type	Description
time_code	INTEGER	time code
order_date	DATE	order date
month_code	SMALLINT	month code
month_name	CHAR(10)	name of month
quarter_code	SMALLINT	quarter code
quarter_name	CHAR(10)	name of quarter
year	INTEGER	year

IDS

The superstores_demo Database

SQL files and user-defined routines (UDRs) that are provided with DB-Access let you derive the **superstores_demo** object-relational database.

The **superstores_demo** database is not ANSI compliant.

This section provides the following **superstores_demo** information:

- The structure of all the tables in the **superstores_demo** database
- A list and definition of the extended data types that **superstores_demo** uses
- A map of table hierarchies
- The primary-foreign key relationships among the columns in the database tables

For information on how to create and populate the **superstores_demo** database, see the *DB-Access User's Manual*. For information on how to work with object-relational databases, see the *Informix Guide to Database Design and Implementation*. For information on the **stores_demo** database on which **superstores_demo** is based, see Appendix A.

Structure of the superstores_demo Tables

The **superstores_demo** database includes the following tables. Although many tables have the same name as **stores_demo** tables, they are different. The tables are listed alphabetically, not in the order in which they are created.

- **call_type**
- **catalog**
- **cust_calls**
- **customer**
  - **retail_customer** *(new)*
  - **whlsale_customer** *(new)*
- **items**
- **location** *(new)*
  - **location_non_us** *(new)*
  - **location_us** *(new)*
- **manufact**
- **orders**
- **region** *(new)*
- **sales_rep** *(new)*
- **state**
- **stock**
- **stock_discount** *(new)*
- **units** *(new)*

This section lists the column names, column data types, and column descriptions for each table in the **superstores_demo** database. The unique identifier for each table (primary key) is shaded and indicated by a key symbol. Columns that represent extended data types are discussed in "User-Defined Routines and Extended Data Types" on page B-24. Primary-foreign key relationships between the tables are outlined in "Referential Relationships" on page B-27.

The call_type Table

The call codes associated with customer calls are stored in the **call_type** table. Figure B-7 shows the columns of the **call_type** table.

Name	Type	Description
call_code	CHAR(1)	call code
codel_descr	CHAR (30)	description of call code

The catalog Table

The **catalog** table describes each item in stock. Retail stores use this table when placing orders with the distributor. Figure B-8 shows the columns of the **catalog** table.

Name	Type	Description
catalog_num	SERIAL(1001)	system-generated catalog number
stock_num	SMALLINT	distributor stock number (foreign key to **stock** table)
manu_code	CHAR(3)	manufacturer code (foreign key to **stock** table)
unit	CHAR(4)	unit by which item is ordered (foreign key to **stock** table)
advert	ROW (picture BLOB, caption LVARCHAR)	picture of item and caption
advert_descr	CLOB	tag line underneath picture

The cust_calls Table

All customer calls for information on orders, shipments, or complaints are logged. The **cust_calls** table contains information about these types of customer calls. Figure B-9 shows the columns of the **cust_calls** table.

Name	Type	Description
customer_num	INTEGER	customer number (foreign key to **customer** table)
call_dtime	DATETIME YEAR TO MINUTE	date and time call received
user_id	CHAR(18)	name of person logging call (default is user login name)
call_code	CHAR(1)	type of call (foreign key to **call_type** table)
call_descr	CHAR(240)	description of call
res_dtime	DATETIME YEAR TO MINUTE	date and time call resolved
res_descr	CHAR(240)	description of how call was resolved

The customer, retail_customer, and whlsale_customer Tables

In this hierarchy, **retail_customer** and **whlsale_customer** are subtables that are created under the **customer** supertable, as Figure B-25 on page B-27 shows.

For information about table hierarchies, see the *Informix Guide to Database Design and Implementation*.

The customer Table

The **customer** table contains information about the retail stores that place orders from the distributor. Figure B-10 shows the columns of the **customer** table.

Figure B-10
The customer Table

Name	Type	Description
customer_num	SERIAL	unique customer identifier
customer_type	CHAR(1)	code to indicate type of customer: ■ R = retail ■ W = wholesale
customer_name	name_t	name of customer
customer_loc	INTEGER	location of customer (foreign key to **location** table)
contact_dates	LIST(DATETIME YEAR TO DAY NOT NULL	dates of contact with customer
cust_discount	percent	customer discount
credit_status	CHAR(1)	customer credit status: ■ D = deadbeat ■ L = lost ■ N = new ■ P = preferred ■ R = regular

The retail_customer Table

The **retail_customer** table contains general information about retail customers. Figure B-11 shows the columns of the **retail_customer** table.

Figure B-11
The retail_customer Table

Name	Type	Description
customer_num	SERIAL	unique customer identifier
customer_type	CHAR(1)	code to indicate type of customer: ■ R = retail ■ W = wholesale
customer_name	name_t	name of customer
customer_loc	INTEGER	location of customer
contact_dates	LIST(DATETIME YEAR TO DAY NOT NULL	dates of contact with customer
cust_discount	percent	customer discount
credit_status	CHAR(1)	customer credit status: ■ D = deadbeat ■ L = lost ■ N = new ■ P = preferred ■ R = regular
credit_num	CHAR(19)	credit card number
expiration	DATE	expiration data of credit card

The whlsale_customer Table

The **whlsale_customer** table contains general information about wholesale customers. Figure B-12 shows the columns of the **whlsale_customer** table.

Figure B-12
The whlsale_customer Table

Name	Type	Description
customer_num	SERIAL	unique customer identifier
customer_type	CHAR(1)	code to indicate type of customer: ■ R = retail ■ W = wholesale
customer_name	name_t	name of customer
customer_loc	INTEGER	location of customer
contact_dates	LIST(DATETIME YEAR TO DAY NOT NULL)	dates of contact with customer
cust_discount	percent	customer discount
credit_status	CHAR(1)	customer credit status: ■ D = deadbeat ■ L = lost ■ N = new ■ P = preferred ■ R = regular
resale_license	CHAR(15)	resale license number
terms_net	SMALLINT	net term in days

The items Table

An order can include one or more items. One row exists in the **items** table for each item in an order. Figure B-13 shows the columns of the **items** table.

Name	Type	Description
item_num	SMALLINT	sequentially assigned item number for an order
order_num	INT8	order number (foreign key to **orders** table)
stock_num	SMALLINT	stock number for item (foreign key to **stock** table)
manu_code	CHAR(3)	manufacturer code for item ordered (foreign key to **stock** table)
unit	CHAR(4)	unit by which item is ordered (foreign key to **stock** table)
quantity	SMALLINT	quantity ordered (value must be > 1)
item_subtotal	MONEY(8,2)	quantity ordered * unit price = total price of item

The location, location_non_us, and location_us Tables

In this hierarchy, **location_non_us** and **location_us** are subtables that are created under the **location** supertable, as shown in the diagram on page B-27. For information about table hierarchies, see the *Informix Guide to Database Design and Implementation*.

The location Table

The **location** table contains general information about the locations (addresses) that the database tracks. Figure B-14 shows the columns of the **location** table.

Figure B-14
The location Table

Name	Type	Description
location_id	SERIAL	unique identifier for location
loc_type	CHAR(2)	code to indicate type of location
company	VARCHAR(20)	name of company
street_addr	LIST(VARCHAR(25) NOT NULL)	street address
city	VARCHAR(25)	city for address
country	VARCHAR(25)	country for address

The location_non_us Table

The **location_non_us** table contains specific address information for locations (addresses) that are outside the United States. Figure B-15 shows the columns of the **location_non_us** table.

Figure B-15
The location_non_us Table

Name	Type	Description
location_id	SERIAL	unique identifier for location
loc_type	CHAR(2)	code to indicate type of location
company	VARCHAR(20)	name of company
street_addr	LIST(VARCHAR(25) NOT NULL)	street address
city	VARCHAR(25)	city for address
country	VARCHAR(25)	country for address
province_code	CHAR(2)	province code
zipcode	CHAR(9)	zip code
phone	CHAR(15)	phone number

The location_us Table

The **location_us** table contains specific address information for locations (addresses) that are in the United States. Figure B-16 shows the columns of the **location_us** table.

Figure B-16
The location_us Table

Name	Type	Description
location_id	SERIAL	unique identifier for location
loc_type	CHAR(2)	code to indicate type of location
company	VARCHAR(20)	name of company
street_addr	LIST(VARCHAR(25) NOT NULL)	street address
city	VARCHAR(25)	city for address
country	VARCHAR(25)	country for address
state_code	CHAR(2)	state code (foreign key to **state** table)
zip	CHAR(9)	zip code
phone	CHAR(15)	phone number

The manufact Table

Information about the manufacturers whose sporting goods are handled by the distributor is stored in the **manufact** table. Figure B-17 shows the columns of the **manufact** table.

Figure B-17
The manufact Table

Name	Type	Description
manu_code	CHAR(3)	manufacturer code
manu_name	VARCHAR(15)	name of manufacturer
lead_time	INTERVAL DAY(3) TO DAY	lead time for shipment of orders
manu_loc	INTEGER	manufacturer location (foreign key to **location** table)
manu_account	CHAR(32)	distributer account number with manufacturer
account_status	CHAR(1)	status of account with manufacturer
terms_net	SMALLINT	distributor terms with manufacturer (in days)
discount	percent	distributor volume discount with manufacturer

The orders Table

The **orders** table contains information about orders placed by the customers of the distributor. Figure B-18 shows the columns of the **orders** table.

Figure B-18
The orders Table

Name	Type	Description
order_num	SERIAL8(1001)	system-generated order number
order_date	DATE	date order entered
customer_num	INTEGER	customer number (foreign key to **customer** table)
shipping	ship_t	special shipping instructions
backlog	BOOLEAN	indicates order cannot be filled because the item is backlogged
po_num	CHAR(10)	customer purchase order number
paid_date	DATE	date order paid

The region Table

The **region** table contains information about the sales regions for the distributor. Figure B-19 shows the columns of the **region** table.

Figure B-19
The region Table

Name	Type	Description
region_num	SERIAL	system-generated region number
region_name	VARCHAR(20) UNIQUE	name of sales region
region_loc	INTEGER	location of region office (foreign key to **location** table)

The sales_rep Table

The **sales_rep** table contains information about the sales representatives for the distributor. Figure B-20 shows the columns of the **sales_rep** table.

Figure B-20
The sales_rep Table

Name	Type	Description
rep_num	SERIAL(101)	system-generated sales rep number
name	name_t	name of sales rep
region_num	INTEGER	region in which sales rep works (foreign key to the **region** table)
home_office	BOOLEAN	home office location of sales rep
sales	SET(ROW (month DATETIME YEAR TO MONTH, amount MONEY) NOT NULL)	amount of monthly sales for rep
commission	percent	commission rate for sales rep

The state Table

The **state** table contains the names and postal abbreviations for the 50 states of the United States as well as sales tax information. Figure B-21 shows the columns of the **state** table.

Figure B-21
The state Table

Name	Type	Description
code	CHAR(2)	state code
sname	CHAR(15)	state name
sales_tax	percent	state sales tax

The stock Table

The **stock** table is a catalog of the items sold by the distributor. Figure B-22 shows the columns of the **stock** table.

Figure B-22
The stock Table

Name	Type	Description
stock_num	SMALLINT	stock number that identifies type of item
manu_code	CHAR(3)	manufacturer code (foreign key to **manufact**)
unit	CHAR(4)	unit by which item is ordered
description	VARCHAR(15)	description of item
unit_price	MONEY(6,2)	unit price
min_reord_qty	SMALLINT	minimum reorder quantity
min_inv_qty	SMALLINT	quantity of stock below which item should be reordered
manu_item_num	CHAR(20)	manufacturer item number
unit_cost	MONEY(6,2)	distributer cost per unit of item from manufacturer
status	CHAR(1)	status of item: ■ A = active ■ D = discontinued ■ N = no order
bin_num	INTEGER	bin number
qty_on_hand	SMALLINT	quantity in stock
bigger_unit	CHAR(4)	stock unit for next larger unit (for same stock_num and manu_code)
per_bigger_unit	SMALLINT	how many of this unit in bigger_unit

The stock_discount Table

The **stock_discount** table contains information about stock discounts. (There is no primary key). Figure B-23 shows the columns of the **stock_discount** table.

Figure B-23
The stock_discount Table

Name	Type	Description
discount_id	SERIAL	system-generated discount identifier
stock_num	SMALLINT	distributor stock number (part of foreign key to **stock** table)
manu_code	CHAR(3)	manufacturer code (part of foreign key to **stock** table)
unit	CHAR(4)	unit by which item is ordered (each, pair, case, and so on) (foreign key to **units** table; part of foreign key to **stock** table)
unit_discount	percent	unit discount during sale period
start_date	DATE	discount start date
end_date	DATE	discount end date

The units Table

The **units** table contains information about the units in which the inventory items can be ordered. Each item in the stock table is available in one or more types of container. Figure B-24 shows the columns of the **units** table.

Name	Type	Description
unit_name	CHAR(4)	units by which an item is ordered (each, pair, case, box)
unit_descr	VARCHAR(15)	description of units

User-Defined Routines and Extended Data Types

The **superstores_demo** database uses *user-defined routines* (UDRs) and extended data types.

A UDR is a routine that you define that can be invoked within an SQL statement or another UDR. A UDR can either return values or not.

The data type system of Dynamic Server is an extensible and flexible data type system that supports the following types of activities:

- Extension of existing data types by redefining some of the behavior for the data types that the database server provides.
- Definition of custom data types by a user.

This section lists the extended data types and UDRs created for the **superstores_demo** database. For information about creating and using UDRs and extended data types, see *Extending Informix Dynamic Server 2000*.

The **superstores_demo** database creates the *distinct* data type, percent, in a UDR, as follows:

```
CREATE DISTINCT TYPE percent AS DECIMAL(5,5);
DROP CAST (DECIMAL(5,5) AS percent);
CREATE IMPLICIT CAST (DECIMAL(5,5) AS percent);
```

The **superstores_demo** database creates the following *named row types*:

- **location** hierarchy:
  - ❏ location_t
  - ❏ loc_us_t
  - ❏ loc_non_us_t
- **customer** hierarchy:
  - ❏ name_t
  - ❏ customer_t
  - ❏ retail_t
  - ❏ whlsale_t
- **orders** table
  - ❏ ship_t

location_t definition

```
location_id SERIAL
loc_type    CHAR(2)
company     VARCHAR(20)
street_addr LIST(VARCHAR(25) NOT NULL)
city        VARCHAR(25)
country     VARCHAR(25)
```

loc_us_t definition

```
state_code  CHAR(2)
zip         ROW(code INTEGER, suffix SMALLINT)
phone       CHAR(18)
```

loc_non_us_t definition

```
province_code   CHAR(2)
zipcode         CHAR(9)
phone           CHAR(15)
```

name_t definition

```
first       VARCHAR(15)
last        VARCHAR(15)
```

customer_t definition

```
customer_num    SERIAL
customer_type   CHAR(1)
customer_name   name_t
customer_loc    INTEGER
contact_dates   LIST(DATETIME YEAR TO DAY NOT NULL)
cust_discount   percent
credit_status   CHAR(1)
```

retail_t definition

```
credit_num   CHAR(19)
expiration   DATE
```

whlsale_t definition

```
resale_license   CHAR(15)
terms_net        SMALLINT
```

ship_t definition

```
date       DATE
weight     DECIMAL(8,2)
charge     MONEY(6,2)
instruct   VARCHAR(40)
```

Table Hierarchies

Figure B-25 shows how the hierarchical tables of the **superstores_demo** database are related.

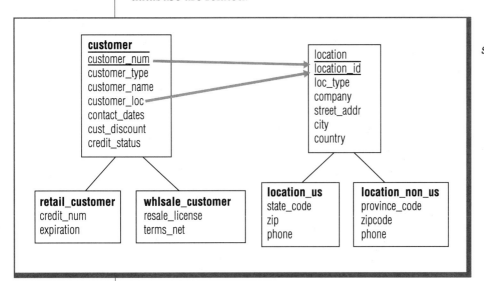

Figure B-25
Hierarchies of superstores_demo Tables

Referential Relationships

The tables of the **superstores_demo** database are linked by the primary-foreign key relationships that are identified in this section. This type of relationship is called a *referential constraint* because a foreign key in one table *references* the primary key in another table.

The customer and orders Tables

The **customer** table contains a **customer_num** column that holds a number that identifies a customer. The **orders** table also contains a **customer_num** column that stores the number of the customer who placed a particular order. In the **orders** table, the **customer_num** column is a foreign key that references the **customer_num** column in the **customer** table.

The orders and items Tables

The **orders** and **items** tables are linked by an **order_num** column that contains an identification number for each order. If an order includes several items, the same order number appears in several rows of the **items** table. In the **items** table, the **order_num** column is a foreign key that references the **order_num** column in the **orders** table.

The items and stock Tables

The **items** table and the **stock** table are joined by three columns: the **stock_num** column, which stores a stock number for an item, the **manu_code** column, which stores a code that identifies the manufacturer, and the **units** column, which identifies the types of unit in which the item can be ordered. You need the stock number, the manufacturer code, and the units to uniquely identify an item. The same stock number and manufacturer code can appear in more than one row of the **items** table, if the same item belongs to separate orders. In the **items** table, the **stock_num**, **manu_code**, and **unit** columns are foreign keys that reference the **stock_num**, **manu_code**, and **unit** columns in the **stock** table.

The stock and catalog Tables

The **stock** table and **catalog** table are joined by three columns: the **stock_num** column, which stores a stock number for an item, the **manu_code** column, which stores a code that identifies the manufacturer, and the **unit** column, which identifies the type of units in which the item can be ordered. You need all three columns to uniquely identify an item. In the **catalog** table, the **stock_num**, **manu_code**, and **unit** columns are foreign keys that reference the **stock_num**, **manu_code**, and **unit** columns in the **stock** table.

The stock and manufact Tables

The **stock** table and the **manufact** table are joined by the **manu_code** column. The same manufacturer code can appear in more than one row of the **stock** table if the manufacturer produces more than one piece of equipment. In the **stock** table, the **manu_code** column is a foreign key that references the **manu_code** column in the **manufact** table.

The cust_calls and customer Tables

The **cust_calls** table and the **customer** table are joined by the **customer_num** column. The same customer number can appear in more than one row of the **cust_calls** table if the customer calls the distributor more than once with a problem or question. In the **cust_calls** table, the **customer_num** column is a foreign key that references the **customer_num** column in the **customer** table.

The call_type and cust_calls Tables

The **call_type** and **cust_calls** tables are joined by the **call_code** column. The same call code can appear in more than one row of the **cust_calls** table because many customers can have the same type of problem. In the **cust_calls** table, the **call_code** column is a foreign key that references the **call_code** column in the **call_type** table.

The state and customer Tables

The **state** table and the **customer** table are joined by a column that contains the state code. This column is called **code** in the **state** table and **state** in the **customer** table. If several customers live in the same state, the same state code appears in several rows of the table. In the **customer** table, the **state** column is a foreign key that references the **code** column in the **state** table.

The customer and location Tables

In the **customer** table, the **customer_loc** column is a foreign key that references the **location_id** of the **location** table. The **customer_loc** and **location_id** columns each uniquely identify the customer location

The manufact and location Tables

The **manu_loc** column in the **manufact** table is a foreign key that references the **location_id** column, which is the primary key in the **location** table. Both **manu_loc** and **location_id** uniquely identify the manufacturer location.

The state and location_us Tables

The **state** and **location_us** tables are joined by the column that contains the state code. The **state_code** column in the **location_us** table is a foreign key that references the **code** column in the **state** table.

The sales_rep and region Tables

The **region_num** column is the primary key in the **region** table. It is a system-generated region number. The **region_num** column in the **sales_rep** table is a foreign key that references and joins the **region_num** column in the region table.

The region and location Tables

The **region_loc** column in the **region** table identifies the regional office location. It is a foreign key that references the **location_id** column in the **location** table, which is a unique identifier for location.

The stock and stock_discount Tables

The **stock** table and the **stock_discount** table are joined by three columns: **stock_num, manu_code,** and **unit.** These columns form the primary key for the **stock** table. The **stock_discount** table has no primary key and references the **stock** table.

The stock and units Tables

The **unit_name** column of the **units** table is a primary key that identifies the kinds of units that can be ordered, such as case, pair, box, and so on. The **unit** column of the **stock** table joins the **unit_name** column of the **units** table.

Glossary

Tip: *Other manuals in the Informix documentation sets, such as the "Informix Storage Manager Administrator's Guide," and the "Informix SNMP Subagent Guide" include a glossary of specialized terms. For additional product-specific information, refer to these glossaries.*

8-bit character
A single-byte character that consists of eight bits, which means that the code point is in the range 128 through 255. Examples from the ISO8859-1 code set include the non-English é, ñ, and ö characters. They can be interpreted correctly only if the software that interprets them is 8-bit clean. *See also* non-ASCII character.

8-bit clean
An operating system or database server that can process character data that contains 8-bit characters. The operating system or database server reads the eighth bit as part of the code value. In other words, it does not ignore the eighth bit or make its own interpretation of the eighth bit.

16-bit code set
A code set (such as JIS X0208) in which approximately 65,000 distinct characters can be encoded.

access method
A group of *routines* that access or manipulate a table or an index. In the output of a SET EXPLAIN statement, access method refers to the type of table access in a *query* (for example, SEQUENTIAL SCAN as opposed to INDEX PATH). *See also* primary access method and secondary access method.

access privileges
The types of operations that a user has permission to perform in a specific database, table, table fragment, or column. Informix maintains its own set of database, table, table fragment, and column access privileges, which are independent of the operating-system access privileges.

active set   The collection of rows that satisfies a query associated with a cursor.

aggregate function   An SQL *function* that returns one value for a group of queried rows; for example, the total number, sum, average, and maximum or minimum of an expression in a query or report. *See also* user-defined aggregate.

aggregate support function   One of a group of *user-defined functions* that the database server uses to calculate a *user-defined aggregate*.

alias   A temporary alternative name for a table in a query; usually used in complex subqueries and required for self-joins. In a form-specification file or any SQL query, alias refers to a single-word alternative name used in place of a more complex table name (for example, *t1* as an alias for *owner.table_name*).

ALS   Legacy acronym for the *Asian Language Support* feature for working with Asian (multibyte) data. Supplanted by *Global Language Support (GLS)*.

ANSI   Acronym for the American National Standards Institute. This group sets standards in many areas, including the computer industry and standards for SQL languages.

ANSI compliant   A database that conforms to certain ANSI standards. Informix databases can be created either as ANSI compliant or not ANSI compliant. An ANSI-compliant database enforces certain ANSI requirements, such as implicit transactions, required owner naming, and unbuffered logging (unbuffered logging only when using Dynamic Server), that are not enforced in databases that are not ANSI compliant.

API   *See* application programming interface (API).

application development tool   Software, such as INFORMIX-NewEra, that you can use to create and maintain a database. The software allows a user to send instructions and data to and receive information from the database server.

application process   The process that manages an ESQL or other program at runtime. It executes the program logic and initiates SQL requests. Memory that is allocated for program variables, program data, and the fetch buffer is part of this process. *See also* database server process.

application-productivity tools   Tools, such as forms and reports, used to write applications.

application program   An *executable file* or logically related set of files.

application programming interface (API)	A group of related software components, usually provided by a third party such as Informix, that a developer uses to create applications that communicate with a third-party product. An API can include a *library* of *functions*, *header files*, graphic user interfaces, and command-line programs. *See also* SQL API and DataBlade API.
arbitrary rule	A series of expressions that you define for *expression-based fragmentation*, using SQL relational and logical operators. Unlike the range rule, the arbitrary rule allows you to use any relational operator and any logical operator to define the expressions. Typically includes the use of the OR logical operator to group data.
archiving	Copying all the data and indexes of a database onto a new medium, usually a tape or a different physical device from the one that stores the database. Archived material is used for recovering from a failure and is usually performed by a database administrator. *See also* backup.
argument	A value that is passed to a *routine* or command. *Compare with* parameter.
array	An ordered set of items of the same type. Individual members of the array are referred to as *elements* and usually are distinguished by an integer argument that gives the position of the element in the array. Informix arrays can have up to three dimensions.
ASCII	Acronym for the American Standards Committee for Information Interchange. ASCII is a coding scheme that assigns numeric values to letters, numbers, punctuation marks, and certain other characters. ASCII describes an ordered set of printable and nonprintable characters used in computers and telecommunication. It contains 128 characters, each of which can be represented with 7 bits of information. *See also* single-byte character.
ASF	Acronym for Associated Services Facility. The code in the ASF portion of Informix products controls the connections between clients and servers. System developers use this term; users of Informix products see this term only in occasional error messages.
Asian Language Support (ALS)	A class of products that operate with multibyte code sets. ALS products support various multibyte code sets whose characters are composed of 8, 16, 24, and 32 bits. ALS servers and tools are available for Version 6.x and earlier family of products. These products might have been developed with the GLS Library or other software written specifically to handle Asian language processing. For more information, see the *Informix Migration Guide*.

attached index

An index that is created without an explicit fragmentation strategy. You create an attached index by omitting both the distribution scheme (specified by the FRAGMENT BY clause) and the storage option (specified by the IN clause) of the CREATE INDEX or ALTER FRAGMENT ON INDEX statements. An attached index can be created on a fragmented table.

The location of the index data varies depending on the database server. In most cases, index pages reside in the same tblspaces as the data pages to which they refer.

For Dynamic Server, index pages for user indexes reside in separate tblspaces, but within the same dbspaces, as the data pages to which they refer. Only the **syscatalogs** indexes reside in the same tblspace as the corresponding data pages.

For Enterprise Decision Server, both user and system-catalog index pages reside in separate tblspaces but in the same dbspaces as the corresponding data pages. *See also* detached index.

audit event

(Not for Enterprise Decision Server) Any database server activity or operation that could potentially access and alter data, which should be recorded and monitored by the database secure auditing facility. Examples of audit events include accessing tables, altering indexes, dropping chunks, granting database access, updating the current row, running database utilities, and so forth. (For a complete list of audit events, see the *Trusted Facility Manual*.)

audit file

(Not for Enterprise Decision Server) A file that contains records of audit events and resides in the specified audit directory. Audit files form an audit trail of information that can be extracted by the database secure auditing facility for analysis by the database administrator.

audit mask

(Not for Enterprise Decision Server) A structure that specifies which events should be audited by (or excluded from auditing by) the database secure auditing facility.

auxiliary statements

The SQL statements that you use to obtain auxiliary information about tables and databases. These statements include INFO, OUTPUT, WHENEVER, and GET DIAGNOSTICS.

B+ tree

A method of organizing an index into a tree structure for efficient record retrieval.

B-tree index   A type of index that uses a balanced tree structure for efficient record retrieval. A B-tree index is balanced when the leaf nodes are all at the same level from the root node. B-tree indexes store a list of rowids for any duplicate key value data in ascending or descending order. *See also* bitmap index and R-tree index.

backup   A duplicate of a computer file on another device or tape to preserve existing work, in case of a computer failure or other mishap. A *backup* refers to duplicating logical-log files while *archiving* refers to duplicating data.

base table   *See* table.

base type   *See* opaque data type.

before-image   The image of a row, page, or other item before any changes are made to it.

big-endian   A hardware-determined storage method in which the most-significant byte of a multibyte number has the lowest address. *See also* little-endian.

bitmap index   A type of index that stores a bitmap for any highly duplicate key value. The bitmap indicates which rows have the duplicate key value. You create a bitmap index with the USING BITMAP keywords in the CREATE INDEX statement. *See also* B-tree index.

blob   A legacy term for binary large object that is now known as and includes TEXT or BYTE data types. These data objects effectively have no maximum size (theoretically as large as 2^{31} bytes). *See also* simple large object.

BLOB   Acronym for binary large object. A data type for a *smart large object* that stores any type of binary data, including images. It can be stored and retrieved in pieces and has database properties such as recovery and transaction rollback. *See also* CLOB.

blobpage   (Not for Enterprise Decision Server) The unit of disk allocation within a blobspace. The database server administrator determines the size of a blobpage. The size can vary, depending on the size of the TEXT or BYTE data that the user inserts.

blobspace   (Not for Enterprise Decision Server) A logical collection of *chunks* that is used to store TEXT and BYTE data.

Boolean   A variable or an expression that can take on the logical values TRUE (1), FALSE (0), or UNKNOWN (if null values are involved).

BOOLEAN	A built-in data type that supports single-byte true/false values. TRUE is represented internally as 0 and externally as t. FALSE is represented internally as 1 and externally as f. A null value is represented as null.
Boolean function	A *function* that returns a Boolean value (true or false). A Boolean function can act as a *filter*.
branch node	An index page that contains pointers to *leaf nodes* and other branch nodes. The database server creates branch nodes when the *root node* and subsequent *leaf nodes* become full.
buffer	A portion of computer memory where a program temporarily stores data. Data typically is read into or written out from buffers to disk.
buffered disk I/O	Disk I/O that the operating system controls instead of an application. With buffered disk I/O, the operating system stores data in the kernel portion of memory before periodically writing the data to disk. *See also* unbuffered disk I/O and disk I/O.
buffered logging	A type of logging that holds transactions in a memory buffer until the buffer is full, regardless of when the transaction is committed or rolled back. Informix database servers provide this option to speed up operations by reducing the number of disk writes.
built-in	Provided by the database server, usually in the system catalog; not defined by the user.
built-in data type	A fundamental *data type* that the database server defines, for example, INTEGER, CHAR, or SERIAL.
byte	The smallest physical computer storage unit. A byte is not necessarily one character. In multibyte code sets, a character is more than one byte.
BYTE	A *data type* for a *simple large object* that stores any type of binary data and can be as large as 2^{31} bytes. *See also* TEXT.
Cartesian product	The set that results when you pair each and every member of one set with each and every member of another set. A Cartesian product results from a multiple-table query when you do not specify the joining conditions among tables. *See also* join.

cascading deletes	A feature that causes deletion of rows from a child table that were associated by foreign key to a row that is deleted from the parent table. When any rows are deleted from the primary-key column of a table, cascading deletes, if enabled, eliminate identical information from any foreign-key column in a related table.
case-sensitivity	The condition of distinguishing between uppercase and lowercase letters. Be careful running Informix programs because certain commands and their options are case-sensitive; that is, they react differently to the same letters presented in uppercase and lowercase characters.
cast	A mechanism that converts one data type to another. *See also* built-in cast, user-defined cast, explicit cast, and implicit cast.
cast function	A *user-defined function* that implements a cast. The function must be registered with the CREATE CAST statement before it can be used.
character	A logical unit of storage for a code point. A character is equal to one or more bytes and can be numeric, alphabetic, or a nonprintable character (control character). *See also* multibyte character and single-byte character.
character set	One or more natural-language alphabets together with additional symbols for digits, punctuation, and diacritical marks. A natural language is a language that people use to communicate with each other, such as English, Chinese, or German. *See also* code set.
character special device	*See* unbuffered disk I/O.
check constraint	A condition that must be met before data can be assigned to a table column during an INSERT or UPDATE statement.
checkpoint	A point in time during a database server operation when the pages on disk are synchronized with the pages in the shared-memory buffer pool. It can be a *full checkpoint* or a *fuzzy checkpoint*.
child table	The referencing table in a referential constraint. *See also* parent table.
chunk	(No blobspace chunks for Enterprise Decision Server) The largest contiguous section of disk space available for a database server. A specified set of chunks defines a *dbspace* or *blobspace*. A database server administrator allocates a chunk to a dbspace or blobspace when that dbspace or blobspace approaches full capacity. A chunk contains a certain number of pages.

client application	A program that requests services from a server program, typically a file server or a database server. For the GLS feature, the term *client application* includes database server utilities.
client computer	The computer on which a client application runs.
client locale	The locale that a client application uses to perform read and write operations on the client computer. The **CLIENT_LOCALE** environment variable can specify a nondefault locale. *See also* locale and server locale.
client/server architecture	A hardware and software design that allows the user interface and database server to reside on separate nodes or platforms on a single computer or over a network.
client/server connection statements	The SQL statements that you use to make connections with databases. These statements include CONNECT, DISCONNECT, and SET CONNECTION.
CLOB	Acronym for character large object. A data type for a *smart large object* that stores large text items, such as PostScript or HTML files. It can be stored and retrieved in pieces and has database properties such as recovery and transaction rollback. *See also* BLOB.
close a cursor	To drop the association between a cursor and active set of rows that results from a query.
close a database	To deactivate the connection between a client and a database. Only one database can be active at a time.
close a file	To release the association between a file and a program.
cluster an index	To rearrange the physical data of a table according to a specific index.
cluster key	The column in a table that logically relates a group of simple large objects or smart large objects that are stored in an optical cluster.
clustersize	The amount of space, specified in kilobytes, that is allocated to an optical cluster on an optical volume.
code point	A bit pattern that represents one character in a *code set*. For example, in the ASCII code set, the *A* character has a code point of 0x00.

code set	A computer representation of a character set that specifies how to map each character in a character set to a unique code point. For example, ASCII, ISO8859-1, Microsoft 1252, and EBCDIC are code sets that can represent the English language. A locale name specifies a code set. *See also* code point and character set.
code-set conversion	The process of converting character data from one code set (the source code set) to another (the target code set). Code-set conversion is useful when the client and server computers use different code sets to represent the same character data.
code-set order	The order of characters within a code set based on their code points. For example, in the ASCII code set, uppercase characters (*A* through *Z*) are ordered before lowercase characters (*a* through *z*). *See also* collation order and localized order.
cogroup	A named group of coservers. At initialization, the database server creates a cogroup that is named **cogroup_all** from all configured *coservers*.
collating sequence	The sequence of values that specifies some logical order in which the character fields in a database are sorted and indexed. A collation sequence depends on either the order of the code set or the locale. Collating sequence is also known as *collation order*.
collation	The process of sorting characters based on a collation order.
collation order	*See* collating sequence and code-set order.
collection	An instance of a *collection data type*; a group of *elements* of the same *data type* stored in a SET, MULTISET, or LIST.
collection cursor	A database *cursor* that has an Informix ESQL/C *collection variable* associated with it and provides access to the individual *elements* of a column whose data type is a *collection data type*.
collection data type	A *complex data type* whose instances are groups of *elements* of the same *data type*, which can be any *opaque data type*, *distinct data type*, *built-in data type*, *collection data type*, or *row type*.
collection-derived table	A table that Informix ESQL/C or SPL creates for a collection column when it encounters the TABLE keyword in an INSERT, DELETE, UPDATE, or SELECT statement. ESQL/C and SPL store this table in a *collection variable* to access *elements* of the collection as rows of the collection-derived table.

collection subquery	A query that takes the result of a subquery and turns it into a expression by using the MULTISET keyword to convert returned values into a MULTISET collection.
collection variable	An Informix ESQL/C *host variable* or *SPL variable* that holds an entire *collection* and provides access, through a *collection cursor*, to the individual *elements* of the collection.
collocated join	A join that occurs locally on the coserver where the data resides. The local coserver sends the data to the other coservers after the join is complete.
column	A data element that contains a particular type of information that occurs in every row of the table. Also known as a *field*. *See also* row.
column expression	An expression that includes a column name and optionally uses *column subscripts* to define a *column substring*.
column subscript	A subscript in a column expression. *See also* subscript.
column substring	A substring in a column expression. *See also* substring.
command file	A system file that contains one or more statements or commands, such as SQL statements.
comment	The information in a program file that is not processed by the computer but documents the program. You use special characters such as a pound sign (#), curly braces ({ }), slash marks (/) and asterisks (*), or a double dash (--) to identify comments, depending on the programming environment.
commit work	To complete a transaction by accepting all changes to the database since the beginning of the transaction. *See also* roll back.
Committed Read	An Informix level of isolation in which a user can view only rows that are currently committed at the moment of the query request; that is, a user cannot view rows that were changed as a part of a currently uncommitted transaction. Committed Read is available through a database server and set with the SET ISOLATION statement. It is the default level of isolation for databases that are not ANSI compliant. *See also* isolation and Read Committed.
compile	To translate source code (in a high-level language) into executable code. *Compare with* execute and link. *See also* source file.
compile-time error	An error that occurs when you *compile* the program source code. This type of error indicates syntax errors in the source code. *Compare with* runtime error.

complex data type

A *data type* that is built from a combination of other data types using an SQL type constructor and whose components can be accessed through SQL statements. *See also* row type and collection data type.

component

In the High-Performance Loader (HPL), the information required to load or unload data is organized in several *components*. The components are format, map, filter, query, project, device array, load job, and unload job.

composite data type

See row type.

composite index

An index constructed on two or more columns of a table. The ordering imposed by the composite index varies least frequently on the first-named column and most frequently on the last-named column.

composite join

A join between two or more tables based on the relationship among two or more columns in each table. *See also* join and simple join.

compressed bitmap

An indexing method that identifies records through a fragment identifier and a record identifier.

concatenate

To append a second string to the end of a first string.

concatenation operator

A symbolic notation composed of two pipe symbols (| |) used in expressions to indicate the joining of two strings.

concurrency

The ability of two or more processes to access the same database simultaneously.

configuration management (CM) coserver

A coserver that Informix designates to run CM software and store CM data.

configuration file

A file read during database server disk or shared-memory initialization that contains the parameters that specify values for configurable behavior. Database server and its archiving tool use configuration files.

connection

A logical association between two applications or between an application and a database environment, created by a CONNECT or DATABASE statement. Database servers can also have connections to one another. *See also* explicit connection, implicit connection, and multiplexed connection.

connection coserver

The coserver to which a client is directly connected. *See also* coserver and participating coserver.

connection redirector	An Enterprise Decision Server feature that is enabled by an option-field setting in the sqlhosts file whereby the database server attempts to establish a client connection with each coserver in a dbserver group until the connection is successful.
constant	Data whose value does not change during the execution of a program or command. In a program, a constant has a name that can be referenced. *Compare with* variable. *See also* literal.
constraint	A restriction on what kinds of data can be inserted or updated in tables. *See also* check constraint, primary-key constraint, referential constraint, not-null constraint, and unique constraint.
constructed data type	*See* complex data type.
constructor	*See* type constructor.
control character	A character whose occurrence in a particular context initiates, modifies, or stops a control function (an operation to control a device, for example, in moving a cursor or in reading data). In a program, you can define actions that use the CTRL key with another key to execute some programming action (for example, entering CTRL-W to obtain on-line Help in Informix products). A control character is sometimes referred to as a *control key. Compare with* printable character.
cooked files	*See* buffered disk I/O.
correlated subquery	A subquery (or inner SELECT) that depends on a value produced by the outer SELECT statement that contains it. Also a nested subquery whose WHERE clause refers to an attribute of a relation that is declared in an outer SELECT. Correlated subqueries reference one or more columns from one or more tables of a parent query and need to be evaluated once for each row in the parent query. *See also* independent subquery and subquery.
correlation name	The prefix that you can use with a column name in a triggered action to refer to an old (before triggering statement) or a new (after triggering statement) column value. The associated column name must belong to the triggering table.
corrupted database	A database whose tables or indexes contain incomplete or invalid data.
corrupted index	An index that does not correspond exactly to its table.

coserver	The functional equivalent of a database server that operates on a single node. *See also* connection coserver and participating coserver.
current row	The most recently retrieved row of the active set of a query.
cursor	An identifier associated with a group of rows or a collection data type. Conceptually, the pointer to the current row or collection element. You can use cursors for SELECT statements or EXECUTE PROCEDURE statements (associating the cursor with the rows returned by a query) or INSERT statements (associating the cursor with a buffer to insert multiple rows as a group). A select cursor is declared for sequential only (regular cursor) or nonsequential (scroll cursor) retrieval of row information. In addition, you can declare a select cursor for update (initiating locking control for updated and deleted rows) or WITH HOLD (completing a transaction does not close the cursor). In ESQL/C, a cursor can be dynamic, meaning that it can be an identifier or a character/string variable.
cursor function	A *user-defined function* that returns one or more rows of data and therefore requires a *cursor* to execute. An *SPL function* is a cursor function when its RETURN statement contains the WITH RESUME keywords. An *external function* is a cursor function when it is defined as an *iterator function. Compare with* noncursor function.
cursor manipulation statements	The SQL statements that control cursors; specifically, the CLOSE, DECLARE, FETCH, FLUSH, OPEN, and PUT statements.
Cursor Stability	An Informix level of isolation available through the SET ISOLATION statement in which the database server must secure a shared lock on a fetched row before the row can be viewed. The database server retains the lock until it receives a request to fetch a new row. *See also* isolation.
data access statements	The SQL statements that you use to grant and revoke permissions and to lock tables.
data definition statements	The SQL statements that you use to create, alter, drop, and rename data objects, including databases, tables, views, synonyms, triggers, and SPL routines.
data dictionary	The collection of tables that keeps track of the structure of the database. Information about the database is maintained in the data dictionary, which is also referred to as the system catalog. *See also* system catalog.

data distribution	A mapping of the data in a column into a set of the column values. The contents of the column are examined and divided into bins, each of which represents a percentage of the data. The organization of column values into bins is called the distribution for that column. Use the UPDATE STATISTICS statement to create data distributions.
data integrity	The process of ensuring that data corruption does not occur when multiple users simultaneously try to alter the same data. Locking and transaction processing are used to control data integrity.
data integrity statements	The SQL statements that you use to control transactions and audits. Data integrity statements also include statements for repairing and recovering tables.
data manipulation statements	The SQL statements that you use to query tables, insert into tables, delete from tables, update tables, and load into and unload from tables.
data partitioning	*See* table fragmentation.
data replication	The ability to allow database objects to have more than one representation at more than one distinct site.
data restriction	Synonym for *constraint*.
data type	A descriptor assigned to each column in a table or program variable, which indicates the type of data the column or program variable is intended to hold. Informix data types are discussed in Chapter 2, "Data Types." Informix data types for Global Language Support are discussed in the *Informix Guide to GLS Functionality*. *See also* built-in data type, complex data type, distinct data type, opaque data type, and user-defined data type.
database	A collection of information (contained in tables) that is useful to a particular organization or used for a specific purpose. See also relational database.
Database Administrator	*See* DBA.
database application	A program that applies database management techniques to implement specific data manipulation and reporting tasks.
database environment	Used in the CONNECT statement, either the database server or the database server and database to which a user connects.

database locale	The locale that a database server uses to interpret NCHAR and NVARCHAR data that is in a particular database. The **DB_LOCALE** environment variable can specify a nondefault database locale. *See also* locale.
database management system	*See* DBMS.
database object	An SQL entity that is recorded in a system catalog table, such as a *table, column, constraint, cursor, index, prepared statement, synonym, trigger, user-defined cast, user-defined data type, user-defined routine,* or *view.*
database server	A software package that manages access to one or more databases for one or more client applications. *See also* relational database server.
database server process	A virtual processor that functions similarly to a CPU in a computer. *See also* application process.
database server utility	A program that performs a specific task. For example, DB-Access, **dbexport**, and **onmode** are Informix database server utilities.
DataBlade API	An *application programming interface* that Informix provides to allow a C *user-defined routine* access to the database server. You can also use the DataBlade API to create client LIBMI applications (for backward compatibility with Illustra applications).
DataBlade module	A group of *database objects* and supporting code that extends an object-relational database to manage new kinds of data or add new features. A DataBlade module can include new data types, *routines, casts, aggregates, access methods,* SQL code, client code, and installation programs.
DBA	Acronym for *Database Administrator*. The DBA is responsible for the contents and use of a database, whereas the database server administrator is responsible for managing one or more database servers.
DBA-privileged	A class of SPL routines that only a user with DBA database privileges creates.
DBMS	Acronym for *database management system*. It is all the components necessary to create and maintain a database, including the application development tools and the database server.
dbserver group	A collection of coservers defined and named by entries in the sqlhosts file. Dbserver groups make multiple coservers into a single logical entity for establishing or changing client/server connections.

dbslice	A named set of dbspaces that can span multiple coservers. A dbslice is managed as a single storage object. *See also* logslice, physslice, and rootslice.
dbspace	A logical collection of one or more chunks. Because chunks represent specific regions of disk space, the creators of databases and tables can control where their data is physically located by placing databases or tables in specific dbspaces. A dbspace provides a link between logical (such as tables) and physical (such as chunks) units of storage. *See also* root dbspace.
DDL	Acronym for data definition language. *See also* data definition statements.
deadlock	A situation in which two or more threads cannot proceed because each is waiting for data locked by the other (or another) thread. The database server monitors and prevents potential deadlock situations by sending an error message to the application whose request for a lock might result in a deadlock.
debug file	A file that receives output used for debugging purposes.
decision-support application	An application that provides information that is used for strategic planning, decision-making, and reporting. It typically executes in a batch environment in a sequential scan fashion and returns a large fraction of the rows scanned. Decision-support queries typically scan the entire database. *See also* online transaction processing application.
decision-support query	A query that a decision-support application generates. It often requires operations such as multiple joins, temporary tables, and extensive calculations, and can benefit significantly from PDQ. *See also* online transaction processing queries.
declaration statement	A programming language statement that describes or defines objects; for example, defining a program variable. *Compare with* procedure. *See also* data definition statements.
default	How a program acts or the values that are assumed if the user does not explicitly specify an action.
default locale	The locale that a product uses unless you specify a different (nondefault) locale. For Informix products, U.S. English is the default locale. *See also* locale.
default value	A value inserted in a *column* or *variable* when an explicit value is not specified. You can assign default values to columns with the ALTER TABLE and CREATE TABLE statements and to variables in *SPL routines*.

delete	To remove any row or combination of rows with the DELETE statement.
delimited identifier	An identifier surrounded by double quotes. The purpose of a delimited identifier is to allow usage of identifiers that are otherwise identical to SQL reserved keywords or that contain nonalphabetical characters. *See also* identifier.
delimiter	A boundary on an input field or the terminator for a column or row. Some files and prepared objects require semicolon (;), comma (,), space, or tab delimiters between statements.
deluxe mode	A method of loading or unloading data that uses regular inserts.
descriptor	A quoted string or embedded variable name that identifies an allocated system-descriptor area or an **sqlda** structure. It is used for the Informix SQL APIs. *See also* identifier.
detached index	The type of index you get when the distribution scheme (specified by the FRAGMENT BY clause) and the storage option (specified by the IN clause) of the CREATE INDEX or ALTER FRAGMENT ON INDEX statements differ from the distribution scheme of the underlying table. Index pages reside in separate dbspaces from the corresponding data pages. *See also* attached index.
device array	A list of I/O devices. *See also* component.
diagnostic area	A data structure that stores diagnostic information about an executed SQL statement.
diagnostics table	A special table that holds information about the integrity violations caused by each row in a violations table. You use the START VIOLATIONS TABLE statement to create violations and diagnostics tables and associate them with a base table.
Dirty Read	An Informix isolation level set with the SET ISOLATION statement that does not account for locks and allows viewing of any existing rows, even rows that currently can be altered from inside an uncommitted transaction. Dirty Read is the lowest level of isolation (no isolation at all), and is thus the most efficient. *See also* Read Uncommitted.
disabled mode	The object mode in which a database object is disabled. When a constraint, index, or trigger is in the disabled mode, the database server acts as if the object does not exist and does not take it into consideration during the execution of data manipulation statements.

disk configuration	The organization of data on a disk; also refers to the process of preparing a disk to store data.
disk I/O	The process of transferring data between memory and disk. The I/O refers to input/output.
display label	A temporary name for a column or expression in a query.
distinct data type	A *data type* that you create with the CREATE DISTINCT TYPE statement. A distinct data type has the same internal storage representation as its source type (an existing *opaque data type, built-in data type, named row type,* or distinct data type) but has a different name. To compare a distinct data type with its source type requires an *explicit cast*. A distinct data type inherits all routines that are defined on its source type.
distribution	*See* data distribution.
distribution scheme	*See* table fragmentation.
DLL	See dynamic link library (DLL).
DML	Acronym for data manipulation language. *See also* data manipulation statements.
dominant table	*See* outer join.
DRDA	Acronym for Distributed Relational Database Architecture. DRDA is an IBM-defined set of protocols that software manufacturers can follow to develop connectivity solutions between heterogeneous relational database management environments.
DSS	Acronym for Decision Support System. *See also* decision-support application.
duplicate index	An index that allows duplicate values in the indexed column.
dynamic link library (DLL)	A *shared-object file* on a Windows system. *See also* shared library.
dynamic management statements	The SQL statements that describe, execute, and prepare statements.
dynamic routine-name specification	The execution of a *user-defined routine* whose name is determined at runtime through an *SPL variable* in the EXECUTE PROCEDURE or EXECUTE FUNCTION statement.

Dynamic Server instance	The set of processes, storage spaces, and shared memory that together comprise a complete database server.
dynamic SQL	The statements and structures that allow a program to form an SQL statement during execution, so that portions of the statement can be determined by user input.
dynamic statements	The SQL statements that are created at the time the program is executed rather than when the program is written. You use the PREPARE statement to create dynamic statements.
EBCDIC	Acronym for Extended Binary Coded Decimal Interchange Code. An 8-bit, 256-element character set.
element	A member of a *collection*. An element can be a single value of any *built-in data type, opaque data type, distinct data type, named row type, unnamed row type*, or *collection data type*.
element type	The *data type* of the *elements* in a *collection*.
embedded SQL	The SQL statements that are placed within a host language. Informix supports embedded SQL in C.
enabled mode	The default object mode of database objects. When a constraint, index, or trigger is in this mode, the database server recognizes the existence of the object and takes the object into consideration while executing data manipulation statements. *See also* object mode.
end-user format	The format in which data appears within a client application when the format is in literal strings or character variables. End-user formats are useful for data types that have a database format that is different from the format to which users are accustomed.
end-user routine	A *user-defined routine* that performs a task within an SQL statement that the existing *built-in* routines do not perform. Examples of tasks include encapsulating multiple SQL statements, creating trigger actions, and restricting who can access *database objects*.
environment variable	A variable that the operating system maintains for each user and made available to all programs that the user runs.
error log	A file that receives error information whenever a program runs.

error message	A message that is associated with a (usually negative) designated number. Informix applications display error messages on the screen or write them to files.
error trapping	*See* exception handling.
escape character	A character that indicates that the following character, normally interpreted by the program, is to be printed as a literal character instead. The escape character is used with the interpreted character to "escape" or ignore the interpreted meaning.
escape key	The keyboard key, usually marked ESC, that is used to terminate one mode and start another mode in most UNIX and DOS systems.
ESQL/C Smart Large-Object API	An *API* of C routines that an Informix ESQL/C client application can use to access *smart large objects* as operating-system files. The ESQL/C Smart Large-Object API is part of the Informix ESQL/C *SQL API*. You can also access smart large objects with a set of functions in the *DataBlade API*.
exception	An error or warning that the database server returns or a state that a SPL statement initiates.
exception handling	The code in a program that anticipates and reacts to runtime errors and warnings. Also referred to as error handling or error trapping.
exclusive access	Sole access to a database or table by a user. Other users are prevented from using it.
exclusive lock	A lock on an object (row, page, table, or database) that is held by a single thread that prevents other processes from acquiring a lock of any kind on the same object.
executable file	A file that contains code that can be executed directly. A C-language object file can be an executable file; it contains the machine-level instructions that correspond to the C-language *source file*.
execute	To run a statement, program, *routine,* or a set of instructions. *See also* executable file.
explicit cast	A *user-defined cast* that a user explicitly invokes with the CAST AS keyword or cast operator (::). *See also* implicit cast.
explicit connection	A connection made to a database environment that uses the CONNECT statement. *See also* implicit connection.

explicit select list	A SELECT statement in which the user explicitly specifies the columns that the query returns.
explicit transaction	A transaction that begins with a BEGIN statement and ends with a COMMIT statement. This type of transaction applies only to non-ANSI databases with logging. *See also* implicit ANSI transaction and singleton implicit transaction.
exponent	The power to which a value is to be raised.
express mode	An Enterprise Decision Server method of loading or unloading data that uses light appends.
expression	Anything from a simple numeric or alphabetic constant to a more complex series of column values, functions, quoted strings, operators, and keywords. A Boolean expression contains a logical operator ($>$, $<$, $=$, $!=$, IS NULL, and so on) and evaluates as TRUE, FALSE, or UNKNOWN. An arithmetic expression contains the operators ($+$, $-$, $\times$, $/$, and so on) and evaluates as a number.
expression-based fragmentation	A distribution scheme that distributes rows to fragments according to a user-specified expression that is defined in the WHERE clause of an SQL statement.
extended data type	A term used to refer to data types that are not built-in; namely *complex data types*, *opaque data types*, and *distinct data types*.
extent	A continuous segment of disk space that a database server allocated to a tbl-space (a table). The user can specify both the initial extent size for a table and the size of all subsequent extents that a database server allocates to the table.
external function	An *external routine* that returns a single value.
external procedure	An *external routine* that does not return a value.
external routine	A *user-defined routine* that is written in an external language that the database supports. These external languages include C and Java. The routine names, parameters, and other information are registered in the system catalog tables of a database. However, the executable code of an external routine is stored outside the database. An external routine can be an *external function* or an *external procedure*.

external space   Storage space that a user-defined access method manages rather than the database server. You can specify the name of an external space instead of the name of a dbspace in the IN clause of the CREATE TABLE and CREATE INDEX statements.

external table   A database table that is not in the current database. It might or might not be in a database that the same database server manages.

extspace   (Not for Enterprise Decision Server) A logical name associated with an arbitrary string that signifies the location of external data. Access its contents with a user-defined access method.

family name   A quoted string constant that specifies a family name in the optical family. *See also* optical family.

fault tolerance   *See* high availability.

fetch   The action of moving a cursor to a new row and retrieving the row values into memory.

fetch buffer   A buffer in the application process that the database server uses to send fetched row data (except TEXT and BYTE data) to the application. *See also* application process.

field   A component of a *named row type* or *unnamed row type* that contains a name and a *data type* and can be accessed in an SQL statement by using dot notation in the form *row type name.field name*. *See also* column.

file   A collection of related information stored together on a system, such as the words in a letter or report, a computer program, or a listing of data.

file server   A network node that manages a set of disks and provides storage services to computers on the network.

filename extension   The part of a filename following the period. For example, DB-Access appends the extension **.sql** to command files.

filter   A set of conditions for selecting rows or records. For an SQL statement, the conditional expression in the WHERE clause is a filter that controls the set of rows that a query evaluates. This filter is sometimes referred to as a *predicate*. The High-Performance Loader (HPL) uses a filter *component* to screen data before loading it into a database.

filtering mode	The object mode of a database object that causes bad rows to be filtered out to the violations table during data manipulation operations. Only constraints and unique indexes can be in the filtering mode. When a constraint or unique index is in this mode, the database server enforces the constraint or the unique index requirement during INSERT, DELETE, and UPDATE operations but filters out rows that would violate the constraint or unique index requirement.
fixchar	A character data type, available in ESQL/C programs, in which the character string is fixed in length, padded with trailing blanks if necessary, and not null-terminated.
fixed-point number	A number where the decimal point is fixed at a specific place regardless of the value of the number.
flag	A command-line option, usually indicated by a minus (-) sign in UNIX systems. For example, in DB-Access the **-e** flag echoes input to the screen.
flexible temporary table	An explicit temporary table that Enterprise Decision Server automatically fragments using a round-robin distribution scheme.
floating-point number	A number with fixed precision (total number of digits) and undefined scale (number of digits to the left of the decimal point). The decimal point *floats* as appropriate to represent an assigned value.
foreign key	A column or set of columns that references a unique or primary key in a table. For every entry in a foreign-key column, there must exist a matching entry in the unique or primary column, if all foreign-key columns contain non-null values.
format	A description of the organization of a data file. *See also* component.
formatting character	A percent sign (%) followed by a letter (c, n, o, or r). When used in a command line, Enterprise Decision Server expands the formatting character to designate multiple coserver numbers (%c), multiple nodes (%n), multiple ordinal numbers designating dbspaces (%d), or a range of dbspaces (%r).
fragment	*See* index fragment and table fragment.
fragment elimination	The process of applying a filter predicate to the fragmentation strategy of a table or index and removing the fragments that do not apply to the operation.

fragmentation	The process of defining groups of rows within a table based on a rule and then storing these groups, or fragments, in separate dbspaces that you specify when you create a table or index fragmentation strategy. *See also* table fragmentation.
full checkpoint	A type of checkpoint where the pages on disk are synchronized with the pages in the shared-memory buffer pool.
function	A *routine* that returns one or more values. *See also* user-defined function.
function cursor	A cursor that is associated with an EXECUTE FUNCTION statement, which executes routines that return values. *See also* cursor function.
function overloading	See routine overloading.
fuzzy checkpoint	A type of checkpoint where only certain pages on disk are synchronized with the pages in the shared-memory buffer pool, and the logical log is used to synchronize the rest of the pages during fast recovery.
gateway	A data communications device that establishes communications between networks.
generalized-key (GK) index	A type of index for static tables with Enterprise Decision Server that can speed certain queries by letting you store the result of an expression as a key in a B-tree or bitmap index. The three categories of GK index are *selective*, *virtual column*, and *join*.
gigabyte	Gigabyte is a unit of storage. A gigabyte equals 1024 megabytes or 1024^3 bytes.
Global Language Support (GLS)	An application environment that lets Informix APIs and database servers handle different languages, cultural conventions, and code sets. For information about the GLS feature, see the *Informix Guide to GLS Functionality*.
global variable	A *variable* or *identifier* whose *scope of reference* is all modules of a program. *Compare with* local variable.
globally-detached index	For Enterprise Decision Server, a type of index that has a fragmentation strategy that is independent of the table fragmentation and where the database server cannot verify that each index row resides on the same coserver as the referenced data row. You can use an expression, system-defined hash, or hybrid distribution scheme to create globally detached indexes for any table. *See also* locally-detached index.

GLS	*See* Global Language Support (GLS).
GLS API	A legacy acronym for Informix GLS. An *API* of C routines that a C-language *external routine* can use to access Informix GLS *locales*. This API also includes functions that obtain culture-specific collation order, time and date formats, numeric formats, and functions that provide a uniform way of accessing character data, regardless of whether the locale supports *single-byte characters* or *multibyte characters*.
hash fragmentation	*See* system-defined hash fragmentation.
hash rule	A user-defined algorithm that maps each row in a table to a set of hash values and that is used to determine the fragment in which a row is stored.
header file	A *source file* that contains *declarations* for *variables*, *constants*, and *macros* that a particular group of modules or programs share.
help message	On-line text displayed automatically or at the request of the user to assist the user in interactive programs. Such messages are stored in help files.
heterogeneous commit	A protocol that governs a group of database servers in which at least one participant is a *gateway* participant. It ensures the all-or-nothing basis of distributed transactions in a heterogeneous environment. *See also* two-phase commit.
hierarchy	A tree-like data structure in which some groups of data are subordinate to others such that only one group (called **root**) exists at the highest level, and each group except root is related to only one parent group on a higher level.
high availability	The ability of a system to resist failure and data loss. High availability includes features such as fast recovery and mirroring. It is sometimes referred to as *fault tolerance*.
High-Performance Loader	The High-Performance Loader (HPL) utility is part of Dynamic Server. The HPL loads and unloads data using parallel access to devices. *See also* external table.
highlight	A rectangular inverse-video area that marks your place on the screen. A highlight often indicates the current option on a menu or the current character in an editing session. If a terminal cannot display highlighting, the current option often appears in angle brackets, and the current character is underlined.

hold cursor   A cursor that is created using the WITH HOLD keywords. A hold cursor remains open past the end of a transaction. It allows uninterrupted access to a set of rows across multiple transactions.

home page   The page that contains the first byte of the data row, specified by the rowid. Even if a data row outgrows its original storage location, the home page does not change. The home page contains a forward pointer to the new location of the data row. *See also* remainder page.

host variable   An SQL API program variable that you use in an embedded statement to transfer information between the SQL API program and the database.

HPL   *See* High-Performance Loader.

hybrid fragmentation   A distribution scheme that lets the user specify two fragmentation methods. Usually one method is used globally and one method is used locally.

identifier   A sequence of letters, digits, and underscores (_) that represents the unqualified name of a database or program object.

implicit ANSI transaction   A transaction that begins implicitly after a COMMIT statement and ends with the next COMMIT statement. This type of transaction applies only to ANSI databases. *See also* explicit transaction and singleton implicit transaction.

implicit cast   A *built-in* or *user-defined cast* that the database server automatically invokes to perform the data conversion. *See also* explicit cast.

implicit connection   A connection made using a database statement (DATABASE, CREATE DATABASE, START DATABASE, DROP DATABASE). *See also* explicit connection.

implicit select list   A SELECT statement that uses the asterisk (*) symbol so that a query returns all columns of the table.

incremental archiving   A system of archiving that allows the option to archive only those parts of the data that have changed since the last archive was created.

independent subquery   A subquery that has no relationship to or dependency on any of its parent queries. It needs to be evaluated only once and the results can be used thereafter. In independent subqueries, both the parent and subquery are parallelized. *See also* correlated subquery and subquery.

index   A structure of entries, each of which contains a value or values and a pointer to the corresponding location in a table or smart large object. An index might improve the performance of database queries by ordering a table according to key column values or by providing access to data inside of large objects.

index fragment	Consists of zero or more index items grouped together, which can be stored in the same dbspace as the associated table fragment or in a separate dbspace. An index fragment also might occupy an sbspace or an *extspace*.
Informix user ID	A login user ID (login user name) that must be valid on all computer systems (operating systems) involved in the client's database access. Often referred to as the client's user ID or user name. The user ID does not need to refer to a fully functional user account on the computer system; only the user identity components of the user account information are significant to Informix database servers. Any given user typically has the same Informix user ID on all networked computer systems involved in the database access.
Informix user password	A user ID password that must be valid on all computer systems (operating systems) involved in the client's database access. When the client specifies an explicit user ID, most computer systems require the Informix user password to validate the user ID.
inheritance	The process that allows an object to acquire the properties of another object. Inheritance allows for incremental modification, so that an object can inherit a general set of properties and add properties that are specific to itself. *See also* type inheritance and table inheritance.
initialize	To prepare for execution. To initialize a *variable*, you assign it a starting value. To initialize the database server, you start its operation.
inmigration	The process by which Optical Subsystem migrates TEXT and BYTE data from the optical storage subsystem into the Dynamic Server environment.
inner join	*See* simple join.
input	The information that is received from an external source (for example, from the keyboard, a file, or another program) and processed by a program.
input parameter	A placeholder within a prepared SQL statement that indicates a value is to be provided at the time the statement is executed.
insert cursor	A cursor for insert operations, associated with an INSERT statement. Allows bulk insert data to be buffered in memory and written to disk.
installation	The loading of software from some magnetic medium (tape, cartridge, or floppy disk) or CD onto a computer and preparing it for use.
interactive	Refers to a program that accepts input from the user, processes the input, and then produces output on the screen, in a file, or on a printer.

internationalization (I18n)

The process of making Informix products easily adaptable to any culture and language. Among other features, internationalized software provides support for culturally specific sorting and for adaptable date, time, and money formats. For more information, see the *Informix Guide to GLS Functionality*.

interquery parallelization

The ability to process multiple queries simultaneously to avoid a performance delay when multiple independent queries access the same table. *See also* intraquery parallelization.

interrupt

A signal from a user or another process that can stop the current process temporarily or permanently. *See also* signal.

interrupt key

A key used to cancel or abort a program or to leave a current menu and return to the menu one level above. On many systems, the interrupt key is CONTROL-C; on other systems, the interrupt key is DEL or CONTROL-Break.

intraquery parallelization

Breaking of a single query into subqueries by a database server using PDQ and then processing the subqueries in parallel. Parallel processing of this type has important implications when each subquery retrieves data from a fragment of a table. Because each partial query operates on a smaller amount of data, the retrieval time is significantly reduced and performance is improved. *See also* interquery parallelization.

IPX/SPX

Acronym for Internetwork Packet Exchange/Sequenced Packet Exchange. It refers to the NetWare network protocol by Novell.

ISAM

Acronym for Indexed Sequential Access Method. An indexed sequential access method allows you to find information in a specific order or to find specific pieces of information quickly through an index. *See also* access method.

ISAM error

Operating system or file access error.

ISO

Acronym for the International Standards Organization. ISO sets worldwide standards for the computer industry, including standards for character input and manipulation, code sets, and SQL syntax.

ISO8859-1

A code set that contains 256 single-byte characters. Characters 0 through 127 are the ASCII characters. Characters 128 through 255 are mostly characters from European languages, for example, é, ñ and ö.

isolation   The level of independence when multiple users attempt to access common data specifically relating to the locking strategy for read-only SQL requests. The various levels of isolation are distinguished primarily by the length of time that shared locks are (or can be) acquired and held. Set the isolation level with the SET ISOLATION or SET TRANSACTION statement.

iterator function   A *cursor function* that is written in an external language such as C or Java.

jagged rows   A query result in which rows differ in the number and type of columns they contain because the query applies to more than one table in a *table hierarchy*.

join   The process of combining information from two or more tables based on some common domain of information. Rows from one table are paired with rows from another table when information in the corresponding rows match on the joining criterion. For example, if a **customer_num** column exists in the **customer** and the **orders** tables, you can construct a query that pairs each **customer** row with all the associated **orders** rows based on the common **customer_num**. *See also* Cartesian product and outer join.

join index   A type of *generalized-key index* that contains keys that are the result of a query that joins multiple tables.

jukebox   A cabinet that consists of one or more optical-disc drives, slots that store optical platters when they are not mounted, and a robotic arm that transfers platters between the slots and the drives. A jukebox is also known as an *autochanger*.

kernel   The part of the operating system that controls processes and the allocation of resources.

key   The pieces of information that are used to locate a row of data. A key defines the pieces of information for which you want to search as well as the order in which you want to process information in a table. For example, you can index the **last_name** column in a **customer** table to find specific customers or to process the customers in alphabetical or reverse alphabetical order by their last names (**last_name** serves as the key).

keyword   A word that has meaning to a program. For example, the word SELECT is a keyword in SQL.

kilobyte   A unit of storage that equals 1024 bytes.

Language Supplement	An Informix product that provides the locale files and error messages to support one or more languages. The International Language Supplement supports several European languages. Informix provides separate Language Supplements for several Asian languages.
large object	A data object that is logically stored in a table column but physically stored independently of the column, due to its size. Large objects can be *simple large objects* (TEXT, BYTE) or *smart large objects* (BLOB, CLOB).
leaf node	An index page that contains index items and horizontal pointers to other leaf nodes. The database server creates leaf nodes when the *root node* becomes full.
level of isolation	*See* isolation.
library	A group of precompiled *routines* designed to perform tasks that are common to a particular kind of application. An *application programming interface* can include a library of routines that you can call from your *application program*. *See also* dynamic link library (DLL), shared library, and shared-object file.
light append	An unbuffered, unlogged insert operation.
link	To combine separately compiled program modules, usually into an executable program. *Compare with* compile and execute.
LIST	A *collection data type* created with the LIST constructor in which *elements* are ordered and duplicates are allowed.
literal	The representation of a data type value in a format that the database server accepts in data-entry operations. For example, 234 is a literal integer and "abcd" is a literal character.
little-endian	A hardware-determined storage method in which the least-significant byte of a multibyte number has the lowest address. *See also* big-endian.
load job	The information required to load data into a relational database using the HPL. This information includes the format, map, filter, device array, project, and special options.
local copy	For Enterprise Decision Server, a replica of a table on a local coserver that is copied to multiple coservers. This allows faster access to the data for OLTP transactions connected to those coservers because you do not have to send the data across the communication links between coservers.

local loopback A connection between the client and database server that uses a network connection even though the client and the database server are on the same computer.

local variable A *variable* or *identifier* whose *scope of reference* is only within the *routine* in which it is defined. *Compare with* global variable.

locale A set of Informix files that specify the linguistic rules for a country, region, culture, or language. Informix products provide pre-defined locales that customers cannot modify. A locale provides the name of the code set that the application data uses, the collation order to use for character data, and the end-user format. *See also* client locale, database locale, default locale, server locale, and server-processing locale.

localized order The order of characters as specified within a particular locale. Localized order can also specify a dictionary or phone-book order. For example, in dictionary order, uppercase characters and lowercase characters are treated the same; one does not take precedence over the other. *See also* collation order.

locally-detached index For Enterprise Decision Server, a type of index that has a fragmentation strategy that is independent of the table fragmentation but where the database server recognizes that each index row resides on the same co-server as the referenced data row. You can use an expression, system-defined hash, or hybrid distribution scheme to create locally detached indexes for any table. *See also* globally-detached index.

lock coupling A method that holds a lock on the child node until a lock is obtained on the parent node during upward movement when updating an R-tree index. Lock coupling is used when an R-tree index is updated if the bounding box of a leaf node has changed. You must propagate the change to the parent node by moving upwards in the tree until you reach a parent node that does not need to be changed.

lock mode An option that describes whether a user who requests a lock on an already locked object is to not wait for the lock and instead receive an error, wait until the object is released to receive the lock, or wait a certain amount of time before receiving an error.

locking	The process of temporarily limiting access to an object (database, table, page, or row) to prevent conflicting interactions among concurrent processes. Locks can be in either exclusive mode, which restricts read and write access to only one user or share mode, which allows read-only access to other users. In addition, update locks exist that begin in share mode but are upgraded to exclusive mode when a row is changed.
locking granularity	The size of a locked object. The size can be a database, table, page, or row.
logical log	An allocation of disk space that the database server manages that contains records of all changes that were performed on a database during the period the log was active. The logical log is used to roll back transactions, recover from system failures, and restore databases from archives. *See also* physical log.
login	The process of identifying oneself to a computer.
login password	*See* Informix user password.
login user ID	*See* Informix user ID.
logslice	A dbslice whose contents are comprised solely of logical-log files. The logical-log files in the logslice can be owned by multiple coservers, one log file per dbspace. *See also* dbslice, rootslice, and physslice.
LVARCHAR	A *built-in data type* that stores varying-length character data of up to 32 kilobytes.
macro	A named set of instructions that the computer substitutes when it encounters the name in source code.
mantissa	The significant digits in a floating-point number.
map	A description of the relation between the records of a data file and the columns of a relational database. *See also* component.
massively parallel processing system	A system composed of multiple computers that are connected to a single high-speed communication subsystem. MPP computers can be partitioned into nodes. *Compare with* symmetric multiprocessing system.
megabyte	A unit of storage that equals 1024 kilobytes or 1024^2 bytes.

Memory Grant Manager (MGM)	(Not for Enterprise Decision Server) A database server component that coordinates the use of memory and I/O bandwidth for decision-support queries. MGM uses the DS_MAX_QUERIES, DS_TOTAL_MEMORY, DS_MAX_SCANS, and PDQPRIORITY configuration parameters to determine what resources can or cannot be granted to a decision-support query.
menu	A screen display that allows you to choose the commands that you want the computer to perform.
MGM	Acronym for Memory Grant Manager.
mirroring	Storing the same data on two chunks simultaneously. If one chunk fails, the data is still usable on the other chunk in the mirrored pair. The database server administrator handles this data storage option.
MODE ANSI	The keywords specified on the CREATE DATABASE statement to make a database ANSI compliant.
monochrome	A term that describes a monitor that can display only one color.
MPP	Acronym for *massively parallel processing system*.
multibyte character	A character that might require from two to four bytes of storage. If a language contains more than 256 characters, the code set must contain multibyte characters. Applications that handle data in a multibyte code set cannot assume that one character requires only one byte of storage. See also single-byte character.
multiplexed connection	A single network connection between a database server and a client application that handled multiple database connections from the client.
MULTISET	A *collection data type* created with the MULTISET constructor in which *elements* are not ordered and duplicates are allowed.
multithreading	Running of multiple threads that are run within the same process. *See* thread.
named row type	A *row type* created with the CREATE ROW TYPE statement that has a defined name and *inheritance* properties and can be used to construct a *typed table*. A named row type is not equivalent to another named row type, even if its field definitions are the same.
national character	A character in a native language character set. Also known as *native character*.
native character	*See* national character.

Native Language Support (NLS)	A class of products that operate with single-byte code sets. An NLS product uses locales and code sets that the operating system supplies. NLS servers and tools are available for the Version 6.x and later family of products. For more information, see the *Informix Migration Guide*.
NLS	Legacy acronym for the *Native Language Support* feature for working with single-byte, non-English data. Supplanted by *Global Language Support* (*GLS*).
node	Within the context of an index for a database, a node is an ordered group of key values having a fixed number of elements. (A key is a value from a data record.) A B+ tree, for example, is a set of nodes that contain keys and pointers that are arranged in a hierarchy. *See also* branch node, leaf node, and root node.
	Within the context of a MPP system, a node is an individual computer. *See also* massively parallel processing system.
	Within the context of a SMP system, a node can either be the entire SMP computer or a fully functioning subsystem that uses a portion of the hardware resources of that SMP system. *See also* symmetric multiprocessing system.
	For Enterprise Decision Server, a node is an individual computer with one or more CPUs that runs a single instance of an operating system within a parallel-processing platform. A node can be a uniprocessor, a cluster of stand-alone computers, an SMP computer, or an independent subsystem configured within an SMP computer.
non-ASCII character	A character with a code point greater than 127. Non-ASCII characters include 8-bit characters and multibyte characters.
noncursor function	A *user-defined function* that returns a single group of values (one row of data) and therefore does not require a *cursor* when it is executed. *Compare with* cursor function.
nonvariant function	A user-defined function that always returns the same value when passed the same arguments. A nonvariant function must not contain SQL statements. *Compare with* variant function.
not-null constraint	A constraint on a column that specifies the column cannot contain null values.
null value	A value that is unknown or not applicable. (A null is not the same as a value of zero or blank.)

object	*See* database object.
object mode	The state of a database object as recorded in the **sysobjstate** system catalog table. A constraint or unique index can be in the enabled, disabled, or filtering mode. A trigger or duplicate index can be in the enabled or disabled mode. You use the SET statement to change the object mode of an object.
object-relational database	A database that adds object-oriented features to a *relational database,* including support for *user-defined data types, user-defined routines,* user-defined *casts,* user-defined *access methods,* and *inheritance.*
OLTP	Acronym for Online Transaction Processing. *See also* online transaction processing application.
online transaction processing application	Characterized by quick, indexed access to a small number of data items. The applications are typically multiuser, and response times are measured in fractions of seconds. See also decision-support application.
online transaction processing queries	The transactions that OLTP applications handle are usually simple and pre-defined. A typical OLTP system is an order-entry system where only a limited number of rows are accessed by a single transaction many times. *See also* decision-support query.
ON-Monitor	(Not for Enterprise Decision Server) An interface that presents a series of screens through which a database server administrator can monitor and modify a database server.
opaque data type	A fundamental *data type* that you define, which contains one or more values encapsulated with an internal length and input and output functions that convert text to and from an internal storage format. Opaque types need *user-defined routines* and *user-defined operators* that work on them. Synonym for *base type* and *user-defined base type.*
opaque-type support function	One of a group of *user-defined functions* that the database server uses to perform operations on *opaque data types* (such as converting between the internal and external representations of the type).
open	The process of making a resource available, such as preparing a file for access, activating a cursor, or initiating a window.
operational table	A logging permanent table that uses light appends for fast update operations. Operational tables do not perform record-by-record logging.

operator	In an SQL statement, a symbol (such as =, >, <,+, -, and *) that invokes an *operator function*. The operands to the operator are *arguments* to the *operator function*.
operator binding	The implicit invocation of an *operator function* when an *operator* is used in an SQL statement.
operator class	An association of *operator-class functions* with a *secondary access method*. The database server uses an operator class to optimize queries and build an index of that secondary access method.
operator-class function	One of the *operator-class support functions* or *operator-class strategy functions* that constitute an *operator class*. For user-defined operator classes, the operator-class functions are *user-defined functions*.
operator-class strategy function	An *operator-class function* that can appear as a *filter* in a query. The query optimizer uses the strategy functions to determine if an *index* of a particular *secondary access method* can be used to process the filter. You register operator-class strategy functions in the STRATEGIES clause of the CREATE OPCLASS statement.
operator-class support function	An *operator-class function* that a *secondary access method* uses to build or search an *index*. You register operator-class support functions in the SUPPORT clause of the CREATE OPCLASS statement.
operator function	A *function* that processes one or more arguments (its operands) and returns a value. Many operator functions have corresponding operators, such as **plus()** and +. You can overload an operator function so that it handles a *user-defined data type*. *See also* routine overloading.
optical cluster	An amount of space, on an optical disc, that is reserved for storing a group of logically related simple large objects or smart large objects.
optical family	A group of optical discs, theoretically unlimited in number.
optical platters	The removable optical discs that store data in an optical storage subsystem.
optical statements	The SQL statements that you use to control optical clustering.
optical volume	One side of a removable Write-Once-Read-Many (WORM) optical disc.

outer join	An asymmetric joining of a dominant (*outer*) table and a subservient table in a query where the values for the outer part of the join are preserved even though no matching rows exist in the subservient table. Any dominant-table rows that do not have a matching row in the subservient table contain null values in the columns selected from the subservient table.
outmigration	The process by which Optical Subsystem migrates TEXT or BYTE data from the Dynamic Server environment to an optical storage subsystem.
output	The result that the computer produces in response to a query or a request for a report.
overloading	*See* routine overloading.
owner-privileged	A class of SPL routines that any user can create who has Resource database privileges.
packed decimal	A storage format that represents either two decimal digits or a sign and one decimal digit in each byte.
pad	Usually, to fill empty places at the beginning or end of a line, string, or field with spaces or blanks when the input is shorter than the field.
page	The physical unit of disk storage and basic unit of memory storage that the database server uses to read from and write to Informix databases. Page size is fixed for a particular operating system and platform. A page is always entirely contained within a chunk. *See also* home page and remainder page.
parallel database query	The execution of SQL queries in parallel rather than sequential order. The tasks a query requires are distributed across several processors. This type of distribution enhances database performance.
parallel-processing platform	A parallel-processing platform is a set of independent computers that operate in parallel and communicate over a high-speed network, bus, or interconnect. *See also* symmetric multiprocessing system and massively parallel processing system.
parallelism	Ability of an Informix database server to process a task in parallel by breaking the task into subtasks and processing the subtasks simultaneously, thus improving performance.

parameter	A variable that is given a value for a specified application. In the signature of a user-defined routine, a parameter serves as a placeholder for an *argument*. The parameter specifies the *data type* of the value that the user-defined routine expects when it receives the associated argument at runtime. *See also* configuration file, input parameter, and routine signature.
parent-child relationship	*See* referential constraint.
parent table	The referenced table in a referential constraint. *See also* child table.
participating coserver	A coserver that controls one or more fragments of a table that Enterprise Decision Server accesses. *See also* coserver and connection coserver.
partition	*See* table fragment.
pattern	An identifiable or repeatable series of characters or symbols.
PDQ	Acronym for *parallel database query*.
PDQ priority	Determines the amount of resources that a database server allocates to process a query in parallel. These resources include memory, threads (such as scan threads), and sort space. The level of parallelism is established by using the **PDQPRIORITY** environment variable or various database server configuration parameters (including PDQPRIORITY and MAX_PDQPRIORITY) or dynamically through the SET PDQPRIORITY statement.
permission	On some operating systems, the right to access files and directories.
phantom row	A row of a table that is initially modified or inserted during a transaction but is subsequently rolled back. Another user can see a phantom row if the isolation level is Informix Dirty Read or ANSI Read Uncommitted. No other isolation level allows the user to see a changed but uncommitted row.
physical log	A set of contiguous disk pages in shared memory where the database server stores an unmodified copy (before-image) of pages before the changed pages are recorded. The pages in the physical log can be any database server page except a blobspace blobpage.
physslice	A dbslice that contains the physical log. *See also* dbslice, logslice, and rootslice.
pointer	A value that specifies the address in memory of the data or *variable*, rather than the contents of the data or variable.

polymorphism	*See* routine overloading and type substitutability.
precision	The total number of significant digits in a real number, both to the right and left of the decimal point. For example, the number 1437.2305 has a precision of 8. *See also* scale.
predefined opaque data type	An opaque data type for which the database server provides the type definition. *See also* BLOB, BOOLEAN, CLOB, LVARCHAR and pointer.
predicate	*See* filter.
predicate lock	A lock held on index keys that qualifies for a predicate. In a predicate lock, exclusive predicates consist of a single key value, and shared predicates consist of a query rectangle and a scan operation such as inclusion or overlap.
prepared statement	An SQL statement that is generated by the PREPARE statement from a character string or from a variable that contains a character string. This feature allows you to form your request while the program is executing without having to modify and recompile the program.
preprocessor	A program that takes high-level programs and produces code that a standard language compiler such as C can compile.
primary access method	An *access method* whose *routines* access a *table* with such operations as inserting, deleting, updating, and scanning. *See also* secondary access method.
primary key	The information from a column or set of columns that uniquely identifies each row in a table. The primary key sometimes is called a *unique key.*
primary-key constraint	Specifies that each entry in a column or set of columns contains a non-null unique value.
printable character	A character that can be displayed on a terminal, screen, or printer. Printable characters include A-Z, a-z, 0-9, and punctuation marks. *Compare with* control character.
privilege	The right to use or change the contents of a database, table, table fragment, or column. *See also* access privileges.
procedure	A *routine* that does not return values. *See also* user-defined procedure.
procedure overloading	*See* routine overloading.
process	A discrete task, generally a program, that the operating system executes.

project   A group of related components that the High-Performance Loader (HPL) uses. *See also* component.

projection   Taking a subset from the columns of a single table. Projection is implemented through the select list in the SELECT clause of a SELECT statement and returns some of the columns and all the rows in a table. *See also* selection and join.

promotable lock A lock that can be changed from a shared lock to an exclusive lock. *See also* update lock.

protocol   A set of rules that govern communication among computers. These rules govern format, timing, sequencing, and error control.

query   A request to the database to retrieve data that meets certain criteria, usually made with the SELECT statement. When used with the High-Performance Loader (HPL), selects records to unload from a relational database. *See also* component.

query optimization information statements   The SQL statements that are used to optimize queries. These statements include SET EXPLAIN, SET OPTIMIZATION, and UPDATE STATISTICS.

query unnesting An execution strategy for nested SQL subqueries whereby Enterprise Decision Server rewrites such subqueries to use modified joins rather than iteration mechanisms. The **sqexplain.out** file reflects the query plan that has been selected after subquery unnesting has occurred.

R-tree index   (Not for Enterprise Decision Server) A type of index that uses a tree structure based on overlapping bounding rectangles to speed access to spatial and multidimensional data types. *See also* bitmap index and B-tree index.

range fragmentation   A distribution scheme that distributes data in table fragments that contain a specified key range. This method can eliminate scans of table fragments that do not contain the required rows, making queries faster.

range rule   A user-defined algorithm for *expression-based fragmentation*. It defines the boundaries of each fragment in a table using SQL relational and logical operators. Expressions in a range rule can use the following restricted set of operators: >, <, >=, <=, and the logical operator AND.

raw device   *See* unbuffered disk I/O.

raw disk   *See* unbuffered disk I/O.

raw table	A nonlogged permanent table that uses *light appends*.
Read Committed	An ANSI level of isolation available through Dynamic Server and set with the SET TRANSACTION statement in which a user can view only rows that are currently committed at the moment of the query request. That is, a user cannot view rows that were changed as a part of a currently uncommitted transaction. It is the default level of isolation for databases that are not ANSI compliant. *See also* isolation and Committed Read.
Read Uncommitted	An ANSI level of isolation set with the SET TRANSACTION statement that does not account for locks and allows viewing of any existing rows, even rows that currently can be altered from inside an uncommitted transaction. Read Uncommitted is the lowest level of isolation (no isolation at all), and is thus the most efficient. *See also* isolation and Dirty Read.
real user ID	*See* Informix user ID.
record	*See* row.
Record-ID	A four-byte RSAM entity, also known as RID, that describes the logical position of the record within a fragment. Not the same as rowid.
recover a database	To restore a database to a former condition after a system failure or other destructive event. The recovery restores the database as it existed immediately before the failure.
referential constraint	The relationship between columns within a table or between tables; also known as a *parent-child relationship*. Referencing columns are also known as *foreign keys*.
registering	In a database, the process of storing information about a *database object* in the *system catalog tables* of a database. Most SQL data definition statements perform some type of registration. For example, the CREATE FUNCTION and CREATE PROCEDURE statements register a *user-defined routine* in a database.
relation	*See* table.
relational database	A database that uses table structures to store data. Data in a relational database is divided across tables in such a way that additions and modifications to the data can be made easily without loss of information.
relational database server	A database server that manages data that is stored in rows and columns.

remainder page   A page that accommodates subsequent bytes of a long data row. If the trailing portion of a data row is less than a full page, it is stored on a remainder page. After the database server creates a remainder page for a long row, it can use the remaining space in the page to store other rows. Each full page that follows the home page is referred to as a big-remainder page. *See also* home page.

remote   A connection that requires a network.

Repeatable Read   An Informix and ANSI level of isolation available with the Informix SET ISOLATION statement or the ANSI SET TRANSACTION statement, which ensures that all data read during a transaction is not modified during the entire transaction. Transactions under ANSI Repeatable Read are also known as Serializable. Informix Repeatable Read is the default level of isolation for ANSI-compliant databases. *See also* isolation and Serializable.

reserved pages   The first 12 pages of the initial chunk of the root dbspace. Each reserved page stores specific control and tracking information that the database server uses.

reserved word   A word in a statement or command that you cannot use in any other context of the language or program without receiving a warning or error message.

restore a database   *See* recover a database.

role   A classification or work task, such as **payroll**, that the DBA assigns. Assignment of roles makes management of privileges convenient.

role separation   (Not for Enterprise Decision Server) A database server installation option that allows different users to perform different administrative tasks.

roll back   The process that reverses an action or series of actions on a database. The database is returned to the condition that existed before the actions were executed. *See also* transaction and commit work.

root dbspace   The initial *dbspace* that the database server creates. It contains reserved pages and internal tables that describe and track all other dbspaces, blobspaces, sbspaces, tblspaces, chunks, and databases.

root node   A single index page that contains node pointers to *branch nodes*. The database server allocates the root node when you create an index for an empty table.

root supertype   The *named row type* at the top of a *type hierarchy*. A root supertype has no *supertype* above it.

rootslice

A dbslice that contains the root dbspaces for all coservers for Enterprise Decision Server. *See also* dbslice, logslice, and physslice.

round-robin fragmentation

A distribution scheme in which the database server distributes rows sequentially and evenly across specified dbspaces.

routine

A group of program statements that perform a particular task. A routine can be a *function* or a *procedure*. All routines can accept *arguments*. *See also* built-in and user-defined routine.

routine modifier

A keyword in the WITH clause of a CREATE FUNCTION, CREATE PROCEDURE, ALTER FUNCTION, ALTER PROCEDURE, or ALTER ROUTINE statement that specifies a particular attribute or usage of a *user-defined routine*.

routine overloading

The ability to assign one name to multiple *user-defined routines* and specify *parameters* of different data types on which each routine can operate. An overloaded routine is uniquely defined by its *routine signature*.

routine resolution

The process that the database server uses to determine which *user-defined routine* to execute based on the *routine signature*. *See also* routine overloading.

routine signature

The information that the database server uses to uniquely identify a *user-defined routine*. The signature includes the type of routine (function or procedure); the routine name; and the number, order, and data types of the parameters. *See also* routine overloading and specific name.

row

A group of related items of information about a single entity across all columns in a database table. In a table of customer information, for example, a row contains information about a single customer. A row is sometimes referred to as a *record* or *tuple*. In an object-relational model, each row of a table stands for one *instance* of the subject of the table, which is one particular example of that entity. In a screen form, a row can refer to a line of the screen. *See also* column.

row type

A *complex data type* that contains one or more related data *fields*, of any *data type,* that form a template for a record. The data in a row type can be stored in a row or column. *See also* named row type and unnamed row type.

row variable

An Informix ESQL/C *host variable* or *SPL variable* that holds an entire *row type* and provides access to the individual *fields* of the row.

rowid In nonfragmented tables, rowid refers to an integer that defines the physical location of a row. Rowids must be explicitly created to be used in fragmented tables and they do not define a physical location for a row. Rowids in fragmented tables are accessed by an index that is created when the rowid is created; this access method is slow. Informix recommends that users creating new applications move toward using primary keys as a method of row identification instead of using rowids.

rule How a database server or a user determines into which fragment rows are placed. The database server determines the rule for *round-robin fragmentation* and *system-defined hash fragmentation*. The user determines the rule for *expression-based fragmentation* and *hybrid fragmentation*. *See also* arbitrary rule and range rule.

runtime environment The hardware and operating-system services available at the time a program runs.

runtime error An error that occurs during program execution. *Compare with* compile-time error.

sbspace (Not for Enterprise Decision Server) A logical storage area that contains one or more chunks that store only BLOB and CLOB data.

scale The number of digits to the right of the decimal place in DECIMAL notation. The number 14.2350 has a scale of 4 (four digits to the right of the decimal point). *See also* precision.

scale up The ability to compensate for an increase in query size by adding a corresponding amount of computer resources so that processing time does not also increase.

scan thread A database server thread that is assigned the task of reading rows from a table. When a query is executed in parallel, the database server allocates multiple scan threads to perform the query in parallel.

schema The structure of a database or a table. The schema for a table lists the names of the columns, their data types, and (where applicable) the lengths, indexing, and other information about the structure of the table.

scope of reference The portion of a *routine* or *application program* in which a *variable* or *identifier* can be accessed. Three possible scopes exist: local (applies only in a single program block), modular (applies throughout a single module), and global (applies throughout the entire program). *See also* local variable and global variable.

scratch table A nonlogging temporary table.

scroll cursor A cursor created with the SCROLL keyword that allows you to fetch rows of the active set in any sequence.

secondary access method An *access method* whose *routines* access an *index* with such operations as inserting, deleting, updating, and scanning. *See also* operator class and primary access method.

secure auditing (Not for Enterprise Decision Server) A facility of Informix database servers that lets a database server administrator keep track of unusual or potentially harmful user activity. Use the **onaudit** utility to enable auditing of events and create audit masks, and the **onshowaudit** utility to extract the audit event information for analysis.

select *See* query.

select cursor A cursor that is associated with a SELECT statement, which lets you scan multiple rows of data, moving data row by row into a set of receiving variables.

selection Taking a horizontal subset of the rows of a single table that satisfies a particular condition. Selection is implemented through the WHERE clause of a SELECT statement and returns some of the rows and all of the columns in a table. *See also* projection and join.

selective index A type of *generalized-key index* that contains keys for only a subset of a table.

selectivity The proportion of rows within the table that a query filter can pass.

self-join A join between a table and itself. A self-join occurs when a table is used two or more times in a SELECT statement (with different aliases) and joined to itself.

semaphore An operating-system communication device that signals a process to awaken.

sequential cursor A cursor that can fetch only the next row in sequence. A sequential cursor can read through a table only once each time the sequential cursor is opened.

Serializable An ANSI level of isolation set with the SET TRANSACTION statement, ensuring all data read during a transaction is not modified during the entire transaction. *See also* isolation and Repeatable Read.

server locale   The locale that a database server uses when it performs its own read and write operations. The **SERVER_LOCALE** environment variable can specify a nondefault locale. *See also* client locale and locale.

server name   The unique name of a database server, assigned by the database server administrator, that an application uses to select a database server.

server number   A unique number between 0 and 255, inclusive, that a database server administrator assigns when a database server is initialized.

server-processing locale   The locale that a database server determines dynamically for a particular connection between a client application and a database. *See also* locale.

session   The structure that is created for an application using the database server.

SET   A *collection data type* created with the SET type constructor, in which *elements* are not ordered and duplicate values can be inserted.

shared library   A *shared-object file* on a UNIX system. *See also* dynamic link library (DLL).

shared lock   A lock that more than one thread can acquire on the same object. Shared locks allow for greater concurrency with multiple users; if two users have shared locks on a row, a third user cannot change the contents of that row until both users (not just the first) release the lock. Shared-locking strategies are used in all levels of isolation except Informix Dirty Read and ANSI Read Uncommitted.

shared memory   A portion of main memory that is accessible to multiple processes. Shared memory allows multiple processes to communicate and access a common data space in memory. Common data does not have to be reread from disk for each process, reducing disk I/O and improving performance. Also used as an Inter-Process Communication (IPC) mechanism to communicate between two processes running on the same computer.

shared-object file   A *library* that is not linked to an application at compile time but instead is loaded into memory by the operating system as needed. Several applications can share access to the loaded shared-object file. *See also* dynamic link library (DLL) *and* shared library.

shelf   The location of an optical platter that is neither on an optical drive nor in a jukebox slot.

shuffling	Shuffling refers to the process that occurs when a database server moves rows or key values from one fragment to another. Shuffling occurs in a variety of circumstances including when you attach, detach, or drop a fragment.
signal	A means of asynchronous communication between two processes. For example, signals are sent when a user or a program wants to interrupt or suspend the execution of a process. *See also* interrupt.
signature	*See* routine signature.
simple join	A join that combines information from two or more tables based on the relationship between one column in each table. Rows that do not satisfy the join criteria are discarded from the result. Also known as an inner join. *See also* composite join.
simple large object	A *large object* that is stored in a *blobspace* or *dbspace* is not recoverable and does not obey transaction isolation modes. Simple large objects include TEXT and BYTE data types. Enterprise Decision Server does not support simple large objects that are stored in a blobspace.
simple predicate	A search condition in the WHERE clause that has one of the following forms: **f(column, constant)**, **f(constant, column)**, or **f(column)**, where **f** is a binary or unary function that returns a Boolean value (TRUE, FALSE, or UNKNOWN).
single-byte character	A character that uses one byte of storage. Because a single byte can store values in the range of 0 to 255, it can uniquely identify 256 characters. When an application handles data in these code sets, it can assume that one character is always stored in one byte. *See also* 8-bit character and multibyte character.
singleton implicit transaction	A single-statement transaction that does not require either a BEGIN WORK or a COMMIT WORK statement. This type of transaction occurs in a non-ANSI logging database. *See also* explicit transaction and implicit ANSI transaction.
singleton select	A SELECT statement that returns a single row.
smart large object	A *large object* that is stored in an *sbspace*, which has read, write, and seek properties similar to a UNIX file, is recoverable, obeys transaction isolation modes, and can be retrieved in segments by an application. Smart large objects include BLOB and CLOB data types.
SMI	Acronym for *system-monitoring interface*.
SMP	*See* symmetric multiprocessing system.

source file	A text file that contains instructions in a high-level language, such as C. A C source file is *compiled* into an *executable file* called an object file. An SPL source file is compiled into its own executable format. *See also* compile.
specific name	A name that you can assign to an overloaded *user-defined routine* to uniquely identify a particular signature of the user-defined routine. *See also* routine overloading and routine signature.
speed up	The ability to add computing hardware to achieve correspondingly faster performance for a DSS query or OLTP operation of a given volume.
SPL	*See* Stored Procedure Language (SPL).
SPL function	An *SPL routine* that returns one or more values.
SPL procedure	An *SPL routine* that does not return a value.
SPL routine	A *user-defined routine* that is written in Stored Procedure Language (*SPL*). Its name, parameters, and other information are registered in the system catalog tables of a database. The database server also stores the executable format in system catalog tables. An SPL routine can be an *SPL procedure* or an *SPL function*.
SPL variable	A *variable* that is created with the DEFINE statement and used in an *SPL routine*.
SQL	Acronym for Structured Query Language. SQL is a database query language that was developed by IBM and standardized by ANSI. Informix relational database management products are based on an extended implementation of ANSI-standard SQL.
SQL API	An *application programming interface* that allows you to embed Structured Query Language (SQL) statements directly in an application. The embedded-language product Informix ESQL/C is an example of an SQL API. *See also* host variable.
SQLCA	Acronym for SQL Communications Area. The SQLCA is a data structure that stores information about the most recently executed SQL statement. The result code returned by the database server to the SQLCA is used for error handling by Informix SQL APIs.

sqlda	Acronym for SQL descriptor area. A dynamic SQL management structure that can be used with the DESCRIBE statement to store information about database columns or host variables used in dynamic SQL statements. The structure contains an **sqlvar_struct** structure for each column; each **sqlvar_struct** structure provides information such as the name, data type, and length of the column. The sqlda structure is an Informix-specific structure for handling dynamic columns. It is available only within an Informix ESQL/C program. *See also* descriptor and system-descriptor area.
sqlhosts	A file that identifies the types of connections the database server supports.
stack operator	Operators that allow programs to manipulate values that are on the stack.
staging-area blobspace	(Not for Enterprise Decision Server) The blobspace where a database server temporarily stores TEXT or BYTE data that is being outmigrated to an optical storage subsystem.
statement	A line or set of lines of program code that describes a single action (for example, a SELECT statement or an UPDATE statement).
statement block	A unit of SPL program code that performs a particular task and is usually marked by the keywords BEGIN and END. The statement block of an *SPL routine* is the smallest *scope of reference* for program variables.
statement identifier	An embedded variable name or SQL statement identifier that represents a data structure defined in a PREPARE statement. It is used for dynamic SQL statement management by Informix SQL APIs.
static table	A nonlogging, read-only permanent table.
status variable	A program variable that indicates the status of some aspect of program execution. Status variables often store error numbers or act as flags to indicate that an error has occurred.
storage space	A *dbspace*, *blobspace*, or *sbspace* that is used to hold data.
stored procedure	A legacy term for an *SPL routine*.
Stored Procedure Language (SPL)	An Informix extension to SQL that provides flow-control features such as sequencing, branching, and looping. *See also* SPL routine.
strategy function	*See* operator-class strategy function.

string	A set of characters (generally alphanumeric) that is manipulated as a single unit. A string might consist of a word (such as 'Smith'), a set of digits representing a number (such as '19543'), or any other collection of characters. Strings generally are surrounded by single quotes. A string is also a character data type, available in Informix ESQL/C programs, in which the character string is stripped of trailing blanks and is null-terminated.
subordinate table	*See* outer join.
subquery	A query that is embedded as part of another SQL statement. For example, an INSERT statement can contain a subquery in which a SELECT statement supplies the inserted values in place of a VALUES clause; an UPDATE statement can contain a subquery in which a SELECT statement supplies the updating values; or a SELECT statement can contain a subquery in which a second SELECT statement supplies the qualifying conditions of a WHERE clause for the first SELECT statement. (Parentheses always delimit a subquery, unless you are referring to a CREATE VIEW statement or unions.) Subqueries are always parallelized. *See also* correlated subquery and independent subquery.
subscript	A subscript is an offset into an array. Subscripts can be used to indicate the start or end position in a CHAR variable.
substring	A portion of a character string.
subtable	A *typed table* that inherits properties (column definitions, constraints, triggers) from a *supertable* above it in the *table hierarchy* and can add additional properties.
subtype	A *named row type* that inherits all representation (data *fields*) and behavior (*routines*) from a *supertype* above it in the *type hierarchy* and can add additional fields and routines. The number of fields in a subtype is always greater than or equal to the number of fields in its supertype.
supertable	A *typed table* whose properties (constraints, storage options, triggers) are inherited by a *subtable* beneath it in the *table hierarchy*. The scope of a query on a supertable is the supertable and its subtables.
supertype	A *named row type* whose representation (data *fields*) and behavior (*routines*) is inherited by a *subtype* below it in the *type hierarchy*.
support function	*See* aggregate support function, opaque-type support function, and operator-class support function.
support routine	*See* support function.

symmetric multiprocessing system	A system composed of multiple computers that are connected to a single high-speed communication subsystem. An SMP has fewer computers than an MPP system and cannot be partitioned into nodes. *Compare with* massively parallel processing system.
synonym	A name that is assigned to a table and used in place of the original name for that table. A synonym does not replace the original table name; instead, it acts as an alias for the table.
sysmaster database	A database on each database server that holds the ON-Archive catalog tables and *system-monitoring interface* (SMI) tables that contain information about the state of the database server. The database server creates the **sysmaster** database when it initializes disk space.
system call	A routine in an operating-system *library* that programs call to obtain information from the operating system.
system catalog	A group of database tables that contain information about the database itself, such as the names of tables or columns in the database, the number of rows in a table, the information about indexes and database privileges, and so on. *See also* data dictionary.
system-defined cast	A *cast* that is built in to the database server. A built-in cast performs automatic conversions between different *built-in data types*.
system-defined hash fragmentation	An Enterprise Decision Server-defined distribution scheme that maps each row in a table to a set of integers and uses a system-defined algorithm to distribute data evenly by hashing a specified key.
system-descriptor area	A dynamic SQL management structure that is used with the ALLOCATE DESCRIPTOR, DEALLOCATE DESCRIPTOR, DESCRIBE, GET DESCRIPTOR, and SET DESCRIPTOR statements to store information about database columns or host variables used in dynamic SQL statements. The structure contains an item descriptor for each column; each item descriptor provides information such as the name, data type, length, scale, and precision of the column. The system-descriptor area is the X/Open standard for handling dynamic columns. *See also* descriptor and sqlda.
system-monitoring interface	A collection of tables and pseudo-tables in the **sysmaster** database that maintains dynamically updated information about the operation of the database server. The tables are constructed in memory but are not recorded on disk. Users can query the SMI tables with the SQL SELECT statement.

table   A rectangular array of data in which each row describes a single entity and each column contains the values for each category of description. For example, a table can contain the names and addresses of customers. Each row corresponds to a different customer and the columns correspond to the name and address items. A table is sometimes referred to as a *base table* to distinguish it from the views, indexes, and other objects defined on the underlying table or associated with it.

table fragment   Zero or more rows that are grouped together and stored in a dbspace that you specify when you create the fragment. A virtual table fragment might reside in an *sbspace* or an *extspace*.

table fragmentation A method of separating a table into potentially balanced fragments to distribute the workload and optimize the efficiency of the database operations. Also known as data partitioning. Table-fragmentation methods (also known as distribution schemes) include *expression-based*, *hybrid*, *range*, *round-robin*, and *system-defined hash*.

table hierarchy   A relationship you can define among *typed tables* in which *subtables* inherit the behavior (constraints, triggers, storage options) from *supertables*. Subtables can add additional constraint definitions, storage options, and triggers.

table inheritance   The property that allows a *typed table* to inherit the behavior (constraints, storage options, triggers) from a *typed table* above it in the *table hierarchy*.

target table   The underlying base table that a violations table and diagnostics table are associated with. You use the START VIOLATIONS TABLE statement to create the association between the target table and the violations and diagnostics tables.

tblspace   The logical collection of *extents* that are assigned to a table. It contains all the disk space that is allocated to a given table or table fragment and includes pages allocated to data and to indexes, pages that store TEXT or BYTE data in the dbspace, and bitmap pages that track page use within the extents.

TCP/IP   The specific name of a particular standard transport layer protocol (TCP) and network layer protocol (IP). A popular network protocol used in DOS, UNIX, and other environments.

temp table   A logging temporary table that support indexes, constraints, and rollback.

temporary   An attribute of any file, index, or table that is used only during a single session. Temporary files or resources are typically removed or freed when program execution terminates or an on-line session ends.

TEXT

A *data type* for a *simple large object* that stores text and can be as large as 2^{31} bytes. *See also* BYTE.

thread

A piece of work or task for a *virtual processor* in the same way that a virtual processor is a task for a CPU. A virtual processor is a task that the operating system schedules for execution on the CPU; a database server thread is a task that a virtual processor schedules internally for processing. Threads are sometimes called *lightweight processes* because they are like processes but make fewer demands on the operating system. *See also* multithreading and user thread.

TLI

Acronym for Transport Layer Interface. It is the interface designed for use by application programs that are independent of a network protocol.

trace

To keep a running list of the values of program variables, arguments, expressions, and so on, in a program or SPL routine.

transaction

A collection of one or more SQL statements that is treated as a single unit of work. If one statement in a transaction fails, the entire transaction can be *rolled back* (canceled). If the transaction is successful, the work is *committed* and all changes to the database from the transaction are accepted. *See also* explicit transaction, implicit ANSI transaction, and singleton implicit transaction.

transaction lock

A lock on an *R-tree index* that is obtained at the beginning of a transaction and held until the end of the transaction.

transaction logging

The process of keeping records of transactions. *See also* logical log.

transaction mode

The method by which constraints are checked during transactions. You use the SET statement to specify whether constraints are checked at the end of each data manipulation statement or after the transaction is committed.

trigger

A mechanism that resides in the database. It specifies that when a particular action (insert, delete, or update) occurs on a particular table, the database server should automatically perform one or more additional actions.

tuple

See row.

two-phase commit

A protocol that ensures that transactions are uniformly committed or rolled back across multiple database servers. It governs the order in which commit transactions are performed and provides a recovery mechanism in case a transaction does not execute. *See also* heterogeneous commit.

type constructor	An SQL keyword that indicates to the database server the type of complex data to create (for example, *LIST, MULTISET, ROW, SET*).
type hierarchy	A relationship that you define among *named row types* in which *subtypes* inherit representation (data *fields*) and behavior (*routines*) from *supertypes* and can add more fields and routines.
type inheritance	The property that allows a *named row type* or *typed table* to inherit representation (data *fields*, columns) and behavior (*routines*, operators, rules) from a named row type above it in the *type hierarchy*.
type substitutability	The ability to use an instance of a subtype when an instance of its supertype is expected.
typed collection variable	An ESQL/C *collection variable* or *SPL variable* that has a defined *collection data type* associated with it and can only hold a *collection* of its defined type. *See also* untyped collection variable.
typed table	A table that is constructed from a *named row type* and whose rows contain instances of that *row type*. A typed table can be used as part of a *table hierarchy*. The columns of a typed table correspond to the *fields* of the named row type.
UDA	*See* user-defined aggregate.
UDR	*See* user-defined routine.
UDT	*See* user-defined data type.
unbuffered disk I/O	Disk I/O that is controlled directly by the database server instead of the operating system. This direct control helps improve performance and reliability for updates to database data. Unbuffered I/O is supported by character-special files on UNIX and by both unbuffered files and the raw disk interface on Windows NT.
Uncommitted Read	*See* Read Uncommitted.
uncorrelated subquery	*See* independent subquery.
unique constraint	Specifies that each entry in a column or set of columns has a unique value.
unique index	An index that prevents duplicate values in the indexed column.
unique key	*See* primary key.

UNIX real user ID	*See* Informix user ID.
unload job	The information required to unload data from a relational database using the HPL. This information includes format, map, query, device array, project, and special options.
unlock	To free an object (database, table, page, or row) that has been locked. For example, a locked table prevents others from adding, removing, updating, or (in the case of an exclusive lock) viewing rows in that table as long as it is locked. When the user or program unlocks the table, others are permitted access again.
unnamed row type	A *row type* created with the ROW constructor that has no defined name and no inheritance properties. Two unnamed row types are equivalent if they have the same number of *fields* and if corresponding fields have the same *data type*, even if the fields have different names.
untyped collection variable	A generic ESQL/C *collection variable* or *SPL variable* that can hold a *collection* of any *collection data type* and takes on the data type of the last collection assigned to it. *See also* typed collection variable.
update	The process of changing the contents of one or more columns in one or more existing rows of a table.
update lock	A promotable lock that is acquired during a SELECT...FOR UPDATE. An update lock behaves like a shared lock until the update actually occurs, and it then becomes an exclusive lock. It differs from a shared lock in that only one update lock can be acquired on an object at a time.
user-defined aggregate	An *aggregate function* that is not provided by the database server (built in) that includes extensions to built-in aggregates and newly defined aggregates. The database server manages all aggregates.
user-defined base type	*See* opaque data type.
user-defined cast	A *cast* that a user creates with the CREATE CAST statement. A user-defined cast typically requires a *cast function*. A user-defined cast can be an *explicit cast* or an *implicit cast*.
user-defined data type	A *data type* that you define for use in a relational database. You can define *opaque data types* and *distinct data types*.

user-defined function	A *user-defined routine* that returns at least one value. You can write a user-defined function in SPL (*SPL function*) or in an external language that the database server supports (*external function*).
user-defined procedure	A *user-defined routine* that does not return a value. You can write a user-defined procedure in SPL (*SPL procedure*) or in an external language that the database server supports (*external procedure*).
user-defined routine	A *routine* that you write and register in the system catalog tables of a database, and that an SQL statement or another routine can invoke. You can write a user-defined routine in SPL (*SPL routine*) or in an external language (*external routine*) that the database server supports.
user ID	*See* Informix user ID.
user ID password	*See* Informix user password.
user name	*See* Informix user ID.
user password	*See* Informix user password.
user thread	A database server thread that services requests from client applications. User threads include session threads (called **sqlexec** threads) that are the primary threads that the database server runs to service client applications. User threads also include a thread to service requests from the **onmode** utility, threads for recovery, and page-cleaner threads. *See* thread.
variable	The *identifier* for a location in memory that stores the value of a program object whose value can change during program execution. *Compare with* constant, macro, and pointer.
variant function	A *user-defined function* that might return different values when passed the same arguments. A variant function can contain SQL statements. *Compare with* nonvariant function.
view	A dynamically controlled picture of the contents in a database that allows a programmer to determine what information the user sees and manipulates. A view represents a virtual table based on a specified SELECT statement.
violations table	A special table that holds rows that fail to satisfy constraints and unique index requirements during data manipulation operations on base tables. You use the START VIOLATIONS TABLE statement to create a violations table and associate it with a base table.

virtual column	A derived column of information, created with an SQL statement, that is not stored in the database. For example, you can create virtual columns in a SELECT statement by arithmetically manipulating a single column, such as multiplying existing values by a constant, or by combining multiple columns, such as adding the values from two columns.
virtual-column index	A type of *generalized-key index* that contains keys that are the result of an expression.
virtual processor	A multithreaded process that makes up the database server and is similar to the hardware processors in the computer. It can serve multiple clients and, where necessary, run multiple threads to work in parallel for a single query.
virtual table	A table whose data you create to access data in an external file, external DBMS, or smart large object. The database server does not manage external data or directly manipulate data within a smart large object. The Virtual-Table Interface allows users to access the external data in a virtual table using SQL DML statements and join the external data with Dynamic Server table data.
VLDB	Acronym for very large database(s).
warning	A message or other indicator about a condition that software (such as the database server or compiler) detects. A condition that results in a warning does not necessarily affect the ability of the code to run. *See also* compile-time error *and* runtime error.
white space	A series of one or more space characters. The GLS locale defines the characters that are considered to be space characters. For example, both the TAB and blank might be defined as space characters in one locale, but certain combinations of the CTRL key and another character might be defined as space characters in a different locale.
wide character	A form of a code set that involves normalizing the size of each multibyte character so that each character is the same size. This size must be equal to or greater than the largest character that an operating system can support, and it must match the size of an integer data type that the C compiler can scale. Some examples of an integer data type that the C compiler can scale are short integer (**short int**), integer (**int**), or long integer (**long int**).

wildcard	A special symbol that represents any sequence of zero or more characters or any single character. In SQL, for example, you can use the asterisk (*), question mark (?), brackets ([]), percent sign (%), and underscore (_) as wildcard characters. (The asterisk, question mark, and brackets are also wildcards in UNIX.)
window	A rectangular area on the screen in which you can take actions without leaving the context of the background program.
WORM	Acronym for Write-Once-Read-Many optical media. When a bit of data is written to a WORM platter, a permanent mark is made on the platter.
X/Open	An independent consortium that produces and develops specifications and standards for open-systems products and technology such as dynamic SQL.
X/Open Portability Guide	A set of specifications that vendors and users can use to build portable software. Any vendor that carries the XPG brand on any particular software product is guaranteeing that the software correctly implements the X/Open Common Applications Environment (CAE) specifications. There are CAE specifications for SQL, XA, ISAM, RDA, and so on.
zoned decimal	A data representation that uses the low-order four bits of each byte to designate a decimal digit (0 through 9) and the high-order four bits to designate the sign of the digit.

Index

location shown in sysblobs
table 1-24
restrictions
in Boolean expression 2-12
with GROUP BY 2-12
with LIKE or MATCHES 2-12
with ORDER BY 2-12
selecting a BYTE column 2-12
setting buffer size 3-31

C

C compiler, setting INFORMIXC
environment variable 3-64
C shell
.cshrc file 3-9
.login file 3-9
call_type table in stores_demo
database, columns in A-9
call_type table in superstores_demo
database, columns in B-10
Cast 2-63 to 2-70
built-in 2-64 to 2-67, 2-68
distinct data type 2-69
explicit 2-68
from BYTE to BLOB data
type 2-13
from TEXT to CLOB data
type 2-45
implicit 2-67, 2-68
precedence of 2-68
syscasts information 1-25
CHAR data type
casts for 2-65
collation 2-14
description of 2-13
multibyte values 2-14
nonprintable characters with 2-14
with numeric values 2-13
Character data types
collength (column length)
information 1-33
list of 2-48
CHARACTER data type. See
CHAR data type.
Character string
as DATETIME values 2-20, 2-56
as INTERVAL values 2-29

CHARACTER VARYING data type
description of 2-15
length 1-33
See also VARCHAR data type.
Check constraint
described in syschecks table 1-26
described in syscoldepend
table 1-29
Checking contents of environment
configuration file 3-12
chkenv utility
description of 3-12
error message for 3-13
Client/server
INFORMIXSQLHOSTS
environment variable 3-73
shared memory communication
segments 3-72, 3-73
specifying default database 3-70
specifying stacksize for client
session 3-74
CLOB data type
attributes in syscolatribs 1-27
casting not available 2-15
code-set conversion of 2-16
collation 2-16
coltype code for 1-32
description of 2-15
inserting data 2-16
multibyte characters with 2-16
COCKPITSERVICE environment
variable 3-27
Code set, ISO 8859-1 Intro-4
Code, sample, conventions
for Intro-12
Collation
with CHAR data type 2-14
with CLOB data type 2-16
with TEXT data type 2-46
with VARCHAR data type 2-48
Collection data type
casting matrix 2-70
description of 2-60
LIST 2-30
MULTISET 2-33
SET 2-42
sysattrtypes information about
elements 1-23

sysxtddesc contents for 1-82
sysxtdtypes information 1-84
Colon
as delimiter in DATETIME 2-19
as delimiter in INTERVAL 2-29
Color, setting INFORMIXTERM
for 3-75
Column
changing data type 2-63
constraints, listed in
sysconstraints table 1-36
defaults, described in sysdefaults
table 1-37
described in syscolumns
table 1-30
in stores_demo
database A-3 to A-10
inserting data into BLOB 2-11
inserting into BYTE 2-12
inserting values into unnamed
row type 2-39
referential constraints in
sysreferences table 1-66
storing numeric values in
VARCHAR 2-47
value, maximum/minimum 1-35
Column-level privilege, described
in syscolauth table 1-28
Command-line conventions
elements of Intro-10
example diagram Intro-11
how to read Intro-11
Comment icons Intro-8
Compiling
environment variable for C
compiler 3-64
ESQL/C programs, environment
variable to change order
of 3-28
multithreaded ESQL/C
applications 3-98
Complex data type 2-59 to 2-62
collection types 2-60
row types 2-61
sysattrtypes information about
members 1-23
Compliance
with industry standards Intro-15

Message file for error
   messages Intro-13
Messages
   ANSI warning 3-30
   error in syserrors 1-41
   optimized transfers 3-84
   reducing requests 3-85
   warning in syserrors 1-41
MINUTE keyword
   as DATETIME field qualifier 2-18
   as INTERVAL field qualifier 2-27
MONEY data type
   casts for 2-65
   description of 2-32
   display format specified with
      DBMONEY 3-44
   international money formats 2-32
   length (syscolumns) 1-33
MONTH keyword
   as DATETIME field qualifier 2-18
   as INTERVAL field qualifier 2-27
Multibyte characters
   with CHAR data type 2-14
   with CLOB data type 2-16
   with TEXT data type 2-46
   with VARCHAR data type 2-48
MULTISET data type, description
   of 2-33

N

Named row data type
   casting permitted 2-70
   defining 2-36
   description of 2-36
   equivalence 2-37
   inheritance 2-37
   typed tables 2-37
   See also Row type.
NCHAR data type, description
   of 2-34
Network environment variable,
   DBPATH 3-46
New features of this
   product Intro-5
NODEFDAC environment
   variable 3-81

Nonprintable characters
   with CHAR data type 2-14
   with TEXT data type 2-46
   with VARCHAR data type 2-47
Not null constraint, described in
   syscoldepend table 1-29
Null value
   allowed or not allowed 1-31
   testing in BYTE expression 2-12
   testing with TEXT data type 2-45
Numeric data types
   casting between 2-65
   casting to characters 2-65
   list of 2-48
NUMERIC data type. *See*
   DECIMAL data type.
NVARCHAR data type
   description of 2-34
   length (syscolumns) 1-33

O

Object mode of database objects,
   described in sysobjstate
   table 1-55
ONCONFIG environment
   variable 3-82
On-line manuals Intro-13
Opaque data type
   cast matrix 2-70
   description of 2-35
   smart large objects with 2-50
   storage of 2-31
   sysxtddesc contents for 1-82
   sysxtdtypeauth contents for 1-83
   sysxtdtypes contents for 1-84
Operator class
   sysams information 1-18
   sysopclasses information 1-56
Operator precedence 2-71
OPTCOMPIND environment
   variable 3-83
Optical cluster, described in
   sysopclstr table 1-57
OPTMSG environment
   variable 3-84
OPTOFC environment
   variable 3-85

OPT_GOAL environment
   variable 3-86
orders table in superstores_demo
   database, columns in B-16, B-17,
   B-18, B-20
Output support function 2-31

P

Parallel database query. *See* PDQ.
Parallel distributed queries, setting
   with PDQPRIORITY
   environment variable 3-88
Parallel sorting, using
   PSORT_NPROCS for 3-92
PATH environment variable 3-87
Pathname
   for C compiler 3-64
   for database server 3-46
   for executable programs 3-87
   for installation 3-68
   for message files 3-42
   for parallel sorting 3-92
   for remote shell 3-49
   specifying with DBPATH 3-46
   specifying with PATH 3-87
PDQ
   OPTCOMPIND environment
      variable 3-83
   PDQPRIORITY environment
      variable 3-88
Platform icons Intro-8
PLCONFIG environment
   variable 3-90
PLOAD_LO_PATH environment
   variable 3-91
PLOAD_SHMBASE environment
   variable 3-91
Precedence
   operator 2-71
   rules for command-line utility
      environment variables 3-18
   rules for environment variables
      for Informix native Windows
      applications 3-19
   rules for environment variables in
      UNIX 3-13

Syntax

Introduction

In This Introduction

This Introduction provides an overview of the information in this book and describes the conventions it uses.

About This Book

This book contains all the syntax descriptions for structured query language (SQL) and Stored Procedure Language (SPL) statements for Version 9.2 of Informix Dynamic Server 2000 and Version 8.3 of Informix Enterprise Decision Server.

This book is a companion volume to the *Informix Guide to SQL: Tutorial, Second Edition* and the *Informix Guide to Designing Databases and Data Warehouses*. The first section, *Reference*, provides reference information for aspects of SQL other than the language statements. The *Informix Guide to SQL: Tutorial, Second Edition* shows how to use basic and advanced SQL and SPL routines to access and manipulate the data in your databases. The *Informix Guide to Designing Databases and Data Warehouses* shows how to use SQL to implement and manage your databases.

Types of Users

This book is written for the following users:

- Database users
- Database administrators
- Database-application programmers

This book assumes that you have the following background:

- A working knowledge of your computer, your operating system, and the utilities that your operating system provides
- Some experience working with relational databases or exposure to database concepts
- Some experience with computer programming

If you have limited experience with relational databases, SQL, or your operating system, refer to the *Getting Started* manual for your database server for a list of supplementary titles.

Software Dependencies

This book assumes that you are using one of the following database servers:

- Informix Enterprise Decision Server, Version 8.3
- Informix Dynamic Server 2000, Version 9.2

Assumptions About Your Locale

Informix products can support many languages, cultures, and code sets. All culture-specific information is brought together in a single environment, called a Global Language Support (GLS) locale.

This manual assumes that you use the U.S. 8859-1 English locale as the default locale. The default is **en_us.8859-1** (ISO 8859-1) on UNIX platforms or **en_us.1252** (Microsoft 1252) for Windows NT environments. This locale supports U.S. English format conventions for dates, times, and currency, and also supports the ISO 8859-1 or Microsoft 1252 code set, which includes the ASCII code set plus many 8-bit characters such as é, è, and ñ.

If you plan to use nondefault characters in your data or your SQL identifiers, or if you want to conform to the nondefault collation rules of character data, you need to specify the appropriate nondefault locale.

For instructions on how to specify a nondefault locale, additional syntax, and other considerations related to GLS locales, see the *Informix Guide to GLS Functionality*.

Demonstration Databases

The DB-Access utility, which is provided with your Informix database server products, includes one or more of the following demonstration databases:

- The **stores_demo** database illustrates a relational schema with information about a fictitious wholesale sporting-goods distributor. Many examples in Informix manuals are based on the **stores_demo** database.

- The **sales_demo** database illustrates a dimensional schema for data-warehousing applications. For conceptual information about dimensional data modeling, see the *Informix Guide to Database Design and Implementation.* ♦

- The **superstores_demo** database illustrates an object-relational schema. The **superstores_demo** database contains examples of extended data types, type and table inheritance, and user-defined routines. ♦

For information about how to create and populate the demonstration databases, see the *DB-Access User's Manual*. For descriptions of the databases and their contents, see the *Informix Guide to SQL: Reference*.

The scripts that you use to install the demonstration databases reside in the **$INFORMIXDIR/bin** directory on UNIX platforms and in the **%INFORMIXDIR%\bin** directory in Windows environments.

New Features

For a comprehensive list of new database server features, see the release notes. This section lists new features relevant to this manual.

New Features in Version 8.3

This book describes new features in Version 8.3 of Enterprise Decision Server. The features fall into the following areas:

- Performance enhancements
- New SQL functionality
- Version 8.3 features from Dynamic Server 7.30

Performance Enhancements

This book describes the following performance enhancements to Version 8.3 of Enterprise Decision Server:

- Insert cursors with simple large objects
- Coarse-grain index locks
- Updates with subquery in SET clause
- Index on aggregates

New SQL Functionality

This book describes the following new SQL functionality in Version 8.3 of Enterprise Decision Server:

- CASE statement in Stored Procedure Language (SPL)
- Creating a table with RANGE fragmentation
- DELETE...USING statement to delete rows based on a table join
- Globally detached indexes
- Load and unload simple large objects to external tables

- MIDDLE function
- Referential integrity for globally detached indexes
- TRUNCATE statement

Version 8.3 Features from Version 7.30

This book describes the following features from Version 7.3 of Dynamic Server in Version 8.3 of Enterprise Decision Server:

- Ability to retain update locks
- ALTER FRAGMENT attach with remainders
- ALTER TABLE to add or drop a foreign key constraint
- ALTER TABLE to add, drop, or modify a column
- Constraints on columns other than the fragmentation column
- COUNT function
- DBINFO provides all Version 7.3 information and adds the coserver ID and dbspace name
- Deferred constraints for all constraint types
- Deferred referential-integrity constraints
- Insert from SPL functions
- NVL and DECODE functions
- REPLACE, SUBSTR, LPAD, and RPAD functions for string manipulation
- RENAME COLUMN statement
- TO_CHAR and TO_DATE functions for date conversion
- Triggers
- UPDATE SET clause subqueries
- UPPER, LOWER, and INITCAP functions for case-insensitive search
- Memory-resident tables
- Violations table

New Features in Version 9.2

This book describes new features in Version 9.2 of Dynamic Server. The features fall into the following areas:

- Extensibility enhancements
- Performance improvements
- Special features
- Version 9.2 features from Version 7.30 of Dynamic Server

Extensibility Enhancements

This book describes the following extensibility enhancements to Version 9.2 of Dynamic Server:

- General enhancements to SQL:
  - Embedded newline characters in quoted strings
  - Nested dot expressions for row types
- Triggers on SELECT statements
- Enhancements to smart large objects:
  - Round-robin fragmentation for smart large objects
  - ALTER TABLE for smart large objects
- Enhancements to collections:
  - Collection constructors that use arbitrary expression elements
  - Collection-derived tables
  - Collection subqueries
- Enhancements to row types:
  - Serial types in row types
  - GRANT, REVOKE UNDER on row types
- Enhancements to user-defined routines (UDRs):
  - GRANT, REVOKE on UDR external languages
  - ALTER FUNCTION, PROCEDURE, ROUTINE statements
  - User-defined aggregates

Performance Improvements

This book describes the following performance improvements to Version 9.2 of Dynamic Server:

- For SQL:
    - Parallel statement-local variables (SLVs)
    - SQL statement cache
- For UDRs:
    - Expensive-function optimization
    - Parallel UDRs
    - User-defined statistics routines

Special Features

This book describes the following special features of Version 9.2 of Dynamic Server:

- Long identifiers:
    - 128-character identifier
    - 32-character user names
- Ability to retain update locks

Version 9.2 Features from Dynamic Server 7.30

This book also describes features first released in Version 7.30. These features fall into the following areas:

- Reliability, availability, and serviceability:
  ALTER FRAGMENT ATTACH, DETACH enhancements
- Performance:
    - Optimizer directives
    - Select first *n* rows
    - SET OPTIMIZATION statement enhancements
    - Memory-resident tables

- Application migration:
    - UPPER, LOWER, and INITCAP functions for case-insensitive search (for built-in types)
    - REPLACE, SUBSTR, LPAD, and RPAD functions for string manipulation (for built-in types)
    - UNION operator in CREATE VIEW statement
    - CASE expression
    - NVL and DECODE functions
    - TO_CHAR and TO_DATE date-conversion functions (for built-in types)
    - EXECUTE PROCEDURE syntax to update triggering columns
    - New arguments to the **dbinfo()** function to obtain the hostname and version of the database server

Documentation Conventions

This section describes the conventions that this manual uses. These conventions make it easier to gather information from this and other volumes in the documentation set.

The following conventions are discussed:

- Typographical conventions
- Icon conventions
- Syntax conventions
- Sample-code conventions

Typographical Conventions

This book uses the following conventions to introduce new terms, illustrate screen displays, describe command syntax, and so forth.

Convention	Meaning
KEYWORD	All primary elements in a programming language statement (keywords) appear in uppercase letters in a serif font.
italics **italics** italics	Within text, new terms and emphasized words appear in italics. Within syntax and code examples, variable values that you are to specify appear in italics.
boldface ***boldface***	Names of program entities (such as classes, events, and tables), environment variables, file and pathnames, and interface elements (such as icons, menu items, and buttons) appear in boldface.
monospace *monospace*	Information that the product displays and information that you enter appear in a monospace typeface.
KEYSTROKE	Keys that you are to press appear in uppercase letters in a sans serif font.
♦	This symbol indicates the end of one or more product- or platform-specific paragraphs.
→	This symbol indicates a menu item. For example, "Choose **Tools→Options**" means choose the **Options** item from the **Tools** menu.

Tip: *When you are instructed to "enter" characters or to "execute" a command, immediately press* RETURN *after the entry. When you are instructed to "type" the text or to "press" other keys, no* RETURN *is required.*

Icon Conventions

Throughout the documentation, you will find text that is identified by several different types of icons. This section describes these icons.

Comment Icons

Comment icons identify three types of information, as the following table describes. This information always appears in italics.

Icon	Label	Description
⚠	*Warning:*	Identifies paragraphs that contain vital instructions, cautions, or critical information
⇨	*Important:*	Identifies paragraphs that contain significant information about the feature or operation that is being described
💡	*Tip:*	Identifies paragraphs that offer additional details or shortcuts for the functionality that is being described

Feature, Product, and Platform Icons

Feature, product, and platform icons identify paragraphs that contain feature-specific, product-specific, or platform-specific information.

Icon	Description
EDS	Identifies information or syntax that is specific to Informix Enterprise Decision Server
C	Identifies information that is specific to C user-defined routines (UDRs)
DB	Identifies information that is specific to DB-Access

(1 of 2)

Icon	Description
E/C	Identifies information that is specific to Informix ESQL/C
Ext	Identifies information that is specific to external routines, that is, UDRs written in both C and Java.
GLS	Identifies information that relates to the Informix Global Language Support (GLS) feature
IDS	Identifies information that is specific to Informix Dynamic Server 2000
Java	Identifies information that is specific to UDRs written in Java
SQLE	Identifies information that is specific to SQL Editor, which is a component of Informix Enterprise Command Center for Dynamic Server
UNIX	Identifies information that is specific to UNIX platforms
WIN NT	Identifies information that is specific to the Windows NT environment

(2 of 2)

These icons can apply to an entire section or to one or more paragraphs within a section. If an icon appears next to a section heading, the information that applies to the indicated feature, product, or platform ends at the next heading at the same or higher level. A ♦ symbol indicates the end of feature-, product-, or platform-specific information that appears in one or more paragraphs within a section.

Compliance Icons

Compliance icons indicate paragraphs that provide guidelines for complying with a standard.

Icon	Description
ANSI	Identifies information that is specific to an ANSI-compliant database
X/O	Identifies functionality that conforms to X/Open
+	Identifies information or syntax that is an Informix extension to ANSI SQL-92 entry-level standard SQL

These icons can apply to an entire section or to one or more paragraphs within a section. If an icon appears next to a section heading, the information that applies to the indicated feature, product, or platform ends at the next heading at the same or higher level. A ♦ symbol indicates the end of feature-, product-, or platform-specific information that appears within one or more paragraphs within a section.

Syntax Conventions

This section describes conventions for syntax diagrams. Each diagram displays the sequences of required and optional keywords, terms, and symbols that are valid in a given statement or segment, as Figure 1 shows.

Figure 1
Example of a Simple Syntax Diagram

Each syntax diagram begins at the upper-left corner and ends at the upper-right corner with a vertical terminator. Between these points, any path that does not stop or reverse direction describes a possible form of the statement.

Syntax elements in a path represent terms, keywords, symbols, and segments that can appear in your statement. The path always approaches elements from the left and continues to the right, except in the case of separators in loops. For separators in loops, the path approaches counterclockwise. Unless otherwise noted, at least one blank character separates syntax elements.

Elements That Can Appear on the Path

You might encounter one or more of the following elements on a path.

Element	Description
KEYWORD	A word in UPPERCASE letters is a keyword. You must spell the word exactly as shown; however, you can use either uppercase or lowercase letters.
(. , ; @ + * - /)	Punctuation and other nonalphanumeric characters are literal symbols that you must enter exactly as shown.
' '	Single quotes are literal symbols that you must enter as shown.
variable	A word in italics represents a value that you must supply. A table immediately following the diagram explains the value.
ADD Clause p. 3-288 / ADD Clause	A reference in a box represents a subdiagram. Imagine that the subdiagram is spliced into the main diagram at this point. When a page number is not specified, the subdiagram appears on the same page.
Back to ADD Clause p. 1-14	A reference in a box in the upper-right corner of a subdiagram refers to the next higher-level diagram of which this subdiagram is a member.
E/C	An icon is a warning that this path is valid only for some products, or only under certain conditions. Characters on the icons indicate what products or conditions support the path. These icons might appear in a syntax diagram:

Element	Description
EDE	This path is valid only for Enterprise Decision Server.
C	This path is valid only for C user-defined routines (UDRs).
DB	This path is valid only for DB-Access.
E/C	This path is valid only for Informix ESQL/C.
Ext	This path is valid only for external routines, that is, UDRs written in C and Java.
GLS	This path is recommended only if you use a nondefault locale.
Java	This path is valid only for UDRs written in Java.
IDS	This path is valid only for Dynamic Server.
SPL	This path is valid only if you are using Informix Stored Procedure Language (SPL).
+	This path is an Informix extension to ANSI SQL-92 entry-level standard SQL. If you initiate Informix extension checking and include this syntax branch, you receive a warning. If you have set the **DBANSIWARN** environment variable at compile time, or have used the **-ansi** compile flag, you receive warnings at compile time. If you have **DBANSIWARN** set at runtime, or if you compiled with the **-ansi** flag, warning flags are set in the **sqlwarn** structure. The Informix extension warnings tend to be conservative. Sometimes the warnings appear even when a syntax path conforms to the ANSI standard.

Element	Description
— ALL -	A shaded option is the default action.
→ ▶	Syntax within a pair of arrows is a subdiagram.
⊣	The vertical line terminates the syntax diagram.
IS ——————NULL NOT	A branch below the main path indicates an optional path. (Any term on the main path is required, unless a branch can circumvent it.)
NOT FOUND ERROR WARNING	A set of multiple branches indicates that a choice among more than two different paths is available.
, *variable* *statement*	A loop indicates a path that you can repeat. Punctuation along the top of the loop indicates the separator symbol for list items. If no symbol appears, a blank space is the separator.
, ⟨3⟩ *size*	A gate (⟨3⟩) on a path indicates that you can only use that path the indicated number of times, even if it is part of a larger loop. You can specify *size* no more than three times within this statement segment.

(3 of 3)

How to Read a Syntax Diagram

Figure 2 shows a syntax diagram that uses most of the path elements that the previous table lists.

Figure 2
Example of a Syntax Diagram

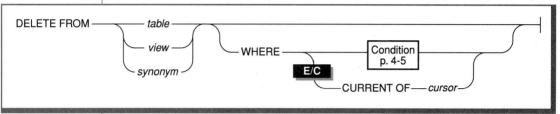

To use this diagram to construct a statement, start at the top left with the keyword DELETE FROM. Follow the diagram to the right, proceeding through the options that you want.

Figure 2 illustrates the following steps:

1. Type `DELETE FROM`.
1. You can delete a table, view, or synonym:

   ■ Type the table name, view name, or synonym, as you desire.

   ■ You can type `WHERE` to limit the rows to delete.

   ■ If you type `WHERE` and you are using DB-Access or the SQL Editor, you must include the Condition clause to specify a condition to delete. To find the syntax for specifying a condition, go to the "Condition" segment on the specified page.

   ■ If you are using ESQL/C, you can include either the Condition clause to delete a specific condition or the CURRENT OF *cursor* clause to delete a row from the table.

1. Follow the diagram to the terminator.

   Your DELETE statement is complete.

Sample-Code Conventions

Examples of SQL code occur throughout this book. Except where noted, the code is not specific to any single Informix application development tool. If only SQL statements are listed in the example, they are not delimited by semicolons. For instance, you might see the code in the following example:

```
CONNECT TO stores_demo
...

DELETE FROM customer
    WHERE customer_num = 121
...

COMMIT WORK
DISCONNECT CURRENT
```

To use this SQL code for a specific product, you must apply the syntax rules for that product. For example, if you are using DB-Access, you must delimit multiple statements with semicolons. If you are using an SQL API, you must use EXEC SQL at the start of each statement and a semicolon (or other appropriate delimiter) at the end of the statement.

Tip: *Ellipsis points in a code example indicate that more code would be added in a full application, but it is not necessary to show it to describe the concept being discussed.*

For detailed directions on using SQL statements for a particular application development tool or SQL API, see the manual for your product.

Additional Documentation

For additional information, you might want to refer to the following types of documentation:

- On-line manuals
- Printed manuals
- On-line help
- Error message documentation
- Documentation notes, release notes, and machine notes
- Related reading

On-Line Manuals

An Answers OnLine CD that contains Informix books in electronic format is provided with your Informix products. You can install the documentation or access it directly from the CD. For information about how to install, read, and print on-line manuals, see the installation insert that accompanies Answers OnLine.

Informix on-line manuals are also available on the following Web site:

```
www.informix.com/answers
```

Printed Manuals

To order printed manuals, call 1-800-331-1763 or send email to moreinfo@informix.com. Please provide the following information when you place your order:

- The documentation that you need
- The quantity that you need
- Your name, address, and telephone number

WIN NT

On-Line Help

Informix provides on-line help with each graphical user interface (GUI) that displays information about those interfaces and the functions that they perform. Use the help facilities that each GUI provides to display the on-line help.

Error Message Documentation

Informix software products provide ASCII files that contain all of the Informix error messages and their corrective actions.

UNIX

To read error messages and corrective actions on UNIX, use one of the following utilities.

Utility	Description
finderr	Displays error messages on line
rofferr	Formats error messages for printing

♦

WIN NT

To read error messages and corrective actions in Windows environments, use the **Informix Find Error** utility. To display this utility, choose **Start→Programs→Informix** from the Task Bar. ♦

Instructions for using the preceding utilities are available in Answers OnLine. Answers OnLine also provides a listing of error messages and corrective actions in HTML format.

Documentation Notes, Release Notes, Machine Notes

In addition to printed documentation, the following sections describe the on-line files that supplement the information in this book. Please examine these files before you begin using your database server. They contain vital information about application and performance issues.

UNIX

On UNIX platforms, the following on-line files appear in the **$INFORMIXDIR/release/en_us/0333** directory. Replace *x.y* in the filenames with the version number of your database server.

On-Line File	Purpose
SQLDOC_*x.y*	The documentation-notes file for your version of this manual describes topics that are not covered in the manual or that were modified since publication.
SERVERS_*x.y*	The release-notes file describes feature differences from earlier versions of Informix products and how these differences might affect current products. This file also contains information about any known problems and their workarounds.
IDS_EDS_8.3 or **IDS_9.2**	The machine-notes file describes any special actions that you must take to configure and use Informix products on your computer. Machine notes are named for the product described.

WIN NT The following items appear in the **Informix** folder. To display this folder, choose **Start→Programs→Informix** from the Task Bar.

Program Group Item	Description
Documentation Notes	This item includes additions or corrections to manuals, along with information about features that might not be covered in the manuals or that have been modified since publication.
Release Notes	This item describes feature differences from earlier versions of Informix products and how these differences might affect current products. This file also contains information about any known problems and their workarounds.

Machine notes do not apply to Windows environments. ♦

Related Reading

For a list of publications that provide an introduction to database servers and operating-system platforms, refer to your *Getting Started* manual.

Compliance with Industry Standards

The American National Standards Institute (ANSI) has established a set of industry standards for SQL. Informix SQL-based products are fully compliant with SQL-92 Entry Level (published as ANSI X3.135-1992), which is identical to ISO 9075:1992. In addition, many features of Informix database servers comply with the SQL-92 Intermediate and Full Level and X/Open SQL CAE (common applications environment) standards.

Informix Welcomes Your Comments

Let us know what you like or dislike about our books. To help us with future versions of our manuals, we want to know about any corrections or clarifications that you would find useful. Include the following information:

- The name and version of the manual that you are using
- Any comments that you have about the manual
- Your name, address, and phone number

Send electronic mail to us at the following address:

doc@informix.com

The **doc** alias is reserved exclusively for reporting errors and omissions in our documentation.

We appreciate your suggestions.

Overview of SQL Syntax

In This Chapter

This chapter provides information about how to use the SQL statements, SPL statements, and segments that are discussed in the later chapters of this book. It is organized into the following sections.

Section	Starting Page	Scope
"How to Enter SQL Statements"	1-4	This section shows how to use the statement diagrams and descriptions to enter SQL statements correctly.
"How to Enter SQL Comments"	1-6	This section shows how to enter comments for SQL statements.
"Categories of SQL Statements"	1-9	This section lists SQL statements by functional category.
"ANSI Compliance and Extensions"	1-13	This section lists SQL statements by degree of ANSI compliance.

How to Enter SQL Statements

The purpose of the statement descriptions in this manual is to help you to enter SQL statements successfully. Each statement description includes the following information:

- A brief introduction that explains the purpose of the statement
- A syntax diagram that shows how to enter the statement correctly
- A syntax table that explains each input parameter in the syntax diagram
- Rules of usage, including examples that illustrate these rules

If a statement consists of multiple clauses, the statement description provides the same set of information for each clause.

Each statement description concludes with references to related information in this manual and other manuals.

The major aids for entering SQL statements include:

- the combination of the syntax diagram and syntax table.
- the examples of syntax that appear in the rules of usage.
- the references to related information.

Using Syntax Diagrams and Syntax Tables

Before you try to use the syntax diagrams in this chapter, it is helpful to read the "Syntax Conventions" on page 14 of the Introduction. This section is the key to understanding the syntax diagrams in the statement descriptions.

The Syntax Conventions section explains the elements that can appear in a syntax diagram and the paths that connect the elements to each other. This section also includes a sample syntax diagram that illustrates the major elements of all syntax diagrams. The narrative that follows the sample diagram shows how to read the diagram in order to enter the statement successfully.

When a syntax diagram within a statement description includes input parameters, the syntax diagram is followed by a syntax table that shows how to enter the parameters without generating errors. Each syntax table includes the following columns:

- The **Elements** column lists the name of each parameter as it appears in the syntax diagram.

- The **Purpose** column briefly states the purpose of the parameter. If the parameter has a default value, it is listed in this column.

- The **Restrictions** column summarizes the restrictions on the parameter, such as acceptable ranges of values.

- The **Syntax** column points to the SQL segment that gives the detailed syntax for the parameter.

Using Examples

To understand the main syntax diagram and subdiagrams for a statement, study the examples of syntax that appear in the rules of usage for each statement. These examples have two purposes:

- To show how to accomplish particular tasks with the statement or its clauses

- To show how to use the syntax of the statement or its clauses in a concrete way

Tip: *An efficient way to understand a syntax diagram is to find an example of the syntax and compare it with the keywords and parameters in the syntax diagram. By mapping the concrete elements of the example to the abstract elements of the syntax diagram, you can understand the syntax diagram and use it more effectively.*

For an explanation of the conventions used in the examples in this manual, see "Sample-Code Conventions" on page 19 of the Introduction.

Using Related Information

For help in understanding the concepts and terminology in the SQL statement description, check the "Related Information" section at the end of each statement.

This section points to related information in this manual and other manuals that helps you to understand the statement in question. The section provides some or all of the following information:

■ The names of related statements that might contain a fuller discussion of topics in this statement

■ The titles of other manuals that provide extended discussions of topics in this statement

Tip: *If you do not have extensive knowledge and experience with SQL, the "Informix Guide to SQL: Tutorial" gives you the basic SQL knowledge that you need to understand and use the statement descriptions in this manual.*

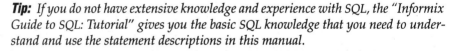

How to Enter SQL Comments

You can add comments to clarify the purpose or effect of particular SQL statements. You can also use comment symbols during program development to disable selected statements without deleting them from your source code.

Your comments can help you or others to understand the role of the statement within a program, SPL routine, or command file. The code examples in this manual sometimes include comments that clarify the role of an SQL statement within the code.

The following table shows the SQL comment symbols that you can enter in your code. A *Y* in a column signifies that you can use the symbol with the product or database type named in the column heading. An *N* in a column signifies that you cannot use the symbol with the product or database type that the column heading names.

Comment Symbol	ESQL/C	SPL Routine	DB-Access	ANSI-Compliant Databases	Databases That Are Not ANSI Compliant	Description
double dash (--)	Y	Y	Y	Y	Y	The double dash precedes the comment. The double dash can comment only a single line. To comment more than one line, you must put the double dash at the beginning of each comment line.
braces ({})	N	Y	Y	Y	Y	Braces enclose the comment. The { precedes the comment, and the } follows the comment. You can use braces for single-line comments or for multiple-line comments. Comments cannot be nested.

ANSI

If the product that you are using supports both comment symbols, your choice of a comment symbol depends on your requirements for ANSI compliance:

- The double dash (--) complies with the ANSI SQL standard.
- Braces ({}) are an Informix extension to the standard.

If ANSI compliance is not an issue, your choice of comment symbols is a matter of personal preference. ♦

DB

In DB-Access, you can use either comment symbol when you enter SQL statements with the SQL editor and when you create SQL command files with the SQL editor or a system editor. An SQL command file is an operating-system file that contains one or more SQL statements. Command files are also known as command scripts. For more information about command files, see the discussion of command scripts in the *Informix Guide to SQL: Tutorial*. For information on how to create and modify command files with the SQL editor or a system editor in DB-Access, see the *DB-Access User's Manual*. ♦

SPL

You can use either comment symbol in any line of an SPL routine. See the discussion of how to comment and document an SPL routine in the *Informix Guide to SQL: Tutorial*. ♦

E/C

In ESQL/C, you can use the double dash (--) to comment SQL statements. For further information on the use of SQL comment symbols and language-specific comment symbols in ESQL/C programs, see the *Informix ESQL/C Programmer's Manual.* ◆

Examples of SQL Comment Symbols

Some simple examples can help to illustrate the different ways to use the SQL comment symbols.

Examples of the Double-Dash Symbol

The following example shows the use of the double dash (--) to comment an SQL statement. In this example, the comment appears on the same line as the statement.

```
SELECT * FROM customer -- Selects all columns and rows
```

In the following example, the user enters the same SQL statement and the same comment as in the preceding example, but the user places the comment on a line by itself:

```
SELECT * FROM customer
    -- Selects all columns and rows
```

In the following example, the user enters the same SQL statement as in the preceding example but now enters a multiple-line comment:

```
SELECT * FROM customer
    -- Selects all columns and rows
    -- from the customer table
```

Examples of the Braces Symbols

DB

SPL

The following example shows the use of braces ({}) to comment an SQL statement. In this example, the comment appears on the same line as the statement.

```
SELECT * FROM customer {Selects all columns and rows}
```

In the following example, the user enters the same SQL statement and the same comment as in the preceding example but places the comment on a line by itself:

```
SELECT * FROM customer
    {Selects all columns and rows}
```

In the following example, the user enters the same SQL statement as in the preceding example but enters a multiple-line comment:

```
SELECT * FROM customer
    {Selects all columns and rows
     from the customer table}
```

GLS

Non-ASCII Characters in SQL Comments

You can enter non-ASCII characters (including multibyte characters) in SQL comments if your locale supports a code set with the non-ASCII characters. For further information on the GLS aspects of SQL comments, see the *Informix Guide to GLS Functionality*.

Categories of SQL Statements

SQL statements are divided into the following categories:

- Data definition statements
- Data manipulation statements
- Cursor manipulation statements
- Cursor optimization statements
- Dynamic management statements
- Data access statements
- Data integrity statements
- Optimization statements
- Routine Definition statements
- Auxiliary statements
- Client/server connection statements
- Optical subsystem statements

The specific statements for each category are as follows.

Data Definition Statements

ALTER FRAGMENT	CREATE TEMPORARY TABLE
ALTER FUNCTION	CREATE TRIGGER
ALTER INDEX	CREATE VIEW
ALTER PROCEDURE	DATABASE
ALTER ROUTINE	DROP AGGREGATE
ALTER TABLE	DROP CAST
CLOSE DATABASE	DROP DATABASE
CREATE AGGREGATE	DROP INDEX
CREATE CAST	DROP PROCEDURE
CREATE DATABASE	DROP ROLE
CREATE DISTINCT TYPE	DROP ROW TYPE
CREATE EXTERNAL TABLE	DROP SYNONYM
CREATE INDEX	DROP TABLE
CREATE OPAQUE TYPE	DROP TRIGGER
CREATE PROCEDURE	DROP VIEW
CREATE PROCEDURE FROM	RENAME COLUMN
CREATE ROLE	RENAME DATABASE
CREATE ROW TYPE	RENAME TABLE
CREATE SCHEMA	TRUNCATE
CREATE SYNONYM	
CREATE TABLE	

Data Manipulation Statements

DELETE	SELECT
INSERT	UNLOAD
LOAD	UPDATE

Cursor Manipulation Statements

CLOSE	FREE
DECLARE	OPEN
FETCH	PUT
FLUSH	SET AUTOFREE

Cursor Optimization Statements

SET AUTOFREE
SET DEFERRED_PREPARE

Dynamic Management Statements

ALLOCATE COLLECTION
ALLOCATE DESCRIPTOR
ALLOCATE ROW
DEALLOCATE COLLECTION
DEALLOCATE DESCRIPTOR
DEALLOCATE ROW
DESCRIBE

EXECUTE
EXECUTE IMMEDIATE
FREE
GET DESCRIPTOR
PREPARE
SET DEFERRED_PREPARE
SET DESCRIPTOR

Data Access Statements

GRANT
GRANT FRAGMENT
LOCK TABLE
REVOKE
REVOKE FRAGMENT
SET ISOLATION

SET LOCK MODE
SET ROLE
SET SESSION AUTHORIZATION
SET TRANSACTION
SET TRANSACTION MODE
UNLOCK TABLE

Data Integrity Statements

BEGIN WORK
COMMIT WORK
ROLLBACK WORK
SET DATABASE OBJECT MODE
SET LOG

SET PLOAD FILE
SET TRANSACTION MODE
START VIOLATIONS TABLE
STOP VIOLATIONS TABLE

Optimization Statements

SET EXPLAIN
SET OPTIMIZATION
SET PDQPRIORITY
SET RESIDENCY

SET SCHEDULE LEVEL
SET STATEMENT CACHE
UPDATE STATISTICS

Routine Definition Statements

ALTER FUNCTION
ALTER PROCEDURE
ALTER ROUTINE
CREATE FUNCTION
CREATE FUNCTION FROM
CREATE PROCEDURE
CREATE PROCEDURE FROM

CREATE ROUTINE FROM
DROP FUNCTION
DROP PROCEDURE
DROP ROUTINE
EXECUTE FUNCTION
EXECUTE PROCEDURE
SET DEBUG FILE TO

Auxiliary Statements

INFO
OUTPUT
GET DIAGNOSTICS

SET DATASKIP
WHENEVER

Client/Server Connection Statements

CONNECT
DISCONNECT

SET CONNECTION

IDS

Optical Subsystem Statements

ALTER OPTICAL CLUSTER
CREATE OPTICAL CLUSTER
DROP OPTICAL CLUSTER

RELEASE
RESERVE
SET MOUNTING TIMEOUT

Important: *Optical Subsystem statements are described in the "Guide to the Optical Subsystem."*

ANSI Compliance and Extensions

The following lists show statements that are compliant with the ANSI SQL-92 standard at the entry level, statements that are ANSI compliant but include Informix extensions, and statements that are Informix extensions to the ANSI standard.

ANSI-Compliant Statements

CLOSE	SET SESSION AUTHORIZATION
COMMIT WORK	SET TRANSACTION
ROLLBACK WORK	

ANSI-Compliant Statements with Informix Extensions

CREATE SCHEMA AUTHORIZATION	GRANT
CREATE TABLE	INSERT
CREATE TEMPORARY TABLE	OPEN
CREATE VIEW	SELECT
DECLARE	SET CONNECTION
DELETE	UPDATE
EXECUTE	WHENEVER
FETCH	

Statements That Are Extensions to the ANSI Standard

ALLOCATE DESCRIPTOR
ALTER FRAGMENT
ALTER FUNCTION
ALTER INDEX
ALTER OPTICAL CLUSTER
ALTER PROCEDURE
ALTER ROUTINE
ALTER TABLE
BEGIN WORK
CLOSE DATABASE
CONNECT
CREATE AGGREGATE
CREATE DATABASE
CREATE EXTERNAL TABLE
CREATE INDEX
CREATE OPTICAL CLUSTER
CREATE PROCEDURE
CREATE PROCEDURE FROM
CREATE ROLE
CREATE SYNONYM
CREATE TRIGGER
DATABASE
DEALLOCATE DESCRIPTOR
DESCRIBE
DISCONNECT
DROP AGGREGATE
DROP DATABASE
DROP INDEX
DROP OPTICAL CLUSTER
DROP PROCEDURE
DROP ROLE
DROP SYNONYM
DROP TABLE
DROP TRIGGER
DROP VIEW
EXECUTE IMMEDIATE
EXECUTE PROCEDURE
FLUSH
FREE
GET DESCRIPTOR
GET DIAGNOSTICS

GRANT FRAGMENT
INFO
LOAD
LOCK TABLE
OUTPUT
PREPARE
PUT
RELEASE
RENAME COLUMN
RENAME DATABASE
RENAME TABLE
RESERVE
REVOKE
REVOKE FRAGMENT
SET AUTOFREE
SET DATABASE OBJECT MODE
SET DATASKIP
SET DEBUG FILE TO
SET DEFERRED_PREPARE
SET DESCRIPTOR
SET EXPLAIN
SET ISOLATION
SET LOCK MODE
SET LOG
SET MOUNTING TIMEOUT
SET OPTIMIZATION
SET PDQPRIORITY
SET PLOAD FILE
SET RESIDENCY
SET ROLE
SET SCHEDULE LEVEL
SET STATEMENT CACHE
SET TRANSACTION
SET TRANSACTION MODE
START VIOLATIONS TABLE
STOP VIOLATIONS TABLE
TRUNCATE
UNLOAD
UNLOCK TABLE
UPDATE STATISTICS

SQL Statements

In This Chapter

This chapter gives comprehensive reference descriptions of SQL statements. The statement descriptions appear in alphabetical order. For an explanation of the structure of statement descriptions, see Chapter 1, "Overview of SQL Syntax."

ALLOCATE COLLECTION

Use the ALLOCATE COLLECTION statement to allocate memory for a collection variable.

Use this statement with ESQL/C.

Syntax

```
ALLOCATE COLLECTION ─────────────── variable ─────────────────┤
```

Element	Purpose	Restrictions	Syntax
variable	Name that identifies a typed or untyped collection variable for which to allocate memory	The variable must be the name of an unallocated ESQL/C collection host variable.	Name must conform to language-specific rules for variable names.

Usage

The ALLOCATE COLLECTION statement allocates memory for a variable that stores collection data. To create a collection variable for an ESQL/C program, perform the following steps:

1. Declare the collection variable as a client collection variable in an ESQL/C program.

    The collection variable can be a typed or untyped collection variable.

2. Allocate memory for the collection variable with the ALLOCATE COLLECTION statement.

The ALLOCATE COLLECTION statement sets **SQLCODE (sqlca.sqlcode)** to zero (0) if the memory allocation was successful and to a negative error code if the allocation failed.

You must explicitly release memory with the DEALLOCATE COLLECTION statement. Once you free the collection variable with the DEALLOCATE COLLECTION statement, you can reuse the collection variable.

Tip: *The ALLOCATE COLLECTION statement allocates memory for an ESQL/C collection variable only. To allocate memory for an ESQL/C row variable, use the ALLOCATE ROW statement.*

Examples

The following example shows how to allocate resources with the ALLOCATE COLLECTION statement for the untyped collection variable, **a_set**:

```
EXEC SQL BEGIN DECLARE SECTION;
    client collection a_set;
EXEC SQL END DECLARE SECTION;
.
.
.

EXEC SQL allocate collection :a_set;
.
.
.
```

The following example uses ALLOCATE COLLECTION to allocate resources for a typed collection variable, **a_typed_set**:

```
EXEC SQL BEGIN DECLARE SECTION;
    client collection set(integer not null) a_typed_set;
EXEC SQL END DECLARE SECTION;
.
.
.

EXEC SQL allocate collection :a_typed_set;
.
.
.
```

Related Information

Related examples: Refer to the collection variable example in PUT

Related statements: ALLOCATE ROW and DEALLOCATE COLLECTION

For a discussion of collection data types, see the *Informix ESQL/C Programmer's Manual.*

ALLOCATE DESCRIPTOR

Use the ALLOCATE DESCRIPTOR statement to allocate memory for a system-descriptor area. This statement creates a place in memory to hold information that a DESCRIBE statement obtains or to hold information about the WHERE clause of a statement.

Use this statement with ESQL/C.

Syntax

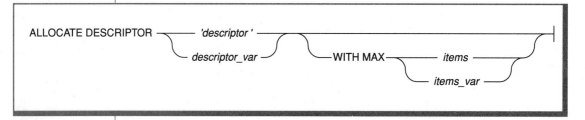

Element	Purpose	Restrictions	Syntax
descriptor	Quoted string that identifies a system-descriptor area	Use single quotes. String must represent the name of an unallocated system-descriptor area.	Quoted String, p. 4-260
descriptor_var	Host-variable name that identifies a system-descriptor area	Variable must contain the name of an unallocated system-descriptor area.	Name must conform to language-specific rules for variable names.
items	Number of item descriptors in the system-descriptor area The default value is 100.	Value must be unsigned INTEGER greater than zero.	Literal Number, p. 4-237
items_var	Host variable that contains the number of items	Data type must be INTEGER or SMALLINT.	Name must conform to language-specific rules for variable names.

Usage

The ALLOCATE DESCRIPTOR statement creates a system-descriptor area. A system-descriptor area contains one or more fields called item descriptors. Each item descriptor holds a data value that the database server can receive or send. The item descriptors also contain information about the data such as type, length, scale, precision, and nullability.

If the name that you assign to a system-descriptor area matches the name of an existing system-descriptor area, the database server returns an error. If you free the descriptor with the DEALLOCATE DESCRIPTOR statement, you can reuse the descriptor.

A system-descriptor area holds information that a DESCRIBE...USING SQL DESCRIPTOR statement obtains or it holds information about the WHERE clause of a dynamically executed statement.

WITH MAX Clause

You can use the WITH MAX clause to indicate the maximum number of item descriptors you need. When you use this clause, the COUNT field is set to the number of *items* you specify. If you do not specify the WITH MAX clause, the default value of the COUNT field is 100. You can change the value of the COUNT field with the SET DESCRIPTOR statement.

The following examples show valid ALLOCATE DESCRIPTOR statements. Each example includes the WITH MAX clause. The first line uses embedded variable names to identify the system-descriptor area and to specify the desired number of item descriptors. The second line uses a quoted string to identify the system-descriptor area and an unsigned integer to specify the desired number of item descriptors.

```
EXEC SQL allocate descriptor :descname with max :occ;

EXEC SQL allocate descriptor 'descl' with max 3;
```

Related Information

Related statements: DEALLOCATE DESCRIPTOR, DECLARE, DESCRIBE, EXECUTE, FETCH, GET DESCRIPTOR, OPEN, PREPARE, PUT, and SET DESCRIPTOR

For more information on system-descriptor areas, refer to the *Informix ESQL/C Programmer's Manual*.

ALLOCATE ROW

Use the ALLOCATE ROW statement to allocate memory for a row variable.

Use this statement with ESQL/C.

Syntax

```
ALLOCATE ROW ───────────────── variable ─────────────────────┤
```

Element	Purpose	Restrictions	Syntax
variable	Name that identifies a typed or untyped row variable for which to allocate memory	The variable must be an unallocated ESQL/C row host variable.	Name must conform to language-specific rules for variable names.

Usage

The ALLOCATE ROW statement allocates memory for a variable that stores row-type data. To create a row variable, perform the following steps in your ESQL/C program:

1. Declare the row variable.

    The row variable can be a typed or untyped row variable.

2. Allocate memory for the row variable with the ALLOCATE ROW statement.

The ALLOCATE ROW statement sets **SQLCODE (sqlca.sqlcode)** to zero (0) if the memory allocation was successful and to a negative error code if the allocation failed.

You must explicitly release memory with the DEALLOCATE ROW statement. Once you free the row variable with the DEALLOCATE ROW statement, you can reuse the row variable.

Tip: *The ALLOCATE ROW statement allocates memory for an ESQL/C row variable only. To allocate memory for an ESQL/C collection variable, use the ALLOCATE COLLECTION statement.*

When you use the same row variable in multiple calls without deallocating it, a memory leak on the client computer results. Because there is no way to determine if a pointer is valid when it is passed, ESQL/C assumes that it is not valid and assigns it to a new memory location.

Example

The following example shows how to allocate resources with the ALLOCATE ROW statement for the typed row variable, **a_row**:

```
EXEC SQL BEGIN DECLARE SECTION;
    row (a int, b int) a_row;
EXEC SQL END DECLARE SECTION;
.
.
.
EXEC SQL allocate row :a_row;
```

Related Information

Related statements: ALLOCATE COLLECTION and DEALLOCATE ROW

For a discussion of complex types, see the *Informix ESQL/C Programmer's Manual*.

ALTER FRAGMENT

Use the ALTER FRAGMENT statement to alter the distribution strategy or storage location of an existing table or index.

Syntax

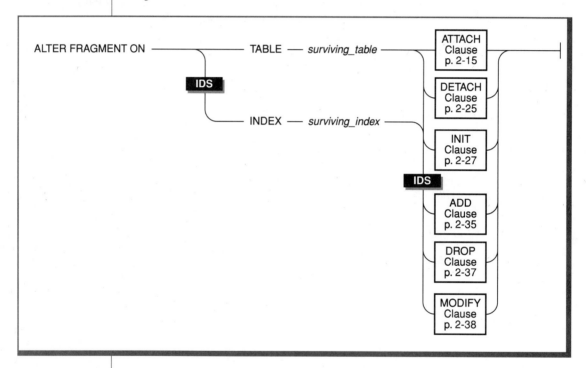

Element	Purpose	Restrictions	Syntax
surviving_index	Index on which you execute the ALTER FRAGMENT statement	The index must exist at the time you execute the statement.	Database Object Name, p. 4-50
surviving_table	Table on which you execute the ALTER FRAGMENT statement	The table must exist at the time you execute the statement.	Database Object Name, p. 4-50
		For more information, see "Restrictions on When You Can Use the ALTER FRAGMENT Statement" on page 2-14.	

Usage

The clauses of the ALTER FRAGMENT statement let you perform the following tasks.

Clause	Purpose
ATTACH	Combines tables that contain identical table structures into a single fragmented table.
DETACH	Detaches a table fragment or slice from a fragmentation strategy and places it in a new table.
INIT	Provides the following options:
	■ Defines and initializes a fragmentation strategy on a table.
	■ Creates a fragmentation strategy for tables.
	■ Changes the order of evaluation of fragment expressions.
	■ Alters the fragmentation strategy of an existing table or index.
	■ Changes the storage location of an existing table.
ADD	Adds an additional fragment to an existing fragmentation list.
DROP	Drops an existing fragment from a fragmentation list.
MODIFY	Changes an existing fragmentation expression.

The ALTER FRAGMENT statement applies only to table or index fragments that are located at the current site (or cluster, for Enterprise Decision Server). No remote information is accessed or updated.

Warning: *This statement can cause indexes to be dropped and rebuilt. Before undertaking alter operations, check corresponding sections in your "Performance Guide" to review effects and strategies*

General Privileges

You must have the Alter or the DBA privilege to change the fragmentation strategy of a table. You must have the Index or the DBA privilege to alter the fragmentation strategy of an index.

Restrictions on When You Can Use the ALTER FRAGMENT Statement

You cannot use the ALTER FRAGMENT statement on a temporary table, an external table, or a view.

If your table or index is not already fragmented, the only clauses available to you are INIT and ATTACH.

IDS

You cannot use ALTER FRAGMENT on a typed table that is part of a table hierarchy. ♦

EDS

You cannot use the ALTER FRAGMENT statement on a generalized-key (GK) index. Also, you cannot use the ALTER FRAGMENT statement on any table that has a dependent GK index defined on it. In addition, you cannot use this statement on a table that has range fragmentation.

If the *surviving_table* has hash fragmentation, the only clauses available are ATTACH and INIT. ♦

How Is the ALTER FRAGMENT Statement Executed?

If your database uses logging, the ALTER FRAGMENT statement is executed within a single transaction. When the fragmentation strategy uses large numbers of records, you might run out of log space or disk space. (The database server requires extra disk space for the operation; it later frees the disk space).

Making More Space

When you run out of log space or disk space, try one of the following procedures to make more space available:

- Turn off logging and turn it back on again at the end of the operation. This procedure indirectly requires a backup of the root dbspace.
- Split the operations into multiple ALTER FRAGMENT statements, moving a smaller portion of records at each time.

For information about log-space requirements and disk-space requirements, see your *Administrator's Guide*. That guide also contains detailed instructions about how to turn off logging. For information about backups, refer to your *Backup and Restore Guide*.

Determining the Number of Rows in the Fragment

You can place as many rows into a fragment as the available space in the dbspace allows.

To find out how many rows are in a fragment

1. Run the UPDATE STATISTICS statement on the table. This step fills the **sysfragments** system catalog table with the current table information.

2. Query the **sysfragments** system catalog table to examine the **npused** and **nrows** fields. The **npused** field gives you the number of data pages used in the fragment, and the **nrows** field gives you the number of rows in the fragment.

ATTACH Clause

Use the ATTACH clause to combine tables that contain identical table structures into a fragmentation strategy.

Important: *Use the CREATE TABLE statement or the INIT clause of the ALTER FRAGMENT statement to create fragmented tables.*

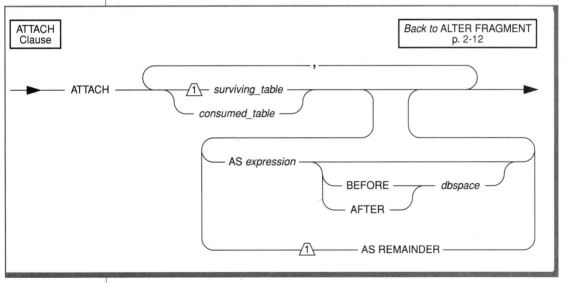

Element	Purpose	Restrictions	Syntax
consumed_table	Table which loses its identity and becomes part of the surviving table	The table must exist at the time you execute the statement.	Database Object Name, p. 4-50
		The table cannot contain serial columns.	
		The table cannot contain unique, referential, or primary-key constraints.	
		The table must be nonfragmented (IDS only).	
		See also, "General Restrictions for the ATTACH Clause" on page 2-17.	
dbspace	Dbspace that specifies where the consumed table expression occurs in the fragmentation list	The dbspace must exist at the time you execute the statement.	Identifier, p. 4-205
	With a hybrid-fragmented table, dbspace identifies a set of dbspaces (EDS only). See "Altering Hybrid-Fragmented Tables" on page 2-19.		
expression	Expression that defines which rows are stored in a fragment	The expression element can contain only columns from the current table and only data values from a single row.	Condition, p. 4-27, and Expression, p. 4-73
		No subqueries, user-defined routines, aggregates, or references to the fields of a row-type column are allowed. In addition, the current, date and/or time built-in functions are not allowed.	
surviving_table	Table that survives the execution of ALTER FRAGMENT	The table must exist at the time you execute the statement.	Database Object Name, p. 4-50
		The table cannot contain any constraints.	
		See also, "General Restrictions for the ATTACH Clause" on page 2-17.	

The ATTACH clause allows you to perform the following tasks:

- Create a single fragmented table by combining two or more identically-structured, nonfragmented tables

  (See "Combining Nonfragmented Tables to Create a Fragmented Table" on page 2-18.)

- Attach one or more tables to a fragmented table

  (See "Attaching a Table to a Fragmented Table" on page 2-19.)

Privileges

You must be the DBA or the owner of the tables that are involved to use the ATTACH clause.

General Restrictions for the ATTACH Clause

Any tables that you attach must have been created previously in separate dbspaces. You cannot attach the same table more than once.

All consumed tables listed in the ATTACH clause must be identical in structure to the surviving table; that is, all column definitions must match. The number, names, data types, and relative position of the columns must be identical.

IDS

You cannot attach a fragmented table to another fragmented table. ♦

EDS

Additional Restrictions on the ATTACH Clause Specific to EDS

In addition to the general restrictions, every consumed table must be of the same usage type as the surviving table. For information about how to specify the usage type of a table, refer to "Usage-Type Options" on page 2-231.

You cannot use the ATTACH clause in certain situations. The attach operation fails:

- if the consumed tables contain data that belongs in some existing fragment of the surviving table.
- if existing data in the surviving table would belong in a new fragment.

In other words, you cannot use the ATTACH clause for data movement among fragments. To perform this task, see the "INIT Clause" on page 2-27.

Using the BEFORE, AFTER, and REMAINDER Options

The BEFORE and AFTER options allow you to place a new fragment either before or after an existing dbspace. You cannot use the BEFORE and AFTER options when the distribution scheme is round-robin.

When you attach a new fragment without an explicit BEFORE or AFTER option, the database server places the added fragment at the end of the fragmentation list, unless a remainder fragment exists. If a remainder fragment exists, the new fragment is placed just before the remainder fragment. You cannot attach a new fragment after the remainder fragment.

EDS

When you create or append to a hybrid-fragmented table, the positioning specification (BEFORE, AFTER, or REMAINDER) applies to an entire dbslice. You can use any dbspace in a dbslice to identify the dbslice for the BEFORE or AFTER position. ♦

Combining Nonfragmented Tables to Create a Fragmented Table

When you transform tables with identical table structures into fragments in a single table, you allow the database server to manage the fragmentation instead of allowing the application to manage the fragmentation. The distribution scheme can be round-robin or expression-based.

To make a single, fragmented table from two or more identically-structured, nonfragmented tables, the ATTACH clause must contain the surviving table in the *attach list*. The attach list is the list of tables in the ATTACH clause.

IDS

To include a **rowid** column in the newly-created single, fragmented table, attach all tables first and then add the **rowid** with the ALTER TABLE statement. ♦

Attaching a Table to a Fragmented Table

To attach a nonfragmented table to an already fragmented table, the nonfragmented table must have been created in a separate dbspace and must have the same table structure as the fragmented table. In the following example, a round-robin distribution scheme fragments the table **cur_acct**, and the table **old_acct** is a nonfragmented table that resides in a separate dbspace. The example shows how to attach **old_acct** to **cur_acct**:

```
ALTER FRAGMENT ON TABLE cur_acct ATTACH old_acct
```

IDS

When you attach one or more tables to a fragmented table, a *consumed table* must be nonfragmented. ♦

EDS

When you attach one or more tables to a fragmented table, a *consumed table* can be nonfragmented or have hash fragmentation.

If you specify a *consumed_table* that has hash fragmentation, the hash column specification must match that of the *surviving_table* and any other *consumed_table* involved in the attach operation. ♦

EDS

Altering Hybrid-Fragmented Tables

When you alter a hybrid-fragmented table with either an ATTACH or DETACH clause, you need specify only one dbspace to identify the entire set of dbspaces that are associated with a given expression in the base fragmentation strategy of the table.

The set of dbspaces associated with an expression in the base fragmentation strategy of the table might have been defined as one or more dbslices or a dbspaces. For more information, see "Fragmenting by HYBRID" on page 2-264.

If you know the name of the dbslice, but not any of the dbspaces that it comprises, you can name the first dbspace in the dbslice by adding .1 to the name of the dbslice. For example, if the dbslice were named **dbsl1**, you could specify `dbsl1.1`.

What Happens?

After the attach executes, all consumed tables no longer exist. Any constraints (CHECK or NOT NULL) that were on the consumed tables also no longer exist.

You must reference the records that were in the consumed tables through the surviving table.

What Happens to Indexes?

In a logging database, when the attach executes, the database server extends any attached index on the surviving table according to the new fragmentation strategy of the surviving table. All rows in the consumed table are subject to these automatically adjusted indexes. For information on whether the database server completely rebuilds the index on the surviving table or reuses an index that was on the consumed table, see your *Performance Guide*.

IDS

In a nonlogging database, when the attach executes, the database server does not extend indexes on the surviving table according to the new fragmentation strategy of the surviving table. To extend the fragmentation strategy of an attached index according to the new fragmentations strategy of the surviving table, you must drop the index and recreate it on the surviving table. ♦

A detached index on the surviving table retains its same fragmentation strategy. That is, a detached index does not automatically adjust to accommodate the new fragmentation of the surviving table.

For more information on what happens to indexes, see the discussion about altering table fragments in your *Performance Guide*.

What Happens to BYTE and TEXT Columns?

IDS

Each BYTE and TEXT column in every table that is named in the ATTACH clause must have the same storage type, either blobspace or tblspace. If the BYTE or TEXT column is stored in a blobspace, the same column in all tables must be in the same blobspace. If the BYTE or TEXT column is stored in a tblspace, the same column must be stored in a tblspace in all tables. ♦

EDS

In Enterprise Decision Server, BYTE and TEXT columns are stored in separate fragments that are created for that purpose. If a table includes a BYTE or TEXT column, the database server creates a separate, additional fragment in the same dbspace as each regular table fragment. BYTE or TEXT columns are stored in the separate fragment that is associated with the regular table fragment where a given row resides.

When an attach occurs, BYTE and TEXT fragments of the consumed table become part of the surviving table and continue to be associated with the same rows and data fragments as they were before the attach. ◆

What Happens to Triggers?

When you attach tables, any triggers that are defined on the consumed table no longer exist, and all rows in the consumed table are subject to the triggers that are defined in the surviving table. That is, triggers on the surviving table survive the ATTACH, but triggers on the consumed table are dropped.

No triggers are activated with the ATTACH clause, but subsequent data-manipulation operations on the new rows can activate triggers.

What Happens to Views?

Views on the surviving table survive the ATTACH, but views on the consumed table are dropped.

What Happens with the Distribution Scheme?

You can attach a nonfragmented table to a table with any type of supported distribution scheme. In general, the resulting table has the same fragmentation strategy as the prior fragmentation strategy of the *surviving_table*. However, when you attach two or more nonfragmented tables, the distribution scheme can either be based on expression or round-robin.

IDS

The following table shows the distribution schemes that can result from different distribution schemes of the tables mentioned in the ATTACH clause.

Prior Distribution Scheme of Surviving Table	Prior Distribution Scheme of Consumed Table	Resulting Distribution Scheme
None	None	Round-robin or expression
Round-robin	None	Round-robin
Expression	None	Expression

♦

EDS

The following table shows the distribution schemes that can result from different distribution schemes of the tables mentioned in the ATTACH clause.

Prior Distribution Scheme of Surviving Table	Prior Distribution Scheme of Consumed Table	Resulting Distribution Scheme
None	None	Round-robin or expression
None	Hash	Hybrid
Round-robin	None	Round-robin
Expression	None	Expression
Hash	None	Hybrid
Hash	Hash	Hybrid
Hybrid	None	Hybrid
Hybrid	Hash	Hybrid

When you attach a nonfragmented table to a table that has hash fragmentation, the resulting table has hybrid fragmentation.

You can attach a table with a hash distribution scheme to a table that currently has no fragmentation, hash fragmentation, or hybrid fragmentation. In any of these situations, the resulting table has a hybrid distribution scheme. ♦

Examples

The following examples illustrate the use of the ATTACH clause to create fragmented tables with different distribution schemes.

Round-Robin Distribution Scheme

The following example combines nonfragmented tables **pen_types** and **pen_makers** into a single, fragmented table, **pen_types**. Table **pen_types** resides in dbspace **dbsp1,** and table **pen_makers** resides in dbspace **dbsp2**. Table structures are identical in each table.

```
ALTER FRAGMENT ON TABLE pen_types
    ATTACH pen_types, pen_makers
```

After you execute the ATTACH clause, the database server fragments the table **pen_types** round-robin into two dbspaces: the dbspace that contained **pen_types** and the dbspace that contained **pen_makers**. Table **pen_makers** is consumed, and no longer exists; all rows that were in table **pen_makers** are now in table **pen_types**.

Expression Distribution Scheme

Consider the following example that combines tables **cur_acct** and **new_acct** and uses an expression-based distribution scheme. Table **cur_acct** was originally created as a fragmented table and has fragments in dbspaces **dbsp1** and **dbsp2**. The first statement of the example shows that table **cur_acct** was created with an expression-based distribution scheme. The second statement of the example creates table **new_acct** in **dbsp3** without a fragmentation strategy. The third statement combines the tables **cur_acct** and **new_acct**. Table structures (columns) are identical in each table.

```
CREATE TABLE cur_acct (a int) FRAGMENT BY EXPRESSION
    a < 5 in dbsp1,
    a >= 5 and a < 10 in dbsp2;

CREATE TABLE new_acct (a int) IN dbsp3;

ALTER FRAGMENT ON TABLE cur_acct ATTACH new_acct AS a>=10;
```

When you examine the **sysfragments** system catalog table after you alter the fragment, you see that table **cur_acct** is fragmented by expression into three dbspaces. For additional information about the **sysfragments** system catalog table, see the *Informix Guide to SQL: Reference*.

In addition to simple range rules, you can use the ATTACH clause to fragment by expression with hash or arbitrary rules. For a discussion of all types of expressions in an expression-based distribution scheme, see "FRAGMENT BY Clause for Tables" on page 2-30.

Warning: *When you specify a date value in a fragment expression, make sure to specify 4 digits instead of 2 digits for the year. When you specify a 4-digit year, the DBCENTURY environment variable has no effect on the distribution scheme. When you specify a 2-digit year, the DBCENTURY environment variable can affect the distribution scheme and can produce unpredictable results. For more information on the DBCENTURY environment variable, see the "Informix Guide to SQL: Reference."*

`EDS`

Hybrid Fragmentation Distribution Scheme

Consider a case where monthly sales data is added to the **sales_info** table defined below. Due to the large amount of data, the table is distributed evenly across multiple coservers with a system-defined hash function. To manage monthly additions of data to the table, it is also fragmented by a date expression. The combined hybrid fragmentation is declared in the following CREATE TABLE statement:

```
CREATE TABLE sales_info (order_num int, sale_date date, ...)
FRAGMENT BY HYBRID (order_num) EXPRESSION
sale_date >= '01/01/1996' AND sale_date < '02/01/1996'
IN sales_slice_9601,
sale_date >= '02/01/1996' AND sale_date < '03/01/1996'
IN sales_slice_9602,
     .
     .
     .
sale_date >= '12/01/1996' AND sale_date < '01/01/1997'
IN sales_slice_9612
```

The data for a new month is originally loaded from an external source. The data is distributed evenly across the name coservers on which the **sales_info** table is defined, using a system-defined hash function on the same column:

```
CREATE TABLE jan_97 (order_num int, sale_date date, ...)
    FRAGMENT BY HASH (order_num) IN sales_slice_9701
INSERT INTO jan_97 SELECT (...) FROM ...
```

Once the data is loaded, you can attach the new table to **sales_info.** You can issue the following ALTER FRAGMENT statement to attach the new table:

```
ALTER FRAGMENT ON TABLE sales_info ATTACH jan_97
    AS sale_date >= '01/01/1997' AND sale_date < '02/01/1997'
```

DETACH Clause

Use the DETACH clause to detach a table fragment from a distribution scheme and place the contents into a new nonfragmented table.

EDS In Enterprise Decision Server, the new table can also be a table with hash fragmentation. ◆

For an explanation of distribution schemes, see "FRAGMENT BY Clause for Tables" on page 2-30.

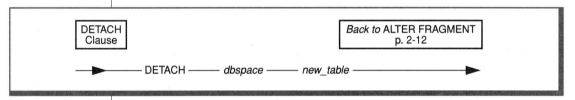

Element	Purpose	Restrictions	Syntax
dbspace	Dbspace that contains the fragment to be detached	The dbspace must exist when you execute the statement.	Identifier, p. 4-205
	With a hybrid-fragmented table, dbspace identifies a set of dbspaces (EDS only). See "Altering Hybrid-Fragmented Tables" on page 2-19.		
new_table	Nonfragmented table that results after you execute the ALTER FRAGMENT statement	The table must not exist before you execute the statement.	Database Object Name, p. 4-50
	In EDS, the table can also be a hash-fragmented table.		

The new table that results from the execution of the DETACH clause does not inherit any indexes or constraints from the original table. Only the data remains.

The new table that results from the execution of the DETACH clause does not inherit any privileges from the original table. Instead this table has the default privileges for any new table. For further information on default table-level privileges, see the GRANT statement on "Table-Level Privileges" on page 2-505.

Restrictions

The DETACH clause cannot be applied to a table if that table is the parent of a referential constraint or if a rowid column is defined on the table.

EDS

In Enterprise Decision Server, you cannot use the DETACH clause if the table has a dependent GK index defined on it. ♦

Detach That Results in a Non-fragmented Table

The following example shows the table **cur_acct** fragmented into two dbspaces, **dbsp1** and **dbsp2**:

```
ALTER FRAGMENT ON TABLE cur_acct DETACH dbsp2 accounts
```

This example detaches **dbsp2** from the distribution scheme for **cur_acct** and places the rows in a new table, **accounts**. Table **accounts** now has the same structure (column names, number of columns, data types, and so on) as table **cur_acct**, but the table **accounts** does not contain any indexes or constraints from the table **cur_acct**. Both tables are now nonfragmented.

The following example shows a table that contains three fragments:

```
ALTER FRAGMENT ON TABLE bus_acct DETACH dbsp3 cli_acct
```

This statement detaches **dbsp3** from the distribution scheme for **bus_acct** and places the rows in a new table, **cli_acct**. Table **cli_acct** now has the same structure (column names, number of columns, data types, and so on) as **bus_acct,** but the table **cli_acct** does not contain any indexes or constraints from the table **bus_acct**. Table **cli_acct** is a nonfragmented table, and table **bus_acct** remains a fragmented table.

EDS

Detach That Results in a Table with Hash Fragmentation

The new table will be a hash-fragmented table if the *surviving_table* had hybrid fragmentation and the detached dbslice has more than one fragment. In a hybrid-fragmented table, you specify the dbslice to be detached by naming *any* dbspace in that slice.

Consider the **sales_info** table discussed in the "Hybrid Fragmentation Distribution Scheme" on page 2-24. Once the January 1997 data is available in the **sales_info** table, you might archive year-old **sales_info** data.

```
ALTER FRAGMENT ON TABLE sales_info
    DETACH sales_slice_9601.1 jan_96
```

In this example, data from January 1996 is detached from the **sales_info** table and placed in a new table called **jan_96**.

INIT Clause

The INIT clause allows you to:

- move a nonfragmented table from one dbspace to another dbspace.
- convert a fragmented table to a nonfragmented table.
- fragment an existing table that is not fragmented without redefining the table.
- convert an existing fragmentation strategy to another fragmentation strategy
- fragment an existing index that is not fragmented without redefining the index
- convert a fragmented index to a nonfragmented index. ♦

Warning: *When you execute the ALTER FRAGMENT statement with this clause, it results in data movement if the table contains any data. If data moves, the potential exits for significant logging, for the transaction being aborted as a long transaction, and for a relatively long exclusive lock being held on the affected tables. Use this statement when it does not interfere with day-to-day operations.*

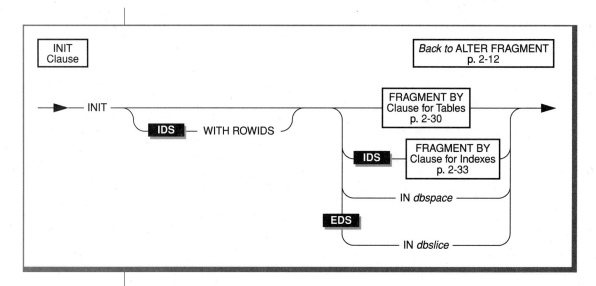

Element	Purpose	Restrictions	Syntax
dbslice	Dbslice that contains the fragmented information	The dbslice must exist at the time you execute the statement.	Identifier, p. 4-205
dbspace	Dbspace that contains the fragmented information	The dbspace must exist at the time you execute the statement.	Identifier, p. 4-205

EDS

You cannot use the INIT clause to change the fragmentation strategy of a table that has a GK index. ♦

For more information about the storage spaces in which you can store a table, see "Using the IN Clause" on page 2-257.

When you use the INIT clause to modify a table, the **tabid** value in system catalog tables changes for the affected table. The **constrid** of all unique and referential constraints on the table also change.

WITH ROWIDS Option

Nonfragmented tables contain a pseudocolumn called the **rowid** column. Fragmented tables do not contain this column unless it is explicitly created.

Use the WITH ROWIDS option to add a new column called the **rowid** column. The database server assigns a unique number to each row that remains stable for the existence of the row. The database server creates an index that it uses to find the physical location of the row. Each row contains an additional 4 bytes to store the **rowid** column after you add the WITH ROWIDS option.

Important: *Informix recommends that you use primary keys, rather than the **rowid** column, as an access method.*

Converting a Fragmented Table to a Nonfragmented Table

You might decide that you no longer want a table to be fragmented. You can use the INIT clause to convert a fragmented table to a nonfragmented table. The following example shows the original fragmentation definition as well as how to use the ALTER FRAGMENT statement to convert the table:

```
CREATE TABLE checks (col1 int, col2 int)
    FRAGMENT BY ROUND ROBIN IN dbsp1, dbsp2, dbsp3;

ALTER FRAGMENT ON TABLE checks INIT IN dbsp1;
```

You must use the IN *dbspace* clause to place the table in a dbspace explicitly.

When you use the INIT clause to change a fragmented table to a nonfragmented table (that is, to rid the table of any fragmentation strategy), all attached indexes become nonfragmented indexes. In addition, constraints that do not use existing user indexes (detached indexes) become nonfragmented indexes. All newly nonfragmented indexes exist in the same dbspace as the new nonfragmented table.

When you use the INIT clause to change a fragmented table to a nonfragmented table, the fragmentation strategy of detached indexes (and constraints that use detached indexes) is not affected.

FRAGMENT BY Clause for Tables

Use the FRAGMENT BY portion of the INIT clause to fragment an existing non-fragmented table or convert an existing fragmentation strategy to another fragmentation strategy.

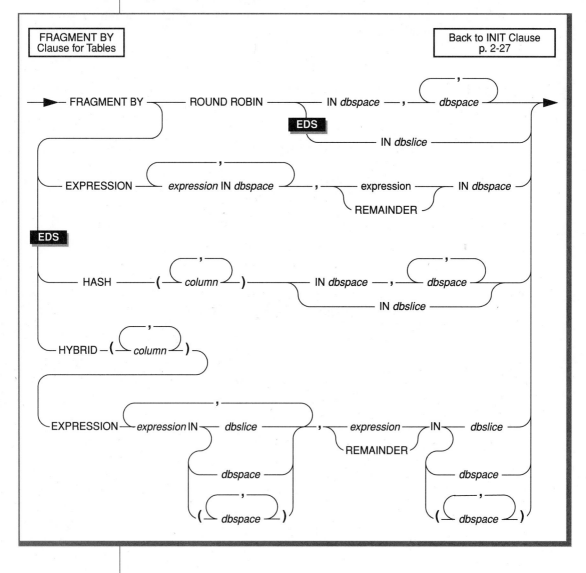

FRAGMENT BY
Clause for Tables

Back to INIT Clause
p. 2-27

Element	Purpose	Restrictions	Syntax
column	Name of the column or columns on which you want to apply the fragmentation strategy In the HYBRID clause, column identifies the column or columns on which you want to apply the hash portion of the hybrid table fragmentation strategy	The column must exist.	Identifier, p. 4-205
dbslice	Dbslice that contains the table fragment	The dbslice must be defined.	Identifier, p. 4-205
dbspace	Dbspace that contains the table fragment	You must specify at least two dbspaces. You can specify a maximum of 2,048 dbspaces.	Identifier, p. 4-205
expression	Expression that defines a table fragment using a range, hash, or arbitrary rule	Each fragment expression can contain only columns from the current table and only data values from a single row. No subqueries, user-defined routines, aggregates, or references to the fields of a row-type column are allowed. In addition, the current, date and/or time built-in functions are not allowed.	Condition, p. 4-27, and Expression, p. 4-73

For more information on the available fragmentation strategies, see the "FRAGMENT BY Clause" on page 2-259.

Changing an Existing Fragmentation Strategy on a Table

You can redefine a fragmentation strategy on a table if you decide that your initial strategy does not fulfill your needs. When you alter a fragmentation strategy, the database server discards the existing fragmentation strategy and moves records to fragments as defined in the new fragmentation strategy.

The following example shows the statement that originally defined the fragmentation strategy on the table **account** and then shows an ALTER FRAGMENT statement that redefines the fragmentation strategy:

```
CREATE TABLE account (col1 int, col2 int)
    FRAGMENT BY ROUND ROBIN IN dbsp1, dbsp2;

ALTER FRAGMENT ON TABLE account
    INIT FRAGMENT BY EXPRESSION
    col1 < 0 in dbsp1,
    col2 >= 0in dbsp2;
```

If an existing dbspace is full when you redefine a fragmentation strategy, you must not use it in the new fragmentation strategy.

Defining a Fragmentation Strategy on a Nonfragmented Table

You can use the INIT clause to define a fragmentation strategy on a nonfragmented table. It does not matter whether the table was created with a storage option.

IDS

When you use the INIT clause to fragment an existing nonfragmented table, all indexes on the table become fragmented in the same way as the table. ♦

EDS

When you use the INIT clause to fragment an existing nonfragmented table, indexes retain their existing fragmentation strategy.

The following example shows the original table definition as well as how to use the ALTER FRAGMENT statement to fragment the table:

```
CREATE TABLE balances (col1 int, col2 int) IN dbsp1;

ALTER FRAGMENT ON TABLE balances INIT
    FRAGMENT BY EXPRESSION
    col1 <= 500 IN dbsp1,
    col1 > 500 and col1 <=1000 IN dbsp2,
    REMAINDER IN dbsp3;
```

♦

IDS

FRAGMENT BY Clause for Indexes

The INIT FRAGMENT BY clause for indexes allows you to fragment an existing index that is not fragmented without redefining the index. You can convert an existing fragmentation strategy to another fragmentation strategy. Any existing fragmentation strategy is discarded and records are moved to fragments as defined in the new fragmentation strategy. You can also convert a fragmented index to a nonfragmented index.

Use the FRAGMENT BY clause for indexes to define the expression-based distribution scheme.

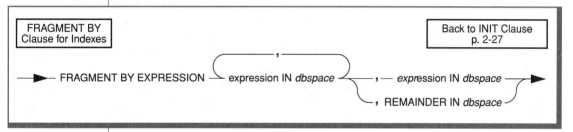

Element	Purpose	Restrictions	Syntax
dbspace	Dbspace that contains the fragmented information	You must specify at least two dbspaces. You can specify a maximum of 2,048 dbspaces.	Identifier, p. 4-205
expression	Expression that defines an index fragment by using a range, hash, or arbitrary rule	Each fragment expression can contain only columns from the current table and only data values from a single row.	Condition, p. 4-27, and Expression, p. 4-73
		No subqueries, user-defined routines, aggregates, or references to the fields of a row-type column are allowed. In addition, the current, date and/or time built-in functions are not allowed.	

Fragmenting Unique and System Indexes

You can fragment unique indexes only if the table uses an expression-based distribution scheme. The columns that are referenced in the fragment expression must be indexed columns. If your ALTER FRAGMENT INIT statement fails to meet either of these restrictions, the INIT fails, and work is rolled back.

You might have an attached unique index on a table fragmented by **Column A**. If you use INIT to change the table fragmentation to **Column B**, the INIT fails because the unique index is defined on **Column A**. To resolve this issue, you can use the INIT clause on the index to detach it from the table fragmentation strategy and fragment it separately.

System indexes (such as those used in referential constraints and unique constraints) use user indexes if the indexes exist. If no user indexes can be used, system indexes remain nonfragmented and are moved to the dbspace where the database was created. To fragment a system index, create the fragmented index on the constraint columns, and then use the ALTER TABLE statement to add the constraint.

Detaching an Index from a Table-Fragmentation Strategy

You can detach an index from a table-fragmentation strategy with the INIT clause, which causes an attached index to become a detached index. This breaks any dependency of the index on the table fragmentation strategy.

IDS

ADD Clause

Use the ADD clause to add another fragment to an existing fragmentation list.

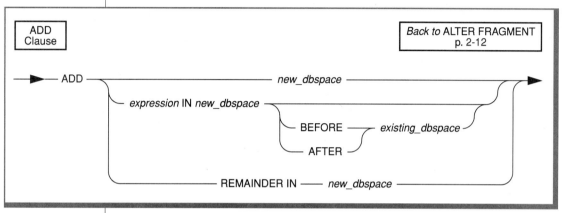

Element	Purpose	Restrictions	Syntax
existing_dbspace	Name of a dbspace in an existing fragmentation list	The dbspace must exist at the time you execute the statement.	Identifier, p. 4-205
expression	Expression that defines the added fragment	The expression can contain only columns from the current table and only data values from a single row.	Condition, p. 4-27, and Expression, p. 4-73
		No subqueries, user-defined routines, aggregates, or references to the fields of a row-type column are allowed. In addition, the current, date and/or time built-in functions are not allowed.	
new_dbspace	Name of dbspace to be added to the fragmentation scheme	The dbspace must exist at the time you execute the statement.	Identifier, p. 4-205

Adding a New Dbspace to a Round-Robin Distribution Scheme

You can add more dbspaces to a round-robin distribution scheme. The following example shows the original round-robin definition:

```
CREATE TABLE book (col1 int, col2 title)
FRAGMENT BY ROUND ROBIN in dbsp1, dbsp4;
```

To add another dbspace, use the ADD clause, as shown in the following example:

```
ALTER FRAGMENT ON TABLE book ADD dbsp3;
```

Adding Fragment Expressions

Adding a fragment expression to the fragmentation list in an expression-based distribution scheme can shuffle records from some existing fragments into the new fragment. When you add a new fragment into the middle of the fragmentation list, all the data existing in fragments after the new one must be re-evaluated. The following example shows the original expression definition:

```
        .
        .
        .
    FRAGMENT BY EXPRESSION
    c1 < 100 IN dbsp1,
    c1 >= 100 and c1 < 200 IN dbsp2,
    REMAINDER IN dbsp3;
```

If you want to add another fragment to the fragmentation list and have this fragment hold rows between 200 and 300, use the following ALTER FRAGMENT statement:

```
ALTER FRAGMENT ON TABLE news ADD
    c1 >= 200 and c1 < 300 IN dbsp4;
```

Any rows that were formerly in the remainder fragment and that fit the criteria c1 >= 200 and c1 < 300 are moved to the new dbspace.

Using the BEFORE and AFTER Options

The BEFORE and AFTER options allow you to place a new fragment either before or after an existing dbspace. You cannot use the BEFORE and AFTER options when the distribution scheme is round-robin.

When you attach a new fragment without an explicit BEFORE or AFTER option, the database server places the added fragment at the end of the fragmentation list, unless a remainder fragment exists. If a remainder fragment exists, the new fragment is placed just before the remainder fragment. You cannot attach a new fragment after the remainder fragment.

Using the REMAINDER Option

You cannot add a remainder fragment when one already exists. When you add a new fragment to the fragmentation list, and a remainder fragment exists, the records in the remainder fragment are retrieved and re-evaluated. Some of these records may move to the new fragment. The remainder fragment always remains the last item in the fragment list.

IDS

DROP Clause

Use the DROP clause to drop an existing fragment from a fragmentation list.

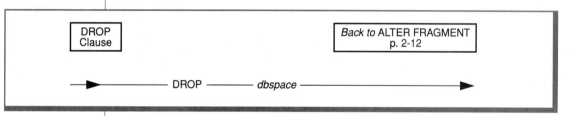

Element	Purpose	Restrictions	Syntax
dbspace	Name of the dbspace that contains the dropped fragment	The dbspace must exist at the time you execute the statement.	Identifier, p. 4-205

You cannot drop one of the fragments when the table contains only two fragments. You cannot drop a fragment in a table that is fragmented with an expression-based distribution scheme if the fragment contains data that cannot be moved to another fragment. If the distribution scheme contains a REMAINDER option, or if the expressions were constructed in an overlapping manner, you can drop a fragment that contains data.

When you want to make a fragmented table nonfragmented, use either the INIT or DETACH clause.

When you drop a fragment from a dbspace, the underlying dbspace is not affected. Only the fragment data within that dbspace is affected. When you drop a fragment all the records located in the fragment move to another fragment. The destination fragment might not have enough space for the additional records. When this happens, follow one of the procedures that are listed in "Making More Space" on page 2-14 to increase your space, and retry the procedure.

The following examples show how to drop a fragment from a fragmentation list. The first line shows how to drop an index fragment, and the second line shows how to drop a table fragment.

```
ALTER FRAGMENT ON INDEX cust_indx DROP dbsp2;

ALTER FRAGMENT ON TABLE customer DROP dbsp1;
```

IDS

MODIFY Clause

Use the MODIFY clause to change an existing fragment expression on an existing dbspace. You can also use the MODIFY clause to move a fragment expression from one dbspace to a different dbspace.

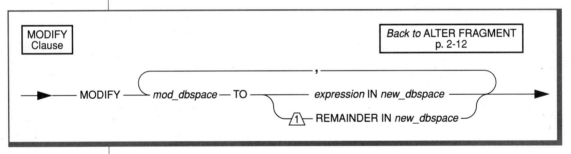

Element	Purpose	Restrictions	Syntax
expression	Modified range, hash, or arbitrary expression	The fragment expression can contain only columns from the current table and only data values from a single row.	Condition, p. 4-27, and Expression, p. 4-73
		No subqueries, user-defined routines, aggregates, or references to the fields of a row-type column are allowed. In addition, the current, date and/or time built-in functions are not allowed.	
mod_ dbspace	Modified dbspace	The dbspace must exist when you execute the statement.	Identifier, p. 4-205
new_dbspace	Dbspace that contains the modified information	The dbspace must exist when you execute the statement.	Identifier, p. 4-205

General Usage

When you use the MODIFY clause, the underlying dbspaces are not affected. Only the fragment data within the dbspaces is affected.

You cannot change a REMAINDER fragment into a nonremainder fragment if records within the REMAINDER fragment do not pass the new expression.

Changing the Expression in an Existing Dbspace

When you use the MODIFY clause to change an expression without changing the dbspace storage for the expression, you must use the same name for the *mod_dbspace* and the *new_dbspace*.

The following example shows how to use the MODIFY clause to change an existing expression:

```
ALTER FRAGMENT ON TABLE cust_acct
    MODIFY dbsp1 to acct_num < 65 IN dbsp1
```

Moving an Expression from One Dbspace to Another

When you use the MODIFY clause to move an expression from one dbspace to another, *mod_dbspace* is the name of the dbspace where the expression was previously located, and *new_dbspace* is the new location for the expression.

The following example shows how to use the MODIFY clause to move an expression from one dbspace to another:

```
ALTER FRAGMENT ON TABLE cust_acct
    MODIFY dbsp1 to acct_num < 35 in dbsp2
```

In this example, the distribution scheme for the **cust_acct** table is modified so that all row items in the column **acct_num** that are less than 35 are now contained in the dbspace **dbsp2**. These items were formerly contained in the dbspace **dbsp1**.

Changing the Expression and Moving it to a New Dbspace

When you use the MODIFY clause to change the expression and move it to a new dbspace, change both the expression and the dbspace name.

What Happens to Indexes?

If your indexes are attached indexes, and you modify the table, the index fragmentation strategy is also modified.

Related Information

Related statements: CREATE TABLE, CREATE INDEX, and ALTER TABLE

For a discussion of fragmentation strategy, refer to the *Informix Guide to Database Design and Implementation*.

For information on how to maximize performance when you make fragment modifications, see your *Performance Guide*.

ALTER FUNCTION

Use the ALTER FUNCTION statement to change the routine modifiers or pathname of a user-defined function.

Syntax

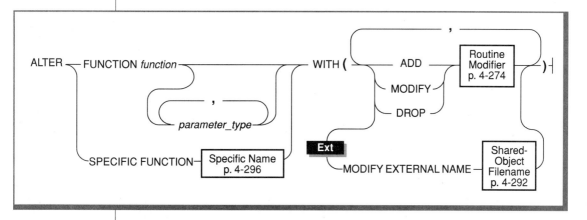

Element	Purpose	Restrictions	Syntax
function	Name of the user-defined function to modify	The function must exist (that is, be registered) in the database.	Database Object Name, p. 4-50
		If the name does not uniquely identify a function, you must enter one or more appropriate values for *parameter_type*.	
parameter_type	Data type of the parameter	The data type (or list of data types) must be the same types (and specified in the same order) as those specified in the CREATE FUNCTION statement when the function was created.	Identifier, p. 4-205

Usage

The ALTER FUNCTION statement allows you to modify a user-defined function to tune its performance. With this statement you can modify characteristics that control how the function executes. You can also add or replace related UDRs that provide alternatives for the optimizer, which can improve performance.

All modifications take effect on the next invocation of the function.

Privileges

To use the ALTER FUNCTION statement, you must be the owner of the UDR or have the DBA privilege.

Keywords That Introduce Modifications

Use the following keywords to introduce the items in the user-defined function that you want to modify.

Keyword	Purpose
ADD	Introduces a routine modifier that you want to add to the user-defined function
MODIFY	Introduces a routine modifier for which you want to modify a value
DROP	Introduces a routine modifier that you want to remove from the user-defined function
MODIFY EXTERNAL NAME (for external functions only)	Introduces a new location for the executable file
WITH	Introduces all modifications

If the routine modifier is a Boolean value, MODIFY sets the value to be T (that is, it is the equivalent of using the keyword ADD to add the routine modifier). For example, both of the following statements alter the **func1** function so that it can be executed in parallel in the context of a parallelizable data query statement.

```
ALTER FUNCTION func1 WITH (MODIFY PARALLELIZABLE)

ALTER FUNCTION func1 WITH (ADD PARALLELIZABLE)
```

For a related example, see "Altering Routine Modifiers Example" on page 2-54.

Related Information

Related Statements: ALTER PROCEDURE, ALTER ROUTINE, CREATE FUNCTION, CREATE PROCEDURE, DROP FUNCTION, DROP PROCEDURE, and DROP ROUTINE

For a discussion on how to create and use SPL routines, see the *Informix Guide to SQL: Tutorial*.

For a discussion of how to create and use external routines, see *Extending Informix Dynamic Server 2000*.

For information about how to create C UDRs, see the *DataBlade API Programmer's Manual*.

ALTER INDEX

Use the ALTER INDEX statement to put the data in a table in the order of an existing index or to release an index from the clustering attribute.

Syntax

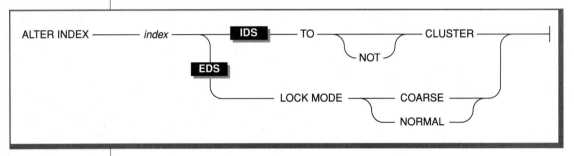

Element	Purpose	Restrictions	Syntax
index	Name of the index to alter	The index must exist.	Database Object Name, p. 4-50

Usage

The ALTER INDEX statement works only on indexes that are created with the CREATE INDEX statement; it does not affect constraints that are created with the CREATE TABLE statement.

You cannot alter the index of a temporary table.

TO CLUSTER Option

The TO CLUSTER option causes the rows in the physical table to reorder in the indexed order.

The following example shows how you can use the ALTER INDEX TO CLUSTER statement to order the rows in the **orders** table physically. The CREATE INDEX statement creates an index on the **customer_num** column of the table. Then the ALTER INDEX statement causes the physical ordering of the rows.

```
CREATE INDEX ix_cust ON orders (customer_num);

ALTER INDEX ix_cust TO CLUSTER;
```

When you reorder, the entire file is rewritten. This process can take a long time, and it requires sufficient disk space to maintain two copies of the table.

While a table is clustering, the table is locked IN EXCLUSIVE MODE. When another process is using the table to which the index name belongs, the database server cannot execute the ALTER INDEX statement with the TO CLUSTER option; it returns an error unless lock mode is set to WAIT. (When lock mode is set to WAIT, the database server retries the ALTER INDEX statement.)

Over time, if you modify the table, you can expect the benefit of an earlier cluster to disappear because rows are added in space-available order, not sequentially. You can recluster the table to regain performance by issuing another ALTER INDEX TO CLUSTER statement on the clustered index. You do not need to drop a clustered index before you issue another ALTER INDEX TO CLUSTER statement on a currently clustered index.

EDS

If you are using Enterprise Decision Server, you cannot use the CLUSTER option on STANDARD tables. ♦

TO NOT CLUSTER Option

The NOT option drops the cluster attribute on the index name without affecting the physical table. Because only one clustered index per table can exist, you must use the NOT option to release the cluster attribute from one index before you assign it to another. The following statements illustrate how to remove clustering from one index and how a second index physically reclusters the table:

```
CREATE UNIQUE INDEX ix_ord
    ON orders (order_num);

CREATE CLUSTER INDEX ix_cust
    ON orders (customer_num);
    .
    .
    .

ALTER INDEX ix_cust TO NOT CLUSTER;

ALTER INDEX ix_ord TO CLUSTER;
```

The first two statements create indexes for the **orders** table and cluster the physical table in ascending order on the **customer_num** column. The last two statements recluster the physical table in ascending order on the **order_num** column.

LOCK MODE Options

Use the lock modes to specify the locking granularity of the index.

When you use the coarse-lock mode, index-level locks are acquired on the index instead of item-level or page-level locks. This mode reduces the number of lock calls on an index.

Use the coarse-lock mode when you know the index is not going to change, that is, when read-only operations are performed on the index.

Use the coarse-lock mode to have the database server place item-level or page-level locks on the index as necessary. Use this mode when the index gets updated frequently.

When the database server executes the command to change the lock mode to coarse, it acquires an exclusive lock on the table for the duration of the command. Any transactions that are currently using a lock of finer granularity must complete before the database server switches to the coarse-lock mode.

Related Information

Related statements: CREATE INDEX and CREATE TABLE

For a discussion of the performance implications of clustered indexes, see your *Performance Guide*.

ALTER PROCEDURE

Use the ALTER PROCEDURE statement to change the routine modifiers or pathname of a previously defined external procedure.

Syntax

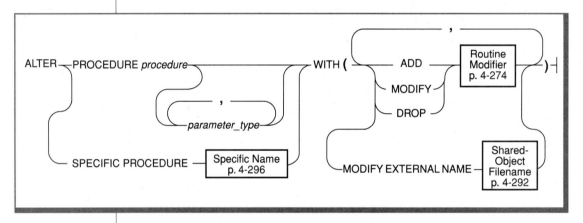

Element	Purpose	Restrictions	Syntax
parameter_type	Data type of the parameter	The data type (or list of data types) must be the same types (and specified in the same order) as those specified in the CREATE PROCEDURE statement when the procedure was created.	Identifier, p. 4-205
procedure	Name of the external procedure to modify	The procedure must exist (that is, be registered) in the database.	Database Object Name, p. 4-50
		If the name does not uniquely identify a procedure, you must enter one or more appropriate values for parameter_type.	

Usage

The ALTER PROCEDURE statement allows you to modify an external procedure to tune its performance. With this statement you can modify characteristics that control how the external procedure executes. You can also add or replace related UDRs that provide alternatives for the optimizer, which can improve performance.

All modifications take effect on the next invocation of the procedure.

Privileges

To use the ALTER PROCEDURE statement, you must be the owner of the UDR or have the DBA privilege.

Keywords That Introduce Modifications

Use the following keywords to introduce the items in the external procedure that you want to modify.

Keyword	Purpose
ADD	Introduces a routine modifier that you want to add to the external procedure
MODIFY	Introduces a routine modifier for which you want to modify a value
DROP	Introduces a routine modifier that you want to remove from the external procedure
MODIFY EXTERNAL NAME (for external routines only)	Introduces a new location for the executable file
WITH	Introduces all modifications

If the routine modifier is a Boolean value, MODIFY sets the value to be T (that is, it is the equivalent of using the keyword ADD to add the routine modifier). For example, both of the following statements alter the **proc1** procedure so that it can be executed in parallel in the context of a parallelizable data query statement.

```
ALTER PROCEDURE proc1 WITH (MODIFY PARALLELIZABLE)

ALTER PROCEDURE proc1 WITH (ADD PARALLELIZABLE)
```

For a related example, see "Altering Routine Modifiers Example" on page 2-54.

Related Information

Related Statements: ALTER FUNCTION, ALTER ROUTINE, CREATE FUNCTION, CREATE PROCEDURE, DROP FUNCTION, DROP PROCEDURE, and DROP ROUTINE

For a discussion on how to create and use SPL routines, see the *Informix Guide to SQL: Tutorial*.

For a discussion of how to create and use external routines, see *Extending Informix Dynamic Server 2000*.

For information about how to create C UDRs, see the *DataBlade API Programmer's Manual*.

ALTER ROUTINE

Use the ALTER ROUTINE statement to change the routine modifiers or pathname of a previously defined user-defined routine (UDR).

Syntax

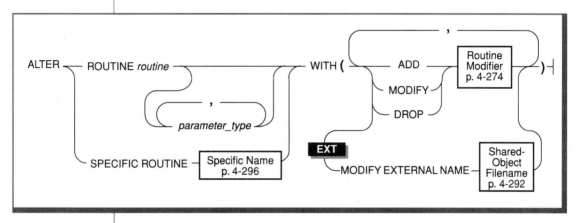

Element	Purpose	Restrictions	Syntax
parameter_type	Data type of the parameter	The data type (or list of data types) must be the same types (and specified in the same order) as those specified when the UDR was created.	Identifier, p. 4-205
routine	Name of the UDR to modify	The UDR must exist (that is, be registered) in the database.	Database Object Name, p. 4-50
		If the name does not uniquely identify a UDR, you must enter one or more appropriate values for *parameter_type*.	

Usage

The ALTER ROUTINE statement allows you to modify a previously-defined UDR to tune its performance. With this statement you can modify characteristics that control how the UDR executes. You can also add or replace related UDRs that provide alternatives for the optimizer, which can improve performance.

This statement is useful when you do not know whether a UDR is a user-defined function or a user-defined procedure. When you use this statement, the database server alters the appropriate user-defined procedure or user-defined function.

All modifications take effect on the next invocation of the UDR.

Privileges

To use the ALTER ROUTINE statement, you must be the owner of the UDR or have the DBA privilege.

Restrictions

When you use this statement, the type of UDR cannot be ambiguous. The UDR that you specify must refer to either a user-defined function or a user-defined procedure. If either of the following conditions exist, the database server returns an error:

- The name (and parameters) that you specify apply to both a user-defined procedure and a user-defined function
- The specific name that you specify applies to both a user-defined function and a user-defined procedure

Keywords That Introduce Modifications

Use the following keywords to introduce the items in the UDR that you want to modify.

Keyword	Purpose
ADD	Introduces a routine modifier that you want to add to the UDR
MODIFY	Introduces a routine modifier for which you want to modify a value
DROP	Introduces a routine modifier that you want to remove from the UDR
MODIFY EXTERNAL NAME (for external UDRs only)	Introduces a new location for the executable file
WITH	Introduces all modifications

If the routine modifier is a Boolean value, MODIFY sets the value to be T (that is, it is the equivalent of using the keyword ADD to add the routine modifier). For example, both of the following statements alter the **func1** UDR so that it can be executed in parallel in the context of a parallelizable data query statement.

```
ALTER ROUTINE func1 WITH (MODIFY PARALLELIZABLE)

ALTER ROUTINE func1 WITH (ADD PARALLELIZABLE)
```

Altering Routine Modifiers Example

Suppose you have an external function **func1** that is set to handle null values and has a cost per invocation set to 40. The following ALTER ROUTINE statement adjusts the settings of the function by dropping the ability to handle null values, tunes the **func1** by changing the cost per invocation to 20, and indicates that the function can execute in parallel.

```
ALTER ROUTINE func1(char, int, boolean)
    WITH (
        DROP HANDLESNULLS,
        MODIFY PERCALL_COST = 20,
        ADD PARALLELIZABLE
        )
```

Note also, that because the name **func1** is not unique to the database, the data type parameters are specified so that the routine signature would be unique. If this function had a Specific Name, for example, **raise_sal**, specified when it was created, you could identify the function with the following first line:

```
ALTER SPECIFIC ROUTINE raise_sal
```

Related Information

Related Statements: ALTER FUNCTION, ALTER PROCEDURE, CREATE FUNCTION, CREATE PROCEDURE, DROP FUNCTION, DROP PROCEDURE, and DROP ROUTINE

For a discussion on how to create and use SPL routines, see the *Informix Guide to SQL: Tutorial*.

For a discussion of how to create and use external routines, see *Extending Informix Dynamic Server 2000*.

For information about how to create C UDRs, see the *DataBlade API Programmer's Manual*.

ALTER TABLE

Use the ALTER TABLE statement to modify the definition of a table.

Syntax

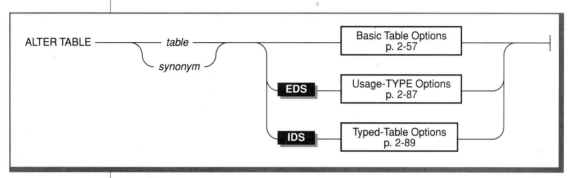

Element	Purpose	Restrictions	Syntax
synonym	Name of the synonym for the table to alter	The synonym and the table to which the synonym points must exist.	Database Object Name, p. 4-50
table	Name of the table to alter	The table must exist.	Database Object Name, p. 4-50

Usage

Altering a table on which a view depends might invalidate the view.

Warning: *The clauses available with this statement have varying performance implications. Before you undertake alter operations, check corresponding sections in your "Performance Guide" to review effects and strategies.*

Restrictions

You cannot alter a temporary table. You also cannot alter a violations or diagnostics table. In addition, you cannot add, drop, or modify a column if the table that contains the column has violations and diagnostics tables associated with it.

EDS

If a table has range fragmentation, the parts of this statement that you can use are the Usage-TYPE options, and the Lock-Mode clause. All other operations return an error.

If you have a static or raw table, the only information that you can alter is the usage type of the table. That is, the Usage-TYPE options are the only part of the ALTER TABLE statement that you can use. ♦

Privileges

To use the ALTER TABLE statement, you must meet one of the following conditions:

- You must have the DBA privilege on the database where the table resides.

- You must own the table.

- You must have the Alter privilege on the specified table and the Resource privilege on the database where the table resides.

- To add a referential constraint, you must have the DBA or References privilege on either the referenced columns or the referenced table.

- To drop a constraint, you must have the DBA privilege or be the owner of the constraint. If you are the owner of the constraint but not the owner of the table, you must have Alter privilege on the specified table. You do not need the References privilege to drop a constraint.

Basic-Table Options

With the ALTER TABLE statement, you can perform basic alter operations such as adding, modifying, or dropping columns and constraints, and changing the extent size and locking granularity of a table. The database server performs the alter operations in the order that you specify. If any of the actions fails, the entire operation is cancelled.

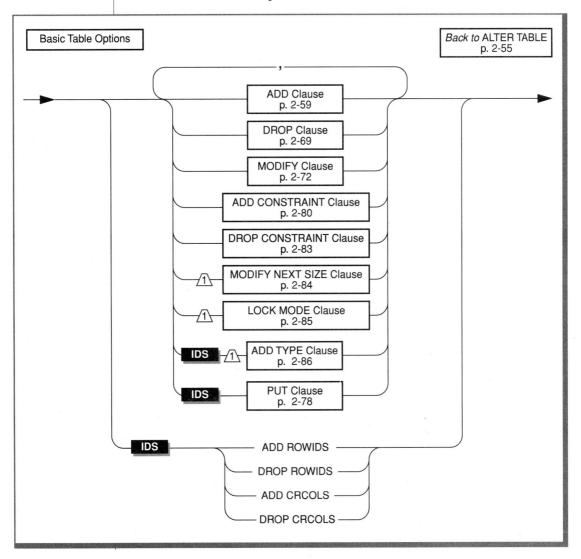

IDS

You can also associate a table with a named-row type or specify a new storage space to store large-object data.

In addition, you can add or drop rowid columns and shadow columns that for Enterprise Replication. However, you cannot specify these options in conjunction with any other alterations. ♦

IDS

Using the ADD ROWIDS Keywords

Use the ADD ROWIDS keywords to add a new column called **rowid** to a fragmented table. (Fragmented tables do not contain the hidden **rowid** column by default.)

When you add a **rowid** column, the database server assigns a unique number to each row that remains stable for the life of the row. The database server creates an index that it uses to find the physical location of the row. After you add the **rowid** column, each row of the table contains an additional 4 bytes to store the **rowid** value.

Tip: *Use the ADD ROWIDS clause only on fragmented tables. In nonfragmented tables, the* **rowid** *column remains unchanged. Informix recommends that you use primary keys as an access method rather than exploiting the* **rowid** *column.*

For additional information about the **rowid** column, refer to your *Administrator's Reference*.

IDS

Using the DROP ROWIDS Keywords

Use the DROP ROWIDS keywords to drop a **rowid** column that you added (with either the CREATE TABLE or ALTER FRAGMENT statement) to a fragmented table. You cannot drop the **rowid** column of a nonfragmented table.

IDS

Using the ADD CRCOLS Keywords

Use the ADD CRCOLS keywords to create the shadow columns, **cdrserver** and **cdrtime**, that Enterprise Replication uses for conflict resolution. You must add these columns before you can use time-stamp or UDR conflict resolution.

For more information, refer to "Using the WITH CRCOLS Option" on page 2-255 and to the *Guide to Informix Enterprise Replication*.

IDS

Using the DROP CRCOLS Keywords

Use the DROP CRCOLS keywords to drop the **cdrserver** and **cdrtime** shadow columns. You cannot drop these columns if Enterprise Replication is in use.

ADD Clause

Use the ADD clause to add a column to a table.

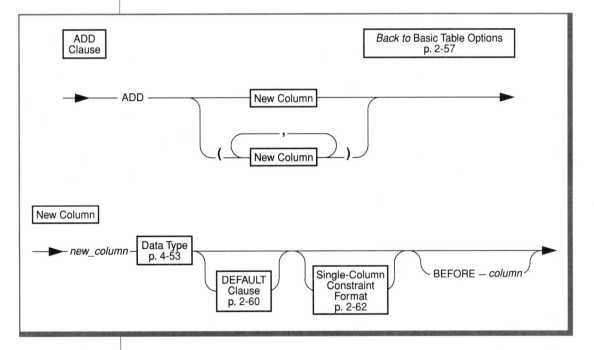

Element	Purpose	Restrictions	Syntax
column	Name of the column before which the new column is to be placed	The column must already exist in the table.	Identifier, p. 4-205
new_column	Name of the column that you are adding	You cannot add a serial column if the table contains data.	Identifier, p. 4-205

The following restrictions apply to the ADD clause:

- You cannot add a serial column to a table if the table contains data.

EDS

- In Enterprise Decision Server, you cannot add a column to a table that has a bit-mapped index. ♦

Using the BEFORE Option

Use the BEFORE option to specify the column before which a new column or list of columns is to be added.

If you do not include the BEFORE option, the database server adds the new column or list of columns to the end of the table definition by default.

In the following example, the BEFORE option directs the database server to add the **item_weight** column before the **total_price** column:

```
ALTER TABLE items
    ADD (item_weight DECIMAL(6,2) NOT NULL
        BEFORE total_price)
```

DEFAULT Clause

Use the DEFAULT clause to specify the default value that the database server should insert in a column when an explicit value for the column is not specified.

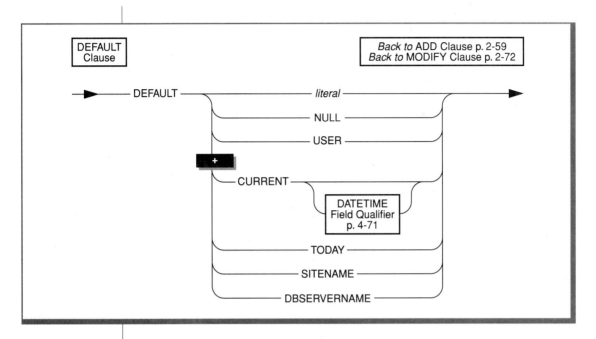

Element	Purpose	Restrictions	Syntax
literal	Literal term that defines alpha or numeric constant characters to use as the default value for the column	Term must be appropriate type for the column. See "Using a Literal as a Default Value" on page 2-235.	Expression, p. 4-73

You cannot place a default on serial columns.

If the table that you are altering already has rows in it when you add a column that contains a default value, the database server inserts the default value for all pre-existing rows.

For more information about the options of the DEFAULT clause, refer to "DEFAULT Clause" on page 2-234.

Example of a Literal Default Value

The following example adds a column to the **items** table. In **items**, the new column **item_weight** has a literal default value:

```
ALTER TABLE items
    ADD item_weight DECIMAL (6, 2) DEFAULT 2.00
    BEFORE total_price
```

In this example, each existing row in the **items** table has a default value of 2.00 for the **item_weight** column.

Single-Column Constraint Format

Use the Single-Column Constraint Format to associate constraints with a particular column.

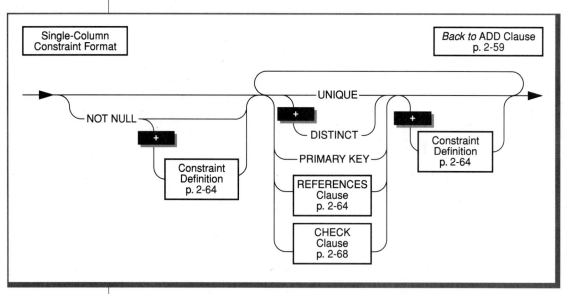

You cannot specify a primary-key or unique constraint on a new column if the table contains data. However, in the case of a unique constraint, the table can contain a *single* row of data. When you want to add a column with a primary-key constraint, the table must be empty when you issue the ALTER TABLE statement.

The following rules apply when you place primary-key or unique constraints on existing columns:

- When you place a primary-key or unique constraint on a column or set of columns, the database server creates an internal B-tree index on the constrained column or set of columns unless a user-created index was defined on the column or set of columns.

- When you place a primary-key or unique constraint on a column or set of columns, and a unique index already exists on that column or set of columns, the constraint shares the index. However, if the existing index allows duplicates, the database server returns an error. You must then drop the existing index before you add the constraint.

- When you place a primary-key or unique constraint on a column or set of columns, and a referential constraint already exists on that column or set of columns, the duplicate index is upgraded to unique (if possible), and the index is shared.

You cannot place a unique constraint on a BYTE or TEXT column, nor can you place referential constraints on these types of columns. You can place a check constraint on a BYTE or TEXT column. However, you can check only for IS NULL, IS NOT NULL, or LENGTH.

When you place a referential constraint on a column or set of columns, and an index already exists on that column or set of columns, the index is upgraded to unique (if possible) and the index is shared.

Using Not-Null Constraints with ADD

If a table contains data, when you add a column with a not-null constraint you must also include a DEFAULT clause. If the table is empty, no additional restrictions exist; that is, you can add a column and apply only the not-null constraint.

The following statement is valid whether or not the table contains data:

```
ALTER TABLE items
    ADD (item_weight DECIMAL(6,2)
    DEFAULT 2.0 NOT NULL
        BEFORE total_price)
```

Constraint Definition

IDS

Use the Constraint Definition portion of the ALTER TABLE statement to assign a name to a constraint and to set the mode of the constraint to disabled, enabled, or filtering. ♦

EDS

In Enterprise Decision Server, use the Constraint Definition portion of the ALTER TABLE statement to assign a name to a constraint. ♦

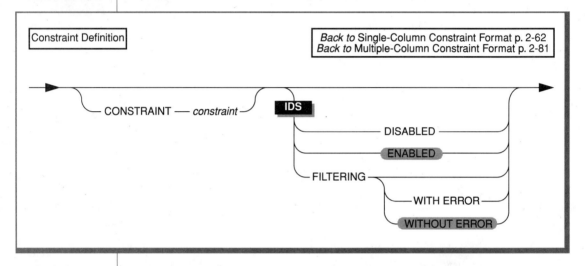

Element	Purpose	Restrictions	Syntax
constraint	Name assigned to the constraint	None.	Identifier, p. 4-205

For more information about constraint-mode options, see "Choosing a Constraint-Mode Option" on page 2-249.

REFERENCES Clause

The REFERENCES clause allows you to place a foreign-key reference on a column. The referenced column can be in the same table as the referencing column, or the referenced column can be in a different table in the same database.

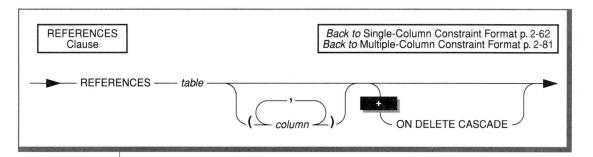

Element	Purpose	Restrictions	Syntax
column	Referenced column or set of columns in the referenced table	See "Restrictions on the Referenced Column" on page 2-66.	Identifier, p. 4-205
	If the referenced table is different from the referencing table, the default is the primary-key column. If the referenced table is the same as the referencing table, there is no default.		
table	Name of the referenced table	The referenced table can be the same table as the referencing table, or it can be a different table. The referenced and referencing tables must reside in the same database.	Database Object Name, p. 4-50

Restrictions on Referential Constraints

You must have the REFERENCES privilege to create a referential constraint.

Restrictions on the Referenced Column

You must observe the following restrictions on the *column* variable (the referenced column) in the REFERENCES clause:

- The referenced and referencing tables must be in the same database.
- The referenced column (or set of columns) must have a unique or primary-key constraint.
- The data types of the referencing and referenced columns must be identical.

  The only exception is that a referencing column must be an integer data type if the referenced column is a serial.
- You cannot place a referential constraint on a BYTE or TEXT column.
- A column-level REFERENCES clause can include only a single column name.
- The maximum number of columns in a table-level REFERENCES clause is 16.

IDS
- The total length of the columns in a table-level REFERENCES clause cannot exceed 390 bytes. ♦

EDS
- The total length of the columns in a table-level REFERENCES clause cannot exceed 255 bytes. ♦

Default Values for the Referenced Column

If the referenced table is different from the referencing table, you do not need to specify the referenced column; the default column is the primary-key column (or columns) of the referenced table. If the referenced table is the same as the referencing table, you must specify the referenced column.

The following example creates a new column in the **cust_calls** table, **ref_order**. The **ref_order** column is a foreign key that references the **order_num** column in the **orders** table.

```
ALTER TABLE cust_calls
    ADD ref_order INTEGER
    REFERENCES orders (order_num)
    BEFORE user_id
```

When you place a referential constraint on a column or set of columns, and a duplicate or unique index already exists on that column or set of columns, the index is shared.

Using the ON DELETE CASCADE Option

Use the ON DELETE CASCADE option to specify whether you want rows deleted in the child table when corresponding rows are deleted in the parent table. If you do not specify cascading deletes, the default behavior of the database server prevents you from deleting data in a table if other tables reference it.

If you specify this option, later when you delete a row in the parent table, the database server also deletes any rows associated with that row (foreign keys) in a child table. The principal advantage to the cascading deletes feature is that it allows you to reduce the quantity of SQL statements you need to perform delete actions.

For example, in the **stores_demo** database, the **stock** table contains the **stock_num** column as a primary key. The **catalog** table refers to the **stock_num** column as a foreign key. The following ALTER TABLE statements drop an existing foreign-key constraint (without cascading delete) and add a new constraint that specifies cascading deletes:

```
ALTER TABLE catalog DROP CONSTRAINT aa

ALTER TABLE catalog ADD CONSTRAINT
    (FOREIGN KEY (stock_num, manu_code) REFERENCES stock
    ON DELETE CASCADE CONSTRAINT ab)
```

With cascading deletes specified on the child table, in addition to deleting a stock item from the **stock** table, the delete cascades to the **catalog** table that is associated with the **stock_num** foreign key. This cascading delete works only if the **stock_num** that you are deleting was not ordered; otherwise, the constraint from the **items** table would disallow the cascading delete. For more information, see "Restrictions on DELETE When Tables Have Cascading Deletes" on page 2-376.

Restrictions

If a table has a trigger with a DELETE trigger event, you cannot define a cascading-delete referential constraint on that table. You receive an error when you attempt to add a referential constraint that specifies ON DELETE CASCADE to a table that has a delete trigger.

For information about syntax restrictions and locking implications when you delete rows from tables that have cascading deletes, see "Considerations When Tables Have Cascading Deletes" on page 2-375.

Locks Held During Creation of a Referential Constraint

When you create a referential constraint, the database server places an exclusive lock on the referenced table. The lock is released after you finish with the ALTER TABLE statement or at the end of a transaction (if you are altering a table in a database with transactions, and you are using transactions).

CHECK Clause

A check constraint designates a condition that must be met *before* data can be inserted into a column.

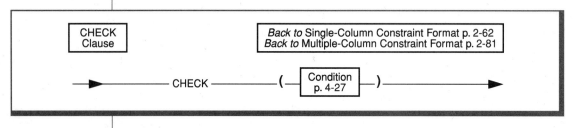

During an insert or update, if a row evaluates to *false* for any check constraint defined on a table, the database server returns an error. The database server does not return an error if a row evaluates to null for a check constraint. In some cases, you might wish to use both a check constraint and a NOT NULL constraint.

Check constraints are defined using *search conditions*. The search condition cannot contain the following items: subqueries, aggregates, host variables, rowids, or user-defined routines. In addition, the search condition cannot contain the following built-in functions: CURRENT, USER, SITENAME, DBSERVERNAME, or TODAY.

You cannot create check constraints for columns across tables. When you are using the ADD or MODIFY clause, the check constraint cannot depend upon values in other columns of the same table. The following example adds a new column, **unit_price**, to the **items** table and includes a check constraint that ensures that the entered value is greater than 0:

```
ALTER TABLE items
    ADD (unit_price MONEY (6.2) CHECK (unit_price > 0) )
```

To create a constraint that checks values in more than one column, use the ADD CONSTRAINT clause. The following example builds a constraint on the column that was added in the previous example. The check constraint now spans two columns in the table.

```
ALTER TABLE items ADD CONSTRAINT
    CHECK (unit_price < total_price)
```

DROP Clause

Use the DROP clause to drop one or more columns from a table.

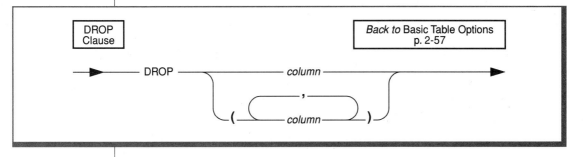

Element	Purpose	Restrictions	Syntax
column	Name of the column that you want to drop	The column must already exist in the table.	Identifier, p. 4-205
		If the column is referenced in a fragment expression, it cannot be dropped. If the column is the last column in the table, it cannot be dropped.	

You cannot issue an ALTER TABLE DROP statement that would drop every column from the table. At least one column must remain in the table.

You cannot drop a column that is part of a fragmentation strategy.

EDS   In Enterprise Decision Server, you cannot use the DROP clause if the table has a dependent GK index. ♦

How Dropping a Column Affects Constraints

When you drop a column, all constraints placed on that column are dropped, as described in the following list:

- All single-column constraints are dropped.
- All referential constraints that reference the column are dropped.
- All check constraints that reference the column are dropped.
- If the column is part of a multiple-column primary-key or unique constraint, the constraints placed on the multiple columns are also dropped. This action, in turn, triggers the dropping of all referential constraints that reference the multiple columns.

Because any constraints that are associated with a column are dropped when the column is dropped, the structure of other tables might also be altered when you use this clause. For example, if the dropped column is a unique or primary key that is referenced in other tables, those referential constraints also are dropped. Therefore the structure of those other tables is also altered.

How Dropping a Column Affects Triggers

In general, when you drop a column from a table, the triggers based on that table remain unchanged. However, if the column that you drop appears in the action clause of a trigger, you can invalidate the trigger.

The following statements illustrate the possible affects on triggers:

```
CREATE TABLE tab1 (i1 int, i2 int, i3 int);
CREATE TABLE tab2 (i4 int, i5 int);
CREATE TRIGGER col1trig UPDATE OF i2 ON tab1 BEFORE(INSERT
INTO tab2 VALUES(1,1));
ALTER TABLE tab2 DROP i4;
```

After the ALTER TABLE statement, **tab2** has only one column. The **col1trig** trigger is invalidated because the action clause as it is currently defined with values for two columns cannot occur.

If you drop a column that occurs in the triggering column list of an UPDATE trigger, the database server drops the column from the triggering column list. If the column is the only member of the triggering column list, the database server drops the trigger from the table. For more information on triggering columns in an UPDATE trigger, see "CREATE TRIGGER" on page 2-296.

If a trigger is invalidated when you alter the underlying table, drop and then recreate the trigger.

How Dropping a Column Affects Views

When you drop a column from a table, the views based on that table remain unchanged. That is, the database server does not automatically drop the corresponding columns from associated views.

The database server does not automatically drop the column because you can change the order of columns in a table by dropping a column and then adding a new column with the same name. In this case, views based on the altered table continue to work. However, they retain their original sequence of columns.

If a view is invalidated when you alter the underlying table, you must rebuild the view.

EDS

How Dropping a Column Affects a Generalized-Key Index

In Enterprise Decision Server, if you drop a column from a table that has a dependent GK index, all GK indexes on the table that refer to the dropped column are dropped. Any GK indexes on other tables that refer to the dropped column are also dropped.

MODIFY Clause

Use the MODIFY clause to change the data type of a column and the length of a character column, to add or change the default value for a column, and to allow or disallow nulls in a column.

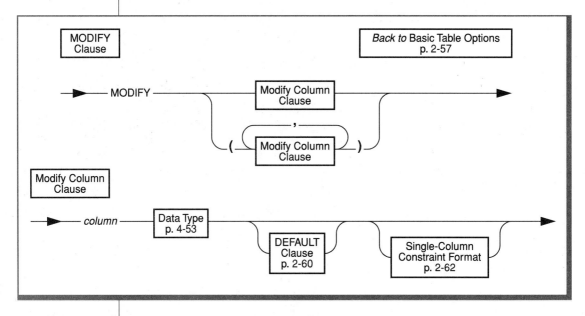

Element	Purpose	Restrictions	Syntax
column	Name of the column that you want to modify	The column must already exist in the table. The data type of the column cannot be a collection data type.	Identifier, p. 4-205

EDS

In Enterprise Decision Server, you cannot use the MODIFY clause if the table has a dependent GK index. ♦

IDS

You cannot change the data type of a column to be a collection type or a row type. ♦

When you modify a column, *all* attributes previously associated with that column (that is, default value, single-column check constraint, or referential constraint) are dropped. When you want certain attributes of the column to remain, such as PRIMARY KEY, you must re-specify those attributes. For example, if you are changing the data type of an existing column, **quantity**, to SMALLINT, and you want to keep the default value (in this case, 1) and non-null attributes for that column, you can issue the following ALTER TABLE statement:

```
ALTER TABLE items
    MODIFY (quantity SMALLINT DEFAULT 1 NOT NULL)
```

Tip: *Both attributes are specified again in the MODIFY clause.*

When you modify a column that has column constraints associated with it, the following constraints are dropped:

- All single-column constraints are dropped.
- All referential constraints that reference the column are dropped.
- If the modified column is part of a multiple-column primary-key or unique constraint, all referential constraints that reference the multiple columns also are dropped.

For example, if you modify a column that has a unique constraint, the unique constraint is dropped. If this column was referenced by columns in other tables, those referential constraints are also dropped. In addition, if the column is part of a multiple-column primary-key or unique constraint, the multiple-column constraints are not dropped, but any referential constraints placed on the column by other tables *are* dropped. For example, a column is part of a multiple-column primary-key constraint. This primary key is referenced by foreign keys in two other tables. When this column is modified, the multiple-column primary-key constraint is not dropped, but the referential constraints placed on it by the two other tables *are* dropped.

Using the MODIFY Clause in Different Situations

The characteristics of the object you are attempting to modify can affect how you handle your modifications.

Altering BYTE and TEXT Columns

You can use the MODIFY clause to change a BYTE column to a TEXT column, and vice versa. However, you cannot use the MODIFY clause to change a BYTE or TEXT column to any other type of column, and vice versa.

IDS

You can also use the MODIFY clause to change a BYTE column to a BLOB column and a TEXT column to a CLOB column. ♦

Altering the Next Serial Number

You can use the MODIFY clause to reset the next value of a serial column. You cannot set the next value below the current maximum value in the column because that action can cause the database server to generate duplicate numbers. However, you can set the next value to any value higher than the current maximum, which creates gaps in the sequence.

The following example sets the next serial number to 1000.

```
ALTER TABLE my_table MODIFY (serial_num serial (1000))
```

As an alternative, you can use the INSERT statement to create a gap in the sequence of a serial column. For more information, see "Inserting Values into Serial Columns" on page 2-543.

IDS

Altering the Next Serial Number of a Typed Table

You can set the initial serial number or modify the next serial number for a row-type field with the MODIFY clause of the ALTER TABLE statement. (You cannot set the start number for a serial field when you create a row type.)

Suppose you have row types **parent**, **child1**, **child2**, and **child3**.

```
CREATE ROW TYPE parent (a int);
CREATE ROW TYPE child1 (s serial) UNDER parent;
CREATE ROW TYPE child2 (b float, s8 serial8) UNDER child1;
CREATE ROW TYPE child3 (d int) UNDER child2;
```

You then create corresponding typed tables:

```
CREATE TABLE OF TYPE parent;
CREATE TABLE OF TYPE child1 UNDER parent;
CREATE TABLE OF TYPE child2 UNDER child1;
CREATE TABLE OF TYPE child3 UNDER child2;
```

To change the next serial and next serial 8 numbers to 75, you can enter the following command:

```
ALTER TABLE child3tab
    MODIFY (s serial(75), s8 serial8(75))
```

When the ALTER TABLE statement executes, the database server updates corresponding serial columns in the **child1**, **child2**, and **child3** tables.

Altering the Structure of Tables

When you use the MODIFY clause, you can also alter the structure of other tables. If the modified column is referenced by other tables, those referential constraints are dropped. You must add those constraints to the referencing tables again, using the ALTER TABLE statement.

When you change the data type of an existing column, all data is converted to the new data type, including numbers to characters and characters to numbers (if the characters represent numbers). The following statement changes the data type of the **quantity** column:

```
ALTER TABLE items MODIFY (quantity CHAR(6))
```

When a primary-key or unique constraint exists, however, conversion takes place only if it does not violate the constraint. If a data-type conversion would result in duplicate values (by changing FLOAT to SMALLFLOAT, for example, or by truncating CHAR values), the ALTER TABLE statement fails.

Modifying Tables for Null Values

You can modify an existing column that formerly permitted nulls to disallow nulls, provided that the column contains no null values. To do this, specify MODIFY with the same column name and data type and the NOT NULL keywords. The NOT NULL keywords create a not-null constraint on the column.

You can modify an existing column that did not permit nulls to permit nulls. To do this, specify MODIFY with the column name and the existing data type, and omit the NOT NULL keywords. The omission of the NOT NULL keywords drops the not-null constraint on the column. If a unique index exists on the column, you can remove it using the DROP INDEX statement.

An alternative method of permitting nulls in an existing column that did not permit nulls is to use the DROP CONSTRAINT clause to drop the not-null constraint on the column.

IDS

Adding a Constraint When Existing Rows Violate the Constraint

If you use the MODIFY clause to add a constraint in the enabled mode and receive an error message because existing rows would violate the constraint, you can take the following steps to add the constraint successfully:

1. Add the constraint in the disabled mode.

   Issue the ALTER TABLE statement again, but this time specify the DISABLED keyword in the MODIFY clause.

2. Start a violations and diagnostics table for the target table with the START VIOLATIONS TABLE statement.

3. Issue a SET statement to switch the database object mode of the constraint to the enabled mode.

   When you issue this statement, existing rows in the target table that violate the constraint are duplicated in the violations table; however, you receive an integrity-violation error message, and the constraint remains disabled.

4. Issue a SELECT statement on the violations table to retrieve the nonconforming rows that are duplicated from the target table.

   You might need to join the violations and diagnostics tables to get all the necessary information.

5. Take corrective action on the rows in the target table that violate the constraint.

6. After you fix all the nonconforming rows in the target table, issue the SET statement again to switch the disabled constraint to the enabled mode.

This time the constraint is enabled, and no integrity-violation error message is returned because all rows in the target table now satisfy the new constraint.

How Modifying a Column Affects a Generalized-Key Index

In Enterprise Decision Server, when you modify a column, all GK indexes that reference the column are dropped if the column is used in the GK index in a way that is incompatible with the new data type of the column.

For example, if a numeric column is changed to a character column, any GK indexes involving that column are dropped if they involve arithmetic expressions.

How Modifying a Column Affects Triggers

If you modify a column that appears in the triggering column list of an UPDATE trigger, the trigger is unchanged.

When you modify a column in a table, the triggers based on that table remain unchanged. However, the column modification might invalidate the trigger.

The following statements illustrate the possible affects on triggers:

```
CREATE TABLE tab1 (i1 int, i2 int, i3 int);
CREATE TABLE tab2 (i4 int, i5 int);
CREATE TRIGGER col1trig UPDATE OF i2 ON tab1 BEFORE(INSERT
INTO tab2 VALUES(1,1));
ALTER TABLE tab2 MODIFY i4 char;
```

After the ALTER TABLE statement, column **i4** accepts only character values. Because character columns accept only values enclosed in quotation marks, the action clause of the **col1trig** trigger is invalidated.

If a trigger is invalidated when you modify the underlying table, drop and then recreate the trigger.

How Modifying a Column Affects Views

When you modify a column in a table, the views based on that table remain unchanged. If a view is invalidated when you alter the underlying table, you must rebuild the view.

IDS

PUT Clause

Use the PUT clause to specify the storage space (an sbspace) for a column that contains smart large objects. You can use this clause to specify storage characteristics for a new column or replace the storage characteristics of an existing column.

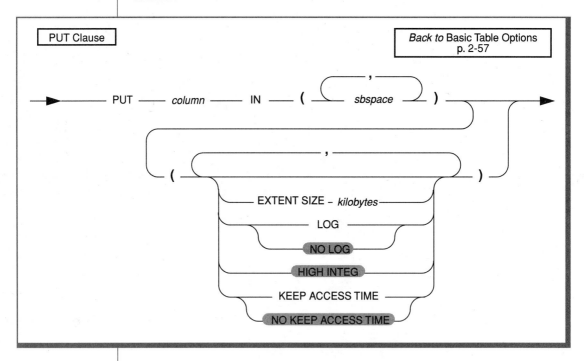

Element	Purpose	Restrictions	Syntax
column	Name of the column to store in the specified sbspace	Column must contain a user-defined type, complex type, BLOB, or CLOB data type.	Identifier, p. 4-205
		The column cannot be in the form *column.field*. That is, the smart large object that you are storing cannot be one field of a row type.	
kilobytes	Number of kilobytes to allocate for the extent size	The number must be an integer value.	Literal Number, p. 4-237
sbspace	Name of an area of storage used for smart large objects	The sbspace must exist.	Identifier, p. 4-205

When you modify the storage characteristics of an existing column, *all* attributes previously associated with the storage space for that column are dropped. When you want certain attributes to remain, you must respecify those attributes. For example, to retain logging, you must respecify the LOG keyword.

When you modify the storage characteristics of a column that holds smart large objects, the database server does not alter smart large objects that already exist. The database server applies the new storage characteristics to only those smart large objects that are inserted after the ALTER TABLE statement takes effect.

For more information on the available storage characteristics, refer to the counterpart of this section in the CREATE TABLE statement, "PUT Clause" on page 2-273. For a discussion of large-object characteristics, refer to "Large-Object Data Types" on page 4-62.

ADD CONSTRAINT Clause

Use the ADD CONSTRAINT clause to specify a constraint on a new or existing column or on a set of columns.

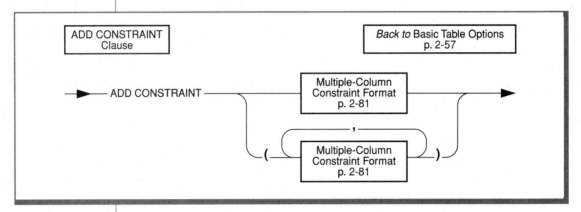

For example, to add a unique constraint to the **fname** and **lname** columns of the **customer** table, use the following statement:

```
ALTER TABLE customer
    ADD CONSTRAINT UNIQUE (lname, fname)
```

To name the constraint, change the preceding statement, as the following example shows:

```
ALTER TABLE customer
    ADD CONSTRAINT UNIQUE (lname, fname) CONSTRAINT u_cust
```

When you do not provide a constraint name, the database server provides one. You can find the name of the constraint in the **sysconstraints** system catalog table. For more information about the **sysconstraints** system catalog table, see the *Informix Guide to SQL: Reference*.

Multiple-Column Constraint Format

Use the Multiple-Column Constraint Format option to assign a constraint to one column or a set of columns.

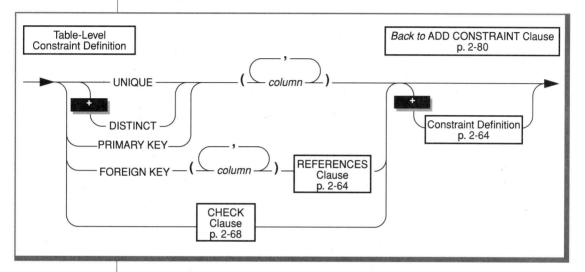

Element	Purpose	Restrictions	Syntax
column	Name of the column or columns on which the constraint is placed	The maximum number of columns is 16, and the total length of the list of columns cannot exceed 255 bytes.	Identifier, p. 4-237

A constraint that involves multiple columns can include no more than 16 column names.

- The total length of the list of columns cannot exceed 390 bytes. ◆
- The total length of the list of columns cannot exceed 255 bytes. ◆

You can assign a name to the constraint and set its mode by means of "Constraint Definition" on page 2-64.

Adding a Primary-Key or Unique Constraint

When you place a primary-key or unique constraint on a column or set of columns, those columns must contain unique values.

When you place a primary-key or unique constraint on a column or set of columns, the database server checks for existing constraints and indexes.

- If a user-created unique index already exists on that column or set of columns, the constraint shares the index.

- If a user-created index that allows duplicates already exists on that column or set of columns, the database server returns an error.

  You must drop the existing index before adding the primary-key or unique constraint.

- If a referential constraint already exists on that column or set of columns, the duplicate index is upgraded to unique (if possible) and the index is shared.

- If no referential constraint or user-created index exists on that column or set of columns, the database server creates an internal B-tree index on the specified columns.

Adding a Referential Constraint

When you place a referential constraint on a column or set of columns, and an index already exists on that column or set of columns, the index is shared.

Privileges Required for Adding Constraints

When you own the table or have the Alter privilege on the table, you can create a check, primary-key, or unique constraint on the table and specify yourself as the owner of the constraint. To add a referential constraint, you must have the References privilege on either the referenced columns or the referenced table. When you have the DBA privilege, you can create constraints for other users.

IDS

Recovery from Constraint Violations

If you use the ADD CONSTRAINT clause to add a constraint in the enabled mode and receive an error message because existing rows would violate the constraint, you can follow a procedure to add the constraint successfully. See "Adding a Constraint When Existing Rows Violate the Constraint" on page 2-76.

DROP CONSTRAINT Clause

Use the DROP CONSTRAINT clause to drop a named constraint.

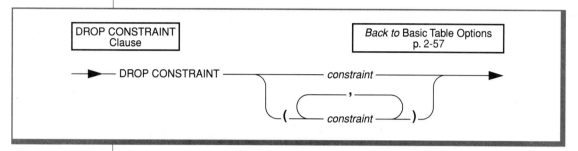

Element	Purpose	Restrictions	Syntax
constraint	Name of the constraint that you want to drop	The constraint must exist.	Database Object Name, p. 4-50

To drop an existing constraint, specify the DROP CONSTRAINT keywords and the name of the constraint. The following statement is an example of dropping a constraint:

```
ALTER TABLE manufact DROP CONSTRAINT con_name
```

If a constraint name is not specified when the constraint is created, the database server generates the name. You can query the **sysconstraints** system catalog table for the name and owner of a constraint. For example, to find the name of the constraint placed on the **items** table, you can issue the following statement:

```
SELECT constrname FROM  sysconstraints
    WHERE tabid = (SELECT tabid FROM systables
        WHERE tabname = 'items')
```

When you drop a primary-key or unique constraint that has a corresponding foreign key, the referential constraints are dropped. For example, if you drop the primary-key constraint on the **order_num** column in the **orders** table and **order_num** exists in the **items** table as a foreign key, that referential relationship is also dropped.

MODIFY NEXT SIZE Clause

Use the MODIFY NEXT SIZE clause to change the size of new extents.

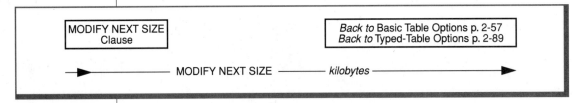

Element	Purpose	Restrictions	Syntax
kilobytes	Length in kilobytes that you want to assign for the next extent for this table	The minimum length is four times the disk-page size on your system. For example, if you have a 2-kilobyte page system, the minimum length is 8 kilobytes. The maximum length is equal to the chunk size.	Expression, p. 4-73

If you want to specify an extent size of 32 kilobytes, use a statement such as the one in the following example:

```
ALTER TABLE customer MODIFY NEXT SIZE 32
```

When you use this clause, the size of existing extents does not change. You cannot change the size of existing extents without unloading all of the data.

Changing the Size of Existing Extents

To change the size of existing extents, you must unload all of the data, modify the extent and next-extent sizes in the CREATE TABLE statement of the database schema, re-create the database, and reload the data. For information about optimizing extents, see your *Administrator's Guide*.

LOCK MODE Clause

Use the LOCK MODE keywords to change the locking granularity of a table.

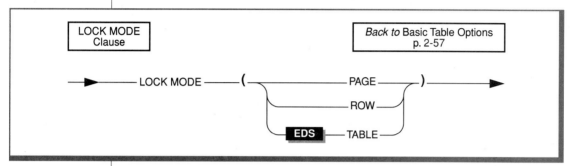

The following table describes the locking-granularity options available.

Locking Granularity Option	Purpose
ROW	Obtains and releases one lock per row.
	Row-level locking provides the highest level of concurrency. However, if you are using many rows at one time, the lock-management overhead can become significant. You can also exceed the maximum number of locks available, depending on the configuration of your database-server.
PAGE	Obtains and releases one lock on a whole page of rows.
	This is the default locking granularity.
	Page-level locking is especially useful when you know that the rows are grouped into pages in the same order that you are using to process all the rows. For example, if you are processing the contents of a table in the same order as its cluster index, page locking is especially appropriate.
TABLE (EDS only)	Places a lock on the entire table.
	This type of lock reduces update concurrency in comparison to row and page locks. A table lock reduces the lock-management overhead for the table
	Multiple read-only transactions can still access the table.

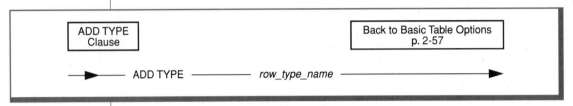

IDS

ADD TYPE Clause

Use the ADD TYPE clause to convert a table that is not based on a named-row type into a typed table.

Element	Purpose	Restrictions	Syntax
row_type_name	Name of the row type being added to the table	The field types of this row type must match the column types of the table.	Data Type, p. 4-53

When you use the ADD TYPE clause, you assign a named-row type to a table whose columns match the fields of the row type.

You cannot add a type to a fragmented table that has rowids.

You cannot combine the ADD TYPE clause with any clause that changes the structure of the table. That is, you cannot use an ADD, DROP, or MODIFY clause in the same statement as the ADD TYPE clause.

Tip: *To change the data type of a column, use the MODIFY clause. The ADD TYPE clause does not allow you to change column data types.*

When you add a named-row type to a table, be sure that:

- the type already exists.
- the fields in the named-row type match the column types in the table.

You must have the Usage privilege to add a type to a table.

EDS

Usage-TYPE Options

In Enterprise Decision Server, use the Usage-TYPE options to specify that the table have particular characteristics that can improve various bulk operations on it.

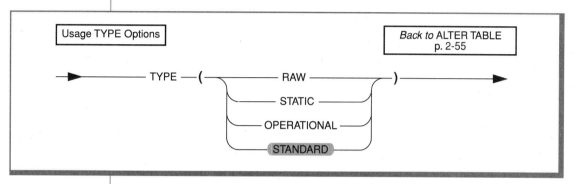

Other than the default option (STANDARD) that is used for OLTP databases, these Usage-TYPE options are used primarily to improve performance in data warehousing databases.

A table can have any of the following usage characteristics.

Option	Purpose
RAW	Non-logging table that cannot have indexes or referential constraints but can be updated
	Use this type for quickly loading data. With this type you take advantage of light appends and avoid the overhead of logging, checking constraints, and building indexes.

Option	Purpose
STATIC	Non-logging table that can contain index and referential constraints but cannot be updated
	Use this type for read-only operations because there is no logging or locking overhead.
OPERATIONAL	Logging table that uses light appends and cannot be restored from archive
	Use this type on tables that are refreshed frequently because light appends allow the quick addition of many rows.
STANDARD	Logging table that allows rollback, recovery, and restoration from archives
	This type is the default.
	Use this type for all the recovery and constraints functionality that you want on your OLTP databases.

For a more detailed description, refer to your *Administrator's Guide*.

Restrictions on the Usage-TYPE Options

The usage-TYPE options have the following restrictions:

- You cannot change the usage type if the table has a dependent GK index.
- You must perform a level-0 archive before the usage type of a table can be altered to STANDARD from any other type.
- If you want to change the usage type of a table to RAW, you must drop all indexes on the table before you do so.
- If you have triggers defined on the table, you cannot change the usage type to RAW or STATIC.

  That is, raw and static tables do not support triggers.
- You cannot use this clause with SCRATCH or TEMP tables.

  That is, you cannot change any of these types of tables to either a SCRATCH or TEMP table. Similarly, you cannot change a SCRATCH or TEMP table to any of these types of tables.

IDS

Typed Tables Options

In Dynamic Server, the database server performs the actions in the ALTER TABLE statement in the order that you specify. If any of the actions fails, the entire operation is cancelled.

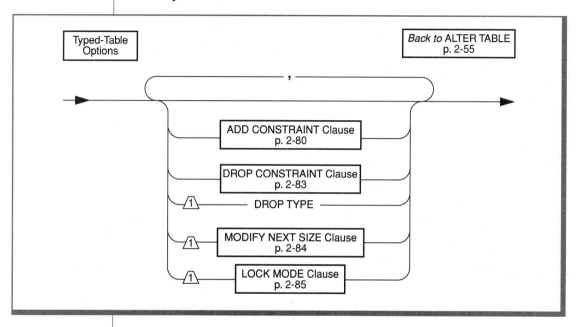

Altering Subtables and Supertables

The following considerations apply to tables that are part of inheritance hierarchies:

■ For subtables, ADD CONSTRAINT and DROP CONSTRAINT are not allowed on inherited constraints.

■ For supertables, ADD CONSTRAINT and DROP CONSTRAINT propagate to all subtables.

DROP TYPE Option

Use the DROP TYPE option to drop the type from a table. DROP TYPE removes the association between a table and a named-row type. You must drop the type from a typed table before you can modify, drop, or change the data type of a column in the table.

If a table is part of a table hierarchy, you cannot drop its type unless it is the last subtype in the hierarchy. That is, you can only drop a type from a table if that table has no subtables. When you drop the type of a subtable, it is automatically removed from the hierarchy. The table rows are deleted from all indexes defined by its supertables.

Related Information

Related statements: CREATE TABLE, DROP TABLE, LOCK TABLE, and SET Database Object Mode

For discussions of data-integrity constraints and the ON DELETE CASCADE option, see the *Informix Guide to SQL: Tutorial*.

For a discussion of database and table creation, see the *Informix Guide to Database Design and Implementation*.

For information on how to maximize performance when you make table modifications, see your *Performance Guide*.

BEGIN WORK

Use the BEGIN WORK statement to start a transaction (a sequence of database operations that the COMMIT WORK or ROLLBACK WORK statement terminates). Use the BEGIN WORK WITHOUT REPLICATION statement to start a transaction that does not replicate to other database servers.

Syntax

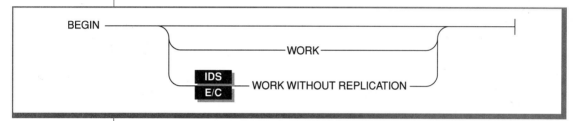

Usage

Each row that an UPDATE, DELETE, or INSERT statement affects during a transaction is locked and remains locked throughout the transaction. A transaction that contains many such statements or that contains statements affecting many rows can exceed the limits that your operating system or the database server configuration imposes on the maximum number of simultaneous locks. If no other user is accessing the table, you can avoid locking limits and reduce locking overhead by locking the table with the LOCK TABLE statement after you begin the transaction. Like other locks, this table lock is released when the transaction terminates. The example of a transaction on "Example of BEGIN WORK" on page 2-93 includes a LOCK TABLE statement.

Important: *You can issue the BEGIN WORK statement only if a transaction is not in progress. If you issue a BEGIN WORK statement while you are in a transaction, the database server returns an error.*

In ESQL/C, if you use the BEGIN WORK statement within a UDR called by a WHENEVER statement, specify WHENEVER SQLERROR CONTINUE and WHENEVER SQLWARNING CONTINUE before the ROLLBACK WORK statement. These statements prevent the program from looping if the ROLLBACK WORK statement encounters an error or a warning. ♦

WORK Keyword

The WORK keyword is optional in a BEGIN WORK statement. The following two statements are equivalent:

```
BEGIN;

BEGIN WORK;
```

ANSI

BEGIN WORK and ANSI-Compliant Databases

In an ANSI-compliant database, you do not need the BEGIN WORK statement because transactions are implicit. A warning is generated if you use a BEGIN WORK statement immediately after one of the following statements:

- DATABASE
- COMMIT WORK
- CREATE DATABASE
- ROLLBACK WORK

An error is generated if you use a BEGIN WORK statement after any other statement.

IDS

E/C

BEGIN WORK WITHOUT REPLICATION

When you use Enterprise Replication for data replication, you can use the BEGIN WORK WITHOUT REPLICATION statement to start a transaction that does not replicate to other database servers.

You cannot execute the BEGIN WORK WITHOUT REPLICATION statement as a stand-alone embedded statement within an ESQL/C application. Instead you must execute this statement indirectly. You can use either of the following methods:

- You can use a combination of the PREPARE and EXECUTE statements to prepare and execute the BEGIN WORK WITHOUT REPLICATION statement.
- You can use the EXECUTE IMMEDIATE statement to prepare and execute the BEGIN WORK WITHOUT REPLICATION statement in a single step.

You cannot use the DECLARE cursor CURSOR WITH HOLD with the BEGIN WORK WITHOUT REPLICATION statement.

For more information about data replication, see the *Guide to Informix Enterprise Replication*.

Example of BEGIN WORK

The following code fragment shows how you might place statements within a transaction. The transaction is made up of the statements that occur between the BEGIN WORK and COMMIT WORK statements. The transaction locks the **stock** table (LOCK TABLE), updates rows in the **stock** table (UPDATE), deletes rows from the **stock** table (DELETE), and inserts a row into the **manufact** table (INSERT). The database server must perform this sequence of operations either completely or not at all. The database server guarantees that all the statements are completely and perfectly committed to disk, or the database is restored to the same state as before the transaction began.

```
BEGIN WORK;
    LOCK TABLE stock;
    UPDATE stock SET unit_price = unit_price * 1.10
        WHERE manu_code = 'KAR';
    DELETE FROM stock WHERE description = 'baseball bat';
    INSERT INTO manufact (manu_code, manu_name, lead_time)
        VALUES ('LYM', 'LYMAN', 14);
COMMIT WORK;
```

Related Information

Related statements: COMMIT WORK, ROLLBACK WORK

For discussions of transactions and locking, see the *Informix Guide to SQL: Tutorial*.

E/C

CLOSE

Use the CLOSE statement when you no longer need to refer to the rows that a select or function cursor produced or when you want to flush and close an insert cursor.

Use this statement with ESQL/C.

Syntax

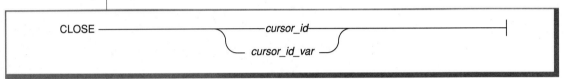

Element	Purpose	Restrictions	Syntax
cursor_id	Name of the cursor to close	The DECLARE statement must have previously declared the cursor.	Identifier, p. 4-205
cursor_id_var	Host variable that holds the value of cursor_id	Host variable must be a character data type. The cursor must be declared. In ANSI-compliant databases, before you can close a cursor, the cursor must be open.	Name must conform to language-specific rules for variable names.

Usage

Closing a cursor makes the cursor unusable for any statements except OPEN or FREE and releases resources that the database server had allocated to the cursor. A CLOSE statement treats a cursor that is associated with an INSERT statement differently than one that is associated with a SELECT or EXECUTE FUNCTION (or EXECUTE PROCEDURE) statement.

You can close a cursor that was never opened or that has already been closed. No action is taken in these cases.

ANSI

In an ANSI-compliant database, the database server returns an error if you close a cursor that was not open. ♦

Closing a Select or Function Cursor

When a cursor identifier is associated with a SELECT or EXECUTE FUNCTION (or EXECUTE PROCEDURE) statement, closing the cursor terminates the SELECT or EXECUTE FUNCTION (or EXECUTE PROCEDURE) statement. The database server releases all resources that it might have allocated to the active set of rows, for example, a temporary table that it used to hold an ordered set. The database server also releases any locks that it might have held on rows that were selected through the cursor. If a transaction contains the CLOSE statement, the database server does not release the locks until you execute COMMIT WORK or ROLLBACK WORK.

After you close a select or function cursor, you cannot execute a FETCH statement that names that cursor until you have reopened it.

Closing an Insert Cursor

When a cursor identifier is associated with an INSERT statement, the CLOSE statement writes any remaining buffered rows into the database. The number of rows that were successfully inserted into the database is returned in the third element of the **sqlerrd** array, **sqlca.sqlerrd[2]**, in the **sqlca** structure. For information on using SQLERRD to count the total number of rows that were inserted, see "Error Checking" on page 2-601.

The SQLCODE field of the **sqlca** structure, **sqlca.sqlcode**, indicates the result of the CLOSE statement for an insert cursor. If all buffered rows are successfully inserted, SQLCODE is set to zero. If an error is encountered, the **sqlca.sqlcode** field in the SQLCODE is set to a negative error message number.

When SQLCODE is zero, the row buffer space is released, and the cursor is closed; that is, you cannot execute a PUT or FLUSH statement that names the cursor until you reopen it.

Tip: *When you encounter an **SQLCODE** error, a corresponding **SQLSTATE** error value also exists. For information about how to get the message text, check the GET DIAGNOSTICS statement.*

If the insert is not successful, the number of successfully inserted rows is stored in **sqlerrd**. Any buffered rows that follow the last successfully inserted row are discarded. Because the insert fails, the CLOSE statement fails also, and the cursor is not closed. For example, a CLOSE statement can fail if insufficient disk space prevents some of the rows from being inserted. In this case, a second CLOSE statement can be successful because no buffered rows exist. An OPEN statement can also be successful because the OPEN statement performs an implicit close.

IDS

Closing a Collection Cursor

You can declare both select and insert cursors on collection variables. Such cursors are called collection cursors. Use the CLOSE statement to deallocate resources that have been allocated for the collection cursor.

For more information on how to use a collection cursor, see the following sections: "Fetching From a Collection Cursor" on page 2-466 and "Inserting into a Collection Cursor" on page 2-599.

Using End of Transaction to Close a Cursor

The COMMIT WORK and ROLLBACK WORK statements close all cursors except those that are declared with hold. It is better to close all cursors explicitly, however. For select or function cursors, this action simply makes the intent of the program clear. It also helps to avoid a logic error if the WITH HOLD clause is later added to the declaration of a cursor.

For an insert cursor, it is important to use the CLOSE statement explicitly so that you can test the error code. Following the COMMIT WORK statement, SQLCODE reflects the result of the COMMIT statement, not the result of closing cursors. If you use a COMMIT WORK statement without first using a CLOSE statement, and if an error occurs while the last buffered rows are being written to the database, the transaction is still committed.

For how to use insert cursors and the WITH HOLD clause, see "DECLARE" on page 2-349.

ANSI

In an ANSI-compliant database, a cursor cannot be closed implicitly. You must issue a CLOSE statement. ◆

Related Information

Related statements: DECLARE, FETCH, FLUSH, FREE, OPEN, PUT, and SET
AUTOFREE

For an introductory discussion of cursors, see the *Informix Guide to SQL:
Tutorial*.

For a more advanced discussion of cursors, see the *Informix ESQL/C
Programmer's Manual*.

CLOSE DATABASE

Use the CLOSE DATABASE statement to close the current database.

Syntax

```
CLOSE DATABASE──────────────────────────────────────────────────┤
```

Usage

When you issue a CLOSE DATABASE statement, you can issue only the following SQL statements immediately after it:

- CONNECT
- CREATE DATABASE
- DATABASE
- DROP DATABASE
- DISCONNECT

  This statement is valid only if an explicit connection existed before you issued the CLOSE DATABASE statement.

Issue the CLOSE DATABASE statement before you drop the current database.

If your database has transactions, and if you have started a transaction, you must issue a COMMIT WORK statement before you use the CLOSE DATABASE statement.

The following example shows how to use the CLOSE DATABASE statement to drop the current database:

```
DATABASE stores_demo
 .
 .
 .
CLOSE DATABASE
DROP DATABASE stores_demo
```

E/C

In ESQL/C, the CLOSE DATABASE statement cannot appear in a multi-statement PREPARE operation.

If you use the CLOSE DATABASE statement within a UDR called by a WHENEVER statement, specify WHENEVER SQLERROR CONTINUE and WHENEVER SQLWARNING CONTINUE before the ROLLBACK WORK statement. This action prevents the program from looping if the ROLLBACK WORK statement encounters an error or a warning.

When you issue the CLOSE DATABASE statement, declared cursors are no longer valid. You must re-declare any cursors that you want to use. ♦

Related Information

Related statements: CONNECT, CREATE DATABASE, DATABASE, DISCONNECT, and DROP DATABASE

COMMIT WORK

Use the COMMIT WORK statement to commit all modifications made to the database from the beginning of a transaction. This statement informs the database server that you reached the end of a series of statements that must succeed as a single unit. The database server takes the required steps to make sure that all modifications made by the transaction are completed correctly and committed to disk.

Syntax

```
COMMIT ─────────────────────────────────────────┤
                        └─ WORK ─┘
```

Usage

Use the COMMIT WORK statement when you are sure you want to keep changes that are made to the database from the beginning of a transaction. Use the COMMIT WORK statement only at the end of a multistatement operation.

The COMMIT WORK statement releases all row and table locks.

E/C

In ESQL/C, the COMMIT WORK statement closes all open cursors except those declared with hold. ◆

WORK Keyword

The WORK keyword is optional in a COMMIT WORK statement. The following two statements are equivalent:

```
COMMIT;

COMMIT WORK;
```

Example

The following example shows a transaction bounded by BEGIN WORK and COMMIT WORK statements. In this example, the user first deletes the row from the **call_type** table where the value of the **call_code** column is 0. The user then inserts a new row in the **call_type** table where the value of the **call_code** column is S. The database server guarantees that both operations succeed or else neither succeeds.

```
BEGIN WORK;
    DELETE FROM call_type WHERE call_code = '0';
    INSERT INTO call_type VALUES ('S', 'order status');
COMMIT WORK;
```

Issuing COMMIT WORK in a Database That Is Not ANSI Compliant

In a database that is not ANSI compliant, if you initiate a transaction with a BEGIN WORK statement, you must issue a COMMIT WORK statement at the end of the transaction. If you fail to issue a COMMIT WORK statement in this case, the database server rolls back the modifications to the database that the transaction made.

However, if you do not issue a BEGIN WORK statement, the database server executes each statement within its own transaction. These single-statement transactions do not require either a BEGIN WORK statement or a COMMIT WORK statement.

ANSI

Issuing COMMIT WORK in an ANSI-Compliant Database

In an ANSI-compliant database, you do not need to mark the beginning of a transaction. You only need to mark the end of each transaction. An implicit transaction is always in effect. A new transaction starts automatically after each COMMIT WORK or ROLLBACK WORK statement.

You must issue an explicit COMMIT WORK statement to mark the end of each transaction. If you fail to do so, the database server rolls back the modifications to the database that the transaction made.

Related Information

Related statements: BEGIN WORK, ROLLBACK WORK, and DECLARE

For a discussion of concepts related to transactions, see the *Informix Guide to SQL: Tutorial*.

CONNECT

Use the CONNECT statement to connect to a database environment.

Syntax

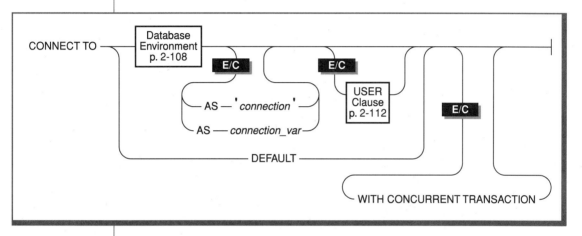

Element	Purpose	Restrictions	Syntax
connection	Quoted string that assigns a name to the connection	Each connection name must be unique.	Quoted String, p. 4-260
connection_var	Host variable that holds the value of connection	Variable must be a fixed-length character data type.	Name must conform to language-specific rules for variable names.

Usage

The CONNECT statement connects an application to a *database environment*. The database environment can be a database, a database server, or a database and a database server. If the application successfully connects to the specified database environment, the connection becomes the current connection for the application. SQL statements fail if no current connection exists between an application and a database server. If you specify a database name, the database server opens the database. You cannot use the CONNECT statement in a PREPARE statement.

An application can connect to several database environments at the same time, and it can establish multiple connections to the same database environment, provided each connection has a unique connection name.

UNIX

On UNIX, the only restriction on establishing multiple connections to the same database environment is that an application can establish only one connection to each local server that uses the shared-memory connection mechanism. To find out whether a local server uses the shared-memory connection mechanism or the local-loopback connection mechanism, examine the **$INFORMIXDIR/etc/sqlhosts** file. For more information on the **sqlhosts** file, refer to your *Administrator's Guide*. ♦

WIN NT

On Windows NT, the local connection mechanism is named pipes. Multiple connections to the local server from one client can exist. ♦

Only one connection is current at any time; other connections are dormant. The application cannot interact with a database through a dormant connection. When an application establishes a new connection, that connection becomes current, and the previous current transaction becomes dormant. You can make a dormant connection current with the SET CONNECTION statement. For more information, see "SET CONNECTION" on page 2-694.

Privileges for Executing the CONNECT Statement

The current user, or PUBLIC, must have the Connect database privilege on the database specified in the CONNECT statement.

The user who executes the CONNECT statement cannot have the same user name as an existing role in the database.

For information on using the USER clause to specify an alternate user name when the CONNECT statement connects to a database server on a remote host, see "USER Clause" on page 2-112.

Connection Identifiers

The optional connection name is a unique identifier that an application can use to refer to a connection in subsequent SET CONNECTION and DISCONNECT statements. If the application does not provide a connection name (or a connection-host variable), it can refer to the connection using the database environment. If the application makes more than one connection to the same database environment, however, each connection must have a unique connection name.

After you associate a connection name with a connection, you can refer to the connection using only that connection name.

The value of a connection name is case sensitive.

Connection Context

Each connection encompasses a set of information that is called the *connection context*. The connection context includes the name of the current user, the information that the database environment associates with this name, and information on the state of the connection (such as whether an active transaction is associated with the connection). The connection context is saved when an application becomes dormant, and this context is restored when the application becomes current again. (For more information on dormant connections, see "Making a Dormant Connection the Current Connection" on page 2-695.)

DEFAULT Option

Use the DEFAULT option to request a connection to a default database server, called a *default connection*. The default database server can be either local or remote. To designate the default database server, set its name in the environment variable **INFORMIXSERVER**. This form of the CONNECT statement does not open a database.

If you select the DEFAULT option for the CONNECT statement, you must use the DATABASE statement or the CREATE DATABASE statement to open or create a database in the default database environment.

The Implicit Connection with DATABASE Statements

If you do not execute a CONNECT statement in your application, the first SQL statement must be one of the following database statements (or a single statement PREPARE for one of the following statements):

- DATABASE
- CREATE DATABASE
- DROP DATABASE

If one of these database statements is the first SQL statement in an application, the statement establishes a connection to a database server, which is known as an *implicit* connection. If the database statement specifies only a database name, the database server name is obtained from the **DBPATH** environment variable. This situation is described in "Locating the Database" on page 2-110.

An application that makes an implicit connection can establish other connections explicitly (using the CONNECT statement) but cannot establish another implicit connection unless the original implicit connection is disconnected. An application can terminate an implicit connection using the DISCONNECT statement.

After *any* implicit connection is made, that connection is considered to be the default connection, regardless of whether the database server is the default specified by the **INFORMIXSERVER** environment variable. This default allows the application to refer to the implicit connection if additional explicit connections are made, because the implicit connection does not have an identifier. For example, if you establish an implicit connection followed by an explicit connection, you can make the implicit connection current by issuing the SET CONNECTION DEFAULT statement. This means, however, that once you establish an implicit connection, you cannot use the CONNECT DEFAULT command because the implicit connection is considered to be the default connection.

The database statements can always be used to open a database or create a new database on the current database server.

WITH CONCURRENT TRANSACTION Option

The WITH CONCURRENT TRANSACTION clause lets you switch to a different connection while a transaction is active in the current connection. If the current connection was *not* established using the WITH CONCURRENT TRANSACTION clause, you cannot switch to a different connection if a transaction is active; the CONNECT or SET CONNECTION statement fails, returning an error, and the transaction in the current connection continues to be active. In this case, the application must commit or roll back the active transaction in the current connection before it switches to a different connection.

The WITH CONCURRENT TRANSACTION clause supports the concept of multiple concurrent transactions, where each connection can have its own transaction and the COMMIT WORK and ROLLBACK WORK statements affect only the current connection. The WITH CONCURRENT TRANSACTION clause does not support global transactions in which a single transaction spans databases over multiple connections. The COMMIT WORK and ROLLBACK WORK statements do not act on databases across multiple connections.

The following example illustrates how to use the WITH CONCURRRENT TRANSACTION clause:

```
main()
{
EXEC SQL connect to 'a@srv1' as 'A';
EXEC SQL connect to 'b@srv2' as 'B' with concurrent transaction;
EXEC SQL connect to 'c@srv3' as 'C' with concurrent transaction;

/*
    Execute SQL statements in connection 'C' , starting a
    transaction
*/

EXEC SQL set connection 'B'; -- switch to connection 'B'

/*
    Execute SQL statements starting a transaction in 'B'.
    Now there are two active transactions, one each in 'B'
    and 'C'.
*/

EXEC SQL set connection 'A'; -- switch to connection 'A'

/*
    Execute SQL statements starting a transaction in 'A'.
    Now there are three active transactions, one each in 'A',
    'B' and 'C'.
*/

EXEC SQL set connection 'C'; -- ERROR, transaction active in 'A'
```

```
/*
    SET CONNECTION 'C' fails (current connection is still 'A')
    The transaction in 'A' must be committed/rolled back since
    connection 'A' was started without the CONCURRENT TRANSACTION
    clause.
*/

EXEC SQL commit work;-- commit tx in current connection ('A')

/*
    Now, there are two active transactions, in 'B' and in 'C',
    which must be committed/rolled back separately
*/

EXEC SQL set connection 'B'; -- switch to connection 'B'
EXEC SQL commit work;           -- commit tx in current connection ('B')

EXEC SQL set connection 'C'; -- go back to connection 'C'
EXEC SQL commit work;        -- commit tx in current connection ('C')

EXEC SQL disconnect all;
}
```

Warning: *When an application uses the WITH CONCURRENT TRANSACTION clause to establish multiple connections to the same database environment, a deadlock condition can occur.*

Database Environment

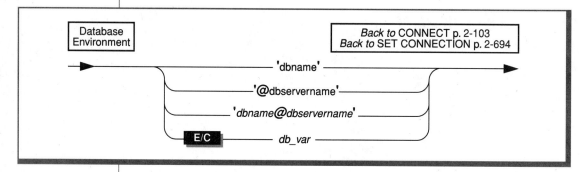

Element	Purpose	Restrictions	Syntax
db_var	Host variable that contains a value representing a database environment	Variable must be a fixed-length character data type. The value stored in this host variable must have one of the database-environment formats listed in the syntax diagram.	Variable name must conform to language-specific rules for variable names.
dbname	Name of the database to which a connection is made	The specified database must already exist.	Identifier, p. 4-205
dbservername	Name of the database server to which a connection is made	The specified database server must exist. You cannot put a space between the @ symbol and dbservername.	Identifier, p. 4-205

Using Quote Marks in the Database Environment

If the **DELIMIDENT** environment variable is set, the quote marks in the database environment must be single. If the **DELIMIDENT** environment variable is not set, surrounding quotes can be single or double.

Restrictions on the dbservername Parameter

When the *dbservername* parameter appears in the specification of a database environment, you must observe the following restrictions.

UNIX

On UNIX, the database server that you specify in *dbservername* must match the name of a database server in the **sqlhosts** file. ♦

WIN NT

On Windows NT, the database server that you specify in *dbservername* must match the name of a database server in the **sqlhosts** subkey in the registry. Informix recommends that you use the **setnet32** utility to update the registry. ♦

Specifying the Database Environment

Using the options in the syntax diagram, you can specify either a server and a database, a database server only, or a database only.

Specifying a Database Server Only

The *@dbservername* option establishes a connection to the named database server only; it does not open a database. When you use this option, you must subsequently use the DATABASE or CREATE DATABASE (or a PREPARE statement for one of these statements and an EXECUTE statement) to open a database.

Specifying a Database Only

The *dbname* option establishes a connection to the default database server or to another database server in the **DBPATH** variable. It also locates and opens the named database. The same is true of the *db_var* option if it specifies only a database name. For the order in which an application connects to different database servers to locate a database, see "Locating the Database" on page 2-110.

Locating the Database

How a database is located and opened depends on whether you specify a database server name in the database environment expression.

Database Server and Database Specified

If you specify both a database server and a database in the CONNECT statement, your application connects to the database server, which locates and opens the database.

If the database server that you specify is not on-line, you receive an error.

Only Database Specified

If you specify only a database in your CONNECT statement, the application obtains the name of a database server from the **DBPATH** environment variable. The database server in the **INFORMIXSERVER** environment variable is always added before the **DBPATH** value.

UNIX

On UNIX, set the **INFORMIXSERVER** and **DBPATH** environment variables as the following example shows:

```
setenv INFORMIXSERVER srvA
setenv DBPATH //srvB://srvC
```

◆

WIN NT

On Windows NT, choose **Start→Programs→Informix→setnet32** from the Task Bar and set the **INFORMIXSERVER** and **DBPATH** environment variables, as the following example shows:

```
set INFORMIXSERVER = srvA
set DBPATH = //srvA://srvB://srvC
```

◆

The resulting **DBPATH** that your application uses is shown in the following example:

```
//srvA://srvB://srvC
```

The application first establishes a connection to the database server specified by **INFORMIXSERVER**. The database server uses parameters that are specified in the configuration file to locate the database.

If the database does not reside on the default database server, or if the default database server is not on-line, the application connects to the next database server in **DBPATH**. In the previous example, that server would be **srvB**.

UNIX

If a directory in **DBPATH** is an NFS-mounted directory, it is expanded to contain the host name of the NFS computer and the complete pathname of the directory on the NFS host. In this case, the host name must be listed in your **sqlhosts** file as a dbservername, and an **sqlexecd** daemon must be running on the NFS host. ◆

USER Clause

The USER clause specifies information that is used to determine whether the application can access the target computer when the CONNECT statement connects to the database server on a remote host. Subsequent to the CONNECT statement, all database operations on the remote host use the specified user name.

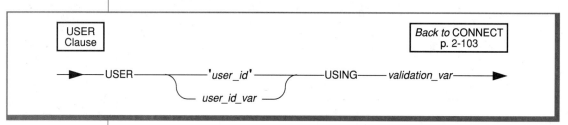

Element	Purpose	Restrictions	Syntax
user_id	Quoted string that is a valid login name for the application	The specified login name must be a valid login name. For additional restrictions see "Restrictions on the User Identifier Parameter" on page 2-113.	Quoted String, p. 4-260
user_id_var	Host variable that holds the value of user_id	Variable must be a fixed-length character data type. The login name stored in this variable is subject to the same restrictions as user_id.	Name must conform to language-specific rules for variable names.
validation_var	Host variable that holds the valid password for the login name specified in *user_id* or *user_id_var*	Variable must be a fixed-length character data type. The password stored in this variable must be a valid password. For additional restrictions see "Restrictions on the Validation Variable Parameter" on page 2-113.	Name must conform to language-specific rules for variable names.

Restrictions on the Validation Variable Parameter

UNIX

On UNIX, the password stored in *validation_var* must be a valid password and must exist in the **/etc/passwd** file. If the application connects to a remote database server, the password must exist in this file on both the local and remote database servers. ◆

WIN NT

On Windows NT, the password stored in *validation_var* must be a valid password and must be the one entered in **User Manager**. If the application connects to a remote database server, the password must exist in the domain of both the client and the server. ◆

Restrictions on the User Identifier Parameter

UNIX

On UNIX, the login name you specify in *user_id* must be a valid login name and must exist in the **/etc/passwd** file. If the application connects to a remote server, the login name must exist in this file on both the local and remote database servers. ◆

WIN NT

On Windows NT, the login name you specify in *user_id* must be a valid login name and must exist in **User Manager**. If the application connects to a remote server, the login name must exist in the domain of both the client and the server. ◆

Rejection of the Connection

The connection is rejected if the following conditions occur:

- The specified user lacks the privileges to access the database named in the database environment.

- The specified user does not have the required permissions to connect to the remote host.

- You supply a USER clause but do not include the USING *validation_var* phrase.

In compliance with the X/Open specification for the CONNECT statement, the ESQL/C preprocessor allows a CONNECT statement that has a USER clause without the USING *validation_var* phrase. However, if the *validation_var* is not present, the database server rejects the connection at runtime. ♦

Use of the Default User ID

If you do not supply the USER clause, the default user ID is used to attempt the connection. The default Informix user ID is the login name of the user running the application. In this case, you obtain network permissions with the standard authorization procedures. For example, on UNIX, the default user ID must match a user ID in the **/etc/hosts.equiv** file. On Windows NT, you must be a member of the domain, or if the database server is installed locally, you must be a valid user on the computer where it is installed.

Related Information

Related Statements: DISCONNECT, SET CONNECTION, DATABASE, and CREATE DATABASE

For more information about **sqlhosts**, refer to your *Administrator's Guide*.

CREATE AGGREGATE

Use the CREATE AGGREGATE statement to create a new aggregate function. User-defined aggregates extend the functionality of the database server because they can perform any kind of aggregate computation that the user wants to implement.

Syntax

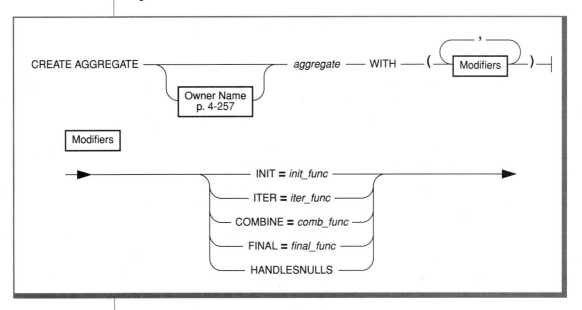

Element	Purpose	Restrictions	Syntax
aggregate	Name of the new aggregate	The name cannot be the same as the name of any built-in aggregate or the name of any UDR.	Identifier, p. 4-205
comb_func	Function that merges one partial result into the other and returns the updated partial result	You must specify the combine function both for parallel queries and for sequential queries.	Database Object Name, p. 4-50

(1 of 2)

Element	Purpose	Restrictions	Syntax
final_func	Function that converts a partial result into the result type	If the final function is omitted, the database server returns the final result of the iterator function.	Database Object Name, p. 4-50
init_func	Function that initializes the data structures required for the aggregate computation	The initialization function must be able to handle null arguments.	Database Object Name, p. 4-50
iter_func	Function that merges a single value with a partial result and returns the updated partial result	You must specify a value for the iterator function. If the initialization function is omitted, the iterator function must be able to handle null arguments.	Database Object Name, p. 4-50

(2 of 2)

Usage

You can specify the INIT, ITER, COMBINE, FINAL, and HANDLESNULLS modifiers in any order.

Important: *You must specify the ITER and COMBINE modifiers in a CREATE AGGREGATE statement. You do not have to specify the INIT, FINAL, and HANDLESNULLS modifiers in a CREATE AGGREGATE statement.*

The ITER, COMBINE, FINAL, and INIT modifiers specify the support functions for a user-defined aggregate. These support functions do not have to exist at the time you create the user-defined aggregate.

If you omit the HANDLESNULLS modifier, rows with null aggregate argument values do not contribute to the aggregate computation. If you include the HANDLESNULLS modifier, you must declare all the support functions to handle null values as well.

Extending the Functionality of Aggregates

The database server provides two ways to extend the functionality of aggregates. You use the CREATE AGGREGATE statement only for the second method.

- **Extensions of built-in aggregates**

  A built-in aggregate is an aggregate that the database server provides, such as COUNT, SUM, or AVG. These aggregates work only with built-in data types. You can extend these aggregates to work with extended data types. To extend a built-in aggregate, you must create user-defined routines that overload the binary operators for that aggregate. For further information on extending built-in aggregates, see the *Extending Informix Dynamic Server 2000* manual.

- **Creation of user-defined aggregates**

  A user-defined aggregate is an aggregate that you define to perform an aggregate computation that is not provided by the database server. You can use user-defined aggregates with built-in data types, extended data types, or both. To create a user-defined aggregate, you use the CREATE AGGREGATE statement. In this statement, you name the new aggregate and specify the support functions that compute the aggregate result. These support functions perform initialization, sequential aggregation, combination of results, and type conversion

Example of Creating a User-Defined Aggregate

In the following example, you create a user-defined aggregate named **average**:

```
CREATE AGGREGATE average
    WITH (
        INIT = average_init,
        ITER = average_iter,
        COMBINE = average_combine,
        FINAL = average_final
        )
```

Before you use the average aggregate in a query, you must also use CREATE FUNCTION statements to create the support functions specified in the CREATE AGGREGATE statement. The following table gives an example of the task that each support function might perform for **average**.

Keyword	Support Function	Purpose
INIT	average_init	Allocates and initializes an extended data type that stores the current sum and the current row count.
ITER	average_iter	For each row, adds the value of the expression to the current sum and increments the current row count by one.
COMBINE	average_combine	Adds the current sum and the current row count of one partial result to the other and returns the updated result.
FINAL	average_final	Returns the ratio of the current sum to the current row count and converts this ratio to the result type.

Parallel Execution

The database server can break up an aggregate computation into several pieces and compute them in parallel. The database server using the INIT and ITER support functions to compute each piece sequentially. Then the database server uses the COMBINE function to combine the partial results from all the pieces into a single result value. Whether an aggregate is parallel is an optimization decision that is transparent to the user.

Related Information

Related statements: DROP AGGREGATE

For information about how to invoke a user-defined aggregate, see the discussion of user-defined aggregates in the Expression segment.

For a description of the **sysaggregates** system catalog table that holds information about user-defined aggregates, see the *Informix Guide to SQL: Reference*.

For a discussion of user-defined aggregates, see *Extending Informix Dynamic Server 2000.*

CREATE CAST

Use the CREATE CAST statement to register a cast that converts data from one data type to another.

Syntax

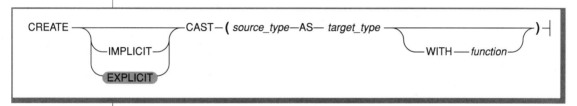

Element	Purpose	Restrictions	Syntax
function	Name of the user-defined function that you register to implement the cast	See "WITH Clause" on page 2-122.	Database Object Name, p. 4-50
source_type	Data type to be converted	The type must exist in the database at the time the cast is registered.	Data Type, p. 4-53
		Either the *source_type* or the *target_type*, but not both, can be a built-in type.	
		Neither type can be a distinct type of the other.	
		The type cannot be a collection data type.	
target_type	Data type that results from the conversion	The type must exist in the database at the time the cast is registered.	Data Type, p. 4-53
		Either the *source_type* or the *target_type*, but not both, can be a built-in type.	
		Neither type can be a distinct type of the other.	
		The type cannot be a collection data type.	

Usage

A cast is a mechanism that the database server uses to convert one data type to another. The database server uses casts to perform the following tasks:

- To compare two values in the WHERE clause of a SELECT, UPDATE, or DELETE statement
- To pass values as arguments to a user-defined routines
- To return values from user-defined routines

To create a cast, you must have the necessary privileges on both the *source data type* and the *target data type*. All users have permission to use the built-in data types. However, to create a cast to or from an opaque type, distinct type, or named-row type requires the Usage privilege on that type.

The CREATE CAST statement registers a cast in the **syscasts** system catalog table. For more information on **syscasts**, see the chapter on system catalog tables in the *Informix Guide to SQL: Reference*.

Source and Target Data Types

The CREATE CAST statement defines a cast that converts a *source data type* to a *target data type*. Both the *source data type* and *target data type* must exist in the database when you execute the CREATE CAST statement to register the cast. The *source data type* and the *target data type* have the following restrictions:

- Either the *source data type* or the *target data type*, but not both, can be a built-in type.
- Neither the *source data type* nor the *target data type* can be a distinct type of the other.
- Neither the *source data type* nor the *target data type* can be a collection data type.

Explicit and Implicit Casts

To process queries with multiple data types often requires casts that convert data from one data type to another. You can use the CREATE CAST statement to create the following kinds of casts:

- Use the CREATE EXPLICIT CAST statement to define an *explicit* cast.
- Use the CREATE IMPLICIT CAST statement to define an *implicit* cast.

Explicit Casts

An explicit cast is a cast that you must specifically invoke, with either the CAST AS keywords or with the cast operator (::). The database server does *not* automatically invoke an explicit cast to resolve data type conversions. The EXPLICIT keyword is optional; by default, the CREATE CAST statement creates an explicit cast.

The following CREATE CAST statement defines an explicit cast from the **rate_of_return** opaque data type to the **percent** distinct data type:

```
CREATE EXPLICIT CAST (rate_of_return AS percent
    WITH rate_to_prcnt)
```

The following SELECT statement explicitly invokes this explicit cast in its WHERE clause to compare the **bond_rate** column (of type **rate_of_return**) to the **initial_APR** column (of type **percent**):

```
SELECT bond_rate FROM bond
WHERE bond_rate::percent > initial_APR
```

Implicit Casts

The database server invokes built-in casts to convert from one built-in data type to another built-in type that is not directly substitutable. For example, the database server performs conversion of a character type such as CHAR to a numeric type such as INTEGER through a built-in cast.

An implicit cast is a cast that the database server can invoke automatically when it encounters data types that cannot be compared with built-in casts. This type of cast enables the database server to handle automatically conversions between other data types.

To define an implicit cast, specify the IMPLICIT keyword in the CREATE CAST statement. For example, the following CREATE CAST statement specifies that the database server should automatically use the **prcnt_to_char()** function when it needs to convert from the CHAR data type to a distinct data type, **percent**:

```
CREATE IMPLICIT CAST (CHAR AS percent WITH prcnt_to_char)
```

This cast provides the database server with only the ability to automatically convert *from* the CHAR data type *to* **percent**. For the database server to convert *from* **percent** *to* CHAR, you need to define another implicit cast, as follows:

```
CREATE IMPLICIT CAST (percent AS CHAR WITH char_to_prcnt)
```

The database server would automatically invoke the **char_to_prcnt()** function to evaluate the WHERE clause of the following SELECT statement:

```
SELECT commission FROM sales_rep
WHERE commission > "25%"
```

Users can also invoke implicit casts explicitly. For more information on how to explicitly invoke a cast function, see "Explicit Casts" on page 2-121.

When a built-in cast does not exist for conversion between data types, you can create user-defined casts to make the necessary conversion.

WITH Clause

The WITH clause of the CREATE CAST statement specifies the name of the user-defined function to invoke to perform the cast. This function is called the cast function. You must specify a *function name* unless the *source data type* and the *target data type* have identical representations. Two data types have identical representations when the following conditions are met:

- Both data types have the same length and alignment
- Both data types are passed by reference or both are passed by value

The cast function must be registered in the same database as the cast at the time the cast is invoked, but need not exist when the cast is created. The CREATE CAST statement does not check permissions on the specified *function name*, or even verify that the cast function exists. Each time a user invokes the cast explicitly or implicitly, the database server verifies that the user has Execute privilege on the cast function.

Related Information

Related statements: CREATE FUNCTION, CREATE DISTINCT TYPE, CREATE OPAQUE TYPE, CREATE ROW TYPE and DROP CAST

For more information about data types, casting, and conversion, see the Data Types segment in this manual and the *Informix Guide to SQL: Reference*.

For examples that show how to create and use casts, see the *Informix Guide to SQL: Tutorial*.

CREATE DATABASE

Use the CREATE DATABASE statement to create a new database.

Syntax

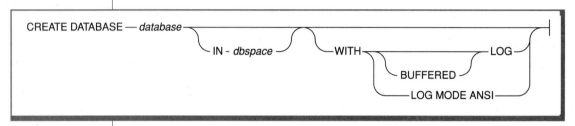

Element	Purpose	Restrictions	Syntax
database	Name of the database to create	The database name must be unique on the server.	Database Name, p. 4-47
dbspace	Name of the dbspace where you want to store the data for this database; default is the root dbspace	The dbspace must already exist.	Identifier, p. 4-205

Usage

This statement is an extension to ANSI-standard syntax. The ANSI standard does not provide any syntax for the construction of a database, that is how a database comes into existence.

The database that you create becomes the current database.

The database name that you use must be unique within the database server environment in which you are working. The database server creates the system catalog tables that describe the structure of the database.

When you create a database, you alone have access to it. The database remains inaccessible to other users until you, as DBA, grant database privileges. For information on how to grant database privileges, see "GRANT" on page 2-500.

E/C

In ESQL/C, the CREATE DATABASE statement cannot appear in a multistatement PREPARE operation. ♦

If you do not specify the dbspace, the database server creates the system catalog tables in the **root** dbspace. The following statement creates the **vehicles** database in the **root** dbspace:

```
CREATE DATABASE vehicles
```

The following statement creates the **vehicles** database in the **research** dbspace:

```
CREATE DATABASE vehicles IN research
```

Logging Options

The logging options of the CREATE DATABASE statement determine the type of logging that is done for the database.

In the event of a failure, the database server uses the log to re-create all committed transactions in your database.

If you do not specify the WITH LOG option, you cannot use transactions or the statements that are associated with databases that have logging (BEGIN WORK, COMMIT WORK, ROLLBACK WORK, SET LOG, and SET ISOLATION).

EDS

If you are using Enterprise Decision Server, the CREATE DATABASE statement always creates a database with unbuffered logging. The database server ignores any logging specifications included in a CREATE DATABASE statement. ♦

Designating Buffered Logging

The following example creates a database that uses a buffered log:

```
CREATE DATABASE vehicles WITH BUFFERED LOG
```

If you use a buffered log, you marginally enhance the performance of logging at the risk of not being able to re-create the last few transactions after a failure. (See the discussion of buffered logging in the *Informix Guide to Database Design and Implementation*.)

| ANSI |

ANSI-Compliant Databases

When you use the LOG MODE ANSI option in the CREATE DATABASE statement, the database that you create is an ANSI-compliant database. The following example creates an ANSI-compliant database:

```
CREATE DATABASE employees WITH LOG MODE ANSI
```

ANSI-compliant databases are set apart from databases that are not ANSI-compliant by the following features:

- All statements are automatically contained in transactions.

  All databases use unbuffered logging.
- Owner-naming is enforced.

  You must use the owner name when you refer to each table, view, synonym, index, or constraint unless you are the owner.
- For databases, the default isolation level is repeatable read.
- Default privileges on objects differ from those in databases that are not ANSI-compliant.

  Users do not receive PUBLIC privilege to tables and synonyms by default.

Other slight differences exist between databases that are ANSI-compliant and those that are not. These differences are noted as appropriate with the related SQL statement. For a detailed discussion of the differences between ANSI-compliant databases and databases that are not ANSI-compliant, see the *Informix Guide to Database Design and Implementation*.

Creating an ANSI-compliant database does not mean that you get ANSI warnings when you run the database. You must use the **-ansi** flag or the **DBANSIWARN** environment variable to receive warnings.

For additional information about **-ansi** and **DBANSIWARN**, see the *Informix Guide to SQL: Reference*.

Related Information

Related statements: CLOSE DATABASE, CONNECT, DATABASE, DROP DATABASE

For discussions of how to create a database and of ANSI-compliant databases, see the *Informix Guide to Database Design and Implementation*.

CREATE DISTINCT TYPE

Use the CREATE DISTINCT TYPE statement to create a new distinct type. A *distinct type* is a data type based on a built-in type or an existing opaque type, a named-row type, or another distinct type. Distinct types are strongly typed. Although the distinct type has the same physical representation as data of its source type, the two types cannot be compared without an explicit cast from one type to the other.

Syntax

CREATE DISTINCT TYPE ————— *distinct_type* ————— AS ————— *source_type* —————|

Element	Purpose	Restrictions	Syntax
distinct_ type	Name of the new data type	In an ANSI-compliant database, the combination of the owner and data type must be unique within the database. In a database that is not ANSI compliant, the name of the data type must be unique within the database.	Data Type, p. 4-53
source_type	Name of an existing data type on which the new type is based	The type must be either a built-in type or a type created with the CREATE DISTINCT TYPE, CREATE OPAQUE TYPE, or CREATE ROW TYPE statement.	Data Type, p. 4-53

Usage

To create a distinct type in a database, you must have the Resource privilege. Any user with the Resource privilege can create a distinct type from one of the built-in data types, which are owned by user **informix**.

Important: *You cannot create a distinct type on the SERIAL or SERIAL8 data type.*

To create a distinct type from an opaque type, a named-row type, or another distinct type, you must be the owner of the type or have the Usage privilege on the type.

Once a distinct type is defined, only the type owner and the DBA can use it. The owner of the type can grant other users the Usage privilege on the type.

A distinct type has the same storage structure as its source type. The following statement creates the distinct type **birthday**, based on the built-in data type, DATE:

```
CREATE DISTINCT TYPE birthday AS DATE
```

Dynamic Server uses the same storage method for the distinct type as it does for the source type of the distinct type. However, a distinct type and its source type cannot be compared in an operation unless one type is explicitly cast to the other type.

Privileges on Distinct Types

To create a distinct type, you must have the Resource privilege on the database. When you create the distinct type, only you, the owner, have Usage privilege on this type. Use the GRANT or REVOKE statements to grant or revoke Usage privilege to other database users.

To find out what privileges exist on a particular type, check the **sysxtdtypes** system catalog table for the owner name and the **sysxtdtypeauth** system catalog table for additional type privileges that might have been granted. For more information on system catalog tables, see the *Informix Guide to SQL: Reference*.

DB

The DB-Access utility can also display privileges on distinct types. ♦

Support Functions and Casts

When you create a distinct type, Dynamic Server automatically defines two explicit casts:

- A cast from the distinct type to its source type
- A cast from the source type to the distinct type

Because the two types have the same representation (the same length and alignment), no support functions are required to implement the casts.

You can create an implicit cast between a distinct type and its source type. However, to create an implicit cast, you must first drop the default explicit cast between the distinct type and its source type.

All support functions and casts that are defined on the source type can be used on the distinct type. However, casts and support functions that are defined on the distinct type are not available to the source type.

Manipulating Distinct Types

When you compare or manipulate data of a distinct type and its source type, you must explicitly cast one type to the other.

You must explicitly cast one type to the other in the following situations:

- To insert or update a column of one type with values of the other type
- To use a relational operator to add, subtract, multiply, divide, compare, or otherwise manipulate two values, one of the source type and one of the distinct type

For example, suppose you create a distinct type, dist_type, that is based on the NUMERIC data type. You then create a table with two columns, one of type dist_type and one of type NUMERIC.

```
CREATE DISTINCT TYPE dist_type AS NUMERIC;
CREATE TABLE t(col1 dist_type, col2 NUMERIC);
```

To directly compare the distinct type and its source type or assign a value of the source type to a column of the distinct type, you must cast one type to the other, as the following examples show:

```
INSERT INTO tab (col1) VALUES (3.5::dist_type);

SELECT col1, col2
    FROM t WHERE (col1::NUMERIC) > col2;

SELECT col1, col2, (col1 + col2::dist_type) sum_col
    FROM tab;
```

Related Information

Related statements: CREATE CAST, CREATE FUNCTION, CREATE OPAQUE TYPE, CREATE ROW TYPE, DROP TYPE and DROP ROW TYPE

For information and examples that show how to use and cast distinct types, see the *Informix Guide to SQL: Tutorial*.

For more information on when you might create a distinct type, see *Extending Informix Dynamic Server 2000*.

CREATE EXTERNAL TABLE

Use the CREATE EXTERNAL TABLE statement to define an external source that is not part of your database so you can use that external source to load and unload data for your database.

Syntax

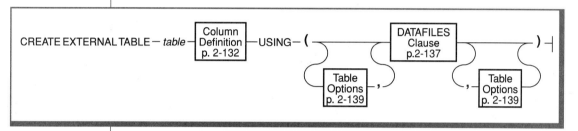

Element	Purpose	Restrictions	Syntax
table	Name of the external table that describes the external data	The name must be different from any existing table, view, or synonym name in the current database.	Database Object Name, p. 4-50

Usage

After you create a table with the CREATE EXTERNAL TABLE statement, you can move data to and from the external source with an INSERT INTO...SELECT statement.

Column Definition

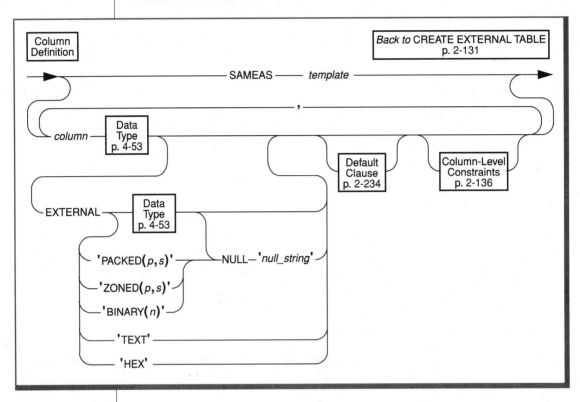

Element	Purpose	Restrictions	Syntax
column	One column name for each column of the external table	For each column, you must specify an Informix data type.	Identifier, p. 4-205
n	Number of 8-bit bytes to represent the integer	For FIXED format binary integers; *big-endian* byte order.	*n*=2 for 16-bit integers; *n*=4 for 32-bit integers
p	Precision (total number of digits)	For FIXED-format files only.	Literal Number, p. 4-237
s	Scale (number of digits after the decimal point)	For FIXED-format files only.	Literal Number, p. 4-237

(1 of 2)

Element	Purpose	Restrictions	Syntax
null_string	Value that is to be interpreted as a null	For restriction information, refer to "Defining Null Values."	Quoted String, p. 4-260
template	Name of a table with the exact column names and definitions for your external table	You cannot skip columns or put data of a different type into any column.	Database Object Name, p. 4-50

Using the SAME AS Clause

When you create a table with the SAMEAS keyword, the column names from the original table are used in the new table. You cannot use indexes in the external table definition.

You cannot use the SAMEAS keyword for FIXED-format files.

Using the EXTERNAL Keyword

Use the EXTERNAL keyword to specify a data type for each column of your external table that has a data type different from the internal table. For example, you might have a VARCHAR column in the internal table that you want to map to a CHAR column in the external table.

You must specify an external type for every column that is in fixed format. You cannot specify an external type for delimited format columns except for BYTE and TEXT columns where your specification is optional. For more information, see "TEXT and HEX External Types" on page 2-135.

Integer Data Types

Besides valid Informix integer data types, you can specify packed decimal, zoned decimal, and IBM-format binary representation of integers.

For packed or zoned decimal, you specify precision (total number of digits in the number) and scale (number of digits that are to the right of the decimal point). Packed decimal representation can store two digits, or a digit and a sign, in each byte. Zoned decimal requires $(p + 1)$ bytes to store p digits and the sign.

Big-Endian Format

The database server also supports two IBM-format binary representations of integers: BINARY(2) for 16-bit integer storage and BINARY(4) for 32-bit integer storage. The most significant byte of each number has the lowest address; that is, binary-format integers are stored big-end first (big-endian format) in the manner of IBM and Motorola processors. Intel processors and some others store binary-format integers little-end first, a storage method that the database server does not support for external data.

Defining Null Values

The packed decimal, zoned decimal, and binary data types do not have a natural null value, so you must define a value that can be interpreted as a null when the database server loads or unloads data from an external file. You can define the *null_string* as a number that will not be used in the set of numbers stored in the data file (for example, -9999.99). You can also define a bit pattern in the field as a hexadecimal pattern, such as 0xffff, that is to be interpreted as a null.

The database server uses the null representation for a fixed-format external table to both interpret values as the data is loaded into the database and to format null values into the appropriate data type when data is unloaded to an external table.

The following examples are of column definitions with null values for a fixed-format external table:

```
i smallint external "binary (2)" null "-32767"
li integer external "binary (4)" null "-99999"
d decimal (5,2) external "packed (5,2)" null "0xffffff"
z decimal (4,2) external "zoned (4,2)" null "0x0f0f0f0f"
zl decimal (3,2) external "zoned (3,2)" null "-1.00"
```

If the packed decimal or zoned decimal is stored with all bits cleared to represent a null value, the *null_string* can be defined as "0x0". The following rules apply to the value assigned to a *null_string*:

- The null representation must fit into the length of the external field.
- If a bit pattern is defined, the *null_string* is not case sensitive.
- If a bit pattern is defined, the *null_string* must begin with "0x".

- For numeric fields, the left-most fields are assigned zeros by the database server if the bit pattern does not fill the entire field.

- If the null representation is not a bit pattern, the null value must be a valid number for that field.

Warning: *If a row that contains a null value is unloaded into an external table and the column that receives the null value has no null value defined, the database server inserts a zero into the column.*

TEXT and HEX External Types

An Informix BYTE or TEXT column can be encoded in either the TEXT or HEX external type. You can use only delimited BYTE and TEXT formats with these external types. Fixed formats are not allowed. In addition, you cannot use these external types with any other type of delimited-format columns (such as character columns).

You do not need to specify these external types. If you do not define an external column specifically, Informix TEXT columns default to TEXT and Informix BYTE columns default to HEX.

The database server interprets two adjacent field delimiters as a null value.

During unloading, the database server escapes delimiters and backslashes (\). During loading, any character that follows a backslash is taken literally. Nonprintable characters are directly embedded in the data file if you choose TEXT format.

User-defined delimiters are limited to one byte each. For information about delimiters if you are using a multibyte locale, see the *Informix Guide to GLS Functionality*.

For more information on BYTE and TEXT data, see your *Administrator's Guide*.

Manipulating Data in Fixed Format Files

For files in FIXED format, you must declare the column name and the EXTERNAL item for each column to set the name and number of characters. For FIXED-format files, the only data type allowed is CHAR. You can use the keyword NULL to specify what string to interpret as a null value.

Column-Level Constraints

Use column-level constraints to limit the type of data that is allowed in a column. Constraints at the column level are limited to a single column.

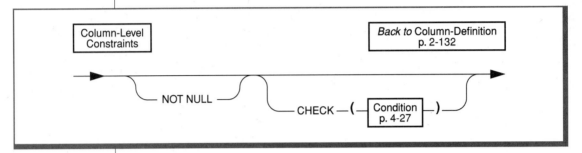

Using the Not-Null Constraint

If you do not indicate a default value for a column, the default is null *unless* you place a not-null constraint on the column. In that case, no default value exists for the column.

If you place a not-null constraint on a column (and no default value is specified), the data in the external table must have a value set for the column when loading through the external table. When no reject file exists and no value is encountered, the database server returns an error and the loading stops. When a reject file exists and no value is encountered, the error is reported in the reject file and the load continues.

Using the CHECK Constraint

Check constraints allow you to designate conditions that must be met *before* data can be assigned to a column during an INSERT or UPDATE statement. When a reject file does not exist and a row evaluates to *false* for any check constraint defined on a table during an insert or update, the database server returns an error. When there is a reject file and a row evaluates to *false* for a check constraint defined on the table, the error is reported in the reject file and the statement continues to execute.

Check constraints are defined with *search conditions*. The search condition cannot contain subqueries, aggregates, host variables, or SPL routines. In addition, it cannot include the following built-in functions: CURRENT, USER, SITENAME, DBSERVERNAME, or TODAY.

When you define a check constraint at the column level, the only column that the check constraint can check against is the column itself. In other words, the check constraint cannot depend upon values in other columns of the table.

DATAFILES Clause

The DATAFILES clause names the external files that are opened when you use external tables.

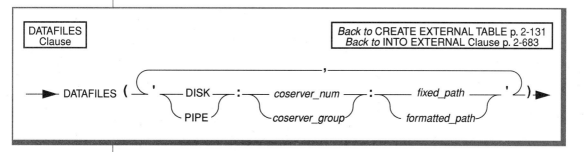

Back to CREATE EXTERNAL TABLE p. 2-131
Back to INTO EXTERNAL Clause p. 2-683

Element	Purpose	Restrictions	Syntax
coserver_group	Name of the coserver group that contains the external data	The coserver group must exist.	Identifier, p. 4-205
coserver_num	Numeric ID of the coserver that contains the external data	The coserver must exist.	Literal Number, p. 4-237
fixed_path	Pathname for describing the input or output files in the external table definition	The specified path must exist.	The pathname must conform to the conventions of your operating system.
formatted_path	Formatted pathname that uses pattern-matching characters	The specified path must exist.	The pathname must conform to the conventions of your operating system.

You can use cogroup names and coserver numbers when you describe the input or output files for the external table definition. You can identify the DATAFILES either by coserver number or by cogroup name. A coserver number contains only digits. A cogroup name is a valid identifier that begins with a letter but otherwise contains any combination of letters, digits, and underscores.

If you use only some of the available coservers for reading or writing files, you can designate these coservers as a cogroup using **onutil** and then use the cogroup name rather than explicitly naming each coserver and file separately. Whenever you use all coservers to manage external files, you can use the predefined *coserver_group*.

For examples of the DATAFILES clause, see the section, "Examples" on page 2-144.

Using Formatting Characters

You can use a formatted pathname to designate a filename. If you use a formatted pathname, you can take advantage of the substitution characters *%c*, *%n*, and *%r(first...last)*.

Formatting String	Purpose
%c	Replaced with the number of the coserver that manages the file
%n	Replaced with the name of the node on which the coserver that manages the file resides
%r(first...last)	Names multiple files on a single coserver

Important: *The formatted pathname option does not support the %o formatting string.*

Table Options

The optional table parameters include additional characteristics that define the table.

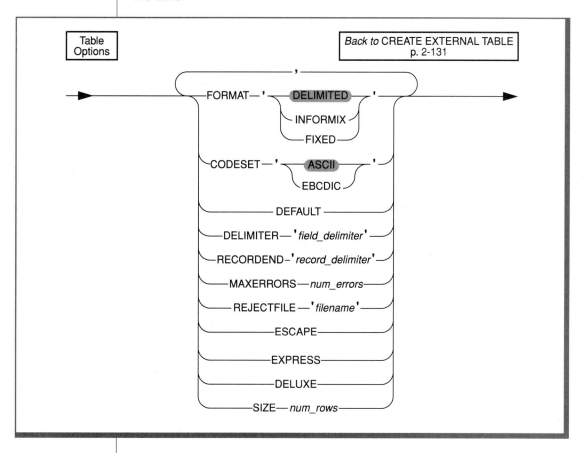

Element	Purpose	Restrictions	Syntax
filename	Full directory path and filename that you want all coservers to use as a destination when they write conversion error messages	If you do not specify REJECTFILE, no reject files are created, and if errors occur, the load task will fail.	Filename must conform to the conventions of your operating system.
field_delimiter	Character to separate fields The default value is the pipe (l) character.	If you use a non-printing character as a delimiter, you must encode it as the octal representation of the ASCII character. For example, ' \006 ' can represent CTRL-F.	Quoted String, p. 4-260
num_errors	Number of errors allowed per coserver before the database server stops the load	If you do not set the MAXERRORS environment variable, the database server processes all data regardless of the number of errors. This parameter is ignored during an unload task.	Literal Number, p. 4-237
num_rows	Approximate number of rows contained in the external table	None.	Literal Number, p. 4-237
quoted_string	ASCII character that represents the escape	Only one character is valid.	Quoted String, p. 4-260
record_delimiter	Character to separate records If you do not set the RECORDEND environment variable, the default value is the newline character (\n).	If you use a non-printing character as a delimiter, you must encode it as the octal representation of the ASCII character. For example, ' \006 ' can represent CTRL-F.	Quoted String, p. 4-260

Use the table options keywords as the following table describes. You can use each keyword whenever you plan to load or unload data unless only one of the two modes is specified.

Keyword	Purpose
CODESET	Specifies the type of code set of the data
DEFAULT (load only)	Specifies that the database server should replace missing values in delimited input files with column defaults (if they are defined) instead of inserting nulls
	This option allows input files to be sparsely populated. The input files do not need to have an entry for every column in the file where a default is the value to be loaded.
DELIMITER	Specifies the character that separates fields in a delimited text file
DELUXE (load only)	Sets a flag that causes the database server to load data in deluxe mode
	Deluxe mode is required for loading into STANDARD tables.
ESCAPE	Directs the database server to recognize ASCII special characters embedded in ASCII-text-based data files
	If you do not specify ESCAPE when you load data, the database server does not check the character fields in text data files for embedded special characters.
	If you do not specify ESCAPE when you unload data, the database server does not create embedded hexadecimal characters in text fields.
EXPRESS	Sets a flag that causes the database server to attempt to load data in express mode
	If you request express mode but indexes or unique constraints exist on the table or the table contains BYTE or TEXT data, or the target table is not RAW or OPERATIONAL, the load stops with an error message reporting the problem.
FORMAT	Specifies the format of the data in the data files
MAXERRORS	Sets the number of errors that are allowed per coserver before the database server stops the load

(1 of 2)

Keyword	Purpose
RECORDEND	Specifies the character that separates records in a delimited text file
REJECTFILE	Sets the full pathname for all coservers to the area where reject files are written for data-conversion errors
	If conversion errors occur and you have not specified REJECTFILE or the reject files cannot be opened, the load job ends abnormally.
	For information on reject-file naming and use of formatting characters, see "Reject Files" on page 2-142.
SIZE	Specifies the approximate number of rows that are contained in the external table
	This option can improve performance if you use the external table in a join query.

(2 of 2)

Important: *Check constraints on external tables are designed to be evaluated only when loading data. The database server cannot enforce check constraints on external tables because the data can be freely altered outside the control of the server. If you want to restrict rows that are written to an external table during unload, use a WHERE clause to filter the rows.*

Reject Files

Rows that have conversion errors during a load or rows that violate check constraints defined on the external table are written to a reject file on the coserver that performs the conversion. Each coserver manages its own reject file. The REJECTFILE keyword determines the name given to the reject file on each coserver.

You can use the formatting characters %c and %n (but not %r) in the filename format. Use the %c formatting characters to make the filenames unique. For more information on formatting characters, see the section "Using Formatting Characters" on page 2-138.

If you perform another load to the same table during the same session, any earlier reject file of the same name is overwritten.

Reject file entries have the following format:

```
coserver-number, filename, record, reason-code,
    field-name: bad-line
```

Element	Purpose
coserver-number	Number of the coserver from which the file is read
filename	Name of the input file
record	Record number in the input file where the error was detected
reason-code	Description of the error
field-name	External field name where the first error in the line occurred, or '<none>' if the rejection is not specific to a particular column
bad-line	Line that caused the error (delimited or fixed-position character files only): up to 80 characters

The reject file writes the *coserver-number, filename, record, field-name* and *reason-code* in ASCII. The bad line information varies with the type of input file. For delimited files or fixed-position character files, up to 80 characters of the bad line are copied directly into the reject file. For Informix internal data files, the bad line is not placed in the reject file, because you cannot edit the binary representation in a file. However, *coserver-number, filename, record, reason-code*, and *field-name* are still reported in the reject file so you can isolate the problem.

The types of errors that cause a row to be rejected are as follows.

Error Text	Explanation
CONSTRAINT *constraint name*	This constraint was violated.
CONVERT_ERR	Any field encounters a conversion error.
MISSING_DELIMITER	No delimiter was found.

(1 of 2)

Error Text	Explanation
MISSING_RECORDEND	No recordend was found.
NOT NULL	A null was found in *field-name*.
ROW_TOO_LONG	The input record is longer than 32 kilobytes.

(2 of 2)

Examples

The examples in this section show how you can name files to use in the DATAFILES field.

Assume that the database server is running on four nodes, and one file is to be read from each node. All files have the same name. The DATAFILES item can then be as follows:

```
DATAFILES ("DISK:cogroup_all:/work2/unload.dir/mytbl")
```

Now, consider a system with 16 coservers where only three coservers have tape drives attached (for example, coservers 2, 5, and 9). If you define a cogroup for these coservers before you run load and unload commands, you can use the cogroup name rather than a list of individual coservers when you execute the commands. To set up the cogroup, run **onutil**.

```
% onutil
1> create cogroup tape_group
2> from coserver.2, coserver.5, coserver.9;
Cogroup successfully created.
```

Then define the file locations for named pipes:

```
DATAFILES ("PIPE:tape_group:/usr/local/TAPE.%c")
```

The filenames expand as follows:

```
DATAFILES ("pipe:2:/usr/local/TAPE.2",
        "pipe:5:/usr/local/TAPE.5",
        "pipe:9:/usr/local/TAPE.9")
```

If, instead, you want to process three files on each of two coservers, define the files as follows:

```
DATAFILES ("DISK:1:/work2/extern.dir/mytbl.%r(1..3)",
        "DISK:2:/work2/extern.dir/mytbl.%r(4..6)")
```

The expanded list is as follows:

```
DATAFILES ("disk:1:/work2/extern.dir/mytbl.1",
           "disk:1:/work2/extern.dir/mytbl.2",
           "disk:1:/work2/extern.dir/mytbl.3",
           "disk:2:/work2/extern.dir/mytbl.4",
           "disk:2:/work2/extern.dir/mytbl.5",
           "disk:2:/work2/extern.dir/mytbl.6")
```

Related Information

Related statements: INSERT, SELECT, and SET PLOAD FILE

For more information on external tables, refer to your *Administrator's Reference*.

CREATE FUNCTION

Use the CREATE FUNCTION statement to create a user-defined function. With this statement, you can register an external function or write and register an SPL function.

Tip: *If you are trying to create a function from text that is in a separate file, use the CREATE FUNCTION FROM statement.*

Syntax

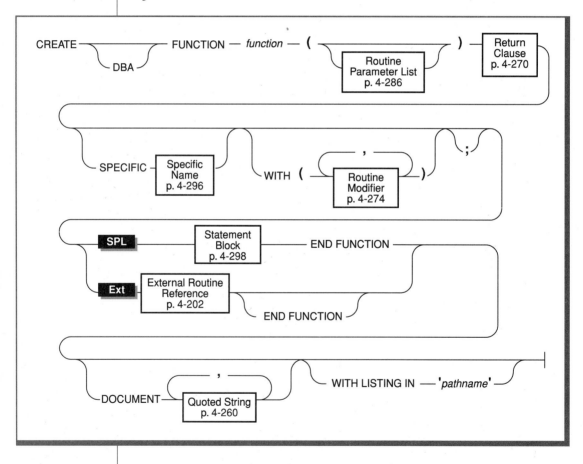

Element	Purpose	Restrictions	Syntax
function	Name of the function to create	You must have the appropriate language privileges. For more information, see "GRANT" on page 2-500.	Database Object Name, p. 4-50
		Also see, "Naming a Function" on page 2-148.	
pathname	Pathname to a file in which compile-time warnings are stored	The specified pathname must exist on the computer where the database resides.	Pathname and filename must conform to the conventions of your operating system.

Usage

The database server supports user-defined functions written in the following languages:

- Stored Procedure Language (*SPL functions*)

  An SPL function can return one or more values.

- One of the external languages (C or Java) that Dynamic Server supports (*external functions*)

  An external function must return exactly one value.

For information on how the manual uses the terms UDR, function, and procedure as well as recommended usage, see "Relationship Between Routines, Functions and Procedures" on page 2-201 and "Using CREATE PROCEDURE Versus CREATE FUNCTION" on page 2-199, respectively.

The entire length of a CREATE FUNCTION statement must be less than 64 kilobytes. This length is the literal length of the statement, including blank space and tabs.

E/C

You can use a CREATE FUNCTION statement only within a PREPARE statement. If you want to create a user-defined function for which the text is known at compile time, you must put the text in a file and specify this file with the CREATE FUNCTION FROM statement. ♦

Privileges Necessary for Using CREATE FUNCTION

You must have the Resource privilege on a database to create a function within that database.

Ext

Before you can create an external function, you must also have the Usage privilege on the language in which you will write the function. For more information, see "GRANT" on page 2-500. ♦

SPL

By default, the Usage privilege on SPL is granted to PUBLIC. You must also have at least the Resource privilege on a database to create an SPL function within that database. ♦

DBA Keyword and Privileges on the Created Function

The level of privilege necessary to execute a UDR depends on whether the UDR is created with the DBA keyword.

If you create a UDR with the DBA keyword, it is known as a DBA-privileged UDR. You need the DBA privilege to create or execute a DBA-privileged UDR.

If you do not use the DBA keyword, the UDR is known as an owner-privileged UDR.

ANSI

If you create an owner-privileged UDR in an ANSI-compliant database, anyone can execute the UDR. ♦

If you create an owner-privileged UDR in a database that is not ANSI compliant, the **NODEFDAC** environment variable prevents privileges on that UDR from being granted to PUBLIC. If this environment variable is set, the owner of a UDR must grant the Execute privilege for that UDR to other users.

Ext

If an external function has a negator function, you must grant the Execute privilege on both the external function and its negator function before users can execute the external function. ♦

Naming a Function

Because Dynamic Server offers *routine overloading*, you can define more than one function with the same name, but different parameter lists. You might want to overload functions in the following situations:

■ You create a user-defined function with the same name as a built-in function (such as **equal()**) to process a new user-defined data type.

■ You create *type hierarchies*, in which subtypes inherit data represen-tation and functions from supertypes.

■ You create *distinct types*, which are data types that have the same internal storage representation as an existing data type, but have different names and cannot be compared to the source type without casting. Distinct types inherit support functions from their source types.

For a brief description of the routine signature which uniquely identifies each user-defined function, see "Routine Overloading and Naming UDRs with a Routine Signature" on page 4-52.

Using the SPECIFIC Clause to Specify a Specific Name

You can specify a specific name for a user-defined function. A specific name is a name that is unique in the database. A specific name is useful when you are overloading a function.

DOCUMENT Clause

The quoted string in the DOCUMENT clause provides a synopsis and description of the UDR. The string is stored in the **sysprocbody** system catalog table and is intended for the user of the UDR.

Anyone with access to the database can query the **sysprocbody** system catalog table to obtain a description of one or all of the UDRs stored in the database.

For example, the following query obtains a description of the SPL function **update_by_pct**, shown in "SPL Functions" on page 2-150:

```
SELECT data FROM sysprocbody b, sysprocedures p
WHERE b.procid = p.procid
        --join between the two catalog tables
    AND p.procname = 'update_by_pct'
        -- look for procedure named update_by_pct
    AND b.datakey  = 'D'-- want user document;
```

The preceding query returns the following text:

```
USAGE: Update a price by a percentage
Enter an integer percentage from 1 - 100
and a part id number
```

A UDR or application program can query the system catalog tables to fetch the DOCUMENT clause and display it for a user.

Ext

You can use a DOCUMENT clause at the end of the CREATE FUNCTION statement, whether or not you use the END FUNCTION keywords. ♦

WITH LISTING IN Clause

The WITH LISTING IN clause specifies a filename where compile time warnings are sent. After you compile a UDR, this file holds one or more warning messages.

If you do not use the WITH LISTING IN clause, the compiler does not generate a list of warnings.

UNIX

If you specify a filename but not a directory, this listing file is created in your home directory on the computer where the database resides. If you do not have a home directory on this computer, the file is created in the root directory (the directory named "/"). ♦

Windows

If you specify a filename but not a directory, this listing file is created in your current working directory if the database is on the local machine. Otherwise, the default directory is **%INFORMIXDIR%\bin**. ♦

SPL

SPL Functions

SPL functions are UDRs written in Stored Procedure Language (SPL) that return one or more values.

To write and register an SPL function, use a CREATE FUNCTION statement. Embed appropriate SQL and SPL statements between the CREATE FUNCTION and END FUNCTION keywords. You can also follow the function with the DOCUMENT and WITH FILE IN options.

SPL functions are parsed, optimized (as far as possible), and stored in the system catalog tables in executable format. The body of an SPL function is stored in the **sysprocbody** system catalog table. Other information about the function is stored in other system catalog tables, including **sysprocedures**, **sysprocplan**, and **sysprocauth**. For more information about these system catalog tables, see the discussion of the system catalog in the *Informix Guide to SQL: Reference.*

You must use the END FUNCTION keywords with an SPL function.

Place a semicolon after the clause that immediately precedes the statement block.

Example of an SPL Function

The following example creates an SPL function:

```
CREATE FUNCTION update_by_pct ( pct INT, pid CHAR(10))
    RETURNING INT;

    DEFINE n INT;

    UPDATE inventory SET price = price + price * (pct/100)
        WHERE part_id = pid;
    LET n = price;
    RETURN price;

END FUNCTION
    DOCUMENT "USAGE: Update a price by a percentage",
            "Enter an integer percentage from 1 - 100",
            "and a part id number"
    WITH LISTING IN '/tmp/warn_file'
```

For more information on writing SPL functions, see the *Informix Guide to SQL: Tutorial.* ◆

Ext

External Functions

External functions are functions you write in an external language that Dynamic Server supports.

To create a C user-defined function, follow these steps:

1. Write the C function.

2. Compile the function and store the compiled code in a shared library (the shared-object file for C).

3. Register the function in the database server with the CREATE FUNCTION statement.

To create a user-defined function written in Java, follow these steps:

1. Write a Java static method, which can use the JDBC functions to interact with the database server.

2. Compile the Java source file and create a jar file (the shared-object file for Java).

3. Execute the **install_jar()** procedure with the EXECUTE PROCEDURE statement to install the jar file in the current database.

4. If the UDR uses user-defined types, create a map between SQL data types and Java classes.

   Use the **setUDTExtName()** procedure that is explained in "EXECUTE PROCEDURE" on page 2-444.

5. Register the UDR with the CREATE FUNCTION statement.

Rather than storing the body of an external routine directly in the database, the database server stores only the pathname of the shared-object file that contains the compiled version of the routine. When the database server executes the external routine, the database server invokes the external object code.

The database server stores information about an external function in several system catalog tables, including **sysprocbody** and **sysprocauth**. For more information on these system catalog tables, see the *Informix Guide to SQL: Reference*.

C

Example of Registering a C User-Defined Function

The following example registers an external C user-defined function named **equal()** in the database. This function takes two arguments of the type **basetype1** and returns a single Boolean value. The external routine reference name specifies the path to the C shared library where the function object code is actually stored. This library contains a C function **basetype1_equal()**, which is invoked during execution of the **equal()** function:

```
CREATE FUNCTION equal ( arg1 basetype1, arg2 basetype1)
RETURNING BOOLEAN;
EXTERNAL NAME
"/usr/lib/basetype1/lib/libbtype1.so(basetype1_equal)"
LANGUAGE C
END FUNCTION
```

Java

Example of Registering a User-Defined Function Written in Java

The following CREATE FUNCTION statement registers the user-defined function, **sql_explosive_reaction()**. This function is discussed in "sqlj.install_jar" on page 2-447:

```
CREATE FUNCTION sql_explosive_reaction(int) RETURNS int
    WITH (class="jvp")
    EXTERNAL NAME "course_jar:Chemistry.explosiveReaction"
    LANGUAGE JAVA
```

This function returns a single value of type INTEGER. The EXTERNAL NAME clause specifies that the Java implementation of the **sql_explosive_reaction()** function is a method called **explosiveReaction()**, which resides in the **Chemistry** Java class that resides in the **course_jar** jar file.

Ownership of Created Database Objects

The user who creates an owner-privileged UDR owns any database objects that are created by the UDR when the UDR is executed, unless another owner is specified for the created database object. In other words, the UDR owner, not the user who executes the UDR, is the owner of any database objects created by the UDR unless another owner is specified in the statement that creates the database object.

For example, assume that user **mike** creates the following user-defined function:

```
CREATE FUNCTION func1 () RETURNING INT;
    CREATE TABLE tab1 (colx INT);
    RETURN 1;
END FUNCTION
```

If user **joan** now executes function **func1**, user **mike**, not user **joan**, is the owner of the newly created table **tab1**.

However, in the case of a DBA-privileged UDR, the user who executes the UDR—not the UDR owner—owns any database objects created by the UDR, unless another owner is specified for the database object within the UDR.

For example, assume that user **mike** creates the following user-defined function:

```
CREATE DBA FUNCTION func2 () RETURNING INT;
    CREATE TABLE tab2 (coly INT);
    RETURN 1;
END FUNCTION
```

If user **joan** now executes function **func2**, user **joan**, not user **mike**, is the owner of the newly created table **tab2**.

Related Information

Related statements: ALTER FUNCTION, ALTER ROUTINE, CREATE PROCEDURE, CREATE FUNCTION FROM, DROP FUNCTION, DROP ROUTINE, GRANT, EXECUTE FUNCTION, PREPARE, REVOKE, and UPDATE STATISTICS

For a discussion on creating and using SPL routines, see the *Informix Guide to SQL: Tutorial*.

For a discussion of how to create and use external routines, see *Extending Informix Dynamic Server 2000*.

For information about how to create C UDRs, see the *DataBlade API Programmer's Manual*.

For more information on the **NODEFDAC** environment variable and the relative system catalog tables (**sysprocedures, sysprocplan, sysprocbody** and **sysprocauth)**, see the *Informix Guide to SQL: Reference*.

CREATE FUNCTION FROM

Use the CREATE FUNCTION FROM statement to access a user-defined function. The actual text of the CREATE FUNCTION statement resides in a separate file.

Syntax

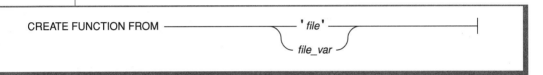

Element	Purpose	Restrictions	Syntax
file	Pathname and filename of the file that contains the full text of a CREATE FUNCTION statement The default pathname is the current directory.	The specified file must exist. The file that you specify can contain only one CREATE FUNCTION statement.	Pathname and filename must conform to the conventions of your operating system.
file_var	Name of a program variable that holds the value of file	The file that is specified in the program variable must exist. The file that you specify can contain only one CREATE FUNCTION statement.	Name must conform to language-specific rules for variable names.

Usage

An ESQL/C program cannot directly create a user-defined function. That is, it cannot contain the CREATE FUNCTION statement. However, you can create these functions within an ESQL/C program with the following steps:

1.   Create a source file with the CREATE FUNCTION statement.

2.   Use the CREATE FUNCTION FROM statement to send the contents of this source file to the database server for execution.

     The file that you specify in the *file* parameter can contain only one CREATE FUNCTION statement.

For example, suppose that the following CREATE FUNCTION statement is in a separate file, called **del_ord.sql**:

```
CREATE FUNCTION delete_order( p_order_num int )
    RETURNING int, int;
    DEFINE item_count int;
    SELECT count(*) INTO item_count FROM items
        WHERE order_num = p_order_num;
    DELETE FROM orders
        WHERE order_num = p_order_num;
    RETURN p_order_num, item_count;
END FUNCTION;
```

In the ESQL/C program, you can access the **delete_order()** SPL function with the following CREATE FUNCTION FROM statement:

```
EXEC SQL create function from 'del_ord.sql';
```

If you are not sure whether the UDR in the file is a user-defined function or a user-defined procedure, use the CREATE ROUTINE FROM statement.

The filename that you provide is relative. If you provide a simple filename (as in the preceding example), the client application looks for the file in the current directory.

Important: *The ESQL/C preprocessor does not process the contents of the file that you specify. It just sends the contents to the database server for execution. Therefore, there is no syntactic check that the file that you specify in CREATE FUNCTION FROM actually contains a CREATE FUNCTION statement. However, to improve readability of the code, Informix recommends that you match these two statements.*

Related Information

Related statements: CREATE FUNCTION, CREATE PROCEDURE, CREATE PROCEDURE FROM, and CREATE ROUTINE FROM

CREATE INDEX

Use the CREATE INDEX statement to create an index for one or more columns in a table, to specify whether or not it allows only unique values, to cluster the physical table in the order of the index, and to designate where the index should be stored.

Syntax

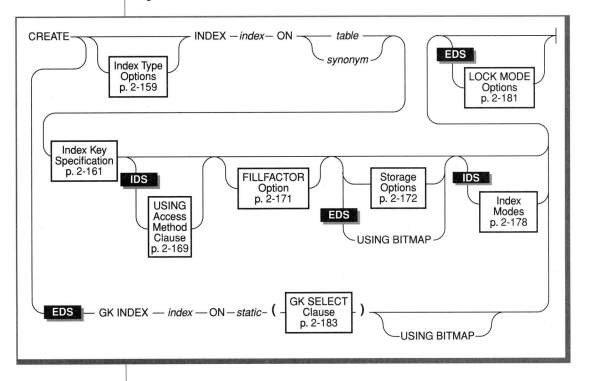

Element	Purpose	Restrictions	Syntax
index	Name of the index to create	The name must be unique within the database.	Database Object Name, p. 4-50
		The first byte of the name cannot be a leading ASCII blank (hex 20).	
synonym	Synonym for the name of the table on which the index is created	The synonym and the table to which the synonym points must already exist.	Database Object Name, p. 4-50
		(IDS) This table cannot be a virtual table.	
static	Name of the table on which a GK index is created	The table must exist. It must be a static table.	Database Object Name, p. 4-50
table	Name of the table on which the index is created	The table must exist. The table can be a regular database table or a temporary table.	Database Object Name, p. 4-50
		(IDS) This table cannot be a virtual table.	

Usage

A *secondary access method* (sometimes referred to as an *index access method*) is a set of database server functions that build, access, and manipulate an index structure such as a B-tree, R-tree, or an index structure that a DataBlade module provides. Typically, a secondary access method speeds up the retrieval of data.

When you issue the CREATE INDEX statement, the table is locked in exclusive mode. If another process is using the table, the database server cannot execute the CREATE INDEX statement and returns an error.

EDS

If you are using Enterprise Decision Server, use the USING BITMAP keywords to store the list of records in each key of the index as a compressed bitmap. The storage option is not compatible with a bitmap index because bitmap indexes must be fragmented in the same way as the table. ♦

Index-Type Options

The index-type options let you specify the characteristics of the index.

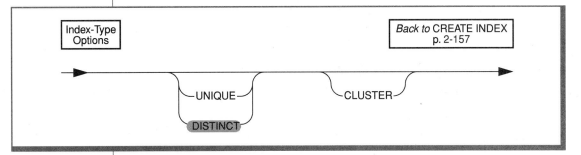

UNIQUE or DISTINCT Option

Use the UNIQUE or DISTINCT keywords to require that the column or set of columns on which the index is based accepts only unique data.

The following example creates a unique index:

```
CREATE UNIQUE INDEX c_num_ix ON customer (customer_num)
```

A unique index prevents duplicates in the **customer_num** column. A column with a unique index can have, at most, one null value. The DISTINCT keyword is a synonym for the keyword UNIQUE, so the following statement accomplishes the same task:

```
CREATE DISTINCT INDEX c_num_ix ON customer (customer_num)
```

The index in either example is maintained in ascending order, which is the default order.

If you do not specify the UNIQUE or DISTINCT keywords in a CREATE INDEX statement, the database server allows duplicate values in the indexed column.

You can also prevent duplicates in a column or set of columns by creating a unique constraint with the CREATE TABLE or ALTER TABLE statement. For more information on creating unique constraints, see the CREATE TABLE or ALTER TABLE statements.

How Indexes Affect Primary-Key, Unique, and Referential Constraints

The database server creates internal B-tree indexes for primary-key, unique, and referential constraints. If a primary-key, unique, or referential constraint is added after the table is created, any user-created indexes on the constrained columns are used, if appropriate. An appropriate index is one that indexes the same columns that are used in the primary-key, referential or unique constraint. If an appropriate user-created index is not available, the database server creates a nonfragmented internal index on the constrained column or columns.

CLUSTER Option

Use the CLUSTER option to reorder the physical table in the order that the index designates. The CREATE CLUSTER INDEX statement fails if a CLUSTER index already exists.

```
CREATE CLUSTER INDEX c_clust_ix ON customer (zipcode)
```

This statement creates an index on the **customer** table that physically orders the table by zip code.

If the CLUSTER option is specified in addition to fragments on an index, the data is clustered only within the context of the fragment and not globally across the entire table.

EDS

If you are using Enterprise Decision Server, you cannot use the CLUSTER option on STANDARD tables. In addition, you cannot use the CLUSTER option and storage options in the same CREATE INDEX statement (see "Storage Options" on page 2-172). When you create a clustered index the **constrid** of any unique or referential constraints on the associated table changes. The **constrid** is stored in the **sysconstraints** system catalog table. ♦

IDS

Some secondary access methods (such as R-tree) do not support clustering. Before you specify CLUSTER for your index, be sure that it uses an access method that supports clustering. ♦

Index-Key Specification

Use the Index-Key Specification portion of the CREATE INDEX statement to specify the key value for the index, an operator class, and whether the index will be sorted in ascending or descending order.

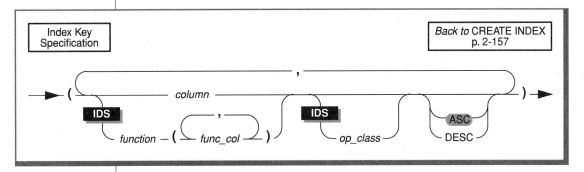

Element	Purpose	Restrictions	Syntax
column	Name of the column or columns used as a key to this index	You must observe restrictions on the location of the columns, the maximum number of columns, the total width of the columns, existing constraints on the columns, and the number of indexes allowed on the same columns. See "Using a Column as the Index Key" on page 2-163.	Identifier, p. 4-205
function	Name of the user-defined function used as a key to this index	This must be a nonvariant function. The return type of the function cannot be BYTE or TEXT. You cannot create an index on built-in algebraic, exponential, log, or hex functions.	DataBase Object Name, p. 4-50

(1 of 2)

Element	Purpose	Restrictions	Syntax
func_col	Name of the column or columns on which the user-defined function acts	See "Using a Column as the Index Key" on page 2-163.	Identifier, p. 4-205
op_class	Operator class associated with this column or function of the index	If you specify a secondary access method in the USING clause that does not have a default operator class, you must specify an operator class here.	Identifier, p. 4-205
		If you use an alternative access method, and if the access method has a default operator class, you can omit the operator class here.	
		If you do not specify an operator class and the secondary access method does not have a default operator class, the database server returns an error.	
		For more information, see "Using an Operator Class" on page 2-168.	

(2 of 2)

The index-key value can be one or more columns that contain built-in data types. When multiple columns are listed, the concatenation of the set of columns is treated as a single composite column for indexing.

IDS

In addition, the index-key value can be one of the following types:

- One or more columns that contain user-defined data types
- One or more values that a user-defined function returns (referred to as a functional index)
- A combination of columns and functions ♦

Using a Column as the Index Key

Observe the following restrictions when you specify a column or columns as the index key:

- All the columns you specify must exist and must belong to the table being indexed.
- The maximum number of columns and the total width of all columns vary with the database server. See "Creating Composite Indexes" on page 2-164.
- You cannot add an ascending index to a column or column list that already has a unique constraint on it. See "Using the ASC and DESC Sort-Order Options" on page 2-164.
- You cannot add a unique index to a column or column list that has a primary-key constraint on it. The reason is that defining the column or column list as the primary key causes the database server to create a unique internal index on the column or column list. So you cannot create another unique index on this column or column list with the CREATE INDEX statement.
- The number of indexes you can create on the same column or same sequence of columns is restricted. See "Restrictions on the Number of Indexes on a Single Column" on page 2-167 and "Restrictions on the Number of Indexes on a Sequence of Columns" on page 2-167.
- You cannot create an index on a column that belongs to an external table.
- The column you specify cannot be a column whose data type is a collection. ♦

IDS

IDS

Using a Function as an Index Key

You can create an index on a user-defined function. You can also create functional indexes within an SPL routine.

A functional index can be a B-tree index, an R-tree index, or a user-defined secondary access method.

Functional indexes are indexed on the value returned by the specified function rather than on the value of a column.

For example, the following statement creates a functional index on table **zones** using the value returned by the function **Area()** as the key:

```
CREATE INDEX zone_func_ind ON zones (Area(length,width));
```

Creating Composite Indexes

Place columns in a composite index in the order from most-frequently used to least-frequently used.

The following example creates a composite index using the **stock_num** and **manu_code** columns of the **stock** table:

```
CREATE UNIQUE INDEX st_man_ix ON stock (stock_num, manu_code
)
```

The index prevents any duplicates of a given combination of **stock_num** and **manu_code**. The index is in ascending order by default.

EDS

You can include up to 16 columns in a composite index. The total width of all indexed columns in a single CREATE INDEX statement cannot exceed 255 bytes. ♦

IDS

A composite index can have up to 16 key parts. An *index key part* is either a table column or the result of a user-defined function on one or more table columns. A composite index can have any of the following items as an index key:

- One or more columns
- One or more values that a user-defined function returns (referred to as a functional index)
- A combination of columns and user-defined functions

The total width of all indexed columns in a single CREATE INDEX statement cannot exceed 390 bytes. ♦

Using the ASC and DESC Sort-Order Options

Use the ASC option to specify an index that is maintained in ascending order. The ASC option is the default ordering scheme. Use the DESC option to specify an index that is maintained in descending order.

You can use these options with B-trees only.

Effects of Unique Constraints on Sort Order Options

When a column or list of columns is defined as unique in a CREATE TABLE or ALTER TABLE statement, the database server implements that UNIQUE CONSTRAINT by creating a unique ascending index. Thus, you cannot use the CREATE INDEX statement to add an ascending index to a column or column list that is already defined as unique.

However, you can create a descending index on such columns, and you can include such columns in composite ascending indexes in different combinations. For example, the following sequence of statements is allowed:

```
CREATE TABLE customer (
    customer_num        SERIAL(101) UNIQUE,
    fname               CHAR(15),
    lname               CHAR(15),
    company             CHAR(20),
    address1            CHAR(20),
    address2            CHAR(20),
    city                CHAR(15),
    state               CHAR(2),
    zipcode             CHAR(5),
    phone               CHAR(18)
    )

CREATE INDEX c_temp1 ON customer (customer_num DESC)
CREATE INDEX c_temp2 ON customer (customer_num, zipcode)
```

In this example, the **customer_num** column has a unique constraint placed on it. The first CREATE INDEX example places an index sorted in descending order on the **customer_num** column. The second CREATE INDEX example includes the **customer_num** column as part of a composite index. For more information on composite indexes, see "Creating Composite Indexes" on page 2-164.

Bidirectional Traversal of Indexes

When you create an index on a column but do not specify the ASC or DESC keywords, the database server stores the key values in ascending order by default.

However, the bidirectional-traversal capability of the database server lets you create just one index on a column and use that index for queries that specify sorting of results in either ascending or descending order of the sort column.

Because of this capability, it does not matter whether you create a single-column index as an ascending or descending index. Whichever storage order you choose for an index, the database server can traverse that index in ascending or descending order when it processes queries.

However, if you create a composite index on a table, the ASC and DESC keywords might be required. For example, if you want to enter a SELECT statement whose ORDER BY clause sorts on multiple columns and sorts each column in a different order and you want to use an index for this query, you need to create a composite index that corresponds to the ORDER BY columns.

For example, suppose that you want to enter the following query:

```
SELECT stock_num, manu_code, description, unit_price
    FROM stock
    ORDER BY manu_code ASC, unit_price DESC
```

This query sorts first in ascending order by the value of the **manu_code** column and then in descending order by the value of the **unit_price** column. To use an index for this query, you need to issue a CREATE INDEX statement that corresponds to the requirements of the ORDER BY clause. For example, you can enter either of the following statements to create the index:

```
CREATE INDEX stock_idx1 ON stock
    (manu_code ASC, unit_price DESC);

CREATE INDEX stock_idx2 ON stock
    (manu_code DESC, unit_price ASC);
```

The composite index that was used for this query (**stock_idx1** or **stock_idx2**) cannot be used for queries in which you specify the same sort direction for the two columns in the ORDER BY clause. For example, suppose that you want to enter the following queries:

```
SELECT stock_num, manu_code, description, unit_price
    FROM stock
    ORDER BY manu_code ASC, unit_price ASC;

SELECT stock_num, manu_code, description, unit_price
    FROM stock
    ORDER BY manu_code DESC, unit_price DESC;
```

If you want to use a composite index to improve the performance of these queries, you need to enter one of the following CREATE INDEX statements. You can use either one of the created indexes (**stock_idx3** or **stock_idx4**) to improve the performance of the preceding queries.

```
CREATE INDEX stock_idx3 ON stock
    (manu_code ASC, unit_price ASC);

CREATE INDEX stock_idx4 ON stock
    (manu_code DESC, unit_price DESC);
```

Restrictions on the Number of Indexes on a Single Column

You can create only one ascending index and one descending index on a single column.

Because of the bidirectional traversal capability of the database server, you do not need to create both indexes in practice. You only need to create one of the indexes. Both of these indexes would achieve exactly the same results for an ascending or descending sort on the **stock_num** column.

Restrictions on the Number of Indexes on a Sequence of Columns

You can create multiple indexes on a sequence of columns, provided that each index has a unique combination of ascending and descending columns. For example, to create all possible indexes on the **stock_num** and **manu_code** columns of the **stock** table, you could create the following indexes:

- The **ix1** index on both columns in ascending order
- The **ix2** index on both columns in descending order
- The **ix3** index on **stock_num** in ascending order and on **manu_code** in descending order
- The **ix4** index on **stock_num** in descending order and on **manu_code** in ascending order

Because of the bidirectional-traversal capability of the database server, you do not need to create these four indexes. You only need to create two indexes:

- The **ix1** and **ix2** indexes achieve exactly the same results for sorts in which the user specifies the same sort direction (ascending or descending) for both columns. Therefore, you only need to create one index of this pair.

- The **ix3** and **ix4** indexes achieve exactly the same results for sorts in which the user specifies different sort directions for the two columns (ascending on the first column and descending on the second column or vice versa). Therefore, you only need to create one index of this pair.

For further information on the bidirectional-traversal capability of the database server, see "Bidirectional Traversal of Indexes" on page 2-165.

IDS

Using an Operator Class

An *operator class* is the set of operators the database server associates with a secondary access method for query optimization and building the index.

Specify an operator class when you create an index if you have one of the following situations:

- A default operator class for the secondary access method does not exist. For example, some of the user-defined access methods do not provide a default operator class.

- You want to use an operator class that is different from the default operator class that the secondary access method provides.

For more information, see "Default Operator Classes" on page 2-197. The following CREATE INDEX statement creates a B-tree index on the **cust_tab** table that uses the **abs_btree_ops** operator class for the **cust_num** key:

```
CREATE INDEX c_num1_ix ON cust_tab (cust_num abs_btree_ops);
```

IDS

USING Access Method Clause

Use the USING clause to specify the secondary access method to use for the new index.

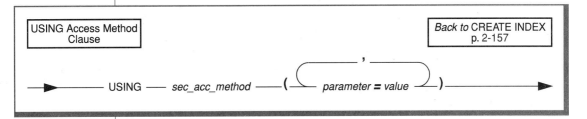

USING Access Method Clause		*Back to* CREATE INDEX p. 2-157

USING —— *sec_acc_method* ——(—— *parameter = value* ——)——

Element	Purpose	Restrictions	Syntax
parameter	Name of the secondary access-method parameter used with this index	The parameter name must be one of the strings allowed for this secondary access method. For more information, refer to the user documentation for your user-defined access method.	Quoted String, p. 4-260
sec_acc_method	Name of the secondary access method used with the index you are creating	The access method can be a B-tree, R-tree, or user-defined access method, such as one that was defined by a DataBlade module. The access method must be a valid access method in the **sysams** system catalog table. The default secondary access method is B-tree.	Identifier, p. 4-205
		If the access method is B-tree, you can create only one index for each unique combination of ascending and descending columnar or functional keys with operator classes. This restriction does not apply to other secondary access methods.	
value	Value of the specified parameter	The parameter value must be one of the quoted strings or literal numbers allowed for this secondary access method.	Quoted String, p. 4-260 or Literal Number, p. 4-237

A *secondary access method* is a set of routines that perform all of the operations needed to make an index available to a server, such as create, drop, insert, delete, update, and scan.

The database server provides the following secondary access methods:

- The generic B-tree index is the built-in secondary access method.

  A B-tree index is good for a query that retrieves a range of data values. The database server implements this secondary access method and registers it as **btree** in the system catalog tables of a database.

- The R-tree secondary access method is a registered secondary access method.

  An R-tree index is good for searches on multi-dimensional data (such as box, circle, and so forth). The database server registers this secondary access method as **rtree** in the system catalog tables of a database. For more information on R-tree indexes, see the *Informix R-Tree Index User's Guide*.

Some user-defined access methods are packaged as DataBlades. For more information about user-defined access methods, refer to your access-method or DataBlade user guides.

By default, the CREATE INDEX statement creates a generic B-tree index. If you want to create an index with a secondary access method other than B-tree, you must specify the name of the secondary access method in the USING clause.

The following example assumes that the database implements the R-tree index. It creates an R-tree index on the **location** column that contains an opaque data type, **point**.

```
CREATE INDEX loc_ix ON TABLE emp (location)
    USING rtree;
SELECT name FROM emp
    WHERE location N_equator_equals point('500, 0');
```

The sample query has a filter on the **location** column.

Some DataBlade modules provide indexes that require specific parameters when you create them.

Example of an Index with Parameters

The following CREATE INDEX statement creates an index that uses the secondary access method **fulltext**, which takes two parameters: WORD_SUPPORT and PHRASE_SUPPORT. It indexes a table **t**, which has two columns: **i**, an integer column, and **data**, a TEXT column.

```
CREATE INDEX tx ON t(data)
USING fulltext (WORD SUPPORT='PATTERN',
PHRASE_SUPPORT='MAXIMUM');
```

FILLFACTOR Option

Use the FILLFACTOR option to provide for expansion of an index at a later date or to create compacted indexes.

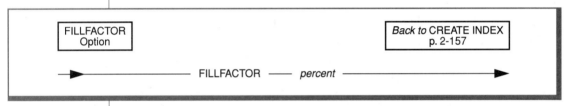

Element	Purpose	Restrictions	Syntax
percent	Percentage of each index page that is filled by index data when the index is created The default value is 90.	Value must be in the range 1 to 100.	Literal Number, p. 4-237

When the index is created, the database server initially fills only that percentage of the nodes specified with the FILLFACTOR value.

The FILLFACTOR option takes effect only when you build an index on a table that contains more than 5,000 rows and uses more than 100 table pages, when you create an index on a fragmented table, or when you create a fragmented index on a nonfragmented table.

The FILLFACTOR can also be set as a parameter in the ONCONFIG file. The FILLFACTOR clause on the CREATE INDEX statement overrides the setting in the ONCONFIG file.

For more information about the ONCONFIG file and the parameters you can use with **ONCONFIG**, see your *Administrator's Guide*.

Providing a Low Percentage Value

If you provide a low percentage value, such as 50, you allow room for growth in your index. The nodes of the index initially fill to a certain percentage and contain space for inserts. The amount of available space depends on the number of keys in each page as well as the percentage value. For example, with a 50-percent FILLFACTOR value, the page would be half full and could accommodate doubling in size. A low percentage value can result in faster inserts and can be used for indexes that you expect to grow.

Providing a High Percentage Value

If you provide a high percentage value, such as 99, your indexes are compacted, and any new index inserts result in splitting nodes. The maximum density is achieved with 100 percent. With a 100-percent FILLFACTOR value, the index has no room available for growth; any additions to the index result in splitting the nodes. A 99-percent FILLFACTOR value allows room for at least one insertion per node. A high percentage value can result in faster selects and can be used for indexes that you do not expect to grow or for mostly read-only indexes.

Storage Options

The storage options let you specify the distribution scheme of an index. You can use the IN clause to specify a storage space to hold the entire index, or you can use the FRAGMENT BY clause to fragment the index across multiple storage spaces

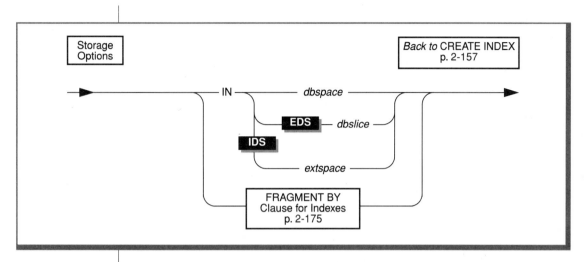

Element	Purpose	Restrictions	Syntax
dbslice	Name of the dbslice that contains all of the index fragments	The dbslice must exist when you execute the statement.	Identifier, p. 4-205
dbspace	Name of the dbspace in which you want to place the index	The dbspace must exist when you execute the statement.	Identifier, p. 4-205
extspace	Name assigned with the **onspaces** command to a storage area outside the database server	The specified *extspace* must already exist.	Refer to the user documentation for your custom access method for more information.

If you do not use the storage options (that is, if you do not specify a distribution scheme), by default the index inherits the distribution scheme as of the table on which it is built. Such an index is called an *attached index.*

An attached index is created in the same dbspace (or dbspaces if the table is fragmented) as the table on which it is built. If the distribution scheme of a table changes, all attached indexes start using the new distribution scheme.

When you specify one of the storage options, you create a *detached index.* Detached indexes are indexes that are created with a specified distribution scheme. Even if the distribution scheme specified for the index is identical to that specified for the table, the index is still considered to be detached. If the distribution scheme of a table changes, all detached indexes continue to use their own distribution scheme.

EDS

For information on locally-detached and globally-detached indexes, see "FRAGMENT BY Clause for Indexes" on page 2-175.

If you are using Enterprise Decision Server. you cannot use the CLUSTER option and storage options in the same CREATE INDEX statement. See "CLUSTER Option" on page 2-160. ◆

IN Clause

Use the IN clause to specify a storage space to hold the entire index. The storage space that you specify must already exist.

Storing an Index in a dbspace

Use the IN *dbspace* clause to specify the dbspace where you want your index to reside. When you use this clause, you create a detached index.

The IN *dbspace* clause allows you to isolate an index. For example, if the **customer** table is created in the **custdata** dbspace, but you want to create an index in a separate dbspace called **custind**, use the following statements:

```
CREATE TABLE customer
    .
    .
    .
    IN custdata EXTENT SIZE 16
CREATE INDEX idx_cust ON customer (customer_num)
    IN custind
```

EDS

Storing an Index in a dbslice

If you are using Enterprise Decision Server, the IN *dbslice* clause allows you to fragment an index across multiple dbspaces. The database server fragments the table by round-robin in the dbspaces that make up the dbslice at the time the table is created.

IDS

Storing an Index in an extspace

In general, you use this option in conjunction with the "USING Access Method Clause" on page 2-169. You can also store an index in an sbspace. For more information, refer to the user documentation for your custom access method.

FRAGMENT BY Clause for Indexes

Use the FRAGMENT BY clause to fragment an index across multiple dbspaces.

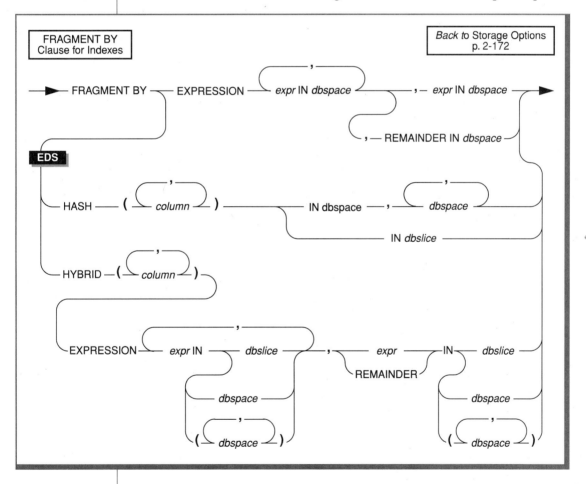

Element	Purpose	Restrictions	Syntax
column	Name of the column on which you want to fragment your index	All specified columns must be in the current table. If you specify a serial column, you cannot specify any other column.	Identifier, p. 4-205
dbslice	Name of the dbslice that contains all of the index fragments	The dbslice must exist when you execute the statement.	Identifier, p. 4-205
dbspace	Name of the dbspace that will contain an index fragment that expr defines	The dbspaces must exist at the time you execute the statement. You can specify a maximum of 2,048 dbspaces.	Identifier, p. 4-205
expr	Expression that defines which index keys are stored in a fragment	Each fragment expression can contain only columns from the current table and only data values from a single row. The columns contained in a fragment expression must be the same as the indexed columns, or a subset of the indexed columns. No subqueries, user-defined routines, aggregates, or references to the fields of a row-type column are allowed. In addition, no built-in current, date and/or time functions are allowed.	Expression, p. 4-73, and Condition, p. 4-27

When you use this clause, you create a detached index.

EDS

You can fragment indexes on any column of a table, even if the table spans multiple coservers. The columns that you specify in the FRAGMENT BY clause do not have to be part of the index key.

Detached indexes can be either locally detached or globally detached. A *locally detached index* is an index in which, for each data tuple in a table, the corresponding index tuple is guaranteed to be on the same coserver. The table and index fragmentation strategies do not have to be identical as long as colocality can be guaranteed. If the data tuple and index tuple colocality does not exist, then the index is a *globally detached index*. For performance implications of globally-detached indexes, see your *Performance Guide*.

For more information on the expression, hash, and hybrid distribution schemes, see "Fragmenting by EXPRESSION" on page 2-262; "Fragmenting by HASH" on page 2-263; and "Fragmenting by HYBRID" on page 2-264, respectively in the CREATE TABLE statement. ♦

Fragmentation of System Indexes

System indexes (such as those used in referential constraints and unique constraints) utilize user indexes if they exist. If no user indexes can be utilized, system indexes remain nonfragmented and are moved to the dbspace where the database was created. To fragment a system index, create the fragmented index on the constraint columns, and then add the constraint using the ALTER TABLE statement.

IDS

Fragmentation of Unique Indexes

You can fragment unique indexes only with a table that uses an expression-based distribution scheme. The columns referenced in the fragment expression must be part of the indexed columns. If your CREATE INDEX statement fails to meet either of these restrictions, the CREATE INDEX fails, and work is rolled back.

Fragmentation of Indexes on Temporary Tables

You can fragment a unique index on a temporary table only if the underlying table uses an expression-based distribution scheme. That is, the CREATE Temporary TABLE statement that defines the temporary table must specify an explicit expression-based distribution scheme.

If you try to create a fragmented, unique index on a temporary table for which you did not specify a fragmentation strategy when you created it, the database server creates the index in the first dbspace that the **DBSPACETEMP** environment variable specifies.

For more information on the default storage characteristics of temporary tables, see "Where Temporary Tables are Stored" on page 2-293.

For more information on the **DBSPACETEMP** environment variable, see the *Informix Guide to SQL: Reference.*

IDS

Index Modes

Use the index modes to control the behavior of the index during insert, delete, and update operations.

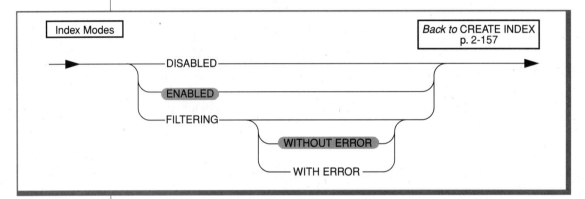

The following table explains the index modes

Mode	Purpose
DISABLED	The database server does not update the index after insert, delete, and update operations that modify the base table.
	The optimizer does not use the index during the execution of queries.
ENABLED	The database server updates the index after insert, delete, and update operations that modify the base table.
	The optimizer uses the index during query execution.
	If an insert or update operation causes a duplicate key value to be added to a unique index, the statement fails.

(1 of 2)

Mode	Purpose
FILTERING	The database server updates a unique index after insert, delete, and update operations that modify the base table. (This option is not available with duplicate indexes.)
	The optimizer uses the index during query execution.
	If an insert or update operation causes a duplicate key value to be added to a unique index in filtering mode, the statement continues processing, but the bad row is written to the violations table associated with the base table. Diagnostic information about the unique-index violation is written to the diagnostics table associated with the base table.

(2 of 2)

If you specify filtering for a unique index, you can also specify one of the following error options.

Error Option	Purpose
WITHOUT ERROR	When a unique-index violation occurs during an insert or update operation, no integrity-violation error is returned to the user.
WITH ERROR	When a unique-index violation occurs during an insert or update operation, an integrity-violation error is returned to the user.

Specifying Modes for Unique Indexes

You must observe the following rules when you specify modes for unique indexes in CREATE INDEX statements:

- You can set the mode of a unique index to enabled, disabled, or filtering.

- If you do not specify a mode, by default the index is enabled.

- For an index set to filtering mode, if you do not specify an error option, the default is WITHOUT ERROR.

- When you add a new unique index to an existing base table and specify the disabled mode for the index, your CREATE INDEX statement succeeds even if duplicate values in the indexed column would cause a unique-index violation.

- When you add a new unique index to an existing base table and specify the enabled or filtering mode for the index, your CREATE INDEX statement succeeds provided that no duplicate values exist in the indexed column that would cause a unique-index violation. However, if any duplicate values exist in the indexed column, your CREATE INDEX statement fails and returns an error.

- When you add a new unique index to an existing base table in the enabled or filtering mode, and duplicate values exist in the indexed column, erroneous rows in the base table are not filtered to the violations table. Thus, you cannot use a violations table to detect the erroneous rows in the base table.

Adding a Unique Index When Duplicate Values Exist in the Column

If you attempt to add a unique index in the enabled mode but receive an error message because duplicate values are in the indexed column, take the following steps to add the index successfully:

1. Add the index in the disabled mode. Issue the CREATE INDEX statement again, but this time specify the DISABLED keyword.

2. Start a violations and diagnostics table for the target table with the START VIOLATIONS TABLE statement.

3. Issue a SET Database Object Mode statement to switch the mode of the index to enabled. When you issue this statement, existing rows in the target table that violate the unique-index requirement are duplicated in the violations table. However, you receive an integrity-violation error message, and the index remains disabled.

4. Issue a SELECT statement on the violations table to retrieve the nonconforming rows that are duplicated from the target table. You might need to join the violations and diagnostics tables to get all the necessary information.

5. Take corrective action on the rows in the target table that violate the unique-index requirement.

6. After you fix all the nonconforming rows in the target table, issue the SET Database Object Mode statement again to switch the disabled index to the enabled mode. This time the index is enabled, and no integrity violation error message is returned because all rows in the target table now satisfy the new unique-index requirement.

Specifying Modes for Duplicate Indexes

You must observe the following rules when you specify modes for duplicate indexes in CREATE INDEX statements:

- You can set a duplicate index to enabled or disabled mode. Filtering mode is available only for unique indexes.
- If you do not specify the mode of a duplicate index, by default the index is enabled.

IDS

How the Database Server Treats Disabled Indexes

Whether a disabled index is a unique or duplicate index, the database server effectively ignores the index during data-manipulation operations.

When an index is disabled, the database server stops updating it and stops using it during queries, but the catalog information about the disabled index is retained. So you cannot create a new index on a column or set of columns if a disabled index on that column or set of columns already exists.

Similarly, you cannot create an active (enabled) unique, foreign-key, or primary-key constraint on a column or set of columns if the indexes on which the active constraint depends are disabled.

EDS

LOCK MODE Options

Use the lock modes to specify the locking granularity of the index.

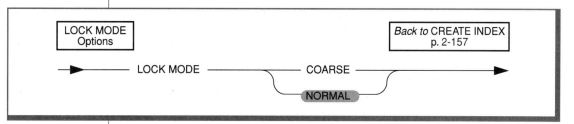

When you use the coarse-lock mode, index-level locks are acquired on the index instead of item-level or page-level locks. This mode reduces the number of lock calls on an index.

Use the coarse-lock mode when you know the index is not going to change, that is, when read-only operations are performed on the index.

If you do not specify a lock mode, the default is normal. That is, the database server places item-level or page-level locks on the index as necessary.

EDS

Generalized-Key Indexes

If you are using Enterprise Decision Server, you can create generalized-key (GK) indexes. Keys in a conventional index consist of one or more columns of the table being indexed. A GK index stores information about the records in a table based on the results of a query. Only tables created with the STATIC type can be used in a GK index.

GK indexes provide a form of pre-computed index capability that allows faster query processing, especially in data-warehousing environments. The optimizer can use the GK index to increase performance.

A GK index is *defined on* a table when that table is the one being indexed. A GK index *depends on* a table when the table appears in the FROM clause of the index. Before you create a GK index, keep the following issues in mind:

- All tables used in a GK index must be static tables. If you try to change the type of a table to non-static while a GK index depends on that table, the database server returns an error.

- Since any table involved in a GK index needs to be a static type, UPDATE, DELETE, INSERT, and LOAD operations may not be performed on such a table until the dependent GK index is dropped and the table type changes.

Key-only index scans are not available with GK indexes.

SELECT Clause for Generalized-Key Index

If you are using Enterprise Decision Server, the options of the GK SELECT clause are a subset of the options of the SELECT statement. The syntax of the GK SELECT clause has the same format as the syntax for "SELECT" on page 2-634.

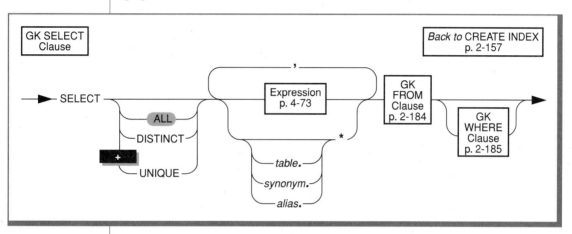

Element	Purpose	Restrictions	Syntax
alias	Temporary name assigned to the table in the FROM clause	You cannot use an alias for a select clause unless you assign the alias to the table in the FROM clause.	Identifier, p. 4-205
		You cannot use an alias for the table on which the index is being built.	
synonym	Name of the synonym from which you want to retrieve data	The synonym and the table to which the synonym points must exist.	Database Object Name, p. 4-50
table	Name of the table from which you want to retrieve data	The table must exist.	Database Object Name, p. 4-50

The following limitations apply to the expression in the GK SELECT clause:

- The expression cannot refer to any SPL routine.
- The expression cannot include the USER, TODAY, CURRENT, DBINFO built-in functions or any function that refers to a time or a time interval.

FROM Clause for Generalized-Key Index

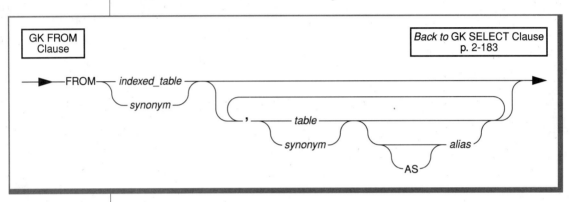

Element	Purpose	Restrictions	Syntax
alias	Temporary name for a table	You cannot use an alias with indexed_table.	Identifier, p. 4-205
indexed_table	Name of the table on which the index is being built	The FROM clause must include the indexed table.	Database Object Name, p. 4-50
synonym	Synonym for the table from which you want to retrieve data	The synonym and the table to which the synonym points must exist.	Database Object Name, p. 4-50
table	Name of the table from which you want to retrieve data	The table must exist.	Database Object Name, p. 4-50

All tables that appear in the FROM clause must be local static tables. That is, no views, non-static, or remote tables are allowed.

The tables that are mentioned in the FROM clause must be *transitively joined on key* to the indexed table. Table **A** is transitively joined on key to table **B** if **A** and **B** are joined with equal joins on the unique-key columns of **A**. For example, suppose tables **A**, **B**, and **C** each have **col1** as a primary key. In the following example, **B** is joined on key to **A** and **C** is joined on key to **B**. **C** is transitively joined on key to **A**.

```
CREATE GK INDEX gki
(SELECT A.col1, A.col2 FROM A, B, C
 WHERE A.col1 = B.col1 AND B.col1 = C.col1)
```

WHERE Clause for Generalized-Key Index

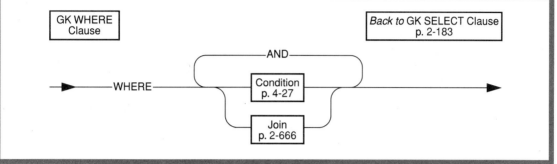

The WHERE clause for a GK index has the following limitations:

- The clause cannot include USER, TODAY, CURRENT, DBINFO built-in functions or any functions that refer to time or a time interval.
- The clause cannot refer to any SPL routine.
- The clause cannot have any subqueries.
- The clause cannot use any aggregate function.
- The clause cannot have any IN, LIKE, or MATCH clauses.

Related Information

Related statements: ALTER INDEX, CREATE OPCLASS, CREATE TABLE, DROP INDEX, and SET Database Object Mode

For a discussion of the structure of indexes, see your *Administrator's Reference*.

For a discussion on the different types of indexes and information about performance issues with indexes, see your *Performance Guide*.

GLS For a discussion of the GLS aspects of the CREATE INDEX statement, see the *Informix Guide to GLS Functionality*. ◆

For information about operator classes, refer to the CREATE OPCLASS statement and *Extending Informix Dynamic Server 2000*.

For information about the indexes provided by DataBlade modules, refer to your DataBlade module user's guide.

CREATE OPAQUE TYPE

Use the CREATE OPAQUE TYPE statement to create an opaque data type.

Syntax

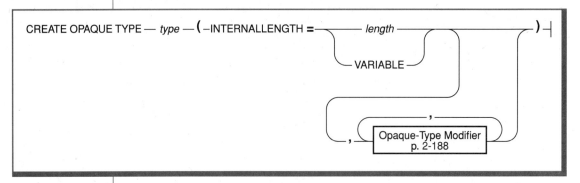

Element	Purpose	Restrictions	Syntax
length	Number of bytes needed by the database server to store a value of this data type	The number must match the positive integer reported when the C language **sizeof()** directive is applied to the type structure.	Literal Number, p. 4-237
type	Name of the new opaque data type	The name you specify must follow the conventions of SQL identifiers. The *type* must be unique within the database. In an ANSI-compliant database, the combination owner.type must be unique within the database.	Identifier, p. 4-205 Data Type, p. 4-53

Usage

The CREATE OPAQUE TYPE statement registers a new opaque type in the database. Dynamic Server stores information on extended data types, including opaque types, in the **sysxtdtypes** system catalog table.

Privileges on Opaque Types

To create an opaque type, you must have the Resource privilege on the database. When you create the opaque type, only you, the owner, have the Usage privilege on this type. Use the GRANT or REVOKE statements to grant or revoke the Usage privilege to other database users.

To find out what privileges exist on a particular type, check the **sysxtdtypes** system catalog table for the owner name and the **sysxtdtypeauth** system catalog table for additional type privileges that might have been granted. For more information on system catalog tables, see the *Informix Guide to SQL: Reference*.

DB

The DB-Access utility can also display privileges on opaque types. ♦

Naming an Opaque Type

The actual name of an opaque type is an SQL identifier. When you create an opaque type, the name must be unique within a database.

ANSI

When you create an opaque type in an ANSI-compliant database, *owner.type_name* must be unique within the database.

The owner name is case sensitive. If you do not put quotes around the owner name, the name of the opaque-type owner is stored in uppercase letters. ♦

INTERNALLENGTH Modifier

The INTERNALLENGTH modifier specifies the size of an opaque type. The way you specify the internal length defines whether the opaque type is fixed length or varying length.

Fixed-Length Opaque Types

A fixed-length opaque type has an internal structure that has a fixed size. To create a fixed-length opaque type, specify the size of the internal structure, in bytes, for the INTERNALLENGTH modifier. The following statement creates a fixed-length opaque type called **fixlen_typ**. The database server allocates 8 bytes for this type.

```
CREATE OPAQUE TYPE fixlen_typ(INTERNALLENGTH=8, CANNOTHASH)
```

Varying-Length Opaque Types

A varying-length opaque type has an internal structure whose size might vary from one instance of the opaque type to another. For example, the internal structure of an opaque type might hold the actual value of a string up to a certain size but beyond this size it might use an LO-pointer to a CLOB to hold the value.

To create a varying-length opaque type, use the VARIABLE keyword for the INTERNALLENGTH modifier. The following statement creates a variable-length opaque type called **varlen_typ**:

```
CREATE OPAQUE TYPE varlen_typ(INTERNALLENGTH=VARIABLE,
    MAXLEN=1024)
```

Opaque-Type Modifier

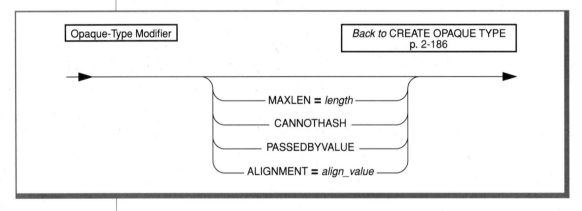

Element	Purpose	Restrictions	Syntax
align_value	Byte boundary on which the database server aligns the opaque type when passing it to a user-defined routine	The alignment must be 1, 2, 4, or 8, depending on the C definition of the opaque type and the hardware and compiler used to build the object file for the type. If alignment is not specified, the system default is 4 bytes.	Literal Number, p. 4-237
length	Maximum length in bytes to allocate for instances of the type in varying-length opaque types If maximum length is not specified for a variable-length type, the default is 2 kilobytes.	The length must be a positive integer less than or equal to 32 kilobytes. Do not specify for fixed-length types. Values that exceed this length return errors.	Literal Number, p. 4-237

Use modifiers to specify the following optional information:

- MAXLEN specifies the maximum length for varying-length opaque types.

- CANNOTHASH specifies that the database server cannot use a hash function on the opaque type.

  You must provide an appropriate hash function for the database server to evaluate GROUP BY clauses on the type.

- PASSEDBYVALUE specifies that an opaque type of 4 bytes or fewer is passed by value.

  By default, opaque types are passed to user-defined routines by reference.

- ALIGNMENT specifies the byte boundary on which the database server aligns the opaque type.

Defining an Opaque Type

To define the opaque type to the database server, you must provide the following information in the C language:

- A data structure that serves as the internal storage of the opaque type

  The internal storage details of the data type are hidden, or opaque. Once you define a new opaque type, the database server can manipulate it without knowledge of the C structure in which it is stored.

- Support functions that allow the database server to interact with this internal structure

  The support functions tell the database server how to interact with the internal structure of the type. These support functions must be written in the C programming language.

- Additional user-defined functions that can be called by other support functions or by end users to operate on the opaque type (optional)

  Possible support functions include operator functions and cast functions. Before you can use these functions in SQL statements, they must be registered with the appropriate DEFINE CAST, CREATE PROCEDURE, or CREATE FUNCTION statement.

The following table summarizes the support functions for an opaque type.

Function	Purpose	Invoked
input	Converts the opaque type from its external LVARCHAR representation to its internal representation	When a client application sends a character representation of the opaque type in an INSERT, UPDATE, or LOAD statement
output	Converts the opaque type from its internal representation to its external LVARCHAR representation	When the database server sends a character representation of the opaque type as a result of a SELECT or FETCH statement
receive	Converts the opaque type from its internal representation on the client computer to its internal representation on the server computer Provides platform-independent results regardless of differences between client and server computer types.	When a client application sends an internal representation of the opaque type in an INSERT, UPDATE, or LOAD statement

(1 of 2)

Function	Purpose	Invoked
send	Converts the opaque type from its internal representation on the server computer to its internal representation on the client computer Provides platform-independent results regardless of differences between client and database server computer types.	When the database server sends an internal representation of the opaque type as a result of a SELECT or FETCH statement
import	Performs any tasks need to convert from the external (character) representation of an opaque type to the internal representation for a bulk copy	When DB-Access (LOAD) or the High Performance Loader initiates a bulk copy from a text file to a database
export	Performs any tasks need to convert from the internal representation of an opaque type to the external (character) representation for a bulk copy	When DB-Access (UNLOAD) or the High Performance Loader initiates a bulk copy from a database to a text file
importbinary	Performs any tasks need to convert from the internal representation of an opaque type on the client computer to the internal representation on the server computer for a bulk copy	When DB-Access (LOAD) or the High Performance Loader initiates a bulk copy from a binary file to a database
exportbinary	Performs any tasks need to convert from the internal representation of an opaque type on the server computer to the internal representation on the client computer for a bulk copy	When DB-Access (UNLOAD) or the High Performance Loader initiates a bulk copy from a database to a binary file
assign()	Performs any processing required before storing the opaque type to disk This support function must be named **assign()**.	When the database server executes an INSERT, UPDATE, and LOAD statement, before it stores the opaque type to disk
destroy()	Performs any processing necessary before removing a row that contains the opaque type This support function must be named **destroy()**.	When the database server executes the DELETE and DROP TABLE statements, before it removes the opaque type from disk
lohandles()	Returns a list of the LO-pointer structures (pointers to smart large objects) in an opaque type	Whenever the database server must search opaque types for references to smart large objects: when the **oncheck** utility runs, when an archive is performed
compare()	Compares two values of the opaque type and returns an integer value to indicate whether the first value is less than, equal to, or greater than the second value	When the database server encounters an ORDER BY, UNIQUE, DISTINCT, or UNION clause in a SELECT statement, or when it executes the CREATE INDEX statement to create a B-tree index

(2 of 2)

Once you write the necessary support functions for the opaque type, use the CREATE FUNCTION statement to register these support functions in the same database as the opaque type. Certain support functions convert other data types to or from the new opaque type. After you create and register these support functions, use the CREATE CAST statement to associate each function with a particular cast. The cast must be registered in the same database as the support function.

When you have written the necessary source code to define the opaque type, you then use the CREATE OPAQUE TYPE statement to register the opaque type in the database.

Related Information

Related statements: CREATE CAST, CREATE DISTINCT TYPE, CREATE FUNCTION, CREATE ROW TYPE, CREATE TABLE, and DROP TYPE

For a summary of an opaque type, see the *Informix Guide to SQL: Reference*.

For information on how to define an opaque type, see *Extending Informix Dynamic Server 2000*.

For information about the GLS aspects of the CREATE OPAQUE TYPE statement, refer to the *Informix Guide to GLS Functionality*.

CREATE OPCLASS

Use the CREATE OPCLASS statement to create an *operator class* for a *secondary access method*.

Syntax

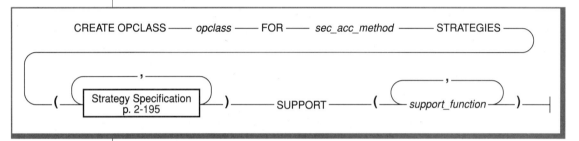

Element	Purpose	Restrictions	Syntax
opclass	Name of the operator class being created	The operator class name must be unique within the database.	Database Object Name, p. 4-50
sec_acc_method	Name of the secondary access method with which the specified operator class is being associated	The secondary access method must already exist and must be registered in the **sysams** system catalog table.	Identifier, p. 4-205
		The database server provides the B-tree and R-tree secondary access method.	
support_function	Name of a support function required by the specified secondary access method	The support functions must be listed in the order expected by the specified access method.	Identifier, p. 4-205

Usage

An *operator class* is the set of operators that Dynamic Server associates with the specified secondary access method for query optimization and building the index. A secondary access method (sometimes referred to as an *index access method*) is a set of database server functions that build, access, and manipulate an index structure such as a B-tree, R-tree, or an index structure that a DataBlade module provides.

You define a new operator class when you want:

- an index to use a different order for the data than the sequence provided by the default operator class.
- a set of operators that is different from any existing operator classes that are associated with a particular secondary access method.

You must have the Resource privilege or be the DBA to create an operator class. The actual name of an operator class is an SQL identifier. When you create an operator class, *opclass name* must be unique within a database.

ANSI

When you create an operator class in an ANSI-compliant database, *owner.opclass_name* must be unique within the database.

The owner name is case sensitive. If you do not put quotes around the owner name, the name of the operator-class owner is stored in uppercase letters. ♦

The following CREATE OPCLASS statement creates a new operator class called **abs_btree_ops** for the **btree** secondary access method:

```
CREATE OPCLASS abs_btree_ops FOR btree
    STRATEGIES (abs_lt, abs_lte, abs_eq, abs_gte,
        abs_gt)
    SUPPORT (abs_cmp)
```

For more information on the **btree** secondary access method, see "Default Operator Classes" on page 2-197.

An operator class has two kinds of operator-class functions:

- Strategy functions

  Specify strategy functions of an operator class in the STRATEGY clause of the CREATE OPCLASS statement. In the preceding CREATE OPCLASS statement, the **abs_btree_ops** operator class has five strategy functions.

- Support functions

  Specify support functions of an operator class in the SUPPORT clause of the CREATE OPCLASS statement. In the preceding CREATE OPCLASS statement, the **abs_btree_ops** operator class has one support function.

STRATEGIES Clause

Strategy functions are functions that end users can invoke within an SQL statement to operate on a data type. The query optimizer uses the strategy functions to determine if a particular index can be used to process a query. If an index exists on a column or user-defined function in a query, and the qualifying operator in the query matches one of the strategy functions in the Strategy Specification list, the optimizer considers using the index for the query. For more information on query plans, see your *Performance Guide*.

When you create a new operator class, you specify the strategy functions for the secondary access method in the STRATEGIES clause. The Strategy Specification lists the name of each strategy function. List these functions in the order that the secondary access method expects. For the specific order of strategy operators for the default operator classes for a B-tree index and an R-tree index, see *Extending Informix Dynamic Server 2000*.

Strategy Specification

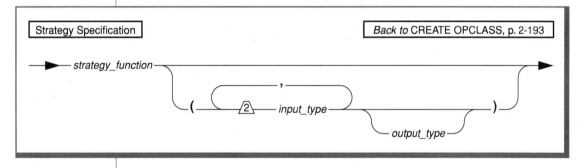

Element	Purpose	Restrictions	Syntax
input_type	Data type of the input argument for the strategy function	This is the data type for which you want to use a specific secondary access method. A strategy function takes two input arguments and one optional output argument.	Data Type, p. 4-53
output_type	Data type of the optional output argument for the strategy function	This is an optional output argument for side effect indexes.	Data Type, p. 4-53
strategy_function	Name of a strategy function to associate with the specified operator class	The operators must be listed in the order expected by the specified secondary access method.	Database Object Name, p. 4-50

The *strategy_function* is an external function. The CREATE OPCLASS statement does not verify that a user-defined function of the name you specify exists. However, for the secondary access method to use the strategy function, the external function must be:

- compiled in a shared library.
- registered in the database with the CREATE FUNCTION statement.

Optionally, you can specify the signature of a strategy function in addition to its name. A strategy function requires two input parameters and an optional output parameter. To specify the function signature, you specify:

- an *input data type* for each of the two input parameters of the strategy function, in the order that the strategy function uses them.
- optionally, one *output data type* for an output parameter of the strategy function.

You can specify user-defined data types as well as built-in types. If you do not specify the function signature, the database server assumes that each strategy function takes two arguments of the same data type and returns a boolean value.

Side-Effect Indexes

Side-effect data is additional data that a strategy function returns when Dynamic Server executes a query containing the strategy function. For example, an image DataBlade module might use a *fuzzy* index to search image data. The index ranks the images according to how closely they match the search criteria. The database server returns the rank value as the side-effect data, along with the qualifying images.

SUPPORT Clause

Support functions are functions that the secondary access method uses internally to build and search the index. You specify the support functions for the secondary access method in the SUPPORT clause of the CREATE OPCLASS statement.

You must list the names of the support functions in the order that the secondary access method expects. For the specific order of support operators for the default operator classes for a B-tree index and an R-tree index, refer to "Default Operator Classes" on page 2-197.

The support function is an external function. The CREATE OPCLASS statement does not verify that a named support function exists. However, for the secondary access method to use a support function, the support function must be:

- compiled in a shared library.
- registered in the database with the CREATE FUNCTION statement.

Default Operator Classes

Each secondary access method has a default operator class that is associated with it. By default, the CREATE INDEX statement creates associates the default operator class with an index. For example, the following CREATE INDEX statement creates a B-tree index on the **zipcode** column and automatically associates the default B-tree operator class with this column:

```
CREATE INDEX zip_ix ON customer(zipcode)
```

For each of the secondary access methods that Dynamic Server provides, it provides a *default operator class*, as follows:

- The default B-tree operator class is a built-in operator class.

  The database server implements the operator-class functions for this operator class and registers it as **btree_ops** in the system catalog tables of a database.

- The default R-tree operator class is a registered operator class.

  The database server registers this operator class as **rtree_ops** in the system catalog tables of a database. The database server does *not* implement the operator-class functions for the default R-tree operator class.

Important: *To use an R-tree index, you must install a spatial DataBlade module such as the Geodetic DataBlade module or any other third-party DataBlade module that implements the R-tree index. These DataBlade modules implement the R-tree operator-class functions.*

For information on the operator-class functions of these operator classes, refer to the chapter on operator classes in *Extending Informix Dynamic Server 2000*.

DataBlade modules can provide other types of secondary access methods. If a DataBlade module provides a secondary access method, it might also provide a default operator class. For more information, refer to your DataBlade module user guide.

Related Information

Related statements: CREATE FUNCTION, CREATE INDEX, and DROP OPCLASS

For information on how to create and extend an operator class, see *Extending Informix Dynamic Server 2000*.

For information about the R-tree index, see the *Informix R-Tree Index User's Guide*.

For information about the GLS aspects of the CREATE OPCLASS statement, refer to the *Informix Guide to GLS Functionality*.

CREATE PROCEDURE

Use the CREATE PROCEDURE statement to create a user-defined procedure.

Tip: *If you are trying to create a procedure from text that is in a separate file, use the CREATE PROCEDURE FROM statement.*

Using CREATE PROCEDURE Versus CREATE FUNCTION

In Enterprise Decision Server, in addition to using this statement to create an SPL procedure, you must use the CREATE PROCEDURE statement to write and register an SPL routine that returns one or more values (that is, an SPL function). Enterprise Decision Server does not support the CREATE FUNCTION statement. ◆

In Dynamic Server, although you can use the CREATE PROCEDURE statement to write and register an SPL routine that returns one or more values (that is, an SPL function), Informix recommends that you use the CREATE FUNCTION statement. To register an external function, you must use the CREATE FUNCTION statement.

Use the CREATE PROCEDURE statement to write and register an SPL procedure or to register an external procedure. ◆

For information on how terms such as user-defined procedures and user-defined functions are used in this manual, see "Relationship Between Routines, Functions and Procedures" on page 2-201.

Syntax

```
CREATE ─────────────── PROCEDURE ─── procedure ───────── ( ──────────── ) ──
         └─ DBA ─┘              └ SPL ┘
                                  └─ function ─┘        └─ Routine
                                                          Parameter List
                                                          p. 4-286 ─┘


──┬─ SPL ─┬────────────────┬─ IDS ──────────────────┬─ IDS ───────────────────────┬──
  │       Return Clause    │  SPECIFIC ─ Specific Name │  SPL                    , │
  │       p. 4-270         │             p. 4-296      │   WITH ( ─ Routine ─── ) │
  └───────────────────────┘                            └─         Modifier        ┘
                                                                  p. 4-274


──┬──────────┬─ SPL ─ Statement ──── END PROCEDURE ─────────────────────────
  │    ;     │        Block
  └──────────┘        p. 4-298
             └─ IDS ─ External Routine ───────────────────
                Ext   Reference
                      p.4-202    └─ END PROCEDURE ─┘


──┬──────────────────────────────────────── WITH LISTING IN 'pathname' ─┬──
  │                              ,                                        │
  └─ DOCUMENT ─── Quoted String ─────┘                                   │
                  p. 4-260
```

Element	Purpose	Restrictions	Syntax
function	Name of the SPL function to create	(EDS) The name must be unique among all SPL routines in the database.	Database Object Name, p. 4-50
		(IDS) See "Naming a Procedure in Dynamic Server" on page 2-203.	
pathname	Pathname to a file in which compile-time warnings are stored	The specified pathname must exist on the computer where the database resides.	The pathname and filename must conform to the conventions of your operating system.
procedure	Name of the user-defined procedure to create	(EDS) The name must be unique among all SPL routines in the database.	Database Object Name, p. 4-50
		(IDS) See "Naming a Procedure in Dynamic Server" on page 2-203.	

Usage

The entire length of a CREATE PROCEDURE statement must be less than 64 kilobytes. This length is the literal length of the CREATE PROCEDURE statement, including blank space and tabs.

E/C

In ESQL/C, you can use a CREATE PROCEDURE statement only within a PREPARE statement. If you want to create a procedure for which the text is known at compile time, you must use a CREATE PROCEDURE FROM statement. ♦

Relationship Between Routines, Functions and Procedures

A *procedure* is a routine that can accept arguments but does not return any values. A *function* is a routine that can accept arguments and returns one or more values.

User-defined routine (UDR) is a generic term that includes both user-defined procedures and user-defined functions.

You can write a UDR in SPL (*SPL routine*) or in an external language (*external routine*) that the database server supports. Consequently, anywhere the term UDR appears in the manual, its significance applies to both SPL routines and external routines. Likewise, the term user-defined procedure applies to SPL procedures and external procedures. Similarly, the term user-defined function applies to SPL functions and external functions.

SPL

In earlier Informix products, the term *stored procedure* was used for both SPL procedures and SPL functions. In this manual, the term *SPL routine* replaces the term stored procedure. When it is necessary to distinguish between an SPL function and an SPL procedure, the manual does so. ♦

IDS

The term *external routine* applies to an external procedure or an external function. When it is necessary to distinguish between an external function and an external procedure, the manual does so. ♦

EDS

Enterprise Decision Server does not support external routines. However, the term user-defined routine (UDR) encompasses both the terms SPL routine and external routine. Therefore, wherever the term UDR appears it is applicable to SPL routines. ♦

Privileges Necessary for Using CREATE PROCEDURE

You must have the Resource privilege on a database to create a user-defined procedure within that database.

Ext

Before you can create an external procedure, you must also have the Usage privilege on the language in which you will write the procedure. For more information, see "GRANT" on page 2-500. ♦

SPL

By default, the Usage privilege on SPL is granted to PUBLIC. You must also have at least the Resource privilege on a database to create an SPL procedure within that database. ♦

DBA Keyword and Privileges on the Created Procedure

The level of privilege necessary to execute a UDR depends on whether the UDR is created with the DBA keyword.

If you create a UDR with the DBA keyword, it is known as a DBA-privileged UDR. You need the DBA privilege to create or execute a DBA-privileged UDR.

If you do not use the DBA keyword, the UDR is known as an owner-privileged UDR.

ANSI

If you create an owner-privileged UDR in an ANSI-compliant database, anyone can execute the UDR. ♦

If you create an owner-privileged UDR in a database that is not ANSI compliant, the **NODEFDAC** environment variable prevents privileges on that UDR from being granted to PUBLIC. If this environment variable is set, the owner of a UDR must grant the Execute privilege for that UDR to other users.

EDS

Naming a Procedure in Enterprise Decision Server

In Enterprise Decision Server, you must specify a unique name for the SPL routine that you create. The name must be unique among all SPL routines in the database.

IDS

Naming a Procedure in Dynamic Server

Because Dynamic Server offers *routine overloading,* you can define more than one user-defined routine (UDR) with the same name, but different parameter lists. You might want to overload UDRs in the following situations:

- You create a UDR with the same name as a built-in routine (such as **equal()**) to process a new user-defined data type.

- You create *type hierarchies*, in which subtypes inherit data represen-tation and UDRs from supertypes.

- You create *distinct types*, which are data types that have the same internal storage representation as an existing data type, but have different names and cannot be compared to the source type without casting. Distinct types inherit UDRs from their source types.

For a brief description of the routine signature that uniquely identifies each UDR, see "Routine Overloading and Naming UDRs with a Routine Signature" on page 4-52.

Using the SPECIFIC Clause to Specify a Specific Name

You can specify a specific name for a user-defined procedure. A specific name is a name that is unique in the database. A specific name is useful when you are overloading a procedure.

DOCUMENT Clause

The quoted string in the DOCUMENT clause provides a synopsis and description of a UDR. The string is stored in the **sysprocbody** system catalog table and is intended for the user of the UDR.

Anyone with access to the database can query the **sysprocbody** system catalog table to obtain a description of one or all the UDRs stored in the database.

For example, to find the description of the SPL procedure **raise_prices**, shown in "SPL Procedures" on page 2-205, enter a query such as the following example:

```
SELECT data FROM sysprocbody b, sysprocedures p
WHERE b.procid = p.procid
        --join between the two catalog tables
    AND p.procname = 'raise_prices'
        -- look for procedure named raise_prices
    AND b.datakey  = 'D';-- want user document
```

The preceding query returns the following text:

```
USAGE: EXECUTE PROCEDURE raise_prices( xxx )
xxx = percentage from 1 - 100
```

A UDR or application program can query the system catalog tables to fetch the DOCUMENT clause and display it for a user.

You can use a DOCUMENT clause at the end of the CREATE PROCEDURE statement, whether or not you use the END PROCEDURE keywords. ♦

Ext

Using the WITH LISTING IN Option

The WITH LISTING IN clause specifies a filename where compile time warnings are sent. After you compile a UDR, this file holds one or more warning messages.

If you do not use the WITH LISTING IN clause, the compiler does not generate a list of warnings.

This listing file is created on the computer where the database resides.

UNIX

If you specify a filename but not a directory, this listing file is created in your home directory on the computer where the database resides. If you do not have a home directory on this computer, the file is created in the root directory (the directory named "/"). ◆

Windows

If you specify a filename but not a directory, this listing file is created in your current working directory if the database is on the local computer. Otherwise, the default directory is **%INFORMIXDIR%\bin**. ◆

SPL

SPL Procedures

SPL procedures are UDRs written in Stored Procedure Language (SPL) that do not return a value.

To write and register an SPL procedure, use a CREATE PROCEDURE statement. Embed appropriate SQL and SPL statements between the CREATE PROCEDURE and END PROCEDURE keywords. You can also follow the procedure with the DOCUMENT and WITH FILE IN options.

SPL procedures are parsed, optimized (as far as possible), and stored in the system catalog tables in executable format. The body of an SPL procedure is stored in the **sysprocbody** system catalog table. Other information about the procedure is stored in other system catalog tables, including **sysprocedures**, **sysprocplan**, and **sysprocauth**.

If the statement block portion of the CREATE PROCEDURE statement is empty, no operation takes place when you call the procedure. You might use such a procedure in the development stage when you want to establish the existence of a procedure but have not yet coded it.

If you specify an optional clause after the parameter list, you must place a semicolon after the clause that immediately precedes the Statement Block.

Example

The following example creates an SPL procedure:

```
CREATE PROCEDURE raise_prices ( per_cent INT )
    UPDATE stock SET unit_price =
        unit_price + (unit_price * (per_cent/100) );
END PROCEDURE
    DOCUMENT "USAGE: EXECUTE PROCEDURE raise_prices( xxx )",
    "xxx = percentage from 1 - 100 "
    WITH LISTING IN '/tmp/warn_file'
```

IDS

Ext

External Procedures

External procedures are procedures you write in an external language that the database server supports.

To create a C user-defined procedure, follow these steps:

1. Write a C function that does not return a value.

2. Compile the C function and store the compiled code in a shared library (the shared-object file for C).

3. Register the C function in the database server with the CREATE PROCEDURE statement.

To create a user-defined procedure written in Java, follow these steps:

1. Write a Java static method, which can use the JDBC functions to interact with the database server.

2. Compile the Java source file and create a jar file (the shared-object file for Java).

3. Execute the **install_jar()** procedure with the EXECUTE PROCEDURE statement to install the jar file in the current database.

4. If the UDR uses user-defined types, create a mapping between SQL data types and Java classes.

    Use the **setUDTExtName()** procedure that is explained in "EXECUTE PROCEDURE" on page 2-444.

5. Register the UDR with the CREATE PROCEDURE statement.

Rather than storing the body of an external routine directly in the database, the database server stores only the pathname of the shared-object file that contains the compiled version of the routine. When the database server executes an external routine, the database server invokes the external object code.

The database server stores information about an external function in several system catalog tables, including **sysprocbody** and **sysprocauth**. For more information on these system catalog tables, see the *Informix Guide to SQL: Reference*.

If an external routine returns a value, you must register it with the CREATE FUNCTION statement.

Example of Registering a C User-Defined Procedure

C

The following example registers a C user-defined procedure named **check_owner()** in the database. This procedure takes one argument of the type **lvarchar**. The external routine reference specifies the path to the C shared library where the procedure object code is stored. This library contains a C function **unix_owner()**, which is invoked during execution of the **check_owner()** procedure.

```
CREATE PROCEDURE check_owner ( owner lvarchar )
EXTERNAL NAME "/usr/lib/ext_lib/genlib.so(unix_owner)"
LANGUAGE C
END PROCEDURE
```

Example of Registering a User-Defined Procedure Written in Java

Java

The following example registers a user-defined procedure named **showusers()**:

```
CREATE PROCEDURE showusers()
    WITH (CLASS = "jvp")
    EXTERNAL NAME 'admin_jar:admin.showusers'
    LANGUAGE JAVA
```

The EXTERNAL NAME clause specifies that the Java implementation of the **showusers()** procedure is a method called **showusers()**, which resides in the **admin** Java class that resides in the **admin_jar** jar file.

Ownership of Created Database Objects

The user who creates an owner-privileged UDR owns any database objects that are created by the UDR when the UDR is executed, unless another owner is specified for the created database object. In other words, the UDR owner, not the user who executes the UDR, is the owner of any database objects created by the UDR unless another owner is specified in the statement that creates the database object.

However, in the case of a DBA-privileged UDR, the user who executes the UDR, not the UDR owner, owns any database objects created by the UDR unless another owner is specified for the database object within the UDR.

For examples of these situations, see the similar section, "Ownership of Created Database Objects" on page 2-153, in the CREATE FUNCTION statement.

Related Information

Related statements: ALTER FUNCTION, ALTER PROCEDURE, ALTER ROUTINE, CREATE FUNCTION, CREATE FUNCTION FROM, CREATE PROCEDURE FROM, DROP FUNCTION, DROP PROCEDURE, DROP ROUTINE, EXECUTE FUNCTION, EXECUTE PROCEDURE, GRANT, EXECUTE PROCEDURE, PREPARE, REVOKE, and UPDATE STATISTICS

For a discussion of how to create and use SPL routines, see the *Informix Guide to SQL: Tutorial*.

For a discussion of how to create and use external routines, see *Extending Informix Dynamic Server 2000*.

For information about how to create C UDRs, see the *DataBlade API Programmer's Manual*.

For more information on the **NODEFDAC** environment variable and the relative system catalog tables (**sysprocedures, sysprocplan, sysprocbody** and **sysprocauth)**, see the *Informix Guide to SQL: Reference*.

CREATE PROCEDURE FROM

Use the CREATE PROCEDURE FROM statement to access a user-defined procedure. The actual text of the CREATE PROCEDURE statement resides in a separate file.

In Enterprise Decision Server, use this statement to access any SPL routine. Enterprise Decision Server does not support the CREATE FUNCTION FROM statement. ♦

Use this statement with ESQL/C.

Syntax

Element	Purpose	Restrictions	Syntax
file	Pathname and filename of the file that contains the full text of a CREATE PROCEDURE statement The default pathname is the current directory.	The specified file must exist. The file must contain only one CREATE PROCEDURE statement.	Pathname and filename must conform to the conventions of your operating system.
file_var	Name of a program variable that holds the value of file	The file that is specified in the program variable must exist. This file must contain only one CREATE PROCEDURE statement.	Name must conform to language-specific rules for variable names.

Usage

You cannot create a user-defined procedure directly in an ESQL/C program. That is, the program cannot contain the CREATE PROCEDURE statement. The following steps describe how you can use a user-defined procedure in an ESQL/C program:

1. Create a source file with the CREATE PROCEDURE statement.

2. Use the CREATE PROCEDURE FROM statement to send the contents of this source file to the database server for execution.

   The file that you specify in the *file* parameter can contain only one CREATE PROCEDURE statement.

For example, suppose that the following CREATE PROCEDURE statement is in a separate file, called **raise_pr.sql**:

```
CREATE PROCEDURE raise_prices( per_cent int )
    UPDATE stock -- increase by percentage;
    SET unit_price = unit_price +
        ( unit_price * (per_cent / 100) );
END PROCEDURE;
```

In the ESQL/C program, you can access the **raise_prices()** SPL procedure with the following CREATE PROCEDURE FROM statement:

```
EXEC SQL create procedure from 'raise_pr.sql';
```

IDS

If you are not sure whether the UDR in the file is a user-defined function or a user-defined procedure, use the CREATE ROUTINE FROM statement. ♦

Default Directory That Holds the File

The filename that you provide is relative.

UNIX

On UNIX, if you specify a simple filename instead of a full pathname in the *file* parameter, the client application looks for the file in your home directory on the computer where the database resides. If you do not have a home directory on this computer, the default directory is the root directory. ♦

WIN NT

On Windows NT, if you specify a filename but not a directory in the *file* parameter, the client application looks for the file in your current working directory if the database is on the local computer. Otherwise, the default directory is **%INFORMIXDIR%\bin**. ♦

Important: *The ESQL/C preprocessor does not process the contents of the file that you specify. It just sends the contents to the database server for execution. Therefore, there is no syntactic check that the file that you specify in CREATE PROCEDURE FROM actually contains a CREATE PROCEDURE statement. However, to improve readability of the code, Informix recommends that you match these two statements.*

Related Information

Related statements: CREATE PROCEDURE, CREATE FUNCTION FROM, and CREATE ROUTINE FROM

CREATE ROLE

Use the CREATE ROLE statement to create a new role.

Syntax

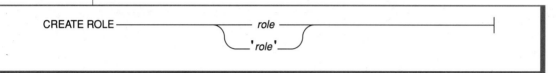

Element	Purpose	Restrictions	Syntax
role	Name assigned to a role created by the DBA	In Dynamic Server, the maximum number of bytes in *role* is 32. In Enterprise Decision Server, the maximum number of bytes in *role* is 8.	Identifier, p. 4-205
		A role name cannot be a user name known to the database server or the operating system of the database server. A role name cannot be in the **username** column of the **sysusers** system catalog table or in the **grantor** or **grantee** columns of the **systabauth, syscolauth, sysprocauth, sysfragauth,** and **sysroleauth** system catalog tables.	
		When a role name is enclosed in quotation marks, the role name is case sensitive.	

Usage

The database administrator (DBA) uses the CREATE ROLE statement to create a new role. A role can be considered as a classification, with privileges on database objects granted to the role. The DBA can assign the privileges of a related work task, such as **engineer**, to a role and then grant that role to users, instead of granting the same set of privileges to every user.

After a role is created, the DBA can use the GRANT statement to grant the role to users or to other roles. When a role is granted to a user, the user must use the SET ROLE statement to enable the role. Only then can the user use the privileges of the role.

The CREATE ROLE statement, when used with the GRANT and SET ROLE statements, allows a DBA to create one set of privileges for a role and then grant the role to many users, instead of granting the same set of privileges to many users.

A role exists until either the DBA or a user to whom the role was granted with the WITH GRANT OPTION uses the DROP ROLE statement to drop the role.

To create the role **engineer**, enter the following statement:

```
CREATE ROLE engineer
```

Related Information

Related statements: DROP ROLE, GRANT, REVOKE, and SET ROLE

For a discussion of how to use roles, see the *Informix Guide to Database Design and Implementation*.

CREATE ROUTINE FROM

Use the CREATE ROUTINE FROM statement to access a user-defined routine (UDR). The actual text of the CREATE FUNCTION or CREATE PROCEDURE statement resides in a separate file.

Syntax

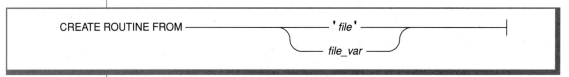

Element	Purpose	Restrictions	Syntax
file	Pathname and filename of the file that contains the full text of a CREATE PROCEDURE or CREATE FUNCTION statement The default pathname is the current directory.	The specified file must exist. The file that you specify can contain only one CREATE FUNCTION or CREATE PROCEDURE statement.	Pathname and filename must conform to the conventions of your operating system.
file_var	Name of a program variable that holds the value of file	The file that is specified in the program variable must exist. The file that you specify can contain only one CREATE FUNCTION or CREATE PROCEDURE statement.	Name must conform to language-specific rules for variable names.

Usage

An Informix ESQL/C program cannot directly define a UDR. That is, it cannot contain the CREATE FUNCTION or CREATE PROCEDURE statement. The following steps describe how you can use a UDR in an ESQL/C program:

1. Create a source file with the CREATE FUNCTION or CREATE PROCEDURE statement.

2. Use the CREATE ROUTINE FROM statement to send the contents of this source file to the database server for execution.

   The file that you specify in the *file* parameter can contain only one CREATE FUNCTION or CREATE PROCEDURE statement.

The filename that you provide is relative. If you provide a simple filename, the client application looks for the file in the current directory.

If you do not know at compile time whether the UDR in the file is a function or a procedure, use the CREATE ROUTINE FROM statement in the ESQL/C program. However, if you do know if the UDR is a function or procedure, Informix recommends that you use the matching statement to access the source file:

- To access user-defined functions, use CREATE FUNCTION FROM
- To access user-defined procedures, use CREATE PROCEDURE FROM

Use of the matching statements improves the readability of the code.

Related Information

Related statements: CREATE FUNCTION, CREATE FUNCTION FROM, CREATE PROCEDURE, and CREATE PROCEDURE FROM

CREATE ROW TYPE

Use the CREATE ROW TYPE statement to create a named-row type.

Syntax

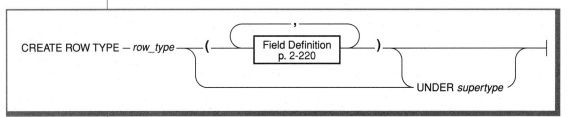

Element	Purpose	Restrictions	Syntax
row_type	Name of the named-row type that you create If you create a named-row type under an existing supertype, this is the name of the subtype.	The name you specify for the named-row type must follow the conventions for SQL identifiers. In an ANSI-compliant database, the combination owner. type must be unique within the database. In a database that is not ANSI compliant, the type name must be unique within the database.	Identifier, p. 4-205
supertype	Name of the supertype in an inheritance hierarchy	The supertype must already exist as a named-row type.	Data type, p. 4-53

Usage

The CREATE ROW TYPE statement creates a named-row type. You can assign a named-row type to a table or view to create a typed table or typed view. You can also assign a named-row type to a column. Although you can assign a row type to a table to define the structure of the table, row types are not the same as table rows. Table rows consist of one or more columns; row types consist of one or more fields, which are defined using the Field Definition syntax.

You can use a named-row type anywhere you can use any other data type. Named-row types are strongly typed. Any two named-row types are not considered equivalent even if they are structurally equivalent. Row types without names are called *unnamed-row types*. Any two unnamed-row types are considered equivalent if they are structurally equivalent. For more information on unnamed-row types, see "Unnamed Row Types" on page 4-68.

Privileges on Named-Row Types

The following table indicates which privileges you must have to create a row type.

Task	Privileges Required
Create a named-row type	Resource privilege on the database
Create a named-row type as a subtype under a supertype	Under privilege on the supertype, as well as the Resource privilege

To find out what privileges exist on a particular type, check the **sysxtdtypes** system catalog table for the owner name and the **sysxtdtypeauth** system catalog table for additional type privileges that might have been granted. For more information on system catalog tables, see the *Informix Guide to SQL: Reference*.

For information about the RESOURCE, UNDER, and ALL privileges, see GRANT.

Privileges on a typed table (a table that is assigned a named-row type) are the same as privileges on any table. For more information, see "Table-Level Privileges" on page 2-505.

To find out what privileges you have on a particular table, check the **systabauth** system catalog table.

Privileges on Named -ow Type Columns

Privileges on named-row type columns are the same as privileges on any column. For more information, see "Table-Level Privileges" on page 2-505.

To find out what privileges you have on a particular column, check the **syscolauth** system catalog table. This table is described in the *Informix Guide to SQL: Reference*.

Inheritance and Named-Row Types

A named-row type can belong to an inheritance hierarchy, as either a subtype or a supertype. You use the UNDER clause in the CREATE ROW TYPE statement to create a named-row type as a subtype. The supertype must also be a named-row type.

When you create a named-row type as a subtype, the subtype inherits all fields of the supertype. In addition, you can add new fields to the subtype that you create. The new fields are specific to the subtype alone.

You cannot substitute a row type in an inheritance hierarchy for its supertype or its subtype. For example, suppose you define a type hierarchy in which **person_t** is the supertype and **employee_t** is the subtype. If a column is of type **person_t**, the column can only contain **person_t** data. It cannot contain **employee_t** data. Likewise, if a column is of type **employee_t**, the column can only contain **employee_t** data. It cannot contain **person_t** data.

Creating a Subtype

In most cases, you add new fields when you create a named-row type as a subtype of another named-row type (supertype). To create the fields of a named-row type, you use the field definition clause (see "Field Definition" on page 2-220).

When you create a subtype, you must use the UNDER keyword to associate the supertype with the named-row type that you want to create. The following statement creates the **employee_t** type under the **person_t** type:

```
CREATE ROW TYPE employee_t
(salary NUMERIC(10,2), bonus NUMERIC(10,2))
UNDER person_t;
```

The **employee_t** type inherits all the fields of **person_t** and has two additional fields: **salary** and **bonus**. However, the **person_t** type is not altered.

Type Hierarchies

When you create a subtype, you create a type hierarchy. In a type hierarchy, each subtype that you create inherits its properties from a single supertype. If you create a named-row type **customer_t** under **person_t**, **customer_t** inherits all the fields of **person_t**. If you create another named-row type, **salesrep_t** under **customer_t**, **salesrep_t** inherits all the fields of **customer_t**. More specifically, **salesrep_t** inherits all the fields that **customer_t** inherited from **person_t** as well as all the fields defined specifically for **customer_t**. For a full discussion of type inheritance, refer to the *Informix Guide to SQL: Tutorial*.

Procedure for Creating a Subtype

Before you create a named-row type as a subtype in an inheritance hierarchy, check the following information:

- Verify that you are authorized to create new data types.

  You must have the Resource privilege on the database. You can find this information in the **sysusers** system catalog table.

- Verify that the supertype exists.

  You can find this information in the **sysxtdtypes** system catalog table.

- Verify that you are authorized to create subtypes to that supertype.

  You must have the Under privilege on the supertype. You can find this information in the **sysusers** system catalog table.

- Verify that the name that you assign to the named-row type is unique within the schema.

  To verify whether the name you want to assign to a new data type is unique within the schema, check the **sysxtdtypes** system catalog table. The name you want to use must not be the name of an existing data type.

- If you are defining fields for the row type, check that no duplicate field names exist in both new and inherited fields.

Important: *When you create a subtype, do not redefine fields that the subtype inherited for its supertype. If you attempt to redefine these fields, the database server returns an error.*

Constraints on Named-Row Types

You cannot apply constraints to named-row types directly. Specify the constraints for the tables that use named-row types when you create or alter the table.

Field Definition

Use the field definition portion of CREATE ROW TYPE to define a new field in a named-row type.

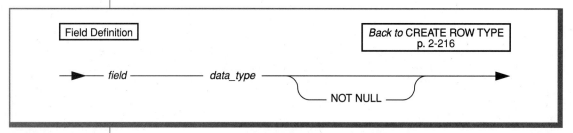

Element	Purpose	Restrictions	Syntax
data_type	Data type of the field	See "Limitations With Serial and Simple-Large-Object Data Types" on page 2-221.	Data type, p. 4-53
field	Name of a field in the row	Name must be unique within the row type and its supertype.	Identifier, p. 4-205

The NOT NULL constraint that you specify on a field of a named-row type also applies to corresponding columns of a table when the named-row type is used to create a typed table.

Limitations With Serial and Simple-Large-Object Data Types

Serial and simple-large-object data types cannot be nested within a table. Therefore, if a row type contains a BYTE, TEXT, SERIAL, or SERIAL8 field, you cannot use the row type to define a column in a table that is not based on a row type. For example, the following code example produces an error:

```
CREATE ROW TYPE serialtype (s serial, s8 serial8);
CREATE TABLE tab1 (col1 serialtype) --INVALID CODE
```

You cannot create a row type that has a BYTE or TEXT value that is stored in a separate storage space. That is, you cannot use the IN clause to specify the storage location. For example, the following example produces an error:

```
CREATE ROW TYPE row1 (field1 byte IN blobspace1) --INVALID
CODE
```

Across a table hierarchy, you can use only one SERIAL and one SERIAL8. That is, if a supertable table contains a SERIAL column, no subtable can contain a SERIAL column. However, a subtable can have a SERIAL8 column (as long as no other subtables contain a SERIAL8 column). Consequently, when you create the named-row types on which the table hierarchy is to be based, they can contain at most one SERIAL and one SERIAL8 field among them.

You cannot set the starting serial value with CREATE ROW TYPE.

To modify the value for a serial field, you must use either the MODIFY clause of the ALTER TABLE statement or the INSERT statement to insert a value that is larger than the current maximum (or default) serial value.

When you use serial fields in row types, you create performance implications across a table hierarchy. When you insert data into a subtable whose supertable (or its supertable) contains the serial counter, the database server must also open the supertable, update the serial value, and close the supertable, thus adding extra overhead.

Related Information

Related statements: DROP ROW TYPE, CREATE TABLE, CREATE CAST, GRANT, and REVOKE

For a discussion of named-row types, see the *Informix Guide to Database Design and Implementation* and the *Informix Guide to SQL: Reference.*

CREATE SCHEMA

Use the CREATE SCHEMA statement to issue a block of CREATE and GRANT statements as a unit. The CREATE SCHEMA statement allows you to specify an owner of your choice for all database objects that the CREATE SCHEMA statement creates.

Use this statement with DB-Access and the SQL Editor.

Syntax

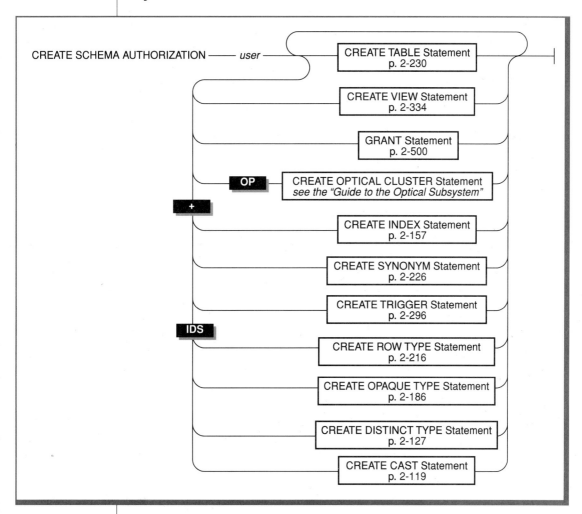

Element	Purpose	Restrictions	Syntax
user	Name of the user who owns the database objects that the CREATE SCHEMA statement creates	If the user who issues the CREATE SCHEMA statement has the Resource privilege, user must be the name of this user. If the user who issues the CREATE SCHEMA statement has the DBA privilege, user can be the name of this user or another user.	Identifier, p. 4-205

Usage

You cannot issue the CREATE SCHEMA statement until you create the affected database.

Users with the Resource privilege can create a schema for themselves. In this case, *user* must be the name of the person with the Resource privilege who is running the CREATE SCHEMA statement. Anyone with the DBA privilege can also create a schema for someone else. In this case, *user* can identify a user other than the person who is running the CREATE SCHEMA statement.

You can put CREATE and GRANT statements in any logical order within the statement, as the following example shows. Statements are considered part of the CREATE SCHEMA statement until a semicolon or an end-of-file symbol is reached.

```
CREATE SCHEMA AUTHORIZATION sarah
    CREATE TABLE mytable (mytime DATE, mytext TEXT)
    GRANT SELECT, UPDATE, DELETE ON mytable TO rick
    CREATE VIEW myview AS
        SELECT * FROM mytable WHERE mytime > '12/31/1997'
    CREATE INDEX idxtime ON mytable (mytime);
```

Creating Database Objects Within CREATE SCHEMA

All database objects that a CREATE SCHEMA statement creates are owned by *user*, even if you do not explicitly name each database object. If you are the DBA, you can create database objects for another user. If you are not the DBA, and you try to create a database object for an owner other than yourself, you receive an error message.

Granting Privileges Within CREATE SCHEMA

You can only grant privileges with the CREATE SCHEMA statement; you cannot revoke or drop privileges.

Creating Database Objects or Granting Privileges Outside CREATE SCHEMA

If you create a database object or use the GRANT statement outside a CREATE SCHEMA statement, you receive warnings if you use the **-ansi** flag or set **DBANSIWARN**.

Related Information

Related statements: CREATE INDEX, CREATE SYNONYM, CREATE TABLE, CREATE VIEW, and GRANT

For a discussion of how to create a database, see the *Informix Guide to Database Design and Implementation*.

CREATE SYNONYM

Use the CREATE SYNONYM statement to provide an alternative name for a
table or view.

Syntax

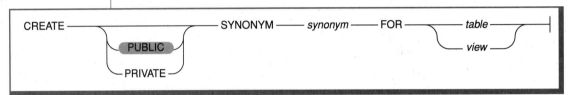

Element	Purpose	Restrictions	Syntax
synonym	Name of the synonym to be created	The synonym name must be unique in the database.	Database Object Name, p. 4-50
table	Name of the table for which the synonym is created	The table must exist.	Database Object Name, p. 4-50
view	Name of the view for which the synonym is created	The view must exist.	Database Object Name, p. 4-50

Usage

Users have the same privileges for a synonym that they have for the table to
which the synonym applies.

The synonym name must be unique; that is, the synonym name cannot be the
same as another database object, such as a table, view, or temporary table.

Once a synonym is created, it persists until the owner executes the DROP
SYNONYM statement. This property distinguishes a synonym from an alias
that you can use in the FROM clause of a SELECT statement. The alias persists
for the existence of the SELECT statement. If a synonym refers to a table or
view in the same database, the synonym is automatically dropped if you
drop the referenced table or view.

You cannot create a synonym for a synonym in the same database.

ANSI

In an ANSI-compliant database, the owner of the synonym (*owner.synonym*) qualifies the name of a synonym. The identifier *owner.synonym* must be unique among all the synonyms, tables, temporary tables, and views in the database. You must specify *owner* when you refer to a synonym that another user owns. The following example shows this convention:

```
CREATE SYNONYM emp FOR accting.employee
```

♦

You can create a synonym for any table or view in any database on your database server. Use the *owner.* convention if the table is part of an ANSI-compliant database. The following example shows a synonym for a table outside the current database. It assumes that you are working on the same database server that contains the **payables** database.

```
CREATE SYNONYM mysum FOR payables:jean.summary
```

Creating a Synonym on a Table in a Remote Database

You can create a synonym for a table or view that exists on any networked database server as well as on the database server that contains your current database. The database server that holds the table must be on-line when you create the synonym. In a network, the database server verifies that the database object referred to by the synonym exists when you create the synonym.

The following example shows how to create a synonym for a database object that is not in the current database:

```
CREATE SYNONYM mysum FOR payables@phoenix:jean.summary
```

The identifier **mysum** now refers to the table **jean.summary**, which is in the **payables** database on the **phoenix** database server. Note that if the **summary** table is dropped from the **payables** database, the **mysum** synonym is left intact. Subsequent attempts to use **mysum** return the error `Table not found`.

IDS

Restrictions

You cannot create synonyms on the following types of remote tables:

- Typed tables (including any table that is part of a table hierarchy)
- Tables that contain any extended data types

PUBLIC and PRIVATE Synonyms

If you use the PUBLIC keyword (or no keyword at all), anyone who has access to the database can use your synonym. If a synonym is public, a user does not need to know the name of the owner of the synonym. Any synonym in a database that is not ANSI compliant *and* was created in an Informix database server earlier than Version 5.0 is a public synonym.

ANSI

In an ANSI-compliant database, synonyms are always private. If you use the PUBLIC or PRIVATE keywords, you receive a syntax error. ♦

If you use the PRIVATE keyword, the synonym can be used only by the owner of the synonym or if the name of the owner is specified explicitly with the synonym. More than one private synonym with the same name can exist in the same database. However, a different user must own each synonym with that name.

You can own only one synonym with a given name; you cannot create both private and public synonyms with the same name. For example, the following code generates an error:

```
CREATE SYNONYM our_custs FOR customer;
CREATE PRIVATE SYNONYM our_custs FOR cust_calls;-- ERROR!!!
```

Synonyms with the Same Name

If you own a private synonym, and a public synonym exists with the same name, when you use the synonym by its unqualified name, the private synonym is used.

If you use DROP SYNONYM with a synonym, and multiple synonyms exist with the same name, the private synonym is dropped. If you issue the DROP SYNONYM statement again, the public synonym is dropped.

Chaining Synonyms

If you create a synonym for a table that is not in the current database, and this table is dropped, the synonym stays in place. You can create a new synonym for the dropped table, with the name of the dropped table as the synonym name, which points to another external or remote table. In this way, you can move a table to a new location and chain synonyms together so that the original synonyms remain valid. (You can chain as many as 16 synonyms in this manner.)

The following steps chain two synonyms together for the **customer** table, which will ultimately reside on the **zoo** database server (the CREATE TABLE statements are not complete):

1. In the **stores_demo** database on the database server that is called **training**, issue the following statement:
   ```
   CREATE TABLE customer (lname CHAR(15)...)
   ```
2. On the database server called **accntg**, issue the following statement:
   ```
   CREATE SYNONYM cust FOR stores_demo@training:customer
   ```
3. On the database server called **zoo**, issue the following statement:
   ```
   CREATE TABLE customer (lname CHAR(15)...)
   ```
4. On the database server called **training**, issue the following statement:
   ```
   DROP TABLE customer
   CREATE SYNONYM customer FOR stores_demo@zoo:customer
   ```

The synonym **cust** on the **accntg** database server now points to the **customer** table on the **zoo** database server.

The following steps show an example of chaining two synonyms together and changing the table to which a synonym points:

1. On the database server called **training**, issue the following statement:
   ```
   CREATE TABLE customer (lname CHAR(15)...)
   ```
2. On the database server called **accntg**, issue the following statement:
   ```
   CREATE SYNONYM cust FOR stores_demo@training:customer
   ```
3. On the database server called **training**, issue the following statement:
   ```
   DROP TABLE customer
   CREATE TABLE customer (lastname CHAR(20)...)
   ```

The synonym **cust** on the **accntg** database server now points to a new version of the **customer** table on the **training** database server.

Related Information

Related statement: DROP SYNONYM

For a discussion of concepts related to synonyms, see the *Informix Guide to Database Design and Implementation*.

CREATE TABLE

Use the CREATE TABLE statement to create a new table in the current database, place data-integrity constraints on columns, designate where the table should be stored, indicate the size of its initial and subsequent extents, and specify how to lock it.

You can use the CREATE TABLE statement to create relational-database tables or *typed tables* (object-relational tables). For information on how to create temporary tables, see "CREATE Temporary TABLE" on page 2-286.

Syntax

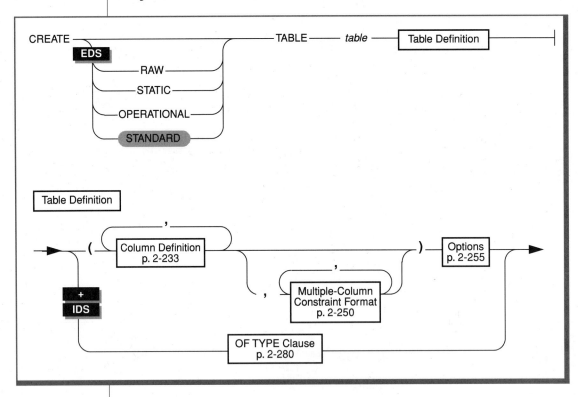

Element	Purpose	Restrictions	Syntax
table	Name assigned to the table. Every table must have a name.	The name must be unique within a database. It must not be used for any other tables or for any views or synonyms within the current database.	Database Object Name, p. 4-50

Usage

When you create a table, the table and columns within that table must have unique names and every table column must have a data type associated with it.

ANSI

In an ANSI-compliant database, the combination *owner.table* must be unique within the database. ♦

DB

In DB-Access, using the CREATE TABLE statement outside the CREATE SCHEMA statement generates warnings if you use the **-ansi** flag or set **DBANSIWARN**. ♦

E/C

In ESQL/C, using the CREATE TABLE statement generates warnings if you use the **-ansi** flag or set **DBANSIWARN**. ♦

For information about the **DBANSIWARN** environment variable, refer to the *Informix Guide to SQL: Reference*.

EDS

Usage-Type Options

In Enterprise Decision Server, use the Usage-TYPE Options to specify that the table has particular characteristics that can improve various bulk operations on it. Other than the default option (STANDARD) that is used for OLTP databases, these usage-type options are used primarily to improve performance in data warehousing databases.

A table can have any of the following usage characteristics.

Option	Purpose
RAW	Non-logging table that cannot have indexes or referential constraints but can be updated
	Use this type for quickly loading data. With this type you take advantage of light appends and avoid the overhead of logging, checking constraints, and building indexes.
STATIC	Non-logging table that can contain index and referential constraints but cannot be updated
	Use this type for read-only operations because no logging or locking overhead occurs.
OPERATIONAL	Logging table that uses light appends and cannot be restored from archive
	Use this type on tables that are refreshed frequently because light appends allow the quick addition of many rows.
STANDARD	Logging table that allows rollback, recovery, and restoration from archives
	This type is the default.
	Use this type for all the recovery and constraints functionality that you want on your OLTP databases.

For a more detailed description of these table types, refer to your Αδμινιστρατορ∏σ Γυιδε.

Column Definition

Use the column definition portion of CREATE TABLE to list the name, data type, default values, and constraints *of a single column.*

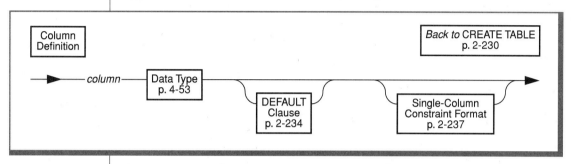

Element	Purpose	Restrictions	Syntax
column	Name of a column in the table	The name must be unique in a table, but you can use the same names in different tables in the same database.	Identifier, p. 4-205

When you name a column, as with any SQL identifier, you can use a reserved word, but syntactic ambiguities can occur. For more information on reserved words for Dynamic Server, see Appendix A, "Reserved Words for Dynamic Server." For more information on reserved words for Enterprise Decision Server, see Appendix B, "Reserved Words for Enterprise Decision Server." For more information on the ambiguities that can occur, see "Using Keywords as Column Names" on page 4-212.

IDS

If you define a column of a table to be of a named-row type, the table does not adopt any constraints of the named row. ◆

DEFAULT Clause

Use the DEFAULT clause to specify the default value that the database server should insert in a column when an explicit value for the column is not specified.

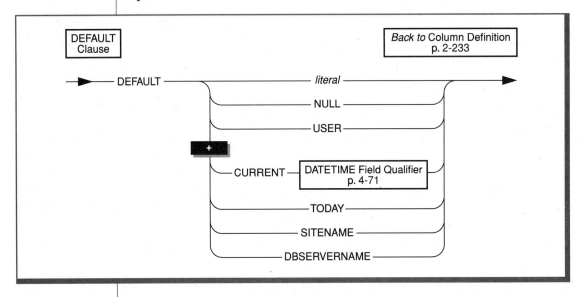

Element	Purpose	Restrictions	Syntax
literal	String of alphabetic or numeric characters	The string must be an appropriate type for the column. See "Using a Literal as a Default Value" on page 2-235	Expression, p. 4-73

If you do not indicate a default value for a column, the default is null *unless* you place a not-null constraint on the column. In that case, no default value exists for the column.

You cannot specify default values for serial columns.

Using a Literal as a Default Value

You can designate a *literal* value as a default value. A literal value is a string of alphabetic or numeric characters. To use a literal value as a default value, you must adhere to the syntax restrictions in the following table.

For Columns of Data Type	Format of Default Value	Syntax Restrictions
BOOLEAN	CHARACTER	't' or 'f' representing true or false The literal must be specified as a quoted string.
CHAR, VARCHAR, NCHAR, NVARCHAR, CHARACTER VARYING, DATE	CHARACTER	Quoted String, p. 4-260
DATETIME	DATETIME	Literal DATETIME, p. 4-231
DECIMAL, MONEY, FLOAT, SMALLFLOAT	DECIMAL	Literal Number, p. 4-237
INTEGER, SMALLINT, DECIMAL, MONEY, FLOAT, SMALLFLOAT, INT8	INTEGER	Literal Number, p. 4-237
INTERVAL	INTERVAL	Literal INTERVAL, p. 4-234
Opaque data types (IDS only)	CHARACTER	Quoted String, p. 4-260 You must use the single-column constraint format to specify the default value.

Date literals must be of the format that the **DBDATE** environment variable specifies. If **DBDATE** is not set, the date literals must be of the *mm/dd/yyyy* format.

Using NULL as a Default Value

If you do not indicate a default value for a column, the default is null *unless* you place a not-null constraint on the column. In this case, no default value exists for the column.

If you specify NULL as the default value for a column, you cannot specify a not-null constraint as part of the column definition.

You cannot designate null as the default value for a column that is part of a primary key.

If the column is BYTE or TEXT data type, null is the only default value that you can designate.

IDS

If the column is BLOB or CLOB data type, null is the only default value that you can designate.

Using a Built-in Function as a Default Value

You can specify a built-in function as the default value for a column. The following table indicates the built-in functions that you can specify, the data type requirements, and the recommended size for their corresponding columns.

Built-In Function Name	Data Type Requirement	Recommended Size of Column
CURRENT	DATETIME column with matching qualifier	Byte value that accommodates the largest DATETIME value for your locale.
DBSERVERNAME	CHAR, VARCHAR, NCHAR, NVARCHAR, or CHARACTER VARYING column	At least 128 bytes (IDS) At least 18 bytes (EDS)
SITENAME	CHAR, VARCHAR, NCHAR, NVARCHAR, or CHARACTER VARYING column	At least 128 bytes (IDS) At least 18 bytes (EDS)
TODAY	DATE column	Byte value that accommodates the largest DATE value for your locale.
USER	CHAR, VARCHAR, NCHAR, NVARCHAR, or CHARACTER VARYING column	At least 32 bytes (IDS) At least 8 bytes (EDS)

Informix recommends a column size because if the column length is too small to store the default value during INSERT and ALTER TABLE operations, the database server returns an error.

IDS

You cannot designate a built-in function (that is, CURRENT, USER, TODAY, SITENAME, or DBSERVERNAME) as the default value for a column that holds opaque or distinct data types. ♦

For more information on these built-in functions, see "Constant Expressions" on page 4-108.

Examples of Default Values in Column Definitions

The following example creates a table called **accounts**. In **accounts**, the **acc_num, acc_type**, and **acc_descr** columns have literal default values. The **acc_id** column defaults to the login name of the user.

```
CREATE TABLE accounts (
    acc_num INTEGER DEFAULT 1,
    acc_type CHAR(1) DEFAULT 'A',
    acc_descr CHAR(20) DEFAULT 'New Account',
    acc_id CHAR(32) DEFAULT USER)
```

Single-Column Constraint Format

Use the Single-Column Constraint Format to associate one or more constraints with a particular column. You can use this portion of CREATE TABLE to perform the following tasks:

- Create one or more data-integrity constraints for a column
- Specify a meaningful name for a constraint
- Specify the constraint-mode that controls the behavior of a constraint during insert, delete, and update operations

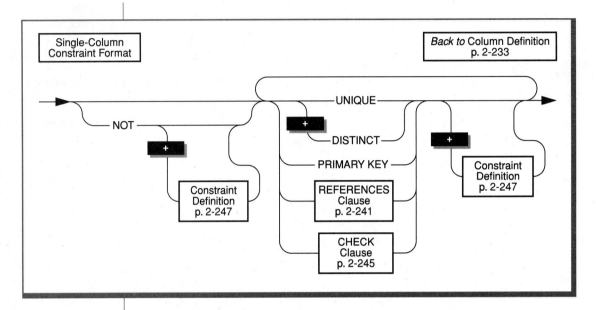

The following example creates a simple table with two constraints, a primary-key constraint named **num** on the **acc_num** column and a unique constraint named **code** on the **acc_code** column:

```
CREATE TABLE accounts (
    acc_num     INTEGER PRIMARY KEY CONSTRAINT num,
    acc_code    INTEGER UNIQUE CONSTRAINT code,
    acc_descr   CHAR(30))
```

The constraints used in this example are defined in the following sections.

Restrictions on Using the Single-Column Constraint Format

When you use the single-column constraint format, you cannot use constraints that involve more than one column. For example, you cannot use the single-column constraint format to define a composite key. For information on multiple-column constraints, see "Multiple-Column Constraint Format" on page 2-250.

Using Large-Object Types in Constraints

You cannot place unique, primary-key, or referential constraints on BYTE or TEXT columns. However, you can check for null or non-null values with a check constraint.

IDS

You cannot place unique, primary-key, or referential constraints on BLOB or CLOB columns. ◆

Using the NOT NULL Constraint

Use the NOT NULL keywords to require that a column receive a value during insert or update operations. If you place a NOT NULL constraint on a column (and no default value is specified), you *must* enter a value into this column when you insert a row or update that column in a row. If you do not enter a value, the database server returns an error.

The following example creates the **newitems** table. In **newitems**, the column **manucode** does not have a default value nor does it allow nulls.

```
CREATE TABLE newitems (
    newitem_num INTEGER,
    manucode CHAR(3) NOT NULL,
    promotype INTEGER,
    descrip CHAR(20))
```

Relationship Between the Default Value and the NOT NULL Constraint

If you do not indicate a default value for a column, the default is null *unless* you place a NOT NULL constraint on the column. In this case, no default value exists for the column.

You cannot specify NULL as the default value for a column and also specify the NOT NULL constraint.

Using the UNIQUE or DISTINCT Constraints

Use the UNIQUE or DISTINCT keyword to require that a column or set of columns accepts only unique data. You cannot insert duplicate values in a column that has a unique constraint. When you create a UNIQUE or DISTINCT constraint, the database server automatically creates an internal index on the constrained column or columns.

Restrictions on Defining Unique Constraints

You cannot place a unique constraint on a column on which you have already placed a primary-key constraint.

You cannot place a unique constraint on a BYTE or TEXT column.

IDS

You cannot place a unique or primary-key constraint on a BLOB or CLOB column.

Opaque types support a unique constraint only where a secondary access method supports uniqueness for that type. The default secondary access method is a generic B-tree, which supports the **equal()** function. Therefore, if the definition of the opaque type includes the **equal()** function, a column of that opaque type can have a unique constraint. ♦

Example That Uses the Single-Column Constraint Format

The following example creates a simple table that has a unique constraint on one of its columns:

```
CREATE TABLE accounts
    (acc_name   CHAR(12),
     acc_num    SERIAL UNIQUE CONSTRAINT acc_num)
```

For an explanation of the constraint name, refer to "Choosing a Constraint Name" on page 2-247.

Using the PRIMARY KEY Constraint

A *primary key* is a column or a set of columns (available when you use the multiple-column constraint format) that contains a non-null, unique value for each row in a table. When you create a PRIMARY KEY constraint, the database server automatically creates an internal index on the column or columns that make up the primary key.

Restrictions for Primary-Key Constraints

You can designate only one primary key for a table. If you define a single column as the primary key, it is unique by definition; you cannot explicitly give the same column a unique constraint.

You cannot place a primary-key constraint on a BYTE or TEXT column.

You cannot place a unique or primary-key constraint on a BLOB or CLOB column.

Opaque types support a primary key constraint only where a secondary access method supports the uniqueness for that type. The default secondary access method is a generic B-tree, which supports the **equal()** function. Therefore, if the definition of the opaque type includes the **equal()** function, a column of that opaque type can have a primary-key constraint. ♦

Example That Uses the Single-Column Constraint Format

In the previous two examples, a unique constraint was placed on the column **acc_num**. The following example creates this column as the primary key for the **accounts** table:

```
CREATE TABLE accounts
    (acc_name CHAR(12),
     acc_num SERIAL PRIMARY KEY CONSTRAINT acc_num)
```

REFERENCES Clause

Use the REFERENCES clause to establish a referential relationship:

- within a table (that is, between two columns of the same table).
- between two tables (in other words, create a foreign key).

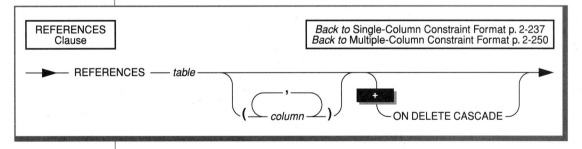

Element	Purpose	Restrictions	Syntax
column	Name of the referenced column or columns	See "Restrictions on Referential Constraints" on page 2-242.	Identifier, p.4-205
table	Name of the referenced table	The referenced table must reside in the same database as the referencing table.	Database Object Name, p. 4-50

The *referencing* column (the column being defined) is the column or set of columns that refers to the referenced column or set of columns. The referencing column or set of columns can contain null and duplicate values. However, the values in the referenced column or set of columns must be unique.

The relationship between referenced and referencing columns is called a *parent-child* relationship, where the parent is the referenced column (primary key) and the child is the referencing column (foreign key). The referential constraint establishes this parent-child relationship.

When you create a referential constraint, the database server automatically creates an internal index on the constrained column or columns.

Restrictions on Referential Constraints

You must have the References privilege to create a referential constraint.

When you use the REFERENCES clause, you must observe the following restrictions:

- The referenced and referencing tables must be in the same database.
- The referenced column (or set of columns when you use the multiple-column constraint format) must have a unique or primary-key constraint.
- The data types of the referencing and referenced columns must be identical.

  The only exception is that a referencing column must be an integer data type if the referenced column is a serial.
- You cannot place a referential constraint on a BYTE or TEXT column.
- When you use the single-column constraint format, you can reference only one column.

EDS

■ When you use the multiple-column constraint format, the maximum number of columns in the REFERENCES clause is 16, and the total length of the columns cannot exceed 255 bytes. ♦

IDS

■ When you use the multiple-column constraint format, the maximum number of columns in the REFERENCES clause is 16, and the total length of the columns cannot exceed 390 bytes.

■ You cannot place a referential constraint on a BLOB or CLOB column. ♦

Default Values for the Referenced Column

If the referenced table is different from the referencing table, you do not need to specify the referenced column; the default column is the primary-key column (or columns) of the referenced table. If the referenced table is the same as the referencing table, you must specify the referenced column.

Referential Relationships Within a Table

You can establish a referential relationship between two columns of the same table. In the following example, the **emp_num** column in the **employee** table uniquely identifies every employee through an employee number. The **mgr_num** column in that table contains the employee number of the manager who manages that employee. In this case, **mgr_num** references **emp_num**. Duplicate values appear in the **mgr_num** column because managers manage more than one employee.

```
CREATE TABLE employee
    (
    emp_num INTEGER PRIMARY KEY,
    mgr_num INTEGER REFERENCES employee (emp_num)
    )
```

Locking Implications of Creating a Referential Constraint

When you create a referential constraint, an exclusive lock is placed on the referenced table. The lock is released when the CREATE TABLE statement is finished. If you are creating a table in a database with transactions, and you are using transactions, the lock is released at the end of the transaction.

Example That Uses the Single-Column Constraint Format

The following example uses the single-column constraint format to create a referential relationship between the **sub_accounts** and **accounts** tables. The **ref_num** column in the **sub_accounts** table references the **acc_num** column (the primary key) in the **accounts** table.

```
CREATE TABLE accounts (
    acc_num INTEGER PRIMARY KEY,
    acc_type INTEGER,
    acc_descr CHAR(20))

CREATE TABLE sub_accounts (
    sub_acc INTEGER PRIMARY KEY,
    ref_num INTEGER REFERENCES accounts (acc_num),
    sub_descr CHAR(20))
```

When you use the single-column constraint format, you do not explicitly specify the **ref_num** column as a foreign key. To use the FOREIGN KEY keyword, use the "Multiple-Column Constraint Format" on page 2-250.

Using the ON DELETE CASCADE Option

Use the ON DELETE CASCADE option to specify whether you want rows deleted in a child table when corresponding rows are deleted in the parent table. If you do not specify cascading deletes, the default behavior of the database server prevents you from deleting data in a table if other tables reference it.

If you specify this option, later when you delete a row in the parent table, the database server also deletes any rows associated with that row (foreign keys) in a child table. The principal advantage to the cascading-deletes feature is that it allows you to reduce the quantity of SQL statements you need to perform delete actions.

For example, the **all_candy** table contains the **candy_num** column as a primary key. The **hard_candy** table refers to the **candy_num** column as a foreign key. The following CREATE TABLE statement creates the **hard_candy** table with the cascading-delete option on the foreign key:

```
CREATE TABLE all_candy
    (candy_num  SERIAL PRIMARY KEY,
     candy_maker CHAR(25));

CREATE TABLE hard_candy
    (candy_num      INT,
     candy_flavor   CHAR(20),
     FOREIGN KEY (candy_num) REFERENCES all_candy
     ON DELETE CASCADE)
```

Because the ON DELETE CASCADE option is specified for the child table, when an item from the **all_candy** table is deleted, the delete cascades to the corresponding rows of the **hard_candy** table.

For information about syntax restrictions and locking implications when you delete rows from tables that have cascading deletes, see "Considerations When Tables Have Cascading Deletes" on page 2-375.

CHECK Clause

Use the CHECK clause to designate conditions that must be met *before* data can be assigned to a column during an INSERT or UPDATE statement.

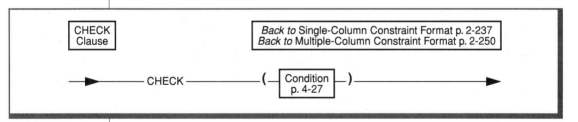

During an insert or update, if a row evaluates to *false* for any check constraint defined on a table, the database server returns an error. The database server does not return an error if a row evaluates to null for a check constraint. In some cases, you might wish to use both a check constraint and a NOT NULL constraint.

You use *search conditions* to define check constraints. The search condition cannot contain the following items: subqueries, aggregates, host variables, rowids, or user-defined routines. In addition, the search condition cannot contain the following built-in functions: CURRENT, USER, SITENAME, DBSERVERNAME, or TODAY.

*When you specify a date value in a search condition, make sure you specify 4 digits instead of 2 digits for the year. When you specify a 4-digit year, the **DBCENTURY** environment variable has no effect on the distribution scheme. When you specify a 2-digit year, the **DBCENTURY** environment variable can affect the distribution scheme and can produce unpredictable results. See the "Informix Guide to SQL: Reference" for more information on the **DBCENTURY** environment variable.*

With a BYTE or TEXT column, you can check for null or not-null values. This constraint is the only constraint allowed on a BYTE or TEXT columns.

IDS

With a BLOB or CLOB column, you can check for null or not-null values. This constraint is the only constraint allowed on a BLOB or CLOB columns.

Restrictions When Using the Single-Column Constraint Format

When you use the single-column constraint format to define a check constraint, the only column that the check constraint can check against is the column itself. In other words, the check constraint cannot depend on values in other columns of the table.

Example

The following example creates the **my_accounts** table which has two columns with check constraints:

```
CREATE TABLE my_accounts (
    chk_id      SERIAL PRIMARY KEY,
    acct1       MONEY CHECK (acct1 BETWEEN 0 AND 99999),
    acct2       MONEY CHECK (acct2 BETWEEN 0 AND 99999))
```

Both **acct1** and **acct2** are columns of MONEY data type whose values must be between 0 and 99999.

If, however, you want to test that **acct1** has a larger balance than **acct2**, you cannot use the single-column constraint format. To create a constraint that checks values in more than one column, you must use the "Multiple-Column Constraint Format" on page 2-250.

Constraint Definition

Use the constraint definition portion of CREATE TABLE for the following purposes:

- To assign a name to a constraint
- To set a constraint to disabled, enabled, or filtering mode ♦

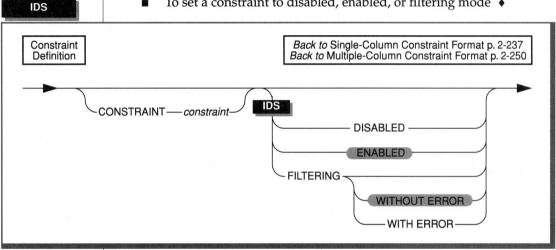

| Constraint Definition | | *Back to* Single-Column Constraint Format p. 2-237
Back to Multiple-Column Constraint Format p. 2-250 |

Element	Purpose	Restrictions	Syntax
constraint	Name of the constraint	The constraint name must be unique in the database.	Database Object Name, p. 4-50

Choosing a Constraint Name

Whenever you use the single- or multiple-column constraint format to place a data restriction on a column, the database server creates a constraint and adds a row for that constraint to the **sysconstraints** system catalog table. The database server also generates an identifier and adds a row to the **sysindexes** system catalog table for each new primary-key, unique, or referential constraint that does not share an index with an existing constraint. Even if you assign a name to a constraint, the database server generates the name that appears in the **sysindexes** table.

If you wish, you can specify a meaningful name for the constraint. The name of a constraint must be unique within the database.

Constraint names appear in error messages having to do with constraint violations. You can use this name when you use the DROP CONSTRAINT clause of the ALTER TABLE statement.

IDS

In addition, you specify a constraint name when you change the mode of constraint with the SET Database Object Mode statement or the SET Transaction Mode statement. ♦

ANSI

When you create a constraint of any type, the *owner.constraint* (the combination of the owner name and constraint name) must be unique within the database. ♦

IDS

The system catalog table that holds information about indexes is the **sysindices** table. ♦

Constraint Names Generated by the Database Server

If you do not specify a constraint name, the database server generates a constraint name using the following template:

```
<constraint_type><tabid>_<constraintid>
```

In this template, *constraint_type* is the letter **u** for unique or primary-key constraints, **r** for referential constraints, **c** for check constraints, and **n** for not-null constraints. In the template, *tabid* and *constraintid* are values from the **tabid** and **constrid** columns of the **systables** and **sysconstraints** system catalog tables, respectively. For example, the constraint name for a unique constraint might look like: **u111_14**.

If the generated name conflicts with an existing identifier, the database server returns an error, and you must then supply a constraint name.

The index name in **sysindexes** (or **sysindices**) is created with the following format:

```
[space]<tabid>_<constraintid>
```

For example, the index name might be something like: **" 111_14"** (quotation marks are used to show the space).

IDS

Choosing a Constraint-Mode Option

Use the constraint-mode options to control the behavior of constraints during insert, delete, and update operations. The following list explains these options.

Mode	Purpose
DISABLED	Does not enforce the constraint during insert, delete, and update operations.
ENABLED	Enforces the constraint during insert, delete, and update operations.
	If a target row causes a violation of the constraint, the statement fails.
	This is the default mode.
FILTERING	Enforces the constraint during insert, delete, and update operations.
	If a target row causes a violation of the constraint, the statement continues processing. The database server writes the row in question to the violations table associated with the target table and writes diagnostic information about the constraint violation to the diagnostics table associated with the target table.

If you choose filtering mode, you can specify the WITHOUT ERROR or WITH ERROR options. The following list explains these options.

Error Option	Purpose
WITHOUT ERROR	Does not return an integrity-violation error when a filtering-mode constraint is violated during an insert, delete, or update operation.
	This is the default error option.
WITH ERROR	Returns an integrity-violation error when a filtering-mode constraint is violated during an insert, delete, or update operation.

For how to set the constraint mode after the table exists, see "SET Database Object Mode" on page 2-700. For information about where the database server stores data that violates a constraint set to filtering, see "START VIOLATIONS TABLE" on page 2-778.

Multiple-Column Constraint Format

Use the multiple-column constraint format to associate one or more columns with a constraint. This alternative to the single-column constraint format allows you to associate multiple columns with a constraint.

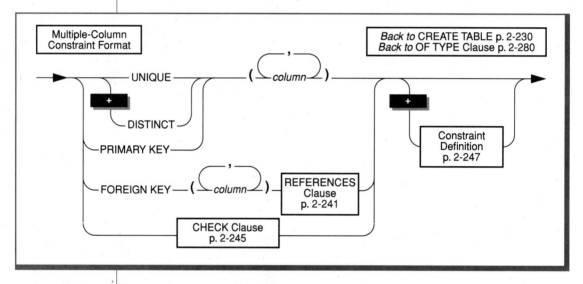

Element	Purpose	Restrictions	Syntax
column	Name of the column or columns on which the constraint is placed	The column must be defined.	Identifier, p.4-205
		The column cannot be a BYTE or TEXT, BLOB or CLOB column.	
		You can include a maximum of 16 columns in a constraint list. The total length of all columns cannot exceed:	
		■ 255 bytes (EDS)	
		■ 390 bytes (IDS)	
		When you define a unique constraint (UNIQUE or DISTINCT keywords), a column cannot appear in the constraint list more than once.	

When you use the multiple-column constraint format, you can perform the following tasks:

- Create one or more data-integrity constraints for a single column or set of columns
- Specify a meaningful name for a constraint
- Specify the constraint-mode option that controls the behavior of a constraint during insert, delete, and update operations

When you use this format, you can create composite primary and foreign keys. You can also define check constraints that involve comparing data in different columns.

Restrictions with the Multiple-Column Constraint Format

When you use the multiple-column constraint format, you cannot define any default values for columns. In addition, you cannot establish a referential relationship between two columns of the same table.

To define a default value for a column or establish a referential relationship between two columns of the same table, refer to "Single-Column Constraint Format" on page 2-237 and "Referential Relationships Within a Table" on page 2-243 respectively.

Using Large-Object Types in Constraints

You cannot place unique, primary-key, or referential (FOREIGN KEY) constraints on BYTE or TEXT columns. However, you can check for null or non-null values with a check constraint.

IDS

You cannot place unique or primary-key constraints on BLOB or CLOB columns. ♦

Location of Information Regarding Specific Constraints

The following table indicates where you can find detailed discussions of specific constraints

Constraint	For more information, see	For an Example, see
CHECK	"CHECK Clause" on page 2-245	"Defining Check Constraints Across Columns" on page 2-253
DISTINCT	"Using the UNIQUE or DISTINCT Constraints" on page 2-239	"Examples that Use the Multiple-Column Constraint Format" on page 2-253
FOREIGN KEY	"Using the FOREIGN KEY Constraint" on page 2-252	"Defining Composite Primary and Foreign Keys" on page 2-254
PRIMARY KEY	"Using the PRIMARY KEY Constraint" on page 2-240	"Defining Composite Primary and Foreign Keys" on page 2-254
UNIQUE	"Using the UNIQUE or DISTINCT Constraints" on page 2-239	"Examples that Use the Multiple-Column Constraint Format" on page 2-253

Using the FOREIGN KEY Constraint

A foreign key *joins* and establishes dependencies between tables, that is, it creates a referential constraint.

A foreign key references a unique or primary key in a table. For every entry in the foreign-key columns, a matching entry must exist in the unique or primary-key columns if all foreign-key columns contain non-null values.

You cannot make BYTE or TEXT columns be foreign keys.

IDS

You cannot make BLOB or CLOB columns be foreign keys. ♦

For more information on referential constraints, see the "REFERENCES Clause" on page 2-241.

Examples that Use the Multiple-Column Constraint Format

The following example creates a simple table with a unique constraint. The example uses the multiple-column constraint format. However, nothing in this example would prohibit you from using the single-column constraint format to define this constraint.

```
CREATE TABLE accounts
    (acc_name    CHAR(12),
     acc_num     SERIAL,
     UNIQUE      (acc_num) CONSTRAINT acc_num)
```

For an explanation of the constraint name, refer to "Choosing a Constraint Name" on page 2-247.

Defining Check Constraints Across Columns

When you use the multiple-column constraint format to define check constraints, a check constraint can apply to more than one column in the table. (However, you cannot create a check constraint for columns across tables.)

The following example includes a comparison of **acct1** and **acct2** two columns in the table.

```
CREATE TABLE my_accounts
    (
    chk_id      SERIAL PRIMARY KEY,
    acct1       MONEY,
    acct2       MONEY,
    CHECK (0 < acct1 AND acct1 < 99999),
    CHECK (0 < acct2 AND acct2 < 99999),
    CHECK (acct1 > acct2)
    )
```

In this example, the **acct1** column must be greater than the **acct2** column, or the insert or update fails.

Defining Composite Primary and Foreign Keys

When you use the multiple-column constraint format, you can create a composite key (that is, you can specify multiple columns for a primary key or foreign key constraint.

The following example creates two tables. The first table has a composite key that acts as a primary key, and the second table has a composite key that acts as a foreign key.

```
CREATE TABLE accounts (
    acc_num INTEGER,
    acc_type INTEGER,
    acc_descr CHAR(20),
    PRIMARY KEY (acc_num, acc_type))

CREATE TABLE sub_accounts (
    sub_acc INTEGER PRIMARY KEY,
    ref_num INTEGER NOT NULL,
    ref_type INTEGER NOT NULL,
    sub_descr CHAR(20),
    FOREIGN KEY (ref_num, ref_type) REFERENCES accounts
        (acc_num, acc_type))
```

In this example, the foreign key of the **sub_accounts** table, **ref_num** and **ref_type**, references the composite key, **acc_num** and **acc_type**, in the **accounts** table. If, during an insert or update, you tried to insert a row into the **sub_accounts** table whose value for **ref_num** and **ref_type** did not exactly correspond to the values for **acc_num** and **acc_type** in an existing row in the **accounts** table, the database server would return an error.

A referential constraint must have a one-to-one relationship between referencing and referenced columns. In other words, if the primary key is a set of columns (a composite key), then the foreign key also must be a set of columns that corresponds to the composite key.

Because of the default behavior of the database server, when you create the foreign key reference, you do not have to reference the composite key columns (**acc_num** and **acc_type**) explicitly.

You can rewrite the references section of the previous example as follows:

```
    . . .
    FOREIGN KEY (ref_num, ref_type) REFERENCES accounts
    . . .
```

Options

The CREATE TABLE options let you specify storage locations, extent size, locking modes, and user-defined access methods.

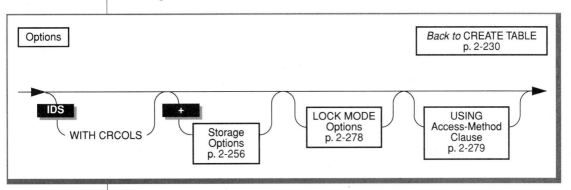

Using the WITH CRCOLS Option

Use the WITH CRCOLS keywords to create two shadow columns that Enterprise Replication uses for conflict resolution. The first column, **cdrserver**, contains the identity of the database server where the last modification occurred. The second column, **cdrtime**, contains the time stamp of the last modification. You must add these columns before you can use time-stamp or user-defined routine conflict resolution.

For most database operations, the **cdrserver** and **cdrtime** columns are hidden. For example, if you include the WITH CRCOLS keywords when you create a table, the **cdrserver** and **cdrtime** columns:

- do not appear when you issue the statement
  ```
  SELECT * from tablename
  ```
- do not appear in DB-Access when you ask for information about the columns of the table.
- are not included in the number of columns (**ncols**) in the **systables** system catalog table entry for *tablename*.

To view the contents of **cdrserver** and **cdrtime**, explicitly name the columns in a SELECT statement, as the following example shows:

```
SELECT cdrserver, cdrtime from tablename
```

For more information about using this option, refer to the *Guide to Informix Enterprise Replication*.

Storage Options

Use the storage option portion of CREATE TABLE to specify the storage space and the size of the extents for the table.

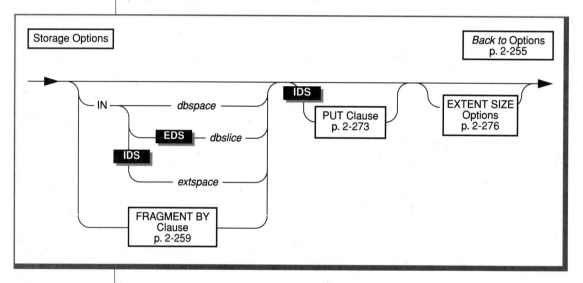

Element	Purpose	Restrictions	Syntax
dbslice	Name of the dbslice in which to store the table	The specified dbslice must already exist.	Identifier, p. 4-205
dbspace	Name of the dbspace in which to store the table	The specified dbspace must already exist.	Identifier, p. 4-205
	If you do not specify a location with either the IN *dbspace* clause or a fragmentation scheme, the default is the dbspace where the current database resides.		
extspace	Name assigned with the **onspaces** command to a storage area outside the database server	The specified *extspace* must already exist.	Refer to the user documentation for your custom access method for more information.

If you use the "USING Access-Method Clause" on page 2-279 to specify an access method, the storage space named must be supported by that access method.

You can specify a dbspace for the table that is different from the storage location specified for the database, or fragment the table into several dbspaces. If you do not specify the IN clause or a fragmentation scheme, the database server stores the table in the dbspace where the current database resides.

You can use the PUT clause to specify storage options for smart large objects. For more information, see "PUT Clause" on page 2-273.

Tip: *If your table has columns that contain simple large objects (TEXT or BYTE), you can specify a separate blobspace for each object. For information on storing simple large objects, refer to "Large-Object Data Types" on page 4-62.* ♦

Using the IN Clause

Use the IN clause to specify a storage space for a table. The storage space that you specify must already exist.

Storing Data in a dbspace

You can use the IN clause to isolate a table. For example, if the **history** database is in the **dbs1** dbspace, but you want the **family** data placed in a separate dbspace called **famdata**, use the following statements:

```
CREATE DATABASE history IN dbs1

CREATE TABLE family
    (
    id_num          SERIAL(101) UNIQUE,
    name            CHAR(40),
    nickname        CHAR(20),
    mother          CHAR(40),
    father          CHAR(40)
    )
    IN famdata
```

For more information about how to store and manage your tables in separate dbspaces, see your *Administrator's Guide*.

EDS

Storing Data in a dbslice

If you are using Enterprise Decision Server, the IN *dbslice* clause allows you to fragment a table across a group of dbspaces that share the same naming convention. The database server fragments the table by round-robin in the dbspaces that make up the dbslice at the time the table is created.

To fragment a table across a dbslice, you can use either the IN *dbslice* syntax or the FRAGMENT BY ROUND ROBIN IN *dbslice* syntax.

IDS

Storing Data in an extspace

In general, you use this option in conjunction with the "USING Access-Method Clause" on page 2-279. Refer to the user documentation for your custom-access method for more information.

FRAGMENT BY Clause

Use the FRAGMENT BY clause to create fragmented tables and specify the distribution scheme.

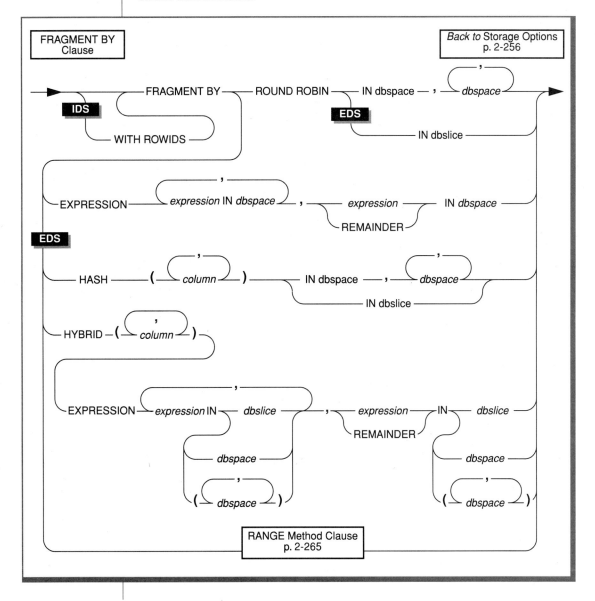

Element	Purpose	Restrictions	Element
column	Name of the column or columns on which you want to apply the fragmentation strategy In the HYBRID clause, column identifies the column or columns on which you want to apply the hash portion of the hybrid table fragmentation strategy.	All specified columns must be in the current table. If you specify a serial column, you cannot specify any other column.	Identifier, p. 4-205
dbslice	Name of the dbslice that contains the dbspaces in which the table fragments reside	The dbslice must exist when you execute the statement.	Identifier, p.4-205
dbspace	Name of the dbspace that contains the table fragment If you do not specify a location with either the IN *dbspace* clause or a fragmentation scheme, the default is the dbspace where the current database resides.	The dbspace must exist when you execute the statement. The minimum number of dbspaces that you can specify is two. The maximum number of dbspaces that you can specify is 2,048.	Identifier, p. 4-205
expression	Expression that defines which rows are stored in a fragment	Each expression can contain only columns from the current table and only data values from a single row. No subqueries, user-defined routines, serial columns, aggregates, or references to the fields of a row-type column are allowed. In addition, the built-in current, date and/or time functions are not allowed.	Expression, p. 4-73

When you fragment a table, the IN keyword introduces the storage space where a table fragment is to be stored.

IDS

Using the WITH ROWIDS Option

Nonfragmented tables contain a hidden column called the **rowid** column. However, fragmented tables do not contain this column. If a table is fragmented, you can use the WITH ROWIDS keywords to add the **rowid** column to the table. The database server assigns to each row in the **rowid** column a unique number that remains stable for the life of the row. The database server uses an index to find the physical location of the row. After you add the **rowid** column, each row contains an additional 4 bytes to store the **rowid**.

Important: *Informix recommends that you use primary keys as an access method rather than the* **rowid** *column.*

You cannot use the WITH ROWIDS clause with typed tables.

Fragmenting by ROUND ROBIN

In a round-robin distribution scheme, specify at least two dbspaces where you want the fragments to be placed. As records are inserted into the table, they are placed in the first available dbspace. The database server balances the load between the specified dbspaces as you insert records and distributes the rows in such a way that the fragments always maintain approximately the same number of rows. In this distribution scheme, the database server must scan all fragments when it searches for a row.

EDS

If you are using Enterprise Decision Server, you can specify the name of a dbslice to fragment a table across a group of dbspaces that share the same naming convention. For a syntax alternative to `FRAGMENT BY ROUND ROBIN IN` *dbslice* that achieves the same results, see "Storing Data in a dbslice" on page 2-258. ♦

IDS

Use the PUT clause to specify round-robin fragmentation for smart large objects. For more information, see "PUT Clause" on page 2-273. ♦

Fragmenting by EXPRESSION

In an *expression-based* distribution scheme, each fragment expression in a rule specifies a storage space. Each fragment expression in the rule isolates data and aids the database server in searching for rows. Specify one of the following rules:

- Range rule

    A range rule specifies fragment expressions that use a range to specify which rows are placed in a fragment, as the following example shows:

    ```
    . . .
        FRAGMENT BY EXPRESSION
        c1 < 100 IN dbsp1,
        c1 >= 100 AND c1 < 200 IN dbsp2,
        c1 >= 200 IN dbsp3
    ```

- Arbitrary rule

    An arbitrary rule specifies fragment expressions based on a predefined SQL expression that typically uses OR clauses to group data, as the following example shows:

    ```
    . . .
        FRAGMENT BY EXPRESSION
        zip_num = 95228 OR zip_num = 95443 IN dbsp2,
        zip_num = 91120 OR zip_num = 92310 IN dbsp4,
        REMAINDER IN dbsp5
    ```

Warning: *When you specify a date value in a fragment expression, make sure you specify 4 digits instead of 2 digits for the year. When you specify a 4-digit year, the **DBCENTURY** environment variable has no effect on the distribution scheme. When you specify a 2-digit year, the **DBCENTURY** environment variable can affect the distribution scheme and can produce unpredictable results. See the "Informix Guide to SQL: Reference" for more information on the **DBCENTURY** environment variable.*

Using the REMAINDER Keyword

Use the REMAINDER keyword to specify the storage space in which to store valid values that fall outside the specified expression or expressions.

If you do not specify a remainder and a row is inserted or updated such that it no longer belongs to any dbspace, the database server returns an error.

Fragmenting by HASH

If you use a hash-distribution scheme, the database server distributes the rows as you insert them so that the fragments maintain approximately the same number of rows. In this distribution scheme, the database server can eliminate fragments when it searches for a row because the hash is known internally.

For example, if you have a very large database, as in a data-warehousing environment, you can fragment your tables across disks that belong to different coservers. If you expect to perform a lot of queries that scan most of the data, you can use a system-defined hash-distribution scheme to balance the I/O processing as follows:

```
CREATE TABLE customer
    (
    cust_id integer,
    descr char(45),
    level char(15),
    sale_type char(10),
    channel char(30),
    corp char(45),
    cust char(45),
    vert_mkt char(30),
    state_prov char(20),
    country char(15),
    org_cust_id char(20)
    )
FRAGMENT BY HASH (cust_id) IN
                customer1_spc,
                customer2_spc,
                customer3_spc,
                customer4_spc,
                customer5_spc,
                customer6_spc,
                customer7_spc,
                customer8_spc
EXTENT SIZE 20 NEXT SIZE 16
    .
    .
    .
```

This example uses eight coservers with one dbspace defined on each coserver.

You can also specify a *dbslice*. When you specify a dbslice, the database server fragments the table across the dbspaces that make up the dbslice.

Serial Columns in Hash-Distribution Schemes

If you choose to fragment on a serial column, the only distribution scheme that you can use is a hash-distribution scheme. In addition, the serial column must be the only column in the hashing key.

The following excerpt is a sample CREATE TABLE statement:

```
CREATE TABLE customer
    (
    cust_id serial,
    .
    .
    .
    )
FRAGMENT BY HASH (cust_id) IN
            customer1_spc,
            customer2_spc
    .
    .
    .
```

You might notice a difference between serial-column values in fragmented and nonfragmented tables. The database server assigns serial values round-robin across fragments so a fragment might contain values from noncontiguous ranges. For example, if there are two fragments, the first serial value is placed in the first fragment, the second serial value is placed in the second fragment, the third value is placed in the first fragment, and so on.

EDS

Fragmenting by HYBRID

The HYBRID clause allows you to apply two distribution schemes to the same table. You can use a combination of hash- and expression-distribution schemes or a combination of range distribution schemes on a table. This section discusses the hash and expression form of hybrid fragmentation. For more information on range fragmentation, see "RANGE Method Clause" on page 2-265.

When you specify hybrid fragmentation, the EXPRESSION clause determines the base fragmentation strategy of the table. In this clause, you associate an expression with a set of dbspaces (dbspace, dbslice, or dbspacelist format) to designate where the data is stored. The hash column (or columns) determines the dbspace within the specified set of dbspaces.

When you specify a dbslice, the database server fragments the table across the dbspaces that make up the dbslice. Similarly, if you specify a dbspacelist, the database server fragments the table across the dbspaces specified in that list.

For example, the following table, **my_hybrid**, distributes rows based on two columns of the table. The value of **col1** determines in which dbslice the row belongs. The hash value of **col2** determines in which dbspace (within the previously determined dbslice) to insert into.

```
CREATE TABLE my_hybrid
    (col1 INT,
    col2 DATE,
    col3 CHAR(10)
    )
    HYBRID (col2)
        EXPRESSION
        col1 < 100 IN dbslice1,
        col1 >= 100 and col1 < 200 IN dbslice2,
        REMAINDER IN dbslice3
```

For more information on an expression-based distribution scheme, see "Fragmenting by EXPRESSION" on page 2-262.

EDS

RANGE Method Clause

You can use a range-fragmentation method as a convenient alternative to fragmenting by the EXPRESSION or HYBRID clauses. This method provides a method to implicitly and uniformly distribute data whose fragmentation column values are dense or naturally uniform.

In a range-fragmented table, the database server assigns each dbspace a contiguous, completely bound and non-overlapping range of integer values over one or two columns. In other words, the database server implicitly clusters rows within the fragments based on the range of the values in the fragmentation column.

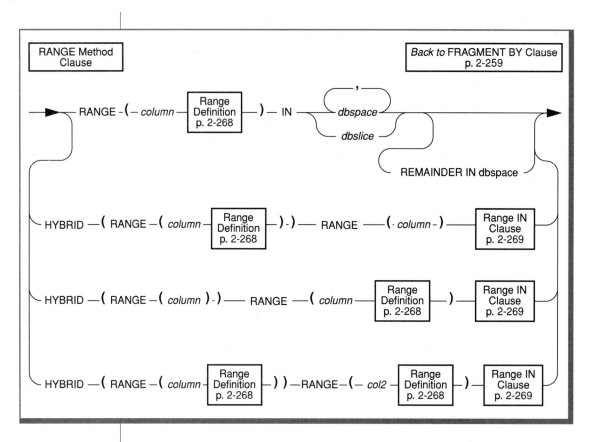

Element	Purpose	Restrictions	Element
column	Name of the column on which you want to apply the fragmentation strategy	The column must be in the current table.	Identifier, p. 4-205
		The column must be of type INT or SMALL INT.	
		If you use one of the hybrid-range fragmentation strategies in which *column* appears twice, both occurrences of *column* must be the same column.	

(1 of 2)

Element	Purpose	Restrictions	Element
col2	Name of the column on which you want to apply the second fragmentation strategy	The column must be of type INT or SMALL INT.	Identifier, p. 4-205
		The column must be in the current table.	
		This column must be a different column from that specified in *column*.	
dbslice	Name of the dbslice that contains the dbspaces in which the table fragments reside	The dbslice must exist when you execute the statement.	Identifier, p.4-205
		If you list more than one dbslice, including a remainder dbslice, each dbslice must contain the same number of dbspaces.	
dbspace	Name of the dbspace that contains the table fragment	The dbspace must exist when you execute the statement.	Identifier, p. 4-205
		Unless you are specifying the dbspace in the REMAINDER option, the minimum number of dbspaces that you can specify is two.	
		The maximum number of dbspaces that you can specify is 2,048.	

(2 of 2)

Range Definition

Use the range definition to specify the minimum and maximum values of the entire range.

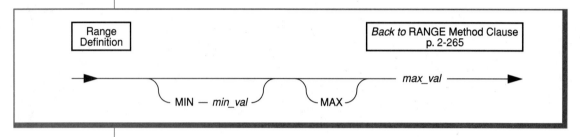

Element	Purpose	Restrictions	Element
max_val	Maximum value in the range	The value must an INT or SMALLINT. The *max_val* must be greater than or equal to the *min_val* if *min_val* is supplied.	Literal Number, p. 4-237
min_val	Minimum value in the range The default is 0.	The value must an INT or SMALLINT. The *min_val* must be less than or equal to the *max_val*.	Literal Number, p. 4-237

You do not have to specify a minimum value.

The database server uses the minimum and maximum values to determine the exact range of values to allocate for each storage space.

Range IN Clause

Use the IN clause to specify the storage spaces across which to distribute the data.

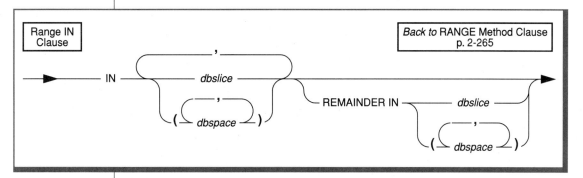

Element	Purpose	Restrictions	Element
dbslice	Name of the dbslice that contains the dbspaces in which the table fragments reside	The dbslice must exist when you execute the statement.	Identifier, p.4-205
		If you list more than one dbslice, including a remainder dbslice, each dbslice must contain the same number of dbspaces.	
dbspace	Name of the dbspace that contains the table fragment	The dbspace must exist when you execute the statement.	Identifier, p. 4-205
		Unless you are specifying the dbspace in the REMAINDER option, the minimum number of dbspaces that you can specify is two.	
		The maximum number of dbspaces that you can specify is 2,048.	

When you use a range fragmentation method, the number of integral values between the minimum and maximum specified values must be equal to or greater than the number of storage spaces specified so that the database server can allocate non-overlapping contiguous ranges across the dbspaces.

For example, the following code returns an error because the allocations for the range cannot be distributed across all specified dbspaces:

```
CREATE TABLE Tab1 (Col1 INT...)
    FRAGMENT BY RANGE (Col1 MIN 5 MAX 7)
        IN db1, db2, db3, db4, db5, db6 -- code returns an
error
```

The error for this example occurs because the specified range contains three values (5, 6, and 7), but six dbspaces are specified; three values cannot be distributed across six dbspaces.

Using the REMAINDER Keyword

Use the REMAINDER keyword to specify the storage space in which to store valid values that fall outside the specified expression or expressions.

If you do not specify a remainder and a row is inserted or updated such that it no longer belongs to any storage space, the database server returns an error.

Restrictions

If you fragment a table with range fragmentation, you cannot perform the following operations on it once it is created:

- You cannot change the fragmentation strategy (ALTER FRAGMENT).
- You cannot rename the columns of the table (RENAME COLUMN).
- You cannot duplicate the table locally (COPY TABLE).
- You cannot alter the table in any way except to change the table type or to change the lock mode.

  That is, the Usage-TYPE Options and the Lock Mode Clause are the only options of the ALTER TABLE statement that you can use on a table that has range fragmentation.

Examples

The following examples illustrate range fragmentation in its simple and hybrid forms.

Simple Range Fragmentation Strategy

The following example shows a simple range fragmentation strategy:

```
CREATE TABLE Tab1 (Col1 INT...)
    FRAGMENT BY RANGE (Col1 MIN 100 MAX 200)
        IN db1, db2, db3, db4
```

In this example, the database server fragments the table according to the following allocations.

Storage Space	Holds Values
db1	100 <= Col1 < 125
db2	125 <= Col1 < 150
db3	150 <= Col1 < 175
db4	175 <= Col1 <200

The previous table shows allocations that can also be made with an expression-based fragmentation scheme:

```
... FRAGMENT BY EXPRESSION
    Col1 >= 100 AND Col1 < 125 IN db1
    Col1 >= 125 AND Col1 < 150 IN db2
    Col1 >= 150 AND Col1 < 175 IN db3
    Col1 >= 175 AND Col1 < 200 IN db4
```

However, as the examples show, the range-fragmentation example requires much less coding to achieve the same results. The same is true for the hybrid-range fragmentation methods in relation to hybrid-expression fragmentation methods.

Column-Major-Range Allocation

The following example demonstrates the syntax for column-major-range allocation, a hybrid-range fragmentation strategy:

```
CREATE TABLE tab2 (col2 INT, colx char (5))
    FRAGMENT BY HYBRID
        ( RANGE (col2 MIN 100 MAX 220))
        RANGE (col2)
        IN dbs11, dbs12, dbs13
```

This type of fragmentation creates a distribution across dbslices and provides a further subdivision within each dbslice (across the dbspaces in the dbslice) such that when a query specifies a value for col1 (for example, WHERE col1 = 127), the query uniquely identifies a dbspace. To take advantage of the additional subdivision, you must specify more than one dbslice.

Row-Major-Range Allocation

The following example demonstrates the syntax for row-major-range allocation, a hybrid-range fragmentation strategy:

```
CREATE TABLE tab3 (col3 INT, colx char (5))
    FRAGMENT BY HYBRID
        ( RANGE (col3) )
        RANGE (col3 MIN 100 MAX 220)
        IN dbs11, dbs12, dbs13
```

This fragmentation strategy is the counterpart to the column-major-range allocation. The advantages and restrictions are equivalent.

Independent-Range Allocation

The following example demonstrates the syntax for an independent-range allocation, a hybrid-range fragmentation strategy:

```
CREATE TABLE tab4 (col4 INT, colx char (5), col5 INT)
    FRAGMENT BY HYBRID
        ( RANGE (col4 MIN 100 MAX 200) )
        RANGE (col5 MIN 500 MAX 800)
        IN dbs11, dbs12, dbs13
```

In this type of range fragmentation, the two columns are independent, and therefore the range allocations are independent. The range allocation for a dbspace on both columns is the conjunctive combination of the range allocation on each of the two independent columns. This type of fragmentation does not provide subdivisions within either column.

With this type of fragmentation, a query that specifies values for both columns (such as, WHERE col4 = 128 and col5 = 650) uniquely identifies the dbspace at the intersection of the two dbslices identified by the columns independently.

IDS

PUT Clause

Use the PUT clause to specify the storage spaces and characteristics for each column that will contain smart large objects.

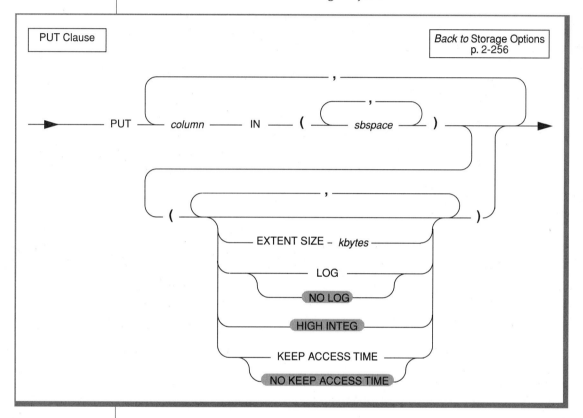

Element	Purpose	Restrictions	Syntax
column	Name of the column to store in the specified sbspace	Column must contain a user-defined type, complex type, BLOB, or CLOB data type.	Identifier, p. 4-205
		The column cannot be in the form *column.field*. That is, the smart large object that you are storing cannot be one field of a row type.	
kbytes	Number of kilobytes to allocate for the extent size	The number must be an integer value.	Literal Number, p. 4-237
sbspace	Name of an area of storage used for smart large objects	The sbspace must exist.	Identifier, p. 4-205

A smart large object is contained in a single sbspace. The SBSPACENAME configuration parameter specifies the system default in which smart large objects are created unless you specify another area.

When you specify more than one sbspace, the database server distributes the smart large objects in a round-robin distribution scheme so that the number of smart large objects in each space is approximately equal. The fragmentation scheme is stored in the **syscolattribs** system catalog table.

When you fragment smart large objects across different sbspaces you can work with smaller sbspaces. If you limit the size of an sbspace, backup and archive operations can perform more quickly. For an example that uses the PUT clause, see "Storage Options" on page 2-256.

Important: *The PUT clause does not affect the storage of simple-large-object data types (BYTE and TEXT). For information on how to store BYTE and TEXT data, see "Large-Object Data Types" on page 4-62.*

Using Options in the PUT Clause

The following table describes the storage options available when you store BLOB and CLOB data.

Option	Purpose
EXTENT SIZE	Specifies the number of kilobytes in a smart-large-object extent.
	The database server might round the EXTENT SIZE up so that the extents are multiples of the sbspace page size.
HIGH INTEG	Produces user-data pages that contain a page header and a page trailer to detect incomplete writes and data corruption.
	This is the default data-integrity behavior.
KEEP ACCESS TIME	Records, in the smart-large-object metadata, the system time at which the corresponding smart large object was last read or written.
	This capability is provided for compatibility with the Illustra interface.
LOG	Follows the logging procedure used with the current database log for the corresponding smart large object.
	This option can generate large amounts of log traffic and increase the risk that the logical log fills up. For an alternative, see "Alternative to Full Logging" on page 2-276.
NO LOG	Turns off logging.
	The NO LOG option is the default logging behavior.
NO KEEP ACCESS TIME	Do not record the system time at which the corresponding smart large object was last read or written.
	This option provides better performance than the KEEP ACCESS TIME option.
	This option is the default tracking behavior.

If a user-defined type or complex type contains more than one large object, the specified large-object storage options apply to all large objects in the type unless the storage options are overridden when the large object is created.

Alternative to Full Logging

Instead of full logging, you might turn off logging when you load the smart large object initially, and then turn logging back on once the smart large object is loaded.

Use the NO LOG option to turn off logging. If you use NO LOG, you can restore the smart-large-object metadata later to a state in which no structural inconsistencies exist. In most cases, no transaction inconsistencies will exist either, but that result is not guaranteed.

Example of Using the PUT Clause

The following statement creates the **greek** table. The data for the table is fragmented into the **dbs1** and **dbs2** dbspaces. However, the PUT clause assigns the smart-large-object data in the **gamma** and **delta** columns to the **sb1** and **sb2** sbspaces, respectively. The TEXT data in the **eps** column is assigned to the **blb1** blobspace.

```
CREATE TABLE greek
(alpha        INTEGER,
beta          VARCHAR(150),
gamma         CLOB,
delta         BLOB,
eps           TEXT IN blb1)
    FRAGMENT BY EXPRESSION
    alpha <= 5 IN dbs1,
    alpha > 5 IN dbs2
    PUT gamma IN (sb1), delta IN (sb2)
```

EXTENT SIZE Options

Use the extent size options to define the size of the extents assigned to the table.

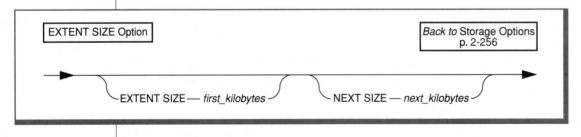

Element	Purpose	Restrictions	Syntax
first_kilobytes	Length in kilobytes of the first extent for the table The default is 16 kilobytes.	The minimum length is four times the disk-page size on your system. For example, if you have a 2-kilobyte page system, the minimum length is 8 kilobytes. The maximum length is equal to the chunk size.	Expression, p.4-73
next_kilobytes	Length in kilobytes for the subsequent extents The default is 16 kilobytes.	The minimum length is four times the disk-page size on your system. For example, if you have a 2-kilobyte page system, the minimum length is 8 kilobytes. The maximum length is equal to the chunk size.	Expression, p.4-73

The following example specifies a first extent of 20 kilobytes and allows the rest of the extents to use the default size:

```
CREATE TABLE emp_info
    (
    f_name      CHAR(20),
    l_name      CHAR(20),
    position    CHAR(20),
    start_date  DATETIME YEAR TO DAY,
    comments    VARCHAR(255)
    )
EXTENT SIZE 20
```

Revising Extent Sizes

If you need to revise the extent sizes of a table, you can modify the extent and next-extent sizes in the generated schema files of an unloaded table. For example, to make a database more efficient, you might unload a table, modify the extent sizes in the schema files and then create and load a new table. For information about optimizing extents, see your *Administrator's Guide*.

LOCK MODE Options

Use the LOCK MODE options to specify the locking granularity of the table.

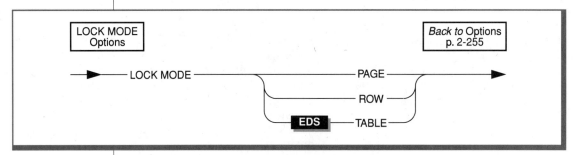

The following table describes the locking-granularity options available.

Locking-Granularity Option	Purpose
ROW	Obtains and releases one lock per row
	Row-level locking provides the highest level of concurrency. However, if you are using many rows at one time, the lock-management overhead can become significant. You can also exceed the maximum number of locks available, depending on the configuration of your database server.
PAGE	Obtains and releases one lock on a whole page of rows
	This is the default locking granularity.
	Page-level locking is especially useful when you know that the rows are grouped into pages in the same order that you are using to process all the rows. For example, if you are processing the contents of a table in the same order as its cluster index, page locking is appropriate.
TABLE (EDS only)	Places a lock on the entire table
	This type of lock reduces update concurrency compared to row and page locks. A table lock reduces the lock-management overhead for the table
	With table locking, multiple read-only transactions can still access the table.

You can change the lock mode of an existing table with the ALTER TABLE statement.

IDS

USING Access-Method Clause

A primary access method is a set of routines that perform all of the operations you need to make a table available to a server, such as create, drop, insert, delete, update, and scan. The database server provides a built-in primary access method.

You store and manage a virtual table either outside of the database server in an extspace or inside the database server in an sbspace. (See "Storage Options" on page 2-256.) You can access a virtual table with SQL statements. Access to a virtual table requires a user-defined primary access method.

DataBlade modules can provide other primary access methods to access virtual tables. When you access a virtual table, the database server calls the routines associated with that access method rather than the built-in table routines. For more information on these other primary access methods, refer to your access method documentation.

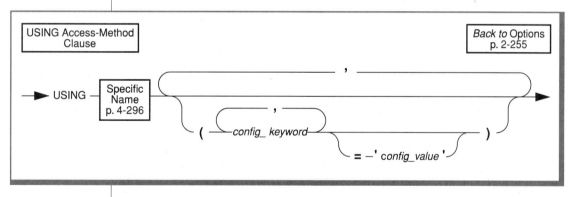

Element	Purpose	Restrictions	Syntax
config_keyword	Configuration keyword associated with the specified access method name	The maximum length is 18 bytes.	
config_value	Value of the specified configuration keyword	The value must be defined by the access method.	Quoted String, p. 4-260
	You can retrieve a list of configuration values for an access method from a table descriptor (mi_am_table_desc) using the MI_TAB_AMPARAM macro.	Not all keywords require configuration values. The maximum length is 236 bytes.	

For example, if an access method called **textfile** exists, you can specify that access method with the following syntax:

```
create table mybook
( ... )
IN myextspace
USING textfile (delimiter=':')
```

The access method must already exist.

IDS

OF TYPE Clause

Use the OF TYPE clause to create a *typed table* for an object-relational database. A typed table is a table that has a named-row type assigned to it.

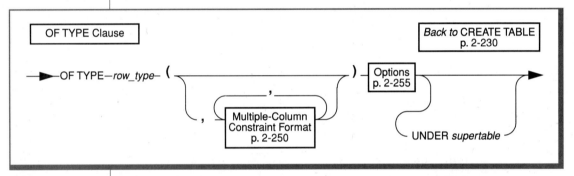

Element	Purpose	Restrictions	Syntax
row_type	Name of the row type on which this table is based	This type must already exist and must be a named-row type. If you are using the UNDER clause, the row_type must be derived from the row type of the supertable.	Data Type, p. 4-53 Identifier, p. 4-205
supertable	Name of the table from which this table inherits its properties	The supertable must already exist as a typed table. A type hierarchy must already exist in which the named-row type of this table is a subtype of the named-row type of the supertable.	Database Object Name, p. 4-50

When you create a typed table, the columns of the table are not named in the CREATE TABLE statement. Instead, the columns are specified when you create the row type. The columns of a typed table correspond to the fields of the named-row type. You cannot add additional columns to a typed table.

For example, suppose you create a named-row type, **student_t,** as follows:

```
CREATE ROW TYPE student_t
    (name        VARCHAR(30),
     average     REAL,
     birthdate   DATETIME YEAR TO DAY)
```

If a table is assigned the type **student_t,** the table is a typed table whose columns are of the same name and data type (and in the same order) as the fields of the type **student_t.**

The following CREATE TABLE statement creates a typed table named **students** whose type is **student_t:**

```
CREATE TABLE students OF TYPE student_t
```

The **students** table has the following columns:

```
name        VARCHAR(30)
average     REAL
birthdate   DATETIME
```

For more information about row types, refer to the CREATE ROW TYPE statement on page 1-194.

Using Large-Object Data in Typed Tables

Informix recommends that you use the BLOB or CLOB data types instead of the BYTE or TEXT data types when you create a typed table that contains columns for large objects. For backward compatibility, you can create a named-row type that contains BYTE or TEXT fields and use that type to recreate an existing (untyped) table as a typed table. However, although you can use a row type that contains BYTE or TEXT fields to create a typed table, you cannot use such a row type as a column. You can use a row type that contains BLOB or CLOB fields in both typed tables and columns.

Using the UNDER Clause

Use the UNDER clause to specify inheritance (that is, define the table as a subtable.) The subtable inherits properties from the supertable which it is under. In addition, you can define new properties specific to the subtable.

Continuing the example shown in "OF TYPE Clause" on page 2-280, the following statements create a typed table, **grad_students**, that inherits all of the columns of the **students** table. In addition, the **grad_students** table has columns for **adviser** and **field_of_study** that correspond to their respective fields in the **grad_student_t** row type:

```
CREATE ROW TYPE grad_student_t
    (adviser         CHAR(25),
     field_of_study CHAR(40))
     UNDER student_t;

CREATE TABLE grad_students OF TYPE grad_student_t
     UNDER students;
```

Properties That a Subtable Inherits

When you use the UNDER clause, the subtable inherits the following properties:

- All columns in the supertable

- All constraints defined on the supertable

- All indexes defined on the supertable

- Referential integrity

- The access method

- The storage option (including fragmentation strategy)

  If a subtable does not define fragments, and if its supertable has fragments defined, then the subtable inherits the fragments of the supertable.

- All triggers defined on the supertable

Tip: *Any heritable attributes that are added to a supertable after subtables have been created will automatically be inherited by existing subtables. You do not need to add all heritable attributes to a supertable before you create its subtables.*

Inheritance occurs in one direction only—from supertable to subtable. Properties of subtables are *not* inherited by supertables.

Restrictions on the Inheritance Hierarchy

No two tables in a table hierarchy can have the same type. For example, the final line of the following code sample is illegal because the tables **tab2** and **tab3** cannot have the same row type (**rowtype2**):

```
          create row type rowtype1 (...);
          create row type rowtype2 (...) under rowtype1;
          create table tab1 of type rowtype1;
          create table tab2 of type rowtype2 under tab1;
Illegal --> create table tab3 of type rowtype2 under tab1;
```

Recording Properties in the System Catalog Tables

Constraints, indexes, and triggers are recorded in the system catalog for the supertable, but not for subtables that inherit them. Fragmentation information is recorded for both supertables and subtables.

For more information about inheritance, refer to the *Informix Guide to SQL: Tutorial*.

Privileges on Tables

The privileges on a table describe both who can access the information in the table and who can create new tables. For more information about privileges, see "GRANT" on page 2-500.

ANSI

In an ANSI-compliant database, no default table-level privileges exist. You must grant these privileges explicitly. ♦

When set to yes, the environment variable **NODEFDAC** prevents default privileges from being granted to PUBLIC on a new table in a database that is not ANSI compliant.

For information about how to prevent privileges from being granted to PUBLIC, see the **NODEFDAC** environment variable in the *Informix Guide to SQL: Reference*. For additional information about privileges, see the *Informix Guide to SQL: Tutorial*.

Default Index Creation Strategy for Constraints

When you create a table with unique or primary-key constraints, the database server creates an internal, unique, ascending index for each constraint.

When you create a table with a referential constraint, the database server creates an internal, nonunique, ascending index for each column specified in the referential constraint.

The database server stores this internal index in the same location that the table uses. If you fragment the table, the database server stores the index fragments in the same dbspaces as the table fragments or in some cases, the database dbspace.

If you require an index fragmentation strategy that is independent of the underlying table fragmentation, do not include the constraint when you create the table. Instead, use the CREATE INDEX statement to create a unique index with the desired fragmentation strategy. Then use the ALTER TABLE statement to add the constraint. The new constraint will use the previously defined index.

Important: *In a database without logging, detached checking is the only kind of constraint checking available. Detached checking means that constraint checking is performed on a row-by-row basis.*

System Catalog Information

When you create a table, the database server adds basic information about the table to the **systables** system catalog table and column information to **syscolumns** table. The **sysblobs** table contains information about the location of dbspaces and simple large objects. The **syschunks** table in the **sysmaster** database contains information about the location of smart large objects.

The **systabauth, syscolauth, sysfragauth, sysprocauth, sysusers,** and **sysxt-dtypeauth** tables contain information about the privileges that various CREATE TABLE options require. The **systables, sysxtdtypes,** and **sysinherits** system catalog tables provide information about table types.

Related Information

Related statements: ALTER TABLE, CREATE INDEX, CREATE DATABASE, CREATE EXTERNAL TABLE, CREATE ROW TYPE, CREATE Temporary TABLE, DROP TABLE, SET Database Object Mode, and SET Transaction Mode

For discussions of database and table creation, including discussions on data types, data-integrity constraints, and tables in hierarchies, see the *Informix Guide to Database Design and Implementation*.

For information about the system catalog tables that store information about objects in the database, see the *Informix Guide to SQL: Reference*.

For information about the **syschunks** table (in the **sysmaster** database) that contains information about the location of smart large objects, see your *Administrator's Reference*.

CREATE Temporary TABLE

Use the CREATE Temporary TABLE statement to create a temporary table in the current database.

Syntax

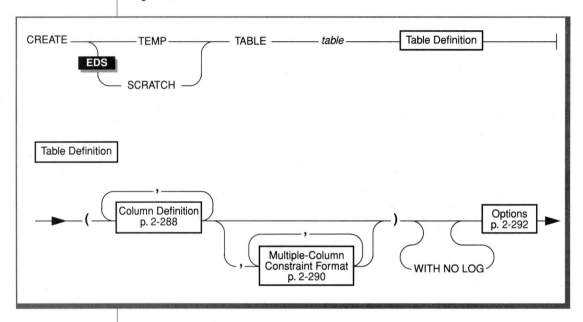

Element	Purpose	Restrictions	Syntax
table	Name assigned to the table	The name must be unique in the database.	Database Object Name, p. 4-50

Usage

If you have the Connect privilege on a database, you can create a temporary table. However, you are the only user who can see the temporary table.

DB

In DB-Access, using the CREATE Temporary TABLE statement outside the CREATE SCHEMA statement generates warnings if you set **DBANSIWARN**. ♦

E/C

The CREATE TABLE statement generates warnings if you use the **-ansi** flag or set the **DBANSIWARN** environment variable. ♦

Using the TEMP Option

Once a TEMP table is created, you can build indexes on the table.

IDS

If your database does not have logging, the table behaves in the same way as a table that uses the WITH NO LOG option. ♦

EDS

Using the SCRATCH Option

Use the INTO SCRATCH clause to reduce the overhead of transaction logging. A scratch table is a nonlogging temporary table that does not support indexes or referential constraints. A scratch table is identical to a TEMP table created with the WITH NO LOG option. Operations on scratch tables are not included in transaction-log operations.

Naming a Temporary Table

A temporary table is associated with a session, not a database. Therefore, when you create a temporary table, you cannot create another temporary table with the same name (even for another database) until you drop the first temporary table or end the session.

The name must be different from existing table, view, or synonym names in the current database; however, it need not be different from other temporary table names used by other users.

ANSI

In an ANSI-compliant database, the combination *owner.table* must be unique in the database. ♦

Using the WITH NO LOG Option

EDS

Informix recommends that you use a scratch table rather than a TEMP…WITH NO LOG table. The behavior of a temporary table that you create with the WITH NO LOG option is the same as that of a scratch table. ♦

Use the WITH NO LOG option to reduce the overhead of transaction logging. If you use the WITH NO LOG option, operations on the temporary table are not included in the transaction-log operations.

You must use the WITH NO LOG option on temporary tables you create in temporary dbspaces.

IDS

If you use the WITH NO LOG option in a database that does not use logging, the WITH NO LOG option is ignored. ♦

Once you turn off logging on a temporary table, you cannot turn it back on; a temporary table is, therefore, always logged or never logged.

The following example shows how to prevent logging temporary tables in a database that uses logging:

```
CREATE TEMP TABLE tab2
    (fname CHAR(15),
     lname CHAR(15))
    WITH NO LOG
```

Column Definition

Use the column definition portion of CREATE Temporary TABLE to list the name, data type, default value, and constraints *of a single column*.

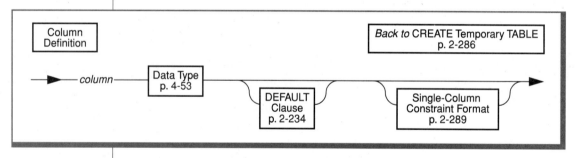

Element	Purpose	Restrictions	Syntax
column	Name of a column in the table	The name must be unique in a table, but you can use the same names in different tables in the same database.	Identifier, p. 4-205

This portion of the CREATE Temporary TABLE statement is almost identical to the corresponding section in the CREATE TABLE statement. The difference is that fewer types of constraints are allowed in a temporary table.

Single-Column Constraint Format

Use the single column constraint format to create one or more data-integrity constraints for a single column in a temporary table.

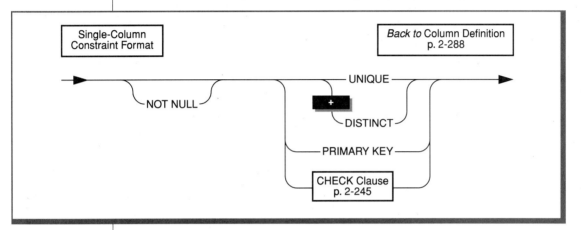

The following table indicates where you can find detailed discussions of specific constraints.

Constraint	For more information, see
CHECK	"CHECK Clause" on page 2-245
DISTINCT	"Using the UNIQUE or DISTINCT Constraints" on page 2-239
NOT NULL	"Using the NOT NULL Constraint" on page 2-239.
PRIMARY KEY	"Using the PRIMARY KEY Constraint" on page 2-240
UNIQUE	"Using the UNIQUE or DISTINCT Constraints" on page 2-239

Constraints you define on temporary tables are always enabled.

Multiple-Column Constraint Format

Use the multiple-column constraint format to associate one or more columns with a constraint. This alternative to the single-column constraint format allows you to associate multiple columns with a constraint.

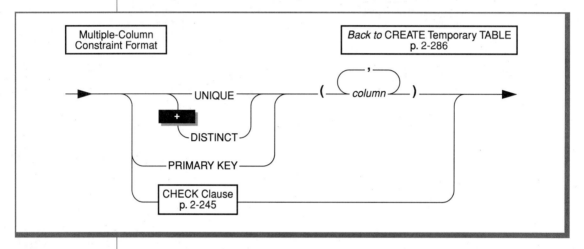

Element	Purpose	Restrictions	Syntax
column	Name of the column or columns on which the constraint is placed	The name must be unique in a table, but you can use the same names in different tables in the same database.	Identifier, p. 4-205

This alternative to the column-level constraints portion of the CREATE TABLE statement allows you to associate multiple columns with a constraint.

Constraints you define on temporary tables are always enabled.

The following table indicates where you can find detailed discussions of specific constraints.

Constraint	For more information, see	For an Example, see
CHECK	"CHECK Clause" on page 2-245	"Defining Check Constraints Across Columns" on page 2-253
DISTINCT	"Using the UNIQUE or DISTINCT Constraints" on page 2-239	"Examples that Use the Multiple-Column Constraint Format" on page 2-253
PRIMARY KEY	"Using the PRIMARY KEY Constraint" on page 2-240	"Defining Composite Primary and Foreign Keys" on page 2-254
UNIQUE	"Using the UNIQUE or DISTINCT Constraints" on page 2-239	"Examples that Use the Multiple-Column Constraint Format" on page 2-253

Options

The CREATE TABLE options let you specify storage locations, locking modes, and user-defined access methods

You cannot specify initial and next extents for a temporary table. Extents for a temporary table are always eight pages.

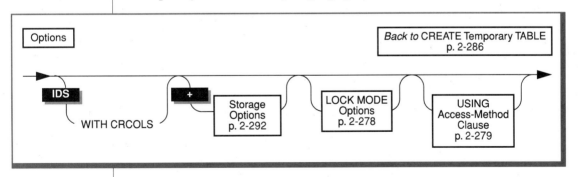

Options

Back to CREATE Temporary TABLE
p. 2-286

IDS

WITH CRCOLS

Storage Options p. 2-292

LOCK MODE Options p. 2-278

USING Access-Method Clause p. 2-279

Storage Options

Use the storage-option portion of the CREATE Temporary Table statement to specify the distribution scheme for the table.

EDS

If you are using Enterprise Decision Server, you can fragment a temporary table across multiple dbspaces that different coservers manage. ♦

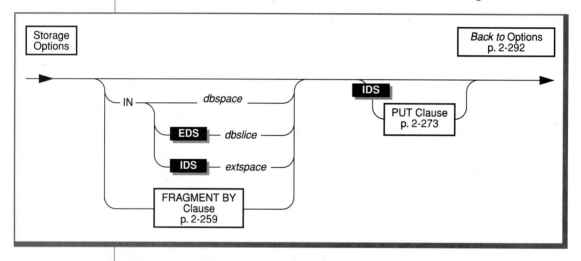

If you plan to create a fragmented, unique index on a temporary table, you must specify an explicit expression-based distribution scheme for a temporary table in the CREATE Temporary TABLE statement.

Element	Purpose	Restrictions	Syntax
dbspace	Name of the dbspace in which to store the table	Specified dbspace must already exist.	Identifier, p. 4-205
	The default for database tables is the dbspace in which the current database resides.		
dbslice	Name of the dbslice in which to store the table	The specified dbslice must already exist.	Identifier, p. 4-205
extspace	Name assigned with the onspaces command to a storage area outside the database server	Specified *extspace* must already exist.	Refer to the user documentation for your custom access method for more information.

Where Temporary Tables are Stored

The distribution scheme that you specify with the CREATE Temporary TABLE statement (either with the IN clause or the FRAGMENT BY clause) takes precedence over the information specified in the **DBSPACETEMP** environment variable and the DBSPSCETEMP configuration parameter.

For temporary tables for which you do not specify an explicit distribution scheme, each temporary table that you create round-robins to a dbspace specified by the **DBSPACETEMP** environment variable or the DBSPACETEMP configuration parameter if the environment variable is not set. For example, if you create three temporary tables, the first one goes into the dbspace called **tempspc1**, the second one goes into **tempspc2**, and the third one goes into **tempspc3**.

This behavior also applies temporary tables that you create with SELECT...INTO TEMP or SELECT...INTO SCRATCH.

For more information on the **DBSPACETEMP** environment variable, see *Informix Guide to SQL: Reference*.

For more information on the DBSPACETEMP configuration parameter, see your *Administrator's Reference*.

Example

The following example shows how to insert data into a temporary table called **result_tmp** to output to a file the results of a user-defined function (**f_one**) that returns multiple rows.

```
CREATE TEMP TABLE result_tmp( ... );
INSERT INTO result_tmp EXECUTE FUNCTION f_one();
UNLOAD TO 'file' SELECT * FROM temp1;
```

EDS

In Enterprise Decision Server, to recreate this example use the CREATE PROCEDURE statement instead of the CREATE FUNCTION statement. ◆

Differences between Temporary Tables and Permanent Tables

Temporary tables differ from permanent tables in a number of ways. Temporary tables:

- have fewer types of constraints available.
- have fewer options that you can specify.
- are not preserved.

  For more information, see "Duration of Temporary Tables" on page 2-294.

- are not visible to other users or sessions.
- do not appear in the system catalogs.

EDS

You can use the following data definition statements on a temporary table from a secondary coserver: CREATE Temporary TABLE, CREATE INDEX, CREATE SCHEMA, DROP TABLE, and DROP INDEX.

DB

You cannot use the INFO statement and the Info Menu option with temporary tables. ♦

Duration of Temporary Tables

The duration of a temporary table depends on whether or not that table is logged.

Logged Temporary Tables

A logged, temporary table exists until one of the following situations occurs:

- The application disconnects.
- A DROP TABLE statement is issued on the temporary table.
- The database is closed.

When any of these events occur, the temporary table is deleted.

Nonlogging Temporary Tables

Nonlogging temporary tables include temp tables created with the WITH NO LOG option and SCRATCH tables.

A nonlogging, temporary table exists until one of the following situations occurs:

- The application disconnects.
- A DROP TABLE statement is issued on the temporary table.

Because these tables do not disappear when the database is closed, you can use a nonlogging temporary table to transfer data from one database to another while the application remains connected.

Related Information

Related statements: ALTER TABLE, CREATE TABLE, CREATE DATABASE, DROP TABLE, and SELECT

For additional information about the **DBANSIWARN** and **DBSPACETEMP** environment variables, refer to the *Informix Guide to SQL: Reference*.

For additional information about the ONCONFIG parameter DBSPACETEMP, see your *Administrator's Guide*.

CREATE TRIGGER

Use the CREATE TRIGGER statement to create a trigger on a table.

Syntax

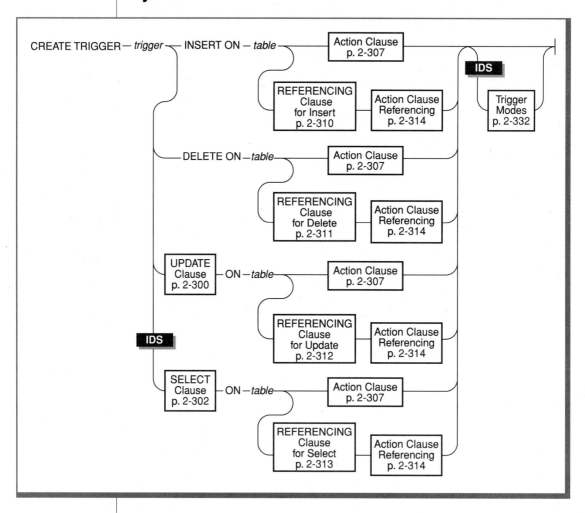

Element	Purpose	Restrictions	Syntax
table	Name of the table that the trigger affects	The name must be different from any existing table, view, or synonym name in the current database.	Database Object Name, p. 4-50
trigger	Name of the trigger	You can specify a trigger for the current database only. The name of the trigger must be unique.	Database Object Name, p. 4-50

Usage

You can use the CREATE TRIGGER statement to define a trigger on a table. A trigger is a database object that automatically sets off a specified set of SQL statements when a specified event occurs.

EDS

You cannot create a trigger on a raw or static table. When you create a trigger on an operational table, the table cannot use light appends. For more information on light appends, see your *Administrator's Guide*.

Information in this statement that discusses nonlogging databases does not apply to Enterprise Decision Server. In Enterprise Decision Server, all databases are logging databases. ♦

Rules for Triggers

You must be either the owner of the table or have the DBA status to create a trigger on a table.

For information about the relationship between the privileges of the trigger owner and the privileges of other users, see "Privileges to Execute Triggered Actions" on page 2-326.

IDS

You can use roles with triggers. Role-related statements (CREATE ROLE, DROP ROLE, and SET ROLE) and SET SESSION AUTHORIZATION statements can be triggered inside a trigger. Privileges that a user has acquired through enabling a role or through a SET SESSION AUTHORIZATION statement are not relinquished when a trigger is executed. ♦

When you create a trigger, the name of the trigger must be unique within a database.

You can create a trigger only on a table in the current database. You cannot create a trigger on a temporary table, a view, or a system catalog table.

You cannot create a trigger inside an SPL routine if the routine is called inside a data manipulation statement. For example, in the following INSERT statement, if the **sp_items** procedure contains a trigger, the database server returns an error:

```
INSERT INTO items EXECUTE PROCEDURE sp_items
```

For a list of data manipulation statements, see "Data Manipulation Statements" on page 1-10.

You cannot use an SPL variable in a CREATE TRIGGER statement.

DB

In DB-Access, if you want to define a trigger as part of a schema, place the CREATE TRIGGER statement inside a CREATE SCHEMA statement. ♦

E/C

If you are embedding the CREATE TRIGGER statement in an ESQL/C program, you cannot use a host variable in the trigger specification. ♦

Trigger Events

The trigger event specifies the type of statement that activates a trigger. The trigger event can be an INSERT, DELETE, UPDATE, or SELECT statement. Each trigger can have only one trigger event. The occurrence of the trigger event is the *triggering statement*.

For each table, you can define only one trigger that is activated by an INSERT statement and only one trigger that is activated by a DELETE statement. For each table, you can define multiple triggers that are activated by UPDATE statements or SELECT statements. For more information about multiple update or select triggers on the same table, see "UPDATE Clause" on page 2-300 and "SELECT Clause" on page 2-302.

You cannot define a DELETE trigger event on a table with a referential constraint that specifies ON DELETE CASCADE.

You are responsible for guaranteeing that the triggering statement returns the same result with and without the triggered actions. For more information on the behavior of triggered actions, see "Action Clause" on page 2-307 and "Triggered Action List" on page 2-315.

A triggering statement from an external database server can activate the trigger. As shown in the following example, an insert trigger on **newtab**, managed by **dbserver1**, is activated by an INSERT statement from **dbserver2**. The trigger executes as if the insert originated on **dbserver1**.

```
-- Trigger on stores_demo@dbserver1:newtab

CREATE TRIGGER ins_tr INSERT ON newtab
REFERENCING new AS post_ins
FOR EACH ROW(EXECUTE PROCEDURE nt_pct (post_ins.mc));

-- Triggering statement from dbserver2

INSERT INTO stores_demo@dbserver1:newtab
    SELECT item_num, order_num, quantity, stock_num,
manu_code,
    total_price FROM items;
```

Trigger Events with Cursors

If the triggering statement uses a cursor, the complete trigger is activated each time the statement executes. That is, each part of the trigger (BEFORE, FOR EACH ROW, and AFTER) is activated for each row that the cursor processes.

This behavior is different from what occurs when a triggering statement does not use a cursor and updates multiple rows. In this case, the set of triggered actions executes only once. For more information on the execution of triggered actions, see "Action Clause" on page 2-307.

Privileges on the Trigger Event

You must have the appropriate Insert, Delete, Update, or Select privilege on the triggering table to execute the INSERT, DELETE, UPDATE, or SELECT statement that is the trigger event. The triggering statement might still fail, however, if you do not have the privileges necessary to execute one of the SQL statements in the action clause. When the triggered actions are executed, the database server checks your privileges for each SQL statement in the trigger definition as if the statement were being executed independently of the trigger. For information on the privileges you need to execute a trigger, see "Privileges to Execute Triggered Actions" on page 2-326.

Performance Impact of Triggers

The INSERT, DELETE, UPDATE, and SELECT statements that initiate triggers might appear to execute slowly because they activate additional SQL statements, and the user might not know that other actions are occurring.

The execution time for a triggering data manipulation statement depends on the complexity of the triggered action and whether it initiates other triggers. Obviously, the elapsed time for the triggering data manipulation statement increases as the number of cascading triggers increases. For more information on triggers that initiate other triggers, see "Cascading Triggers" on page 2-327.

UPDATE Clause

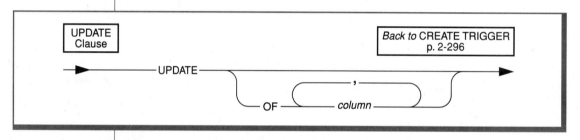

Element	Purpose	Restrictions	Syntax
column	Name of a column or columns that activate the trigger The default is all the columns in the table on which you create the trigger.	The specified columns must belong to the table on which you create the trigger. If you define more than one update trigger on a table, the column lists of the triggering statements must be mutually exclusive.	Identifier, p. 4-205

If the trigger event is an UPDATE statement, the trigger executes when any column in the triggering column list is updated.

If the trigger event is an UPDATE statement and you do not specify the OF *column* option in the definition of the trigger event, the trigger executes when any column in the triggering table is updated.

If the triggering UPDATE statement updates more than one of the triggering columns in a trigger, the trigger executes only once.

Defining Multiple Update Triggers

If you define more than one update trigger event on a table, the column lists of the triggers must be mutually exclusive. The following example shows that **trig3** is illegal on the **items** table because its column list includes **stock_num**, which is a triggering column in **trig1**. Multiple update triggers on a table cannot include the same columns.

```
CREATE TRIGGER trig1 UPDATE OF item_num, stock_num ON items
REFERENCING OLD AS pre NEW AS post
FOR EACH ROW(EXECUTE PROCEDURE proc1());

CREATE TRIGGER trig2 UPDATE OF manu_code ON items
BEFORE(EXECUTE PROCEDURE proc2());

-- Illegal trigger: stock_num occurs in trig1
CREATE TRIGGER trig3 UPDATE OF order_num, stock_num ON items
BEFORE(EXECUTE PROCEDURE proc3());
```

When an UPDATE Statement Activates Multiple Triggers

When an UPDATE statement updates multiple columns that have different triggers, the column numbers of the triggering columns determine the order of trigger execution. Execution begins with the smallest triggering column number and proceeds in order to the largest triggering column number. The following example shows that table **taba** has four columns (**a**, **b**, **c**, **d**):

```
CREATE TABLE taba (a int, b int, c int, d int)
```

Define **trig1** as an update on columns **a** and **c**, and define **trig2** as an update on columns **b** and **d**, as shown in the following example:

```
CREATE TRIGGER trig1 UPDATE OF a, c ON taba
    AFTER (UPDATE tabb SET y = y + 1);

CREATE TRIGGER trig2 UPDATE OF b, d ON taba
    AFTER (UPDATE tabb SET z = z + 1);
```

The triggering statement is shown in the following example:

```
UPDATE taba SET (b, c) = (b + 1, c + 1)
```

Then **trig1** for columns **a** and **c** executes first, and **trig2** for columns **b** and **d** executes next. In this case, the smallest column number in the two triggers is column 1 (**a**), and the next is column 2 (**b**).

SELECT Clause

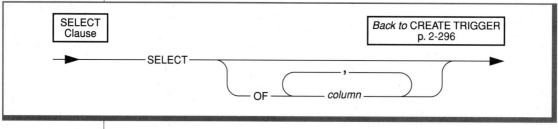

Element	Purpose	Restrictions	Syntax
column	Name of a column or columns that activate the trigger The default is all the columns in the table on which you create the trigger.	The specified columns must belong to the table on which you create the trigger. If you define more than one select trigger on a table, the column lists of the triggering statements must be mutually exclusive.	Identifier, p. 4-205

If the trigger event is a SELECT statement, the trigger executes when any column in the triggering column list is selected.

If the trigger event is a SELECT statement and you do not specify the OF *column* option in the definition of the trigger event, the trigger executes when any column in the triggering table is selected.

If the triggering SELECT statement selects more than one of the triggering columns in a trigger, the trigger executes only once.

The triggered action of a select trigger cannot include UPDATE, INSERT, or DELETE actions on the triggering table. However, the triggered action of a select trigger can include UPDATE, INSERT, and DELETE actions on tables other than the triggering table.

The following example shows how a select trigger is defined within a CREATE TRIGGER statement:

```
CREATE TRIGGER mytrig
    SELECT OF cola ON mytab
    REFERENCING OLD AS pre
    FOR EACH ROW (INSERT INTO newtab('for each action'))
```

Circumstances When a Select Trigger is Activated

A SELECT statement on the triggering table activates a select trigger in the following circumstances:

- The SELECT statement is a standalone SELECT statement.
- The SELECT statement occurs within a UDR called in a select list.
- The SELECT statement is a subquery in a select list.
- The SELECT statement occurs within a UDR called by EXECUTE PROCEDURE. ◆
- The SELECT statement occurs within a UDR called by EXECUTE PROCEDURE or EXECUTE FUNCTION.
- The SELECT statement selects data from a supertable in a table hierarchy. In this case the SELECT statement activates select triggers for the supertable and all the subtables in the hierarchy. ◆

For information on the conditions when a SELECT statement on the triggering table does not activate a select trigger, see "Circumstances When a Select Trigger is Not Activated" on page 2-305.

Standalone SELECT Statements

A select trigger is activated if the triggering column appears in the select list of a standalone SELECT statement. For example, assume that a select trigger was defined such that it will execute whenever column **col1** of table **tab1** is selected. Both of the following standalone SELECT statements will activate the select trigger.

```
SELECT * FROM tab1;
SELECT col1 FROM tab1;
```

SELECT Statements within UDRs in the Select List

A select trigger is activated by a UDR if the UDR contains a SELECT statement within its statement block and if the UDR appears in the select list of a SELECT statement. For example, assume that a UDR named **my_rtn** contains the following SELECT statement in its statement block:

```
SELECT col1 FROM tab1
```

Now suppose that the following SELECT statement invokes the **my_rtn** UDR in its select list:

```
SELECT my_rtn() FROM tab2
```

This SELECT statement activates the select trigger defined on column **col1** of table **tab1** when the **my_rtn** UDR is executed.

UDRs Called by EXECUTE PROCEDURE and EXECUTE FUNCTION

A select trigger is activated by a UDR if the UDR contains a SELECT statement within its statement block and the UDR is called by an EXECUTE PROCEDURE or EXECUTE FUNCTION statement. For example, assume that the user-defined procedure named **my_rtn** contains the following SELECT statement in its statement block:

```
SELECT col1 FROM tab1
```

Now suppose that the following EXECUTE PROCEDURE statement invokes the **my_rtn** procedure:

```
EXECUTE PROCEDURE my_rtn()
```

This EXECUTE PROCEDURE statement activates the select trigger defined on column **col1** of table **tab1** when the SELECT statement within the statement block is executed.

Subqueries in the Select List

A select trigger is activated by a subquery if the subquery appears in the select list of a SELECT statement. For example, if a select trigger was defined on **col1** of **tab1**, the subquery in the following SELECT statement activates the select trigger:

```
SELECT (SELECT col1 FROM tab1 WHERE col1=1),
    colx, col y
    FROM tabz
```

Select Triggers in Table Hierarchies

A subtable inherits the select triggers that are defined on its supertable. When you select from a supertable, the SELECT statement activates the select triggers on the supertable and the inherited select triggers on the subtables in the table hierarchy. For example, assume that table **tab1** is the supertable and table **tab2** is the subtable in a table hierarchy. If the select trigger **trig1** is defined on table **tab1**, a SELECT statement on table **tab1** activates the select trigger **trig1** for the rows in table **tab1** and the inherited select trigger **trig1** for the rows in table **tab2**.

If you add a select trigger to a subtable, this select trigger can override the select trigger that the subtable inherits from its supertable. For example, if the select trigger **trig1** is defined on column **col1** in supertable **tab1**, the subtable **tab2** inherits this trigger. But if you define a select trigger named **trig2** on column **col1** in subtable **tab2**, and a SELECT statement selects from **col1** in supertable **tab1**, this SELECT statement activates trigger **trig1** for the rows in table **tab1** and trigger **trig2** (not trigger **trig1**) for the rows in table **tab2**. In other words, the trigger that you add to the subtable overrides the trigger that the subtable inherits from the supertable.

Circumstances When a Select Trigger is Not Activated

A SELECT statement on the triggering table does not activate a select trigger in certain circumstances:

- If a subquery or UDR containing the triggering SELECT statement appears in any clause of a SELECT statement other than the select list, the select trigger is not activated.

  For example, if the subquery or UDR appears in the WHERE clause or HAVING clause of a SELECT statement, the SELECT statement within the subquery or UDR does not activate the select trigger.

- If a SELECT statement contains a built-in aggregate or user-defined aggregate in its select list, the select trigger is not activated. For example, the following SELECT statement does not activate a select trigger defined on **col1** of **tab1**:

```
SELECT MIN(col1) FROM tab1
```

- If the triggered action of a select trigger executes a UDR that has a triggering SELECT statement, the select trigger on this SELECT statement is not activated. Cascading select triggers are not supported.

- If a SELECT statement includes the UNION or UNION ALL operator, this statement does not activate a select trigger.

- The SELECT clause of an INSERT statement does not activate a select trigger.

- If the select list of a SELECT statement includes the DISTINCT or UNIQUE keywords, the SELECT statement does not activate a select trigger.

- Select triggers are not supported on scroll cursors.

Select Triggers and FOR EACH ROW Actions

If the triggered action of a select trigger is a FOR EACH ROW action, and a row appears more than once in the result of the triggering SELECT statement, the database server executes the FOR EACH ROW action for each instance of the row. For example, the same row can appear more than once in the result of a SELECT statement that joins two tables. For more information on FOR EACH ROW actions, see "FOR EACH ROW Actions" on page 2-308.

Action Clause

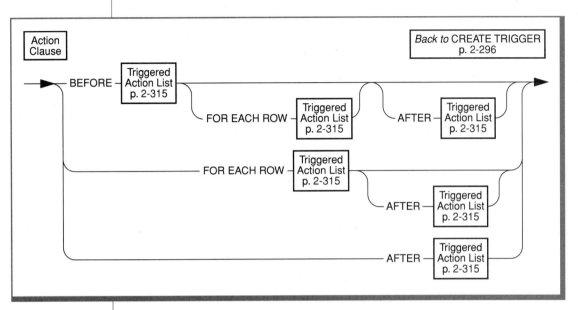

The action clause defines the characteristics of triggered actions and specifies the time when these actions occur. You must define at least one triggered action, using the keywords BEFORE, FOR EACH ROW, or AFTER to indicate when the action occurs relative to the triggering statement. You can specify triggered actions for all three options on a single trigger, but you must order them in the following sequence: BEFORE, FOR EACH ROW, and AFTER. You cannot follow a FOR EACH ROW triggered action list with a BEFORE triggered action list. If the first triggered action list is FOR EACH ROW, an AFTER action list is the only option that can follow it. For more information on the action clause when a REFERENCING clause is present, see "Action Clause Referencing" on page 2-314.

BEFORE Actions

The BEFORE triggered action or actions execute once before the triggering statement executes. If the triggering statement does not process any rows, the BEFORE triggered actions still execute because the database server does not yet know whether any row is affected.

FOR EACH ROW Actions

The FOR EACH ROW triggered action or actions execute once for each row that the triggering statement affects. The triggered SQL statement executes after the triggering statement processes each row.

If the triggering statement does not insert, delete, update, or select any rows, the FOR EACH ROW triggered actions do not execute.

EDS

You cannot have FOR EACH ROW actions on tables that have globally-detached indexes. ♦

AFTER Actions

An AFTER triggered action or actions execute once after the action of the triggering statement is complete. If the triggering statement does not process any rows, the AFTER triggered actions still execute.

Actions of Multiple Triggers

When an UPDATE statement activates multiple triggers, the triggered actions merge. Assume that **taba** has columns **a**, **b**, **c**, and **d**, as shown in the following example:

```
CREATE TABLE taba (a int, b int, c int, d int)
```

Next, assume that you define **trig1** on columns **a** and **c**, and **trig2** on columns **b** and **d**. If both triggers have triggered actions that are executed BEFORE, FOR EACH ROW, and AFTER, then the triggered actions are executed in the following sequence:

1. BEFORE action list for trigger (**a**, **c**)
2. BEFORE action list for trigger (**b**, **d**)
3. FOR EACH ROW action list for trigger (**a**, **c**)
4. FOR EACH ROW action list for trigger (**b**, **d**)
5. AFTER action list for trigger (**a**, **c**)
6. AFTER action list for trigger (**b**, **d**)

The database server treats the triggers as a single trigger, and the triggered action is the merged-action list. All the rules governing a triggered action apply to the merged list as one list, and no distinction is made between the two original triggers.

Guaranteeing Row-Order Independence

In a FOR EACH ROW triggered-action list, the result might depend on the order of the rows being processed. You can ensure that the result is independent of row order by following these suggestions:

- Avoid selecting the triggering table in the FOR EACH ROW section.

  If the triggering statement affects multiple rows in the triggering table, the result of the SELECT statement in the FOR EACH ROW section varies as each row is processed. This condition also applies to any cascading triggers. See "Cascading Triggers" on page 2-327.

- In the FOR EACH ROW section, avoid updating a table with values derived from the current row of the triggering table.

  If the triggered actions modify any row in the table more than once, the final result for that row depends on the order in which rows from the triggering table are processed.

- Avoid modifying a table in the FOR EACH ROW section that is selected by another triggered statement in the same FOR EACH ROW section, including any cascading triggered actions.

  If you modify a table in this section and refer to it later, the changes to the table might not be complete when you refer to it. Consequently, the result might differ, depending on the order in which rows are processed.

The database server does not enforce rules to prevent these situations because doing so would restrict the set of tables from which a triggered action can select. Furthermore, the result of most triggered actions is independent of row order. Consequently, you are responsible for ensuring that the results of the triggered actions are independent of row order.

REFERENCING Clause for Insert

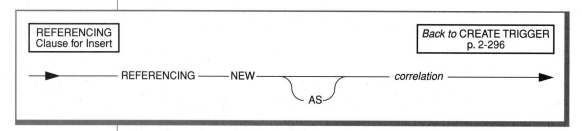

| REFERENCING Clause for Insert | | Back to CREATE TRIGGER p. 2-296 |

REFERENCING ── NEW ──┬── correlation ──────
                     └─ AS ─┘

Element	Purpose	Restrictions	Syntax
correlation	Name that you assign to a new column value so that you can refer to it within the triggered action The new column value in the triggering table is the value of the column after execution of the triggering statement.	The correlation name must be unique within the CREATE TRIGGER statement.	Identifier, p. 4-205

Once you assign a correlation name, you can use it only inside the FOR EACH ROW triggered action. See "Action Clause Referencing" on page 2-314.

To use the correlation name, precede the column name with the correlation name, followed by a period. For example, if the new correlation name is **post**, refer to the new value for the column **fname** as **post.fname**.

If the trigger event is an INSERT statement, using the old correlation name as a qualifier causes an error because no value exists before the row is inserted. For the rules that govern how to use correlation names, see "Using Correlation Names in Triggered Actions" on page 2-319.

You can use the INSERT REFERENCING clause only if you define a FOR EACH ROW triggered action.

The following example illustrates the use of the INSERT REFERENCING clause. This example inserts a row into **backup_table1** for every row that is inserted into **table1**. The values that are inserted into **col1** and **col2** of **backup_table1** are an exact copy of the values that were just inserted into **table1**.

```
CREATE TABLE table1 (col1 INT, col2 INT);
CREATE TABLE backup_table1 (col1 INT, col2 INT);
CREATE TRIGGER before_trig
    INSERT ON table1
    REFERENCING NEW as new
    FOR EACH ROW
    (
    INSERT INTO backup_table1 (col1, col2)
    VALUES (new.col1, new.col2)
    );
```

As the preceding example shows, the advantage of the INSERT REFERENCING clause is that it allows you to refer to the data values that the trigger event in your triggered action produces.

REFERENCING Clause for Delete

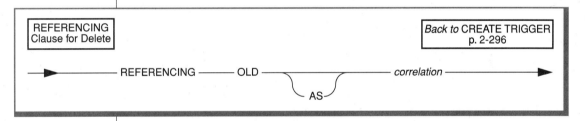

REFERENCING
Clause for Delete

Back to CREATE TRIGGER
p. 2-296

REFERENCING —— OLD —— AS —— correlation

Element	Purpose	Restrictions	Syntax
correlation	Name that you assign to an old column value so that you can refer to it within the triggered action	The correlation name must be unique within the CREATE TRIGGER statement.	Identifier, p. 4-205
	The old column value in the triggering table is the value of the column before execution of the triggering statement.		

Once you assign a correlation name, you can use it only inside the FOR EACH ROW triggered action. See "Action Clause Referencing" on page 2-314.

You use the correlation name to refer to an old column value by preceding the column name with the correlation name and a period (.). For example, if the old correlation name is **pre**, refer to the old value for the column **fname** as **pre.fname**.

If the trigger event is a DELETE statement, using the new correlation name as a qualifier causes an error because the column has no value after the row is deleted. For the rules governing the use of correlation names, see "Using Correlation Names in Triggered Actions" on page 2-319.

You can use the DELETE REFERENCING clause only if you define a FOR EACH ROW triggered action.

EDS

The OLD correlation value cannot be a byte or text value. That is, you cannot refer to a byte or text column. ♦

REFERENCING Clause for Update

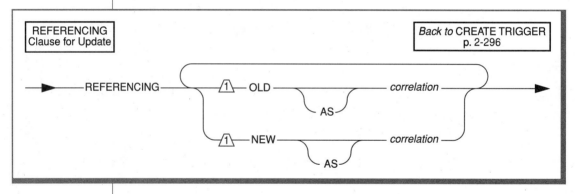

Element	Purpose	Restrictions	Syntax
correlation	Name that you assign to an old or new column value so that you can refer to it within the triggered action The old column value in the triggering table is the value of the column before execution of the triggering statement. The new column value in the triggering table is the value of the column after executing the triggering statement.	You can specify a correlation name for an old column value only (OLD option), for a new column value only (NEW option), or for both the old and new column values. Each correlation name you specify must be unique within the CREATE TRIGGER statement.	Identifier, p. 4-205

Once you assign a correlation name, you can use it only inside the FOR EACH ROW triggered action. See "Action Clause Referencing" on page 2-314.

Use the correlation name to refer to an old or new column value by preceding the column name with the correlation name and a period (.). For example, if the new correlation name is **post,** you refer to the new value for the column **fname** as **post.fname.**

If the trigger event is an UPDATE statement, you can define both old and new correlation names to refer to column values before and after the triggering update. For the rules that govern the use of correlation names, see "Using Correlation Names in Triggered Actions" on page 2-319.

You can use the UPDATE REFERENCING clause only if you define a FOR EACH ROW triggered action.

EDS

The OLD correlation value cannot be a byte or text value. That is, you cannot refer to a byte or text column. ♦

IDS

REFERENCING CLAUSE FOR Select

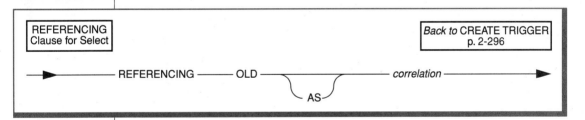

Element	Purpose	Restrictions	Syntax
correlation	Name that you assign to an old column value so that you can refer to it within the triggered action	The correlation name must be unique within the CREATE TRIGGER statement.	Identifier, p. 4-205

Once you assign a correlation name, you can use it only inside the FOR EACH ROW triggered action. See "Action Clause Referencing" on page 2-314.

You use the correlation name to refer to an old column value by preceding the column name with the correlation name and a period (.). For example, if the old correlation name is **pre**, refer to the old value for the column **fname** as **pre.fname**.

If the trigger event is a SELECT statement, using the new correlation name as a qualifier causes an error because the column does not have a new value after the column is selected. For the rules governing the use of correlation names, see "Using Correlation Names in Triggered Actions" on page 2-319.

You can use the SELECT REFERENCING clause only if you define a FOR EACH ROW triggered action.

EDS

The OLD correlation value cannot be a byte or text value. That is, you cannot refer to a byte or text column. ♦

Action Clause Referencing

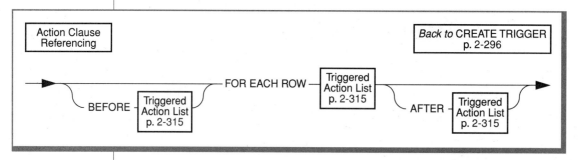

If the CREATE TRIGGER statement contains an INSERT REFERENCING clause, a DELETE REFERENCING clause, an UPDATE REFERENCING clause, or a SELECT REFERENCING clause, you *must* include a FOR EACH ROW triggered-action list in the action clause. You can also include BEFORE and AFTER triggered-action lists, but they are optional. For information on the BEFORE, FOR EACH ROW, and AFTER triggered-action lists, see "Action Clause" on page 2-307.

EDS

You cannot have FOR EACH ROW actions on tables that have globally-detached indexes. ♦

Triggered Action List

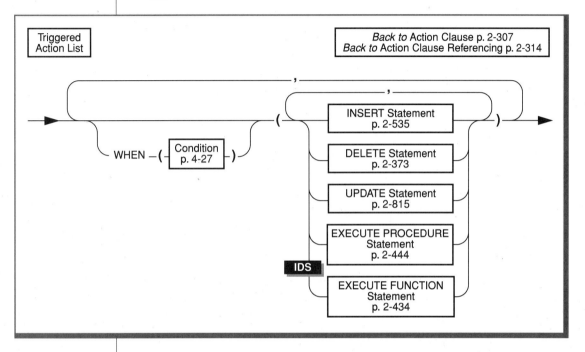

Triggered Action List

Back to Action Clause p. 2-307
Back to Action Clause Referencing p. 2-314

WHEN — (Condition p. 4-27)

INSERT Statement
p. 2-535

DELETE Statement
p. 2-373

UPDATE Statement
p. 2-815

EXECUTE PROCEDURE
Statement
p. 2-444

IDS

EXECUTE FUNCTION
Statement
p. 2-434

The triggered action consists of an optional WHEN condition and the action statements. Database objects that are referenced in the triggered action, that is, tables, columns, and UDRs, must exist when the CREATE TRIGGER statement is executed. This rule applies only to database objects that are referenced directly in the trigger definition.

Warning: *When you specify a date expression in the WHEN condition or in an action statement, make sure to specify 4 digits instead of 2 digits for the year. When you specify a 4-digit year, the **DBCENTURY** environment variable has no effect on how the database server interprets the date expression. When you specify a 2-digit year, the **DBCENTURY** environment variable can affect how the database server interprets the date expression, so the triggered action might produce unpredictable results. See the "Informix Guide to SQL: Reference" for more information on the **DBCENTURY** environment variable.*

WHEN Condition

The WHEN condition lets you make the triggered action dependent on the outcome of a test. When you include a WHEN condition in a triggered action, if the triggered action evaluates to true, the actions in the triggered action list execute in the order in which they appear. If the WHEN condition evaluates to false or unknown, the actions in the triggered action list are not executed. If the triggered action is in a FOR EACH ROW section, its search condition is evaluated for each row.

For example, the triggered action in the following trigger executes only if the condition in the WHEN clause is true:

```
CREATE TRIGGER up_price
UPDATE OF unit_price ON stock
REFERENCING OLD AS pre NEW AS post
FOR EACH ROW WHEN(post.unit_price > pre.unit_price * 2)
    (INSERT INTO warn_tab VALUES(pre.stock_num,
        pre.order_num, pre.unit_price, post.unit_price,
        CURRENT))
```

An SPL routine that executes inside the WHEN condition carries the same restrictions as a UDR that is called in a data-manipulation statement. That is, the called SPL routine cannot contain certain SQL statements. For information on which statements are restricted, see "Restrictions on an SPL Routine Called in a Data Manipulation Statement" on page 4-302. ♦

Action Statements

The triggered-action statements can be INSERT, DELETE, UPDATE, EXECUTE FUNCTION, or EXECUTE PROCEDURE statements. If a triggered-action list contains multiple statements, these statements execute in the order in which they appear in the list.

UDRs as Triggered Actions

You can use both user-defined functions and user-defined procedures as triggered actions.

IDS

Use the EXECUTE FUNCTION statement to execute any user-defined function. Use the EXECUTE PROCEDURE statement to execute any user-defined procedure. ♦

EDS

Use the EXECUTE PROCEDURE statement to execute any SPL routine. ♦

For restrictions that apply to using SPL routines as triggered actions, see "Rules for SPL Routines" on page 326.

Achieving a Consistent Result

To guarantee that the triggering statement returns the same result with and without the triggered actions, make sure that the triggered actions in the BEFORE and FOR EACH ROW sections do not modify any table referenced in the following clauses:

- WHERE clause
- SET clause in the UPDATE statement
- SELECT clause
- EXECUTE PROCEDURE clause or EXECUTE FUNCTION clause in a multiple-row INSERT statement

Using Reserved Words

If you use the INSERT, DELETE, UPDATE, or EXECUTE reserved words as an identifier in any of the following clauses inside a triggered action list, you must qualify them by the owner name, the table name, or both:

- FROM clause of a SELECT statement
- INTO clause of the EXECUTE PROCEDURE or EXECUTE FUNCTION statement
- GROUP BY clause
- SET clause of the UPDATE statement

You get a syntax error if these keywords are *not* qualified when you use these clauses inside a triggered action.

If you use the keyword as a column name, it must be qualified by the table name—for example, **table.update**. If both the table name and the column name are keywords, they must be qualified by the owner name—for example, **owner.insert.update**. If the owner name, table name, and column name are all keywords, the owner name must be in quotes—for example, **'delete'.insert.update**. The only exception is when these keywords are the first table or column name in the list, and you do not have to qualify them. For example, **delete** in the following statement does not need to be qualified because it is the first column listed in the INTO clause:

```
CREATE TRIGGER t1 UPDATE OF b ON tab1
    FOR EACH ROW (EXECUTE PROCEDURE p2()
    INTO delete, d)
```

The following statements show examples in which you must qualify the column name or the table name:

- FROM clause of a SELECT statement

```
CREATE TRIGGER t1 INSERT ON tab1
    BEFORE (INSERT INTO tab2 SELECT * FROM tab3,
    'owner1'.update)
```

- INTO clause of an EXECUTE PROCEDURE statement

```
CREATE TRIGGER t3 UPDATE OF b ON tab1
    FOR EACH ROW (EXECUTE PROCEDURE p2() INTO
    d, tab1.delete)
```

- GROUP BY clause of a SELECT statement

```
CREATE TRIGGER t4 DELETE ON tab1
    BEFORE (INSERT INTO tab3 SELECT deptno, SUM(exp)
    FROM budget GROUP BY deptno, budget.update)
```

- SET clause of an UPDATE statement

```
CREATE TRIGGER t2 UPDATE OF a ON tab1
    BEFORE (UPDATE tab2 SET a = 10, tab2.insert = 5)
```

Using Correlation Names in Triggered Actions

The following rules apply when you use correlation names in triggered actions:

- You can use the correlation names for the old and new column values only in statements in the FOR EACH ROW triggered-action list. You can use the old and new correlation names to qualify any column in the triggering table in either the WHEN condition or the triggered SQL statements.

- The old and new correlation names refer to all rows affected by the triggering statement.

- You cannot use the correlation name to qualify a column name in the GROUP BY, the SET, or the COUNT DISTINCT clause.

- The scope of the correlation names is the entire trigger definition. This scope is statically determined, meaning that it is limited to the trigger definition; it does not encompass cascading triggers or columns that are qualified by a table name in a UDR that is a triggered action.

When to Use Correlation Names

In an SQL statement in a FOR EACH ROW triggered action, you must qualify all references to columns in the triggering table with either the old or new correlation name, unless the statement is valid independent of the triggered action.

In other words, if a column name inside a FOR EACH ROW triggered action list is not qualified by a correlation name, even if it is qualified by the triggering table name, it is interpreted as if the statement is independent of the triggered action. No special effort is made to search the definition of the triggering table for the non-qualified column name.

For example, assume that the following DELETE statement is a triggered action inside the FOR EACH ROW section of a trigger:

```
DELETE FROM tab1 WHERE col_c = col_c2
```

For the statement to be valid, both **col_c** and **col_c2** must be columns from **tab1**. If **col_c2** is intended to be a correlation reference to a column in the triggering table, it must be qualified by either the old or the new correlation name.   If **col_c2** is not a column in **tab1** and is not qualified by either the old or new correlation name, you get an error.

When a column is not qualified by a correlation name, and the statement is valid independent of the triggered action, the column name refers to the current value in the database. In the triggered action for trigger **t1** in the following example, **mgr** in the WHERE clause of the correlated subquery is an unqualified column from the triggering table. In this case, **mgr** refers to the current column value in **empsal** because the INSERT statement is valid independent of the triggered action.

```
CREATE DATABASE db1;
CREATE TABLE empsal (empno INT, salary INT, mgr INT);
CREATE TABLE mgr (eno INT, bonus INT);
CREATE TABLE biggap (empno INT, salary INT, mgr INT);

CREATE TRIGGER t1 UPDATE OF salary ON empsal
AFTER (INSERT INTO biggap SELECT * FROM empsal WHERE salary <
    (SELECT bonus FROM mgr WHERE eno = mgr));
```

In a triggered action, an unqualified column name from the triggering table refers to the current column value, but only when the triggered statement is valid independent of the triggered action.

Qualified Versus Unqualified Value

The following table summarizes the value retrieved when you use the column name qualified by the old correlation name and the column name qualified by the new correlation name.

Trigger Event	old.col	new.col
INSERT	No value (error)	Inserted value
UPDATE (column updated)	Original value	Current value (N)
UPDATE (column not updated)	Original value	Current value (U)
DELETE	Original value	No value (error)

Refer to the following key when you read the table.

Term	Purpose
Original value	Value before the triggering statement
Current value	Value after the triggering statement
(N)	Cannot be changed by triggered action
(U)	Can be updated by triggered statements; value may be different from original value because of preceding triggered actions

Outside a FOR EACH ROW triggered-action list, you cannot qualify a column from the triggering table with either the old correlation name or the new correlation name; it always refers to the current value in the database.

Reentrancy of Triggers

In some cases a trigger can be reentrant. In these cases the triggered action can reference the triggering table. In other words, both the trigger event and the triggered action can operate on the same table. The following list summarizes the situations in which triggers can be reentrant and the situations in which triggers cannot be reentrant:

- If the trigger event is an UPDATE statement, the triggered action cannot be an INSERT or DELETE statement that references the table that was updated by the trigger event.

- If the trigger event is an UPDATE statement, the triggered action cannot be an UPDATE statement that references a column that was updated by the trigger event.

    However, if the trigger event is an UPDATE statement, and the triggered action is also an UPDATE statement, the triggered action can update a column that was not updated by the trigger event.

    For example, assume that the following UPDATE statement, which updates columns **a** and **b** of **tab1**, is the triggering statement:

    ```
    UPDATE tab1 SET (a, b) = (a + 1, b + 1)
    ```

Now consider the 1vbtriggered actions in the following example. The first UPDATE statement is a valid triggered action, but the second one is not because it updates column **b** again.

```
UPDATE tab1 SET c = c + 1; -- OK
UPDATE tab1 SET b = b + 1;-- ILLEGAL
```

■ If the trigger event is an UPDATE statement, the triggered action can be an EXECUTE PROCEDURE or EXECUTE FUNCTION statement with an INTO clause that references a column that was updated by the trigger event or any other column in the triggering table.

When an EXECUTE PROCEDURE or EXECUTE FUNCTION statement is the triggered action, you can specify the INTO clause for an UPDATE trigger only when the triggered action occurs in the FOR EACH ROW section. In this case, the INTO clause can contain only column names from the triggering table. The following statement illustrates the appropriate use of the INTO clause:

```
CREATE TRIGGER upd_totpr UPDATE OF quantity ON items
REFERENCING OLD AS pre_upd NEW AS post_upd
FOR EACH ROW(EXECUTE PROCEDURE
    calc_totpr(pre_upd.quantity,
    post_upd.quantity, pre_upd.total_price)
    INTO total_price)
```

The column that follows the INTO keyword can be a column in the triggering table that was updated by the trigger event, or a column in the triggering table that was not updated by the trigger event.

When the INTO clause appears in the EXECUTE PROCEDURE or EXECUTE FUNCTION statement, the database server updates the columns named there with the values returned from the UDR. The database server performs the update immediately upon returning from the UDR.

■ If the trigger event is an INSERT statement, the triggered action cannot be an INSERT or DELETE statement that references the triggering table.

■ If the trigger event is an INSERT statement, the triggered action can be an UPDATE statement that references a column in the triggering table. However, this column cannot be a column for which a value was supplied by the trigger event.

If the trigger event is an INSERT, and the triggered action is an UPDATE on the triggering table, the columns in both statements must be mutually exclusive. For example, assume that the trigger event is an INSERT statement that inserts values for columns **cola** and **colb** of table **tab1**:

```
INSERT INTO tab1 (cola, colb) VALUES (1,10)
```

Now consider the triggered actions. The first UPDATE statement is valid, but the second one is not because it updates column **colb** even though the trigger event already supplied a value for column **colb**:

```
UPDATE tab1 SET colc=100; --OK
UPDATE tab1 SET colb=100; --ILLEGAL
```

■ If the trigger event is an INSERT statement, the triggered action can be an EXECUTE PROCEDURE or EXECUTE FUNCTION statement with an INTO clause that references a column that was supplied by the trigger event or a column that was not supplied by the trigger event.

When an EXECUTE PROCEDURE or EXECUTE FUNCTION statement is the triggered action, you can specify the INTO clause for an INSERT trigger only when the triggered action occurs in the FOR EACH ROW section. In this case, the INTO clause can contain only column names from the triggering table. The following statement illustrates the appropriate use of the INTO clause:

```
CREATE TRIGGER ins_totpr INSERT ON items
REFERENCING NEW as new_ins
FOR EACH ROW (EXECUTE PROCEDURE
    calc_totpr(0, new_ins.quantity, 0)
    INTO total_price).
```

The column that follows the INTO keyword can be a column in the triggering table that was supplied by the trigger event, or a column in the triggering table that was not supplied by the trigger event.

When the INTO clause appears in the EXECUTE PROCEDURE or EXECUTE FUNCTION statement, the database server updates the columns named there with the values returned from the UDR. The database server performs the update immediately upon returning from the UDR.

- If the triggered action is a SELECT statement, the SELECT statement can reference the triggering table. The SELECT statement can be a triggered statement in the following instances:

  ❑ The SELECT statement appears in a subquery in the WHEN clause or a triggered-action statement.

  ❑ The triggered action is a UDR, and the SELECT statement appears inside the UDR.

Reentrancy and Cascading Triggers

The cases when a trigger cannot be reentrant apply recursively to all cascading triggers, which are considered part of the initial trigger. In particular, this rule means that a cascading trigger cannot update any columns in the triggering table that were updated by the original triggering statement, including any nontriggering columns affected by that statement. For example, assume the following UPDATE statement is the triggering statement:

```
UPDATE tab1 SET (a, b) = (a + 1, b + 1)
```

Then in the cascading triggers shown in the following example, **trig2** fails at runtime because it references column **b**, which is updated by the triggering UPDATE statement:

```
CREATE TRIGGER trig1 UPDATE OF a ON tab1-- Valid
    AFTER (UPDATE tab2 set e = e + 1);

CREATE TRIGGER trig2 UPDATE of e ON tab2-- Invalid
    AFTER (UPDATE tab1 set b = b + 1);
```

Now consider the following SQL statements. When the final UPDATE statement is executed, column **a** is updated and the trigger **trig1** is activated. The triggered action again updates column **a** with an EXECUTE PROCEDURE INTO statement.

```
CREATE TABLE temp1 (a int, b int, e int);
INSERT INTO temp1 VALUES (10, 20, 30);

CREATE PROCEDURE proc(val int)
RETURNING int,int;
RETURN val+10, val+20;
END PROCEDURE;
```

```
CREATE TRIGGER trig1 UPDATE OF a ON temp1
FOR EACH ROW (EXECUTE PROCEDURE proc(50) INTO a, e);

CREATE TRIGGER trig2 UPDATE OF e ON temp1
FOR EACH ROW (EXECUTE PROCEDURE proc(100) INTO a, e);

UPDATE temp1 SET (a,b) = (40,50);
```

EDS

In Enterprise Decision Server, to recreate this example use the CREATE PROCEDURE statement instead of the CREATE FUNCTION statement. ♦

Several questions arise from this example of cascading triggers. First, should the update of column **a** activate trigger **trig1** again? The answer is no. Because the trigger was activated, it is stopped from being activated a second time. Whenever the triggered action is an EXECUTE PROCEDURE INTO statement or EXECUTE FUNCTION INTO statement, the only triggers that are activated are those that are defined on columns that are mutually exclusive from the columns in that table updated until then (in the cascade of triggers). Other triggers are ignored.

Another question that arises from the example is whether trigger **trig2** should be activated. The answer is yes. The trigger **trig2** is defined on column **e**. Until now, column **e** in table **temp1** has not been modified. Trigger **trig2** is activated.

A final question that arises from the example is whether triggers **trig1** and **trig2** should be activated after the triggered action in **trig2** is performed. The answer is no. Neither trigger is activated. By this time columns **a** and **e** have been updated once, and triggers **trig1** and **trig2** have been executed once. The database server ignores these triggers instead of firing them.

For more information about cascading triggers, see "Cascading Triggers" on page 2-327.

Rules for SPL Routines

In addition to the rules listed in "Reentrancy of Triggers" on page 2-321, the following rules apply to an SPL routine that is used as a triggered action:

- The SPL routine cannot be a cursor function (that is, a function that returns more than one row) in a place where only one row is expected.

- You cannot use the old or new correlation name inside the SPL routine.

  If you need to use the corresponding values in the routine, you must pass them as parameters. The routine should be independent of triggers, and the old or new correlation name do not have any meaning outside the trigger.

When you use an SPL routine as a triggered action, the database objects that the routine references are not checked until the routine is executed.

Privileges to Execute Triggered Actions

If you are not the trigger owner, but the privileges of the trigger owner include the WITH GRANT OPTION privilege, you inherit the privileges of the owner as well as the WITH GRANT OPTION privilege for each triggered SQL statement. You have these privileges in addition to your privileges.

If the triggered action is a UDR you must have the Execute privilege on the UDR or the owner of the trigger must have the Execute privilege and the WITH GRANT OPTION privilege.

While executing the UDR, you do not carry the privileges of the trigger owner; instead you receive the privileges granted with the UDR, as follows:

1. Privileges for a DBA UDR

   When a UDR is registered with the CREATE DBA keywords and you are granted the Execute privilege on the UDR, the database server automatically grants you temporary DBA privileges while the UDR executes. These DBA privileges are available only when you are executing the UDR.

2. Privileges for a UDR without DBA restrictions

If the UDR owner has the WITH GRANT OPTION right for the necessary privileges on the underlying database objects, you inherit these privileges when you are granted the Execute privilege. In this case, all the non-qualified database objects that the UDR references are qualified by the name of the UDR owner.

If the UDR owner does not have the WITH GRANT OPTION right, you have your original privileges on the underlying database objects when the UDR executes.

For more information on privileges on SPL routines, refer to the *Informix Guide to SQL: Tutorial.*

Creating a Triggered Action That Anyone Can Use

To create a trigger that is executable by anyone who has the privileges to execute the triggering statement, you can ask the DBA to create a DBA-privileged UDR and grant you the Execute privilege with the WITH GRANT OPTION right. You then use the DBA-privileged UDR as the triggered action. Anyone can execute the triggered action because the DBA-privileged UDR carries the WITH GRANT OPTION right. When you activate the UDR, the database server applies privilege-checking rules for a DBA.

Cascading Triggers

The database server allows triggers other than select triggers to cascade, meaning that the triggered actions of one trigger can activate another trigger. For further information on the restriction against cascading select triggers, see "Circumstances When a Select Trigger is Not Activated" on page 2-305.

The maximum number of triggers in a cascading sequence is 61; the initial trigger plus a maximum of 60 cascading triggers. When the number of cascading triggers in a series exceeds the maximum, the database server returns error number -748, as the following example shows:

```
Exceeded limit on maximum number of cascaded triggers.
```

The following example illustrates a series of cascading triggers that enforce referential integrity on the **manufact**, **stock**, and **items** tables in the **stores_demo** database. When a manufacturer is deleted from the **manufact** table, the first trigger, **del_manu**, deletes all the items from that manufacturer from the **stock** table. Each delete in the **stock** table activates a second trigger, **del_items**, that deletes all the **items** from that manufacturer from the **items** table. Finally, each delete in the **items** table triggers the SPL routine **log_order**, which creates a record of any orders in the **orders** table that can no longer be filled.

```
CREATE TRIGGER del_manu
DELETE ON manufact
REFERENCING OLD AS pre_del
FOR EACH ROW(DELETE FROM stock
    WHERE manu_code = pre_del.manu_code);

CREATE TRIGGER del_stock
DELETE ON stock
REFERENCING OLD AS pre_del
FOR EACH ROW(DELETE FROM items
    WHERE manu_code = pre_del.manu_code);

CREATE TRIGGER del_items
DELETE ON items
REFERENCING OLD AS pre_del
FOR EACH ROW(EXECUTE PROCEDURE log_order(pre_del.order_num));
```

When you are not using logging, referential integrity constraints on both the **manufact** and **stock** tables prohibit the triggers in this example from executing. When you use logging, however, the triggers execute successfully because constraint checking is deferred until all the triggered actions are complete, including the actions of cascading triggers. For more information about how constraints are handled when triggers execute, see "Constraint Checking" on page 2-329.

The database server prevents loops of cascading triggers by not allowing you to modify the triggering table in any cascading triggered action, except an UPDATE statement, which does not modify any column that the triggering UPDATE statement updated, or an INSERT statement. INSERT trigger statements can have UPDATE triggered actions on the same table.

Constraint Checking

When you use logging, the database server defers constraint checking on the triggering statement until after the statements in the triggered-action list execute. The database server effectively executes a SET CONSTRAINTS ALL DEFERRED statement before it executes the triggering statement. After the triggered action is completed, it effectively executes a SET CONSTRAINTS *constraint* IMMEDIATE statement to check the constraints that were deferred. This action allows you to write triggers so that the triggered action can resolve any constraint violations that the triggering statement creates. For more information, see "SET Database Object Mode" on page 2-700.

Consider the following example, in which the table **child** has constraint **r1**, which references the table **parent**. You define trigger **trig1** and activate it with an INSERT statement. In the triggered action, **trig1** checks to see if **parent** has a row with the value of the current **cola** in **child**; if not, it inserts it.

```
CREATE TABLE parent (cola INT PRIMARY KEY);
CREATE TABLE child (cola INT REFERENCES parent CONSTRAINT r1);
CREATE TRIGGER trig1 INSERT ON child
    REFERENCING NEW AS new
    FOR EACH ROW
    WHEN((SELECT COUNT (*) FROM parent
        WHERE cola = new.cola) = 0)
-- parent row does not exist
    (INSERT INTO parent VALUES (new.cola));
```

When you insert a row into a table that is the child table in a referential constraint, the row might not exist in the parent table. The database server does not immediately return this error on a triggering statement. Instead, it allows the triggered action to resolve the constraint violation by inserting the corresponding row into the parent table. As the previous example shows, you can check within the triggered action to see whether the parent row exists, and if so, bypass the insert.

For a database without logging, the database server does *not* defer constraint checking on the triggering statement. In this case, it immediately returns an error if the triggering statement violates a constraint.

You cannot use the SET Transaction Mode statement in a triggered action. The database server checks this restriction when you activate a trigger, because the statement could occur inside a UDR.

EDS

Rows that cause constraint violations might appear in the violations table even if a later trigger action corrects the violation. ♦

Preventing Triggers from Overriding Each Other

When you activate multiple triggers with an UPDATE statement, a trigger can possibly override the changes that an earlier trigger made. If you do not want the triggered actions to interact, you can split the UPDATE statement into multiple UPDATE statements, each of which updates an individual column. As another alternative, you can create a single update trigger for all columns that require a triggered action. Then, inside the triggered action, you can test for the column being updated and apply the actions in the desired order. This approach, however, is different than having the database server apply the actions of individual triggers, and it has the following disadvantages:

- If the trigger has a BEFORE action, it applies to all columns because you cannot yet detect whether a column has changed.

- If the triggering UPDATE statement sets a column to the current value, you cannot detect the update, so the triggered action is skipped. You might want to execute the triggered action even though the value of the column has not changed.

Client/Server Environment

The statements inside the triggered action can affect tables in external databases. The following example shows an update trigger on **dbserver1**, which triggers an update to **items** on **dbserver2**:

```
CREATE TRIGGER upd_nt UPDATE ON newtab
REFERENCING new AS post
FOR EACH ROW(UPDATE stores_demo@dbserver2:items
    SET quantity = post.qty WHERE stock_num = post.stock
    AND manu_code = post.mc)
```

If a statement from an external database server initiates the trigger, however, and the triggered action affects tables in an external database, the triggered actions fail. For example, the following combination of triggered action and triggering statement results in an error when the triggering statement executes:

```
-- Triggered action from dbserver1 to dbserver3:

CREATE TRIGGER upd_nt UPDATE ON newtab
REFERENCING new AS post
FOR EACH ROW(UPDATE stores_demo@dbserver3:items
    SET quantity = post.qty WHERE stock_num = post.stock
    AND manu_code = post.mc);

-- Triggering statement from dbserver2:

UPDATE stores_demo@dbserver1:newtab
    SET qty = qty * 2 WHERE s_num = 5
    AND mc = 'ANZ';
```

Logging and Recovery

You can create triggers for databases, with and without logging. However, when the database does not have logging, you cannot roll back when the triggering statement fails. In this case, you are responsible for maintaining data integrity in the database.

If the trigger fails and the database has transactions, all triggered actions and the triggering statement are rolled back because the triggered actions are an extension of the triggering statement. The rest of the transaction, however, is not rolled back.

The row action of the triggering statement occurs before the triggered actions in the FOR EACH ROW section. If the triggered action fails for a database without logging, the application must restore the row that was changed by the triggering statement to its previous value.

When you use a UDR as a triggered action, if you terminate the UDR in an exception-handling section, any actions that modify data inside that section are rolled back along with the triggering statement. In the following partial example, when the exception handler traps an error, it inserts a row into the table **logtab**:

```
ON EXCEPTION IN (-201)
    INSERT INTO logtab values (errno, errstr);
    RAISE EXCEPTION -201
END EXCEPTION
```

When the RAISE EXCEPTION statement returns the error, however, the database server rolls back this insert because it is part of the triggered actions. If the UDR is executed outside a triggered action, the insert is not rolled back.

The UDR that implements a triggered action cannot contain any BEGIN WORK, COMMIT WORK, or ROLLBACK WORK statements. If the database has logging, you must either begin an explicit transaction before the triggering statement, or the statement itself must be an implicit transaction. In any case, another transaction-related statement cannot appear inside the UDR.

You can use triggers to enforce referential actions that the database server does not currently support. For any database without logging, you are responsible for maintaining data integrity when the triggering statement fails.

IDS

Trigger Modes

Use the trigger-modes to enable or disable a trigger when you create it.

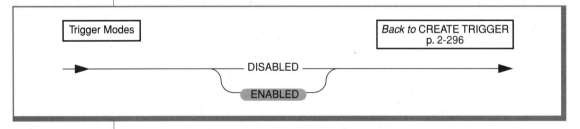

You can create triggers in the following modes.

Mode	Purpose
DISABLED	When a trigger is created in disabled mode, the database server does not execute the triggered action when the trigger event (an insert, delete, select, or update operation) takes place. In effect, the database server ignores the trigger even though its catalog information is maintained.
ENABLED	When a trigger is created in enabled mode, the database server executes the triggered action when the trigger event (an insert, delete, select, or update operation) takes place.

Specifying Modes for Triggers

You must observe the following rules when you specify the mode for a trigger in the CREATE TRIGGER statement:

- If you do not specify a mode, the trigger is enabled by default.
- You can use the SET Database Object Mode statement to switch the mode of a disabled trigger to the enabled mode. Once the trigger is re-enabled, the database server executes the triggered action whenever the trigger event takes place. However, the re-enabled trigger does not perform retroactively. The database server does not attempt to execute the trigger for rows that were inserted, deleted, or updated after the trigger was disabled and before it was enabled; therefore, be cautious about disabling a trigger. If disabling a trigger will eventually destroy the semantic integrity of the database, do not disable the trigger.
- You cannot create a trigger on a violations table or a diagnostics table.

Related Information

Related statements: DROP TRIGGER, CREATE PROCEDURE, EXECUTE PROCEDURE, and SET Database Object Mode

For a task-oriented discussion of triggers, see the *Informix Guide to SQL: Tutorial.*

For performance implications of triggers, see your *Performance Guide.*

CREATE VIEW

Use the CREATE VIEW statement to create a new view that is based on existing tables and views in the database.

Syntax

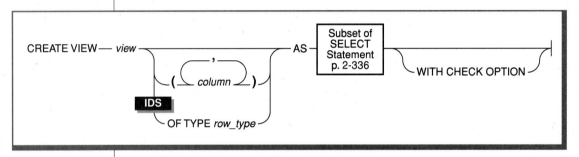

Element	Purpose	Restrictions	Syntax
column	Name of a column in the view	See "Naming View Columns" on page 2-337.	Identifier, p. 4-205
row_type	Name of a named-row type that you use to specify the type of a typed view	You must have Usage privileges on the named-row type or be its owner or the DBA. The named-row type must exist before you can assign it to a view.	Data Type, p. 4-53
view	Name of the view	The name must be unique in the database.	Database Object Name, p. 4-50

Usage

You can create typed or untyped views. If you omit the OF TYPE clause, the rows in the view are considered to be untyped and default to an unnamed-row type. The following statement creates a view that is based on the **person** table. When you create a view without an OF TYPE clause, the view is referred to as an *untyped view*.

```
CREATE VIEW v1 AS SELECT *
FROM person
```

Typed views, like typed tables, are based on a named-row type. Each column in the view corresponds to a field in the named-row type. The following statement creates a typed view that is based on the table **person**. To create a typed view, you must include an OF TYPE clause. When you create a typed view, the named-row type that you specify immediately after the OF TYPE keywords must already exist.

```
CREATE VIEW v2 OF TYPE person_t AS SELECT *
FROM person
```

Except for the statements in the following list, you can use a view in any SQL statement where you can use a table:

ALTER FRAGMENT	DROP INDEX
ALTER INDEX	DROP TABLE
ALTER TABLE	DROP TRIGGER
CREATE INDEX	LOCK TABLE
CREATE TABLE	RENAME TABLE
CREATE TRIGGER	UNLOCK TABLE

The view behaves like a table that is called *view*. It consists of the set of rows and columns that the SELECT statement returns each time the SELECT statement is executed by using the view. The view reflects changes to the underlying tables with one exception. If a SELECT * clause defines the view, the view has only the columns in the underlying tables at the time the view is created. New columns that are subsequently added to the underlying tables with the ALTER TABLE statement do not appear in the view.

The view name must be unique; that is, a view name cannot have the same name as another database object, such as a table, synonym, or temporary table.

The view inherits the data types of the columns in the tables from which the view is derived. The database server determines data types of virtual columns from the nature of the expression.

To create a view, you must have the Select privilege on all columns from which the view is derived.

The SELECT statement is stored in the **sysviews** system catalog table. When you subsequently refer to a view in another statement, the database server performs the defining SELECT statement while it executes the new statement.

DB

In DB-Access, if you create a view outside the CREATE SCHEMA statement, you receive warnings if you use the **-ansi** flag or set **DBANSIWARN**. ♦

Restrictions

You cannot create a view on a temporary table.

IDS

You cannot create a view on the following types of tables in a remote database:

- Typed tables (including any table that is part of a table hierarchy)
- Tables that contain any extended data types

♦

Subset of SELECT Statement Allowed in CREATE VIEW

In CREATE VIEW, the FROM clause of the SELECT statement cannot contain the name of a temporary table.

Do not use display labels in the select list. Display labels in the select list are interpreted as column names.

The SELECT statement in CREATE VIEW cannot include the following clauses:

- FIRST
- INTO TEMP
- ORDER BY

For a complete description of SELECT syntax and usage, see "SELECT" on page 2-634.

Union Views

The SELECT statement in CREATE VIEW can contain a UNION or UNION ALL operator. A view that contains a UNION or UNION ALL operator in its SELECT statement is known as a union view. Observe the following restrictions on union views:

- If a CREATE VIEW statement defines a union view, you cannot specify the WITH CHECK OPTION keywords in the CREATE VIEW statement.

- All restrictions that apply to UNION or UNION ALL operations in standalone SELECT statements also apply to UNION and UNION ALL operations in the SELECT statement of a union view. For a list of these restrictions, see "Restrictions on a Combined SELECT" on page 2-689.

For an example of a CREATE VIEW statement that defines a union view, see "Naming View Columns."

Naming View Columns

The number of columns that you specify in the *column* parameter must match the number of columns returned by the SELECT statement that defines the view.

If you do not specify a list of columns, the view inherits the column names of the underlying tables. In the following example, the view **herostock** has the same column names as the ones in the SELECT statement:

```
CREATE VIEW herostock AS
    SELECT stock_num, description, unit_price, unit,
unit_descr
        FROM stock WHERE manu_code = 'HRO'
```

If the SELECT statement returns an expression, the corresponding column in the view is called a *virtual* column. You must provide a name for virtual columns. In the following example, the user must specify the *column* parameter because the select list of the SELECT statement contains an aggregate expression.

```
CREATE VIEW newview (firstcol, secondcol) AS
    SELECT sum(cola), colb
        FROM oldtab
```

You must also provide a column name in cases where the selected columns have duplicate column names when the table prefixes are stripped. For example, when both **orders.order_num** and **items.order_num** appear in the SELECT statement, you must provide two separate column names to label them in the CREATE VIEW statement, as the following example shows:

```
CREATE VIEW someorders (custnum,ocustnum,newprice) AS
    SELECT orders.order_num,items.order_num,
           items.total_price*1.5
      FROM orders, items
      WHERE orders.order_num = items.order_num
      AND items.total_price > 100.00
```

You must also provide column names in the *column* parameter when the SELECT statement includes a UNION or UNION ALL operator and the names of the corresponding columns in the SELECT statements are not identical. In the following example, the user must specify the *column* parameter since the second column in the first SELECT statement has a different name from the second column in the second SELECT statement.

```
CREATE VIEW myview (cola, colb) AS
    SELECT colx, coly from firsttab
    UNION
    SELECT colx, colz from secondtab
```

If you must provide names for some of the columns in a view, then you must provide names for all the columns; that is, the column list must contain an entry for every column that appears in the view.

Using a View in the SELECT Statement

You can define a view in terms of other views, but you must abide by the restrictions on creating views that are discussed in the *Informix Guide to Database Design and Implementation.* For further information, see that manual.

WITH CHECK OPTION Keywords

The WITH CHECK OPTION keywords instruct the database server to ensure that all modifications that are made through the view to the underlying tables satisfy the definition of the view.

The following example creates a view that is named **palo_alto**, which uses all the information in the **customer** table for customers in the city of Palo Alto. The database server checks any modifications made to the **customer** table through **palo_alto** because the WITH CHECK OPTION is specified.

```
CREATE VIEW palo_alto AS
    SELECT * FROM customer
        WHERE city = 'Palo Alto'
        WITH CHECK OPTION
```

You can insert into a view a row that does not satisfy the conditions of the view (that is, a row that is not visible through the view). You can also update a row of a view so that it no longer satisfies the conditions of the view. For example, if the view was created without the WITH CHECK OPTION keywords, you could insert a row through the view where the city is Los Altos, or you could update a row through the view by changing the city from Palo Alto to Los Altos.

To prevent such inserts and updates, you can add the WITH CHECK OPTION keywords when you create the view. These keywords ask the database server to test every inserted or updated row to ensure that it meets the conditions that are set by the WHERE clause of the view. The database server rejects the operation with an error if the row does not meet the conditions.

However, even if the view was created with the WITH CHECK OPTION keywords, you can perform inserts and updates through the view to change columns that are not part of the view definition. A column is not part of the view definition if it does not appear in the WHERE clause of the SELECT statement that defines the view.

Updating Through Views

If a view is built on a single table, the view is *updatable* if the SELECT statement that defined it did not contain any of the following items:

- Columns in the select list that are aggregate values
- Columns in the select list that use the UNIQUE or DISTINCT keyword
- A GROUP BY clause
- A UNION operator

In an updatable view, you can update the values in the underlying table by inserting values into the view.

In addition, if a view is built on a table that has a derived value for a column, that column is not updatable through the view. However, other columns in the view can be updated.

Important: *You cannot update or insert rows in a remote table through views with check options.*

Related Information

Related statements: CREATE TABLE, DROP VIEW, GRANT, SELECT, and SET SESSION AUTHORIZATION

For a discussion of views, see the *Informix Guide to Database Design and Implementation.*

DATABASE

Use the DATABASE statement to select an accessible database as the current database.

Syntax

DATABASE —————— *database* ————————————⌐
                                    └ EXCLUSIVE ┘

Element	Purpose	Restrictions	Syntax
database	Name of the database to select	The database must exist.	Database Name, p. 4-47

Usage

You can use the DATABASE statement to select any database on your database server. To select a database on another database server, specify the name of the database server with the database name.

If you specify the name of the current database server or another database server with the database name, the database server name cannot be uppercase.

Issuing a DATABASE statement when a database is already open closes the current database before opening the new one. Closing the current database releases any cursor resources held by the database server, which invalidates any cursors you have declared up to that point. If the user identity was changed through a SET SESSION AUTHORIZATION statement, the original user name is restored.

The current user (or PUBLIC) must have the Connect privilege on the database specified in the DATABASE statement. The current user cannot have the same user name as an existing role in the database.

E/C

Using the DATABASE Statement with ESQL/C

In ESQL/C, you cannot include the DATABASE statement in a multistatement PREPARE operation.

You can determine the characteristics of a database a user selects by checking the warning flag after a DATABASE statement in the **sqlca** structure.

If the database has transactions, the second element of the **sqlwarn** structure (the **sqlca.sqlwarn.sqlwarn1** field) contains a W after the DATABASE statement executes.

ANSI

In an ANSI-compliant database, the third element of the **sqlwarn** structure (the **sqlca.sqlwarn.sqlwarn2** field) contains the letter W after the DATABASE statement executes. ♦

IDS

The fourth element of the **sqlwarn** structure (the **sqlca.sqlwarn.sqlwarn3** field) contains the letter W after the DATABASE statement executes.

If the database is running in secondary mode, the seventh element of the **sqlwarn** structure (the **sqlca.sqlwarn.sqlwarn6** field) contains the letter W after the DATABASE statement executes. ♦

EXCLUSIVE Keyword

The EXCLUSIVE keyword opens the database in exclusive mode and prevents access by anyone but the current user. To allow others access to the database, you must execute the CLOSE DATABASE statement and then reopen the database without the EXCLUSIVE keyword.

The following statement opens the **stores_demo** database on the **training** database server in exclusive mode:

```
DATABASE stores_demo@training EXCLUSIVE
```

If another user has already opened the database, exclusive access is denied, an error is returned, and no database is opened.

Related Information

Related statements: CLOSE DATABASE and CONNECT

For discussions of how to use different data models to design and implement a database, see the *Informix Guide to Database Design and Implementation*.

DEALLOCATE COLLECTION

Use the DEALLOCATE COLLECTION statement to release memory for a collection variable that was previously allocated with the ALLOCATE COLLECTION statement.

Use this statement with ESQL/C.

Syntax

DEALLOCATE COLLECTION ———————— **:** *variable* ——————————

Element	Purpose	Restrictions	Syntax
variable	Name that identifies a typed or untyped collection variable for which to deallocate memory	The variable must be the name of an ESQL/C collection variable that has already been allocated.	Name must conform to language-specific rules for variable names.

Usage

The DEALLOCATE COLLECTION statement frees all the memory that is associated with the ESQL/C collection variable that *variable* identifies. You must explicitly release memory resources for a collection variable with DEALLOCATE COLLECTION. Otherwise, deallocation occurs automatically at the end of the program.

The DEALLOCATE COLLECTION statement releases resources for both typed and untyped collection variables.

Tip: *The DEALLOCATE COLLECTION statement deallocates memory for an ESQL/C collection variable only. To deallocate memory for an ESQL/C row variable, use the DEALLOCATE ROW statement.*

If you deallocate a nonexistent collection variable or a variable that is not an ESQL/C collection variable, an error results. Once you deallocate a collection variable, you can use the ALLOCATE COLLECTION to reallocate resources and you can then reuse a collection variable.

Example

The following example shows how to deallocate resources with the
DEALLOCATE COLLECTION statement for the untyped collection variable,
a_set:

```
EXEC SQL BEGIN DECLARE SECTION;
    client collection a_set;
EXEC SQL END DECLARE SECTION;
   .
   .
   .
EXEC SQL allocate collection :a_set;
   .
   .
   .
EXEC SQL deallocate collection :a_set;
```

Related Information

Related example: refer to the collection variable example in PUT.

Related statements: ALLOCATE COLLECTION and DEALLOCATE ROW

For a discussion of collection data types, see the *Informix ESQL/C Programmer's
Manual.*

DEALLOCATE DESCRIPTOR

Use the DEALLOCATE DESCRIPTOR statement to free a previously allocated, system-descriptor area.

Use this statement with ESQL/C.

Syntax

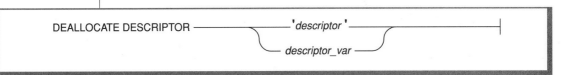

Element	Purpose	Restrictions	Syntax
descriptor	Quoted string that identifies a system-descriptor area	System-descriptor area must already be allocated. The surrounding quotes must be single.	Quoted String, p. 4-260
descriptor_var	Host variable name that identifies a system-descriptor area	System-descriptor area must already be allocated.	Name must conform to language-specific rules for variable names.

Usage

The DEALLOCATE DESCRIPTOR statement frees all the memory that is associated with the system-descriptor area that *descriptor* or *descriptor_var* identifies. It also frees all the item descriptors (including memory for data items in the item descriptors).

You can reuse a descriptor or descriptor variable after it is deallocated. Deallocation occurs automatically at the end of the program.

If you deallocate a nonexistent descriptor or descriptor variable, an error results.

You cannot use the DEALLOCATE DESCRIPTOR statement to deallocate an **sqlda** structure. You can use it only to free the memory that is allocated for a system-descriptor area.

The following examples show valid DEALLOCATE DESCRIPTOR statements. The first line uses an embedded-variable name, and the second line uses a quoted string to identify the allocated system-descriptor area.

```
EXEC SQL deallocate descriptor :descname;

EXEC SQL deallocate descriptor 'descl';
```

Related Information

Related statements: ALLOCATE DESCRIPTOR, DECLARE, DESCRIBE, EXECUTE, FETCH, GET DESCRIPTOR, OPEN, PREPARE, PUT, and SET DESCRIPTOR

For more information on system-descriptor areas, refer to the *Informix ESQL/C Programmer's Manual*.

DEALLOCATE ROW

Use the DEALLOCATE ROW statement to release memory for a row variable that was previously allocated with the ALLOCATE ROW statement.

Use this statement with ESQL/C.

Syntax

DEALLOCATE ROW ———————————— **:** *variable* ————————————┤

Element	Purpose	Restrictions	Syntax
variable	Name that identifies a typed or untyped row variable for which to deallocate memory	The variable must be an ESQL/C row variable that has already been allocated.	Name must conform to language-specific rules for variable names.

Usage

The DEALLOCATE ROW statement frees all the memory that is associated with the ESQL/C row variable that *variable* identifies. You must explicitly release memory resources for a row variable with DEALLOCATE ROW. Otherwise, deallocation occurs automatically at the end of the program.

The DEALLOCATE COLLECTION statement releases resources for both typed and untyped **row** variables.

Tip: *The DEALLOCATE ROW statement deallocates memory for an ESQL/C row variable only. To deallocate memory for an ESQL/C collection variable, use the DEALLOCATE COLLECTION statement.*

If you deallocate a nonexistent row variable or a variable that is not an ESQL/C **row** variable, an error results. Once you deallocate a row variable, you can use the ALLOCATE ROW statement to reallocate resources, and you can then reuse a **row** variable.

Example

The following example shows how to deallocate resources for the row variable, **a_row**, with the DEALLOCATE ROW statement:

```
EXEC SQL BEGIN DECLARE SECTION;
    row (a int, b int) a_row;
EXEC SQL END DECLARE SECTION;
.
.

.
EXEC SQL allocate row :a_row;
.

.
EXEC SQL deallocate row :a_row;
```

Related Information

Related statements: ALLOCATE ROW and DEALLOCATE COLLECTION

For a discussion of row types, see the *Informix Guide to SQL: Tutorial*.

For a discussion of complex data types, see the *Informix ESQL/C Programmer's Manual*.

E/C

DECLARE

Use the DECLARE statement to associate a cursor with a group of rows.

Use this statement with ESQL/C.

Syntax

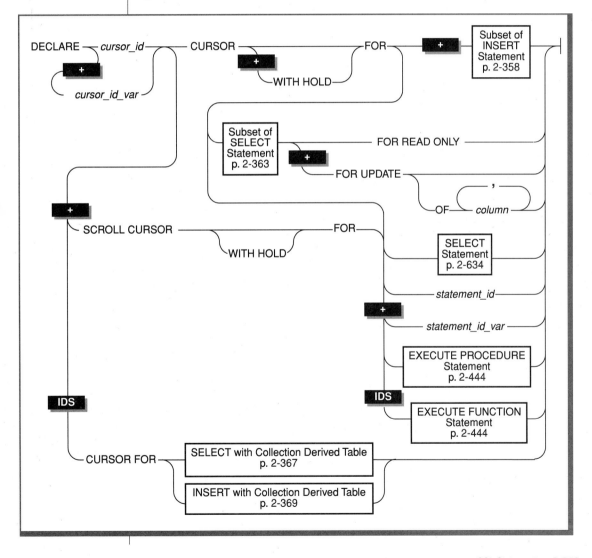

Element	Purpose	Restrictions	Syntax
column	Name of the column to update through the cursor	The specified column must exist, but it does not have to be in the select list of the SELECT clause.	Identifier, p. 4-205
cursor_id	Name that the DECLARE statement assigns to the cursor and that refers to the cursor in other statements	You cannot specify a cursor name that a previous DECLARE statement in the same program has specified.	Identifier, p. 4-205
cursor_id_var	Embedded variable that holds the value of *cursor_id*	Variable must be a character data type.	Name must conform to language-specific rules for variable names.
statement_id	Statement identifier that is a data structure that represents the text of a prepared statement	The statement_id must have already been specified in a PREPARE statement in the same program.	Identifier, p. 4-205
statement_id_var	Embedded variable that holds the value of *statement_id*	Variable must be a character data type.	Name must conform to language-specific rules for variable names.

Usage

A *cursor* is an identifier that you associate with a group of rows. The DECLARE statement associates the cursor with one of the following database objects:

- With an SQL statement, such as SELECT, EXECUTE FUNCTION (OR EXECUTE PROCEDURE), or INSERT

  Each of these SQL statements creates a different type of cursor. For more information, see Overview of Cursor Types, page 2-352.

- With the statement identifier (*statement id* or *statement id variable*) of a prepared statement.

  You can prepare one of the previous SQL statements and associate the prepared statement with a cursor. For more information, see "Associating a Cursor With a Prepared Statement" on page 2-366.

IDS

- With a collection variable in an ESQL/C program

  The name of the collection variable appears in the FROM clause of a SELECT or the INTO clause of an INSERT. For more information, see "Associating a Cursor With a Collection Variable" on page 2-367. ◆

The DECLARE statement assigns an identifier to the cursor, specifies its uses, and directs the preprocessor to allocate storage to hold the cursor.

The DECLARE statement must precede any other statement that refers to the cursor during the execution of the program.

The maximum length of a DECLARE statement is 64 kilobytes.

The number of prepared items in a single program is limited by the available memory. These items include both statement identifiers that are named in PREPARE statements (*statement_id* or *statement_id_var*) and declared cursors. To avoid exceeding the limit, use a FREE statement to release some statements or cursors.

A program can consist of one or more source-code files. By default, the scope of a cursor is global to a program, so a cursor declared in one file can be referenced from another file. In a multiple-file program, if you want to limit the scope of cursors to the files in which they are declared, you must preprocess all the files with the **-local** command-line option.

To declare multiple cursors, use a single statement identifier. For instance, the following ESQL/C example does not return an error:

```
EXEC SQL prepare id1 from 'select * from customer';
EXEC SQL declare x cursor for id1;
EXEC SQL declare y scroll cursor for id1;
EXEC SQL declare z cursor with hold for id1;
```

If you include the **-ansi** compilation flag (or if **DBANSIWARN** is set), warnings are generated for statements that use dynamic cursor names or dynamic statement identifier names and statements that use derived table names. Some error checking is performed at runtime. The following list indicates the typical checks:

- Illegal use of cursors (that is, normal cursors used as scroll cursors)
- Use of undeclared cursors
- Bad cursor or statement names (empty)

Checks for multiple declarations of a cursor of the same name are performed at compile time only if the cursor or statement is an identifier. The following example uses a host variable to hold the cursor name.

```
EXEC SQL declare x cursor for
    select * from customer;
. . .
stcopy("x", s);
EXEC SQL declare :s cursor for
    select * from customer;
```

Overview of Cursor Types

Functionally, you can declare the following types of cursors with the DECLARE statement:

- A *select cursor* is a cursor that is associated with A SELECT statement.
- A *function cursor* is a cursor that is associated with an EXECUTE FUNCTION (OR EXECUTE PROCEDURE) statement
- An *insert cursor* is a cursor that is associated with an INSERT statement.

Any of these cursor types can have cursor characteristics: sequential, scroll, and hold. These characteristics determine the structure of the cursor. For more information, see "Cursor Characteristics" on page 2-360. In addition, a select or function cursor can have a cursor mode: read-only or update. For more information, see "Select Cursor or Function Cursor" on page 2-353.

The following table summarizes types of cursors that are available.

Cursor Type	Cursor Mode		Cursor Characteristic		
	Read-Only	Update	Sequential	Scroll	Hold
Select and Function	✔		✔		
	✔		✔		✔
		✔	✔		
		✔	✔		✔
	✔			✔	
	✔			✔	✔
Insert			✔		
			✔		✔

A cursor can also be associated with a statement identifier, enabling you to use a cursor with an INSERT, SELECT, EXECUTE FUNCTION (or EXECUTE PROCEDURE) statement that is prepared dynamically and to use different statements with the same cursor at different times. In this case, the type of cursor depends on the statement that is prepared at the time the cursor is opened. For more information, see "Associating a Cursor With a Prepared Statement" on page 2-366.

The following sections describe each of these cursor types.

Tip: *Cursors for functions behave the same as select cursors that are enabled as update cursors.*

Select Cursor or Function Cursor

When an SQL statement returns more than one group of values to an ESQL/C program, you must declare a cursor to save the multiple groups, or rows, of data and to access these rows one at a time. You must associate the following SQL statements with cursors:

- When you associate a SELECT statement with a cursor, the cursor is called a *select cursor.*

  A select cursor is a data structure that represents a specific location within the active set of rows that the SELECT statement retrieved.

- When you associate an EXECUTE FUNCTION (or EXECUTE PROCEDURE) statement with a cursor, the cursor is called a *function cursor.*

  The function cursor represents the columns or values that a user-defined function returns. Function cursors behave the same as select cursors, which are enabled as update cursors.

EDS

In Enterprise Decision Server, to create a function cursor, you must use the EXECUTE PROCEDURE statement. Enterprise Decision Server does not support the EXECUTE FUNCTION statement. ♦

IDS

In Dynamic Server, for backward compatibility, if an SPL function was created with the CREATE PROCEDURE statement, you can create a function cursor with the EXECUTE PROCEDURE statement. With external functions, you must use the EXECUTE FUNCTION statement. ♦

When you associate a SELECT or EXECUTE FUNCTION (or EXECUTE PROCEDURE) statement with a cursor, the statement can include an INTO clause. However, if you prepare the SELECT or EXECUTE FUNCTION (or EXECUTE PROCEDURE) statement, you must omit the INTO clause in the PREPARE statement and use the INTO clause of the FETCH statement to retrieve the values from the collection cursor.

A select or function cursor enables you to scan returned rows of data and to move data row by row into a set of receiving variables, as the following steps describe:

1. DECLARE

   Use a DECLARE statement to define a cursor and associate it with a statement.

2. OPEN

   Use the OPEN statement to open the cursor. The database server processes the query until it locates or constructs the first row of the active set.

3. FETCH

   Use the FETCH statement to retrieve successive rows of data from the cursor.

4. CLOSE

   Use the CLOSE statement to close the cursor when the active set is no longer needed.

5. FREE

   Use the FREE statement to release the resources that are allocated for the declared cursor.

Using the FOR READ ONLY Option

Use the FOR READ ONLY keywords to define a cursor as a read-only cursor. A cursor declared to be read-only cannot be used to update (or delete) any row that it fetches.

The need for the FOR READ ONLY keywords depends on whether your database is an ANSI-compliant database or a database that is not ANSI compliant.

In a database that is not ANSI compliant, the cursor that the DECLARE statement defines is a read-only cursor by default. So you do not need to specify the FOR READ ONLY keywords if you want the cursor to be a read-only cursor. The only advantage of specifying the FOR READ ONLY keywords explicitly is for better program documentation.

ANSI

In an ANSI-compliant database, the cursor associated with a SELECT statement through the DECLARE statement is an update cursor by default, provided that the SELECT statement conforms to all of the restrictions for update cursors listed in "Subset of SELECT Statement Associated with Cursors" on page 2-363. If you want a select cursor to be read only, you must use the FOR READ ONLY keywords when you declare the cursor. ♦

The database server can use less stringent locking for a read-only cursor than for an update cursor.

The following example creates a read-only cursor:

```
EXEC SQL declare z_curs cursor for
    select * from customer_ansi
    for read only;
```

Using the FOR UPDATE Option

Use the FOR UPDATE option to declare an update cursor. You can use the update cursor to modify (update or delete) the current row.

ANSI

In an ANSI-compliant database, you can use a select cursor to update or delete data as long as the cursor was not declared with the FOR READ ONLY keywords and it follows the restrictions on update cursors that are described in "Subset of SELECT Statement Associated with Cursors" on page 2-363. You do not need to use the FOR UPDATE keywords when you declare the cursor. ♦

The following example declares an update cursor:

```
EXEC SQL declare new_curs cursor for
    select * from customer_notansi
    for update;
```

In an update cursor, you can update or delete rows in the active set. After you create an update cursor, you can update or delete the currently selected row by using an UPDATE or DELETE statement with the WHERE CURRENT OF clause. The words CURRENT OF refer to the row that was most recently fetched; they take the place of the usual test expressions in the WHERE clause.

An update cursor lets you perform updates that are not possible with the UPDATE statement because the decision to update and the values of the new data items can be based on the original contents of the row. Your program can evaluate or manipulate the selected data before it decides whether to update. The UPDATE statement cannot interrogate the table that is being updated.

You can specify particular columns that can be updated.

Using FOR UPDATE with a List of Columns

When you declare an update cursor, you can limit the update to specific columns by including the OF keyword and a list of columns. You can modify only those named columns in subsequent UPDATE statements. The columns need not be in the select list of the SELECT clause.

The following example declares an update cursor and specifies that this cursor can update only the **fname** and **lname** columns in the **customer_notansi** table:

```
EXEC SQL declare name_curs cursor for
    select * from customer_notansi
    for update of fname, lname;
```

ANSI

By default, a select cursor in a database that is ANSI compliant is an update cursor. Therefore, the FOR UPDATE keywords are optional. However, if you want an update cursor to be able to modify only some of the columns in a table, you must specify these columns in the FOR UPDATE option. ♦

The principal advantage to specifying columns is documentation and preventing programming errors. (The database server refuses to update any other columns.) An additional advantage is speed, when the SELECT statement meets the following criteria:

■ The SELECT statement can be processed using an index.

■ The columns that are listed are not part of the index that is used to process the SELECT statement.

If the columns that you intend to update are part of the index that is used to process the SELECT statement, the database server must keep a list of each row that is updated to ensure that no row is updated twice. When you use the OF keyword to specify the columns that can be updated, the database server determines whether to keep the list of updated rows. If the database server determines that the list is unnecessary, then eliminating the work of keeping the list results in a performance benefit. If you do not use the OF keyword, the database server keeps the list of updated rows, although it might be unnecessary.

The following example contains ESQL/C code that uses an update cursor with a DELETE statement to delete the current row. Whenever the row is deleted, the cursor remains between rows. After you delete data, you must use a FETCH statement to advance the cursor to the next row before you can refer to the cursor in a DELETE or UPDATE statement.

```
EXEC SQL declare q_curs cursor for
    select * from customer where lname matches :last_name
        for update;

EXEC SQL open q_curs;
for (;;)
{
    EXEC SQL fetch q_curs into :cust_rec;
    if (strncmp(SQLSTATE, "00", 2) != 0)
        break;

    /* Display customer values and prompt for answer */
    printf("\n%s %s", cust_rec.fname, cust_rec.lname);
    printf("\nDelete this customer? ");
    scanf("%s", answer);

    if (answer[0] == 'y')
        EXEC SQL delete from customer where current of q_curs;
    if (strncmp(SQLSTATE, "00", 2) != 0)
        break;
}
printf("\n");
EXEC SQL close q_curs;
```

Locking with an Update Cursor

When you use the FOR UPDATE keywords you notify the database server that updating is possible and cause it to use more stringent locking than with a select cursor. You declare an update cursor to let the database server know that the program might update (or delete) any row that it fetches as part of the SELECT statement. The update cursor employs *promotable* locks for rows that the program fetches. Other programs can read the locked row, but no other program can place a promotable or write lock. Before the program modifies the row, the row lock is promoted to an exclusive lock.

Although it is possible to declare an update cursor with the WITH HOLD keywords, the only reason to do so is to break a long series of updates into smaller transactions. You must fetch and update a particular row in the same transaction.

If an operation involves fetching and updating a very large number of rows, the lock table that the database server maintains can overflow. The usual way to prevent this overflow is to lock the entire table that is being updated. If this action is impossible, an alternative is to update through a hold cursor and to execute COMMIT WORK at frequent intervals. However, you must plan such an application very carefully because COMMIT WORK releases all locks, even those that are placed through a hold cursor.

Subset of INSERT Statement Associated with a Sequential Cursor

As indicated in the diagram for "DECLARE" on page 349, to create an insert cursor, you associate a sequential cursor with a restricted form of the INSERT statement. The INSERT statement must include a VALUES clause; it cannot contain an embedded SELECT statement.

The following example contains ESQL/C code that declares an insert cursor:

```
EXEC SQL declare ins_cur cursor for
    insert into stock values
    (:stock_no,:manu_code,:descr,:u_price,:unit,:u_desc);
```

The insert cursor simply inserts rows of data; it cannot be used to fetch data. When an insert cursor is opened, a buffer is created in memory to hold a block of rows. The buffer receives rows of data as the program executes PUT statements. The rows are written to disk only when the buffer is full. You can use the CLOSE, FLUSH, or COMMIT WORK statement to flush the buffer when it is less than full. This topic is discussed further under the PUT and CLOSE statements. You must close an insert cursor to insert any buffered rows into the database before the program ends. You can lose data if you do not close the cursor properly.

For a complete description of INSERT syntax and usage, see "INSERT" on page 535.

Insert Cursor

When you associate an INSERT statement with a cursor, the cursor is called an *insert cursor*. An insert cursor is a data structure that represents the rows that the INSERT statement is to add to the database. The insert cursor simply inserts rows of data; it cannot be used to fetch data. To create an insert cursor, you associate a cursor with a restricted form of the INSERT statement. The INSERT statement must include a VALUES clause; it cannot contain an embedded SELECT statement.

Create an insert cursor if you want to add multiple rows to the database in an INSERT operation. An insert cursor allows bulk insert data to be buffered in memory and written to disk when the buffer is full, as the following steps describe:

1. Use a DECLARE statement to define an insert cursor for the INSERT statement.

2. Open the cursor with the OPEN statement. The database server creates the insert buffer in memory and positions the cursor at the first row of the insert buffer.

3. Put successive rows of data into the insert buffer with the PUT statement.

4. The database server writes the rows to disk only when the buffer is full. You can use the CLOSE, FLUSH, or COMMIT WORK statement to flush the buffer when it is less than full. This topic is discussed further under the PUT and CLOSE statements.

5. Close the cursor with the CLOSE statement when the insert cursor is no longer needed. You must close an insert cursor to insert any buffered rows into the database before the program ends. You can lose data if you do not close the cursor properly.

6. Free the cursor with the FREE statement. The FREE statement releases the resources that are allocated for an insert cursor.

An insert cursor increases processing efficiency (compared with embedding the INSERT statement directly). This process reduces communication between the program and the database server and also increases the speed of the insertions.

In addition to select and function cursors, insert cursors can also have the sequential cursor characteristic. To create an insert cursor, you associate a sequential cursor with a restricted form of the INSERT statement. (For more information, see "Insert Cursor" on page 2-359.) The following example contains Informix ESQL/C code that declares a sequential insert cursor:

```
EXEC SQL declare ins_cur cursor for
    insert into stock values
    (:stock_no,:manu_code,:descr,:u_price,:unit,:u_desc);
```

Cursor Characteristics

Structurally, you can declare a cursor as a *sequential* cursor (the default condition), a *scroll* cursor (using the SCROLL keyword), or a *hold* cursor (using the WITH HOLD keywords). The following sections explain these structural characteristics.

A select or function cursor can be either a sequential or a scroll cursor. An insert cursor can only be a sequential cursor. Select, function, and insert cursors can optionally be hold cursors. For a graphical representation of this information, see "Overview of Cursor Types" on page 2-352.

Creating a Sequential Cursor by Default

If you use only the CURSOR keyword, you create a sequential cursor, which can fetch only the next row in sequence from the active set. The sequential cursor can read through the active set only once each time it is opened. If you are using a sequential cursor for a select cursor, on each execution of the FETCH statement, the database server returns the contents of the current row and locates the next row in the active set.

The following example creates a read-only sequential cursor in a database that is not ANSI compliant and an update sequential cursor in an ANSI-compliant database:

```
EXEC SQL declare s_cur cursor for
    select fname, lname into :st_fname, :st_lname
    from orders where customer_num = 114;
```

In addition to select and function cursors, insert cursors can also have the sequential cursor characteristic. To create an insert cursor, you associate a sequential cursor with a restricted form of the INSERT statement. (For more information, see "Insert Cursor" on page 2-359.) The following example declares a sequential insert cursor:

```
EXEC SQL declare ins_cur cursor for
    insert into stock values
    (:stock_no,:manu_code,:descr,:u_price,:unit,:u_desc);
```

Using the SCROLL Keyword to Create a Scroll Cursor

Use the SCROLL keyword to create a scroll cursor, which can fetch rows of the active set in any sequence.

The database server retains the active set of the cursor as a temporary table until the cursor is closed. You can fetch the first, last, or any intermediate rows of the active set as well as fetch rows repeatedly without having to close and reopen the cursor. (See FETCH.)

On a multiuser system, the rows in the tables from which the active-set rows were derived might change after the cursor is opened and a copy is made in the temporary table. If you use a scroll cursor within a transaction, you can prevent copied rows from changing either by setting the isolation level to Repeatable Read or by locking the entire table in share mode during the transaction. (See SET ISOLATION and LOCK TABLE.)

The following example creates a scroll cursor for a SELECT:

```
DECLARE sc_cur SCROLL CURSOR FOR
    SELECT * FROM orders
```

Restrictions

You can create scroll cursors for select and function cursors but *not* for insert cursors. Scroll cursors cannot be declared as FOR UPDATE.

Using the WITH HOLD Keywords to Create a Hold Cursor

Use the WITH HOLD keywords to create a hold cursor. A hold cursor allows uninterrupted access to a set of rows across multiple transactions. Ordinarily, all cursors close at the end of a transaction. A hold cursor does not close; it remains open after a transaction ends.

A hold cursor can be either a sequential cursor or a scroll cursor.

You can use the WITH HOLD keywords to declare select and function cursors (sequential and scroll), and insert cursors. These keywords follow the CURSOR keyword in the DECLARE statement. The following example creates a sequential hold cursor for a SELECT:

```
DECLARE hld_cur CURSOR WITH HOLD FOR
    SELECT customer_num, lname, city FROM customer
```

You can use a select hold cursor as the following ESQL/C code example shows. This code fragment uses a hold cursor as a *master* cursor to scan one set of records and a sequential cursor as a *detail* cursor to point to records that are located in a different table. The records that the master cursor scans are the basis for updating the records to which the detail cursor points. The COMMIT WORK statement at the end of each iteration of the first WHILE loop leaves the hold cursor **c_master** open but closes the sequential cursor **c_detail** and releases all locks. This technique minimizes the resources that the database server must devote to locks and unfinished transactions, and it gives other users immediate access to updated rows.

```
EXEC SQL BEGIN DECLARE SECTION;
    int p_custnum,
    int save_status;
    long p_orddate;
EXEC SQL END DECLARE SECTION;

EXEC SQL prepare st_1 from
    'select order_date
        from orders where customer_num = ? for update';
EXEC SQL declare c_detail cursor for st_1;

EXEC SQL declare c_master cursor with hold for
    select customer_num
        from customer where city = 'Pittsburgh';

EXEC SQL open c_master;
if(SQLCODE==0) /* the open worked */
    EXEC SQL fetch c_master into :p_custnum; /* discover first customer */
while(SQLCODE==0) /* while no errors and not end of pittsburgh customers */
    {
    EXEC SQL begin work; /* start transaction for customer p_custnum */
    EXEC SQL open c_detail using :p_custnum;
    if(SQLCODE==0) /* detail open succeeded */
```

```
        EXEC SQL fetch c_detail into :p_orddate; /* get first order */
    while(SQLCODE==0) /* while no errors and not end of orders */
        {
        EXEC SQL update orders set order_date = '08/15/94'
            where current of c_detail;
        if(status==0) /* update was ok */
            EXEC SQL fetch c_detail into :p_orddate; /* next order */
        }
    if(SQLCODE==SQLNOTFOUND) /* correctly updated all found orders */
        EXEC SQL commit work; /* make updates permanent, set status */
    else /* some failure in an update */
        {
        save_status = SQLCODE; /* save error for loop control */
        EXEC SQL rollback work;
        SQLCODE = save_status; /* force loop to end */
        }
    if(SQLCODE==0) /* all updates, and the commit, worked ok */
        EXEC SQL fetch c_master into :p_custnum; /* next customer? */
    }
EXEC SQL close c_master;
```

Use either the CLOSE statement to close the hold cursor explicitly or the CLOSE DATABASE or DISCONNECT statements to close it implicitly. The CLOSE DATABASE statement closes all cursors.

Using an Insert Cursor with Hold

If you associate a hold cursor with an INSERT statement, you can use transactions to break a long series of PUT statements into smaller sets of PUT statements. Instead of waiting for the PUT statements to fill the buffer and trigger an automatic write to the database, you can execute a COMMIT WORK statement to flush the row buffer. If you use a hold cursor, the COMMIT WORK statement commits the inserted rows but leaves the cursor open for further inserts. This method can be desirable when you are inserting a large number of rows, because pending uncommitted work consumes database server resources.

Subset of SELECT Statement Associated with Cursors

As indicated in the diagram for "DECLARE" on page 349, not all SELECT statements can be associated with a read-only or update cursor. If the DECLARE statement includes one of these options, you must observe certain restrictions on the SELECT statement that is included in the DECLARE statement (either directly or as a prepared statement).

If the DECLARE statement includes the FOR READ ONLY option, the SELECT statement must conform to the following restrictions:

- The SELECT statement cannot have a FOR READ ONLY option.
- The SELECT statement cannot have a FOR UPDATE option.

For a complete description of SELECT syntax and usage, see "SELECT" on page 634.

If the DECLARE statement includes the FOR UPDATE option, the SELECT statement must conform to the following restrictions:

- The statement can select data from only one table.
- The statement cannot include any aggregate functions.
- The statement cannot include any of the following clauses or keywords: DISTINCT, FOR READ ONLY, FOR UPDATE, GROUP BY, INTO TEMP, ORDER BY, UNION, or UNIQUE.

| EDS |
- In Enterprise Decision Server, the statement cannot include the INTO EXTERNAL and INTO SCRATCH clauses. ♦

Examples of Cursors in Non-ANSI Databases

In a database that is not ANSI compliant, a cursor associated with a SELECT statement is a read-only cursor by default. The following example declares a read-only cursor in a non-ANSI database:

```
EXEC SQL declare cust_curs cursor for
    select * from customer_notansi;
```

If you want to make it clear in the program code that this cursor is a read-only cursor, you can specify the FOR READ ONLY option as shown in the following example:

```
EXEC SQL declare cust_curs cursor for
    select * from customer_notansi
    for read only;
```

If you want this cursor to be an update cursor, you need to specify the FOR UPDATE option in your DECLARE statement. The following example declares an update cursor:

```
EXEC SQL declare new_curs cursor for
    select * from customer_notansi
    for update;
```

If you want an update cursor to be able to modify only some of the columns in a table, you need to specify these columns in the FOR UPDATE option. The following example declares an update cursor and specifies that this cursor can update only the **fname** and **lname** columns in the **customer_notansi** table:

```
EXEC SQL declare name_curs cursor for
    select * from customer_notansi
    for update of fname, lname;
```

Examples of Cursors in ANSI-compliant Databases

In an ANSI-compliant database, a cursor associated with a SELECT statement is an update cursor by default. The following example declares an update cursor in an ANSI-compliant database:

```
EXEC SQL declare x_curs cursor for
    select * from customer_ansi;
```

If you want to make it clear in the program documentation that this cursor is an update cursor, you can specify the FOR UPDATE option as shown in the following example:

```
EXEC SQL declare x_curs cursor for
    select * from customer_ansi
    for update;
```

If you want an update cursor to be able to modify only some of the columns in a table, you must specify these columns in the FOR UPDATE option. The following example declares an update cursor and specifies that this cursor can update only the **fname** and **lname** columns in the **customer_ansi** table:

```
EXEC SQL declare y_curs cursor for
    select * from customer_ansi
    for update of fname, lname;
```

If you want a cursor to be a read-only cursor, you must override the default behavior of the DECLARE statement by specifying the FOR READ ONLY option in your DECLARE statement. The following example declares a read-only cursor:

```
EXEC SQL declare z_curs cursor for
    select * from customer_ansi
    for read only;
```

Associating a Cursor With a Prepared Statement

The PREPARE statement lets you assemble the text of an SQL statement at runtime and pass the statement text to the database server for execution. If you anticipate that a dynamically prepared SELECT, EXECUTE FUNCTION (or EXECUTE PROCEDURE) statement that returns values could produce more than one row of data, the prepared statement must be associated with a cursor. (See PREPARE.)

The result of a PREPARE statement is a statement identifier (*statement id* or *id variable*), which is a data structure that represents the prepared statement text. To declare a cursor for the statement text, associate a cursor with the statement identifier.

You can associate a sequential cursor with any prepared SELECT or EXECUTE FUNCTION (or EXECUTE PROCEDURE) statement. You cannot associate a scroll cursor with a prepared INSERT statement or with a SELECT statement that was prepared to include a FOR UPDATE clause.

After a cursor is opened, used, and closed, a different statement can be prepared under the same statement identifier. In this way, it is possible to use a single cursor with different statements at different times. The cursor must be redeclared before you use it again.

The following example contains ESQL/C code that prepares a SELECT statement and declares a sequential cursor for the prepared statement text. The statement identifier **st_1** is first prepared from a SELECT statement that returns values; then the cursor **c_detail** is declared for **st_1**.

```
EXEC SQL prepare st_1 from
    'select order_date
        from orders where customer_num = ?';
EXEC SQL declare c_detail cursor for st_1;
```

If you want to use a prepared SELECT statement to modify data, add a FOR UPDATE clause to the statement text that you wish to prepare, as the following ESQL/C example shows:

```
EXEC SQL prepare sel_1 from
    'select * from customer for update';
EXEC SQL declare sel_curs cursor for sel_1;
```

IDS

Associating a Cursor With a Collection Variable

The DECLARE statement allows you to declare a cursor for an ESQL/C collection variable. Such a cursor is called a *collection cursor*. You use a collection variable to access the elements of a collection (SET, MULTISET, LIST) column. Use a cursor when you want to access one or more elements in a collection variable.

The Collection Derived Table segment identifies the collection variable for which to declare the cursor. For more information, see "Collection Derived Table" on page 4-9.

Select With Collection Derived Table

The diagram for "DECLARE" on page 349 refers to this section.

To declare a select cursor for a collection variable, include the Collection Derived Table segment with the SELECT statement that you associate with the collection cursor. A select cursor allows you to select one or more elements *from* the collection variable.

For a complete description of SELECT syntax and usage, see "SELECT" on page 634.

Restrictions

When you declare a select cursor for a collection variable, the DECLARE statement has the following restrictions:

- It can not include the FOR READ ONLY keywords that specify the read-only cursor mode.

  The select cursor is an update cursor.
- It cannot include the SCROLL or WITH HOLD keywords.

  The select cursor must be a sequential cursor.

In addition, the SELECT statement that you associate with the collection cursor has the following restrictions:

- It cannot include the following clauses or options: WHERE, GROUP BY, ORDER BY, HAVING, INTO TEMP, and WITH REOPTIMIZATION.
- It cannot contain expressions in the select list.

- If the collection contains elements of opaque, distinct, built-in, or other collection data types, the select list must be an asterisk (*).
- Column names in the select list must be simple column names.

  These columns cannot use the following syntax:

  ```
  database@server:table.column --INVALID SYNTAX
  ```
- It *must* contain the name of the collection variable in the FROM clause.

  You cannot specify an input parameter (the question-mark (?) symbol) for the collection variable. Likewise you cannot use the virtual table format of the Collection Derived Table segment.

Using a SELECT Cursor with a Collection Variable

A collection cursor that includes a SELECT statement with the Collection Derived Table clause allows you to access the elements in a collection variable.

To select more than one element, follow these general steps:

1. Create a client collection variable in your ESQL/C program.
2. Declare the collection cursor for the SELECT statement with the DECLARE statement.

   If you want to modify the elements of the collection variable, declare the select cursor as an update cursor with the FOR UPDATE keywords. You can then use the WHERE CURRENT OF clause of the DELETE and UPDATE statements to delete or update elements of the collection.
3. Open this cursor with the OPEN statement.
4. Fetch the elements from the collection cursor with the FETCH statement and the INTO clause.
5. If necessary, perform any updates or deletes on the fetched data and save the modified collection variable in the collection column.

   Once the collection variable contains the correct elements, use the UPDATE or INSERT statement to save the contents of the collection variable in the actual collection column (SET, MULTISET, or LIST).
6. Close the collection cursor with the CLOSE statement.

Example

The following DECLARE statement declares a select cursor for a collection variable:

```
EXEC SQL BEGIN DECLARE SECTION;
    client collection set(integer not null) a_set;
EXEC SQL END DECLARE SECTION;
...
EXEC SQL declare set_curs cursor for
    select * from table(:a_set);
```

For an extended code example that uses a collection cursor for a SELECT statement, see "Fetching From a Collection Cursor" on page 2-466.

Insert With a Collection Derived Table

The diagram for "DECLARE" on page 349 refers to this section.

To declare an insert cursor for a collection variable, include the Collection Derived Table segment with the INSERT statement that you associate with the collection cursor. An insert cursor allows you to insert one or more elements in the collection.

For a complete description of INSERT syntax and usage, see "INSERT" on page 535.

Restrictions

The insert cursor must be a sequential cursor, that is the DECLARE statement cannot contain the WITH HOLD keywords.

When you declare an insert cursor for a collection variable, the Collection-Derived Table clause of the INSERT statement *must* contain the name of the collection variable. You cannot specify an input parameter (the question-mark (?) symbol) for the collection variable. However, you can use an input parameter in the VALUES clause of the INSERT statement. This parameter indicates that the collection element is to be provided later by the FROM clause of the PUT statement.

Using an INSERT Cursor with a Collection Variable

A collection cursor that includes an INSERT statement with the Collection-Derived Table clause allows you to insert more than one element into a collection variable.

To insert more than one element, follow these general steps:

1. Create a client collection variable in your ESQL/C program.

2. Declare the collection cursor for the INSERT statement with the DECLARE statement.

3. Open the cursor with the OPEN statement.

4. Put the elements into the collection cursor with the PUT statement and the FROM clause.

5. Once the collection variable contains all the elements, you then use the UPDATE statement or the INSERT statement on a table name to save the contents of the collection variable in a collection column (SET, MULTISET, or LIST).

6. Close the collection cursor with the CLOSE statement.

Example

For example, the following DECLARE statement declares an insert cursor for the **a_set** collection variable:

```
EXEC SQL BEGIN DECLARE SECTION;
    client collection multiset(smallint not null) a_mset;
    int an_element;
EXEC SQL END DECLARE SECTION;
. . .
EXEC SQL declare mset_curs cursor for
    insert into table(:a_mset)
    values (?);
EXEC SQL open mset_curs;
while (1)
{
. . .
    EXEC SQL put mset_curs from :an_element;
. . .
}
```

To insert the elements into the collection variable, use the PUT statement with the FROM clause. For a code example that uses a collection cursor for an INSERT statement, see "Inserting into a Collection Cursor" on page 2-599.

Using Cursors with Transactions

To roll back a modification, you must perform the modification within a transaction. A transaction in a database that is not ANSI compliant begins only when the BEGIN WORK statement is executed.

ANSI

In an ANSI-compliant database, transactions are always in effect. ♦

The database server enforces the following guidelines for select and update cursors. These guidelines ensure that modifications can be committed or rolled back properly:

- Open an insert or update cursor within a transaction.
- Include PUT and FLUSH statements within one transaction.
- Modify data (update, insert, or delete) within one transaction.

The database server lets you open and close a hold cursor for an update outside a transaction; however, you should fetch all the rows that pertain to a given modification and then perform the modification all within a single transaction. You cannot open and close hold or update cursors outside a transaction.

The following example uses an update cursor within a transaction:

```
EXEC SQL declare q_curs cursor for
    select customer_num, fname, lname from customer
    where lname matches :last_name
        for update;
EXEC SQL open q_curs;
EXEC SQL begin work;
EXEC SQL fetch q_curs into :cust_rec; /* fetch after begin */
EXEC SQL update customer set lname = 'Smith'
    where current of q_curs;
/* no error */
EXEC SQL commit work;
```

When you update a row within a transaction, the row remains locked until the cursor is closed or the transaction is committed or rolled back. If you update a row when no transaction is in effect, the row lock is released when the modified row is written to disk.

If you update or delete a row outside a transaction, you cannot roll back the operation.

In a database that uses transactions, you cannot open an insert cursor outside a transaction unless it was also declared with the WITH HOLD keywords.

Related Information

Related statements: CLOSE, DELETE, EXECUTE PROCEDURE, FETCH, FREE, INSERT, OPEN, PREPARE, PUT, SELECT, and UPDATE

For discussions of cursors and data modification, see the *Informix Guide to SQL: Tutorial.*

For more advanced issues related to cursors or information about using cursors with collection variables, see the *Informix ESQL/C Programmer's Manual.*

DELETE

Use the DELETE statement to delete one or more rows from a table, or one or more elements in an SPL or ESQL/C collection variable.

Syntax

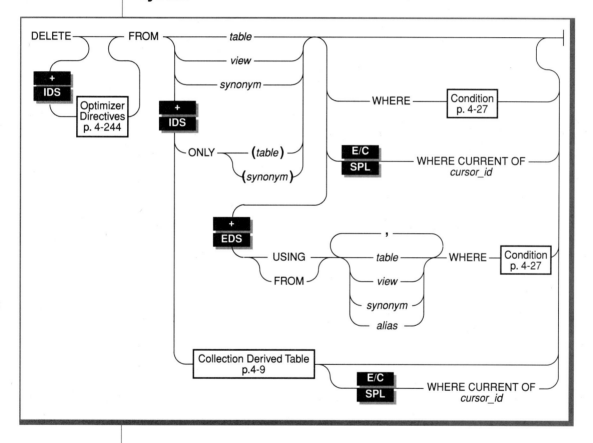

Element	Purpose	Restrictions	Syntax
alias	Temporary name for a table	You cannot use an alias with indexed_table.	Identifier, p. 4-205
cursor_id	Name of the cursor whose current row is to be deleted	The cursor must have been previously declared in a DECLARE statement with a FOR UPDATE clause.	Identifier, p. 4-205
synonym	Name of the synonym that contains the row or rows to be deleted	The synonym and the table to which the synonym points must exist.	Database Object Name, p. 4-50
table	Name of the table that contains the row or rows to be deleted	The table must exist.	Database Object Name, p. 4-50
view	Name of the view that contains the row or rows to be deleted	The view must exist.	Database Object Name, p. 4-50

Usage

If you use the DELETE statement without a WHERE clause (either to introduce a condition or to indicate the active set of the cursor), the database server deletes all the rows in the table.

If you use the DELETE statement outside a transaction in a database that uses transactions, each DELETE statement that you execute is treated as a single transaction.

The database server locks each row affected by a DELETE statement within a transaction for the duration of the transaction. The type of lock that the database server uses is determined by the lock mode of the table, as set by a CREATE TABLE or ALTER TABLE statement, as follows:

- If the lock mode is ROW, the database server acquires one lock for each row affected by the delete.

EDS

- In Enterprise Decision Server, if the lock mode is PAGE, the database server acquires one lock for each page affected by the delete. ◆

If the number of rows affected is very large and the lock mode is ROW, you might exceed the limits your operating system places on the maximum number of simultaneous locks. If this occurs, you can either reduce the scope of the DELETE statement or lock the table in exclusive mode before you execute the statement.

If you specify a view name, the view must be updatable. For an explanation of an updatable view, see "Updating Through Views" on page 2-339.

DB

If you omit the WHERE clause while you are working within the SQL menu, DB-Access prompts you to verify that you want to delete all rows from a table. You do not receive a prompt if you run the DELETE statement within a command file. ♦

ANSI

In an ANSI-compliant database, statements are always in an implicit transaction. Therefore, you cannot have a DELETE statement outside a transaction. ♦

IDS

Using the ONLY Keyword

If you use the DELETE statement to remove rows of a supertable, rows from both the supertable and its subtables can be deleted. To delete rows from the supertable only, you must use the ONLY keyword prior to the table name, as the following example shows:

```
DELETE FROM ONLY(super_tab)
WHERE name = "johnson"
```

Warning: *If you use the DELETE statement on a supertable without the ONLY keyword and without a WHERE clause, all rows of the supertable and its subtables are deleted.*

You cannot specify the ONLY keyword if you plan to use the WHERE CURRENT OF clause to delete the current row of the active set of a cursor.

Considerations When Tables Have Cascading Deletes

When you use the ON DELETE CASCADE option of the REFERENCES clause on either the CREATE TABLE or ALTER TABLE statement, you specify that you want deletes to cascade from one table to another. For example, in the **stores_demo** database, the **stock** table contains the column **stock_num** as a primary key. The **catalog** and **items** tables each contain the column **stock_num** as foreign keys with the ON DELETE CASCADE option specified. When a delete is performed from the **stock** table, rows are also deleted in the **catalog** and **items** tables, which are referred through the foreign keys.

To have deletes cascade to a table that has a referential constraint on a parent table, you need the DELETE privilege only on the parent table that you mention in the DELETE statement.

If a delete without a WHERE clause is performed on a table that one or more child tables reference with cascading deletes, the database server deletes all rows from that table and from any affected child tables.

For an example of how to create a referential constraint that uses cascading deletes, see "Using the ON DELETE CASCADE Option" on page 2-244.

Restrictions on DELETE When Tables Have Cascading Deletes

If you have a parent table with two child tables that reference it, one child with cascading deletes specified and one child without cascading deletes, and you attempt to delete a row from the parent table that applies to both child tables, the delete statement fails, and no rows are deleted from either the parent or child tables.

You cannot use a child table in a correlated subquery to delete a row from a parent table.

Locking and Logging Implications of Cascading Deletes

During deletes, the database server places locks on all qualifying rows of the referenced and referencing tables.

IDS

You must turn logging on when you perform the deletes. If logging is turned off in a database, even temporarily, deletes do not cascade because if logging is turned off, you cannot roll back any actions. For example, if a parent row is deleted, and the system fails before the child rows are deleted, the database will have dangling child records, which violates referential integrity. However, when logging is turned back on, subsequent deletes cascade. ♦

Using the WHERE Keyword to Introduce a Condition

Use the WHERE keyword to introduce a condition that separates from the table one or more rows that you want to delete. The WHERE conditions are the same as the conditions in the SELECT statement. For example, the following statement deletes all the rows of the **items** table where the order number is less than 1034:

```
DELETE FROM items
    WHERE order_num < 1034
```

DB

If you include a WHERE clause that selects all rows in the table, DB-Access gives no prompt and deletes all rows. ♦

IDS

If you are deleting from a supertable in a table hierarchy, a subquery in the WHERE clause cannot reference a subtable.

If you are deleting from a subtable in a table hierarchy, a subquery in the WHERE clause can reference the supertable if it references only the supertable. That is, the subquery must use the SELECT...FROM ONLY (*supertable*)... syntax. ♦

E/C

SPL

Using the WHERE CURRENT OF Keywords

Use the WHERE CURRENT OF clause to delete the current row of the active set of a cursor.

When you use the WHERE CURRENT OF clause, THE DELETE statement removes the row of the active set at the current position of the cursor. After the deletion, no current row exists; you cannot use the cursor to delete or update a row until you reposition the cursor with a FETCH statement.

You access the current row of the active set of a cursor with an update cursor. Before you can use the THIS clause, you must create a cursor with the FOREACH statement (SPL) or the DECLARE statement with the FOR UPDATE clause (ESQL/C). ♦

ANSI

All select cursors are potentially update cursors in an ANSI-compliant database. You can use this clause with any select cursor. ♦

IDS

You cannot use this clause if you are selecting from only one table in a table hierarchy. That is, you cannot use this option if you use the ONLY keyword.

You use this clause to delete an element from a collection. However, you actually delete the current row of the collection derived table that a collection variable holds. For more information, see "Collection Derived Table" on page 4-9. ♦

Using the USING or FROM Keyword to Introduce a Join Condition

If you want to delete information from a table based on information contained in one or more other tables, use the USING keyword or a second FROM keyword to introduce the list of tables that you want to join in the WHERE clause.

When you use this syntax, the WHERE clause can include any complex join.

If you do not list a join in the WHERE clause, the database server ignores the tables listed after the introductory keyword (either USING or FROM). That is, the query performs as if the list of tables was not included.

Although you can use a second FROM keyword to introduce the list of tables, Informix recommends that you use the USING keyword for more readable code.

When you use a delete join, the entire operation occurs as a single transaction. For example if a delete join query is supposed to delete 100 rows and an error occurs after the 50th row, the first 50 rows that are already deleted will reappear in the table. ♦

Restrictions

When you introduce a list of tables that you want to join in the WHERE clause, the following restrictions for the DELETE statement exist:

- You must list the target table (the one from which rows are to be deleted) and any table that will be part of a join after the USING (or second FROM) keyword.

- The WHERE clause cannot contain outer joins.

- The target table cannot be a static or external table.

- The statement cannot contain cursors.

■ If the target table is a view, the view must be updatable.

That is, the SELECT statement that defines the view cannot contain any of the following syntax:

❑ Aggregate expressions

❑ UNIQUE or DISTINCT

❑ UNION

❑ GROUP BY

Example

The following example deletes those rows from the **lineitem** table whose corresponding rows in the **order** table show that nothing was ordered (that is, a **qty** of less than one).

```
DELETE FROM lineitem
USING order o, lineitem l
WHERE o.qty < 1 AND o.order_num = l.order_num
```

When to Use

A delete join makes it easier to incorporate new data into a database. For example, you can:

1. Store new values in a temporary table.

2. Use a delete join (DELETE...USING statement) to remove any records from the temporary table that already exist in the table into which you want to insert the new records.

3. Insert the remaining records into the table.

In addition, you can use this syntax instead of deleting from the results of a SELECT statement that includes a join.

IDS

Deleting Rows That Contain Opaque Data Types

Some opaque data types require special processing when they are deleted. For example, if an opaque data type contains spatial or multirepresentational data, it might provide a choice of how to store the data: inside the internal structure or, for very large objects, in a smart large object.

This processing is accomplished by calling a user-defined support function called **destroy()**. When you use the DELETE statement to delete a row that contains one of these opaque types, the database server automatically invokes the **destroy()** function for the type. The **destroy()** support function can decide how to remove the data, regardless of where it is stored. For more information on the **destroy()** support function, see *Extending Informix Dynamic Server 2000*.

Deleting Rows That Contain Collection Data Types

When a row contains a column that is a collection data type (LIST, MULTISET, or SET), you can search for a particular element in the collection, and delete the row or rows in which the element is found. For example, the following statement deletes any rows from the **new_tab** table in which the **set_col** column contains the element jimmy smith:

```
DELETE FROM new_tab
WHERE 'jimmy smith' IN set_col
```

You can also use a collection variable to delete values in a collection column. With a collection variable you can delete one or more individual elements in a collection. For more information, see "Collection Derived Table" on page 4-9. ♦

SQLSTATE VALUES When Deleting from an ANSI Database

If you delete from a table in an ANSI-compliant database with a DELETE statement that contains a WHERE clause and no rows are found, that database server issues a warning. You can detect this warning condition in either of the following ways:

- The GET DIAGNOSTICS statement sets the **RETURNED_SQLSTATE** field to the value 02000. In an SQL API application, the **SQLSTATE** variable contains this same value.

- In an SQL API application, the **sqlca.sqlcode** and **SQLCODE** variables contain the value 100.

The database server also sets **SQLSTATE** and **SQLCODE** to these values if the DELETE... WHERE... is a part of a multistatement prepare and the database server returns no rows. ♦

SQLSTATE VALUES When Deleting from a Non-ANSI Database

In a database that is not ANSI compliant, the database server does not return a warning when it finds no matching rows for a WHERE clause in a DELETE statement. The **SQLSTATE** code is 00000 and the **SQLCODE** code is zero (0). However, if the DELETE...WHERE... is a part of a multistatement prepare, and no rows are returned, the database server does issue a warning. It sets **SQLSTATE** to 02000 and **SQLCODE** value to 100.

Related Information

Related Statements: DECLARE, FETCH, GET DIAGNOSTICS, INSERT, OPEN, SELECT, and UPDATE

For discussions of the DELETE statement, SPL routines, statement modification, cursors, and the SQLCODE code, see the *Informix Guide to SQL: Tutorial*.

For information on how to access row and collections with ESQL/C host variables, see the chapter on complex data types in the *Informix ESQL/C Programmer's Manual*.

For a discussion of the GLS aspects of the DELETE statement, see the *Informix Guide to GLS Functionality*.

DESCRIBE

Use the DESCRIBE statement to obtain information about a prepared statement before you execute it.

Use this statement with ESQL/C.

Syntax

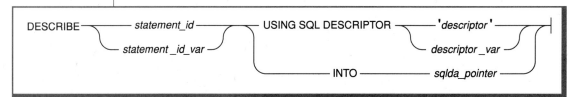

Element	Purpose	Restrictions	Syntax
descriptor	Quoted string that identifies a system-descriptor area	System-descriptor area must already be allocated.	Quoted String, p. 4-260
descriptor_var	Host variable that identifies a system-descriptor area	Variable must contain the name of an allocated system-descriptor area.	Name must conform to language-specific rules for variable names.
sqlda_pointer	Pointer to an **sqlda** structure	You cannot begin an **sqlda** pointer with a dollar sign ($) or a colon (:). You must use an **sqlda** structure if you are using dynamic SQL statements.	See the discussion of **sqlda** structure in the *Informix ESQL/C Programmer's Manual*.
statement_id	Statement identifier for a prepared SQL statement	The statement identifier must be defined in a previous PREPARE statement.	PREPARE, p. 2-579
statement_id_var	Host variable that contains a statement identifier for a prepared SQL statement	The statement identifier must be defined in a previous PREPARE statement. The variable must be a character data type.	Name must conform to language-specific rules for variable names.

Usage

The DESCRIBE statement allows you to determine, at runtime, the following information about a prepared statement:

- The DESCRIBE statement returns the prepared statement type.

- The DESCRIBE statement can determine whether an UPDATE or DELETE statement contains a WHERE clause.

IDS

- For a SELECT, EXECUTE FUNCTION (or EXECUTE PROCEDURE), INSERT, or UPDATE statement, the DESCRIBE statement also returns the number, data types and size of the values, and the name of the column or expression that the query returns. ♦

EDS

- For a SELECT, EXECUTE PROCEDURE, or INSERT statement, the DESCRIBE statement also returns the number, data types and size of the values, and the name of the column or expression that the query returns. ♦

With this information, you can write code to allocate memory to hold retrieved values and display or process them after they are fetched.

Describing the Statement Type

The DESCRIBE statement takes a statement identifier from a PREPARE statement as input. When the DESCRIBE statement executes, the database server sets the value of the SQLCODE field of the **sqlca** to indicate the statement type (that is, the keyword with which the statement begins). If the prepared statement text contains more than one SQL statement, the DESCRIBE statement returns the type of the first statement in the text.

SQLCODE is set to zero to indicate a SELECT statement *without* an INTO TEMP clause. This situation is the most common. For any other SQL statement, SQLCODE is set to a positive integer.

You can test the number against the constant names that are defined. In ESQL/C, the constant names are defined in the **sqlstype.h** header file.

The DESCRIBE statement uses the SQLCODE field differently from any other statement, possibly returning a nonzero value when it executes successfully. You can revise standard error-checking routines to accommodate this behavior, if desired.

Checking for Existence of a WHERE Clause

If the DESCRIBE statement detects that a prepared statement contains an UPDATE or DELETE statement without a WHERE clause, the DESCRIBE statement sets the **sqlca.sqlwarn.sqlwarn4** variable to W.

When you do not specify a WHERE clause in either a DELETE or UPDATE statement, the database server performs the delete or update action on the entire table. Check the **sqlca.sqlwarn.sqlwarn4** variable to avoid unintended global changes to your table.

Describing a Statement with Runtime Parameters

If the prepared statement contains parameters for which the number of parameters or parameter data types is to be supplied at runtime, you can describe these input values. If the prepared statement text includes one of the following statements, the DESCRIBE statement returns a description of each column or expression that is included in the list:

- EXECUTE FUNCTION (or EXECUTE PROCEDURE)
- INSERT
- SELECT (without an INTO TEMP clause)

IDS

- UPDATE

    The **IFX_UPDDESC** environment variable must be set before you can DESCRIBE an UPDATE statement. For more information, see the *Informix Guide to SQL: Reference.* ♦

The description includes the following information:

- The data type of the column, as defined in the table
- The length of the column, in bytes
- The name of the column or expression

If the prepared statement is an INSERT or an UPDATE statement, the DESCRIBE statement returns only the dynamic parameters in that statement, that is, only those parameters that are expressed with a question mark (?).

You can store descriptions in a system-descriptor area or in a pointer to an **sqlda** structure.

Using the USING SQL DESCRIPTOR Clause

Use the USING SQL DESCRIPTOR clause to store the description of a statement list in a previously allocated system-descriptor area.

A system-descriptor area conforms to the X/Open standards. ♦

When you describe one of the previously mentioned statements into a system descriptor area, the database server updates the system-descriptor area in the following ways:

- It sets the COUNT field in the system-descriptor area to the number of values in the statement list. If COUNT is greater than the number of item descriptors in the system-descriptor area, the system returns an error.

- It sets the TYPE, LENGTH, NAME, SCALE, PRECISION, and NULLABLE fields in system-descriptor area.

  If the column has an opaque data type, the database server sets the EXTYPEID, EXTYPENAME, EXTYPELENGTH, EXTYPEOWNER-LENGTH, and EXTYPEOWNERNAME fields of the item descriptor. ♦

- It allocates memory for the DATA field for each item descriptor, based on the TYPE and LENGTH information.

After a DESCRIBE statement is executed, the SCALE and PRECISION fields contain the scale and precision of the column, respectively. If SCALE and PRECISION are set in the SET DESCRIPTOR statement, and TYPE is set to DECIMAL or MONEY, the LENGTH field is modified to adjust for the scale and precision of the decimal value. If TYPE is not set to DECIMAL or MONEY, the values for SCALE and PRECISION are not set, and LENGTH is unaffected.

You can modify the system-descriptor-area information with the SET DESCRIPTOR statement. You must modify the system-descriptor area to show the address in memory that is to receive the described value. You can change the data type to another compatible type. This change causes data conversion to take place when the data is fetched.

You can use the system-descriptor area in statements that support a USING SQL DESCRIPTOR clause, such as EXECUTE, FETCH, OPEN, and PUT.

The following examples show the use of a system descriptor in a DESCRIBE statement. In the first example, the descriptor is a quoted string; in the second example, it is an embedded variable name.

```
main()
{
. . .
EXEC SQL allocate descriptor 'desc1' with max 3;
EXEC SQL prepare curs1 FROM 'select * from tab';
EXEC SQL describe curs1 using sql descriptor 'desc1';
}


EXEC SQL describe curs1 using sql descriptor :desc1var;
```

Using the INTO sqlda pointer Clause

Use the INTO *sqlda_pointer* clause to allocate memory for an **sqlda** structure, and store its address in an **sqlda** pointer. The DESCRIBE statement fills in the allocated memory with descriptive information.

The DESCRIBE statement sets the **sqlda.sqld** field to the number of values in the statement list. The **sqlda** structure also contains an array of data descriptors (**sqlvar** structures), one for each value in the statement list. After a DESCRIBE statement is executed, the **sqlda.sqlvar** structure has the **sqltype**, **sqllen**, and **sqlname** fields set.

IDS

If the column has an opaque data type, DESCRIBE...INTO sets the **sqlxid**, **sqltypename, sqltypelen, sqlownerlen,** and **sqlownername** fields of the item descriptor. ♦

The DESCRIBE statement allocates memory for an **sqlda** pointer once it is declared in a program. However, the application program must designate the storage area of the **sqlda.sqlvar.sqldata** fields.

IDS

Describing a Collection Variable

The DESCRIBE statement can provide information about a collection variable when you use the USING SQL DESCRIPTOR or INTO clause.

You must perform the DESCRIBE statement *after* you open the select or insert cursor. Otherwise, DESCRIBE cannot get information about the collection variable because it is the OPEN...USING statement that specifies the name of the collection variable to use.

The following ESQL/C code fragment shows how to dynamically select the elements of the **:a_set** collection variable into a system-descriptor area called **desc1**:

```
EXEC SQL BEGIN DECLARE SECTION;
        client collection a_set;
        int i, set_count;
        int element_type, element_value;
EXEC SQL END DECLARE SECTION;

EXEC SQL allocate collection :a_set;
EXEC SQL allocate descriptor 'desc1';

EXEC SQL select set_col into :a_set from table1;

EXEC SQL prepare set_id from
        'select * from table(?)'
EXEC SQL declare set_curs cursor for set_id;
EXEC SQL open set_curs using :a_set;
EXEC SQL describe set_id using sql descriptor 'desc1';

do
{
        EXEC SQL fetch set_curs using sql descriptor
'desc1';
        ...
        EXEC SQL get descriptor 'desc1' :set_count =
count;
        for (i = 1; i <= set_count; i++)
        {
            EXEC SQL get descriptor 'desc1' value :i
                :element_type = TYPE;
            switch
            {
                case SQLINTEGER:
                    EXEC SQL get descriptor 'desc1' value
:i
                    :element_value = data;
                ...
            } /* end switch */
        } /* end for */
} while (SQLCODE == 0);

EXEC SQL close set_curs;
EXEC SQL free set_curs;
EXEC SQL free set_id;
EXEC SQL deallocate collection :a_set;
EXEC SQL deallocate descriptor 'desc1';
```

Related Information

Related statements: ALLOCATE DESCRIPTOR, DEALLOCATE DESCRIPTOR, DECLARE, EXECUTE, FETCH, GET DESCRIPTOR, OPEN, PREPARE, PUT, and SET DESCRIPTOR

For a task-oriented discussion of the DESCRIBE statement, see the *Informix Guide to SQL: Tutorial*.

For more information about how to use a system-descriptor area and **sqlda**, refer to the *Informix ESQL/C Programmer's Manual*.

DISCONNECT

Use the DISCONNECT statement to terminate a connection between an application and a database server.

Syntax

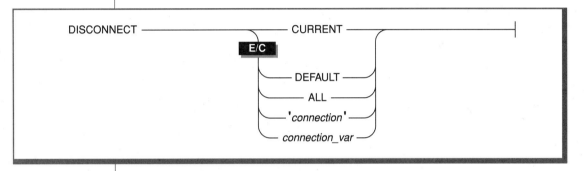

Element	Purpose	Restrictions	Syntax
connection	String that identifies a connection to be terminated	Specified connection must match a connection name assigned by the CONNECT statement.	Quoted String, p. 4-260
connection_var	Host variable that holds the value of connection	Variable must be a fixed-length character data type The specified connection must match a connection name assigned by the CONNECT statement.	Name must conform to language-specific rules for variable names.

Usage

The DISCONNECT statement lets you terminate a connection to a database server. If a database is open, it closes before the connection drops. Even if you made a connection to a specific database only, that connection to the database server is terminated by the DISCONNECT statement.

You cannot use the PREPARE statement for the DISCONNECT statement.

E/C

In ESQL/C, if you disconnect a specific connection with *connection* or *connection_var*, DISCONNECT generates an error if the specified connection is not a current or dormant connection.

A DISCONNECT statement that does not terminate the current connection does not change the context of the current environment (the connection context). ♦

DEFAULT Option

Use the DEFAULT option to identify the default connection for a DISCONNECT statement. The default connection is one of the following connections:

- An explicit default connection (a connection established with the CONNECT TO DEFAULT statement)
- An implicit default connection (any connection made with the DATABASE or CREATE DATABASE statements)

You can use DISCONNECT to disconnect the default connection. For more information, see "DEFAULT Option" on page 2-105 and "The Implicit Connection with DATABASE Statements" on page 2-106.

If the DATABASE statement does not specify a database server, as shown in the following example, the default connection is made to the default database server:

```
EXEC SQL database 'stores_demo';
   .
   .
   .
EXEC SQL disconnect default;
```

If the DATABASE statement specifies a database server, as shown in the following example, the default connection is made to that database server:

```
EXEC SQL database 'stores_demo@mydbsrvr';
   .
   .
   .
EXEC SQL disconnect default;
```

In either case, the DEFAULT option of DISCONNECT disconnects this default connection. See "DEFAULT Option" on page 2-105 and "The Implicit Connection with DATABASE Statements" on page 2-106 for more information about the default database server and implicit connections.

CURRENT Keyword

Use the CURRENT keyword with the DISCONNECT statement as a shorthand form of identifying the current connection. The CURRENT keyword replaces the current connection name. For example, the DISCONNECT statement in the following excerpt terminates the current connection to the database server **mydbsrvr**:

```
CONNECT TO 'stores_demo@mydbsrvr'
.
.
.
DISCONNECT CURRENT
```

When a Transaction is Active

When a transaction is active, the DISCONNECT statement generates an error. The transaction remains active, and the application must explicitly commit it or roll it back. If an application terminates without issuing a DISCONNECT statement (because of a system failure or program error, for example), active transactions are rolled back.

Disconnecting in a Thread-Safe Environment

If you issue the DISCONNECT statement in a thread-safe ESQL/C application, keep in mind that an active connection can only be disconnected from within the thread in which it is active. Therefore, one thread cannot disconnect the active connection of another thread. The DISCONNECT statement generates an error if such an attempt is made.

However, once a connection becomes dormant, any other thread can disconnect this connection unless an ongoing transaction is associated with the dormant connection (the connection was established with the WITH CONCURRENT TRANSACTION clause of CONNECT). If the dormant connection was not established with the WITH CONCURRENT TRANSACTION clause, DISCONNECT generates an error when it tries to disconnect it.

For an explanation of connections in a thread-safe ESQL/C application, see "SET CONNECTION" on page 2-694. ♦

Specifying the ALL Option

Use the keyword ALL to terminate all connections established by the application up to that time. For example, the following DISCONNECT statement disconnects the current connection as well as all dormant connections:

```
DISCONNECT ALL
```

E/C

In ESQL/C, the ALL keyword has the same effect on multithreaded applications that it has on single-threaded applications. Execution of the DISCONNECT ALL statement causes all connections in all threads to be terminated. However, the DISCONNECT ALL statement fails if any of the connections is in use or has an ongoing transaction associated with it. If either of these conditions is true, none of the connections is disconnected. ♦

Related Information

Related statements: CONNECT, DATABASE, and SET CONNECTION

For information on multithreaded applications, see the *Informix ESQL/C Programmer's Manual.*

DROP AGGREGATE

Use the DROP AGGREGATE statement to drop a user-defined aggregate that you created with the CREATE AGGREGATE statement.

Syntax

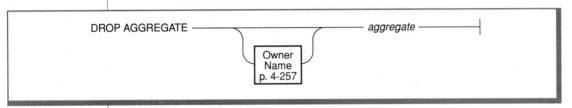

Element	Purpose	Restrictions	Syntax
aggregate	Name of the user-defined aggregate to be dropped	The user-defined aggregate must have been previously created with the CREATE AGGREGATE statement.	Identifier, p. 4-205

Usage

The support functions defined for a user-defined aggregate do not depend on the aggregate for their existence. When you drop a user-defined aggregate, you do not drop the support functions that you defined for the aggregate in the CREATE AGGREGATE statement.

The database server does not track dependency of SQL statements on user-defined aggregates that you use in the statements. For example, you can drop a user-defined aggregate that is used in an SPL routine.

In the following example, the user drops the aggregate named **my_avg**.

```
DROP AGGREGATE my_avg
```

Related Information

Related statements: CREATE AGGREGATE

For information about how to invoke a user-defined aggregate, see the discussion of user-defined aggregates in the Expression segment.

For a description of the **sysaggregates** system catalog table that holds information about user-defined aggregates, see the *Informix Guide to SQL: Reference*.

For a discussion of user-defined aggregates, see *Extending Informix Dynamic Server 2000*.

DROP CAST

Use the DROP CAST statement to remove a previously defined cast from the database.

Syntax

DROP CAST ─────────── (─ *source_type* ─── AS ─── *target_type* ─) ───────────────┤

Element	Purpose	Restrictions	Syntax
source_type	Data type on which the cast operates	The type must exist at the time the cast is dropped.	Data Type, p. 4-53
target_type	Data type that results when the cast is invoked	The type must exist at the time the cast is dropped.	Data Type, p. 4-53

Usage

You must be the owner of the cast or have the DBA privilege to use the DROP CAST statement.

What Happens When You Drop a Cast

When you drop a cast, the cast definition is removed from the database. Once you drop a cast, it cannot be invoked either explicitly or implicitly. Dropping a cast has no effect on the user-defined function associated with the cast. Use the DROP FUNCTION statement to remove the user-defined function from the database.

Warning: *Do not drop the built-in casts, which are owned by user* **informix**. *The database server uses built-in casts for automatic conversions between built-in data types.*

A cast that is defined on a particular data type can also be used on any distinct types created from that type. When you drop the cast, you can no longer invoke it for the distinct types. Dropping a cast that is defined for a distinct type has no effect on casts for its source type.

When you create a distinct type, the database server automatically defines an explicit cast from the distinct type to its source type and another explicit cast from the source type to the distinct type. When you drop the distinct type, the database server automatically drops these two casts.

Related Information

Related statements: CREATE CAST and DROP FUNCTION

For more information about data types, refer to the *Informix Guide to SQL: Reference.*

DROP DATABASE

Use the DROP DATABASE statement to delete an entire database, including all system catalog tables, indexes, and data.

Syntax

```
DROP DATABASE ─────────────────┤ Database Name ├─────────────────┤
                                │   p. 4-47     │
```

Usage

This statement is an extension to ANSI-standard syntax. The ANSI standard does not provide any syntax for the destruction of a database.

You must have the DBA privilege or be user **informix** to run the DROP DATABASE statement successfully. Otherwise, the database server issues an error message and does not drop the database.

You cannot drop the current database or a database that is being used by another user. All the database users must first execute the CLOSE DATABASE statement.

The DROP DATABASE statement cannot appear in a multistatement PREPARE statement.

During a DROP DATABASE operation, the database server acquires a lock on each table in the database and holds the locks until the entire operation is complete. Configure your database server with enough locks to accommodate this fact. For example, if the database to be dropped has 2500 tables, but less than 2500 locks were configured for your server, your DROP DATABASE statement will fail. For further information on how to configure the number of locks available to the database server, see the discussion of the LOCKS configuration parameter in your *Administrator's Reference*.

The following statement drops the **stores_demo** database:

```
DROP DATABASE stores_demo
```

In DB-Access, use this statement with caution. DB-Access does not prompt you to verify that you want to delete the entire database. ♦

You can use a simple database name in a program or host variable, or you can use the full database server and database name. See "Database Name" on page 4-47 for more information. ♦

Related Information

Related statements: CLOSE DATABASE, CREATE DATABASE, and CONNECT

DROP FUNCTION

Use the DROP FUNCTION statement to remove a user-defined function from the database.

Syntax

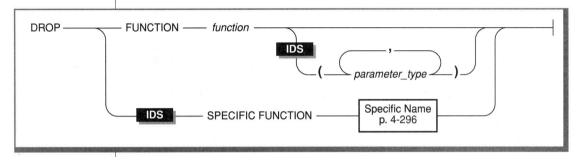

Element	Purpose	Restrictions	Syntax
function	Name of the user-defined function to drop	The function must exist (that is, be registered) in the database.	Database Object Name, p. 4-50
		If the name does not uniquely identify a function, you must enter one or more appropriate values for *parameter_type*.	
parameter_type	Data type of the parameter	The data type (or list of data types) must be the same types (and specified in the same order) as those specified in the CREATE FUNCTION statement when the function was created.	Identifier, p. 4-205

Usage

Dropping a user-defined function removes the text and executable versions of the function from the database.

If you do not know if a UDR is a user-defined function or a user-defined procedure, you can drop the UDR by using the DROP ROUTINE statement.

To use the DROP FUNCTION statement, you must be the owner of the user-defined function or have the DBA privilege.

Examples

If you use parameter data types to identify a user-defined function, they follow the function name, as in the following example:

```
DROP FUNCTION compare(int, int)
```

If you use the specific name for the user-defined function, you must use the keyword SPECIFIC, as in the following example:

```
DROP SPECIFIC FUNCTION compare_point
```

SPL

Dropping SPL Functions

Because you cannot change the text of an SPL function, you must drop it and then re-create it. Make sure that you have a copy of the SPL function text somewhere outside the database, in case you want to re-create it after it is dropped.

You cannot drop an SPL function from within the same SPL function.

Related Information

Related statements: ALTER FUNCTION, CREATE FUNCTION, CREATE FUNCTION FROM, DROP FUNCTION, DROP ROUTINE, and EXECUTE FUNCTION

DROP INDEX

Use the DROP INDEX statement to remove an index.

Syntax

```
DROP INDEX ──────────────────── index ────────────────────┤
```

Element	Purpose	Restrictions	Syntax
index	Name of the index to drop	The index must exist.	Database Object Name, p. 4-50

Usage

You must be the owner of the index or have the DBA privilege to use the DROP INDEX statement.

The following example drops the index **o_num_ix** that **joed** owns. The **stores_demo** database must be the current database.

```
DROP INDEX stores_demo:joed.o_num_ix
```

Effect of DROP INDEX on Constraints

You cannot use the DROP INDEX statement on a column or columns to drop a unique constraint that is created with a CREATE TABLE statement; you must use the ALTER TABLE statement to remove indexes that are created as constraints with a CREATE TABLE or ALTER TABLE statement.

The index is not actually dropped if it is shared by constraints. Instead, it is renamed in the **sysindexes** system catalog table with the following format:

```
[space]<tabid>_<constraint id>
```

In this example, *tabid* and *constraint_id* are from the **systables** and **sysconstraints** system catalog tables, respectively. The **idxname** (index name) column in the **sysconstraints** table is then updated to reflect this change. For example, the renamed index name might be something like: "121_13" (quotes used to show the spaces).

If this index is a unique index with only referential constraints sharing it, the index is downgraded to a duplicate index after it is renamed.

Related Information

Related statements: ALTER TABLE, CREATE INDEX, and CREATE TABLE

For information on the performance characteristics of indexes, see your *Performance Guide*.

DROP OPCLASS

Use the DROP OPCLASS statement to remove an existing operator class from the database.

Syntax

DROP OPCLASS ——————— *opclass* ——————— RESTRICT ——————|

Element	Purpose	Restrictions	Syntax
opclass	Name of the operator class being dropped	The operator class must have been created with the CREATE OPCLASS statement.	Identifier, p. 4-205

Usage

You must be the owner of the operator class or have the DBA privilege to use the DROP OPCLASS statement.

The RESTRICT keyword causes DROP OPCLASS to fail if the database contains indexes defined on the operator class you plan to drop. Therefore, before you drop the operator class, you must use DROP INDEX to drop dependent indexes.

The following DROP OPCLASS statement drops an operator class called **abs_btree_ops**:

```
DROP OPCLASS abs_btree_ops RESTRICT
```

Related Information

Related statement: CREATE OPCLASS

For information on how to create or extend an operator class, see *Extending Informix Dynamic Server 2000*.

DROP PROCEDURE

Use the DROP PROCEDURE statement to remove a user-defined procedure from the database.

Syntax

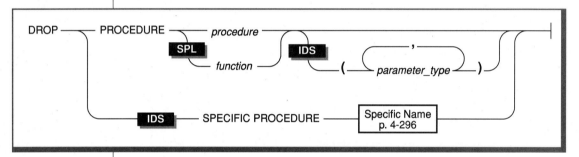

Element	Purpose	Restrictions	Syntax
function	Name of the SPL function to drop	The SPL function must exist (that is, be registered) in the database.	Database Object Name, p.4-50
		(IDS) If the name does not uniquely identify an SPL function, you must enter one or more appropriate values for *parameter_type*.	
parameter_type	The data type of the parameter	The data type (or list of data types) must be the same types (and specified in the same order) as those specified in the CREATE PROCEDURE statement when the procedure was created.	Identifier, p. 4-205
procedure	Name of the user-defined procedure to drop	The procedure must exist (that is, be registered) in the database.	Database Object Name, p.4-50
		(IDS) If the name does not uniquely identify a procedure, you must enter one or more appropriate values for *parameter_type*.	

Usage

Dropping a user-defined procedure removes the text and executable versions of the procedure.

To use the DROP PROCEDURE statement, you must be the owner of the procedure or have the DBA privilege.

EDS

In Enterprise Decision Server, use the DROP PROCEDURE statement to drop any SPL routine. Enterprise Decision Server does not support the DROP FUNCTION statement. ♦

IDS

In Dynamic Server, for backward compatibility, you can use the DROP PROCEDURE statement to drop an SPL function that was created with the CREATE PROCEDURE statement.

If you do not know whether a UDR is a user-defined procedure or a user-defined function, you can use the DROP ROUTINE statement. For more information, see "DROP ROUTINE" on page 2-408. ♦

Examples

If you use parameter data types to identify a user-defined procedure, they follow the procedure name, as in the following example:

```
DROP PROCEDURE compare(int, int)
```

If you use the specific name for the user-defined procedure, you must use the keyword SPECIFIC, as in the following example:

```
DROP SPECIFIC PROCEDURE compare_point
```

SPL

Dropping SPL Procedures

Because you cannot change the text of an SPL procedure, you must drop it and then recreate it. Make sure that you have a copy of the SPL procedure text somewhere outside the database, in case you want to re-create it after it is dropped.

You cannot drop an SPL procedure from within the same SPL procedure.

IDS

For backward compatibility, you can use this statement to drop an SPL function that was created with the CREATE PROCEDURE statement. ♦

Related Information

Related statements: CREATE PROCEDURE, CREATE PROCEDURE FROM, DROP FUNCTION, DROP ROUTINE, and EXECUTE PROCEDURE

DROP ROLE

Use the DROP ROLE statement to remove a previously created role.

Syntax

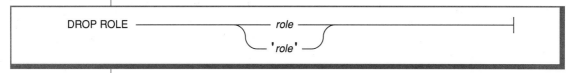

Element	Purpose	Restrictions	Syntax
role	Name of the role to drop	The role name must have been created with the CREATE ROLE statement.	Identifier, p. 4-205
		When a role name is enclosed in quotation marks, the role name is case sensitive.	

Usage

Either the DBA or a user to whom the role was granted with the WITH GRANT OPTION can issue the DROP ROLE statement.

After a role is dropped, the privileges associated with that role, such as table-level privileges or fragment-level privileges, are dropped, and a user cannot grant or enable a role. If a user is using the privileges of a role when the role is dropped, the user automatically loses those privileges.

The following statement drops the role **engineer**:

```
DROP ROLE engineer
```

Related Information

Related statements: CREATE ROLE, GRANT, REVOKE, and SET ROLE

For a discussion of how to use roles, see the *Informix Guide to SQL: Tutorial*.

DROP ROUTINE

Use the DROP ROUTINE statement to remove a user-defined routine (UDR) from the database.

Syntax

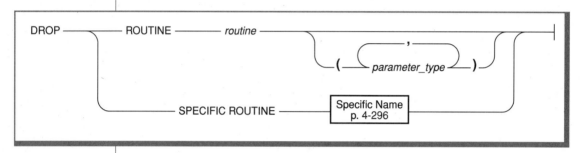

Element	Purpose	Restrictions	Syntax
parameter_type	Data type of the parameter	The data type (or list of data types) must be the same types (and specified in the same order) as those specified when the UDR was created.	Identifier, p. 4-205
routine	Name of the UDR to drop	The UDR must exist (that is, be registered) in the database.	Database Object Name, p. 4-50
		If the name does not uniquely identify a UDR, you must enter one or more appropriate values for *parameter_type*.	

Usage

Dropping a UDR removes the text and executable versions of the UDR from the database.

This statement is useful when you do not know whether a UDR is a user-defined function or a user-defined procedure. When you use this statement, the database server drops the appropriate user-defined function or user-defined procedure.

To use the DROP ROUTINE statement, you must be the owner of the UDR or have the DBA privilege.

Restrictions

When you use this statement, the type of UDR cannot be ambiguous. The UDR that you specify must refer to either a user-defined function or a user-defined procedure. If either of the following conditions exist, the database server returns an error:

- The name (and parameters) that you specify apply to both a user-defined procedure and a user-defined function
- The specific name that you specify applies to both a user-defined function and a user-defined procedure

Examples

If you use parameter data types to identify a UDR, they follow the UDR name, as in the following example:

```
DROP ROUTINE compare(int, int)
```

If you use the specific name for the UDR, you must use the keyword SPECIFIC, as in the following example:

```
DROP SPECIFIC ROUTINE compare_point
```

SPL

Dropping SPL Routines

Because you cannot change the text of an SPL routine, you must drop it and then re-create it. Make sure that you have a copy of the SPL function text somewhere outside the database, in case you want to re-create it after it is dropped.

You cannot drop an SPL routine from within the same SPL routine.

Related Information

Related statements: CREATE FUNCTION, CREATE PROCEDURE, DROP FUNCTION, DROP PROCEDURE, EXECUTE FUNCTION, and EXECUTE PROCEDURE

DROP ROW TYPE

Use the DROP ROW TYPE statement to remove an existing named-row type from the database.

Syntax

```
DROP ROW TYPE ──────────── row_type ──────────── RESTRICT ───────────┤
```

Element	Purpose	Restrictions	Syntax
row_type	Name of the named-row type to be dropped	The type must have been created with the CREATE ROW TYPE statement. The named-row type must already exist. The named-row type cannot be dropped if it is currently used in any columns, tables or inheritance hierarchies.	Data Type, p. 4-53 Identifier, p. 4-205 The named-row type can be of the form *owner.type.*

Usage

You must be the owner of the row type or have the DBA privilege to use the DROP ROW TYPE statement.

You cannot drop a named-row type if the row type name is in use. You cannot drop a named-row type when any of the following conditions are true:

- Any existing tables or columns are using the row type.
- The row type is a supertype in an inheritance hierarchy.
- A view is defined on the row type.

To drop a named-row type column from a table, use ALTER TABLE.

The DROP ROW TYPE statement does *not* drop unnamed-row types.

The Restrict Keyword

The RESTRICT keyword is required with the DROP ROW TYPE statement. RESTRICT causes DROP ROW TYPE to fail if dependencies on that named-row type exist.

The DROP ROW TYPE statement fails and returns an error message if:

- the named-row type is used for an existing table or column.

  Check the **systables** and **syscolumns** system catalog tables to find out whether any tables or types use the named-row type.

- the named-row type is the supertype in an inheritance hierarchy.

  Look in the **sysinherits** system catalog table to see which types have child types.

Example

The following statement drops the row type named **employee_t**:

```
DROP ROW TYPE employee_t RESTRICT
```

Related Information

Related statement: CREATE ROW TYPE

For a description of the system catalog tables, see the *Informix Guide to SQL: Reference*.

For a discussion of named-row types, see the *Informix Guide to SQL: Tutorial*.

DROP SYNONYM

Use the DROP SYNONYM statement to remove a previously defined synonym.

Syntax

DROP SYNONYM ─────────────────── *synonym* ───────────────┤

Element	Purpose	Restrictions	Syntax
synonym	Name of the synonym to drop	The synonym and the table to which the synonym points must exist.	Database Object Name, p. 4-50

Usage

You must be the owner of the synonym or have the DBA privilege to use the DROP SYNONYM statement.

The following statement drops the synonym **nj_cust**, which **cathyg** owns:

```
DROP SYNONYM cathyg.nj_cust
```

If a table is dropped, any synonyms that are in the same database as the table and that refer to the table are also dropped.

If a synonym refers to an external table, and the table is dropped, the synonym remains in place until you explicitly drop it using DROP SYNONYM. You can create another table or synonym in place of the dropped table and give the new database object the name of the dropped table. The old synonym then refers to the new database object. For a complete discussion of synonym chaining, see the CREATE SYNONYM statement.

Related Information

Related statement: CREATE SYNONYM

For a discussion of synonyms, see the *Informix Guide to SQL: Tutorial*.

DROP TABLE

Use the DROP TABLE statement to remove a table, along with its associated indexes and data.

Syntax

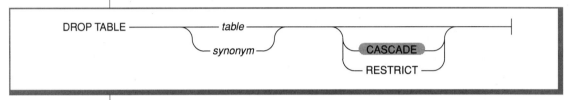

Element	Purpose	Restrictions	Syntax
synonym	Name of the synonym to drop	The synonym and the table to which the synonym points must exist.	Database Object Name, p. 4-50
table	Name of the table to drop	The table must exist.	Database Object Name, p. 4-50

Usage

You must be the owner of the table or have the DBA privilege to use the DROP TABLE statement.

EDS

If you are using Enterprise Decision Server, you cannot drop a table that includes a dependent GK index unless the dependent index is entirely dependent on the affected table. ◆

DB

If you issue a DROP TABLE statement, DB-Access does not prompt you to verify that you want to delete an entire table. ◆

Effects of the DROP TABLE Statement

Use the DROP TABLE statement with caution. When you remove a table, you also delete the data stored in it, the indexes or constraints on the columns (including all the referential constraints placed on its columns), any local synonyms assigned to it, any triggers created for it, and any authorizations you have granted on the table. You also drop all views based on the table and any violations and diagnostics tables associated with the table.

When you drop a table, you do not remove any synonyms for the table that were created in an external database. If you want to remove external synonyms to the dropped table, you must do so manually with the DROP SYNONYM statement.

Specifying CASCADE Mode

The CASCADE mode means that a DROP TABLE statement removes related database objects, including referential constraints built on the table, views defined on the table, and any violations and diagnostics tables associated with the table.

IDS

If the table is the supertable in an inheritance hierarchy, CASCADE drops all of the subtables as well as the supertable. ♦

The CASCADE mode is the default mode of the DROP TABLE statement. You can also specify this mode explicitly with the CASCADE keyword.

Specifying RESTRICT Mode

With the RESTRICT keyword, you can control the success or failure of the drop operation for supertables, for tables that have referential constraints and views defined on them, or for tables that have violations and diagnostics tables associated them. Using the RESTRICT option causes the drop operation to fail and an error message to be returned if any of the following conditions are true:

- Existing referential constraints reference *table name.*
- Existing views are defined on *table name.*
- Any violations and diagnostics tables are associated with table name.

IDS

- The table name is the supertable in an inheritance hierarchy. ♦

IDS

Dropping a Table with Rows That Contain Opaque Data Types

Some opaque data types require special processing when they are deleted. For example, if an opaque data type contains spatial or multi-representational data, it might provide a choice of how to store the data: inside the internal structure or, for very large objects, in a smart large object.

The database server removes opaque types by calling a user-defined support function called **destroy()**. When you execute the DROP TABLE statement on a table whose rows contain an opaque type, the database server automatically invokes the **destroy()** function for the type. The **destroy()** function can perform certain operations on columns of the opaque data type before the table is dropped. For more information about the **destroy()** support function, see *Extending Informix Dynamic Server 2000*.

Tables That Cannot Be Dropped

Observe the following restrictions on the types of tables that you can drop:

- You cannot drop any system catalog tables.
- You cannot drop a table that is not in the current database.
- You cannot drop a violations or diagnostics table. Before you can drop such a table, you must first issue a STOP VIOLATIONS TABLE statement on the base table with which the violations and diagnostics tables are associated.

EDS

- If you are using Enterprise Decision Server, you cannot drop a table that appears in the FROM clause of a GK index. ♦

Examples of Dropping a Table

The following example deletes two tables. Both tables are within the current database and are owned by the current user. Neither table has a violations or diagnostics table associated with it. Neither table has a referential constraint or view defined on it.

```
DROP TABLE customer;
DROP TABLE stores_demo@accntg:joed.state;
```

Related Information

Related statements: CREATE TABLE and DROP DATABASE

For a discussion of the data integrity of tables, see the *Informix Guide to SQL: Tutorial*.

For a discussion of how to create a table, see the *Informix Guide to Database Design and Implementation*.

DROP TRIGGER

Use the DROP TRIGGER statement to remove a trigger definition from a database.

Syntax

DROP TRIGGER ———————————————— *trigger* ————————————————————|

Element	Purpose	Restrictions	Syntax
trigger	Name of the trigger to drop	The trigger must exist.	Identifier, p. 4-205

Usage

You must be the owner of the trigger or have the DBA privilege to drop the trigger.

Dropping a trigger removes the text of the trigger definition and the executable trigger from the database.

The following statement drops the **items_pct** trigger:

```
DROP TRIGGER items_pct
```

If a DROP TRIGGER statement appears inside an SPL routine that is called by a data manipulation statement, the database server returns an error.

Related Information

Related statements: CREATE TRIGGER

DROP TYPE

Use the DROP TYPE statement to remove an existing distinct or opaque data type from the database.

Syntax

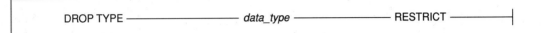

Element	Purpose	Restrictions	Syntax
data_type	Distinct or opaque data type to be removed from the database	The type must have been created with the CREATE DISTINCT TYPE or CREATE OPAQUE TYPE statement. Do not remove built-in types.	Data Type, p. 4-53 The distinct type or opaque type can be of the form *owner.type*.

Usage

To drop a distinct or opaque type with the DROP TYPE statement, you must be the owner of the data type or have the DBA privilege.

When you use the DROP TYPE statement, you remove the type definition from the database (in the **sysxtdtypes** system catalog table). In general, this statement does not remove any definitions for casts or support functions associated with that data type.

Important: *When you drop a distinct type, the database server automatically drops the two explicit casts between the distinct type and the type on which it is based.*

You cannot drop a distinct or opaque type if the database contains any casts, columns, or user-defined functions whose definitions reference the type.

The following statement drops the **new_type** type:

```
DROP TYPE new_type RESTRICT
```

Related Information

Related statements: CREATE DISTINCT TYPE, CREATE OPAQUE TYPE, CREATE ROW TYPE, DROP ROW TYPE, and CREATE TABLE

DROP VIEW

Use the DROP VIEW statement to remove a view from a database.

Syntax

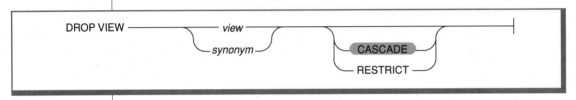

Element	Purpose	Restrictions	Syntax
synonym	Name of the synonym to drop	The synonym and the view to which the synonym points must exist.	Database Object Name, p. 4-50
view	Name of the view to drop	The view must exist.	Database Object Name, p. 4-50

Usage

You must be the owner of the view or have the DBA privilege to drop the view.

When you drop a view or its synonym, you also drop all views that were defined in terms of that view. You can also specify this default condition with the CASCADE keyword.

When you use the RESTRICT keyword in the DROP VIEW statement, the drop operation fails if any existing views are defined on *view*, which would be abandoned in the drop operation.

You can query the **sysdepend** system catalog table to determine which views, if any, depend on another view.

The following statement drops the view that is named **cust1**:

```
DROP VIEW cust1
```

Related Information

Related statements: CREATE VIEW and DROP TABLE

For a discussion of views, see the *Informix Guide to SQL: Tutorial*.

EXECUTE

Use the EXECUTE statement to run a previously prepared statement or set of statements.

Use this statement with ESQL/C.

Syntax

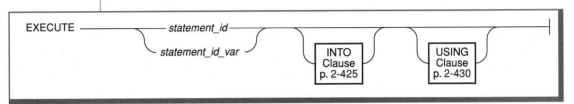

Element	Purpose	Restrictions	Syntax
statement_id	Identifier for a prepared SQL statement	You must have defined the statement identifier in a previous PREPARE statement.	PREPARE, p. 2-579
		After you release the database server resources (using a FREE statement), you cannot use the statement identifier with a DECLARE cursor or with the EXECUTE statement until you prepare the statement again.	
statement_id_var	Host variable that identifies an SQL statement	You must have defined the host variable in a previous PREPARE statement	PREPARE, p. 2-579
		The host variable must be a character data type.	

Usage

The EXECUTE statement passes a prepared SQL statement to the database server for execution. The following example shows an EXECUTE statement within an ESQL/C program:

```
EXEC SQL prepare del_1 from
    'delete from customer
        where customer_num = 119';
EXEC SQL execute del_1;
```

Once prepared, an SQL statement can be executed as often as needed.

If the statement contained question mark (?) placeholders, you use the USING clause to provide specific values for them before execution. For more information, see the "USING Clause" on page 2-430.

You can execute any prepared statement except those in the following list:

■ A prepared SELECT statement that returns more than one row

When you use a prepared SELECT statement to return multiple rows of data, you must use a cursor to retrieve the data rows. As an alternative, you can EXECUTE a prepared SELECT INTO TEMP statement to achieve the same result.

For more information on cursors, see "DECLARE" on page 2-349.

■ A prepared EXECUTE FUNCTION (or EXECUTE PROCEDURE) statement for an SPL function that returns more than one row

When you prepare an EXECUTE FUNCTION (or EXECUTE PROCEDURE) statement for an SPL function that returns multiple rows, you must use a cursor to retrieve the data rows.

For more information on how to execute a SELECT or an EXECUTE FUNCTION (or EXECUTE PROCEDURE) statement, see "PREPARE" on page 2-579.

If you create or drop a trigger after you prepared a triggering INSERT, DELETE, or UPDATE statement, the prepared statement returns an error when you execute it.

Scope of Statement Identifiers

A program can consist of one or more source-code files. By default, the scope of a statement identifier is global to the program, so a statement identifier created in one file can be referenced from another file.

In a multiple-file program, if you want to limit the scope of a statement identifier to the file in which it is executed, you can preprocess all the files with the **-local** command-line option.

The sqlca Record and EXECUTE

Following an EXECUTE statement, the **sqlca** can reflect two results:

- The **sqlca** can reflect an error within the EXECUTE statement. For example, when an UPDATE ...WHERE... statement within a prepared statement processes zero rows, the database server sets **sqlca** to 100.

- The **sqlca** can reflect the success or failure of the executed statement.

Error Conditions with EXECUTE

If a prepared statement fails to access any rows, the database server returns zero (0). In a multistatement prepare, if any statement in the following list fails to access rows, the database server returns SQLNOTFOUND (100):

- INSERT INTO *table* SELECT...WHERE...
- SELECT INTO TEMP...WHERE...
- DELETE...WHERE
- UPDATE...WHERE...

ANSI

In an ANSI-compliant database, if you prepare and execute any of the statements in the preceding list, and no rows are returned, the database server returns SQLNOTFOUND (100). ♦

INTO Clause

Use the INTO clause to save the return values of the following SQL statements:

- A prepared singleton SELECT statement that returns only one row of column values for the columns in the select list
- A prepared EXECUTE FUNCTION (or EXECUTE PROCEDURE) statement for an SPL function that returns only one group of values

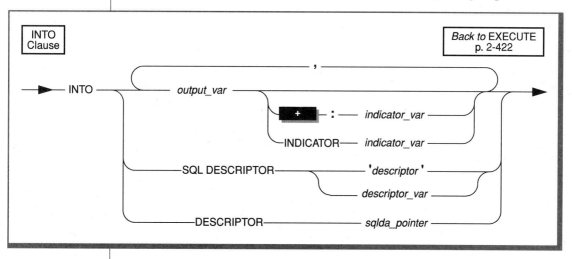

Element	Purpose	Restrictions	Syntax
descriptor	Quoted string that identifies a system-descriptor area	System-descriptor area must already be allocated.	Quoted String, p. 4-260
descriptor_var	Host variable that identifies the system-descriptor area	System-descriptor area must already be allocated.	Quoted String, p. 4-260

Element	Purpose	Restrictions	Syntax
indicator_var	Host variable that receives a return code if null data is placed in the corresponding output _var	Variable cannot be DATETIME or INTERVAL data type.	Variable name must conform to language-specific rules for variable names.
output_var	Host variable whose contents replace a question-mark (?) placeholder in a prepared statement	Variable must be a character data type.	Variable name must conform to language-specific rules for variable names.
sqlda_pointer	Pointer to an **sqlda** structure that defines the data type and memory location of values that correspond to the question-mark (?) placeholder in a prepared statement	You cannot begin *sqlda_pointer* with a dollar sign ($) or a colon (:). You must use an **sqlda** structure if you are using dynamic SQL statements.	DESCRIBE, p. 2-382

The INTO clause provides a concise and efficient alternative to more complicated and lengthy syntax. In addition, by placing values into variables that can be displayed, the INTO clause simplifies and enhances your ability to retrieve and display data values. For example, if you use the INTO clause, you do not have to use a cursor to retrieve values from a table.

You can store the returned values into output variables, output SQL descriptors, or output **sqlda** pointers.

Restrictions with the INTO Clause

If you execute a prepared SELECT statement that returns more than one row of data or a prepared EXECUTE FUNCTION (or EXECUTE PROCEDURE) statement for an SPL function that returns more than one group of return values, you receive an error message. In addition, if you prepare and declare a statement, and then attempt to execute that statement, you receive an error message.

You cannot select a null value from a table column and place that value into an output variable. If you know in advance that a table column contains a null value, after you select the data, check the indicator variable that is associated with the column to determine if the value is null.

The following list describes the procedure for how to use the INTO clause with the EXECUTE statement:

1. Declare the output variables that the EXECUTE statement uses.

2. Use the PREPARE statement to prepare your SELECT statement or to prepare your EXECUTE FUNCTION (or EXECUTE PROCEDURE) statement.

3. Use the EXECUTE statement, with the INTO clause, to execute your SELECT statement or to execute your EXECUTE FUNCTION (or EXECUTE PROCEDURE) statement.

Storage Location for Returned Values

You can specify any of the following items to replace the question-mark placeholders in a statement before you execute it:

■ A host variable name (if the number and data type of the question marks are known at compile time)

■ A system descriptor that identifies a system

■ A descriptor that is a pointer to an **sqlda** structure

Saving Values In Host or Program Variables

If you know the number of return values to be supplied at runtime and their data types, you can define the values that the SELECT or EXECUTE FUNCTION (or EXECUTE PROCEDURE) statement returns as host variables in your program. You use these host variables with the INTO keyword, followed by the names of the variables. These variables are matched with the return values in a one-to-one correspondence, from left to right.

You must supply one variable name for each value that the SELECT or EXECUTE FUNCTION (or EXECUTE PROCEDURE) returns. The data type of each variable must be compatible with the corresponding return value of the prepared statement.

Saving Values in a System-Descriptor Area

If you do not know the number of return values to be supplied at runtime or their data types, you can associate output values with a system-descriptor area. A system-descriptor area describes the data type and memory location of one or more values.

X/O

A system-descriptor area conforms to the X/Open standards. ♦

To specify a system-descriptor area as the location of output values, use the INTO SQL DESCRIPTOR clause of the EXECUTE statement. Each time that the EXECUTE statement is run, the values that the system-descriptor area describes are stored in the system-descriptor area.

The following example shows how to use the system-descriptor area to execute prepared statements in Informix ESQL/C:

```
EXEC SQL allocate descriptor 'desc1';
...
sprintf(sel_stmt, "%s %s %s",
    "select fname, lname from customer",
    "where customer_num =",
    cust_num);
EXEC SQL prepare sel1 from :sel_stmt;
EXEC SQL execute sel1 into sql descriptor 'desc1';
```

The COUNT field corresponds to the number of values that the prepared statement returns. The value of COUNT must be less than or equal to the value of the occurrences that were specified when the system-descriptor area was allocated with the ALLOCATE DESCRIPTOR statement. You can obtain the value of a field with the GET DESCRIPTOR statement and set the value with the SET DESCRIPTOR statement.

For further information, refer to the discussion of the system-descriptor area in the *Informix ESQL/C Programmer's Manual*.

E/C

Saving Values in an sqlda Structure

If you do not know the number of output values to be returned at runtime or their data types, you can associate output values from an **sqlda** structure. An **sqlda** structure lists the data type and memory location of one or more return values. To specify an **sqlda** structure as the location of return values, use the INTO DESCRIPTOR clause of the EXECUTE statement. Each time the EXECUTE statement is run, the database server places the returns values that the **sqlda** structure describes into the **sqlda** structure.

The following example shows how to use an **sqlda** structure to execute a prepared statement in Informix ESQL/C:

```
struct sqlda *pointer2;
...
sprintf(sel_stmt, "%s %s %s",
    "select fname, lname from customer",
    "where customer_num =",
    cust_num);
EXEC SQL prepare sel1 from :sel_stmt;
EXEC SQL describe sel1 into pointer2;
EXEC SQL execute sel1 into descriptor pointer2;
```

The **sqld** value specifies the number of output values that are described in occurrences of **sqlvar**. This number must correspond to the number of values that the SELECT or EXECUTE FUNCTION (or EXECUTE PROCEDURE) statement returns.

For more information, refer to the **sqlda** discussion in the *Informix ESQL/C Programmer's Manual*.

Examples

The following example shows how to use the INTO clause with an EXECUTE statement in ESQL/C:

```
EXEC SQL prepare sel1 from 'select fname, lname from customer
    where customer_num =123';
EXEC SQL execute sel1 into :fname, :lname using :cust_num;
```

The following example shows how to use the INTO clause to return multiple rows of data:

```
EXEC SQL BEGIN DECLARE SECTION;
int customer_num =100;
char fname[25];
EXEC SQL END DECLARE SECTION;

EXEC SQL prepare sel1 from 'select fname from customer
    where customer_num=?';
for ( ;customer_num < 200; customer_num++)
    {
    EXEC SQL execute sel1 into :fname using customer_num;
    printf("Customer number is %d\n", customer_num);
    printf("Customer first name is %s\n\n", fname);
    }
```

USING Clause

Use the USING clause to specify the values that are to replace question-mark (?) placeholders in the prepared statement. Providing values in the EXECUTE statement that replace the question-mark placeholders in the prepared statement is sometimes called *parameterizing* the prepared statement.

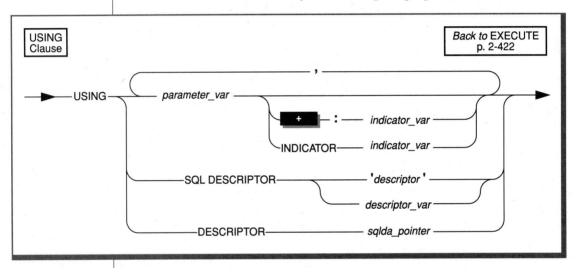

Element	Purpose	Restrictions	Syntax
descriptor	Quoted string that identifies a system-descriptor area	System-descriptor area must already be allocated	Quoted String, p. 4-260
		Make sure surrounding quotation marks are single.	
descriptor_var	Host variable that identifies a system-descriptor area	System-descriptor area must already be allocated	Name must conform to language-specific rules for variable names.

(1 of 2)

Element	Purpose	Restrictions	Syntax
indicator_var	Host variable that receives a return code if null data is placed in the corresponding parameter_var This variable receives truncation information if truncation occurs.	Variable cannot be DATETIME or INTERVAL data type	Name must conform to language-specific rules for variable names.
parameter_var	Host variable whose contents replace a question-mark (?) placeholder in a prepared statement	Variable must be a character data type	Name must conform to language-specific rules for variable names.
sqlda_pointer	Pointer to an **sqlda** structure that defines the data type and memory location of values that correspond to the question-mark (?) placeholder in a prepared statement	You cannot begin *sqlda_pointer* with a dollar sign ($) or a colon (:). You must use an **sqlda** structure if you are using dynamic SQL statements.	DESCRIBE, p. 2-382

(2 of 2)

If you know the number of parameters to be supplied at runtime and their data types, you can define the parameters that are needed by the statement as host variables in your program.

If you do not know the number of parameters to be supplied at runtime or their data types, you can associate input values from a system-descriptor area or an **sqlda** structure. Both of these descriptor structures describe the data type and memory location of one or more values to replace question-mark (?) placeholders.

Supplying Parameters Through Host or Program Variables

You pass parameters to the database server by opening the cursor with the USING keyword, followed by the names of the variables. These variables are matched with prepared statement question-mark (?) placeholders in a one-to-one correspondence, from left to right. You must supply one storage parameter variable for each placeholder. The data type of each variable must be compatible with the corresponding value that the prepared statement requires.

The following example executes the prepared UPDATE statement in ESQL/C:

```
stcopy ("update orders set order_date = ? where po_num = ?", stm1);
EXEC SQL prepare statement_1 from :stm1;
EXEC SQL execute statement_1 using :order_date, :po_num;
```

Supplying Parameters Through a System Descriptor

You can create a system-descriptor area that describes the data type and memory location of one or more values and then specify the descriptor in the USING SQL DESCRIPTOR clause of the EXECUTE statement.

Each time that the EXECUTE statement is run, the values that the system-descriptor area describes are used to replace question-mark (?) placeholders in the PREPARE statement.

The COUNT field corresponds to the number of dynamic parameters in the prepared statement. The value of COUNT must be less than or equal to the number of item descriptors that were specified when the system-descriptor area was allocated with the ALLOCATE DESCRIPTOR statement.

The following example shows how to use system descriptors to execute a prepared statement in ESQL/C:

```
EXEC SQL execute prep_stmt using sql descriptor 'descl';
```

E/C

Supplying Parameters Through an sqlda Structure

You can specify the **sqlda** pointer in the USING DESCRIPTOR clause of the EXECUTE statement.

Each time the EXECUTE statement is run, the values that the descriptor structure describes are used to replace question-mark (?) placeholders in the PREPARE statement.

The **sqld** value specifies the number of input values that are described in occurrences of **sqlvar**. This number must correspond to the number of dynamic parameters in the prepared statement.

The following example shows how to use an **sqlda** structure to execute a prepared statement in ESQL/C:

```
EXEC SQL execute prep_stmt using descriptor pointer2
```

Related Information

Related statements: ALLOCATE DESCRIPTOR, DEALLOCATE DESCRIPTOR, DECLARE, EXECUTE IMMEDIATE, FETCH, GET DESCRIPTOR, PREPARE, PUT, and SET DESCRIPTOR

For a task-oriented discussion of the EXECUTE statement, see the *Informix Guide to SQL: Tutorial*.

For more information about concepts relating to the EXECUTE statement, refer to the *Informix ESQL/C Programmer's Manual*.

EXECUTE FUNCTION

Use the EXECUTE FUNCTION statement to execute a user-defined function.

Syntax

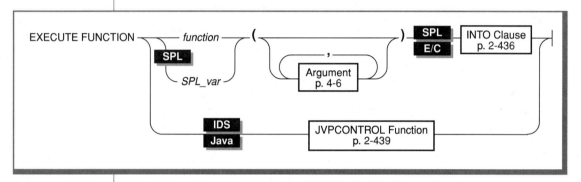

Element	Purpose	Restrictions	Syntax
function	Name of the user-defined function to execute	The function must exist.	Database Object Name, p. 4-50
SPL_var	Variable created with the DEFINE statement that contains the name of an SPL routine to be executed	The SPL variable must be CHAR, VARCHAR, NCHAR, or NVARCHAR data type. The name assigned to *SPL_var* must be non-null and the name of an existing SPL function.	Identifier, p. 4-205

Usage

The EXECUTE FUNCTION statement invokes the named user-defined function, specifies its arguments, and determines where the results are returned.

An external function returns exactly one value.

An SPL function can return one or more values.

You cannot use EXECUTE FUNCTION to execute any type of user-defined procedure. Instead, use the EXECUTE PROCEDURE statement to execute procedures.

Privileges

You must have the Execute privilege on the user-defined function.

If a user-defined function has a companion function, any user who executes the function must have the Execute privilege on both the function and its companion. For example, if a function has a negator function, any user who executes the function must have the Execute privilege on both the function and its negator.

For more information, see "GRANT" on page 2-500.

How EXECUTE FUNCTION Works

For a user-defined function to be executed with the EXECUTE FUNCTION statement, the following conditions must exist:

- The qualified function name or the function signature (the function name with its parameter list) must be unique within the name space or database.

- The function must exist.

- The function must not have any OUT parameters.

If an EXECUTE FUNCTION statement specifies fewer arguments than the called user-defined function expects, the unspecified arguments are said to be *missing*. Missing arguments are initialized to their corresponding parameter default values, if you specified default values. The syntax of specifying default values for parameters is described in "Routine Parameter List" on page 4-286.

The EXECUTE FUNCTION statement returns an error under the following conditions:

- It specifies more arguments than the called user-defined function expects.
- One or more arguments are missing and do not have default values.

  In this case, the arguments are initialized to the value of UNDEFINED.
- The fully qualified function name or the signature is not unique.
- No function with the specified name or signature that you specify is found.
- You use it to try to execute a user-defined procedure.

INTO Clause

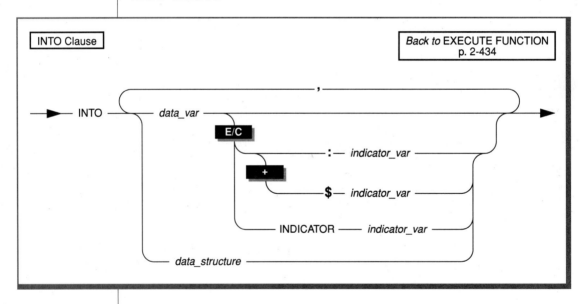

Element	Purpose	Restrictions	Syntax
data_structure	Structure that was declared as a host variable	The individual elements of the structure must be matched appropriately to the data type of values being selected.	Name must conform to language-specific rules for variable names.
data_var	Variable that receives the value returned by a user-defined function	If you issue this statement within an ESQL/C program, *data_var* must be a host variable.	Name must conform to language-specific rules for variable names.
		If you issue this statement within an SPL routine, *data_var* must be an SPL variable.	For the syntax of SPL variables, see Identifier, p. 4-205.
		If you issue this statement within a CREATE TRIGGER statement, *data_var* must be column names within the triggering table or another table.	For the syntax of column names, see Identifier, p. 4-205.
indicator_var	Program variable that receives a return code if null data is placed in the corresponding data_var	This parameter is optional, but you should use an indicator variable if the possibility exists that the value of the corresponding data_var is null.	Name must conform to language-specific rules for variable names.

You must specify an INTO clause with EXECUTE FUNCTION to name the variables that receive the values that a user-defined function returns. If the function returns more than one value, the values are returned into the list of variables in the order in which you specify them.

If the EXECUTE FUNCTION statement stands alone (that is, it is not part of a DECLARE statement and does not use the INTO clause), it must execute a noncursor function. A noncursor function returns only one row of values. The following example shows a SELECT statement in Informix ESQL/C:

```
EXEC SQL execute function cust_num(fname, lname,
company_name)
    into :c_num;
```

E/C

INTO Clause with Indicator Variables

You should use an indicator variable if the possibility exists that data returned from the user-defined function statement is null. See the *Informix ESQL/C Programmer's Manual* for more information about indicator variables.

INTO Clause with Cursors

If the EXECUTE FUNCTION statement executes a user-defined function that returns more than one row of values, it must execute a cursor function. A cursor function can return one or more rows of values and must be associated with a function cursor to execute.

If the SPL function returns more than one row or a collection data type, you must access the rows or collection elements with a cursor.

Ext

To return more than one row of values, an external function must be defined as an iterator function. For more information on how to write iterator functions, see the *DataBlade API Programmer's Manual.* ♦

SPL

To return more than one row of values, an SPL function must include the WITH RESUME keywords in its RETURN statement. For more information on how to write SPL functions, see the *Informix Guide to SQL: Tutorial.* ♦

E/C

In an Informix ESQL/C program, use the DECLARE statement to declare the function cursor and the FETCH statement to fetch the rows individually from the function cursor. You can put the INTO clause in the FETCH statement rather than in the EXECUTE FUNCTION statement, but you cannot put it in both. The following Informix ESQL/C code examples show different ways you can use the INTO clause:

- Using the INTO clause in the EXECUTE FUNCTION statement

```
EXEC SQL declare f_curs cursor for
    execute function get_orders(customer_num)
    into :ord_num, :ord_date;
EXEC SQL open f_curs;
while (SQLCODE == 0)
    EXEC SQL fetch f_curs;
EXEC SQL close f_curs;
```

- Using the INTO clause in the FETCH statement

```
EXEC SQL declare f_curs cursor for
    execute function get_orders(customer_num);
EXEC SQL open f_curs;
while (SQLCODE == 0)
    EXEC SQL fetch f_curs into :ord_num, :ord_date;
EXEC SQL close f_curs;
```

♦

SPL

In an SPL routine, if a SELECT returns more than one row, you must use the FOREACH statement to access the rows individually. The INTO clause of the SELECT statement holds the fetched values. For more information, see "FOREACH" on page 3-30. ♦

E/C

Alternatives to Preparing an *EXECUTE FUNCTION...INTO* Statement

You cannot prepare an EXECUTE FUNCTION statement that has an INTO clause. You can prepare the EXECUTE FUNCTION without the INTO clause, declare a function cursor for the prepared statement, open the cursor, and then use the FETCH statement with an INTO clause to fetch the return values into the program variables.

Alternatively, you can declare a cursor for the EXECUTE FUNCTION statement without first preparing the statement and include the INTO clause in the EXECUTE FUNCTION when you declare the cursor. Then open the cursor, and fetch the return values from the cursor without using the INTO clause of the FETCH statement.

SPL

Dynamic Routine-Name Specification of SPL Functions

Dynamic routine-name specification simplifies the writing of an SPL function that calls another SPL routine whose name is not known until runtime. To specify the name of an SPL routine in the EXECUTE FUNCTION statement, instead of listing the explicit name of an SPL routine, you can use an SPL variable to hold the routine name.

For more information about how to execute SPL functions dynamically, see the *Informix Guide to SQL: Tutorial*.

Java

The jvpcontrol Function

The **jvpcontrol()** function is a built-in iterative function that you use to obtain information about a Java VP class.

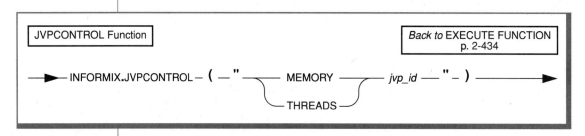

Element	Purpose	Restrictions	Syntax
jvp_id	Name of the Java virtual processor (JVP) class for which you want information	The named Java virtual processor class must exist.	Identifier, p. 4-205

You must associate this function with the equivalent of a cursor in the Java language.

Using the Memory Keyword

When you specify the MEMORY keyword, the **jvpcontrol** function returns the memory usage on the JVP class that you specify. The following example requests information about the memory usage of the JVP class named **4**.

```
EXECUTE FUNCTION INFORMIX.JVPCONTROL ("MEMORY 4");
```

Using the Threads Keyword

When you specify the THREADS keyword, the **jvpcontrol** function returns a list of the threads running on the JVP class that you specify. The following example requests information about the threads running on the JVP class named **4**.

```
EXECUTE FUNCTION INFORMIX.JVPCONTROL ("THREADS 4");
```

Related Information

Related statements: CALL, CREATE FUNCTION, CREATE FUNCTION FROM, DROP FUNCTION, DROP ROUTINE, EXECUTE PROCEDURE, and FOREACH

EXECUTE IMMEDIATE

Use the EXECUTE IMMEDIATE statement to perform the functions of the PREPARE, EXECUTE, and FREE statements.

Use this statement with ESQL/C.

Syntax

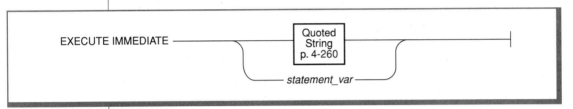

Element	Purpose	Restrictions	Syntax
statement_var	Host variable whose value is a character string that consists of one or more SQL statements	The host variable must have been defined within the program.	Name must conform to language-specific rules for variable names.
		The variable must be character data type.	
		For additional restrictions, see "EXECUTE IMMEDIATE and Restricted Statements" on page 2-442 and "Restrictions on Allowed Statements" on page 2-443.	

Usage

The EXECUTE IMMEDIATE statement makes it easy to execute dynamically a single simple SQL statement that is constructed during program execution. For example, you can obtain the name of a database from program input, construct the DATABASE statement as a program variable, and then use EXECUTE IMMEDIATE to execute the statement, which opens the database.

The quoted string is a character string that includes one or more SQL statements. The string, or the contents of *statement_var*, is parsed and executed if correct; then all data structures and memory resources are released immediately. In the usual method of dynamic execution, these functions are distributed among the PREPARE, EXECUTE, and FREE statements.

The maximum length of an EXECUTE IMMEDIATE statement is 64 kilobytes.

EXECUTE IMMEDIATE and Restricted Statements

You cannot use the EXECUTE IMMEDIATE statement to execute the following SQL statements. Although the EXECUTE PROCEDURE statement appears on this list, the restriction applies only to EXECUTE PROCEDURE statements that return values.

CLOSE	OPEN
CONNECT	OUTPUT
DECLARE	PREPARE
DISCONNECT	SELECT
EXECUTE	SET AUTOFREE
EXECUTE FUNCTION	SET CONNECTION
EXECUTE PROCEDURE	SET DEFERRED_PREPARE
FETCH	SET DESCRIPTOR
GET DESCRIPTOR	WHENEVER
GET DIAGNOSTICS	

In addition, you cannot use the EXECUTE IMMEDIATE statement to execute the following statements in text that contains multiple statements that are separated by semicolons.

CLOSE DATABASE	DROP DATABASE
CREATE DATABASE	SELECT
DATABASE	(except SELECT INTO TEMP)

Use a PREPARE and either a cursor or the EXECUTE statement to execute a dynamically constructed SELECT statement.

Restrictions on Allowed Statements

The following restrictions apply to the statement that is contained in the quoted string or in the statement variable:

- The statement cannot contain a host-language comment.

- Names of host-language variables are not recognized as such in prepared text. The only identifiers that you can use are names defined in the database, such as table names and columns.

- The statement cannot reference a host variable list or a descriptor; it must not contain any question-mark (?) placeholders, which are allowed with a PREPARE statement.

- The text must not include any embedded SQL statement prefix, such as the dollar sign ($) or the keywords EXEC SQL. Although it is not required, the SQL statement terminator (;) can be included in the statement text.

- A SELECT or INSERT statement cannot contain a Collection Derived Table clause. EXECUTE IMMEDIATE cannot process input host variables, which are required for a collection variable. Use the EXECUTE statement or a cursor to process prepared accesses to collection variables.

IDS

Examples of the EXECUTE IMMEDIATE Statement

The following examples show EXECUTE IMMEDIATE statements in ESQL/C. Both examples use host variables that contain a CREATE DATABASE statement. The first example uses the SQL statement terminator (;) inside the quoted string.

```
sprintf(cdb_text1, "create database %s;", usr_db_id);
EXEC SQL execute immediate :cdb_text;

sprintf(cdb_text2, "create database %s", usr_db_id);
EXEC SQL execute immediate :cdb_text;
```

Related Information

Related statements: EXECUTE, FREE, and PREPARE

For a discussion of quick execution, see the *Informix Guide to SQL: Tutorial*.

EXECUTE PROCEDURE

Use the EXECUTE PROCEDURE statement to execute a user-defined procedure.

Syntax

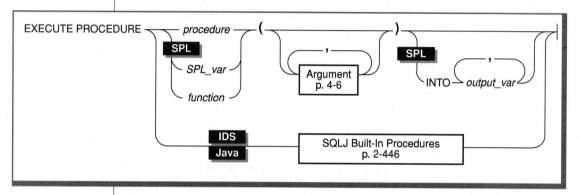

Element	Purpose	Restrictions	Syntax
function	Name of the SPL function to execute	The function must exist.	Database Object Name, p. 4-50
output_var	Host variable or program variable that receives the value returned by a user-defined function	If you issue this statement within a CREATE TRIGGER statement, the output_var must be column names within the triggering table or another table.	Name must conform to language-specific rules for variable names.
			For the syntax of SPL variables, see Identifier, p. 4-205.
			For the syntax of column names, see Identifier, p. 4-205.

Element	Purpose	Restrictions	Syntax
procedure	Name of the user-defined procedure to execute	The procedure must exist.	Database Object Name, p. 4-50
SPL_var	Variable created with the DEFINE statement that contains the name of an SPL routine to be executed	The SPL variable must be CHAR, VARCHAR, NCHAR, or NVARCHAR data type.	Identifier, p.4-205
		The name assigned to *SPL_var* must be non-null and the name of an existing SPL routine.	

Usage

The EXECUTE PROCEDURE statement invokes the named user-defined procedure and specifies its arguments.

IDS

In Dynamic Server, for backward compatibility, you can use the EXECUTE PROCEDURE statement to execute an SPL function that was created with the CREATE PROCEDURE statement. ♦

EDS

In Enterprise Decision Server, use the EXECUTE PROCEDURE statement to execute any SPL routine. Enterprise Decision Server does not support the EXECUTE FUNCTION statement. ♦

E/C

In ESQL/C, if the EXECUTE PROCEDURE statement returns more than one row, it must be enclosed within an SPL FOREACH loop or accessed through a cursor. ♦

SPL

Using the INTO Clause

Use the INTO clause to specify where to store the values that the SPL function returns.

If an SPL function returns more than one value, the values are returned into the list of variables in the order in which you specify them. If an SPL function returns more than one row or a collection data type, you must access the rows or collection elements with a cursor.

You cannot prepare an EXECUTE PROCEDURE statement that has an INTO clause. For more information, see "Alternatives to Preparing an EXECUTE FUNCTION...INTO Statement" on page 2-439.

SPL

Dynamic Routine-Name Specification of SPL Procedures

Dynamic routine-name specification simplifies the writing of an SPL routine that calls another SPL routine whose name is not known until runtime. To specify the name of an SPL routine in the EXECUTE PROCEDURE statement, instead of listing the explicit name of an SPL routine, you can use an SPL variable to hold the routine name.

If the SPL variable names an SPL routine that returns a value (an SPL function), include the INTO clause of EXECUTE PROCEDURE to specify a *receiving variable* (or variables) to hold the value (or values) that the SPL function returns.

For more information on how to execute SPL procedures dynamically, see the *Informix Guide to SQL: Tutorial*. ◆

Causes of Errors

The EXECUTE PROCEDURE statement returns an error under the following conditions:

- It has more arguments than the called procedure expects.
- One or more arguments are missing and do not have default values. In this case the arguments are initialized to the value of UNDEFINED.
- The fully qualified procedure name or the signature is not unique.
- No procedure with the specified name or signature is found.

IDS

Java

SQLJ Driver Built-In Procedures

Use the SQLJ Driver built-in procedures for one of the following tasks:

- to install, replace, or remove a set of Java classes
- to specify a path for Java class resolution for Java classes that are included in a Jar file
- to map or remove the mapping between a user-defined type and the Java type to which it corresponds

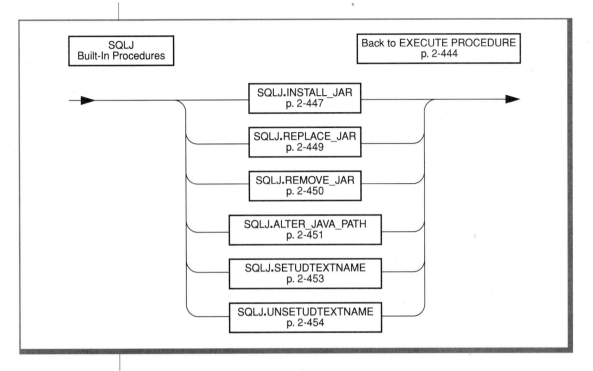

The SQLJ built-in procedures are stored in the **sysprocedures** catalog table. They are grouped under the **sqlj** schema.

Tip: *For any Java static method, the first built-in procedure that you execute must be the **install_jar()** procedure. You must install the jar file before you can create a UDR or map a user-defined data type to a Java type. Similarly, you cannot use any of the other SQLJ built-in procedures until you have used **install_jar()**.*

sqlj.install_jar

Use the **install_jar()** procedure to install a Java jar file in the current database and assign it a jar identifier.

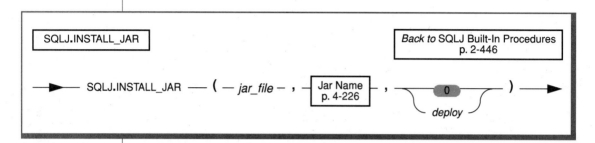

Element	Purpose	Restrictions	Syntax
deploy	Integer that causes the procedure to search for deployment descriptor files in the jar file	None.	Literal Number, p. 4-237
jar_file	URL of the jar file that contains the UDR written in Java	The maximum length of the URL is 255 bytes.	Quoted String, p. 4-260

For example, consider a Java class **Chemistry** which contains the following static method **explosiveReaction()**:

```
public static int explosiveReaction(int ingredient);
```

Suppose that the **Chemistry** class resides in the following jar file on the server computer:

```
/students/data/Courses.jar
```

You can install all classes in the **Courses.jar** jar file in the current database with the following call to the **install_jar()** procedure:

```
EXECUTE PROCEDURE
    sqlj.install_jar("file://students/data/Courses.jar",
    "course_jar")
```

The **install_jar()** procedure assigns the jar ID, **course_jar**, to the **Courses.jar** file that it has installed in the current database.

After you define jar ID in the database, you can use that jar ID when you create and execute a UDR written in Java.

Using Deployment Descriptor Files

When you specify a nonzero number for the third argument, the database server searches through any included deployment descriptor files. For example, you might want to included descriptor files that include SQL statements to register and grant privileges on UDRs in the jar file.

sqlj.replace_jar

Use the **replace_jar()** procedure to replace a previously installed jar file with a new version. When you use this syntax, you provide only the new jar file and assign it to the jar ID for which you want to replace the file.

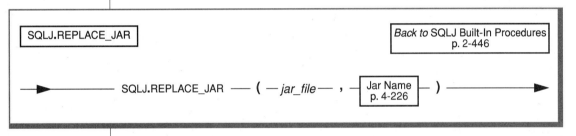

SQLJ.REPLACE_JAR

Back to SQLJ Built-In Procedures p. 2-446

SQLJ.REPLACE_JAR — (— jar_file — , — Jar Name p. 4-226 —) —

Element	Purpose	Restrictions	Syntax
jar_file	URL of the jar file that contains the UDR written in Java	The maximum length of the URL is 255 bytes.	Quoted String, p. 4-260

If you attempt to replace a jar file that is referenced by one or more UDRs, the database server generates an error. You must drop the referencing UDRs before replacing the jar file.

For example, the following call replaces the **Courses.jar** file, which had previously been installed for the **course_jar** identifier, with the **Subjects.jar** file:

```
EXECUTE PROCEDURE
    sqlj.replace_jar("file://students/data/Subjects.jar",
    "course_jar")
```

Before you replace the **Course.jar** file, you must drop the user-defined function **sql_explosive_reaction()** with the DROP FUNCTION (or DROP ROUTINE) statement.

sqlj.remove_jar

Use the **remove_jar()** procedure to remove a previously installed jar file from the current database.

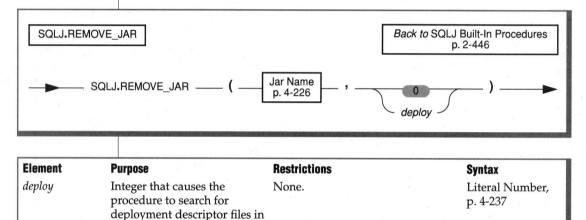

SQLJ.REMOVE_JAR			
		Back to SQLJ Built-In Procedures p. 2-446	

SQLJ.REMOVE_JAR ── (── | Jar Name p. 4-226 | , ── 0 / *deploy* ──) ──►

Element	Purpose	Restrictions	Syntax
deploy	Integer that causes the procedure to search for deployment descriptor files in the jar file	None.	Literal Number, p. 4-237

If you attempt to remove a jar file that is referenced by one or more UDRs, the database server generates an error. You must drop the referencing UDRs before replacing the jar file.

For example, the following SQL statements remove the jar file associated with the **course_jar** jar id:

```
DROP FUNCTION sql_explosive_reaction;
EXECUTE PROCEDURE sqlj.remove_jar("course_jar")
```

Using Deployment Descriptor Files

When you specify a nonzero number for the second argument, the database server searches through any included deployment descriptor files. For example, you might want to include descriptor files that include SQL statements that revoke privileges on the UDRs in the associated jar file and to drop them from the database.

sqlj.alter_java_path

Use the **alter_java_path()** procedure to specify the *jar-file path* to use when the routine manager resolves related Java classes for the jar file of a UDR written in Java.

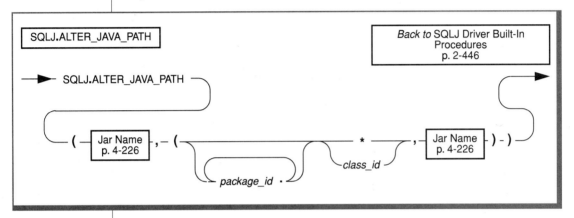

Element	Purpose	Restrictions	Syntax
class_id	Name of the Java class that contains the method to implement the UDR	The Java class must exist in the jar file that *jar_id* identifies. The fully qualified identifier of *package_id.class_id* must not exceed 255 bytes.	Name must conform to language-specific rules for Java identifiers.
package_id	Name of the package that contains the Java class	The fully qualified identifier of *package_id.class_id* must not exceed 255 bytes.	Name must conform to language-specific rules for Java identifiers.

The jar IDs that you specify, (the jar ID for which you are altering the jar-file path and the resolution jar ID) must have been installed with the **sqlj.install_jar** procedure.

When you invoke a UDR written in Java, the routine manager attempts to load the Java class in which the UDR resides. At this time, it must resolve the references that this Java class makes to other Java classes. The three types of such class references are:

1. References to Java classes that the JVPCLASSPATH configuration parameter specifies (such as Java system classes like **java.util.Vector**)
2. References to classes which are in the same jar file as the UDR
3. References to classes which are outside the jar file that contains the UDR

The routine manager implicitly resolves classes of type 1 and 2 in the preceding list. However, to resolve type 3 references, the routine manager examines all the jar files in the jar-file path that the latest call to **alter_java_path()** has specified. The routine manager throws an exception if it cannot resolve a class reference.

The routine manager checks the jar-file path for class references *after* it performs the implicit type 1 and type 2 resolutions. If you want a Java class to be loaded from the jar file that the jar-file path specifies, make sure the Java class is *not* present in the JVPCLASSPATH configuration parameter. Otherwise, the system loader picks up that Java class first, which might result in a different class being loaded than what you expect.

Suppose that the **install_jar()** procedure and the CREATE FUNCTION statement have been executed as described in preceding sections. The following SQL statement invokes **sql_explosive_reaction()** function in the **course_jar** jar file:

```
EXECUTE PROCEDURE alter_java_path("course_jar",
    "(professor/*, prof_jar)");
EXECUTE FUNCTION sql_explosive_reaction(10000)
```

The routine manager attempts to load the class **Chemistry**. It uses the path that the call to **alter_java_path()** specifies to resolve any class references. Therefore, it checks the classes that are in the **professor** package of the jar file that **prof_jar** identifies.

sqlj.setUDTExtName

Use the **setUDTExtName()** procedure to define the mapping between a user-defined data type and a Java class.

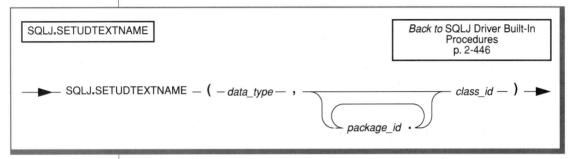

Element	Purpose	Restrictions	Syntax
class_id	Name of the Java class that contains the Java data type	The fully qualified identifier of package_id.class_id must not exceed 255 bytes.	Name must conform to language-specific rules for Java identifiers.
data_type	Name of user-defined type for which you want to create a mapping	You must have registered the type of one of the following statements: ■ CREATE DISTINCT TYPE ■ CREATE OPAQUE TYPE ■ CREATE ROW TYPE The name must not exceed 255 bytes.	Identifier, p. 4-205
package_id	Name of the package that contains the Java class	The fully qualified identifier of *package_id.class_id* must not exceed 255 bytes.	Name must conform to language-specific rules for Java identifiers.

To look up the Java class for a user-defined data type, the database server searches in the jar-file path, which the **alter_java_path()** procedure has specified. For more information on the jar-file path, see"sqlj.alter_java_path" on page 2-451.

On the client side, the driver looks into the **CLASSPATH** path on the client environment before it asks the database server for the name of the Java class.

The **setUDTExtName** procedure is an extension to the *SQLJ:SQL Routines using the Java Programming Language* specification.

sqlj.unsetUDTExtName

Use the **remove_jar()** procedure to remove the mapping from a user-defined data type to a Java class.

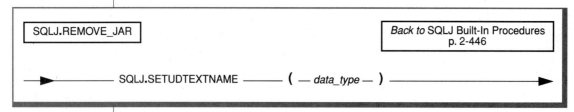

| SQLJ.REMOVE_JAR | | Back to SQLJ Built-In Procedures p. 2-446 |

SQLJ.SETUDTEXTNAME (— data_type —)

Element	Purpose	Restrictions	Syntax
data_type	Name of user-defined type for which you want to remove the mapping	The data type must exist.	Identifier, p. 4-205

This procedure removes the SQL-to-Java mapping, and consequently removes any cached copy of the Java class from database server shared memory.

The **unsetUDTExtName** procedure is an extension to the *SQLJ:SQL Routines using the Java Programming Language* specification.

Related Information

Related statements: CREATE FUNCTION, CREATE PROCEDURE, EXECUTE FUNCTION, GRANT, CALL, FOREACH, and LET

E/C

FETCH

Use the FETCH statement to move a cursor to a new row in the active set and to retrieve the row values from memory.

Use this statement with ESQL/C.

Syntax

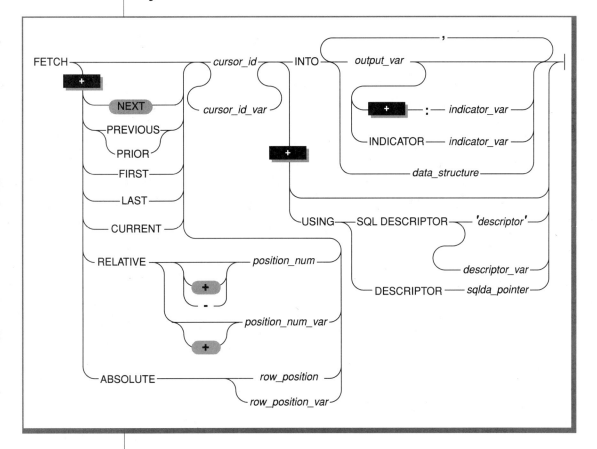

Element	Purpose	Restrictions	Syntax
cursor_id	Name of a cursor from which rows are to be retrieved	The cursor must have been created in an earlier DECLARE statement and opened in an earlier OPEN statement.	Identifier, p. 4-205
cursor_id_var	Host variable name that holds the value of *cursor_id*	The identified cursor must have been created in an earlier DECLARE statement and opened in an earlier OPEN statement.	Name must conform to language-specific rules for variable names.
		The host variable must be a character data type.	
data_structure	Structure that was declared as a host variable	The individual members of the data structure must be matched appropriately to the type of values that are being fetched.	Name must conform to language-specific rules for data-structure names.
		If you use a program array, you must list both the array name and a specific element of the array in *data_structure*.	
descriptor	String that identifies the system-descriptor area into which you fetch the contents of a row	The system-descriptor area must have been allocated with the ALLOCATE DESCRIPTOR statement.	Quoted String, p. 4-260
descriptor_var	Host variable name that holds the value of *descriptor*	The identified system-descriptor area must have been allocated with the ALLOCATE DESCRIPTOR statement.	Name must conform to language-specific rules for variable names.

(1 of 2)

Element	Purpose	Restrictions	Syntax
indicator_var	Host variable that receives a return code if null data is placed in the corresponding output_var	This parameter is optional, but use an indicator variable if the possibility exists that the value of output_var is null.	Name must conform to language-specific rules for variable names.
		If you specify the indicator variable without the INDICATOR keyword, you cannot put a space between *output_var* and *indicator_var*.	
		For information about rules for placing a prefix before the *indicator_var*, see the *Informix ESQL/C Programmer's Manual*.	
		The host variable cannot be a DATETIME or INTERVAL data type.	
output_var	Host variable that receives one value from the fetched row	The host variable must have a data type that is appropriate for the value that is fetched into it.	Name must conform to language-specific rules for variable names.
position_num	Integer value that gives the relative position of the desired row in relation to the current row in the active set of rows	A value of 0 fetches the current row.	Literal Number, p. 4-237
position_num_var	Host variable that contains position_num	A value of 0 fetches the current row.	Name must conform to language-specific rules for variable names.
row_position	Integer value that gives the position of the desired row in the active set of rows	The value of row_ position must be 1 or higher.	Literal Number, p. 4-237
row_position_var	Host variable that contains row_ position	The value of *row_ position* must be 1 or higher.	Name must conform to language-specific rules for variable names.
sqlda_pointer	Pointer to an **sqlda** structure that receives the values from the fetched row	You cannot begin an **sqlda** pointer with a dollar sign ($) or a colon (:).	See the discussion of **sqlda** structure in the *Informix ESQL/C Programmer's Manual*.

(2 of 2)

Usage

The way the database server creates and stores members of the active set and then fetches rows from the active set differs depending on whether the cursor is a sequential cursor or a scroll cursor.

X/O

In X/Open mode, if a cursor-direction value (such as NEXT or RELATIVE) is specified, a warning message is issued, indicating that the statement does not conform to X/Open standards. ♦

FETCH with a Sequential Cursor

A sequential cursor can fetch only the next row in sequence from the active set. The sole cursor-position option that is available to a sequential cursor is the default value, NEXT. A sequential cursor can read through a table only once each time it is opened. The following ESQL/C example illustrates the FETCH statement with a sequential cursor:

```
EXEC SQL FETCH seq_curs into :fname, :lname;
EXEC SQL FETCH NEXT seq_curs into ;fname, :lname;
```

When the program opens a sequential cursor, the database server processes the query to the point of locating or constructing the first row of data. The goal of the database server is to tie up as few resources as possible.

Because the sequential cursor can retrieve only the next row, the database server can frequently create the active set one row at a time. On each FETCH operation, the database server returns the contents of the current row and locates the next row. This one-row-at-a-time strategy is not possible if the database server must create the entire active set to determine which row is the first row (as would be the case if the SELECT statement included an ORDER BY clause).

FETCH with a Scroll Cursor

A scroll cursor can fetch any row in the active set, either by specifying an absolute row position or a relative offset. Use the following cursor-position options to specify a particular row that you want to retrieve.

Cursor-Position Option	Purpose
NEXT	Retrieves the next row in the active set
PREVIOUS	Retrieves the previous row in the active set
PRIOR	Retrieves the previous row in the active set. (Synonymous with PREVIOUS.)
FIRST	Retrieves the first row in the active set
LAST	Retrieves the last row in the active set
CURRENT	Retrieves the current row in the active set (the same row as returned by the preceding FETCH statement from the scroll cursor)
RELATIVE	Retrieves the *n*th row, relative to the current cursor position in the active set, where *position_num* (or *position_num_var*) supplies *n*
	A negative value indicates the nth row prior to the current cursor position. If *position_num* is 0, the current row is fetched.
ABSOLUTE	Retrieves the *n*th row in the active set, where *row_position* (or *row_position_var*) supplies *n*
	Absolute row positions are numbered from 1.

The following ESQL/C examples illustrate the FETCH statement with a scroll cursor:

```
EXEC SQL fetch previous q_curs into :orders;

EXEC SQL fetch last q_curs into :orders;

EXEC SQL fetch relative -10 q_curs into :orders;

printf("Which row? ");
scanf("%d",row_num);
EXEC SQL fetch absolute :row_num q_curs into :orders;
```

Tip: *Do not confuse row-position values with rowid values. A rowid value is based on the position of a row in its table and remains valid until the table is rebuilt. A row-position value (a value introduced by the ABSOLUTE keyword) is based on the position of the row in the active set of the cursor; the next time the cursor is opened, different rows might be selected.*

How the Database Server Stores Rows

The database server must retain all the rows in the active set for a scroll cursor until the cursor closes, because it cannot be sure which row the program asks for next. When a scroll cursor opens, the database server implements the active set as a temporary table although it might not fill this table immediately.

The first time a row is fetched, the database server copies it into the temporary table as well as returning it to the program. When a row is fetched for the second time, it can be taken from the temporary table. This scheme uses the fewest resources in case the program abandons the query before it fetches all the rows. Rows that are never fetched are usually not created or are saved in a temporary table.

Specifying Where Values Go in Memory

Each value from the select list of the query or the output of the executed user-defined function must be returned into a memory location. You can specify these destinations in one of the following ways:

- Use the INTO clause of a SELECT statement.
- Use the INTO clause of an EXECUTE FUNCTION (or EXECUTE PROCEDURE) statement.
- Use the INTO clause of a FETCH statement.
- Use a system-descriptor area.
- Use an **sqlda** structure.

Using the INTO Clause of SELECT, EXECUTE FUNCTION, or EXECUTE PROCEDURE

When you associate a SELECT, or EXECUTE FUNCTION (OR EXECUTE PROCEDURE) statement with the cursor (a function cursor), the statement can contain an INTO clause to specify the program variables that are to receive the return values.

You can use this method only when you write the SELECT or EXECUTE FUNCTION (or EXECUTE PROCEDURE) statement as part of the cursor declaration (see "DECLARE" on page 2-349).

In this case, the FETCH statement cannot contain an INTO clause.

The following example uses the INTO clause of the SELECT statement to specify program variables in ESQL/C:

```
EXEC SQL declare ord_date cursor for
    select order_num, order_date, po_num
        into :o_num, :o_date, :o_po;
EXEC SQL open ord_date;
EXEC SQL fetch next ord_date;
```

Use an indicator variable if the returned data might be null.

If you prepare a SELECT statement, the SELECT *cannot* include the INTO clause so you must use the INTO clause of the FETCH statement.

When you create a SELECT statement dynamically, you cannot use an INTO clause because you cannot name host variables in a prepared statement. If you are certain of the number and data type of values in the select list, you can use an INTO clause in the FETCH statement. However, if user input generated the query, you might not be certain of the number and data type of values that are being selected. In this case, you must use a system descriptor or **sqlda** pointer structure

Using the INTO Clause of FETCH

When the SELECT or EXECUTE FUNCTION (or EXECUTE PROCEDURE) statement omits the INTO clause, you must specify the destination of the data whenever a row is fetched. For example, to dynamically execute a SELECT or EXECUTE FUNCTION (or EXECUTE PROCEDURE) statement, the SELECT or EXECUTE FUNCTION (or EXECUTE PROCEDURE) cannot include its INTO clause in the PREPARE statement. Therefore, the FETCH statement must include an INTO clause to retrieve data into a set of variables. This method lets you store different rows in different memory locations.

In the following ESQL/C example, a series of complete rows is fetched into a program array. The INTO clause of each FETCH statement specifies an array element as well as the array name.

```
EXEC SQL BEGIN DECLARE SECTION;
    char wanted_state[2];
    short int row_count = 0;
    struct customer_t{
    {
        int     c_no;
        char    fname[15];
        char    lname[15];
    } cust_rec[100];
EXEC SQL END DECLARE SECTION;

main()
{
    EXEC SQL connect to'stores_demo';
    printf("Enter 2-letter state code: ");
    scanf ("%s", wanted_state);

    EXEC SQL declare cust cursor for
        select * from customer where state = :wanted_state;

    EXEC SQL open cust;

    EXEC SQL fetch cust into :cust_rec[row_count];
    while (SQLCODE == 0)
    {
        printf("\n%s %s", cust_rec[row_count].fname,
            cust_rec[row_count].lname);

        row_count++;
        EXEC SQL fetch cust into :cust_rec[row_count];
    }
    printf ("\n");
    EXEC SQL close cust;
    EXEC SQL free cust;
}
```

You can fetch into a program-array element only by using an INTO clause in the FETCH statement. When you are declaring a cursor, do not refer to an array element within the SQL statement.

Tip: *If you are certain of the number and data type of values in the select list, you can use an INTO clause in the FETCH statement.*

Using a System-Descriptor Area

You can use a system-descriptor area to store output values when you do not know the number of return values or their data types that a SELECT or EXECUTE FUNCTION (or EXECUTE PROCEDURE) statement returns at runtime. A system-descriptor area describes the data type and memory location of one or more return values.

The keywords USING SQL DESCRIPTOR introduce the name of the system-descriptor area into which you fetch the contents of a row or the return values of a user-defined function. You can then use the GET DESCRIPTOR statement to transfer the values that the FETCH statement returns from the system-descriptor area into host variables.

The following example shows a valid FETCH...USING SQL DESCRIPTOR statement:

```
EXEC SQL allocate descriptor 'desc';
...
EXEC SQL declare selcurs cursor for
    select * from customer where state = 'CA';
EXEC SQL describe selcurs using sql descriptor 'desc';
EXEC SQL open selcurs;
while (1)
    {
    EXEC SQL fetch selcurs using sql descriptor 'desc';
    ...
```

You can also use an **sqlda** structure to dynamically supply parameters. However, a system-descriptor area conforms to the X/Open standards.

Using an sqlda Structure

You can use a pointer to an **sqlda** structure that stores the output values when you do not know the number of return values or their data types that a SELECT or EXECUTE FUNCTION (or EXECUTE PROCEDURE) statement returns at runtime. This structure contains data descriptors that specify the data type and memory location for one selected value. The keywords USING DESCRIPTOR introduce the name of the **sqlda** pointer structure.

Tip: *If you are certain of the number and data type of values in the select list, you can use an INTO clause in the FETCH statement. For more information, see "Using the INTO Clause of FETCH" on page 2-462.*

To specify an **sqlda** structure as the location of parameters, follow these steps:

1. Declare an **sqlda** pointer variable.
2. Use the DESCRIBE statement to fill in the **sqlda** structure.
3. Allocate memory to hold the data values.
4. Use the USING DESCRIPTOR clause of the FETCH statement to name the **sqlda** structure as the location into which you fetch the return values.

The following example shows a FETCH USING DESCRIPTOR statement:

```
struct sqlda *sqlda_ptr;
...
EXEC SQL declare selcurs2 cursor for
    select * from customer where state = 'CA';
EXEC SQL describe selcurs2 into sqlda_ptr;
...
EXEC SQL open selcurs2;
while (1)
    {
    EXEC SQL fetch selcurs2 using descriptor sqlda_ptr;
    ...
```

The **sqld** value specifies the number of output values that are described in occurrences of the **sqlvar** structures of the **sqlda** structure. This number must correspond to the number of return values from the prepared statement.

Fetching a Row for Update

The FETCH statement does not ordinarily lock a row that is fetched. Thus, another process can modify (update or delete) the fetched row immediately after your program receives it. A fetched row is locked in the following cases:

- When you set the isolation level to Repeatable Read, each row you fetch is locked with a read lock to keep it from changing until the cursor closes or the current transaction ends. Other programs can also read the locked rows.

- When you set the isolation level to Cursor Stability, the current row is locked.

- In an ANSI-compliant database, an isolation level of Repeatable Read is the default; you can set it to something else. ♦

- When you are fetching through an update cursor (one that is declared FOR UPDATE), each row you fetch is locked with a promotable lock. Other programs can read the locked row, but no other program can place a promotable or write lock; therefore, the row is unchanged if another user tries to modify it using the WHERE CURRENT OF clause of an UPDATE or DELETE statement.

When you modify a row, the lock is upgraded to a write lock and remains until the cursor is closed or the transaction ends. If you do not modify the row, the behavior of the database server depends on the isolation level you have set. The database server releases the lock on an unchanged row as soon as another row is fetched, unless you are using Repeatable Read isolation (see "SET ISOLATION" on page 2-736).

Important: *You can hold locks on additional rows even when Repeatable Read isolation is not in use or is unavailable. Update the row with unchanged data to hold it locked while your program is reading other rows. You must evaluate the effect of this technique on performance in the context of your application, and you must be aware of the increased potential for deadlock.*

When you use explicit transactions, be sure that a row is both fetched and modified within a single transaction; that is, both the FETCH statement and the subsequent UPDATE or DELETE statement must fall between a BEGIN WORK statement and the next COMMIT WORK statement.

IDS

Fetching From a Collection Cursor

A collection cursor allows you to access the individual elements of an ESQL/C collection variable. To declare a collection cursor, use the DECLARE statement and include the Collection Derived Table segment in the SELECT statement that you associate with the cursor. Once you open the collection cursor with the OPEN statement, the cursor allows you to access the elements of the collection variable.

To fetch elements, one at a time, from a collection cursor, use the FETCH statement and the INTO clause. The FETCH statement identifies the collection cursor that is associated with the collection variable. The INTO clause identifies the host variable that holds the element value that is fetched from the collection cursor. The data type of the host variable in the INTO clause must match the element type of the collection.

Suppose you have a table called **children** with the following structure:

```
CREATE TABLE children
(
    age         SMALLINT,
    name        VARCHAR(30),
    fav_colors  SET(VARCHAR(20) NOT NULL),
)
```

The following ESQL/C code fragment shows how to fetch elements from the **child_colors** collection variable:

```
EXEC SQL BEGIN DECLARE SECTION;
    client collection child_colors;
    varchar one_favorite[21];
    char child_name[31] = "marybeth";
EXEC SQL END DECLARE SECTION;

EXEC SQL allocate collection :child_colors;

/* Get structure of fav_colors column for untyped
 * child_colors collection variable */
EXEC SQL select fav_colors into :child_colors
    from children
    where name = :child_name;
/* Declare select cursor for child_colors collection
 * variable */
EXEC SQL declare colors_curs cursor for
    select * from table(:child_colors);
EXEC SQL open colors_curs;

do
{
    EXEC SQL fetch colors_curs into :one_favorite;
    ...
} while (SQLCODE == 0)

EXEC SQL close colors_curs;
EXEC SQL free colors_curs;
EXEC SQL deallocate collection :child_colors;
```

Once you have fetched a collection element, you can modify the element with the UPDATE or DELETE statements. For more information, see the UPDATE and DELETE statements in this manual. You can also insert new elements into the collection variable with an INSERT statement. For more information, see the INSERT statement.

Checking the Result of FETCH

You can use the **SQLSTATE** variable to check the result of each FETCH statement. The database server sets the **SQLSTATE** variable after each SQL statement. If a row is returned successfully, the **SQLSTATE** variable contains the value 00000. If no row is found, the database server sets the **SQLSTATE** code to 02000, which indicates no data found, and the current row is unchanged. The following conditions set the **SQLSTATE** code to 02000, indicating no data found:

- The active set contains no rows.

- You issue a FETCH NEXT statement when the cursor points to the last row in the active set or points past it.

- You issue a FETCH PRIOR or FETCH PREVIOUS statement when the cursor points to the first row in the active set.

- You issue a FETCH RELATIVE *n* statement when no *n*th row exists in the active set.

- You issue a FETCH ABSOLUTE *n* statement when no *n*th row exists in the active set.

The database server copies the **SQLSTATE** code from the **RETURNED_SQLSTATE** field of the system-diagnostics area. You can use the GET DIAGNOSTICS statement to examine the **RETURNED_SQLSTATE** field directly. The system-diagnostics area can also contain additional error information.

You can also use SQLCODE of **sqlca** to determine the same results.

Related Information

Related statements: ALLOCATE DESCRIPTOR, CLOSE, DEALLOCATE DESCRIPTOR, DECLARE, DESCRIBE, GET DESCRIPTOR, OPEN, PREPARE, SET DEFERRED_PREPARE, and SET DESCRIPTOR

For a task-oriented discussion of the FETCH statement, see the *Informix Guide to SQL: Tutorial*.

For more information about concepts relating to the FETCH statement, see the *Informix ESQL/C Programmer's Manual*.

FLUSH

Use the FLUSH statement to force rows that a PUT statement buffered to be written to the database.

Use this statement with ESQL/C.

Syntax

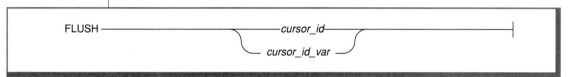

Element	Purpose	Restrictions	Syntax
cursor_id	Name of a cursor	A DECLARE statement must have previously created the cursor.	Identifier, p. 4-205
cursor_id_var	Host variable that holds the value of cursor_id	Host variable must be a character data type. A DECLARE statement must have previously created the cursor.	Name must conform to language-specific rules for variable names.

Usage

The PUT statement adds a row to a buffer, and the buffer is written to the database when it is full. Use the FLUSH statement to force the insertion when the buffer is not full.

If the program terminates without closing the cursor, the buffer is left unflushed. Rows placed into the buffer since the last flush are lost. Do not expect the end of the program to close the cursor and flush the buffer automatically.

The following example shows a FLUSH statement:

```
FLUSH icurs
```

Error Checking FLUSH Statements

The **sqlca** structure contains information on the success of each FLUSH statement and the number of rows that are inserted successfully. The result of each FLUSH statement is contained in the fields of the **sqlca**: **sqlca.sqlcode**, SQLCODE and **sqlca.sqlerrd[2]**.

When you use data buffering with an insert cursor, you do not discover errors until the buffer is flushed. For example, an input value that is incompatible with the data type of the column for which it is intended is discovered only when the buffer is flushed. When an error is discovered, rows in the buffer that are located after the error are *not* inserted; they are lost from memory.

The **SQLCODE** field is set either to an error code or to zero (0) if no error occurs. The third element of the **sqlerrd** array is set to the number of rows that are successfully inserted into the database:

- If a block of rows is successfully inserted into the database, **SQLCODE** is set to zero (0) and **sqlerrd** to the count of rows.

- If an error occurs while the FLUSH statement is inserting a block of rows, **SQLCODE** shows which error, and **sqlerrd** contains the number of rows that were successfully inserted. (Uninserted rows are discarded from the buffer.)

Tip: *When you encounter an* **SQLCODE** *error, a corresponding* **SQLSTATE** *error value also exists. For information about how to get the message text, check the GET DIAGNOSTICS statement.*

Counting Total and Pending Rows

To count the number of rows actually inserted into the database as well as the number not yet inserted, perform the following steps:

1. Prepare two integer variables, for example, **total** and **pending**.
2. When the cursor opens, set both variables to 0.
3. Each time a PUT statement executes, increment both **total** and **pending**.
4. Whenever a FLUSH statement executes or the cursor is closed, subtract the third field of the SQLERRD array from **pending**.

Related Information

Related statements: CLOSE, DECLARE, OPEN, and PREPARE

For a task-oriented discussion of FLUSH, see the *Informix Guide to SQL: Tutorial*.

For information about the **sqlca** structure, see the *Informix ESQL/C Programmer's Manual*.

FREE

Use the FREE statement to release resources that are allocated to a prepared statement or to a cursor.

Use this statement with ESQL/C.

Syntax

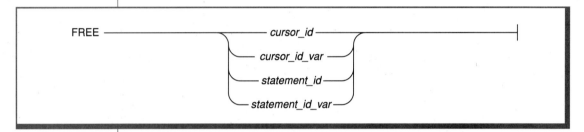

Element	Purpose	Restrictions	Syntax
cursor_id	Name of a cursor	A DECLARE statement must have previously created the cursor.	Identifier, p. 4-205
cursor_id_var	Host variable that holds the value of cursor_id	Variable must be a character data type. Cursor must have been previously created by a DECLARE statement.	Name must conform to language-specific rules for variable names.
statement_id	String that identifies an SQL statement	The statement identifier must be defined in a previous PREPARE statement.	PREPARE, p. 2-579
		After you release the database-server resources, you cannot use the statement identifier with a DECLARE cursor or with the EXECUTE statement until you prepare the statement again.	
statement_id_var	Host variable that identifies an SQL statement	The statement identifier must be defined in a previous PREPARE statement.	PREPARE, p. 2-579
		The host variable must be a character data type.	

Usage

The FREE statement releases the resources that the database server and application-development tool allocated for a prepared statement or a declared cursor.

Freeing a Statement

If you prepared a statement (but did not declare a cursor for it), FREE *statement_id* (or *statement_id_var*) releases the resources in both the application development tool and the database server.

If you declared a cursor for a prepared statement, FREE *statement_id* (or *statement_id_var*) releases only the resources in the application development tool; the cursor can still be used. The resources in the database server are released only when you free the cursor.

After you free a statement, you cannot execute it or declare a cursor for it until you prepare it again.

The following ESQL/C example shows the sequence of statements that is used to free an implicitly prepared statement:

```
EXEC SQL prepare sel_stmt from 'select * from orders';
  .
  .
  .
EXEC SQL free sel_stmt;
```

The following ESQL/C example shows the sequence of statements that are used to release the resources of an explicitly prepared statement. The first FREE statement in this example frees the cursor. The second FREE statement in this example frees the prepared statement.

```
sprintf(demoselect, "%s %s",
    "select * from customer ",
    "where customer_num between 100 and 200");
EXEC SQL prepare sel_stmt from :demoselect;
EXEC SQL declare sel_curs cursor for sel_stmt;
EXEC SQL open sel_curs;
  .
  .
  .
EXEC SQL close sel_curs;
EXEC SQL free sel_curs;
EXEC SQL free sel_stmt;
```

Freeing a Cursor

If you declared a cursor for a prepared statement, freeing the cursor releases only the resources in the database server. To release the resources for the statement in the application-development tool, use FREE *statement_id* (or *statement_id_var*).

If a cursor is not declared for a prepared statement, freeing the cursor releases the resources in both the application-development tool and the database server.

After a cursor is freed, it cannot be opened until it is declared again. The cursor should be explicitly closed before it is freed.

For an example of a FREE statement that frees a cursor, see the second example in "Freeing a Statement" on page 2-473.

Related Information

Related statements: CLOSE, DECLARE, EXECUTE, EXECUTE IMMEDIATE, OPEN, PREPARE, and SET AUTOFREE

For a task-oriented discussion of the FREE statement, see the *Informix Guide to SQL: Tutorial*.

GET DESCRIPTOR

Use the GET DESCRIPTOR statement to accomplish the following separate tasks:

- Determine how many items are described in a system-descriptor area
- Determine the characteristics of each column or expression that is described in the system-descriptor area
- Copy a value from the system-descriptor area into a host variable after a FETCH statement

Use this statement with ESQL/C.

Syntax

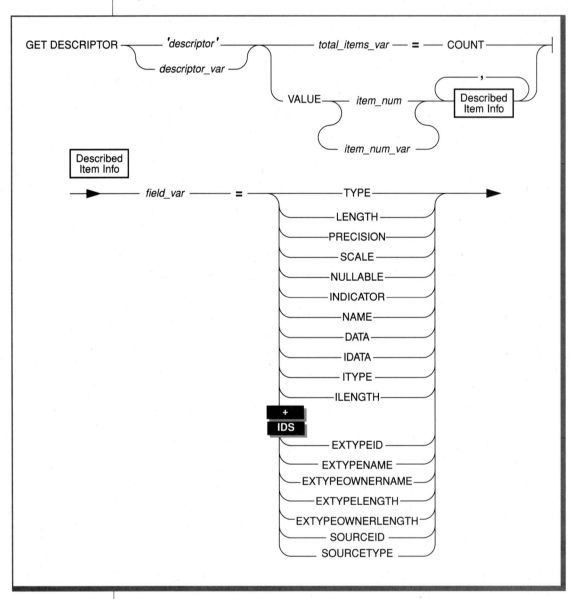

Element	Purpose	Restrictions	Syntax
descriptor	Quoted string that identifies a system-descriptor area from which information is to be obtained	The system-descriptor area must have been allocated in an ALLOCATE DESCRIPTOR statement.	Quoted String, p. 4-260
descriptor_var	Embedded variable name that holds the value of descriptor	The system-descriptor area identified in descriptor_var must have been allocated in an ALLOCATE DESCRIPTOR statement.	Name must conform to language-specific rules for variable names.
field_var	Host variable that receives the contents of the specified field from the system-descriptor area	The *field_var* must be an appropriate type to receive the value of the specified field from the system-descriptor area.	Name must conform to language-specific rules for variable names.
item_num	Unsigned integer that represents one of the items described in the system-descriptor area	The value of *item_num* must be greater than zero (0) and less than the number of item descriptors that were specified when the system-descriptor area was allocated with the ALLOCATE DESCRIPTOR statement.	Literal Number, p. 4-237
item_num_ var	Host variable that holds the value of item_num	The item_num_ var must be an integer data type.	Name must conform to language-specific rules for variable names.
total_items_var	Host variable that indicates how many items are described in the system-descriptor area	The host variable must be an integer data type.	Name must conform to language-specific rules for variable names.

Usage

IDS

Use the GET DESCRIPTOR statement after you have described EXECUTE FUNCTION, INSERT, SELECT, or UPDATE statements with the DESCRIBE...USING SQL DESCRIPTOR statement. ◆

EDS

Use the GET DESCRIPTOR statement after you have described EXECUTE PROCEDURE, INSERT, or SELECT statements with the DESCRIBE...USING SQL DESCRIPTOR statement. ◆

The host variables that are used in the GET DESCRIPTOR statement must be declared in the BEGIN DECLARE SECTION of a program.

If an error occurs during the assignment to any identified host variable, the contents of the host variable are undefined.

Using the COUNT Keyword

Use the COUNT keyword to determine how many items are described in the system-descriptor area.

The following ESQL/C example shows how to use a GET DESCRIPTOR statement with a host variable to determine how many items are described in the system-descriptor area called **desc1**:

```
main()
{
EXEC SQL BEGIN DECLARE SECTION;
int h_count;
EXEC SQL END DECLARE SECTION;

EXEC SQL allocate descriptor 'desc1' with max 20;

/* This section of program would prepare a SELECT or INSERT
 * statement into the s_id statement id.
 */
EXEC SQL describe s_id using sql descriptor 'desc1';

EXEC SQL get descriptor 'desc1' :h_count = count;
...
}
```

Using the VALUE Clause

Use the VALUE clause to obtain information about a described column or expression or to retrieve values that the database server returns in a system descriptor area.

The *item_num* must be greater than zero (0) and less than the number of item descriptors that were specified when the system-descriptor area was allocated with the ALLOCATE DESCRIPTOR statement.

Using the VALUE Clause After a DESCRIBE

After you describe a SELECT, EXECUTE FUNCTION (or EXECUTE PROCEDURE), INSERT, or UPDATE statement, the characteristics of each column or expression in the select list of the SELECT statement, the characteristics of the values returned by the EXECUTE FUNCTION (or EXECUTE PROCEDURE) statement, or the characteristics of each column in a INSERT or UPDATE statement are returned to the system-descriptor area. Each value in the system-descriptor area describes the characteristics of one returned column or expression.

The following ESQL/C example shows how to use a GET DESCRIPTOR statement to obtain data type information from the **demodesc** system-descriptor area:

```
EXEC SQL get descriptor 'demodesc' value :index
        :type = TYPE,
        :len = LENGTH,
        :name = NAME;
printf("Column %d: type = %d, len = %d, name = %s\n",
        index, type, len, name);
```

The value that the database server returns into the TYPE field is a defined integer. To evaluate the data type that is returned, test for a specific integer value. For additional information about integer data type values, see "Setting the TYPE or ITYPE Field" on page 2-724.

In X/Open mode, the X/Open code is returned to the TYPE field. You cannot mix the two modes because errors can result. For example, if a particular data type is not defined under X/Open mode but is defined for Informix products, executing a GET DESCRIPTOR statement can result in an error.

In X/Open mode, a warning message appears if ILENGTH, IDATA, or ITYPE is used. It indicates that these fields are not standard X/Open fields for a system-descriptor area. ♦

If the TYPE of a fetched value is DECIMAL or MONEY, the database server returns the precision and scale information for a column into the **PRECISION** and **SCALE** fields after a DESCRIBE statement is executed. If the TYPE is *not* DECIMAL or MONEY, the **SCALE** and **PRECISION** fields are undefined.

Using the VALUE Clause After a FETCH

Each time your program fetches a row, it must copy the fetched value into host variables so that the data can be used. To accomplish this task, use a GET DESCRIPTOR statement after each fetch of each value in the select list. If three values exist in the select list, you need to use three GET DESCRIPTOR statements after each fetch (assuming you want to read all three values). The item numbers for each of the three GET DESCRIPTOR statements are 1, 2, and 3.

The following ESQL/C example shows how you can copy data from the **DATA** field into a host variable (**result**) after a fetch. For this example, it is predetermined that all returned values are the same data type.

```
EXEC SQL get descriptor 'demodesc' :desc_count = count;
   .
   .
   .
EXEC SQL fetch democursor using sql descriptor 'demodesc';
for (i = 1; i <= desc_count; i++)
    {
    if (sqlca.sqlcode != 0) break;
    EXEC SQL get descriptor 'demodesc' value :i :result = DATA;
    printf("%s ", result);
    }
printf("\n");
```

Fetching a Null Value

When you use GET DESCRIPTOR after a fetch, and the fetched value is null, the **INDICATOR** field is set to -1 (null). The value of DATA is undefined if INDICATOR indicates a null value. The host variable into which DATA is copied has an unpredictable value.

Using LENGTH or ILENGTH

If your **DATA** or **IDATA** field contains a character string, you must specify a value for **LENGTH**. If you specify LENGTH=0, **LENGTH** is automatically set to the maximum length of the string. The **DATA** or **IDATA** field might contain a literal character string or a character string that is derived from a character variable of CHAR or VARCHAR data type. This provides a method to determine the length of a string in the **DATA** or **IDATA** field dynamically.

If a DESCRIBE statement precedes a GET DESCRIPTOR statement, **LENGTH** is automatically set to the maximum length of the character field that is specified in your table.

This information is identical for **ILENGTH**. Use **ILENGTH** when you create a dynamic program that does not comply with the X/Open standard.

IDS

Describing an Opaque-Type Column

The DESCRIBE statement sets the following item-descriptor fields when the column to fetch has an opaque type as its data type:

- The EXTYPEID field stores the extended ID for the opaque type.

  This integer value corresponds to a value in the **extended_id** column of the **sysxtdtypes** system catalog table.

- The EXTYPENAME field stores the name of the opaque type.

  This character value corresponds to a value in the **name** column of the row with the matching **extended_id** value in the **sysxtdtypes** system catalog table.

- The EXTYPELENGTH field stores the length of the opaque-type name.

  This integer value is the length, in bytes, of the name of the opaque type.

- The EXTYPEOWNERNAME field stores the name of the opaque-type owner.

  This character value corresponds to a value in the **owner** column of the row with the matching **extended_id** value in the **sysxtdtypes** system catalog table.

- The EXTYPEOWNERLENGTH field stores the length of the value in the EXTTYPEOWNERNAME field.

  This integer value is the length, in bytes, of the owner name for the opaque type.

Use these field names with the GET DESCRIPTOR statement to obtain information about an opaque column.

Describing a Distinct-Type Column

The DESCRIBE statement sets the following item-descriptor fields when the column to fetch has a distinct type as its data type:

- The SOURCEID field stores the extended identifier for the source data type.

  This integer value corresponds to a value in the **source** column for the row of the **sysxtdtypes** system catalog table whose **extended_id** value matches that of the distinct type you are setting. This field is only set if the source data type is an opaque data type.

- The SOURCETYPE field stores the data type constant for the source data type.

  This value is the data type constant (from the **sqltypes.h** file) for the data type of the source type for the distinct type. The codes for the SOURCETYPE field are listed in the description of the TYPE field in the SET DESCRIPTOR statement. (For more information, see "Setting the TYPE or ITYPE Field" on page 2-724). This integer value must correspond to the value in the **type** column for the row of the **sysxtdtypes** system catalog table whose **extended_id** value matches that of the distinct type you are setting.

Use these field names with the GET DESCRIPTOR statement to obtain information about a distinct-type column.

Related Information

Related statements: ALLOCATE DESCRIPTOR, DEALLOCATE DESCRIPTOR, DECLARE, DESCRIBE, EXECUTE, FETCH, OPEN, PREPARE, PUT, and SET DESCRIPTOR

For more information on concepts relating to the GET DESCRIPTOR statement, see the *Informix ESQL/C Programmer's Manual*.

For more information on the **sysxtdtypes** system catalog table, see of the *Informix Guide to SQL: Reference*.

GET DIAGNOSTICS

Use the GET DIAGNOSTICS statement to return diagnostic information about executing an SQL statement. The GET DIAGNOSTICS statement uses one of two clauses, as described in the following list:

- The Statement clause determines count and overflow information about errors and warnings generated by the most recent SQL statement.

- The EXCEPTION clause provides specific information about errors and warnings generated by the most recent SQL statement.

Use this statement with ESQL/C.

Syntax

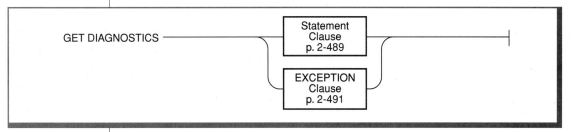

Usage

The GET DIAGNOSTICS statement retrieves selected status information from the diagnostics area and retrieves either count and overflow information or information on a specific exception.

The GET DIAGNOSTICS statement never changes the contents of the diagnostics area.

Using the SQLSTATE Error Status Code

When an SQL statement executes, an error status code is automatically generated. This code represents `success`, `failure`, `warning`, or `no data found`. This error status code is stored in a variable called **SQLSTATE**.

Class and Subclass Codes

THE **SQLSTATE** status code is a a five-character string that can contain only digits and capital letters.

The first two characters of the **SQLSTATE** status code indicate a class. The last three characters of the **SQLSTATE** code indicate a subclass. Figure 2-1 shows the structure of the **SQLSTATE** code. This example uses the value 08001, where 08 is the class code and 001 is the subclass code. The value 08001 represents the error `unable to connect with database environment`.

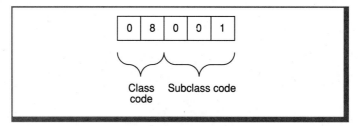

Figure 2-1
Structure of the
SQLSTATE Code

The following table is a quick reference for interpreting class code values.

SQLSTATE Class Code Value	Outcome
00	Success
01	Success with warning
02	No data found
> 02	Error or warning

Support for ANSI Standards

All status codes returned to the **SQLSTATE** variable are ANSI compliant except in the following cases:

- **SQLSTATE** codes with a class code of 01 and a subclass code that begins with an I are Informix-specific warning messages.
- **SQLSTATE** codes with a class code of IX and any subclass code are Informix-specific error messages.
- **SQLSTATE** codes whose class code begins with a digit in the range 5 to 9 or with a capital letter in the range I to Z indicate conditions that are currently undefined by ANSI. The only exception is that **SQLSTATE** codes whose class code is IX are Informix-specific error messages.

List of SQLSTATE Codes

The following table describes the class codes, subclass codes, and the meaning of all valid warning and error codes associated with the **SQLSTATE** error status code.

Class	Subclass	Purpose
00	000	Success
01	000	Success with warning
01	002	Disconnect error. Transaction rolled back
01	003	Null value eliminated in set function
01	004	String data, right truncation
01	005	Insufficient item descriptor areas
01	006	Privilege not revoked
01	007	Privilege not granted

(1 of 4)

Class	Subclass	Purpose
01	I01	Database has transactions
01	I03	ANSI-compliant database selected
01	I04	Informix database server selected
01	I05	Float to decimal conversion was used
01	I06	Informix extension to ANSI-compliant standard syntax
01	I07	UPDATE or DELETE statement does not have a WHERE
01	I08	clause
01	I09	An ANSI keyword was used as a cursor name
01	I10	Number of items in the select list is not equal to the number in the into list
01	I11	Database server running in secondary mode
		Dataskip is turned on
02	000	No data found
07	000	Dynamic SQL error
07	001	USING clause does not match dynamic parameters
07	002	USING clause does not match target specifications
07	003	Cursor specification cannot be executed
07	004	USING clause is required for dynamic parameters
07	005	Prepared statement is not a cursor specification
07	006	Restricted data type attribute violation
07	008	Invalid descriptor count
07	009	Invalid descriptor index
08	000	Connection exception
08	001	Server rejected the connection
08	002	Connection name in use
08	003	Connection does not exist
08	004	Client unable to establish connection
08	006	Transaction rolled back
08	007	Transaction state unknown
08	S01	Communication failure

Class	Subclass	Purpose
0A	000	Feature not supported
0A	001	Multiple server transactions
21	000	Cardinality violation
21	S01	Insert value list does not match column list
21	S02	Degree of derived table does not match column list
22	000	Data exception
22	001	String data, right truncation
22	002	Null value, no indicator parameter
22	003	Numeric value out of range
22	005	Error in assignment
22	027	Data exception trim error
22	012	Division by zero (0)
22	019	Invalid escape character
22	024	Unterminated string
22	025	Invalid escape sequence
23	000	Integrity constraint violation
24	000	Invalid cursor state
25	000	Invalid transaction state
2B	000	Dependent privilege descriptors still exist
2D	000	Invalid transaction termination
26	000	Invalid SQL statement identifier
2E	000	Invalid connection name
28	000	Invalid user-authorization specification
33	000	Invalid SQL descriptor name
34	000	Invalid cursor name
35	000	Invalid exception number

(3 of 4)

Class	Subclass	Purpose
37	000	Syntax error or access violation in PREPARE or EXECUTE IMMEDIATE
3C	000	Duplicate cursor name
40	000	Transaction rollback
40	003	Statement completion unknown
42	000	Syntax error or access violation
S0	000	Invalid name
S0	001	Base table or view table already exists
S0	002	Base table not found
S0	011	Index already exists
S0	021	Column already exists
S1	001	Memory allocation failure
IX	000	Informix reserved error message

(4 of 4)

Using SQLSTATE in Applications

You can use a variable, called **SQLSTATE**, that you do not have to declare in your program. **SQLSTATE** contains the error code that is essential for error handling, which is generated every time your program executes an SQL statement. **SQLSTATE** is created automatically. You can examine the **SQLSTATE** variable to determine whether an SQL statement was successful. If the **SQLSTATE** variable indicates that the statement failed, you can execute a GET DIAGNOSTICS statement to obtain additional error information.

For an example of how to use an **SQLSTATE** variable in a program, see "Using GET DIAGNOSTICS for Error Checking" on page 2-498.

Statement Clause

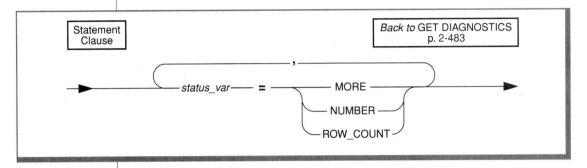

Element	Purpose	Restrictions	Syntax
status_var	Host variable that receives status information about the most recent SQL statement Receives information for the specified status field name.	Data type must match that of the requested field.	Name must conform to language-specific rules for variable names.

When retrieving count and overflow information, GET DIAGNOSTICS can deposit the values of the three statement fields into a corresponding host variable. The host-variable data type must be the same as that of the requested field. These three fields are represented by the following keywords.

Field Name Keyword	Field Data Type	Field Contents	ESQL/C Host Variable Data Type
MORE	Character	Y or N	char[2]
NUMBER	Integer	1 to 35,000	int
ROW_COUNT	Integer	0 to 999,999,999	int

Using the MORE Keyword

Use the MORE keyword to determine if the most recently executed SQL statement performed the following actions:

- Stored all the exceptions it detected in the diagnostics area.

  The GET DIAGNOSTICS statement returns a value of N.
- Detected more exceptions than it stored in the diagnostics area.

  The GET DIAGNOSTICS statement returns a value of Y.

The value of MORE is always N.

Using the NUMBER Keyword

Use the NUMBER keyword to count the number of exceptions that the most recently executed SQL statement placed into the diagnostics area. The **NUMBER** field can hold a value from 1 to 35,000, depending on how many exceptions are counted.

Using the ROW_COUNT Keyword

Use the ROW_COUNT keyword to count the number of rows the most recently executed statement processed. ROW_COUNT counts the following number of rows:

- Inserted into a table
- Updated in a table
- Deleted from a table

EXCEPTION Clause

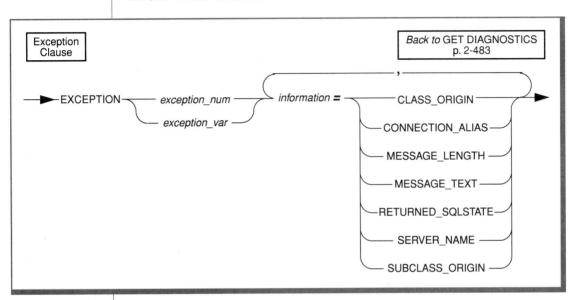

Element	Purpose	Restrictions	Syntax
exception_num	Literal integer value that specifies the exception number for a GET DIAGNOSTICS statement The *exception_num* literal indicates one of the exception values from the number of exceptions returned by the NUMBER field in the Statement clause.	Integer value is limited to a range from 1 to 35,000.	Literal Number, p. 4-237
exception_var	Host variable that specifies an exception number for a GET DIAGNOSTICS statement	Variable must contain an integer value limited to a range from 1 to 35,000. Variable data type must be INT or SMALLINT.	Variable name must conform to language-specific rules for variable names.
information	Host variable that receives EXCEPTION information about the most recent SQL statement Receives information for a specified exception field name.	Data type must match that of the requested field.	Variable name must conform to language-specific rules for variable names.

When retrieving exception information, GET DIAGNOSTICS deposits the values of each of the seven fields into corresponding host variables. These fields are located in the diagnostics area and are derived from an exception raised by the most recent SQL statement.

The host-variable data type must be the same as that of the requested field. The seven exception information fields are represented by the keywords described in the following table.

Field Name Keyword	Field Data Type	Field Contents	ESQL/C Host Variable Data Type
RETURNED_SQLSTATE	Character	SQLSTATE value	char[6]
CLASS_ORIGIN	Character	String	char[255]
SUBCLASS_ORIGIN	Character	String	char[255]
MESSAGE_TEXT	Character	String	char[255]
MESSAGE_LENGTH	Integer	Numeric value	int
SERVER_NAME	Character	String	char[255]
CONNECTION_NAME	Character	String	char[255]

The application specifies the exception by number, using either an unsigned integer or an integer host variable (an exact numeric with a scale of 0). An exception with a value of 1 corresponds to the **SQLSTATE** value set by the most recent SQL statement other than GET DIAGNOSTICS. The association between other exception numbers and other exceptions raised by that SQL statement is undefined. Thus, no set order exists in which the diagnostic area can be filled with exception values. You always get at least one exception, even if the **SQLSTATE** value indicates success.

If an error occurs within the GET DIAGNOSTICS statement (that is, if an illegal exception number is requested), the Informix internal **SQLCODE** and **SQLSTATE** variables are set to the value of that exception. In addition, the GET DIAGNOSTICS fields are undefined.

Using the RETURNED_SQLSTATE Keyword

Use the RETURNED_SQLSTATE keyword to determine the **SQLSTATE** value that describes the exception.

Using the CLASS_ORIGIN Keyword

Use the CLASS_ORIGIN keyword to retrieve the class portion of the **RETURNED_SQLSTATE** value. If the International Standards Organization (ISO) standard defines the class, the value of CLASS_ORIGIN is equal to ISO 9075. Otherwise, the value of CLASS_ORIGIN is defined by Informix and cannot be ISO 9075. ANSI SQL and ISO SQL are synonymous.

Using the SUBCLASS_ORIGIN Keyword

Use the SUBCLASS_ORIGIN keyword to define the source of the subclass portion of the **RETURNED_SQLSTATE** value. If the ISO international standard defines the subclass, the value of SUBCLASS_ORIGIN is equal to ISO 9075.

Using the MESSAGE_TEXT Keyword

Use the MESSAGE_TEXT keyword to determine the message text of the exception (for example, an error message).

Using the MESSAGE_LENGTH Keyword

Use the MESSAGE_LENGTH keyword to determine the length of the current MESSAGE_TEXT string.

Using the SERVER_NAME Keyword

Use the SERVER_NAME keyword to determine the name of the database server associated with the actions of a CONNECT or DATABASE statement.

When the SERVER_NAME Field Is Updated

The GET DIAGNOSTICS statement updates the **SERVER_NAME** field when the following situations occur:

- a CONNECT statement successfully executes.
- a SET CONNECTION statement successfully executes.
- a DISCONNECT statement successfully executes at the current connection.
- a DISCONNECT ALL statement fails.

When the SERVER_NAME Field Is Not Updated

The **SERVER_NAME** field is not updated when:

- a CONNECT statement fails.
- a DISCONNECT statement fails (this does not include the DISCONNECT ALL statement).
- a SET CONNECTION statement fails.

The **SERVER_NAME** field retains the value set in the previous SQL statement. If any of the preceding conditions occur on the first SQL statement that executes, the **SERVER_NAME** field is blank.

The Contents of the SERVER_NAME Field

The **SERVER_NAME** field contains different information after you execute the following statements.

Executed Statement	SERVER_NAME Field Contents
CONNECT	Contains the name of the database server to which you connect or fail to connect
	Field is blank if you do not have a current connection or if you make a default connection.
SET CONNECTION	Contains the name of the database server to which you switch or fail to switch
DISCONNECT	Contains the name of the database server from which you disconnect or fail to disconnect
	If you disconnect and then you execute a DISCONNECT statement for a connection that is not current, the **SERVER_NAME** field remains unchanged.
DISCONNECT ALL	Sets the field to blank if the statement executes successfully
	If the statement does not execute successfully, the **SERVER_NAME** field contains the names of all the database servers from which you did not disconnect. However, this information does not mean that the connection still exists.

If the CONNECT statement is successful, the **SERVER_NAME** field is set to one of the following values:

- The **INFORMIXSERVER** value if the connection is to a default database server (that is, the CONNECT statement does not list a database server).
- The name of the specific database server if the connection is to a specific database server.

The DATABASE Statement

When you execute a DATABASE statement, the **SERVER_NAME** field contains the name of the server on which the database resides.

Using the CONNECTION_NAME Keyword

Use the CONNECTION_NAME keyword to specify a name for the connection used in your CONNECT or DATABASE statements.

When the CONNECTION_NAME Keyword Is Updated

GET DIAGNOSTICS updates the **CONNECTION_NAME** field when the following situations occur:

- a CONNECT statement successfully executes.
- a SET CONNECTION statement successfully executes.
- a DISCONNECT statement successfully executes at the current connection. GET DIAGNOSTICS fills the **CONNECTION_NAME** field with blanks because no current connection exists.
- a DISCONNECT ALL statement fails.

When CONNECTION_NAME Is Not Updated

The **CONNECTION_NAME** field is not updated when the following situations occur:

- a CONNECT statement fails.
- a DISCONNECT statement fails (this does not include the DISCONNECT ALL statement).
- a SET CONNECTION statement fails.

The **CONNECTION_NAME** field retains the value set in the previous SQL statement. If any of the preceding conditions occur on the first SQL statement that executes, the **CONNECTION_NAME** field is blank.

The Contents of the CONNECTION_NAME Field

The **CONNECTION_NAME** field contains different information after you execute the following statements.

Executed Statement	CONNECTION_NAME Field Contents
CONNECT	Contains the name of the connection, specified in the CONNECT statement, to which you connect or fail to connect
	The field is blank if you do not have a current connection or if you make a default connection.
SET CONNECTION	Contains the name of the connection, specified in the CONNECT statement, to which you switch or fail to switch
DISCONNECT	Contains the name of the connection, specified in the CONNECT statement, from which you disconnect or fail to disconnect
	If you disconnect, and then you execute a DISCONNECT statement for a connection that is not current, the CONNECTION_NAME field remains unchanged.
DISCONNECT ALL	Contains no information if the statement executes successfully
	If the statement does not execute successfully, the CONNECTION_NAME field contains the names of all the connections, specified in your CONNECT statement, from which you did not disconnect. However, this information does not mean that the connection still exists.

If the CONNECT is successful, the **CONNECTION_NAME** field is set to the following values:

- The name of the database environment as specified in the CONNECT statement if the CONNECT does not include the AS clause
- The name of the connection (identifier after the AS keyword) if the CONNECT includes the AS clause

DATABASE Statement

When you execute a DATABASE statement, the **CONNECTION_NAME** field is blank.

Using GET DIAGNOSTICS for Error Checking

The GET DIAGNOSTICS statement returns information held in various fields of the diagnostic area. For each field in the diagnostic area that you want to access, you must supply a host variable with a compatible data type.

The following example illustrates how to use the GET DIAGNOSTICS statement to display error information. The example shows an ESQL/C error display routine called **disp_sqlstate_err()**.

```
void disp_sqlstate_err()
{
int j;

EXEC SQL BEGIN DECLARE SECTION;
    int exception_count;
    char overflow[2];
    int exception_num=1;
    char class_id[255];
    char subclass_id[255];
    char message[255];
    int messlen;
    char sqlstate_code[6];
    int i;
EXEC SQL END DECLARE SECTION;

    printf("---------------------------------");
    printf("------------------------\n");
    printf("SQLSTATE: %s\n",SQLSTATE);
    printf("SQLCODE: %d\n", SQLCODE);
    printf("\n");

    EXEC SQL get diagnostics :exception_count = NUMBER,
        :overflow = MORE;
    printf("EXCEPTIONS:  Number=%d\t", exception_count);
    printf("More? %s\n", overflow);
    for (i = 1; i <= exception_count; i++)
```

```
{
    EXEC SQL get diagnostics  exception :i
        :sqlstate_code = RETURNED_SQLSTATE,
        :class_id = CLASS_ORIGIN, :subclass_id = SUBCLASS_ORIGIN,
        :message = MESSAGE_TEXT, :messlen = MESSAGE_LENGTH;
    printf("- - - - - - - - - - - - - - - - - - -\n");
    printf("EXCEPTION %d: SQLSTATE=%s\n", i,
        sqlstate_code);
    message[messlen-1] ='\0';
    printf("MESSAGE TEXT: %s\n", message);

    j = stleng(class_id);
    while((class_id[j] == '\0') ||
          (class_id[j] == ' '))
        j--;
    class_id[j+1] = '\0';
    printf("CLASS ORIGIN: %s\n",class_id);

    j = stleng(subclass_id);
    while((subclass_id[j] == '\0') ||
          (subclass_id[j] == ' '))
        j--;
    subclass_id[j+1] = '\0';
    printf("SUBCLASS ORIGIN: %s\n",subclass_id);
}

printf("--------------------------------");
printf("------------------------\n");
}
```

Related Information

For a task-oriented discussion of error handling and the **SQLSTATE** variable, see the *Informix Guide to SQL: Tutorial.*

For a discussion of concepts related to the GET DIAGNOSTICS statement and the **SQLSTATE** variable, see the *Informix ESQL/C Programmer's Manual.*

GRANT

Use the GRANT statement to:

- authorize others to use, develop, or administrate a database that you create.
- allow others to view, alter, or drop a table, synonym, or view that you create.
- allow others to use a data type or execute a user-defined routine (UDR) that you create.
- give a role name and its privileges to one or more users.

Syntax

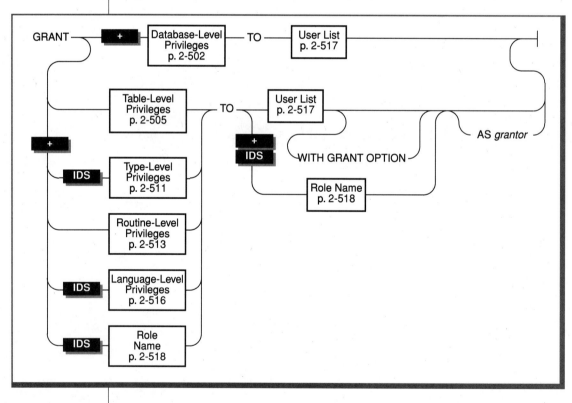

Element	Purpose	Restrictions	Syntax
grantor	Name that identifies who can REVOKE the effects of the current GRANT By default, the login of the person who issues the GRANT statement identifies the grantor. To override the default, include the AS keyword followed by the login of your appointed grantor.	If you specify someone else as the grantor of the specified privilege, you cannot later revoke that privilege.	The name must conform to the conventions of your operating system.

Usage

The GRANT statement extends privileges to other users that would normally accrue only to the DBA or to the creator of an object. Later GRANT statements do not affect privileges already granted to a user.

You can grant privileges to a previously created role. You can grant a role to individual users or to another role.

Privileges you grant remain in effect until you cancel them with a REVOKE statement. Only the grantor of a privilege can revoke that privilege. The grantor is normally the person who issues the GRANT statement. To transfer the right to revoke, name another user as grantor when you issue a GRANT statement.

The keyword PUBLIC extends a GRANT to all users. If you want to restrict privileges to a particular user that **public** already has, you must first revoke the right of **public** to those privileges.

When database-level privileges collide with table-level privileges, the more restrictive privileges take precedence.

Database-Level Privileges

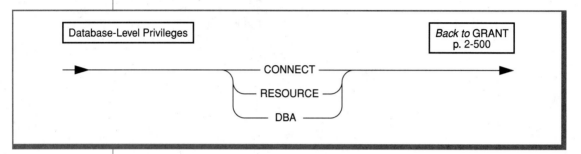

Database-Level Privileges

Back to GRANT
p. 2-500

CONNECT

RESOURCE

DBA

When you create a database with the CREATE DATABASE statement, you are the owner. As the database owner, you automatically receive all database-level privileges. The database remains inaccessible to other users until you, as DBA, grant database privileges.

As database owner, you also automatically receive table-level privileges on all tables in the database. For more information about table-level privileges, see "Table-Level Privileges" on page 2-505.

Database access levels are, from lowest to highest, Connect, Resource, and DBA. Use the corresponding keyword to grant a level of access privilege.

Privilege	Functions
CONNECT	Lets you query and modify data. You can modify the database schema if you own the database object you want to modify. Any user with the Connect privilege can perform the following functions:
	▪ Connect to the database with the CONNECT statement or another connection statement
	▪ Execute SELECT, INSERT, UPDATE, and DELETE statements, provided the user has the necessary table-level privileges
	▪ Create views, provided the user has the Select privilege on the underlying tables
	▪ Create synonyms
	▪ Create temporary tables and create indexes on the temporary tables
	▪ Alter or drop a table or an index, provided the user owns the table or index (or has Alter, Index, or References privileges on the table)
	▪ Grant privileges on a table or view, provided the user owns the table (or was given privileges on the table with the WITH GRANT OPTION keyword)
RESOURCE	Lets you extend the structure of the database. In addition to the capabilities of the Connect privilege, the holder of the Resource privilege can perform the following functions:
	▪ Create new tables
	▪ Create new indexes
	▪ Create new UDRs
	▪ Create new data types

(1 of 2)

Privilege	Functions
DBA	Has all the capabilities of the Resource privilege and can perform the following functions: ■ Grant any database-level privilege, including the DBA privilege, to another user ■ Grant any table-level privilege to another user ■ Grant any table-level privilege to a role ■ Grant a role to a user or to another role ■ Execute the SET SESSION AUTHORIZATION statement ■ Use the NEXT SIZE keywords to alter extent sizes in the system catalog ■ Insert, delete, or update rows of any system catalog table except **systables** ■ Drop any database object, regardless of its owner ■ Create tables, views, and indexes, and specify another user as owner of the database objects ■ Restrict the Execute privilege to DBAs when registering a UDR ■ Execute the DROP DATABASE statement ■ Execute the DROP DISTRIBUTIONS option of the UPDATE STATISTICS statement

(2 of 2)

User **informix** has the privilege required to alter tables in the system catalog, including the **systables** table.

Warning: *Although the user **informix** and DBAs can modify most system catalog tables (only user **informix** can modify **systables**), Informix strongly recommends that you do not update, delete, or alter any rows in them. Modifying the system catalog tables can destroy the integrity of the database.*

The following example uses the PUBLIC keyword to grant the Connect privilege on the currently active database to all users:

```
GRANT CONNECT TO PUBLIC
```

Table-Level Privileges

When you create a table with the CREATE TABLE statement, you are the table owner and automatically receive all table-level privileges. You cannot transfer table ownership to another user, but you can grant table-level privileges to another user or to a role.

A person with the database-level DBA privilege automatically receives all table-level privileges on every table in that database.

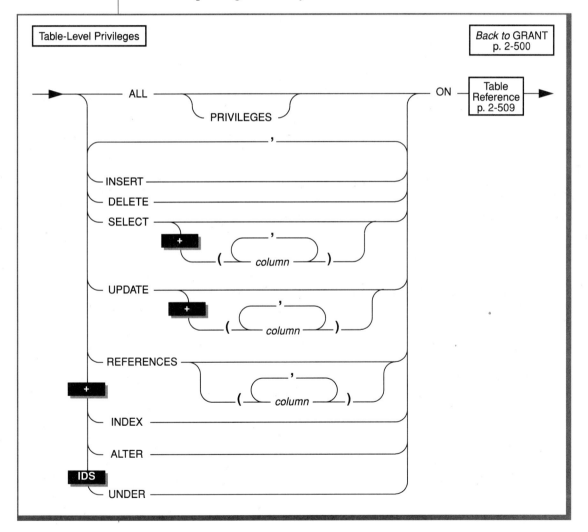

Element	Purpose	Restrictions	Syntax
column	Name of the column or columns to which a Select, Update, or References privilege is granted	The specified column or columns must exist.	Identifier, p. 4-205
	If you omit *column name*, the privilege applies to all columns in the specified table.		

The table that follows lists keywords for granting table-level privileges.

Privilege	Purpose
INSERT	Lets you insert rows
DELETE	Lets you delete rows
SELECT	Lets you name any column in SELECT statements
	You can restrict the Select privilege to one or more columns by listing them.
UPDATE	Lets you name any column in UPDATE statements
	You can restrict the Update privilege to one or more columns by listing them.
REFERENCES	Lets you reference columns in referential constraints
	You must have the Resource privilege to take advantage of the References privilege. (However, you can add a referential constraint during an ALTER TABLE statement. This action does not require that you have the Resource privilege on the database.) You can restrict the References privilege to one or more columns by listing them.
	You need only the References privilege to indicate cascading deletes. You do not need the Delete privilege to place cascading deletes on a table.
INDEX	Lets you create permanent indexes
	You must have Resource privilege to use the Index privilege. (Any user with the Connect privilege can create an index on temporary tables.)

(1 of 2)

Privilege	Purpose
ALTER	Lets you add or delete columns, modify column data types, add or delete constraints, change the locking mode of the table from PAGE to ROW, or add or drop a corresponding row type name for your table.
	Also lets you set the database object mode of unique indexes and constraints to the enabled, disabled, or filtering mode. In addition, this privilege lets you set the database object mode of nonunique indexes and triggers to the enabled or disabled modes.
	You must have the Resource privilege to use the Alter privilege. In addition, you also need the Usage privilege for any user-defined type affected by the ALTER TABLE statement.
UNDER (IDS only)	Lets you create subtables under a typed table.
ALL	Provides all privileges
	The PRIVILEGES keyword is optional.

(2 of 2)

You can narrow the scope of a Select, Update, or References privilege by naming the specific columns to which the privilege applies.

Specify keyword PUBLIC as *user* if you want a GRANT statement to apply to all users.

Examples

Some simple examples can help to illustrate how table-level privileges are granted with the GRANT statement.

Examples of Granting Delete, Select, and Update Privileges

The following statement grants the privilege to delete and select values in any column in the table **customer** to users **mary** and **john**. It also grants the Update privilege, but only for columns **customer_num**, **fname**, and **lname**.

```
GRANT DELETE, SELECT, UPDATE (customer_num, fname, lname)
    ON customer TO mary, john
```

To grant the same privileges as those above to all authorized users, use the keyword PUBLIC as shown in the following example:

```
GRANT DELETE, SELECT, UPDATE (customer_num, fname, lname)
        ON customer TO PUBLIC
```

Example of Granting the UNDER Privilege

Suppose a user named **mary** has created a typed table named **tab1**. By default, only user **mary** can create subtables under the **tab1** table. If **mary** wants to grant the ability to create subtables under the **tab1** table to a user named **john**, **mary** must enter the following GRANT statement:

```
GRANT UNDER ON tab1 TO john
```

After receiving the UNDER privilege on table **tab1**, user **john** can create one or more subtables under **tab1**.

Behavior of the ALL Keyword

The ALL keyword grants all table-level privileges to the specified user. If any or all of the table-level privileges do not exist for the grantor, the GRANT statement with the ALL keyword succeeds, but the following SQLSTATE warning is returned:

```
01007 - Privilege not granted.
```

For example, assume that the user **ted** has the Select and Insert privileges on the **customer** table with the authority to grant those privileges to other users. User **ted** wants to grant all table-level privileges to user **tania**. So user **ted** issues the following GRANT statement:

```
GRANT ALL ON customer TO tania
```

This statement executes successfully but returns SQLSTATE code 01007 for the following reasons:

- The statement succeeds in granting the Select and Insert privileges to user **tania** because user **ted** has those privileges and the right to grant those privileges to other users.
- The other privileges implied by the ALL keyword were not grantable by user **ted** and, therefore, were not granted to user **tania**.

Effect of the All Keyword on the UNDER Privilege

If you grant all table-level privileges with the ALL keyword, the grant includes the Under privilege only if the table is a typed table. The grant of ALL privileges does not include the Under privilege if the table is not based on a row type.

If the table owner grants ALL privileges on a traditional relational table and later changes that table to a typed table, the table owner must explicitly grant the Under privilege to allow other users to create subtables under it.

Table Reference

You grant table-level privileges directly by referencing the table name or an existing synonym. You can also grant table-level privileges on a view.

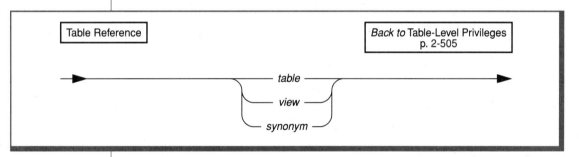

Element	Purpose	Restrictions	Syntax
synonym	Synonym for the table on which privileges are granted	The synonym must exist.	Database Object Name, p. 4-50
table	Table on which privileges are granted	The table must exist.	Database Object Name, p. 4-50
view	View on which privileges are granted	The view must exist.	Database Object Name, p. 4-50

The table, view, or synonym on which you grant privileges must reside in the current database.

Privileges on Table Name and Synonym Name

Normally, when you create a table in a database that is *not* ANSI compliant, **public** receives Select, Insert, Delete, Under, and Update privileges for that table and its synonyms. (The **NODEFDAC** environment variable, when set to yes, prevents **public** from automatically receiving table-level privileges.)

To allow access to only certain users, explicitly revoke those privileges **public** automatically receives and then grant only those you want, as the following example shows:

```
REVOKE ALL ON customer FROM PUBLIC;
GRANT ALL ON customer TO john, mary;
GRANT SELECT (fname, lname, company, city)
    ON customer TO PUBLIC
```

ANSI

If you create a table in an ANSI-compliant database, only you, as table owner, have any table-level privileges until you explicitly grant privileges to others. ♦

As explained in the next section, "Privileges on a View," **public** does *not* automatically receive any privileges for a view that you create.

Privileges on a View

You must have at least the Select privilege on a table or columns to create a view on that table.

For views that reference only tables in the current database, if the owner of a view loses the Select privilege on any table underlying the view, the view is dropped.

You have the same privileges for the view that you have for the table or tables contributing data to the view. For example, if you create a view from a table to which you have only Select privileges, you can select data from your view but you cannot delete or update data.

For detailed information on how to create a view, see "CREATE VIEW" on page 2-334.

When you create a view, only you have access to table data through that view. Even users who have privileges on the base table of the view do not automatically receive privileges for the view.

You can grant (or revoke) privileges on a view only if you are the owner of the underlying tables or if you received these privileges on the table with the right to grant them (the WITH GRANT OPTION keyword). You must explicitly grant those privileges within your authority; **public** does not automatically receive privileges on a view.

The creator of a view can explicitly grant Select, Insert, Delete, and Update privileges for the view to other users or to a role name. You cannot grant Index, Alter, Under, or References privileges on a view (or the All privilege because All includes Index, References, and Alter).

IDS

Type-Level Privileges

You can specify two privileges on data types:

- You can specify the Usage privilege on a user-defined data type.
- You can specify the Under privilege on a named-row type.

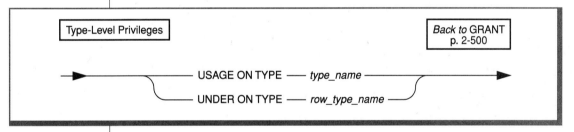

Element	Purpose	Restrictions	Syntax
row_type_name	Name of the named-row type on which the Under privilege is granted	The specified named-row type must exist.	Data Type, p. 4-53
type_name	The name of the user-defined data type on which the Usage privilege is granted	The specified data type must exist.	Data Type, p. 4-53

To find out what privileges exist on a particular type, check the **sysxtdtypes** system catalog table for the owner name and the **sysxtdtypeauth** system catalog table for additional type privileges that might have been granted. For more information on system catalog tables, see the *Informix Guide to SQL: Reference*.

USAGE Privilege

You own a user-defined data type that you create. As owner, you automatically receive the Usage privilege on that data type and can grant the Usage privilege to others so that they can reference the type name or reference data of that type in SQL statements. DBAs can also grant the Usage privilege for user-defined data types.

If you grant the Usage privilege to a user or role that has Alter privileges, that person can add a column to the table that contains data of your user-defined type.

Without a GRANT statement, any user can create SQL statements that contain built-in data types. By contrast, a user must receive an explicit Usage privilege from a GRANT statement to use a distinct data type, even if the distinct type is based on a built-in type.

For more information about user-defined types, see "CREATE OPAQUE TYPE" on page 2-186, "CREATE DISTINCT TYPE" on page 2-127, the discussion of data types in the *Informix Guide to SQL: Reference*, and the discussion of data types in the *Informix Guide to Database Design and Implementation*.

UNDER Privilege

You own a named-row type that you create. If you want other users to be able to create subtypes under this named-row type, you must grant these users the Under privilege on your named-row type.

For example, suppose that you have created a row type named **rtype1**:

```
CREATE ROW TYPE rtype1
    (cola INT, colb INT)
```

If you want another user named **kathy** to be able to create a subtype under this named-row type, you must grant the Under privilege on this named-row type to user **kathy**:

```
GRANT UNDER on rtype1 to kathy
```

Now user **kathy** can create another row type under the **rtype1** row type even though **kathy** is not the owner of the **rtype1** row type:

```
CREATE ROW TYPE rtype2
    (colc INT, cold INT)
    UNDER rtype1
```

For more information about named-row types, see "CREATE ROW TYPE" on page 2-216, the discussion of data types in the *Informix Guide to SQL: Reference*, and the discussion of data types in the *Informix Guide to Database Design and Implementation*.

Routine-Level Privileges

When you create a user-defined routine (UDR) with the CREATE FUNCTION or CREATE PROCEDURE statement, you own, and automatically receive the Execute privilege on that UDR.

The Execute privilege allows you to invoke the UDR with an EXECUTE FUNCTION or EXECUTE PROCEDURE statement, whichever is appropriate, or with a CALL statement in an SPL routine. The Execute privilege also allows you to use a user-defined function in an expression, as in the following example:

```
SELECT * FROM table WHERE in_stock(partnum) < 20
```

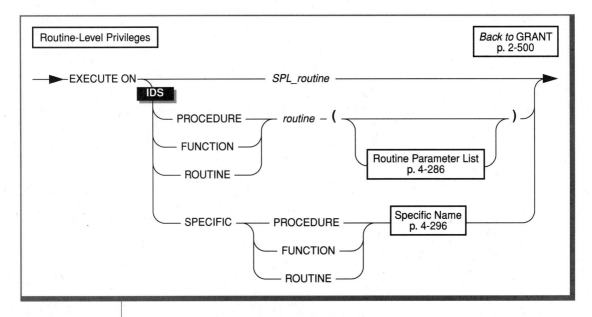

Element	Purpose	Restrictions	Syntax
routine	Name of a user-defined routine created with the CREATE FUNCTION or CREATE PROCEDURE statement	The identifier must refer to an existing user-defined routine. In an ANSI-compliant database, specify the owner as the prefix to the routine name.	Database Object Name, p. 4-50
SPL_routine	Name of an SPL routine that was created with the CREATE PROCEDURE statement	The SPL routine must exist. The SPL routine cannot be overloaded. That is, the name must be unique in the database.	Database Object Name, p. 4-50

The requirement to grant the Execute privilege explicitly depends on the following conditions:

- If you have DBA-level privileges, you can use the DBA keyword of CREATE FUNCTION or CREATE PROCEDURE to restrict the default Execute privilege to users with the DBA database-level privilege. You must explicitly grant the Execute privilege on that UDR to users who do not have the DBA privilege.

- If you have the Resource database-level privilege, but not the DBA privilege, you cannot use the DBA keyword when you create a UDR:

  □ When you create a UDR in a database that is *not* ANSI compliant, **public** can execute that UDR. You do not need to issue a GRANT statement for the Execute privilege.

  □ The **NODEFDAC** environment variable, when set to `yes`, prevents **public** from executing your UDR until you explicitly grant the Execute privilege.

ANSI

- In an ANSI-compliant database, the creator of a UDR must explicitly grant the Execute privilege on that UDR. ♦

IDS

Because of routine overloading, you can grant the Execute privilege on more than one UDR at a time. The following table explains the purpose of the keywords that you specify.

KEYWORD	Purpose
SPECIFIC	Grants the Execute privilege for the UDR identified by *specific name*
FUNCTION	Grants the Execute privilege for all user-defined functions with the specified *routine name* (and parameter types that match *routine parameter list*, if supplied)
PROCEDURE	Grants the Execute privilege for all user-defined procedures with the specified *routine name* (and parameter types that match *routine parameter list*, if supplied)
ROUTINE	Grants the Execution privilege for all user-defined functions and all user-defined procedures with the specified *routine name* (and parameter types that match *routine parameter list*, if supplied)

If both a user-defined function and a user-defined procedure have the same name and list of parameter types, you can grant the Execute privilege to both with the keyword ROUTINE. To limit the Execute privilege to one version of the same routine name, use the FUNCTION, PROCEDURE, or SPECIFIC keyword.

To limit the Execute privilege to a UDR that accepts particular data types as arguments, include the routine parameter list or use the SPECIFIC keyword to introduce the specific name of a particular UDR.

Tip: *If an external function has a negator function, you must grant the Execute privilege on both the external function and its negator function before users can execute the external function.*

◆

IDS

Language-Level Privileges

A user must have the Usage privilege on a language to register a user-defined routine (UDR) that is written in that language.

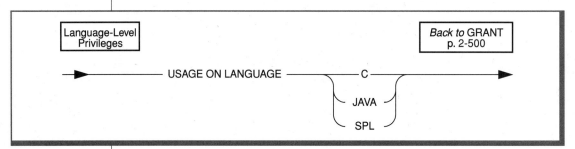

When a user executes a CREATE FUNCTION or CREATE PROCEDURE statement to register a UDR, the database server verifies that the user has the Usage privilege on the language in which the UDR is written.For information on other privileges that these statements require, see "CREATE FUNCTION" on page 2-146 and "CREATE PROCEDURE" on page 2-199.

Usage Privilege on External Languages

Only user **informix** or a user who was granted the Usage privilege WITH GRANT OPTION can grant the Usage privilege on an external language to another user. If user **informix** grants the Usage privilege on an external language to the DBA WITH GRANT OPTION, the DBA can then grant the Usage privilege on the external language to another user.

In the following example, user **informix** grants the Usage privilege on both available external languages (C and Java) to user **joy**:

```
GRANT USAGE ON LANGUAGE C TO joy;
GRANT USAGE ON LANGUAGE JAVA TO joy;
```

Usage Privilege on the Stored Procedure Language

Only user **informix**, the DBA, or a user who was granted the Usage privilege WITH GRANT OPTION can grant the Usage privilege on the Stored Procedure Language (SPL) to another user.

The Usage privilege on SPL is granted to PUBLIC by default.

In the following example, assume that the default Usage privilege on SPL was revoked from PUBLIC and the DBA wants to grant the Usage privilege on SPL to the role named **developers**:

```
GRANT USAGE ON LANGUAGE SPL TO developers
```

User List

You can grant privileges to an individual user or a list of users. You can also use the PUBLIC keyword to grant privileges to all users.

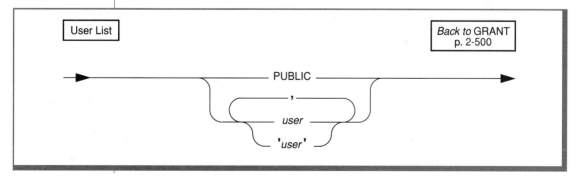

Element	Purpose	Restrictions	Syntax
user	The login name to receive the role or privilege granted	Put quotes around user to ensure that the name of the user is stored exactly as you type it. Use the single keyword PUBLIC for user to grant a role or privilege to all authorized users.	The name must conform to the conventions of your operating system.

The following example grants the table-level privilege Insert on **table1** to the user named **mary** in a database that is not ANSI compliant:

```
GRANT INSERT ON table1 TO mary
```

ANSI

In an ANSI-compliant database, if you do not use quotes around *user*, the name of the user is stored in uppercase letters. ♦

IDS

Role Name

You can identify one or more users by a name that describes their function, or *role*. You create the role, then grant the role to one or more users. You can also grant a role to another role.

After you create and grant a role, you can grant certain privileges to the one or more users associated with that role name.

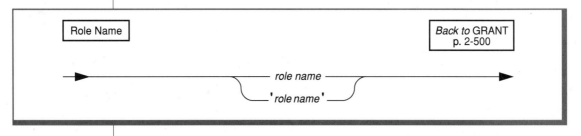

Element	Purpose	Restrictions	Syntax
role name	Name of the role that is granted, or the name of the role to which a privilege or another role is granted	The role must have been created with the CREATE ROLE statement. When a role name is enclosed in quotation marks, the role name is case sensitive.	Identifier, p. 4-205

Granting a Role to a User or Another Role

You must add a role name to the database before anyone can use that role name in a GRANT statement. For more information, see "CREATE ROLE" on page 2-212.

A DBA has the authority to grant a new role to another user. If a user receives a role WITH GRANT OPTION, that user can grant the role to other users or to another role. Users keep a role granted to them until a REVOKE statement breaks the association between their login names and the role name.

Important: *CREATE ROLE and GRANT do not activate the role. A role has no effect until the SET ROLE statement enables it. A role grantor or a role grantee can issue the SET ROLE.*

The following example shows the sequence required to grant and activate the role **payables** to a group of employees who perform account payables functions. First the DBA creates role **payables**, then grants it to **maryf**.

```
CREATE ROLE payables;
GRANT payables TO maryf WITH GRANT OPTION
```

The DBA or **maryf** can activate the role with the following statement:

```
SET ROLE payables
```

User **maryf** has the WITH GRANT OPTION authorization to grant **payables** to other employees who pay accounts.

```
GRANT payables TO charly, gene, marvin, raoul
```

If you grant privileges for one role to another role, the recipient role has a combined set of privileges. The following example grants the role **petty_cash** to the role **payables**:

```
CREATE ROLE petty_cash;
SET ROLE petty_cash;
GRANT petty_cash TO payables
```

If you attempt to grant a role to itself, either directly or indirectly, the database server generates an error.

Granting a Privilege to a Role

You can grant table-, type-, and routine-level privileges to a role if you have the authority to grant these same privileges to login names or PUBLIC. A role cannot have database-level privileges.

When you grant a privilege to a role:

- you can specify the AS *grantor* clause

  In this way, the people who have the role can revoke these same privileges. For more information, see "AS grantor Clause" on page 2-521.

- you cannot include the WITH GRANT OPTION clause.

  A role cannot, in turn, grant the same table-, type-, or routine-level privileges to another user.

The following example grants the table-level privilege Insert on the **supplier** table to the role **payables**:

```
GRANT INSERT ON supplier TO payables
```

Anyone granted the role of **payables** can now insert into **supplier**.

WITH GRANT OPTION Keywords

Using the WITH GRANT OPTION keyword conveys the specified privilege to *user* along with the right to grant those same privileges to other users. You create a chain of privileges that begins with you and extends to *user* as well as to whomever *user* conveys the right to grant privileges. If you use the WITH GRANT OPTION keyword, you can no longer control the dissemination of privileges.

If you revoke from *user* the privilege that you granted using the WITH GRANT OPTION keyword, you sever the chain of privileges. That is, when you revoke privileges from *user*, you automatically revoke the privileges of all users who received privileges from *user* or from the chain that *user* created (unless *user*, or the users who received privileges from *user*, were granted the same set of privileges by someone else). The following examples illustrate this situation. You, as the owner of the table **items**, issue the following statements to grant access to the user **mary**:

```
REVOKE ALL ON items FROM PUBLIC;
GRANT SELECT, UPDATE ON items TO mary WITH GRANT OPTION
```

The user **mary** uses her new privilege to grant users **cathy** and **paul** access to the table.

```
GRANT SELECT, UPDATE ON items TO cathy;
GRANT SELECT ON items TO paul
```

Later you issue the following statement to cancel access privileges for the user **mary** on the **items** table:

```
REVOKE SELECT, UPDATE ON items FROM mary
```

This single statement effectively revokes all privileges on the **items** table from the users **mary**, **cathy**, and **paul**.

If you want to create a chain of privileges with another user as the source of the privilege, use the AS *grantor* clause.

AS grantor Clause

When you grant privileges, by default, you are the one who can revoke those privileges. The AS *grantor* clause lets you establish another user as the source of the privileges you are granting. When you use this clause, the login provided in the AS grantor clause replaces your login in the appropriate system catalog table.

You can use this clause only if you have the DBA privilege on the database.

Once you use this clause, only the specified *grantor* can REVOKE the effects of the current GRANT. Even a DBA cannot revoke a privilege unless that DBA is listed in the appropriate system catalog table as the source who granted the privilege.

The following example illustrates this situation. You are the DBA and you grant all privileges on the **items** table to the user **tom**, along with the right to grant all privileges:

```
REVOKE ALL ON items FROM PUBLIC;
GRANT ALL ON items TO tom WITH GRANT OPTION
```

The following example illustrates a different situation. You also grant Select and Update privileges to the user **jim**, but you specify that the grant is made as the user **tom**. (The records of the database server show that the user **tom** is the grantor of the grant in the **systabauth** system catalog table, rather than you.)

```
GRANT SELECT, UPDATE ON items TO jim AS tom
```

Later, you decide to revoke privileges on the **items** table from the user **tom**, so you issue the following statement:

```
REVOKE ALL ON items FROM tom
```

When you try to revoke privileges from the user **jim** with a similar statement, however, the database server returns an error, as the following example shows:

```
REVOKE SELECT, UPDATE ON items FROM jim

580: Cannot revoke permission.
```

You get an error because the database server record shows the original grantor as the user **tom**, and you cannot revoke the privilege. Although you are the DBA, you cannot revoke a privilege that another user granted.

Related Information

Related statements: GRANT FRAGMENT, REVOKE, AND REVOKE FRAGMENT

For information about roles, see the following statements: CREATE ROLE, DROP ROLE, and SET ROLE.

In the *Informix Guide to Database Design and Implementation*, see the discussion of privileges.

For a discussion of how to embed GRANT and REVOKE statements in programs, see the *Informix Guide to SQL: Tutorial*.

GRANT FRAGMENT

Use the GRANT FRAGMENT statement to grant Insert, Update, and Delete privileges on individual fragments of a fragmented table.

Syntax

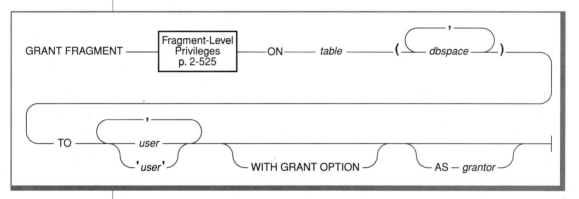

Element	Purpose	Restrictions	Syntax
dbspace	Name of the dbspace where the fragment is stored Use this parameter to specify the fragment or fragments on which privileges are to be granted. No default value exists.	You must specify at least one dbspace. The specified dbspaces must exist.	Identifier, p. 4-205
grantor	Name of the user who is to be listed as the grantor of the specified privileges in the **grantor** column of the **sysfragauth** system catalog table The user who issues the GRANT FRAGMENT statement is the default grantor of the privileges.	The user specified in *grantor* must be a valid user.	The name must conform to the conventions of your operating system.

(1 of 2)

Element	Purpose	Restrictions	Syntax
table	Name of the table that contains the fragment or fragments on which privileges are to be granted No default value exists.	The specified table must exist and must be fragmented by expression.	Database Object Name, p. 4-50
user	Name of the user or users to whom the specified privileges are to be granted No default value exists.	If you enclose user in quotation marks, the name of the user is stored exactly as you typed it. In an ANSI-compliant database, the name of the user is stored as uppercase letters if you do not use quotes around user.	The name must conform to the conventions of your operating system.

(2 of 2)

Usage

The GRANT FRAGMENT statement is similar to the GRANT statement. Both statements grant privileges to users. The difference between the two statements is that you use GRANT to grant privileges on a table while you use GRANT FRAGMENT to grant privileges on table fragments.

Use the GRANT FRAGMENT statement to grant the Insert, Update, or Delete privilege on one or more fragments of a table to one or more users.

The GRANT FRAGMENT statement is valid only for tables that are fragmented according to an expression-based distribution scheme. For an explanation of expression-based distribution schemes, see "Syntax" on page 2-12.

Fragment-Level Privileges

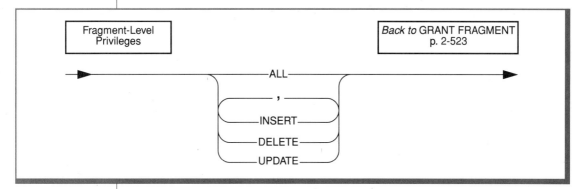

Fragment-Level Privileges

Back to GRANT FRAGMENT
p. 2-523

The following table defines each of the fragment-level privileges.

Privilege	Purpose
ALL	Provides Insert, Delete, and Update privileges on a fragment
INSERT	Lets you insert rows in the fragment
DELETE	Lets you delete rows in the fragment
UPDATE	Lets you update rows in the fragment and to name any column of the table in an UPDATE statement

Definition of Fragment-Level Authority

When a fragmented table is created in an ANSI-compliant database, the table owner implicitly receives all table-level privileges on the new table, but no other users receive privileges.

When a fragmented table is created in a database that is not ANSI compliant, the table owner implicitly receives all table-level privileges on the new table, and other users (that is, PUBLIC) receive the following default set of privileges on the table: Select, Update, Insert, Delete, and Index. The privileges granted to PUBLIC are explicitly recorded in the **systabauth** system catalog table.

A user who has table privileges on a fragmented table has the privileges implicitly on all fragments of the table. These privileges are not recorded in the **sysfragauth** system catalog table.

Whether or not the database is ANSI compliant, you can use the GRANT FRAGMENT statement to grant explicit Insert, Update, and Delete privileges on one or more fragments of a table that is fragmented by expression. The privileges granted by the GRANT FRAGMENT statement are explicitly recorded in the **sysfragauth** system catalog table.

The Insert, Update, and Delete privileges that are conferred on table fragments by the GRANT FRAGMENT statement are collectively known as fragment-level privileges or fragment-level authority.

Role of Fragment-Level Authority in Command Validation

Fragment-level authority lets users execute INSERT, DELETE, and UPDATE statements on table fragments even if they lack Insert, Update, and Delete privileges on the table as a whole. Users who lack privileges at the table level can insert, delete, and update rows in authorized fragments because of the algorithm by which the database server validates commands. This algorithm consists of the following checks:

1. When a user executes an INSERT, DELETE, or UPDATE statement, the database server first checks whether the user has the table authority necessary for the operation attempted. If the table authority exists, the command continues processing.

2. If the table authority does not exist, the database server checks whether the table is fragmented by expression. If the table is not fragmented by expression, the database server returns an error to the user. This error indicates that the user does not have the privilege to execute the command.

3. If the table is fragmented by expression, the database server checks whether the user has the fragment authority necessary for the operation attempted. If the fragment authority exists, the command continues processing. If the fragment authority does not exist, the database server returns an error to the user. This error indicates that the user does not have the privilege to execute the command.

Duration of Fragment-Level Authority

The duration of fragment-level authority is tied to the duration of the fragmentation strategy for the table as a whole.

If you drop a fragmentation strategy by means of a DROP TABLE statement or the INIT, DROP, or DETACH clauses of an ALTER FRAGMENT statement, you also drop any authorities that exist for the affected fragments. Similarly, if you drop a dbspace, you also drop any authorities that exist for the fragment that resides in that dbspace.

Tables that are created as a result of a DETACH or INIT clause of an ALTER FRAGMENT statement do not keep the authorities that the former fragment or fragments had when they were part of the fragmented table. Instead, such tables assume the default table authorities.

If a table with fragment authorities defined on it is changed to a table with a round-robin strategy or some other expression strategy, the fragment authorities are also dropped, and the table assumes the default table authorities.

Granting Privileges on One Fragment or a List of Fragments

You can grant fragment-level privileges on one fragment of a table or on a list of fragments.

Granting Privileges on One Fragment

The following statement grants the Insert, Update, and Delete privileges on the fragment of the **customer** table in **dbsp1** to the user **larry**:

```
GRANT FRAGMENT ALL ON customer (dbsp1) TO larry
```

Granting Privileges on More Than One Fragment

The following statement grants the Insert, Update, and Delete privileges on the fragments of the **customer** table in **dbsp1** and **dbsp2** to the user **millie**:

```
GRANT FRAGMENT ALL ON customer (dbsp1, dbsp2) TO millie
```

Granting Privileges on All Fragments of a Table

If you want to grant privileges on all fragments of a table to the same user or users, you can use the GRANT statement instead of the GRANT FRAGMENT statement. However, you can also use the GRANT FRAGMENT statement for this purpose.

Assume that the **customer** table is fragmented by expression into three fragments, and these fragments reside in the dbspaces named **dbsp1**, **dbsp2**, and **dbsp3**. You can use either of the following statements to grant the Insert privilege on all fragments of the table to the user **helen**:

```
GRANT FRAGMENT INSERT ON customer (dbsp1, dbsp2, dbsp3)
TO helen;

GRANT INSERT ON customer TO helen;
```

Granting Privileges to One User or a List of Users

You can grant fragment-level privileges to a single user or to a list of users.

Granting Privileges to One User

The following statement grants the Insert, Update, and Delete privileges on the fragment of the **customer** table in **dbsp3** to the user **oswald**:

```
GRANT FRAGMENT ALL ON customer (dbsp3) TO oswald
```

Granting Privileges to a List of Users

The following statement grants the Insert, Update, and Delete privileges on the fragment of the **customer** table in **dbsp3** to the users **jerome** and **hilda**:

```
GRANT FRAGMENT ALL ON customer (dbsp3) TO jerome, hilda
```

Granting One Privilege or a List of Privileges

When you specify fragment-level privileges in a GRANT FRAGMENT statement, you can specify one privilege, a list of privileges, or all privileges.

Granting One Privilege

The following statement grants the Update privilege on the fragment of the **customer** table in **dbsp1** to the user **ed**:

```
GRANT FRAGMENT UPDATE ON customer (dbsp1) TO ed
```

Granting a List of Privileges

The following statement grants the Update and Insert privileges on the fragment of the **customer** table in **dbsp1** to the user **susan**:

```
GRANT FRAGMENT UPDATE, INSERT ON customer (dbsp1) TO susan
```

Granting All Privileges

The following statement grants the Insert, Update, and Delete privileges on the fragment of the **customer** table in **dbsp1** to the user **harry**:

```
GRANT FRAGMENT ALL ON customer (dbsp1) TO harry
```

WITH GRANT OPTION Clause

By including the WITH GRANT OPTION clause in the GRANT FRAGMENT statement, you convey the specified fragment-level privileges to a user and the right to grant those same privileges to other users.

The following statement grants the Update privilege on the fragment of the **customer** table in **dbsp3** to the user **george** and gives this user the right to grant the Update privilege on the same fragment to other users:

```
GRANT FRAGMENT UPDATE ON customer (dbsp3) TO george
    WITH GRANT OPTION
```

AS grantor Clause

The AS *grantor* clause is optional in a GRANT FRAGMENT statement. Use this clause to specify the grantor of the privilege.

Including the AS grantor Clause

When you include the AS *grantor* clause in the GRANT FRAGMENT statement, you specify that the user who is named as *grantor* is listed as the grantor of the privilege in the **grantor** column of the **sysfragauth** system catalog table.

In the following example, the DBA grants the Delete privilege on the fragment of the **customer** table in **dbsp3** to the user **martha**. In the GRANT FRAGMENT statement, the DBA uses the AS *grantor* clause to specify that the user **jack** is listed as the grantor of the privilege in the **sysfragauth** system catalog table.

```
GRANT FRAGMENT DELETE ON customer (dbsp3) TO martha AS jack
```

Omitting the AS grantor Clause

When a GRANT FRAGMENT statement does not include the AS *grantor* clause, the user who issues the statement is the default grantor of the privileges that are specified in the statement.

In the following example, the user grants the Update privilege on the fragment of the **customer** table in **dbsp3** to the user **fred**. Because this statement does not specify the AS *grantor* clause, the user who issues the statement is listed by default as the grantor of the privilege in the **sysfragauth** system catalog table.

```
GRANT FRAGMENT UPDATE ON customer (dbsp3) TO fred
```

Consequences of the AS grantor Clause

If you omit the AS *grantor* clause, or if you specify your own user name in the *grantor* parameter, you can later revoke the privilege that you granted to the specified user. However, if you specify someone other than yourself as the grantor of the specified privilege to the specified user, only that grantor can revoke the privilege from the user.

For example, if you grant the Delete privilege on the fragment of the **customer** table in **dbsp3** to user **martha** but specify user **jack** as the grantor of the privilege, user **jack** can revoke that privilege from user **martha**, but you cannot revoke that privilege from user **martha**.

Related Information

Related statements: GRANT and REVOKE FRAGMENT

For a discussion of fragment-level and table-level privileges, see the *Informix Guide to Database Design and Implementation*.

INFO

Use the INFO statement to display a variety of information about databases and tables.

Use this statement with DB-Access.

Syntax

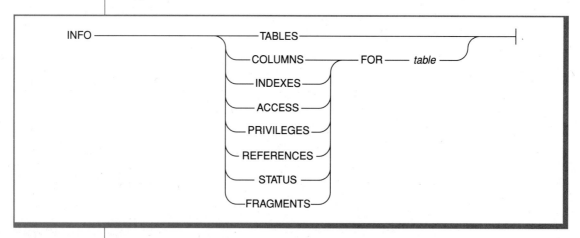

Element	Purpose	Restrictions	Syntax
table	Name of the table for which you want to find information	The table must exist.	Database Object Name, p. 4-50

Usage

You can use the keywords of the INFO statement to display the following types of information.

INFO Keyword	Information Displayed
TABLES	Table names in the current database
COLUMNS	Column information for a specified table
INDEXES	Index information for a specified table
FRAGMENTS	Fragmentation strategy for a specified table
ACCESS	Access privileges for a specified table
PRIVILEGES	Access privileges for a specified table
REFERENCES	References privileges for the columns of a specified table
STATUS	Status information for a specified table

TABLES Keyword

Use the TABLES keyword to display a list of the tables in the current database. The TABLES keyword does not display the system catalog tables.

The name of a table can appear in one of the following ways:

- If you are the owner of the **cust_calls** table, it appears as **cust_calls**.
- If you are *not* the owner of the **cust_calls** table, the owner's name precedes the table name, such as **'june'.cust_calls**.

COLUMNS Keyword

Use the COLUMNS keyword to display the names and data types of the columns in a specified table and whether null values are allowed.

INDEXES Keyword

Use the INDEXES keyword to display the name, owner, and type of each index in a specified table, whether the index is clustered, and the names of the columns that are indexed.

FRAGMENTS Keyword

Use the FRAGMENTS keyword to display the dbspace names where fragments are located for a specified table. If the table is fragmented with an expression-based distribution scheme, the INFO statement also shows the expressions.

ACCESS Keyword

Use the ACCESS or PRIVILEGES keywords to display user-access privileges for a specified table.

REFERENCES Keyword

Use the REFERENCES keyword to display the References privilege for users for the columns of a specified table.

If you want information about database-level privileges, you must use a SELECT statement to access the **sysusers** system catalog table.

STATUS Keyword

Use the STATUS keyword to display information about the owner, row length, number of rows and columns, creation date, and status of audit trails for a specified table.

Related Information

Related statements: GRANT and REVOKE

For a description of the Info option on the SQL menu or the TABLE menu in DB-Access, see the *DB-Access User's Manual*.

INSERT

Use the INSERT statement to insert one or more new rows into a table or view or one or more elements into an SPL or ESQL/C collection variable.

Syntax

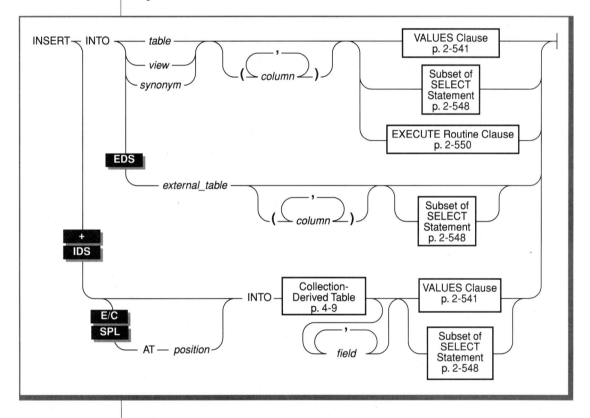

Element	Purpose	Restrictions	Syntax
column	Name of a column that receives a new column value, or a list of columns that receive new values If you specify a column list, values are inserted into columns in the order in which you list the columns. If you do not specify a column list, values are inserted into columns in the column order that was established when the table was created or last altered.	The number of columns you specify must equal the number of values supplied in the VALUES clause or by the SELECT statement, either implicitly or explicitly. If you omit a column from the column list, and the column does not have a default value associated with it, the database server places a null value in the column when the INSERT statement is executed.	Identifier, p. 4-205
external_table	Name of the external table on which you want to insert data	The external table must exist.	Database Object Name, p. 4-50
field	Name of a field of a named or unnamed row type	The row type must already be defined in the database.	"Field Definition" on page 2-220 and "Unnamed Row Types" on page 4-68
position	Position at which you want to insert an element in a LIST	The position can be a literal number or an SPL variable of type INT or SMALLINT.	Literal Number, p. 4-237
synonym	Name of the synonym on which you want to insert data	The synonym and the table to which the synonym points must exist.	Database Object Name, p. 4-50
table	Name of the table on which you want to insert data	The table must exist.	Database Object Name, p. 4-50
view	Name of the view on which you want to insert data	The view must exist.	Database Object Name, p. 4-50

Usage

To insert data into a table, you must either own the table or have the Insert privilege for the table (see "GRANT" on page 2-500). To insert data into a view, you must have the required Insert privilege, and the view must meet the requirements explained in "Inserting Rows Through a View."

If you insert data into a table that has data integrity constraints associated with it, the inserted data must meet the constraint criteria. If it does not, the database server returns an error.

If you are using effective checking, and the checking mode is set to IMMEDIATE, all specified constraints are checked at the end of each INSERT statement. If the checking mode is set to DEFERRED, all specified constraints are *not* checked until the transaction is committed.

Specifying Columns

If you do not explicitly specify one or more columns, data is inserted into columns using the column order that was established when the table was created or last altered. The column order is listed in the **syscolumns** system catalog table.

In ESQL/C, you can use the DESCRIBE statement with an INSERT statement to determine the column order and the data type of the columns in a table. ♦

The number of columns specified in the INSERT INTO clause must equal the number of values supplied in the VALUES clause or by the SELECT statement, either implicitly or explicitly. If you specify columns, the columns receive data in the order in which you list them. The first value following the VALUES keyword is inserted into the first column listed, the second value is inserted into the second column listed, and so on.

Using the AT Clause

Use the AT clause to insert LIST elements at a specified position in a collection variable. By default, Dynamic Server adds a new element at the end of a LIST collection. If you specify a position that is greater than the number of elements in the list, the database server adds the element to the end of the list. You must specify a position value of at least 1 because the first element in the list is at position 1.

The following SPL example shows how you can insert a value at a specific position in a list:

```
CREATE PROCEDURE test3()

    DEFINE a_list LIST(SMALLINT NOT NULL);

    SELECT list_col INTO a_list FROM table1
        WHERE id = 201;
    INSERT AT 3 INTO TABLE(a_list) VALUES( 9 );

    UPDATE table1
        VALUES list_col = a_list
        WHERE id = 201;

END PROCEDURE;
```

Suppose that before this INSERT, **a_list** contained the elements {1,8,4,5,2}. After this INSERT, **a_list** contains the elements {1,8,9,4,5,2}. The new element 9 was inserted at position 3 in the list. For more information on inserting values into collection variables, see "Collection Derived Table" on page 4-9.

Inserting Rows Through a View

You can insert data through a *single-table* view if you have the Insert privilege on the view. To do this, the defining SELECT statement can select from only one table, and it cannot contain any of the following components:

- DISTINCT keyword
- GROUP BY clause
- Derived value (also referred to as a virtual column)
- Aggregate value

Columns in the underlying table that are unspecified in the view receive either a default value or a null value if no default is specified. If one of these columns does not specify a default value, and a null value is not allowed, the insert fails.

You can use data-integrity constraints to prevent users from inserting values into the underlying table that do not fit the view-defining SELECT statement. For further information, see "WITH CHECK OPTION Keywords" on page 2-338.

If several users are entering sensitive information into a single table, the built-in USER function can limit their view to only the specific rows that each user inserted. The following example contains a view and an INSERT statement that achieve this effect:

```
CREATE VIEW salary_view AS
    SELECT lname, fname, current_salary
        FROM salary
        WHERE  entered_by = USER

INSERT INTO salary
    VALUES ('Smith', 'Pat', 75000, USER)
```

Inserting Rows with a Cursor

In ESQL/C, if you associate a cursor with an INSERT statement, you must use the OPEN, PUT, and CLOSE statements to carry out the INSERT operation. For databases that have transactions but are not ANSI-compliant, you must issue these statements within a transaction.

If you are using a cursor that is associated with an INSERT statement, the rows are buffered before they are written to the disk. The insert buffer is flushed under the following conditions:

- The buffer becomes full.

- A FLUSH statement executes.

- A CLOSE statement closes the cursor.

- In a database that is not ANSI-compliant, an OPEN statement implicitly closes and then reopens the cursor.

- A COMMIT WORK statement ends the transaction.

When the insert buffer is flushed, the client processor performs appropriate data conversion before it sends the rows to the database server. When the database server receives the buffer, it converts any user-defined data types and then begins to insert the rows one at a time into the database. If an error is encountered while the database server inserts the buffered rows into the database, any buffered rows that follow the last successfully inserted rows are discarded.

Inserting Rows into a Database Without Transactions

If you are inserting rows into a database without transactions, you must take explicit action to restore inserted rows after a failure. For example, if the INSERT statement fails after you insert some rows, the successfully inserted rows remain in the table. You cannot recover automatically from a failed insert.

Inserting Rows into a Database with Transactions

If you are inserting rows into a database with transactions, and you are using explicit transactions, use the ROLLBACK WORK statement to undo the insertion. If you do not execute BEGIN WORK before the insert, and the insert fails, the database server automatically rolls back any database modifications made since the beginning of the insert.

ANSI

If you are inserting rows into an ANSI-compliant database, transactions are implicit, and all database modifications take place within a transaction. In this case, if an INSERT statement fails, use the ROLLBACK WORK statement to undo the insertions.

If you are using an explicit transaction, and the update fails, the database server automatically undoes the effects of the update. ♦

EDS

If you are using Enterprise Decision Server, tables that you create with the RAW usage type are never logged. Thus, raw tables are not recoverable, even though the database uses logging. For information about raw tables, refer to the *Informix Guide to SQL: Reference*. ♦

Rows that you insert with a transaction remain locked until the end of the transaction. The end of a transaction is either a COMMIT WORK statement, where all modifications are made to the database, or a ROLLBACK WORK statement, where none of the modifications are made to the database. If many rows are affected by a *single* INSERT statement, you can exceed the maximum number of simultaneous locks permitted. To prevent this situation, either insert fewer rows per transaction or lock the page (or the entire table) before you execute the INSERT statement.

VALUES Clause

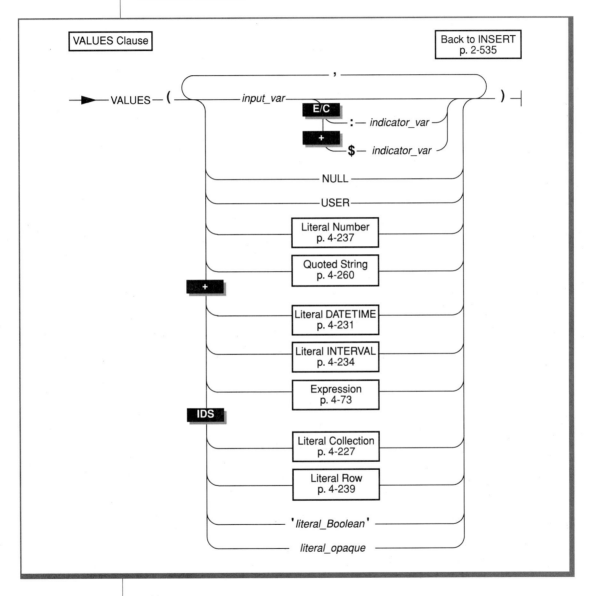

Element	Purpose	Restrictions	Syntax
indicator_var	Program variable that indicates when an SQL statement in an ESQL/C program returns a null value to *input_var*	For restrictions that apply to indicator variables in ESQL/C, see the *Informix ESQL/C Programmer's Manual.*	Name must conform to language-specific rules for variable names.
input_var	Host or program variable that specifies a value to be inserted into a column This variable can be a collection variable.	You can specify in input_var any other value option listed in the VALUES clause (NULL, Literal Number, and so on). If you specify a quoted string in *input_var*, the string can be longer than the 32-kilobyte maximum that applies to your specified quoted strings.	Name must conform to language-specific rules for variable names.
literal_opaque (IDS only)	Literal representation for an opaque data type	Must be a literal that is recognized by the input support function for the associated opaque type.	The literal representation is defined by the developer of the opaque type.
literal_Boolean	Literal representation of a Boolean value	A literal Boolean value can only be 't' (TRUE) or 'f' (FALSE) and must be specified as a quoted string.	Quoted String, p. 4-260

When you use the VALUES clause, you can insert only one row at a time. Each value that follows the VALUES keyword is assigned to the corresponding column listed in the INSERT INTO clause (or in column order if a list of columns is not specified).

If you are inserting a quoted string into a column, the maximum length of the string is 256 bytes. If you insert a quoted string that is longer than 256 bytes, the database server returns an error.

E/C

In ESQL/C, if you are using variables, you can insert quoted strings longer than 256 bytes into a table. ♦

For discussions on the keywords that you can use in the VALUES clause, refer to "Constant Expressions" on page 4-108.

Considering Data Types

When you use the INSERT statement, the value that you insert into a column does not have to be of the same data type as the column that receives it. However, these two data types must be compatible. Two data types are compatible if the database server has some way to cast one data type to another. A *cast* is the mechanism by which the database server converts one data type to another.

The database server makes every effort to perform data conversion. If the data cannot be converted, the INSERT operation fails.

Data conversion also fails if the target data type cannot hold the value that is specified. For example, you cannot insert the integer 123456 into a column defined as a SMALLINT data type because this data type cannot hold a number that large.

For a summary of the casting that the database server provides, see the *Informix Guide to SQL: Reference*. For information on how to create a user-defined cast, see the CREATE CAST statement in this manual and *Extending Informix Dynamic Server 2000*.

Inserting Values into Serial Columns

You can insert consecutive numbers, explicit values, or explicit values that reset the serial sequence value in a serial column:

- To insert a consecutive serial value

  Specify a zero for the serial column in the INSERT statement. When a serial column is set to zero, the database server assigns the next highest value.

- To insert an explicit value

  Specify the nonzero value after you first verify that the value does not duplicate one already in the table. If the serial column is uniquely indexed or has a unique constraint, and you try to insert a value that duplicates one already in the table, the database server returns an error.

  If the value is greater than the current maximum value, you will create a gap in the sequence.

- To create a gap in the sequence (reset the serial value)

  Specify a positive value that is greater than the current maximum value in the column.

  As an alternative, you can use the MODIFY clause of the ALTER TABLE statement to reset the next value of a serial column. For more information, see "Altering the Next Serial Number" on page 2-74.

Null values are not allowed in serial columns.

IDS

If you are inserting a serial value into a table that is part of a table hierarchy, the database server updates all tables in the hierarchy that contain the serial counter with the value that you insert (either a zero (0) for the next highest value or a specific number). ♦

IDS

Inserting Values into Opaque-Type Columns

Some opaque data types require special processing when they are inserted. For example, if an opaque data type contains spatial or multirepresentational data, it might provide a choice of how to store the data: inside the internal structure or, for very large objects, in a smart large object.

This processing is accomplished by calling a user-defined support function called **assign()**. When you execute the INSERT statement on a table whose rows contains one of these opaque types, the database server automatically invokes the **assign()** function for the type. The **assign()** function can make the decision of how to store the data. For more information about the **assign()** support function, see *Extending Informix Dynamic Server 2000*.

IDS

Inserting Values into Collection Columns

You can use the VALUES clause to insert values into a collection column. For more information, see "Collection Constructors" on page 4-118.

E/C

SPL

You can also use a collection variable to insert values into a collection column. With a collection variable you can insert one or more individual elements in a collection. For more information, see "Collection Derived Table" on page 4-9. ♦

Regardless of what method you use to insert values into a collection column, you cannot insert null elements into the collection column. Thus expressions that you use cannot evaluate to null. If the collection that you are attempting to insert contains a null element, the database server returns an error.

Example

For example, suppose you define the **tab1** table as follows:

```
CREATE TABLE tab1
(
    int1 INTEGER,
    list1 LIST(ROW(a INTEGER, b CHAR(5)) NOT NULL),
    dec1 DECIMAL(5,2)
)
```

The following INSERT statement inserts a row into **tab1**:

```
INSERT INTO tab1 VALUES
    (
    10,
    LIST{ROW(1,'abcde'),
        ROW(POW(3,3), '=27'),
        ROW(ROUND(ROOT(126)), '=11')},
    100
    )
```

The collection column, **list1**, in this example has three elements. Each element is an unnamed row type with an INTEGER field and a CHAR(5) field. The first element is composed of two literal values, an integer (1) and a quoted string (abcde). The second and third elements also use a quoted string to indicate the value for the second field. However, they each designate the value for the first field with an expression rather than a literal value.

IDS

Inserting Values into Row-Type Columns

You can use the VALUES clause to insert literal and nonliteral values in a named row type or unnamed row type column. For example, suppose you define the following named row type and table:

```
CREATE ROW TYPE address_t
(
    street CHAR(20),
    city CHAR(15),
    state CHAR(2),
    zipcode CHAR(9)
);

CREATE TABLE employee
(
    name ROW ( fname CHAR(20), lname CHAR(20)),
    address address_t
);
```

The following INSERT statement inserts *literal* values in the **name** and **address** columns of the **employee** table:

```
INSERT INTO employee VALUES
    (
        ROW('John', 'Williams'),
        ROW('103 Baker St', 'Tracy','CA', 94060)::address_t
    )
```

The INSERT statement uses ROW constructors to generate values for the **name** column (an unnamed row type) and the **address** column (a named row type). When you specify a value for a named row type, you must use the CAST AS keyword or the double colon (::) operator, in conjunction with the name of the named row type, to cast the value to the named row type.

For more information on the syntax for ROW constructors, see "Constructor Expressions" on page 4-116 in the Expression segment. For information on literal values for named row types and unnamed row types, see "Literal Row" on page 4-239.

E/C

You can use ESQL/C host variables to insert *non-literal* values as:

- an entire row type into a column.

  Use a **row** variable as a variable name in the VALUES clause to insert values for all fields in a row column at one time.

- individual fields of a row type.

  To insert nonliteral values in a row-type column, you can first insert the elements in a **row** variable and then specify the **collection** variable in the SET clause of an UPDATE statement.

When you use a row variable in the VALUES clause, the row variable must contain values for each field value. For information on how to insert values in a row variable, see "Inserting into a Row Variable" on page 2-551. ♦

Using Expressions in the VALUES Clause

You can insert any type of expression except a column expression into a column. For example, you can insert built-in functions that return the current date, date and time, login name of the current user, or database server name where the current database resides.

The TODAY keyword returns the system date. The CURRENT keyword returns the system date and time. The USER keyword returns a string that contains the login account name of the current user. The SITENAME or DBSERVERNAME keyword returns the database server name where the current database resides. The following example shows how to use built-in functions to insert data:

```
INSERT INTO cust_calls (customer_num, call_dtime, user_id,
                        call_code, call_descr)
    VALUES (212, CURRENT, USER, 'L', '2 days')
```

For more information, see "Expression" on page 4-73.

Inserting Nulls with the VALUES Clause

When you execute an INSERT statement, a null value is inserted into any column for which you do not provide a value as well as for all columns that do not have default values associated with them, which are not listed explicitly. You also can use the NULL keyword to indicate that a column should be assigned a null value. The following example inserts values into three columns of the **orders** table:

```
INSERT INTO orders (orders_num, order_date, customer_num)
    VALUES (0, NULL, 123)
```

In this example, a null value is explicitly entered in the **order_date** column, and all other columns of the **orders** table that are *not* explicitly listed in the INSERT INTO clause are also filled with null values.

Subset of SELECT Statement

As indicated in the diagram for "INSERT" on page 2-535, not all clauses and options of the SELECT statement are available for you to use in an INSERT statement.

The following SELECT clauses and options are not supported:

- FIRST
- INTO TEMP
- ORDER BY
- UNION ♦

For a complete description of SELECT syntax and usage, see "SELECT" on page 634.

If this statement has a WHERE clause that does not return rows, **sqlca** returns SQLNOTFOUND (100) for ANSI-compliant databases. In databases that are not ANSI compliant, **sqlca** returns (0). When you insert as a part of a multi-statement prepare, and no rows are inserted, **sqlca** returns SQLNOTFOUND (100) for both ANSI databases and databases that are not ANSI compliant.

IDS

If you are inserting values into a supertable in a table hierarchy, the subquery can reference a subtable.

If you are inserting values into a subtable in a table hierarchy, the subquery can reference the supertable if it references only the supertable. That is, the subquery must use the SELECT...FROM ONLY (*supertable*)...syntax. ♦

EDS

Using External Tables

In Enterprise Decision Server, when you create a SELECT statement as a part of a load or unload operation that involves an external table, keep the following restrictions in mind:

- Only one external table is allowed in the FROM clause.
- The SELECT subquery cannot contain an INTO clause, but it can include any valid SQL expression.

When you move data from a database into an external table, the SELECT statement must define all columns in the external table. The SELECT statement must not contain a FIRST, FOR UPDATE, INTO, INTO SCRATCH, or INTO TEMP clause. However, you can use an ORDER BY clause to produce files that are ordered within themselves.

E/C

Using INSERT as a Dynamic Management Statement

In ESQL/C, you can use the INSERT statement to handle situations where you need to write code that can insert data whose structure is unknown at the time you compile. For more information, refer to the dynamic management section of the *Informix ESQL/C Programmer's Manual*.

EXECUTE Routine Clause

You can specify the EXECUTE FUNCTION (or EXECUTE PROCEDURE) statement to insert values that a user-defined function returns.

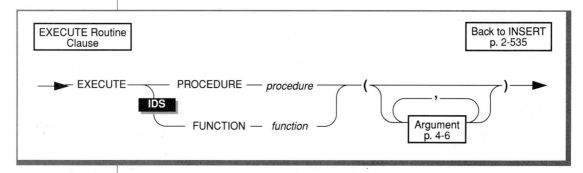

Element	Purpose	Restrictions	Syntax
function	Name of the user-defined function to use to insert the data	The function must exist.	Database Object Name, p. 4-50
procedure	Name of the user-defined procedure to use to insert the data	The procedure must exist.	Database Object Name, p. 4-50

When you use a user-defined function to insert column values, the return values of the function must have a one-to-one correspondence with the listed columns. That is, each value that the function returns must be of the data type expected by the corresponding column in the column list.

IDS

For backward compatibility, you can use the EXECUTE PROCEDURE keywords to execute an SPL function that was created with the CREATE PROCEDURE statement. ♦

If the called SPL routine scans or updates the target table of the insert, the database returns an error. That is, the SPL routine cannot select data from the table into which you are inserting rows.

If a called SPL routine contains certain SQL statements, the database server returns an error. For information on which SQL statements cannot be used in an SPL routine that is called within a data manipulation statement, see "Restrictions on an SPL Routine Called in a Data Manipulation Statement" on page 4-302.

Number of Allowed Return Values

SPL

An SPL function can return one or more values. Make sure that the number of values that the function returns matches the number of columns in the table or the number of columns that you list in the column list of the INSERT statement. The columns into which you insert the values must have compatible data types with the values that the SPL function returns. ♦

Ext

An external function can only return *one* value. Make sure that you specify only one column in the column list of the INSERT statement. This column must have a compatible data type with the value that the external function returns. The external function can be an iterator function. ♦

Example

The following example shows how to insert data into a temporary table called **result_tmp** in order to output to a file the results of a user-defined function (**f_one**) that returns multiple rows.

```
CREATE TEMP TABLE result_tmp( ... );
INSERT INTO result_tmp EXECUTE FUNCTION f_one();
UNLOAD TO 'file' SELECT * FROM foo_tmp;
```

IDS
E/C
SPL

Inserting into a Row Variable

The INSERT statement does not support a row variable in the Collection Derived Table segment. However, you can use the UPDATE statement to insert new field values into a row variable. For example, the following ESQL/C code fragment inserts a new row into the **rectangles** table (which "Inserting Values into Row-Type Columns" on page 2-546 defines):

```
EXEC SQL BEGIN DECLARE SECTION;
    row (x int, y int, length float, width float) myrect;
EXEC SQL END DECLARE SECTION;

...
EXEC SQL update table(:myrect)
    set x=7, y=3, length=6, width=2;
EXEC SQL insert into rectangles values (12, :myrect);
```

For more information, see "Updating a Row Variable" on page 2-832.

Related Information

Related statements: CLOSE, CREATE EXTERNAL TABLE, DECLARE, DESCRIBE, EXECUTE, FLUSH, FOREACH, OPEN, PREPARE, PUT, and SELECT

For a task-oriented discussion of inserting data into tables and for information on how to access row and collections with SPL variables, see the *Informix Guide to SQL: Tutorial*.

For a discussion of the GLS aspects of the INSERT statement, see the *Informix Guide to GLS Functionality*.

For information on how to access row and collections with ESQL/C host variables, see the chapter on complex types in the *Informix ESQL/C Programmer's Manual*.

LOAD

Use the LOAD statement to insert data from an operating-system file into an existing table or view.

Use this statement with DB-Access and the SQL Editor.

Syntax

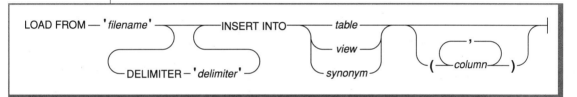

Element	Purpose	Restrictions	Syntax
column	Name of a column or columns that receive data values from the load file during the load operation	You must specify the columns that receive data if you are not loading data into all columns. You must also specify columns if the order of the fields in the load file does not match the default order of the columns in the table (the order established when the table was created).	Identifier, p. 4-205
delimiter	Quoted string that identifies the character to use to separate the data values in each line of the load file The default delimiter is the character set in the **DBDELIMITER** environment variable. If **DBDELIMITER** has not been set, the default delimiter is the pipe (l).	You cannot use any of the following characters as a delimiter: backslash (\), newline character (=CTRL-J), and hexadecimal numbers (0-9, a-f, A-F).	Quoted String, p. 4-260

(1 of 2)

Element	Purpose	Restrictions	Syntax
filename	Quoted string that identifies the pathname and filename of the load file	See "LOAD FROM File" on page 2-554.	Pathname and filename must conform to the naming conventions of your operating system.
	The load file contains the data to be loaded into the specified table or view. The default pathname for the load file is the current directory.		
synonym	Name of the synonym for the table in which you want to insert data	The synonym and the table to which the synonym points must exist.	Database Object Name, p. 4-50
table	Name of the table in which you want to insert data	The table must exist.	Database Object Name, p. 4-50
view	Name of the view in which you want to insert data	The view must exist.	Database Object Name, p. 4-50

(2 of 2)

Usage

The LOAD statement appends new rows to the table. It does not overwrite existing data.

You cannot add a row that has the same key as an existing row.

To use the LOAD statement, you must have Insert privileges for the table where you want to insert data. For information on database-level and table-level privileges, see the GRANT statement.

LOAD FROM File

The LOAD FROM file contains the data to add to a table. You can use the file that the UNLOAD statement creates as the LOAD FROM file.

If you do not include a list of columns in the INSERT INTO clause, the fields in the file must match the columns that are specified for the table in number, order, and data type.

Each line of the file must have the same number of fields. You must define field lengths that are less than or equal to the length that is specified for the corresponding column. Specify only values that can convert to the data type of the corresponding column. The following table indicates how the database server expects you to represent the data types in the LOAD FROM file (when you use the default locale, U.S. English).

Type of Data	Input Format
blank	One or more blank characters between delimiters.
	You can include leading blanks in fields that do not correspond to character columns.
Boolean	A 't' or 'T' indicates a TRUE value, and an 'f' or 'F' indicates a FALSE value.
collections	Collection must have its values surrounded by braces ({}) and a field delimiter separating each element.
	For more information, see "Loading Complex Types" on page 2-560.
datE	Character string in the following format: *mm/dd/year*.
	You must state the month as a two-digit number. You can use a two-digit number for the year if the year is in the 20th century. (You can specify another century algorithm with the **DBCENTURY** environment variable.) The value must be an actual date; for example, February 30 is illegal. You can use a different date format if you indicate this format with the **GL_DATE** or **DBDATE** environment variable.
	For more information about these environment variables, see the *Informix Guide to GLS Functionality*.
MONEY	Value that can include currency notation: a leading currency symbol ($), a comma (,) as the thousands separator, and a period (.) as the decimal separator.
	You can use a different currency notation if you indicate this notation with the **DBMONEY** environment variable.
	For more information on this environment variable, see the *Informix Guide to GLS Functionality*.
NULL	Nothing between the delimiters.

(1 of 2)

Type of Data	Input Format
row types (named and unnamed)	Row type must have its values surrounded by parentheses and a field delimiter separating each element. For more information, see "Loading Complex Types" on page 2-560.
simple large objects (TEXT, BYTE)	TEXT and BYTE columns are loaded directly from the LOAD TO file. For more information, see "Loading Simple Large Objects" on page 2-558.
smart large objects (CLOB, BLOB)	CLOB and BLOB columns are loaded from a separate operating-system file. The field for the CLOB or BLOB column in the LOAD FROM file contains the name of this separate file. For more information, see "Loading Smart Large Objects" on page 2-559.
time	Character string in the following format: *year-month-day hour:minute:second.fraction*. You cannot use type specification or qualifiers for DATETIME or INTERVAL values. The year must be a four-digit number, and the month must be a two-digit number. You can specify a different date and time format with the **GL_DATETIME** or **DBTIME** environment variable. For more information on these environment variables, see the *Informix Guide to GLS Functionality*.
user-defined data formats (opaque types)	Associated opaque type must have an import support function defined if special processing is required to copy the data in the LOAD FROM file to the internal format of the opaque type. An import binary support function might also be required if the data is in binary format. The data in the LOAD FROM file must correspond to the format that the import or importbinary support function expects. The associated opaque type must have an assign support function if special processing is required before the data is written in the database. For more information, see "Loading Opaque-Type Columns" on page 2-560.

For more information on **DB** environment variables, refer to the *Informix Guide to SQL: Reference*. For more information on **GL** environment variables, refer to the *Informix Guide to GLS Functionality*.

GLS

If you are using a nondefault locale, the formats of DATE, DATETIME, MONEY, and numeric column values in the LOAD FROM file must be compatible with the formats that the locale supports for these data types. For more information, see the *Informix Guide to GLS Functionality*. ♦

The following example shows the contents of a hypothetical input file named **new_custs**:

```
0|Jeffery|Padgett|Wheel Thrills|3450 El Camino|Suite 10|Palo
Alto|CA|94306||
0|Linda|Lane|Palo Alto Bicycles|2344 University||Palo
Alto|CA|94301|(415)323-6440
```

This data file conveys the following information:

- Indicates a serial field by specifying a zero (0)
- Uses the pipe (|), the default delimiter
- Assigns null values to the **phone** field for the first row and the **address2** field for the second row. The null values are shown by two delimiter with nothing between them.

The following statement loads the values from the **new_custs** file into the **customer** table owned by **jason**:

```
LOAD FROM 'new_custs' INSERT INTO jason.customer
```

If you include any of the following special characters as part of the value of a field, you must precede the character with a backslash (\):

- Backslash
- Delimiter
- Newline character anywhere in the value of a VARCHAR or NVARCHAR column
- Newline character at end of a value for a TEXT value

Do not use the backslash character (\) as a field separator. It serves as an escape character to inform the LOAD statement that the next character is to be interpreted as part of the data.

Loading Character Data

The fields that correspond to character columns can contain more characters than the defined maximum allows for the field. The extra characters are ignored.

If you are loading files that contain VARCHAR data types, note the following information:

- If you give the LOAD statement data in which the character fields (including VARCHAR) are longer than the column size, the excess characters are disregarded.
- Use the backslash (\) to escape embedded delimiter and backslash characters in all character fields, including VARCHAR.
- Do not use the following characters as delimiting characters in the LOAD FROM file: 0 to 9, a to f, A to F, backslash, newline character.

Loading Simple Large Objects

The database server loads simple large objects (BYTE and TEXT columns) directly from the LOAD FROM file. Keep the following restrictions in mind when you load BYTE and TEXT data:

- You cannot have leading and trailing blanks in BYTE fields.
- Use the backslash (\) to escape embedded delimiter and backslash characters in TEXT fields.
- Data being loaded into a BYTE column must be in ASCII-hexadecimal form. BYTE columns cannot contain preceding blanks.
- Do not use the following characters as delimiting characters in the LOAD FROM file: 0 to 9, a to f, A to F, backslash, newline character.

GLS

For TEXT columns, the database server handles any required code-set conversions for the data. For more information, see the *Informix Guide to GLS Functionality.* ♦

If you are unloading files that contain simple-large-object data types, objects smaller than 10 kilobytes are stored temporarily in memory. You can adjust the 10-kilobyte setting to a larger setting with the **DBBLOBBUF** environment variable. Simple large objects that are larger than the default or the setting of the **DBBLOBBUF** environment variable are stored in a temporary file. For additional information about the **DBBLOBBUF** environment variable, see the *Informix Guide to SQL: Reference*.

Loading Smart Large Objects

The database server loads smart large objects (BLOB and CLOB columns) from a separate operating-system file on the client computer. For more information on the structure of this file, see "Unloading Smart Large Objects" on page 2-809.

In a LOAD FROM file, a CLOB or BLOB column value appears as follows:

```
start_off,length,client_path
```

In this format, start_off is the starting offset (in hexadecimal) of the smart-large-object value within the client file, *length* is the length (in hexadecimal) of the BLOB or CLOB value, and *client_path* is the pathname for the client file. No spaces can appear between these values.

For example, to load a CLOB value that is 512 bytes long and is at offset 256 in the **/usr/apps/clob9ce7.318** file, the database server expects the CLOB value to appear as follows in the LOAD FROM file:

```
|100,200,/usr/apps/clob9ce7.318|
```

If the whole client file is to be loaded, a CLOB or BLOB column value appears as follows in the LOAD FROM file:

```
client_path
```

For example, to load a CLOB value that occupies the entire file **/usr/apps/clob9ce7.318**, the database server expects the CLOB value to appear as follows in the LOAD FROM file:

```
|/usr/apps/clob9ce7.318|
```

For CLOB columns, the database server handles any required code-set conversions for the data. For more information, see the *Informix Guide to GLS Functionality*. ◆

IDS

Loading Complex Types

In a LOAD FROM file, complex types appear as follows:

- Collections are introduced with the appropriate constructor (SET, MULTISET, or LIST), and their elements are enclosed in braces ({}) and separated with a comma, as follows:

  ```
  constructor{val1 , val2 , ... }
  ```

  For example, to load the SET values {1, 3, 4} into a column whose data type is SET(INTEGER NOT NULL), the corresponding field of the LOAD FROM file appears as:

  ```
  |SET{1 , 3 , 4}|
  ```

- Row types (named and unnamed) are introduced with the ROW constructor and their fields are enclosed with parentheses and separated with a comma, as follows:

  ```
  ROW(val1 , val2 , ... )
  ```

  For example, to load the ROW values (1, 'abc'), the corresponding field of the LOAD FROM file appears as:

  ```
  |ROW(1 , abc)|
  ```

IDS

Loading Opaque-Type Columns

Some opaque data types require special processing when they are inserted. For example, if an opaque data type contains spatial or multirepresentational data, it might provide a choice of how to store the data: inside the internal structure or, for very large objects, in a smart large object.

This processing is accomplished by calling a user-defined support function called **assign()**. When you execute the LOAD statement on a table whose rows contain one of these opaque types, the database server automatically invokes the **assign()** function for the type. The **assign()** function can make the decision of how to store the data. For more information about the **assign()** support function, see the *Extending Informix Dynamic Server 2000* manual.

DELIMITER Clause

Use the DELIMITER clause to specify the delimiter that separates the data contained in each column in a row in the input file. You can specify TAB (CTRL-I) or <blank> (= ASCII 32) as the delimiter symbol. You cannot use the following items as the delimiter symbol:

- Backslash (\)
- Newline character (CTRL-J)
- Hexadecimal numbers (0 to 9, a to f, A to F)

If you omit this clause, the database server checks the **DBDELIMITER** environment variable. For information about how to set the **DBDELIMITER** environment variable, see the *Informix Guide to SQL: Reference.*

If the **DBDELIMITER** environment variable has not been set, the default delimiter is the pipe (|).

The following example identifies the semicolon (;) as the delimiting character. The example uses Windows NT file-naming conventions.

```
LOAD FROM 'C:\data\loadfile' DELIMITER ';'
    INSERT INTO orders
```

INSERT INTO Clause

Use the INSERT INTO clause to specify the table, synonym, or view in which to load the new data. You must specify the column names only if one of the following conditions is true:

- You are not loading data into all columns.
- The input file does not match the default order of the columns (determined when the table was created).

The following example identifies the **price** and **discount** columns as the only columns in which to add data. The example uses Windows NT file-naming conventions.

```
LOAD FROM 'C:\tmp\prices' DELIMITER ','
    INSERT INTO norman.worktab(price,discount)
```

Related Information

Related statements: UNLOAD and INSERT

For a task-oriented discussion of the LOAD statement and other utilities for moving data, see the *Informix Migration Guide*.

For a discussion of the GLS aspects of the LOAD statement, see the *Informix Guide to GLS Functionality*.

LOCK TABLE

Use the LOCK TABLE statement to control access to a table by other processes.

Syntax

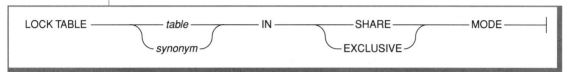

Element	Purpose	Restrictions	Syntax
synonym	Name of the synonym for the table to be locked	The synonym and the table to which the synonym points must exist.	Database Object Name, p. 4-50
table	Name of the table to be locked	The table cannot be locked in exclusive mode by another process before you execute the LOCK TABLE statement.	Database Object Name, p. 4-50
		The table cannot be locked in share mode by another process before you execute a LOCK TABLE EXCLUSIVE statement.	

Usage

You can lock a table if you own the table or have the Select privilege on the table or on a column in the table, either from a direct grant or from a grant to PUBLIC. The LOCK TABLE statement fails if the table is already locked in exclusive mode by another process, or if an exclusive lock is attempted while another user has locked the table in share mode.

The SHARE keyword locks a table in shared mode. Shared mode allows other processes *read* access to the table but denies *write* access. Other processes cannot update or delete data if a table is locked in shared mode.

The EXCLUSIVE keyword locks a table in exclusive mode. Exclusive mode denies other processes both read and write access to the table.

Exclusive-mode locking automatically occurs when you execute the ALTER INDEX, ALTER TABLE, CREATE INDEX, DROP INDEX, RENAME COLUMN, RENAME TABLE, START VIOLATIONS TABLE, and STOP VIOLATIONS TABLE statements.

Databases with Transactions

If your database was created with transactions, the LOCK TABLE statement succeeds only if it executes within a transaction. You must issue a BEGIN WORK statement before you can execute a LOCK TABLE statement.

ANSI

Transactions are implicit in an ANSI-compliant database. The LOCK TABLE statement succeeds whenever the specified table is not already locked by another process. ♦

The following guidelines apply to the use of the LOCK TABLE statement within transactions:

- You cannot lock system catalog tables.
- You cannot switch between shared and exclusive table locking within a transaction. For example, once you lock the table in shared mode, you cannot upgrade the lock mode to exclusive.
- If you issue a LOCK TABLE statement before you access a row in the table, no row locks are set for the table. In this way, you can override row-level locking and avoid exceeding the maximum number of locks that are defined in the database server configuration.
- All row and table locks release automatically after a transaction is completed. Note that the UNLOCK TABLE statement fails in a database that uses transactions.

The following example shows how to change the locking mode of a table in a database that was created with transaction logging:

```
BEGIN WORK
LOCK TABLE orders IN EXCLUSIVE MODE
  . . .
COMMIT WORK
BEGIN WORK
LOCK TABLE orders IN SHARE MODE
  . . .
COMMIT WORK
```

Databases Without Transactions

In a database that was created without transactions, table locks set by using the LOCK TABLE statement are released after any of the following occurrences:

- An UNLOCK TABLE statement executes.
- The user closes the database.
- The user exits the application.

To change the lock mode on a table, release the lock with the UNLOCK TABLE statement and then issue a new LOCK TABLE statement.

The following example shows how to change the lock mode of a table in a database that was created without transactions:

```
LOCK TABLE orders IN EXCLUSIVE MODE
  .
  .
  .
UNLOCK TABLE orders
  .
  .
  .
LOCK TABLE orders IN SHARE MODE
```

Related Information

Related statements: BEGIN WORK, COMMIT WORK, ROLLBACK WORK, SET ISOLATION, SET LOCK MODE, and UNLOCK TABLE

For a discussion of concurrency and locks, see the *Informix Guide to SQL: Tutorial*.

<table>
<tr><td>E/C</td></tr>
</table>

OPEN

Use the OPEN statement to activate a cursor.

Use this statement with ESQL/C.

Syntax

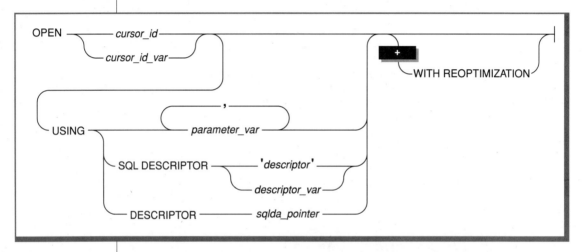

Element	Purpose	Restrictions	Syntax
cursor_id	Name of a cursor	Cursor must have been previously created by a DECLARE statement.	Identifier, p. 4-205
cursor_id_var	Host variable that holds the value of cursor_id	Host variable must be a character data type.	Name must conform to language-specific rules for variable names
		Cursor must have been previously created by a DECLARE statement.	
descriptor	Quoted string that identifies the system-descriptor area	System-descriptor area must already be allocated.	Quoted String, p. 4-260

(1 of 2)

Element	Purpose	Restrictions	Syntax
descriptor_var	Host variable that identifies the system-descriptor area	System-descriptor area must already be allocated.	Quoted String, p. 4-260
parameter_var	Host variable whose contents replace a question-mark (?) placeholder in a prepared statement	Variable must be a character or collection data type.	Name must conform to language-specific rules for variable names.
sqlda_pointer	Pointer to an **sqlda** structure that defines the type and memory location of values that correspond to the question-mark (?) placeholder in a prepared statement	You cannot begin *sqlda_pointer* with a dollar sign ($) or a colon (:). You must use an **sqlda** structure if you are using dynamic SQL statements.	DESCRIBE, p. 2-382

(2 of 2)

Usage

The OPEN statement activates the following types of cursors:

- A select cursor: a cursor that is associated with a SELECT statement
- A function cursor: a cursor that is associated with the EXECUTE FUNCTION (or EXECUTE PROCEDURE) statement
- An insert cursor: a cursor that is associated with the INSERT statement

IDS

- A collection cursor: a select or insert cursor that operates on a collection variable ♦

The specific actions that the database server takes differ, depending on the statement with which the cursor is associated.

When you associate one of the previous statements with a cursor directly (that is, you do not prepare the statement and associate the statement identifier with the cursor) the OPEN statement implicitly prepares the statement.

ANSI

In an ANSI-compliant database, you receive an error code if you try to open a cursor that is already open. ♦

Opening a Select Cursor

When you open either a select cursor or an update cursor that is created with the SELECT... FOR UPDATE syntax, the SELECT statement is passed to the database server along with any values that are specified in the USING clause. The database server processes the query to the point of locating or constructing the first row of the active set.

Example of Opening a Select Cursor

The following example illustrates a simple OPEN statement in ESQL/C:

```
EXEC SQL declare s_curs cursor for
    select * from orders;
EXEC SQL open s_curs;
```

Opening an Update Cursor Inside a Transaction

If you are working in a database with explicit transactions, you must open an update cursor within a transaction. This requirement is waived if you declared the cursor using the WITH HOLD option.

Opening a Function Cursor

When you open a function cursor, the EXECUTE FUNCTION (or EXECUTE PROCEDURE) statement is passed to the database server along with any values that are specified in the USING Clause. The values in the USING Clause are passed as arguments to the user-defined function. This user-defined function must be declared to accept values. (If the statement was previously prepared, the statement was passed to the database server when it was prepared.) The database server executes the function to the point where it returns the first set of values.

Example of Opening a Function Cursor

The following example illustrates a simple OPEN statement in ESQL/C:

```
EXEC SQL declare s_curs cursor for
    execute function new_func(arg1,arg2)
    into :ret_val1, :ret_val2;
EXEC SQL open s_curs;
```

EDS

In Enterprise Decision Server, to recreate this example use the CREATE PROCEDURE statement instead of the CREATE FUNCTION statement. ♦

Reopening a Select or Function Cursor

The database server evaluates the values that are named in the USING clause of the OPEN statement only when it opens the select or function cursor. While the cursor is open, subsequent changes to program variables in the USING clause do not change the active set of the cursor.

ANSI

In an ANSI-compliant database, you receive an error code if you try to open a cursor that is already open. ◆

In a non-ANSI database, a subsequent OPEN statement closes the cursor and then reopens it. When the database server reopens the cursor, it creates a new active set that is based on the current values of the variables in the USING clause. If the program variables have changed since the previous OPEN statement, reopening the cursor can generate an entirely different active set.

Even if the values of the variables are unchanged, the values in the active set can be different, in the following situations:

- If the user-defined function takes a different execution path from the previous OPEN statement on a function cursor
- If data in the table was modified since the previous OPEN statement on a select cursor

The database server can process most queries dynamically. For these queries, the database server does not pre-fetch all rows when it opens the select or function cursor. Therefore, if other users are modifying the table at the same time that the cursor is being processed, the active set might reflect the results of these actions.

However, for some queries, the database server evaluates the entire active set when it opens the cursor. These queries include those with the following features:

- Queries that require sorting: those with an ORDER BY clause or with the DISTINCT or UNIQUE keyword
- Queries that require hashing: those with a join or with the GROUP BY clause

For these queries, any changes that other users make to the table while the cursor is being processed are not reflected in the active set.

Errors Associated with Select and Function Cursors

Because the database server is seeing the query for the first time, it might detect errors. In this case, the database server does not actually return the first row of data, but it sets a return code in the **sqlca.sqlcode, SQLCODE** field of the **sqlca**. The return code value is either negative or zero, as the following table describes.

Return Code Value	Purpose
Negative	Shows an error is detected in the SELECT statement
Zero	Shows the SELECT statement is valid

If the SELECT, SELECT…FOR UPDATE, EXECUTE FUNCTION (or EXECUTE PROCEDURE) statement is valid, but no rows match its criteria, the first FETCH statement returns a value of 100 (SQLNOTFOUND), which means no rows were found.

Tip: *When you encounter an **SQLCODE** error, a corresponding **SQLSTATE** error value also exists. For information about how to get the message text, check the GET DIAGNOSTICS statement.*

Opening an Insert Cursor

When you open an insert cursor, the cursor passes the INSERT statement to the database server, which checks the validity of the keywords and column names. The database server also allocates memory for an insert buffer to hold new data. (See "DECLARE" on page 2-349.)

An OPEN statement for a cursor that is associated with an INSERT statement cannot include a USING clause.

Example of Opening an Insert Cursor

The following ESQL/C example illustrates an OPEN statement with an insert cursor:

```
EXEC SQL prepare s1 from
    'insert into manufact values ('npr', 'napier')';
EXEC SQL declare in_curs cursor for s1;
EXEC SQL open in_curs;
EXEC SQL put in_curs;
EXEC SQL close in_curs;
```

Reopening an Insert Cursor

When you reopen an insert cursor that is already open, you effectively flush the insert buffer; any rows that are stored in the insert buffer are written into the database table. The database server first closes the cursor, which causes the flush and then reopens the cursor. For information about how to check errors and count inserted rows, see "Error Checking" on page 2-601.

ANSI

In an ANSI-compliant database, you receive an error code if you try to open a cursor that is already open. ♦

IDS

Opening a Collection Cursor

You can declare both select and insert cursors on collection variables. Such cursors are called collection cursors. You must use the OPEN statement to activate these cursors.

Use the name of a collection variable in the USING clause of the OPEN statement. For more information on the use of OPEN...USING with a collection variable, see "Fetching From a Collection Cursor" on page 2-466 and "Inserting into a Collection Cursor" on page 2-599.

USING Clause

The USING clause of the OPEN statement is required when the cursor is associated with a prepared statement that includes question-mark (?) place-holders, as follows:

- A SELECT statement that contains input parameters in its WHERE clause
- An EXECUTE FUNCTION (or EXECUTE PROCEDURE) statement that contains input parameters as arguments of its user-defined function
- An INSERT statement that contains input parameters in its VALUES clause

You can supply values for these parameters in one of the following ways:

- You can specify one or more host variables
- You can specify a system-descriptor area
- You can specify a pointer to an **sqlda** structure

(For more information, see "PREPARE" on page 2-579.)

Specifying Host Variables

If you know the number of parameters to be supplied at runtime and their data types, you can define the parameters that are needed by the statement as host variables in your program. You pass parameters to the database server by opening the cursor with the USING keyword, followed by the names of the variables. These variables are matched with the SELECT or EXECUTE FUNCTION (or EXECUTE PROCEDURE) statement question-mark (?) parameters in a one-to-one correspondence, from left to right.

You cannot include indicator variables in the list of variable names. To use an indicator variable, you must include the SELECT or EXECUTE FUNCTION (or EXECUTE PROCEDURE) statement as part of the DECLARE statement.

You must supply one host variable name for each placeholder. The data type of each variable must be compatible with the corresponding type that the prepared statement requires.

Examples of Specifying Host Variables with Select and Function Cursors

The following example illustrates an ESQL/C code fragment that opens a select cursor and specifies host variables in the USING clause:

```
sprintf (select_1, "%s %s %s %s %s",
    "SELECT o.order_num, sum(total price)",
    "FROM orders o, items i",
    "WHERE o.order_date > ? AND o.customer_num - ?",
    "AND o.order_num = i.order_num",
    "GROUP BY o.order_num");
EXEC SQL prepare statement_1 from :select_1;
EXEC SQL declare q_curs cursor for statement_1;
EXEC SQL open q_curs using :o_date, :o.customer_num;
```

The following example illustrates the USING clause of the OPEN statement with an EXECUTE FUNCTION statement in an ESQL/C code fragment:

```
stcopy ("EXECUTE FUNCTION one_func(?, ?)", exfunc_stmt);
EXEC SQL prepare exfunc_id from :exfunc_stmt;
EXEC SQL declare func_curs cursor for exfunc_id;
EXEC SQL open func_curs using :arg1, :arg2;
```

EDS

In Enterprise Decision Server, to recreate this example use the CREATE PROCEDURE statement instead of the CREATE FUNCTION statement. ♦

Specifying a System Descriptor Area

If you do not know the number of parameters to be supplied at runtime or their data types, you can associate input values from a system-descriptor area. A system-descriptor area describes the data type and memory location of one or more values to replace question-mark (?) placeholders.

X/O

A system-descriptor area conforms to the X/Open standards. ♦

Use the SQL DESCRIPTOR keywords to introduce the name of a system descriptor area as the location of the parameters.

The COUNT field in the system-descriptor area corresponds to the number of dynamic parameters in the prepared statement. The value of COUNT must be less than or equal to the number of item descriptors that were specified when the system-descriptor area was allocated with the ALLOCATE DESCRIPTOR statement. You can obtain the value of a field with the GET DESCRIPTOR statement and set the value with the SET DESCRIPTOR statement.

Example of Specifying a System Descriptor Area

The following example shows the OPEN...USING SQL DESCRIPTOR statement:

```
EXEC SQL allocate descriptor 'desc1';
...
EXEC SQL open selcurs using sql descriptor 'desc1';
```

As the example indicates, the system descriptor area must be allocated before you reference it in the OPEN statement.

Specifying a Pointer to an sqlda Structure

If you do not know the number of parameters to be supplied at runtime, or their data types, you can associate input values from an **sqlda** structure. An **sqlda** structure lists the data type and memory location of one or more values to replace question-mark (?) placeholders.

Use the DESCRIPTOR keyword to introduce a pointer to the **sqlda** structure as the location of the parameters.

The **sqlda** value specifies the number of input values that are described in occurrences of **sqlvar**. This number must correspond to the number of dynamic parameters in the prepared statement.

Example of Specifying a Pointer to an sqlda Structure

The following example shows an OPEN...USING DESCRIPTOR statement:

```
struct sqlda *sdp;
...
EXEC SQL open selcurs using descriptor sdp;
```

Using the WITH REOPTIMIZATION Option

Use the WITH REOPTIMIZATION option to reoptimize your query-design plan.

When you prepare a SELECT or EXECUTE FUNCTION (or EXECUTE PROCEDURE) statement, the database server uses a query-design plan to optimize that query. If you later modify the data that is associated with the prepared statement, you can compromise the effectiveness of the query-design plan for that statement. In other words, if you change the data, you can deoptimize your query. To ensure optimization of your query, you can prepare the statement again or open the cursor again using the WITH REOPTI-MIZATION option.

Informix recommends that you use the WITH REOPTIMIZATION option because it provides the following advantages over preparing a statement again:

- Rebuilds only the query-design plan rather than the entire statement
- Uses fewer resources
- Reduces overhead
- Requires less time

The WITH REOPTIMIZATION option forces the database server to optimize the query-design plan before it processes the OPEN cursor statement.

The following example shows the WITH REOPTIMIZATION option:

```
EXEC SQL open selcurs using descriptor sdp with
reoptimization;
```

Relationship Between OPEN and FREE

The database server allocates resources to prepared statements and open cursors. If you execute a FREE *statement_id* or FREE *statement_id_var* statement, you can still open the cursor associated with the freed statement ID. However, if you release resources with a FREE *cursor_id* or FREE *cursor_id_var* statement, you cannot use the cursor unless you declare the cursor again.

Similarly, if you use the SET AUTOFREE statement for one or more cursors, when the program closes the specific cursor, the database server automatically frees the cursor-related resources. In this case, you cannot use the cursor unless you declare the cursor again.

Related Information

Related statements: ALLOCATE DESCRIPTOR, DEALLOCATE DESCRIPTOR, DESCRIBE, CLOSE, DECLARE, EXECUTE, FETCH, FLUSH, FREE, GET DESCRIPTOR, PREPARE, PUT, SET AUTOFREE, SET DEFERRED_PREPARE, and SET DESCRIPTOR

For a task-oriented discussion of the OPEN statement, see the *Informix Guide to SQL: Tutorial*.

For more information on system-descriptor areas and the **sqlda** structure, refer to the *Informix ESQL/C Programmer's Manual*.

OUTPUT

Use the OUTPUT statement to send query results directly to an operating-system file or to pipe query results to another program.

Use this statement with DB-Access.

Syntax

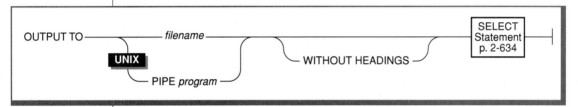

Element	Purpose	Restrictions	Syntax
filename	Pathname and filename of an operating-system file where the results of the query are written The default pathname is the current directory.	You can specify a new or existing file in filename. If the specified file exists, the results of the query overwrite the current contents of the file.	The pathname and filename must conform to the conventions of your operating system.
program	Name of a program where the results of the query are sent	The program must exist and must be known to the operating system. The program must be able to read the results of a query.	The name of the program must conform to the conventions of your operating system.

Usage

You can use the OUTPUT statement to direct the results of a query to an operating-system file or to a program. You can also specify whether column headings should be omitted from the query output.

Sending Query Results to a File

You can send the results of a query to an operating-system file by specifying the full pathname for the file. If the file already exists, the output overwrites the current contents.

The following examples show how to send the result of a query to an operating-system file. The example uses UNIX file-naming conventions.

```
OUTPUT TO /usr/april/query1
    SELECT * FROM cust_calls WHERE call_code = 'L'
```

Displaying Query Results Without Column Headings

You can display the results of a query without column headings by using the WITHOUT HEADINGS keywords.

UNIX

Sending Query Results to Another Program

In the UNIX environment, you can use the keyword PIPE to send the query results to another program, as the following example shows:

```
OUTPUT TO PIPE more
    SELECT customer_num, call_dtime, call_code
        FROM cust_calls
```

Related Information

Related statements: SELECT and UNLOAD

PREPARE

Use the PREPARE statement to parse, validate, and generate an execution plan for SQL statements at runtime.

Use this statement with ESQL/C.

Syntax

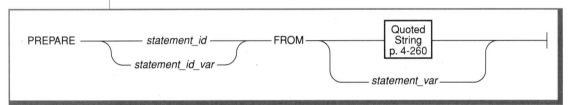

Element	Purpose	Restrictions	Syntax
statement_id	Identifier that represents the data structure of an SQL statement or sequence of SQL statements	After you release the database-server resources (using a FREE statement), you cannot use the statement identifier with a DECLARE cursor or with the EXECUTE statement until you prepare the statement again.	Identifier, p. 4-205
statement_id_var	Host variable that contains the statement identifier	This variable must be a character data type.	Name must conform to language-specific rules for variable names.
statement_var	Host variable whose value is a character string that consists of one or more SQL statements	This variable must be a character data type. For restrictions on the statements in the character string, see "Restricted Statements in Single-Statement Prepares" on page 2-584 and "Restricted Statements in Multi-Statement Prepares" on page 2-591. A statement variable name cannot be used if the SQL statement contains the Collection Derived Table segment.	Name must conform to language-specific rules for variable names.

Usage

The PREPARE statement permits your program to assemble the text of an SQL statement at runtime and make it executable. This dynamic form of SQL is accomplished in three steps:

1. A PREPARE statement accepts statement text as input, either as a quoted string or stored within a character variable. Statement text can contain question-mark (?) placeholders to represent values that are to be defined when the statement is executed.

2. An EXECUTE or OPEN statement can supply the required input values and execute the prepared statement once or many times.

3. Resources allocated to the prepared statement can be released later using the FREE statement.

The number of prepared items in a single program is limited by the available memory. These items include both statement identifiers that are named in PREPARE statements (*statement_id* or *statement_id_var*) and declared cursors. To avoid exceeding the limit, use a FREE statement to release some statements or cursors.

Restrictions

For information on statements that you cannot use in a prepared statement, see "Restricted Statements in Single-Statement Prepares" on page 2-584 and "Restricted Statements in Multi-Statement Prepares" on page 2-591.

The maximum length of a PREPARE statement is 64 kilobytes.

Using a Statement Identifier

A PREPARE statement sends the statement text to the database server. The database server analyzes the statement text. If the text contains no syntax errors, the database server translates it to an internal form. This translated statement is saved for later execution in a data structure that the PREPARE statement allocates. The name of the structure is the value that is assigned to the statement identifier in the PREPARE statement. Subsequent SQL statements refer to the structure by using the same statement identifier that was used in the PREPARE statement.

A subsequent FREE statement releases the resources that were allocated to the statement. After you release the database-server resources, you cannot use the statement identifier with a DECLARE cursor or with the EXECUTE statement until you prepare the statement again.

Scope of Statement Identifiers

A program can consist of one or more source-code files. By default, the scope of a statement identifier is global to the program. Therefore, a statement identifier that is prepared in one file can be referenced from another file.

In a multiple-file program, if you want to limit the scope of a statement identifier to the file in which it is prepared, preprocess all the files with the **-local** command-line option.

Releasing a Statement Identifier

A statement identifier can represent only one SQL statement or sequence of statements at a time. You can execute a new PREPARE statement with an existing statement identifier if you wish to bind a given statement identifier to a different SQL statement text.

The PREPARE statement supports dynamic statement-identifier names, which allow you to prepare a statement identifier as an identifier or as a host character-string variable.

The first example shows a statement identifier that was prepared as a host variable. The second example shows a statement identifier that was prepared as a character-string constant:

```
stcopy ("query2", stmtid);
EXEC SQL prepare :stmtid from
    'select * from customer';

EXEC SQL prepare query2 from
    'select * from customer';
```

A statement-identifier variable must be a character data type. In C, it must be defined as char.

Statement Text

The PREPARE statement can take statement text either as a quoted string or as text that is stored in a program variable. The following restrictions apply to the statement text:

- The text can contain only SQL statements. It cannot contain statements or comments *from* the host programming language.

- The text can contain comments that are preceded by a double dash (--) or enclosed in braces ({ }).

  These comment symbols represent SQL comments. For more information on SQL comment symbols, see "How to Enter SQL Comments" on page 1-6.

- The text can contain either a single SQL statement or a sequence of statements that are separated by semicolons.

  For more information on how to prepare a single SQL statement, see "Restricted Statements in Single-Statement Prepares" on page 2-584. For more information on how to prepare a sequence of SQL statements, see "Preparing Sequences of Multiple SQL Statements" on page 2-590.

- Names of host-language variables are not recognized as such in prepared text.

  Therefore, you cannot prepare a SELECT statement that contains an INTO clause or an EXECUTE FUNCTION (or EXECUTE PROCEDURE) that contains an INTO clause because the INTO clause requires a host-language variable.

- The only identifiers that you can use are names that are defined in the database, such as names of tables and columns.

  For more information on how to use identifiers in statement text, see "Preparing Statements with SQL Identifiers" on page 2-587.

- Use a question mark (?) as a placeholder to indicate where data is supplied when the statement executes.

  For more information on how to use question marks as placeholders, see "Preparing Statements That Receive Parameters" on page 2-585.

- The text cannot include an embedded SQL statement prefix or terminator, such as a dollar sign ($) or the words EXEC SQL.

The following ESQL/C example shows a PREPARE statement that takes statement text as a quoted string:

```
EXEC SQL prepare new_cust from
    'insert into customer(fname,lname) values(?,?)';
```

IDS

If the prepared statement contains the Collection Derived Table segment on an ESQL/C collection variable, some additional limitations exist on how you can assemble the text for the PREPARE statement. For information about dynamic SQL, see the *Informix ESQL/C Programmer's Manual.* ◆

Preparing and Executing User-Defined Routines

The way to prepare a user-defined routine (UDR) depends on whether the UDR is a user-defined procedure or a user-defined function:

- To prepare a user-defined procedure, prepare the EXECUTE PROCEDURE statement that executes the procedure.

  To execute the prepared procedure, use the EXECUTE statement.

- To prepare a user-defined function, prepare the EXECUTE FUNCTION (or EXECUTE PROCEDURE) statement that executes the function.

  You cannot include the INTO clause of EXECUTE FUNCTION (or EXECUTE PROCEDURE) in the PREPARE statement.

  The way to execute a prepared user-defined function depends on whether the function returns only one group of values or multiple groups of values. Use the EXECUTE statement for user-defined functions that return only one group of values. To execute user-defined functions that return more than one group of return values, you must associate the EXECUTE FUNCTION (or EXECUTE PROCEDURE) statement with a cursor.

Restricted Statements in Single-Statement Prepares

In general, you can prepare any database manipulation statement.

IDS

You can prepare any single SQL statement except the following statements.

ALLOCATE COLLECTION	FLUSH
ALLOCATE DESCRIPTOR	FREE
ALLOCATE ROW	GET DESCRIPTOR
CLOSE	GET DIAGNOSTICS
CONNECT	INFO
CREATE FUNCTION FROM	LOAD
CREATE PROCEDURE FROM	OPEN
CREATE ROUTINE FROM	OUTPUT
DEALLOCATE COLLECTION	PREPARE
DEALLOCATE DESCRIPTOR	PUT
DEALLOCATE ROW	SET AUTOFREE
DECLARE	SET CONNECTION
DESCRIBE	SET DEFERRED_PREPARE
DISCONNECT	SET DESCRIPTOR
EXECUTE	UNLOAD
EXECUTE IMMEDIATE	WHENEVER
FETCH	

♦

EDS

You can prepare any single SQL statement except the following statements

ALLOCATE DESCRIPTOR	GET DESCRIPTOR
CLOSE	GET DIAGNOSTICS
CONNECT	INFO
CREATE PROCEDURE FROM	LOAD
DEALLOCATE DESCRIPTOR	OPEN
DECLARE	OUTPUT
DESCRIBE	PREPARE
DISCONNECT	PUT
EXECUTE	SET CONNECTION
EXECUTE IMMEDIATE	SET DEFERRED_PREPARE
FETCH	SET DESCRIPTOR
FLUSH	UNLOAD
FREE	WHENEVER

♦

You can prepare a SELECT statement. If the SELECT statement includes the INTO TEMP clause, you can execute the prepared statement with an EXECUTE statement. If it does not include the INTO TEMP clause, the statement returns rows of data. Use DECLARE, OPEN, and FETCH cursor statements to retrieve the rows.

A prepared SELECT statement can include a FOR UPDATE clause. This clause is used with the DECLARE statement to create an update cursor. The following example shows a SELECT statement with a FOR UPDATE clause in ESQL/C:

```
sprintf(up_query, "%s %s %s",
    "select * from customer ",
    "where customer_num between ? and ? ",
    "for update");
EXEC SQL prepare up_sel from :up_query;

EXEC SQL declare up_curs cursor for up_sel;

EXEC SQL open up_curs using :low_cust,:high_cust;
```

Preparing Statements When Parameters Are Known

In some prepared statements, all necessary information is known at the time the statement is prepared. The following example in ESQL/C shows two statements that were prepared from constant data:

```
sprintf(redo_st, "%s %s",
    "drop table workt1; ",
    "create table workt1 (wtk serial, wtv float)" );
EXEC SQL prepare redotab from :redo_st;
```

Preparing Statements That Receive Parameters

In some statements, parameters are unknown when the statement is prepared because a different value can be inserted each time the statement is executed. In these statements, you can use a question-mark (?) placeholder where a parameter must be supplied when the statement is executed.

The PREPARE statements in the following ESQL/C examples show some uses of question-mark (?) placeholders:

```
EXEC SQL prepare s3 from
    'select * from customer where state matches ?';

EXEC SQL prepare in1 from
    'insert into manufact values (?,?,?)';

sprintf(up_query, "%s %s",
    "update customer set zipcode = ?"
    "where current of zip_cursor");
EXEC SQL prepare update2 from :up_query;

EXEC SQL prepare exfunc from
    'execute function func1 (?, ?)';
```

You can use a placeholder to defer evaluation of a value until runtime only for an expression. You cannot use a question-mark (?) placeholder to represent an SQL identifier except as noted in "Preparing Statements with SQL Identifiers" on page 2-587.

The following example of an ESQL/C code fragment prepares a statement from a variable that is named **demoquery**. The text in the variable includes one question-mark (?) placeholder. The prepared statement is associated with a cursor and, when the cursor is opened, the USING clause of the OPEN statement supplies a value for the placeholder.

```
EXEC SQL BEGIN DECLARE SECTION;
    char queryvalue [6];
    char demoquery  [80];
EXEC SQL END DECLARE SECTION;

EXEC SQL connect to 'stores_demo';
sprintf(demoquery, "%s %s",
        "select fname, lname from customer ",
        "where lname > ? ");
EXEC SQL prepare quid from :demoquery;
EXEC SQL declare democursor cursor for quid;
stcopy("C", queryvalue);
EXEC SQL open democursor using :queryvalue;
```

The USING clause is available in both OPEN (for statements that are associated with a cursor) and EXECUTE (all other prepared statements) statements.

You can use a question-mark (?) placeholder to represent the name of an ESQL/C or SPL collection variable.

Preparing Statements with SQL Identifiers

In general, you cannot use question-mark (?) placeholders for SQL identifiers. You must specify these identifiers in the statement text when you
prepare the statement.

However, in a few special cases, you can use the question-mark (?) placeholder for an SQL identifier. These cases are as follows:

- You can use the question-mark (?) placeholder for the database name
  in the DATABASE statement.

- You can use the question-mark (?) placeholder for the dbspace name
  in the IN *dbspace* clause of the CREATE DATABASE statement.

- You can use the question-mark (?) placeholder for the cursor name in
  statements that use cursor names.

Obtaining SQL Identifiers from User Input

If a prepared statement requires identifiers, but the identifiers are unknown
when you write the prepared statement, you can construct a statement that
receives SQL identifiers from user input.

The following ESQL/C example prompts the user for the name of a table and
uses that name in a SELECT statement. Because the table name is unknown
until runtime, the number and data types of the table columns are also
unknown. Therefore, the program cannot allocate host variables to receive
data from each row in advance. Instead, this program fragment describes the
statement into an **sqlda** descriptor and fetches each row with the descriptor.
The fetch puts each row into memory locations that the program provides
dynamically.

If a program retrieves all the rows in the active set, the FETCH statement
would be placed in a loop that fetched each row. If the FETCH statement
retrieves more than one data value (column), another loop exists after the
FETCH, which performs some action on each data value.

```
#include <stdio.h>
EXEC SQL include sqlda;
EXEC SQL include sqltypes;

char *malloc( );

main()
{
    struct sqlda *demodesc;
    char tablename[19];
    int i;
EXEC SQL BEGIN DECLARE SECTION;
    char demoselect[200];
EXEC SQL END DECLARE SECTION;

/*  This program selects all the columns of a given tablename.
        The tablename is supplied interactively. */

EXEC SQL connect to 'stores_demo';

printf( "This program does a select * on a table\n" );
printf( "Enter table name: " );
scanf( "%s", tablename );

sprintf(demoselect, "select * from %s", tablename );

EXEC SQL prepare iid from :demoselect;
EXEC SQL describe iid into demodesc;

/* Print what describe returns */

for ( i = 0;  i < demodesc->sqld; i++ )
    prsqlda (demodesc->sqlvar + i);

/* Assign the data pointers. */

for ( i = 0;  i < demodesc->sqld; i++ )
    {
    switch (demodesc->sqlvar[i].sqltype & SQLTYPE)
        {
        case SQLCHAR:
            demodesc->sqlvar[i].sqltype = CCHARTYPE;
            /* make room for null terminator */
            demodesc->sqlvar[i].sqllen++;
            demodesc->sqlvar[i].sqldata =
                malloc( demodesc->sqlvar[i].sqllen );
            break;

        case SQLSMINT:    /* fall through */
        case SQLINT:      /* fall through */
        case SQLSERIAL:
            demodesc->sqlvar[i].sqltype = CINTTYPE;
            demodesc->sqlvar[i].sqldata =
                malloc( sizeof( int ) );
            break;

        /*  And so on for each type.  */

        }
    }
```

```
/* Declare and open cursor for select . */
EXEC SQL declare d_curs cursor for iid;
EXEC SQL open d_curs;

/* Fetch selected rows one at a time into demodesc. */

for( ; ; )
    {
    printf( "\n" );
    EXEC SQL fetch d_curs using descriptor demodesc;
    if ( sqlca.sqlcode != 0 )
        break;
    for ( i = 0;  i < demodesc->sqld; i++ )
        {
        switch (demodesc->sqlvar[i].sqltype)
            {
            case CCHARTYPE:
                printf( "%s: \"%s\n", demodesc->sqlvar[i].sqlname,
                    demodesc->sqlvar[i].sqldata );
                break;
            case CINTTYPE:
                printf( "%s: %d\n", demodesc->sqlvar[i].sqlname,
                    *((int *) demodesc->sqlvar[i].sqldata) );
                break;

            /* And so forth for each type... */

            }
        }
    }
EXEC SQL close d_curs;
EXEC SQL free d_curs;


/*  Free the data memory.  */

for ( i = 0;  i < demodesc->sqld; i++ )
    free( demodesc->sqlvar[i].sqldata );
free( demodesc );

printf ("Program Over.\n");
}


prsqlda(sp)
    struct sqlvar_struct *sp;

    {
    printf ("type = %d\n", sp->sqltype);
    printf ("len = %d\n", sp->sqllen);
    printf ("data = %lx\n", sp->sqldata);
    printf ("ind = %lx\n", sp->sqlind);
    printf ("name = %s\n", sp->sqlname);
    }
```

Preparing Sequences of Multiple SQL Statements

You can execute several SQL statements as one action if you include them in the same PREPARE statement. Multistatement text is processed as a unit; actions are not treated sequentially. Therefore, multistatement text cannot include statements that depend on actions that occur in a previous statement in the text. For example, you cannot create a table and insert values into that table in the same prepared block.

If a statement in a multistatement prepare returns an error, the whole prepared statement stops executing. The database server does not execute any remaining statements.

In most situations, compiled products return error-status information on the error, but do not indicate which statement in the sequence causes an error. You can use the **sqlca.sqlerrd[4]** field in the **sqlca** to find the offset of the errors.

In a multistatement prepare, if no rows are returned from a WHERE clause in the following statements, the database server returns the error, SQLNOTFOUND (100):

- UPDATE...WHERE...
- SELECT INTO TEMP...WHERE...
- INSERT INTO...WHERE...
- DELETE FROM...WHERE...

In the following example, four SQL statements are prepared into a single ESQL/C string that is called **query**. Individual statements are delimited with semicolons. A single PREPARE statement can prepare the four statements for execution, and a single EXECUTE statement can execute the statements that are associated with the **qid** statement identifier.

```
sprintf (query,  "%s %s %s %s %s %s %s",
    "update account set balance = balance + ? ",
        "where acct_number = ?;",
    "update teller set balance = balance + ? ",
        "where teller_number = ?;",
    "update branch set balance = balance + ? ",
        "where branch_number = ?;",
    "insert into history values (?, ?);";
EXEC SQL prepare qid from :query;

EXEC SQL begin work;
EXEC SQL execute qid using
        :delta, :acct_number, :delta, :teller_number,
        :delta, :branch_number, :timestamp, :values;
EXEC SQL commit work;
```

In the preceding code fragment, the semicolons (;) are required as SQL statement-terminator symbols between each SQL statement in the text that **query** holds.

Restricted Statements in Multi-Statement Prepares

In addition to the statements listed as exceptions in "Restricted Statements in Single-Statement Prepares" on page 2-584, you cannot use the following statements in text that contains multiple statements that are separated by semicolons.

CLOSE DATABASE	DROP DATABASE
CREATE DATABASE	SELECT (with one exception)
DATABASE	

In addition, the following types of statements are not allowed in a multistatement prepare:

- Statements that can cause the current database to close during the execution of the multistatement sequence
- Statements that include references to TEXT or BYTE host variables

Using the SELECT Statement in a Multistatement Prepare

In general, you cannot use the SELECT statement in a multistatement prepare. The only form of the SELECT statement allowed in a multistatement prepare is a SELECT statement with an INTO temporary table clause.

Using Prepared Statements for Efficiency

To increase performance efficiency, you can use the PREPARE statement and an EXECUTE statement in a loop to eliminate overhead that redundant parsing and optimizing cause. For example, an UPDATE statement that is located within a WHILE loop is parsed each time the loop runs. If you prepare the UPDATE statement outside the loop, the statement is parsed only once, eliminating overhead and speeding statement execution. The following example shows how to prepare an ESQL/C statement to improve performance:

```
EXEC SQL BEGIN DECLARE SECTION;
    char disc_up[80];
    int cust_num;
EXEC SQL END DECLARE SECTION;

main()
{
    sprintf(disc_up, "%s %s",
        "update customer ",
        "set discount = 0.1 where customer_num = ?");
    EXEC SQL prepare up1 from :disc_up;

    while (1)
        {
        printf("Enter customer number (or 0 to quit): ");
        scanf("%d", cust_num);
        if (cust_num == 0)
            break;
        EXEC SQL execute up1 using :cust_num;
        }
}
```

Related Information

Related statements: CLOSE, DECLARE, DESCRIBE, EXECUTE, FREE, OPEN, SET AUTOFREE, and SET DEFERRED_PREPARE

For information about basic concepts relating to the PREPARE statement, see the *Informix Guide to SQL: Tutorial*.

For information about more advanced concepts relating to the PREPARE statement, see the *Informix ESQL/C Programmer's Manual*.

PUT

Use the PUT statement to store a row in an insert buffer for later insertion into the database.

Use this statement with ESQL/C.

Syntax

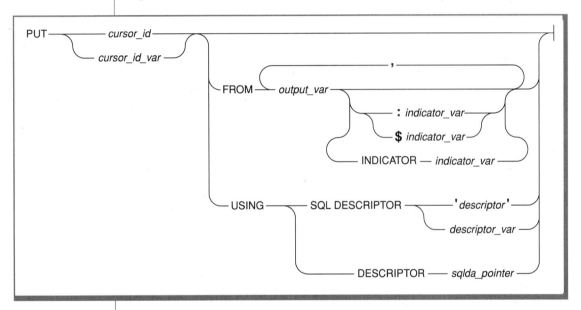

Element	Purpose	Restrictions	Syntax
cursor_id	Name of a cursor	The cursor must be open.	Identifier, p. 4-205
cursor_id_var	Host variable that holds the value of cursor_id	Host variable must be a character data type. The cursor must be open.	Name must conform to language-specific rules for variable names.

(1 of 2)

Element	Purpose	Restrictions	Syntax
descriptor	Quoted string that identifies the system-descriptor area that defines the type and memory location of values that correspond to the question-mark (?) placeholder in a prepared INSERT statement	System-descriptor area must already be allocated.	Quoted String, p. 4-260
descriptor_var	Host variable name that identifies the system-descriptor area	System-descriptor area must already be allocated.	Quoted String, p. 4-260
indicator_var	Host variable that receives a return code if null data is placed in the corresponding output_var	Variable cannot be a DATETIME or INTERVAL data type. This parameter is optional, but use an indicator variable if the possibility exists that *output_var* might contain null-value data. If you specify the indicator variable without the INDICATOR keyword, you cannot put a space between *output_var* and *indicator_var*.	Name must conform to language-specific rules for variable names.
output_var	Host variable whose contents replace a question-mark (?) placeholder in a prepared INSERT statement	Variable must be a character data type.	Name must conform to language-specific rules for variable names.
sqlda_pointer	Pointer to an **sqlda** structure that defines the type and memory location of values that correspond to the question-mark (?) placeholder in a prepared INSERT statement	You cannot begin an **sqlda** pointer with a dollar sign ($) or a colon (:).	DESCRIBE, p. 2-382.

(2 of 2)

Usage

Each PUT statement stores a row in an insert buffer that was created when the cursor was opened. If the buffer has no room for the new row when the statement executes, the buffered rows are written to the database in a block and the buffer is emptied. As a result, some PUT statement executions cause rows to be written to the database, and some do not.

You can use the FLUSH statement to write buffered rows to the database without adding a new row. The CLOSE statement writes any remaining rows before it closes an insert cursor.

If the current database uses explicit transactions, you must execute a PUT statement within a transaction.

The following example uses a PUT statement in ESQL/C:

```
EXEC SQL prepare ins_mcode from
    'insert into manufact values(?,?)';
EXEC SQL declare mcode cursor for ins_mcode;
EXEC SQL open mcode;
EXEC SQL put mcode from :the_code, :the_name;
```

X/O

The PUT statement is not an X/Open SQL statement. Therefore, you get a warning message if you compile a PUT statement in X/Open mode. ♦

Supplying Inserted Values

The values that reside in the inserted row can come from one of the following sources:

- Constant values that are written into the INSERT statement
- Program variables that are named in the INSERT statement
- Program variables that are named in the FROM clause of the PUT statement
- Values that are prepared in memory addressed by an **sqlda** structure or a system-descriptor area and then named in the USING clause of the PUT statement

Using Constant Values in INSERT

The VALUES clause of the INSERT statement lists the values of the inserted columns. One or more of these values might be constants (that is, numbers or character strings).

When *all* the inserted values are constants, the PUT statement has a special effect. Instead of creating a row and putting it in the buffer, the PUT statement merely increments a counter. When you use a FLUSH or CLOSE statement to empty the buffer, one row and a repetition count are sent to the database server, which inserts that number of rows.

In the following ESQL/C example, 99 empty customer records are inserted into the **customer** table. Because all values are constants, no disk output occurs until the cursor closes. (The constant zero for **customer_num** causes generation of a SERIAL value.)

```
int count;
EXEC SQL declare fill_c cursor for
    insert into customer(customer_num) values(0);
EXEC SQL open fill_c;
for (count = 1; count <= 99; ++count)
    EXEC SQL put fill_c;
EXEC SQL close fill_c;
```

Naming Program Variables in INSERT

When you associate the INSERT statement with a cursor (in the DECLARE statement), you create an insert cursor. In the INSERT statement, you can name program variables in the VALUES clause. When each PUT statement is executed, the contents of the program variables at that time are used to populate the row that is inserted into the buffer.

If you are creating an insert cursor (using DECLARE with INSERT), you must use only program variables in the VALUES clause. Variable names are not recognized in the context of a prepared statement; you associate a prepared statement with a cursor through its statement identifier.

The following ESQL/C example illustrates the use of an insert cursor. The code includes the following statements:

- The DECLARE statement associates a cursor called **ins_curs** with an INSERT statement that inserts data into the **customer** table. The VALUES clause names a data structure that is called **cust_rec**; the ESQL/C preprocessor converts **cust_rec** to a list of values, one for each component of the structure.

- The OPEN statement creates a buffer.

- A user-defined function that is not defined in the example obtains customer information from an interactive user and leaves it in **cust_rec**.

- The PUT statement composes a row from the current contents of the **cust_rec** structure and sends it to the row buffer.

- The CLOSE statement inserts into the **customer** table any rows that remain in the row buffer and closes the insert cursor.

```
int keep_going = 1;
EXEC SQL BEGIN DECLARE SECTION
    struct cust_row { /* fields of a row of customer table */ } cust_rec;
EXEC SQL END DECLARE SECTION

EXEC SQL declare ins_curs cursor for
      insert into customer values (:cust_row);
EXEC SQL open ins_curs;
while ( (sqlca.sqlcode == 0) && (keep_going) )
    {
    keep_going = get_user_input(cust_rec); /* ask user for new customer */
    if (keep_going )                       /* user did supply customer info */
        {
        cust_rec.customer_num = 0;        /* request new serial value */
        EXEC SQL put ins_curs;
        }
    if (sqlca.sqlcode == 0)                /* no error from PUT */
        keep_going = (prompt_for_y_or_n("another new customer") =='Y')
    }
EXEC SQL close ins_curs;
```

Use an indicator variable if the data to be inserted by the INSERT statement might be null.

Naming Program Variables in PUT

When the INSERT statement is prepared (see "PREPARE" on page 2-579), you cannot use program variables in its VALUES clause. However, you can represent values using a question-mark (?) placeholder. List the names of program variables in the FROM clause of the PUT statement to supply the missing values. The following ESQL/C example lists host variables in a PUT statement:

```
char answer [1] = 'y';
EXEC SQL BEGIN DECLARE SECTION;
    char ins_comp[80];
    char u_company[20];
EXEC SQL END DECLARE SECTION;

main()
{
    EXEC SQL connect to 'stores_demo';
    EXEC SQL prepare ins_comp from
        'insert into customer (customer_num, company) values (0, ?)';
    EXEC SQL declare ins_curs cursor for ins_comp;
    EXEC SQL open ins_curs;

    while (1)
        {
        printf("\nEnter a customer: ");
        gets(u_company);
        EXEC SQL put ins_curs from :u_company;
        printf("Enter another customer (y/n) ? ");
```

```
        if (answer = getch() != 'y')
            break;
        }
    EXEC SQL close ins_curs;
    EXEC SQL disconnect all;
}
```

Using the USING Clause

If you do not know the number of parameters to be supplied at runtime or their data types, you can associate input values from a system-descriptor area or an **sqlda** structure. Both of these descriptor structures describe the data type and memory location of one or more values to replace question-mark (?) placeholders.

Each time the PUT statement executes, the values that the descriptor structure describes are used to replace question-mark (?) placeholders in the INSERT statement. This process is similar to using a FROM clause with a list of variables, except that your program has full control over the memory location of the data values.

Specifying a System Descriptor Area

Use the SQL DESCRIPTOR option to introduce the name of a system descriptor area.

The COUNT field in the system-descriptor area corresponds to the number of dynamic parameters in the prepared statement. The value of COUNT must be less than or equal to the number of item descriptors that were specified when the system-descriptor area was allocated with the ALLOCATE DESCRIPTOR statement. You can obtain the value of a field with the GET DESCRIPTOR statement and set the value with the SET DESCRIPTOR statement.

X/O

A system-descriptor area conforms to the X/Open standards. ♦

Example of Specifying a System Descriptor Area

The following ESQL/C example shows how to associate values from a system-descriptor area:

```
    EXEC SQL allocate descriptor 'descl';
    ...
    EXEC SQL put selcurs using sql descriptor 'descl';
```

Specifying an sqlda Structure

Use the DESCRIPTOR option to introduce the name of a pointer to an **sqlda** structure.

The following ESQL/C example shows how to associate values from an **sqlda** structure:

```
EXEC SQL put selcurs using descriptor pointer2;
```

Inserting into a Collection Cursor

A collection cursor allows you to access the individual elements of a collection variable. To declare a collection cursor, use the DECLARE statement and include the Collection Derived Table segment in the INSERT statement that you associate with the cursor. Once you open the collection cursor with the OPEN statement, the cursor allows you to put elements in the collection variable.

To put elements, one at a time, into the insert cursor, use the PUT statement and the FROM clause. The PUT statement identifies the collection cursor that is associated with the collection variable. The FROM clause identifies the element value to be inserted into the cursor. The data type of any host variable in the FROM clause must match the element type of the collection.

Important: *The collection variable stores the elements of the collection. However, it has no intrinsic connection with a database column. Once the collection variable contains the correct elements, you must then save the variable into the actual collection column with the INSERT or UPDATE statement.*

Suppose you have a table called **children** with the following structure:

```
CREATE TABLE children
(
    age          SMALLINT,
    name         VARCHAR(30),
    fav_colors   SET(VARCHAR(20)),
)
```

The following ESQL/C code fragment shows how to use an insert cursor to put elements into a collection variable called **child_colors**:

```
EXEC SQL BEGIN DECLARE SECTION;
    client collection child_colors;
    char *favorites[]
    (
        "blue",
        "purple",
        "green",
        "white",
        "gold",
        0
    );

    int a = 0;
    char child_name[21];
EXEC SQL END DECLARE SECTION;

EXEC SQL allocate collection :child_colors;

/* Get structure of fav_colors column for untyped
 * child_colors collection variable */
EXEC SQL select fav_colors into :child_colors
    from children
    where name = :child_name;

/* Declare insert cursor for child_colors collection
 * variable and open this cursor */
EXEC SQL declare colors_curs cursor for
    insert into table(:child_colors)
    values (?);
EXEC SQL open colors_curs;

/* Use PUT to gather the favorite-color values
 * into a cursor */
while (fav_colors[a])
{
    EXEC SQL put colors_curs from :favorites[:a];
    a++
    ...
}

/* Flush cursor contents to collection variable */
EXEC SQL flush colors_curs;
EXEC SQL update children set fav_colors = :child_colors;

EXEC SQL close colors_curs;
EXEC SQL deallocate collection :child_colors;
```

After the FLUSH statement executes, the collection variable, **child_colors**, contains the elements {"blue", "purple", "green", "white", "gold"}. The UPDATE statement at the end of this code fragment saves the new collection into the **fav_colors** column of the database. Without this UPDATE statement, the collection column never has the new collection added.

Writing Buffered Rows

When the OPEN statement opens an insert cursor, an insert buffer is created. The PUT statement puts a row into this insert buffer. The block of buffered rows is inserted into the database table as a block only when necessary; this process is called *flushing the buffer*. The buffer is flushed after any of the following events:

- The buffer is too full to hold the new row at the start of a PUT statement.
- A FLUSH statement executes.
- A CLOSE statement closes the cursor.
- An OPEN statement executes, naming the cursor.

  When the OPEN statement is applied to an open cursor, it closes the cursor before reopening it; this implied CLOSE statement flushes the buffer.
- A COMMIT WORK statement executes.
- The buffer contains BYTE or TEXT data (flushed after a single PUT statement).

If the program terminates without closing an insert cursor, the buffer remains unflushed. Rows that were inserted into the buffer since the last flush are lost. Do not rely on the end of the program to close the cursor and flush the buffer.

Error Checking

The **sqlca** structure contains information on the success of each PUT statement as well as information that lets you count the rows that were inserted. The result of each PUT statement is contained in the following fields of the **sqlca**: **sqlca.sqlcode**, **SQLCODE** and **sqlca.sqlerrd[2]**.

Data buffering with an insert cursor means that errors are not discovered until the buffer is flushed. For example, an input value that is incompatible with the data type of the column for which it is intended is discovered only when the buffer is flushed. When an error is discovered, rows in the buffer that are located after the error are *not* inserted; they are lost from memory.

The SQLCODE field is set to 0 if no error occurs; otherwise, it is set to an error code. The third element of the **sqlerrd** array is set to the number of rows that are successfully inserted into the database:

- If a row is put into the insert buffer, and buffered rows are *not* written to the database, SQLCODE and **sqlerrd** are set to 0 (SQLCODE because no error occurred, and **sqlerrd** because no rows were inserted).

- If a block of buffered rows is written to the database during the execution of a PUT statement, SQLCODE is set to 0 and **sqlerrd** is set to the number of rows that was successfully inserted into the database.

- If an error occurs while the buffered rows are written to the database, SQLCODE indicates the error, and **sqlerrd** contains the number of successfully inserted rows. (The uninserted rows are discarded from the buffer.)

Tip: *When you encounter an **SQLCODE** error, a corresponding **SQLSTATE** error value also exists. For information about how to get the message text, check the GET DIAGNOSTICS statement.*

Counting Total and Pending Rows

To count the number of rows that were actually inserted in the database as well as the number not yet inserted, perform the following steps:

1. Prepare two integer variables (for example, **total** and **pending**).
2. When the cursor is opened, set both variables to 0.
3. Each time a PUT statement executes, increment both **total** and **pending**.
4. Whenever a PUT or FLUSH statement executes, or the cursor closes, subtract the third field of the **SQLERRD** array from **pending**.

At any time, (**total** - **pending**) represents the number of rows that were actually inserted. If all commands are successful, **pending** contains zero after the cursor is closed. If an error occurs during a PUT, FLUSH, or CLOSE statement, the value that remains in **pending** is the number of uninserted (discarded) rows.

Related Information

Related statements: ALLOCATE DESCRIPTOR, CLOSE, DEALLOCATE DESCRIPTOR, FLUSH, DECLARE, GET DESCRIPTOR, OPEN, PREPARE, and SET DESCRIPTOR

For a task-oriented discussion of the PUT statement, see the *Informix Guide to SQL: Tutorial*.

For further information about error checking, the system-descriptor area, and the **sqlda** structure, see the *Informix ESQL/C Programmer's Manual*.

RENAME COLUMN

Use the RENAME COLUMN statement to change the name of a column.

Syntax

```
RENAME COLUMN ———— table — · —old_column———— TO ——— new_column ————|
```

Element	Purpose	Restrictions	Syntax
new_column	New name to be assigned to the column	If you rename a column that appears within a trigger definition, the new column name replaces the old column name in the trigger definition only if certain conditions are met. For more information on this restriction, see "How Triggers Are Affected" on page 2-605.	Identifier, p. 4-205
old_column	Current name of the column you want to rename	The column must exist within the table.	Identifier, p. 4-205
table	Name of the table in which the column exists	The table must exist.	Database Object Name, p. 4-50

Usage

You can rename a column of a table if any of the following conditions are true:

- You own the table.
- You have the DBA privilege on the database.
- You have the Alter privilege on the table.

EDS

You cannot rename the columns of a fragmented table if the table is fragmented by range. For more information on tables fragmented by range, see "RANGE Method Clause" on page 2-265. ♦

How Views and Check Constraints Are Affected

If you rename a column that appears in a view, the text of the view in the **sysviews** system catalog table is updated to reflect the new column name.

If you rename a column that appears in a check constraint, the text of the check constraint in the **syschecks** system catalog table is updated to reflect the new column name.

How Triggers Are Affected

If you rename a column that appears within a trigger, it is replaced with the new name only in the following instances:

- When it appears as part of a correlation name inside the FOR EACH ROW action clause of a trigger
- When it appears as part of a correlation name in the INTO clause of an EXECUTE FUNCTION (or EXECUTE PROCEDURE) statement
- When it appears as a triggering column in the UPDATE clause

When the trigger executes, if the database server encounters a column name that no longer exists in the table, it returns an error.

Example of RENAME COLUMN

The following example assigns the new name of **c_num** to the **customer_num** column in the **customer** table:

```
RENAME COLUMN customer.customer_num TO c_num
```

Related Information

Related statements: ALTER TABLE, CREATE TABLE, and RENAME TABLE

RENAME DATABASE

Use the RENAME DATABASE statement to change the name of a database.

Syntax

```
RENAME DATABASE ——————— old_database ——————— TO ——————— new_database ———————|
```

Element	Purpose	Restrictions	Syntax
new_database	New name for the database	Name must be unique.	Database Name, p. 4-47
		You cannot rename the current database.	
		The database to be renamed must not be opened by any users when the RENAME DATABASE command is issued.	
old_database	Current name of the database	The database must exist.	Database Name, p. 4-47

Usage

You can rename a database if either of the following statements is true:

- You created the database.
- You have the DBA privilege on the database.

You can only rename local databases. You can rename a local database from inside an SPL routine.

Related Information

Related statement: CREATE DATABASE

RENAME TABLE

Use the RENAME TABLE statement to change the name of a table.

Syntax

RENAME TABLE ———————— *old_table* ———————— TO ————————— *new_table* ——————————|

Element	Purpose	Restrictions	Syntax
new_table	New name for the table	You cannot use the owner. convention in the new name of the table.	Identifier, p. 4-205
old_table	Current name of the table	The table must exist.	Identifier, p. 4-205

Usage

You can rename a table if any of the following statements are true:

- You own the table.
- You have the DBA privilege on the database.
- You have the Alter privilege on the table.

You cannot change the table owner by renaming the table. You can use the *owner.* convention in the old name of the table, but an error occurs during compilation if you try to use the *owner.* convention in the new name of the table.

EDS

If you are using Enterprise Decision Server, you cannot rename a table that contains a dependent GK index. ◆

ANSI

In an ANSI-compliant database, you must use the *owner.* convention in the old name of the table if you are referring to a table that you do not own. ◆

You cannot use the RENAME TABLE statement to move a table from the current database to another database or to move a table from another database to the current database. The table that you want to rename must reside in the current database. The renamed table that results from the statement remains in the current database.

Renaming Tables That Views Reference

If a view references the table that was renamed, and the view resides in the same database as the table, the database server updates the text of the view in the **sysviews** system catalog table to reflect the new table name. For further information on the **sysviews** system catalog table, see the *Informix Guide to SQL: Reference*.

Renaming Tables That Have Triggers

If you rename a table that has a trigger, it produces the following results:

- The database server replaces the name of the table in the trigger definition.
- The table name is *not* replaced where it appears inside any triggered actions.
- The database server returns an error if the new table name is the same as a correlation name in the REFERENCING clause of the trigger definition.

When the trigger executes, the database server returns an error if it encounters a table name for which no table exists.

Example of Renaming a Table

The following example reorganizes the **items** table. The intent is to move the **quantity** column from the fifth position to the third. The example illustrates the following steps:

1. Create a new table, **new_table**, that contains the column **quantity** in the third position.

2. Fill the table with data from the current **items** table.

3. Drop the old **items** table.

4. Rename **new_table** with the name **items**.

The following example uses the RENAME TABLE statement as the last step:

```
CREATE TABLE new_table
    (
    item_num    SMALLINT,
    order_num   INTEGER,
    quantity    SMALLINT,
    stock_num   SMALLINT,
    manu_code   CHAR(3),
    total_price MONEY(8)
    );
INSERT INTO new_table
    SELECT item_num, order_num, quantity, stock_num,
           manu_code, total_price
    FROM items;
DROP TABLE items;
RENAME TABLE new_table TO items;
```

Related Information

Related statements: ALTER TABLE, CREATE TABLE, DROP TABLE, and RENAME COLUMN.

REVOKE

Use the REVOKE statement to cancel any of the following items for specific users or for a role:

- Privileges on a database
- Privileges on a table, synonym, or view
- Privileges on a user-defined data type or user-defined routine (UDR)
- A role name

Syntax

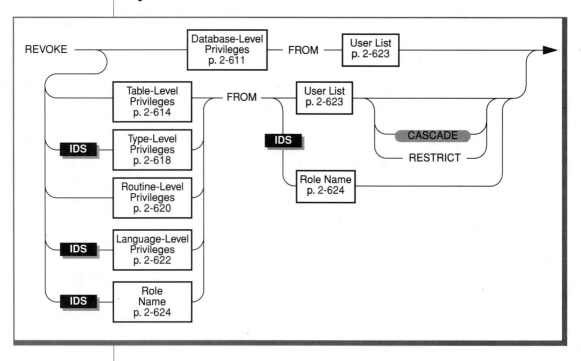

Usage

You can revoke privileges if:

- you granted them and did not name another user as grantor.
- the GRANT statement named you as grantor.
- you own an object on which PUBLIC has privileges by default.
- you have database-level DBA privileges.

You cannot revoke privileges from yourself. You cannot revoke privileges you granted if you named another user as grantor, nor can you revoke the status as grantor from the other user.

Database-Level Privileges

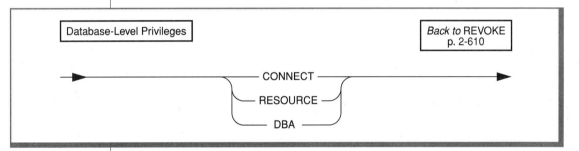

Three concentric layers of privileges, Connect, Resource, and DBA, authorize increasing power over database access and control. Only a user with the DBA privilege can grant or revoke database-level privileges.

Because of the hierarchical organization of the privileges (as outlined in the privilege definitions that are described later in this section), if you revoke either the Resource or the Connect privilege from a user with the DBA privilege, the statement has no effect. If you revoke the DBA privilege from a user who has the DBA privilege, the user retains the Connect privilege on the database. To deny database access to a user with the DBA or Resource privilege, you must first revoke the DBA or the Resource privilege and then revoke the Connect privilege in a separate REVOKE statement.

Similarly, if you revoke the Connect privilege from a user with the Resource privilege, the statement has no effect. If you revoke the Resource privilege from a user, the user retains the Connect privilege on the database.

The following table lists the appropriate keyword for each database-level privilege.

Privilege	Purpose
CONNECT	Lets you query and modify data. You can modify the database schema if you own the database object that you want to modify. Any user with the Connect privilege can perform the following functions:
	■ Connect to the database with the CONNECT statement or another connection statement
	■ Execute SELECT, INSERT, UPDATE, and DELETE statements, provided that the user has the necessary table-level privileges
	■ Create views, provided that the user has the Select privilege on the underlying tables
	■ Create synonyms
	■ Create temporary tables, and create indexes on the temporary tables
	■ Alter or drop a table or an index, provided that the user owns the table or index (or has the Alter, Index, or References privilege on the table)
	■ Grant privileges on a table, provided that the user owns the table (or was given privileges on the table with the WITH GRANT OPTION keyword)
RESOURCE	Lets you extend the structure of the database. In addition to the capabilities of the Connect privilege, the holder of the Resource privilege can perform the following functions:
	■ Create new tables
	■ Create new indexes
	■ Create new UDRs
	■ Create new data types

(1 of 2)

Privilege	Purpose
DBA	Has all the capabilities of the Resource privilege and can perform the following functions in addition to t: ■ Grant any database-level privilege, including the DBA privilege, to another user ■ Grant any table-level privilege to another user ■ Grant any table-level privilege to a role ■ Grant a role to a user or to another role ■ Restrict the Execute privilege to DBAs when registering a UDR ■ Execute the SET SESSION AUTHORIZATION statement ■ Use the NEXT SIZE keywords to alter extent sizes in the system catalog tables ■ Drop any database object, regardless of who owns it ■ Create tables, views, and indexes as well as specify another user as owner of the database objects ■ Execute the DROP DATABASE statement ■ Insert, delete, or update rows of any system catalog table except **systables**

(2 of 2)

 Warning: *Although the user **informix** and DBAs can modify most system catalog tables (only the user **informix** can modify **systables**), Informix strongly recommends that you do not update, delete, or insert any rows in these tables. Modifying the system catalog tables can destroy the integrity of the database. Informix does support use of the ALTER TABLE statement to modify the size of the next extent of system catalog tables.*

Table-Level Privileges

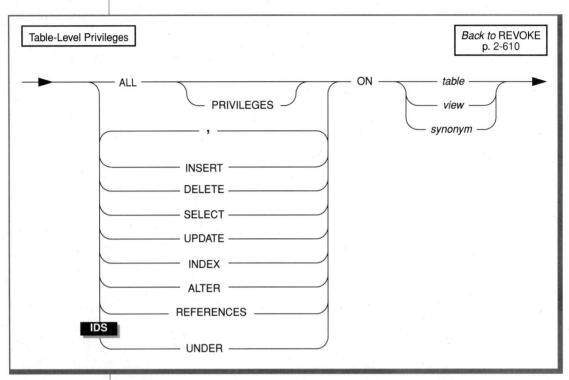

Element	Purpose	Restrictions	Syntax
synonym	Synonym for the table on which privileges are revoked	The synonym must exist.	Database Object Name, p. 4-50
table	Table on which privileges are revoked	The table must exist.	Database Object Name, p. 4-50
view	View on which privileges are revoked	The view must exist.	Database Object Name, p. 4-50

In one REVOKE statement, you can list one or more of the following keywords to specify the privileges you want to revoke from the same users.

Privilege	Purpose
INSERT	Lets you insert rows
DELETE	Lets you delete rows
SELECT	Lets you display data obtained from a SELECT statement
UPDATE	Lets you change column values
INDEX	Lets you create permanent indexes
	You must have the Resource privilege to take advantage of the Index privilege. (Any user with the Connect privilege can create indexes on temporary tables.)
ALTER	Lets you add or delete columns, modify column data types, add or delete constraints, change the locking mode of a table from PAGE to ROW, or add or drop a corresponding row type name for your table.
	This privilege also lets you set the database object mode of unique indexes and constraints to the enabled, disabled, or filtering mode. In addition, this privilege lets you set the database object mode of non-unique indexes and triggers to the enabled or disabled modes.
REFERENCES	Lets you reference columns in referential constraints
	You must have the Resource privilege to take advantage of the References privilege. (However, you can add a referential constraint during an ALTER TABLE statement. This method does not require that you have the Resource privilege on the database.) Revoke the References privilege to disallow cascading deletes.
UNDER (IDS only)	Lets you create subtables under a typed table.
ALL	Provides all the preceding privileges.
	The PRIVILEGES keyword is optional.

If a user receives the same privilege from two different grantors and one grantor revokes the privilege, the grantee still has the privilege until the second grantor also revokes the privilege. For example, if both you and a DBA grant the Update privilege on your table to **ted**, both you and the DBA must revoke the Update privilege to prevent **ted** from updating your table.

When to Use REVOKE Before GRANT

You can use combinations of REVOKE and GRANT to replace PUBLIC with specific users as the grantees and to remove some columns from table-level privileges.

Replacing PUBLIC With Specified Users

If a table owner grants a privilege to PUBLIC, the owner cannot revoke the same privilege from any particular user. For example, assume PUBLIC has default Select privileges on your **customer** table. You issue the following statement in an attempt to exclude **ted** from accessing your table:

```
REVOKE ALL ON customer FROM ted
```

The REVOKE statement results in ISAM error message 111, No record found, because the system catalog tables (**syscolauth** or **systabauth**) contain no table-level privilege entry for a user named **ted**. The REVOKE does not prevent **ted** from having all the table-level privileges given to PUBLIC on the **customer** table.

To restrict table-level privileges, first revoke the privileges with the PUBLIC keyword, then re-grant them to the appropriate users. The following example revokes the Index and Alter privileges from all users for the **customer** table and grants these privileges specifically to user **mary**:

```
REVOKE INDEX, ALTER ON customer FROM PUBLIC
GRANT INDEX, ALTER ON customer TO mary
```

Restricting Access to Specific Columns

The REVOKE statement has no syntax for revoking privileges on particular column names. When you revoke the Select, Update, or References privilege from a user, you revoke the privilege for all columns in the table. If you want a user to have some access to some, but not all the columns previously granted, issue a new GRANT statement to restore the appropriate privileges.

In the following example, **mary** first receives the ability to reference four columns in **customer**, then the table owner restricts references to two columns:

```
GRANT REFERENCES (fname, lname, company, city) ON
    customer TO mary
REVOKE REFERENCES ON customer FROM mary
GRANT REFERENCES (company, city)
    ON customer TO mary
```

The following example shows how to restrict Select privileges for PUBLIC to certain columns:

```
REVOKE SELECT ON customer FROM PUBLIC
GRANT SELECT (fname, lname, company, city)
    ON customer TO PUBLIC
```

Behavior of the ALL Keyword

The ALL keyword revokes all table-level privileges. If any or all of the table-level privileges do not exist for the revokee, the REVOKE statement with the ALL keyword executes successfully but returns the following SQLSTATE code:

```
01006--Privilege not revoked
```

For example, assume that the user **hal** has the Select and Insert privileges on the **customer** table. User **jocelyn** wants to revoke all seven table-level privileges from user **hal**. So user **jocelyn** issues the following REVOKE statement:

```
REVOKE ALL ON customer FROM hal
```

This statement executes successfully but returns SQLSTATE code 01006. The SQLSTATE warning is returned with a successful statement as follows:

- The statement succeeds in revoking the Select and Insert privileges from user **hal** because user **hal** had those privileges.

- SQLSTATE code 01006 is returned because the other privileges implied by the ALL keyword did not exist for user **hal**; therefore, these privileges were not revoked.

Tip: *The ALL keyword instructs the database server to revoke everything possible, including nothing. If the user from whom privileges are revoked has no privileges on the table, the REVOKE ALL statement still succeeds because it revokes everything possible from the user (in this case, no privileges at all).*

Effect of ALL Keyword on UNDER Privilege

If you revoke ALL privileges on a typed table, the Under privilege is included in the privileges that are revoked. If you revoke ALL privileges on a table that is not based on a row type, the Under privilege is not included in the privileges that are revoked. (The Under privilege cannot be granted on a traditional relational table.)

IDS

Type-Level Privileges

You can revoke two privileges on data types:

- You can revoke the Usage privilege on a user-defined data type.
- You can revoke the Under privilege on a named-row type.

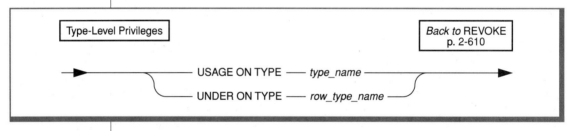

Element	Purpose	Restrictions	Syntax
row_type_name	Name of the named-row type for which the Under privilege is revoked	The specified named-row type must exist.	Data Type, p. 4-53
type_name	Name of the user-defined data type for which the Usage privilege is revoked	The specified data type must exist.	Data Type, p. 4-53

Usage Privilege

Any user can reference a built-in data type in an SQL statement, but not a distinct data type based on a built-in data type. The creator of a user-defined data type or a DBA must explicitly grant the Usage privilege on that new type, including a distinct data type based on a built-in data type.

REVOKE with the USAGE ON TYPE keywords removes the Usage privilege that you granted earlier to another user or role.

Under Privilege

You own a named-row type that you create. If you want other users to be able to create subtypes under this named-row type, you must grant these users the Under privilege on your named-row type. If you later want to remove the ability of these users to create subtypes under the named-row type, you must revoke the Under privilege from these users. A REVOKE statement with the UNDER ON TYPE keywords removes the Under privilege that you granted earlier to these users.

For example, suppose that you have created a row type named **rtype1**:

```
CREATE ROW TYPE rtype1
    (cola INT, colb INT)
```

If you want another user named **kathy** to be able to create a subtype under this named-row type, you must grant the Under privilege on this named-row type to user **kathy**:

```
GRANT UNDER on rtype1 to kathy
```

Now user **kathy** can create another row type under the **rtype1** row type even though **kathy** is not the owner of the **rtype1** row type:

```
CREATE ROW TYPE rtype2
    (colc INT, cold INT)
    UNDER rtype1
```

If you later want to remove the ability of user **kathy** to create subtypes under the **rtype1** row type, enter the following statement:

```
REVOKE UNDER on rtype1 FROM kathy
```

Routine-Level Privileges

If you revoke the EXECUTE privilege on a user-defined routine (UDR) from a user, that user can no longer execute that UDR in any way. For information on the ways a user can execute a UDR, see "Routine-Level Privileges" on page 2-513.

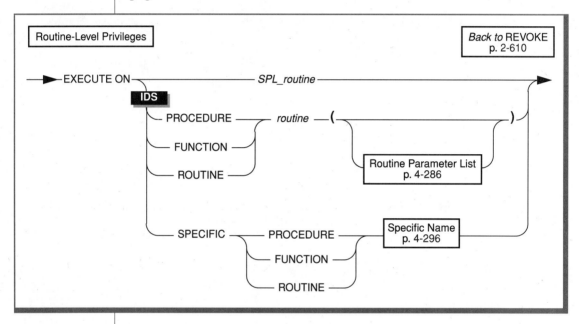

Element	Purpose	Restrictions	Syntax
routine	Name given to a user-defined routine in a CREATE FUNCTION or CREATE PROCEDURE statement	The identifier must refer to an existing UDR. In an ANSI-compliant database, specify the owner as the prefix to the routine name.	Database Object Name, p. 4-50
SPL_routine	Name given to an SPL routine that was created with the CREATE PROCEDURE statement	The SPL routine must exist. The SPL routine cannot be overloaded. That is, the name must be unique in the database.	Database Object Name, p. 4-50

When you create a UDR under any of the following circumstances, you must explicitly grant the Execute privilege before you can revoke it:

ANSI

- You create a UDR in an ANSI-compliant database. ♦
- You have DBA-level privileges and use the DBA keyword with CREATE to restrict the Execute privilege to users with the DBA database-level privilege.
- The **NODEFDAC** environment variable is set to `yes` to prevent PUBLIC from receiving any privileges that are not explicitly granted.

IDS

Any negator function for which you grant the Execute privilege requires a separate, explicit REVOKE statement. ♦

When you create a UDR without any of the preceding conditions in effect, PUBLIC can execute your UDR without a GRANT statement. To limit who executes your UDR, revoke the privilege using the keywords FROM PUBLIC and then grant it to a user list (see "User List" on page 2-623) or role (see "Role Name" on page 2-624).

IDS

If two or more UDRs have the same name, use the appropriate keyword from the following list to specify which of those UDRs a user can no longer execute.

PRIVILEGE	Purpose
SPECIFIC	Prevents a user from executing the UDR identified by *specific name*.
FUNCTION	Prevents execution of any function with the specified *routine name* (and parameter types that match *routine parameter list*, if supplied).
PROCEDURE	Prevents execution of any procedure with the specified *routine name* (and parameter types that match *routine parameter list*, if supplied).
ROUTINE	Prevents execution of both functions and procedures with the specified *routine name* (and parameter types that match *routine parameter list*, if supplied).

♦

IDS

Language-Level Privileges

A user must have the Usage privilege on a language to register a user-defined routine (UDR) that is written in that language.

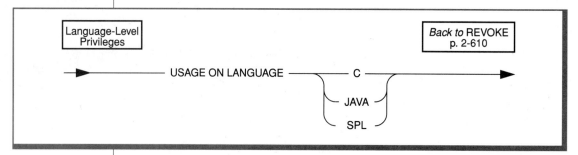

When a user executes a CREATE FUNCTION or CREATE PROCEDURE statement to register a UDR, the database server verifies that the user has the Usage privilege on the language in which the UDR is written. If the user does not have the Usage privilege, the statement fails.

If you want to revoke the Usage privilege on a language from a user or role, issue a REVOKE USAGE ON LANGUAGE statement.

The effect of issuing this statement is that the user or role can no longer register UDRs that are written in the specified language. For example, if you revoke the default Usage privilege on the SPL language from PUBLIC, the ability to create SPL routines is taken away from all users:

```
REVOKE USAGE ON LANGUAGE SPL FROM PUBLIC
```

You can now issue a GRANT USAGE ON LANGUAGE statement to grant Usage privilege on the SPL language to a restricted group such as the role named **developers**:

```
GRANT USAGE ON LANGUAGE SPL TO developers
```

User List

In the user list, you identify who loses the privileges you are revoking. The user list can consist of the logins for a single user or multiple users, separated by commas. If you use the PUBLIC keyword as the user list, the REVOKE statement revokes privileges from all users.

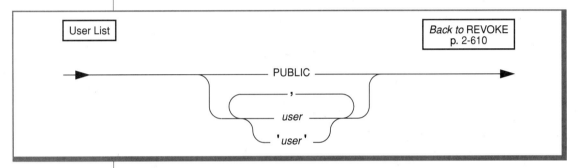

Element	Purpose	Restrictions	Syntax
user	Login name of the user who is to lose the role or privilege that was granted	Put quotes around *user* to ensure that the name of the user is stored exactly as you type it. Use the single keyword PUBLIC for *user* to revoke a role or privilege from all authorized users.	The name must conform to the conventions of your operating system.

When the user list contains specific logins, you can combine the REVOKE statement with the GRANT statement to selectively secure tables, columns, UDRs, types, and so forth. For examples, see "When to Use REVOKE Before GRANT" on page 2-616.

Spell the user names in the list exactly as they were spelled in the GRANT statement. In a database that is not ANSI compliant, you can optionally use quotes around each user in the list.

ANSI

In an ANSI-compliant database, if you do not use quotes around *user*, the name of the user is stored in uppercase letters. ◆

IDS

Role Name

Only the DBA or a user granted a role with the WITH GRANT OPTION can revoke a role or its privileges. Users cannot revoke roles from themselves.

When you revoke a role that was granted with the WITH GRANT OPTION, both the role and grant option are revoked. "Revoking Privileges Granted WITH GRANT OPTION" on page 2-625 explains revoking such a role.

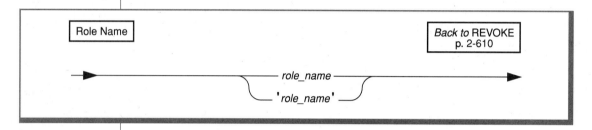

Element	Purpose	Restrictions	Syntax
role_name	Name of the role that: ■ loses a privilege assigned to it ■ loses the use of another role ■ a user or another role loses	The role must have been created with the CREATE ROLE statement and granted with the GRANT statement. When a role name is enclosed in quotation marks, the role name is case sensitive.	Identifier, p. 4-205

The following examples show the effects of REVOKE with *role name*:

■ Remove users or another role name from inclusion in the role

```
REVOKE accounting FROM mary
REVOKE payroll FROM accounting
```

■ Remove one or more privileges from a role

```
REVOKE UPDATE ON employee FROM accounting
```

When you revoke table-level privileges from a role, you cannot use the RESTRICT or CASCADE clauses.

Revoking Privileges Granted WITH GRANT OPTION

If you revoke from *user* the privileges that you granted using the WITH GRANT OPTION keywords, you sever the chain of privileges granted by that *user*.

Thus, when you revoke privileges from users or a role, you also revoke the same privilege resulting from GRANT statements:

- issued by your grantee.
- allowed because your grantee used the WITH GRANT OPTION clause.
- allowed because subsequent grantees granted the same privilege using the WITH GRANT OPTION clause.

The following examples illustrate this situation. You, as the owner of the table **items**, issue the following statements to grant access to the user **mary**:

```
REVOKE ALL ON items FROM PUBLIC
GRANT SELECT, UPDATE ON items TO mary WITH GRANT OPTION
```

The user **mary** uses her new privilege to grant users **cathy** and **paul** access to the table.

```
GRANT SELECT, UPDATE ON items TO cathy
GRANT SELECT ON items TO paul
```

Later you revoke privileges on the **items** table to user **mary**.

```
REVOKE SELECT, UPDATE ON items FROM mary
```

This single statement effectively revokes all privileges on the **items** table from the users **mary**, **cathy**, and **paul**.

The CASCADE keyword has the same effect as this default condition.

Effect of CASCADE Keyword on UNDER Privileges

If you revoke the Under privilege on a typed table with the CASCADE option, the Under privilege is removed from the specified user, and any subtables created under the typed table by that user are dropped from the database.

However, if you revoke the Under privilege on a named-row type with the CASCADE option, and the row type is in use, the REVOKE statement fails. This exception to the normal behavior of the CASCADE option results from the fact that the database server supports the DROP ROW TYPE statement with the RESTRICT keyword only.

For example, assume that user **jeff** creates a row type named **rtype1** and grants the Under privilege on that row type to user **mary**. User **mary** now creates a row type named **rtype2** under row type **rtype1** and grants the Under privilege on row type **rtype2** to user **andy.** Then user **andy** creates a row type named **rtype3** under row type **rtype2**. Now user **jeff** tries to revoke the Under privilege on row type **rtype1** from user **mary** with the CASCADE option. The REVOKE statement fails because row type **rtype2** is still in use by row type **rtype3**.

Controlling the Scope of REVOKE with the RESTRICT Option

The RESTRICT keyword causes the REVOKE statement to fail when any of the following dependencies exist:

- A view depends on a Select privilege that you attempt to revoke.
- A foreign-key constraint depends on a References privilege that you attempt to revoke.
- You attempt to revoke a privilege from a user who subsequently granted this privilege to another user or users.

A REVOKE statement does not fail if it pertains to a user who has the right to grant the privilege to any other user but does not exercise that right, as the following example shows:

Assume that the user **clara** uses the WITH GRANT OPTION clause to grant the Select privilege on the **customer** table to the user **ted**.

Assume that user **ted**, in turn, grants the Select privilege on the **customer** table to user **tania**. The following REVOKE statement issued by **clara** fails because **ted** used his authority to grant the Select privilege:

```
REVOKE SELECT ON customer FROM ted RESTRICT
```

By contrast, if user **ted** does not grant the Select privilege to **tania** or any other user, the same REVOKE statement succeeds.

Even if **ted** does grant the Select privilege to another user, either of the following statements succeeds:

```
REVOKE SELECT ON customer FROM ted CASCADE
REVOKE SELECT ON customer FROM ted
```

Effect of Uncommitted Transactions

When a REVOKE statement is executed, an exclusive row lock is placed on the entry in the **systables** system catalog table for the table from which privileges were revoked. This lock is released only after the transaction that contains the REVOKE statement is complete. When another transaction attempts to prepare a SELECT statement against this table, the transaction fails because the entry for this table in **systables** is exclusively locked. The attempt to prepare the SELECT statement will not succeed until the first transaction was committed.

Related Information

Related Statements: GRANT, GRANT FRAGMENT, and REVOKE FRAGMENT

For information about roles, see the following statements: CREATE ROLE, DROP ROLE, and SET ROLE.

In the *Informix Guide to Database Design and Implementation*, see the discussion of privileges.

For a discussion of how to embed GRANT and REVOKE statements in programs, see the *Informix Guide to SQL: Tutorial*.

REVOKE FRAGMENT

Use the REVOKE FRAGMENT statement to revoke privileges that were granted on individual fragments of a fragmented table. You can use this statement to revoke the Insert, Update, and Delete fragment-level privileges from users.

Syntax

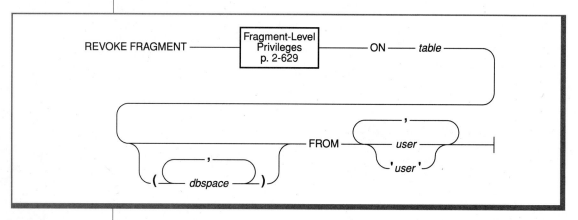

Element	Purpose	Restrictions	Syntax
dbspace	Name of the dbspace where the fragment is stored Use this parameter to specify the fragment or fragments on which privileges are to be revoked. If you do not specify a fragment, the REVOKE statement applies to all fragments in the specified table that have the specified privileges.	The specified dbspace or dbspaces must exist.	Identifier, p. 4-205
table	Name of the table that contains the fragment or fragments on which privileges are to be revoked No default value exists.	The specified table must exist and must be fragmented by expression.	Database Object Name, p. 4-50
user	Name of the user or users from whom the specified privileges are to be revoked No default value exists.	The user must be a valid user.	The name must conform to the conventions of your operating system.

Usage

Use the REVOKE FRAGMENT statement to revoke the Insert, Update, or Delete privilege on one or more fragments of a fragmented table from one or more users.

The REVOKE FRAGMENT statement is only valid for tables that are fragmented according to an expression-based distribution scheme. For an explanation of an expression-based distribution scheme, see "Syntax" on page 2-12.

You can specify one fragment or a list of fragments in the REVOKE FRAGMENT statement. To specify a fragment, name the dbspace in which the fragment resides.

You do not have to specify a particular fragment or a list of fragments in the REVOKE FRAGMENT statement. If you do not specify any fragments in the statement, the specified users lose the specified privileges on all fragments for which the users currently have those privileges.

Fragment-Level Privileges

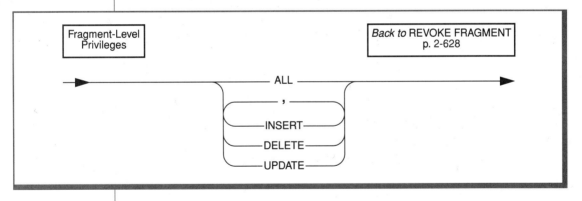

You can revoke fragment-level privileges individually or in combination. List the keywords that correspond to the privileges that you are revoking from *user*. The following table defines each of the fragment-level privileges.

Privilege	Purpose
ALL	Provides insert, delete, and update privileges on a fragment
INSERT	Lets you insert rows in the fragment
DELETE	Lets you delete rows in the fragment
UPDATE	Lets you update rows in the fragment and to name any column of the table in an UPDATE statement

If you specify the ALL keyword in a REVOKE FRAGMENT statement, the specified users lose all fragment-level privileges that they currently have on the specified fragments.

For example, assume that a user currently has the Update privilege on one fragment of a table. If you use the ALL keyword to revoke all current privileges on this fragment from this user, the user loses the Update privilege that he or she had on this fragment.

Examples of the REVOKE FRAGMENT Statement

The examples that follow are based on the **customer** table. All the examples assume that the **customer** table is fragmented by expression into three fragments that reside in the dbspaces that are named **dbsp1**, **dbsp2**, and **dbsp3**.

Revoking One Privilege

The following statement revokes the Update privilege on the fragment of the **customer** table in **dbsp1** from the user **ed**:

```
REVOKE FRAGMENT UPDATE ON customer (dbsp1) FROM ed
```

Revoking More Than One Privilege

The following statement revokes the Update and Insert privileges on the fragment of the **customer** table in **dbsp1** from the user **susan**:

```
REVOKE FRAGMENT UPDATE, INSERT ON customer (dbsp1) FROM susan
```

Revoking All Privileges

The following statement revokes all privileges currently granted to the user **harry** on the fragment of the **customer** table in **dbsp1**.:

```
REVOKE FRAGMENT ALL ON customer (dbsp1) FROM harry
```

Revoking Privileges on More Than One Fragment

The following statement revokes all privileges currently granted to the user **millie** on the fragments of the **customer** table in **dbsp1** and **dbsp2**:

```
REVOKE FRAGMENT ALL ON customer (dbsp1, dbsp2) FROM millie
```

Revoking Privileges from More Than One User

The following statement revokes all privileges currently granted to the users **jerome** and **hilda** on the fragment of the **customer** table in **dbsp3**:

```
REVOKE FRAGMENT ALL ON customer (dbsp3) FROM jerome, hilda
```

Revoking Privileges Without Specifying Fragments

The following statement revokes all current privileges from the user **mel** on all fragments for which this user currently has privileges:

```
REVOKE FRAGMENT ALL ON customer FROM mel
```

Related Information

Related statements: GRANT FRAGMENT and REVOKE

For a discussion of fragment-level and table-level privileges, see the *Informix Guide to Database Design and Implementation.*

ROLLBACK WORK

Use the ROLLBACK WORK statement to cancel a transaction deliberately and undo any changes that occurred since the beginning of the transaction. The ROLLBACK WORK statement restores the database to the state that it was in before the transaction began.

Syntax

```
ROLLBACK ─────────────────────────────────────────────┤
                              └─ WORK ─┘
```

Usage

The ROLLBACK WORK statement is valid only in databases with transactions.

In a database that is not ANSI-compliant, start a transaction with a BEGIN WORK statement. You can end a transaction with a COMMIT WORK statement or cancel the transaction with a ROLLBACK WORK statement. The ROLLBACK WORK statement restores the database to the state that existed before the transaction began.

Use the ROLLBACK WORK statement only at the end of a multistatement operation.

The ROLLBACK WORK statement releases all row and table locks that the cancelled transaction holds. If you issue a ROLLBACK WORK statement when no transaction is pending, an error occurs.

ANSI

In an ANSI-compliant database, transactions are implicit. Transactions start after each COMMIT WORK or ROLLBACK WORK statement, so no BEGIN WORK statement is required. If you issue a ROLLBACK WORK statement when no transaction is pending, the statement is accepted but has no effect. ♦

E/C

In ESQL/C, the ROLLBACK WORK statement closes all open cursors except those that are declared with hold. Hold cursors remain open after a transaction is committed or rolled back.

If you use the ROLLBACK WORK statement within an SPL routine that a WHENEVER statement calls, specify WHENEVER SQLERROR CONTINUE and WHENEVER SQLWARNING CONTINUE before the ROLLBACK WORK statement. This step prevents the program from looping if the ROLLBACK WORK statement encounters an error or a warning. ♦

WORK Keyword

The WORK keyword is optional in a ROLLBACK WORK statement. The following two statements are equivalent:

```
ROLLBACK;

ROLLBACK WORK;
```

Related Information

Related statements: BEGIN WORK and COMMIT WORK

For a discussion of transactions and ROLLBACK WORK, see the *Informix Guide to SQL: Tutorial*.

SELECT

Use the SELECT statement to query a database or the contents of an SPL or ESQL/C collection variable.

Syntax

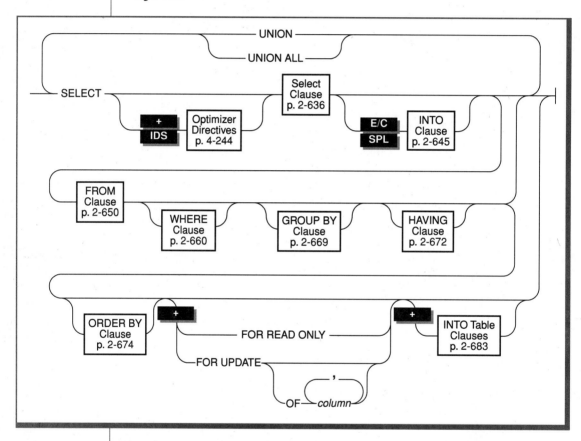

Element	Purpose	Restrictions	Syntax
column	Name of a column that can be updated after a fetch	The specified column must be in the table, but it does not have to be in the select list of the SELECT clause.	Identifier, p. 4-205

Usage

You can query the tables in the current database, a database that is not current, or a database that is on a different database server from your current database.

The SELECT statement includes many basic clauses. Each clause is described in the following list.

Clause	Purpose
SELECT	Names a list of items to be read from the database
INTO	Specifies the program variables or host variables that receive the selected data
FROM	Names the tables that contain the selected columns
WHERE	Sets conditions on the selected rows
GROUP BY	Combines groups of rows into summary results
HAVING	Sets conditions on the summary results
ORDER BY	Orders the selected rows
FOR UPDATE	Specifies that the values returned by the SELECT statement can be updated after a fetch
FOR READ ONLY	Specifies that the values returned by the SELECT statement cannot be updated after a fetch
INTO TEMP	Creates a temporary table in the current database and puts the results of the query into the table
INTO SCRATCH	Creates an unlogging temporary table in the current database and puts the results of the query into the table
INTO EXTERNAL	Loads an external table with the results of the query

SELECT Clause

The SELECT clause contains the list of database objects or expressions to be selected, as shown in the following diagram

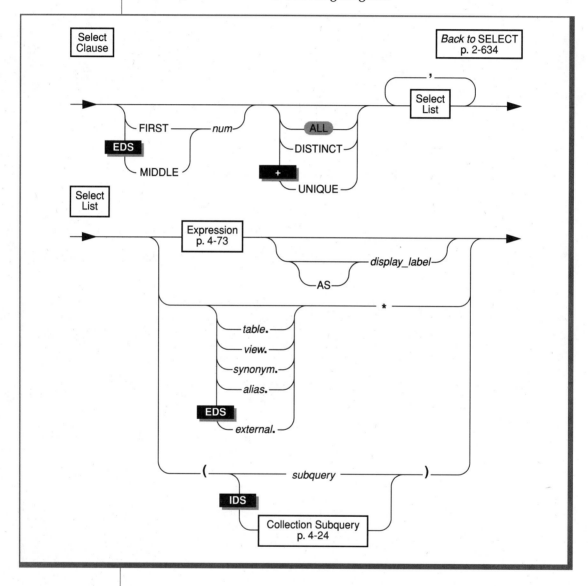

Element	Purpose	Restrictions	Syntax
*	Symbol that signifies that all columns in the specified table or view are to be selected	Use this symbol whenever you want to retrieve all the columns in the table or view in their defined order. If you want to retrieve all the columns in some other order, or if you want to retrieve a subset of the columns, you must specify the columns explicitly in the SELECT list.	The asterisk (*) is a literal value that has a special meaning in this statement.
alias	Temporary alternative name assigned to the table or view in the FROM clause For more information on aliases, see "FROM Clause" on page 2-650.	You cannot use an alias for a SELECT clause unless you assign the alias to the table or view in the FROM clause.	Identifier, p. 4-205
display_label	Temporary name that you assign to a column For more information on how the label is displayed, see "Using a Display Label" on page 2-644.	For restrictions that apply to when you use a display label, see "Using a Display Label" on page 2-644.	Identifier, p. 4-205
external	Name of the external table from which you want to retrieve data	The external table must exist.	Database Object Name, p. 4-50
num	Integer that indicates the number of rows to return	The value must be greater than zero (0). If the value is greater than the number of rows that match the selection criteria of the query, all matching rows are returned.	Literal Number, p. 4-237
subquery	Embedded query	The subquery cannot contain either the FIRST or the ORDER BY clause.	SELECT, p. 2-634
synonym	Name of the synonym from which you want to retrieve data	The synonym and the table to which the synonym points must exist.	Database Object Name, p. 4-50
table	Name of the table from which you want to retrieve data	The table must exist.	Database Object Name, p. 4-50
view	Name of the view from which you want to retrieve data	The view must exist.	Database Object Name, p. 4-50

In the SELECT clause, specify exactly what data is being selected as well as whether you want to omit duplicate values.

Using the FIRST Option

The FIRST option allows you to specify a maximum number of rows to retrieve that match conditions specified in the SELECT statement. Rows that match the selection criteria, but fall outside the specified number, are not returned.

The following example retrieves at most 10 rows from a table:

```
SELECT FIRST 10 a, b FROM tab1;
```

When you use this option with an ORDER BY clause, you can retrieve the first number of rows according to the order criteria. For example, the following query finds the ten highest-paid employees.

```
SELECT FIRST 10 name, salary
FROM emp
ORDER BY salary DESC
```

EDS

If you are using Enterprise Decision Server, you can also use the FIRST option to select the first rows that result from a union query. In the following example, the FIRST option is applied to the result of the UNION expression.

```
SELECT FIRST 10 a, b FROM tab1 UNION SELECT a, b FROM tab2
```

♦

Restrictions on the First Option

The FIRST option is not allowed in the following situations:

- When you define a view
- In nested SELECT statements
- In subqueries
- In the SELECT clause of an INSERT statement
- When your SELECT statement is selecting data and inserting it into another table, such as a temporary, scratch, or external table
- In statements that allow embedded SELECT statements to be used as expressions

IDS

- As part of a UNION query ♦

IDS

Using FIRST as a Column Name with Dynamic Server

Although FIRST is a keyword, the database server can also interpret it as a column name. If an integer does not follow the keyword, the database server interprets FIRST as the name of a column. For example, if a table has columns **first**, **second**, and **third**, the following query would return data from the column named **first**:

```
SELECT first
from T
```

EDS

Using the MIDDLE Option

The MIDDLE option, like the FIRST option, allows you to specify a maximum number of rows to retrieve that match conditions specified in the SELECT statement. However, whereas the FIRST option returns the first number of specified rows that match the selection criteria, the MIDDLE option returns the middle number of rows.

The syntax and restrictions for this option are the same as those for the FIRST option. For more information see "Using the FIRST Option" on page 2-638.

Allowing Duplicates

You can apply the ALL, UNIQUE, or DISTINCT keywords to indicate whether duplicate values are returned, if any exist. If you do not specify any keywords, all the rows are returned by default.

Keyword	Purpose
ALL	Specifies that all selected values are returned, regardless of whether duplicates exist
	ALL is the default state.
DISTINCT	Eliminates duplicate rows from the query results
UNIQUE	Eliminates duplicate rows from the query results
	UNIQUE is a synonym for DISTINCT.

For example, the following query lists the **stock_num** and **manu_code** of all items that have been ordered, excluding duplicate items:

```
SELECT DISTINCT stock_num, manu_code FROM items
```

You can use the DISTINCT or UNIQUE keywords once in each level of a query or subquery. For example, the following query uses DISTINCT in both the query and the subquery:

```
SELECT DISTINCT stock_num, manu_code FROM items
    WHERE order_num = (SELECT DISTINCT order_num FROM orders
        WHERE customer_num = 120)
```

Expressions in the Select List

You can use any basic type of expression (column, constant, built-in function, aggregate function, and user-defined routine), or combination thereof, in the select list. The expression types are described in "Expression" on page 4-73.

The following sections present examples of using each type of simple expression in the select list.

You can combine simple numeric expressions by connecting them with arithmetic operators for addition, subtraction, multiplication, and division. However, if you combine a column expression and an aggregate function, you must include the column expression in the GROUP BY clause.

You cannot use variable names (for example, a host variable in an ESQL/C application) in the select list by themselves. You can include a variable name in the select list, however, if an arithmetic or concatenation operator connects it to a constant.

Selecting Columns

Column expressions are the most commonly used expressions in a SELECT statement. For a complete description of the syntax and use of column expressions, see "Column Expressions" on page 4-91.

The following examples show column expressions within a select list:

```
SELECT orders.order_num, items.price FROM orders, items

SELECT customer.customer_num ccnum, company FROM customer

SELECT catalog_num, stock_num, cat_advert [1,15] FROM catalog

SELECT lead_time - 2 UNITS DAY FROM manufact
```

Selecting Constants

If you include a constant expression in the select list, the same value is returned for each row that the query returns. For a complete description of the syntax and use of constant expressions, see "Constant Expressions" on page 4-108.

The following examples show constant expressions within a select list:

```
SELECT 'The first name is', fname FROM customer

SELECT TODAY FROM cust_calls

SELECT SITENAME FROM systables WHERE tabid = 1

SELECT lead_time - 2 UNITS DAY FROM manufact

SELECT customer_num + LENGTH('string') from customer
```

Selecting Built-In Function Expressions

A built-in function expression uses a function that is evaluated for each row in the query. All built-in function expressions require arguments. This set of expressions contains the time functions and the length function when they are used with a column name as an argument.

The following examples show built-in function expressions within a select list:

```
SELECT EXTEND(res_dtime, YEAR TO SECOND) FROM cust_calls

SELECT LENGTH(fname) + LENGTH(lname) FROM customer

SELECT HEX(order_num) FROM orders

SELECT MONTH(order_date) FROM orders
```

Selecting Aggregate Expressions

An aggregate function returns one value for a set of queried rows. The aggregate functions take on values that depend on the set of rows that the WHERE clause of the SELECT statement returns. In the absence of a WHERE clause, the aggregate functions take on values that depend on all the rows that the FROM clause forms.

The following examples show aggregate functions in a select list:

```
SELECT SUM(total_price) FROM items WHERE order_num = 1013

SELECT COUNT(*) FROM orders WHERE order_num = 1001

SELECT MAX(LENGTH(fname) + LENGTH(lname)) FROM customer
```

Selecting User-Defined Function Expressions

User-defined functions extend the range of functions that are available to you and allow you to perform a subquery on each row that you select.

The following example calls the **get_orders** user-defined function for each **customer_num** and displays the output of the function under the n_orders label:

```
SELECT customer_num, lname,
    get_orders(customer_num) n_orders
        FROM customer
```

SPL

If a called SPL routine contains certain SQL statements, the database server returns an error. For information on which SQL statements cannot be used in an SPL routine that is called within a data manipulation statement, see "Restrictions on an SPL Routine Called in a Data Manipulation Statement" on page 4-302. ♦

For the complete syntax of user-defined function expressions, see "User-Defined Functions" on page 4-179.

Selecting Expressions That Use Arithmetic Operators

You can combine numeric expressions with arithmetic operators to make complex expressions. You cannot combine expressions that contain aggregate functions with column expressions. The following examples show expressions that use arithmetic operators within a select list:

```
SELECT stock_num, quantity*total_price FROM customer

SELECT price*2 doubleprice FROM items

SELECT count(*)+2 FROM customer

SELECT count(*)+LENGTH('ab') FROM customer
```

IDS

Selecting Row Fields

You can select a particular field of a row-type column (named or unnamed row type) with dot notation, which uses a period (.) as a separator between the row and field names. For example, suppose you have the following table structure:

```
CREATE ROW TYPE one (a INTEGER, b FLOAT);
CREATE ROW TYPE two (c one, d CHAR(10));
CREATE ROW TYPE three (e CHAR(10), f two);

CREATE TABLE new_tab OF TYPE two;
CREATE TABLE three_tab OF TYPE three;
```

The following expressions are valid in the select list:

```
SELECT t.c FROM new_tab t;
SELECT f.c.a FROM three_tab;
SELECT f.d FROM three_tab;
```

You can also enter an asterisk in place of a field name to signify that all fields of the row-type column are to be selected. For example, if the **my_tab** table has a row-type column named **rowcol** that contains four fields, the following SELECT statement retrieves all four fields of the **rowcol** column:

```
SELECT rowcol.* FROM my_tab
```

You can also retrieve all fields from a row-type column by specifying the column name without any dot notation. The following SELECT statement has the same effect as the preceding SELECT statement:

```
SELECT rowcol FROM my_tab
```

You can use dot notation not only with row-type columns but with expressions that evaluate to row-type values. For more information on the use of dot notation with row-type columns and expressions, see "Column Expressions" on page 4-91 in the Expression segment.

Using a Display Label

You can assign a display label to any column in your select list.

DB

In DB-Access, a display label appears as the heading for that column in the output of the SELECT statement. ♦

E/C

In ESQL/C, the value of *display_label* is stored in the **sqlname** field of the **sqlda** structure. For more information on the **sqlda** structure, see the *Informix ESQL/C Programmer's Manual*. ♦

Using the AS Keyword

If your display label is also an SQL reserved word, you can use the AS keyword with the display label to clarify the use of the word. If you want to use the word UNITS, YEAR, MONTH, DAY, HOUR, MINUTE, SECOND, or FRACTION as your display label, you must use the AS keyword with the display label. The following example shows how to use the AS keyword with **minute** as a display label:

```
SELECT call_dtime AS minute FROM cust_calls
```

For a list of SQL reserved words, see Appendix A, "Reserved Words for Dynamic Server."

Usage Restrictions with Certain Database Objects

If you are creating a temporary table, you must supply a display label for any columns that are not simple column expressions. The display label is used as the name of the column in the temporary table.

If you are using the SELECT statement in creating a view, do not use display labels. Specify the desired label names in the CREATE VIEW column list instead.

INTO Clause

Use the INTO clause in an SPL routine or an ESQL/C program to specify the program variables or host variables to receive the data that the SELECT statement retrieves. The following diagram shows the syntax of the INTO clause.

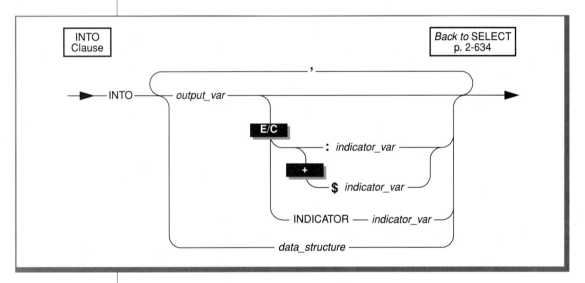

Element	Purpose	Restrictions	Syntax
data_structure	Structure that was declared as a host variable	The individual elements of the structure must be matched appropriately to the data type of values being selected.	Name must conform to language-specific rules for data structures.
indicator_var	Program variable that receives a return code if null data is placed in the corresponding output_var	This parameter is optional, but you should use an indicator variable if the possibility exists that the value of the corresponding output_var is null.	Name must conform to language-specific rules for variable names.

(1 of 2)

Element	Purpose	Restrictions	Syntax
output_var	Program variable or host variable This variable receives the value of the corresponding item in the select list of the SELECT clause. This variable can be a collection variable.	The order of receiving variables in the INTO clause must match the order of the corresponding items in the select list of the SELECT clause. The number of receiving variables must be equal to the number of items in the select list. The data type of each receiving variable should agree with the data type of the corresponding column or expression in the select list. For the actions that the database server takes when the data type of the receiving variable does not match that of the selected item, see "Warnings in ESQL/C" on page 2-649.	Name must conform to language-specific rules for variable names.

You must specify an INTO clause with SELECT to name the variables that receive the values that the query returns. If the query returns more than one value, the values are returned into the list of variables in the order in which you specify them.

If the SELECT statement stands alone (that is, it is not part of a DECLARE statement and does not use the INTO clause), it must be a singleton SELECT statement. A *singleton* SELECT statement returns only one row.

The following example shows a singleton SELECT statement in ESQL/C:

```
EXEC SQL select fname, lname, company_name
    into :p_fname, :p_lname, :p_coname
    where customer_num = 101;
```

SPL

In an SPL routine, if a SELECT returns more than one row, you must use the FOREACH statement to access the rows individually. The INTO clause of the SELECT statement holds the fetched values. For more information, see "FOREACH" on page 3-30. ♦

E/C

INTO Clause with Indicator Variables

In ESQL/C, if the possibility exists that data returned from the SELECT statement is null, use an indicator variable in the INTO clause. For more information about indicator variables, see the *Informix ESQL/C Programmer's Manual*.

INTO Clause with Cursors

If the SELECT statement returns more than one row, you must use a cursor in a FETCH statement to fetch the rows individually. You can put the INTO clause in the FETCH statement rather than in the SELECT statement, but you should not put it in both.

The following ESQL/C code examples show different ways you can use the INTO clause. As both examples show, first you must use the DECLARE statement to declare a cursor.

Using the INTO clause in the SELECT statement

```
EXEC SQL declare q_curs cursor for
    select lname, company
        into :p_lname, :p_company
        from customer;
EXEC SQL open q_curs;
while (SQLCODE == 0)
    EXEC SQL fetch q_curs;
EXEC SQL close q_curs;
```

Using the INTO clause in the FETCH statement

```
EXEC SQL declare q_curs cursor for
    select lname, company
    from customer;
EXEC SQL open q_curs;
while (SQLCODE == 0)
    EXEC SQL fetch q_curs into :p_lname, :p_company;
EXEC SQL close q_curs;
```

E/C

Preparing a SELECT...INTO Query

In ESQL/C, you cannot prepare a query that has an INTO clause. You can prepare the query without the INTO clause, declare a cursor for the prepared query, open the cursor, and then use the FETCH statement with an INTO clause to fetch the cursor into the program variable. Alternatively, you can declare a cursor for the query without first preparing the query and include the INTO clause in the query when you declare the cursor. Then open the cursor, and fetch the cursor without using the INTO clause of the FETCH statement.

E/C

Using Array Variables with the INTO Clause

In ESQL/C, if you use a DECLARE statement with a SELECT statement that contains an INTO clause, and the program variable is an array element, you can identify individual elements of the array with integer constants or with variables. The value of the variable that is used as a subscript is determined when the cursor is declared, so afterward the subscript variable acts as a constant.

The following ESQL/C code example declares a cursor for a SELECT...INTO statement using the variables **i** and **j** as subscripts for the array **a**. After you declare the cursor, the INTO clause of the SELECT statement is equivalent to INTO a[5], a[2].

```
i = 5
j = 2
EXEC SQL declare c cursor for
    select order_num, po_num into :a[i], :a[j] from orders
        where order_num =1005 and po_num =2865
```

You can also use program variables in the FETCH statement to specify an element of a program array in the INTO clause. With the FETCH statement, the program variables are evaluated at each fetch rather than when you declare the cursor.

Error Checking

If the data type of the receiving variable does not match that of the selected item, the data type of the selected item is converted, if possible. If the conversion is impossible, an error occurs, and a negative value is returned in the status variable, **sqlca.sqlcode, SQLCODE**. In this case, the value in the program variable is unpredictable.

ANSI

In an ANSI-compliant database, if the number of variables that are listed in the INTO clause differs from the number of items in the SELECT clause, you receive an error. ♦

E/C

Warnings in ESQL/C

In ESQL/C, if the number of variables that are listed in the INTO clause differs from the number of items in the SELECT clause, a warning is returned in the **sqlwarn** structure: **sqlca.sqlwarn.sqlwarn3**. The actual number of variables that are transferred is the lesser of the two numbers. For information about the **sqlwarn** structure, see the *Informix ESQL/C Programmer's Manual*.

FROM Clause

The FROM clause lists the table or tables from which you are selecting the data. The following diagrams show the syntax of the FROM clause.

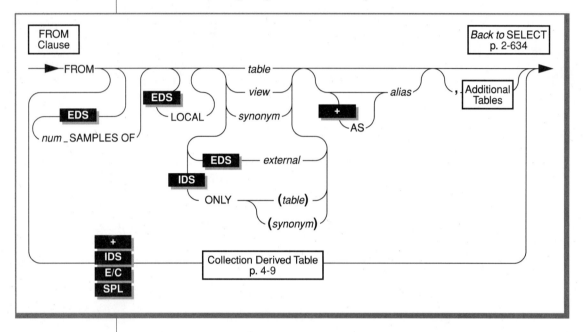

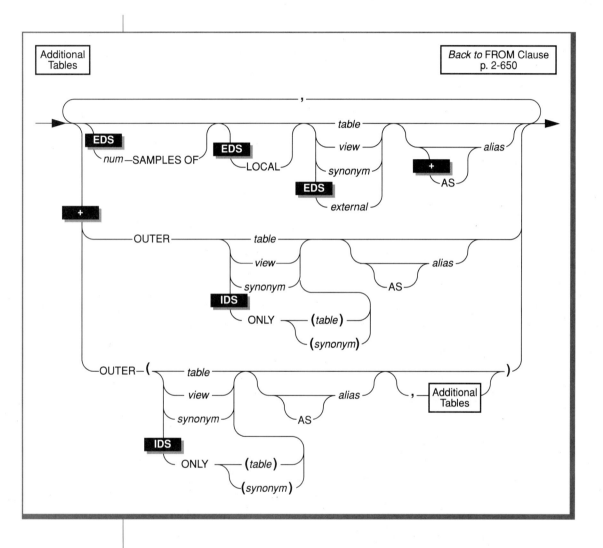

Element	Purpose	Restrictions	Syntax
alias	Temporary alternative name for a table or view within the scope of a SELECT statement You can use aliases to make a query shorter.	If the SELECT statement is a self-join, you must list the table name twice in the FROM clause and assign a different alias to each occurrence of the table name. If you use a potentially ambiguous word as an alias, you must precede the alias with the keyword AS. For further information on this restriction, see "AS Keyword with Aliases" on page 2-653.	Identifier, p. 4-205
external	Name of the external table from which you want to retrieve data	The external table must exist.	Database Object Name, p. 4-50
num	Number of sample rows to return	The value must be an unsigned integer greater than 0. If the value specified is greater than the number of rows in the table, the whole table is scanned.	Literal Number, p. 4-237
synonym	Name of the synonym from which you want to retrieve data	The synonym and the table to which the synonym points must exist.	Database Object Name, p. 4-50
table	Name of the table from which you want to retrieve data	The table must exist.	Database Object Name, p. 4-50
view	Name of the view from which you want to retrieve data	The view must exist.	Database Object Name, p. 4-50

Use the keyword OUTER to form outer joins. Outer joins preserve rows that otherwise would be discarded by simple joins. If you have a complex outer join, that is, the query has more than one outer join, you must embed the additional outer join or joins in parentheses as the syntax diagram shows. For more information on outer joins, see the *Informix Guide to SQL: Tutorial*.

When one of the tables to be joined is a collection, the FROM clause cannot have a join. This restriction applies when you use a collection variable to hold your collection derived table. For more information, see "Collection Derived Table" on page 4-9.

You can supply an alias for a table name or view name in the FROM clause. If you do so, you must use the alias to refer to the table or view in other clauses of the SELECT statement. Aliases are especially useful with a self-join. For more information about self-joins, see "WHERE Clause" on page 2-660.

The following example shows typical uses of the FROM clause. The first query selects all the columns and rows from the **customer** table. The second query uses a join between the **customer** and **orders** table to select all the customers who have placed orders.

```
SELECT * FROM customer

SELECT fname, lname, order_num
    FROM customer, orders
    WHERE customer.customer_num = orders.customer_num
```

The following example is the same as the second query in the preceding example, except that it establishes aliases for the tables in the FROM clause and uses them in the WHERE clause:

```
SELECT fname, lname, order_num
    FROM customer c, orders o
    WHERE c.customer_num = o.customer_num
```

The following example uses the OUTER keyword to create an outer join and produce a list of all customers and their orders, regardless of whether they have placed orders:

```
SELECT c.customer_num, lname, order_num
    FROM customer c, OUTER orders o
    WHERE c.customer_num = o.customer_num
```

AS Keyword with Aliases

To use potentially ambiguous words as an alias for a table or view, you must precede them with the keyword AS. Use the AS keyword if you want to use the words ORDER, FOR, AT, GROUP, HAVING, INTO, UNION, WHERE, WITH, CREATE, or GRANT as an alias for a table or view.

If you do not assign an alias name to a collection derived table, the database server assigns an implementation-dependent name to it.

IDS

Using the ONLY Keyword

If you use the SELECT statement to query a supertable, rows from both the supertable and its subtables are returned. To query rows from the supertable only, you must include the ONLY keyword in the FROM clause, as shown in the following example:

```
SELECT *
FROM ONLY(super_tab)
```

EDS

Restrictions on Using External Tables in Joins and Subqueries

In Enterprise Decision Server, when you use external tables in joins or subqueries, the following restrictions apply:

- Only one external table is allowed in a query.
- The external table cannot be the outer table in an outer join.
- For subqueries that cannot be converted to joins, you can use an external table in the main query, but not the subquery.
- You cannot do a self join on an external table.

For more information on subqueries, refer to your *Performance Guide*.

EDS

LOCAL Keyword

In Enterprise Decision Server, the LOCAL table feature allows client applications to read data only from the *local* fragments of a table. In other words, it allows the application to read only the fragments that reside on the coserver to which the client is connected.

This feature provides application partitioning. An application can connect to multiple coservers, execute a LOCAL read on each coserver, and assemble the final result on the client machine.

You qualify the name of a table with the LOCAL keyword to indicate that you want to retrieve rows from fragments only on the local coserver. The LOCAL keyword has no effect on data that is retrieved from nonfragmented tables.

When a query involves a join, you must plan carefully if you want to extract data that the client can aggregate. The simplest way to ensure that a join will retrieve data suitable for aggregation is to limit the number of LOCAL tables to one. The client can then aggregate data with respect to that table.

The following example shows a query that returns data suitable for aggregation by the client:

```
SELECT x.col1, y.col2
    FROM LOCAL tab1 x, tab2 y{can be aggregated by client}
    INTO TEMP t1
    WHERE x.col1 = y.col1;{tab1 is local}
```

The following example shows data that the client cannot aggregate:

```
SELECT x.col1, y.col2
    FROM LOCAL tab1 x, LOCAL tab2 y{cannot be aggregated by
                            client}
    INTO SCRATCH s4
    WHERE x.col1 = y.col1;{tab1 and tab2 are local}
```

The client must submit exactly the same query to each coserver to retrieve data that can be aggregated.

EDS

Sampled Queries: the SAMPLES OF Option

In Enterprise Decision Server, *sampled queries* are supported. Sampled queries are queries that are based on *sampled tables*. A sampled table is the result of randomly selecting a specified number of rows from the table, rather than all rows that match the selection criteria.

You can use a sampled query to gather quickly an approximate profile of data within a large table. If you use a sufficiently large sample size, you can examine trends in the data by sampling the data instead of scanning all the data. In such cases, sampled queries can provide better performance than scanning the data.

To indicate that a table is to be sampled, specify the number of samples to return in the SAMPLES OF option of the FROM clause within the SELECT statement. You can run sampled queries against tables and synonyms, but not against views. Sampled queries are not supported in the INSERT, DELETE, UPDATE, or other SQL statements.

A sampled query has at least one sampled table. You do not need to sample all tables in a sampled query. You can specify the SAMPLES OF option for some tables in the FROM clause but not specify it for other tables.

The sampling method is known as *sampling without replacement*. This term means that a sampled row is not sampled again. The database server applies selection criteria *after* samples are selected. Therefore, the database server uses the selection criteria to restrict the sample set, not the rows from which it takes the sample.

If a table is fragmented, the database server divides the specified number of samples among the fragments. The number of samples from a fragment is proportional to the ratio of the size of a fragment to the size of the table. In other words, the database server takes more samples from larger fragments.

Important: *You must run* UPDATE STATISTICS LOW *before you run the query with the* SAMPLES OF *option. If you do not run* UPDATE STATISTICS, *the* SAMPLE *clause is ignored, and all data is returned. For better results, Informix recommends that you run* UPDATE STATISTICS MEDIUM *before you run the query with the* SAMPLES OF *option.*

The results of a sampled query will contain a certain amount of deviation from a complete scan of all rows. However, you can reduce this expected error to an acceptable level by increasing the proportion of sampled rows to actual rows. When you use sampled queries in joins, the expected error increases dramatically; you must use larger samples in each table to retain an acceptable level of accuracy.

For example, you might want to generate a list of how many of each part is sold from the **parts_sold** table, which is known to contain approximately 100,000,000 rows. The following query provides a sampling ratio of one percent and returns an approximate result:

```
SELECT part_number, COUNT(*) * 100 AS how_many
    FROM 1000000 SAMPLES OF parts_sold
    GROUP BY part_number;
```

IDS

Selecting From a Collection Variable

The SELECT statement in conjunction with the Collection Derived Table segment allows you to select elements from a collection variable.

The Collection Derived Table segment identifies the collection variable from which to select the elements. For more information, see "Collection Derived Table" on page 4-9.

Using Collection Variables with SELECT

When you want to modify the contents of a collection, you can use the SELECT statement with a collection variable in different ways:

- You can select the contents (if any) of a collection column into a collection variable.

  You can assign the data type of the column to the collection variable if the collection is of type COLLECTION (that is, an untyped collection variable).

- You can select the contents from a collection variable to determine the data that you might want to update.

- You can select the contents from a collection variable INTO another variable in order to update certain collection elements.

  The INTO clause identifies the variable for the element value that is selected from the collection variable. The type of the host variable in the INTO clause must be compatible with the element type of the collection.

E/C

- You can use a collection cursor to select one or more elements from an ESQL/C collection variable. For more information, including restrictions on the SELECT statement that you use, see "Associating a Cursor With a Collection Variable" on page 2-367 in the DECLARE statement. ◆

SPL

- You can use a collection cursor to select one or more elements from an SPL collection variable. For more information, including restrictions on the SELECT statement that you use, see "Using a SELECT...INTO Statement" on page 3-33 of the FOREACH statement. ◆

For more information, see the Collection Derived Table segment and the INSERT, UPDATE, or DELETE statements.

Selecting From a Row Variable

The SELECT statement with the Collection Derived Table segment allows you to select fields from a **row** variable. The Collection Derived Table segment identifies the **row** variable from which to select the fields. For more information, see "Collection Derived Table" on page 4-9.

To select fields, follow these steps:

1. Create a **row** variable in your ESQL/C program.

2. Optionally, fill the **row** variable with field values.

   You can select a row-type column into the **row** variable with the SELECT statement (without the Collection Derived Table segment). Or you can insert field values into the **row** variable with the UPDATE statement and the Collection Derived Table segment.

3. Select row fields from the **row** variable with the SELECT statement and the Collection Derived Table segment.

4. Once the **row** variable contains the correct field values, you can then use the INSERT or UPDATE statement on a table or view name to save the contents of the **row** variable in a row column (named and unnamed).

The SELECT statement and the Collection Derived Table segment allow you to select a particular field or group of fields in the **row** variable. The INTO clause identifies the variable that holds the field value selected from the **row** variable. The data type of the host variable in the INTO clause must be compatible with the field type.

For example, the following code fragment puts the value of the **width** field into the **rect_width** host variable:

```
EXEC SQL BEGIN DECLARE SECTION;
    row (x int, y int, length float, width float) myrect;
    double rect_width;
EXEC SQL END DECLARE SECTION;
...
EXEC SQL select rect into :myrect from rectangles
    where area = 200;
EXEC SQL select width into :rect_width from table(:myrect);
```

The SELECT statement on a **row** variable has the following restrictions:

- No expressions are allowed in the select list.
- Row columns cannot be specified in a comparison condition in a WHERE clause.
- The select list must be an asterisk (*) if the row-type contains fields of opaque, distinct, or built-in data types.
- Column names in the select list must be simple column names.

    These columns cannot use the syntax *database@server:table.column*

- The following SELECT clauses are not allowed: GROUP BY, HAVING, INTO TEMP, ORDER BY, and WHERE.
- The FROM clause has no provisions to do a join.

You can modify the **row** variable with the Collection Derived Table segment of the UPDATE statements. (The INSERT and DELETE statements do not support a row variable in the Collection Derived Table segment.) The **row** variable stores the fields of the row. However, it has no intrinsic connection with a database column. Once the **row** variable contains the correct field values, you must then save the variable into the row column with one of the following SQL statements:

- To update the row column in the table with the row variable, use an UPDATE statement on a table or view name and specify the row variable in the SET clause.

    For more information, see "Updating Row-Type Columns" on page 2-826.

- To insert a row in a column, use the INSERT statement on a table or view name and specify the row variable in the VALUES clause.

    For more information, see "Inserting Values into Row-Type Columns" on page 2-546.

For more information on how to use SPL row variables, see the *Informix Guide to SQL: Tutorial*. For more information on how to use ESQL/C **row** variables, see the discussion of complex data types in the *Informix ESQL/C Programmer's Manual*.

WHERE Clause

Use the WHERE clause to specify search criteria and join conditions on the data that you are selecting.

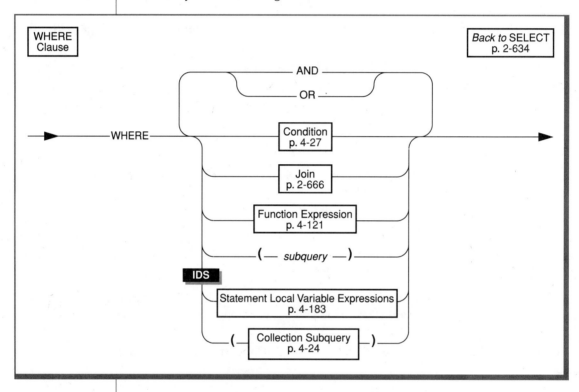

Element	Purpose	Restrictions	Syntax
subquery	Embedded query	The subquery cannot contain either the FIRST or the ORDER BY clause.	SELECT, p. 2-634

Using a Condition in the WHERE Clause

You can use the following kinds of simple conditions or comparisons in the WHERE clause:

- Relational-operator condition
- BETWEEN
- IN
- IS NULL
- LIKE or MATCHES

You also can use a SELECT statement within the WHERE clause; this is called a *subquery*. The following list contains the kinds of subquery WHERE clauses:

- IN
- EXISTS
- ALL, ANY, SOME

Examples of each type of condition are shown in the following sections. For more information about each kind of condition, see "Condition" on page 27.

You cannot use an aggregate function in the WHERE clause unless it is part of a subquery or if the aggregate is on a correlated column originating from a parent query and the WHERE clause is within a subquery that is within a HAVING clause.

Relational-Operator Condition

For a complete description of the relational-operator condition, see "Relational-Operator Condition" on page 4-32.

A relational-operator condition is satisfied when the expressions on either side of the relational operator fulfill the relation that the operator set up. The following SELECT statements use the greater than (>) and equal (=) relational operators:

```
SELECT order_num FROM orders
    WHERE order_date > '6/04/98'

SELECT fname, lname, company
    FROM customer
    WHERE city[1,3] = 'San'
```

BETWEEN Condition

For a complete description of the BETWEEN condition, see "BETWEEN Condition" on page 4-33.

The BETWEEN condition is satisfied when the value to the left of the BETWEEN keyword lies in the inclusive range of the two values on the right of the BETWEEN keyword. The first two queries in the following example use literal values after the BETWEEN keyword. The third query uses the built-in CURRENT function and a literal interval. It looks for dates between the current day and seven days earlier.

```
SELECT stock_num, manu_code FROM stock
    WHERE unit_price BETWEEN 125.00 AND 200.00

SELECT DISTINCT customer_num, stock_num, manu_code
    FROM orders, items
    WHERE order_date BETWEEN '6/1/97' AND '9/1/97'

SELECT * FROM cust_calls WHERE call_dtime
    BETWEEN (CURRENT - INTERVAL(7) DAY TO DAY) AND CURRENT
```

IN Condition

For a complete description of the IN condition, see "IN Subquery" on page 4-41.

The IN condition is satisfied when the expression to the left of the IN keyword is included in the list of values to the right of the keyword. The following examples show the IN condition:

```
SELECT lname, fname, company
    FROM customer
    WHERE state IN ('CA','WA', 'NJ')

SELECT * FROM cust_calls
    WHERE user_id NOT IN (USER )
```

IS NULL Condition

For a complete description of the IS NULL condition, see "IS NULL Condition" on page 4-36.

The IS NULL condition is satisfied if the column contains a null value. If you use the NOT option, the condition is satisfied when the column contains a value that is not null. The following example selects the order numbers and customer numbers for which the order has not been paid:

```
SELECT order_num, customer_num FROM orders
    WHERE paid_date IS NULL
```

LIKE or MATCHES Condition

For a complete description of the LIKE or MATCHES condition, see "LIKE and MATCHES Condition" on page 4-36.

The LIKE or MATCHES condition is satisfied when either of the following tests is true:

- The value of the column that precedes the LIKE or MATCHES keyword matches the pattern that the quoted string specifies. You can use wildcard characters in the string.

- The value of the column that precedes the LIKE or MATCHES keyword matches the pattern that is specified by the column that follows the LIKE or MATCHES keyword. The value of the column on the right serves as the matching pattern in the condition.

The following SELECT statement returns all rows in the **customer** table in which the **lname** column begins with the literal string 'Baxter'. Because the string is a literal string, the condition is case sensitive.

```
SELECT * FROM customer WHERE lname LIKE 'Baxter%'
```

The following SELECT statement returns all rows in the **customer** table in which the value of the **lname** column matches the value of the **fname** column:

```
SELECT * FROM customer WHERE lname LIKE fname
```

The following examples use the LIKE condition with a wildcard. The first SELECT statement finds all stock items that are some kind of ball. The second SELECT statement finds all company names that contain a percent sign (%). The backslash (\) is used as the standard escape character for the wildcard percent sign (%). The third SELECT statement uses the ESCAPE option with the LIKE condition to retrieve rows from the **customer** table in which the **company** column includes a percent sign (%). The z is used as an escape character for the wildcard percent sign (%).

```
SELECT stock_num, manu_code FROM stock
    WHERE description LIKE '%ball'

SELECT * FROM customer
    WHERE company LIKE '%\%%'

SELECT * FROM customer
    WHERE company LIKE '%z%%' ESCAPE 'z'
```

The following examples use MATCHES with a wildcard in several SELECT statements. The first SELECT statement finds all stock items that are some kind of ball. The second SELECT statement finds all company names that contain an asterisk (*). The backslash (\) is used as the standard escape character for the wildcard asterisk (*). The third statement uses the ESCAPE option with the MATCHES condition to retrieve rows from the **customer** table where the **company** column includes an asterisk (*). The z character is used as an escape character for the wildcard asterisk (*).

```
SELECT stock_num, manu_code FROM stock
    WHERE description MATCHES '*ball'

SELECT * FROM customer
    WHERE company MATCHES '*\**'

SELECT * FROM customer
    WHERE company MATCHES '*z**' ESCAPE 'z'
```

IN Subquery

For a complete description of the IN subquery, see "IN Condition" on page 4-34.

With the IN subquery, more than one row can be returned, but only one column can be returned. The following example shows the use of an IN subquery in a SELECT statement:

```
SELECT DISTINCT customer_num FROM orders
    WHERE order_num NOT IN
        (SELECT order_num FROM items
            WHERE stock_num = 1)
```

EXISTS Subquery

For a complete description of the EXISTS subquery, see "EXISTS Subquery" on page 4-42.

With the EXISTS subquery, one or more columns can be returned.

The following example of a SELECT statement with an EXISTS subquery returns the stock number and manufacturer code for every item that has never been ordered (and is therefore not listed in the **items** table). It is appropriate to use an EXISTS subquery in this SELECT statement because you need the correlated subquery to test both **stock_num** and **manu_code** in the **items** table.

```
SELECT stock_num, manu_code FROM stock
    WHERE NOT EXISTS
        (SELECT stock_num, manu_code FROM items
            WHERE stock.stock_num = items.stock_num AND
                stock.manu_code = items.manu_code)
```

The preceding example would work equally well if you use a SELECT * in the subquery in place of the column names because you are testing for the existence of a row or rows.

ALL, ANY, SOME Subquery

For a complete description of the ALL, ANY, SOME subquery, see "ALL, ANY, SOME Subquery" on page 4-43.

In the following example, the SELECT statements return the order number of all orders that contain an item whose total price is greater than the total price of every item in order number 1023. The first SELECT statement uses the ALL subquery, and the second SELECT statement produces the same result by using the MAX aggregate function.

```
SELECT DISTINCT order_num FROM items
    WHERE total_price > ALL (SELECT total_price FROM items
        WHERE order_num = 1023)

SELECT DISTINCT order_num FROM items
    WHERE total_price > SELECT MAX(total_price) FROM items
        WHERE order_num = 1023)
```

The following SELECT statements return the order number of all orders that contain an item whose total price is greater than the total price of at least one of the items in order number 1023. The first SELECT statement uses the ANY keyword, and the second SELECT statement uses the MIN aggregate function.

```
SELECT DISTINCT order_num FROM items
    WHERE total_price > ANY (SELECT total_price FROM items
        WHERE order_num = 1023)

SELECT DISTINCT order_num FROM items
    WHERE total_price > (SELECT MIN(total_price) FROM items
        WHERE order_num = 1023)
```

You can omit the keywords ANY, ALL, or SOME in a subquery if you know that the subquery returns exactly one value. If you omit ANY, ALL, or SOME, and the subquery returns more than one value, you receive an error. The subquery in the following example returns only one row because it uses an aggregate function:

```
SELECT order_num FROM items
    WHERE stock_num = 9 AND quantity =
        (SELECT MAX(quantity) FROM items WHERE stock_num = 9)
```

Using a Join in the WHERE Clause

You join two tables when you create a relationship in the WHERE clause between at least one column from one table and at least one column from another table. The effect of the join is to create a temporary composite table where each pair of rows (one from each table) that satisfies the join condition is linked to form a single row. You can create two-table joins, multiple-table joins, and self-joins.

The following diagram shows the syntax for a join.

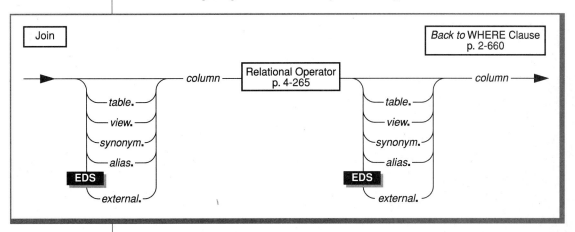

Element	Purpose	Restrictions	Syntax
alias	Temporary alternative name assigned to the table or view in the FROM clause For more information on aliases for tables and views, see "FROM Clause" on page 2-650.	If the tables to be joined are the same table (that is, if the join is a self-join), you must refer to each instance of the table in the WHERE clause by the alias assigned to that table instance in the FROM clause.	Identifier, p. 4-205
column	Name of a column from one of the tables or views to be joined Rows from the tables or views are joined when there is a match between the values of the specified columns.	When the specified columns have the same name in the tables or views to be joined, you must distinguish the columns by preceding each column name with the name or alias of the table or view in which the column resides.	Identifier, p. 4-205
external	Name of the external table from which you want to retrieve data	The external table must exist.	Database Object Name, p. 4-50
synonym	Name of the synonym to be joined	The synonym and the table to which the synonym points must exist.	Database Object Name, p. 4-50
table	Name of the table to be joined	The table must exist.	Database Object Name, p. 4-50
view	Name of the view to be joined	The view must exist.	Database Object Name, p. 4-50

Two-Table Joins

The following example shows a two-table join:

```
SELECT order_num, lname, fname
    FROM customer, orders
    WHERE customer.customer_num = orders.customer_num
```

Tip: *You do not have to specify the column where the two tables are joined in the SELECT list.*

Multiple-Table Joins

A multiple-table join is a join of more than two tables. Its structure is similar to the structure of a two-table join, except that you have a join condition for more than one pair of tables in the WHERE clause. When columns from different tables have the same name, you must distinguish them by preceding the name with its associated table or table alias, as in *table.column*. For the full syntax of a table name, see "Database Object Name" on page 4-50.

The following multiple-table join yields the company name of the customer who ordered an item as well as the stock number and manufacturer code of the item:

```
SELECT DISTINCT company, stock_num, manu_code
    FROM customer c, orders o, items i
    WHERE c.customer_num = o.customer_num
        AND o.order_num = i.order_num
```

Self-Joins

You can join a table to itself. To do so, you must list the table name twice in the FROM clause and assign it two different table aliases. Use the aliases to refer to each of the *two* tables in the WHERE clause.

The following example is a self-join on the **stock** table. It finds pairs of stock items whose unit prices differ by a factor greater than 2.5. The letters x and y are each aliases for the **stock** table.

```
SELECT x.stock_num, x.manu_code, y.stock_num, y.manu_code
    FROM stock x, stock y
    WHERE x.unit_price > 2.5 * y.unit_price
```

EDS

If you are using Enterprise Decision Server, you cannot use a self-join with an external table. ♦

Outer Joins

The following outer join lists the company name of the customer and all associated order numbers, if the customer has placed an order. If not, the company name is still listed, and a null value is returned for the order number.

```
SELECT company, order_num
    FROM customer c, OUTER orders o
    WHERE c.customer_num = o.customer_num
```

EDS

If you are using Enterprise Decision Server, you cannot use an external table as the outer table in an outer join. ♦

For more information about outer joins, see the *Informix Guide to SQL: Tutorial*.

GROUP BY Clause

Use the GROUP BY clause to produce a single row of results for each group. A group is a set of rows that have the same values for each column listed.

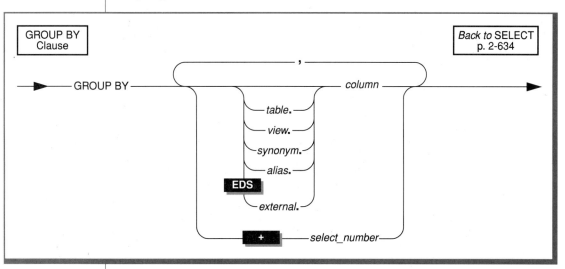

Element	Purpose	Restrictions	Syntax
alias	Temporary alternative name assigned to a table or view in the FROM clause For more information on aliases for tables and views, see "FROM Clause" on page 2-650.	You cannot use an alias for a table or view in the GROUP BY clause unless you have assigned the alias to the table or view in the FROM clause.	Identifier, p. 4-205
column	Name of a stand-alone column in the select list of the SELECT clause or the name of one of the columns joined by an arithmetic operator in the select list The SELECT statement returns a single row of results for each group of rows that have the same value in *column*.	See "Relationship of the GROUP BY Clause to the SELECT Clause" on page 2-671.	Identifier, p. 4-205
external	Name of the external table from which you want to retrieve data	The external table must exist.	Database Object Name, p. 4-50
select_number	Integer that identifies a column or expression in the select list of the SELECT clause by specifying its order in the select list The SELECT statement returns a single row of results for each group of rows that have the same value in the column or expression identified by *select_number*.	See "Using Select Numbers" on page 2-672.	Literal Number, p. 4-237
synonym	Name of the synonym where the column or columns exist	The synonym and the table to which the synonym points must exist.	Database Object Name, p. 4-50
table	Name of the table where the column or columns exist	The table must exist.	Database Object Name, p. 4-50
view	Name of the view where the column or columns exist	The view must exist.	Database Object Name, p. 4-50

Relationship of the GROUP BY Clause to the SELECT Clause

A GROUP BY clause restricts what you can enter in the SELECT clause. If you use a GROUP BY clause, each column that you select must be in the GROUP BY list. If you use an aggregate function and one or more column expressions in the select list, you must put all the column names that are not used as part of an aggregate or time expression in the GROUP BY clause. Do not put constant expressions or BYTE or TEXT column expressions in the GROUP BY list.

If you are selecting a BYTE or TEXT column, you cannot use the GROUP BY clause. In addition, you cannot use ROWID in a GROUP BY clause.

IDS

If your select list includes a column with a user-defined data type, the type must either use the built-in bit-hashing function or have its own user-defined hash function. Otherwise, you cannot use a GROUP BY clause. ◆

The following example names one column that is not in an aggregate expression. The **total_price** column should not be in the GROUP BY list because it appears as the argument of an aggregate function. The COUNT and SUM keywords are applied to each group, not the whole query set.

```
SELECT order_num, COUNT(*), SUM(total_price)
    FROM items
    GROUP BY order_num
```

If a column stands alone in a column expression in the select list, you must use it in the GROUP BY clause. If a column is combined with another column by an arithmetic operator, you can choose to group by the individual columns or by the combined expression using a specific number.

Using Select Numbers

You can use one or more integers in the GROUP BY clause to stand for column expressions. In the following example, the first SELECT statement uses select numbers for **order_date** and **paid_date - order_date** in the GROUP BY clause. Note that you can group only by a combined expression using the select-number notation. In the second SELECT statement, you cannot replace the 2 with the expression **paid_date - order_date**.

```
SELECT order_date, COUNT(*), paid_date - order_date
    FROM orders
    GROUP BY 1, 3

SELECT order_date, paid_date - order_date
    FROM orders
    GROUP BY order_date, 2
```

Nulls in the GROUP BY Clause

Each row that contains a null value in a column that is specified by a GROUP BY clause belongs to a single group (that is, all null values are grouped together).

HAVING Clause

Use the HAVING clause to apply one or more qualifying conditions to groups.

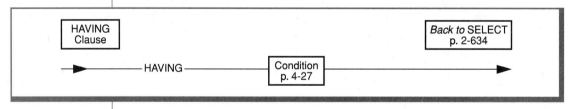

In the following examples, each condition compares one calculated property of the group with another calculated property of the group or with a constant. The first SELECT statement uses a HAVING clause that compares the calculated expression COUNT(*) with the constant 2. The query returns the average total price per item on all orders that have more than two items. The second SELECT statement lists customers and the call months if they have made two or more calls in the same month.

```
SELECT order_num, AVG(total_price) FROM items
    GROUP BY order_num
    HAVING COUNT(*) > 2

SELECT customer_num, EXTEND (call_dtime, MONTH TO MONTH)
    FROM cust_calls
    GROUP BY 1, 2
    HAVING COUNT(*) > 1
```

You can use the HAVING clause to place conditions on the GROUP BY column values as well as on calculated values. The following example returns the **customer_num, call_dtime** (in full year-to-fraction format), and **cust_code**, and groups them by **call_code** for all calls that have been received from customers with **customer_num** less than 120:

```
SELECT customer_num, EXTEND (call_dtime), call_code
    FROM cust_calls
    GROUP BY call_code, 2, 1
    HAVING customer_num < 120
```

The HAVING clause generally complements a GROUP BY clause. If you use a HAVING clause without a GROUP BY clause, the HAVING clause applies to all rows that satisfy the query. Without a GROUP BY clause, all rows in the table make up a single group. The following example returns the average price of all the values in the table, as long as more than ten rows are in the table:

```
SELECT AVG(total_price) FROM items
    HAVING COUNT(*) > 10
```

ORDER BY Clause

Use THE ORDER BY clause to sort query results by the values that are contained in one or more columns.

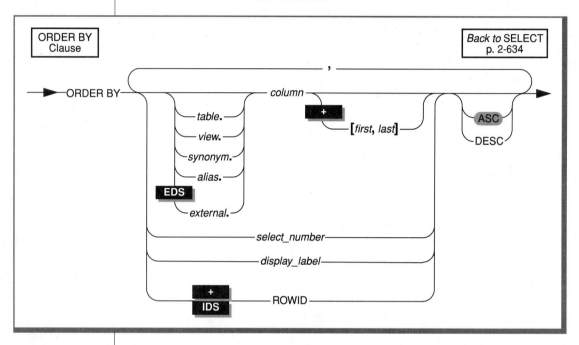

Element	Purpose	Restrictions	Syntax
alias	Alias assigned to a table or view in the FROM clause. For more information on aliases for tables and views, see "FROM Clause" on page 2-650.	You cannot specify an alias for a table or view in the ORDER BY clause unless you have assigned the alias to the table or view in the FROM clause.	Identifier, p. 4-205

(1 of 3)

Element	Purpose	Restrictions	Syntax
column	Name of a column in the specified table or view The query results are sorted by the values contained in this column.	A column specified in the ORDER BY clause must be listed explicitly or implicitly in the select list of the SELECT clause. If you want to order the query results by a derived column, you must supply a display label for the derived column in the select list and specify this label in the ORDER BY clause. Alternatively, you can omit a display label for the derived column in the select list and specify the derived column by means of a select number in the ORDER BY clause. This cannot be a column whose data type is a collection.	Identifier, p. 4-205
display_label	Temporary name that you assign to a column in the select list of the SELECT clause You can use a display label in place of the column name in the ORDER BY clause.	You cannot specify a display label in the ORDER BY clause unless you have specified this display label for a column in the select list.	Identifier, p. 4-205
external	Name of the external table from which you want to retrieve data	The external table must exist.	Database Object Name, p. 4-50
first	Position of the first character in the portion of the column that is used to sort the query results	The column must be one of the following character types: BYTE, CHAR, NCHAR, NVARCHAR, TEXT, or VARCHAR.	Literal Number, p. 4-237
last	Position of the last character in the portion of the column that is used to sort the query results	The column must be one of the following character types: BYTE, CHAR, NCHAR, NVARCHAR, TEXT, or VARCHAR.	Literal Number, p. 4-237
select_number	Integer that identifies a column in the select list of the SELECT clause by specifying its order in the select list You can use a select number in place of a column name in the ORDER BY clause.	You must specify select numbers in the ORDER BY clause when SELECT statements are joined by UNION or UNION ALL keywords or compatible columns in the same position have different names.	Literal Number, p. 4-237

(2 of 3)

Element	Purpose	Restrictions	Syntax
synonym	Name of the synonym that contains the specified column	The synonym and the table to which the synonym points must exist.	Database Object Name, p. 4-50
table	Name of the table that contains the specified column	The table must exist.	Database Object Name, p. 4-50
view	Name of the view that contains the specified column	The view must exist.	Database Object Name, p. 4-50

(3 of 3)

You can perform an ORDER BY operation on a column or on an aggregate expression when you use SELECT * or a display label in your SELECT statement.

The following query explicitly selects the order date and shipping date from the **orders** table and then rearranges the query by the order date. By default, the query results are listed in ascending order.

```
SELECT order_date, ship_date FROM orders
    ORDER BY order_date
```

In the following query, the **order_date** column is selected implicitly by the SELECT * statement, so you can use **order_date** in the ORDER BY clause:

```
SELECT * FROM orders
    ORDER BY order_date
```

Ordering by a Column Substring

You can order by a column substring instead of ordering by the entire length of the column. The column substring is the portion of the column that the database server uses for the sort. You define the column substring by specifying column subscripts (the *first* and *last* parameters). The column subscripts represent the starting and ending character positions of the column substring.

The following example shows a SELECT statement that queries the **customer** table and specifies a column substring in the ORDER BY column. The column substring instructs the database server to sort the query results by the portion of the **lname** column contained in the sixth through ninth positions of the column:

```
SELECT * from customer
    ORDER BY lname[6,9]
```

Assume that the value of **lname** in one row of the **customer** table is Greenburg. Because of the column substring in the ORDER BY clause, the database server determines the sort position of this row by using the value burg, not the value Greenburg.

You can specify column substrings only for columns that have a character data type. If you specify a column substring in the ORDER BY clause, the column must have one of the following data types: BYTE, CHAR, NCHAR, NVARCHAR, TEXT, or VARCHAR.

GLS

For information on the GLS aspects of using column substrings in the ORDER BY clause, see the *Informix Guide to GLS Functionality*. ◆

Ordering by a Derived Column

You can order by a derived column by supplying a display label in the SELECT clause, as shown in the following example:

```
SELECT paid_date - ship_date span, customer_num
    FROM orders
    ORDER BY span
```

Ascending and Descending Orders

You can use the ASC and DESC keywords to specify ascending (smallest value first) or descending (largest value first) order. The default order is ascending.

For DATE and DATETIME data types, *smallest* means earliest in time and *largest* means latest in time. For standard character data types, the ASCII collating sequence is used. For a listing of the collating sequence, see "Collating Order for English Data" on page 4-267.

Nulls in the ORDER BY Clause

Nulls are ordered as less than values that are not null. Using the ASC order, the null value comes before the not-null value; using DESC order, the null comes last.

Nested Ordering

If you list more than one column in the ORDER BY clause, your query is ordered by a nested sort. The first level of sort is based on the first column; the second column determines the second level of sort. The following example of a nested sort selects all the rows in the **cust_calls** table and orders them by **call_code** and by **call_dtime** within **call_code**:

```
SELECT * FROM cust_calls
    ORDER BY call_code, call_dtime
```

Using Select Numbers

In place of column names, you can enter one or more integers that refer to the position of items in the SELECT clause. You can use a select number to order by an expression. For instance, the following example orders by the expression **paid_date - order_date** and **customer_num**, using select numbers in a nested sort:

```
SELECT order_num, customer_num, paid_date - order_date
    FROM orders
    ORDER BY 3, 2
```

Select numbers are required in the ORDER BY clause when SELECT statements are joined by the UNION or UNION ALL keywords or compatible columns in the same position have different names.

IDS

Ordering by Rowids

You can specify the **rowid** column as a column in the ORDER BY clause. The **rowid** column is a hidden column in nonfragmented tables and in fragmented tables that were created with the WITH ROWIDS clause. The **rowid** column contains a unique internal record number that is associated with a row in a table. Informix recommends, however, that you utilize primary keys as an access method rather than exploiting the **rowid** column.

If you want to specify the **rowid** column in the ORDER BY clause, enter the keyword ROWID in lowercase or uppercase letters.

You cannot specify the **rowid** column in the ORDER BY clause if the table from which you are selecting is a fragmented table that does not have a **rowid** column.

You cannot specify the **rowid** column in the ORDER BY clause unless you have included the **rowid** column in the select list of the SELECT clause.

For further information on how to use the **rowid** column in column expressions, see "Expression" on page 4-73.

E/C

ORDER BY Clause with DECLARE

In ESQL/C, you cannot use a DECLARE statement with a FOR UPDATE clause to associate a cursor with a SELECT statement that has an ORDER BY clause.

Placing Indexes on ORDER BY Columns

When you include an ORDER BY clause in a SELECT statement, you can improve the performance of the query by creating an index on the column or columns that the ORDER BY clause specifies. The database server uses the index that you placed on the ORDER BY columns to sort the query results in the most efficient manner. For more information on how to create indexes that correspond to the columns of an ORDER BY clause, see "Using the ASC and DESC Sort-Order Options" on page 2-164 under the CREATE INDEX statement.

FOR UPDATE Clause

Use the FOR UPDATE clause when you prepare a SELECT statement, and you intend to update the values returned by the SELECT statement when the values are fetched. Preparing a SELECT statement that contains a FOR UPDATE clause is equivalent to preparing the SELECT statement without the FOR UPDATE clause and then declaring a FOR UPDATE cursor for the prepared statement.

The FOR UPDATE keyword notifies the database server that updating is possible, causing it to use more-stringent locking than it would with a select cursor. You cannot modify data through a cursor without this clause. You can specify particular columns that can be updated.

After you declare a cursor for a SELECT... FOR UPDATE statement, you can update or delete the currently selected row using an UPDATE OR DELETE statement with the WHERE CURRENT OF clause. The words CURRENT OF refer to the row that was most recently fetched; they replace the usual test expressions in the WHERE clause.

To update rows with a particular value, your program might contain statements such as the sequence of statements shown in the following example:

```
EXEC SQL BEGIN DECLARE SECTION;
    char fname[ 16];
    char lname[ 16];
    EXEC SQL END DECLARE SECTION;
  .
  .
  .

  EXEC SQL connect to 'stores_demo';
  /* select statement being prepared contains a for update clause */
  EXEC SQL prepare x from 'select fname, lname from customer for update';
  EXEC SQL declare xc cursor for x;

  for (;;)
    {
    EXEC SQL fetch xc into $fname, $lname;
    if (strncmp(SQLSTATE, '00', 2) != 0) break;
    printf("%d %s %s\n",cnum, fname, lname );
    if (cnum == 999)--update rows with 999 customer_num
        EXEC SQL update customer set fname = 'rosey' where current of xc;
    }

  EXEC SQL close xc;
  EXEC SQL disconnect current;
```

A SELECT...FOR UPDATE statement, like an update cursor, allows you to perform updates that are not possible with the UPDATE statement alone, because both the decision to update and the values of the new data items can be based on the original contents of the row. The UPDATE statement cannot interrogate the table that is being updated.

Syntax That is Incompatible with the FOR UPDATE Clause

A SELECT statement that uses a FOR UPDATE clause must conform to the following restrictions:

- The statement can select data from only one table.
- The statement cannot include any aggregate functions.
- The statement cannot include any of the following clauses or keywords: DISTINCT, FOR READ ONLY, GROUP BY, INTO SCRATCH, INTO TEMP, INTO EXTERNAL, ORDER BY, UNION, or UNIQUE.

For information on how to declare an update cursor for a SELECT statement that does not include a FOR UPDATE clause, see "Using the FOR UPDATE Option" on page 2-355.

FOR READ ONLY Clause

Use the FOR READ ONLY clause to specify that the select cursor declared for the SELECT statement is a read-only cursor. A read-only cursor is a cursor that cannot modify data. This section provides the following information about the FOR READ ONLY clause:

- When you must use the FOR READ ONLY clause
- Syntax restrictions on a SELECT statement that uses a FOR READ ONLY clause

Using the FOR READ ONLY Clause in Read-Only Mode

Normally, you do not need to include the FOR READ ONLY clause in a SELECT statement. A SELECT statement is a read-only operation by definition, so the FOR READ ONLY clause is usually unnecessary. However, in certain special circumstances, you must include the FOR READ ONLY clause in a SELECT statement.

ANSI

If you have used the High-Performance Loader (HPL) in express mode to load data into the tables of an ANSI-compliant database, and you have not yet performed a level-0 backup of this data, the database is in read-only mode. When the database is in read-only mode, the database server rejects any attempts by a select cursor to access the data unless the SELECT or the DECLARE includes a FOR READ ONLY clause. This restriction remains in effect until the user has performed a level-0 backup of the data.

When the database is an ANSI-compliant database, select cursors are update cursors by default. An update cursor is a cursor that can be used to modify data. These update cursors are incompatible with the read-only mode of the database. For example, the following SELECT statement against the **customer_ansi** table fails:

```
EXEC SQL declare ansi_curs cursor for
    select * from customer_ansi;
```

The solution is to include the FOR READ ONLY clause in your select cursors. The read-only cursor that this clause specifies is compatible with the read-only mode of the database. For example, the following SELECT FOR READ ONLY statement against the **customer_ansi** table succeeds:

```
EXEC SQL declare ansi_read cursor for
    select * from customer_ansi for read only;
```

♦

DB

DB-Access executes all SELECT statements with select cursors. Therefore, you must include the FOR READ ONLY clause in all SELECT statements that access data in a read-only ANSI-mode database. The FOR READ ONLY clause causes DB-Access to declare the cursor for the SELECT statement as a read-only cursor. ♦

For more information on level-0 backups, see your *Backup and Restore Guide*. For more information on select cursors, read-only cursors, and update cursors, see "DECLARE" on page 2-349.

IDS

For more information on the express mode of the HPL, see the *Guide to the High-Performance Loader*. ♦

Syntax That Is Incompatible with the FOR READ ONLY Clause

You cannot include both the FOR READ ONLY clause and the FOR UPDATE clause in the same SELECT statement. If you attempt to do so, the SELECT statement fails.

For information on how to declare a read-only cursor for a SELECT statement that does not include a FOR READ ONLY clause, see "DECLARE" on page 2-349.

INTO Table Clauses

Use the INTO Table clauses to specify a table to receive the data that the SELECT statement retrieves.

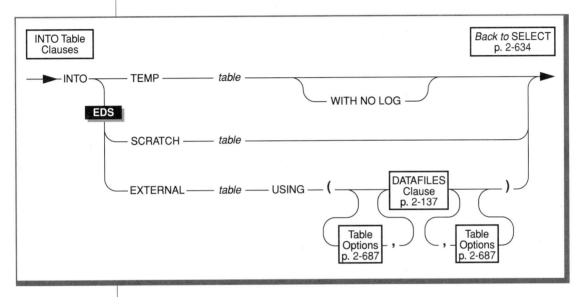

Element	Purpose	Restrictions	Syntax
table	Name of a table that contains the results of the SELECT statement The column names of the temporary table are those that are named in the select list of the SELECT clause.	The name must be different from any existing table, view, or synonym name in the current database, but it does not have to be different from other temporary table names used by other users. You must have the Connect privilege on a database to create a temporary table in that database. If you use the INTO TEMP clause to create a temporary table, you must supply a display label for all expressions in the select list other than simple column expressions.	Database Object Name, p. 4-50

Naming Columns

The column names of the temporary, scratch, or external table are those that are named in the SELECT clause. You must supply a display label for all expressions other than simple column expressions. The display label for a column or expression becomes the column name in the temporary, scratch or external table. If you do not provide a display label for a column expression, the table uses the column name from the select list.

The following INTO TEMP example creates the **pushdate** table with two columns, **customer_num** and **slowdate**:

```
SELECT customer_num, call_dtime + 5 UNITS DAY slowdate
    FROM cust_calls INTO TEMP pushdate
```

Results When No Rows are Returned

When you use an INTO Table clause combined with the WHERE clause, and no rows are returned, the **SQLNOTFOUND** value is 100 in ANSI-compliant databases and 0 in databases that are not ANSI compliant. If the SELECT INTO TEMP...WHERE... statement is a part of a multistatement prepare and no rows are returned, the **SQLNOTFOUND** value is 100 for both ANSI-compliant databases and databases that are not ANSI-compliant.

E/C

Restrictions with INTO Table Clauses in ESQL/C

In ESQL/C, do not use the INTO clause with an INTO Table clause. If you do, no results are returned to the program variables and the **sqlca.sqlcode**, SQLCODE variable is set to a negative value.

INTO TEMP Clause

Use the INTO TEMP clause to create a temporary table that contains the query results. The initial and next extents for a temporary table are always eight pages. The temporary table must be accessible by the built-in RSAM access method of the database server; you cannot specify an alternate access method.

If you use the same query results more than once, using a temporary table saves time. In addition, using an INTO TEMP clause often gives you clearer and more understandable SELECT statements. However, the data in the temporary table is static; data is not updated as changes are made to the tables used to build the temporary table.

You can put indexes on a temporary table.

A logged, temporary table exists until one of the following situations occurs:

- The application disconnects.
- A DROP TABLE statement is issued on the temporary table.
- The database is closed.

IDS

If your database does not have logging, the table behaves in the same way as a table that uses the WITH NO LOG option. ♦

Using the WITH NO LOG Option

Use the WITH NO LOG option to reduce the overhead of transaction logging. (Operations on nonlogging temporary tables are not included in the transaction-log operations.)

A nonlogging, temporary table exists until one of the following situations occurs:

- The application disconnects.
- A DROP TABLE statement is issued on the temporary table.

Because nonlogging temp tables do not disappear when the database is closed, you can use a nonlogging temp table to transfer data from one database to another while the application remains connected.

The behavior of a temporary table that you create with the WITH NO LOG option is the same as that of a scratch table.

For more information about temporary tables, see "CREATE Temporary TABLE" on page 2-286.

EDS

INTO SCRATCH Clause

If you are using Enterprise Decision Server, use the INTO SCRATCH clause to reduce the overhead of transaction logging. (Operations on scratch tables are not included in transaction-log operations.)

A scratch table does not support indexes or constraints.

A scratch table exists until one of the following situations occurs:

- The application disconnects.
- A DROP TABLE statement is issued on the temporary table.

Because scratch tables do not disappear when the database is closed, you can use a scratch table to transfer data from one database to another while the application remains connected.

A scratch table is identical to a temporary table that is created with the WITH NO LOG option.

For more information about scratch tables, see "CREATE Temporary TABLE" on page 2-286.

EDS

INTO EXTERNAL Clause

If you are using Enterprise Decision Server, use the INTO EXTERNAL clause to build a SELECT statement that unloads data from your database into an external table.

When you use the INTO EXTERNAL clause to unload data, you create a default external table description. This clause is especially useful for unloading Informix-internal data files because you can use the external table description when you subsequently reload the files.

To obtain the same effect for text tables, issue a CREATE EXTERNAL...SAMEAS statement. Then issue an INSERT INTO...SELECT statement.

Table Options

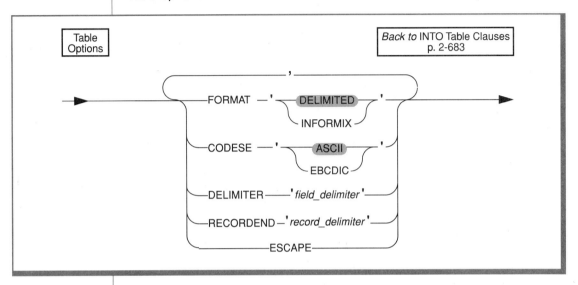

Element	Purpose	Restrictions	Syntax
field_delimiter	Character to separate fields The default value is the pipe (I) character.	If you use a non-printing character as a delimiter, you must encode it as the octal representation of the ASCII character. For example, ' \006 ' can represent CTRL-F.	Quoted String, p. 4-260
record_delimiter	Character to separate records If you do not set the RECORDEND environment variable, the default value is the newline character (\n).	If you use a non-printing character as a delimiter, you must encode it as the octal representation of the ASCII character. For example, ' \006 ' can represent CTRL-F.	Quoted String, p. 4-260

The following table describes the keywords that apply to unloading data. If you want to specify additional table options in the external-table description for the purpose of reloading the table later, see "Table Options" on page 2-139. In the SELECT...INTO EXTERNAL statement, you can specify all table options that are discussed in the CREATE EXTERNAL TABLE statement except the fixed-format option.

You can use the INTO EXTERNAL clause when the format type of the created data file is either DELIMITED text or text in Informix internal data format. You cannot use it for a fixed-format unload.

Keyword	Purpose
CODESET	Specifies the type of code set
DELIMITER	Specifies the character that separates fields in a delimited text file
ESCAPE	Directs the database server to recognize ASCII special characters embedded in ASCII-text-based data files
	If you do not specify ESCAPE when you load data, the database server does not check the character fields in text data files for embedded special characters.
	If you do not specify ESCAPE when you unload data, the database server does not create embedded hexadecimal characters in text fields.
FORMAT	Specifies the format of the data in the data files
RECORDEND	Specifies the character that separates records in a delimited text file

For more information on external tables, see "CREATE EXTERNAL TABLE" on page 2-131.

UNION Operator

Place the UNION operator between two SELECT statements to combine the queries into a single query. You can string several SELECT statements together using the UNION operator. Corresponding items do not need to have the same name.

Restrictions on a Combined SELECT

Several restrictions apply on the queries that you can connect with a UNION operator, as the following list describes:

E/C

- In ESQL/C, you cannot use an INTO clause in a query unless you are sure that the compound query returns exactly one row, and you are not using a cursor. In this case, the INTO clause must be in the first SELECT statement. ♦

- The number of items in the SELECT clause of each query must be the same, and the corresponding items in each SELECT clause must have compatible data types.

- The columns in the SELECT clause of each query cannot be BYTE or TEXT columns. This restriction does not apply to UNION ALL operations.

- If you use an ORDER BY clause, it must follow the last SELECT clause, and you must refer to the item ordered by integer, not by identifier. Ordering takes place after the set operation is complete.

IDS

- You cannot use a UNION operator inside a subquery. ♦

To put the results of a UNION operator into a temporary table, use an INTO TEMP clause in the final SELECT statement.

Duplicate Rows in a Combined SELECT

If you use the UNION operator alone, the duplicate rows are removed from the complete set of rows. That is, if multiple rows contain identical values in each column, only one row is retained. If you use the UNION ALL operator, all the selected rows are returned (the duplicates are not removed). The following example uses the UNION ALL operator to join two SELECT statements without removing duplicates. The query returns a list of all the calls that were received during the first quarter of 1997 and the first quarter of 1998.

```
SELECT customer_num, call_code FROM cust_calls
    WHERE call_dtime BETWEEN
        DATETIME (1997-1-1) YEAR TO DAY
        AND DATETIME (1997-3-31) YEAR TO DAY

UNION ALL

SELECT customer_num, call_code FROM cust_calls
    WHERE call_dtime BETWEEN
        DATETIME (1998-1-1)YEAR TO DAY
        AND DATETIME (1998-3-31) YEAR TO DAY
```

If you want to remove duplicates, use the UNION operator without the keyword ALL in the query. In the preceding example, if the combination 101 B were returned in both SELECT statements, a UNION operator would cause the combination to be listed once. (If you want to remove duplicates within each SELECT statement, use the DISTINCT keyword in the SELECT clause, as described in "SELECT Clause" on page 2-636.)

Related Information

For task-oriented discussions of the SELECT statement, see the *Informix Guide to SQL: Tutorial*.

For a discussion of the GLS aspects of the SELECT statement, see the *Informix Guide to GLS Functionality*.

For information on how to access row and collections with ESQL/C host variables, see the discussion of complex data types in the *Informix ESQL/C Programmer's Manual*.

SET AUTOFREE

Use the SET AUTOFREE statement to specify that the database server will free the memory allocated for a cursor automatically, as soon as the cursor is closed.

Use this statement with ESQL/C.

Syntax

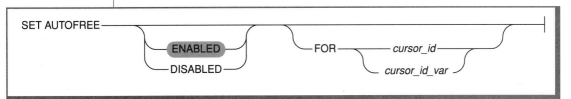

Element	Purpose	Restrictions	Syntax
cursor_id	Name of a cursor for which the Autofree feature is enabled or disabled	The cursor must be declared within the program.	Identifier, p. 4-205
cursor_id_var	Host variable that holds the value of cursor_*id*	The host variable must store the name of a cursor that is declared within the program.	Name must conform to language-specific rules for variable names.

Usage

When the Autofree feature is enabled for a cursor, you do not need to explicitly use a FREE statement to free the cursor memory in the database server once the cursor is closed.

You can specify the ENABLED or DISABLED options for the SET AUTOFREE statement. If you do not specify either option, the default is ENABLED. The following example shows how to enable the Autofree feature for all subsequent cursors in the program by default:

```
EXEC SQL set autofree;
```

Restrictions

The SET AUTOFREE statement that enables the Autofree feature must appear before the OPEN statement that opens a cursor. If a cursor is already open, the SET AUTOFREE statement does not affect its behavior.

After a cursor is autofree enabled, you cannot open the cursor a second time.

Globally Affecting Cursors with SET AUTOFREE

If you do not specify a *cursor _id* or *cursor_id_var*, the SET AUTOFREE statement affects all subsequent cursors in the program.

The following example shows how to enable the Autofree feature for all subsequent cursors:

```
EXEC SQL set autofree enabled;
```

Using the FOR Clause to Specify a Specific Cursor

If you specify a *cursor _id* or *cursor_id_var*, the SET AUTOFREE statement affects only the cursor that you specify after the FOR keyword.

This option allows you to override a global setting for all cursors. For example, if you issue a SET AUTOFREE ENABLED statement for all cursors in a program, you can issue a subsequent SET AUTOFREE DISABLED FOR statement for a particular cursor.

In the following example, the first statement enables the Autofree feature for all cursors, while the second statement disables the Autofree feature for the cursor named **x1**:

```
EXEC SQL set autofree enabled;
EXEC SQL set autofree disabled for x1;
```

Associated and Detached Statements

When a cursor is automatically freed, its associated prepared statement (or associated statement) is also freed.

The term *associated statement* has a special meaning in the context of the Autofree feature. A cursor is associated with a prepared statement if it is the first cursor that you declare with the prepared statement, or if it is the first cursor that you declare with the statement after the statement is detached.

The term *detached statement* has a special meaning in the context of the Autofree feature. A prepared statement is detached if you do not declare a cursor with the statement, or if the cursor with which the statement is associated was freed.

If the Autofree feature is enabled for a cursor that has an associated prepared statement, the database server frees memory allocated to the prepared statement as well as the memory allocated for the cursor. Suppose that you enable the Autofree feature for the following cursor:

```
/*Cursor associated with a prepared statement */
EXEC SQL prepare sel_stmt 'select * from customer';
EXEC SQL declare sel_curs2 cursor for sel_stmt;
```

When the database server closes the **sel_curs2** cursor, it automatically performs the equivalent of the following FREE statements:

```
FREE sel_curs2;
FREE sel_stmt;
```

Because the **sel_stmt** statement is freed automatically, you cannot declare a new cursor on it unless you prepare the statement again.

Closing Cursors Implicitly

A potential problem exists with cursors that have the Autofree feature enabled. In a non-ANSI-compliant database, if you do not close a cursor explicitly and then open it again, the cursor is closed implicitly. This implicit closing of the cursor triggers the Autofree feature. The second time the cursor is opened, the database server generates an error message (cursor not found) because the cursor is already freed.

Related Information

Related statements: CLOSE, DECLARE, FETCH, FREE, OPEN, and PREPARE

For more information on the Autofree feature, see the *Informix ESQL/C Programmer's Manual*.

E/C

SET CONNECTION

Use the SET CONNECTION statement to reestablish a connection between an application and a database environment and make the connection current. You can also use the SET CONNECTION statement with the DORMANT option to put the current connection in a dormant state.

Use this statement with ESQL/C.

Syntax

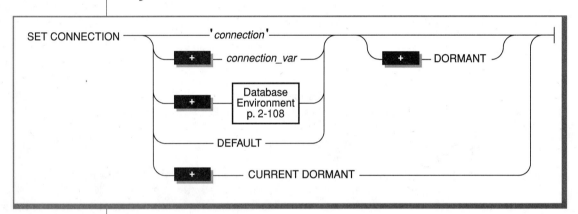

Element	Purpose	Restrictions	Syntax
connection	Quoted string that identifies the name that you assigned to a specific connection It is the connection assigned by the CONNECT statement when the initial connection was made.	The database must already exist. If you use the SET CONNECTION statement with the DORMANT option, *connection* must represent the current connection. If you use the SET CONNECTION statement without the DORMANT option, *connection* must represent a dormant connection.	Quoted String, p. 4-260
connection_var	Host variable that contains the value of connection	Variable must be the character data type.	Name must conform to language-specific rules for variable names.

Usage

You can use the SET CONNECTION statement to change the state of a connection in the following ways:

- Make a dormant connection current
- Make the current connection dormant

You cannot use the SET CONNECTION statement in the statement text of a prepared statement.

Making a Dormant Connection the Current Connection

The SET CONNECTION statement, with no DORMANT option, makes the specified dormant connection the current one. The connection that the application specifies must be dormant. The connection that is current when the statement executes becomes dormant. A dormant connection is a connection that is established but is not current.

The SET CONNECTION statement in the following example makes connection `con1` the current connection and makes `con2` a dormant connection:

```
CONNECT TO 'stores_demo' AS 'con1'
...
CONNECT TO 'demo' AS 'con2'
...
SET CONNECTION 'con1'
```

A dormant connection has a *connection context* associated with it. When an application makes a dormant connection current, it reestablishes that connection to a database environment and restores its connection context. (For more information on connection context, see the CONNECT statement on page 2-103.) Reestablishing a connection is comparable to establishing the initial connection, except that it typically avoids authenticating the permissions for the user again, and it saves reallocating resources associated with the initial connection. For example, the application does not need to reprepare any statements that have previously been prepared in the connection, nor does it need to redeclare any cursors.

Making a Current Connection Dormant

The SET CONNECTION statement with the DORMANT option makes the specified current connection a dormant connection. For example, the following SET CONNECTION statement makes connection `con1` dormant:

```
SET CONNECTION 'con1' DORMANT
```

The SET CONNECTION statement with the DORMANT option generates an error if you specify a connection that is already dormant. For example, if connection `con1` is current and connection `con2` is dormant, the following SET CONNECTION statement returns an error message:

```
SET CONNECTION 'con2' DORMANT
```

However, the following SET CONNECTION statement executes successfully:

```
SET CONNECTION 'con1' DORMANT
```

Dormant Connections in a Single-Threaded Environment

In a single-threaded ESQL/C application (an application that does not use threads), the DORMANT option makes the current connection dormant. The availability of the DORMANT option makes single-threaded ESQL/C applications upwardly compatible with thread-safe ESQL/C applications. However, a single-threaded environment can have only one active connection while the program executes.

Dormant Connections in a Thread-Safe Environment

In a thread-safe ESQL/C application, the DORMANT option makes an active connection dormant. Another thread can now use the connection by issuing the SET CONNECTION statement without the DORMANT option. A thread-safe environment can have many threads (concurrent pieces of work performing particular tasks) in one ESQL/C application, and each thread can have one active connection.

An active connection is associated with a particular thread. Two threads cannot share the same active connection. Once a thread makes an active connection dormant, that connection is available to other threads. A dormant connection is still established but is not currently associated with any thread. For example, if the connection named con1 is active in the thread named thread_1, the thread named thread_2 cannot make connection con1 its active connection until thread_1 has made connection con1 dormant.

The following code fragment from a thread-safe ESQL/C program shows how a particular thread within a thread-safe application makes a connection active, performs work on a table through this connection, and then makes the connection dormant so that other threads can use the connection:

```
thread_2()
{    /* Make con2 an active connection */
     EXEC SQL connect to 'db2' as 'con2';
     /*Do insert on table t2 in db2*/
     EXEC SQL insert into table t2 values(10);
     /* make con2 available to other threads */
     EXEC SQL set connection 'con2' dormant;
}
   .
   .
   .
```

If a connection to a database environment is initiated with the WITH CONCURRENT TRANSACTION clause of the CONNECT statement, any thread that subsequently connects to that database environment can use an ongoing transaction. In addition, if an open cursor is associated with such a connection, the cursor remains open when the connection is made dormant. Threads within a thread-safe ESQL/C application can use the same cursor by making the associated connection current even though only one thread can use the connection at any given time.

For a detailed discussion of thread-safe ESQL/C applications and the use of the SET CONNECTION statement in these applications, see the *Informix ESQL/C Programmer's Manual*.

Identifying the Connection

If the application did not use a connection name in the initial CONNECT statement, you must use a database environment (such as a database name or a database pathname) as the connection name. For example, the following SET CONNECTION statement uses a database environment for the connection name because the CONNECT statement does not use a connection name. For information about quoted strings that contain a database environment, see "Database Environment" on page 2-108.

```
CONNECT TO 'stores_demo'
.
.
.
CONNECT TO 'demo'
.
.
.
SET CONNECTION 'stores_demo'
```

If a connection to a database server was assigned a connection name, however, you must use the connection name to reconnect to the database server. An error is returned if you use a database environment rather than the connection name when a connection name exists.

DEFAULT Option

Use the DEFAULT option to identify the default connection for a SET CONNECTION statement. The default connection is one of the following connections:

- An explicit default connection (a connection established with the CONNECT TO DEFAULT statement)

- An implicit default connection (any connection established with the DATABASE or CREATE DATABASE statements)

You can use SET CONNECTION without a DORMANT option to reestablish the default connection or with the DORMANT option to make the default connection dormant. For more information, see "DEFAULT Option" on page 2-105 and "The Implicit Connection with DATABASE Statements" on page 2-106.

CURRENT Keyword

Use the CURRENT keyword with the DORMANT option of the SET CONNECTION statement as a shorthand form of identifying the current connection. The CURRENT keyword replaces the current connection name. If the current connection is con1, the following two statements are equivalent:

```
SET CONNECTION 'con1' DORMANT;

SET CONNECTION CURRENT DORMANT;
```

When a Transaction is Active

When you issue a SET CONNECTION statement without the DORMANT option, the SET CONNECTION statement implicitly puts the current connection in the dormant state. When you issue a SET CONNECTION statement (with the DORMANT option), the SET CONNECTION statement explicitly puts the current connection in the dormant state. In either case, the statement can fail if a connection that becomes dormant has an uncommitted transaction.

If the connection that becomes dormant has an uncommitted transaction, the following conditions apply:

- If the connection was established with the WITH CONCURRENT TRANSACTION clause of the CONNECT statement, the SET CONNECTION statement succeeds and puts the connection in a dormant state.

- If the connection was established without the WITH CONCURRENT TRANSACTION clause of the CONNECT statement, the SET CONNECTION statement fails and cannot set the connection to a dormant state and the transaction in the current connection continues to be active. The statement generates an error and the application must decide whether to commit or roll back the active transaction.

Related Information

Related statements: CONNECT, DISCONNECT, and DATABASE

For a discussion of the SET CONNECTION statement and thread-safe applications, see the *Informix ESQL/C Programmer's Manual*.

SET Database Object Mode

Use the SET Database Object Mode statement to change the mode of constraints, indexes, and triggers.

To specify whether constraints are checked at the statement level or at the transaction level, see "SET Transaction Mode" on page 2-774.

Syntax

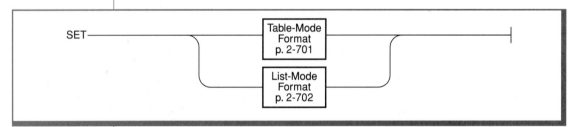

Usage

When you change the mode of constraints, indexes, or triggers, the change is persistent. The setting remains in effect until you change the mode of the database object again.

The **sysobjstate** system catalog table lists all of the database objects in the database and the current mode of each database object. For information on the **sysobjstate** system catalog table, see the *Informix Guide to SQL: Reference*.

Privileges Required for Changing Database Object Modes

To change the mode of a constraint, index, or trigger, you must have the necessary privileges. Specifically, you must meet one of the following requirements:

- You must have the DBA privilege on the database.
- You must be the owner of the table on which the database object is defined and must have the Resource privilege on the database.
- You must have the Alter privilege on the table on which the database object is defined and the Resource privilege on the database.

Table-Mode Format

Use the table-mode format to change the mode of all database objects of a given type that have been defined on a particular table.

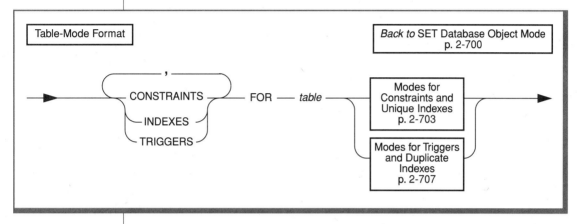

Element	Purpose	Restrictions	Syntax
table	Name of the table on which the database objects reside	The table must be a local table. You cannot set database objects defined on a temporary table to disabled or filtering modes.	Database Object Name, p. 4-47

For example, to disable all constraints that are defined on the **cust_subset** table, enter the following statement:

```
SET CONSTRAINTS FOR cust_subset DISABLED
```

When you use the table-mode format, you can change the modes of more than one database object type with a single SET Database Object Mode statement. For example, to enable all constraints, indexes, and triggers that are defined on the **cust_subset** table, enter the following statement:

```
SET CONSTRAINTS, INDEXES, TRIGGERS FOR cust_subset
     ENABLED
```

List-Mode Format

Use the list-mode format to change the mode for a particular constraint, index, or trigger.

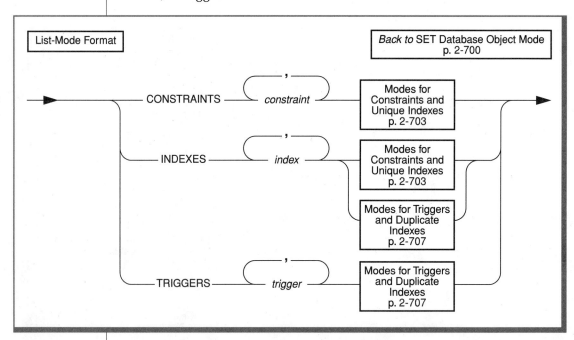

Element	Purpose	Restrictions	Syntax
constraint	Name of the constraint whose mode is to be set	Each constraint in the list must be a local constraint.	Database Object Name, p. 4-47
		All constraints in the list must be defined on the same table.	
index	Name of the index whose mode is to be set	Each index in the list must be a local index.	Database Object Name, p. 4-47
		All indexes in the list must be defined on the same table.	
trigger	Name of the trigger whose mode is to be set	Each trigger in the list must be a local trigger.	Database Object Name, p. 4-47
		All triggers in the list must be defined on the same table.	

For example, to change the mode of the unique index **unq_ssn** on the **cust_subset** table to filtering, enter the following statement:

```
SET INDEXES unq_ssn FILTERING
```

You can also use the list-mode format to change the mode for a list of constraints, indexes, or triggers that are defined on the same table. Assume that four triggers are defined on the **cust_subset** table: **insert_trig**, **update_trig**, **delete_trig**, and **execute_trig**. Also assume that all four triggers are enabled. To disable all triggers except **execute_trig**, enter the following statement:

```
SET TRIGGERS insert_trig, update_trig, delete_trig DISABLED
```

Modes for Constraints and Unique Indexes

You can specify a disabled, enabled, or filtering mode for a constraint or a unique index.

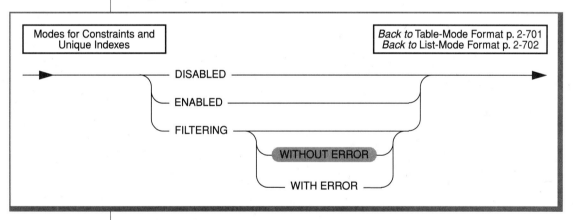

If you do not specify the mode for a constraint in a CREATE TABLE, ALTER TABLE, or SET Database Object Mode statement, the constraint is enabled by default.

If you do not specify the mode for an index in the CREATE INDEX or SET Database Object Mode statement, the index is enabled by default.

Definitions of Database Object Modes

You can use database object modes to control the effects of INSERT, DELETE, and UPDATE statements. Your choice of mode affects the tables whose data you are manipulating, the behavior of the database objects defined on those tables, and the behavior of the data manipulation statements themselves.

Enabled Mode

Constraints, indexes, and triggers are enabled by default. The CREATE TABLE, ALTER TABLE, CREATE INDEX, and CREATE TRIGGER statements create database objects in the enabled mode unless you specify another mode in the statement.

When a database object is enabled, the database server recognizes the existence of the database object and takes the database object into consideration while it executes an INSERT, DELETE, OR UPDATE statement. Thus, an enabled constraint is enforced, an enabled index updated, and an enabled trigger is executed when the trigger event takes place. When you enable constraints and unique indexes, if a violating row exists, the data manipulation statement fails (that is no rows change) and the database server returns an error message.

Disabled Mode

When a database object is disabled, the database server does not take it into consideration during the execution of an INSERT, DELETE, OR UPDATE statement. A disabled constraint is not enforced, a disabled index is not updated, and a disabled trigger is not executed when the trigger event takes place. When you disable constraints and unique indexes, any data manipulation statement that violates the restriction of the constraint or unique index succeeds, (that is the target row is changed) and the database server does not return an error message.

You can use the disabled mode to add a new constraint or new unique index to an existing table, even if some rows in the table do not satisfy the new integrity specification. For information on adding a new constraint, see "Adding a Constraint When Existing Rows Violate the Constraint"in the ALTER TABLE statement. For information on adding a new unique index, see "Adding a Unique Index When Duplicate Values Exist in the Column" in the CREATE INDEX statement.

Filtering Mode

When a constraint or unique index is in filtering mode, the INSERT, DELETE, OR UPDATE statement succeeds, but the database server enforces the constraint or the unique-index requirement by writing any failed rows to the violations table associated with the target table. Diagnostic information about the constraint violation or unique-index violation is written to the diagnostics table associated with the target table.

How Filtering Mode Affects Data Manipulation Statements

Filtering mode has the following specific effects on INSERT, UPDATE, and DELETE statements:

- A constraint violation or unique-index violation during an INSERT statement causes the database server to make a copy of the nonconforming record and write it to the violations table. The database server does not write the nonconforming record to the target table. If the INSERT statement is not a singleton insert, the rest of the insert operation proceeds with the next record.

- A constraint violation or unique-index violation during an UPDATE statement causes the database server to make a copy of the existing record that was to be updated and write it to the violations table. The database server also makes a copy of the new record and writes it to the violations table. The database server does not update the actual record in the target table. If the UPDATE statement is not a singleton update, the rest of the update operation proceeds with the next record.

- A constraint violation or unique-index violation during a DELETE statement causes the database server to make a copy of the record that was to be deleted and write it to the violations table. The database server does not delete the actual record in the target table. If the DELETE statement is not a singleton delete, the rest of the delete operation proceeds with the next record.

In all of these cases, the database server sends diagnostic information about each constraint violation or unique-index violation to the diagnostics table associated with the target table.

For detailed information on the structure of the records that the database server writes to the violations and diagnostics tables, see "Structure of the Violations Table" on page 2-785 and "Structure of the Diagnostics Table" on page 2-793.

Starting and Stopping the Violations and Diagnostics Tables

You must use the START VIOLATIONS TABLE statement to start the violations and diagnostics tables for the target table on which the database objects are defined, either before you set any database objects that are defined on the table to the filtering mode, or after you set database objects to filtering, but before any users issue INSERT, DELETE, or UPDATE statements.

If you want to stop the database server from filtering bad records to the violations table and sending diagnostic information about each bad record to the diagnostics table, you must issue a STOP VIOLATIONS TABLE statement.

For further information on these statements, see "START VIOLATIONS TABLE" on page 2-778 and "STOP VIOLATIONS TABLE" on page 2-800.

Error Options for Filtering Mode

When you set the mode of a constraint or unique index to filtering, you can specify one of two error options. These error options control whether the database server displays an integrity-violation error message when it encounters bad records during execution of data manipulation statements.

- The WITHOUT ERROR option is the default error option. The WITHOUT ERROR option signifies that when the database server executes an INSERT, DELETE, or UPDATE statement, and one or more of the target rows causes a constraint violation or unique-index violation, no integrity-violation error message is returned to the user.

- The WITH ERROR option signifies that when the database server executes an INSERT, DELETE, or UPDATE statement, and one or more of the target rows causes a constraint violation or unique-index violation, the database server returns an integrity-violation error message.

Net Effect of Filtering Mode on the Database

The net effect of the filtering mode is that the contents of the target table always satisfy all constraints on the table and any unique-index requirements on the table. In addition, the database server does not lose any data that violates a constraint or unique-index requirement because bad records are sent to the violations table and diagnostic information about those records is sent to the diagnostics table.

Furthermore, when filtering mode is in effect, insert, delete, and update operations on the target table do not fail when the database server encounters bad records. These operations succeed in adding all the good records to the target table. So filtering mode is especially appropriate for large-scale batch updates of tables. The user can fix records that violate constraints and unique-index requirements after the fact. The user does not have to fix the bad records before the batch update or lose the bad records during the batch update.

Modes for Triggers and Duplicate Indexes

You can specify the disabled or enabled modes for triggers or duplicate indexes.

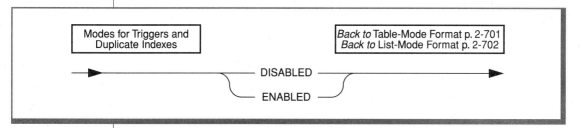

If you do not specify the mode for a trigger in the CREATE TRIGGER or SET Database Object Mode statement, the trigger is enabled by default.

If you do not specify the mode for an index in the CREATE INDEX or SET Database Object Mode statement, the index is enabled by default.

Related Information

Related statements: ALTER TABLE, CREATE TABLE, CREATE INDEX, CREATE TRIGGER, START VIOLATIONS TABLE and STOP VIOLATIONS TABLE

For a discussion of object modes and violation detection and examples that show how database object modes work when users execute data manipulation statements on target tables or add new constraints and indexes to target tables, see the *Informix Guide to SQL: Tutorial*.

For information on the system catalog tables associated with the SET Database Object Mode statement, see the **sysobjstate** and **sysviolations** tables in the *Informix Guide to SQL: Reference*.

SET DATASKIP

Use the SET DATASKIP statement to instruct the database server to skip a dbspace that is unavailable during the course of processing a transaction.

Syntax

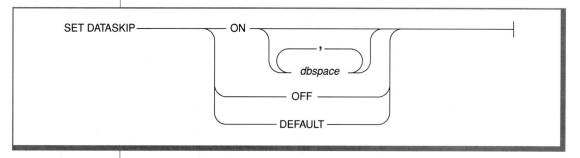

Element	Purpose	Restrictions	Syntax
dbspace	Name of the skipped dbspace	The dbspace must exist at the time the statement is executed.	Identifier, p. 4-205

Usage

The SET DATASKIP statement allows you to control whether the database server skips a dbspace that is unavailable (for example, due to a media failure) in the course of processing a transaction.

E/C

In ESQL/C, you receive a warning if a dbspace is skipped. The warning flag **sqlca.sqlwarn.sqlwarn6** is set to W if a dbspace is skipped. For more information about this topic, see the *Informix ESQL/C Programmer's Manual*. ♦

IDS

This statement applies only to tables that are fragmented across dbspaces. It does not apply to blobspaces or sbspaces. ♦

When you SET DATASKIP ON without specifying a dbspace, you are telling the database server to skip any dbspaces in the fragmentation list that are unavailable. You can use the **onstat -d** or **-D** utility to determine if a dbspace is down.

When you SET DATASKIP ON *dbspace*, you are telling the database server to skip the specified dbspace if it is unavailable.

Use the SET DATASKIP OFF statement to turn off the dataskip feature.

When the setting is DEFAULT, the database server uses the setting for the dataskip feature from the ONCONFIG file. The setting of the dataskip feature can be changed at runtime.

Under What Circumstances Is a Dbspace Skipped?

The database server skips a dbspace when SET DATASKIP is set to ON and the dbspace is unavailable.

The database server cannot skip a dbspace under certain conditions. The following list outlines those conditions:

- Referential constraint checking

  When you want to delete a parent row, the child rows must also be available for deletion. The child rows must exist in an available fragment.

  When you want to insert a new child row, the parent row must be found in the available fragments.

- Updates

  When you perform an update that moves a record from one fragment to another, both fragments must be available.

- Inserts

  When you try to insert records in a expression-based fragmentation strategy and the dbspace is unavailable, an error is returned. When you try to insert records in a round-robin fragment-based strategy, and a dbspace is down, the database server inserts the rows into any available dbspace. When no dbspace is available, an error is returned.

- Indexing

  When you perform updates that affect the index, such as when you insert or delete records, or when you update an indexed field, the index must be available.

  When you try to create an index, the dbspace you want to use must be available.

- Serial keys

  The first fragment is used to store the current serial-key value internally. This is not visible to you except when the first fragment becomes unavailable and a new serial key value is required, which happens during insert statements.

Related Information

For additional information about the dataskip feature, see your *Administrator's Guide*.

SET DEBUG FILE TO

Use the SET DEBUG FILE TO statement to name the file that is to hold the run-time trace output of an SPL routine.

Syntax

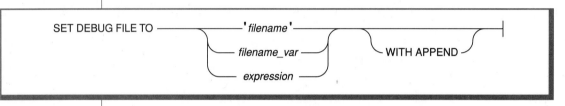

Element	Purpose	Restrictions	Syntax
expression	Expression that evaluates to a filename	The filename that is derived from the expression must be usable. The same restrictions apply to the derived filename as to the filename parameter.	Expression, p. 4-73
filename	Quoted string that identifies the pathname of the file that contains the output of the TRACE statement For information on the default actions that are taken if you omit the pathname, see "Location of the Output File" on page 2-714.	You can specify a new or existing file. If you specify an existing file, you must include the WITH APPEND keywords if you want to preserve the current contents of the file intact. For further information, see "Using the WITH APPEND Option" on page 2-713.	Quoted String, p. 4-260. Name must conform to the naming conventions of your operating system.
filename_var	Host variable that holds the value of filename	The host variable must be a character data type.	Name must conform to language-specific rules for variable names.

Usage

This statement indicates that the output of the TRACE statement in the SPL routine goes to the file that *filename* indicates. Each time the TRACE statement is executed, the trace data is added to this output file.

Using the WITH APPEND Option

The output file that you specify in the SET DEBUG TO file statement can be a new file or existing file.

If you specify an existing file, the current contents of the file are purged when you issue the SET DEBUG TO FILE statement. The first execution of a TRACE command sends trace output to the beginning of the file.

However, if you include the WITH APPEND option, the current contents of the file are preserved when you issue the SET DEBUG TO FILE statement. The first execution of a TRACE command adds trace output to the end of the file.

If you specify a new file in the SET DEBUG TO FILE statement, it makes no difference whether you include the WITH APPEND option. The first execution of a TRACE command sends trace output to the beginning of the new file whether you include or omit the WITH APPEND option.

Closing the Output File

To close the file that the SET DEBUG FILE TO statement opened, issue another SET DEBUG FILE TO statement with another filename. You can then edit the contents of the first file.

Redirecting Trace Output

You can use the SET DEBUG FILE TO statement outside an SPL routine to direct the trace output of the SPL routine to a file. You also can use this statement inside an SPL routine to redirect its own output.

Location of the Output File

If you invoke a SET DEBUG FILE TO statement with a simple filename on a local database, the output file is located in your current directory. If your current database is on a remote database server, the output file is located in your home directory on the remote database server. If you provide a full pathname for the debug file, the file is placed in the directory and file that you specify on the remote database server. If you do not have write permissions in the directory, you get an error.

Example of the SET DEBUG FILE TO Statement

The following example sends the output of the SET DEBUG FILE TO statement to a file called **debug.out**:

```
SET DEBUG FILE TO 'debug' || '.out'
```

Related Information

Related statement: TRACE

For a task-oriented discussion of SPL routines, see the *Informix Guide to SQL: Tutorial*.

SET DEFERRED_PREPARE

Use the SET DEFERRED_PREPARE statement to defer sending a PREPARE statement to the database server until the OPEN or EXECUTE statement is sent.

Use this statement with ESQL/C.

Syntax

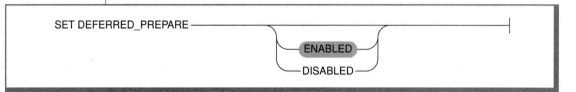

Usage

The SET DEFERRED_PREPARE statement causes the application program to delay sending the PREPARE statement to the database server until the OPEN or EXECUTE statement is executed. In effect, the PREPARE statement is bundled with the other statement so that one round trip of messages instead of two is sent between the client and the server.

The Deferred-Prepare feature works with the following sequences:

- PREPARE, DECLARE, OPEN statement blocks that operate with the FETCH or PUT statements
- PREPARE, EXECUTE statement blocks or the EXECUTE IMMEDIATE statement

SET DEFERRED_PREPARE Options

You can specify the ENABLED or DISABLED options for the SET DEFERRED_PREPARE statement. If you do not specify either option, the default is ENABLED. The following example shows how to enable the Deferred-Prepare feature by default:

```
EXEC SQL set deferred_prepare;
```

ENABLED Option

Use the ENABLED option to enable the Deferred-Prepare feature within the application. The following example shows how to use the ENABLED option:

```
EXEC SQL set deferred_prepare enabled;
```

When you enter a SET DEFERRED_PREPARE ENABLED statement in your application, the Deferred-Prepare feature is enabled for all PREPARE statements in the application. The application then exhibits the following behavior:

- The sequence PREPARE, DECLARE, OPEN sends the PREPARE statement to the database server with the OPEN statement.

- If a prepared statement contains syntax errors, the database server does not return error messages to the application until the application declares a cursor for the prepared statement and opens the cursor.

- The sequence PREPARE, EXECUTE sends the PREPARE statement to the database server with the EXECUTE statement. If a prepared statement contains syntax errors, the database server does not return error messages to the application until the application attempts to execute the prepared statement.

DESCRIBE Restriction with the ENABLED Option

If you use the Deferred-Prepare feature in a PREPARE, DECLARE, OPEN statement block that contains a DESCRIBE statement, the DESCRIBE statement must follow the OPEN statement rather than the PREPARE statement. If the DESCRIBE statement follows the PREPARE statement, the DESCRIBE statement results in an error.

DISABLED Option

Use the DISABLED option to disable the Deferred-Prepare feature within the application. The following example shows how to use the DISABLED option:

```
EXEC SQL set deferred_prepare disabled;
```

When you disable the Deferred-Prepare feature, the application sends each PREPARE statement to the database server when the PREPARE statement is executed.

Example of SET DEFERRED_PREPARE

The following code fragment shows a SET DEFERRED PREPARE statement with a PREPARE, EXECUTE statement block. In this case, the database server executes the PREPARE and EXECUTE statements all at once.

```
EXEC SQL BEGIN DECLARE SECTION;
    int a;
EXEC SQL END DECLARE SECTION;
EXEC SQL allocate descriptor 'desc';
EXEC SQL create database test;
EXEC SQL create table x (a int);

/* Enable Deferred-Prepare feature */
EXEC SQL set deferred_prepare enabled;

/* Prepare an INSERT statement */
EXEC SQL prepare ins_stmt from 'insert into x values(?)';

a = 2;
EXEC SQL EXECUTE ins_stmt using :a;
if (SQLCODE)
    printf("EXECUTE : SQLCODE is %d\n", SQLCODE);
```

Using Deferred-Prepare with OPTOFC

You can use the Deferred-Prepare and Open-Fetch-Close Optimization (OPTOFC) features together in your application. The OPTOFC feature delays sending the OPEN message to the database server until the FETCH message is sent.

The following situations occur if you enable the Deferred-Prepare and OPTOFC features at the same time:

- If the text of a prepared statement contains syntax errors, the error messages are not returned to the application until the first FETCH statement is executed.

- A DESCRIBE statement cannot be executed until after the FETCH statement.

- You must issue an ALLOCATE DESCRIPTOR statement before a DESCRIBE or GET DESCRIPTOR statement can be executed.

  The database server performs an internal execution of a SET DESCRIPTOR statement which sets the TYPE, LENGTH, DATA, and other fields in the system descriptor area. You can specify a GET DESCRIPTOR statement after the FETCH statement to see the data that is returned.

Related Information

Related statements: DECLARE, DESCRIBE, EXECUTE, OPEN, and PREPARE

For a task-oriented discussion of the PREPARE statement and dynamic SQL, see the *Informix Guide to SQL: Tutorial*.

For more information about concepts relating to the SET DEFERRED_PREPARE statement, see the *Informix ESQL/C Programmer's Manual*.

SET DESCRIPTOR

Use the SET DESCRIPTOR statement to assign values to a system-descriptor area.

Use this statement with ESQL/C.

Syntax

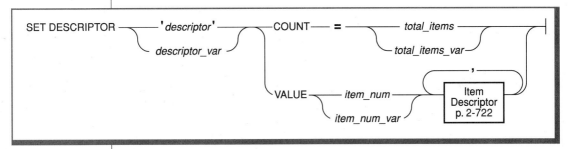

Element	Purpose	Restrictions	Syntax
descriptor	String that identifies the system-descriptor area to which values are assigned	The system-descriptor area must have been previously allocated with the ALLOCATE DESCRIPTOR statement.	Quoted String, p. 4-260
descriptor_var	Host variable that holds the value of descriptor	The same restrictions apply to descriptor_var as apply to *descriptor*.	Name must conform to language-specific rules for variable names.
item_num	Unsigned integer that specifies one of the item descriptors in the system-descriptor area	The value must be greater than 0 and less than (or equal to) the number of item descriptors that were specified when the system-descriptor area was allocated with the ALLOCATE DESCRIPTOR statement.	Literal Number, p. 4-237

(1 of 2)

Element	Purpose	Restrictions	Syntax
item_num_var	Host variable that holds the value of item_num	The same restrictions apply to item_num_var as apply to *item_num*.	Name must conform to language-specific rules for variable names.
total_items	Unsigned integer that specifies how many items are actually described in the system-descriptor area	The value must be greater than 0 and less than (or equal to) the number of item descriptors that were specified when the system-descriptor area was allocated with the ALLOCATE DESCRIPTOR statement.	Literal Number, p. 4-237
total_items_var	Host variable that holds a literal integer that specifies how many items are actually described in the system-descriptor area	The same restrictions apply to total_items_var as apply to *total_items*.	Name must conform to language-specific rules for variable names.

(2 of 2)

Usage

The SET DESCRIPTOR statement can be used after you have described SELECT, EXECUTE FUNCTION (OR EXECUTE PROCEDURE), and INSERT statements with the DESCRIBE...USING SQL DESCRIPTOR statement. The SET DESCRIPTOR statement can assign values to a system-descriptor area in the following instances:

- To set the COUNT field of a system-descriptor area to match the number of items for which you are providing descriptions in the system-descriptor area

- To set the item descriptor for each value for which you are providing descriptions in the system-descriptor area

- To modify the contents of an item-descriptor field

If an error occurs during the assignment to any identified system-descriptor fields, the contents of all identified fields are set to 0 or null, depending on the variable type.

Using the COUNT Clause

Use the COUNT clause to set the number of items that are to be used in the system-descriptor area.

If you allocate a system-descriptor area with more items than you are using, you need to set the COUNT field to the number of items that you are actually using. The following example shows the sequence of statements in ESQL/C that can be used in a program:

```
EXEC SQL BEGIN DECLARE SECTION;
    int count;
EXEC SQL END DECLARE SECTION;

EXEC SQL allocate descriptor 'desc_100'; /*allocates for 100 items*/

count = 2;
EXEC SQL set descriptor 'desc_100' count = :count;
```

Using the VALUE Clause

Use the VALUE clause to assign values from host variables into fields of a system-descriptor area. You can assign values for items for which you are providing a description (such as parameters in a WHERE clause), or you can modify values for items after you use a DESCRIBE statement to fill the fields for a SELECT or INSERT statement.

Item Descriptor

Use the Item Descriptor portion of the SET DESCRIPTOR statement to set value for a particular field in a system-descriptor area.

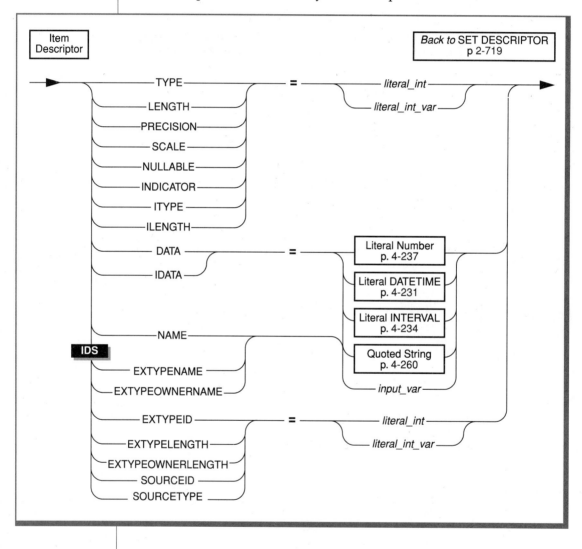

Element	Purpose	Restrictions	Syntax
input_var	Host variable that contains the information for the specified field in the specified item descriptor	The information that is contained in input_var must be appropriate for the specified field.	Name must conform to language-specific rules for variable names.
literal_int	Positive, nonzero integer that assigns a value to the specified field in the specified item descriptor	The restrictions that apply to literal_int vary with the field type (item_descriptor) you specify in the VALUE clause (TYPE, LENGTH, and so on).	Literal Number, p. 4-237
		For information on the codes that are allowed for the TYPE field and their meaning, see "Setting the TYPE or ITYPE Field" on page 2-724.	
		For the restrictions that apply to other field types, see the individual headings for field types under "Using the VALUE Clause" on page 2-721.	
literal_int_var	Host variable that contains the value of literal_int	The same restrictions apply to literal_int_var as apply to *literal_int*.	Name must conform to language-specific rules for variable names.

Setting the TYPE or ITYPE Field

Use the following integer constants to set the value of TYPE for each item.

SQL Data Type	Integer Value	X-Open Integer Value
CHAR	0	1
SMALLINT	1	4
INTEGER	2	5
FLOAT	3	6
SMALLFLOAT	4	-
DECIMAL	5	3
SERIAL	6	-
DATE	7	-
MONEY	8	-
DATETIME	10	-
BYTE	11	-
TEXT	12	-
VARCHAR	13	-
INTERVAL	14	-
NCHAR	15	-
NVARCHAR	16	-

IDS

The following table includes additional integer constants that represent data types available with the Dynamic Server.

SQL Data Type	Integer Value
INT8	17
SERIAL8	18
SET	19
MULTISET	20
LIST	21
ROW	22
COLLECTION	23
Varying-length opaque type	40
Fixed-length opaque type	41
LVARCHAR (client-side only)	43
BOOLEAN	45

These TYPE constants are the same values that appear in the **coltype** column in the **syscolumns** system catalog table.

For code that is easier to maintain, use the predefined constants for these SQL data types instead of their actual integer values. These constants are defined in the **sqltypes.h** header file. However, you cannot use the actual constant name in the SET DESCRIPTOR statement. Instead, assign the constant to an integer host variable and specify the host variable in the SET DESCRIPTOR statement file.

The following example shows how you can set the TYPE field in ESQL/C:

```
main()
{
EXEC SQL BEGIN DECLARE SECTION;
    int itemno, type;
EXEC SQL END DECLARE SECTION;
...
EXEC SQL allocate descriptor 'desc1' with max 5;
...
type = SQLINT; itemno = 3;
EXEC SQL set descriptor 'desc1' value :itemno type = :type;
}
```

This information is identical for **ITYPE**. Use **ITYPE** when you create a dynamic program that does not comply with the X/Open standard.

Compiling Without the -xopen Option

If you compile without the **-xopen** option, the regular Informix SQL code is assigned for TYPE. You must be careful not to mix normal and X/Open modes because errors can result. For example, if a particular type is not defined under X/Open mode but is defined under normal mode, executing a SET DESCRIPTOR statement can result in an error.

Setting the TYPE Field in X/Open Programs

In X/Open mode, you must use the X/Open set of integer codes for the data type in the TYPE field.

If you use the ILENGTH, IDATA, or ITYPE fields in a SET DESCRIPTOR statement, a warning message appears. The warning indicates that these fields are not standard X/Open fields for a system-descriptor area.

For code that is easier to maintain, use the predefined constants for these X/Open SQL data types instead of their actual integer value. These constants are defined in the **sqlxtype.h** header file.

Using DECIMAL or MONEY Data Types

If you set the **TYPE** field for a DECIMAL or MONEY data type, and you want to use a scale or precision other than the default values, set the **SCALE** and **PRECISION** fields. You do not need to set the **LENGTH** field for a DECIMAL or MONEY item; the **LENGTH** field is set accordingly from the **SCALE** and **PRECISION** fields.

Using DATETIME or INTERVAL Data Types

If you set the **TYPE** field for a DATETIME or INTERVAL value, you can set the **DATA** field as a literal DATETIME or INTERVAL or as a character string. If you use a character string, you must set the **LENGTH** field to the encoded qualifier value.

To determine the encoded qualifiers for a DATETIME or INTERVAL character string, use the datetime and interval macros in the **datetime.h** header file.

If you set DATA to a host variable of DATETIME or INTERVAL, you do not need to set **LENGTH** explicitly to the encoded qualifier integer.

Setting the DATA or IDATA Field

When you set the **DATA** or **IDATA** field, you must provide the appropriate type of data (character string for CHAR or VARCHAR, integer for INTEGER, and so on).

When any value other than DATA is set, the value of DATA is undefined. You cannot set the **DATA** or **IDATA** field for an item without setting TYPE for that item. If you set the **TYPE** field for an item to a character type, you must also set the **LENGTH** field. If you do not set the **LENGTH** field for a character item, you receive an error.

Setting the LENGTH or ILENGTH Field

If your **DATA** or **IDATA** field contains a character string, you must specify a value for **LENGTH**. If you specify LENGTH=0, **LENGTH** sets automatically to the maximum length of the string. The **DATA** or **IDATA** field can contain a 368-literal character string or a character string derived from a character variable of CHAR or VARCHAR data type. This provides a method to determine the length of a string in the **DATA** or **IDATA** field dynamically.

If a DESCRIBE statement precedes a SET DESCRIPTOR statement, **LENGTH** is automatically set to the maximum length of the character field that is specified in your table.

This information is identical for **ILENGTH**. Use **ILENGTH** when you create a dynamic program that does not comply with the X/Open standard.

Setting the INDICATOR Field

If you want to put a null value into the system-descriptor area, set the **INDICATOR** field to -1, and do not set the **DATA** field.

If you set the **INDICATOR** field to 0 to indicate that the data is not null, you must set the **DATA** field.

IDS

Setting Opaque-Type Fields

The following item-descriptor fields provide information about a column that has an opaque type as its data type:

- The **EXTYPEID** field stores the extended identifier for the opaque type.

  This integer value must correspond to a value in the **extended_id** column of the **sysxtdtypes** system catalog table.

- The **EXTYPENAME** field stores the name of the opaque type.

  This character value must correspond to a value in the **name** column of the row with the matching **extended_id** value in the **sysxtdtypes** system catalog table.

- The **EXTYPELENGTH** field stores the length of the opaque-type name.

  This integer value is the length, in bytes, of the string in the **EXTYPENAME** field.

- The **EXTYPEOWNERNAME** field stores the name of the opaque-type owner.

  This character value must correspond to a value in the **owner** column of the row with the matching **extended_id** value in the **sysxtdtypes** system catalog table.

- The **EXTYPEOWNERLENGTH** field stores the length of the value in the **EXTTYPEOWNERNAME** field.

  This integer value is the length, in bytes, of the string in the **EXTYPEOWNERNAME** field.

For more information on the **sysxtdtypes** system catalog table, see the *Informix Guide to SQL: Reference*.

Setting Distinct-Type Fields

The following item-descriptor fields provide information about a column that has an distinct type as its data type:

- The **SOURCEID** field stores the extended identifier for the source data type.

  Set this field if the source type of the distinct type is an opaque data type. This integer value must correspond to a value in the **source** column for the row of the **sysxtdtypes** system catalog table whose **extended_id** value matches that of the distinct type you are setting.

- The **SOURCETYPE** field stores the data-type constant for the source data type.

  This value is the data-type constant for the built-in data type that is the source type for the distinct type. The codes for the **SOURCETYPE** field are the same as those for the TYPE field (page 2-724). This integer value must correspond to the value in the **type** column for the row of the **sysxtdtypes** system catalog table whose **extended_id** value matches that of the distinct type you are setting.

For more information on the **sysxtdtypes** system catalog table, see the *Informix Guide to SQL: Reference*.

Modifying Values Set by the DESCRIBE Statement

You can use a DESCRIBE statement to modify the contents of a system-descriptor area after it is set.

After you use a DESCRIBE statement on a SELECT or an INSERT statement, you must check to determine whether the **TYPE** field is set to either 11 or 12 to indicate a TEXT or BYTE data type. If **TYPE** contains an 11 or a 12, you must use the SET DESCRIPTOR statement to reset **TYPE** to 116, which indicates FILE type.

Related Information

Related statements: ALLOCATE DESCRIPTOR, DEALLOCATE DESCRIPTOR, DECLARE, DESCRIBE, EXECUTE, FETCH, GET DESCRIPTOR, OPEN, PREPARE, and PUT

For more information on system-descriptor areas, refer to the *Informix ESQL/C Programmer's Manual*.

SET EXPLAIN

Use the SET EXPLAIN statement to display the query plan the optimizer chooses, an estimate of the number of rows returned, and a relative cost of the query.

Syntax

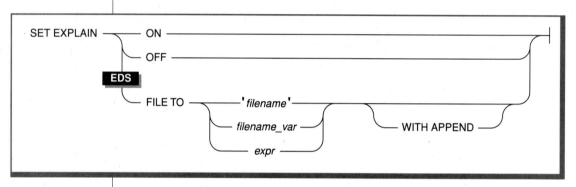

Element	Purpose	Restrictions	Syntax
expr	Expression that evaluates to a filename	The filename that is derived from the expression must be usable. The same restrictions apply to the derived filename as to the filename parameter.	Expression, p. 4-73
filename	Quoted string that identifies the path and filename of the file that contains the output of the SET EXPLAIN FILE TO statement For information on the default actions that are taken if you omit the pathname, see "Location of the Output File" on page 2-714.	You can specify a new or existing file. If you specify an existing file, you must include the WITH APPEND keywords if you want to preserve the current contents of the file intact. For further information, see "Using the WITH APPEND Option" on page 2-713.	Quoted String, p. 4-260. Name must conform to the naming conventions of your operating system.
filename_var	Host variable that holds the value of filename	The host variable must be a character data type.	Name must conform to language-specific rules for variable names.

Usage

The SET EXPLAIN statement provides various measurements of the work involved in performing a query.

Option	Purpose
ON	Generates measurements for each subsequent query and writes the results to an output file in the current directory. If the file already exists, new explain output is appended to the existing file.
OFF	Terminates the SET EXPLAIN statement so that measurements for subsequent queries are no longer generated or written to the output file.
FILE TO	Generates measurements for each subsequent query and allows you to specify the location for the explain output file. If the file already exists, new explain output overwrites the contents of the file unless you use the WITH APPEND option.

Persistence and Default Behavior

When you issue a SET EXPLAIN ON statement, the output is directed to the appropriate file until you issue a SET EXPLAIN OFF statement or until the program ends. If you do not enter a SET EXPLAIN statement, the default behavior is OFF. The database server does not generate measurements for queries.

Execution of the SET EXPLAIN Statement

The SET EXPLAIN statement executes during the database server optimization phase, which occurs when you initiate a query. For queries that are associated with a cursor, if the query is prepared and does not have host variables, optimization occurs when you prepare it. Otherwise, optimization occurs when you open the cursor.

Using the FILE TO option

When you execute a SET EXPLAIN FILE TO statement, explain output is implicitly turned on. The default filename for the output is **sqexplain.out** until changed by a SET EXPLAIN FILE TO statement. Once changed, the filename remains set until the end of the session or until changed by another SET EXPLAIN FILE TO statement.

The filename may be any valid combination of optional path and filename. If no path component is specified, the file is placed in your current directory. The permissions for the file are owned by the current user.

Using the WITH APPEND Option

The output file that you specify in the SETEXPLAIN statement can be a new file or an existing file.

If you specify an existing file, the current contents of the file are purged when you issue the SET EXPLAIN FILE TO statement. The first execution of a FILE TO command sends output to the beginning of the file.

However, if you include the WITH APPEND option, the current contents of the file are preserved when you issue the SET EXPLAIN FILE TO statement. The execution of a WITH APPEND command appends output to the end of the file.

If you specify a new file in the SET EXPLAIN FILE TO statement, it makes no difference whether you include the WITH APPEND option. The first execution of the command sends output to the beginning of the new file.

Default Name and Location of the Output File

UNIX

On UNIX, when you issue a SET EXPLAIN ON statement, the plan that the optimizer chooses for each subsequent query is written to the **sqexplain.out** file by default.

If the output file does not exist when you issue the SET EXPLAIN ON statement, the database server creates the output file. If the output file already exists when you issue the SET EXPLAIN ON statement, subsequent output is appended to the file.

If the client application and the database server are on the same computer, the **sqexplain.out** file is stored in your current directory. If you are using a version 5.x or earlier client application and the **sqexplain.out** file does not appear in the current directory, check your home directory for the file. When the current database is on another computer, the **sqexplain.out** file is stored in your home directory on the remote host. ♦

WIN NT

On Windows NT, when you issue a SET EXPLAIN ON statement, the plan that the optimizer chooses for each subsequent query is written to the file **%INFORMIXDIR%\sqexpln*username*.out** where *username* is the user login. ♦

SET EXPLAIN Output

By examining the SET EXPLAIN output file, you can determine if steps can be taken to improve the performance of the query.

The following table contains terms that can appear in the output file and their significance.

Term	Significance
Query	Displays the executed query. Indicates whether SET OPTIMIZATION was set to high.
	If you SET OPTIMIZATION to LOW, the output of SET EXPLAIN displays the following uppercase string as the first line:
	QUERY:{LOW}
	If you SET OPTIMIZATION to HIGH, the output of SET EXPLAIN displays the following uppercase string as the first line:
	QUERY:
Directives followed	Lists the directives set for the executed query.
	If the syntax for a directive is incorrect, the query is processed without the directive. In that case, the output will show DIRECTIVES NOT FOLLOWED in addition to DIRECTIVES FOLLOWED.
	For more information on the directives specified after this term, see the "Optimizer Directives" on page 4-244 or "SET OPTIMIZATION" on page 2-747.
Estimated Cost	An estimate of the amount of work for the query.
	The optimizer uses an estimate to compare the cost of one path with another. The estimated cost is a number the optimizer assigns to the selected access method. The estimated cost does not translate directly into time, and cannot be used to compare different queries. However, it can be used to compare changes made for the same query. When data distributions are used, a query with a higher estimate generally takes longer to run than one with a smaller estimate.
	In the case of a query and a subquery, two estimated cost figures are returned; the query figure also contains the subquery cost. The subquery cost is shown only so you can see the cost that is associated with the subquery.
Estimated # of Rows Returned	An estimate of the number of rows to be returned.
	This number is based on the information in the system catalog tables
Numbered List	The order in which tables are accessed, followed by the access method used (index path or sequential scan).
	When a query involves table inheritance, all of the tables are listed under the supertable in the order they were accessed.

(1 of 2)

Term	Significance
Index Keys	The columns used as filters or indexes; the column name used for the index path or filter is indicated.
	The notation *(Key Only)* indicates that all of the desired columns are part of the index key, so a key-only read of the index could be substituted for a read of the actual table.
	The *Lower Index Filter* shows the key value where the index read begins. If the filter condition contains more than one value, an *Upper Index Filter* would be shown for the key value where the index read stops.
Join Method	When the query involves a join between two tables, the join method the optimizer used (Nested Loop or Dymanic Hash) is shown at the bottom of the output for that query.
	When the query involves a dynamic join of two tables, if the output contains the words *Build Outer*, the hash table is built on the first table listed (called the build table).
	If the words *Build Outer* do not appear, the hash table is built on the second table listed.

(2 of 2)

Related Information

Related statements: SET OPTIMIZATION and UPDATE STATISTICS

For discussions of SET EXPLAIN and of analyzing the output of the optimizer, see your *Performance Guide*.

SET ISOLATION

Use the SET ISOLATION statement to define the degree of concurrency among processes that attempt to access the same rows simultaneously.

The SET ISOLATION statement is an Informix extension to the ANSI SQL-92 standard. If you want to set isolation levels through an ANSI-compliant statement, use the SET TRANSACTION statement instead. For a comparison of these two statements, see "SET TRANSACTION" on page 2-768.

Syntax

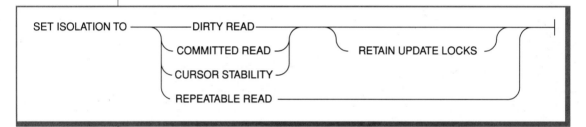

Usage

The database isolation level affects read concurrency when rows are retrieved from the database. The database server uses shared locks to support different levels of isolation among processes attempting to access data.

The update or delete process always acquires an exclusive lock on the row that is being modified. The level of isolation does not interfere with rows that you are updating or deleting. If another process attempts to update or delete rows that you are reading with an isolation level of Repeatable Read, that process is denied access to those rows.

E/C

In ESQL/C, cursors that are currently open when you execute the SET ISOLATION statement might or might not use the new isolation level when rows are later retrieved. The isolation level in effect could be any level that was set from the time the cursor was opened until the time the application actually fetches a row. The database server might have read rows into internal buffers and internal temporary tables using the isolation level that was in effect at that time. To ensure consistency and reproducible results, close open cursors before you execute the SET ISOLATION statement. ♦

Informix Isolation Levels

The following definitions explain the critical characteristics of each isolation level, from the lowest level of isolation to the highest.

Using the Dirty Read Option

Use the Dirty Read option to copy rows from the database whether or not there are locks on them. The program that fetches a row places no locks and it respects none. Dirty Read is the only isolation level available to databases that do not have transactions.

This isolation level is most appropriate for static tables that are used for queries, that is, tables where data is not being modified, since it provides no isolation. With Dirty Read, the program might return a phantom row, which is an uncommitted row that was inserted or modified within a transaction that has subsequently rolled back. No other isolation level allows access to a phantom row.

Using the Committed Read Option

Use the Committed Read option to guarantee that every retrieved row is committed in the table at the time that the row is retrieved. This option does not place a lock on the fetched row. Committed Read is the default level of isolation in a database with logging that is not ANSI compliant.

Committed Read is appropriate to use when each row of data is processed as an independent unit, without reference to other rows in the same or other tables.

Using the Cursor Stability Option

Use the Cursor Stability option to place a shared lock on the fetched row, which is released when you fetch another row or close the cursor. Another process can also place a shared lock on the same row, but no process can acquire an exclusive lock to modify data in the row. Such row stability is important when the program updates another table based on the data it reads from the row.

If you set the isolation level to Cursor Stability, but you are not using a transaction, the Cursor Stability isolation level acts like the Committed Read isolation level.

Using the Repeatable Read Option

Use the Repeatable Read option to place a shared lock on every row that is selected during the transaction. Another process can also place a shared lock on a selected row, but no other process can modify any selected row during your transaction or insert a row that meets the search criteria of your query during your transaction. If you repeat the query during the transaction, you reread the same information. The shared locks are released only when the transaction commits or rolls back. Repeatable Read is the default isolation level in an ANSI-compliant database.

Repeatable Read isolation places the largest number of locks and holds them the longest. Therefore, it is the level that reduces concurrency the most.

Default Isolation Levels

The default isolation level for a particular database is established when you create the database according to database type. The following list describes the default isolation level for each database type.

Isolation Level	Database Type
Dirty Read	Default level of isolation in a database without logging
Committed Read	Default level of isolation in a database with logging that is not ANSI compliant
Repeatable Read	Default level of isolation in an ANSI-compliant database

The default level remains in effect until you issue a SET ISOLATION statement. After a SET ISOLATION statement executes, the new isolation level remains in effect until one of the following events occurs:

- You enter another SET ISOLATION statement.
- You open another database that has a default isolation level different from the isolation level that your last SET ISOLATION statement specified.
- The program ends.

Using the RETAIN UPDATE LOCKS Option

Use the RETAIN UPDATE LOCKS option to affect the behavior of the database server when it handles a SELECT... FOR UPDATE statement.

In a database with the isolation level set to Dirty Read, Committed Read, or Cursor Stability, the database server places an update lock on a fetched row of a SELECT... FOR UPDATE statement. When you turn on the RETAIN UPDATE LOCKS option, the database server retains the update lock until the end of the transaction rather than release it at the next subsequent FETCH or when the cursor is closed. This option prevents other users from placing an exclusive lock on the updated row before the current user reaches the end of the transaction.

You can use this option to achieve the same locking effects but avoid the overhead of dummy updates or the repeatable read isolation level.

You can turn this option on or off at any time during the current session.

You can turn the option off by resetting the isolation level without using the RETAIN UPDATE LOCKS keywords.

For more information on update locks, see "Locking Considerations" on page 2-819.

Turning the Option Off In the Middle of a Transaction

If you turn the RETAIN UPDATE LOCKS option off in the middle of a transaction, several update locks might still exist.

Switching off the feature does not directly release any update lock. When you turn this option off, the database server reverts to normal behavior for the three isolation levels. That is, a FETCH statement releases the update lock placed on a row by the immediately preceding FETCH statement, and a closed cursor releases the update lock on the current row.

Update locks placed by earlier FETCH statements are not released unless multiple update cursors are present within the same transaction. In this case, a subsequent FETCH could also release older update locks of other cursors.

Effects of Isolation Levels

You cannot set the database isolation level in a database that does not have logging. Every retrieval in such a database occurs as a Dirty Read.

You can issue a SET ISOLATION statement from a client computer only after a database is opened.

The data obtained during retrieval of a BYTE or TEXT column can vary, depending on the database isolation level. Under Dirty Read or Committed Read levels of isolation, a process is permitted to read a BYTE or TEXT column that is either deleted (if the delete is not yet committed) or in the process of being deleted. Under these isolation levels, an application can read a deleted data when certain conditions exist. For information about these conditions, see the *Administrator's Guide*.

DB

When you use DB-Access, as you use higher levels of isolation, lock conflicts occur more frequently. For example, if you use Cursor Stability, more lock conflicts occur than if you use Committed Read. ♦

E/C

In ESQL/C, if you use a scroll cursor in a transaction, you can force consistency between your temporary table and the database table either by setting the isolation level to Repeatable Read or by locking the entire table during the transaction.

If you use a scroll cursor with hold in a transaction, you cannot force consistency between your temporary table and the database table. A table-level lock or locks that are set by Repeatable Read are released when the transaction is completed, but the scroll cursor with hold remains open beyond the end of the transaction. You can modify released rows as soon as the transaction ends, but the retrieved data in the temporary table might be inconsistent with the actual data. ♦

Related Information

Related statements: CREATE DATABASE, SET LOCK MODE, and SET TRANSACTION

For a discussion of setting the isolation level, see the *Informix Guide to SQL: Tutorial*.

SET LOCK MODE

Use the SET LOCK MODE statement to define how the database server handles a process that tries to access a locked row or table.

Syntax

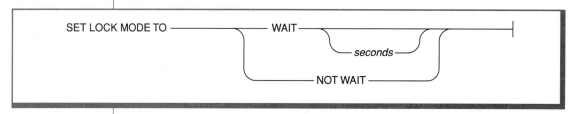

Element	Purpose	Restrictions	Syntax
seconds	Maximum number of seconds that a process waits for a lock to be released If the lock is still held at the end of the waiting period, the database server ends the operation and returns an error code to the process.	In a networked environment, the DBA establishes a default value for the waiting period by using the ONCONFIG parameter DEADLOCK_TIMEOUT. If you specify a value for *seconds*, the value applies only when the waiting period is shorter than the system default.	Literal Number, p. 4-237

Usage

You can direct the response of the database server in the following ways when a process tries to access a locked row or table.

Lock Mode	Effect
NOT WAIT	Database server ends the operation immediately and returns an error code. This condition is the default.
WAIT	Database server suspends the process until the lock releases.
WAIT *seconds*	Database server suspends the process until the lock releases or until the end of a waiting period, which is specified in seconds. If the lock remains after the waiting period, the database server ends the operation and returns an error code.

In the following example, the user specifies that the process should be suspended until the lock is released:

```
SET LOCK MODE TO WAIT
```

In the following example, the user specifies that if the process requests a locked row the operation should end immediately and an error code should be returned:

```
SET LOCK MODE TO NOT WAIT
```

In the following example, the user places an upper limit of 17 seconds on the length of any wait:

```
SET LOCK MODE TO WAIT 17
```

WAIT Clause

The WAIT clause causes the database server to suspend the process until the lock is released or until a specified number of seconds have passed without the lock being released.

The database server protects against the possibility of a deadlock when you request the WAIT option. Before the database server suspends a process, it checks whether suspending the process could create a deadlock. If the database server discovers that a deadlock could occur, it ends the operation (overruling your instruction to wait) and returns an error code. In the case of either a suspected or actual deadlock, the database server returns an error.

Cautiously use the unlimited waiting period that was created when you specify the WAIT option without *seconds*. If you do not specify an upper limit, and the process that placed the lock somehow fails to release it, suspended processes could wait indefinitely. Because a true deadlock situation does not exist, the database server does not take corrective action.

In a networked environment, the DBA uses the ONCONFIG parameter DEADLOCK_TIMEOUT to establish a default value for *seconds*. If you use a SET LOCK MODE statement to set an upper limit, your value applies only when your waiting period is shorter than the system default. The number of seconds that the process waits applies only if you acquire locks within the current database server and a remote database server within the same transaction.

Related Information

Related statements: LOCK TABLE, SET ISOLATION, SET TRANSACTION and UNLOCK TABLE

For a discussion on how to set the lock mode, see the *Informix Guide to SQL: Tutorial*.

SET LOG

Use the SET LOG statement to change your database logging mode from buffered transaction logging to unbuffered transaction logging or vice versa.

Syntax

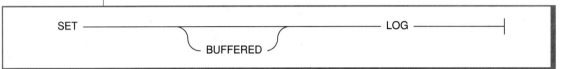

Usage

You activate transaction logging when you create a database or add logging to an existing database. These transaction logs can be buffered or unbuffered.

Buffered logging is a type of logging that holds transactions in a memory buffer until the buffer is full, regardless of when the transaction is committed or rolled back. The database server provides this option to speed up operations by reducing the number of disk writes. You gain a marginal increase in efficiency with buffered logging, but you incur some risk. In the event of a system failure, the database server cannot recover the completed transactions that were buffered in memory.

The SET LOG statement in the following example changes the transaction logging mode to buffered logging:

```
SET BUFFERED LOG
```

Unbuffered logging is a type of logging that does not hold transactions in a memory buffer. As soon as a transaction ends, the database server writes the transaction to disk. If a system failure occurs when you are using unbuffered logging, you recover all completed transactions. The default condition for transaction logs is unbuffered logging.

The SET LOG statement in the following example changes the transaction logging mode to unbuffered logging:

```
SET LOG
```

The SET LOG statement redefines the mode for the current session only. The default mode, which the database administrator sets with the **ondblog** utility, remains unchanged.

The buffering option does not affect retrievals from external tables. For distributed queries, a database with logging can retrieve only from databases with logging, but it makes no difference whether the databases use buffered or unbuffered logging.

ANSI

An ANSI-compliant database cannot use buffered logs.

You cannot change the logging mode of ANSI-compliant databases. If you created a database with the WITH LOG MODE ANSI keywords, you cannot later use the SET LOG statement to change the logging mode to buffered or unbuffered transaction logging. ♦

Related Information

Related statement: CREATE DATABASE

SET OPTIMIZATION

Use the SET OPTIMIZATION statement to specify the time the optimizer spends to determine the query plan or to specify the optimization goals of the query.

Syntax

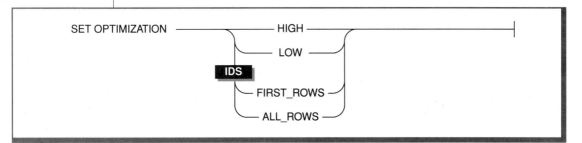

Usage

You can execute a SET OPTIMIZATION statement at any time. The optimization level carries across databases on the current database server.

When you issue a SET OPTIMIZATION statement, the option that you specify is persistent. That is, the new optimization level remains in effect until you issue another SET OPTIMIZATION statement or until the program ends.

The default database-server optimization level for the time the optimizer spends determining the query plan is HIGH.

The default database-server optimization level for the optimization goal of the query is ALL_ROWS.

Although you can set only one option at a time, you can issue two SET OPTIMIZATION statements: one that specifies the time the optimizer spends to determine the query plan and one that specifies the optimization goal of the query. ◆

HIGH and LOW Options

The HIGH and LOW options relate to the time the optimizer spends to determine the query plan:

- HIGH

  This option directs the optimizer to use a sophisticated, cost-based algorithm that examines all reasonable query-plan choices and selects the best overall alternative.

  For large joins, this algorithm can incur more overhead than you desire. In extreme cases, you can run out of memory.

- LOW

  This option directs the optimizer to use a less sophisticated, but faster, optimization algorithm. This algorithm eliminates unlikely join strategies during the early stages of optimization and reduces the time and resources spent during optimization.

  When you specify a low level of optimization, the database server might not select the optimal strategy because the strategy was eliminated from consideration during the early stages of the algorithm.

IDS

FIRST_ROWS and ALL_ROWS Options

The FIRST_ROWS and ALL_ROWS options relate to the optimization goal of the query:

- FIRST_ROWS

  This option directs the optimizer to choose the query plan that returns the first result record as soon as possible.

- ALL_ROWS

  This option directs the optimizer to choose the query plan which returns all the records as quickly as possible.

You can also specify the optimization goal of a specific query with the optimization-goal directive. For more information on how to use a directive to specify the optimization goal of a query, see "Optimizer Directives" on page 4-244.

Optimizing SPL Routines

For SPL routines that remain unchanged or change only slightly, you might want to set the SET OPTIMIZATION statement to HIGH when you create the SPL routine. This step stores the best query plans for the SPL routine. Then execute a SET OPTIMIZATION LOW statement before you execute the SPL routine. The SPL routine then uses the optimal query plans and runs at the more cost-effective rate.

Examples

The following example shows optimization across a network. The **central** database (on the **midstate** database server) is to have LOW optimization; the **western** database (on the **rockies** database server) is to have HIGH optimization.

```
CONNECT TO 'central@midstate';
SET OPTIMIZATION LOW;
SELECT * FROM customer;
CLOSE DATABASE;
CONNECT TO 'western@rockies';
SET OPTIMIZATION HIGH;
SELECT * FROM customer;
CLOSE DATABASE;
CONNECT TO 'wyoming@rockies';
SELECT * FROM customer;
```

The **wyoming** database is to have HIGH optimization because it resides on the same database server as the **western** database. The code does not need to respecify the optimization level for the **wyoming** database because the **wyoming** database resides on the **rockies** database server like the **western** database.

IDS

The following example directs the optimizer to use the most time to determine a query plan and to then return the first rows of the result as soon as possible.

```
SET OPTIMIZATION LOW;
SET OPTIMIZATION FIRST_ROWS;
SELECT lname, fname, bonus
FROM sales_emp, sales
WHERE sales.empid = sales_emp.empid AND bonus > 5,000
ORDER BY bonus DESC
```

◆

Related Information

Related statements: SET EXPLAIN and UPDATE STATISTICS

IDS

For information on other methods by which you can alter the query plan of the optimizer, see "Optimizer Directives" on page 4-244. ♦

For more information on how to optimize queries, see your *Performance Guide*.

SET PDQPRIORITY

The SET PDQPRIORITY statement allows an application to set the query priority level dynamically within an application.

Syntax

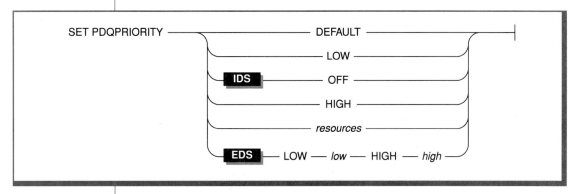

Element	Purpose	Restrictions	Syntax
high	Integer value that specifies the desired resource allocation	You must specify a value in the range 1 to 100. The *high* value must be greater than or equal to the *low* value.	Literal Number, p. 4-237
low	Integer value that specifies the minimum acceptable resource allocation	You must specify a value in the range 1 to 100.	Literal Number, p. 4-237
resources	Integer value that specifies the query priority level and the percent of resources the database server uses to process the query	Value must be from -1 to 100. For information on the specific meanings of certain values, see "Allocating Database Server Resources" on page 2-753.	Literal Number, p. 4-237

Usage

The priority set with the SET PDQPRIORITY statement overrides the environment variable **PDQPRIORITY**. However, no matter what priority value you set with the SET PDQPRIORITY statement, the ONCONFIG configuration parameter MAX_PDQPRIORITY determines the actual priority value that the database server uses for your queries.

For example, assume that the DBA sets the MAX_PDQPRIORITY parameter to 50. Then a user enters the following SET PDQPRIORITY statement to set the query priority level to 80 percent of resources:

```
SET PDQPRIORITY 80
```

When it processes the query, the database server uses the value of the MAX_PDQPRIORITY parameter to factor the query priority level set by the user. The database server silently processes the query with a priority level of 40. This priority level represents 50 percent of the 80 percent of resources that the user specifies.

IDS

Set PDQ priority to a value that is less than the quotient of 100 divided by the maximum number of prepared statements. For example, if two prepared statements are active, you should set PDQ priority to less than 50. ◆

EDS

In Enterprise Decision Server, set PDQ priority to a value greater than 0 when you need more memory for database operations such as sorts, groups, and index builds. For guidelines on which values to use, see your *Performance Guide.* ◆

SET PDQPRIORITY Keywords

The following table shows the keywords that you can enter for the SET PDQPRIORITY statement.

Keyword	Purpose
DEFAULT	Uses the value that is specified in the PDQPRIORITY environment variable
LOW	Signifies that data is fetched from fragmented tables in parallel
	In Dynamic Server, when you specify LOW, the database server uses no other forms of parallelism.
OFF	Indicates that PDQ is turned off (Dynamic Server only)
	The database server uses no parallelism. OFF is the default setting if you use neither the PDQPRIORITY environment variable nor the SET PDQPRIORITY statement.
HIGH	Signifies that the database server determines an appropriate value to use for PDQPRIORITY
	This decision is based on several factors, including the number of available processors, the fragmentation of the tables being queried, the complexity of the query, and so on. Informix reserves the right to change the performance behavior of queries when HIGH is specified in future releases.

Allocating Database Server Resources

You can specify any integer in the range from -1 to 100 to indicate a query priority level as the percent of resources the database server uses to process the query.

Resources include the amount of memory and the number of processors. The higher the number you specify in this parameter, the more resources the database server uses. Although the use of more resources by a database server usually indicates better performance for a given query, using too many resources can cause contention among the resources and remove resources from other queries, which results in degraded performance.

With the *resources* option, the following values are numeric equivalents of the keywords that indicate query priority level.

Value	Equivalent Keyword-Priority Level
-1	DEFAULT
0	OFF (Dynamic Server only)
1	LOW (Dynamic Server only)

IDS

The following statements are equivalent. The first statement uses the keyword LOW to establish a low query-priority level. The second statement uses a value of 1 in the *resources* parameter to establish a low query-priority level.

```
SET PDQPRIORITY LOW;

SET PDQPRIORITY 1;
```

EDS

Using a Range of Values

In Enterprise Decision Server, when you specify a range of values in SET PDQPRIORITY, you allow the Resource Grant Manager (RGM) some discretion when allocating resources. The largest value in the range is the desired resource allocation, while the smallest value is the minimum acceptable resource allocation for the query. If the minimum PDQ priority exceeds the available system resources, the RGM blocks the query. Otherwise, the RGM chooses the largest PDQ priority in the range specified in SET PDQPRIORITY that does not exceed available resources.

Related Information

For information about configuration parameters and about the Resource Grant Manager, see your *Administrator's Guide* and your *Performance Guide*.

For information about the **PDQPRIORITY** environment variable, see the *Informix Guide to SQL: Reference*.

SET PLOAD FILE

Use the SET PLOAD FILE statement to prepare a log file for a session of loading or unloading data from or to an external table. The log file records summary statistics about each load or unload job. The log file also lists any reject files created during a load job.

Syntax

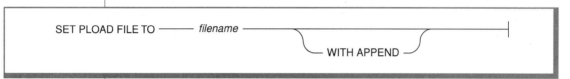

Element	Purpose	Restrictions	Syntax
filename	Name for the log file If you do not specify a log filename, log information is written to /**dev**/**null**.	If the file cannot be opened for writing, an error results.	IDENTIFIER P. 4-205

Usage

The WITH APPEND option allows you to append new log information to the existing log file.

Each time a session closes, the log file for that session also closes. If you issue more than one SET PLOAD FILE statement within a session, each new statement closes a previously opened log file and opens a new log file.

If you invoke a SET PLOAD FILE statement with a simple filename on a local database, the output file is located in your current directory. If your current database is on a remote database server, then the output file is located in your home directory on the remote database server, on the coserver where the initial connection was made. If you provide a full pathname for the file, it is placed in the directory and file specified on the remote server.

Related Information

Related Statements: CREATE EXTERNAL TABLE

SET Residency

Use the SET Residency statement to specify that one or more fragments of a table or index be resident in shared memory as long as possible.

Syntax

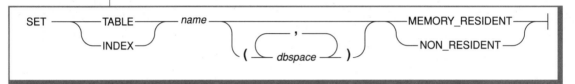

Element	Purpose	Restrictions	Syntax
dbspace	Name of the dbspace in which the fragment resides	The dbspace must exist.	Identifier, p. 4-205
name	Name of the table or index for which you want to change the resident state	The table or index must exist.	Database Object Name, p. 4-50

Usage

The SET Residency statement allows you to specify the tables, indexes, and data fragments that you want to remain in the buffer as long as possible. When a free buffer is requested, pages that are declared MEMORY_RESIDENT are considered last for page replacement.

The default resident state for database objects is nonresident. The resident state is persistent for the time the database server is up. That is, each time the database server is started you must specify the database objects that you want to remain in shared memory.

After a table, index, or data fragment is set to MEMORY_RESIDENT, the resident state remains in effect until one of the following events occurs:

- You use the SET Residency statement to set the database object to NON_RESIDENT.
- The database object is dropped.
- The database server is taken off-line.

You must be user **informix** to set or change the residency status of a database object.

Residency and the Changing Status of Fragments

If new fragments are added to a resident table, the fragments are not marked automatically as resident. You must issue the SET Residency statement for each new fragment or reissue the statement for the entire table.

Similarly, if a resident fragment is detached from a table, the residency status of the fragment remains unchanged. If you want the residency status to change to nonresident, you must issue the SET Residency statement to declare the specific fragment (or the entire table) as nonresident.

Examples

The following example shows how to set the residency status of an entire table.

```
SET TABLE tab1 MEMORY_RESIDENT
```

For fragmented tables or indexes, you can specify residency for individual fragments as the following example shows.

```
SET INDEX index1 (dbspace1, dbspace2) MEMORY_RESIDENT;
SET TABLE tab1 (dbspace1) NON_RESIDENT
```

This example specifies that the **tab1** fragment in **dbspace1** is not to remain in shared memory while the **index1** fragments in **dbspace1** and **dbspace2** are to remain in shared memory as long as possible.

Related Information

Related statements: SYNTAX

For information on how to monitor the residency status of tables, indexes and fragments, refer to your *Administrator's Guide*.

SET ROLE

Use the SET ROLE statement to enable the privileges of a role.

Syntax

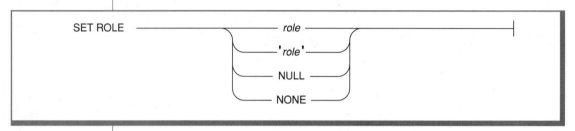

Element	Purpose	Restrictions	Syntax
role	Name of the role that you want to enable	The role must have been created with the CREATE ROLE statement. When a role name is enclosed in quotation marks, the role name is case sensitive.	Identifier, p. 4-205

Usage

Any user who is granted a role can enable the role using the SET ROLE statement. You can only enable one role at a time. If you execute the SET ROLE statement after a role is already set, the new role replaces the old role.

All users are, by default, assigned the role NULL or NONE (NULL and NONE are synonymous). The roles NULL and NONE have no privileges. When you set the role to NULL or NONE, you disable the current role.

When you set a role, you gain the privileges of the role, in addition to the privileges of PUBLIC and your own privileges. If a role is granted to another role, you gain the privileges of both roles, in addition to those of PUBLIC and your own privileges. After a SET ROLE statement executes successfully, the role remains effective until the current database is closed or the user executes another SET ROLE statement. Additionally, the user, not the role, retains ownership of all the database objects, such as tables, that were created during a session.

The scope of a role is within the current database only. You cannot use the privileges you acquire from a role to access data in another database. For example, if you have privileges from a role in the database named **acctg**, and you execute a distributed query over the databases named **acctg** and **inventory**, your query cannot access the data in the **inventory** database unless your were granted privileges in the **inventory** database.

Your cannot execute the SET ROLE statement while in a transaction. If the SET ROLE statement is executed while a transaction is active, an error occurs.

If the SET ROLE statement is executed as a part of a trigger or SPL routine, and the owner of the trigger or SPL routine was granted the role with the WITH GRANT OPTION, the role is enabled even if you are not granted the role.

The following example sets the role **engineer**:

```
SET ROLE engineer
```

The following example sets a role and then relinquishes the role after it performs a SELECT operation:

```
EXEC SQL set role engineer;
EXEC SQL select fname, lname, project
        into :efname, :elname, :eproject
        from projects
        where project_num > 100 and lname = 'Larkin';
printf ("%s is working on %s\n", efname, eproject);
EXEC SQL set role null;
```

Related Information

Related statements: CREATE ROLE, DROP ROLE, GRANT, and REVOKE

For a discussion of how to use roles, see the *Informix Guide to SQL: Tutorial*.

SET SCHEDULE LEVEL

The SET SCHEDULE LEVEL statement specifies the scheduling level of a query when queries are waiting to be processed.

Syntax

SET SCHEDULE LEVEL ──────────── *level* ──────────────┤

Element	Purpose	Restrictions	Syntax
level	Integer value that determines the scheduling priority of a query	The value must be between 1 and 100. If the value falls outside the range of 1 and 100, the database server uses the default value of 50.	Literal Number, p. 4-237

Usage

The highest priority level is 100. That is, a query at level 100 is more important than a query at level 1. In general, the Resource Grant Manager (RGM) processes a query with a higher scheduling level before a query with a lower scheduling level. The exact behavior of the RGM is influenced by the setting of the DS_ADM_POLICY configuration parameter.

Related Information

Related statement: SET PDQPRIORITY

For information about the Resource Grant Manager, see your *Administrator's Guide*.

For information about the DS_ADM_POLICY configuration parameter, see your *Administrator's Reference*.

SET SESSION AUTHORIZATION

The SET SESSION AUTHORIZATION statement lets you change the user name under which database operations are performed in the current session. This statement is enabled by the DBA privilege, which you must obtain from the DBA before the start of your current session. The new identity remains in effect in the current database until you execute another SET SESSION AUTHORIZATION statement or until you close the current database.

Syntax

SET SESSION AUTHORIZATION TO ───────────── '*user*' ─────────────┤

Element	Purpose	Restrictions	Syntax
user	User name under which database operations are to be performed in the current session	You must specify a valid user name. You must put quotation marks around the user name.	Identifier, p. 4-205

Usage

The SET SESSION AUTHORIZATION statement allows a user with the DBA privilege to bypass the privileges that protect database objects. You can use this statement to gain access to a table and adopt the identity of a table owner to grant access privileges. You must obtain the DBA privilege before you start a session in which you use this statement. Otherwise, this statement returns an error.

When you use this statement, the user name to which the authorization is set must have the Connect privilege on the current database. Additionally, the DBA cannot set the authorization to PUBLIC or to any defined role in the current database.

After SET SESSION AUTHORIZATION is executed, all owner-privileged UDRs created while using the new identity will be given RESTRICTED mode. For more information on RESTRICTED mode, see the **sysprocedures** system catalog table in the *Informix Guide to SQL: Reference*.

Setting a session to another user causes a change in a user name in the current active database server. In other words, these users are, as far as this database server process is concerned, completely dispossessed of any privileges that they might have while accessing the database server through some administrative utility. Additionally, the new session user is not able to initiate an administrative operation (execute a utility, for example) by virtue of the acquired identity.

After the SET SESSION AUTHORIZATION statement successfully executes, the user must use the SET ROLE statement to assume a role granted to the current user. Any role enabled by a previous user is relinquished.

Restriction on Scope of SET SESSION AUTHORIZATION

When you assume the identity of another user by executing the SET SESSION AUTHORIZATION statement, you can perform operations in the current database only. You cannot perform an operation on a database object outside the current database, such as a remote table. In addition, you cannot execute a DROP DATABASE or RENAME DATABASE statement, even if the database is owned by the real or effective user.

Using SET SESSION AUTHORIZATION to Obtain Privileges

You can use the SET SESSION AUTHORIZATION statement either to obtain access to the data directly or to grant the database-level or table-level privileges needed for the database operation to proceed. The following example shows how to use the SET SESSION AUTHORIZATION statement to obtain table-level privileges:

```
SET SESSION AUTHORIZATION TO 'cathl';
GRANT ALL ON customer TO mary;
SET SESSION AUTHORIZATION TO 'mary';
UPDATE customer
    SET fname = 'Carl'
    WHERE lname = 'Pauli';
```

SET SESSION AUTHORIZATION and Transactions

If your database is not ANSI compliant, you must issue the SET SESSION AUTHORIZATION statement outside a transaction. If you issue the statement within a transaction, you receive an error message.

ANSI

In an ANSI-compliant database, you can execute the SET SESSION AUTHORIZATION statement as long as you have not executed a statement that initiates an implicit transaction. Such statements either acquire locks or log data (for example, CREATE TABLE or SELECT). Statements that do not initiate an implicit transaction are statements that do not acquire locks or log data (for example, SET EXPLAIN and SET ISOLATION).

The COMMIT WORK and DATABASE statements do not initiate implicit transactions. So, in an ANSI-compliant database, you can execute the SET SESSION AUTHORIZATION statement immediately after a DATABASE statement or a COMMIT WORK statement. ♦

Related Information

Related statements: CONNECT, DATABASE, GRANT, and SET ROLE

SET STATEMENT CACHE

Use the SET STATEMENT CACHE statement to turn caching on or off for the current session.

Syntax

Usage

You can use the SET STATEMENT CACHE statement to turn caching in the SQL statement cache ON or OFF for the current session. The SQL statement cache is a mechanism that stores identical statements that are repeatedly executed in a buffer.

This mechanism allows qualifying statements to bypass the optimization stage and parsing stage, and avoid recompiling, which reduces memory consumption and improves query processing time.

Precedence and Default Behavior

The SET STATEMENT CACHE statement takes precedence over the **STMT_CACHE** environment variable and the STMT_CACHE configuration parameter. However, you must enable the SQL statement cache (either by setting the STMT_CACHE configuration parameter or using the **onmode** utility) before a SET STATEMENT CACHE statement can execute successfully.

When you issue a SET STATMENT CACHE ON statement, the SQL statement cache remains in effect until you issue a SET STATEMENT CACHE OFF statement or until the program ends. If you do not enter a SET STATEMENT CACHE statement, the default behavior is OFF.

Turning the Cache On

Use the ON option to enable the SQL statement cache.

When the SQL statement cache is enabled, each statement that you execute passes through the SQL statement cache to determine if a matching cache entry is present. If so, the database server uses the cached entry to execute the statement.

If the statement does not have a matching entry, the database server tests to see if it qualifies for entry into the cache. For information on the conditions a statement must meet to enter into the cache, see "Statement Qualification" on page 766.

Restrictions on Matching Entries in the SQL Statement Cache

When the database server considers whether or not a statement is identical to a statement in the SQL statement cache, the following items must match:

- Case
- Comments
- Query text strings
- White space
- Optimization settings
  - SET OPTIMIZATION statement options
  - Optimizer directives
  - Settings of the **OPTCOMPIND** environment variable or the OPTCOMPIND ONCONFIG configuration parameter

Host variable names, however, are insignificant. For example, the following select statements are considered identical:

```
SELECT * FROM tab1 WHERE x = :x AND y = :y;

SELECT * FROM tab1 WHERE x = :p AND y = :q;
```

In the previous example, although the host names are different, the statements qualify because the case, query text strings, and white space match.

Turning the Cache OFF

Use the OFF option to disable the SQL statement cache. When you turn caching off for your session, no SQL statement cache code is executed for that session.

The SQL statement cache is designed to save memory in environments where identical queries are executed repeatedly and where schema changes are infrequent. If this is not the case, you might want to turn the SQL statement cache off to avoid the overhead of caching.

For example, if you have little cache cohesion, that is, when relatively few matches but many new entries into the cache exist, the cache management overhead is high. In this case, turn the SQL statement cache off.

In addition, if you know that you are executing many statements that do not qualify for the SQL statement cache, you might want to disable it and avoid the overhead of testing to see if each statement qualifies for entry into the cache.

Statement Qualification

A statement that can be cached in the SQL statement cache (and consequently, one that can match a statement that already appears in the SQL statement cache), must meet the following conditions:

- It must be a SELECT, INSERT, UPDATE, or DELETE statement.
- It must contain only built-in data types (excluding BLOB, BOOLEAN, BYTE, CLOB, LVARCHAR, or TEXT).
- It must contain only built-in operators.
- It cannot contain user-defined routines.
- It cannot contain temporary or remote tables.
- It cannot contain subqueries in the select list.
- It cannot be part of a multi-statement PREPARE.
- It cannot have user-permission restrictions on target columns.
- In an ANSI-compliant database, it must contain fully qualified object names.
- It cannot require re-optimization.

Related Information

For information on optimization settings, see "SET OPTIMIZATION" on page 2-747 and "Optimizer Directives" on page 4-244.

For information about the **STMT_CACHE** environment variable, see the *Informix Guide to SQL: Reference*.

For more information about the STMT_CACHE onconfig parameter and the **onmode** utility, see your *Administrator's Reference*.

For more information on the performance implications of this feature, see your *Performance Guide*.

SET TRANSACTION

Use the SET TRANSACTION statement to define isolation levels and to define the access mode of a transaction (read-only or read-write).

Syntax

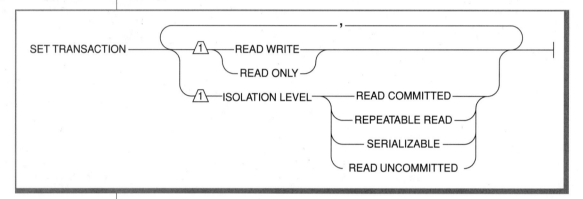

Usage

You can use SET TRANSACTION only in databases with logging.

You can issue a SET TRANSACTION statement from a client computer only after a database is opened.

The database isolation level affects concurrency among processes that attempt to access the same rows simultaneously from the database. The database server uses shared locks to support different levels of isolation among processes that are attempting to read data as the following list shows:

- Read Uncommitted
- Read Committed
- (ANSI) Repeatable Read
- Serializable

The update or delete process always acquires an exclusive lock on the row that is being modified. The level of isolation does not interfere with rows that you are updating or deleting; however, the access mode does affect whether you can update or delete rows. If another process attempts to update or delete rows that you are reading with an isolation level of Serializable or (ANSI) Repeatable Read, that process will be denied access to those rows.

Comparing *SET TRANSACTION* with *SET ISOLATION*

The SET TRANSACTION statement complies with ANSI SQL-92. This statement is similar to the Informix SET ISOLATION statement; however, the SET ISOLATION statement is not ANSI compliant and does not provide access modes. In fact, the isolation levels that you can set with the SET TRANSACTION statement are almost parallel to the isolation levels that you can set with the SET ISOLATION statement, as the following table shows.

SET TRANSACTION Isolation Level	SET ISOLATION Isolation Level
Read Uncommitted	Dirty Read
Read Committed	Committed Read
Not supported	Cursor Stability
(ANSI) Repeatable Read	(Informix) Repeatable Read
Serializable	(Informix) Repeatable Read

Another difference between the SET TRANSACTION and SET ISOLATION statements is the behavior of the isolation levels within transactions. You can issue the SET TRANSACTION statement only once for a transaction. Any cursors that are opened during that transaction are guaranteed to get that isolation level (or access mode if you are defining an access mode). With the SET ISOLATION statement, after a transaction is started, you can change the isolation level more than once within the transaction. The following examples illustrate this difference in the behavior of the SET ISOLATION and SET TRANSACTION statements:

SET ISOLATION

```
EXEC SQL BEGIN WORK;
EXEC SQL SET ISOLATION TO DIRTY READ;
EXEC SQL SELECT ... ;
EXEC SQL SET ISOLATION TO REPEATABLE READ;
EXEC SQL INSERT ... ;
EXEC SQL COMMIT WORK;
    -- Executes without error
```

SET TRANSACTION

```
EXEC SQL BEGIN WORK;
EXEC SQL SET TRANSACTION ISOLATION LEVEL SERIALIZABLE;
EXEC SQL SELECT ... ;
EXEC SQL SET TRANSACTION ISOLATION LEVEL READ COMMITTED;
    -- Produces error 876: Cannot issue SET TRANSACTION
    -- in an active transaction.
```

Another difference between SET ISOLATION and SET TRANSACTION is the duration of isolation levels. The isolation level set by SET ISOLATION remains in effect until another SET ISOLATION statement is issued. The isolation level set by SET TRANSACTION only remains in effect until the transaction terminates. Then the isolation level is reset to the default for the database type.

Informix Isolation Levels

The following definitions explain the critical characteristics of each isolation level, from the lowest level of isolation to the highest.

Using the Read Uncommitted Option

Use the Read Uncommitted option to copy rows from the database whether or not locks are present on them. The program that fetches a row places no locks and it respects none. Read Uncommitted is the only isolation level available to databases that do not have transactions.

This isolation level is most appropriate for static tables that are used for queries, that is, tables where data is not being modified, since it provides no isolation. With Read Uncommitted, the program might return a phantom row, which is an uncommitted row that was inserted or modified within a transaction that has subsequently rolled back. No other isolation level allows access to a phantom row.

Using the Read Committed Option

Use the Read Committed option to guarantee that every retrieved row is committed in the table at the time that the row is retrieved. This option does not place a lock on the fetched row. Read Committed is the default level of isolation in a database with logging that is not ANSI compliant.

Read Committed is appropriate to use when each row of data is processed as an independent unit, without reference to other rows in the same or other tables.

Using the Repeatable Read Option

Use the Serializable option to place a shared lock on every row that is selected during the transaction. Another process can also place a shared lock on a selected row, but no other process can modify any selected row during your transaction or insert a row that meets the search criteria of your query during your transaction. If you repeat the query during the transaction, you reread the same information. The shared locks are released only when the transaction commits or rolls back. Serializable is the default isolation level in an ANSI-compliant database.

Serializable isolation places the largest number of locks and holds them the longest. Therefore, it is the level that reduces concurrency the most.

Default Isolation Levels

The default isolation level for a particular database is established according to database type when you create the database. The default isolation level for each database type is described in the following table.

Informix	ANSI	Purpose
Dirty Read	Read Uncommitted	Default level of isolation in a database without logging
Committed Read	Read Committed	Default level of isolation in a database with logging that is not ANSI compliant
Repeatable Read	Serializable	Default level of isolation in an ANSI-compliant database

The default isolation level remains in effect until you issue a SET TRANSACTION statement within a transaction. After a COMMIT WORK statement completes the transaction or a ROLLBACK WORK statement cancels the transaction, the isolation level is reset to the default.

Access Modes

Informix database servers support access modes. Access modes affect read and write concurrency for rows within transactions. Use access modes to control data modification.

You can specify that a transaction is read-only or read-write through the SET TRANSACTION statement. By default, transactions are read-write. When you specify that a transaction is read-only, certain limitations apply. Read-only transactions cannot perform the following actions:

- Insert, delete, or update table rows
- Create, alter, or drop any database object such as schemas, tables, temporary tables, indexes, or SPL routines
- Grant or revoke privileges
- Update statistics
- Rename columns or tables

You can execute SPL routines in a read-only transaction as long as the SPL routine does not try to perform any restricted statement.

Effects of Isolation Levels

You cannot set the database isolation level in a database that does not have logging. Every retrieval in such a database occurs as a Read Uncommitted.

The data that is obtained during retrieval of BYTE or TEXT data can vary, depending on the database isolation levels. Under Read Uncommitted or Read Committed isolation levels, a process is permitted to read a BYTE or TEXT column that is either deleted (if the delete is not yet committed) or in the process of being deleted. Under these isolation levels, an application can read a deleted BYTE or TEXT column when certain conditions exist. For information about these conditions, see the *Administrator's Guide*.

E/C

In ESQL/C, if you use a scroll cursor in a transaction, you can force consistency between your temporary table and the database table either by setting the isolation level to Serializable or by locking the entire table during the transaction.

If you use a scroll cursor with hold in a transaction, you cannot force consistency between your temporary table and the database table. A table-level lock or locks set by Serializable are released when the transaction is completed, but the scroll cursor with hold remains open beyond the end of the transaction. You can modify released rows as soon as the transaction ends, so the retrieved data in the temporary table might be inconsistent with the actual data. ◆

Related Information

Related statements: CREATE DATABASE, SET ISOLATION, and SET LOCK MODE

For a discussion of isolation levels and concurrency issues, see the *Informix Guide to SQL: Tutorial*.

SET Transaction Mode

Use the SET Transaction Mode statement to specify whether constraints are checked at the statement level or at the transaction level.

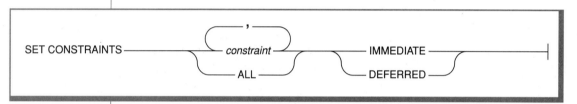

IDS

To change the mode of constraints to on, off, or filtering, see "SET Database Object Mode" on page 2-700. ♦

Syntax

SET CONSTRAINTS ───── constraint ───── IMMEDIATE ─────┤
              └──── ALL ────┘   └──── DEFERRED ────┘

Element	Purpose	Restrictions	Syntax
constraint	Constraint whose transaction mode is to be changed, or a list of constraint names No default value exists.	The specified constraint must exist in a database with logging. You cannot change the transaction mode of a constraint to deferred mode unless the constraint is currently in the enabled mode. All constraints in a list of constraints must exist in the same database.	Database Object Name, p. 4-50

Usage

When you set the transaction mode of a constraint, the effect of the SET Transaction Mode statement is limited to the transaction in which it is executed. The setting that the SET Transaction Mode statement produces is effective only during the transaction.

You use the IMMEDIATE keyword to set the transaction mode of constraints to statement-level checking. You use the DEFERRED keyword to set the transaction mode to transaction-level checking.

You can set the transaction mode of constraints only in a database with logging.

Statement-Level Checking

When you set the transaction mode to immediate, statement-level checking is turned on, and all specified constraints are checked at the end of each INSERT, UPDATE, or DELETE statement. If a constraint violation occurs, the statement is not executed. Immediate is the default transaction mode of constraints.

Transaction-Level Checking

When you set the transaction mode of constraints to deferred, statement-level checking is turned off, and all specified constraints are not checked until the transaction is committed. If a constraint violation occurs while the transaction is being committed, the transaction is rolled back.

Tip: *If you defer checking a primary-key constraint, checking the not-null constraint for that column or set of columns is also deferred.*

Duration of Transaction Modes

The duration of the transaction mode that the SET Transaction Mode statement specifies is the transaction in which the SET Transaction Mode statement is executed. You cannot execute this statement outside a transaction. Once a COMMIT WORK or ROLLBACK WORK statement is successfully completed, the transaction mode of all constraints reverts to IMMEDIATE.

Switching Transaction Modes

To switch from transaction-level checking to statement-level checking, you can use the SET Transaction Mode statement to set the transaction mode to immediate, or you can use a COMMIT WORK or ROLLBACK WORK statement in your transaction.

Specifying All Constraints or a List of Constraints

You can specify all constraints in the database in your SET Transaction Mode statement, or you can specify a single constraint or list of constraints.

Specifying All Constraints

If you specify the ALL keyword, the SET Transaction Mode statement sets the transaction mode for all constraints in the database. If any statement in the transaction requires that any constraint on any table in the database be checked, the database server performs the checks at the statement level or the transaction level, depending on the setting that you specify in the SET Transaction Mode statement.

Specifying a List of Constraints

If you specify a single constraint name or a list of constraints, the SET Transaction Mode statement sets the transaction mode for the specified constraints only. If any statement in the transaction requires checking of a constraint that you did not specify in the SET Transaction Mode statement, that constraint is checked at the statement level regardless of the setting that you specified in the SET Transaction Mode statement for other constraints.

When you specify a list of constraints, the constraints do not have to be defined on the same table, but they must exist in the same database.

Specifying Remote Constraints

You can set the transaction mode of local constraints or remote constraints. That is, the constraints that are specified in the SET Transaction Mode statement can be constraints that are defined on local tables or constraints that are defined on remote tables.

Examples of Setting the Transaction Mode for Constraints

The following example shows how to defer checking constraints within a
transaction until the transaction is complete. The SET Transaction Mode
statement in the example specifies that any constraints on any tables in the
database are not checked until the COMMIT WORK statement is encountered.

```
BEGIN WORK
SET CONSTRAINTS ALL DEFERRED
.
.
.
COMMIT WORK
```

The following example specifies that a list of constraints is not checked until
the transaction is complete:

```
BEGIN WORK
SET CONSTRAINTS update_const, insert_const DEFERRED
.
.
.
COMMIT WORK
```

Related Information

Related Statements: ALTER TABLE and CREATE TABLE

START VIOLATIONS TABLE

Use the START VIOLATIONS TABLE statement to create a violations table and a diagnostics table for a specified target table. The database server associates the violations and diagnostics tables with the target table by recording the relationship among the three tables in the **sysviolations** system catalog table.

In Enterprise Decision Server, the START VIOLATIONS TABLE statement creates a violations table but not a diagnostics table. ◆

Syntax

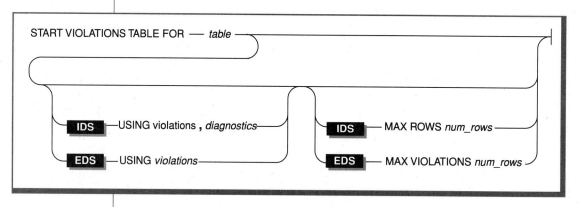

Element	Purpose	Restrictions	Syntax
diagnostics	Name of the diagnostics table to be associated with the target table	The name of the diagnostics table cannot match the name of any existing table in the database.	Database Object Name, p. 4-50

(1 of 2)

Element	Purpose	Restrictions	Syntax
num_rows	Maximum number of rows that the database server can insert into the diagnostics table when a single statement is executed on the target table (IDS)	The value that you specify must be an integer in the range from 1 to the maximum value of the INTEGER data type.	Literal Number, p. 4-237
	Maximum number of rows that any single coserver can insert into the violations table when a single statement is executed on the target table (EDS)		
table	Name of the target table for which a violations table and diagnostics table are to be created	If you do not include the USING clause in the statement, the name of the target table must be 124 characters or less (IDS).	Database Object Name, p. 4-50
		If you do not include the USING clause in the statement, the name of the target table must be 14 characters or less (EDS).	
		The target table cannot have a violations and diagnostics table associated with it before you execute the statement.	
		The target table cannot be a system catalog table.	
		The target table must be a local table.	
violations	Name of the violations table to be associated with the target table	The name of the violations table cannot match the name of any existing table in the database.	Database Object Name, p. 4-50

(2 of 2)

Usage

The START VIOLATIONS TABLE statement creates the special violations table that holds rows that fail to satisfy constraints and unique indexes during insert, update, and delete operations on target tables. This statement also creates the special diagnostics table that contains information about the integrity violations caused by each row in the violations table.

EDS

In Enterprise Decision Server, the START VIOLATIONS TABLE statement creates a violations table but not a diagnostics table. ♦

Relationship of **START VIOLATIONS TABLE** and **SET** Database Object Mode Statements

The START VIOLATIONS TABLE statement is closely related to the SET Database Object Mode statement. If you use the SET Database Object Mode statement to set the constraints or unique indexes defined on a table to the filtering database object mode, but you do not use the START VIOLATIONS TABLE statement to start the violations and diagnostics tables for this target table, any rows that violate a constraint or unique-index requirement during an insert, update, or delete operation are not filtered out to a violations table. Instead you receive an error message indicating that you must start a violations table for the target table.

Similarly, if you use the SET Database Object Mode statement to set a disabled constraint or disabled unique index to the enabled or filtering database object mode, but you do not use the START VIOLATIONS TABLE statement to start the violations and diagnostics tables for the table on which the database objects are defined, any existing rows in the table that do not satisfy the constraint or unique-index requirement are not filtered out to a violations table. If, in these cases, you want the ability to identify existing rows that do not satisfy the constraint or unique-index requirement, you must issue the START VIOLATIONS TABLE statement to start the violations and diagnostics tables before you issue the SET Database Object Mode statement to set the database objects to the enabled or filtering database object mode.

EDS

In Enterprise Decision Server, the SET Database Object Mode statement is not supported, and the concept of database object modes does not exist. Instead, once you use the START VIOLATIONS TABLE statement to create a violations table and associate it with a target table, the existence of this violations table causes all violations of constraints and unique-index requirements by insert, delete, and update operations to be recorded in the violations table.

In other words, once you issue a START VIOLATIONS TABLE statement, all constraints and unique indexes in a database on Enterprise Decision Server behave like filtering-mode constraints and filtering-mode unique indexes in a database on Dynamic Server. For an explanation of the behavior of filtering-mode constraints and filtering-mode unique indexes, see "Filtering Mode" on page 2-705. ♦

Effect of Violations Table on Concurrent Transactions

A transaction must issue the START VIOLATIONS TABLE statement in isolation. That is, no other transaction can be in progress on a target table when a transaction issues a START VIOLATIONS TABLE statement on that table. However, any transactions that start on the target table after the first transaction has issued the START VIOLATIONS TABLE statement will behave the same way as the first transaction with respect to the violations and diagnostics tables. That is, any constraint and unique-index violations by these subsequent transactions will be recorded in the violations and diagnostics tables.

For example, if transaction A operates on table **tab1** and issues a START VIOLATIONS TABLE statement on table **tab1**, the database server starts a violations table named **tab1_vio** and filters any constraint or unique-index violations on table **tab1** by transaction A to table **tab1_vio**. If transactions B and C start on table **tab1** after transaction A has issued the START VIOLATIONS TABLE statement, the database server also filters any constraint and unique-index violations by transactions B and C to table **tab1_vio**.

However, the result is that all three transactions do not receive error messages about constraint and unique-index violations even though transactions B and C do not expect this behavior. For example, if transaction B issues an INSERT or UPDATE statement that violates a check constraint on table **tab1**, the database server does not issue a constraint violation error to transaction B. Instead, the database server filters the bad row to the violations table without notifying transaction B that a data-integrity violation occurred.

IDS

You can prevent this situation from arising in Dynamic Server by specifying the WITH ERRORS option when you set database objects to the FILTERING mode in a SET Database Object Mode, CREATE TABLE, ALTER TABLE, or CREATE INDEX statement. When multiple transactions operate on a table and the WITH ERRORS option is in effect, any transaction that violates a constraint or unique-index requirement on a target table receives a data-integrity error message. ♦

IDS

In Enterprise Decision Server, once a transaction issues a START VIOLATIONS TABLE statement, you have no way to make the database server issue data-integrity violation messages to that transaction or to any other transactions that start subsequently on the same target table. ♦

Stopping the Violations and Diagnostics Tables

After you use a START VIOLATIONS TABLE statement to create an association between a target table and the violations and diagnostics tables, the only way to drop the association between the target table and the violations and diagnostics tables is to issue a STOP VIOLATIONS TABLE statement for the target table. For more information, see "STOP VIOLATIONS TABLE" on page 2-800.

USING Clause

IDS

You can use the USING clause to assign explicit names to the violations and diagnostics tables.

If you omit the USING clause, the database server assigns names to the violations and diagnostics tables. The system-assigned name of the violations table consists of the name of the target table followed by the string `vio`. The system-assigned name of the diagnostics table consists of the name of the target table followed by the string `dia`.

If you omit the USING clause, the maximum length of the target table is 124 characters.♦

EDS

You can use the USING clause to assign an explicit name to the violations table.

If you omit the USING clause, the database server assigns a name to the violations table. The system-assigned name of the violations table consists of the name of the target table followed by the string `vio`.

If you omit the USING clause, the maximum length of the target table is 14 characters. ♦

IDS

Use of the MAX ROWS Clause

You can use the MAX ROWS clause to specify the maximum number of rows that the database server can insert into the diagnostics table when a single statement is executed on the target table.

If you do not include the MAX ROWS clause in the START VIOLATIONS TABLE statement, no upper limit exists on the number of rows that can be inserted into the diagnostics table when a single statement is executed on the target table.

EDS

Use of the MAX VIOLATIONS Clause

You can use the MAX VIOLATIONS clause to specify the maximum number of rows that any single coserver can insert into the violations table when a single statement is executed on the target table. Each coserver where the violations table resides has this limit. The first coserver to reach this limit raises an error and causes the statement to fail.

If you do not include the MAX VIOLATIONS clause in a START VIOLATIONS TABLE statement, no upper limit exists on the number of rows that can be inserted into the violations table when a single statement is executed on the target table.

Examples of START VIOLATIONS TABLE Statements

The following examples show different ways to execute the START VIOLATIONS TABLE statement.

Starting Violations and Diagnostics Tables Without Specifying Their Names

The following statement starts violations and diagnostics tables for the target table named **cust_subset**. The violations table is named **cust_subset_vio** by default, and the diagnostics table is named **cust_subset_dia** by default.

```
START VIOLATIONS TABLE FOR cust_subset
```

Starting Violations and Diagnostics Tables and Specifying Their Names

The following statement starts a violations and diagnostics table for the target table named **items**. The USING clause assigns explicit names to the violations and diagnostics tables. The violations table is to be named **exceptions**, and the diagnostics table is to be named **reasons**.

```
START VIOLATIONS TABLE FOR items
USING exceptions, reasons
```

IDS

Specifying the Maximum Number of Rows in the Diagnostics Table

The following statement starts violations and diagnostics tables for the target table named **orders**. The MAX ROWS clause specifies the maximum number of rows that can be inserted into the diagnostics table when a single statement, such as an INSERT statement, is executed on the target table.

```
START VIOLATIONS TABLE FOR orders MAX ROWS 50000
```

EDS

Specifying the Maximum Number of Rows in the Violations Table

The following statement starts a violations table for the target table named **orders**. The MAX VIOLATIONS clause specifies the maximum number of rows that any single coserver can insert into the violations table when a single statement, such as an INSERT statement, is executed on the target table.

```
START VIOLATIONS TABLE FOR orders MAX VIOLATIONS 50000
```

Privileges Required for Starting Violations Tables

To start a violations and diagnostics table for a target table, you must meet one of the following requirements:

- You must have the DBA privilege on the database.
- You must be the owner of the target table and have the Resource privilege on the database.
- You must have the Alter privilege on the target table and the Resource privilege on the database.

Structure of the Violations Table

When you issue a START VIOLATIONS TABLE statement for a target table, the violations table that the statement creates has a predefined structure. This structure consists of the columns of the target table and three additional columns.

The following table shows the structure of the violations table.

Column Name	Type	Purpose
Same columns as the target table, in the same order that they appear in the target table	These columns of the violations table match the data type of the corresponding columns in the target table, except that SERIAL columns in the target table are converted to INTEGER data types in the violations table.	Table definition of the target table is reproduced in the violations table so that rows that violate constraints or unique-index requirements during insert, update, and delete operations can be filtered to the violations table. Users can examine these bad rows in the violations table, analyze the related rows that contain diagnostics information in the diagnostics table, and take corrective actions.
informix_tupleid	SERIAL	Contains the unique serial identifier that is assigned to the nonconforming row.
informix_optype	CHAR(1)	Indicates the type of operation that caused this bad row. This column can have the following values: I = Insert D = Delete O = Update (with this row containing the original values) N = Update (with this row containing the new values) S = SET Database Object Mode statement (IDS)
informix_recowner	CHAR(8)	Identifies the user who issued the statement that created this bad row.

Relationship Between the Violations and Diagnostics Tables

Users can take advantage of the relationships among the target table, violations table, and diagnostics table to obtain complete diagnostic information about rows that have caused data-integrity violations during INSERT, DELETE, and UPDATE statements.

Each row of the violations table has at least one corresponding row in the diagnostics table. The row in the violations table contains a copy of the row in the target table for which a data-integrity violation was detected. The row in the diagnostics table contains information about the nature of the data-integrity violation caused by the bad row in the violations table. The row in the violations table has a unique serial identifier in the **informix_tupleid** column. The row in the diagnostics table has the same serial identifier in its **informix_tupleid** column.

A given row in the violations table can have more than one corresponding row in the diagnostics table. The multiple rows in the diagnostics table all have the same serial identifier in their **informix_tupleid** column so that they are all linked to the same row in the violations table. Multiple rows can exist in the diagnostics table for the same row in the violations table because a bad row in the violations table can cause more than one data-integrity violation.

For example, a bad row can violate a unique-index requirement for one column, a not-null constraint for another column, and a check constraint for yet another column. In this case, the diagnostics table contains three rows for the single bad row in the violations table. Each of these diagnostic rows identifies a different data-integrity violation that the nonconforming row in the violations table caused.

By joining the violations and diagnostics tables, the DBA or target-table owner can obtain complete diagnostic information about any or all bad rows in the violations table. You can use SELECT statements to perform these joins interactively, or you can write a program to perform them within transactions.

Initial Privileges on the Violations Table

When you issue the START VIOLATIONS TABLE statement to create the violations table, the database server uses the set of privileges granted on the target table as a basis for granting privileges on the violations table. However, the database server follows different rules when it grants each type of privilege.

The following table explains the circumstances under which the database server grants each privilege on the violations table. The first column lists each privilege. The second column explains the conditions under which the database server grants that privilege to a user.

Privilege	Condition for Granting the Privilege
Insert	User has the Insert privilege on the violations table if the user has any of the following privileges on the target table: the Insert privilege, the Delete privilege, or the Update privilege on any column.
Delete	User has the Delete privilege on the violations table if the user has any of the following privileges on the target table: the Insert privilege, the Delete privilege, or the Update privilege on any column.
Select	User has the Select privilege on the **informix_tupleid**, **informix_optype**, and **informix_recowner** columns of the violations table if the user has the Select privilege on any column of the target table.
	User has the Select privilege on any other column of the violations table if the user has the Select privilege on the same column in the target table.
Update	User has the Update privilege on the **informix_tupleid**, **informix_optype**, and **informix_recowner** columns of the violations table if the user has the Update privilege on any column of the target table.
	However, even if the user has the Update privilege on the **informix_tupleid** column, the user cannot update this column because this column is a SERIAL column.
	User has the Update privilege on any other column of the violations table if the user has the Update privilege on the same column in the target table.

(1 of 2)

Privilege	Condition for Granting the Privilege
Index	User has the Index privilege on the violations table if the user has the Index privilege on the target table.
	The user cannot create a globally detached index on the violations table even if the user has the Index privilege on the violations table (EDS).
Alter	Alter privilege is not granted on the violations table. (Users cannot alter violations tables.)
References	References privilege is not granted on the violations table. (Users cannot add referential constraints to violations tables.)

(2 of 2)

The following rules apply to ownership of the violations table and privileges on the violations table:

- When the violations table is created, the owner of the target table becomes the owner of the violations table.

- The owner of the violations table automatically receives all table-level privileges on the violations table, including the Alter and References privileges. However, the database server prevents the owner of the violations table from altering the violations table or adding a referential constraint to the violations table.

- You can use the GRANT and REVOKE statements to modify the initial set of privileges on the violations table.

- When you issue an INSERT, DELETE, or UPDATE statement on a target table that has a filtering-mode unique index or constraint defined on it, you must have the Insert privilege on the violations and diagnostics tables.

  If you do not have the Insert privilege on the violations and diagnostics tables, the database server executes the INSERT, DELETE, or UPDATE statement on the target table provided that you have the necessary privileges on the target table. The database server does not return an error concerning the lack of insert permission on the violations and diagnostics tables unless an integrity violation is detected during the execution of the INSERT, DELETE, or UPDATE statement.

Similarly, when you issue a SET Database Object Mode statement to set a disabled constraint or disabled unique index to the enabled or filtering mode, and a violations table and diagnostics table exist for the target table, you must have the Insert privilege on the violations and diagnostics tables.

If you do not have the Insert privilege on the violations and diagnostics tables, the database server executes the SET Database Object Mode statement provided that you have the necessary privileges on the target table. The database server does not return an error concerning the lack of insert permission on the violations and diagnostics tables unless an integrity violation is detected during the execution of the SET Database Object Mode statement.

- The grantor of the initial set of privileges on the violations table is the same as the grantor of the privileges on the target table. For example, if the user **henry** was granted the Insert privilege on the target table by both the user **jill** and the user **albert**, the Insert privilege on the violations table is granted to user **henry** both by user **jill** and by user **albert**.

- Once a violations table is started for a target table, revoking a privilege on the target table from a user does not automatically revoke the same privilege on the violations table from that user. Instead you must explicitly revoke the privilege on the violations table from the user.

- If you have fragment-level privileges on the target table, you have the corresponding fragment-level privileges on the violations table.

Example of Privileges on the Violations Table

The following example illustrates how the initial set of privileges on a violations table is derived from the current set of privileges on the target table.

For example, assume that you have a table named **cust_subset** that holds customer data. This table consists of the following columns: **ssn** (customer social security number), **fname** (customer first name), **lname** (customer last name), and **city** (city in which the customer lives).

The following set of privileges exists on the **cust_subset** table:

- User **barbara** has the Insert and Index privileges on the table. She also has the Select privilege on the **ssn** and **lname** columns.

- User **carrie** has the Update privilege on the **city** column. She also has the Select privilege on the **ssn** column.

- User **danny** has the Alter privilege on the table.

Now user **alvin** starts a violations table named **cust_subset_viols** and a diagnostics table named **cust_subset_diags** for the **cust_subset** table, as follows:

```
START VIOLATIONS TABLE FOR cust_subset
    USING cust_subset_viols, cust_subset_diags
```

The database server grants the following set of initial privileges on the **cust_subset_viols** violations table:

- User **alvin** is the owner of the violations table, so he has all table-level privileges on the table.

- User **barbara** has the Insert, Delete, and Index privileges on the violations table.

  User **barbara** has the Select privilege on the following columns of the violations table: the **ssn** column, the **lname** column, the **informix_tupleid** column, the **informix_optype** column, and the **informix_recowner** column.

- User **carrie** has the Insert and Delete privileges on the violations table.

  User **carrie** has the Update privilege on the following columns of the violations table: the **city** column, the **informix_tupleid** column, the **informix_optype** column, and the **informix_recowner** column. However, user **carrie** cannot update the **informix_tupleid** column because this column is a SERIAL column.

  User **carrie** has the Select privilege on the following columns of the violations table: the **ssn** column, the **informix_tupleid** column, the **informix_optype** column, and the **informix_recowner** column.

- User **danny** has no privileges on the violations table.

Using the Violations Table

The following rules concern the structure and use of the violations table:

- Every pair of update rows in the violations table has the same value in the **informix_tupleid** column to indicate that both rows refer to the same row in the target table.

- If the target table has columns named **informix_tupleid**, **informix_optype**, or **informix_recowner**, the database server attempts to generate alternative names for these columns in the violations table by appending a digit to the end of the column name (for example, **informix_tupleid1**). If this attempt fails, the database server returns an error, and the violations table is not started for the target table.

- When a table functions as a violations table, it cannot have triggers or constraints defined on it.

- When a table functions as a violations table, users can create indexes on the table, even though the existence of an index affects performance. Unique indexes on the violations table cannot be set to the filtering database object mode.

- If a target table has a violations and diagnostics table associated with it, dropping the target table in cascade mode (the default mode) causes the violations and diagnostics tables to be dropped also. If the target table is dropped in the restricted mode, the existence of the violations and diagnostics tables causes the DROP TABLE statement to fail.

- Once a violations table is started for a target table, you cannot use the ALTER TABLE statement to add, modify, or drop columns in the target table, violations table, or diagnostics table. Before you can alter any of these tables, you must issue a STOP VIOLATIONS TABLE statement for the target table.

- The database server does not clear out the contents of the violations table before or after it uses the violations table during an Insert, Update, Delete, or SET Database Object Mode operation.

- If a target table has a filtering-mode constraint or unique index defined on it and a violations table associated with it, users cannot insert into the target table by selecting from the violations table. Before you insert rows into the target table by selecting from the violations table, you must take one of the following steps:

  ❏ You can set the database object mode of the constraint or unique index to the enabled or disabled database object mode.

  ❏ You can issue a STOP VIOLATIONS TABLE statement for the target table.

  If it is inconvenient to take either of these steps, but you still want to copy records from the violations table into the target table, a third option is to select from the violations table into a temporary table and then insert the contents of the temporary table into the target table.

- If the target table that is specified in the START VIOLATIONS TABLE statement is fragmented, the violations table has the same fragmentation strategy as the target table. Each fragment of the violations table is stored in the same dbspace as the corresponding fragment of the target table.

- Once a violations table is started for a target table, you cannot use the ALTER FRAGMENT statement to alter the fragmentation strategy of the target table or the violations table.

- If the target table specified in the START VIOLATIONS TABLE statement is not fragmented, the database server places the violations table in the same dbspace as the target table.

- If the target table has BYTE or TEXT columns, BYTE or TEXT data in the violations table is created in the same blobspace as the BYTE or TEXT data in the target table.

Example of a Violations Table

To start a violations and diagnostics table for the target table named **customer** in the demonstration database, enter the following statement:

```
START VIOLATIONS TABLE FOR customer
```

Because your START VIOLATIONS statement does not include a USING clause, the violations table is named **customer_vio** by default. The **customer_vio** table includes the following columns:

```
customer_num
fname
lname
company
address1
address2
city
state
zipcode
phone
informix_tupleid
informix_optype
informix_recowner
```

The **customer_vio** table has the same table definition as the **customer** table except that the **customer_vio** table has three additional columns that contain information about the operation that caused the bad row.

IDS

Structure of the Diagnostics Table

When you issue a START VIOLATIONS TABLE statement for a target table, the diagnostics table that the statement creates has a predefined structure. This structure is independent of the structure of the target table.

The following table shows the structure of the diagnostics table.

Column Name	Type	Purpose
informix_tupleid	INTEGER	Implicitly refers to the values in the **informix_tupleid** column in the violations table
		However, this relationship is not declared as a foreign-key to primary-key relationship.
objtype	CHAR(1)	Identifies the type of the violation
		This column can have the following values.
		C = Constraint violation
		I = Unique-index violation

(1 of 2)

Column Name	Type	Purpose
objowner	CHAR(8)	Identifies the owner of the constraint or index for which an integrity violation was detected.
objname	CHAR(18)	Contains the name of the constraint or index for which an integrity violation was detected.

(2 of 2)

Initial Privileges on the Diagnostics Table

When the START VIOLATIONS TABLE statement creates the diagnostics table, the database server uses the set of privileges granted on the target table as a basis for granting privileges on the diagnostics table. However, the database server follows different rules when it grants each type of privilege.

The following table explains the circumstances under which the database server grants each privilege on the diagnostics table. The first column lists each privilege. The second column explains the conditions under which the database server grants that privilege to a user.

Privilege	Condition for Granting the Privilege
Insert	User has the Insert privilege on the diagnostics table if the user has any of the following privileges on the target table: the Insert privilege, the Delete privilege, or the Update privilege on any column
Delete	User has the Delete privilege on the diagnostics table if the user has any of the following privileges on the target table: the Insert privilege, the Delete privilege, or the Update privilege on any column
Select	User has the Select privilege on the diagnostics table if the user has the Select privilege on any column in the target table
Update	User has the Update privilege on the diagnostics table if the user has the Update privilege on any column in the target table

(1 of 2)

Privilege	Condition for Granting the Privilege
Index	User has the Index privilege on the diagnostics table if the user has the Index privilege on the target table
Alter	Alter privilege is not granted on the diagnostics table (Users cannot alter diagnostics tables.)
References	References privilege is not granted on the diagnostics table (Users cannot add referential constraints to diagnostics tables.)

(2 of 2)

The following rules concern privileges on the diagnostics table:

- When the diagnostics table is created, the owner of the target table becomes the owner of the diagnostics table.

- The owner of the diagnostics table automatically receives all table-level privileges on the diagnostics table, including the Alter and References privileges. However, the database server prevents the owner of the diagnostics table from altering the diagnostics table or adding a referential constraint to the diagnostics table.

- You can use the GRANT and REVOKE statements to modify the initial set of privileges on the diagnostics table.

- When you issue an INSERT, DELETE, or UPDATE statement on a target table that has a filtering-mode unique index or constraint defined on it, you must have the Insert privilege on the violations and diagnostics tables.

  If you do not have the Insert privilege on the violations and diagnostics tables, the database server executes the INSERT, DELETE, or UPDATE statement on the target table provided that you have the necessary privileges on the target table. The database server does not return error concerning the lack of insert permission on the violations and diagnostics tables unless an integrity violation is detected during the execution of the INSERT, DELETE, or UPDATE statement.

Similarly, when you issue a SET Database Object Mode statement to set a disabled constraint or disabled unique index to the enabled or filtering mode, and a violations table and diagnostics table exist for the target table, you must have the Insert privilege on the violations and diagnostics tables.

If you do not have the Insert privilege on the violations and diagnostics tables, the database server executes the SET Database Object Mode statement provided that you have the necessary privileges on the target table. The database server does not return an error concerning the lack of insert permission on the violations and diagnostics tables unless an integrity violation is detected during the execution of the SET Database Object MODE statement.

- The grantor of the initial set of privileges on the diagnostics table is the same as the grantor of the privileges on the target table. For example, if the user **jenny** was granted the Insert privilege on the target table by both the user **wayne** and the user **laurie**, both user **wayne** and user **laurie** grant the Insert privilege on the diagnostics table to user **jenny**.

- Once a diagnostics table is started for a target table, revoking a privilege on the target table from a user does not automatically revoke the same privilege on the diagnostics table from that user. Instead you must explicitly revoke the privilege on the diagnostics table from the user.

- If you have fragment-level privileges on the target table, you have the corresponding table-level privileges on the diagnostics table.

Example of Privileges on the Diagnostics Table

The following example illustrates how the initial set of privileges on a diagnostics table is derived from the current set of privileges on the target table.

For example, assume that you have a table called **cust_subset** that **holds customer data.** This table consists of the following columns: **ssn** (social security number), **fname** (first name), **lname** (last name), and **city** (city in which the customer lives).

The following set of privileges exists on the **cust_subset** table:

- User **alvin** is the owner of the table.
- User **barbara** has the Insert and Index privileges on the table. She also has the Select privilege on the **ssn** and **lname** columns.
- User **carrie** has the Update privilege on the **city** column. She also has the Select privilege on the **ssn** column.
- User **danny** has the Alter privilege on the table.

Now user **alvin** starts a violations table named **cust_subset_viols** and a diagnostics table named **cust_subset_diags** for the **cust_subset** table, as follows:

```
START VIOLATIONS TABLE FOR cust_subset
    USING cust_subset_viols, cust_subset_diags
```

The database server grants the following set of initial privileges on the **cust_subset_diags** diagnostics table:

- User **alvin** is the owner of the diagnostics table, so he has all table-level privileges on the table.
- User **barbara** has the Insert, Delete, Select, and Index privileges on the diagnostics table.
- User **carrie** has the Insert, Delete, Select, and Update privileges on the diagnostics table.
- User **danny** has no privileges on the diagnostics table.

Using the Diagnostics Table

For information on the relationship between the diagnostics table and the violations table, see "Relationship Between the Violations and Diagnostics Tables" on page 2-786.

The following issues concern the structure and use of the diagnostics table:

- The MAX ROWS clause of the START VIOLATIONS TABLE statement sets a limit on the number of rows that can be inserted into the diagnostics table when you execute a single statement, such as an INSERT or SET Database Object Mode statement, on the target table.
- The MAX ROWS clause limits the number of rows only for operations in which the table functions as a diagnostics table.

- When a table functions as a diagnostics table, it cannot have triggers or constraints defined on it.

- When a table functions as a diagnostics table, users can create indexes on the table, even though the existence of an index affects performance. You cannot set unique indexes on the diagnostics table to the filtering database object mode.

- If a target table has a violations and diagnostics table associated with it, dropping the target table in the cascade mode (the default mode) causes the violations and diagnostics tables to be dropped also. If the target table is dropped in the restricted mode, the existence of the violations and diagnostics tables causes the DROP TABLE statement to fail.

- Once a violations table is started for a target table, you cannot use the ALTER TABLE statement to add, modify, or drop columns in the target table, violations table, or diagnostics table. Before you can alter any of these tables, you must issue a STOP TABLE VIOLATIONS statement for the target table.

- The database server does not clear out the contents of the diagnostics table before or after it uses the diagnostics table during an Insert, Update, Delete, or Set operation.

- If the target table that is specified in the START VIOLATIONS TABLE statement is fragmented, the diagnostics table is fragmented with a round-robin strategy over the same dbspaces in which the target table is fragmented.

Example of a Diagnostics Table

To start a violations and diagnostics table for the target table named **stock** in the demonstration database, enter the following statement:

```
START VIOLATIONS TABLE FOR stock
```

Because your START VIOLATIONS TABLE statement does not include a USING clause, the diagnostics table is named **stock_dia** by default. The **stock_dia** table includes the following columns:

```
informix_tupleid
objtype
objowner
objname
```

This list of columns shows an important difference between the diagnostics table and violations table for a target table. Whereas the violations table has a matching column for every column in the target table, the columns of the diagnostics table do not match any columns in the target table. The diagnostics table created by any START VIOLATIONS TABLE statement always has the same columns with the same column names and data types.

Related Information

Related statements: SET DATABASE OBJECT MODE and STOP VIOLATIONS TABLE

For a discussion of object modes and violation detection, see the *Informix Guide to SQL: Tutorial*.

STOP VIOLATIONS TABLE

Use the STOP VIOLATIONS TABLE statement to drop the association between a target table and the special violations and diagnostics tables.

EDS

In Enterprise Decision Server, the diagnostics table does not exist. The STOP VIOLATIONS TABLE statement drops the association between the target table and the violations table. ♦

Syntax

```
STOP VIOLATIONS TABLE FOR ──────────── table ──────────────┤
```

Element	Purpose	Restrictions	Syntax
table	Name of the target table whose association with the violations and diagnostics table is to be dropped	The target table must have a violations and diagnostics table associated with it before you can execute the statement.	Database Object Name, p. 4-50
	No default value exists.	The target table must be a local table.	

Usage

The STOP VIOLATIONS TABLE statement drops the association between the target table and the violations and diagnostics tables. After you issue this statement, the former violations and diagnostics tables continue to exist, but they no longer function as violations and diagnostics tables for the target table. They now have the status of regular database tables instead of violations and diagnostics tables for the target table. You must issue the DROP TABLE statement to drop these two tables explicitly.

When Insert, Delete, and Update operations cause data-integrity violations for rows of the target table, the nonconforming rows are no longer filtered to the former violations table, and diagnostics information about the data-integrity violations is not placed in the former diagnostics table.

Example of Stopping a Violations and Diagnostics Table

Assume that a target table named **cust_subset** has an associated violations table named **cust_subset_vio** and an associated diagnostics table named **cust_subset_dia**. To drop the association between the target table and the violations and diagnostics tables, enter the following statement:

```
STOP VIOLATIONS TABLE FOR cust_subset
```

Example of Dropping a Violations and Diagnostics Table

After you execute the STOP VIOLATIONS TABLE statement in the preceding example, the **cust_subset_vio** and **cust_subset_dia** tables continue to exist, but they are no longer associated with the **cust_subset** table. Instead they now have the status of regular database tables. To drop these two tables, enter the following statements:

```
DROP TABLE cust_subset_vio;
DROP TABLE cust_subset_dia;
```

Privileges Required for Stopping a Violations Table

To stop a violations and diagnostics table for a target table, you must meet one of the following requirements:

- You must have the DBA privilege on the database.
- You must be the owner of the target table and have the Resource privilege on the database.
- You must have the Alter privilege on the target table and the Resource privilege on the database.

Related Information

Related statements: SET DATABASE OBJECT MODE and START VIOLATIONS TABLE

For a discussion of database object modes and violation detection, see the *Informix Guide to SQL: Tutorial*.

TRUNCATE

Use the TRUNCATE statement to quickly remove all rows from a table and also remove all corresponding index data.

Syntax

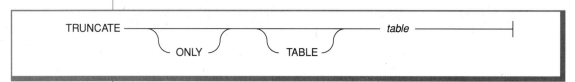

Element	Purpose	Restrictions	Syntax
table	Name of the table from which to remove all data	The table must exist.	Database Object Name, p. 4-50

Usage

You must be the owner of the table or have the DBA privilege to use this statement.

The TRUNCATE statement does not automatically reset the serial value of a column. To reset the serial value of a column, you must do so explicitly, either before or after you run the TRUNCATE statement.

Restrictions

The statement will not succeed if any of the following conditions exist:

- One or more cursors are open on the table
- Referential constraints exist on the table and any of the referencing tables has at least one row
- A shared or exclusive lock on the table already exists

- The statement references one of the following types of tables:
  - ❑ external
  - ❑ system catalog
  - ❑ violations
- It is issued inside a transaction

Using the ONLY and TABLE Keywords

The ONLY and TABLE keywords do not affect the performance of this statement.

The ONLY keyword is compatible with the future implementation of this statement in Dynamic Server. It has no significance in Enterprise Decision Server.

The TABLE keyword provides descriptive coding.

Example

The following statement deletes all rows and related index data from the **cust** table:

```
TRUNCATE TABLE cust
```

After the Statement Executes

Information about the success of this statement appears in the logical-log files. For more information about logical-log files, see your *Administrator's Guide*.

Because the TRUNCATE statement does not alter the schema, the database server does not automatically update statistics. After you use this statement, you might want to issue an UPDATE STATISTICS statement.

If the table was fragmented, after the statement executes, each fragment has a space allocated for it that is the same size as that of the first extent size. The fragment size of any indexes also correspond to the size of the first extents.

When You Might Use This Statement

This statement performs similar operations to those that you can perform with the DELETE statement or a combination of DROP TABLE and CREATE TABLE.

Using this statement can be faster than removing all rows from a table with the DELETE statement because it does not activate any DELETE triggers. In addition, when you use this statement, the database server creates a log entry for the entire TRUNCATE statement rather than for each deleted row.

You might also use this statement instead of dropping a table and then recreating it. When you drop and recreate a table, you have to regrant privileges on the table. In addition, you must recreate any indexes, constraints, and triggers defined on the table. The TRUNCATE statement leaves these database objects and privileges intact.

Related Information

Related Statements: DELETE, DROP TABLE

For more information about the performance implications of this statement, see your *Performance Guide*.

UNLOAD

Use the UNLOAD statement to write the rows retrieved in a SELECT statement to an operating-system file.

Use this statement with DB-Access and SQL Editor.

Syntax

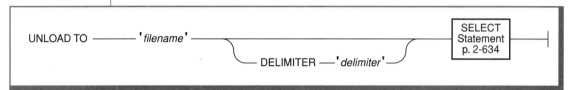

Element	Purpose	Restrictions	Syntax
delimiter	Quoted string that identifies the character to use as the delimiter in the output file If you do not specify a delimiter, the database server uses the setting in the **DBDELIMITER** environment variable. If **DBDELIMITER** has not been set, the default delimiter is the pipe (I).	You cannot use the following items as the delimiter: backslash (\), newline character (=CTRL-J), hexadecimal numbers (0 to 9, a to f, A to F).	Quoted String, p. 4-260
filename	Quoted string that specifies the pathname and filename of an operating-system file The output file receives the selected rows from the table during the unload operation. The default pathname for the output file is the current directory.	See "UNLOAD TO File" on p. 2-806.	The pathname and filename must conform to the naming conventions of your operating system.

Usage

To use the UNLOAD statement, you must have the Select privilege on all columns selected in the SELECT statement. For information on database-level and table-level privileges, see "GRANT" on page 2-500.

The SELECT statement can consist of a literal SELECT statement or the name of a character variable that contains a SELECT statement. (See "SELECT" on page 2-634.)

UNLOAD TO File

The UNLOAD TO file contains the selected rows retrieved from the table. You can use the UNLOAD TO file as the LOAD FROM file in a LOAD statement.

The following table shows types of data and their output format in the UNLOAD TO file (when the locale is the default locale, U.S. English).

Data Type	Output Format
boolean	BOOLEAN data is represented as a 't' for a TRUE value and an 'f' for a FALSE value.
character	If a character field contains the delimiter, Informix products automatically escape it with a backslash (\) to prevent interpretation as a special character. (If you use a LOAD statement to insert the rows into a table, backslashes are automatically stripped.) Trailing blanks are automatically clipped.
collections	A collection is unloaded with its values surrounded by braces ({}) and a field delimiter separating each element. For more information, see "Unloading Complex Types" on page 2-811.
date	DATE values are represented as *mm*/*dd*/*yyyy*, where *mm* is the month (January = 1, and so on), *dd* is the day, and *yyyy* is the year. If you have set the **GL_DATE** or **DBDATE** environment variable, the UNLOAD statement uses the specified date format for DATE values.

(1 of 3)

Data Type	Output Format
MONEY	MONEY values are unloaded with no leading currency symbol. They use the comma (,) as the thousands separator and the period (.) as the decimal separator. If you have set the **DBMONEY** environment variable, the UNLOAD statement uses the specified currency format for MONEY values.
NULL	NULL columns are unloaded by placing no characters between the delimiters.
number	Number data types are displayed with no leading blanks. INTEGER or SMALLINT zero are represented as 0, and FLOAT, SMALLFLOAT, DECIMAL, or MONEY zero are represented as 0.00.
row types (named and unnamed)	A row type is unloaded with its values surrounded by parentheses and a field delimiter separating each element. For more information, see "Unloading Complex Types" on page 2-811.
simple large objects (TEXT, BYTE)	TEXT and BYTE columns are unloaded directly into the UNLOAD TO file. For more information, see "Unloading Simple Large Objects" on page 2-809.
smart large objects (CLOB, BLOB)	CLOB and BLOB columns are unloaded into a separate operating-system file on the client computer. The field for the CLOB or BLOB column in the UNLOAD TO file contains the name of this separate file. For more information, see "Unloading Smart Large Objects" on page 2-809.
time	DATETIME and INTERVAL values are represented in character form, showing only their field digits and delimiters. No type specification or qualifiers are included in the output. The following pattern is used: *yyyy-mm-dd hh:mi:ss.fff*, omitting fields that are not part of the data. If you have set the **GL_DATETIME** or **DBTIME** environment variable, the UNLOAD statement uses the specified format for DATETIME values.

(2 of 3)

Data Type	Output Format
user-defined data formats (opaque types)	The associated opaque type must have an export support function defined if special processing is required to copy the data in the internal format of the opaque type to the format in the UNLOAD TO file. An export binary support function might also be required if the data is in binary format. The data in the UNLOAD TO file would correspond to the format that the export or exportbinary support function returns.

(3 of 3)

For more information on **DB** environment variables, refer to the *Informix Guide to SQL: Reference*. For more information on **GL** environment variables, refer to the *Informix Guide to GLS Functionality*.

GLS

If you are using a nondefault locale, the formats of DATE, DATETIME, MONEY, and numeric column values in the UNLOAD TO file are determined by the formats that the locale supports for these data types. For more information, see the *Informix Guide to GLS Functionality*. ♦

The following statement unloads rows from the **customer** table where the value of **customer_num** is greater than or equal to 138, and puts them in a filenamed **cust_file**:

```
UNLOAD TO 'cust_file' DELIMITER '!'
    SELECT * FROM customer WHERE customer_num> = 138
```

The output file, **cust_file**, appears as shown in the following example:

```
138!Jeffery!Padgett!Wheel Thrills!3450 El Camino!Suite
10!Palo Alto!CA!94306!!
139!Linda!Lane!Palo Alto Bicycles!2344 University!!Palo
Alto!CA!94301!(415)323-5400
```

Unloading VARCHAR Columns

If you are unloading files that contain VARCHAR columns, note the following information:

- Trailing blanks are retained in VARCHAR fields.
- Do not use the following characters as delimiters in the UNLOAD TO file: 0 to 9, a to f, A to F, newline character, or backslash.

Unloading Simple Large Objects

The database server unloads simple large objects (BYTE and TEXT columns) directly into the UNLOAD TO file. BYTE data are written in hexadecimal dump format with no added spaces or new lines. Consequently, the logical length of an UNLOAD TO file that contains BYTE items can be very long and very difficult to print or edit.

If you are unloading files that contain simple-large-object data types, do not use the following characters as delimiters in the UNLOAD TO file: 0 to 9, a to f, A to F, newline character, or backslash.

GLS

For TEXT columns, the database server handles any required code-set conversions for the data. For more information, see the *Informix Guide to GLS Functionality*. ♦

If you are unloading files that contain simple-large-object data types, objects smaller than 10 kilobytes are stored temporarily in memory. You can adjust the 10-kilobyte setting to a larger setting with the **DBBLOBBUF** environment variable. Simple large objects that are larger than the default or the setting of the **DBBLOBBUF** environment variable are stored in a temporary file. For additional information about the **DBBLOBBUF** environment variable, see the *Informix Guide to SQL: Reference*.

IDS

Unloading Smart Large Objects

The database server unloads smart large objects (BLOB and CLOB columns) into a separate operating-system file on the client computer. It creates this file in the same directory as the UNLOAD TO file. The filename of this file has one of the following formats:

- For a BLOB value:
    blob########
- For a CLOB value:
    clob########

In the preceding formats, the pound (#) symbols represent the digits of the unique hexadecimal smart-large-object identifier. The database server uses the hexadecimal ID for the first smart large object in the file. The maximum number of digits for a smart-large-object identifier is 17. However, most smart large objects would have an identifier with significantly fewer digits.

When the database server unloads the first smart large object, it creates the appropriate BLOB or CLOB client file with the hexadecimal identifier of the smart large object. It appends any additional BLOB or CLOB values to the appropriate file until the file size reaches a limit of 2 gigabytes. If additional smart-large-object values are present, the database server creates another BLOB or CLOB client file whose filename contains the hexadecimal identifier of the next smart large object to unload.

Each BLOB or CLOB value is appended to the appropriate file. The database server might create several files if the values are extremely large or there are many values.

In an UNLOAD TO file, a BLOB or CLOB column value appears as follows:

```
start_off,length,client_path
```

In this format, start_off is the starting offset (in hexadecimal) of the smart-large-object value within the client file, *length* is the length (in hexadecimal) of the BLOB or CLOB value, and *client_path* is the pathname for the client file. No spaces can appear between these values.

For example, if a CLOB value is 512 bytes long and is at offset 256 in the **/usr/apps/clob9ce7.318** file, the CLOB value appears as follows in the UNLOAD TO file:

```
|100,200,/usr/apps/clob9ce7.318|
```

If a BLOB or CLOB column value occupies an entire client file, the CLOB or BLOB column value appears as follows in the UNLOAD TO file:

```
client_path
```

For example, if a CLOB value occupies the entire file **/usr/apps/clob9ce7.318**, the CLOB value appears as follows in the UNLOAD TO file:

```
|/usr/apps/clob9ce7.318|
```

GLS

For CLOB columns, the database server handles any required code-set conversions for the data. For more information, see the *Informix Guide to GLS Functionality.* ♦

IDS

Unloading Complex Types

In an UNLOAD TO file, complex types appear as follows:

- Collections are introduced with the appropriate constructor (SET, MULTISET, LIST), and have their elements enclosed in braces ({}) and separated with a comma, as follows:

    ```
    constructor{val1 , val2 , ... }
    ```

    For example, to unload the SET values {1, 3, 4} from a column of the SET (INTEGER NOT NULL) data type, the corresponding field of the UNLOAD TO file appears as follows:

    ```
    |SET{1 , 3 , 4}|
    ```

- Row types (named and unnamed) are introduced with the ROW constructor and have their fields enclosed with parentheses and separated with a comma, as follows:

    ```
    ROW(val1 , val2 ,... )
    ```

    For example, to unload the ROW values (1, 'abc'), the corresponding field of the UNLOAD TO file appears as follows:

    ```
    |ROW(1 , abc)|
    ```

DELIMITER Clause

Use the DELIMITER clause to identify the delimiter that separates the data contained in each column in a row in the output file. If you omit this clause, DB-Access checks the **DBDELIMITER** environment variable. If **DBDELIMITER** has not been set, the default delimiter is the pipe (|).

You can specify the TAB (CTRL-I) or <blank> (ASCII 32) as the delimiter symbol. You cannot use the following as the delimiter symbol:

- Backslash (\)
- Newline character (CTRL-J)
- Hexadecimal numbers (0 to 9, a to f, A to F)

Do not use the backslash (\) as a field separator or UNLOAD delimiter. It serves as an escape character to inform the UNLOAD statement that the next character is to be interpreted as part of the data.

The following statement specifies the semicolon (;) as the delimiter:

```
UNLOAD TO 'cust.out' DELIMITER ';'
    SELECT fname, lname, company, city
        FROM customer
```

Related Information

Related statements: LOAD and SELECT

For information about setting the **DBDELIMITER** environment variable, see the *Informix Guide to SQL: Reference*.

For a discussion of the GLS aspects of the UNLOAD statement, see the *Informix Guide to GLS Functionality*.

For a task-oriented discussion of the UNLOAD statement and other utilities for moving data, see the *Informix Migration Guide*.

UNLOCK TABLE

Use the UNLOCK TABLE statement in a database without transactions to unlock a table that you previously locked with the LOCK TABLE statement. The UNLOCK TABLE statement fails in a database that uses transactions.

Syntax

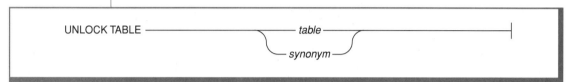

Element	Purpose	Restrictions	Syntax
synonym	Name of the synonym for the table you want to unlock	The synonym and the table to which the synonym points must exist.	Database Object Name, p. 4-50
table	Name of the table that you want to unlock	The table must be in a database without transactions.	Database Object Name, p. 4-50
		The table must be one that you previously locked with the LOCK TABLE statement. You cannot unlock a table that another process locked.	

Usage

You can lock a table if you own the table or if you have the Select privilege on the table, either from a direct grant to yourself or from a grant to **public**. You can only unlock a table that you locked. You cannot unlock a table that another process locked. Only one lock can apply to a table at a time.

The table name either is the name of the table you are unlocking or a synonym for the table. Do not specify a view or a synonym of a view.

To change the lock mode of a table in a database without transactions, use the UNLOCK TABLE statement to unlock the table, then issue a new LOCK TABLE statement. The following example shows how to change the lock mode of a table in a database that was created without transactions:

```
LOCK TABLE items IN EXCLUSIVE MODE
    .
    .
    .
UNLOCK TABLE items
    .
    .
    .
LOCK TABLE items IN SHARE MODE
```

The UNLOCK TABLE statement fails if it is issued within a transaction. Table locks set within a transaction are released automatically when the transaction completes.

ANSI

If you are using an ANSI-compliant database, do not issue an UNLOCK TABLE statement. The UNLOCK TABLE statement fails if it is issued within a transaction, and a transaction is always in effect in an ANSI-compliant database. ♦

Related Information

Related statements: BEGIN WORK, COMMIT WORK, LOCK TABLE, and ROLLBACK WORK

For a discussion of concurrency and locks, see the *Informix Guide to SQL: Tutorial*.

UPDATE

Use the UPDATE statement to change the values in one or more columns of one or more rows in a table or view.

IDS

With Dynamic Server, you can also use this statement to change the values in one or more elements in an ESQL/C collection variable. ♦

Syntax

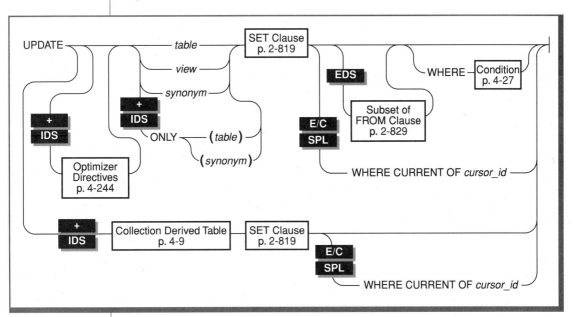

Element	Purpose	Restrictions	Syntax
cursor_id	Name of the cursor to use The current row of the active set for this cursor is updated when the UPDATE statement is executed.	You cannot update a row with a cursor if that row includes aggregates. The specified cursor (as defined in the SELECT...FOR UPDATE portion of a DECLARE statement) can contain only column names.	Identifier, p. 4-205

(1 of 2)

Element	Purpose	Restrictions	Syntax
synonym	Name of the synonym that contains the rows to update	The synonym and the table to which the synonym points must exist.	Database Object Name, p. 4-50
table	Name of the table that contains the rows to update	The table must exist.	Database Object Name, p. 4-50
view	Name of the view that contains the rows to update	The view must exist.	Database Object Name, p. 4-50

(2 of 2)

Usage

Use the UPDATE statement to update any of the following types of objects:

- A row in a table: a single row, a group of rows, or all rows in a table
- An element in a collection variable
- An ESQL/C **row** variable: a field or all fields

IDS

For information on how to update elements of a collection variable, see "Collection Derived Table" on page 4-9. The other sections of this UPDATE statement describe how to update a row in a table. ♦

To update data in a table, you must either own the table or have the Update privilege for the table (see "GRANT" on page 2-500). To update data in a view, you must have the Update privilege, and the view must meet the requirements that are explained in "Updating Rows Through a View" on page 2-817.

If you omit the WHERE clause, all rows of the target table are updated.

If you are using effective checking, and the checking mode is set to IMMEDIATE, all specified constraints are checked at the end of each UPDATE statement. If the checking mode is set to DEFERRED, all specified constraints are *not* checked until the transaction is committed.

EDS

In Enterprise Decision Server, if the UPDATE statement is constructed in such a way that a single row might be updated more than once, the database server returns an error. However, if the new value is the same in every update, the database server allows the update operation to take place without reporting an error. ♦

DB

If you omit the WHERE clause and are in interactive mode, DB-Access does not run the UPDATE statement until you confirm that you want to change all rows. However, if the statement is in a command file, and you are running from the command line, the statement executes immediately. ♦

IDS

Using the ONLY Keyword

If you use the UPDATE statement to update rows of a supertable, rows from both the supertable and its subtables can be updated. To update rows from the supertable only, you must use the ONLY keyword prior to the table name, as the following example shows:

```
UPDATE ONLY(am_studies_super)
WHERE advisor = "johnson"
SET advisor = "camarillo"
```

Warning: *If you use the UPDATE statement on a supertable without the ONLY keyword and without a WHERE clause, all rows of the supertable and its subtables are updated.*

You cannot use the ONLY keyword if you plan to use the WHERE CURRENT OF clause to update the current row of the active set of a cursor.

Updating Rows Through a View

You can update data through a *single-table* view if you have the Update privilege on the view (see "GRANT" on page 2-500). However, certain restrictions exist. For a view to be updatable, the SELECT statement that defines the view must not contain any of the following items:

- Columns in the select list that are aggregate values
- Columns in the select list that use the UNIQUE or DISTINCT keyword
- A GROUP BY clause
- A UNION operator

In addition, if a view is built on a table that has a derived value for a column, that column is not updatable through the view. However, other columns in the view can be updated.

In an updatable view, you can update the values in the underlying table by inserting values into the view.

You can use data-integrity constraints to prevent users from updating values in the underlying table when the update values do not fit the SELECT statement that defined the view. For more information, see "WITH CHECK OPTION Keywords" on page 2-338.

Because duplicate rows can occur in a view even though the underlying table has unique rows, be careful when you update a table through a view. For example, if a view is defined on the **items** table and contains only the **order_num** and **total_price** columns, and if two items from the same order have the same total price, the view contains duplicate rows. In this case, if you update one of the two duplicate total price values, you have no way to know which item price is updated.

Important: *If you are using a view with a check option, you cannot update rows to a remote table.*

Updating Rows in a Database Without Transactions

If you are updating rows in a database without transactions, you must take explicit action to restore updated rows. For example, if the UPDATE statement fails after updating some rows, the successfully updated rows remain in the table. You cannot automatically recover from a failed update.

Updating Rows in a Database with Transactions

If you are updating rows in a database with transactions, and you are using transactions, you can undo the update using the ROLLBACK WORK statement. If you do not execute a BEGIN WORK statement before the update, and the update fails, the database server automatically rolls back any database modifications made since the beginning of the update.

You can create temporary tables with the WITH NO LOG option. These tables are never logged and are not recoverable.

EDS

In Enterprise Decision Server, tables that you create with the RAW table type are never logged. Thus, RAW tables are not recoverable, even if the database uses logging. For information about RAW tables, refer to the *Informix Guide to SQL: Reference.* ◆

ANSI

If you are updating rows in an ANSI-compliant database, transactions are implicit, and all database modifications take place within a transaction. In this case, if an UPDATE statement fails, you can use the ROLLBACK WORK statement to undo the update.

If you are within an explicit transaction, and the update fails, the database server automatically undoes the effects of the update. ♦

Locking Considerations

When a row is selected with the intent to update, the update process acquires an update lock. Update locks permit other processes to read, or *share*, a row that is about to be updated but do not let those processes update or delete it. Just before the update occurs, the update process *promotes* the shared lock to an exclusive lock. An exclusive lock prevents other processes from reading or modifying the contents of the row until the lock is released.

An update process can acquire an update lock on a row or a page that has a shared lock from another process, but you cannot promote the update lock from shared to exclusive (and the update cannot occur) until the other process releases its lock.

If the number of rows affected by a single update is very large, you can exceed the limits placed on the maximum number of simultaneous locks. If this occurs, you can reduce the number of transactions per UPDATE statement, or you can lock the page or the entire table before you execute the statement.

SET Clause

Use the SET clause to identify the columns to update and assign values to each column. The clause supports the following formats:

- A single-column format, which pairs a single column to a single expression
- A multiple-column format, which lists multiple columns and sets them equal to corresponding expressions

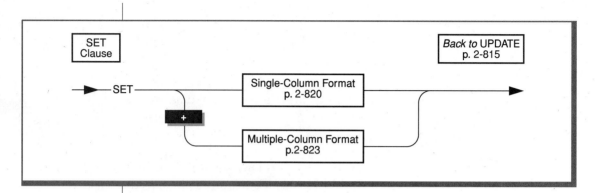

Single-Column Format

Use the single-column format of the SET clause to pair a single column to a single expression.

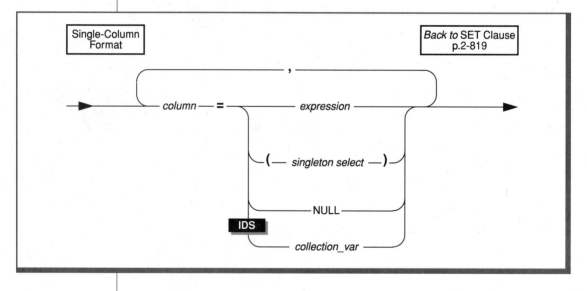

Element	Purpose	Restrictions	Syntax
column	Name of the column that you want to update	You cannot update SERIAL or SERIAL8 columns.	Identifier, p. 4-205
		You can use this syntax to update a row column.	
		An expression list can include an SQL subquery that returns a single row of multiple values as long as the number of columns named in the column list equals the number of values that the expressions in the expression list produce.	
collection_var	Name of the host or program collection variable	The collection variable must exist.	Name must conform to language-specific rules for variable names.
expression	Expression that evaluates to a value	The expression cannot contain aggregate functions.	Expression, p. 4-73
singleton select	Subquery that returns exactly one row	The values that the subquery returns must correspond to the columns named in the column list.	SELECT, p. 2-634

You can include any number of single-columns to single-expressions in the UPDATE statement. For information on how to specify values of a row type column in a SET clause, see "Updating Row-Type Columns" on page 2-826.

The following examples illustrate the single-column format of the SET clause.

```
UPDATE customer
    SET address1 = '1111 Alder Court',
        city = 'Palo Alto',
        zipcode = '94301'
    WHERE customer_num = 103;

UPDATE stock
    SET unit_price = unit_price * 1.07;
```

Using a Subquery to Update a Column

You can update a column with the value that a subquery returns.

```
UPDATE orders
    SET ship_charge =
        (SELECT SUM(total_price) * .07
            FROM items
            WHERE orders.order_num = items.order_num)
        WHERE orders.order_num = 1001
```

IDS

If you are updating a supertable in a table hierarchy, the SET clause cannot include a subquery that references a subtable.

If you are updating a subtable in a table hierarchy, a subquery in the SET clause can reference the supertable if it references only the supertable. That is, the subquery must use the SELECT…FROM ONLY (*supertable*)…syntax. ♦

Updating a Column to NULL

You can use the NULL keyword to modify a column value when you use the UPDATE statement. For example, for a customer whose previous address required two address lines but now requires only one, you would use the following entry:

```
UPDATE customer
    SET address1 = '123 New Street',
    SET address2 = null,
    city = 'Palo Alto',
    zipcode = '94303'
    WHERE customer_num = 134
```

Updating the Same Column Twice

You can specify the same column more than once in the SET clause. If you do so, the column is set to the last value that you specified for the column. In the following example, the user specifies the **fname** column twice in the SET clause. For the row where the customer number is 101, the user sets **fname** first to gary and then to harry. After the UPDATE statement executes, the value of **fname** is harry.

```
UPDATE customer
    SET fname = "gary", fname = "harry"
        WHERE customer_num = 101
```

Multiple-Column Format

Use the multiple-column format of the SET clause to list multiple columns and set them equal to corresponding expressions.

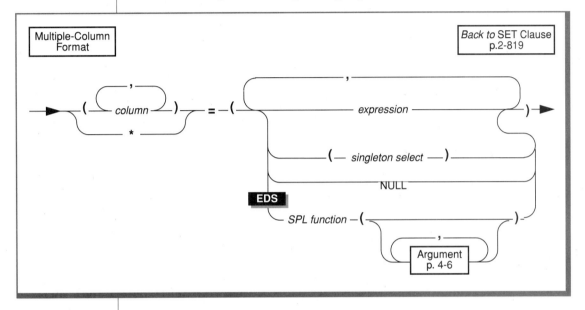

Element	Purpose	Restrictions	Syntax
*	Character that indicates all columns in the specified table or view are to be updated	The restrictions that apply to the multiple columns equal to multiple expressions format discussed under *column* also apply to the asterisk (*).	The asterisk (*) is a literal value with a special meaning in this statement.
column	Name of the column that you want to update	You cannot update SERIAL or SERIAL8 columns.	Identifier, p. 4-205
		You cannot use this syntax to update a row column.	
		The number of columns in the column list must be equal to the number of values supplied through expressions, subqueries and so on.	

(1 of 2)

Element	Purpose	Restrictions	Syntax
expression	Expression that evaluates to a value	The expression cannot contain aggregate functions.	Expression, p. 4-73
singleton select	Subquery that returns exactly one row	The values that the subquery returns must correspond to the columns named in the column list	SELECT, p. 2-634
SPL function	Name of an SPL routine that returns one or more values.	The values that the function returns must have a one-to-one correspondence to the columns named in the column list.	Identifier, p. 4-205

The multiple-column format of the SET clause offers the following options for listing a series of columns you intend to update:

- Explicitly list each column, placing commas between columns and enclosing the set of columns in parentheses.
- Implicitly list all columns in the table by using an asterisk (*).

You must list each expression explicitly, placing commas between expressions and enclosing the set of expressions in parentheses. The number of columns in the column list must be equal to the number of expressions in the expression list, unless the expression list includes an SQL subquery.

The following examples show the multiple-column format of the SET clause:

```
UPDATE customer
    SET (fname, lname) = ('John', 'Doe')
    WHERE customer_num = 101


UPDATE manufact
    SET * = ('HNT', 'Hunter')
    WHERE manu_code = 'ANZ'
```

Using a Subquery to Update Column Values

An expression list can include an SQL subquery that returns a single row of multiple values as long as the number of columns named, explicitly or implicitly, equals the number of values produced by the expression or expressions that follow the equal sign.

The following examples show the use of subqueries:

```
UPDATE items
    SET (stock_num, manu_code, quantity) =
        ( (SELECT stock_num, manu_code FROM stock
            WHERE description = 'baseball'), 2)
    WHERE item_num = 1 AND order_num = 1001


UPDATE table1
    SET (col1, col2, col3) =
        ((SELECT MIN (ship_charge),
            MAX (ship_charge) FROM orders),
            '07/01/1997')
    WHERE col4 = 1001
```

IDS

If you are updating the supertable in a table hierarchy, the SET clause cannot include a subquery that references one of its subtables.

If you are updating a subtable in a table hierarchy, a subquery in the SET clause can reference the supertable if it references only the supertable. That is, the subquery must use the SELECT...FROM ONLY (*supertable*)... syntax. ♦

EDS

Using an SPL Function to Update Column Values

When you use an SPL function to update column values, the return values of the function must have a one-to-one correspondence with the listed columns. That is, each value that the SPL function returns must be of the data type expected by the corresponding column in the column list.

If the called SPL routine contains certain SQL statements, the database server returns an error. For information on which SQL statements cannot be used in an SPL routine that is called within a data manipulation statement, see "Restrictions on an SPL Routine Called in a Data Manipulation Statement" on page 4-302.

In the following example, the SPL function **p2()** updates the **i2** and **c2** columns of the **t2** table.

```
CREATE PROCEDURE p2()
RETURNING int, char(20);
RETURN 3, 'three';
END PROCEDURE;

UPDATE t2 SET (i2, c2) = (p2())
WHERE i2 = 2;
```

In Enterprise Decision Server, you create an SPL function with the CREATE PROCEDURE statement. The CREATE FUNCTION statement is not available.

IDS

Updating Row-Type Columns

You use the SET clause to update a named row-type or unnamed row-type column. For example, suppose you define the following named row type and a table that contains columns of both named and unnamed row types:

```
CREATE ROW TYPE address_t
(
    street CHAR(20),
    city CHAR(15),
    state CHAR(2)
);

CREATE TABLE empinfo
(
    emp_id INT
    name ROW ( fname CHAR(20), lname CHAR(20)),
    address address_t
);
```

To update an unnamed row type, specify the ROW constructor before the parenthesized list of field values. The following statement updates the **name** column (an unnamed row type) of the **empinfo** table:

```
UPDATE empinfo
SET name = ROW('John','Williams')
WHERE emp_id =455
```

To update a named row type, specify the ROW constructor before the parenthesized list of field values and use the cast operator (::) to cast the row value as a named row type. The following statement updates the **address** column (a named row type) of the **empinfo** table:

```
UPDATE empinfo
SET address = ROW('103 Baker St','Tracy','CA')::address_t
WHERE emp_id = 3568
```

For more information on the syntax for ROW constructors, see "Constructor Expressions" on page 4-116. See also "Literal Row" on page 4-239.

E/C

The row-column SET clause can only support literal values for fields. To use a variable to specify a field value, you must select the row into a row variable, use host variables for the individual field values, then update the row column with the row variable. For more information, see "Updating a Row Variable" on page 2-832. ♦

E/C

You can use ESQL/C host variables to insert *non-literal* values as:

- an entire row type into a column.

  Use a **row** variable as a variable name in the SET clause to update all fields in a row column at one time.
- individual fields of a row type.

  To insert non-literal values into a row-type column, you can first update the elements in a **row** variable and then specify the **collection** variable in the SET clause of an UPDATE statement.

When you use a row variable in the SET clause, the **row** variable must contain values for each field value. For information on how to insert values into a row variable, see "Updating a Row Variable" on page 2-832. ♦

To update only some of the fields in a row, you can perform one of the following operations:

- Specify the field names with field projection for all fields whose values remain unchanged.

  For example, the following UPDATE statement changes only the **street** and **city** fields of the **address** column of the **empinfo** table:

  ```
  UPDATE empinfo
  SET address = ROW('23 Elm St', 'Sacramento',
                    address.state)
     WHERE emp_id = 433
  ```

  The **address.state** field remains unchanged.

E/C

- Select the row into a row variable and update the desired fields.

  For more information, see "Updating a Row Variable" on page 2-832. ♦

IDS

Updating Collection Columns

You can use the SET clause to update values in a collection column. For more information, see "Collection Constructors" on page 4-118.

E/C

SPL

You can also use a collection variable to update values in a collection column. With a collection variable you can insert one or more individual elements in a collection. For more information, see "Collection Derived Table" on page 4-9. ♦

Example

For example, suppose you define the **tab1** table as follows:

```
CREATE TABLE tab1
(
    int1 INTEGER,
    list1 LIST(ROW(a INTEGER, b CHAR(5)) NOT NULL),
    dec1 DECIMAL(5,2)
)
```

The following UPDATE statement updates a row in **tab1**:

```
UPDATE tab1
    SET list1 = LIST{ROW(2, 'zyxwv'),
    ROW(POW(2,6), '=64'),
        ROW(ROUND(ROOT(146)), '=12')},
    where int1 = 10
```

The collection column, **list1**, in this example has three elements. Each element is an unnamed row type with an INTEGER field and a CHAR(5) field. The first element is composed of two literal values, an integer (2) and a quoted string ('zyxwv'). The second and third elements also use a quoted string to indicate the value for the second field. However, they each designate the value for the first field with an expression rather than a literal value.

IDS

Updating Values in Opaque-Type Columns

Some opaque data types require special processing when they are updated. For example, if an opaque data type contains spatial or multirepresentational data, it might provide a choice of how to store the data: inside the internal structure or, for very large objects, in a smart large object.

This processing is accomplished by calling a user-defined support function called **assign()**. When you execute the UPDATE statement on a table whose rows contain one of these opaque types, the database server automatically invokes the **assign()** function for the type. The **assign()** function can make the decision of how to store the data. For more information about the **assign()** support function, see *Extending Informix Dynamic Server 2000*.

EDS

Subset of FROM Clause

In Enterprise Decision Server, you can use a join to determine which column values to update by supplying a FROM clause. You can use columns from any table that is listed in the FROM clause in the WHERE clause to provide values for the columns and rows to update.

As indicated in the diagram for "UPDATE" on page 2-815, you can use only a subset of the FROM clause. You cannot use the LOCAL keyword or the SAMPLES OF segment of the FROM clause with the UPDATE statement.

The following example shows how you can use a FROM clause to introduce tables to be joined in the WHERE clause.

```
UPDATE tab1
SET tab1.a = tab2.a
FROM tab1, tab2, tab3
WHERE tab1.b = tab2.b AND tab2.c =tab3.c
```

For a complete description of the FROM Clause, see the "FROM Clause" on page 650.

WHERE Clause

The WHERE clause lets you limit the rows that you want to update. If you omit the WHERE clause, every row in the table is updated.

The WHERE clause consists of a standard search condition. (For more information, see the "WHERE Clause" on page 2-660). The following example illustrates a WHERE condition within an UPDATE statement. In this example, the statement updates three columns (**state**, **zipcode**, and **phone**) in each row of the **customer** table that has a corresponding entry in a table of new addresses called **new_address**.

```
UPDATE customer
    SET (state, zipcode, phone) =
        ((SELECT state, zipcode, phone FROM new_address N
            WHERE N.cust_num =
                    customer.customer_num))
        WHERE customer_num IN
            (SELECT cust_num FROM new_address)
```

ANSI

SQLSTATE VALUES When Updating an ANSI Database

If you update a table in an ANSI-compliant database with an UPDATE statement that contains the WHERE clause and no rows are found, the database server issues a warning. You can detect this warning condition in either of the following ways:

- The GET DIAGNOSTICS statement sets the **RETURNED_SQLSTATE** field to the value 02000. In an SQL API application, the **SQLSTATE** variable contains this same value.

- In an SQL API application, the **sqlca.sqlcode** and **SQLCODE** variables contain the value 100.

The database server also sets **SQLSTATE** and **SQLCODE** to these values if the UPDATE... WHERE... is a part of a multistatement prepare and the database server returns no rows. ◆

SQLSTATE VALUES When Updating a Non-ANSI Database

In a database that is not ANSI compliant, the database server does not return a warning when it finds no matching rows for the WHERE clause of an UPDATE statement. The **SQLSTATE** code is 00000 and the **SQLCODE** code is zero (0). However, if the UPDATE... WHERE... is a part of a multistatement prepare, and no rows are returned, the database server does issue a warning. It sets **SQLSTATE** to 02000 and the **SQLCODE** value to 100.

E/C

SPL

IDS

E/C

SPL

Using the WHERE CURRENT OF Clause

Use the WHERE CURRENT OF clause to update the current row of the active set of a cursor in the current element of a collection cursor (ESQL/C only).

The UPDATE statement does not advance the cursor to the next row, so the current row position remains unchanged.

You cannot use this clause if you are selecting from only one table in a table hierarchy. That is, you cannot use this option if you use the ONLY keyword. ♦

To use the CURRENT OF keywords, you must have previously used the DECLARE statement to define the *cursor* with the FOR UPDATE option.

If the DECLARE statement that created the cursor specified one or more columns in the FOR UPDATE clause, you are restricted to updating only those columns in a subsequent UPDATE...WHERE CURRENT OF statement. The advantage to specifying columns in the FOR UPDATE clause of a DECLARE statement is speed. The database server can usually perform updates more quickly if columns are specified in the DECLARE statement. ♦

Before you can use the CURRENT OF keywords, you must declare a cursor with the FOREACH statement. ♦

Tip: *You can use an update cursor to perform updates that are not possible with the UPDATE statement.*

The following ESQL/C example illustrates the CURRENT OF form of the WHERE clause. In this example, updates are performed on a range of customers who receive 10-percent discounts (assume that a new column, **discount**, is added to the **customer** table). The UPDATE statement is prepared outside the WHILE loop to ensure that parsing is done only once.

```
char answer [1] = 'y';
EXEC SQL BEGIN DECLARE SECTION;
    char fname[32],lname[32];
    int low,high;
EXEC SQL END DECLARE SECTION;

main()
{
    EXEC SQL connect to 'stores_demo';
    EXEC SQL prepare sel_stmt from
        'select fname, lname from customer \
            where cust_num between ? and ? for update';
    EXEC SQL declare x cursor for sel_stmt;
    printf("\nEnter lower limit customer number: ");
```

```
scanf("%d", &low);
printf("\nEnter upper limit customer number: ");
scanf("%d", &high);
EXEC SQL open x using :low, :high;
EXEC SQL prepare u from
    'update customer set discount = 0.1 \
    where current of x';

while (1)
    {
    EXEC SQL fetch x into :fname, :lname;
    if ( SQLCODE == SQLNOTFOUND)
        break;
    }
printf("\nUpdate %.10s %.10s (y/n)?", fname, lname);
if (answer = getch() == 'y')
    EXEC SQL execute u;
EXEC SQL close x;
}
```

IDS

E/C

Updating a Row Variable

The UPDATE statement with the Collection Derived Table segment allows you to update fields in a **row** variable. The Collection Derived Table segment identifies the **row** variable in which to update the fields. For more information, see "Collection Derived Table" on page 4-9.

To update fields, follow these steps:

1. Create a **row** variable in your ESQL/C program.

2. Optionally, select a row-type column into the **row** variable with the SELECT statement (without the Collection Derived Table segment).

3. Update fields of the **row** variable with the UPDATE statement and the Collection Derived Table segment.

4. Once the **row** variable contains the correct fields, you then use the UPDATE or INSERT statement on a table or view name to save the row variable in the row column (named or unnamed).

The UPDATE statement and the Collection Derived Table segment allow you to update a particular field or group of fields in the **row** variable. You specify the new field values in the SET clause. For example, the following UPDATE changes the **x** and **y** fields in the **myrect** ESQL/C **row** variable:

```
EXEC SQL BEGIN DECLARE SECTION;
    row (x int, y int, length float, width float) myrect;
EXEC SQL END DECLARE SECTION;
    .
    .
    .
EXEC SQL select into :myrect from rectangles
    where area = 64;
EXEC SQL update table(:myrect)
    set x=3, y=4;
```

Suppose that after the SELECT statement, the **myrect2** variable has the values x=0, y=0, length=8, and width=8. After the UPDATE statement, the **myrect2** variable has field values of x=3, y=4, length=8, and width=8.

You cannot use a **row** variable in the Collection Derived Table segment of an INSERT statement. However, you can use the UPDATE statement and the Collection Derived Table segment to insert new field values into a **row** host variable, as long as you specify a value for every field in the row. For example, the following code fragment inserts new field values into the **myrect** row variable and then inserts this **row** variable into the database:

```
EXEC SQL update table(:myrect)
    set x=3, y=4, length=12, width=6;
EXEC SQL insert into rectangles
    values (72, :myrect);
```

If the row variable is an untyped variable, you must use a SELECT statement *before* the UPDATE so that ESQL/C can determine the data types of the fields. An UPDATE of a field or fields in a row variable cannot include a WHERE clause.

The row variable stores the fields of the row. However, it has no intrinsic connection with a database column. Once the row variable contains the correct field values, you must then save the variable into the row column with one of the following SQL statements:

- To update the row column in the table with contents of the **row** variable, use an UPDATE statement on a table or view name and specify the **row** variable in the SET clause.

    For more information, see "Updating Row-Type Columns" on page 2-826.

- To insert a row in a column, use the INSERT statement on a table or view name and specify the **row** variable in the VALUES clause.

    For more information, see "Inserting Values into Row-Type Columns" on page 2-546.

For more information on how to use SPL row variables, see the *Informix Guide to SQL: Tutorial*. For more information on how to use ESQL/C **row** variables, see the discussion of complex data types in the *Informix ESQL/C Programmer's Manual*. ♦

Related Information

Related statements: DECLARE, INSERT, OPEN, SELECT, and FOREACH

For a task-oriented discussion of the UPDATE statement, see the *Informix Guide to SQL: Tutorial*.

For a discussion of the GLS aspects of the UPDATE statement, see the *Informix Guide to GLS Functionality*.

For information on how to access row and collections with ESQL/C host variables, see the discussion of complex data types in the *Informix ESQL/C Programmer's Manual*.

UPDATE STATISTICS

Use the UPDATE STATISTICS statement to:

- determine the distribution of column values.
- update the system catalog tables that the server uses to optimize queries.
- force reoptimization of SPL routines.
- convert existing table indexes when you upgrade the database server.

Syntax

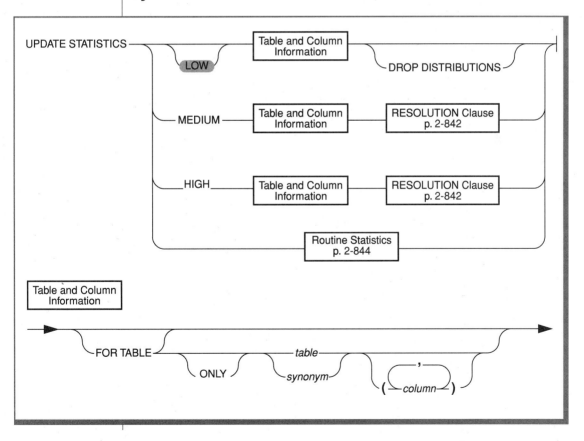

Element	Purpose	Restrictions	Syntax
column	Name of a column in the specified table	The column must exist.	Identifier, p. 4-205
		If you use the LOW keyword and want the UPDATE STATISTICS statement to do minimal work, specify a column name that is not part of an index.	
		If you use the MEDIUM or HIGH keywords, *column* cannot be a BYTE or TEXT column.	
synonym	Name of synonym for table for which statistics are updated	The synonym and the table to which the synonym points must reside in the current database.	Database Object Name, p. 4-50
table	Name of table for which statistics are updated	The table must reside in the current database.	Database Object Name, p. 4-50

Usage

You cannot update the statistics used by the optimizer for a table or UDR that is external to the current database. That is, you cannot update statistics on remote database objects.

Scope of UPDATE STATISTICS

If you do not specify any clause that begins with the FOR keyword, statistics are updated for every table and SPL routine in the current database, including the system catalog tables. Similarly, if you use a clause that begins with the FOR keyword, but do not specify a table or SPL routine name, the database server updates the statistics for all tables, including temporary tables, or all SPL routines in the current database.

If you use the FOR TABLE clause without a specific table name to build distributions on all of the tables in the database, distributions will also be built on all of the temporary tables in your session.

Updating Statistics for Tables

Although a change to the database might obsolete the corresponding statistics in the **systables**, **syscolumns**, **sysindexes**, and **sysdistrib** system catalog tables, the database server does not automatically update them.

Issue an UPDATE STATISTICS statement in the following situations to ensure that the stored distribution information reflects the state of the database:

- You perform extensive modifications to a table.
- An application changes the distribution of column values.

  The UPDATE STATISTICS statement reoptimizes queries on the modified objects.

- You upgrade a database for use with a newer database server.

  The UPDATE STATISTICS statement converts the old indexes to conform to the newer database server index format and implicitly drops the old indexes.

  You can choose to convert the indexes table by table or for the entire database at one time. Follow the conversion guidelines in the *Informix Migration Guide*.

If your application makes many modifications to the data in a particular table, update the system catalog table data for that table routinely with the UPDATE STATISTICS statement to improve query efficiency. The term *many modifications* is relative to the resolution of the distributions. If the data changes do not change the distribution of column values, you do not need to execute UPDATE STATISTICS.

EDS

In Enterprise Decision Server, the UPDATE STATISTICS statement does not update, maintain, or collect statistics on indexes. The statement does not update the **syscolumns** and **sysindexes** tables. Any information about indexes, the **syscolumns,** and the **sysindexes** tables in the following pages does not apply to Enterprise Decision Server. ◆

IDS

Using the ONLY Keyword

Use the ONLY keyword to collect data for one table in a hierarchy of typed tables. If you do not specify the ONLY keyword and the table that you specify has subtables, the database server creates distributions for that table and every table under it in the hierarchy.

For example, assume your database has the typed table hierarchy that appears in Figure 2-2, which shows a supertable named **employee** that has a subtable named **sales_rep**. The **sales_rep** table, in turn, has a subtable named **us_sales_rep.**

Figure 2-2

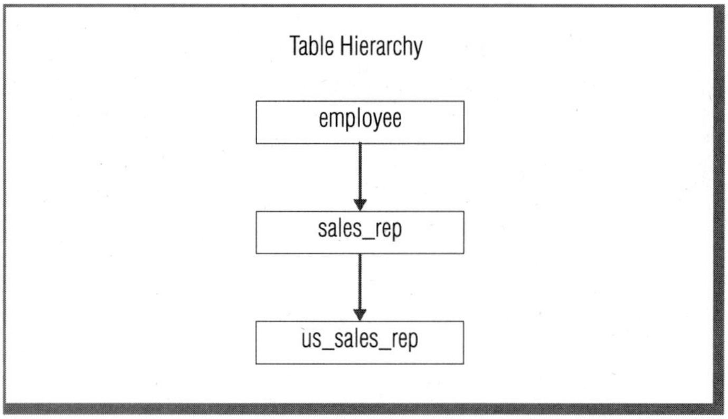

Table Hierarchy

When the following statement executes, the database server generates statistics on both the sales_rep and **us_sales_rep** tables:

```
UPDATE STATISTICS FOR TABLE sales_rep
```

In contrast, the following example generates statistical data for each column in table **sales_rep** but does not act on tables **employee** or **us_sales_rep**:

```
UPDATE STATISTICS FOR TABLE ONLY sales_rep
```

Because neither of the previous examples mentioned the level at which to update the statistical data, the database server uses the low mode by default.

Examining Index Pages

In Dynamic Server, when you execute the UPDATE STATISTICS statement in any mode, the database server reads through index pages to:

- compute statistics for the query optimizer.
- locate pages that have the delete flag marked as 1.

If pages are found with the delete flag marked as 1, the corresponding keys are removed from the B-tree cleaner list.

This operation is particularly useful if a system crash causes the B-tree cleaner list (which exists in shared memory) to be lost. To remove the B-tree items that have been marked as deleted but are not yet removed from the B-tree, run the UPDATE STATISTICS statement. For information on the B-tree cleaner list, see your *Administrator's Guide*.

Using the LOW Mode Option

Use the LOW mode option to generate and update statistical data regarding table, row, and page count statistics in the **systables** system catalog table.

If you do not specify a mode, the database server uses low by default.

IDS

In Dynamic Server, the LOW mode option updates index and column statistics for specified columns also. The database server generates and updates this statistical data in the **syscolumns**, and **sysindexes** tables.

When you use the low mode, the database server generates the least amount of information about the column. If you want the UPDATE STATISTICS statement to do minimal work, specify a column that is not part of an index.

The following example updates statistics on the **customer_num** column of the **customer** table.

```
UPDATE STATISTICS LOW FOR TABLE customer (customer_num)
```

Because the low mode does not update data in the **sysdistrib** system catalog table, all distributions associated with the **customer** table remain intact, even those that already exist on the **customer_num** column. ◆

Using the DROP DISTRIBUTIONS Option

Use the DROP DISTRIBUTIONS option to force the removal of distribution information from the **sysdistrib** system catalog table.

When you specify the DROP DISTRIBUTIONS option, the database server removes the distribution data that exists for the column or columns you specify. If you do not specify any columns, the database server removes all the distribution data for that table.

You must have the DBA privilege or be the owner of the table to use this option.

The following example shows how to remove distributions for the **customer_num** column in the **customer** table:

```
UPDATE STATISTICS LOW
FOR TABLE customer (customer_num) DROP DISTRIBUTIONS
```

As the example shows, you drop the distribution data at the same time you update the statistical data that the LOW mode option generates.

Using the MEDIUM Mode Option

Use the MEDIUM mode option to update the same statistics that you can perform with the low mode and also generate statistics about the distribution of data values for each specified column. The database server places distribution information in the **sysdistrib** system catalog table

If you use the MEDIUM mode option, the database server scans tables at least once and takes longer to execute on a given table than the LOW mode option.

The constructed distribution is statistically significant. When you use the MEDIUM mode option, the data for the distributions is obtained by sampling a percentage of data rows. Because the data obtained by sampling is usually much smaller than the actual number of rows, this mode executes more quickly than the HIGH mode.

Because the data is obtained by sampling, the results might vary (that is, different sample rows might produce different distribution results). If the results vary significantly, you can adjust the resolution percent or confidence level to obtain more consistent results.

If you do not specify a RESOLUTION clause, the default percentage of data distributed to every bin is 2.5. If you do not specify a value for *confidence_level*, the default confidence is 0.95. This value can be roughly interpreted to mean that 95 percent of the time, the estimate is equivalent to that obtained from high distributions.

You must have the DBA privilege or be the owner of the table to create medium distributions.

For more on the similarities between the Medium and High Modes, see the "Resolution Clause" on page 2-842.

Using the HIGH Mode Option

Use the HIGH mode option to update the same statistics that you can perform with the low mode and also generate statistics about the distribution of data values for each specified column. The database server places distribution information in the **sysdistrib** system catalog table.

The constructed distribution is exact. Because of the time required to gather this information, this mode executes more slowly than the LOW and MEDIUM modes.

You must have the DBA privilege or be the owner of the table to create high distributions.

If you do not specify a RESOLUTION clause, the default percentage of data distributed to every bin is 0.5.

If you use the HIGH mode option to update statistics, the database server can take considerable time to gather the information across the database, particularly a database with large tables. The HIGH keyword might scan each table several times (for each column). To minimize processing time, specify a table name and column names within that table.

For more on the similarities between the Medium and High Modes, see the "Resolution Clause."

Resolution Clause

Use the Resolution clause to adjust the size of the distribution bin, designate whether or not to avoid calculating data on indexes, and with the Medium mode, to adjust the confidence level.

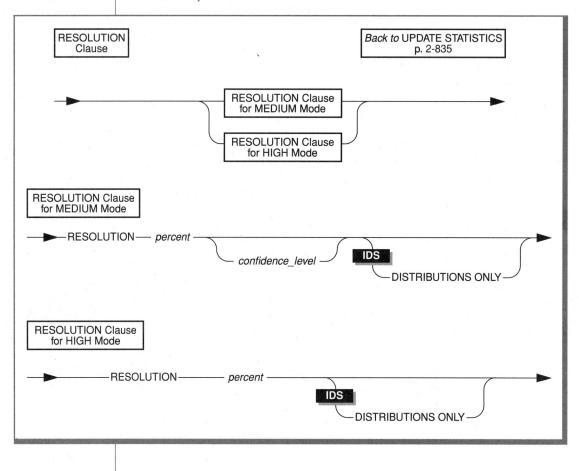

Element	Purpose	Restrictions	Syntax
confidence_level	Expected fraction of times that the sampling entailed by the MEDIUM keyword should produce the same results as the exact methods entailed by the HIGH keyword	The minimum confidence level is 0.80. The maximum confidence level is 0.99.	Literal Number, p. 4-237
	The default confidence level is 0.95. This can be roughly interpreted as meaning that 95 percent of the time, the estimate produced by the MEDIUM keyword is equivalent to using high distributions.		
percent	Percentage of samples in each bin of a distribution	The minimum resolution possible for a table is 1/*nrows*, where *nrows* is the number of rows in the table.	Literal Number, p. 4-237
	For MEDIUM mode, the default value is 2.5.		
	For HIGH mode, the default value is 0.5		

A *distribution* is a mapping of the data in a column into a set of column values. The contents of the column are divided into bins or ranges, each of which contains an equal portion of the column data. For example, if one bin holds 2 percent of the data, 50 of these 2-percent bins hold all the data. A bin contains the particular range of data values that reflects the appropriate percentage of entries in the column.

The optimizer estimates the effect of a WHERE clause by examining, for each column included in the WHERE clause, the proportionate occurrence of data values contained in the column.

You cannot create distributions for BYTE or TEXT columns. If you include a BYTE or TEXT column in an UPDATE STATISTICS statement that specifies medium or high distributions, no distributions are created for those columns. Distributions are constructed for other columns in the list, and the statement does not return an error.

The amount of space that the **DBUPSPACE** environment variable specifies determines the number of times the database server scans the designated table to construct a distribution.

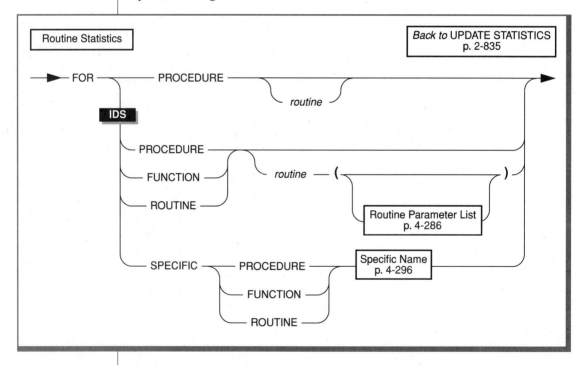

IDS

Using the DISTRIBUTIONS ONLY Option to Suppress Index Information

In Dynamic Server, when you specify the DISTRIBUTIONS ONLY option, you do not update index information. This option does not affect existing index information.

Use this option to avoid the examination of index information that can consume considerable processing time.

This option does not affect the recalculation of information on tables, such as the number of pages used, the number of rows, and fragment information. UPDATE STATISTICS needs this data to construct accurate column distributions and requires little time and system resources to collect it.

Routine Statistics

Use the Routine Statistics portion of the UPDATE STATISTICS statement to update the optimized execution plans for SPL routines in the **sysprocplan** system catalog table.

Element	Purpose	Restrictions	Syntax
routine	Name given to the SPL routine in a CREATE FUNCTION or CREATE PROCEDURE statement If you omit *routine*, the statistics for all SPL routines in the current database are updated.	The SPL routine must reside in the current database. In an ANSI-compliant database, specify the owner as the prefix to the routine name.	Database Object Name, p. 4-50

The following table explains the keywords that you can use when you update routine statistics.

KEYWORD	Purpose
SPECIFIC	Reoptimizes the execution plan for an SPL routine identified by *specific name*.
FUNCTION	Reoptimizes the execution plan for any SPL function with the specified routine name (and parameter types that match *routine parameter list*, if supplied).
PROCEDURE	Reoptimizes the execution plan for any SPL procedure with the specified routine name (and parameter types that match *routine parameter list*, if supplied).
ROUTINE	Reoptimizes the execution plan for SPL functions and SPL procedures with the specified routine name (and parameter types that match *routine parameter list*, if supplied).

The **sysprocplan** system catalog table stores execution plans for SPL routines. Two actions update the **sysprocplan** system catalog table:

- Execution of an SPL routine that uses a modified table
- The UPDATE STATISTICS statement

If you change a table that an SPL routine references, you can run UPDATE STATISTICS to reoptimize on demand, rather than waiting until the next time an SPL routine that uses the table executes.

```
IDS
```

Updating Statistics for Columns that Contain a User-Defined Type

To collect statistics for a column that holds a user-defined data type, you must specify either medium or high mode. When you execute UPDATE STATISTICS, the database server does not collect values for the **colmin** and **colmax** columns of the **syscolumns** table for columns that hold user-defined data types.

To drop statistics for a column that holds one of these data types, you must execute UPDATE STATISTICS in the low mode and use the DROP DISTRIBU-TIONS option. When you use this option, the database server removes the row in the **sysdistrib** system catalog table that corresponds to the **tableid** and **column**. In addition, the database server removes any large objects that might have been created for storing the statistics information.

Requirements

UPDATE STATISTICS collects statistics for opaque data types only if you have defined user-defined routines for **statcollect()**, **statprint()**, and the selectivity functions. You must have usage permissions on these routines.

In some cases, UPDATE STATISTICS also requires an sbspace as specified by the SYSSBSPACENAME onconfig parameter. For information about the statistics routines, refer to the *DataBlade API Programmer's Manual*. For information about SYSSBSPACENAME, refer to your *Administrator's Reference*.

```
IDS
```

Updating Statistics When You Upgrade the Database Server

When you upgrade a database to use with a newer database server, you can use the UPDATE STATISTICS statement to convert the indexes to the form that the newer database server uses. You can choose to convert the indexes one table at a time or for the entire database at one time. Follow the conversion guidelines that are outlined in the *Informix Migration Guide*.

When you use the UPDATE STATISTICS statement to convert the indexes to use with a newer database server, the indexes are implicitly dropped and re-created. The only time that an UPDATE STATISTICS statement causes table indexes to be implicitly dropped and recreated is when you upgrade a database for use with a newer database server.

Performance

The more specific you make the list of objects that UPDATE STATISTICS examines, the faster it completes execution. Limiting the number of columns distributed speeds the update. Similarly, precision affects the speed of the update. If all other keywords are the same, LOW works fastest, but HIGH examines the most data.

Related Information

Related statements: SET EXPLAIN and SET OPTIMIZATION

For a discussion of the performance implications of UPDATE STATISTICS, see your *Performance Guide*.

For a discussion of how to use the **dbschema** utility to view distributions created with UPDATE STATISTICS, see the *Informix Migration Guide*.

E/C

WHENEVER

Use the WHENEVER statement to trap exceptions that occur during the execution of SQL statements.

Use this statement with ESQL/C.

Syntax

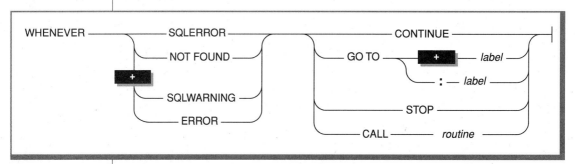

Element	Purpose	Restrictions	Syntax
label	Statement label to which program control transfers when an exception occurs	Label must be a paragraph name or a procedure name.	Label must conform to language-specific rules for statement labels.
routine	Name of the user-defined routine (UDR) that is called when an exception occurs	UDR must exist at compile time.	Database Object Name, p. 4-50.

Usage

The WHENEVER statement is equivalent to placing an exception-checking routine after every SQL statement. The following table summarizes the types of exceptions for which you can check with the WHENEVER statement.

Type of Exception	WHENEVER Clause	For More Information
Errors	SQLERROR	2-851
Warnings	SQLWARNING	2-851
Not Found Condition End of Data Condition	NOT FOUND	2-852

If you do not use the WHENEVER statement in a program, the program does not automatically abort when an exception occurs. Your program must explicitly check for exceptions and take whatever corrective action you desire. If you do not check for exceptions, the program simply continues running. However, as a result of the errors, the program might not perform its intended purpose.

In addition to specifying the type of exception for which to check, the WHENEVER statement also specifies what action to take when the specified exception occurs. The following table summarizes possible actions that WHENEVER can specify.

Type of Action	WHENEVER Keyword	For More Information
Continue program execution	CONTINUE	2-852
Stop program execution	STOP	2-853
Transfer control to a specified label	GOTO GO TO	2-853
Transfer control to a named user-defined routine	CALL	2-854

The Scope of WHENEVER

The ESQL/C preprocessor, not the database server, handles the interpretation of the WHENEVER statement. When the preprocessor encounters a WHENEVER statement in an ESQL/C source file, it inserts the appropriate code into the preprocessed code after each SQL statement based on the exception and the action that WHENEVER lists. The preprocessor defines the scope of a WHENEVER statement as being from the point that it encounters the statement in the source module until it encounters one of the following conditions:

- The next WHENEVER statement with the same exception condition (SQLERROR, SQLWARNING, and NOT FOUND) in the same source module
- The end of the source module

Whichever condition the preprocessor encounters first as it sequentially processes the source module marks the end of the scope of the WHENEVER statement.

The following ESQL/C example program has three WHENEVER statements, two of which are WHENEVER SQLERROR statements. Line 4 uses STOP with SQLERROR to override the default CONTINUE action for errors. Line 8 specifies the CONTINUE keyword to return the handling of errors to the default behavior. For all SQL statements between lines 4 and 8, the preprocessor inserts code that checks for errors and halts program execution if an error occurs. Therefore, any errors that the INSERT statement on line 6 generates cause the program to stop.

After line 8, the preprocessor does not insert code to check for errors after SQL statements. Therefore, any errors that the INSERT statement (line 10), the SELECT statement (line 11), and DISCONNECT statement (line 12) generate are ignored. However, the SELECT statement does not stop program execution if it does not locate any rows; the WHENEVER statement on line 7 tells the program to continue if such an exception occurs.

```
1   main()
2   {

3   EXEC SQL connect to 'test';

4   EXEC SQL WHENEVER SQLERROR STOP;

5   printf("\n\nGoing to try first insert\n\n");
```

```
6    EXEC SQL insert into test_color values ('green');

7    EXEC SQL WHENEVER NOT FOUND CONTINUE;
8    EXEC SQL WHENEVER SQLERROR CONTINUE;

9    printf("\n\nGoing to try second insert\n\n");
10   EXEC SQL insert into test_color values ('blue');
11   EXEC SQL select paint_type from paint where color='red';
12   EXEC SQL disconnect all;
13   printf("\n\nProgram over\n\n");
14   }
```

SQLERROR Keyword

If you use the SQLERROR keyword, any SQL statement that encounters an error is handled as the WHENEVER SQLERROR statement directs. If an error occurs, the **sqlcode** variable (**sqlca.sqlcode, SQLCODE**) is less than zero (0) and the SQLSTATE variable has a class code with a value greater than 02.

The following statement causes a program to stop execution if an SQL error exists:

```
WHENEVER SQLERROR STOP
```

If you do not use any WHENEVER SQLERROR statements in a program, the default for WHENEVER SQLERROR is CONTINUE.

ERROR Keyword

ERROR is a synonym for SQLERROR.

SQLWARNING Keyword

If you use the SQLWARNING keyword, any SQL statement that generates a warning is handled as the WHENEVER SQLWARNING statement directs. If a warning occurs, the first field of the warning structure in SQLCA (**sqlca.sqlwarn.sqlwarn0**) is set to W, and the SQLSTATE variable has a class code of 01.

In addition to setting the first field of the warning structure, a warning also sets an additional field to W. The field that is set indicates the type of warning that occurred.

The following statement causes a program to stop execution if a warning condition exists:

```
WHENEVER SQLWARNING STOP
```

If you do not use any WHENEVER SQLWARNING statements in a program, the default for WHENEVER SQLWARNING is CONTINUE.

NOT FOUND Keywords

If you use the NOT FOUND keywords, exception handling for SELECT and FETCH statements is treated differently than for other SQL statements. The NOT FOUND keyword checks for the following cases:

- The **End of Data** condition: a FETCH statement that attempts to get a row beyond the first or last row in the active set
- The **Not Found** condition: a SELECT statement that returns no rows

In each case, the **sqlcode** variable is set to 100, and the SQLSTATE variable has a class code of 02. For the name of the **sqlcode** variable in each Informix product, see the table in "SQLERROR Keyword" on page 2-851.

The following statement calls the **no_rows()** function each time the NOT FOUND condition exists:

```
WHENEVER NOT FOUND CALL no_rows
```

If you do not use any WHENEVER NOT FOUND statements in a program, the default for WHENEVER NOT FOUND is CONTINUE.

CONTINUE Keyword

Use the CONTINUE keyword to instruct the program to ignore the exception and to continue execution at the next statement after the SQL statement. The default action for all exceptions is CONTINUE. You can use this keyword to turn off a previously specified option.

STOP Keyword

Use the STOP keyword to instruct the program to stop execution when the specified exception occurs. The following statement halts execution of an ESQL/C program each time that an SQL statement generates a warning:

```
EXEC SQL WHENEVER SQLWARNING STOP;
```

GOTO Keywords

Use the GOTO clause to transfer control to the statement that the label identifies when a particular exception occurs. The GOTO keyword is the ANSI-compliant syntax of the clause. The GO TO keywords are a non-ANSI synonym for GOTO.

The following example shows a WHENEVER statement in ESQL/C code that transfers control to the label **missing** each time that the NOT FOUND condition occurs:

```
query_data()
    .
    .
    .
    EXEC SQL WHENEVER NOT FOUND GO TO missing;
    .
    .
    .
    EXEC SQL fetch lname into :lname;
    .
    .
    .
    missing:
        printf("No Customers Found\n");
    .
    .
    .
```

You must define the labeled statement in *each* program block that contains SQL statements. If your program contains more than one user-defined function, you might need to include the labeled statement and its code in *each* function. When the preprocessor reaches the function that does not contain the labeled statement, it tries to insert the code associated with the labeled statement. However, if you do not define this labeled statement within the function, the preprocessor generates an error.

To correct this error, either put a labeled statement with the same label name in each user-defined function, issue another WHENEVER statement to reset the error condition, or use the CALL clause to call a separate function.

CALL Clause

Use the CALL clause to transfer program control to the named UDR when a particular exception occurs. Do not include parentheses after the UDR name. The following WHENEVER statement causes the program to call the **error_recovery()** function if the program detects an error:

```
EXEC SQL WHENEVER SQLERROR CALL error_recovery;
```

When the named function completes, execution resumes at the next statement after the line that is causing the error. If you want to halt execution when an error occurs, include statements that terminate the program as part of the named function.

Observe the following restrictions on the named function:

- You cannot pass arguments to the named function nor can you return values from the named function. If the named function needs external information, use global variables or the GOTO clause of WHENEVER to transfer control to a label that calls the named function.

- You cannot specify the name of an SPL routine in the CALL clause. To call an SPL routine, use the CALL clause to execute a function that contains the EXECUTE FUNCTION (or EXECUTE PROCEDURE) statement.

- Make sure that all functions that the WHENEVER...CALL statement affects can find a declaration of the named function.

Related Information

Related Statements: EXECUTE FUNCTION, EXECUTE PROCEDURE and FETCH

For discussions on exception handling and error checking, see the *Informix ESQL/C Programmer's Manual*.

SPL Statements

In This Chapter

You can use Stored Procedure Language (SPL) statements to write SPL routines (formerly referred to as stored procedures), and you can store these routines in the database. SPL routines are effective tools for controlling SQL activity.

This chapter contains descriptions of the SPL statements. The description of each statement includes the following information:

- A brief introduction that explains the purpose of the statement
- A syntax diagram that shows how to enter the statement correctly
- A syntax table that explains each input parameter in the syntax diagram
- Rules of usage, including examples that illustrate these rules

If a statement is composed of multiple clauses, the statement description provides the same set of information for each clause.

For task-oriented information about using SPL routines, see the *Informix Guide to SQL: Tutorial*.

EDS

In Enterprise Decision Server, to create an SPL function you must use the CREATE PROCEDURE statement. Enterprise Decision Server does not support the CREATE FUNCTION statement. ◆

IDS

In Dynamic Server, for backward compatibility, you can create an SPL function with the CREATE PROCEDURE statement. For external functions, you must use the CREATE FUNCTION statement. Informix recommends that you use the CREATE FUNCTION statement as you create all new user-defined functions. ◆

CALL

Use the CALL statement to execute a user-defined routine (UDR) from within an SPL routine.

Syntax

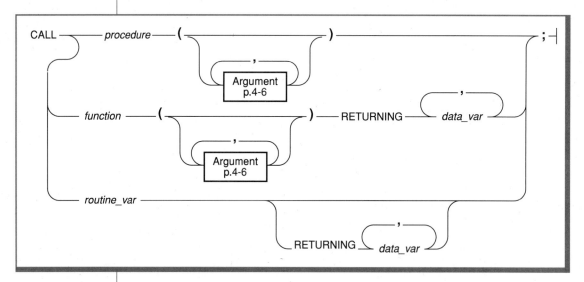

Element	Purpose	Restrictions	Syntax
data_var	Name of a variable that receives the value or values a function returns	The data type of *data_var* must be appropriate for the value the function returns.	Identifier, p. 4-205
function	Name of the user-defined function to call	The function must exist.	Database Object Name, p. 4-50
procedure	Name of the user-defined procedure to call	The procedure must exist.	Database Object Name, p. 4-50
routine_var	Name of a variable that is set to the name of a UDR	The routine_var must have the data type CHAR, VARCHAR, NCHAR, or NVARCHAR.	Identifier, p. 4-205
		The name you assign to *routine_var* must be non-null and the name of an existing UDR.	

Usage

The CALL statement invokes a UDR. The CALL statement is identical in behavior to the EXECUTE PROCEDURE and EXECUTE FUNCTION statements, but you can only use CALL from within an SPL routine. You can use CALL in an ESQL/C program or with DB-Access, but only if you place the statement within an SPL routine executed by the program or DB-Access.

If you CALL a user-defined function, specify a RETURNING clause.

Specifying Arguments

If a CALL statement contains more arguments than the called UDR expects, you receive an error.

If a CALL statement specifies fewer arguments than the called UDR expects, the arguments are said to be missing. The database server initializes missing arguments to their corresponding default values. (See "CREATE PROCEDURE" on page 2-199 and "CREATE FUNCTION" on page 2-146.) This initialization occurs before the first executable statement in the body of the UDR.

If missing arguments do not have default values, the database server initializes the arguments to the value of UNDEFINED. An attempt to use any variable that has the value of UNDEFINED results in an error.

In each UDR call, you have the option of specifying parameter names for the arguments you pass to the UDR. Each of the following examples are valid for a UDR that expects character arguments named t, n, and d, in that order:

```
CALL add_col (t='customer', n = 'newint', d ='integer');
CALL  add_col('customer','newint','integer');
```

The syntax of specifying arguments is described in more detail in "Argument" on page 4-6.

Receiving Input from the Called UDR

The RETURNING clause specifies the data variable that receives values that a
a called function returns.

The following example shows two UDR calls:

```
CREATE PROCEDURE not_much()
    DEFINE i, j, k INT;
    CALL no_args (10,20);
    CALL yes_args (5) RETURNING i, j, k;
END PROCEDURE
```

The first routine call (**no_args**) expects no returned values. The second
routine call is to a function (**yes_args**), which expects three returned values.
The **not_much()** procedure declares three integer variables (**i**, **j**, and **k**) to
receive the returned values from **yes_args**.

EDS

CASE

Use the CASE statement when you need to take one of many branches depending on the value of an SPL variable or a simple expression. The CASE statement is a fast alternative to the IF statement.

Syntax

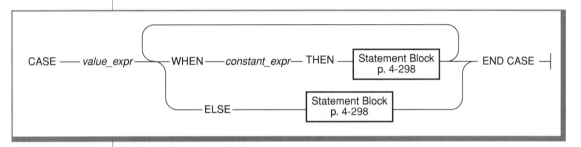

Element	Purpose	Restrictions	Syntax
constant_expr	Constant expression that specifies a literal value	The constant expression can be any of the following literals: a literal number, quoted string, literal datetime, or literal interval. The data type of the constant expression must be compatible with the data type of value_expr.	Constant Expressions, p. 4-108
value_expr	Expression that evaluates to a value	The expression can be an SPL variable or any other type of expression that evaluates to a value.	Expression, p. 4-73

Usage

You can use the CASE statement to create a set of conditional branches within an SPL routine.

Both the WHEN and ELSE clauses are optional, but you must supply one or the other. If you do not specify either a WHEN clause or an ELSE clause, you receive a syntax error.

How the Database Server Executes a CASE Statement

The database server executes the CASE statement in the following way:

- The database server evaluates the *value_expr* parameter.
- If the resulting value matches a literal value specified in the *constant_expr* parameter of a WHEN clause, the database server executes the statement block that follows the THEN keyword in that WHEN clause.
- If the value resulting from the evaluation of the *value_expr* parameter matches the *constant_expr* parameter in more than one WHEN clause, the database server executes the statement block that follows the THEN keyword in the first matching WHEN clause in the CASE statement.
- After the database server executes the statement block that follows the THEN keyword, it executes the statement that follows the CASE statement in the SPL routine.
- If the value of the *value_expr* parameter does not match the literal value specified in the *constant_expr* parameter of any WHEN clause, and if the CASE statement includes an ELSE clause, the database server executes the statement block that follows the ELSE keyword.
- If the value of the *value_expr* parameter does not match the literal value specified in the *constant_expr* parameter of any WHEN clause, and if the CASE statement does not include an ELSE clause, the database server executes the statement that follows the CASE statement in the SPL routine.
- If the CASE statement includes an ELSE clause but not a WHEN clause, the database server executes the statement block that follows the ELSE keyword.

Computation of the Value Expression in CASE

The database server computes the value of the *value_expr* parameter only one time. It computes this value at the start of execution of the CASE statement. If the value expression specified in the *value_expr* parameter contains SPL variables and the values of these variables change subsequently in one of the statement blocks within the CASE statement, the database server does not recompute the value of the *value_expr* parameter. So a change in the value of any variables contained in the *value_expr* parameter has no effect on the branch taken by the CASE statement.

Valid Statements in the Statement Block

The statement block that follows the THEN or ELSE keywords can include any SQL statement or SPL statement that is allowed in the statement block of an SPL routine. For further information on the statement block of an SPL routine, see "Statement Block" on page 4-298.

Example of CASE Statement

In the following example, the CASE statement initializes one of a set of SPL variables (named **j**, **k**, **l**, and **m**) to the value of an SPL variable named **x**, depending on the value of another SPL variable named **i**:

```
CASE i
    WHEN 1 THEN
        LET j = x;
    WHEN 2 THEN
        LET k = x;
    WHEN 3 THEN
        LET l = x;
    WHEN 4 THEN
        LET m = x;
    ELSE
        RAISE EXCEPTION 100;  --illegal value
END CASE
```

CONTINUE

Use the CONTINUE statement to start the next iteration of the innermost FOR, WHILE, or FOREACH loop.

Syntax

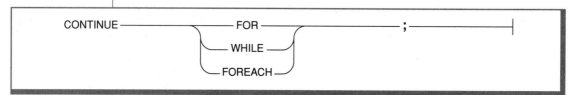

Usage

When you encounter a CONTINUE statement, the SPL routine skips the rest of the statements in the innermost loop of the indicated type. Execution continues at the top of the loop with the next iteration. In the following example, the **loopskip** function inserts values 3 through 15 into the table **testtable**. The function also returns values 3 through 9 and 13 through 15 in the process. The function does not return the value 11 because it encounters the CONTINUE FOR statement. The CONTINUE FOR statement causes the function to skip the RETURN WITH RESUME statement.

```
CREATE FUNCTION loop_skip()
    RETURNING INT;
    DEFINE i INT;
    .
    .
    .
    FOR i IN (3 TO 15 STEP 2)
        INSERT INTO testtable values(i, null, null);
        IF i = 11
            CONTINUE FOR;
        END IF;
        RETURN i WITH RESUME;
    END FOR;

END FUNCTION;
```

The CONTINUE statement generates errors if it cannot find the identified loop.

DEFINE

Use the DEFINE statement to declare variables that an SPL routine uses and to assign them data types.

Syntax

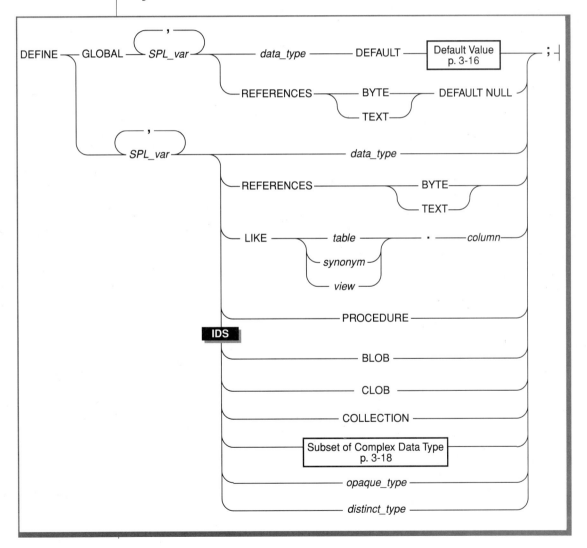

Element	Purpose	Restrictions	Syntax
column	Name of a column in the table	The column must exist in the table by the time you run the SPL routine.	Identifier, p. 4-205
data_type	Data type of the values that the variable holds Variables of INT and INT8 data types hold data from SERIAL and SERIAL8 columns, respectively.	For global variables, the data type can be any built-in data type except SERIAL, SERIAL8, TEXT, BYTE, CLOB, or BLOB. For local variables, the data type can be any built-in data type except SERIAL, SERIAL8, TEXT, or BYTE.	Identifier, p. 4-205
distinct_type	Name of a distinct type	The distinct type must be defined in the database by the time you run the SPL routine.	Identifier, p. 4-205
opaque_type	Name of an opaque type	The opaque type must be defined in the database by the time you run the SPL routine.	Identifier, p. 4-205
SPL_var	Name of the SPL variable that is being defined	The name must be unique within the statement block.	Identifier, p. 4-205
synonym	Name of a synonym	The synonym and the table to which it refers must exist.	Database Object Name, p. 4-50
table	Name of a table	The table must exist.	Database Object Name, p. 4-50
view	Name of a view	The view must exist.	Database Object Name, p. 4-50

Usage

The DEFINE statement is not an executable statement. The DEFINE statement must appear after the routine header and before any other statements.

If you define a local variable (by using DEFINE without the GLOBAL keyword), the scope of the variable is the statement block in which it is defined. You can use the variable anywhere within the statement block. You can also use the same variable name outside the statement block with a different definition.

If you define a variable with the GLOBAL keyword, the variable is global in scope and is available outside the statement block and to other SPL routines.

Referencing TEXT and BYTE Variables

The REFERENCES keyword lets you use BYTE and TEXT variables. BYTE and TEXT variables do not contain the actual data but are simply pointers to the data. The REFERENCES keyword is a reminder that the SPL variable is just a pointer. Use the SPL variables for BYTE and TEXT data types exactly as you would any other variable.

Redeclaration or Redefinition

If you define the same variable twice within the same statement block, you receive an error. You can redefine a variable within a nested block, in which case it temporarily hides the outer declaration. The following example produces an error:

```
CREATE PROCEDURE example1()
    DEFINE n INT; DEFINE j INT;
    DEFINE n CHAR (1); -- redefinition produces an error
    .
    .
    .
```

The database server allows the redeclaration in the following example. Within the nested statement block, n is a character variable. Outside the block, n is an integer variable.

```
CREATE PROCEDURE example2()
    DEFINE n INT; DEFINE j INT;
    .
    .
    .
    BEGIN
    DEFINE n CHAR (1); -- character n masks integer variable
                       -- locally
    .
    .
    .
    END
```

Declaring GLOBAL Variables

The GLOBAL keyword indicates that the variables that follow are available to other SPL routines through the global environment. The data types of these variables must match the data types of variables in the *global environment*. The global environment is the memory that is used by all the SPL routines that run within a given DB-Access or SQL API session. The values of global variables are stored in memory.

SPL routines that are running in the current session share global variables. Because the database server does not save global variables in the database, the global variables do not remain when the current session closes. The data types of global variables you use in your SPL routine must match the data types of variables in the global environment.

Databases do not share global variables. The database server and any application development tools do not share global variables.

The first declaration of a global variable establishes the variable in the global environment; subsequent global declarations simply bind the variable to the global environment and establish the value of the variable at that point. The following example shows two SPL procedures, **proc1** and **proc2**; each has defined the global variable **gl_out**:

- SPL procedure **proc1**

```
CREATE PROCEDURE proc1()
      .
      .
      .
      DEFINE GLOBAL gl_out INT DEFAULT 13;
      .
      .
      .
      LET gl_out = gl_out + 1;
END PROCEDURE;
```

- SPL procedure **proc2**

```
CREATE PROCEDURE proc2()
  .
  .
  .
DEFINE GLOBAL gl_out INT DEFAULT 23;
DEFINE tmp INT;
  .
  .
  .
LET tmp = gl_out
  .
  .
  .
END PROCEDURE;
```

If proc1 is called first, **gl_out** is set to 13 and then incremented to 14. If **proc2** is then called, it sees that the value of **gl_out** is already defined, so the default value of 23 is not applied. Then, **proc2** assigns the existing value of 14 to **tmp**. If **proc2** had been called first, **gl_out** would have been set to 23, and 23 would have been assigned to **tmp**. Later calls to **proc1** would not apply the default of 13.

Default Value

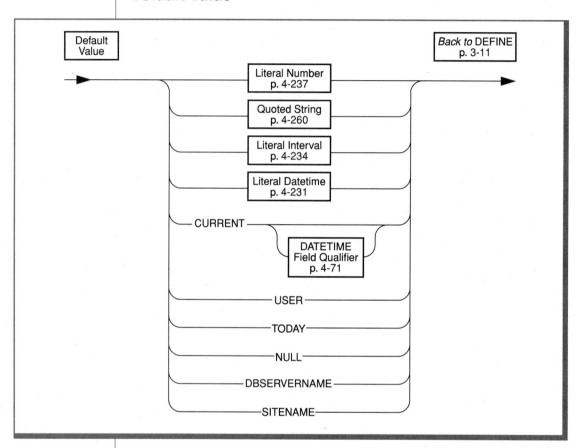

You can provide a literal value or a null value as the default for a global variable. You can also use a call to a built-in function to provide the default value. The following example uses the SITENAME function to provide a default value. It also defines a global BYTE variable.

```
CREATE PROCEDURE gl_def()
    DEFINE GLOBAL gl_site CHAR(200) DEFAULT SITENAME;
    DEFINE GLOBAL gl_byte REFERENCES BYTE DEFAULT NULL;
    .
    .
    .
END PROCEDURE
```

SITENAME or DBSERVERNAME

If you use the value returned by SITENAME or DBSERVERNAME as the default, the variable must be defined as a CHAR, VARCHAR, NCHAR, or NVARCHAR data type.

IDS

If you are using Dynamic Server, Informix recommends that the size of the variable be at least 128 bytes long. You risk getting an error message during INSERT and ALTER TABLE operations if the length of the variable is too small to store the default value. ◆

EDS

If you are using Enterprise Decision Server, Informix recommends that the length of the variable be at least 18 bytes. You risk getting an error message during INSERT and ALTER TABLE operations if the length of the variable is too small to store the default value. ◆

USER

If you use the value returned by USER as the default, the variable must be defined as a CHAR, VARCHAR, NCHAR, or NVARCHAR data type.

IDS

If you are using Dynamic Server, Informix recommends that the length of the variable be at least 32 bytes. You risk getting an error message during INSERT and ALTER TABLE operations if the length of the variable is too small to store the default value. ◆

EDS

If you are using Enterprise Decision Server, Informix recommends that the length of the variable be at least 8 bytes. You risk getting an error message during INSERT and ALTER TABLE operations if the length of the variable is too small to store the default value. ◆

CURRENT

If you use CURRENT as the default, the variable must be a DATETIME value. If the YEAR TO FRACTION keyword has qualified your variable, you can use CURRENT without qualifiers. If your variable uses another set of qualifiers, you must provide the same qualifiers when you use CURRENT as the default value. The following example defines a DATETIME variable with qualifiers and uses CURRENT with matching qualifiers:

```
DEFINE GLOBAL d_var DATETIME YEAR TO MONTH
       DEFAULT CURRENT YEAR TO MONTH;
```

TODAY

If you use TODAY as the default, the variable must be a DATE value.

BYTE and TEXT

The only default value possible for a BYTE or TEXT variable is null. The following example defines a TEXT global variable that is called **l_blob**:

```
CREATE PROCEDURE use_text()
    DEFINE i INT;
    DEFINE GLOBAL l_blob REFERENCES TEXT DEFAULT NULL;
END PROCEDURE
```

IDS

Subset of Complex Data Type

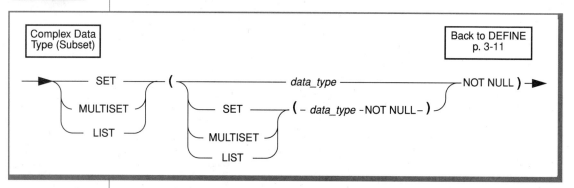

Element	Purpose	Restrictions	Syntax
data_type	Data type of the elements of a collection	The data type must match the data type of the elements of the collection the variable will contain.	Identifier, p. 4-205
		The data type can be any data type except a SERIAL, SERIAL8, TEXT, BYTE, CLOB, or BLOB.	

Declaring Local Variables

Nonglobal (local) variables do not allow defaults. The following example shows typical definitions of local variables:

```
CREATE PROCEDURE def_ex()
    DEFINE i INT;
    DEFINE word CHAR(15);
    DEFINE b_day DATE;
    DEFINE c_name LIKE customer.fname;
    DEFINE b_text REFERENCES TEXT ;
END PROCEDURE
```

IDS

Declaring Collection Variables

A variable of type COLLECTION, SET, MULTISET, and LIST is a collection variable and holds a collection fetched from the database. You cannot define a collection variable as global (with the GLOBAL keyword) or with a default value.

A variable defined with the type COLLECTION is an untyped collection variable. An untyped collection variable is generic and can hold a collection of any type.

A variable defined with the type SET, MULTISET, or LIST is a typed collection variable. A typed collection variable can hold only a collection of its type.

You must use the NOT NULL keywords when you define the elements of a typed collection variable, as in the following examples:

```
DEFINE a SET ( INT NOT NULL );

DEFINE b MULTISET ( ROW ( b1 INT,
                          b2 CHAR(50)
                        ) NOT NULL );

DEFINE c LIST( SET( INTEGER NOT NULL ) NOT NULL );
```

Note that with variable **c**, both the INTEGER values in the SET and the SET values in the LIST are defined as NOT NULL.

You can define collection variables with nested complex types to hold matching nested complex type data. Any type or depth of nesting is allowed. You can nest row types within collection types, collection types within row types, collection types within collection types, row types within collection and row types, and so on.

If you define a variable of COLLECTION type, the variable acquires varying type assignments if it is reused within the same statement block, as in the following example:

```
DEFINE a COLLECTION;
LET a = setB;
    .
    .
    .
LET a = listC;
```

In this example, **varA** is a generic collection variable that changes its data type to the data type of the currently assigned collection. The first LET statement makes **varA** a SET variable. The second LET statement makes **varA** a LIST variable.

IDS

Declaring Row Variables

Row variables hold data from named or unnamed row types. You can define a generic row variable, a named row variable, or an unnamed row variable.

A generic row variable, defined with the ROW keyword, can hold data from any row type. A named row variable holds data from the named row type specified in the variable definition. The following statements show examples of generic row variables and named row variables:

```
DEFINE d ROW;                 -- generic row variable

DEFINE rectv rectangle_t;-- named row variable
```

A named row variable holds named row types of the same type in the variable definition.

To define a variable that will hold data stored in an unnamed row type, use the ROW keyword followed by the fields of the row type, as in:

```
DEFINE area ROW ( x int, y char(10) );
```

Unnamed row types are type-checked only by structural equivalence. Two unnamed row types are considered equivalent if they have the same number of fields, and if the fields have the same type definitions. Therefore, you could fetch either of the following row types into the variable **area** defined above:

```
ROW ( a int, b char(10) )
ROW ( area int, name char(10) )
```

Row variables can have fields, just as row types have fields. To assign a value to a field of a row variable, use the SQL dot notation *variableName.fieldName*, followed by an expression, as in the following example:

```
CREATE ROW TYPE rectangle_t (start point_t, length real,
    width real);

DEFINE r rectangle_t;
        -- Define a variable of a named row type
LET r.length = 45.5;
        -- Assign a value to a field of the variable
```

When you assign a value to a row variable, you can use any allowed expression described in EXPRESSION.

IDS

Declaring Opaque-Type Variables

Opaque-type variables hold data retrieved from opaque types, which you create with the CREATE OPAQUE TYPE statement. An opaque-type variable can only hold data of the opaque type on which it is defined.

The following example defines a variable of the opaque type **point**, which holds the **x** and **y** coordinates of a two-dimensional point:

```
DEFINE b point;
```

Declaring Variables LIKE Columns

If you use the LIKE clause, the database server assigns the variable the same data type as a column in a table, synonym, or view.

The data types of variables that are defined as database columns are resolved at run time; therefore, *column* and *table* do not need to exist at compile time.

Declaring a Variable LIKE a SERIAL Column

You can use the LIKE keyword to declare that a variable is like a SERIAL column. For example, if the column **serialcol** in the **mytab** table has the SERIAL data type, you can create the following SPL function:

```
CREATE FUNCTION func1()
DEFINE local_var LIKE mytab.serialcol;
RETURN;
END FUNCTION;
```

The variable **local_var** is treated as an INTEGER variable.

Declaring Variables as the PROCEDURE Type

The PROCEDURE keyword indicates that in the current scope, the variable is a call to a UDR.

IDS

The DEFINE statement does not have a FUNCTION keyword. Use the PROCEDURE keyword, whether you are calling a user-defined procedure or a user-defined function. ♦

Defining a variable of PROCEDURE type indicates that in the current statement scope, the variable is not a call to a built-in function. For example, the following statement defines **length** as an SPL routine, not as the built-in LENGTH function:

```
DEFINE length PROCEDURE;
  .
  .
  .
LET x = length (a,b,c)
```

This definition disables the built-in LENGTH function within the scope of the statement block. You would use such a definition if you had already created a user-defined routine with the name **length**.

If you create an SPL routine with the same name as an aggregate function (SUM, MAX, MIN, AVG, COUNT) or with the name **extend**, you must qualify the routine name with the owner name.

Declaring Variables for BYTE and TEXT Data

The keyword REFERENCES indicates that the variable does not contain a BYTE or TEXT value but is a pointer to the BYTE or TEXT value. Use the variable as though it holds the data.

The following example defines a local BYTE variable:

```
CREATE PROCEDURE use_byte()
    DEFINE i INT;
    DEFINE l_byte REFERENCES BYTE;
END PROCEDURE --use_byte
```

If you pass a variable of BYTE or TEXT data type to an SPL routine, the data is passed to the database server and stored in the root dbspace or dbspaces that the **DBSPACETEMP** environment variable specifies, if it is set. You do not need to know the location or name of the file that holds the data. BYTE or TEXT manipulation requires only the name of the BYTE or TEXT variable as it is defined in the routine.

EXIT

Use the EXIT statement to stop the execution of a FOR, WHILE, or FOREACH loop.

Syntax

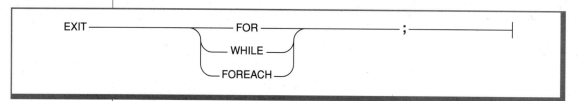

Usage

The EXIT statement causes the innermost loop of the indicated type (FOR, WHILE, or FOREACH) to terminate. Execution resumes at the first statement outside the loop.

If the EXIT statement cannot find the identified loop, it fails.

If the EXIT statement is used outside all loops, it generates errors.

The following example uses an EXIT FOR statement. In the FOR loop, when j becomes 6, the IF condition i = 5 in the WHILE loop is true. The FOR loop stops executing, and the SPL procedure continues at the next statement outside the FOR loop (in this case, the END PROCEDURE statement). In this example, the procedure ends when j equals 6.

```
CREATE PROCEDURE ex_cont_ex()
    DEFINE i,s,j, INT;

    FOR j = 1 TO 20
        IF j > 10 THEN
            CONTINUE FOR;
        END IF

        LET i,s = j,0;
        WHILE i > 0
            LET i = i -1;
            IF i = 5 THEN
                EXIT FOR;
            END IF
        END WHILE
    END FOR
END PROCEDURE
```

FOR

Use the FOR statement to initiate a controlled (definite) loop when you want to guarantee termination of the loop. The FOR statement uses expressions or range operators to establish a finite number of iterations for a loop.

Syntax

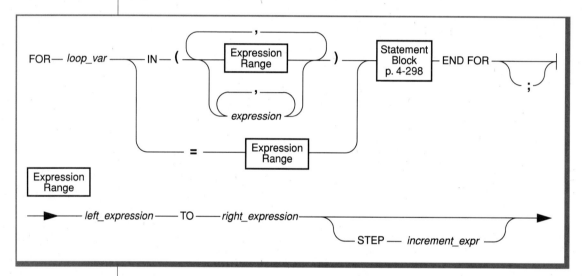

Element	Purpose	Restrictions	Syntax
expression	Numeric or character value against which loop_var is compared to determine if the loop should be executed	The data type of *expression* must match the data type of *loop_var*. You can use the output of a SELECT statement as an *expression*.	Expression, p. 4-73
increment_expr	Positive or negative value by which loop_var is incremented The default is +1 or -1, depending on *left_expression* and *right_expression*.	The increment expression cannot evaluate to 0.	Expression, p. 4-73

(1 of 2)

Element	Purpose	Restrictions	Syntax
left_expression	Starting expression of a range	The value of left_expression must match the data type of *loop_var*. It must be either INT or SMALLINT.	Expression, p. 4-73
loop_var	Value of this variable determines how many times the loop executes	You must have already defined this variable, and the variable must be valid within this statement block.	Identifier, p. 4-205
		If you are using loop_var with a range of values and the TO keyword, you must define *loop_var* explicitly as either INT or SMALLINT.	
right_expression	Ending expression in the range The size of right_expression relative to *left_expression* determines if the range is stepped through positively or negatively.	The value of *right_expression* must match the data type of *loop_var*. It must be either INT or SMALLINT.	Expression, p. 4-73

(2 of 2)

Usage

The database server computes all expressions before the FOR statement executes. If one or more of the expressions are variables, and their values change during the loop, the change has no effect on the iterations of the loop.

The FOR loop terminates when *loop_var* is equal to the values of each element in the expression list or range in succession or when it encounters an EXIT FOR statement.

The database server generates an error if an assignment within the body of the FOR statement attempts to modify the value of *loop_var*.

Using the TO Keyword to Define a Range

The TO keyword implies a range operator. The range is defined by
left_expression and *right_expression*, and the STEP *increment_expr* option
implicitly sets the number of increments. If you use the TO keyword, *loop_var*
must be an INT or SMALLINT data type. The following example shows two
equivalent FOR statements. Each uses the TO keyword to define a range. The
first statement uses the IN keyword, and the second statement uses an equal
sign (=). Each statement causes the loop to execute five times.

```
FOR index_var IN (12 TO 21 STEP 2)
    -- statement block
END FOR

FOR index_var = 12 TO 21 STEP 2
    -- statement block
END FOR
```

If you omit the STEP option, the database server gives *increment_expr* the
value of -1 if *right_expression* is less than *left_expression*, or +1 if
right_expression is more than *left_expression*. If *increment_expr* is specified, it
must be negative if *right_expression* is less than *left_expression*, or positive if
right expression is more than *left_expression*. The two statements in the
following example are equivalent. In the first statement, the STEP increment
is explicit. In the second statement, the STEP increment is implicitly 1.

```
FOR index IN (12 TO 21 STEP 1)
    -- statement block
END FOR

FOR index = 12 TO 21
    -- statement block
END FOR
```

The database server initializes the value of *loop_var* to the value of
left_expression. In subsequent iterations, the server adds *increment_expr* to the
value of *loop_var* and checks *increment_expr* to determine whether the value
of *loop_var* is still between *left_expression* and *right_expression*. If so, the next
iteration occurs. Otherwise, an exit from the loop takes place. Or, if you
specify another range, the variable takes on the value of the first element in
the next range.

Specifying Two or More Ranges in a Single FOR Statement

The following example shows a statement that traverses a loop forward and backward and uses different increment values for each direction:

```
FOR index_var IN (15 to 21 STEP 2, 21 to 15 STEP -3)
    -- statement body
END FOR
```

Using an Expression List as the Range

The database server initializes the value of *loop_var* to the value of the first expression specified. In subsequent iterations, *loop_var* takes on the value of the next expression. When the server has evaluated the last expression in the list and used it, the loop stops.

The expressions in the IN list do not have to be numeric values, as long as you do not use range operators in the IN list. The following example uses a character expression list:

```
FOR c IN ('hello', (SELECT name FROM t), 'world', v1, v2)
    INSERT INTO t VALUES (c);
    END FOR
```

The following FOR statement shows the use of a numeric expression list:

```
FOR index IN (15,16,17,18,19,20,21)
    -- statement block
END FOR
```

Mixing Range and Expression Lists in the Same FOR Statement

If *loop_var* is an INT or SMALLINT value, you can mix ranges and expression lists in the same FOR statement. The following example shows a mixture that uses an integer variable. Values in the expression list include the value that is returned from a SELECT statement, a sum of an integer variable and a constant, the values that are returned from an SPL function named **p_get_int**, and integer constants.

```
CREATE PROCEDURE for_ex ()
    DEFINE i, j INT;
    LET j = 10;
    FOR i IN (1 TO 20, (SELECT c1 FROM tab WHERE id = 1),
    j+20 to j-20, p_get_int(99),98,90 to 80 step -2)
        INSERT INTO tab VALUES (i);
    END FOR
END PROCEDURE
```

FOREACH

Use a FOREACH loop to select and manipulate more than one row.

Syntax

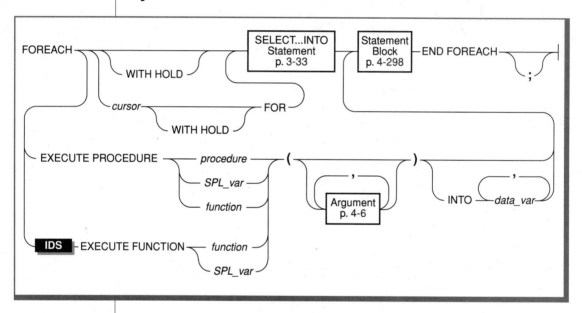

Element	Purpose	Restrictions	Syntax
cursor	Identifier that you supply as a name for the FOREACH loop	Each cursor name within a routine must be unique.	Identifier, p. 4-205
data_var	Name of an SPL variable in the calling SPL routine that will receive the value or values the called function returns	The data type of *data_var* must be appropriate for the value that is being returned.	Identifier, p. 4-205
function	Name of the SPL function you want to execute	The function must exist.	Database Object Name, p. 4-50

(1 of 2)

Element	Purpose	Restrictions	Syntax
procedure	Name of the SPL procedure you want to execute	The procedure must exist.	Database Object Name, p. 4-50
SPL_var	Name of an SPL variable in the calling SPL routine that contains the name of a routine to be executed	The data type of *SPL_var* must be CHAR, VARCHAR, NCHAR, or NVARCHAR.	Identifier, p. 4-205

(2 of 2)

Usage

A FOREACH loop is the procedural equivalent of using a cursor. When a FOREACH statement executes, the database server takes the following actions:

1. It declares and implicitly opens a cursor.

2. It obtains the first row from the query that is contained within the FOREACH loop, or it obtains the first set of values from the called routine.

3. It assigns to each variable in the variable list the value of the corresponding value from the active set that the SELECT statement or the called routine creates.

4. It executes the statement block.

5. It fetches the next row from the SELECT statement or called routine on each iteration, and it repeats steps 3 and 4.

6. It terminates the loop when it finds no more rows that satisfy the SELECT statement or called routine. It closes the implicit cursor when the loop terminates.

Because the statement block can contain additional FOREACH statements, cursors can be nested. No limit exists to the number of cursors that can be nested.

An SPL routine that returns more than one row, collection element, or set of values is called a cursor function. An SPL routine that returns only one row or value is a noncursor function.

The following SPL procedure illustrates FOREACH statements with a
SELECT...INTO clause, with an explicitly named cursor, and with a procedure
call:

```
CREATE PROCEDURE foreach_ex()
    DEFINE i, j INT;

    FOREACH SELECT c1 INTO i FROM tab ORDER BY 1
        INSERT INTO tab2 VALUES (i);
    END FOREACH

    FOREACH cur1 FOR SELECT c2, c3 INTO i, j FROM tab
        IF j > 100 THEN
            DELETE FROM tab WHERE CURRENT OF cur1;
            CONTINUE FOREACH;
        END IF
        UPDATE tab SET c2 = c2 + 10 WHERE CURRENT OF cur1;
    END FOREACH

    FOREACH EXECUTE PROCEDURE bar(10,20) INTO i
        INSERT INTO tab2 VALUES (i);
    END FOREACH
END PROCEDURE;  -- foreach_ex
```

A select cursor is closed when any of the following situations occur:

- The cursor returns no further rows.

- The cursor is a select cursor without a HOLD specification, and a
  transaction completes using COMMIT or ROLLBACK statements.

- An EXIT statement executes, which transfers control out of the
  FOREACH statement.

- An exception occurs that is not trapped inside the body of the
  FOREACH statement. (See "ON EXCEPTION" on page 3-45.)

- A cursor in the calling routine that is executing this cursor routine
  (within a FOREACH loop) closes for any reason.

Using a SELECT...INTO Statement

As indicated in the diagram for "FOREACH" on page 3-30, not all clauses and options of the SELECT statement are available for you to use in a FOREACH statement.

The SELECT statement in the FOREACH statement must include the INTO clause. It can also include UNION and ORDER BY clauses, but it cannot use the INTO TEMP clause. For a complete description of SELECT syntax and usage, see "SELECT" on page 634.

The type and count of each variable in the variable list must match each value that the SELECT...INTO statement returns.

Using Hold Cursors

The WITH HOLD keyword specifies that the cursor should remain open when a transaction closes (is committed or rolled back).

Updating or Deleting Rows Identified by Cursor Name

Use the WHERE CURRENT OF *cursor* clause to update or delete the current row of *cursor*.

IDS

Using Collection Variables

The FOREACH statement allows you to declare a cursor for an SPL collection variable. Such a cursor is called a *collection cursor*. You use a collection variable to access the elements of a collection (SET, MULTISET, LIST) column. Use a cursor when you want to access one or more elements in a collection variable.

Restrictions

When you use a collection cursor to fetch individual elements from a collection variable the FOREACH statement has the following restrictions:

- It cannot contain the WITH HOLD keywords.
- It must contain a restricted select statement within the FOREACH loop.

In addition, the SELECT statement that you associate with the collection cursor has the following restrictions:

- Its general structure is SELECT... INTO... FROM TABLE. The statement selects one element at a time from a collection variable named after the TABLE keyword into another variable called an *element variable*.

- It cannot contain an expression in the select list.

- It cannot include the following clauses or options: WHERE, GROUP BY, ORDER BY, HAVING, INTO TEMP, and WITH REOPTIMIZATION.

- The data type of the element variable must be the same as the element type of the collection.

- The data type of the element variable can be any opaque, distinct, or collection data type, or any built-in data type except SERIAL, SERIAL8, TEXT, BYTE, CLOB or BLOB.

- If the collection contains opaque, distinct, built-in, or collection types, the select list must be an asterisk (*).

- If the collection contains row types, the select list can be a list of one or more field names.

Examples

The following excerpt from an SPL routine shows how to fill a collection variable and then how to use a cursor to access individual elements:

```
DEFINE a SMALLINT;
DEFINE b SET(SMALLINT NOT NULL);

SELECT numbers INTO b FROM table1
    WHERE id = 207;

FOREACH cursor1 FOR
    SELECT * INTO a FROM TABLE(b);
    .
    .
    .
END FOREACH;
```

In this example, the SELECT statement selects one element at a time from the collection variable **b** into the element variable **a**. The select list is an asterisk, because the collection variable **b** contains a collection of built-in types. The variable **b** is used with the TABLE keyword as a Collection Derived Table. For more information, see "Collection Derived Table" on page 4-9.

The next example also shows how to fill a collection variable and then how to use a cursor to access individual elements. This example, however, uses a list of row type fields in its select list.

```
        .
        .
        .
    DEFINE employees employee_t;
    DEFINE n VARCHAR(30);
    DEFINE s INTEGER;

    SELECT emp_list into employees FROM dept_table
        WHERE dept_no = 1057;

    FOREACH cursor1 FOR
        SELECT name,salary
            INTO n,s FROM TABLE( employees ) AS e;
    .
    .
    .
    END FOREACH;
        .
        .
        .
```

In this example, the collection variable **employees** contains a collection of row types. Each row type contains the fields **name** and **salary**. The collection query selects one name and salary combination at a time, placing **name** into **n** and **salary** into **s**. The AS keyword names **e** as an alias for the collection derived table **employees**. The alias exists as long as the SELECT statement executes.

Modifying Elements in a Collection Variable

To update an element of a collection, you must first declare a cursor with the FOREACH statement. Then, within the FOREACH loop, select elements one at a time from the collection variable, using the collection variable as a collection derived table in a SELECT query.

When the cursor is positioned on the element to be updated, you can use the WHERE CURRENT OF clause, as follows:

- The UPDATE statement with the WHERE CURRENT OF clause updates the value in the current element of the collection variable.

- The DELETE statement with the WHERE CURRENT OF clause deletes the current element from the collection variable.

Calling a UDR in the FOREACH Loop

In general, use the following guidelines for calling another UDR from an SPL routine:

- To call a user-defined procedure, use EXECUTE PROCEDURE *procedure name*.

- To call a user-defined function, use EXECUTE FUNCTION *function name* (or EXECUTE PROCEDURE *function name* if the user-defined function was created with the CREATE PROCEDURE statement).

EDS

In Enterprise Decision Server, you must use EXECUTE PROCEDURE. Enterprise Decision Server does not support the EXECUTE FUNCTION statement. ♦

IDS

In Dynamic Server, if you use EXECUTE PROCEDURE, the database server looks first for a user-defined procedure of the name you specify. If it finds the procedure, the server executes it. If it does not find the procedure, it looks for a user-defined function of the same name to execute. If the database server finds neither a function nor a procedure, it issues an error message.

If you use EXECUTE FUNCTION, the database server looks for a user-defined function of the name you specify. If it does not find a function of that name, the server issues an error message. ♦

A called SPL function can return zero (0) or more values or rows.

The type and count of each variable in the variable list must match each value that the function returns.

IF

Use an IF statement to create a branch within an SPL routine.

Syntax

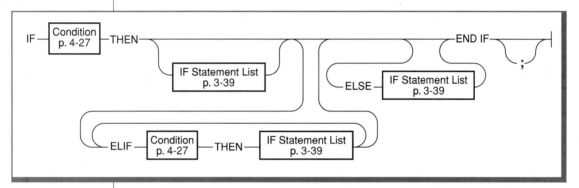

Usage

The condition that the IF clause states is evaluated. If the result is true, the statements that follow the THEN keyword execute. If the result is false, and an ELIF clause exists, the statements that follow the ELIF clause execute. If no ELIF clause exists, or if the condition in the ELIF clause is not true, the statements that follow the ELIF keyword execute.

In the following example, the SPL function uses an IF statement with both an ELIF clause and an ELSE clause. The IF statement compares two strings and displays a 1 to indicate that the first string comes before the second string alphabetically, or a -1 if the first string comes after the second string alphabetically. If the strings are the same, a zero (0) is returned.

```
CREATE FUNCTION str_compare (str1 CHAR(20), str2 CHAR(20))
    RETURNING INT;
    DEFINE result INT;

    IF str1 > str2 THEN
        LET result =1;
    ELIF str2 > str1 THEN
        :LET result = -1;
    ELSE
        LET result = 0;
    END IF
    RETURN result;
END FUNCTION -- str_compare
```

ELIF Clause

Use the ELIF clause to specify one or more additional conditions to evaluate.

If you specify an ELIF clause, and the IF condition is false, the ELIF condition is evaluated. If the ELIF condition is true, the statements that follow the ELIF clause execute.

ELSE Clause

The ELSE clause executes if no true previous condition exists in the IF clause or any of the ELIF clauses.

Conditions in an IF Statement

Conditions in an IF statement are evaluated in the same way as conditions in a WHILE statement.

If any expression that the condition contains evaluates to null, the condition automatically becomes untrue. Consider the following points:

1. If the expression x evaluates to null, then x is not true by definition. Furthermore, not(x) is also *not* true.

2. IS NULL is the sole operator that can yield true for x. That is, x IS NULL is true, and x IS NOT NULL is not true.

An expression within the condition that has an UNKNOWN value (due to the use of an uninitialized variable) causes an immediate error. The statement terminates and raises an exception.

IF Statement List

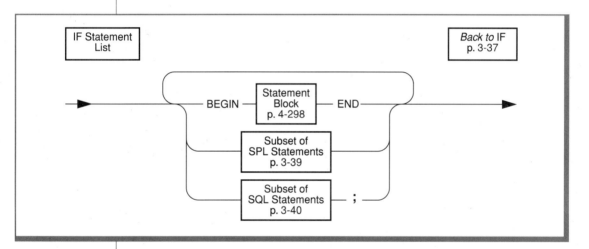

Subset of SPL Statements Allowed in the IF Statement List

You can use any of the following SPL statements in the IF statement list:

CALL	LET
CONTINUE	RAISE EXCEPTION
EXIT	RETURN
FOR	SYSTEM
FOREACH	TRACE
IF	WHILE

The preceding diagram for the "IF Statement List" refers to this section.

SQL Statements Not Allowed in an IF Statement

You can use any SQL statement in the IF statement list except those in the following list:

ALLOCATE DESCRIPTOR	FREE
CLOSE DATABASE	GET DESCRIPTOR
CONNECT	GET DIAGNOSTICS
CREATE DATABASE	INFO
CREATE PROCEDURE	LOAD
DATABASE	OPEN
DEALLOCATE DESCRIPTOR	OUTPUT
DECLARE	PREPARE
DESCRIBE	PUT
DISCONNECT	SET CONNECTION
EXECUTE	SET DESCRIPTOR
EXECUTE IMMEDIATE	UNLOAD
FETCH	WHENEVER
FLUSH	

You can use a SELECT statement only if you use the INTO TEMP clause to put the results of the SELECT statement into a temporary table.

The diagram for the "IF Statement List" on page 3-39 refers to this section.

LET

Use the LET statement to assign values to variables or to call a user-defined function from an SPL routine and assign the return value or values to variables.

Syntax

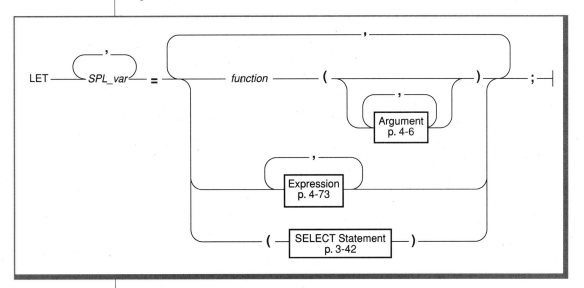

Element	Purpose	Restrictions	Syntax
function	Name of the SPL function you want to call	The function must exist.	Database Object Name, p. 4-50
SPL_var	SPL variable that receives the value the function returns or is set to the result of the expression	The SPL variable must be defined and must be valid in the statement block.	Identifier, p. 4-205

Usage

If you assign a value to a single variable, it is called a *simple assignment*; if you assign values to two or more variables, it is called a *compound assignment*.

You can also assign the value of an expression to a variable. At run time, the value of the SPL expression is computed first. The resulting value is cast to the data type of *variable*, if possible, and the assignment occurs. If conversion is not possible, an error occurs, and the value of *variable name* is undefined.

A compound assignment assigns multiple expressions to multiple variables.The data types of expressions in the expression list does not need to match the data types of the corresponding variables in the variable list, because the database server automatically converts the data types. (For a detailed discussion of casting, see the *Informix Guide to SQL: Reference*.)

The following example shows several LET statements that assign values to SPL variables:

```
LET a   = c + d ;
LET a,b = c,d ;
LET expire_dt = end_dt + 7 UNITS DAY;
LET name = 'Brunhilda';
LET sname = DBSERVERNAME;
LET this_day = TODAY;
```

You cannot use multiple values to operate on other values. For example, the following statement is illegal:

```
LET a,b = (c,d) + (10,15); -- ILLEGAL EXPRESSION
```

Using a SELECT Statement in a LET Statement

The diagram for "LET" on page 3-41 refers to this section.

The examples in this section use a SELECT statement in a LET statement. You can use a SELECT statement to assign values to one or more variables on the left side of the equals (=) operator, as the following example shows:

```
LET a,b = (SELECT c1,c2 FROM t WHERE id = 1);
LET a,b,c = (SELECT c1,c2 FROM t WHERE id = 1), 15;
```

You cannot use a SELECT statement to make multiple values operate on other values. The following example is illegal:

```
LET a,b = (SELECT c1,c2 FROM t) + (10,15); -- ILLEGAL CODE
```

Because a LET statement is equivalent to a SELECT...INTO statement, the two statements in the following example have the same results: a=c and b=d:

```
CREATE PROCEDURE proof()
    DEFINE a, b, c, d INT;
    LET a,b = (SELECT c1,c2 FROM t WHERE id = 1);
    SELECT c1, c2 INTO c, d FROM t WHERE id = 1
END PROCEDURE
```

If the SELECT statement returns more than one row, you must enclose the SELECT statement in a FOREACH loop.

For a complete description of SELECT syntax and usage, see "SELECT" on page 2-634.

Calling a Function in a LET Statement

You can call a user-defined function in a LET statement and assign the return values to an SPL variable. The SPL variable receives the returned values from the called function.

An SPL function can return multiple values (that is, values from multiple columns in the same row) into a list of variable names. In other words, the function can have multiple values in its RETURN statement and the LET statement can have multiple variables to receive the returned values.

When you call the function, you must specify all the necessary arguments to the function unless the arguments of the function have default values. If you name one of the parameters in the called function, with syntax such as **name = 'smith'**, you must name all of the parameters.

An SPL function that selects and returns more than one row must be enclosed in a FOREACH loop.

The following two example show valid LET statements.

```
LET a, b, c = func1(name = 'grok', age = 17);
LET a, b, c = 7, func2('orange', 'green');
```

The following LET statement is not legal, because it tries to add the output of two functions and then assign the sum to two variables, *a* and *b*. You can easily split this LET statement into two legal LET statements.

```
LET a, b = func1() + func2(); -- ILLEGAL CODE
```

A function called in a LET statement can have an argument of COLLECTION, SET, MULTISET, or LIST. You can assign the value returned by the function to a variable, for example:

```
LET d = function1(collection1);
LET a = function2(set1);
```

In the first statement, the SPL function **function1** accepts **collection1** (that is, any collection data type) as an argument and returns its value to the variable **d**. In the second statement, the SPL function **function2** accepts **set1** as an argument and returns a value to the variable **a**.

ON EXCEPTION

Use the ON EXCEPTION statement to specify the actions that are taken for a particular error or a set of errors.

Syntax

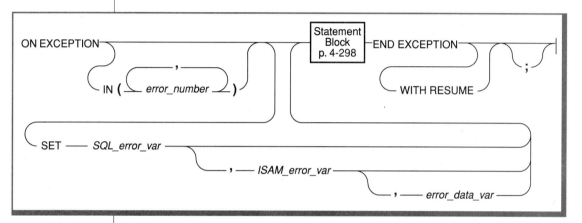

Element	Purpose	Restrictions	Syntax
error_data_var	SPL variable that contains a string returned by an SQL error or a user-defined exception	Must be a character data type to receive the error information. Must be valid in the current statement block.	Identifier, p. 4-205
error_number	SQL error number, or an error number created by a RAISE EXCEPTION statement, that is to be trapped	Must be of integer data type. Must be valid in the current statement block.	Literal number, p. 4-237
ISAM_error_var	Variable that receives the ISAM error number of the exception raised	Must be of integer data type. Must be valid in the current statement block.	Identifier, p. 4-205
SQL_error_var	Variable that receives the SQL error number of the exception raised	Must be a character data type. Must be valid in the current statement block.	Identifier, p. 4-205

Usage

The ON EXCEPTION statement, together with the RAISE EXCEPTION statement, provides an error-trapping and error-recovery mechanism for SPL. The ON EXCEPTION statement defines a list of errors that you want to trap as the SPL routine executes and specifies the action (within the statement block) to take when the trap is triggered. If the IN clause is omitted, all errors are trapped.

You can use more than one ON EXCEPTION statement within a given statement block.

The scope of an ON EXCEPTION statement is the statement block that follows the ON EXCEPTION statement and all the statement blocks that are nested within that following statement block.

The exceptions that are trapped can be either system- or user-defined.

When an exception is trapped, the error status is cleared.

If you specify a variable to receive an ISAM error, but no accompanying ISAM error exists, a zero (0) returns to the variable. If you specify a variable to receive the returned error text, but none exists, an empty string goes into the variable.

An ON EXCEPTION statement does not work in a UDR that is called by a trigger.

Placement of the ON EXCEPTION Statement

ON EXCEPTION is a declarative statement, not an executable statement. For this reason, you must use the ON EXCEPTION statement before any executable statement and after any DEFINE statement in an SPL routine.

The following example shows the correct placement of an ON EXCEPTION statement. The **add_salesperson** function inserts a set of values into a table. If the table does not exist, it is created, and the values are inserted. The function also returns the total number of rows in the table after the insert occurs.

```
CREATE FUNCTION add_salesperson(last CHAR(15),
               first CHAR(15))
     RETURNING INT;
     DEFINE x INT;
     ON EXCEPTION IN (-206) -- If no table was found, create one
          CREATE TABLE emp_list
               (lname CHAR(15),fname CHAR(15), tele CHAR(12));
          INSERT INTO emp_list VALUES -- and insert values
               (last, first, '800-555-1234');
     END EXCEPTION WITH RESUME
     INSERT INTO emp_list VALUES (last, first, '800-555-1234')
     LET x = SELECT count(*) FROM emp_list;
     RETURN x;
END FUNCTION
```

When an error occurs, the database server searches for the last declaration of the ON EXCEPTION statement, which traps the particular error code. The ON EXCEPTION statement can have the error number in the IN clause or have no IN clause. If the database server finds no pertinent ON EXCEPTION statement, the error code passes back to the caller (the SPL routine, application, or interactive user), and execution aborts.

The following example uses two ON EXCEPTION statements with the same error number so that error code 691 can be trapped in two levels of nesting:

```
CREATE PROCEDURE delete_cust (cnum INT)
     ON EXCEPTION  IN (-691)     -- children exist
          BEGIN -- Begin-end is necessary so that other DELETEs
               -- don't get caught in here.
               ON EXCEPTION IN (-691)
                    DELETE FROM another_child WHERE num = cnum;
                    DELETE FROM orders WHERE customer_num = cnum;
               END EXCEPTION -- for 691

          DELETE FROM orders WHERE customer_num = cnum;
          END

        DELETE FROM cust_calls WHERE customer_num = cnum;
        DELETE FROM customer WHERE customer_num = cnum;
     END EXCEPTION
        DELETE FROM customer WHERE customer_num = cnum;
END PROCEDURE
```

Using the IN Clause to Trap Specific Exceptions

A trap is triggered if either the SQL error code or the ISAM error code matches an exception code in the list of error numbers. The search through the list begins from the left and stops with the first match.

You can use a combination of an ON EXCEPTION statement without an IN clause and one or more ON EXCEPTION statements with an IN clause to set up default trapping. When an error occurs, the database server searches for the last declaration of the ON EXCEPTION statement that traps the particular error code.

```
CREATE PROCEDURE ex_test ()
    DEFINE error_num INT;
    .
    .
    .
    ON EXCEPTION
    SET error_num
    -- action C
    END EXCEPTION

    ON EXCEPTION IN (-300)
    -- action B
    END EXCEPTION
    ON EXCEPTION IN (-210, -211, -212)
    SET error_num
    -- action A
    END EXCEPTION
    .
    .
    .
```

A summary of the sequence of statements in the previous example would be:

1. Test for an error.

2. If error -210, -211, or -212 occurs, take action A.

3. If error -300 occurs, take action B.

4. If any other error occurs, take action C.

Receiving Error Information in the SET Clause

If you use the SET clause, when an exception occurs, the SQL error code and (optionally) the ISAM error code are inserted into the variables that are specified in the SET clause. If you provided an *error_data_var*, any error text that the database server returns is put into the *error_data_var*. Error text includes information such as the offending table or column name.

Forcing Continuation of the Routine

The first example in "Placement of the ON EXCEPTION Statement" on page 3-46 uses the WITH RESUME keyword to indicate that after the statement block in the ON EXCEPTION statement executes, execution is to continue at the LET x = SELECT COUNT(*) FROM emp_list statement, which is the line following the line that raised the error. For this function, the result is that the count of salespeople names occurs even if the error occurred.

Continuing Execution After an Exception Occurs

If you do not include the WITH RESUME keyword in your ON EXCEPTION statement, the next statement that executes after an exception occurs depends on the placement of the ON EXCEPTION statement, as the following scenarios describe:

- If the ON EXCEPTION statement is inside a statement block with a BEGIN and an END keyword, execution resumes with the first statement (if any) after that BEGIN...END block. That is, it resumes after the scope of the ON EXCEPTION statement.

- If the ON EXCEPTION statement is inside a loop (FOR, WHILE, FOREACH), the rest of the loop is skipped, and execution resumes with the next iteration of the loop.

- If no statement or block, but only the SPL routine, contains the ON EXCEPTION statement, the routine executes a RETURN statement with no arguments to terminate. That is, the routine returns a successful status and no values.

Errors Within the ON EXCEPTION Statement Block

To prevent an infinite loop, if an error occurs during execution of the statement block of an error trap, the search for another trap does not include the current trap.

RAISE EXCEPTION

Use the RAISE EXCEPTION statement to simulate the generation of an error.

Syntax

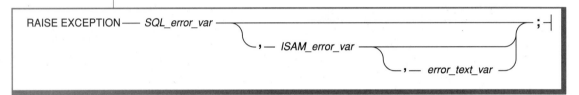

Element	Purpose	Restrictions	Syntax
error_text_var	SPL variable that contains the error text	The SPL variable must be a character data type and must be valid in the statement block.	Identifier, p. 4-205
ISAM_error_var	Variable or expression that represents an ISAM error number The default value is 0.	The variable or expression must evaluate to a SMALLINT value. You can place a minus sign before the error number.	Expression, p. 4-73
SQL_error_var	Variable or expression that represents an SQL error number	The variable or expression must evaluate to a SMALLINT value. You can place a minus sign before the error number.	Expression, p. 4-73

Usage

Use the RAISE EXCEPTION statement to simulate an error or to generate an error with a custom message. An ON EXCEPTION statement can trap the generated error.

If you omit the *ISAM_error_var* parameter, the database server sets the ISAM error code to zero (0) when the exception is raised. If you want to use the *error_text_var* parameter but not specify a value for *ISAM_error_var*, you can specify zero (0) as the value of *ISAM_error_var*.

The statement can raise either system-generated exceptions or user-generated exceptions.

For example, the following statement raises the error number -208 and inserts the text a missing file into the variable of the system-generated error message:

```
RAISE EXCEPTION -208, 0, 'a missing file';
```

Special Error Numbers

The special error number -746 allows you to produce a customized message. For example, the following statement raises the error number -746 and returns the quoted text:

```
RAISE EXCEPTION -746, 0, 'You broke the rules';
```

In the following example, a negative value for alpha raises exception -746 and provides a specific message describing the problem. The code should contain an ON EXCEPTION statement that traps for an exception of -746.

```
FOREACH SELECT c1 INTO alpha FROM sometable
IF alpha < 0 THEN
RAISE EXCEPTION -746, 0, 'a < 0 found' -- emergency exit
END IF
END FOREACH
```

When the SPL routine executes and the IF condition is met, the database server returns the following error:

```
-746: a < 0 found.
```

For more information about the scope and compatibility of exceptions, see "ON EXCEPTION" on page 3-45.

RETURN

Use the RETURN statement to designate the values that the SPL function returns to the calling module.

Syntax

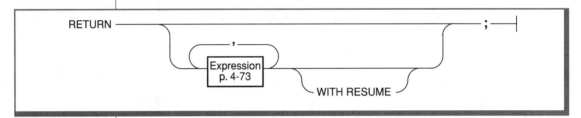

Usage

The RETURN statement returns zero (0) or more values to the calling process.

IDS

In Dynamic Server, for backward compatibility, you can use this statement inside a CREATE PROCEDURE statement to create an SPL function. However, Informix recommends that you only use this statement inside the CREATE FUNCTION statement to create new user-defined functions. ♦

All the RETURN statements in the SPL function must be consistent with the RETURNING clause of the CREATE FUNCTION (or CREATE PROCEDURE) statement, which defines the function.

The number and data type of values in the RETURN statement, if any, must match in number and data type the data types that are listed in the RETURNING clause of the CREATE FUNCTION (or CREATE PROCEDURE) statement. You can choose to return no values even if you specify one or more values in the RETURNING clause. If you use a RETURN statement without any expressions, but the calling UDR or program expects one or more return values, it is equivalent to returning the expected number of null values to the calling program.

In the following example, the SPL function includes two acceptable RETURN statements. A program that calls this function should check if no values are returned and act accordingly.

```
CREATE FUNCTION two_returns (stockno INT)
    RETURNING CHAR (15);
    DEFINE des CHAR(15);
    ON EXCEPTION (-272)
-- if user doesn't have select privs...
        RETURN;
-- return no values.
    END EXCEPTION;
    SELECT DISTINCT descript INTO des FROM stock
            WHERE stocknum = stockno;
    RETURN des;
END FUNCTION
```

A RETURN statement without any expressions exits only if the SPL function is declared not to return values; otherwise it returns nulls.

IDS

In an SPL program, you can use an external function as an expression in a RETURN statement provided that the external function is not an iterator function. An *iterator function* is an external function that returns one or more rows of data and therefore requires a cursor to execute. ♦

WITH RESUME Keyword

If you use the WITH RESUME keyword, after the RETURN statement executes the next invocation of the SPL function (upon the next FETCH OR FOREACH statement) starts from the statement that follows the RETURN statement. If a function executes a RETURN WITH RESUME statement, the calling UDR or program must call the function within a FOREACH loop.

E/C

If an SPL routine executes a RETURN WITH RESUME statement, a FETCH statement in an ESQL/C application can call it. ♦

The following example shows a cursor function that another UDR can call. After the RETURN I WITH RESUME statement returns each value to the calling UDR or program, the next line of **sequence** executes the next time **sequence** is called. If **backwards** equals zero (0), no value is returned to the calling UDR or program, and execution of **sequence** stops.

```
CREATE FUNCTION sequence (limit INT, backwards INT)
    RETURNING INT;
    DEFINE i INT;

    FOR i IN (1 TO limit)
        RETURN i WITH RESUME;
    END FOR

    IF backwards = 0 THEN
        RETURN;
    END IF

    FOR i IN (limit TO 1 STEP -1)
        RETURN i WITH RESUME;
    END IF
END FUNCTION -- sequence
```

SYSTEM

Use the SYSTEM statement to make an operating-system command run from within an SPL routine.

Syntax

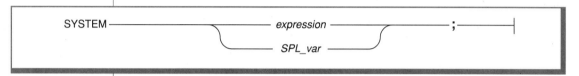

Element	Purpose	Restrictions	Syntax
expression	Any expression that is a user-executable operating-system command	You cannot specify that the command run in the background.	Operating-system dependent
SPL_var	An SPL variable that contains a valid operating-system command	The SPL variable must be of CHAR, VARCHAR, NCHAR, NVARCHAR, or CHARACTER VARYING data type.	Identifier, p. 4-205

Usage

If the supplied expression is not a character expression, *expression* is converted to a character expression before the operating-system command is made. The complete character expression passes to the operating system and executes as an operating-system command.

The operating-system command that the SYSTEM statement specifies cannot run in the background. The database server waits for the operating system to complete execution of the command before it continues to the next statement in the SPL routine.

Your SPL routine cannot use a value or values that the command returns.

If the operating-system command fails (that is, if the operating system returns a nonzero status for the command), an exception is raised that contains the returned operating-system status as the ISAM error code and an appropriate SQL error code.

In DBA- and owner-privileged SPL routines that contain SYSTEM statements, the operating-system command runs with the permissions of the user who is executing the routine.

Specifying Environment Variables in SYSTEM Statements

When the operating-system command that SYSTEM specifies is executed, no guarantee exists that the environment variables that the user application set are passed to the operating system. To ensure that the environment variables that the application set are carried forward to the operating system, enter a SYSTEM command that sets the environment variables before you enter the SYSTEM command that causes the operating-system command to execute.

For information on the operating-system commands that set environment variables, see the *Informix Guide to SQL: Reference*.

UNIX

Examples of the SYSTEM Statement on UNIX

The following example shows a SYSTEM statement in an SPL routine. The SYSTEM statement in this example causes the UNIX operating system to send a mail message to the system administrator.

```
CREATE PROCEDURE sensitive_update()
   .
   .
   .
   LET mailcall = 'mail headhoncho < alert';
   -- code that evaluates if operator tries to execute a
   -- certain command, then sends email to system
   -- administrator
   SYSTEM mailcall;
   .
   .
   .
END PROCEDURE; -- sensitive_update
```

You can use a double-pipe symbol (| |) to concatenate expressions with a SYSTEM statement, as the following example shows:

```
CREATE PROCEDURE sensitive_update2()
    DEFINE user1 char(15);
    DEFINE user2 char(15);
    LET user1 = 'joe';
    LET user2 = 'mary';
    .
    .
    .
    -- code that evaluates if operator tries to execute a
    -- certain command, then sends email to system
    -- administrator
    SYSTEM 'mail -s violation' ||user1 || ' ' || user2
                      || '< violation_file';
    .
    .
    .
END PROCEDURE; --sensitive_update2
```

WIN NT

Example of the SYSTEM Statement on Windows NT

The following example shows a SYSTEM statement in an SPL routine. The first SYSTEM statement in this routine causes the Windows NT operating system to send an error message to a temporary file and to put the message in a system log that is sorted alphabetically. The second SYSTEM statement causes the operating system to delete the temporary file.

```
CREATE PROCEDURE test_proc()
    .
    .
    .
    SYSTEM 'type errormess101 > %tmp%tmpfile.txt |
          sort >> %SystemRoot%systemlog.txt';
    SYSTEM 'del %tmp%tmpfile.txt';
    .
    .
    .
END PROCEDURE; --test_proc
```

The expressions that follow the SYSTEM statements in this example contain two variables, **%tmp%** and **%SystemRoot%**. Both of these variables are defined by the Windows NT operating system.

TRACE

Use the TRACE statement to control the generation of debugging output.

Syntax

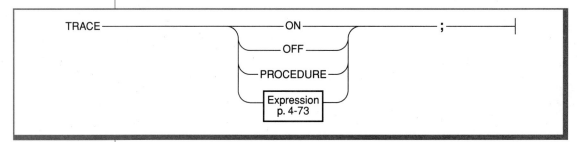

Usage

The TRACE statement generates output that is sent to the file that the SET DEBUG FILE TO statement specifies.

Tracing prints the current values of the following items:

- Variables
- Routine arguments
- Return values
- SQL error codes
- ISAM error codes

The output of each executed TRACE statement appears on a separate line.

If you use the TRACE statement before you specify a DEBUG file to contain the output, an error is generated.

Any routine that the SPL routine calls inherits the trace state. That is, a called routine assumes the same trace state (ON, OFF, or PROCEDURE) as the calling routine. The called routine can set its own trace state, but that state is not passed back to the calling routine.

A routine that is executed on a remote database server does not inherit the trace state.

TRACE ON

If you specify the keyword ON, all statements are traced. The values of variables (in expressions or otherwise) are printed before they are used. To turn tracing ON implies tracing both routine calls and statements in the body of the routine.

TRACE OFF

If you specify the keyword OFF, all tracing is turned off.

TRACE PROCEDURE

If you specify the keyword PROCEDURE, only the routine calls and return values, but not the body of the routine, are traced.

The TRACE statement does not have ROUTINE or FUNCTION keywords. Therefore, use the TRACE PROCEDURE keywords even if the SPL routine you want to trace is a function.

Displaying Expressions

You can use the TRACE statement with a quoted string or an expression to display values or comments in the output file. If the expression is not a literal expression, the expression is evaluated before it is written to the output file.

You can use the TRACE statement with an expression even if you used a TRACE OFF statement earlier in a routine. However, you must first use the SET DEBUG statement to establish a trace-output file.

The following example uses a TRACE statement with an expression after using a TRACE OFF statement. The example uses UNIX file-naming conventions.

```
CREATE PROCEDURE tracing ()
    DEFINE i INT;
BEGIN
    ON EXCEPTION IN (1)
    END EXCEPTION; -- do nothing
    SET DEBUG FILE TO '/tmp/foo.trace';
    TRACE OFF;
    TRACE 'Forloop starts';
    FOR i IN (1 TO 1000)
        BEGIN
            TRACE 'FOREACH starts';
            FOREACH SELECT...INTO a FROM t
                IF <some condition> THEN
                    RAISE EXCEPTION 1     -- emergency exit
                END IF
            END FOREACH

            -- return some value
        END
    END FOR

    -- do something
END;
END PROCEDURE
```

Example Showing Different Forms of TRACE

The following example shows several different forms of the TRACE
statement. The example uses Windows NT file-naming conventions.

```
CREATE PROCEDURE testproc()
    DEFINE i INT;

    SET DEBUG FILE TO 'C:\tmp\test.trace';
    TRACE OFF;
    TRACE 'Entering foo';

    TRACE PROCEDURE;
    LET i = test2();

    TRACE ON;
    LET i = i + 1;

    TRACE OFF;
    TRACE 'i+1 = ' || i+1;
    TRACE 'Exiting testproc';

    SET DEBUG FILE TO 'C:\tmp\test2.trace';

END PROCEDURE
```

Looking at the Traced Output

To see the traced output, use an editor or utility to display or read the
contents of the file.

WHILE

Use the WHILE statement to establish a loop with variable end conditions.

Syntax

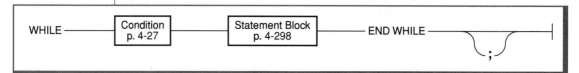

Usage

The condition is evaluated once at the beginning of the loop, and subsequently at the beginning of each iteration. The statement block is executed as long as the condition remains true. The loop terminates when the condition evaluates to not true.

If any expression within the condition evaluates to null, the condition automatically becomes not true unless you are explicitly testing for the IS NULL condition.

If an expression within the condition has an unknown value because it references uninitialized SPL variables, an immediate error results. In this case, the loop terminates, and an exception is raised.

Example of WHILE Loops in an SPL Routine

The following example illustrates the use of WHILE loops in an SPL routine.
In the SPL procedure, **simp_while**, the first WHILE loop executes a DELETE
statement. The second WHILE loop executes an INSERT statement and increments the value of an SPL variable.

```
CREATE PROCEDURE simp_while()
    DEFINE i INT;
    WHILE EXISTS (SELECT fname FROM customer
        WHERE customer_num > 400)
        DELETE FROM customer WHERE id_2 = 2;
    END WHILE;

    LET i = 1;
    WHILE i < 10
        INSERT INTO tab_2 VALUES (i);
        LET i = i + 1;
    END WHILE;
END PROCEDURE
```

Segments

In This Chapter

Segments are language elements, such as table names and expressions, that occur repeatedly in the syntax diagrams for SQL and SPL statements. These language elements are discussed separately in this section for the sake of clarity, ease of use, and comprehensive treatment.

Whenever a segment occurs within the syntax diagram for an SQL or SPL statement, the diagram references the description of the segment in this section.

Scope of Segment Descriptions

The description of each segment includes the following information:

- A brief introduction that explains the purpose of the segment
- A syntax diagram that shows how to enter the segment correctly
- A syntax table that explains each input parameter in the syntax diagram
- Rules of usage, including examples that illustrate these rules

If a segment consists of multiple parts, the segment description provides the same set of information for each part. Some segment descriptions conclude with references to related information in this and other manuals.

Use of Segment Descriptions

The syntax diagram within each segment description is not a stand-alone diagram. Instead it is a subdiagram that is subordinate to the syntax diagram for an SQL or SPL statement.

Syntax diagrams for SQL or SPL statements refer to segment descriptions in two ways:

- A subdiagram-reference box in the syntax diagram for a statement can refer to a segment name and the page number on which the segment description begins.
- The syntax column of the table beneath a syntax diagram can refer to a segment name and the page number on which the segment description begins.

First look up the syntax for the statement, and then turn to the segment description to find out the complete syntax for the segment.

For example, if you want to enter a CREATE VIEW statement that includes a database name and database server name in the view name, first look up the syntax diagram for the CREATE VIEW statement. The table beneath the diagram refers to the Database Object Name segment for the syntax for *view*.

The subdiagram for the Database Object Name segment shows you how to qualify the simple name of a view with the name of the database or with the name of both the database and the database server. Use the syntax in the subdiagram to enter a CREATE VIEW statement that includes the database name and database server name in the view name. The following example creates the **name_only** view in the **sales** database on the **boston** database server:

```
CREATE VIEW sales@boston:name_only AS
        SELECT customer_num, fname, lname FROM customer
```

Segments in This Section

This section describes the following segments.

Argument
Collection Derived Table
Collection Subquery
Condition
Database Name
Database Object Name
Data Type
DATETIME Field Qualifier
Expression
External Routine Reference
Identifier
INTERVAL Field Qualifier
Jar Name
Literal Collection

Literal DATETIME
Literal INTERVAL
Literal Number
Literal Row
Optimizer Directives
Owner Name
Quoted String
Relational Operator
Return Clause
Routine Modifier
Routine Parameter List
Shared-Object Filename
Specific Name
Statement Block

Argument

Use the Argument segment to pass a specific value to a routine parameter.
Use the Argument segment wherever you see a reference to an argument in
a syntax diagram.

Syntax

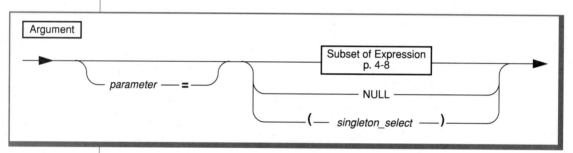

Element	Purpose	Restrictions	Syntax
parameter	Name of a routine parameter for which you supply an argument	The parameter name must match the parameter name that you specified in a corresponding CREATE FUNCTION or CREATE PROCEDURE statement.	Expression, p. 4-73
singleton_select	Embedded query that returns exactly one value of the proper data type and length	This can be any SELECT statement as long as it returns only one value.	SELECT, p. 2-634

Usage

A parameter list for a user-defined routine (UDR) is defined in the CREATE
PROCEDURE or CREATE FUNCTION statement. If the UDR has a parameter
list, you can enter arguments when you execute the UDR. An argument is a
specific data element that matches the data type of one of the parameters for
the UDR.

When you execute a UDR, you can enter arguments in one of two ways:

- With a parameter name (in the form *parameter name = expression),*
  even if the arguments are not in the same order as the parameters

- With no parameter name, if the arguments are in the same order as
  the parameters

If you use a parameter name for one argument, you must use a parameter
name for all the arguments.

In the following example, both statements are valid for a user-defined
procedure that expects three character arguments, **t, d,** and **n:**

```
EXECUTE PROCEDURE add_col (t ='customer', d ='integer', n
='newint');

EXECUTE PROCEDURE add_col ('customer','newint','integer') ;
```

Comparing Arguments to the Parameter List

When you create or register a UDR with CREATE PROCEDURE or CREATE
FUNCTION, you specify a parameter list with the names and data types of the
parameters the UDR expects.

If you attempt to execute a UDR with more arguments than the UDR expects,
you receive an error.

If you execute a UDR with fewer arguments than the UDR expects, the
arguments are said to be *missing.* The database server initializes missing
arguments to their corresponding default values. This initialization occurs
before the first executable statement in the body of the UDR.

If missing arguments do not have default values, the database server
initializes the arguments to the value UNDEFINED. However, you cannot use
a variable with a value of UNDEFINED within the UDR. If you do, the
database server issues an error.

Subset of Expressions Allowed as an Argument

The diagram for "Argument" on page 4-6 refers to this section.

You can use any expression as an argument, except an aggregate expression. If you use a subquery or function call, the subquery or function must return a single value of the appropriate data type and size. For a complete description of syntax and usage, see "Expression" on page 4-73.

Collection Derived Table

Use the Collection Derived Table segment to:

- access the elements of a collection as you would the rows of a table.
- specify a collection variable to access instead of a table name.
- specify a row variable to access instead of a table name.

Syntax

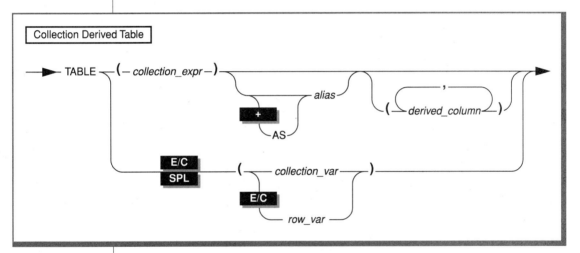

Element	Purpose	Restrictions	Syntax
alias	Temporary name for a collection derived table within the scope of a SELECT statement If you do not assign an alias, the database server assigns an implementation-dependent alias name.	If you use a potentially ambiguous word as an alias, you must precede the alias with the keyword AS. For further information on this restriction, see "AS Keyword with Aliases" on page 2-653.	Identifier, p. 4-205
collection_expr	Any expression that evaluates to a single collection For example, column references, scalar subquery, dotted expression, functions, operators (through overloading), collection subqueries, literal collections, collection constructors, cast functions, and so on.	See "Restrictions with the Collection-Expression Format" on page 4-11.	Expression, p. 4-73
collection_var	Name of a typed or untyped collection variable that holds the collection derived table	The variable must have been declared in an ESQL/C program or defined in an SPL routine. For more information, see the *Informix ESQL/C Programmer's Manual* or DEFINE, respectively.	Name must conform to language-specific rules for variable names.
derived_column	Temporary name for a derived column in a table If you do not assign a derived-column name, the behavior of the database server differs based on the data type of the elements in the underlying collection. For more information, see "Row Type of the Resulting Collection Derived Table" on page 4-13.	If the underlying collection is not a row type, you can specify only one derived-column name.	Identifier, p. 4-205
row_var	Name of an ESQL/C row variable that holds the collection derived table	The variable must be declared as row variable in an ESQL/C program. For more information, see the *Informix ESQL/C Programmer's Manual*.	Name must conform to language-specific rules for variable names.

Usage

A *collection derived table* is a virtual table in which the values in the rows of the table are equivalent to the elements of a collection. In other words, a collection derived table appears as a table in an SQL statement.

The TABLE keyword table converts a collection into a virtual table. You can use the collection expression format to query a collection column or you can use the collection variable or row variable format to manipulate the data in a collection column.

Accessing a Collection Through a Virtual Table

When you use the collection expression format of the Collection Derived Table segment to access the elements of a collection, you can select elements of the collection directly through a virtual table. You can use this format only in the FROM clause of a SELECT statement. The FROM clause can be in either a query or a subquery.

With this format you can use joins, aggregates, WHERE clause, expressions, the ORDER BY clause and other operations not available to you when you use the collection-variable format. This format reduces the need for multiple cursors and temporary tables.

Restrictions with the Collection-Expression Format

When you uses the collection-expression format, certain restrictions apply:

- A collection derived table is read-only.
    - ❑ It cannot be the target of insert, update, or delete statements.

      To perform insert, update, and delete operations you must use the collection-variable format.
    - ❑ It cannot be the underlying table of an updatable cursor or view.
- You cannot use the WITH ORDINALITY keywords to introduce a new column whose value is the ordinality of a row in the list expression.
- If the collection is a list, the resulting collection derived table does not preserve the order of the elements in the list.
- The underlying collection expression cannot evaluate to null.

- The collection expression cannot contain column references to tables that appear in the same FROM clause. That is, the collection derived table must be independent of other tables in the FROM clause.

  For example, the following statement returns an error because the collection derived table, **table (parents.children)**, refers to the table **parents**, which is also referenced in the FROM clause:

  ```
  SELECT COUNT(*)
  FROM parents, TABLE(parents.children) c_table
  WHERE parents.id = 1001
  ```

  To counter this restriction, you might write a query that contains a subquery in the select list:

  ```
  SELECT (SELECT COUNT(*)
      FROM TABLE(parents.children) c_table)
  FROM parents
  WHERE parents.id = 1001
  ```

Additional Restrictions that Apply to ESQL/C

E/C

In addition to the restrictions outlined in the previous section, the following restrictions apply when you use the collection-expression format with ESQL/C.

- You cannot use the format `TABLE(?)`

  The type of the underlying collection variable must be determined statically. To counter this restriction, you can explicitly cast the variable to a typed collection type (SET, MULTISET, or LIST) that the database server recognizes. For example,

  ```
  TABLE(CAST(? AS type))
  ```

- You cannot use the format `TABLE(:`*hostvar*`)`

  To counter this restriction, you must explicitly cast the variable to a typed collection type (SET, MULTISET, or LIST) that the database server recognizes. For example

  ```
  TABLE(CAST(:hostvar AS type))
  ```

- You cannot use the untyped collection-host variable, COLLECTION.

Row Type of the Resulting Collection Derived Table

Although a collection derived table appears to contain columns of individual data types, the resulting columns are, in fact, fields of a row type. The type of row type as well as the column name depends on several factors.

If the data type of the elements of the underlying collection expression is *type*, the database server determines the row type of the collection derived table by the following rules:

- If *type* is a row type, and no derived column list is specified, then the row type of the collection derived table is *type*.

- If *type* is a row type and a derived column list is specified, then the row type of the collection derived table is an unnamed row type whose column types are the same as those of *type* and whose column names are taken from the derived column list.

- If *type* is not a row type, the row type of the collection derived table is an unnamed row type that contains one column of type, and whose name is specified in the derived column list. If a name is not specified, the database server assigns an implementation-dependent name to the column.

The extended examples shown in the following table illustrate these rules. The table uses the following schema for its examples.

```
CREATE ROW TYPE person (name CHAR(255), id INT);
CREATE TABLE parents
    (
    name CHAR(255),
    id INT,
    children LIST (person NOT NULL)
    );
CREATE TABLE parents2
    (
    name CHAR(255),
    id INT,
    children_ids LIST (INT NOT NULL)
    );
```

Type	Derived-Column List Specified	Resulting Row Type of the Collection Derived Table	Example
Row Type	No	*Type*	SELECT (SELECT c_table.name FROM TABLE(parents.children c_table WHERE c_table.id = 1002) FROM parents WHERE parents.id = 1001 In this example, the row type of **c_table** is **parents**.
Row Type	Yes	Unnamed row type of which the column type is *Type* and the column name is the name provided in the derived-column list	SELECT (SELECT c_table.c_name FROM TABLE(parents.children) c_table(c._name, c_id) WHERE c_table.c_id = 1002) FROM parents WHERE parents.id = 1001 In this example, the row type of **c_table** is **row(c_name CHAR(255), c_id INT)**.
Not a row type	No	Unnamed row type that contains one column of *Type* that is assigned an implementation-dependent name	See the following example. Using the following example, if you do not specify **c_id**, the database server assigns a name to the derived column. Thus the row type of **c_table** is **row(server_defined_name INT)**.
Not a row type	Yes	Unnamed row type that contains one column of *Type* whose name is the name provided in the derived-column list.	SELECT(SELECT c_table.c_id FROM TABLE(parents2.child_ids) c_table (c_id) WHERE c_table.c_id = 1002) FROM parents WHERE parents.id = 1001 In this example, the row type of **c_table** is **row(c_id INT)**.

Example of a Collection Expression

The following example uses a collection expression to create a collection derived table:

```
CREATE TABLE wanted(person_id int);
CREATE FUNCTION wanted_person_count
(person_set SET(person NOT NULL))
RETURNS INT;
RETURN( SELECT COUNT (*)
FROM TABLE (person_set) c_table, wanted
WHERE c_tabel.id = wanted.person_id);
END FUNCTION;
```

Accessing a Collection Through a Collection Variable

When you use the collection-variable format of the Collection Derived Table segment, you use a host or program variable to access and manipulate the elements of a collection.

This format allows you to modify the contents of a variable as you would a table in the database and then update the actual table with the contents of the collection variable.

You can use the collection-variable format (the TABLE keyword preceding a collection variable) in place of the name of a table, synonym, or view name in the following SQL statements:

- The FROM clause of the SELECT statement to access an element of the collection variable

- The INTO clause of the INSERT statement to add a new element to the collection variable

- The DELETE statement to remove an element from the collection variable

- The UPDATE statement to modify an existing element in the collection variable

- The DECLARE statement to declare a select or insert cursor to access multiple elements of an ESQL/C collection-host variable.

E/C

- The FETCH statement to retrieve a single element from a collection-host variable that is associated with a select cursor.

- The PUT statement to retrieve a single element from a collection-host variable that is associated with an insert cursor. ♦

SPL

- The FOREACH statement to declare a cursor to access multiple elements of an SPL collection variable and to retrieve a single element from this collection variable. ♦

IDS

Using a Collection Variable to Manipulate Collection Elements

When you use data manipulation statements (SELECT, INSERT, UPDATE or DELETE) in conjunction with a collection variable you can modify one or more elements in a collection.

To modify elements in a collection, follow these general steps:

1. Create a collection variable in your SPL routine or ESQL/C program.

    For information on how to declare a collection variable in ESQL/C, see the *Informix ESQL/C Programmer's Manual*. For information on how to define a collection variable in SPL, see "DEFINE" on page 3-11.

E/C

2. In ESQL/C, allocate memory for the collection; see "ALLOCATE COLLECTION" on page 2-6. ♦

3. Optionally, use a SELECT statement to select a collection column into the collection variable.

    If the collection variable is an untyped COLLECTION variable, you must perform a SELECT from the collection column before you use the variable in the Collection Derived Table segment. The SELECT statement allows the database server to obtain the collection type.

4. Use the appropriate data manipulation statement with the Collection Derived-Table segment to add, delete, or update collection elements in the collection variable.

   To insert more than one element or to update or delete a *particular* element or in the collection, you must use a cursor for the collection variable.

   ■ For more information on how to use an update cursor with ESQL/C, see "DECLARE" on page 2-349.

   ■ For more information on how to use an update cursor with SPL, see "FOREACH" on page 3-30.

5. After the collection variable contains the correct elements, use an INSERT or UPDATE statement on the table or view that holds the actual collection column to save the changes that the collection variable holds.

   ■ With the UPDATE statement, specify the collection variable in the SET clause.

   ■ With the INSERT statement, specify the collection variable in the VALUES clause.

The collection variable stores the elements of the collection. However, it has no intrinsic connection with a database column. Once the collection variable contains the correct elements, you must then save the variable into the actual collection column of the table with either an INSERT or an UPDATE statement.

Example of Deleting from a Collection in ESQL/C

Suppose that the **set_col** column of a row in the **table1** table is defined as a SET and for one row contains the values {1,8,4,5,2}. The following ESQL/C code fragment uses an update cursor and a DELETE statement with a WHERE CURRENT OF clause to delete the element whose value is 4:

```
EXEC SQL BEGIN DECLARE SECTION;
    client collection set(smallint not null) a_set;
    int an_int;
EXEC SQL END DECLARE SECTION;
...
EXEC SQL allocate collection :a_set;
EXEC SQL select set_col into :a_set from table1
    where int_col = 6;

EXEC SQL declare set_curs cursor for
    select * from table(:a_set)
    for update;

EXEC SQL open set_curs;
while (i<coll_size)
{
    EXEC SQL fetch set_curs into :an_int;
    if (an_int = 4)
    {
        EXEC SQL delete from table(:a_set)
            where current of set_curs;
        break;
    }
    i++;
}

EXEC SQL update table1 set set_col = :a_set
    where int_col = 6;

EXEC SQL deallocate collection :a_set;
EXEC SQL close set_curs;
EXEC SQL free set_curs;
```

After the DELETE statement executes, this collection variable contains the elements {1,8,5,2}. The UPDATE statement at the end of this code fragment saves the modified collection into the **set_col** column of the database. Without this UPDATE statement, the collection column never has element 4 deleted.

For information on how to use collection-host variables in an ESQL/C program, see the discussion of complex data types in the *Informix ESQL/C Programmer's Manual.*

Example of Deleting from a Collection

Suppose that the **set_col** column of a row in the **table1** table is defined as a SET and one row contains the values {1,8,4,5,2}. The following SPL code fragment uses a FOREACH loop and a DELETE statement with a WHERE CURRENT OF clause to delete the element whose value is 4:

```
CREATE_PROCEDURE test6()

    DEFINE a SMALLINT;
    DEFINE b SET(SMALLINT NOT NULL);

    SELECT set_col INTO b FROM table1
        WHERE id = 6;
        -- Select the set in one row from the table
        -- into a collection variable

    FOREACH cursor1 FOR
        SELECT * INTO a FROM TABLE(b);
            -- Select each element one at a time from
            -- the collection derived table b into a
        IF a = 4 THEN
            DELETE FROM TABLE(b)
                WHERE CURRENT OF cursor1;
                -- Delete the element if it has the value 4
            EXIT FOREACH;
        END IF;
    END FOREACH;

    UPDATE table1 SET set_col = b
        WHERE id = 6;
        -- Update the base table with the new collection

END PROCEDURE;
```

This SPL routine defines two variables, **a** and **b**, each to hold a set of SMALLINT values. The first SELECT statement selects a SET column from one row of **table1** into **b**. Then, the routine declares a cursor that selects one element at a time from **b** into **a**. When the cursor is positioned on the element with the value 4, the DELETE statement deletes that element from **b**. Last, the UPDATE statement updates the row of **table1** with the new collection that is stored in **b**.

For information on how to use collection variables in an SPL routine, see the *Informix Guide to SQL: Tutorial*. ♦

Example of Updating a Collection

Suppose that the **set_col** column of a table called **table1** is defined as a SET and that it contains the values {1,8,4,5,2}. The following ESQL/C program changes the element whose value is 4 to a value of 10.

```
main
{
    EXEC SQL BEGIN DECLARE SECTION;
        int a;
        collection b;
    EXEC SQL END DECLARE SECTION;

    EXEC SQL allocate collection :b;
    EXEC SQL select set_col into :b from table1
        where int_col = 6;

    EXEC SQL declare set_curs cursor for
        select * from table(:b)
        for update;

    EXEC SQL open set_curs;
    while (SQLCODE != SQLNOTFOUND)
    {
        EXEC SQL fetch set_curs into :a;
        if (a = 4)
        {
            EXEC SQL update table(:b)(x)
                set x = 10
                where current of set_curs;
            break;
        }
    }

    EXEC SQL update table1 set set_col = :b
        where int_col = 6;

    EXEC SQL deallocate collection :b;
    EXEC SQL close set_curs;
    EXEC SQL free set_curs;
}
```

After you execute this ESQL/C program, the **set_col** column in **table1** contains the values {1,8,10,5,2}.

This ESQL/C program defines two **collection** variables, **a** and **b**, and selects a SET from **table1** into **b**. The WHERE clause ensures that only one row is returned. Then, the program defines a collection cursor, which selects elements one at a time from **b** into **a**. When the program locates the element with the value 4, the first UPDATE statement changes that element value to 10 and exits the loop.

In the first UPDATE statement, **x** is a derived column name used to update the current element in the collection derived table. The second UPDATE statement updates the base table **table1** with the new collection. For information on how to use **collection** host variables in an ESQL/C program, see the discussion of complex data types in the *Informix ESQL/C Programmer's Manual*.

Example of Inserting a Value into a Multiset Collection

Suppose the ESQL/C host variable **a_multiset** has the following declaration:

```
EXEC SQL BEGIN DECLARE SECTION;
    client collection multiset(integer not null) a_multiset;
EXEC SQL END DECLARE SECTION;
```

The following INSERT statement adds a new MULTISET element of 142,323 to **a_multiset**:

```
EXEC SQL allocate collection :a_multiset;
EXEC SQL select multiset_col into :a_multiset from table1
    where id = 107;
EXEC SQL insert into table(:a_multiset) values (142323);
EXEC SQL update table1 set multiset_col = :a_multiset
    where id = 107;

EXEC SQL deallocate collection :a_multiset;
```

When you insert elements into a client-collection variable, you cannot specify a SELECT statement or an EXECUTE FUNCTION statement in the VALUES clause of the INSERT. However, when you insert elements into a server-collection variable, the SELECT and EXECUTE FUNCTION statements are valid in the VALUES clause. For more information on client- and server-collection variables, see the *Informix ESQL/C Programmer's Manual*.

Accessing a Nested Collection

If the element of the collection is itself a complex type (**collection** or **row** type), the collection is a *nested collection*. For example, suppose the ESQL/C collection variable, **a_set**, is a nested collection that is defined as follows:

```
EXEC SQL BEGIN DECLARE SECTION;
    client collection set(list(integer not null)) a_set;
    client collection list(integer not null) a_list;
    int an_int;
EXEC SQL END DECLARE SECTION;
```

To access the elements (or fields) of a nested collection, use a collection or row variable that matches the element type (**a_list** and **an_int** in the preceding code fragment) and a select cursor.

Accessing a Row Variable

The TABLE keyword can make an ESQL/C **row** variable a collection derived table, that is, a row appears as a table in an SQL statement. For a **row** variable, you can think of the collection derived table as a table of one row, with each field of the row type being a column of the table row.

Use the TABLE keyword in place of the name of a table, synonym, or view name in the following SQL statements:

- The FROM clause of the SELECT statement to access a field of the row variable

- The UPDATE statement to modify an existing field in the row variable

The DELETE and INSERT statements do not support a row variable in the Collection Derived Table segment.

For example, suppose an ESQL/C host variable **a_row** has the following declaration:

```
EXEC SQL BEGIN DECLARE SECTION;
    row(x int, y int, length float, width float) a_row;
EXEC SQL END DECLARE SECTION;
```

The following ESQL/C code fragment adds the fields in the **a_row** variable to the **row_col** column of the **tab_row** table:

```
EXEC SQL update table(:a_row)
    set x=0, y=0, length=10, width=20;
EXEC SQL update rectangles set rect = :a_row;
```

Related Information

Related statements: DECLARE, DELETE, DESCRIBE, FETCH, INSERT, PUT, SELECT, UPDATE, DEFINE, and FOREACH

For information on how to use collection variables in an SPL routine, see the *Informix Guide to SQL: Tutorial*.

For information on how to use collection or row variables in an ESQL/C program, see the chapter on complex data types in the *Informix ESQL/C Programmer's Manual*.

IDS

Collection Subquery

You can use a collection subquery to create a multiset collection from the results of a subquery.

Syntax

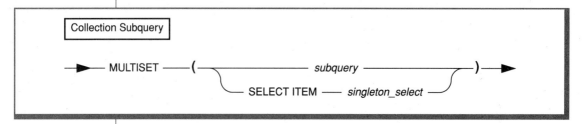

Collection Subquery

→ MULTISET ─── (─── subquery ───) →
              └─ SELECT ITEM ── *singleton_select* ─┘

Element	Purpose	Restrictions	Syntax
singleton_select	Subquery that returns exactly one row	The subquery cannot repeat the SELECT keyword. The subquery cannot contain either the FIRST or the ORDER BY clause.	SELECT, p. 2-634
subquery	Embedded query	The subquery cannot contain either the FIRST or the ORDER BY clause.	SELECT, p. 2-634

Usage

The following table indicates the significance of the keywords in the collection-subquery syntax.

Keywords	Purpose
MULTISET	Indicates a collection of elements with the following qualities: ■ The collection can contain duplicate values. ■ Elements have no specific order associated with them.
SELECT ITEM	When you use the SELECT ITEM keywords, only one expression is allowed in the projection list. Do not repeat the SELECT keyword in the singleton subquery.

You can use a collection subquery in the following locations:

- The SELECT and WHERE clauses of the SELECT statement
- The VALUES clause of the INSERT statement
- The SET clause of the UPDATE statement
- Wherever you can use a collection expression (that is, any expression that evaluates to a single collection)
- As an argument passed to a user-defined routine

Restrictions

The following restrictions apply to a collection subquery:

- It cannot contain duplicate column (field) names in the select list
- It cannot contain aliases for table names in the select list

   However, you can use aliases for column (field) names. See collection-subquery examples in "Row Structure of Results from a Collection Subquery" on page 4-25.

- It is read-only.
- It cannot be opened twice.
- It cannot contain null values.
- It cannot contain syntax that attempts to seek within the subquery.

Row Structure of Results from a Collection Subquery

A collection subquery evaluates to a multiset of unnamed row types. The fields of the unnamed row type are elements in the projection list of the subquery.

The following table includes examples that access the schema created with the following statements:

```
CREATE ROW TYPE rt1 (a INT);
CREATE ROW TYPE rt2 (x int, y rt1);
CREATE TABLE tab1 (col1 rt1, col2 rt2);
CREATE TABLE tab2 OF TYPE rt1;
CREATE TABLE tab3 (a ROW(x INT));
```

The following table includes possible collection subqueries and corresponding collections that result.

Collection Subquery	Resulting Collections
...MULTISET (SELECT * FROM tab1)...	MULTISET(ROW(col1 rt1, col2 rt2))
...MULTISET (SELECT col2.y FROM tab1)...	MULTISET(ROW(y rt1))
...MULTISET (SELECT * FROM tab2)...	MULTISET(ROW(a int))
...MULTISET(SELECT p FROM tab2 p)...	MULTISET(ROW(p rt1))
...MULTISET (SELECT * FROM tab3)...	MULTISET(ROW(a ROW(x int)))

Example

```
SELECT f(MULTISET(select * FROM tab 1 WHERE tab1.x = t.y))
FROM t
WHERE t.name = 'john doe';
```

Condition

Use a condition to test data to determine whether it meets certain qualifica-
tions. Use the Condition segment wherever you see a reference to a condition
in a syntax diagram.

Syntax

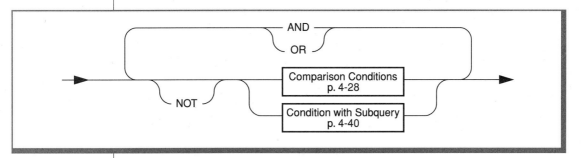

Usage

A condition is a collection of one or more search conditions, optionally
connected by the logical operators AND or OR. Search conditions fall into the
following categories:

- Comparison conditions (also called filters or Boolean expressions)
- Conditions with a subquery

Restrictions on a Condition

A condition can contain only an aggregate function if it is used in the HAVING
clause of a SELECT statement or the HAVING clause of a subquery. You cannot
use an aggregate function in a comparison condition that is part of a WHERE
clause in a DELETE, SELECT, or UPDATE statement unless the aggregate is on
a correlated column that originates from a parent query and the WHERE
clause is within a subquery that is within a HAVING clause.

NOT Operator Option

If you preface a condition with the keyword NOT, the test is true only if the condition that NOT qualifies is false. If the condition that NOT qualifies is unknown (uses a null in the determination), the NOT operator has no effect. The following truth table shows the effect of NOT. The letter T represents a true condition, F represents a false condition, and a question mark (?) represents an unknown condition. Unknown values occur when part of an expression that uses an arithmetic operator is null.

NOT	
T	F
F	T
?	?

Comparison Conditions (Boolean Expressions)

Five kinds of comparison conditions exist: Relational Operator, BETWEEN, IN, IS NULL, and LIKE and MATCHES. Comparison conditions are often called Boolean expressions because they evaluate to a simple true or false result. Their syntax is summarized in the following diagram and explained in detail after the diagram.

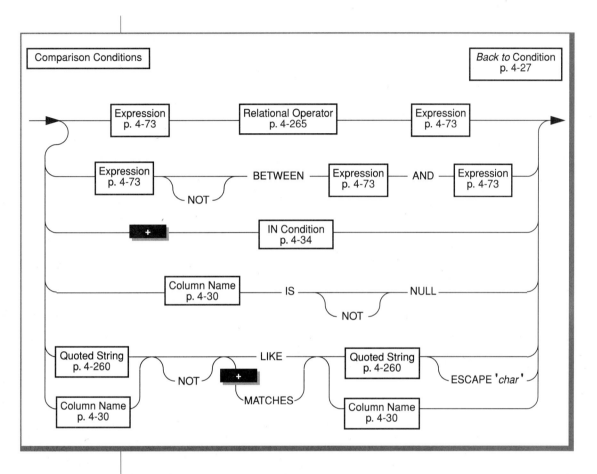

Element	Purpose	Restrictions	Syntax
char	A single ASCII character that is to be used as the escape character within the quoted string in a LIKE or MATCHES condition	See "ESCAPE with LIKE" on page 4-39 and "ESCAPE with MATCHES" on page 4-40.	Quoted String, p. 4-260

Refer to the following sections for more information on the use of the different types of comparison conditions:

- For relational-operator conditions, refer to "Relational-Operator Condition" on page 4-32.

- For the BETWEEN condition, refer to "BETWEEN Condition" on page 4-33.

- For the IN condition, refer to "IN Condition" on page 4-34.

- For the IS NULL condition, refer to "IS NULL Condition" on page 4-36.

- For the LIKE and MATCHES condition, refer to "LIKE and MATCHES Condition" on page 4-36.

For a discussion of the different types of comparison conditions in the context of the SELECT statement, see "Using a Condition in the WHERE Clause" on page 2-661.

 Warning: *When you specify a date value in a comparison condition, make sure to specify 4 digits instead of 2 digits for the year. When you specify a 4-digit year, the* **DBCENTURY** *environment variable has no effect on how the database server interprets the comparison condition. When you specify a 2-digit year, the* **DBCENTURY** *environment variable can affect how the database server interprets the comparison condition, so the comparison condition might not work as you intended. For more information on the* **DBCENTURY** *environment variable, see the "Informix Guide to SQL: Reference."*

Column Name

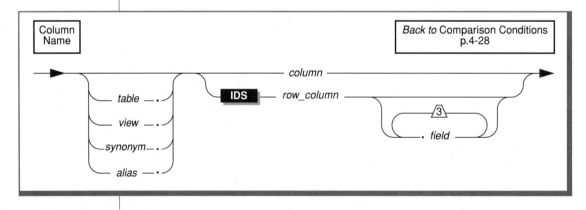

Element	Purpose	Restrictions	Syntax
alias	Temporary alternative name for a table or view within the scope of a SELECT statement	You must have defined the alias in the FROM clause of the SELECT statement.	Identifier, p. 4-205
column	Name of a column that is used in an IS NULL condition or in a LIKE or MATCHES condition. See "IS NULL Condition" on page 4-36 and "LIKE and MATCHES Condition" on page 4-36 for more information on the meaning of *column name* in these conditions.	The column must exist in the specified table.	Identifier, p. 4-205
field	Name of the field that you want to compare in the row column	The field must be a component of the row type that *row-column name* or *field name* (for nested rows) specifies.	Identifier, p. 4-205
row_column	Name of the row column that you specify	The data type of the column must be a named row type or an unnamed row type.	Identifier, p. 4-205
synonym	Name of a view	The synonym must exist within the database.	Database Object Name, p. 4-50
table	Name of a table	The table must exist within the database.	Database Object Name, p. 4-50
view	Name of a synonym	The view must exist within the database.	Database Object Name, p.4-50

Quotation Marks in Conditions

When you compare a column expression with a constant expression in any type of comparison condition, observe the following rules:

- If the column has a numeric data type, do not surround the constant expression with quotation marks.

- If the column has a character data type, surround the constant expression with quotation marks.

- If the column has a date data type, surround the constant expression with quotation marks. Otherwise, you might get unexpected results.

The following example shows the correct use of quotation marks in comparison conditions. The **ship_instruct** column has a character data type. The **order_date** column has a date data type. The **ship_weight** column has a numeric data type.

```
SELECT * FROM orders
    WHERE ship_instruct = 'express'
    AND order_date > '05/01/98'
    AND ship_weight < 30
```

Relational-Operator Condition

Some relational-operator conditions are shown in the following examples:

```
city[1,3] = 'San'

o.order_date > '6/12/98'

WEEKDAY(paid_date) = WEEKDAY(CURRENT-31 UNITS day)

YEAR(ship_date) < YEAR (TODAY)

quantity <= 3

customer_num <> 105

customer_num != 105
```

If either expression is null for a row, the condition evaluates to false. For example, if the **paid_date** column has a null, you cannot use either of the following statements to retrieve that row:

```
SELECT customer_num, order_date FROM orders
    WHERE paid_date = ''

SELECT customer_num, order_date FROM orders
    WHERE NOT PAID !=''
```

An IS NULL condition finds a null value, as shown in the following example. The IS NULL condition is explained fully in "IS NULL Condition" on page 4-36.

```
SELECT customer_num, order_date FROM orders
    WHERE paid_date IS NULL
```

BETWEEN Condition

For a BETWEEN test to be true, the value of the expression on the left of the BETWEEN keyword must be in the inclusive range of the values of the two expressions on the right of the BETWEEN keyword. Null values do not satisfy the condition. You cannot use NULL for either expression that defines the range.

Some BETWEEN conditions are shown in the following examples:

```
order_date BETWEEN '6/1/97' and '9/7/97'

zipcode NOT BETWEEN '94100' and '94199'

EXTEND(call_dtime, DAY TO DAY) BETWEEN
    (CURRENT - INTERVAL(7) DAY TO DAY) AND CURRENT

lead_time BETWEEN INTERVAL (1) DAY TO DAY
    AND INTERVAL (4) DAY TO DAY

unit_price BETWEEN loprice AND hiprice
```

IN Condition

The IN condition is satisfied when the expression to the left of the word IN is included in the list of items.

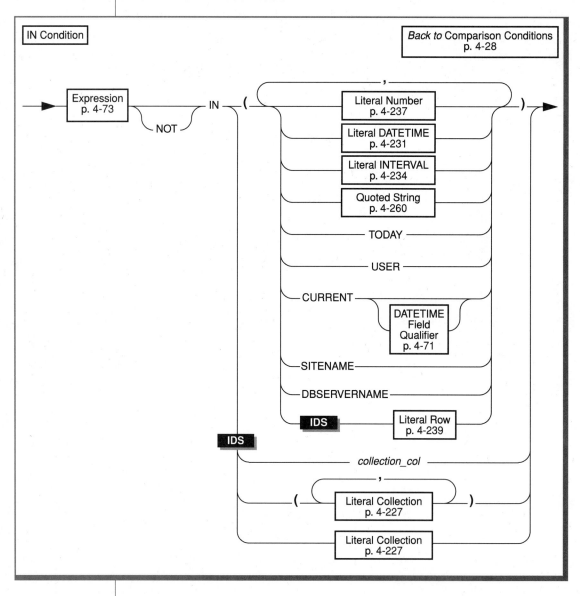

Element	Purpose	Restrictions	Syntax
collection_col	Name of a collection column that is used in an IN condition	The column must exist in the specified table.	Identifier, p. 4-205

The NOT option produces a search condition that is satisfied when the expression is not in the list of items. Null values do not satisfy the condition.

The following examples show some IN conditions:

```
WHERE state IN ('CA', 'WA', 'OR')

WHERE manu_code IN ('HRO', 'HSK')

WHERE user_id NOT IN (USER)

WHERE order_date NOT IN (TODAY)
```

E/C

In ESQL/C, the built-in TODAY function is evaluated at execution time; the built-in CURRENT function is evaluated when a cursor opens or when the query executes, if it is a singleton SELECT statement. ♦

The built-in USER function is case sensitive; it perceives **minnie** and **Minnie** as different values.

IDS

Using the IN Operator with Collection Data Types

You can use the IN operator to determine if an element is contained in a collection. The collection you search can be a simple or nested collection. In a nested collection type, the element type of the collection is also a collection type.

When you use the IN operator to search for an element in a collection, the expression to the left or right of the IN keyword cannot contain a BYTE or TEXT data type.

Suppose you create the following table that contains two collection columns:

```
CREATE TABLE tab_col1
(
set_num SET(INT NOT NULL),
list_name LIST(SET(CHAR(10) NOT NULL) NOT NULL)
);
```

The following partial examples show how you might use the IN operator for search conditions on the collection columns of the **tab_coll** table:

```
WHERE 5 IN set_num

WHERE 5.0::INT IN set_num

WHERE "5" NOT IN set_num

WHERE set_num IN ("SET{1,2,3}", "SET{7,8,9}")

WHERE "SET{'john', 'sally', 'bill'}" IN list_name

WHERE list_name IN ("LIST{""SET{'bill','usha'}"",
                           ""SET{'ann' 'moshi'}""}",
                     "LIST{""SET{'bob','ramesh'}"",
                           ""SET{'bomani' 'ann'}""}")
```

In general, when you use the IN operator on a collection data type, the database server checks whether the value on the left of the IN operator is an element in the set of values on the right of the IN operator.

IS NULL Condition

The IS NULL condition is satisfied if the column contains a null value. If you use the IS NOT NULL option, the condition is satisfied when the column contains a value that is not null. The following example shows an IS NULL condition:

```
WHERE paid_date IS NULL
```

LIKE and MATCHES Condition

A LIKE or MATCHES condition tests for matching character strings. The condition is true, or satisfied, when either of the following tests is true:

- The value of the column on the left matches the pattern that the quoted string specifies. You can use wildcard characters in the string. Null values do not satisfy the condition.

- The value of the column on the left matches the pattern that the column on the right specifies. The value of the column on the right serves as the matching pattern in the condition.

You can use the single quote (') only with the quoted string to match a literal quote; you cannot use the ESCAPE clause. You can use the quote character as the escape character in matching any other pattern if you write it as ' ' ' '.

Important: *You cannot specify a row-type column in a LIKE or MATCHES condition. A row-type column is a column that is defined on a named row type or unnamed row type.*

NOT Option

The NOT option makes the search condition successful when the column on the left has a value that is not null and does not match the pattern that the quoted string specifies. For example, the following conditions exclude all rows that begin with the characters Baxter in the **lname** column:

```
WHERE lname NOT LIKE 'Baxter%'
WHERE lname NOT MATCHES 'Baxter*'
```

LIKE Option

If you use the keyword LIKE, you can use the following wildcard characters in the quoted string.

Wildcard	Purpose
%	Matches zero or more characters
_	Matches any single character
\	Removes the special significance of the next character (used to match % or _ by writing \% or _)

Using the backslash (\) as an escape character is an Informix extension to ANSI-compliant SQL.

ANSI

In an ANSI-compliant database, you can only use an escape character to escape a percent sign (%), an underscore (_), or the escape character itself. ♦

The following condition tests for the string `tennis`, alone or in a longer string, such as `tennis ball` or `table tennis paddle`:

```
WHERE description LIKE '%tennis%'
```

The following condition tests for all descriptions that contain an underscore. The backslash (\) is necessary because the underscore (_) is a wildcard character.

```
WHERE description LIKE '%\_%'
```

The LIKE operator has an associated operator function called **like()**. You can define a **like()** function to handle your own user-defined data types. For more information, see the *Extending Informix Dynamic Server 2000* manual.

MATCHES Option

If you use the keyword MATCHES, you can use the following wildcard characters in the quoted string.

Wildcard	Purpose
*	Matches zero or more characters.
?	Matches any single character.
[...]	Match any\r of the enclosed characters, including character ranges as in [a - z]. Characters inside the square brackets cannot be escaped.
^	As the first character within the square brackets matches any character that is not listed. Hence [^abc] matches any character that is not a, b, or c.
\	Removes the special significance of the next character (used to match * or ? by writing * or \?).

The following condition tests for the string `tennis`, alone or in a longer string, such as `tennis ball` or `table tennis paddle`:

```
WHERE description MATCHES '*tennis*'
```

The following condition is true for the names `Frank` and `frank`:

```
WHERE fname MATCHES '[Ff]rank'
```

The following condition is true for any name that begins with either `F` or `f`:

```
WHERE fname MATCHES '[Ff]*'
```

The following condition is true for any name that ends with the letters `a`, `b`, `c`, or `d`:

```
WHERE fname MATCHES '*[a-d]'
```

The MATCHES operator has an associated operator function called **matches()**. You can define a **matches()** function to handle your own user-defined data types. For more information, see the *Extending Informix Dynamic Server 2000* manual.

ESCAPE with LIKE

The ESCAPE clause lets you include an underscore (_) or a percent sign (%) in the quoted string and avoid having them be interpreted as wildcards. If you choose to use `z` as the escape character, the characters `z_` in a string stand for the underscore character (_). Similarly, the characters `z%` represent the percent sign (%). Finally, the characters `zz` in the string stand for the single character `z`. The following statement retrieves rows from the **customer** table in which the **company** column includes the underscore character:

```
SELECT * FROM customer
    WHERE company LIKE '%z_%' ESCAPE 'z'
```

You can also use a single-character host variable as an escape character. The following statement shows the use of a host variable as an escape character:

```
EXEC SQL BEGIN DECLARE SECTION;
    char escp='z';
    char fname[20];
EXEC SQL END DECLARE SECTION;
EXEC SQL select fname from customer
    into :fname
    where company like '%z_%' escape :escp;
```

ESCAPE with MATCHES

The ESCAPE clause lets you include a question mark (?), an asterisk (*), and a left or right square bracket ([]) in the quoted string and avoid having them be interpreted as wildcards. If you choose to use *z* as the escape character, the characters *z*? in a string stand for the question mark (?). Similarly, the characters *z** stand for the asterisk (*). Finally, the characters *zz* in the string stand for the single character *z*.

The following example retrieves rows from the **customer** table in which the value of the **company** column includes the question mark (?):

```
SELECT * FROM customer
    WHERE company MATCHES '*z?*' ESCAPE 'z'
```

Stand-Alone Condition

A stand-alone condition can be any expression that is not explicitly listed in the syntax for the comparison condition. Such an expression is valid only if its result is of the Boolean type. For example, the following example returns a value of the Boolean type:

```
funcname(x)
```

Condition with Subquery

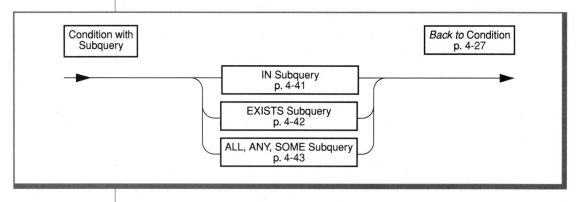

You can use a SELECT statement within a condition; this combination is called a subquery. You can use a subquery in a SELECT statement to perform the following functions:

- Compare an expression to the result of another SELECT statement
- Determine whether an expression is included in the results of another SELECT statement
- Ask whether another SELECT statement selects any rows

The subquery can depend on the current row that the outer SELECT statement is evaluating; in this case, the subquery is a *correlated subquery.*

The kinds of subquery conditions are shown in the following sections with their syntax. For a discussion of the different kinds of subquery conditions in the context of the SELECT statement, see "Using a Condition in the WHERE Clause" on page 2-661.

A subquery can return a single value, no value, or a set of values depending on the context in which it is used. If a subquery returns a value, it must select only a single column. If the subquery simply checks whether a row (or rows) exists, it can select any number of rows and columns. A subquery cannot contain BYTE or TEXT data types, nor can it contain an ORDER BY clause. For a complete description of SELECT syntax and usage, see "SELECT" on page 2-634.

IN Subquery

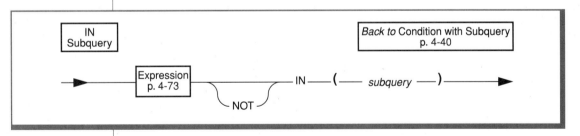

Element	Purpose	Restrictions	Syntax
subquery	Embedded query	The subquery cannot contain either the FIRST or the ORDER BY clause.	SELECT, p. 2-634

An IN subquery condition is true if the value of the expression matches one or more of the values that the subquery selects. The subquery must return only one column, but it can return more than one row. The keyword IN is equivalent to the =ANY sequence. The keywords NOT IN are equivalent to the !=ALL sequence. See "ALL, ANY, SOME Subquery" on page 4-43.

The following example of an IN subquery finds the order numbers for orders that do not include baseball gloves (stock_num = 1):

```
WHERE order_num NOT IN
      (SELECT order_num FROM items WHERE stock_num = 1)
```

Because the IN subquery tests for the presence of rows, duplicate rows in the subquery results do not affect the results of the main query. Therefore, you can put the UNIQUE or DISTINCT keyword into the subquery with no effect on the query results, although eliminating testing duplicates can reduce the time needed for running the query.

EXISTS Subquery

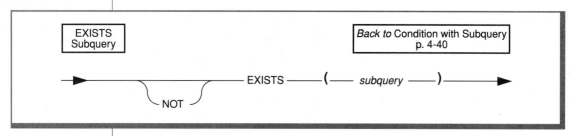

Element	Purpose	Restrictions	Syntax
subquery	Embedded query	The subquery cannot contain either the FIRST or the ORDER BY clause.	SELECT, p. 2-634

An EXISTS subquery condition evaluates to true if the subquery returns a row. With an EXISTS subquery, one or more columns can be returned. The subquery always contains a reference to a column of the table in the main query. If you use an aggregate function in an EXISTS subquery, at least one row is always returned.

The following example of a SELECT statement with an EXISTS subquery returns the stock number and manufacturer code for every item that has never been ordered (and is therefore not listed in the **items** table). You can appropriately use an EXISTS subquery in this SELECT statement because you use the subquery to test both **stock_num** and **manu_code** in **items**.

```
SELECT stock_num, manu_code FROM stock
    WHERE NOT EXISTS (SELECT stock_num, manu_code FROM items
        WHERE stock.stock_num = items.stock_num AND
        stock.manu_code = items.manu_code)
```

The preceding example works equally well if you use SELECT * in the subquery in place of the column names because the existence of the whole row is tested; specific column values are not tested.

ALL, ANY, SOME Subquery

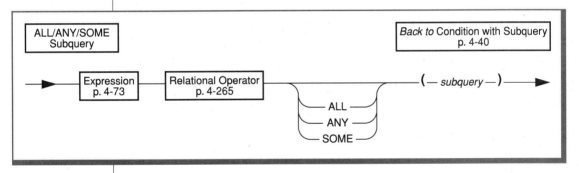

Element	Purpose	Restrictions	Syntax
subquery	Embedded query	The subquery cannot contain either the FIRST or the ORDER BY clause.	SELECT, p. 2-634

You use the ALL, ANY, and SOME keywords to specify what makes the search condition true or false. A search condition that is true when the ANY keyword is used might not be true when the ALL keyword is used, and vice versa.

Using the ALL Keyword

The ALL keyword denotes that the search condition is true if the comparison is true for every value that the subquery returns. If the subquery returns no value, the condition is true.

In the following example of the ALL subquery, the first condition tests whether each **total_price** is greater than the total price of every item in order number 1023. The second condition uses the MAX aggregate function to produce the same results.

```
total_price > ALL (SELECT total_price FROM items
                       WHERE order_num = 1023)

total_price > (SELECT MAX(total_price) FROM items
                       WHERE order_num = 1023)
```

Using the NOT keyword with an ALL subquery tests whether an expression is not true for at least one element returned by the subquery. For example, the following condition is true when the expression **total_price** is not greater than all the selected values. That is, it is true when **total_price** is not greater than the highest total price in order number 1023.

```
NOT total_price > ALL (SELECT total_price FROM items
                           WHERE order_num = 1023)
```

Using the ANY or SOME Keywords

The ANY keyword denotes that the search condition is true if the comparison is true for at least one of the values that is returned. If the subquery returns no value, the search condition is false. The SOME keyword is an alias for ANY.

The following conditions are true when the total price is greater than the total price of at least one of the items in order number 1023. The first condition uses the ANY keyword; the second uses the MIN aggregate function.

```
total_price > ANY (SELECT total_price FROM items
                       WHERE order_num = 1023)

total_price > (SELECT MIN(total_price) FROM items
                       WHERE order_num = 1023)
```

Using the NOT keyword with an ANY subquery tests whether an expression is not true for all elements returned by the subquery. For example, the following condition is true when the expression **total_price** is not greater than any selected value. That is, it is true when **total_price** is greater than none of the total prices in order number 1023.

```
NOT total_price > ANY (SELECT total_price FROM items
                       WHERE order_num = 1023)
```

Omitting the ANY, ALL, or SOME Keywords

You can omit the keywords ANY, ALL, or SOME in a subquery if you know that the subquery will return exactly one value. If you omit the ANY, ALL, or SOME keywords, and the subquery returns more than one value, you receive an error. The subquery in the following example returns only one row because it uses an aggregate function:

```
SELECT order_num FROM items
    WHERE stock_num = 9 AND quantity =
        (SELECT MAX(quantity) FROM items WHERE stock_num = 9)
```

Conditions with AND or OR

You can combine simple conditions with the logical operators AND or OR to form complex conditions. The following SELECT statements contain examples of complex conditions in their WHERE clauses:

```
SELECT customer_num, order_date FROM orders
    WHERE paid_date > '1/1/97' OR paid_date IS NULL

SELECT order_num, total_price FROM items
    WHERE total_price > 200.00 AND manu_code LIKE 'H%'

SELECT lname, customer_num FROM customer
    WHERE zipcode BETWEEN '93500' AND '95700'
    OR state NOT IN ('CA', 'WA', 'OR')
```

The following truth tables show the effect of the AND and OR operators. The letter T represents a true condition, F represents a false condition, and the question mark (?) represents an unknown value. Unknown values occur when part of an expression that uses a logical operator is null.

AND	T	F	?		OR	T	F	?
T	T	F	?		T	T	T	T
F	F	F	F		F	T	F	?
?	?	F	?		?	T	?	?

If the Boolean expression evaluates to UNKNOWN, the condition is not satisfied.

Consider the following example within a WHERE clause:

```
WHERE ship_charge/ship_weight < 5
    AND order_num = 1023
```

The row where **order_num** = 1023 is the row where **ship_weight** is null. Because **ship_weight** is null, **ship_charge/ship_weight** is also null; therefore, the truth value of **ship_charge/ship_weight** < 5 is UNKNOWN. Because **order_num** = 1023 is TRUE, the AND table states that the truth value of the entire condition is UNKNOWN. Consequently, that row is not chosen. If the condition used an OR in place of the AND, the condition would be true.

Related Information

For discussions of comparison conditions in the SELECT statement and of conditions with a subquery, see the *Informix Guide to SQL: Tutorial*.

For information on the GLS aspects of conditions, see the *Informix Guide to GLS Functionality*.

Database Name

Use the Database Name segment to specify the name of a database. Use the Database Name segment whenever you see a reference to a database name in a syntax diagram.

Syntax

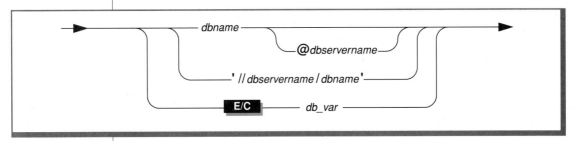

Element	Purpose	Restrictions	Syntax
dbname	Name of the database itself This simple name does not include the pathname or the database server name.	A database name must be unique among the database names on the same database server. In Dynamic Server, *dbname* can have a maximum of 128 bytes. In Enterprise Decision Server, *dbname* can have a maximum of 18 bytes.	Identifier, p. 4-205

(1 of 2)

Element	Purpose	Restrictions	Syntax
dbservername	Name of the database server on which the database that is named in dbname resides.	The database server that is specified in *dbservername* must exist.	Identifier, p. 4-205
		You cannot put a space between the @ symbol and *dbservername*.	
		In Dynamic Server, *dbservername* can have a maximum of 128 bytes. In Enterprise Decision Server, *dbservername* can have a maximum of 18 bytes.	
db_var	Host variable that contains a value representing a database environment	Variable must be a fixed-length character data type.	Name must conform to language-specific rules for variable names.

(2 of 2)

Usage

Database names are not case sensitive. You cannot use delimited identifiers for a database name.

GLS

If you are using a nondefault locale, you can use characters from the code set of your locale in the names of databases.

If you are using a multibyte code set, keep in mind that the maximum length of the database name refers to the number of bytes, not the number of characters.

For further information on the GLS aspects of naming databases, see the *Informix Guide to GLS Functionality*. ♦

Specifying the Database Server

You can choose a database on another database server as your current database by specifying a database server name. The database server that *dbservername* specifies must match the name of a database server that is listed in your **sqlhosts** information.

Using the @ Symbol

The @ symbol is a literal character that introduces the database server name. If you specify a database server name, do not put any spaces between the @ symbol and the database server name. You can either put a space between dbname and the @ symbol, or omit the space.

The following examples show valid database specifications:

```
empinfo@personnel
empinfo @personnel
```

In these examples, **empinfo** is the name of the database and **personnel** is the name of the database server.

Using a Path-Type Naming Method

If you use a path-type naming method, do not put spaces between the quotes, slashes, and names, as the following example shows:

```
'//personnel/empinfo'
```

In this example, **empinfo** is the name of the database and **personnel** is the name of the database server.

E/C

Using a Host Variable

You can use a host variable within an ESQL/C application to contain a value that represents a database environment.

Database Object Name

Use the Database Object Name segment to specify the name of a constraint, index, trigger, table, synonym, user-defined routine (UDR), or view. Use this segment whenever you see a reference to database object name.

Syntax

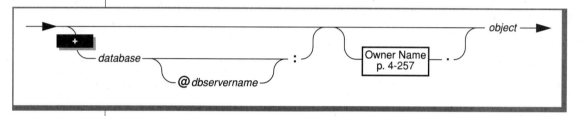

Element	Purpose	Restrictions	Syntax
database	Name of the database where the database object resides	The database must exist.	Identifier, p. 4-205
dbservername	Name of the database server where the database resides	The database server must exist. You cannot put a space between the @ symbol and dbservername.	Identifier, p. 4-205
object	Name of a database object in the database	If you are creating the database object, character limitations exist. For more information, see "Identifier" on page 4-205. If you are accessing the database object, the database object must exist. See also, "Usage."	Identifier, p. 4-205

Usage

If you are creating or renaming a database object, the name that you specify must be unique in relation to other database objects of the same type in the database. For example, a new constraint name must be unique among constraint names that exist in the database.

A new name for a table, synonym, or view, must be unique among all the tables, synonyms, views, and temporary tables that already exist in the database.

IDS

In Dynamic Server, the uniqueness requirement does not apply to UDR names. For more information, see "Routine Overloading and Naming UDRs with a Routine Signature" on page 4-52. ♦

ANSI

In an ANSI-compliant database, the *ownername.object* combination must be unique in a database.

A database object name must include the owner name for a database object that you do not own. For example, if you specify a table that you do not own, you must specify the owner of the table also. The owner of all the system catalog tables is **informix**. ♦

GLS

If you are using a nondefault locale, you can use characters from the code set of your locale in database object names. For more information, see the *Informix Guide to GLS Functionality*. ♦

Specifying a Database Object on a Remote Database Server

To specify an object on a remote database server, you must use a *fully qualified identifier*. A fully qualified identifier includes the names of the database, database server, and owner in addition to the database object name.

The following example shows a fully qualified table name:

```
empinfo@personnel:markg.emp_names
```

In this example, the name of the database is **empinfo**. The name of the database server is **personnel**. The name of the owner of the table is **markg**. The name of the table is **emp_names**.

IDS

Restrictions with UDRs on Remote Database Servers

If a UDR exists on a remote database server, you must specify a fully qualified identifier for the UDR. In addition, the UDR must meet the following requirements:

- All of the arguments passed to the UDR are of built-in data types.
- All of the parameters that the UDR accepts are of built-in data types.
- Any values that a user-defined function returns are of built-in data types.

In other words, you cannot specify a remote UDR if any of its parameters or return values are opaque, distinct, collection, or row types.

IDS

Routine Overloading and Naming UDRs with a Routine Signature

Because of routine overloading, the name of a UDR (that is, a user-defined function or a user-defined procedure) does not have to be unique to the database. You can define more than one UDR with the same name as long as the *routine signature* for each UDR is different.

UDRs are uniquely identified by their signature. The signature of a UDR includes the following items:

- The type (function or procedure)
- The name
- The quantity, data type, and order of the parameters

ANSI
- In an ANSI database, the owner name. ♦

For any given UDR, at least one item in the signature must be unique among all the UDRs stored in a name space or database.

Specifying an Existing UDR

When you are specifying the name of an existing UDR, if the name you specify does not uniquely identify the UDR, you must also specify the parameter data types after the UDR name. You must specify the parameter data types in the same order that they were specified when the UDR was created. The database server then uses routine resolution to identify the instance of the UDR to alter, drop, or execute.

As an alternative you can specify the specific name for the UDR if one was given to it when it was created.

For more information about routine resolution, see *Extending Informix Dynamic Server 2000.*

Data Type

The Data Type segment specifies the data type of a column or value. Use the Data Type segment whenever you see a reference to a data type in a syntax diagram.

Syntax

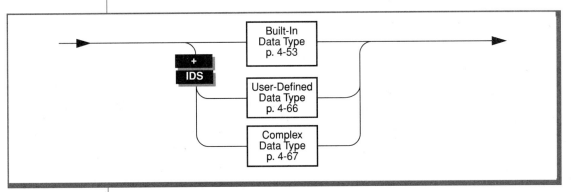

Usage

The following sections summarize each of the categories of data types that the various database server configurations support. For more information, see the discussion of all data types in the *Informix Guide to SQL: Reference*.

Built-In Data Type

Built-in data types are data types that are fundamental to the database server. These data types are built into the database server in the sense that the knowledge for how to interpret and transfer these data types is part of the database server software.

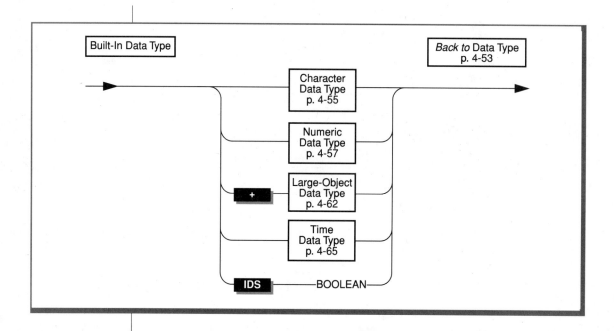

The database server supports the following categories of built-in data types:

- Character data types
- Numeric data types
- Large-object data types
- Time data types

In addition, Dynamic Server supports the BOOLEAN data type.

Character Data Types

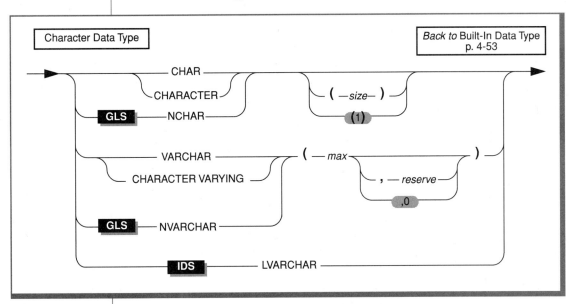

Element	Purpose	Restrictions	Syntax
max	Maximum size of a CHARACTER VARYING, VARCHAR or NVARCHAR column in bytes	You must specify an integer value between 1 and 255 bytes, inclusive. If you place an index on the column, the largest value you can specify for *max* is 254 bytes.	Literal Number, p. 4-237
reserve	Amount of space in bytes reserved for a CHARACTER VARYING, VARCHAR or NVARCHAR column even if the actual number of bytes stored in the column is less than *reserve* The default value of reserve is 0.	You must specify an integer value between 0 and 255 bytes. However, the value you specify for *reserve* must be less than the value you specify for *max*.	Literal Number, p. 4-237
size	Number of bytes in the CHAR or NCHAR column	You must specify an integer value between 1 and 32,767 bytes, inclusive.	Literal Number, p. 4-237

The following table summarizes the available character data types.

Data Type	Purpose
CHAR	Stores single-byte or multibyte text strings of up to 32,767 bytes of text data and supports code-set collation of text data.
CHARACTER	Synonym for CHAR.
CHARACTER VARYING	ANSI-compliant synonym for VARCHAR.
LVARCHAR (IDS)	Stores variable-length strings that are potentially more than 255 bytes, but no more than 2 kilobytes in length.
NCHAR	Stores single-byte or multibyte text strings of up to 32,767 bytes of text data and supports localized collation of the text data.
NVARCHAR	Stores single-byte or multibyte text strings of varying length and up to 255 bytes of text data; it supports localized collation of the text data.
VARCHAR	Stores single-byte or multibyte text strings of varying length and up to 255 bytes of text data; it supports code-set collation of the text data.

The TEXT and CLOB data types also support character data. For more information, see "Large-Object Data Types" on page 4-62.

Fixed- and Varying-Length Data Types

The database server supports storage of fixed-length and varying-length character data. A fixed-length column requires the defined number of bytes regardless of the actual size of the character data. The CHAR data type is a fixed-length character data type. For example, a CHAR(25) column requires 25 bytes of storage for all its column values, so the string "This is a text string" uses 25 bytes of storage. Use the VARCHAR data type to specify varying-length character data.

A varying-length column requires only the number of bytes that its data uses. The VARCHAR and LVARCHAR data types are varying-length character data types. For example, a VARCHAR(25) column reserves up to 25 bytes of storage for the column value, but the string "This is a text string" uses only 21 bytes of the reserved 25 bytes.

The VARCHAR data type can store up to 255 bytes of varying data while the LVARCHAR data type can store up to 2 kilobytes of text data.

NCHAR and NVARCHAR Data Types

The character data types CHAR, LVARCHAR, and VARCHAR support code-set collation of the text data. That is, the database server collates text data in columns of these types by the order that their characters are defined in the code set.

To accommodate locale-specific order of characters, use the NCHAR and NVARCHAR data types. The NCHAR data type is the fixed-length character data type that supports localized collation. The NVARCHAR data type is the varying-length character data type that can store up to 255 bytes of text data and supports localized collation.

For more information, see the *Informix Guide to GLS Functionality*.

Numeric Data Types

Numeric data types allow the database server to store numbers such as integers and real numbers in a column.

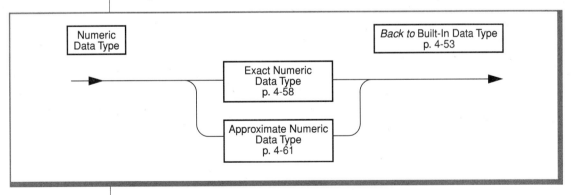

These data types fall into the following two categories:

- Exact numeric data types
- Approximate numeric data types

Exact Numeric Data Types

An exact numeric data type stores a numeric value with a specified precision and scale.

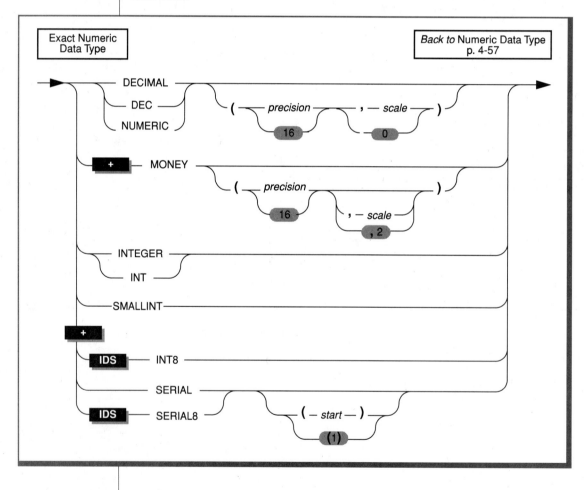

Element	Purpose	Restrictions	Syntax
precision	Total number of significant digits	You must specify an integer between 1 and 32, inclusive.	Literal Number, p. 4-237
scale	Number of digits to the right of the decimal point	You must specify an integer between 1 and *precision*.	Literal Number, p. 4-237
start	Starting number for values in a SERIAL or SERIAL8 column	For SERIAL columns you must specify a number greater than 0 and less than 2,147,483,647.	Literal Number, p. 4-237
		For SERIAL8 columns you must specify a number greater than 0 and less than 9,223,372,036,854,775,807.	

The precision of a number is the number of digits that the data type stores. The scale is the number of digits to the right of the decimal separator.

The following table summarizes the exact numeric data types available.

Data Type	Purpose
DEC(p,s)	Synonym for DECIMAL(p,s).
DECIMAL(p,s)	Stores fixed-point decimal (real) values in the range. The *p* parameter indicates the precision of the decimal value and the *s* parameter indicates the scale. If no precision is specified, the system default of 16 is used. If no scale is specified, the system default of 0 is used.
INT	Synonym for INTEGER.
INTEGER	Stores a 4-byte integer value. These values can be in the range $-((2^{**}31)-1)$ to $(2^{**}31)-1$ (the values -2,147,483,647 to 2,147,483,647).
INT8 (IDS)	Stores an 8-byte integer value. These values can be in the range $-((2^{**}63)-1)$ to $(2^{**}63)-1$ (the values -9,223,372,036,854,775,807 to 9,223,372,036,854,775,807).
MONEY(p,s)	Stores fixed-point currency values. Has the same internal data type as a fixed-point DECIMAL value.
NUMERIC(p,s)	ANSI-compliant synonym for DECIMAL(p,s).

(1 of 2)

Data Type	Purpose
SERIAL	Stores a 4-byte integer value that the database server generates. These values can be in the range -((2**31)-1) to (2**31)-1 (the values -2,147,483,647 to 2,147,483,647).
	If you want to insert an explicit value in a serial column, you can use any nonzero number. However, you cannot start or reset the value (begin the sequence) of a serial column with a negative number.
	A serial column is not unique by definition. A unique index must exist on the column to ensure unique values. (The index can also be in the form of a primary key or unique constraint.) With such an index, values in serial columns are guaranteed to be unique but not contiguous.
SERIAL8 (IDS)	Stores an 8-byte integer value that the database server generates. These values can be in the range -((2**63)-1) to (2**63)-1 (the values -9,223,372,036,854,775,807 to 9,223,372,036,854,775,807).
	If you want to insert an explicit value in a serial column, you can use any nonzero number. However, you cannot start or reset the value (begin the sequence) of a serial column with a negative number.
	A serial column is not unique by definition. A unique index must exist on the column to ensure unique values. (The index can also be in the form of a primary key or unique constraint.) With such an index, values in serial columns are guaranteed to be unique but not contiguous.
SMALLINT	Stores a 2-byte integer value. These values can be in the range -((2**15)-1) to (2**15)-1 (-32,767 to 32,767).

(2 of 2)

Approximate Numeric Data Types

An approximate numeric data type represents numeric values approximately.

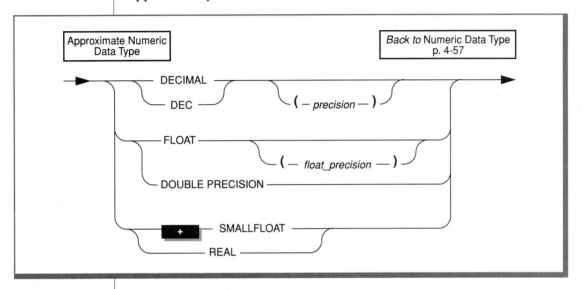

Element	Purpose	Restrictions	Syntax
float_precision	The float precision is ignored.	You must specify a positive integer.	Literal Number, p. 4-237
precision	Total number of significant digits	You must specify an integer between 1 and 32, inclusive.	Literal Number, p. 4-237
	The default is 16.		

Use approximate numeric data types for very large and very small numbers that can tolerate some degree of rounding during arithmetic operations.

The following table summarizes the approximate numeric data types available.

Data Type	Purpose
DECIMAL(p)	Stores floating-point decimal (real) values in the range. The *p* parameter indicates the precision of the decimal value. If no precision is specified, the system default of 16 is used.
DOUBLE PRECISION	ANSI-compliant synonym for FLOAT.
FLOAT	Stores double-precision floating-point numbers with up to 16 significant digits.
REAL	ANSI-compliant synonym for SMALLFLOAT.
SMALL-FLOAT	Stores single-precision floating-point numbers with approximately 8 significant digits.

Large-Object Data Types

Large-object data types allow the database server to store extremely large column values such as images and documents independently of the column.

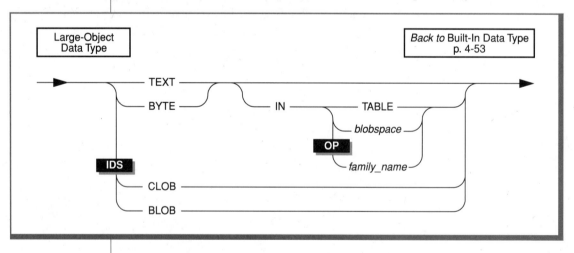

Element	Purpose	Restrictions	Syntax
blobspace	Name of an existing blobspace	The blobspace must exist.	Identifier, p. 4-205
family_name	Quoted string constant that specifies a family name or variable name in the optical family	The family name or variable name must exist.	Quoted String, p. 4-260. For additional information about optical families, see the *Guide to the Optical Subsystem*.

These data types fall into the following two categories:

- Simple-large-object data types: TEXT and BYTE
- Smart-large-object data types: CLOB and BLOB

Simple-Large-Object Data Types

A simple-large-object data type stores text or binary data in blobspaces or in tables. (For information on how to create blobspaces, see your *Administrator's Guide*.) The database server can access a simple-large-object value in one piece. These data types are not recoverable.

The following table summarizes the available simple-large-object data types.

Data Type	Purpose
TEXT	Stores text data of up to 2^{31} bytes.
BYTE	Stores text data of up to 2^{31} bytes.

IDS

Storing BYTE and TEXT data

When you specify a BYTE or TEXT data type, you can specify the location in which it is stored.

You can store data for a BYTE or TEXT column with the table or in a separate blobspace. The following example shows how blobspaces and dbspaces are specified. The user creates the **resume** table. The data for the table is stored in the **employ** dbspace. The data in the **vita** column is stored with the table, but the data associated with the **photo** column is stored in a blobspace named **photo_space**.

```
CREATE TABLE resume
    (
    fname           CHAR(15),
    lname           CHAR(15),
    phone           CHAR(18),
    recd_date       DATETIME YEAR TO HOUR,
    contact_date    DATETIME YEAR TO HOUR,
    comments        VARCHAR(250, 100),
    vita            TEXT IN TABLE,
    photo           BYTE IN photo_space
    )
    IN employ
```

If you are creating a named row type that includes a BYTE or TEXT column, you cannot use the IN clause to specify a separate storage space.

IDS

Smart-Large-Object Data Types

A smart-large-object data type stores text or binary data in sbspaces. (For information about how to create sbspaces, see your *Administrator's Guide*.) The database server can provide random access to a smart-large-object value. That is, it can access any portion of the smart-large-object value. These data types are recoverable.

The following table summarizes the smart-large-object data types that Dynamic Server supports.

Data Type	Purpose
BLOB	Stores binary data of up to 4 terabytes ($4*2^{40}$ bytes).
CLOB	Stores text data of up to 4 terabytes ($4*2^{40}$ bytes).

For more information, see the entries for these data types in the *Informix Guide to SQL: Reference*. For information about the built-in functions you use to import, export, and copy smart large objects, see "Smart-Large-Object Functions" on page 4-146 and the *Informix Guide to SQL: Tutorial*.

Time Data Types

The time data types allow the database server to store increments of time.

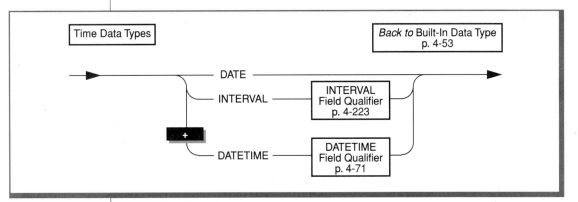

The following table summarizes the time data types available.

Data Type	Purpose
DATE	Stores a date value (*mm/dd/yy*) as a Julian date.
DATETIME	Stores a date and time value (*mm/dd/yy hh:mm:ss.fff*) in an internal format.
INTERVAL	Stores a unit of time such as seconds, hours/minutes, or year/month/day.

<table>
<tr><td>IDS</td></tr>
</table>

User-Defined Data Type

A user-defined data type is a data type that a user defines for the database server.

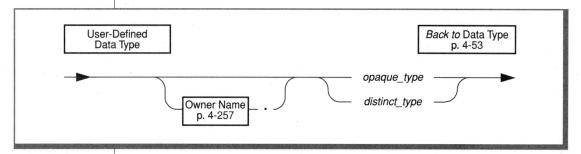

Element	Purpose	Restrictions	Syntax
distinct_type	Name of a distinct data type that has the same structure as an existing data type	The name must be different from all other data types in the database.	Identifier, p. 4-205
opaque_type	Name of the opaque data type	The name must be different from all other data types in the database.	Identifier, p. 4-205

Dynamic Server supports the following categories of user-defined data types:

- Opaque data types
- Distinct data types

Opaque Data Types

An opaque data type is a user-defined data type that can be used in the same way as a built-in data type. To create an opaque type, you must use the CREATE OPAQUE TYPE statement. Because an opaque type is encapsulated, you create support functions to access the individual components of an opaque type. The internal storage details of the type are hidden, or opaque.

For complete information about how to create an opaque type and its support functions, see *Extending Informix Dynamic Server 2000*.

Distinct Data Types

A distinct data type is a user-defined data type that is based on an existing built-in type, opaque type, named row type, or distinct type. To create a distinct type, you must use the CREATE DISTINCT TYPE statement. For more information, see the CREATE DISTINCT TYPE statement.

IDS

Complex Data Type

Complex data types are data types that you create from built-in types, opaque types, distinct types, or other complex types.

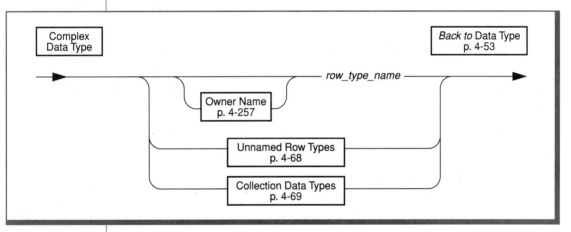

Element	Purpose	Restrictions	Syntax
row_type_name	Name of a row type created with the CREATE ROW TYPE statement	The row type must already exist.	Identifier, p. 4-205 Data type, p. 4-53

When you create a complex type, you define the components of the complex type. However, unlike an opaque type, a complex type is not encapsulated. You can use SQL to access the individual components of a complex data type.

Dynamic Server supports the following categories of complex data types:

- Row types
  - ❏ Named row types
  - ❏ Unnamed row types

- Collection data types
  - ❑ SET
  - ❑ MULTISET
  - ❑ LIST

Named Row Types

You can assign a named row type to a table or a column. To use a named row type to create a typed table or define a column, the named row type must already exist. To create a named row type, see "CREATE ROW TYPE" on page 2-216.

Unnamed Row Types

An unnamed row type is a group of fields that you create with the ROW constructor. You can use an unnamed row type to define a column. The syntax that you use to define a column as an unnamed row type is shown in the following diagram.

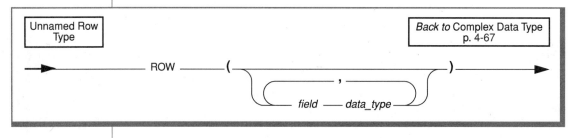

Element	Purpose	Restrictions	Syntax
data_type	Data type of the field	The field can be any data type except BYTE or TEXT.	Data Type, p. 4-53
field	Name of a field in the row	The name must be unique within the row type.	Identifier, p. 4-205

An unnamed row type is identified by its structure. For the syntax you use to specify row values for an unnamed row type, see "Expression" on page 4-73.

Collection Data Types

The syntax you use to define a column as a collection type is shown in the following diagram.

For the syntax you use to specify collection values for a collection data type, see "Collection Constructors" on page 4-118.

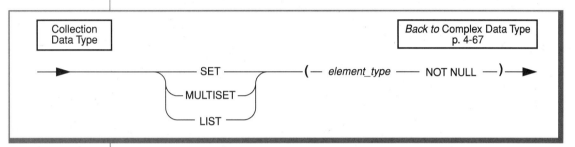

Element	Purpose	Restrictions	Syntax
element_type	Data type of the elements of the collection	The element type can be any data type except TEXT, BYTE, SERIAL, or SERIAL8. See also, "Defining the Element Type" on page 4-70.	Data Type, p. 4-53

Privileges on a collection type are those of the column. You cannot specify privileges on specific elements of a collection.

SET Collection Types

A SET is an unordered collection of elements in which each element is unique. You define a column as a SET collection type when you want to store collections whose elements contain no duplicate values and no specific order associated with them.

MULTISET Collection Types

A MULTISET is an unordered collection of elements in which elements can have duplicate values. You define a column as a MULTISET collection type when you want to store collections whose elements might not be unique and have no specific order associated with them.

LIST Collection Types

A LIST is an ordered collection of elements that allows duplicate elements. A LIST differs from a MULTISET in that each element in a LIST collection has an ordinal position in the collection. You define a column as a LIST collection type when you want to store collections whose elements might not be unique but have a specific order associated with them.

Defining the Element Type

The element type can be any data type except TEXT, BYTE, SERIAL, or SERIAL8. You can nest collection types. That is, an element type can be a collection type.

Every element in the collection must be of the same type. For example, if the element type of a collection type is INTEGER, every element in the collection must be of type INTEGER.

If the element type of a collection is an unnamed row type, the unnamed row type cannot contain fields that hold unnamed row types. That is, a collection cannot contain nested unnamed row types.

When you define a column as a collection type, you must specify that the elements of the collection cannot be null. That is, you must use the NOT NULL keywords after you specify the element type.

Related Information

For more information about choosing a data type for your database, see the *Informix Guide to Database Design and Implementation*.

For more information about the specific qualities of individual data types, see the chapter on data types in the *Informix Guide to SQL: Reference*.

For more information about multi-byte data types, see the discussion of the NCHAR and NVARCHAR data types and the GLS aspects of other character data types in the *Informix Guide to GLS Functionality*.

DATETIME Field Qualifier

Use a DATETIME field qualifier to specify the largest and smallest unit of time in a DATETIME column or value. Use the DATETIME Field Qualifier segment whenever you see a reference to a DATETIME field qualifier in a syntax diagram.

Syntax

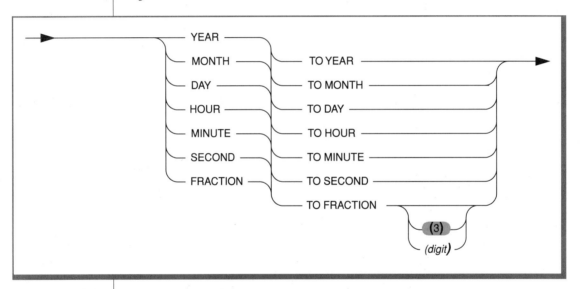

Element	Purpose	Restrictions	Syntax
digit	Single integer that specifies the precision of a decimal fraction of a second. The default precision is 3 digits (a thousandth of a second).	You must specify an integer between 1 and 5, inclusive.	Literal Number, p. 4-237

Usage

Specify the largest unit for the first DATETIME value; after the word TO, specify the smallest unit for the value. The keywords imply that the following values are used in the DATETIME column.

Unit of Time	Purpose
YEAR	Specifies a year, numbered from A.D. 1 to 9999
MONTH	Specifies a month, numbered from 1 to 12
DAY	Specifies a day, numbered from 1 to 31, as appropriate to the month in question
HOUR	Specifies an hour, numbered from 0 (midnight) to 23
MINUTE	Specifies a minute, numbered from 0 to 59
SECOND	Specifies a second, numbered from 0 to 59
FRACTION	Specifies a fraction of a second, with up to five decimal places The default scale is three digits (thousandth of a second).

The following examples show DATETIME qualifiers:

```
DAY TO MINUTE

YEAR TO MINUTE

DAY TO FRACTION(4)

MONTH TO MONTH
```

Related Information

For an explanation of the DATETIME field qualifier, see the discussion of the DATETIME data type in the *Informix Guide to SQL: Reference*.

Expression

An expression is one or more pieces of data that is contained in a table or derived from data in the table. Typically you use expressions to express values in data manipulation statements. Use the Expression segment whenever you see a reference to an expression in a syntax diagram.

For an alphabetical listing of the built-in functions in this segment, see "List of Expressions" on page 4-76.

Expression

Syntax

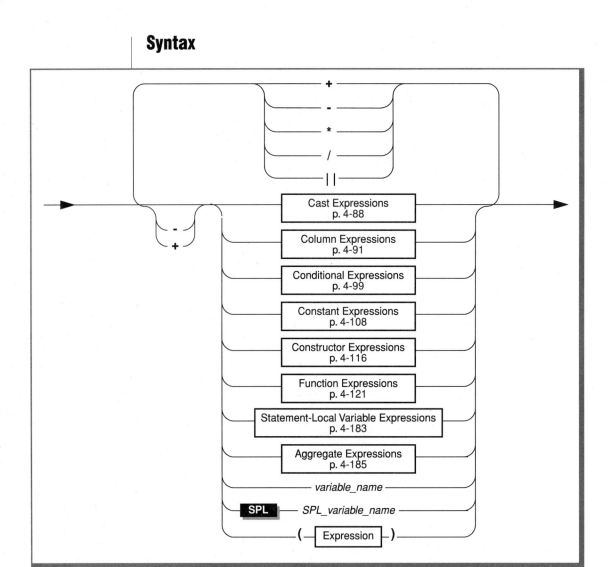

Element	Purpose	Restrictions	Syntax
SPL_variable_ name	Variable that is stored in an SPL routine The value stored in the variable is one of the expression types shown in the syntax diagram.	The expression that is stored in *SPL_variable_name* must conform to the rules for expressions of that type.	Identifier, p. 4-205
variable_name	Host variable or program variable The value stored in the variable is one of the expression types shown in the syntax diagram.	The expression that is stored in *variable_name* must conform to the rules for expressions of that type.	Name must conform to language-specific rules for variable names.

Usage

This segment describes SQL expressions. The following table shows the different types of SQL expressions as shown in the diagram for "Syntax" on page 4-74 and states the purpose of each type.

Expression Type	Purpose
Arithmetic operators	Provide support for arithmetic operations on two items (binary operators) or one item (unary operators) of an expression
Concatenation operator	Provides the ability to concatenate two string values
Cast operators	Provide the ability to explicit cast from one data type to another
Column expressions	Provide the ability to use full or partial column values in data manipulation statements
Conditional expressions	Provide the ability to return values that depend on the outcome of conditional tests
Constant expressions	Provide the ability to use literal values in data manipulation statements
Constructor expressions	Provide the ability to dynamically create values for complex data types

(1 of 2)

Expression Type	Purpose
Function expressions	Provide the ability to call built-in functions or user-defined functions in data manipulation statements
Statement-Local-Variable expressions	Specify how you can use a defined statement-local variable (SLV) elsewhere in an SQL statement
Aggregate functions	Provide the ability to use built-in aggregate functions or user-defined aggregate functions in data manipulation statements

(2 of 2)

You can also use host variables or SPL variables as expressions. For a complete list of SQL expressions, see "List of Expressions" on page 4-76.

List of Expressions

Each category of SQL expression includes many individual expressions. The following table lists all the SQL expressions in alphabetical order and states the purpose of each expression. The columns in this table have the following meanings:

- The **Name** column gives the name of each expression.
- The **Purpose** column shows the purpose of each expression.
- The **Syntax** column refers to the page that describes the syntax of the expression.
- The **Usage** column refers to the page that describes the usage of the expression.

Each expression listed in the following table is supported on all database servers unless otherwise noted. When an expression is not supported on all database servers, the **Name** column notes in parentheses the database server or servers that do support the expression.

Name	Purpose	Syntax	Usage
ABS function	Returns the absolute value of a given expression	p. 4-123	p. 4-125
ACOS function	Returns the arc cosine of a numeric expression	p. 4-159	p. 4-161
Addition operator (+)	Adds two expressions to make a complex expression	p. 4-74	p. 4-85
ASIN function	Returns the arc sine of a numeric expression	p. 4-159	p. 4-161
ATAN function	Returns the arc tangent of a numeric expression	p. 4-159	p. 4-161
ATAN2 function	Computes the angular component of the polar coordinates (r, θ) associated with (x, y)	p. 4-159	p. 4-162
AVG function	Returns the average of all values in the specified column or expression	p. 4-185	p. 4-194
CARDINALITY function (IDS)	Returns the number of elements in a collection column (SET, MULTISET, or LIST)	p. 4-129	p. 4-129
CASE expression	Returns one of several possible results, depending on which of several conditional tests evaluates to true	p. 4-100	p. 4-100
CAST expression (IDS)	Provides the ability to cast an expression to another data type	p. 4-88	p. 4-88
Cast operator	See Double-colon cast operator.	p. 4-88	p. 4-88
CHARACTER_LENGTH function	See CHAR_LENGTH function.	p. 4-143	p. 4-145
CHAR_LENGTH function	Returns the number of logical characters (not bytes) in a character column	p. 4-143	p. 4-145
Column expression	Complete or partial column value from a table	p. 4-91	p. 4-91
Concatenation operator	Concatenates the output of two expressions	p. 4-74	p. 4-87
Constant expression	Expression that evaluates to a constant value	p. 4-108	p. 4-108
COS function	Returns the cosine of a radian expression	p. 4-159	p. 4-160

(1 of 9)

Expression

Name	Purpose	Syntax	Usage
COUNT (as a set of functions)	Provides a set of functions for counting column values and expressions	p. 4-185	p. 4-189
	You invoke each function by specifying the appropriate argument after the COUNT keyword. Each form of the COUNT function is listed below.		
COUNT (ALL *column*) function	See COUNT (*column*) function.	p. 4-185	p. 4-190
COUNT (*column*) function	Returns the number of non-null values in a specified column	p. 4-185	p. 4-190
COUNT DISTINCT function	Returns the number of unique non-null values in a specified column	p. 4-185	p. 4-190
COUNT UNIQUE function	See COUNT DISTINCT function.	p. 4-185	p. 4-190
COUNT (*) function	Returns the number of rows that satisfy a query. If you do not specify a WHERE clause, this function returns the total number of rows in the table.	p. 4-185	p. 4-189
CURRENT function	Shows the current instant by returning a DATETIME value consisting of the date and the time of day	p. 4-108	p. 4-112
DATE function	Returns a DATE value that corresponds to the non-date expression with which you call it	p. 4-152	p. 4-154
DAY function	Returns an integer that represents the day of the month	p. 4-152	p. 4-155
DBINFO (as a set of functions)	Provides a set of functions for retrieving different types of database information	p. 4-130	p. 4-131
	You invoke each function by specifying the appropriate DBINFO option. Each DBINFO option is listed below.		
DBINFO ('coserverid' string followed by a column name qualified by a table name and the 'currentrow' string) (EDS)	Returns the coserver ID of the coserver where each row of a specified table is located	p. 4-130	p. 4-139

Name	Purpose	Syntax	Usage
DBINFO ('coserverid' string with no other arguments) (EDS)	Returns the coserver ID of the coserver to which the user who entered the query is connected	p. 4-130	p. 4-139
DBINFO ('dbhostname' option)	Returns the hostname of the database server to which a client application is connected	p. 4-130	p. 4-136
DBINFO ('dbspace' string followed by a column name qualified by a table name and the 'currentrow' string) (EDS)	Returns the name of the dbspace where each row of a specified table is located	p. 4-130	p. 4-140
DBINFO ('dbspace' string followed by a tblspace number)	Returns the name of a dbspace corresponding to a tblspace number	p. 4-130	p. 4-133
DBINFO ('serial8' option) (IDS)	Returns the last SERIAL8 value inserted in a table	p. 4-130	p. 4-138
DBINFO ('sessionid' option)	Returns the session ID of the current session	p. 4-130	p. 4-135
DBINFO ('sqlca.sqlerrd1' option)	Returns the last serial value inserted in a table	p. 4-130	p. 4-133
DBINFO ('sqlca.sqlerrd2' option)	Returns the number of rows processed by selects, inserts, deletes, updates, EXECUTE PROCEDURE statements, and EXECUTE FUNCTION statements	p. 4-130	p. 4-134
DBINFO ('version' option)	Returns the exact version of the database server to which a client application is connected	p. 4-130	p. 4-136
DBSERVERNAME function	Returns the name of the database server	p. 4-108	p. 4-111
DECODE function	Evaluates one or more expression pairs and compares the *when* expression in each pair against a specified value expression	p. 4-105	p. 4-105
	When the DECODE function finds a match between the *when* expression in an expression pair and the specified value expression, it returns the value of the *then* expression in that expression pair.		

(3 of 9)

Name	Purpose	Syntax	Usage
Division operator (/)	Divides one expression by another to make a complex expression	p. 4-74	p. 4-85
Double-colon cast operator (::) (IDS)	Provides the ability to cast an expression to another data type	p. 4-88	p. 4-88
EXP function	Returns the exponent of a numeric expression	p. 4-141	p. 4-141
EXTEND function	Adjusts the precision of a DATETIME or DATE value	p. 4-152	p. 4-156
FILETOBLOB function (IDS)	Creates a BLOB value for data that is stored in a specified operating-system file	p. 4-146	p. 4-147
FILETOCLOB function (IDS)	Creates a CLOB value for data that is stored in a specified operating-system file	p. 4-146	p. 4-147
HEX function	Returns the hexadecimal encoding of an integer expression	p. 4-142	p. 4-142
Host variable	See Variable.	p. 4-74	p. 4-74
IFX_ALLOW_NEWLINE function	Sets a newline mode that allows newline characters in a quoted strings or disallows newline characters in quoted strings within a given session	p. 4-177	p. 4-177
IFX_REPLACE_MODULE function (IDS)	Replaces a loaded shared library with a new version that has a different name or location	p. 4-145	p. 4-145
INITCAP function	Converts a source expression so that every word in the source expression begins with an initial capital letter and all remaining letters in each word are lowercase	p. 4-174	p. 4-177
LENGTH function	Returns the number of bytes in a character column, not including any trailing spaces	p. 4-143	p. 4-144

Name	Purpose	Syntax	Usage
LIST collection constructor (IDS)	Enables you to specify values for collection columns	p. 4-118	p. 4-118
	The LIST constructor indicates a collection of elements with the following qualities:		
	■ The collection can contain duplicate values.		
	■ Elements have ordered positions.		
Literal BOOLEAN (as an expression)	Provides a literal representation of a BOOLEAN value	p. 4-108	p. 4-108
Literal collection (as an expression) (IDS)	Provides a constant value in data manipulation statements	p. 4-108	p. 4-115
Literal DATETIME (as an expression)	Provides a constant value in data manipulation statements	p. 4-108	p. 4-114
Literal INTERVAL (as an expression)	Provides a constant value in data manipulation statements	p. 4-108	p. 4-114
Literal number (as an expression)	Provides a constant value in data manipulation statements	p. 4-108	p. 4-110
Literal opaque type (as an expression) (IDS)	Provides a literal representation of an opaque data type	p. 4-108	p. 4-108
Literal row (as an expression) (IDS)	Provides a constant value in data manipulation statements	p. 4-108	p. 4-115
LOCOPY function (IDS)	Creates a copy of a smart large object	p. 4-146	p. 4-150
LOGN function	Returns the natural log of a numeric expression	p. 4-141	p. 4-142
LOG10 function	Returns the log of a value to the base 10	p. 4-141	p. 4-142
LOTOFILE function (IDS)	Copies a smart large object to an operating-system file	p. 4-146	p. 4-149
LOWER function	Converts a source expression to lowercase characters	p. 4-174	p. 4-176

(5 of 9)

Name	Purpose	Syntax	Usage
LPAD function	Returns a copy of a source string that is left-padded by a specified number of pad characters	p. 4-172	p. 4-172
MAX function	Returns the largest value in the specified column or expression	p. 4-185	p. 4-194
MDY function	Returns a DATE value with three expressions that evaluate to integers representing the month, day, and year	p. 4-152	p. 4-157
MIN function	Returns the lowest value in the specified column or expression	p. 4-185	p. 4-194
MOD function	Returns the modulus or remainder value for two numeric expressions	p. 4-123	p. 4-126
MONTH function	Returns an integer that corresponds to the month portion of its DATE or DATETIME argument	p. 4-152	p. 4-155
Multiplication operator (*)	Multiplies two expressions to make a complex expression	p. 4-74	p. 4-85
MULTISET collection constructor (IDS)	Enables you to specify values for collection columns The MULTISET constructor indicates a collection of elements with the following qualities: ■ The collection can contain duplicate values. ■ Elements have no specific order associated with them.	p. 4-118	p. 4-118
NVL function	Evaluates an expression and returns the value of the expression if the value of the expression is not null If the value of the expression is null, the NVL function returns a specified result.	p. 4-104	p. 4-104
OCTET_LENGTH function	Returns the number of bytes in a character column, including any trailing spaces	p. 4-143	p. 4-144
POW function	Raises a base value to a specified power	p. 4-123	p. 4-126
Procedure-call expression	See User-defined function.	p. 4-179	p. 4-179

(6 of 9)

Name	Purpose	Syntax	Usage
Program variable	See Variable.	p. 4-74	p. 4-74
Quoted string (as an expression)	Provides a constant value in data manipulation statements	p. 4-108	p. 4-109
RANGE function	Computes the range for a sample of a population	p. 4-185	p. 4-195
REPLACE function	Replaces specified characters in a source string with different characters	p. 4-170	p. 4-170
ROOT function	Returns the root value of a numeric expression	p. 4-123	p. 4-126
ROUND function	Returns the rounded value of an expression	p. 4-123	p. 4-127
ROW constructor (IDS)	Enables you to specify values for columns that are named row types	p. 4-116	p. 4-116
RPAD function	Returns a copy of a source string that is right-padded by a specified number of pad characters	p. 4-173	p. 4-173
SET collection constructor (IDS)	Enables you to specify values for collection columns The SET constructor indicates a collection of elements with the following qualities: ■ The collection must contain unique values. ■ Elements have no specific order associated with them.	p. 4-118	p. 4-118
SIN function	Returns the sine of a radian expression	p. 4-159	p. 4-161
SITENAME function	See DBSERVERNAME function.	p. 4-108	p. 4-111
SPL routine expression	See User-defined functions.	p. 4-179	p. 4-179
SPL variable	SPL variable that stores an expression	p. 4-74	p. 4-74
SQRT function	Returns the square root of a numeric expression	p. 4-123	p. 4-128
Statement-Local-Variable expression	Specifies how you can use a defined statement-local variable (SLV) elsewhere in an SQL statement	p. 4-183	p. 4-183

Name	Purpose	Syntax	Usage
STDEV function	Computes the standard deviation for a sample of a population	p. 4-185	p. 4-196
SUBSTR function	Returns a subset of a source string	p. 4-168	p. 4-168
SUBSTRING function	Returns a subset of a source string	p. 4-166	p. 4-166
Subtraction operator (-)	Subtracts one expression from another to make a complex expression	p. 4-74	p. 4-85
SUM function	Returns the sum of all values in the specified column or expression	p. 4-185	p. 4-195
TAN function	Returns the tangent of a radian expression	p. 4-159	p. 4-161
TO_CHAR function	Converts a DATE or DATETIME value to a character string	p. 4-152	p. 4-157
TO_DATE function	Converts a character string to a DATETIME value	p. 4-152	p. 4-158
TODAY function	Returns the system date	p. 4-108	p. 4-112
TRIM function	Removes leading or trailing (or both) pad characters from a string	p. 4-164	p. 4-164
TRUNC function	Returns the truncated value of a numeric expression	p. 4-123	p. 4-128
UNITS keyword	Enables you to display a simple interval or increase or decrease a specific interval or datetime value	p. 4-108	p. 4-114
UPPER function	Converts a source expression to uppercase characters	p. 4-174	p. 4-176
User-defined aggregate (IDS)	An aggregate that you write (as opposed to the built-in aggregates provided by the database server)	p. 4-199	p. 4-199
User-defined function	A function that you write (as opposed to the built-in functions provided by the database server)	p. 4-179	p. 4-179
USER function	Returns a string that contains the login name of the current user	p. 4-108	p. 4-110

(8 of 9)

Name	Purpose	Syntax	Usage
Variable	host variable or program variable that stores an expression	p. 4-74	p. 4-74
VARIANCE function	Returns the variance for a sample of values as an unbiased estimate of the variance of a population	p. 4-185	p. 4-196
WEEKDAY function	Returns an integer that represents the day of the week	p. 4-152	p. 4-155
YEAR function	Returns a four-digit integer that represents the year	p. 4-152	p. 4-156
* sign	See Multiplication operator.	p. 4-74	p. 4-85
+ sign	See Addition operator.	p. 4-74	p. 4-85
- sign	See Subtraction operator.	p. 4-74	p. 4-85
/ sign	See Division operator.	p. 4-74	p. 4-85
:: symbol	See Double-colon cast operator.	p. 4-88	p. 4-88

(9 of 9)

The following sections describe the syntax and usage of each expression that appears in the preceding table.

Using Arithmetic Operators with Expressions

You can combine expressions with arithmetic operators to make complex expressions. To combine expressions, connect them with the following binary arithmetic operators.

Arithmetic Operation	Arithmetic Operator	Operator Function
Addition	+	**plus()**
Subtraction	-	**minus()**
Multiplication	*	**times()**
Division	/	**divide()**

The following examples use binary arithmetic operators:

```
quantity * total_price

price * 2

COUNT(*) + 2
```

If you combine a DATETIME value with one or more INTERVAL values, all the fields of the INTERVAL value must be present in the DATETIME value; no implicit EXTEND function is performed. In addition, you cannot use YEAR to MONTH intervals with DAY to SECOND intervals.

The binary arithmetic operators have associated operator functions, as the preceding table shows. Connecting two expressions with a binary operator is equivalent to invoking the associated operator function on the expressions. For example, the following two statements both select the product of the **total_price** column and 2. In the first statement, the * operator implicitly invokes the **times()** function.

```
SELECT (total_price * 2) FROM items
    WHERE order_num = 1001

SELECT times(total_price, 2) FROM items
    WHERE order_num = 1001
```

You cannot combine expressions that use aggregate functions with column expressions.

The database server provides the operator functions associated with the relational operators for all built-in data types. You can define new versions of these binary arithmetic operator functions to handle your own user-defined data types. For more information, see *Extending Informix Dynamic Server 2000*.

Informix also provides the following unary arithmetic operators:.

Arithmetic Operation	Arithmetic Operator	Operator Function
Positive	+	**positive()**
Negative	-	**negate()**

The unary arithmetic operators have the associated operator functions that the preceding table shows. You can define new versions of these arithmetic operator functions to handle your own user-defined data types. For more information on how to write versions of operator functions, see *Extending Informix Dynamic Server 2000*.

If any value that participates in an arithmetic expression is null, the value of the entire expression is null, as shown in the following example:

```
SELECT order_num, ship_charge/ship_weight FROM orders
    WHERE order_num = 1023
```

If either **ship_charge** or **ship_weight** is null, the value returned for the expression **ship_charge/ship_weight** is also null. If the expression **ship_charge/ship_weight** is used in a condition, its truth value is unknown.

Using the Concatenation Operator with Expressions

You can use the concatenation operator (| |) to concatenate two expressions. For example, the following examples are some possible concatenated-expression combinations. The first example concatenates the **zipcode** column to the first three letters of the **lname** column. The second example concatenates the suffix **.dbg** to the contents of a host variable called **file_variable**. The third example concatenates the value returned by the **TODAY** function to the string Date.

```
lname[1,3] || zipcode

:file_variable || '.dbg'

'Date:' || TODAY
```

E/C

You cannot use the concatenation operator in an embedded-language-only statement. The ESQL/C-only statements appear in the following list:

ALLOCATE COLLECTION	FETCH
ALLOCATE DESCRIPTOR	FLUSH
ALLOCATE ROW	FREE
CLOSE	GET DESCRIPTOR
CREATE FUNCTION FROM	GET DIAGNOSTICS
CREATE PROCEDURE FROM	OPEN
CREATE ROUTINE FROM	PREPARE
DEALLOCATE COLLECTION	PUT
DEALLOCATE DESCRIPTOR	SET CONNECTION
DEALLOCATE ROW	SET DESCRIPTOR
DECLARE	WHENEVER
DESCRIBE	
EXECUTE	
EXECUTE IMMEDIATE	

You can use the concatenation operator in the SELECT, INSERT, EXECUTE FUNCTION (or EXECUTE PROCEDURE) statement in the DECLARE statement.

You can use the concatenation operator in the SQL statement or statements in the PREPARE statement. ♦

The concatenation operator (| |) has an associated operator function called **concat()**. You can define a **concat()** function to handle your own string-based user-defined data types. For more information, see *Extending Informix Dynamic Server 2000*.

IDS

Cast Expressions

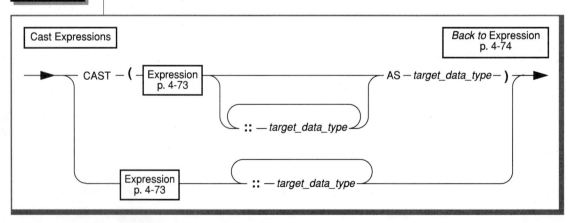

Cast Expressions

Back to Expression
p. 4-74

CAST — (— Expression p. 4-73 — AS — target_data_type —)

:: — target_data_type

Expression p. 4-73 — :: — target_data_type

Element	Purpose	Restrictions	Syntax
target_data_type	Data type that results after the cast is applied	See "Rules for the Target Data Type" on page 4-89.	Data type, p. 4-53

You can use the CAST AS keywords or the double-colon cast operator (::) to cast an expression to another data type. Both the operator and the keywords invoke a cast from the data type of the expression to the target data type. To invoke an explicit cast you must use either the cast operator or the CAST AS keywords. If you use the cast operator or CAST AS keywords, but no explicit or implicit cast was defined to perform the conversion between two data types, the statement returns an error.

Rules for the Target Data Type

You must observe the following rules and restrictions regarding the *target data type* parameter.

- The target data type must be either a built-in type, a user-defined type, or a named row type in the database.
- The target data type cannot be an unnamed row type or a collection data type.
- The target data type can be a BLOB data type under the following conditions:
  - The source expression (the expression to be cast to another data type) is a BYTE data type.
  - The source expression is a user-defined type and the user has defined a cast from the user-defined type to the BLOB type.
- The target data type can be a CLOB data type under the following conditions:
  - The source expression is a TEXT data type.
  - The source expression is a user-defined type and the user has defined a cast from the user-defined type to the CLOB type.

- You cannot cast a BLOB data type to a BYTE data type.
- You cannot cast a CLOB data type to a TEXT data type.
- An explicit or implicit cast must exist that can convert the data type of the source expression to the target data type.

Examples of Cast Expressions

The following examples show two different ways to convert the sum of x and y to a user-defined data type, **user_type**. The two methods produce identical results. Both require the existence of an explicit or implicit cast from the type returned by $x + y$ to the user-defined type.

```
CAST (x + y) AS user_type
(x + y)::user_type
```

The following examples show two different ways of finding the integer equivalent of the expression **expr**. Both require the existence of an implicit or explicit cast from the data type of **expr** to the INTEGER data type.

```
CAST expr AS INTEGER
expr::INTEGER
```

In the following example, the user casts a BYTE column to the BLOB type and copies the BLOB data to an operating-system file:

```
SELECT LOTOFILE(mybytecol::blob, 'fname', 'client')
    FROM mytab
    WHERE pkey = 12345
```

In the following example, the user casts a TEXT column to a CLOB value and then updates a CLOB column in the same table to have the CLOB value derived from the TEXT column:

```
UPDATE newtab SET myclobcol = mytextcol::clob
```

Column Expressions

The possible syntax for column expressions is shown in the following
diagram.

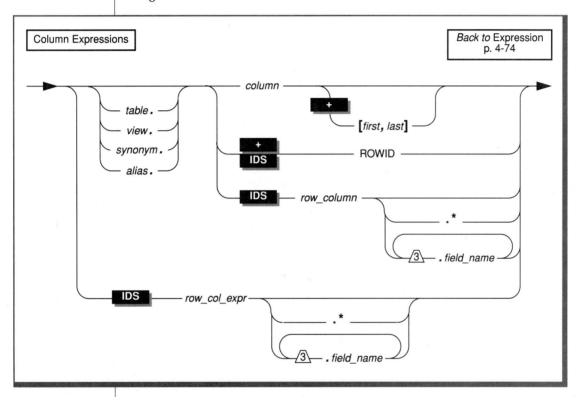

Expression

Element	Purpose	Restrictions	Syntax
*	Signifies that all fields of a row column or of the row type data returned by a row-column expression are selected	You can use the asterisk (*) notation only in the select list of a SELECT statement.	The asterisk (*) is a literal value that you enter from the keyboard.
alias	Temporary alternative name for a table or view within the scope of a SELECT statement This alternative name is established in the FROM clause of the SELECT statement.	The restrictions depend on the clause of the SELECT statement in which alias occurs.	Identifier, p. 4-205
column	Name of the column that you are specifying	The restrictions depend on the statement in which column occurs.	Identifier, p. 4-205
field_name	Name of the row field that you are accessing in the row column or row-column expression	The field must be a member of the row that row-column name or row_col_expr or field name (for nested rows) specifies.	Identifier, p. 4-205
first	Position of the first character in the portion of the column that you are selecting	The column must be one of the following types: BYTE, CHAR, NCHAR, NVARCHAR, TEXT, or VARCHAR.	Literal Number, p. 4-237
last	Position of the last character in the portion of the column that you are selecting	The column must be one of the following types: BYTE, CHAR, NCHAR, NVARCHAR, TEXT, or VARCHAR.	Literal Number, p. 4-237
row_col_expr	Expression that evaluates to row-type values	The result of the expression must be of row type.	Expression, p. 4-73
row_column	Name of the row column that you specify	The data type of the column must be a named row type or an unnamed row type.	Identifier, p. 4-205
synonym	Name of the synonym in which the specified column occurs	The synonym and the table to which the synonym points must exist.	Database Object Name, p. 4-50
table	Name of the table in which the specified column occurs	The table must exist.	Database Object Name, p. 4-50
view	Name of the view in which the specified column occurs	The view must exist.	Database Object Name, p. 4-50

The following examples show column expressions:

```
company

items.price

cat_advert [1,15]
```

Use a table or alias name whenever it is necessary to distinguish between columns that have the same name but are in different tables. The SELECT statements that the following example shows use **customer_num** from the **customer** and **orders** tables. The first example precedes the column names with table names. The second example precedes the column names with table aliases.

```
SELECT * FROM customer, orders
    WHERE customer.customer_num = orders.customer_num

SELECT * FROM customer c, orders o
    WHERE c.customer_num = o.customer_num
```

Using Dot Notation

Dot notation allows you to qualify an SQL identifier with another SQL identifier. You separate the identifiers with the period (.) symbol. For example, you can qualify a column name with any of the following SQL identifiers:

- Table name: *table_name.column_name*
- View name: *view_name.column_name*
- Synonym name: *syn_name.column_name*

The previous forms of dot notation are called *column projections*.

You can also use dot notation to directly access the fields of a row column, as follows:

```
row-column name.field name
```

This use of dot notation is called a *field projection*. For example, suppose you have a column called **rect** with the following definition:

```
CREATE TABLE rectangles
(
    area float,
    rect ROW(x int, y int, length float, width float)
)
```

The following SELECT statement uses dot notation to access field **length** of the **rect** column:

```
SELECT rect.length FROM rectangles
    WHERE area = 64
```

Selecting All Fields of a Column with Asterisk Notation

If you want to select all fields of a column that has a row type, you can specify the column name without dot notation. For example, you can select all fields of the **rect** column as follows:

```
SELECT rect FROM rectangles
    WHERE area = 64
```

You can also use asterisk notation to project all the fields of a column that has a row type. For example, if you want to use asterisk notation to select all fields of the **rect** column, you can enter the following statement:

```
SELECT rect.* FROM rectangles
    WHERE area = 64
```

Asterisk notation is a shorthand form of dot notation that is easier than specifying each field of the **rect** column individually:

```
SELECT rect.x, rect.y, rect.length,
    rect.width
    FROM rectangles
    WHERE area = 64
```

Asterisk notation is not necessary with row-type columns because you can specify just the column name itself to project all of its fields. However, asterisk notation is quite helpful with row-type expressions such as subqueries and user-defined functions that return row-type values. For further information see "Using Dot Notation with Row-Type Expressions" on page 4-96.

You can use asterisk notation with columns and expressions of row type in the select list of a SELECT statement only. You cannot use asterisk notation with columns and expressions of row type in any other clause of a SELECT statement.

Selecting Nested Fields

When the row type that defines a column itself contains other row types, the column contains nested fields. You use dot notation to access these nested fields within a column. For example, assume that the **address** column of the **employee** table contains the fields **street**, **city**, **state**, and **zip**. In addition, the **zip** field contains the nested fields: **z_code** and **z_suffix**. A query on the **zip** field returns values for the **z_code** and **z_suffix** fields. However, you can specify that a query returns only specific nested fields. The following example shows how to use dot notation to construct a SELECT statement that returns rows for the **z_code** field of the **address** column only.

```
SELECT address.zip.z_code
    FROM employee
```

Rules of Precedence

The database server uses the following precedence rules to interpret dot notation:

1. schema *name_a* . table *name_b* . column *name_c* . field *name_d*
2. table name_a . column *name_b* . field *name_c* . field *name_d*
3. column name_a . field *name_b* . field *name_c* . field *name_d*

When the meaning of a particular identifier is ambiguous, the database server uses precedence rules to determine which database object the identifier specifies. Consider the following two tables:

```
CREATE TABLE b (c ROW(d INTEGER, e CHAR(2));
CREATE TABLE c (d INTEGER);
```

In the following SELECT statement, the expression `c.d` references column **d** of table **c** (rather than field **d** of column **c** in table **b**) because a table identifier has a higher precedence than a column identifier:

```
SELECT *
FROM b,c
WHERE c.d = 10
```

For more information about precedence rules and how to use dot notation with row columns, see the *Informix Guide to SQL: Tutorial*.

Using Dot Notation with Row-Type Expressions

You can use dot notation whenever a column has a row data type. However, in addition to column expressions, you can use dot notation with any expression that evaluates to a row type. For example, you can use dot notation in a subquery in an INSERT statement if the subquery returns a single row of values. Assume that you have created a row type named **row_t**:

```
CREATE ROW TYPE row_t (part_id INT, amt INT)
```

Also assume that you have created a typed table named **tab1** that is based on the **row_t** row type:

```
CREATE TABLE tab1 OF TYPE row_t
```

Assume also that you have inserted the following values into table **tab1**:

```
INSERT INTO tab1 VALUES (ROW(1,7));
INSERT INTO tab1 VALUES (ROW(2,10));
```

Finally, assume that you have created another table named **tab2**:

```
CREATE TABLE tab2 (colx INT)
```

Now you can use dot notation to insert the value from just the **part_id** column of table **tab1** into the **tab2** table:

```
INSERT INTO tab2
    VALUES ((SELECT t FROM tab1 t
        WHERE part_id = 1).part_id)
```

The asterisk form of dot notation is not necessary when you want to select all fields of a row type column because you can just specify the column name itself to select all of its fields. However, the asterisk form of dot notation can be quite helpful when you use a subquery as in the preceding example or when you call a user-defined function to return row type values.

Suppose that you create a user-defined function named **new_row** that returns row type values, and you want to call this function to insert the row type values into a table. Asterisk notation makes it easy to specify that all the row type values produced by the **new_row** function are to be inserted into the table:

```
INSERT INTO mytab2 SELECT new_row (mycol).* FROM mytab1
```

Limitations on Dot Notation

References to the fields of a row-type column or a row-type expression are not allowed in fragment expressions. A fragment expression is an expression that defines a table fragment or an index fragment in statements like CREATE TABLE, CREATE INDEX, and ALTER FRAGMENT.

Using Subscripts on Character Columns

You can use subscripts on **CHAR**, **VARCHAR**, **NCHAR**, **NVARCHAR**, **BYTE**, and **TEXT** columns. The subscripts indicate the starting and ending character positions that are contained in the expression. Together the column subscripts define a column substring. The column substring is the portion of the column that is contained in the expression.

For example, if a value in the **lname** column of the **customer** table is Greenburg, the following expression evaluates to burg:

```
lname[6,9]
```

GLS

For information on the GLS aspects of column subscripts and substrings, see the *Informix Guide to GLS Functionality.* ♦

IDS

Using Rowids

In Dynamic Server, you can use the **rowid** column that is associated with a table row as a property of the row. The **rowid** column is essentially a hidden column in nonfragmented tables and in fragmented tables that were created with the WITH ROWIDS clause. The **rowid** column is unique for each row, but it is not necessarily sequential. Informix recommends, however, that you use primary keys as an access method rather than exploiting the **rowid** column.

The following examples show possible uses of the ROWID keyword in a SELECT statement:

```
SELECT *, ROWID FROM customer

SELECT fname, ROWID FROM customer
ORDER BY ROWID

SELECT HEX(rowid) FROM customer
WHERE customer_num = 106
```

The last SELECT statement example shows how to get the page number (the first six digits after 0x) and the slot number (the last two digits) of the location of your row.

You cannot use the ROWID keyword in the select list of a query that contains an aggregate function.

IDS

Using Smart Large Objects

The SELECT, UPDATE, and INSERT statements do not manipulate the values of smart large objects directly. Instead, they use a *handle value*, which is a type of pointer, to access the BLOB or CLOB value, as follows:

- The SELECT statement returns a handle value to the BLOB or CLOB value that the select list specifies.

  SELECT does not return the actual data for the BLOB or CLOB column that the select list specifies. Instead, it returns a handle value to the column data.

- The INSERT and UPDATE statements accept a handle value for a BLOB or CLOB to be inserted or updated.

  INSERT and UPDATE do not send the actual data for the BLOB or CLOB column to the database server. Instead, they accept a handle value to this data as the column value.

To access the data of a smart-large-object column, you must use one of the following application programming interfaces (APIs):

- From within an Informix ESQL/C program, use the ESQL/C library functions that access smart large objects.

  For more information, see the *Informix ESQL/C Programmer's Manual*.

- From within a C program such as a DataBlade module, use the Client and Server API.

  For more information, see your *DataBlade Developers Kit User's Guide*.

You cannot use the name of a smart-large-object column in expressions that involve arithmetic operators. For example, operations such as addition or subtraction on the smart-large-object handle value have no meaning.

When you select a smart-large-object column, you can assign the handle value to any number of columns: all columns with the same handle value share the CLOB or BLOB value across several columns. This storage arrangement reduces the amount of disk space that the CLOB or BLOB data takes. However, when several columns share the same smart-large-object value, the following conditions result:

- The chance of lock contention on a CLOB or BLOB column increases.

  If two columns share the same smart-large-object value, the data might be locked by either column that needs to access it.

- The CLOB or BLOB value can be updated from a number of points

To remove these constraints, you can create separate copies of the BLOB or CLOB data for each column that needs to access it. You can use the **LOCOPY** function to create a copy of an existing smart large object. You can also use the built-in functions **LOTOFILE**, **FILETOCLOB**, and **FILETOBLOB** to access smart-large-object values. For more information on these functions, see "Smart-Large-Object Functions" on page 4-146. For more information on the BLOB and CLOB data types, see the *Informix Guide to SQL: Reference*.

Conditional Expressions

Conditional expressions return values that depend on the outcome of conditional tests. The following diagram shows the syntax for Conditional Expressions.

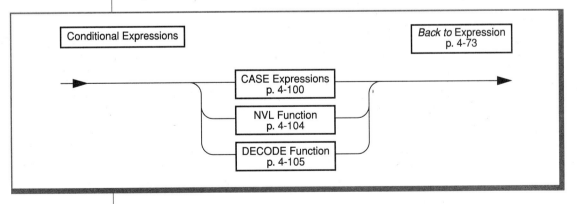

CASE Expressions

The CASE expression allows an SQL statement such as the SELECT statement to return one of several possible results, depending on which of several condition tests evaluates to true. The CASE expression has two forms as the following diagram shows: generic CASE expressions and linear CASE expressions.

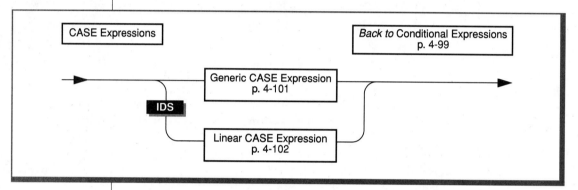

Using CASE Expressions

You can use a generic or linear CASE expression wherever you can use a column expression in an SQL statement (for example, in the select list of a SELECT statement.) You must include at least one WHEN clause in the CASE expression. Subsequent WHEN clauses and the ELSE clause are optional.

The expressions in the search condition or the result value expression can contain subqueries.

You can nest a CASE expression in another CASE expression.

When a CASE expression appears in an aggregate expression, you cannot use aggregate functions in the CASE expression.

Generic CASE Expressions

A generic CASE expression tests for a true condition in a WHEN clause and when it finds a true condition it returns the result specified in the THEN clause.

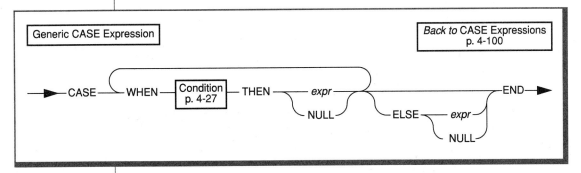

Element	Purpose	Restrictions	Syntax
expr	Expression that returns a result value of a certain data type	The data type of *expr* in a THEN clause must be compatible with the data types of other value expressions in other THEN clauses.	Expression, p. 4-73

The database server processes the WHEN clauses in the order that they appear in the statement. As soon as the database server finds a WHEN clause whose search condition evaluates to true, it takes the corresponding result value expression as the overall result of the CASE expression, and it stops processing the CASE expression.

If no WHEN condition evaluates to true, the database server takes the result of the ELSE clause as the overall result. If no WHEN condition evaluates to true, and no ELSE clause was specified, the resulting value is null. You can use the IS NULL condition to handle null results. For information on how to handle null values, see "IS NULL Condition" on page 4-36.

The following example shows the use of a generic CASE expression in the select list of a SELECT statement. In this example the user retrieves the name and address of each customer as well as a calculated number that is based on the number of problems that exist for that customer.

```
SELECT cust_name,
    CASE
    WHEN number_of_problems = 0
        THEN 100
    WHEN number_of_problems > 0 AND number_of_problems < 4
        THEN number_of_problems * 500
    WHEN number_of_problems >= 4 and number_of_problems <= 9
        THEN number_of_problems * 400
    ELSE
        (number_of_problems * 300) + 250
    END,
    cust_address
FROM custtab
```

In a generic CASE expression, all the results should be of the same type, or they should evaluate to a common compatible type. If the results in all the WHEN clauses are not of the same type, or if they do not evaluate to values of mutually compatible types, an error occurs.

IDS

Linear CASE Expressions

A linear CASE expression tests for a match between the value expression that follows the CASE keyword and a value expression in a WHEN clause.

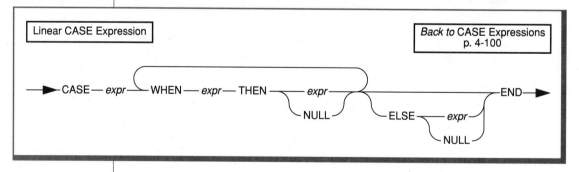

Linear CASE Expression

Back to CASE Expressions
p. 4-100

Element	Purpose	Restrictions	Syntax
expr	Expression that evaluates to a value of a certain data type or that returns a result value of a certain data type	The data type of the *expr* that follows the WHEN keyword in a WHEN clause must be compatible with the data type of the value expression that follows the CASE keyword.	Expression, p. 4-73
		The data type of *expr* in a THEN clause must be compatible with the data types of other value expressions in other THEN clauses.	

First the database server evaluates the value expression that follows the CASE keyword. Then the database server processes the WHEN clauses in the order that they appear in the CASE expression. As soon as the database server finds a WHEN clause where the value expression after the WHEN keyword evaluates to the same value as the value expression that follows the CASE keyword, it takes the value expression that follows the THEN keyword as the overall result of the CASE expression. Then the database server stops processing the CASE expression.

If none of the value expressions that follow the WHEN keywords evaluates to the same value as the value expression that follows the CASE keyword, the database server takes the result value expression of the ELSE clause as the overall result of the CASE expression. If all of the value expressions that follow the WHEN keyword in all the WHEN clauses do not evaluate to the same value as the value expression that follows the CASE keyword, and the user did not specify an ELSE clause, the resulting value is null.

The following example shows a linear CASE expression in the select list of a SELECT statement. For each movie in a table of movie titles, the SELECT statement displays the title of the movie, the cost of the movie, and the type of movie. The statement uses a CASE expression to derive the type of each movie.

```
SELECT title,
    CASE movie_type
        WHEN 1 THEN 'HORROR'
        WHEN 2 THEN 'COMEDY'
        WHEN 3 THEN 'ROMANCE'
        WHEN 4 THEN 'WESTERN'
        ELSE 'UNCLASSIFIED'
    END,
    our_cost
FROM movie_titles
```

In linear CASE expressions, the types of value expressions in all the WHEN clauses have to be compatible with the type of the value expression that follows the CASE keyword.

NVL Function

The **NVL** expression returns different results depending on whether its first argument evaluates to null.

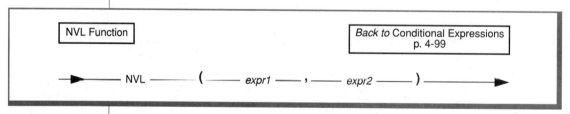

Element	Purpose	Restrictions	Syntax
expr1 *expr2*	Any expression that evaluates to a value of a certain data type or that returns a result value of a certain data type	The expression cannot be a host variable or a BYTE or TEXT data type. The *expression1* and *expression2* values must evaluate to a compatible data type.	Expression, p. 4-73

NVL evaluates *expression1*. If *expression1* is not null, NVL returns the value of *expression1*. If *expression1* is null, NVL returns the value of *expression2*. The expressions *expression1* and *expression2* can be of any data type, as long as they evaluate to a common compatible type.

Suppose that the **addr** column of the **employees** table has null values in some rows, and the user wants to be able to print the label Address unknown for these rows. The user enters the following SELECT statement to display the label Address unknown when the **addr** column has a null value.

```
SELECT fname, NVL (addr, 'Address unknown') AS address
    FROM employees
```

DECODE Function

The **DECODE** expression is similar to the CASE expression in that it can print different results depending on the values found in a specified column.

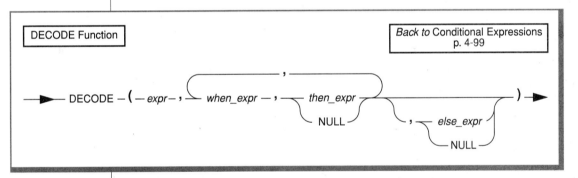

Element	Purpose	Restrictions	Syntax
expr *else_expr* *then_expr* *when_expr*	Expression that evaluates to a value of a certain data type or that returns a result value of a certain data type	The data type of *when_expr* must be compatible with the data type of *expr*. The data type of *then_expr* must be compatible with the data type of *else_expr*. You cannot specify NULL for the *when_expr*. The database server does not decode undefined values.	Expression, p. 4-73

The expressions *expr*, *when_expr*, and *then_expr* are required. DECODE evaluates *expr* and compares it to *when_expr*. If the value of *when_expr* matches the value of *expr*, DECODE returns *then_expr*.

The expressions *when_expr* and *then_expr* are an expression pair, and you can specify any number of expression pairs in the **DECODE** function. In all cases, **DECODE** compares the first member of the pair against *expr* and returns the second member of the pair if the first member matches *expr*.

If no expression matches *expr*, **DECODE** returns *else_expr*. However, if no expression matches *expr* and the user did not specify *else_expr*, **DECODE** returns NULL.

You can specify any data type as input, but two limitations exist.

- All occurrences of the parameter *when_expr* must have the same data type, or they must evaluate to a common compatible type. Similarly, all occurrences of *when_expr* must have the same data type as *expr*, or they must evaluate to a common compatible type.

- All occurrences of the parameter *then_expr* must have the same data type, or they must evaluate to a common compatible type. Similarly, all occurrences of *then_expr* must have the same data type as *else_expr*, or they must evaluate to a common compatible type.

Suppose that a user wants to convert descriptive values in the **evaluation** column of the **students** table to numeric values in the output. The following table shows the contents of the **students** table.

firstname	evaluation
Edward	Great
Joe	Not done
Mary	Good
Jim	Poor

The user now enters a SELECT statement with the **DECODE** function to convert the descriptive values in the **evaluation** column to numeric equivalents.

```
SELECT firstname, DECODE(evaluation,
     'Poor', 0,
     'Fair', 25,
     'Good', 50,
     'Very Good', 75,
     'Great', 100,
     -1) as grade
FROM students
```

The following table shows the output of this SELECT statement.

firstname	grade
Edward	100
Joe	-1
Mary	50
Jim	0

Constant Expressions

The following diagram shows the possible syntax for constant expressions.

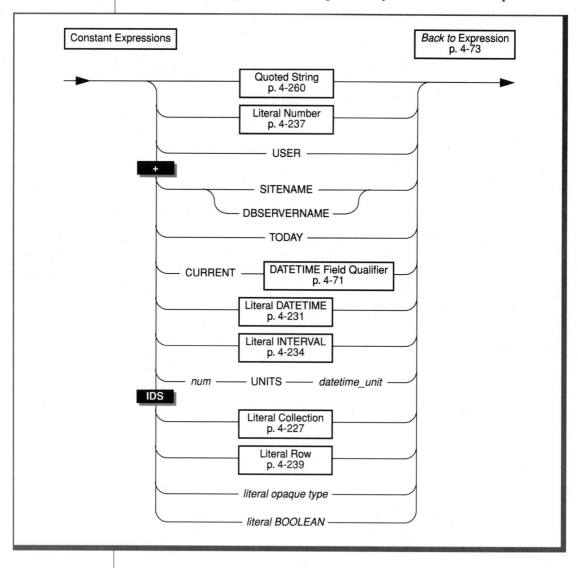

Element	Purpose	Restrictions	Syntax
datetime_unit	Unit that specifies an interval precision; that is, YEAR, MONTH, DAY, HOUR, MINUTE, SECOND, or FRACTION	The datetime unit must be one of the keywords that is listed in the Purpose column.	See the Restrictions column.
		You can enter the keyword in uppercase or lowercase letters.	
	If the unit is YEAR, the expression is a year-month interval; otherwise, the expression is a day-time interval.	You cannot put quotation marks around the keyword.	
literal BOOLEAN	Literal representation of a BOOLEAN value	A literal BOOLEAN can be only *t* (TRUE) or *f* (FALSE).	Quoted string, p. 4-260
literal opaque type	Literal representation for an opaque data type	The literal must be recognized by the input support function of the associated opaque type.	Defined by the developer of the opaque type.
num	Literal number that you use to specify the number of datetime units	If *num* is not an integer, it is rounded down to the nearest whole number when it is used.	Literal Number, p. 4-237
	For more information on this parameter, see "UNITS Keyword" on page 4-114.	The value that you specify for *n* must be appropriate for the datetime unit that you choose.	

Quoted String as an Expression

The following examples show quoted strings as expressions:

```
SELECT 'The first name is ', fname FROM customer

INSERT INTO manufact VALUES ('SPS', 'SuperSport')

UPDATE cust_calls SET res_dtime = '1997-1-1 10:45'
    WHERE customer_num = 120 AND call_code = 'B'
```

For more information, see "Quoted String" on page 4-260.

Literal Number as an Expression

The following examples show literal numbers as expressions:

```
INSERT INTO items VALUES (4, 35, 52, 'HRO', 12, 4.00)

INSERT INTO acreage VALUES (4, 5.2e4)

SELECT unit_price + 5 FROM stock

SELECT -1 * balance FROM accounts
```

For more information, see "Literal Number" on page 4-237.

USER Function

The **USER** function returns a string that contains the login name of the current user (that is, the person running the process).

The following statements show how you might use the **USER** function:

```
INSERT INTO cust_calls VALUES
    (221,CURRENT,USER,'B','Decimal point off', NULL, NULL)

SELECT * FROM cust_calls WHERE user_id = USER

UPDATE cust_calls SET user_id = USER WHERE customer_num = 220
```

The **USER** function does not change the case of a user ID. If you use **USER** in an expression and the present user is **Robertm**, the USER function returns **Robertm**, not **robertm**.

If you specify USER as the default value for a column, the column must have a CHAR, VARCHAR, NCHAR, or NVARCHAR data type.

IDS

If you specify **USER** as the default value for a column, Informix recommends that the size of the column be at least 32 bytes long. You risk getting an error message during INSERT and ALTER TABLE operations if the length of the column is too small to store the default value. ♦

EDS

If you specify USER as the default value for a column, Informix recommends that the size of the column be at least 8 bytes long. You risk getting an error message during INSERT and ALTER TABLE operations if the length of the column is too small to store the default value. ♦

ANSI

In an ANSI-compliant database, if you do not use quotes around the owner name, the name of the table owner is stored as uppercase letters. If you use the USER keyword as part of a condition, you must be sure that the way the user name is stored agrees with the values that the **USER** function returns, with respect to case. ♦

DBSERVERNAME and SITENAME Functions

The **DBSERVERNAME** function returns the database server name, as defined in the ONCONFIG file for the installation where the current database resides or as specified in the **INFORMIXSERVER** environment variable. The two function names, **DBSERVERNAME** and **SITENAME** are synonymous. You can use the **DBSERVERNAME** function to determine the location of a table, to put information into a table, or to extract information from a table. You can insert **DBSERVERNAME** into a simple character field or use it as a default value for a column.

If you specify **DBSERVERNAME** as a default value for a column, the column must have a CHAR, VARCHAR, NCHAR, or NVARCHAR data type.

IDS

If you specify **DBSERVERNAME** as the default value for a column, Informix recommends that the size of the column be at least 128 bytes long. You risk getting an error message during INSERT and ALTER TABLE operations if the length of the column is too small to store the default value. ♦

EDS

If you specify **DBSERVERNAME** as the default value for a column, Informix recommends that the size of the column be at least 18 bytes long. You risk getting an error message during INSERT and ALTER TABLE operations if the length of the column is too small to store the default value. ♦

In the following example, the first statement returns the name of the database server where the **customer** table resides. Because the query is not restricted with a WHERE clause, it returns **DBSERVERNAME** for every row in the table. If you add the DISTINCT keyword to the SELECT clause, the query returns **DBSERVERNAME** once. The second statement adds a row that contains the current site name to a table. The third statement returns all the rows that have the site name of the current system in **site_col**. The last statement changes the company name in the **customer** table to the current system name.

```
SELECT DBSERVERNAME FROM customer

INSERT INTO host_tab VALUES ('1', DBSERVERNAME)

SELECT * FROM host_tab WHERE site_col = DBSERVERNAME

UPDATE customer SET company = DBSERVERNAME
    WHERE customer_num = 120
```

TODAY Function

Use the **TODAY** function to return the system date as a DATE data type. If you specify **TODAY** as a default value for a column, it must be a DATE column.

The following examples show how you might use the **TODAY** function in an INSERT, UPDATE, or SELECT statement:

```
UPDATE orders (order_date) SET order_date = TODAY
    WHERE order_num = 1005

INSERT INTO orders VALUES
    (0, TODAY, 120, NULL, N, '1AUE217', NULL, NULL, NULL,
NULL)

SELECT * FROM orders WHERE ship_date = TODAY
```

CURRENT Function

The **CURRENT** function returns a DATETIME value with the date and time of day, showing the current instant.

If you do not specify a datetime qualifier, the default qualifier is YEAR TO FRACTION(3). The USEOSTIME configuration parameter specifies whether or not the database server uses subsecond precision when it obtains the current time from the operating system. For more information on the USEOSTIME configuration parameter, see your *Administrator's Reference*.

You can use the **CURRENT** function in any context in which you can use a literal DATETIME (see "Literal DATETIME" on page 4-231). If you specify **CURRENT** as the default value for a column, it must be a DATETIME column and the qualifier of **CURRENT** must match the column qualifier, as the following example shows:

```
CREATE TABLE new_acct (col1 int, col2 DATETIME YEAR TO DAY
    DEFAULT CURRENT YEAR TO DAY)
```

If you use the **CURRENT** keyword in more than one place in a single statement, identical values can be returned at each point of the call. You cannot rely on the **CURRENT** function to provide distinct values each time it executes.

The returned value comes from the system clock and is fixed when any SQL statement starts. For example, any call to **CURRENT** from inside the SPL function that an EXECUTE FUNCTION (or EXECUTE PROCEDURE) statement names returns the value when the SPL function starts.

The **CURRENT** function is always evaluated in the database server where the current database is located. If the current database is in a remote database server, the returned value is from the remote host.

The **CURRENT** function might not execute in the physical order in which it appears in a statement. You should not use the **CURRENT** function to mark the start, end, or a specific point in the execution of a statement.

If your platform does not provide a system call that returns the current time with subsecond precision, the **CURRENT** function returns a zero for the FRACTION field.

In the following example, the first statement uses the **CURRENT** function in a WHERE condition. The second statement uses the **CURRENT** function as the input for the **DAY** function. The last query selects rows whose **call_dtime** value is within a range from the beginning of 1997 to the current instant.

```
DELETE FROM cust_calls WHERE
    res_dtime < CURRENT YEAR TO MINUTE

SELECT * FROM orders WHERE DAY(ord_date) < DAY(CURRENT)

SELECT * FROM cust_calls WHERE call_dtime
    BETWEEN '1997-1-1 00:00:00' AND CURRENT
```

For more information, see "DATETIME Field Qualifier" on page 4-71.

Literal DATETIME as an Expression

The following examples show literal DATETIME as an expression:

```
SELECT DATETIME (1997-12-6) YEAR TO DAY FROM customer

UPDATE cust_calls SET res_dtime = DATETIME (1998-07-07 10:40)
        YEAR TO MINUTE
    WHERE customer_num = 110
    AND call_dtime = DATETIME (1998-07-07 10:24) YEAR TO
MINUTE

SELECT * FROM cust_calls
    WHERE call_dtime
    = DATETIME (1998-12-25 00:00:00) YEAR TO SECOND
```

For more information, see "Literal DATETIME" on page 4-231.

Literal INTERVAL as an Expression

The following examples show literal INTERVAL as an expression:

```
INSERT INTO manufact VALUES ('CAT', 'Catwalk Sports',
    INTERVAL (16) DAY TO DAY)

SELECT lead_time + INTERVAL (5) DAY TO DAY FROM manufact
```

The second statement in the preceding example adds five days to each value of **lead_time** selected from the **manufact** table.

For more information, see "Literal INTERVAL" on page 4-234.

UNITS Keyword

The UNITS keyword enables you to display a simple interval or increase or decrease a specific interval or datetime value.

If n is not an integer, it is rounded down to the nearest whole number when it is used.

In the following example, the first SELECT statement uses the UNITS keyword to select all the manufacturer lead times, increased by five days. The second SELECT statement finds all the calls that were placed more than 30 days ago. If the expression in the WHERE clause returns a value greater than 99 (maximum number of days), the query fails. The last statement increases the lead time for the ANZA manufacturer by two days.

```
SELECT lead_time + 5 UNITS DAY FROM manufact

SELECT * FROM cust_calls
    WHERE (TODAY - call_dtime) > 30 UNITS DAY

UPDATE manufact SET lead_time = 2 UNITS DAY + lead_time
    WHERE manu_code = 'ANZ'
```

IDS

Literal Collection as an Expression

The following examples show literal collections as expressions:

```
INSERT INTO tab_a (set_col) VALUES ("SET{6, 9, 3, 12, 4}")

INSERT INTO TABLE(a_set) VALUES (9765)

UPDATE table1 SET set_col = "LIST{3}"

SELECT set_col FROM table1
    WHERE SET{17} IN (set_col)
```

For more information, see "Literal Collection" on page 4-227. For syntax that allows you to use expressions that evaluate to element values, see "Collection Constructors" on page 4-118.

IDS

Literal Row as an Expression

The following examples show literal rows as expressions:

```
INSERT INTO employee VALUES
    (ROW('103 Baker St', 'San Francisco',
        'CA', 94500))

UPDATE rectangles
    SET rect = ROW(8, 3, 7, 20)
    WHERE area = 140

EXEC SQL update table(:a_row)
    set x=0, y=0, length=10, width=20;

SELECT row_col FROM tab_b
    WHERE ROW(17, 'abc') IN (row_col)
```

For more information, see "Literal Row" on page 4-239. For syntax that allows you to use expressions that evaluate to field values, see "ROW Constructors" on page 4-116.

IDS

Constructor Expressions

A *constructor* is a function that the database server uses to create an instance of a particular data type. The database server supports ROW and collection constructors.

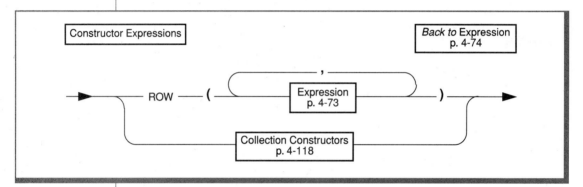

ROW Constructors

You use ROW constructors to generate values for row-type columns. Suppose you create the following named row type and a table that contains the named row type **row_t** and an unnamed row type:

```
CREATE ROW TYPE row_t ( x INT, y INT);
CREATE TABLE new_tab
(
col1 row_t,
col2 ROW( a CHAR(2), b INT )
)
```

When you define a column as a named row type or unnamed row type, you must use a ROW constructor to generate values for the row column. To create a value for either a named row type or unnamed row type, you must complete the following steps:

- Begin the expression with the ROW keyword.
- Specify a value for each field of the row type.
- Enclosed the field values within parentheses.

The format of the value for each field must be compatible with the data type of the row field to which it is assigned.

You can use any kind of expression as a value with a ROW constructor, including literals, functions, and variables. The following examples show the use of different types of expressions with ROW constructors to specify values:

```
ROW(5, 6.77, 'HMO')

ROW(col1.lname, 45000)

ROW('john davis', TODAY)

ROW(USER, SITENAME)
```

The following statement uses literal numbers and quoted strings with ROW constructors to insert values into **col1** and **col2** of the **new_tab** table:

```
INSERT INTO new_tab
VALUES
(
ROW(32, 65)::row_t,
ROW('CA', 34)
)
```

When you use a ROW constructor to generate values for a named row type, you must explicitly cast the row value to the appropriate named row type. The cast is necessary to generate a value of the named row type. To cast the row value as a named row type, you can use the cast operator (::) or the CAST AS keywords, as shown in the following examples:

```
ROW(4,5)::row_t
CAST (ROW(3,4) AS row_t)
```

You can use a ROW constructor to generate row type values not only in INSERT and UPDATE statements but also in SELECT statements. In the following example, the WHERE clause of a SELECT statement specifies a row type value that is cast as type **person_t**

```
SELECT *
FROM person_tab
WHERE col1 = ROW('charlie','hunter')::person_t
```

For further information on using ROW constructors in INSERT and UPDATE statements, see the INSERT and UPDATE statements in this manual. For information on named row types, see the CREATE ROW TYPE statement. For information on unnamed row types, see the discussion of the ROW data type in the *Informix Guide to SQL: Reference*. For task-oriented information on named row types and unnamed row types, see the *Informix Guide to Database Design and Implementation*.

Collection Constructors

Use a collection constructor to specify values for a collection column.

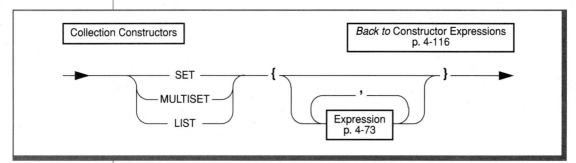

You can use collection constructors in the WHERE clause of the SELECT statement and the VALUES clause of the INSERT statement. You can also pass collection constructors to UDRs.

The following table differentiates the types of collections that you can construct.

Keyword	Purpose
SET	Indicates a collection of elements with the following qualities: ■ The collection must contain unique values. ■ Elements have no specific order associated with them.
MULTISET	Indicates a collection of elements with the following qualities: ■ The collection can contain duplicate values. ■ Elements have no specific order associated with them.
LIST	Indicates a collection of elements with the following qualities: ■ The collection can contain duplicate values. ■ Elements have ordered positions.

You can use any kind of expression with a collection constructor, including literals, functions, and variables. When you use a collection constructor with a list of arbitrary expressions, the database server evaluates each expression to its equivalent literal form and uses the literal values to construct the collection.

You specify an empty collection with a set of empty braces ({}).

The element type of the collection can be any built-in or extended data type.

Restrictions on Collection Constructors

Elements of a collection cannot be null, therefore if an expression element evaluates to a null value the database server returns an error.

The element type of each expression must be homogeneous, that is, they must be exactly the same type. This can be accomplished by casting the entire collection constructor expression to a collection type, or by casting individual element expressions to the same type.

If the database server cannot determine the collection type and the element types are not homogeneous, then the collection constructor will return an error. In the case of host variables, this determination is made at bind time when the client informs the database server the element type of the host variable.

Examples of Collection Constructors

The following extended example illustrates that you can construct collection with many various expressions as long as the resulting values are of the same type.

```
CREATE FUNCTION f (a int RETURNS int;
RETURN a+1;
END FUNCTION;

CREATE TABLE tab1 (x SET(INT NOT NULL));

INSERT INTO tab1 VALUES
(
SET{10,
    1+2+3,
    f(10)-f(2),
    SQRT(100) +POW(2,3),
```

```
            (SELECT tabid FROM systables
                WHERE tabname = 'sysusers'),
            'T'::BOOLEAN::INT}
    )

    SELECT * FROM tab1 WHERE
    x=SET{10,
        1+2+3,
        f(10)-f(2),
        SQRT(100) +POW(2,3),
        (SELECT tabid FROM systables
            WHERE tabname = 'sysusers'),
        'T'::BOOLEAN::INT}
    }
```

This example assumes that a cast from BOOLEAN to INT exists.

For information about a more restrictive, but still-supported syntax for how to specify values for a collection column, see "Literal Collection" on page 4-227.

Function Expressions

A function expression can call built-in functions or user-defined functions, as the following diagram shows.

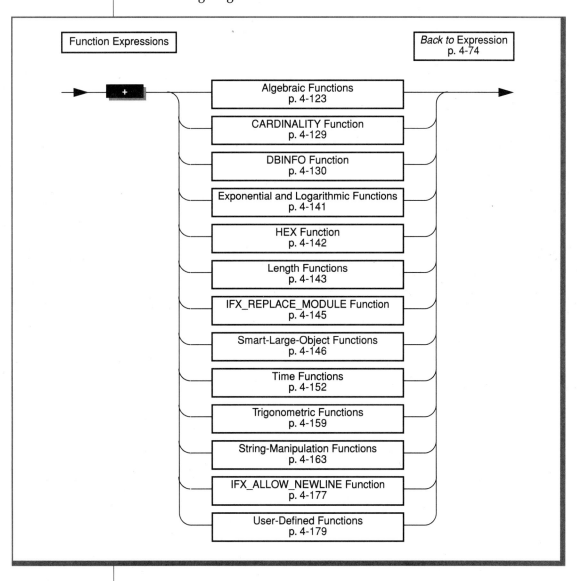

Function Expressions

Back to Expression
p. 4-74

Algebraic Functions
p. 4-123

CARDINALITY Function
p. 4-129

DBINFO Function
p. 4-130

Exponential and Logarithmic Functions
p. 4-141

HEX Function
p. 4-142

Length Functions
p. 4-143

IFX_REPLACE_MODULE Function
p. 4-145

Smart-Large-Object Functions
p. 4-146

Time Functions
p. 4-152

Trigonometric Functions
p. 4-159

String-Manipulation Functions
p. 4-163

IFX_ALLOW_NEWLINE Function
p. 4-177

User-Defined Functions
p. 4-179

Examples of Function Expressions

The following examples show function expressions:

```
EXTEND (call_dtime, YEAR TO SECOND)

MDY (12, 7, 1900 + cur_yr)

DATE (365/2)

LENGTH ('abc') + LENGTH (pvar)

HEX (customer_num)

HEX (LENGTH(123))

TAN (radians)

ABS (-32)

EXP (3)

MOD (10,3)
```

Algebraic Functions

An algebraic function takes one or more arguments, as the following diagram shows.

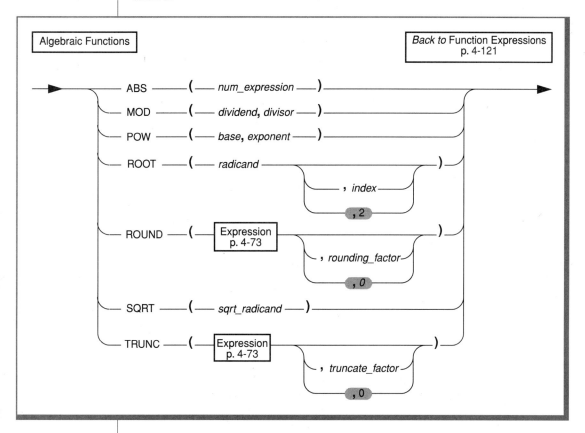

Element	Purpose	Restrictions	Syntax
base	Value to be raised to the power that is specified in exponent The base value is the first argument that is supplied to the POW function.	You can enter in *base* any real number or any expression that evaluates to a real number.	Expression, p. 4-73

(1 of 3)

Expression

Element	Purpose	Restrictions	Syntax
dividend	Value to be divided by the value in divisor The *dividend* value is the first argument supplied to the MOD function.	You can enter in *dividend* any real number or any expression that evaluates to a real number.	Expression, p. 4-73
divisor	Value by which the value in dividend is to be divided The *divisor* value is the second argument that is supplied to the MOD function.	You can enter in *divisor* any real number except zero or any expression that evaluates to a real number other than zero.	Expression, p. 4-73
exponent	Power to which the value that is specified in base is to be raised The *exponent* value is the second argument that is supplied to the POW function.	You can enter in *exponent* any real number or any expression that evaluates to a real number.	Expression, p. 4-73
index	Type of root to be returned, where 2 represents square root, 3 represents cube root, and so on The *index* value is the second argument that is supplied to the ROOT function. The default value of *index* is 2.	You can enter in *index* any real number except zero or any expression that evaluates to a real number other than zero.	Expression, p. 4-73
num_expression	Numeric expression for which an absolute value is to be returned The expression serves as the argument for the ABS function.	The value of *num_expression* can be any real number.	Expression, p. 4-73
radicand	Expression whose root value is to be returned The radicand value is the first argument that is supplied to the ROOT function.	You can enter in *radicand* any real number or any expression that evaluates to a real number.	Expression, p. 4-73

(2 of 3)

Element	Purpose	Restrictions	Syntax
rounding_factor	Number of digits to which a numeric expression is to be rounded The rounding_factor value is the second argument that is supplied to the ROUND function. The default value of *rounding_factor* is zero. This default means that the numeric expression is rounded to zero digits or the ones place.	The value you specify in *rounding factor* must be an integer between +32 and -32, inclusive.	Literal Number, p. 4-237
sqrt_radicand	Expression whose square root value is to be returned The sqrt_radicand value is the argument that is supplied to the SQRT function.	You can enter in *sqrt_radicand* any real number or any expression that evaluates to a real number.	Expression, p. 4-73
truncate_factor	Position to which a numeric expression is to be truncated The truncate_factor value is the second argument that is supplied to the TRUNC function. The default value of *truncate_factor* is zero. This default means that the numeric expression is truncated to zero digits or the ones place.	The value you specify in *truncate_factor* must be an integer between +32 and -32, inclusive. For more information on this restriction, see "TRUNC Function" on page 4-128.	Literal Number, p. 4-237

(3 of 3)

ABS Function

The **ABS** function gives the absolute value for a given expression. The function requires a single numeric argument. The value returned is the same as the argument type. The following example shows all orders of more than $20 paid in cash (+) or store credit (-). The **stores_demo** database does not contain any negative balances; however, you might have negative balances in your application.

```
SELECT order_num, customer_num, ship_charge
  FROM orders WHERE ABS(ship_charge) > 20
```

MOD Function

The **MOD** function returns the modulus or remainder value for two numeric expressions. You provide integer expressions for the dividend and divisor. The divisor cannot be 0. The value returned is INT8. The following example uses a 30-day billing cycle to determine how far into the billing cycle today is:

```
SELECT MOD(today - MDY(1,1,year(today))),30) FROM orders
```

POW Function

The **POW** function raises the *base* to the *exponent*. This function requires two numeric arguments. The return type is FLOAT. The following example returns all the information for circles whose areas ($\pi\, r^2$) are less than 1,000 square units:

```
SELECT * FROM circles WHERE (3.1416 * POW(radius,2)) < 1000
```

If you want to use *e*, the base of natural logarithms, as the base, see the "EXP Function" on page 4-141.

ROOT Function

The **ROOT** function returns the root value of a numeric expression. This function requires at least one numeric argument (the *radicand* argument) and allows no more than two (the *radicand* and *index* arguments). If only the *radicand* argument is supplied, the value 2 is used as a default value for the *index* argument. The value 0 cannot be used as the value of *index*. The value that the **ROOT** function returns is FLOAT. The first SELECT statement in the following example takes the square root of the expression. The second SELECT statement takes the cube root of the expression.

```
SELECT ROOT(9) FROM angles          -- square root of 9

SELECT ROOT(64,3) FROM angles       -- cube root of 64
```

The **SQRT** function uses the form SQRT(x)=ROOT(x) if no index is given.

ROUND Function

The **ROUND** function returns the rounded value of an expression. The expression must be numeric or must be converted to numeric.

If you omit the digit indication, the value is rounded to zero digits or to the ones place. The digit limitation of 32 (+ and -) refers to the entire decimal value.

Positive-digit values indicate rounding to the right of the decimal point; negative-digit values indicate rounding to the left of the decimal point, as Figure 4-1 shows.

Figure 4-1
ROUND Function

Expression:

ROUND (24,536.8746, -2) = 24,500.00

ROUND (24,536.8746, 0) = 24,537.00

ROUND (24,536.8746, 2) = 24,536.87

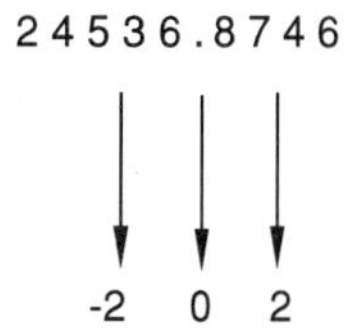

```
2 4 5 3 6 . 8 7 4 6
      -2  0  2
```

The following example shows how you can use the **ROUND** function with a column expression in a SELECT statement. This statement displays the order number and rounded total price (to zero places) of items whose rounded total price (to zero places) is equal to 124.00.

```
SELECT order_num , ROUND(total_price) FROM items
    WHERE ROUND(total_price) = 124.00
```

If you use a MONEY data type as the argument for the **ROUND** function and you round to zero places, the value displays with .00. The SELECT statement in the following example rounds an INTEGER value and a MONEY value. It displays 125 and a rounded price in the form xxx.00 for each row in **items**.

```
SELECT ROUND(125.46), ROUND(total_price) FROM items
```

SQRT Function

The **SQRT** function returns the square root of a numeric expression.

The following example returns the square root of 9 for each row of the **angles** table:

```
SELECT SQRT(9) FROM angles
```

TRUNC Function

The **TRUNC** function returns the truncated value of a numeric expression.

The expression must be numeric or a form that can be converted to a numeric expression. If you omit the digit indication, the value is truncated to zero digits or to the one's place. The digit limitation of 32 (+ and -) refers to the entire decimal value.

Positive digit values indicate truncating to the right of the decimal point; negative digit values indicate truncating to the left of the decimal point, as Figure 4-2 shows.

Figure 4-2
TRUNC Function

If you use a MONEY data type as the argument for the **TRUNC** function and you truncate to zero places, the .00 places are removed. For example, the following SELECT statement truncates a MONEY value and an INTEGER value. It displays 125 and a truncated price in integer format for each row in **items**.

```
SELECT TRUNC(125.46), TRUNC(total_price) FROM items
```

IDS

CARDINALITY Function

The **CARDINALITY** function returns the number of elements in a collection column (SET, MULTISET, LIST).

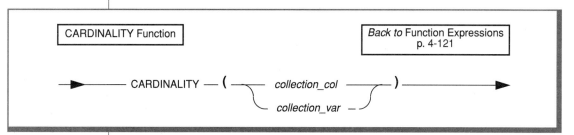

Element	Purpose	Restrictions	Syntax
collection_col	Name of an existing collection column	You must specify an integer or an expression that evaluates to an integer.	Expression, p. 4-73
collection_var	Name of a host or program collection variable	The collection variable must exist.	Name must conform to language-specific rules for variable names.

Suppose that the **set_col** SET column contains the following value:

```
{3, 7, 9, 16, 0}
```

The following SELECT statement returns 5 as the number of elements in the **set_col** column:

```
SELECT CARDINALITY(set_col)
    FROM table1
```

If the collection contains duplicate elements, **CARDINALITY** counts each individual element.

DBINFO Function

The following diagram shows the syntax of the **DBINFO** function.

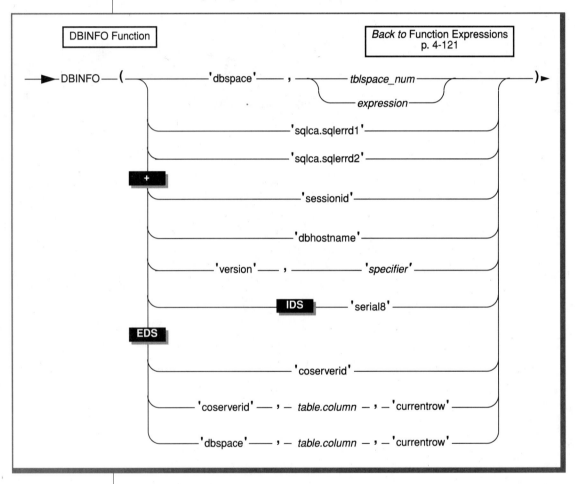

Element	Purpose	Restrictions	Syntax
column	Name of a column in the table that you specify in *table*.	The specified column must exist in the table that you specify in *table*.	Database Object Name, p. 4-50
expression	Expression that evaluates to *tblspace_num*	The expression can contain SPL variables, host variables, column names, or subqueries, but it must evaluate to a numeric value.	Expression, p. 4-73
specifier	Literal value that specifies which part of the version string is to be returned	For the set of values that you can provide for *specifier*, see "Using the 'version' Option" on page 4-136.	Expression, p. 4-73
table	Table for which you want to display the dbspace name or coserver ID corresponding to each row	The specified table must match the name of a table in the FROM clause of the query	Database Object Name, p. 4-50
tblspace_num	Tblspace number (partition number) of a table	The specified tblspace number must exist. That is, it must occur in the **partnum** column of the **systables** table for the database.	Literal Number, p. 4-237

DBINFO Options

The **DBINFO** function is actually a set of functions that return different types of information about the database. You invoke each function by specifying a particular option after the **DBINFO** keyword. You can use any **DBINFO** option anywhere within SQL statements and within UDRs.

Expression

The following table shows the different types of database information that you can retrieve with the **DBINFO** options. The **Option** column shows the name of each **DBINFO** option. The **Purpose** column shows the type of database information that the option retrieves. The next three columns give the names of the database servers on which each option is supported. A check mark in these columns shows that the given database server supports the given option. The **Page** column shows the page where you can find more information about a given option.

Option	Purpose	Page
'dbspace' *tblspace_num*	Returns the name of a dbspace corresponding to a tblspace number	4-133
'sqlca.sqlerrd1'	Returns the last serial value inserted in a table	4-133
'sqlca.sqlerrd2'	Returns the number of rows processed by selects, inserts, deletes, updates, EXECUTE PROCEDURE statements, and EXECUTE FUNCTION statements	4-134
'sessionid'	Returns the session ID of the current session	4-135
'dbhostname'	Returns the hostname of the database server to which a client application is connected	4-136
'version'	Returns the exact version of the database server to which a client application is connected	4-136
'serial8' (IDS)	Returns the last SERIAL8 value inserted in a table	4-138
'coserverid' (EDS)	Returns the coserver ID of the coserver to which the user who entered the query is connected	4-139
'coserverid' *table.column* 'currentrow' (EDS)	Returns the coserver ID of the coserver where each row of a specified table is located	4-139
'dbspace' *table.column* 'currentrow' (EDS)	Returns the name of the dbspace where each row of a specified table is located	4-140

Using the 'dbspace' Option Followed by a Tblspace Number

The **'dbspace'** option returns a character string that contains the name of the dbspace corresponding to a tblspace number. You must supply an additional parameter, either *tblspace_num* or an expression that evaluates to *tblspace_num*. The following example uses the **'dbspace'** option. First, it queries the **systables** system catalog table to determine the *tblspace_num* for the table **customer**, then it executes the function to determine the dbspace name.

```
SELECT tabname, partnum FROM systables
    where tabname = 'customer'
```

If the statement returns a partition number of 1048892, you insert that value into the second argument to find which dbspace contains the **customer** table, as shown in the following example:

```
SELECT DBINFO ('dbspace', 1048892) FROM systables
    where tabname = 'customer'
```

If the table for which you want to know the dbspace name is fragmented, you must query the **sysfragments** system catalog table to find out the tblspace number of each table fragment. Then you must supply each tblspace number in a separate **DBINFO** query to find out all the dbspaces across which a table is fragmented.

Using the 'sqlca.sqlerrd1' Option

The **'sqlca.sqlerrd1'** option returns a single integer that provides the last serial value that is inserted into a table. To ensure valid results, use this option immediately following a singleton INSERT statement that inserts a single row with a serial value into a table.

Tip: *To obtain the value of the last SERIAL8 value that is inserted into a table, use the* ***'serial8'*** *option of* **DBINFO**. *For more information, see "Using the 'serial8' Option" on page 4-138.*

The following example uses the **'sqlca.sqlerrd1'** option:

```
EXEC SQL create table fst_tab (ordernum serial, partnum int);
EXEC SQL create table sec_tab (ordernum serial);

EXEC SQL insert into fst_tab VALUES (0,1);
EXEC SQL insert into fst_tab VALUES (0,4);
EXEC SQL insert into fst_tab VALUES (0,6);

EXEC SQL insert into sec_tab values
(dbinfo('sqlca.sqlerrd1'));
```

This example inserts a row that contains a primary-key serial value into the **fst_tab** table, and then uses the **DBINFO** function to insert the same serial value into the **sec_tab** table. The value that the **DBINFO** function returns is the serial value of the last row that is inserted into **fst_tab**.

Using the 'sqlca.sqlerrd2' Option

The **'sqlca.sqlerrd2'** option returns a single integer that provides the number of rows that SELECT, INSERT, DELETE, UPDATE, EXECUTE PROCEDURE, and EXECUTE FUNCTION statements processed. To ensure valid results, use this option after SELECT, EXECUTE PROCEDURE, and EXECUTE FUNCTION statements have completed executing. In addition, to ensure valid results when you use this option within cursors, make sure that all rows are fetched before the cursors are closed.

The following example shows an SPL routine that uses the **'sqlca.sqlerrd2'** option to determine the number of rows that are deleted from a table:

```
CREATE FUNCTION del_rows (pnumb int)
RETURNING int;

DEFINE nrows int;

DELETE FROM fst_tab WHERE part_number = pnumb;
LET nrows = DBINFO('sqlca.sqlerrd2');
RETURN nrows;

END FUNCTION
```

Using the 'sessionid' Option

The **'sessionid'** option of the **DBINFO** function returns the session ID of your current session.

When a client application makes a connection to the database server, the server starts a session with the client and assigns a session ID for the client. The session ID serves as a unique identifier for a given connection between a client and a database server. The database server stores the value of the session ID in a data structure in shared memory that is called the session control block. The session control block for a given session also includes the user ID, the process ID of the client, the name of the host computer, and a variety of status flags.

When you specify the **'sessionid'** option, the database server retrieves the session ID of your current session from the session control block and returns this value to you as an integer. Some of the System-Monitoring Interface (SMI) tables in the **sysmaster** database include a column for session IDs, so you can use the session ID that the **DBINFO** function obtained to extract information about your own session from these SMI tables. For further information on the session control block, see the *Administrator's Guide*. For further information on the **sysmaster** database and the SMI tables, see the *Administrator's Reference*.

In the following example, the user specifies the **DBINFO** function in a SELECT statement to obtain the value of the current session ID. The user poses this query against the **systables** system catalog table and uses a WHERE clause to limit the query result to a single row.

```
SELECT DBINFO('sessionid') AS my_sessionid
    FROM systables
    WHERE tabname = 'systables'
```

In the preceding example, the SELECT statement queries against the **systables** system catalog table. However, you can obtain the session ID of the current session by querying against any system catalog table or user table in the database. For example, you can enter the following query to obtain the session ID of your current session:

```
SELECT DBINFO('sessionid') AS user_sessionid
    FROM customer
    where customer_num = 101
```

You can use the **DBINFO 'sessionid'** option not only in SQL statements but also in SPL routines. The following example shows an SPL function that returns the value of the current session ID to the calling program or routine:

```
CREATE FUNCTION get_sess()
RETURNING INT;
RETURN DBINFO('sessionid');
END FUNCTION;
```

Using the 'dbhostname' Option

You can use the **'dbhostname'** option to retrieve the hostname of the database server to which a database client is connected. This option retrieves the physical computer name of the computer on which the database server is running.

In the following example, the user enters the **'dbhostname'** option of **DBINFO** in a SELECT statement to retrieve the hostname of the database server to which DB-Access is connected:

```
SELECT DBINFO('dbhostname')
    FROM systables
    WHERE tabid = 1
```

The following table shows the result of this query.

(constant)
rd_lab1

Using the 'version' Option

You can use the **'version'** option of the **DBINFO** function to retrieve the exact version number of the database server against which the client application is running. This option retrieves the exact version string from the message log. The value of the full version string is the same as that displayed by the **-V** option of the **oninit** utility.

You use the *specifier* parameter of the **'version'** option to specify which part of the version string you want to retrieve. The following table lists the values you can enter in the *specifier* parameter, shows which part of the version string is returned for each *specifier* value, and gives an example of what is returned by each value of *specifier*. Each example returns part of the complete version string `Dynamic Server Version 9.20.UC1`.

Value of specifier Parameter	Part of Version String Returned	Example of Return Value
'server-type'	Type of server	`Dynamic Server`
'major'	Major version number of the current server version	`9`
'minor'	Minor version number of the current server version	`20`
'os'	Operating-system identifier within the version string: T = Windows NT U = UNIX 32 bit running on a 32-bit operating system H = UNIX 32 bit running on a 64-bit operating system F = UNIX 64 bit running on a 64-bit operating system	`U`
'level'	Interim release level of the current server version	`C1`
'full'	Complete version string as it would be returned by **oninit -V**	`Dynamic Server Version 9.20.UC1`

The following example shows how to use the **'version'** option of **DBINFO** in a SELECT statement to retrieve the major version number of the database server that the DB-Access client is connected to.

```
SELECT DBINFO('version', 'major')
    FROM systables
    WHERE tabid = 1
```

The following table shows the result of this query.

(constant)
7

IDS

Using the 'serial8' Option

The **'serial8'** option returns a single integer that provides the last SERIAL8 value that is inserted into a table. To ensure valid results, use this option immediately following an INSERT statement that inserts a SERIAL8 value.

Tip: *To obtain the value of the last SERIAL value that is inserted into a table, use the 'sqlca.sqlerrd1' option of DBINFO(). For more information, see "Using the 'sqlca.sqlerrd1' Option" on page 4-133.*

The following example uses the 'serial8' option:

```
EXEC SQL create table fst_tab
    (ordernum serial8, partnum int);
EXEC SQL create table sec_tab (ordernum serial8);

EXEC SQL insert into fst_tab VALUES (0,1);
EXEC SQL insert into fst_tab VALUES (0,4);
EXEC SQL insert into fst_tab VALUES (0,6);

EXEC SQL insert into sec_tab
    select dbinfo('serial8')
    from sec_tab where partnum = 6;
```

This example inserts a row that contains a primary-key SERIAL8 value into the **fst_tab** table, and then uses the **DBINFO** function to insert the same SERIAL8 value into the **sec_tab** table. The value that the **DBINFO** function returns is the SERIAL8 value of the last row that is inserted into **fst_tab**. The subquery in the last line contains a WHERE clause so that a single value is returned.

EDS

Using the 'coserverid' Option with No Other Arguments

The **'coserverid'** option with no other arguments returns a single integer that corresponds to the coserver ID of the coserver to which the user who entered the query is connected.

Suppose that you use the following statement to create the **mytab** table:

```
CREATE TABLE mytab (mycol INT)
    FRAGMENT BY EXPRESSION
        mycol < 5 in rootdbs.1
        mycol > 5 in rootdbs.2
```

Also suppose that the dbspace named **rootdbs.1** resides on coserver 1, and the dbspace named **rootdbs.2** resides on coserver 2.

Also suppose that you use the following statements to insert rows into the **mytab** table:

```
INSERT INTO mytab VALUES ('1');
INSERT INTO mytab VALUES ('6');
```

Finally, suppose that you are logged on to coserver 1 when you make the following query. This query displays the values of all columns in the row where the value of the **mycol** column is 1. This query also displays the coserver ID of the coserver to which you are logged on when you enter the query.

```
SELECT *, DBINFO ('coserverid') AS cid
    FROM mytab
    WHERE mycol = 1
```

The following table shows the result of this query.

mycol	cid
1	1

EDS

Using the 'coserverid' Option Followed by Table and Column Names

Use the **'coserverid'** option followed by the table name and column name and the **'currentrow'** string to find out the coserver ID where each row in a specified table is located. This option is especially useful when you fragment a table across multiple coservers.

In the following example, the user asks to see all columns and rows of the **mytab** table as well as the coserver ID of the coserver where each row resides. For a description of the **mytab** table, see "Using the 'coserverid' Option with No Other Arguments" on page 4-139.

```
SELECT *, DBINFO ('coserverid', mytab.mycol, 'currentrow')
    AS cid
    FROM mytab
```

The following table shows the result of this query.

mycol	cid
1	1
6	2

The column that you specify in the **DBINFO** function can be any column in the specified table.

EDS

Using the 'dbspace' Option Followed by Table and Column Names

Use the **'dbspace '** option followed by the table name and column name and the **'currentrow'** string to find out the name of the dbspace where each row in a specified table is located. This option is especially useful when you fragment a table across multiple dbspaces.

In the following example, the user asks to see all columns and rows of the **mytab** table as well as the name of the dbspace where each row resides. For a description of the **mytab** table, see "Using the 'coserverid' Option with No Other Arguments" on page 4-139.

```
SELECT *, DBINFO ('dbspace', mytab.mycol, 'currentrow')
    AS dbsp
    FROM mytab
```

The following table shows the result of this query.

mycol	dbspace
1	rootdbs.1
6	rootdbs.2

The column that you specify in the **DBINFO** function can be any column in the specified table.

Exponential and Logarithmic Functions

Exponential and logarithmic functions take at least one argument. The return type is FLOAT. The following example shows exponential and logarithmic functions.

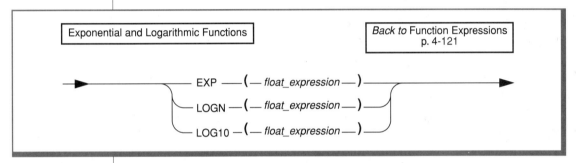

Element	Purpose	Restrictions	Syntax
float_expression	Expression that serves as an argument to the **EXP**, **LOGN**, or **LOG10** functions For information on the meaning of *float_expression* in these functions, see the individual heading for each function on the following pages.	The domain of the expression is the set of real numbers, and the range of the expression is the set of positive real numbers.	Expression, p. 4-73

EXP Function

The **EXP** function returns the exponent of a numeric expression. The following example returns the exponent of 3 for each row of the **angles** table:

```
SELECT EXP(3) FROM angles
```

For this function, the base is always *e*, the base of natural logarithms, as the following example shows.

```
e=exp(1)=2.718281828459
```

When you want to use the base of natural logarithms as the base value, use the **EXP** function. If you want to specify a particular value to raise to a specific power, see the "POW Function" on page 4-126.

LOGN Function

The **LOGN** function returns the natural log of a numeric expression. The logarithmic value is the inverse of the exponential value. The following SELECT statement returns the natural log of population for each row of the **history** table:

```
SELECT LOGN(population) FROM history WHERE country='US'
    ORDER BY date
```

LOG10 Function

The **LOG10** function returns the log of a value to base 10. The following example returns the log base 10 of distance for each row of the **travel** table:

```
SELECT LOG10(distance) + 1 digits FROM travel
```

HEX Function

The **HEX** function returns the hexadecimal encoding of an integer expression.

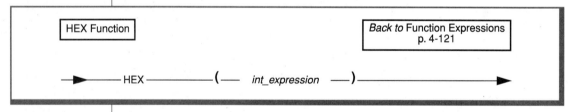

| HEX Function | | Back to Function Expressions p. 4-121 |

HEX ── (── *int_expression* ──)

Element	Purpose	Restrictions	Syntax
int_expression	Numeric expression for which you want to know the hexadecimal equivalent	You must specify an integer or an expression that evaluates to an integer.	Expression, p. 4-73

The following example displays the data type and column length of the columns of the **orders** table in hexadecimal format. For MONEY and DECIMAL columns, you can then determine the precision and scale from the lowest and next-to-the-lowest bytes. For VARCHAR and NVARCHAR columns, you can determine the minimum space and maximum space from the lowest and next to the lowest bytes. For more information about encoded information, see the *Informix Guide to SQL: Reference*.

```
SELECT colname, coltype, HEX(collength)
    FROM syscolumns C, systables T
    WHERE C.tabid = T.tabid AND T.tabname = 'orders'
```

The following example lists the names of all the tables in the current database and their corresponding tblspace number in hexadecimal format. This example is particularly useful because the two most significant bytes in the hexadecimal number constitute the dbspace number. They identify the table in **oncheck** output (in Dynamic Server) and in **onutilcheck** output (in Enterprise Decision Server).

```
SELECT tabname, HEX(partnum) FROM systables
```

The **HEX** function can operate on an expression, as the following example shows:

```
SELECT HEX(order_num + 1) FROM orders
```

Length Functions

You can use length functions to determine the length of a column, string, or variable.

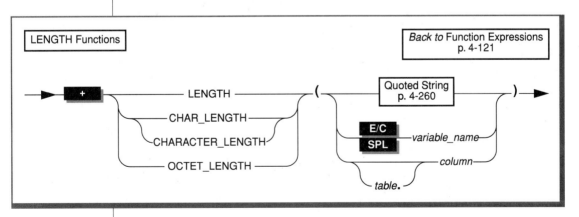

Segments **4-143**

Element	Purpose	Restrictions	Syntax
column	Name of a column in the specified table	The column must have a character data type.	Identifier, p. 4-205
table	Name of the table in which the specified column occurs	The table must exist.	Database Object Name, p. 4-50
variable_name	Host variable or SPL variable that contains a character string	The host variable or procedure variable must have a character data type.	Name must conform to language-specific rules for variable names.

The following list names the list functions:

- **LENGTH**
- **OCTET_LENGTH**
- **CHAR_LENGTH** (also known as **CHARACTER_LENGTH**)

Each of these functions has a distinct purpose.

The LENGTH Function

The **LENGTH** function returns the number of bytes in a character column, not including any trailing spaces. With BYTE or TEXT columns, the **LENGTH** function returns the full number of bytes in the column, including trailing spaces.

The following example illustrates the use of the **LENGTH** function:

```
SELECT customer_num, LENGTH(fname) + LENGTH(lname),
    LENGTH('How many bytes is this?')
    FROM customer WHERE LENGTH(company) > 10
```

E/C

In ESQL/C, you can use the **LENGTH** function to return the length of a character variable. ♦

GLS

For information on GLS aspects of the **LENGTH** function, see the *Informix Guide to GLS Functionality*. ♦

The OCTET_LENGTH Function

The **OCTET_LENGTH** function returns the number of bytes in a character column, including any trailing spaces. For a discussion of the **OCTET_LENGTH** function, see the *Informix Guide to GLS Functionality*.

The CHAR_LENGTH Function

The **CHAR_LENGTH** function returns the number of characters (not bytes) in a character column. The **CHARACTER_LENGTH** function is a synonym for the **CHAR_LENGTH** function. For a discussion of the **CHAR_LENGTH** function, see the *Informix Guide to GLS Functionality*.

IFX_REPLACE_MODULE Function

The **IFX_REPLACE_MODULE** function replaces a loaded shared library with a new version that has a different name or location.

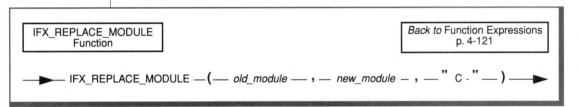

Element	Purpose	Restrictions	Syntax
new_module	Full pathname of the new shared library to replace the shared library that old_module specifies.	The shared library must exist with the specified pathname.	Quoted String, p. 4-260
old_module	Full pathname of the shared library to replace with the shared library that new_module specifies.	The shared library must exist with the specified pathname.	Quoted String, p. 4-260

The **IFX_REPLACE_MODULE** function returns an integer value to indicate the status of the update, as follows:

- Zero (0) to indicate success
- A negative integer to indicate an error

Expression

UNIX

For example, to replace the **circle.so** shared library that resides in the **/usr/apps/opaque_types** directory with one that resides in the **/usr/apps/shared_libs** directory, you can use the following EXECUTE FUNCTION statement to execute the **IFX_REPLACE_MODULE** function:

```
EXECUTE FUNCTION
ifx_replace_module("/usr/apps/opaque_types/circle.so",
    "/usr/apps/shared_libs/circle.so", "c")  ♦
```

WIN NT

For example, to replace the **circle.so** shared library that resides in the C:**usr****apps****opaque_types** directory with one that resides in the C:**usr****apps****shared_libs** directory, you can use the following EXECUTE FUNCTION statement to execute the **IFX_REPLACE_MODULE** function:

```
EXECUTE FUNCTION
ifx_replace_module("C:\usr\apps\opaque_types\circle.so",
    "C:\usr\apps\shared_libs\circle.so", "c")  ♦
```

E/C

To execute the **IFX_REPLACE_MODULE** function in an Informix ESQL/C application, you must associate the function with a cursor. ♦

For more information on how to use **IFX_REPLACE_MODULE** to update a shared library, see the chapter on how to design a UDR in *Extending Informix Dynamic Server 2000.*

IDS

Smart-Large-Object Functions

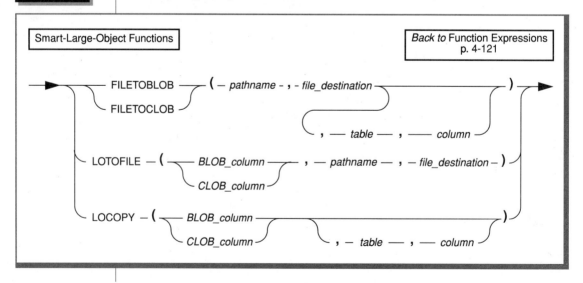

Element	Purpose	Restrictions	Syntax
BLOB_column	Name of a column of type BLOB	If you specify *table* and *column*, a BLOB column must exist in that table.	Identifier, p. 4-205
CLOB_column	Name of a column of type CLOB	If you specify *table* and *column*, a CLOB column must exist in that table.	Identifier, p. 4-205
column	Name of a column within table whose storage characteristics are used for the copy of the BLOB or CLOB value	This column must have CLOB or BLOB as its data type.	Quoted String, p. 4-260
file_destination	String that indicates the computer on which to put or get the smart large object	The only valid values are the strings `server` or `client`.	Quoted String, p. 4-260
pathname	Directory path and filename to locate the smart large object	The pathname must exist on the computer designated by file destination.	Quoted String, p. 4-260
table	Name of the table that contains column, whose storage characteristics are used for the copy of the BLOB or CLOB value	The table must exist in the database and it must contain a CLOB or BLOB column.	Quoted String, p. 4-260

FILETOBLOB and FILETOCLOB Functions

The **FILETOBLOB** function creates a BLOB value for data that is stored in a specified operating-system file. Similarly, the **FILETOCLOB** function creates a CLOB value for data that is stored in an operating-system file. These functions determine the operating-system file to use from the following parameters:

- The *pathname* parameter identifies the directory path and name of the source file.

- The *file destination* parameter identifies the computer, client or server, on which this file resides:

  □ Set *file destination* to `client` to identify the client computer as the location of the source file. The *pathname* can be either a full pathname or relative to the current directory.

  □ Set *file destination* to `server` to identify the server computer as the location of the source file. The *pathname* must be a full pathname.

The *table* and *column* parameters are optional:

- If you omit *table* and *column*, the **FILETOBLOB** function creates a BLOB value with the system-specified storage defaults, and the **FILETOCLOB** function creates a CLOB value with the system-specified storage defaults.

  These functions obtain the system-specific storage characteristics from either the ONCONFIG file or the sbspace. For more information on system-specified storage defaults, see the *Administrator's Guide*.

- If you specify *table* and *column*, the **FILETOBLOB** and **FILETOCLOB** functions use the storage characteristics from the specified column for the BLOB or CLOB value that they create.

The **FILETOBLOB** function returns a handle value (a pointer) to the new BLOB value. Similarly, the **FILETOCLOB** function returns a handle value to the new CLOB value. Neither of these functions actually stores the smart-large-object value into a column in the database. You must assign the BLOB or CLOB value to the appropriate column.

GLS

The **FILETOCLOB** function performs any code-set conversion that might be required when it copies the file from the client or server computer to the database. ♦

The following INSERT statement uses the **FILETOCLOB** function to create a CLOB value from the value in the **haven.rsm** file:

```
INSERT INTO candidate (cand_num, cand_lname, resume)
    VALUES (0, 'Haven', FILETOCLOB('haven.rsm', 'client'))
```

In the preceding example, the **FILETOCLOB** function reads the **haven.rsm** file in the current directory on the client computer and returns a handle value to a CLOB value that contains the data in this file. Because the **FILETOCLOB** function does not specify a table and column name, this new CLOB value has the system-specified storage characteristics. The INSERT statement then assigns this CLOB value to the **resume** column in the **candidate** table.

LOTOFILE Function

The **LOTOFILE** function copies a smart large object to an operating-system file. The first parameter specifies the BLOB or CLOB column to copy. The function determines the operating-system file to create from the following parameters:

- The *pathname* parameter identifies the directory path and name of the source file.
- The *file destination* parameter identifies the computer, client or server, on which this file resides:
  - Set *file destination* to `client` to identify the client computer as the location of the source file. The *pathname* can be either a full pathname or relative to the current directory.
  - Set *file destination* to `server` to identify the server computer as the location of the source file. The pathname must be a full pathname.

By default, the **LOTOFILE** function generates a filename of the form:

```
file.hex_id
```

In this format, *file* is the filename you specify in *pathname* and *hex_id* is the unique hexadecimal smart-large-object identifier. The maximum number of digits for a smart-large-object identifier is 17; however most smart large objects would have an identifier with significantly fewer digits.

UNIX

For example, suppose you specify a *pathname* value as follows:

```
'/tmp/resume'
```

If the CLOB column has an identifier of **203b2**, the **LOTOFILE** function would create the file:

```
/tmp/resume.203b2   ◆
```

WIN NT

For example, suppose you specify a *pathname* value as follows:

```
'C:\tmp\resume'
```

If the CLOB column has an identifier of **203b2**, the **LOTOFILE** function would create the file:

```
C:\tmp\resume.203b2   ◆
```

To change the default filename, you can specify the following wildcards in the filename of the *pathname*:

UNIX

- One or more contiguous question mark (?) characters in the filename can generate a unique filename.

  The **LOTOFILE** function replaces each question mark with a hexadecimal digit from the identifier of the BLOB or CLOB column.

  For example, suppose you specify a *pathname* value as follows:

  ```
  '/tmp/resume??.txt'
  ```

  The **LOTOFILE** function puts 2 digits of the hexadecimal identifier into the name. If the CLOB column has an identifier of **203b2**, the **LOTOFILE** function would create the file:

  ```
  /tmp/resume20.txt
  ```
  ◆

  If you specify more than 17 question marks, the **LOTOFILE** function ignores them.

- An exclamation point (!) at the end of the filename indicates that the filename does not need to be unique.

WIN NT

  For example, suppose you specify a pathname value as follows:

  ```
  'C:\tmp\resume.txt!'
  ```

  The **LOTOFILE** function does not use the smart-large-object identifier in the filename so it generates the following file:

  ```
  C:\tmp\resume.txt
  ```
  ◆

If the filename you specify already exists, **LOTOFILE** returns an error.

GLS

The **LOTOFILE** function performs any code-set conversion that might be required when it copies a CLOB value from the database to a file on the client or server computer. ◆

LOCOPY Function

The **LOCOPY** function creates a copy of a smart large object. The first parameter specifies the BLOB or CLOB column to copy. The *table* and *column* parameters are optional:

- If you omit *table* and *column*, the **LOCOPY** function creates a smart large object with system-specified storage defaults and copies the data in the BLOB or CLOB column into it.

The **LOCOPY** function obtains the system-specific storage defaults from either the **ONCONFIG** file or the sbspace. For more information on system-specified storage defaults, see the *Administrator's Guide*.

■ When you specify *table* and *column*, the **LOCOPY** function uses the storage characteristics from the specified *column* for the BLOB or CLOB value that it creates.

The **LOCOPY** function returns a handle value (a pointer) to the new BLOB or CLOB value. This function does *not* actually store the new smart-large-object value into a column in the database. You must assign the BLOB or CLOB value to the appropriate column.

The following ESQL/C code fragment copies the CLOB value in the **resume** column of the **candidate** table to the **resume** column of the **interview** table:

```
/* Insert a new row in the interviews table and get the
 * resulting SERIAL value (from sqlca.sqlerrd[1])
 */
EXEC SQL insert into interviews (intrv_num, intrv_time)
    values (0, '09:30');
intrv_num = sqlca.sqlerrd[1];

/* Update this interviews row with the candidate number
 * and resume from the candidate table. Use LOCOPY to
 * create a copy of the CLOB value in the resume column
 * of the candidate table.
 */
EXEC SQL update interviews
    SET (cand_num, resume) =
      (SELECT cand_num,
          LOCOPY(resume, 'candidate', 'resume')
        FROM candidate
        WHERE cand_lname = 'Haven')
    WHERE intrv_num = :intrv_num;
```

In the preceding example, the **LOCOPY** function returns a handle value for the copy of the CLOB **resume** column in the **candidate** table. Because the **LOCOPY** function specifies a table and column name, this new CLOB value has the storage characteristics of this **resume** column. If you omit the table (candidate) and column (resume) names, the **LOCOPY** function uses the system-defined storage defaults for the new CLOB value. The UPDATE statement then assigns this new CLOB value to the **resume** column in the **interviews** table.

Expression

Time Functions

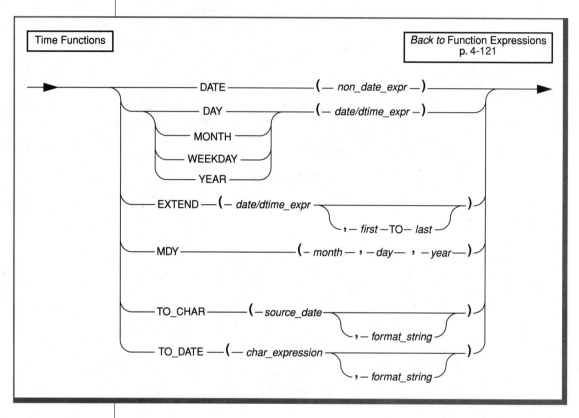

Element	Purpose	Restrictions	Syntax
char_expression	Expression to be converted to a DATE or DATETIME value	The expression must be of a character data type. It can be a constant, host variable, expression, or column.	Expression, p. 4-73
date/dtime_expr	Expression that serves as an argument in the following functions: DAY, MONTH, WEEKDAY, YEAR, and EXTEND	The expression must evaluate to a DATE or DATETIME value.	Expression, p. 4-73
day	Expression that represents the number of the day of the month	The expression must evaluate to an integer not greater than the number of days in the specified month.	Expression, p. 4-73
first	Qualifier that specifies the first field in the result If you do not specify first and *last* qualifiers, the default value of *first* is YEAR.	The qualifier can be any DATETIME qualifier, as long as it is larger than *last*.	DATETIME Field Qualifier, p. 4-71
format_string	String that represents the format of the DATE or DATETIME value	This string must have a character data type. The string must contain a valid date format, according to the formats allowed in the GL_DATE and GL_DATETIME environment variables. The string can be a column, host variable, expression, or constant.	Quoted String, p. 4-260
last	Qualifier that specifies the last field in the result If you do not specify first and *last* qualifiers, the default value of *last* is FRACTION(3).	The qualifier can be any DATETIME qualifier, as long as it is smaller than *first*.	DATETIME Field Qualifier, p. 4-71
month	Expression that represents the number of the month	The expression must evaluate to an integer between 1 and 12, inclusive.	Expression, p. 4-73

(1 of 2)

Element	Purpose	Restrictions	Syntax
non_date_expr	Expression whose value is to be converted to a DATE data type	You can specify any expression that can be converted to a DATE data type. Usually you specify an expression that evaluates to a CHAR, DATETIME, or INTEGER value.	Expression, p. 4-73
source_date	Expression that represents a date that is to be converted to a character string	This value must be of type DATETIME or DATE. It can be a host variable, expression, column, or constant.	Expression, p. 4-73
year	Expression that represents the year	The expression must evaluate to a four-digit integer. You cannot use a two-digit abbreviation.	Expression, p. 4-73

(2 of 2)

DATE Function

The **DATE** function returns a DATE value that corresponds to the non-date expression with which you call it. The argument can be any expression that can be converted to a DATE value, usually a CHAR, DATETIME, or INTEGER value. The following WHERE clause specifies a CHAR value for the non-date expression:

```
WHERE order_date < DATE('12/31/97')
```

When the **DATE** function interprets a CHAR non-date expression, it expects this expression to conform to any DATE format that the **DBDATE** environment specifies. For example, suppose **DBDATE** is set to Y2MD/ when you execute the following query:

```
SELECT DISTINCT DATE('02/01/1998') FROM ship_info
```

This SELECT statement generates an error because the **DATE** function cannot convert this non-date expression. The **DATE** function interprets the first part of the date string (02) as the year and the second part (01) as the month. For the third part (1998), the **DATE** function encounters four digits when it expects a two-digit day (valid day values must be between 01 and 31). It therefore cannot convert the value. For the SELECT statement to execute successfully with the Y2MD/ value for **DBDATE**, the non-date expression would need to be '98/02/01'. For information on the format of **DBDATE**, see the *Informix Guide to SQL: Reference*.

When you specify a positive INTEGER value for the non-date expression, the **DATE** function interprets the value as the number of days after the default date of December 31, 1899. If the integer value is negative, the **DATE** function interprets the value as the number of days before December 31, 1899. The following WHERE clause specifies an INTEGER value for the non-date expression:

```
WHERE order_date  <  DATE(365)
```

The database server searches for rows with an **order_date** value less than December 31, 1900 (12/31/1899 plus 365 days).

DAY Function

The **DAY** function returns an integer that represents the day of the month. The following example uses the **DAY** function with the **CURRENT** function to compare column values to the current day of the month:

```
WHERE DAY(order_date) > DAY(CURRENT)
```

MONTH Function

The **MONTH** function returns an integer that corresponds to the month portion of its type DATE or DATETIME argument. The following example returns a number from 1 through 12 to indicate the month when the order was placed:

```
SELECT order_num, MONTH(order_date) FROM orders
```

WEEKDAY Function

The **WEEKDAY** function returns an integer that represents the day of the week; zero (0) represents Sunday, one represents Monday, and so on. The following lists all the orders that were paid on the same day of the week, which is the current day:

```
SELECT * FROM orders
    WHERE WEEKDAY(paid_date) = WEEKDAY(CURRENT)
```

YEAR Function

The **YEAR** function returns a four-digit integer that represents the year. The following example lists orders in which the **ship_date** is earlier than the beginning of the current year:

```
SELECT order_num, customer_num FROM orders
    WHERE year(ship_date) < YEAR(TODAY)
```

Similarly, because a DATE value is a simple calendar date, you cannot add or subtract a DATE value with an INTERVAL value whose *last* qualifier is smaller than DAY. In this case, convert the DATE value to a DATETIME value.

EXTEND Function

The **EXTEND** function adjusts the precision of a DATETIME or DATE value. The expression cannot be a quoted string representation of a DATE value.

If you do not specify *first* and *last* qualifiers, the default qualifiers are YEAR TO FRACTION(3).

If the expression contains fields that are not specified by the qualifiers, the unwanted fields are discarded.

If the *first* qualifier specifies a larger (that is, more significant) field than what exists in the expression, the new fields are filled in with values returned by the **CURRENT** function. If the *last* qualifier specifies a smaller field (that is, less significant) than what exists in the expression, the new fields are filled in with constant values. A missing MONTH or DAY field is filled in with 1, and the missing HOUR to FRACTION fields are filled in with 0.

In the following example, the first EXTEND call evaluates to the **call_dtime** column value of YEAR TO SECOND. The second statement expands a literal DATETIME so that an interval can be subtracted from it. You must use the **EXTEND** function with a DATETIME value if you want to add it to or subtract it from an INTERVAL value that does not have all the same qualifiers. The third example updates only a portion of the datetime value, the hour position. The **EXTEND** function yields just the *hh:mm* part of the datetime. Subtracting 11:00 from the hours and minutes of the datetime yields an INTERVAL value of the difference, plus or minus, and subtracting that from the original value forces the value to 11:00.

```
EXTEND (call_dtime, YEAR TO SECOND)

EXTEND (DATETIME (1989-8-1) YEAR TO DAY, YEAR TO MINUTE)
     - INTERVAL (720) MINUTE (3) TO MINUTE

UPDATE cust_calls SET call_dtime = call_dtime -
(EXTEND(call_dtime, HOUR TO MINUTE) - DATETIME (11:00) HOUR
TO MINUTE) WHERE customer_num = 106
```

MDY Function

The **MDY** function returns a type DATE value with three expressions that evaluate to integers representing the month, day, and year. The first expression must evaluate to an integer representing the number of the month (1 to 12).

The second expression must evaluate to an integer that represents the number of the day of the month (1 to 28, 29, 30, or 31, as appropriate for the month.)

The third expression must evaluate to a four-digit integer that represents the year. You cannot use a two-digit abbreviation for the third expression. The following example sets the **paid_date** associated with the order number 8052 equal to the first day of the present month:

```
UPDATE orders SET paid_date = MDY(MONTH(TODAY), 1,
YEAR(TODAY))
     WHERE po_num = '8052'
```

TO_CHAR Function

The **TO_CHAR** function converts a DATE or DATETIME value to a character string. The character string contains the date that was specified in the *source_date* parameter, and represents this date in the format that was specified in the *format_string* parameter.

You can use this function only with built-in data types. ♦

If the value of the *source_date* parameter is null, the result of the function is a null value.

If you omit the *format_string* parameter, the **TO_CHAR** function uses the default date format to format the character string. The default date format is specified by environment variables such as **GL_DATETIME** and **GL_DATE**.

The *format_string* parameter does not have to imply the same qualifiers as the *source_date* parameter. When the implied formatting mask qualifier in *format_string* is different from the qualifier in *source_date*, the **TO_CHAR** function extends the DATETIME value as if it had called the **EXTEND** function.

In the following example, the user wants to convert the **begin_date** column of the **tab1** table to a character string. The **begin_date** column is defined as a DATETIME YEAR TO SECOND data type. The user uses a SELECT statement with the **TO_CHAR** function to perform this conversion.

```
SELECT TO_CHAR(begin_date, '%A %B %d, %Y %R')
    FROM tab1
```

The symbols in the *format_string* parameter in this example have the following meanings. For a complete list of format symbols and their meanings, see the **GL_DATE** and **GL_DATETIME** environment variables in the *Informix Guide to GLS Functionality*.

Symbol	Meaning
%A	Full weekday name as defined in the locale
%B	Full month name as defined in the locale
%d	Day of the month as a decimal number
%Y	Year as a 4-digit decimal number
%R	Time in 24-hour notation

The result of applying the specified *format_string* to the **begin_date** column is as follows:

```
Wednesday July 23, 1997 18:45
```

TO_DATE Function

The **TO_DATE** function converts a character string to a DATETIME value. The function evaluates the *char_expression* parameter as a date according to the date format you specify in the *format_string* parameter, and returns the equivalent date.

IDS

You can use this function only with built-in data types. ♦

If the value of the *char_expression* parameter is null, the result of the function is a null value.

If you omit the *format_string* parameter, the **TO_DATE** function applies the default DATETIME format to the DATETIME value. The default DATETIME format is specified by the **GL_DATETIME** environment variable.

In the following example, the user wants to convert a character string to a DATETIME value in order to update the **begin_date** column of the **tab1** table with the converted value. The **begin_date** column is defined as a DATETIME YEAR TO SECOND data type. The user uses an UPDATE statement that contains a **TO_DATE** function to accomplish this result.

```
UPDATE tab1
    SET begin_date = TO_DATE('Wednesday July 23, 1997 18:45',
    '%A %B %d, %Y %R');
```

The *format_string* parameter in this example tells the **TO_DATE** function how to format the converted character string in the **begin_date** column. For a table that shows the meaning of each format symbol in this format string, see "TO_CHAR Function" on page 4-157.

Trigonometric Functions

A trigonometric function takes an argument, as the following diagram shows.

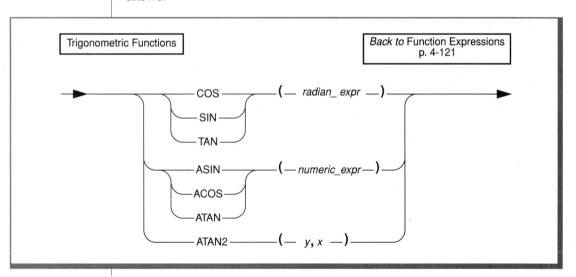

Element	Purpose	Restrictions	Syntax
numeric_expr	Numeric expression that serves as an argument to the ASIN, ACOS, or ATAN functions	The expression must evaluate to a value between -1 and 1, inclusive.	Expression, p. 4-73
radian_expr	Expression that evaluates to the number of radians For further information, see "Formulas for Radian Expressions" on page 4-160.	The expression must evaluate to a numeric value.	Expression, p. 4-73
x	Expression that represents the x coordinate of the rectangular coordinate pair (x, y)	The expression must evaluate to a numeric value.	Expression, p. 4-73
y	Expression that represents the y coordinate of the rectangular coordinate pair (x, y)	The expression must evaluate to a numeric value.	Expression, p. 4-73

Formulas for Radian Expressions

The **COS**, **SIN**, and **TAN** functions take the number of radians (*radian_expr*) as an argument.

If you are using degrees and want to convert degrees to radians, use the following formula:

```
# degrees * p/180= # radians
```

If you are using radians and want to convert radians to degrees, use the following formula:

```
# radians * 180/p = # degrees
```

COS Function

The **COS** function returns the cosine of a radian expression. The following example returns the cosine of the values of the degrees column in the **anglestbl** table. The expression passed to the **COS** function in this example converts degrees to radians.

```
SELECT COS(degrees*180/3.1416) FROM anglestbl
```

SIN Function

The **SIN** function returns the sine of a radian expression. The following example returns the sine of the values in the **radians** column of the **anglestbl** table:

```
SELECT SIN(radians) FROM anglestbl
```

TAN Function

The **TAN** function returns the tangent of a radian expression. The following example returns the tangent of the values in the **radians** column of the **anglestbl** table:

```
SELECT TAN(radians) FROM anglestbl
```

ACOS Function

The **ACOS** function returns the arc cosine of a numeric expression. The following example returns the arc cosine of the value (-0.73) in radians:

```
SELECT ACOS(-0.73) FROM anglestbl
```

ASIN Function

The **ASIN** function returns the arc sine of a numeric expression. The following example returns the arc sine of the value (-0.73) in radians:

```
SELECT ASIN(-0.73) FROM anglestbl
```

ATAN Function

The **ATAN** function returns the arc tangent of a numeric expression. The following example returns the arc tangent of the value (-0.73) in radians:

```
SELECT ATAN(-0.73) FROM anglestbl
```

ATAN2 Function

The **ATAN2** function computes the angular component of the polar coordinates (r, θ) associated with (x, y). The following example compares *angles* to θ for the rectangular coordinates $(4, 5)$:

```
WHERE angles > ATAN2(4,5)       --determines θ for (4,5) and
                                  compares to angles
```

You can determine the length of the radial coordinate *r* using the expression shown in the following example:

```
SQRT(POW(x,2) + POW(y,2))       --determines  r  for  (x,y)
```

You can determine the length of the radial coordinate *r* for the rectangular coordinates $(4,5)$ using the expression shown in the following example:

```
SQRT(POW(4,2) + POW(5,2))       --determines  r  for  (4,5)
```

String-Manipulation Functions

String-manipulation functions perform various operations on strings of characters. The syntax for string-manipulation functions is as follows.

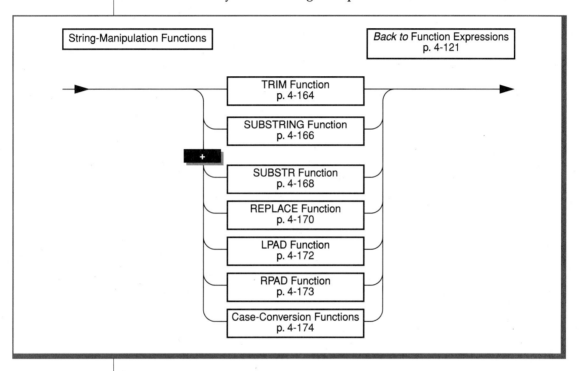

TRIM Function

Use the **TRIM** function to remove leading or trailing (or both) pad characters from a string.

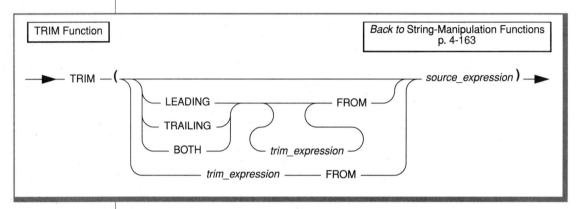

Element	Purpose	Restrictions	Syntax
trim_expression	Expression that evaluates to a single character or null	This expression must be a character expression.	Quoted String, p. 4-260
source_expression	Arbitrary character string expression, including a column or another TRIM function	This expression cannot be a host variable.	Quoted String, p. 4-260

The **TRIM** function returns a VARCHAR string that is identical to the character string passed to it, except that any leading or trailing pad characters, if specified, are removed. If no trim specification (LEADING, TRAILING, or BOTH) is specified, then BOTH is assumed. If no *trim_expression* is used, a single space is assumed. If either the *trim_expression* or the *source_expression* evaluates to null, the result of the **TRIM** function is null. The maximum length of the resultant string must be 255 or less, because the VARCHAR data type supports only 255 characters.

Some generic uses for the **TRIM** function are shown in the following example:

```
SELECT TRIM (c1) FROM tab;
SELECT TRIM (TRAILING '#' FROM c1) FROM tab;
SELECT TRIM (LEADING FROM c1) FROM tab;
UPDATE c1='xyz' FROM tab WHERE LENGTH(TRIM(c1))=5;
SELECT c1, TRIM(LEADING '#' FROM TRIM(TRAILING '%' FROM
    '###abc%%%')) FROM tab;
```

GLS

When you use the DESCRIBE statement with a SELECT statement that uses the **TRIM** function in the select list, the described character type of the trimmed column depends on the database server you are using and the data type of the *source_expression*. For further information on the GLS aspects of the **TRIM** function in ESQL/C, see the *Informix Guide to GLS Functionality*. ◆

Fixed Character Columns

The **TRIM** function can be specified on fixed-length character columns. If the length of the string is not completely filled, the unused characters are padded with blank space. Figure 4-3 shows this concept for the column entry '##A2T##', where the column is defined as CHAR(10).

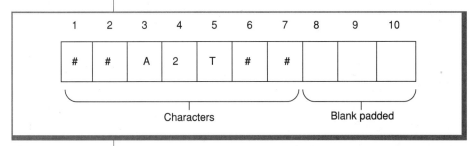

Figure 4-3
Column Entry in a Fixed-Length Character Column

If you want to trim the pound sign (#) *trim_expression* from the column, you need to consider the blank padded spaces as well as the actual characters. For example, if you specify the trim specification BOTH, the result from the trim operation is A2T##, because the **TRIM** function does not match the blank padded space that follows the string. In this case, the only pound signs (#) trimmed are those that precede the other characters. The SELECT statement is shown, followed by Figure 4-4, which presents the result.

```
SELECT TRIM(LEADING '#' FROM col1) FROM taba
```

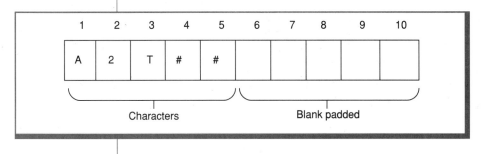

Figure 4-4
Result of TRIM Operation

The following SELECT statement removes all occurrences of the pound sign (#):

```
SELECT TRIM(BOTH '#' FROM TRIM(TRAILING ' ' FROM col1)) FROM taba
```

SUBSTRING Function

The **SUBSTRING** function returns a subset of a source string.

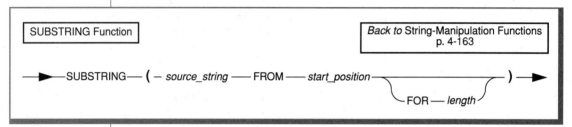

Element	Purpose	Restrictions	Syntax
length	Number of characters to be returned from source_string	This parameter must be an integer. This parameter can be an expression, constant, column, or host variable.	Literal Number, p. 4-237
source_string	String that serves as input to the SUBSTRING function	This parameter can be any data type that can be converted to a character data type. This parameter can be an expression, constant, column, or host variable.	Expression, p. 4-73
start_position	Column position in source_string where the SUBSTRING function starts to return characters	This parameter must be an integer. This parameter can be an expression, constant, column, or host variable. This parameter can be preceded by a plus sign (+), a minus sign (-), or no sign.	Literal Number, p. 4-237

IDS   You can use this function only with built-in data types. ♦

The subset begins at the column position that *start_position* specifies. The following table shows how the database server determines the starting position of the returned subset based on the input value of the *start_position*.

Value of Start_Position	How the Database Server Determines the Starting Position of the Return Subset
Positive	Counts forward from the first character in *source_string*
	For example, if *start_position* = 1, the first character in the *source_string* is the first character in the return subset.
Zero (0)	Counts from one position before (that is, left of) the first character in *source_string*
	For example, if *start_position* = 0 and *length* = 1, the database server returns null, whereas if *length* = 2, the database server returns the first character in *source_string*.
Negative	Counts backward from one position before (that is, left of) the first character in *source_string*
	For example, if *start_position* = -1, the starting position of the return subset is two positions (0 and -1) before the first character in *source_string*.

The size of the subset is specified by *length*. The *length* parameter refers to the number of logical characters rather than to the number of bytes. If you omit the *length* parameter, the **SUBSTRING** function returns the entire portion of *source_ string* that begins at *start_position*.

In the following example, the user specifies that the subset of the source string that begins in column position 3 and is two characters long should be returned.

```
SELECT SUBSTRING('ABCDEFG' FROM 3 FOR 2)
    FROM mytable
```

The following table shows the output of this SELECT statement.

(constant)
CD

In the following example, the user specifies a negative *start_position* for the return subset.

```
SELECT SUBSTRING('ABCDEFG' FROM -3 FOR 7)
    FROM mytable
```

The database server starts at the -3 position (four positions before the first character) and counts forward for 7 characters. The following table shows the output of this SELECT statement.

(constant)
ABC

SUBSTR Function

The **SUBSTR** function has the same purpose as the **SUBSTRING** function (to return a subset of a source string), but it uses different syntax.

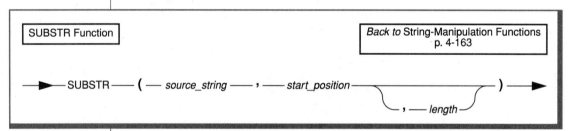

Element	Purpose	Restrictions	Syntax
length	Number of characters to be returned from source_string	This parameter must be an integer. This parameter can be an expression, constant, column, or host variable.	Literal Number, p. 4-237
source_string	String that serves as input to the SUBSTR function	This parameter can be any data type that can be converted to a character data type. This parameter can be an expression, constant, column, or host variable.	Expression, p. 4-73
start_position	Column position in source_string where the SUBSTR function starts to return characters	This parameter must be an integer. This parameter can be an expression, constant, column, or host variable. This parameter can be preceded by a plus sign (+), a minus sign (-), or no sign.	Literal Number, p. 4-237

IDS You can use this function only with built-in data types. ♦

The **SUBSTR** function returns a subset of *source_string*. The subset begins at the column position that *start_position* specifies. The following table shows how the database server determines the starting position of the returned subset based on the input value of the *start_position*.

Value of Start_Position	How the Database Server Determines the Starting Position of the Return Subset
Positive	Counts forward from the first character in *source_string*
Zero (0)	Counts forward from the first character in *source_string* (that is, treats a *start_position* of 0 as equivalent to 1)
Negative	Counts backward from the last character in *source_string*
	A value of -1, returns the last character in *source_string*.

The *length* parameter specifies the number of characters (not bytes) in the subset. If you omit the *length* parameter, the **SUBSTR** function returns the entire portion of *source_ string* that begins at *start_position*.

In the following example, the user specifies that the subset of the source string to be returned begins at a starting position 3 characters back from the end of the string. Because the source string is 7 characters long, the starting position is the fifth column of source_string. Because the user does not specify a value for *length*, the database server returns the entire portion of the source string that begins in column position 5.

```
SELECT SUBSTR('ABCDEFG', -3)
    FROM mytable
```

The following table shows the output of this SELECT statement.

(constant)
EFG

REPLACE Function

The **REPLACE** function replaces specified characters within a source string with different characters.

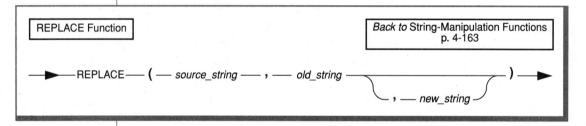

Element	Purpose	Restrictions	Syntax
new_string	Character or characters that replace old_string in the return string	This parameter can be any data type that can be converted to a character data type. The parameter can be an expression, column, constant, or host variable.	Expression, p. 4-73
old_string	Character or characters in source_string that are to be replaced by *new_string*	This parameter can be any data type that can be converted to a character data type. The parameter can be an expression, column, constant, or host variable.	Expression, p. 4-73
source_string	String of characters that serves as input to the REPLACE function	This parameter can be any data type that can be converted to a character data type. The parameter can be an expression, column, constant, or host variable.	Expression, p. 4-73

IDS

You can use this function only with built-in data types. ◆

The **REPLACE** function returns a copy of *source_string* in which every occurrence of *old_string* is replaced by *new_string*. If you omit the *new_string* option, every occurrence of *old_string* is omitted from the return string.

In the following example, the user replaces every occurrence of x z in the source string with t.

```
SELECT REPLACE('Mighxzy xzime', 'xz', 't')
    FROM mytable
```

The following table shows the output of this SELECT statement.

(constant)

Mighty time

LPAD Function

The **LPAD** function returns a copy of *source_string* that is left-padded to the total number of characters specified by *length*.

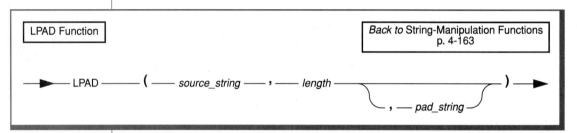

Element	Purpose	Restrictions	Syntax
length	Integer value that indicates the total number of characters in the return string	This parameter can be an expression, constant, column, or host variable.	Literal Number, p. 4-237
pad_string	String that specifies the pad character or characters	This parameter can be any data type that can be converted to a character data type. The parameter can be an expression, column, constant, or host variable.	Expression, p. 4-73
source_string	String that serves as input to the LPAD function	This parameter can be any data type that can be converted to a character data type. The parameter can be an expression, column, constant, or host variable.	Expression, p. 4-73

IDS   You can use this function only with built-in data types. ♦

The *pad_string* parameter specifies the pad character or characters to be used for padding the source string. The sequence of pad characters occurs as many times as necessary to make the return string reach the length specified by *length*. The sequence of pad characters in *pad_string* is truncated if it is too long to fit into *length*. If you omit the *pad_string* parameter, the default value is a single blank.

In the following example, the user specifies that the source string is to be left-padded to a total length of 16 characters. The user also specifies that the pad characters are a sequence consisting of a dash and an underscore (-_).

```
SELECT LPAD('Here we are', 16, '-_')
    FROM mytable
```

The following table shows the output of this SELECT statement.

(constant)

-_-_-Here we are

RPAD Function

The **RPAD** function returns a copy of *source_string* that is right-padded to the total number of characters that *length* specifies.

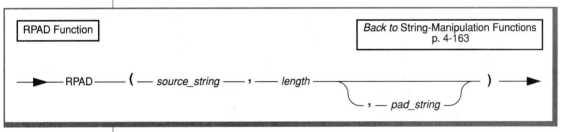

Element	Purpose	Restrictions	Syntax
length	Integer value that indicates the total number of characters in the return string	This parameter can be an expression, constant, column, or host variable.	Literal Number, p. 4-237
pad_string	String that specifies the pad character or characters	This parameter can be any data type that can be converted to a character data type. The parameter can be an expression, column, constant, or host variable.	Expression, p. 4-73
source_string	String that serves as input to the RPAD function	This parameter can be any data type that can be converted to a character data type. The parameter can be an expression, column, constant, or host variable.	Expression, p. 4-73

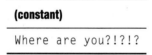

You can use this function only with built-in data types. ♦

The *pad_string* parameter specifies the pad character or characters to be used to pad the source string. The sequence of pad characters occurs as many times as necessary to make the return string reach the length that *length* specifies. The sequence of pad characters in *pad_string* is truncated if it is too long to fit into *length*. If you omit the *pad_string* parameter, the default value is a single blank.

In the following example, the user specifies that the source string is to be right-padded to a total length of 18 characters. The user also specifies that the pad characters to be used are a sequence consisting of a question mark and an exclamation point (?!)

```
SELECT RPAD('Where are you', 18, '?!')
    FROM mytable
```

The following table shows the output of this SELECT statement.

(constant)
Where are you?!?!?

Case-Conversion Functions

The case-conversion functions enable you to perform case-insensitive searches in your queries and specify the format of the output. The case-conversion functions are **UPPER**, **LOWER**, and **INITCAP**. The following diagram shows the syntax of these case-conversion functions.

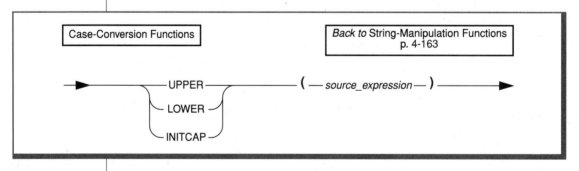

Element	Purpose	Restrictions	Syntax
source_expression	Column name, function, quoted string, host variable, or any expression that evaluates to a character string	This expression must be a character data type. If you use a host variable, the variable must be declared with a length long enough to handle the converted string.	Expression, p. 4-73

The input type of *source_expression* must be a character data type. When the column is described, the data type the database server returns is the same as the input type. For example, if the input type is CHAR, the output type is also CHAR.

IDS

You can use these functions only with built-in data types. ◆

GLS

The byte length returned from the describe of a column with a case-conversion function is the input byte length of the source string. If you use a case-conversion function with a multibyte *source_expression*, the conversion might increase or decrease the length of the string. If the byte length of the result string exceeds the byte length of *source_expression*, the database server truncates the result string to fit into the byte length of *source_expression*. ◆

If *source_expression* is null, the result of a case-conversion function is also null.

The database server treats a case-conversion function as an SPL routine in the following instances:

- If it has no argument
- If it has one argument, and that argument is a named argument
- If it has more than one argument
- If it appears in a SELECT list with a host variable as an argument

If none of the conditions in the preceding list are met, the database server treats a case-conversion function as a system function.

The following example shows how you can use all the case-conversion functions in the same query to specify multiple output formats for the same value:

```
Input value:

SAN Jose

Query:

SELECT City, LOWER(City), Lower("City"),
    UPPER (City), INITCAP(City)
        FROM Weather;

Query output:

SAN Jose    san jose    city    SAN JOSE    San Jose
```

UPPER Function

The **UPPER** function returns a copy of the *source_expression* in which every lowercase alphabetical character in the *source_expression* is replaced by a corresponding uppercase alphabetic character.

The following example shows how to use the **UPPER** function to perform a case-insensitive search on the **lname** column for all employees with the last name of **curran**:

```
SELECT title, INITCAP(fname), INITCAP(lname) FROM employees
WHERE UPPER (lname) = "CURRAN"
```

Because the **INITCAP** function is specified in the select list, the database server returns the results in a mixed-case format. For example, the output of one matching row might read: `accountant James Curran`.

LOWER Function

The **LOWER** function returns a copy of the *source_expression* in which every uppercase alphabetic character in the *source_expression* is replaced by a corresponding lowercase alphabetic character.

The following example shows how to use the **LOWER** function to perform a case-insensitive search on the **City** column. This statement directs the database server to replace all instances (that is, any variation) of the words san jose, with the mixed-case format, San Jose.

```
UPDATE Weather SET City = "San Jose"
WHERE LOWER (City) = "san jose";
```

INITCAP Function

The **INITCAP** function returns a copy of the *source_expression* in which every word in the *source_expression* begins with uppercase letter. With this function, a word begins after any character other than a letter. Thus, in addition to a blank space, symbols such as commas, periods, colons, and so on, introduce a new word.

For an example of the **INITCAP** function, see "UPPER Function" on page 4-176.

IFX_ALLOW_NEWLINE Function

The **IFX_ALLOW_NEWLINE** function sets a newline mode that allows newline characters in quoted strings or disallows newline characters in quoted strings within a given session.

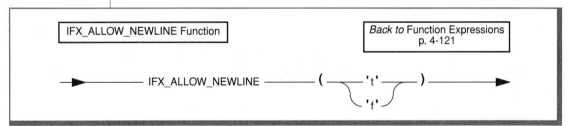

If you enter 't' as the argument of this function, you enable newline characters in quoted strings in the session. If you enter 'f' as the argument of this function, you disallow newline characters in quoted strings in the session.

You can set the newline mode for all sessions by setting the ALLOW_NEWLINE parameter in the ONCONFIG file to a value of 0 (newline characters not allowed) or to a value of 1 (newline characters allowed). If you do not set this configuration parameter, the default value is 0. Each time you start a session, the new session inherits the newline mode set in the ONCONFIG file. To change the newline mode for the session, execute the **IFX_ALLOW_NEWLINE** function. Once you have set the newline mode for a session, the mode remains in effect until the end of the session or until you execute the **IFX_ALLOW_NEWLINE** function again within the session.

In the following example, assume that you did not specify any value for the ALLOW_NEWLINE parameter in the ONCONFIG file, so by default newline characters are not allowed in quoted strings in any session. After you start a new session, you can enable newline characters in quoted strings in that session by executing the **IFX_ALLOW_NEWLINE** function:

```
EXECUTE PROCEDURE IFX_ALLOW_NEWLINE('t')
```

E/C

The newline mode that is set by the ALLOW_NEWLINE parameter in the ONCONFIG file or by the execution of the **IFX_ALLOW_NEWLINE** function in a session applies only to quoted-string literals in SQL statements. The newline mode does not apply to quoted strings contained in host variables in SQL statements. Host variables can contain newline characters within string data regardless of the newline mode currently in effect. For example, you can use a host variable to insert data containing newline characters into a column even if the ALLOW_NEWLINE parameter in the ONCONFIG file is set to 0. ♦

For further information on how the **IFX_ALLOW_NEWLINE** function affects quoted strings, see "Quoted String" on page 4-260. For further information on the ALLOW_NEWLINE parameter in the ONCONFIG file, see the *Administrator's Reference*.

User-Defined Functions

A user-defined function is a function that you write in SPL or in a language external to the database, such as C or Java.

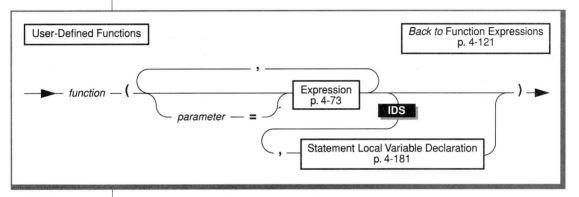

Element	Purpose	Restrictions	Syntax
function	Name of the called function	The function must exist.	Database Object Name, p. 4-50
parameter	Name of a parameter for which you supply an argument to the function The parameter name is originally specified in a CREATE FUNCTION statement.	If you use the *parameter* = option for any argument in the called function, you must use it for all arguments.	Identifier, p. 4-205

You can call user-defined functions within SQL statements. Unlike built-in functions, user-defined functions can only be used by the creator of the function, the DBA, and the users who have been granted the Execute privilege on the function. For more information, see "GRANT" on page 2-500.

The following examples show some user-defined function expressions. The first example omits the *parameter* option when it lists the function argument:

```
read_address('Miller')
```

This second example uses the *parameter* option to specify the argument value:

```
read_address(lastname = 'Miller')
```

When you use the *parameter* option, the *parameter* name must match the name of the corresponding parameter in the function registration. For example, the preceding example assumes that the **read_address()** function had been registered as follows:

```
CREATE FUNCTION read_address(lastname CHAR(20))
RETURNING address_t ...
```

IDS

A statement-local variable (SLV) enables you to transmit a value from a user-defined function call to another part of the SQL statement. To use an SLV with a call to a user-defined function, follow these steps:

- Write an OUT parameter for the user-defined function.

   For more information on how to write a user-defined function with an OUT parameter, see *Extending Informix Dynamic Server 2000*.

- When you register the user-defined function, specify the OUT keyword in front of the OUT parameter.

   For more information, see "Specifying an OUT Parameter for a User-Defined Function" on page 4-290.

- Declare the SLV in a function expression that calls the user-defined function with the OUT parameter.

   The call to the user-defined function must be made within a WHERE clause. See "Statement-Local Variable Declaration" on page 4-181 for information about the syntax to declare the SLV.

- Use the SLV that the user-defined function has initialized within the SQL statement.

   Once the call to the user defined function has initialized the SLV, you can use this value in other parts of the SQL statement. See "Statement-Local Variable Expressions" on page 4-183 for information about the use of an SLV within an SQL statement.

IDS

Statement-Local Variable Declaration

The Statement-Local Variable Declaration declares a statement-local variable (SLV) in a call to a user-defined function that defines an OUT parameter.

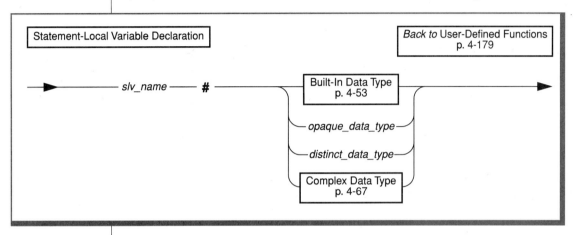

Element	Purpose	Restrictions	Syntax
distinct_data_type	Name of a distinct data type	The distinct data type must already exist in the database.	Identifier, p. 4-205
opaque_data_type	Name of an opaque data type	The opaque data type must already exist in the database.	Identifier, p. 4-205
slv_name	Name of a statement local variable you are defining	The *slv_name* exists only for the life of the statement. The *slv_name* must be unique within the statement.	Identifier, p. 4-205

You declare an SLV in a user-defined function call so that a user-defined function can assign the value of its OUT parameter to the SLV. The call to the user-defined function *must* exist in the WHERE clause of the SQL statement. For example, if you register a function with the following CREATE FUNCTION statement, you can use its **y** parameter as a statement-local variable in a WHERE clause:

```
CREATE FUNCTION find_location(a FLOAT, b FLOAT, OUT y INTEGER)
RETURNING VARCHAR(20)
EXTERNAL NAME "/usr/lib/local/find.so"
LANGUAGE C
```

In this example, **find_location()** accepts two FLOAT values that represent a latitude and a longitude and returns the name of the nearest city, along with an extra value of type INTEGER that represents the population rank of the city.

You can now call **find_location()** in a WHERE clause:

```
SELECT zip_code_t FROM address
    WHERE address.city = find_location(32.1, 35.7, rank # INT)
    AND rank < 101;
```

The function expression passes two FLOAT values to **find_location()** and declares an SLV named **rank** of type INT. In this case, **find_location()** will return the name of the city nearest latitude 32.1 and longitude 35.7 (which may be a heavily populated area) whose population rank is between 1 and 100. The statement will then return the zip code that corresponds to that city.

The WHERE clause of the SQL statement *must* produce an SLV that is used within other parts of the statement. The following SELECT statement is *illegal* because the select list produces the SLV:

```
-- illegal SELECT statement
SELECT title, contains(body, 'dog and cat', rank # INT), rank
    FROM documents
```

The data type you use when you declare the SLV in a statement must be the same as the data type of the OUT parameter in the CREATE FUNCTION statement. If you use different but compatible data types, such as INTEGER and FLOAT, the database server automatically performs the cast between the data types.

SLVs shared the name space with UDR variables and the column names of the table involved in the SQL statement. Therefore, the database uses the following precedence to resolve ambiguous situations:

- UDR variables
- Column names
- SLVs

Once the user-defined function assigns its OUT parameter to the SLV, you can use this SLV value in other parts of the SQL statement. For more information, see "Statement-Local Variable Expressions" on page 4-183.

IDS

Statement-Local Variable Expressions

The Statement-Local Variable Expression specifies how you can use a defined statement-local variable (SLV) elsewhere in an SQL statement.

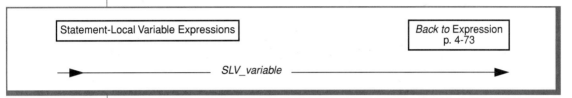

Element	Purpose	Restrictions	Syntax
SLV_variable	Statement-local variable (SLV) that was defined in a call to a user-defined function within the same SQL statement.	The *SLV_variable* exists only for the life of the statement. Its name must be unique within the statement.	Identifier, p. 4-205

You define an SLV in the call to a user-defined function in the WHERE clause of the SQL statement. This user-defined function must be defined with an OUT parameter. The call to the user-defined function assigns the value of the OUT parameter to the SLV. For more information, see "Statement-Local Variable Declaration" on page 4-181.

Once the user-defined function assigns its OUT parameter to the SLV, you can use this value in other parts of the SQL statement. You can use the value of this OUT parameter elsewhere in the statement, subject to the following scoping rules:

- The SLV is *read-only* throughout the query (or subquery) in which it is defined.
- The scope of an SLV extends from the query in which the SLV is defined down into all nested subqueries.

  In other words, if a query contains a subquery, an SLV that is visible in the query is also visible to all subqueries of that query.
- In nested queries, the scope of an SLV does *not* extend upwards.

  In other words, if a query contains a subquery and the SLV is defined in the subquery, it is *not* visible to the parent query.

- In queries that involve UNION, the SLV is only visible in the query in which it is defined.

  The SLV is not visible to all other queries involved in the UNION.

- For INSERT, DELETE, and UPDATE statements, an SLV is not visible outside the SELECT portion of the statement.

  Within this SELECT portion, all the above scoping rules apply.

Important: *A statement-local variable is valid only for the life of a single SQL statement.*

The following SELECT statement calls the **find_location()** function in a WHERE clause and defines the **rank** SLV. In this example, **find_location()** accepts two values that represent a latitude and a longitude and returns the name of the nearest city, along with an extra value of type INTEGER that represents the population rank of the city.

```
SELECT zip_code_t FROM address
    WHERE address.city = find_location(32.1, 35.7, rank # INT)
    AND rank < 101;
```

When execution of the **find_location()** function completes successfully, the function has initialized the **rank** SLV. The SELECT then uses this **rank** value in a second WHERE-clause condition. In this example, the Statement-Local Variable Expression is the variable **rank** in the second WHERE-clause condition:

```
rank < 101
```

If the user-defined function that initializes the SLV is *not* executed in an iteration of the statement, the SLV has a value of null. SLV values do *not* persist across iterations of the statement. At the start of each iteration, the database server sets the SLV value to null.

Each user-defined function can have only *one* OUT parameter and *one* SLV. However, a single SQL statement can invoke multiple functions that have OUT parameters. For example, the following partial statement calls two user-defined functions with OUT parameters, whose values are referenced with the SLV names **out1** and **out2**:

```
SELECT...
    WHERE func_2(x, out1 # INTEGER) < 100
    AND (out1 = 12 OR out1 = 13)
    AND func_3(a, out2 # FLOAT) = "SAN FRANCISCO"
    AND out2 = 3.1416;
```

For more information on how to write a user-defined function with an OUT parameter, see *Extending Informix Dynamic Server 2000*.

Aggregate Expressions

An aggregate expression uses an aggregate function to summarize selected database data.

You cannot use an aggregate expression in a condition that is part of a WHERE clause unless you use the aggregate expression within a subquery.

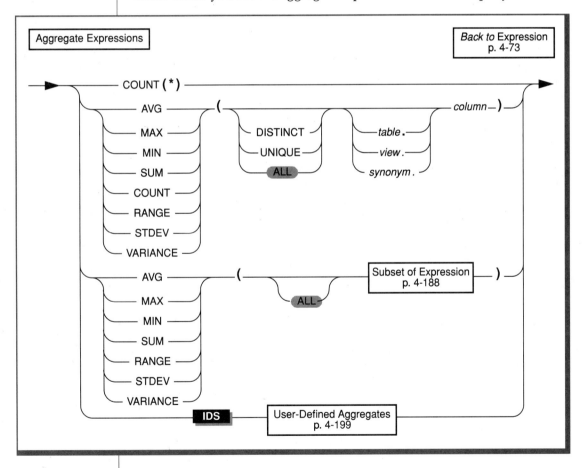

Element	Purpose	Restrictions	Syntax
column	Name of the column to which the specified aggregate function is applied	If you specify an aggregate expression and one or more columns in the SELECT clause of a SELECT statement, you must put all the column names that are not used within the aggregate expression or a time expression in the GROUP BY clause. You cannot apply an aggregate function to a BYTE or TEXT column. For other general restrictions, see "Subset of Expressions Allowed in an Aggregate Expression" on page 4-188. For restrictions that depend on the keywords that precede *column*, see the headings for individual keywords on the following pages.	Identifier, p. 4-205
synonym	Name of the synonym in which the specified column occurs	The synonym and the table to which the synonym points must exist.	Database Object Name, p. 4-50
table	Name of the table in which the specified column occurs	The table must exist.	Database Object Name, p. 4-50
view	Name of the view in which the specified column occurs	The view must exist.	Database Object Name, p. 4-50

An aggregate function returns one value for a set of queried rows. The following examples show aggregate functions in SELECT statements:

```
SELECT SUM(total_price) FROM items WHERE order_num = 1013

SELECT COUNT(*) FROM orders WHERE order_num = 1001

SELECT MAX(LENGTH(fname) + LENGTH(lname)) FROM customer
```

If you use an aggregate function and one or more columns in the select list, you must put all the column names that are not used as part of an aggregate or time expression in the GROUP BY clause.

Types of Aggregate Expressions

You can use two types of aggregate expressions in SQL statements: built-in aggregates and user-defined aggregates. The built-in aggregates include all the aggregates shown in the syntax diagram in "Aggregate Expressions" on page 4-185 except for the "User-Defined Aggregates" category. User-defined aggregates are any new aggregates that the user creates with the CREATE AGGREGATE statement.

Built-in Aggregates

Built-in aggregates are aggregate expressions that are provided by the database server, such as AVG, SUM, and COUNT. By default, these aggregates work only with built-in data types, such as INTEGER and FLOAT.

You can extend these built-in aggregates to work with extended data types. To extend built-in aggregates, you must create UDRs that overload several binary operators.

Once you have overloaded the binary operators for a built-in aggregate, you can use that aggregate with an extended data type in an SQL statement. For example, if you have overloaded the **plus** operator for the SUM aggregate to work with a specified row type and assigned this row type to the **complex** column of the **complex_tab** table, you can apply the SUM aggregate to the **complex** column:

```
SELECT SUM(complex) FROM complex_tab
```

For further information on extending built-in aggregates, see the *Extending Informix Dynamic Server 2000* manual.

For information on invoking built-in aggregates, see the descriptions of individual built-in aggregates in the following pages.

User-Defined Aggregates

A user-defined aggregate is an aggregate that you define to perform an aggregate computation that is not provided by the database server. For example, you can create a user-defined aggregate named SUMSQ that returns the sum of the squared values of a specified column. User-defined aggregates can work with built-in data types or extended data types or both, depending on how you define the support functions for the user-defined aggregate.

To create a user-defined aggregate, use the CREATE AGGREGATE statement. In this statement you name the new aggregate and specify the support functions for the aggregate. Once you have created the new aggregate and its support functions, you can use the aggregate in SQL statements. For example, if you have created the SUMSQ aggregate and specified that it works with the FLOAT data type, you can apply the SUMSQ aggregate to a FLOAT column named **digits** in the **test** table:

```
SELECT SUMSQ(digits) FROM test
```

For further information on creating user-defined aggregates, see "CREATE AGGREGATE" on page 2-115 and the discussion of user-defined aggregates in the *Extending Informix Dynamic Server 2000* manual.

For information on invoking user-defined aggregates, see "User-Defined Aggregates" on page 4-199.

Subset of Expressions Allowed in an Aggregate Expression

As indicated in the diagrams for "Aggregate Expressions" on page 4-185 and "User-Defined Aggregates" on page 4-199, not all expressions are available for you to use when you use an aggregate expression. The argument of an aggregate function cannot itself contain an aggregate function. You cannot use the aggregate functions in the following situations:

- MAX(AVG(order_num))
- An aggregate function in a WHERE clause, unless it is contained in a subquery, or if the aggregate is on a correlated column that originates from a parent query and the WHERE clause is within a subquery that is within a HAVING clause
- An aggregate function on a BYTE or TEXT column

You cannot use a collection column as an argument to the following aggregate functions:

- AVG
- SUM
- MIN
- MAX

For the full syntax of expressions, see "Expression" on page 4-73.

Including or Excluding Duplicates in the Row Set

The DISTINCT keyword causes the function to be applied only to unique values from the named column. The UNIQUE keyword is a synonym for the DISTINCT keyword.

The ALL keyword is the opposite of the DISTINCT keyword. If you specify the ALL keyword, all the values that are selected from the named column or expression, including any duplicate values, are used in the calculation.

Overview of COUNT Functions

The **COUNT** function is actually a set of functions that enable you to count column values and expressions in different ways. You invoke each form of the **COUNT** function by specifying a particular argument after the COUNT keyword. Each form of the **COUNT** function is explained in the following subsections. For a comparison of the different forms of the **COUNT** function, see "Comparison of the Different COUNT Functions" on page 4-191.

COUNT(*) Function

The **COUNT (*)** function returns the number of rows that satisfy the WHERE clause of a SELECT statement. The following example finds how many rows in the **stock** table have the value HRO in the **manu_code** column:

```
SELECT COUNT(*) FROM stock WHERE manu_code = 'HRO'
```

If the SELECT statement does not have a WHERE clause, the **COUNT (*)** function returns the total number of rows in the table. The following example finds how many rows are in the **stock** table:

```
SELECT COUNT(*) FROM stock
```

If the SELECT statement contains a GROUP BY clause, the **COUNT (*)** function reflects the number of values in each group. The following example is grouped by the first name; the rows are selected if the database server finds more than one occurrence of the same name:

```
SELECT fname, COUNT(*) FROM customer
    GROUP BY fname
    HAVING COUNT(*) > 1
```

If the value of one or more rows is null, the **COUNT (*)** function includes the null columns in the count unless the WHERE clause explicitly omits them.

COUNT DISTINCT and COUNT UNIQUE Functions

The **COUNT DISTINCT** function return the number of unique values in the column or expression, as the following example shows. If the **COUNT DISTINCT** function encounters nulls, it ignores them.

```
SELECT COUNT (DISTINCT item_num) FROM items
```

Nulls are ignored unless every value in the specified column is null. If every column value is null, the **COUNT DISTINCT** function returns a zero (0) for that column.

The UNIQUE keyword has exactly the same meaning as the DISTINCT keyword when the UNIQUE keyword is used with the COUNT keyword. The UNIQUE keyword returns the number of unique non-null values in the column or expression.

The following example uses the **COUNT UNIQUE** function, but it is equivalent to the preceding example that uses the **COUNT DISTINCT** function:

```
SELECT COUNT (UNIQUE item_num) FROM items
```

COUNT column Function

The **COUNT** *column* function returns the total number of non-null values in the column or expression, as the following example shows:

```
SELECT COUNT (item_num) FROM items
```

You can include the ALL keyword before the specified column name for clarity, but the query result is the same whether you include the ALL keyword or omit it.

The following example shows how to include the ALL keyword in the **COUNT** *column* function:

```
SELECT COUNT (ALL item_num) FROM items
```

Comparison of the Different COUNT Functions

You can use the different forms of the **COUNT** function to retrieve different types of information about a table. The following table summarizes the meaning of each form of the **COUNT** function.

COUNT Function	Description
COUNT (*)	Returns the number of rows that satisfy the query
	If you do not specify a WHERE clause, this function returns the total number of rows in the table.
COUNT DISTINCT or COUNT UNIQUE	Returns the number of unique non-null values in the specified column
COUNT (*column*) or COUNT (ALL *column*)	Returns the total number of non-null values in the specified column

Some examples can help to show the differences among the different forms of the **COUNT** function. The following examples pose queries against the **orders** table in the demonstration database. Most of the examples query against the **ship_instruct** column in this table. For information on the structure of the **orders** table and the data in the **ship_instruct** column, see the description of the demonstration database in the *Informix Guide to SQL: Reference*.

Examples of the Count(*) Function

In the following example, the user wants to know the total number of rows in the **orders** table. So the user uses the **COUNT(*)** function in a SELECT statement without a WHERE clause.

```
SELECT COUNT(*) AS total_rows FROM orders
```

The following table shows the result of this query.

total_rows
23

In the following example, the user wants to know how many rows in the **orders** table have a null value in the **ship_instruct** column. The user uses the **COUNT(*)** function in a SELECT statement with a WHERE clause, and specifies the IS NULL condition in the WHERE clause.

```
SELECT COUNT (*) AS no_ship_instruct
     FROM orders
     WHERE ship_instruct IS NULL
```

The following table shows the result of this query.

no_ship_instruct
2

In the following example, the user wants to know how many rows in the **orders** table have the value express in the **ship_instruct** column. So the user specifies the **COUNT (*)** function in the select list and the equals (=) relational operator in the WHERE clause.

```
SELECT COUNT (*) AS ship_express
     FROM ORDERS
     WHERE ship_instruct = 'express'
```

The following table shows the result of this query.

ship_express
6

Examples of the COUNT column Function

In the following example the user wants to know how many non-null values are in the **ship_instruct** column of the **orders** table. The user enters the COUNT *column* function in the select list of the SELECT statement.

```
SELECT COUNT(ship_instruct) AS total_notnulls
     FROM orders
```

The following table shows the result of this query.

total_notnulls
21

The user can also find out how many non-null values are in the **ship_instruct** column by including the ALL keyword in the parentheses that follow the COUNT keyword.

```
SELECT COUNT (ALL ship_instruct) AS all_notnulls
    FROM orders
```

The following table shows that the query result is the same whether you include or omit the ALL keyword.

all_notnulls
21

Examples of the COUNT DISTINCT Function

In the following example, the user wants to know how many unique non-null values are in the **ship_instruct** column of the **orders** table. The user enters the **COUNT DISTINCT** function in the select list of the SELECT statement.

```
SELECT COUNT(DISTINCT ship_instruct) AS unique_notnulls
    FROM orders
```

The following table shows the result of this query.

unique_notnulls
16

AVG Function

The **AVG** function returns the average of all values in the specified column or expression. You can apply the **AVG** function only to number columns. If you use the DISTINCT keyword, the average (mean) is greater than only the distinct values in the specified column or expression. The query in the following example finds the average price of a helmet:

```
SELECT AVG(unit_price) FROM stock WHERE stock_num = 110
```

Nulls are ignored unless every value in the specified column is null. If every column value is null, the **AVG** function returns a null for that column.

MAX Function

The **MAX** function returns the largest value in the specified column or expression. Using the DISTINCT keyword does not change the results. The query in the following example finds the most expensive item that is in stock but has not been ordered:

```
SELECT MAX(unit_price) FROM stock
    WHERE NOT EXISTS (SELECT * FROM items
        WHERE stock.stock_num = items.stock_num AND
        stock.manu_code = items.manu_code)
```

Nulls are ignored unless every value in the specified column is null. If every column value is null, the **MAX** function returns a null for that column.

MIN Function

The **MIN** function returns the lowest value in the column or expression. Using the DISTINCT keyword does not change the results. The following example finds the least expensive item in the **stock** table:

```
SELECT MIN(unit_price) FROM stock
```

Nulls are ignored unless every value in the specified column is null. If every column value is null, the **MIN** function returns a null for that column.

SUM Function

The **SUM** function returns the sum of all the values in the specified column or expression, as shown in the following example. If you use the DISTINCT keyword, the sum is for only distinct values in the column or expression.

```
SELECT SUM(total_price) FROM items WHERE order_num = 1013
```

Nulls are ignored unless every value in the specified column is null. If every column value is null, the **SUM** function returns a null for that column.

You cannot use the **SUM** function with a character column.

RANGE Function

The **RANGE** function computes the range for a sample of a population. It computes the difference between the maximum and the minimum values, as follows:

```
range(expr) = max(expr) - min(expr)
```

You can apply the **RANGE** function to only numeric columns. The following query finds the range of ages for a population:

```
SELECT RANGE(age) FROM u_pop
```

As with other aggregates, the **RANGE** function applies to the rows of a group when the query includes a GROUP BY clause, as shown in the following example:

```
SELECT RANGE(age) FROM u_pop
    GROUP BY birth
```

Because DATE data types are stored internally as integers, you can use the **RANGE** function on columns of type DATE. When used with a DATE column, the return value is the number of days between the earliest and latest dates in the column.

Nulls are ignored unless every value in the specified column is null. If every column value is null, the **RANGE** function returns a null for that column.

Important: *All computations for the RANGE function are performed in 32-digit precision, which should be sufficient for many sets of input data. The computation, however, loses precision or returns incorrect results when all of the input data values have 16 or more digits of precision.*

STDEV Function

The **STDEV** function computes the standard deviation for a population. It is the square root of the **VARIANCE** function.

You can apply the **STDEV** function only to numeric columns. The following query finds the standard deviation on a population:

```
SELECT STDEV(age) FROM u_pop WHERE u_pop.age > 0
```

As with the other aggregates, the **STDEV** function applies to the rows of a group when the query includes a GROUP BY clause, as shown in the following example:

```
SELECT STDEV(age) FROM u_pop
    GROUP BY birth
    WHERE STDEV(age) > 0
```

Nulls are ignored unless every value in the specified column is null. If every column value is null, the **STDEV** function returns a null for that column.

Important: *All computations for the **STDEV** function are performed in 32-digit precision, which should be sufficient for many sets of input data. The computation, however, loses precision or returns incorrect results when all of the input data values have 16 or more digits of precision.*

Although DATE data is stored internally as an integer, you cannot use this function on columns of type DATE.

VARIANCE Function

The **VARIANCE** function returns the population variance. It computes the following value:

```
(SUM(Xi²) - (SUM(Xi)²)/N)/N
```

In this formula, Xi is each value in the column and N is the total number of values in the column.

You can apply the **VARIANCE** function only to numeric columns.

The following query finds the variance on a population:

```
SELECT VARIANCE(age) FROM u_pop WHERE u_pop.age > 0
```

As with the other aggregates, the **VARIANCE** function applies to the rows of a group when the query includes a GROUP BY clause, as shown in the following example:

```
SELECT VARIANCE(age) FROM u_pop
    GROUP BY birth
    WHERE VARIANCE(age) > 0
```

When you use the **VARIANCE** function, nulls are ignored unless every value in the specified column is null. If every column value is null, the **VARIANCE** function returns a null for that column. If the total number of values in the column is equal to one, the **VARIANCE** function returns a zero variance. If you want to omit this special case, you can adjust the query construction. For example, you might include a **HAVING COUNT(*) > 1** clause.

Important: *All computations for the **VARIANCE** function are performed in 32-digit precision, which should be sufficient for many sets of input data. The computation, however, loses precision or returns incorrect results when all of the input data values have 16 or more digits of precision.*

Although DATE data is stored internally as an integer, you cannot use this function on columns of type DATE.

Summary of Aggregate Function Behavior

An example can help to summarize the behavior of the aggregate functions. Assume that the **testtable** table has a single INTEGER column that is named **a_number**. The contents of this table are as follows.

a_number
2
2
2
3
3
4
(null)

You can use aggregate functions to obtain different types of information about the **a_number** column and the **testtable** table. In the following example, the user specifies the **AVG** function to obtain the average of all the non-null values in the **a_number** column:

```
SELECT AVG(a_number) AS average_number
       FROM testtable
```

The following table shows the result of this query.

average_number
2.66666666666667

You can use the other aggregate functions in SELECT statements that are similar to the one shown in the preceding example. If you enter a series of SELECT statements that have different aggregate functions in the select list and do not have a WHERE clause, you receive the results that the following table shows.

Function	Results
COUNT (*)	7
COUNT (DISTINCT)	3
COUNT (ALL a_number)	6
COUNT (a_number)	6
AVG	2.66666666666667
AVG (DISTINCT)	3.00000000000000
MAX	4
MAX(DISTINCT)	4
MIN	2
MIN(DISTINCT)	2
SUM	16

(1 of 2)

Function	Results
SUM(DISTINCT)	9
RANGE	2
STDEV	0.74535599249993
VARIANCE	0.55555555555556

E/C

Error Checking in ESQL/C

Aggregate functions always return one row; if no rows are selected, the function returns a null. You can use the **COUNT (*)** function to determine whether any rows were selected, and you can use an indicator variable to determine whether any selected rows were empty. Fetching a row with a cursor associated with an aggregate function always returns one row; hence, 100 for end of data is never returned into the **sqlcode** variable for a first fetch attempt.

You can also use the GET DIAGNOSTICS statement for error checking. ♦

IDS

User-Defined Aggregates

You can create your own aggregate expressions with the CREATE AGGREGATE statement and then invoke these aggregates wherever you can invoke the built-in aggregates. The following diagram shows the syntax for invoking a user-defined aggregate.

Expression

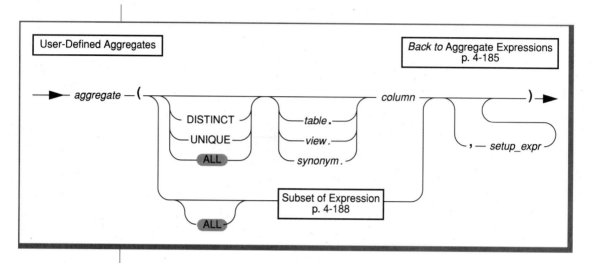

Element	Purpose	Restrictions	Syntax
aggregate	Name of the user-defined aggregate to invoke	The user-defined aggregate and the support functions defined for the aggregate must exist.	Identifier, p. 4-205
column	Name of a column within table whose storage characteristics are used for the copy of the BLOB or CLOB value	This column must have CLOB or BLOB as its data type.	Quoted String, p. 4-260
setup_expr	Set-up expression that customizes the aggregate for a particular invocation	Any columns referenced in the set-up expression must be listed in the GROUP BY clause of the query. The set-up expression cannot be a lone host variable.	Expression, p. 4-73
synonym	Name of the synonym in which the specified column occurs	The synonym and the table to which the synonym points must exist.	Database Object Name, p. 4-50
table	Name of the table in which the specified column occurs	The table must exist.	Database Object Name, p. 4-50
view	Name of the view in which the specified column occurs	The view must exist.	Database Object Name, p. 4-50

Use the DISTINCT or UNIQUE keywords to specify that the user-defined aggregate is to be applied only to unique values in the named column or expression. Use the ALL keyword to specify that the aggregate is to be applied to all values in the named column or expression. If you omit the DISTINCT, UNIQUE, and ALL keywords, ALL is the default value. For further information on the DISTINCT, UNIQUE, and ALL keywords, see "Including or Excluding Duplicates in the Row Set" on page 4-189.

When you specify a set-up expression, this value is passed to the **INIT** support function that was defined for the user-defined aggregate in the CREATE AGGREGATE statement.

In the following example, you apply the user-defined aggregate named **my_avg** to all values of the **quantity** column in the **items** table:

```
SELECT my_avg(quantity) FROM items
```

In the following example, you apply the user-defined aggregate named **my_sum** to unique values of the **quantity** column in the **items** table. You also supply the value 5 as a set-up expression. This value might specify that the initial value of the sum that **my_avg** will compute is 5.

```
SELECT my_sum(DISTINCT quantity, 5) FROM items
```

For further information on user-defined aggregates, see "CREATE AGGREGATE" on page 2-115 and the discussion of user-defined aggregates in *Extending Informix Dynamic Server 2000*.

Related Information

For a discussion of expressions in the context of the SELECT statement, see the *Informix Guide to SQL: Tutorial*.

For discussions of column expressions, length functions, and the **TRIM** function, see the *Informix Guide to GLS Functionality*.

External Routine Reference

Use an External Routine Reference when you write an external routine.

Syntax

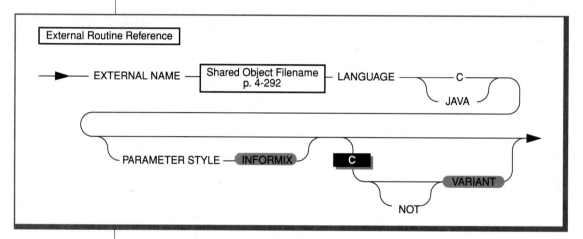

Usage

The External Routine Reference provides the following information about an external routine:

- The pathname to the executable object code, stored in a shared-object file

  For C, this file is either a DLL or a shared library, depending on your operating system.

  For Java, this file is a jar file. Before you can create a UDR written in Java, you must assign a jar identifier to the external jar file with the **sqlj.install_jar** procedure. For more information, see "sqlj.install_jar" on page 2-447.

- The name of the language in which the UDR is written

- The parameter style of the UDR

- The **VARIANT** or **NOT VARIANT** option, if you specify one

  This option applies only to C user-defined functions. ♦

Parameter Style

By default, the parameter style is INFORMIX. If you specify an OUT parameter, the OUT argument is passed by reference.

VARIANT or NOT VARIANT

The **VARIANT** and **NOT VARIANT** options apply only to user-defined functions written in C.

A function is *variant* if it returns different results when it is invoked with the same arguments or if it modifies a database or variable state. For example, a function that returns the current date or time is a variant function.

By default, user-defined functions are variant. If you specify **NOT VARIANT** when you create or modify a function, the function cannot contain any SQL statements.

If the function is nonvariant, the database server might cache the return variant functions. For more information on functional indexes, see "CREATE INDEX" on page 2-157.

To register a nonvariant function, add the NOT VARIANT option in this clause or in the Routine Modifier clause that is discussed in "Routine Modifier" on page 4-274. However, if you specify the modifier in both places, you must use the same modifier in both clauses.

Example of a C User-Defined Function

The following example registers an external function named **equal()** that takes two values of **point** data type as arguments. In this example, **point** is an opaque type that specifies the **x** and **y** coordinates of a two-dimensional point.

```
CREATE FUNCTION equal( a point, b point )
RETURNING BOOLEAN;
EXTERNAL NAME
"/usr/lib/point/lib/libbtype1.so(point1_equal)"
LANGUAGE C
END FUNCTION
```

The function returns a single value of type BOOLEAN. The external name specifies the path to the C shared object file where the object code of the function is stored. The external name indicates that the library contains another function, **point1_equal**, which is invoked while **equal(point, point)** is executing.

Identifier

An identifier specifies the simple name of a database object, such as a column, table, index, or view. Use the Identifier segment whenever you see a reference to an identifier in a syntax diagram.

Syntax

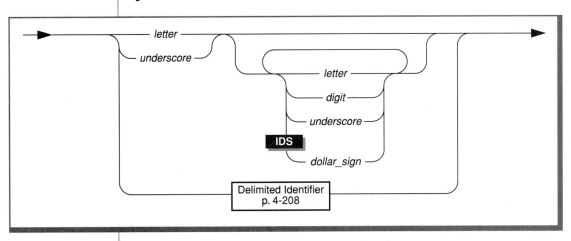

Element	Purpose	Restrictions	Syntax
digit	Integer that forms part of the identifier	You must specify a number between 0 and 9, inclusive. The first character of an identifier cannot be a number.	Literal Number, p. 4-237
dollar_sign	Dollar sign symbol ($) that forms part of the identifier	The dollar-sign symbol cannot be the first character of an identifier. Informix recommends that you do not use the dollar-sign symbol in identifiers because this symbol is a special character and the use of this symbol in an identifier might cause conflicts with other syntax elements.	A dollar sign symbol ($) is a literal value that you enter from the keyboard.

(1 of 2)

Element	Purpose	Restrictions	Syntax
letter	Letter that forms part of the identifier	If you are using the default locale, a letter must be an alphabetical uppercase or lowercase character in the range of A to Z or a to z (in the ASCII code set). If you are using a nondefault locale, *letter* must be an alphabetic character that the locale supports. For further information, see "Support for Non-ASCII Characters in Identifiers" on page 4-208.	Letters are literal values that you enter from the keyboard.
underscore	Underscore character (_) that forms part of the identifier	You cannot substitute a space character, dash, hyphen, or any other nonalphanumeric character for the underscore character.	Underscore character (_) is a literal value that you enter from the keyboard.

(2 of 2)

Usage

The elements of an identifier cannot be separated by blanks. To include a space character in an identifier, you must specify a delimited identifier. For more information, see "Delimited Identifiers" on page 4-208.

IDS

An identifier can contain up to 128 bytes, inclusive. For example, the following table name is valid: **employee_information**. ♦

EDS

An identifier can contain up to 18 bytes, inclusive. For example, the following table name is valid: **employee_info**. ♦

GLS

If you are using a multibyte code set, keep in mind that the maximum length of an identifier refers to the number of bytes, not the number of characters. For further information on the GLS aspects of identifiers, see the *Informix Guide to GLS Functionality*. ♦

IDS

E/C

The database server checks the internal version number of the client application and the setting of the **IFX_LONGID** environment variable to determine whether a client application is capable of handling long identifiers (identifiers that are up to 128 bytes in length). For further information on the **IFX_LONGID** environment variable, see the *Informix Guide to SQL: Reference*. ♦

Use of Uppercase Characters

You can specify the name of a database object with uppercase characters, but the database server shifts the name to lowercase characters unless the **DELIMIDENT** environment variable is set and the name of the database object is enclosed in double quotes. When these conditions are true, the database server treats the name of the database object as a delimited identifier and preserves the uppercase characters in the name. For further information on delimited identifiers, see "Delimited Identifiers" on page 4-208.

Use of Reserved Words as Identifiers

Although you can use almost any word as an identifier, syntactic ambiguities can result from using reserved words as identifiers in SQL statements. The statement might fail or might not produce the expected results. For a discussion of the syntactic ambiguities that can result from using reserved words as identifiers and an explanation of workarounds for these problems, see "Potential Ambiguities and Syntax Errors" on page 4-211.

IDS For a list of all the reserved words in the Informix implementation of SQL in Dynamic Server, see Appendix A, "Reserved Words for Dynamic Server". ♦

EDS For a list of all the reserved words in the Informix implementation of SQL in Enterprise Decision Server, see Appendix B, "Reserved Words for Enterprise Decision Server". ♦

Delimited identifiers provide the easiest and safest way to use a reserved word as an identifier without causing syntactic ambiguities. No workarounds are necessary when you use a reserved word as a delimited identifier. For the syntax and usage of delimited identifiers, see "Delimited Identifiers" on page 4-208.

Tip: *If you receive an error message that seems unrelated to the statement that caused the error, check to determine whether the statement uses a reserved word as an undelimited identifier.*

GLS

Support for Non-ASCII Characters in Identifiers

If you are using a nondefault locale, you can use any alphabetic character that your locale recognizes as a *letter* in an SQL identifier name. You can use a non-ASCII character as a letter as long as your locale supports it. This feature enables you to use non-ASCII characters in the names of database objects such as indexes, tables, and views. For a list of SQL identifiers that support non-ASCII characters, see the *Informix Guide to GLS Functionality*.

Delimited Identifiers

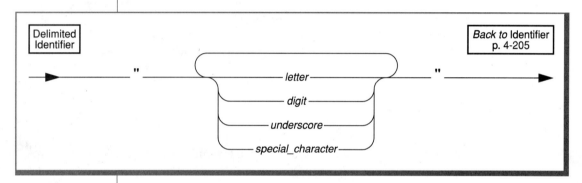

Element	Purpose	Restrictions	Syntax
digit	Integer that forms part of the delimited identifier	You must specify a number between 0 and 9, inclusive.	Literal Number, p. 4-237
letter	Letter that forms part of the delimited identifier	Letters in delimited identifiers are case-sensitive. If you are using the default locale, a letter must be an uppercase or lowercase character in the range a to z (in the ASCII code set). If you are using a nondefault locale, *letter* must be an alphabetic character that the locale supports. For more information, see "Support for Non-ASCII Characters in Delimited Identifiers" on page 4-209.	Letters are literal values that you enter from the keyboard.

(1 of 2)

Element	Purpose	Restrictions	Syntax
special_character	Nonalphanumeric character, such as #, $, or a space, that forms part of the delimited identifier	If you are using the ASCII code set, you can specify any ASCII nonalphanumeric character.	Nonalphanumeric characters are literal values that you enter from the keyboard.
underscore	Underscore (_) that forms part of the delimited identifier	You can use a dash (--), hyphen (-), or any other appropriate character in place of the underscore character.	Underscore (_) is a literal value that you enter from the keyboard.

(2 of 2)

Delimited identifiers allow you to specify names for database objects that are otherwise identical to SQL reserved keywords, such as TABLE, WHERE, DECLARE, and so on. The only database object for which you cannot use delimited identifiers is database name.

Delimited identifiers are case sensitive.

Delimited identifiers are compliant with the ANSI standard.

When you create a database object, avoid including one or more trailing blanks in a delimited identifier. In other words, immediately follow the last non-blank character of the name with the end quote.

Support for Nonalphanumeric Characters

You can use delimited identifiers to specify nonalphanumeric characters in the names of database objects. However, you cannot use delimited identifiers to specify nonalphanumeric characters in the names of storage objects such as dbspaces and blobspaces.

GLS

Support for Non-ASCII Characters in Delimited Identifiers

When you are using a nondefault locale whose code set supports non-ASCII characters, you can specify non-ASCII characters in most delimited identifiers. The rule is that if you can specify non-ASCII characters in the undelimited form of the identifier, you can also specify non-ASCII characters in the delimited form of the same identifier. For a list of identifiers that support non-ASCII characters and for information on non-ASCII characters in delimited identifiers, see the *Informix Guide to GLS Functionality*.

Effect of DELIMIDENT Environment Variable

To use delimited identifiers, you must set the **DELIMIDENT** environment variable. When you set the **DELIMIDENT** environment variable, database objects enclosed in double quotes (") are treated as identifiers and database objects enclosed in single quotes (') are treated as strings. If the **DELIMIDENT** environment variable is not set, values enclosed in double quotes are also treated as strings.

If the **DELIMIDENT** environment variable is set, the SELECT statement in the following example must be in single quotes in order to be treated as a quoted string:

```
PREPARE ... FROM 'SELECT * FROM customer'
```

If a delimited identifier name is used in the SELECT statement that defines a view, then the **DELIMIDENT** environment variable must be set in order for the view to be accessed, even if the view name itself contains no special characters.

Examples of Delimited Identifiers

The following example shows how to create a table with a case-sensitive table name:

```
CREATE TABLE "Power_Ranger" (...)
```

The following example shows how to create a table whose name includes a space character. If the table name were not enclosed in double quotes ("), you could not use a space character in the name.

```
CREATE TABLE "My Customers" (...)
```

The following example shows how to create a table that uses a keyword as the table name:

```
CREATE TABLE "TABLE" (...)
```

Using Double Quotes Within a Delimited Identifier

If you want to include a double-quote (") in a delimited identifier, you must precede the double-quote (") with another double-quote ("), as shown in the following example:

```
CREATE TABLE "My""Good""Data" (...)
```

Potential Ambiguities and Syntax Errors

Although you can use almost any word as an SQL identifier, syntactic ambiguities can occur. An ambiguous statement might not produce the desired results. The following sections outline some potential pitfalls and workarounds.

Using Functions as Column Names

The following two examples show a workaround for using a built-in function as a column name in a SELECT statement. This workaround applies to the aggregate functions (AVG, COUNT, MAX, MIN, SUM) as well as the function expressions (algebraic, exponential and logarithmic, time, hex, length, dbinfo, trigonometric, and trim functions).

Using **avg** as a column name causes the following example to fail because the database server interprets **avg** as an aggregate function rather than as a column name:

```
SELECT avg FROM mytab -- fails
```

If the **DELIMIDENT** environment variable is set, you could use **avg** as a column name as shown in the following example:

```
SELECT "avg" from mytab -- successful
```

The workaround in the following example removes ambiguity by including a table name with the column name:

```
SELECT mytab.avg FROM mytab
```

If you use the keyword TODAY, CURRENT, or USER as a column name, ambiguity can occur, as shown in the following example:

```
CREATE TABLE mytab (user char(10),
    CURRENT DATETIME HOUR TO SECOND,TODAY DATE)

INSERT INTO mytab VALUES('josh','11:30:30','1/22/98')

SELECT user,current,today FROM mytab
```

The database server interprets **user**, **current**, and **today** in the SELECT statement as the built-in functions USER, CURRENT, and TODAY. Thus, instead of returning josh, 11:30:30,1/22/89, the SELECT statement returns the current user name, the current time, and the current date.

If you want to select the actual columns of the table, you must write the SELECT statement in one of the following ways:

```
SELECT mytab.user, mytab.current, mytab.today FROM mytab;

EXEC SQL select * from mytab;
```

Using Keywords as Column Names

Specific workarounds exist for using a keyword as a column name in a SELECT statement or other SQL statement. In some cases, more than one suitable workaround might be available.

Using ALL, DISTINCT, or UNIQUE as a Column Name

If you want to use the ALL, DISTINCT, or UNIQUE keywords as column names in a SELECT statement, you can take advantage of a workaround.

First, consider what happens when you try to use one of these keywords without a workaround. In the following example, using **all** as a column name causes the SELECT statement to fail because the database server interprets **all** as a keyword rather than as a column name:

```
SELECT all FROM mytab -- fails
```

You need to use a workaround to make this SELECT statement execute successfully. If the **DELIMIDENT** environment variable is set, you can use **all** as a column name by enclosing **all** in double quotes. In the following example, the SELECT statement executes successfully because the database server interprets **all** as a column name:

```
SELECT "all" from mytab -- successful
```

The workaround in the following example uses the keyword ALL with the column name **all**:

```
SELECT ALL all FROM mytab
```

The rest of the examples in this section show workarounds for using the keywords UNIQUE or DISTINCT as a column name in a CREATE TABLE statement.

Using **unique** as a column name causes the following example to fail because the database server interprets **unique** as a keyword rather than as a column name:

```
CREATE TABLE mytab (unique INTEGER) -- fails
```

The workaround in the following example uses two SQL statements. The first statement creates the column **mycol**; the second renames the column **mycol** to **unique**.

```
CREATE TABLE mytab (mycol INTEGER)

RENAME COLUMN mytab.mycol TO unique
```

The workaround in the following example also uses two SQL statements. The first statement creates the column **mycol**; the second alters the table, adds the column **unique**, and drops the column **mycol**.

```
CREATE TABLE mytab (mycol INTEGER)

ALTER TABLE mytab
    ADD (unique integer)
    DROP (mycol)
```

Using INTERVAL or DATETIME as a Column Name

The examples in this section show workarounds for using the keyword INTERVAL (or DATETIME) as a column name in a SELECT statement.

Using **interval** as a column name causes the following example to fail because the database server interprets **interval** as a keyword and expects it to be followed by an INTERVAL qualifier:

```
SELECT interval FROM mytab -- fails
```

If the **DELIMIDENT** environment variable is set, you could use **interval** as a column name, as shown in the following example:

```
SELECT "interval" from mytab -- successful
```

The workaround in the following example removes ambiguity by specifying a table name with the column name:

```
SELECT mytab.interval FROM mytab;
```

The workaround in the following example includes an owner name with the table name:

```
SELECT josh.mytab.interval FROM josh.mytab;
```

IDS

Using rowid as a Column Name

Every nonfragmented table has a virtual column named **rowid**. To avoid ambiguity, you cannot use **rowid** as a column name. Performing the following actions causes an error:

- Creating a table or view with a column named **rowid**
- Altering a table by adding a column named rowid
- Renaming a column to rowid

You can, however, use the term rowid as a table name.

```
CREATE TABLE rowid (column INTEGER,
    date DATE, char CHAR(20))
```

Important: *Informix recommends that you use primary keys as an access method rather than exploiting the* **rowid** *column.*

Using Keywords as Table Names

The examples in this section show workarounds that involve owner naming when you use the keyword STATISTICS or OUTER as a table name. This workaround also applies to the use of STATISTICS or OUTER as a view name or synonym.

Using **statistics** as a table name causes the following example to fail because the database server interprets it as part of the UPDATE STATISTICS syntax rather than as a table name in an UPDATE statement:

```
UPDATE statistics SET mycol = 10
```

The workaround in the following example specifies an owner name with the table name, to avoid ambiguity:

```
UPDATE josh.statistics SET mycol = 10
```

Using **outer** as a table name causes the following example to fail because the database server interprets **outer** as a keyword for performing an outer join:

```
SELECT mycol FROM outer -- fails
```

The workaround in the following example uses owner naming to avoid ambiguity:

```
SELECT mycol FROM josh.outer
```

Workarounds That Use the Keyword AS

In some cases, although a statement is not ambiguous and the syntax is correct, the database server returns a syntax error. The preceding pages show existing syntactic workarounds for several situations. You can use the AS keyword to provide a workaround for the exceptions.

You can use the AS keyword in front of column labels or table aliases.

The following example uses the AS keyword with a column label:

```
SELECT column-name AS display-label FROM table-name
```

The following example uses the AS keyword with a table alias:

```
SELECT select-list FROM table-name AS table-alias
```

Using AS with Column Labels

The examples in this section show workarounds that use the AS keyword with a column label. The first two examples show how you can use the keyword UNITS (or YEAR, MONTH, DAY, HOUR, MINUTE, SECOND, or FRACTION) as a column label.

Using **units** as a column label causes the following example to fail because the database server interprets it as a DATETIME qualifier for the column named **mycol**:

```
SELECT mycol units FROM mytab
```

The workaround in the following example includes the AS keyword:

```
SELECT mycol AS units FROM mytab;
```

The following examples show how the AS or FROM keyword can be used as a column label.

Using **as** as a column label causes the following example to fail because the database server interprets **as** as identifying **from** as a column label and thus finds no required FROM clause:

```
SELECT mycol as from mytab -- fails
```

The following example repeats the AS keyword:

```
SELECT mycol AS as from mytab
```

Using **from** as a column label causes the following example to fail because the database server expects a table name to follow the first **from**:

```
SELECT mycol from FROM mytab -- fails
```

The following example uses the AS keyword to identify the first **from** as a column label:

```
SELECT mycol AS from FROM mytab
```

Using AS with Table Aliases

The examples in this section show workarounds that use the AS keyword with a table alias. The first pair shows how to use the ORDER, FOR, GROUP, HAVING, INTO, UNION, WITH, CREATE, GRANT, or WHERE keyword as a table alias.

Using **order** as a table alias causes the following example to fail because the database server interprets **order** as part of an ORDER BY clause:

```
SELECT * FROM mytab order -- fails
```

The workaround in the following example uses the keyword AS to identify **order** as a table alias:

```
SELECT * FROM mytab AS order;
```

The following two examples show how to use the keyword WITH as a table alias.

Using **with** as a table alias causes the following example to fail because the database server interprets the keyword as part of the WITH CHECK OPTION syntax:

```
EXEC SQL select * from mytab with; -- fails
```

The workaround in the following example uses the keyword AS to identify **with** as a table alias:

```
EXEC SQL select * from mytab as with;
```

The following two examples show how to use the keyword CREATE (or GRANT) as a table alias.

Using **create** as a table alias causes the following example to fail because the database server interprets the keyword as part of the syntax to create an entity such as a table, synonym, or view:

```
EXEC SQL select * from mytab create; -- fails
```

The workaround in the following example uses the keyword AS to identify **create** as a table alias:

```
EXEC SQL select * from mytab as create;
```

Fetching Keywords as Cursor Names

In a few situations, no workaround exists for the syntactic ambiguity that occurs when a keyword is used as an identifier in an SQL program.

In the following example, the FETCH statement specifies a cursor named **next**. The FETCH statement generates a syntax error because the preprocessor interprets **next** as a keyword, signifying the next row in the active set and expects a cursor name to follow **next**. This occurs whenever the keyword NEXT, PREVIOUS, PRIOR, FIRST, LAST, CURRENT, RELATIVE, or ABSOLUTE is used as a cursor name.

```
/* This code fragment fails */
EXEC SQL declare next cursor for
    select customer_num, lname from customer;

EXEC SQL open next;
EXEC SQL fetch next into :cnum, :lname;
```

Using Keywords as Variable Names in UDRs

If you use any of the following keywords as identifiers for variables in a user-defined routine (UDR), you can create ambiguous syntax.

CURRENT	OFF
DATETIME	ON
GLOBAL	PROCEDURE
INTERVAL	SELECT
NULL	

Using CURRENT, DATETIME, INTERVAL, and NULL in INSERT

A UDR cannot insert a variable using the CURRENT, DATETIME, INTERVAL, or NULL keyword as the name.

For example, if you define a variable called **null**, when you try to insert the value **null** into a column, you receive a syntax error, as shown in the following example:

```
CREATE PROCEDURE problem()
    .
    .
    .
DEFINE null INT;
LET null = 3;
INSERT INTO tab VALUES (null); -- error, inserts NULL, not 3
```

Using NULL and SELECT in a Condition

If you define a variable with the name *null* or *select*, using it in a condition that uses the IN keyword is ambiguous. The following example shows three conditions that cause problems: in an IF statement, in a WHERE clause of a SELECT statement, and in a WHILE condition:

```
CREATE PROCEDURE problem()
    .
    .
    .
DEFINE x,y,select, null, INT;
DEFINE pfname CHAR[15];
LET x = 3; LET select = 300;
LET null = 1;
IF x IN (select, 10, 12) THEN LET y = 1; -- problem if

IF x IN (1, 2, 4) THEN
SELECT customer_num, fname INTO y, pfname FROM customer
    WHERE customer IN (select , 301 , 302, 303); -- problem in

WHILE x IN (null, 2) -- problem while
    .
    .
    .
END WHILE;
```

You can use the variable *select* in an IN list if you ensure it is not the first element in the list. The workaround in the following example corrects the IF statement shown in the preceding example:

```
IF x IN (10, select, 12) THEN LET y = 1; -- problem if
```

No workaround exists to using *null* as a variable name and attempting to use it in an IN condition.

Using ON, OFF, or PROCEDURE with TRACE

If you define an SPL variable called *on*, *off*, or *procedure*, and you attempt to use it in a TRACE statement, the value of the variable does not trace. Instead, the TRACE ON, TRACE OFF, or TRACE PROCEDURE statements execute. You can trace the value of the variable by making the variable into a more complex expression. The following example shows the ambiguous syntax and the workaround:

```
DEFINE on, off, procedure INT;

TRACE on;          --ambiguous
TRACE 0+ on;       --ok
TRACE off;         --ambiguous
TRACE ''||off;     --ok

TRACE procedure;--ambiguous
TRACE 0+procedure;--ok
```

Using GLOBAL as a Variable Name

If you attempt to define a variable with the name *global*, the define operation fails. The syntax shown in the following example conflicts with the syntax for defining global variables:

```
DEFINE global INT; -- fails;
```

If the **DELIMIDENT** environment variable is set, you could use **global** as a variable name, as shown in the following example:

```
DEFINE "global" INT; -- successful
```

Using EXECUTE, SELECT, or WITH as Cursor Names

Do not use an EXECUTE, SELECT, or WITH keyword as the name of a cursor. If you try to use one of these keywords as the name of a cursor in a FOREACH statement, the cursor name is interpreted as a keyword in the FOREACH statement. No workaround exists.

The following example does not work:

```
DEFINE execute INT;
FOREACH execute FOR SELECT col1 -- error, looks like
                            -- FOREACH EXECUTE PROCEDURE
        INTO var1 FROM tab1; --
```

SELECT Statements in WHILE and FOR Statements

If you use a SELECT statement in a WHILE or FOR loop, and if you need to enclose it in parentheses, enclose the entire SELECT statement in a BEGIN…END statement block. The SELECT statement in the first WHILE statement in the following example is interpreted as a call to the procedure **var1**; the second WHILE statement is interpreted correctly:

```
DEFINE var1, var2 INT;
WHILE var2 = var1
    SELECT col1 INTO var3 FROM TAB -- error, seen as call
var1()
    UNION
    SELECT co2 FROM tab2;
END WHILE

WHILE var2 = var1
    BEGIN
        SELECT col1 INTO var3 FROM TAB -- ok syntax
        UNION
        SELECT co2 FROM tab2;
    END
END WHILE
```

SET Keyword in the ON EXCEPTION Statement

If you use a statement that begins with the keyword SET inside the statement ON EXCEPTION, you must enclose it in a BEGIN…END statement block. The following list shows some of the SQL statements that begin with the keyword SET.

SET	SET LOCK MODE
SET DEBUG FILE	SET LOG
SET EXPLAIN	SET OPTIMIZATION
SET ISOLATION	SET PDQPRIORITY

The following examples show incorrect and correct use of a SET LOCK MODE statement inside an ON EXCEPTION statement.

The following ON EXCEPTION statement returns an error because the SET LOCK MODE statement is not enclosed in a BEGIN…END statement block:

```
ON EXCEPTION IN (-107)
    SET LOCK MODE TO WAIT; -- error, value expected, not 'lock'
END EXCEPTION
```

The following ON EXCEPTION statement executes successfully because the SET LOCK MODE statement is enclosed in a BEGIN...END statement block:

```
ON EXCEPTION IN (-107)
    BEGIN
    SET LOCK MODE TO WAIT; -- ok
    END
END EXCEPTION
```

Related Information

For a discussion of owner naming, see your *Performance Guide*.

For a discussion of identifiers that support non-ASCII characters and a discussion of non-ASCII characters in delimited identifiers, see the *Informix Guide to GLS Functionality*.

INTERVAL Field Qualifier

The INTERVAL field qualifier specifies the units for an INTERVAL value. Use the INTERVAL Field Qualifier segment whenever you see a reference to an INTERVAL field qualifier in a syntax diagram.

Syntax

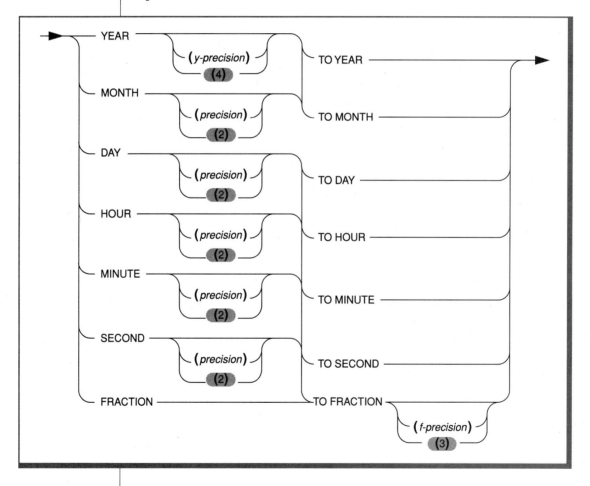

Element	Purpose	Restrictions	Syntax
f-precision	Maximum number of digits used in the fraction field	The maximum value that you can specify in *f-precision* is 5.	Literal Number, p. 4-237
	The default value of f-precision is 3.		
precision	Number of digits in the largest number of months, days, hours, or minutes that the interval can hold	The maximum value that you can specify in *precision* is 9.	Literal Number, p. 4-237
	The default value of precision is 2.		
y-precision	Number of digits in the largest number of years that the interval can hold	The maximum value that you can specify in *y-precision* is 9.	Literal Number, p. 4-237
	The default value of y-precision is 4.		

Usage

The next two examples show INTERVAL data types of the YEAR TO MONTH type. The first example can hold an interval of up to 999 years and 11 months, because it gives 3 as the precision of the year field. The second example uses the default precision on the year field, so it can hold an interval of up to 9,999 years and 11 months.

```
YEAR (3) TO MONTH

YEAR TO MONTH
```

When you want a value to contain only one field, the first and last qualifiers are the same. For example, an interval of whole years is qualified as YEAR TO YEAR or YEAR (5) TO YEAR, for an interval of up to 99,999 years.

The following examples show several forms of INTERVAL qualifiers:

```
YEAR(5) TO MONTH

DAY (5) TO FRACTION(2)

DAY TO DAY

FRACTION TO FRACTION (4)
```

Related Information

For information about how to specify INTERVAL field qualifiers and use INTERVAL data in arithmetic and relational operations, see the discussion of the INTERVAL data type in the *Informix Guide to SQL: Reference*.

IDS

Jar Name

Use the Jar Name segment to specify the name of a jar ID. Use this segment whenever you see a reference to Jar Name in a syntax diagram.

Syntax

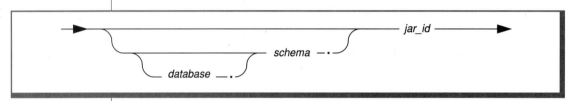

Element	Purpose	Restrictions	Syntax
database	Name of the database in which to install or access jar_id The default is the current database.	The fully qualified identifier of database.package.jar_id must not exceed 255 bytes.	Identifier, p. 4-205
jar_id	Name of the jar file that contains the Java class which you want to access	The *jar_id* must correspond to a jar identifier in the current database. The fully qualified identifier of *database.package.jar_id* must not exceed 255 bytes.	Identifier, p. 4-205
schema	Name of the schema The default is the current schema.	The fully qualified identifier of *database.package.jar_id* must not exceed 255 bytes.	Identifier, p. 4-205

If a Jar name is specified as a character string value to the **sqlj.install_jar**, **sqlj.replace_jar**, or **sqlj.remove_jar** procedures, then any identifiers in the jar name that are delimited identifiers will include the surrounding double quote characters.

Before you can access a *jar_id* in any way (including its use in a CREATE FUNCTION or CREATE PROCEDURE statement), it must be defined in the current database with the **install_jar()** procedure. For more information, see "EXECUTE PROCEDURE" on page 2-444.

IDS

Literal Collection

Use the Literal Collection segment to specify values for a collection column. For syntax that allows you to use expressions that evaluate to element values, see "Collection Constructors" on page 4-118.

Syntax

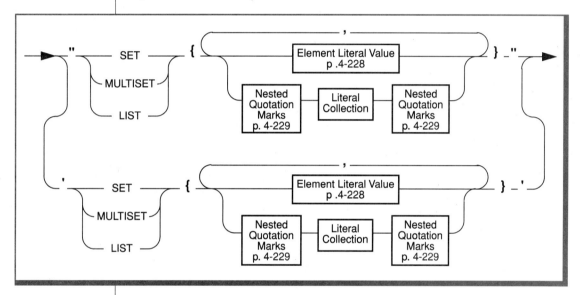

Usage

You can specify literal collection values for each of the collection data types: SET, MULTISET, or LIST.

To specify a single literal-collection value, specify the collection type and the literal values. The following SQL statement inserts four integer values into the **set_col** column that is declared as SET(INT NOT NULL):

```
INSERT INTO table1 (set_col) VALUES ("SET{6, 9, 9, 4}")
```

You specify an empty collection with a set of empty braces ({}). The following INSERT statement inserts an empty list into a collection column **list_col** that is declared as LIST(INT NOT NULL):

```
INSERT INTO table2 (list_col) VALUES ("LIST{}")
```

SQLE

If you are passing a literal collection as an argument to an SPL routine, make sure that there is a space between the parentheses that surround the arguments and the quotation marks that indicate the beginning and end of the literal collection. ♦

If you specify a collection as a literal value in a literal row string you need not include the quotation marks around the collection itself. Only the outermost quotation marks that delineate the row string literal are necessary. No quotation marks need surround the nested collection type. For an example, see "Literals for Nested Rows" on page 4-243.

Element Literal Value

The diagram for "Literal Collection" on page 4-227 refers to this section.

Elements of a collection can be literal values for the data types in the following table.

For a Collection of Type	Literal Value Syntax
BOOLEAN	't' or 'f', representing true or false The literal must be specified as a quoted string.
CHAR, VARCHAR, NCHAR, NVARCHAR, CHARACTER VARYING, DATE	Quoted String, p. 4-260
DATETIME	Literal DATETIME, p. 4-231
DECIMAL, MONEY, FLOAT, INTEGER, INT8, SMALLFLOAT, SMALLINT	Literal Number, p.4-237
INTERVAL	Literal INTERVAL, p. 4-234

(1 of 2)

For a Collection of Type	Literal Value Syntax
Opaque data types	Quoted String, p. 4-260
	The string must be a literal that is recognized by the input support function for the associated opaque type.
Row Type	"Literal Row" on page 4-239
	When the collection element type is a named row type, you do not have to cast the values that you insert to the named row type.

(2 of 2)

Important: *You cannot specify the simple-large-object data types (BYTE and TEXT) as the element type for a collection.*

Quoted strings must be specified with a different type of quotation mark than the quotation marks that encompass the collection so that the database server can parse the quoted strings. Therefore, if you use double quotation marks to specify the collection, use single quotation marks to specify individual, quoted-string elements.

Nested Quotation Marks

The diagram for "Literal Collection" on page 4-227 refers to this section.

A *nested collection* is a collection that is the element type for another collection.

Whenever you nest collection literals, you use nested quotation marks. In these cases, you must follow the rule for nesting quotation marks. Otherwise, the server cannot correctly parse the strings.

The general rule is that you must double the number of quotation marks for each new level of nesting. For example, if you use double quotation marks for the first level, you must use two double quotation marks for the second level, four double quotation marks for the third level, eight for the fourth level, sixteen for the fifth level, and so on. Likewise, if you use single quotes for the first level, you must use two single quotation marks for the second level and four single quotation marks for the third level.

There is no limit to the number of levels you can nest, as long as you follow this rule.

Example of Nested Quotation Marks

The following example illustrates the case for two levels of nested collection literals, using double quotation marks. Table **tab5** is a one-column table whose column, **set_col**, is a nested collection type.

The following statement creates the **tab5** table:

```
CREATE TABLE tab5 (set_col SET(SET(INT NOT NULL) NOT NULL));
```

The following statement inserts values into the table **tab5**:

```
INSERT INTO tab5 VALUES (
"SET{""SET{34, 56, 23, 33}""}"
)
```

For any individual literal value, the opening quotation marks and the closing quotation marks must match. In other words, if you open a literal with two double quotes, you must close that literal with two double quotes (""a literal value"").

E/C

To specify nested quotation marks within an SQL statement in an ESQL/C program, you use the C escape character for every double quote inside a single-quote string. Otherwise, the ESQL/C preprocessor cannot correctly interpret the literal collection value. For example, the preceding INSERT statement on the **tab5** table would appear in an ESQL/C program as follows:

```
EXEC SQL insert into tab5
    values ('set{\"set{34, 56, 23, 33}\"}');
```

For more information, see the chapter on complex data types in the *Informix ESQL/C Programmer's Manual.* ♦

If the collection is a nested collection, you must include the collection-constructor syntax for each level of collection type. Suppose you define the following column:

```
nest_col SET(MULTISET (INT NOT NULL) NOT NULL)
```

The following statement inserts three elements into the **nest_col** column:

```
INSERT INTO tabx (nest_col)
    VALUES ("SET{'MULTISET{1, 2, 3}'}")
```

To learn how to use quotation marks in INSERT statements, see "Nested Quotation Marks" on page 4-229.

Literal DATETIME

The literal DATETIME segment specifies a literal DATETIME value. Use the literal DATETIME segment whenever you see a reference to a literal DATETIME in a syntax diagram.

Syntax

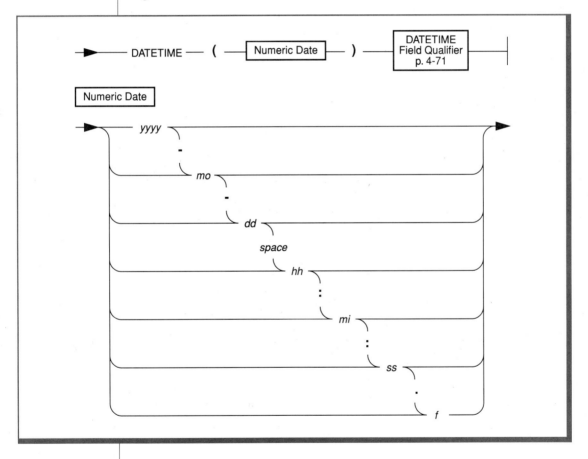

Element	Purpose	Restrictions	Syntax
dd	Day expressed in digits	You can specify up to 2 digits.	Literal Number, p. 4-237
f	Decimal fraction of a second expressed in digits	You can specify up to 5 digits.	Literal Number, p. 4-237
hh	Hour expressed in digits	You can specify up to 2 digits.	Literal Number, p. 4-237
mi	Minute expressed in digits	You can specify up to 2 digits.	Literal Number, p. 4-237
mo	Month expressed in digits	You can specify up to 2 digits.	Literal Number, p. 4-237
space	Space character	You cannot specify more than 1 space character.	The space character is a literal value that you enter by pressing the space bar on the keyboard.
ss	Second expressed in digits	You can specify up to 2 digits.	Literal Number, p. 4-237
yyyy	Year expressed in digits	You can specify up to 4 digits. If you specify 2 digits, the database server uses the setting of the DBCENTURY environment variable to extend the year value. If the DBCENTURY environment variable is not set, the database server uses the current century to extend the year value.	Literal Number, p. 4-237

Usage

You must specify both a numeric date and a DATETIME field qualifier for this date in the Literal DATETIME segment. The DATETIME field qualifier must correspond to the numeric date you specify. For example, if you specify a numeric date that includes a year as the largest unit and a minute as the smallest unit, you must specify YEAR TO MINUTE as the DATETIME field qualifier.

The following examples show literal DATETIME values:

```
DATETIME (97-3-6) YEAR TO DAY

DATETIME (09:55:30.825) HOUR TO FRACTION

DATETIME (97-5) YEAR TO MONTH
```

The following example shows a literal DATETIME value used with the EXTEND function:

```
EXTEND (DATETIME (1997-8-1) YEAR TO DAY, YEAR TO MINUTE)
    - INTERVAL (720) MINUTE (3) TO MINUTE
```

Related Information

For discussions of the DATETIME data type and the **DBCENTURY** environment variable, see the *Informix Guide to SQL: Reference*.

For a discussion of customizing DATETIME values for a locale, see the *Informix Guide to GLS Functionality*.

Literal INTERVAL

The Literal INTERVAL segment specifies a literal INTERVAL value. Use the Literal INTERVAL segment whenever you see a reference to a literal INTERVAL in a syntax diagram.

Syntax

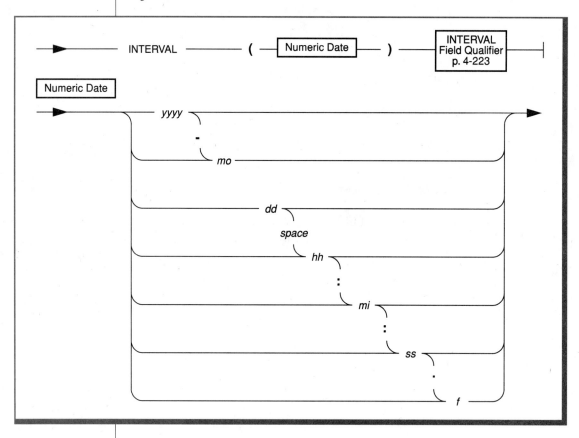

Element	Purpose	Restrictions	Syntax
dd	Number of days	The maximum number of digits allowed is 2, unless this is the first field and the precision is specified differently by the INTERVAL field qualifier.	Literal Number, p. 4-237
f	Decimal fraction of a second	You can specify up to 5 digits, depending on the precision given to the fractional portion in the INTERVAL field qualifier.	Literal Number, p. 4-237
hh	Number of hours	The maximum number of digits allowed is 2, unless this is the first field and the precision is specified differently by the INTERVAL field qualifier.	Literal Number, p. 4-237
mi	Number of minutes	The maximum number of digits allowed is 2, unless this is the first field and the precision is specified differently by the INTERVAL field qualifier.	Literal Number, p. 4-237
mo	Number of months	The maximum number of digits allowed is 2, unless this is the first field and the precision is specified differently by the INTERVAL field qualifier.	Literal Number, p. 4-237
space	Space character	You cannot use any other character in place of the space character.	The space character is a literal value that you enter by pressing the space bar on the keyboard.
ss	Number of seconds	The maximum number of digits allowed is 2, unless this is the first field and the precision is specified differently by the INTERVAL field qualifier.	Literal Number, p. 4-237
yyyy	Number of years	The maximum number of digits allowed is 4, unless this is the first field and the precision is specified differently by the INTERVAL field qualifier.	Literal Number, p. 4-237

Usage

The following examples show literal INTERVAL values:

```
INTERVAL (3-6) YEAR TO MONTH
INTERVAL (09:55:30.825) HOUR TO FRACTION
INTERVAL (40 5) DAY TO HOUR
```

Related Information

For information on how to use INTERVAL data in arithmetic and relational operations, see the discussion of the INTERVAL data type in the *Informix Guide to SQL: Reference*.

Literal Number

A literal number is an integer or noninteger (floating) constant. Use the Literal Number segment whenever you see a reference to a literal number in a syntax diagram.

Syntax

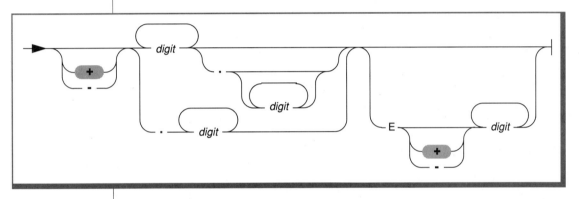

Element	Purpose	Restrictions	Syntax
digit	Digit that forms part of the literal number	You must specify a value between 0 and 9, inclusive.	Digits are literal values that you enter from the keyboard.

Usage

Literal numbers do not contain embedded commas; you cannot use a comma to indicate a decimal point. You can precede literal numbers with a plus or a minus sign.

Integers

Integers do not contain decimal points. The following examples show some integers:

```
10          -27          25567
```

Floating and Decimal Numbers

Floating and decimal numbers contain a decimal point and/or exponential notation. The following examples show floating and decimal numbers:

```
123.456      1.23456E2    123456.0E-3
```

The digits to the right of the decimal point in these examples are the decimal portions of the numbers.

The E that occurs in two of the examples is the symbol for exponential notation. The digit that follows E is the value of the exponent. For example, the number 3E5 (or 3E+5) means 3 multiplied by 10 to the fifth power, and the number 3E-5 means 3 multiplied by 10 to the minus fifth power.

Literal Numbers and the MONEY Data Type

When you use a literal number as a MONEY value, do not precede it with a money symbol or include commas.

Related Information

For discussions of numeric data types, such as DECIMAL, FLOAT, INTEGER, and MONEY, see the *Informix Guide to SQL: Reference.*

IDS

Literal Row

The Literal Row segment specifies the syntax for literal values of named row types and unnamed row types. For syntax that allows you to use expressions that evaluate to field values, see "ROW Constructors" on page 4-116.

Syntax

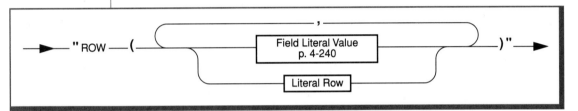

Usage

You can specify literal values for named row types and unnamed row types. The literal row value is introduced with a ROW constructor. The entire literal row value must be enclosed in quotes.

The format of the value for each field of the row type must be compatible with the data type of the corresponding field.

Field Literal Value

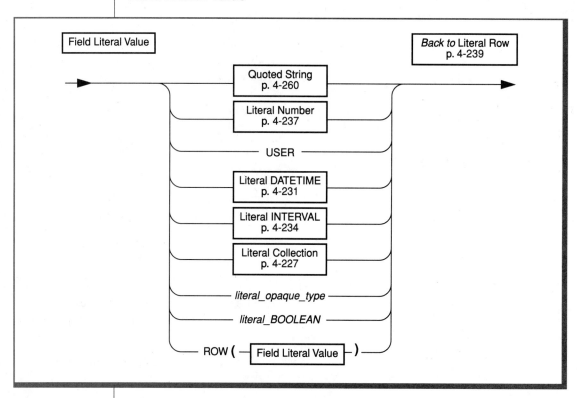

Element	Purpose	Restrictions	Syntax
literal_opaque_type	Literal representation for an opaque data type	Must be a literal that is recognized by the input support function for the associated opaque type.	Defined by the developer of the opaque type.
literal_BOOLEAN	Literal representation of a BOOLEAN value	A literal BOOLEAN value can only be 't' (TRUE) or 'f' (FALSE) and must be specified as a quoted string.	Quoted String, p. 4-260

Fields of a row can be literal values for the data types in the following table.

For a Field of Type	Literal Value Syntax
BOOLEAN	't' or 'f', representing true or false The literal must be specified as a quoted string.
CHAR, VARCHAR, LVARCHAR, NCHAR, NVARCHAR, CHARACTER VARYING, DATE	Quoted String, p. 4-260
DATETIME	Literal DATETIME, p. 4-231
DECIMAL, MONEY, FLOAT, INTEGER, INT8, SMALLFLOAT, SMALLINT	Literal Number, p.4-237
INTERVAL	Literal INTERVAL, p. 4-234
Opaque data types	Quoted String, p. 4-260 The string must be a literal that is recognized by the input support function for the associated opaque type.
Collection type (SET, MULTISET, LIST)	"Literal Collection" on page 4-227 For information on a literal collection value as a column value or as a collection-variable value, see "Nested Quotation Marks" on page 4-229. For information on literal collection value as literal for a row type, see "Literals for Nested Rows" on page 4-243.
Another row type (named or unnamed)	For information on a row type value as literal a row type, see "Literals for Nested Rows" on page 4-243

Important: *You cannot specify the simple-large-object data types (BYTE and TEXT) as the field type for a row.*

Literals of an Unnamed Row Type

To specify a literal value for an unnamed row type, introduce the literal row with the ROW constructor and enclose the values in parentheses. For example, suppose you define the **rectangles** table, as follows:

```
CREATE TABLE rectangles
(
    area FLOAT,
    rect ROW(x INTEGER, y INTEGER, length FLOAT, width FLOAT),
)
```

The following INSERT statement inserts values into the **rect** column of the **rectangles** table:

```
INSERT INTO rectangles (rect)
    VALUES ("ROW(7, 3, 6.0, 2.0)")
```

Literals of a Named Row Type

To specify a literal value for a named row, type, introduce the literal row with the ROW type constructor and enclose the literal values for each field in parentheses. In addition, you can cast the row literal to the appropriate named row type to ensure that the row value is generated as a named row type. The following statements create the named row type **address_t** and the **employee** table:

```
CREATE ROW TYPE address_t
(
street CHAR(20),
city CHAR(15),
state CHAR(2),
zipcode CHAR(9)
);

CREATE TABLE employee
(
    name CHAR(30),
    address address_t
);
```

The following INSERT statement inserts values into the **address** column of the **employee** table:

```
INSERT INTO employee (address)
VALUES (
"ROW('103 Baker St', 'Tracy','CA', 94060)"::address_t)
```

Literals for Nested Rows

If the literal value is for a nested row, specify the ROW type constructor for each row level. However, only the outermost row is enclosed in quotes. For example, suppose you create the following **emp_tab** table:

```
CREATE TABLE emp_tab
(
    emp_name CHAR(10),
    emp_info ROW( stats ROW(x INT, y INT, z FLOAT))
);
```

The following INSERT statement adds a row to the **emp_tab** table:

```
INSERT INTO emp_tab
VALUES ('joe boyd', "ROW(ROW(8,1,12.0))" )
```

Similarly, if the row string literal contains a nested collection, only the outermost quotation marks that delineate the row string literal are necessary. No quotation marks need surround the nested collection type.

Related Information

Related statements: CREATE ROW TYPE, INSERT, UPDATE, and SELECT

For information on ROW constructors, see the Expression segment. See also the Collection Literal segment.

IDS

Optimizer Directives

The Optimizer Directives segment specifies keywords that you can use to partially or fully specify the query plan of the optimizer. Use this segment whenever you see a reference to Optimizer Directives in a syntax diagram.

Syntax

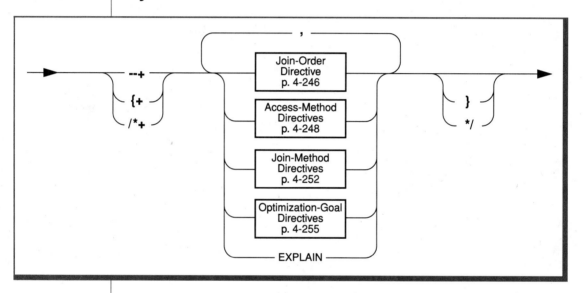

Usage

Use one or more optimizer directives to partially or fully specify the query plan of the optimizer.

When you use an optimizer directive, the scope of the optimizer directive is for the current query only.

By default, optimizer directives are enabled. To obtain information about how specified directives are processed, view the output of the SET EXPLAIN statement. To disable optimizer directives, you must set either the **IFX_DIRECTIVES** environment variable to 0 or OFF or the DIRECTIVES parameter in the **ONCONFIG** file to 0.

Optimizer Directives as Comments

An optimizer directive or a string of optimizer directives immediately follows the DELETE, SELECT, or UPDATE keyword in the form of a comment.

After the comment symbol, the first character in a directive is always a plus (+) sign. No space is allowed between the comment symbol and the plus sign.

You can use any of the following comment styles:

- A double dash (--)

  The double dash needs no closing symbol because it sets off only one comment line of text. When you use this style, include only the optimizer directive information on the comment line.

- Braces ({})
- C-language style comments, slash and asterisk (/* */).

  In ESQL/C, the **-keep** command option to the **esql** compiler must be specified when you use C-style comments.

For more information on SQL comment symbols, see "How to Enter SQL Comments" on page 1-6.

If you use multiple directives in one query, you must separate them. You can separate directives with a space, a comma, or any character that you choose. However, Informix recommends that you separate directives with a comma.

Syntax errors that appear in an optimizer directive do not cause a working query to break. The output of the SET EXPLAIN statement contains information related to such errors.

Restrictions on Optimizer Directives

In general, you can specify optimizer directives for any query block in a DELETE, SELECT, or UPDATE statement. However, you cannot use optimizer directives when your statement includes one of the following items:

- Distributed queries, that is, queries that access one or more remote tables
- In ESQL/C, statements that contain the WHERE CURRENT OF cursor clause ♦

Using the Join-Order Directive

Use the ORDERED join-order directive to force the optimizer to join tables in the order in which they appear in the FROM clause.

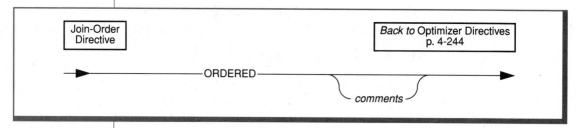

Element	Purpose	Restrictions	Syntax
comments	Any text that explains the purpose of the directive or other significant information	Text must appear inside the comment symbols.	Character string

For example, the following query forces the database server to join the **dept** and **job** tables, and then join the result with the **emp** table.

```
SELECT --+ ORDERED
    name, title, salary, dname
FROM dept, job, emp
Where title = 'clerk'
AND loc = 'Palo Alto'
AND emp.dno = dept.dno
AND emp.job= job.job
```

Because no predicates occur between the **dept** table and the **job** table, this query forces a Cartesian product.

Using the Ordered Directive with Views

When your query involves a view, the placement of the ORDERED join-order directive determines whether you are specifying a partial- or total-join order.

- Specifying partial-join order when you create a view

  If you use the ORDERED join-order directive when you create a view, the base tables are joined contiguously in the order specified in the view definition.

  For all subsequent queries on the view, the database server joins the base tables contiguously in the order specified in the view definition. When used in a view, the ORDERED directive does not affect the join order of other tables named in the FROM clause in a query.

- Specifying total-join order when you query a view

  When you specify the ORDERED join-order directive in a query that uses a view, all tables are joined in the order specified, even those tables that form views. If a view is included in the query, the base tables are joined contiguously in the order specified in the view definition.

For examples that use the ORDERED join-order directive with views, refer to your *Performance Guide.*

Access-Method Directives

Use the access-method directive to specify the manner in which the optimizer should search the tables.

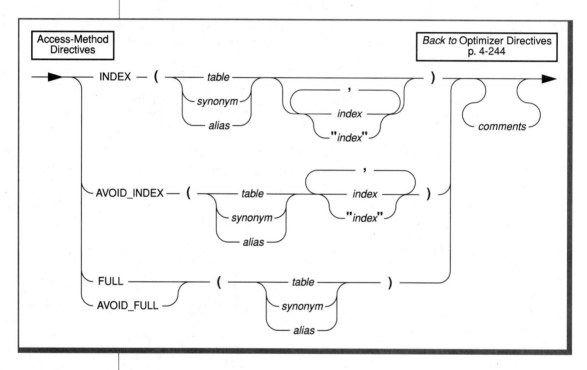

Element	Purpose	Restrictions	Syntax
alias	Temporary alternative name assigned to the table or view in the FROM clause	When an alias is declared in the FROM clause, the alias also must be used in the optimizer directive.	Identifier, p. 4-205
comments	Any text that explains the purpose of the directive or other significant information	Text must appear outside the parenthesis, but inside the comment symbols.	Character string

(1 of 2)

Element	Purpose	Restrictions	Syntax
index	Name of the index for which you want to specify a query plan directive	The index must be defined on the specified table. With the AVOID _INDEX directive, at least one index must be specified.	Database Object Name, p. 4-50
synonym	Name of the synonym for which you want to specify a query plan directive	The synonym and the table to which the synonym points must exist.	Database Object Name, p. 4-50
table	Name of the table for which you want to specify a query plan directive	The table must exist.	Database Object Name, p. 4-50

(2 of 2)

You can separate the elements that appear within the parentheses with either one or more spaces or by commas.

The following table lists the purpose of each of the access-method directives and how it affects the query plan of the optimizer.

Keywords	Purpose	Optimizer Action
AVOID_FULL	Do not perform a full-table scan on the listed table.	The optimizer considers the various indexes it can scan. If no index exists, the optimizer performs a full table scan.
AVOID_INDEX	Do not use any of the indexes listed.	The optimizer considers the remaining indexes and a full table scan. If all indexes for a particular table are specified, the optimizer uses a full table scan to access the table.

(1 of 2)

Keywords	Purpose	Optimizer Action
FULL	Perform a full-table scan.	Even if an index exists on a column, the optimizer uses a full table scan to access the table.
INDEX	Use the index specified to access the table.	If more than one index is specified, the optimizer chooses the index that yields the least cost.
		If no indexes are specified, then all the available indexes are considered.

(2 of 2)

Prohibiting a Full Scan of a Table

Both the AVOID_FULL and INDEX keywords specify that the optimizer should avoid a full scan of a table. However, Informix recommends that you use the AVOID_FULL keyword to specify the intent to avoid a full scan on the table. In addition to specifying that the optimizer not use a full-table scan, the negative directive allows the optimizer to use indexes that are created after the access-method directive is specified.

Using Multiple Access-Method Directives on the Same Table

In general, you can specify only one access-method directive per table. However, you can specify both AVOID_FULL and AVOID_INDEX for the same table. When you specify both of these access-method directives, the optimizer avoids performing a full scan of the table and it avoids using the specified index or indexes.

This combination of negative directives allows the optimizer to use indexes that are created after the access-method directives are specified.

Examples that Uses an Access-Method Directive

Suppose that you have a table named **emp**, that contains the following indexes: **loc_no, dept_no**, and **job_no**. When you perform a SELECT that uses the table in the FROM clause you might direct the optimizer to access the table in one of the following ways:

Example Using a Positive Directive

```
SELECT {+INDEX(emp dept_no)}
```

In this example the access-method directive forces the optimizer to scan the index on the **dept_no** column.

Example Using Negative Directives

```
SELECT {+AVOID_INDEX(emp loc_no, job_no), AVOID_FULL(emp)}
```

This example includes multiple access-method directives. These access-method directives also force the optimizer to scan the index on the **dept_no** column. However, if a new index, **emp_no** is created for table **emp**, the optimizer can consider it.

Join-Method Directives

Use join-method directives to influence how the database server joins tables in a query.

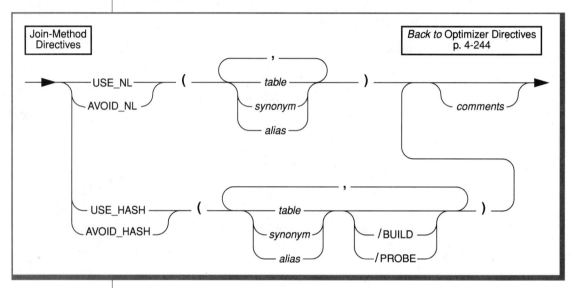

Element	Purpose	Restrictions	Syntax
alias	Temporary alternative name assigned to the table or view in the FROM clause	When an alias is declared in the from clause, the alias also must be used in the optimizer directive.	Identifier, p. 4-205
comments	Any text that explains the purpose of the directive or other significant information	Text must appear outside the parenthesis, but inside the comment symbols.	Character string
synonym	Name of the synonym for which you want to specify a query plan directive	The synonym and the table to which the synonym points must exist.	Database Object Name, p. 4-50
table	Name of the table for which you want to specify a query plan directive	The table must exist.	Database Object Name, p. 4-50

You can separate the elements that appear within the parentheses with either one or more spaces or by commas.

The following table lists the purpose of each of the join-method directives

Keyword	Purpose
USE_NL	Uses the listed tables as the inner table in a nested-loop join. If *n* tables are specified in the FROM clause, then at most *n-1* tables can be specified in the USE_NL join-method directive.
USE_HASH	Uses a hash join to access the listed table. You can also choose whether the table will be used to create the hash table, or to probe the hash table.
AVOID_NL	Does not use the listed table as the inner table in a nested loop join. A table listed with this directive can still participate in a nested loop join as the outer table.
AVOID_HASH	Does not access the listed table using a hash join. Optionally, you can allow a hash join, but restrict the table from being the one that is probed, or the table from which the hash table is built.

A join-method directive takes precedence over the join method forced by the OPTCOMPIND configuration parameter.

Specifying the Role of the Table in a Hash Join

When you specify that you want to avoid or use a hash join, you can also specify the role of each table:

- BUILD

  When used with USE_HASH, this keyword indicates that the specified table be used to construct a hash table. When used with AVOID_HASH, this keyword indicates that the specified table *not* be used to construct a hash table.

- PROBE

  When used with USE_HASH, this keyword indicates that the specified table be used to probe the hash table. When used with AVOID_HASH, this keyword indicates that the specified table *not* be used to probe the hash table. You can specify multiple probe tables as long as there is at least one table for which you do not specify PROBE.

If neither the BUILD nor PROBE keyword is specified, the optimizer uses cost to determine the role of the table.

Example Using Join Method Directives

In the following example, the USE_HASH join-method directive forces the optimizer to construct a hash table on the **dept** table and consider only the hash table to join the **dept** table with the other tables. Because no other directives are specified, the optimizer can choose the least expensive join methods for the other joins in the query.

```
SELECT /*+ USE_HASH (dept /BUILD)
    Force the optimizer to use the dept table to
    construct a hash table */
name, title, salary, dname
FROM emp, dept, job
WHERE loc = 'Phoenix'
AND emp.dno = dept.dno
AND emp.job = job.job
```

Optimization-Goal Directives

Use optimization-goal directives to specify the measure that is used to determine the performance of a query result.

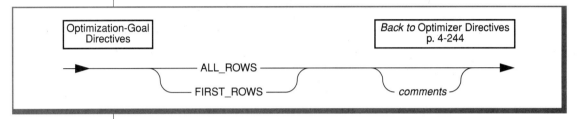

Element	Purpose	Restrictions	Syntax
comments	Any text that explains the purpose of the directive or other significant information	Text must appear outside the parenthesis, but inside the comment symbols.	Character string

The two optimization-goal directives are:

- FIRST_ROWS

  This directive tells the optimizer to choose a plan that optimizes the process of finding only the first screenful of rows that satisfies the query.

  Use this option to decrease initial response time for queries that use an interactive mode or that require the return of only a few rows.

- ALL_ROWS

  This directive tells the optimizer to choose a plan that optimizes the process of finding all rows that satisfy the query.

  This form of optimization is the default.

An optimization-goal directive takes precedence over the **OPT_GOAL** environment variable and the OPT_GOAL configuration parameter.

Restrictions on Optimization-Goal Directives

You cannot use an optimization-goal directive in the following instances:

- In a view definition
- In a subquery

Example of an Optimization-Goal Directive

The following query returns the names of the employees who earned the top fifty bonuses. The optimization-goal directive directs the optimizer to return the first screenful of rows as fast as possible.

```
SELECT {+FIRST_ROWS
    Return the first screenful of rows as fast as possible}
FIRST 50 lname, fname, bonus
FROM emp
ORDER BY bonus DESC
```

For information about how to set the optimization goal for an entire session, see the SET OPTIMIZATION statement.

Directive-Mode Directive

Use the EXPLAIN directive-mode directive to turn SET EXPLAIN ON for a particular query. You can use this directive to test and debug query plans. Information about the query plan is printed to the **sqexplain.out** file. This directive is redundant when SET EXPLAIN ON is already specified.

You cannot use the EXPLAIN directive-mode directive in two situations:

- In a view definition
- In a subquery

Related Information

For information about the **sqexplain.out** file, see SET EXPLAIN.

For information about how to set optimization settings for an entire session, see SET OPTIMIZATION.

For a discussion about optimizer directives and performance, see your *Performance Guide*.

For information on the **IFX_DIRECTIVES** environment variable, see the *Informix Guide to SQL: Reference*.

For information on the DIRECTIVES parameter in the **ONCONFIG** file, see your *Administrator's Reference*.

Owner Name

The owner name segment specifies the name of the owner of a database object in a database. Use this segment whenever you see a reference to Owner Name in a syntax diagram.

Syntax

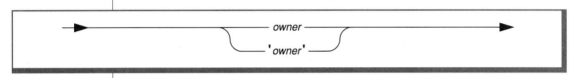

Element	Purpose	Restrictions	Syntax
owner	User name of the owner of a database object in a database	In Dynamic Server, the maximum length of *owner* is 32 bytes. In Enterprise Decision Server, the maximum length of *owner* is 8 bytes.	Name must conform to the conventions of your operating system.
		If you are using an ANSI-compliant database, you must enter the *owner* for a database object that you do not own.	

Usage

In databases that are not ANSI compliant, the owner name is optional. You do not need to specify *owner* when you create database objects or use data access statements. If you do not specify *owner* when you create a database object, the database server assigns your login name as the owner of the object in most cases. For exceptions to this rule, see "Ownership of Created Database Objects" on page 2-153 in CREATE FUNCTION and "Ownership of Created Database Objects" on page 2-208 in CREATE PROCEDURE.

If you specify *owner* in data-access statements, the database server checks it for correctness. Without quotation marks, *owner* is case insensitive.

The following example shows four queries that can access data successfully from the table **kaths.tab1**:

```
SELECT * FROM tab1
SELECT * FROM kaths.tab1
SELECT * FROM KATHS.tab1
SELECT * FROM Kaths.tab1
```

Using Quotation Marks

When you use quotation marks, *owner* is case sensitive. In other words, quotation marks signal the database server to read or store the name exactly as typed. This case sensitivity applies when you create or access a database object.

Suppose you have a table whose owner is Sam. You can use one of the following two statements to access data in the table.

```
SELECT * FROM table1
SELECT * FROM 'Sam'.table1
```

The first query succeeds because the owner name is not required. The second query succeeds because the specified owner name matches the owner name as it is stored in the database.

Accessing Information from the System Catalog Tables

If you use the owner name as one of the selection criteria to access database object information from one of the system catalog tables, the owner name is case sensitive. Because this type of query requires that you use quotation marks, you must type the owner name exactly as it is stored in the system catalog table. Of the following two examples, only the second successfully accesses information on the table **Kaths.table1**.

```
SELECT * FROM systables WHERE tabname = 'table1' AND owner
= 'kaths'
SELECT * FROM systables WHERE tabname = 'table1' AND owner
= 'Kaths'
```

User **informix** is the owner of the system catalog tables.

Tip: *The* USER *keyword returns the login name exactly as it is stored on the system. If the owner name is stored differently from the login name (for example, a mixed-case owner name and an all lowercase login name), the* owner = USER *syntax fails.*

ANSI

ANSI-Compliant Databases Restrictions and Case Sensitivity

If you specify the owner name when you create or rename a database object in an ANSI-compliant database, you must include the owner name in data access statements. You must include the owner name when you access a database object that you do not own.

The following table describes how the database server reads and stores *owner* when you create, rename, or access a database object.

Owner Name Specification Method	What the Database Server Does
Do not specify	Reads or stores owner exactly as the login name is stored in the system
	Users must specify *owner* for a database object or database they do not own.
Specify without quotation marks	Reads or stores *owner* in uppercase letters
Enclose within quotation marks	Reads or stores *owner* exactly as typed
	For more information on how the database server handles this specification method, see "Using Quotation Marks" on page 4-258 and "Accessing Information from the System Catalog Tables" on page 4-258.

Because the database server automatically upshifts *owner* if it is not enclosed in quotation marks, case-sensitive errors can cause queries to fail.

For example, if you are the user **nancy**, and you use the following statement, the resulting view has the name **nancy.njcust**.

```
CREATE VIEW 'nancy'.njcust AS
    SELECT fname, lname FROM customer WHERE state = 'NJ'
```

The following SELECT statement fails because it tries to match the name **NANCY.njcust** to the actual owner and table name of **nancy.njcust**.

```
SELECT * FROM nancy.njcust
```

Tip: *When you use the owner name as one of the selection criteria in a query, (for example,* WHERE owner = 'kaths')*, make sure that the quoted string matches the owner name as it is stored in the database. If the database server cannot find the database object or database, you might need to modify the query so that the quoted string uses uppercase letters (for example,* WHERE owner = 'KATHS')*.*

Quoted String

A quoted string is a string constant that is surrounded by quotation marks. Use the Quoted String segment whenever you see a reference to a quoted string in a syntax diagram.

Syntax

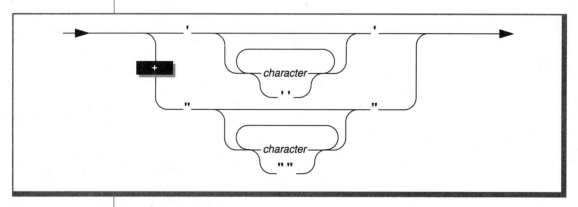

Element	Purpose	Restrictions	Syntax
character	Forms part of the quoted string	The character or characters in the quoted string cannot be surrounded by double quotes if the DELIMIDENT environment variable is set.	Characters are literal values that you enter from the keyboard.

Usage

You use quoted strings to specify string constants in data manipulation statements and other SQL statements. For example, you can use a quoted string in an INSERT statement to insert a value into a column with a character data type.

Restrictions on Specifying Characters in Quoted Strings

You must observe the following restrictions when you specify *character* in quoted strings:

- If you are using the ASCII code set, you can specify any printable ASCII character, including a single quote or double quote. For restrictions that apply to using quotes in quoted strings, see "Using Quotes in Strings" on page 4-262.

- If you are using a nondefault locale, you can specify non-ASCII characters, including multibyte characters, that the code set of your locale supports. For further information, see the discussion of quoted strings in the *Informix Guide to GLS Functionality*. ♦

- If you enable newline characters for quoted strings, you can embed newline characters in quoted strings. For further information on how to enable newline characters for quoted strings, see "Newline Characters in Quoted Strings" on page 4-262.

- When you set the **DELIMIDENT** environment variable, you cannot use double quotes to delimit a quoted string. When **DELIMIDENT** is set, a string enclosed in double quotes is an identifier, not a quoted string. When **DELIMIDENT** is not set, a string enclosed in double quotes is a quoted string, not an identifier. For further information, see "Using Quotes in Strings" on page 4-262.

- You can enter DATETIME and INTERVAL data as quoted strings. For the restrictions that apply to entering DATETIME and INTERVAL data in quoted-string format, see "DATETIME and INTERVAL Values as Strings" on page 4-263.

- Quoted strings that are used with the LIKE or MATCHES keyword in a search condition can include wildcard characters that have a special meaning in the search condition. For further information, see "LIKE and MATCHES in a Condition" on page 4-263.

- When you insert a value that is a quoted string, you must observe a number of restrictions. For further information, see "Inserting Values as Quoted Strings" on page 4-264.

GLS

Newline Characters in Quoted Strings

By default, the string constant must be written on a single line; that is, you cannot use embedded newline characters in a quoted string. However, you can override this default behavior in one of two ways:

- To enable newline characters in quoted strings in all sessions, set the ALLOW_NEWLINE parameter to 1 in the ONCONFIG file.
- To enable newline characters in quoted strings for a particular session, execute the built-in function, **IFX_ALLOW_NEWLINE**, within the session.

In the following example, the user enables newline characters in quoted strings for a particular session:

```
EXECUTE PROCEDURE IFX_ALLOW_NEWLINE('T')
```

If newline characters in quoted strings are not enabled for a session, the following statement is illegal and results in an error:

```
SELECT 'The quick brown fox
    jumped over the old gray fence'
    FROM customer
    WHERE customer_num = 101
```

However, if you enable newline characters in quoted strings for the session, the statement in the preceding example is legal and executes successfully.

For more information on the **IFX_ALLOW_NEWLINE** function, see "IFX_ALLOW_NEWLINE Function" on page 4-177. For more information on the ALLOW_NEWLINE parameter in the ONCONFIG file, see your *Administrator's Reference*.

Using Quotes in Strings

The single quote has no special significance in string constants delimited by double quotes. Likewise, the double quote has no special significance in strings delimited by single quotes. For example, the following strings are valid:

```
"Nancy's puppy jumped the fence"
'Billy told his kitten, "No!"'
```

If your string is delimited by double quotes, you can include a double quote in the string by preceding the double quote with another double quote, as shown in the following string:

```
"Enter ""y"" to select this row"
```

When the **DELIMIDENT** environment variable is set, double quotes delimit identifiers, not strings. For more information on delimited identifiers, see "Delimited Identifiers" on page 4-208.

DATETIME and INTERVAL Values as Strings

You can enter DATETIME and INTERVAL data in the literal forms described in the "Literal DATETIME" on page 4-231 and "Literal INTERVAL" on page 4-234, or you can enter them as quoted strings. Valid literals that are entered as character strings are converted automatically into DATETIME or INTERVAL values. The following INSERT statements use quoted strings to enter INTERVAL and DATETIME data:

```
INSERT INTO cust_calls(call_dtime) VALUES ('1997-5-4 10:12:11')

INSERT INTO manufact(lead_time) VALUES ('14')
```

The format of the value in the quoted string must exactly match the format specified by the qualifiers of the column. For the first case in the preceding example, the **call_dtime** column must be defined with the qualifiers YEAR TO SECOND for the INSERT statement to be valid.

LIKE and MATCHES in a Condition

Quoted strings with the LIKE or MATCHES keyword in a condition can include wildcard characters. For a complete description of how to use wildcard characters, see "Condition" on page 4-27.

Inserting Values as Quoted Strings

If you are inserting a value that is a quoted string, you must adhere to the following conventions:

- Enclose CHAR, VARCHAR, NCHAR, NVARCHAR, DATE, DATETIME, and INTERVAL values in quotation marks.

- Set DATE values in the *mm/dd/yyyy* format or in the format specified by the **DBDATE** environment variable, if set.

- You cannot insert strings longer than 256 bytes. ♦

- You cannot insert strings longer than 32 kilobytes. ♦

- Numbers with decimal values must contain a decimal point. You cannot use a comma as a decimal indicator.

- You cannot precede MONEY data with a dollar sign ($) or include commas.

- You can include NULL as a placeholder only if the column accepts null values.

EDS

IDS

Related Information

For a discussion of the **DELIMIDENT** environment variable, see the *Informix Guide to SQL: Reference*.

For a discussion of the GLS aspects of quoted strings, see the *Informix Guide to GLS Functionality*.

Relational Operator

A relational operator compares two expressions quantitatively. Use the Relational Operator segment whenever you see a reference to a relational operator in a syntax diagram.

Syntax

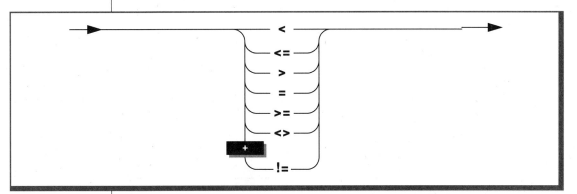

Each operator shown in the syntax diagram has a particular meaning.

Relational Operator	Meaning
<	Less than
<=	Less than or equal to
>	Greater than
=	Equal to
>=	Greater than or equal to
<>	Not equal to
!=	Not equal to

Usage

For DATE and DATETIME expressions, *greater than* means later in time.

For INTERVAL expressions, *greater than* means a longer span of time.

For CHAR, VARCHAR, and LVARCHAR expressions, *greater than* means *after* in code-set order.

GLS

Locale-based collation order is used for NCHAR and NVARCHAR expressions. So for NCHAR and NVARCHAR expressions, *greater than* means *after* in the locale-based collation order. For more information on locale-based collation order and the NCHAR and NVARCHAR data types, see the *Informix Guide to GLS Functionality*. ◆

Using Operator Functions in Place of Relational Operators

Each relational operator is bound to a particular operator function, as shown in the table below. The operator function accepts two values and returns a boolean value of true, false, or unknown.

Relational Operator	Associated Operator Function
<	lessthan()
<=	lessthanorequal()
>	greater than()
>=	greaterthanorequal()
=	equal()
<>	notequal()
!=	notequal()

Connecting two expressions with a binary operator is equivalent to invoking the operator function on the expressions. For example, the following two statements both select orders with a shipping charge of $18.00 or more. The >= operator in the first statement implicitly invokes the **greaterthanorequal()** operator function.

```
SELECT order_num FROM orders
    WHERE ship_charge >= 18.00

SELECT order_num FROM orders
    WHERE greaterthanorequal(ship_charge, 18.00)
```

The database server provides the operator functions associated with the relational operators for all built-in data types. When you develop a user-defined data type, you must define the operator functions for that type for users to be able to use the relational operator on the type.

Collating Order for English Data

If you are using the default locale (U.S. English), the database server uses the code-set order of the default code set when it compares the character expressions that precede and follow the relational operator.

UNIX

On UNIX, the default code set is the ISO8859-1 code set, which consists of the following sets of characters:

- The ASCII characters have code points in the range of 0 to 127.

    This range contains control characters, punctuation symbols, English-language characters, and numerals.

- The 8-bit characters have code points in the range 128 to 255.

    This range includes many non-English-language characters (such as é, â, ö, and ñ) and symbols (such as £, ©, and ¿). ♦

WIN NT

In Windows NT, the default code set is Microsoft 1252. This code set includes both the ASCII code set and a set of 8-bit characters. ♦

The following table shows the ASCII code set. The **Num** column shows the ASCII code numbers, and the **Char** column shows the ASCII character corresponding to each ASCII code number. ASCII characters are sorted according to their ASCII code number. Thus lowercase letters follow uppercase letters, and both follow numerals. In this table, the caret symbol (^) stands for the CTRL key. For example, ^X means CTRL-X.

Num	Char	Num	Char	Num	Char	Num	Char	Num	Char	Num	Char	Num	Char
0	^@	20	^T	40	(	60	<	80	P	100	d	120	x
1	^A	21	^U	41	)	61	=	81	Q	101	e	121	y
2	^B	22	^V	42	*	62	>	82	R	102	f	122	z
3	^C	23	^W	43	+	63	?	83	S	103	g	123	{
4	^D	24	^X	44	,	64	@	84	T	104	h	124		
5	^E	25	^Y	45	-	65	A	85	U	105	i	125	}
6	^F	26	^Z	46	.	66	B	86	V	106	j	126	~
7	^G	27	esc	47	/	67	C	87	W	107	k	127	del
8	^H	28	^\	48	0	68	D	88	X	108	l		
9	^I	29	^]	49	1	69	E	89	Y	109	m		
10	^J	30	^^	50	2	70	F	90	Z	110	n		
11	^K	31	^_	51	3	71	G	91	[	111	o		
12	^L	32		52	4	72	H	92	\	112	p		
13	^M	33	!	53	5	73	I	93	]	113	q		
14	^N	34	"	54	6	74	J	94	^	114	r		
15	^O	35	#	55	7	75	K	95	_	115	s		
16	^P	36	$	56	8	76	L	96	`	116	t		
17	^Q	37	%	57	9	77	M	97	a	117	u		
18	^R	38	&	58	:	78	N	98	b	118	v		
19	^S	39	'	59	;	79	O	99	c	119	w		

GLS

Support for ASCII Characters in Nondefault Code Sets

Most code sets in nondefault locales (called nondefault code sets) support the ASCII characters. If you are using a nondefault locale, the database server uses ASCII code-set order for any ASCII data in CHAR and VARCHAR expressions, as long as the nondefault code set supports these ASCII characters.

Related Information

For a discussion of relational operators in the SELECT statement, see the *Informix Guide to SQL: Tutorial*.

For a discussion of the GLS aspects of relational operators, see the *Informix Guide to GLS Functionality*.

Return Clause

The Return Clause specifies the data type of a value or values that a user-defined function returns. Use this segment whenever you see reference to the Return Clause in a syntax diagram.

Syntax

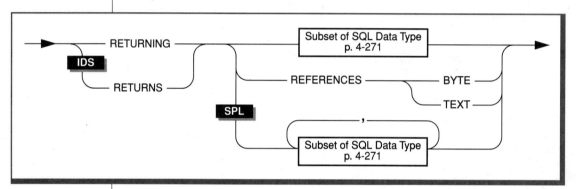

Usage

IDS

For backward compatibility, you can continue to create SPL functions with the CREATE PROCEDURE statement (that is include a Return Clause with the CREATE PROCEDURE statement). However, Informix recommends that you use the CREATE FUNCTION statement to create an SPL routine that returns one or more values. ♦

Once you use the return clause to indicate the type of values that are to be returned, you can use the RETURN SPL statement at any point in the statement block to return SPL variables that correspond to the values in the return clause.

Limits on Return Values

SPL

For an SPL function, you can specify more than one data type in the return clause. ♦

Ext

For an external function, you can specify only one data type in the return clause. However, an external function can return more than one row of data if it is an iterator function. For more information, see "ITERATOR" on page 4-279. ♦

Subset of SQL Data Types

As indicated in the diagram for the "Return Clause" on page 4-270, not all data types are available in a return clause. For more information on data types, see "Data Type" on page 4-53.

SPL

The default precision of a DECIMAL returned by an SPL function is 16 digits. If you want a function to return a different number of significant digits, you must specify the precision in the Return clause. ♦

EDS

A user-defined function can return values of any built-in data type *except* SERIAL, TEXT, or BYTE. ♦

IDS

A user-defined function can return values of any built-in data type *except* those listed in the following table.

Data Type	C	Java	SPL
BLOB	✔		✔
BYTE	✔	✔	✔
COLLECTION		✔	
CLOB	✔		✔
LIST		✔	
MULTISET		✔	
ROW		✔	✔
SET		✔	✔
SERIAL	✔	✔	✔
SERIAL8	✔	✔	✔
TEXT	✔	✔	✔

If you use a complex type in the return clause, the calling user-defined routine must define variables of the appropriate complex types to hold the values that the C or SPL user-defined function returns.

User-defined functions can return a value or values of defined opaque or distinct data types. ♦

Using the REFERENCES Clause to Point to a Simple Large Object

A user-defined function cannot return a BYTE or TEXT value (collectively called *simple large objects*) directly. A user-defined function can, however, use the REFERENCES keyword to return a descriptor that contains a pointer to a BYTE or TEXT object.

The following example shows how to select a text column within an SPL routine and then return the value:

```
CREATE FUNCTION sel_text()
    RETURNING REFERENCES text;

DEFINE blob_var REFERENCES text;

SELECT blob_col INTO blob_var
    FROM blob_table
    WHERE key-col = 10;
RETURN blob_var

END FUNCTION
```

EDS

In Enterprise Decision Server, to recreate this example use the CREATE PROCEDURE statement instead of the CREATE FUNCTION statement. ♦

Cursor and Noncursor Functions

A *cursor* function allows the fetching of the return values one by one by iterating on the generated result set of return values. Such a function is an implicitly iterated function.

A function that returns only one set of values (such as one or more columns from a single row of a table) is a *noncursor* function.

The return clause can occur in a cursor function or in a noncursor function. In the following example, the return clause can return zero (0) or one value if it occurs in a noncursor function. However, if this clause is associated with a cursor function, it returns more than one row from a table, and each returned row contains zero or one value.

```
RETURNING INT;
```

In the following example, the return clause can return zero (0) or two values if it occurs in a noncursor function. However, if this clause is associated with a cursor function, it returns more than one row from a table and each returned row contains zero or two values.

```
RETURNING INT, INT;
```

In both of the preceding examples, the receiving function or program must be written appropriately to accept the information that the function returns.

IDS

Routine Modifier

A routine modifier specifies characteristics of how a user-defined routine (UDR) behaves. Use the Routine Modifier segment whenever you see a reference to a routine modifier in a syntax diagram.

Syntax

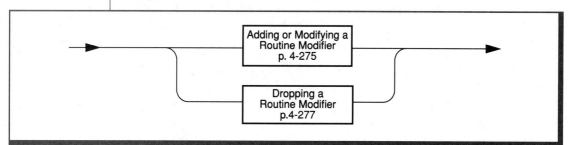

Some modifiers are available only with user-defined functions. For information on whether or not a specific routine modifier applies only to user-defined functions (that is, if it does not apply to user-defined procedures), see the textual description for the modifier.

The options in this segment do not apply to SPL procedures.

Adding or Modifying a Routine Modifier

Use this portion of the Routine Modifier segment to add or modify values for routine modifiers for a UDR.

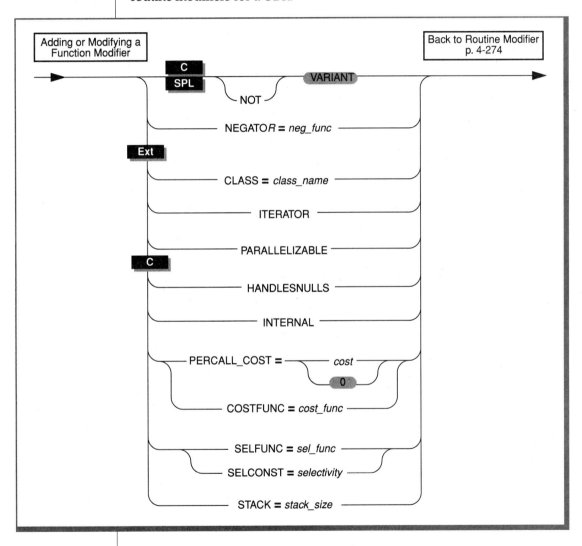

Element	Purpose	Restrictions	Syntax
class_name	Name of the virtual processor (VP) class in which to run the external routine	A C UDR must run in either the CPU VP or in a user-defined VP class.	Quoted String, p. 4-260
	The default for C UDRs is CPU VP. The default for UDRs written in Java is JVP.	If you specify a user-defined VP class, the class must be defined before the UDR runs. A UDR written in Java must run in a JVP	
cost	CPU use cost for each invocation of a C UDR The default is 0.	The *cost* must be a positive integer with a value between 1 (lowest cost) and 2^{31}-1 (highest cost).	Literal Number, p. 4-237
cost_func	Name of a companion user-defined function to invoke	To execute *cost_func*, you must have the Execute privilege on both the function you are invoking directly and the companion function.	Identifier, p. 4-205
		Both functions must have the same owner.	
neg_func	Name of a negator function that can be invoked instead of the current function	To execute *neg_func*, you must have the Execute privilege on both the function you are invoking directly and the companion function.	Identifier, p. 4-205
		Both functions must have the same owner.	
sel_func	Name of a companion user-defined function to invoke	To execute *sel_func*, you must have the Execute privilege on both the function you are invoking directly and the companion function.	Identifier, p. 4-205
		Both functions must have the same owner.	
selectivity	CPU use cost for each invocation of a C UDR The default is 0.	The *selectivity* must be a positive float with a value between 1 (lowest cost) and 2^{31}-1 (highest cost).	Literal Number, p. 4-237
stack_size	Size (in bytes) of the thread stack for threads that execute the C UDR	The *stack_size* must be a positive integer.	Literal Number, p. 4-237
		Usually, this stack size is larger than the stack size that the STACKSIZE configuration parameter specifies.	

You can add these modifiers in any order. If you list the same modifier more than once, the last setting overrides previous values.

Dropping a Routine Modifier

Use this portion of the Routine Modifier segment to drop an existing modifier from a UDR.

When you drop an existing modifier, the database server sets the value of the modifier to the default value, if a default exists.

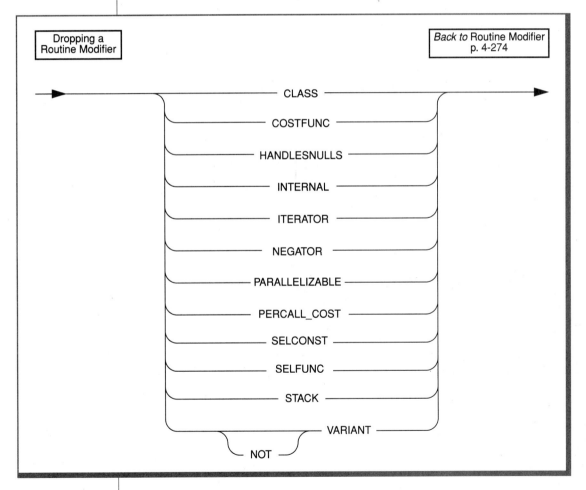

Modifier Descriptions

The following sections describe the modifiers that you can use to help the database server optimally execute a UDR.

EXT

CLASS

Use the CLASS modifier to specify the name of a virtual-processor (VP) class in which to run an external routine.

C

You can execute C UDRs in the following types of VP classes:

- The CPU virtual-processor class (CPU VP)
- A user-defined virtual-processor class

If you do not use the CLASS modifier to specify a VP class, the UDR runs in the CPU VP.

User-defined VP classes protect the database server from ill-behaved C UDRs. An ill-behaved C UDR has at least one of the following characteristics:

- It runs in the CPU VP for a long time without yielding.
- It is not thread safe.
- It calls an unsafe operating-system routine.

A well-behaved C UDR has none of these characteristics. Execute only well-behaved C UDRs in the CPU VP.

Warning: *Execution of an ill-behaved C UDR in the CPU VP can cause serious interference with the operation of the database server. In addition, the UDR itself might not produce correct results. For a more detailed discussion of ill-behaved UDRs, see the DataBlade API Programmer's Manual.* ♦

Java

By default, a UDR written in Java runs in a Java virtual processor class (JVP). Therefore, the CLASS routine modifier is optional for a a UDR written in Java. However, Informix recommends that you use the CLASS routine modifier when you register a UDR written in Java to improve readability of your SQL statements. ♦

C	

COSTFUNC

Use the COSTFUNC modifier to specify the cost of a C UDR. The *cost* of the UDR is an estimate of the time required to execute it.

Occasionally, the cost of a UDR depends on the inputs to the UDR. In that case, you can use a user-defined function that calculates a cost that depends on the input value.

C	

HANDLESNULLS

Use the HANDLESNULLS modifier to specify that a C UDR can handle null values that are passed to it as arguments. If you do not specify HANDLESNULLS for a C UDR, and if you pass an argument with a null value to it, the C UDR does not execute and returns a null value.

By default, a C UDR does *not* handle null values. ♦

SPL	

The HANDLESNULLS modifier is not available for SPL routines because SPL routines handle null values by default. ♦

Ext	

INTERNAL

Use the INTERNAL modifier with an external routine to specify that an SQL or SPL statement cannot call the external routine.

An external routine that is specified as INTERNAL is not considered during routine resolution. Use the INTERNAL modifier for external routines that define access methods, language managers, and so on.

By default, an external routine is *not* internal; that is, an SQL or SPL statement can call the routine.

Ext	

ITERATOR

Use the ITERATOR modifier with external functions to specify that the function is an *iterator function*. An iterator function is a function that returns a single element per function call to return a set of data; that is, it is called with an initial call and zero or more subsequent calls until the set is complete.

An iterator function is similar to an SPL function that contains the RETURN WITH RESUME statement.

By default, an external function is *not* an iterator function.

| E/C |

An iterator function requires a cursor. The cursor allows the client application to retrieve the values one at a time with the FETCH statement. ♦

For more information on how to write iterator functions, see the *DataBlade API Programmer's Manual*.

NEGATOR

Use the NEGATOR modifier with user-defined functions that return Boolean values.

The NEGATOR modifier names a companion user-defined function, called a *negator function*, to the current function. A negator function takes the same arguments as its companion function, in the same order, but returns the Boolean complement. That is, if a function returns TRUE for a given set of arguments, its negator function returns FALSE when passed the same arguments, in the same order.

For example, the following functions are negator functions:

```
equal(a,b)
notequal(a,b)
```

Both functions take the same arguments, in the same order, but return complementary Boolean values.

When it is more efficient to do so, the optimizer can use the negator function instead of the function you specify.

To invoke a user-defined function that has a negator function, you must have the Execute privilege on both functions. In addition, the function must have the same owner as its negator function.

| Ext |

PARALLELIZABLE

Use the PARALLELIZABLE modifier to indicate that an external routine can be executed in parallel in the context of a parallelizable data query (PDQ) statement.

By default, an external routine is non-parallelizable; that is, it executes in sequence.

If your UDR has a complex type as either a parameter or a return value, you cannot use the parallelizable modifier.

If you specify the PARALLELIZABLE modifier for an external routine that cannot be parallelizable, the database server returns a runtime error.

C

A C UDR that calls only PDQ thread-safe DataBlade API functions is parallelizable. The following categories of DataBlade API functions are PDQ thread safe:

- Data handling

  An exception in this category is that collection manipulation functions (**mi_collection_***) are not PDQ thread safe.

- Session, thread, and transaction management
- Function execution
- Memory management
- Exception handling
- Callbacks
- Miscellaneous

For details of the DataBlade API functions included in each category, see the *DataBlade API Programmer's Manual*.

If your UDR calls a function that is not included in one of these categories, it is not PDQ thread safe and therefore not parallelizable. ♦

Java

To parallelize UDR calls, the database server must have multiple instances of JVPs. UDRs written in Java that open a JDBC connection are not parallelizable. ♦

C

PERCALL_COST

Use the PERCALL_COST modifier to specify the approximate CPU usage cost that a C UDR incurs each time it executes. The optimizer uses the cost you specify to determine the order in which to evaluate SQL predicates in the UDR for best performance.

For example, the following query has two predicates joined by a logical AND:

```
SELECT * FROM tab1 WHERE func1() = 10 AND func2() = 'abc';
```

In this example, if one predicate returns FALSE, the optimizer need not evaluate the other predicate. The optimizer uses the cost you specify to order the predicates so that the least expensive predicate is evaluated first.

The CPU usage cost must be an integer between 1 and 2^{31}-1, with 1 the lowest cost and 2^{31}-1 the most expensive. To calculate an approximate cost per call, add the following two figures:

- The number of lines of code that execute each time the C UDR is called
- The number of predicates that require an I/O access

The default cost per execution is 0. When you drop the PERCALL_COST modifier, the cost per execution returns to 0.

SELCONST

Use the SELCONST modifier to specify the selectivity of a C UDR. The *selectivity* of the UDR is an estimate of the fraction of the rows that will be selected by the query. That is, the number of times the UDR will need to be executed.

The value of selectivity constant, **selconst,** is a floating-point number between 0 and 1 that represents the fraction of the rows for which you expect the UDR to return TRUE.

SELFUNC

Use the SELFUNC modifier with a C UDR to name a companion user-defined function, called a *selectivity function,* to the current UDR. The selectivity function provides selectivity information about the current UDR to the optimizer.

The *selectivity* of a UDR is an estimate of the fraction of the rows that will be selected by the query. That is, it is an estimate of the number of times the UDR will execute.

Concept of Selectivity

Selectivity refers to the number of rows that would qualify for a query that does a search based on an equality predicate. The fewer the number of rows that qualify, the more selective the query.

For example, the following query has a search condition based on the **customer_num** column in the **customer** table:

```
SELECT * FROM customer
WHERE customer_num = 102;
```

Since each row in the table has a different customer number, this is a highly selective query.

In contrast, the following query is not selective:

```
SELECT * FROM customer
WHERE state = 'CA';
```

Since most of the rows in the **customer** table are for customers in California, more than half of the rows in the table would be returned.

Restrictions on the SELFUNC Modifier

The selectivity function that you specify must satisfy the following criteria:

- It must take the same number of arguments as the current C UDR.
- The data type of each argument must be SELFUNC_ARG.
- It must return a value of type FLOAT between 0 and 1, which represents the percentage of selectivity of the function. (1 is highly selective; 0 is not at all selective.)
- It can be written in any language the database server supports.

A user who invokes the C UDR must have the Execute privilege both on that UDR and on the selectivity function that the SELFUNC modifier specifies.

Both the C UDR and the selectivity function must have the same owner.

For information on C language macros that you can use to extract information about the arguments to the selectivity function, see the *DataBlade API Programmer's Manual*.

C

STACK

Use the STACK modifier with a C UDR to override the default stack size that the STACKSIZE configuration parameter specifies.

The STACK modifier specifies the size of the thread stack, which a user thread uses to hold information such as routine arguments and function return values.

A UDR needs to have enough stack space for all its local variables. For a particular UDR, you might need to specify a stack size larger than the default size to prevent stack overflow.

When a UDR that includes the STACK modifier executes, the database server allocates a thread-stack size of the specified number of bytes. Once the UDR completes execution, subsequent UDRs execute in threads with a stack size that the STACKSIZE configuration parameter specifies (unless any of these subsequent UDRs have also specified the STACK modifier).

For more information about the thread stack, see your *Administrator's Guide* and the *DataBlade API Programmer's Manual*.

C
SPL

VARIANT and NOT VARIANT

Use the VARIANT and NOT VARIANT modifiers with C user-defined functions and SPL functions. A function is *variant* if it returns different results when it is invoked with the same arguments or if it modifies a database or variable state. For example, a function that returns the current date or time is a variant function.

By default, user-defined functions are variant. If you specify NOT VARIANT when you create or modify a user-defined function, the function cannot contain any SQL statements.

If the user-defined function is nonvariant, the database server might cache the return values of expensive functions. You can create functional indexes only on nonvariant functions. For more information on functional indexes, see "CREATE INDEX" on page 2-157.

C

You can specify VARIANT or NOT VARIANT in this clause or in the EXTERNAL Routine Reference. For more information, see "External Routine Reference" on page 4-202. However, if you specify the modifier in both places, you must use the same modifier in both clauses. ♦

Related Information

For more information on user-defined routines, see *Extending Informix Dynamic Server 2000* and the *DataBlade API Programmer's Manual.*

For more information about how these modifiers can affect performance, see your *Performance Guide.*

Routine Parameter List

Use the appropriate part of the Routine Parameter List segment whenever you see a reference to a Routine Parameter List in a syntax diagram.

Syntax

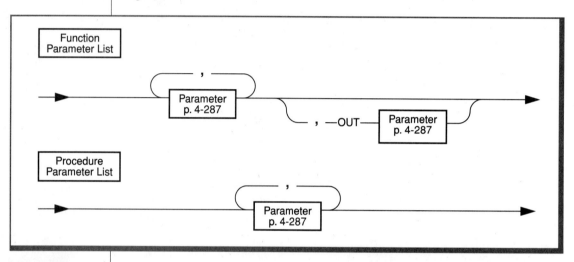

IDS

In Dynamic Server, although you can use the Function Parameter List with a CREATE PROCEDURE statement to write and register an SPL routine that returns one or more values (that is, an SPL function), Informix recommends that you use the Function Parameter List only with the CREATE FUNCTION statement.

EDS

In Enterprise Decision Server, you can use the Function Parameter List with the CREATE PROCEDURE statement because the database server does not support the CREATE FUNCTION statement. ♦

Parameter

A parameter is one item in a Function Parameter List or Procedure Parameter List.

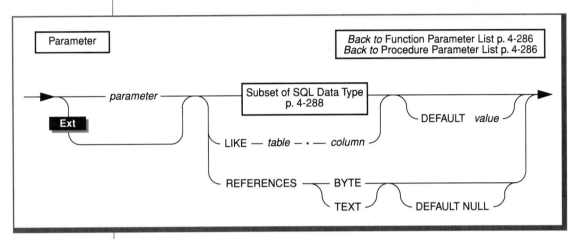

Element	Purpose	Restrictions	Syntax
column	Name of a column whose data type is assigned to the parameter	The column must exist in the specified table.	Identifier, p. 4-205
parameter	Name of a parameter the UDR can accept	The parameter name is required for SPL routines.	Identifier, p. 4-205
table	Name of the table that contains *column*	The table must exist in the database.	Identifier, p. 4-205
value	Default value that a UDR uses if you do not supply a value for the parameter when you call the UDR	This value must be a literal. If *value* is a literal, the value must have the same data type as *parameter*. If *value* is a literal and its type is an opaque type, an input function must be defined on the type.	Literal Number, p. 4-237

Usage

To define a parameter when creating a UDR, specify its name and its data type. You can specify the data type directly or use the LIKE or REFERENCES clause to identify the data type.

IDS The name is optional for external routines. ♦

SPL

Limits on Parameters

You can define any number of parameters for an SPL routine. However, the total length of all the parameters passed to an SPL routine must be less than 32 kilobytes.

Subset of SQL Data Types

As indicated in the diagram for "Parameter" on page 4-287, not all data types are available for you to use as a parameter.

A UDR can define a parameter of any data type defined in the database, except SERIAL, SERIAL8, TEXT, BYTE, CLOB, or BLOB.

In addition to the allowable built-in types, a parameter can be a complex type or user-defined data type.

Java

Complex types are not yet allowed as parameter data types for UDRs written in Java. ♦

For more information on data types, see "Data Type" on page 4-53.

Using the LIKE Clause

Use the LIKE clause to specify that the data type of a parameter is the same as a column defined in the database and changes with the column definition. If you define a parameter with LIKE, the data type of the parameter changes as the data type of the column changes.

IDS

Restriction on Routine Overloading

If you use the LIKE clause to define any of the parameters for the UDR, you cannot overload the UDR. The database server does not consider such a UDR in the routine resolution process.

For example, suppose you create the following user-defined procedure:

```
CREATE PROCEDURE cost (a LIKE tab.col, b INT)
  .
  .
  .
END PROCEDURE;
```

You cannot create another user-defined procedure named **cost()** in the same database with two arguments. However, you can create a user-defined procedure named **cost()** with a number of arguments other than two.

To circumvent this restriction with the LIKE clause, you might want to use user-defined data types to achieve the same purpose.

Using the REFERENCES Clause

Use the REFERENCES clause to specify that a parameter contains BYTE or TEXT data. The REFERENCES keyword allows you to use a pointer to a BYTE or TEXT object as a parameter.

If you use the DEFAULT NULL option in the REFERENCES clause, and you call the UDR without a parameter, a null value is used.

Using the DEFAULT Clause

Use the DEFAULT keyword followed by an expression to specify a default value for a parameter. If you provide a default value for a parameter, and the UDR is called with fewer arguments than were defined for that UDR, the default value is used. If you do not provide a default value for a parameter, and the UDR is called with fewer arguments than were defined for that UDR, the calling application receives an error.

The following example shows a CREATE FUNCTION statement that specifies a default value for a parameter. This function finds the square of the *i* parameter. If the function is called without specifying the argument for the *i* parameter, the database server uses the default value 0 for the *i* parameter.

```
CREATE FUNCTION square_w_default
    (i INT DEFAULT 0) {Specifies default value of i}
RETURNING INT; {Specifies return of INT value}

    DEFINE j INT; {Defines routine variable j}
    LET j = i * i; {Finds square of i and assigns it to j}
    RETURN j; {Returns value of j to calling module}
END FUNCTION;
```

EDS

In Enterprise Decision Server, to recreate this example use the CREATE PROCEDURE statement instead of the CREATE FUNCTION statement.

Warning: *When you specify a date value as the default value for a parameter, make sure to specify 4 digits instead of 2 digits for the year. When you specify a 4-digit year, the **DBCENTURY** environment variable has no effect on how the database server interprets the date value. When you specify a 2-digit year, the **DBCENTURY** environment variable can affect how the database server interprets the date value, so the UDR might not use the default value that you intended. For more information on the **DBCENTURY** environment variable, see the "Informix Guide to SQL: Reference."*

Specifying an OUT Parameter for a User-Defined Function

When you register a user-defined function, you can specify that the last parameter in the list is an OUT parameter. The OUT parameter corresponds to a value the function returns indirectly, through a pointer. The value the function returns through the pointer is an extra value, in addition to the value it returns explicitly.

Once you register a user-defined function with an OUT parameter, you can use the function with a statement-local variable (SLV) in an SQL statement. You can only mark one parameter as OUT, and it must be the last parameter.

If you specify an OUT parameter, and you use Informix-style parameters, the argument is passed to the OUT parameter by reference. The OUT parameter is not significant in determining the routine signature.

For example, the following declaration of a C user-defined function allows you to return an extra value through the **y** parameter:

```
int my_func( int x, int *y );
```

You would register the C user-defined function with a CREATE FUNCTION statement similar to the following example:

```
CREATE FUNCTION my_func( x INT, OUT y INT )
RETURNING INT
EXTERNAL NAME "/usr/lib/local_site.so"
LANGUAGE C
END FUNCTION;
```

Java

For example, the following declaration of a Java method allows you to return an extra value by passing an array:

```
public static String allVarchar(String arg1, String[] arg2)
throws SQLException
{
arg2[0] = arg1;
return arg1;
}
```

You would register the user-defined function with a CREATE FUNCTION statement similar to the following example:

```
CREATE FUNCTION all_varchar(varchar(10), OUT varchar(7))
RETURNING varchar(7)
WITH (class = "jvp")
EXTERNAL NAME
'informix.testclasses.jlm.Param.allVarchar(java.lang.String,
java.lang.String[])'
LANGUAGE JAVA;
```

Shared-Object Filename

Use a shared-object filename to supply a pathname to an executable object file when you register or alter an external routine.

Syntax

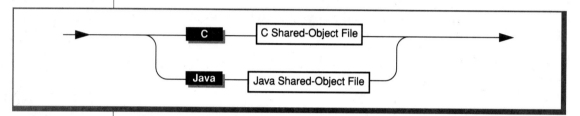

C Shared-Object File

To specify the location of a C shared-object file, specify the path to the executable file within a quoted pathname or a variable that holds the full pathname of the executable file.

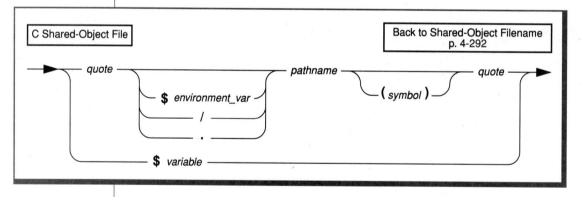

Element	Purpose	Restrictions	Syntax
environment_var	Platform-independent location indicator	The environment_var must begin with a dollar sign ($).	Identifier, p. 4-205
pathname	Pathname to the dynamically loadable executable file	An absolute pathname must begin with a slash mark (\).	Identifier, p. 4-205
		A relative pathname need not begin with a period (.).	
		Each directory name must end with a slash mark (\).	
		The filename at the end of the pathname must end in **.so** and must refer to an executable file in a shared object library.	
quote	Either a single (') or double (") quotation mark symbol	The opening and closing quotation marks must match.	A quotation mark is a literal symbol (either ' or ") that you enter from the keyboard.
symbol	Optional entry point to the dynamically loadable executable file	Use a symbol only if the entry point has a different name than the UDR you are registering with CREATE FUNCTION or CREATE PROCEDURE.	Identifier, p. 4-205
		You must enclose a symbol in parentheses.	
variable	Platform-independent location indicator that contains the full pathname to the executable file	You must begin the variable name with a dollar sign ($).	Identifier, p. 4-205

You can omit a pathname, and enter just a filename, if you want to refer to an internal function.

A relative pathname need not begin with a period, and is relative to the current directory at the time the CREATE or ALTER statement is run.

If you use a *symbol*, it refers to an optional entry point in the executable object file. Use a symbol only if the entry point has a name other than the name of the UDR that you are registering.

You can include spaces or tabs within a Quoted Pathname.

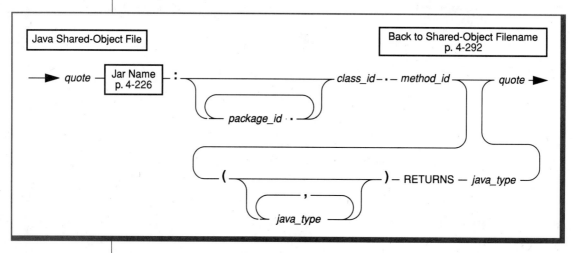

Java Shared-Object File

Java

To specify the name of a Java shared-object file, specify the name of the static Java method to which the UDR corresponds and the location of the Java binary that defines the method.

Element	Purpose	Restrictions	Syntax
class_id	Name of the Java class that contains the method to implement the UDR	The Java class must exist in the jar file that Jar Name identifies.	Name must conform to language-specific rules for Java identifiers.
java_type	Name of a Java data type for a parameter in the Java-method signature	The Java data type must be defined in a JDBC class or by an SQL-to-Java mapping. For more information on mapping user-defined data types to Java data types, see "sqlj.setUDTExtName" on page 2-453.	Name must conform to language-specific rules for Java identifiers.

(1 of 2)

Element	Purpose	Restrictions	Syntax
method_id	Name of the Java method that implements the UDR	The method must exist in the Java class that *java_class_name* specifies.	Name must conform to language-specific rules for Java identifiers.
package_id	Name of the package that contains the Java class		Name must conform to language-specific rules for Java identifiers.
quote	Either a single (') or double (") quotation mark	The opening and closing quotation marks must match	A quotation mark is a literal symbol (either ' or ") that you enter from the keyboard.

(2 of 2)

Before you can create a UDR written in Java, you must assign a jar identifier to the external jar file with the sqlj.install_jar procedure. For more information, see "sqlj.install_jar" on page 2-447.

You can include the Java signature of the method that implements the UDR in the shared-object filename.

- If you do *not* specify the Java signature, the routine manager determines the *implicit* Java signature from the SQL signature in the CREATE FUNCTION or CREATE PROCEDURE statement.

  It maps SQL data types to the corresponding Java data types with the JDBC and SQL-to-Java mappings. For information on mapping user-defined data types to Java data types, see "sqlj.setUDTExtName" on page 2-453.

- If you do specify the Java signature, the routine manager uses this *explicit* Java signature as the name of the Java method to use.

For example, if the Java method **explosiveReaction()** implements the Java UDR **sql_explosive_reaction()** (as discussed in "sqlj.install_jar" on page 2-447), its shared-object filename could be:

```
course_jar:Chemistry.explosiveReaction
```

The preceding shared-object filename provides an implicit Java signature. The following shared-object filename is the equivalent with an explicit Java signature:

```
course_jar:Chemistry.explosiveReaction(int)
```

IDS

Specific Name

Use a specific name to give a UDR a name that is unique in the database or name space. Use the specific name segment whenever you see a reference to specific name in a syntax diagram.

Syntax

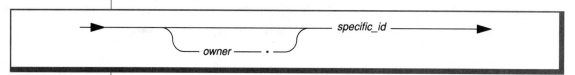

Element	Purpose	Restrictions	Syntax
owner	Name of the owner of the UDR	The *owner* must be the same *owner* used in the function name or procedure name for this UDR.	Identifier, p. 4-205
		For more information, see "Restrictions on the Owner Name" on page 4-297.	
specific_id	Unique name of the UDR	The specific identifier can be up to 128 characters long.	Identifier, p. 4-205
		The *specific_id* must be unique within the database. For implementation differences between ANSI and non-ANSI databases, see "Restrictions on the Specific_ID" on page 4-297.	

Usage

A specific name is a unique identifier that you define in a CREATE PROCEDURE or CREATE FUNCTION statement to serve as an alternative name for a UDR.

Because you can overload routines, a database can have more than one UDR with the same name and different parameter lists. You can assign a UDR a specific name that uniquely identifies the specific UDR.

If you give a UDR a specific name when you create it, you can later use the specific name when you alter, drop, grant or revoke privileges, or update statistics on that UDR. Otherwise, you need to include the parameter data types with the UDR name if the name alone does not uniquely identify the UDR.

Restrictions on the Owner Name

When you give a UDR a specific name, the *owner* must be the same *owner* used in the function name or procedure name for the UDR you create. That is, whether or not you specify the owner name in either the UDR name or the specific name or both, the owner names must match.

When you do not specify an owner name, the database server uses the user ID of the person creating the UDR. Therefore, if you specify the owner name in one location and not the other, the owner name that you specify must match your user ID.

Restrictions on the Specific_ID

In a non-ANSI database, the *specific_id* must be unique within the database. In other words, two specific names cannot have the same *specific_id*, even if they have two different owners.

ANSI

In an ANSI-compliant database, you can use the same specific identifier for two UDRs within the same database if the UDRs have different owners. The combination *owner.specific_id* must be unique. In other words, the specific name of the UDR must be unique for the owner.

The specific name must be unique within the schema. ♦

Statement Block

Use a statement block to specify the operations to take place when the SPL routine is called. Use the statement block segment whenever you see a reference to statement block in a syntax diagram.

Syntax

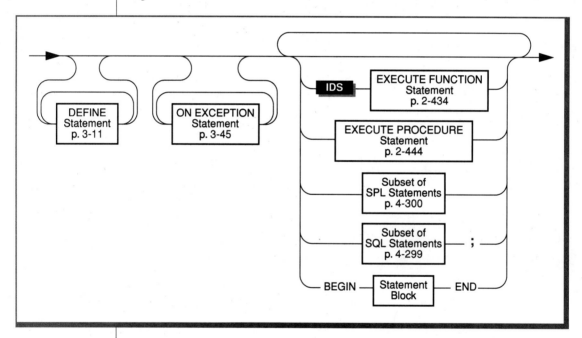

Usage

If the statement block portion of the statement is empty, no operation takes place when you call the SPL routine.

Warning: *When you specify a date value in an expression in any statement in the statement block, make sure to specify 4 digits instead of 2 digits for the year. When you specify a 4-digit year, the **DBCENTURY** environment variable has no effect on how the database server interprets the date value. When you specify a 2-digit year, the **DBCENTURY** environment variable can affect how the database server interprets the date value, so the routine might produce unpredictable results. For more information on the **DBCENTURY** environment variable, see the Informix Guide to SQL: Reference.*

SQL Statements Not Allowed in the Statement Block

The diagram for the "Statement Block" on page 4-298 refers to this section.

The following table lists the SQL statements that are *not* allowed in an SPL routine.

ALLOCATE COLLECTION	EXECUTE
ALLOCATE DESCRIPTOR	EXECUTE IMMEDIATE
ALLOCATE ROW	FETCH
CLOSE	FLUSH
CLOSE DATABASE	FREE
CONNECT	GET DESCRIPTOR
CREATE DATABASE	INFO
CREATE FUNCTION	LOAD
CREATE FUNCTION FROM	OPEN
CREATE PROCEDURE	OUTPUT
CREATE PROCEDURE FROM	PREPARE
DATABASE	PUT
DEALLOCATE COLLECTION	SET CONNECTION
DEALLOCATE DESCRIPTOR	SET DESCRIPTOR
DEALLOCATE ROW	UNLOAD
DECLARE	UPDATE STATISTICS
DESCRIBE	WHENEVER
DISCONNECT	

For example, you cannot close the current database or select a new database within an SPL routine. Likewise you cannot drop the current SPL routine within the routine. You can, however, drop another SPL routine.

You can use a SELECT statement in only two cases:

- You can use the INTO TEMP clause to put the results of the SELECT statement into a temporary table.
- You can use the SELECT... INTO form of the SELECT statement to put the resulting values into SPL variables.

If an SPL routine is later to be called as part of a data manipulation statement, additional restrictions exist. For more information, see "Restrictions on an SPL Routine Called in a Data Manipulation Statement" on page 4-302.

Subset of SPL Statements Allowed in the Statement Block

The diagram for the "Statement Block" on page 4-298 refers to this section.

You can use any of the following SPL statements in the statement block:

CALL	LET
CONTINUE	RAISE EXCEPTION
EXIT	RETURN
FOR	SYSTEM
FOREACH	TRACE
IF	WHILE

Using the BEGIN-END Keywords to Define a Statement Block

You can use the BEGIN-END keywords to limit the scope of SPL variables and exception handlers. Variable declarations and exception handlers defined inside a BEGIN-END statement block are local to that statement block and are not accessible from outside the statement block.

The following code sample demonstrates the use of a BEGIN-END statement block to define the scope of a variable:

```
CREATE DATABASE demo;

CREATE TABLE tracker (
    who_submitted CHAR(80),
-- Show which part of code was running.
    value INT,
-- Show value of the variable.
    sequential_order SERIAL
-- Show order in which statements were executed.
    );

CREATE PROCEDURE demo_local_var()
DEFINE var1 INT;
DEFINE var2 INT;
    LET var1 = 1;
    LET var2 = 2;
    INSERT INTO tracker (who_submitted, value)
    VALUES ('var1 param before sub-block', var1);

BEGIN
    DEFINE var1 INT;    -- same name as global parameter.
    LET var1 = var2;
    INSERT INTO tracker (who_submitted, value)
    VALUES ('var1 var defined inside the "IF/BEGIN".', var1);
END

INSERT INTO tracker (who_submitted, value)
    VALUES ('var1 param after sub-block (unchanged!)', var1);
END PROCEDURE;

EXECUTE PROCEDURE demo_local_var();

SELECT sequential_order, who_submitted, value
 FROM tracker
 ORDER BY sequential_order;
```

This example defines three independent variables, two of which are named **var1**. (The example uses two different variables with the same name to illustrate how a statement block limits the scope of a variable. In general, using the same name for different variables is not a good idea.)

Because of the statement block, only one **var1** variable is in scope at a time.

The **var1** variable that is defined inside the statement block is the only **var1** variable that can be referenced from within the statement block.

The **var1** variable that is defined outside the statement block can not be referenced from within the statement block. Because this variable is out of scope, it is unaffected by the change in value to the **var1** variable that takes place inside the BEGIN-END statement block. After all the statements run, the outer **var1** still has a value of 1.

The **var2** variable shows that an inner statement block does not lose access to outer variables that were not explicitly superseded. The outer variable **var2** is still in scope from within the statement block because it was not superseded by a block-specific variable.

Restrictions on an SPL Routine Called in a Data Manipulation Statement

IDS

If an SPL routine is called as part of an INSERT, UPDATE, DELETE, or SELECT statement, the routine cannot execute any statement in the following list.

ALTER ACCESS METHOD	DROP INDEX
ALTER FRAGMENT	DROP OPCLASS
ALTER INDEX	DROP OPTICAL CLUSTER
ALTER OPTICAL CLUSTER	DROP ROLE
ALTER TABLE	DROP ROW TYPE
BEGIN WORK	DROP SYNONYM
COMMIT WORK	DROP TABLE
CREATE ACCESS METHOD	DROP TRIGGER
CREATE AGGREGATE	DROP TYPE
CREATE DISTINCT TYPE	DROP VIEW
CREATE OPAQUE TYPE	RENAME COLUMN
CREATE OPCLASS	RENAME TABLE
CREATE ROLE	ROLLBACK WORK
CREATE ROW TYPE	SET CONSTRAINTS
CREATE TRIGGER	
DROP ACCESS METHOD	
DROP AGGREGATE	

♦

EDS

If an SPL routine is called as part of an INSERT, UPDATE, DELETE, or SELECT statement, the routine can execute *only* the following statements:

SELECT	SET EXPLAIN
SET PLOAD FILE	SET OPTIMIZATION
SET DEBUG FILE TO	

♦

However, if the SPL routine is called within a statement that is not a data manipulation statement (namely EXECUTE FUNCTION or EXECUTE PROCEDURE), the routine can execute any statement that does not appear in the list that appears in "SQL Statements Not Allowed in the Statement Block" on page 4-299.

Use of Transactions in SPL Routines

You can use the BEGIN WORK and COMMIT WORK statements in SPL routines. You can start a transaction, finish a transaction, or start and finish a transaction in an SPL routine. If you start a transaction in a routine that is executed remotely, you must finish the transaction before the routine exits.

IDS

Support for Roles and User Identity

You can use roles with SPL routines. You can execute role-related statements (CREATE ROLE, DROP ROLE, and SET ROLE) and SET SESSION AUTHORIZATION statements within an SPL routine. You can also grant privileges to roles with the GRANT statement within an SPL routine. Privileges that a user has acquired through enabling a role or by a SET SESSION AUTHORIZATION statement are not relinquished when an SPL routine is executed.

For further information about roles, see the CREATE ROLE, DROP ROLE, GRANT, REVOKE, and SET ROLE statements.

Reserved Words for Dynamic Server 2000

This appendix lists the reserved words in the Informix implementation of SQL in Dynamic Server. Although you can use almost any word as an SQL identifier, syntactic ambiguities can occur. An ambiguous statement might not produce the desired results.

To avoid using a reserved word, Informix recommends that you qualify the word with an owner name or modify the word. For example, rather than name a database object ORDER, you might name it o_order or yatin.order. For a discussion of additional workarounds for particular reserved words, see "Identifier" on page 4-205.

A

ABSOLUTE
ACCESS
ACCESS_METHOD
ADD
AFTER
AGGREGATE
ALIGNMENT
ALL
ALL_ROWS
ALLOCATE
ALTER
AND
ANSI
ANY
APPEND
AS
ASC
AT
ATTACH
AUDIT
AUTHORIZATION
AUTO
AUTOFREE
AVG

B

BEFORE
BEGIN
BETWEEN
BINARY
BOOLEAN
BOTH

BUFFERED
BUILTIN
BY
BYTE

C

CACHE
CALL
CANNOTHASH
CARDINALITY
CASCADE
CASE
CAST
CHAR
CHAR_LENGTH
CHARACTER
CHARACTER_LENGTH
CHECK
CLASS
CLIENT
CLOSE
CLUSTER
CLUSTERSIZE
COARSE
COBOL
CODESET
COLLECTION
COLUMN
COMMIT
COMMITTED
coMMUTATOR
CONCURRENT
CONNECT

CONNECTION
CONST
CONSTRAINT
CONSTRAINTS
CONSTRUCTOR
CONTINUE
COPY
COSTFUNC
COUNT
CRCOLS
CREATE
CURRENT
CURSOR

D

DATABASE
DATAFILES
DATASKIP
DATE
DATETIME
DAY
DBA
dbDATE
DBMONEY
DBPASSWORD
DEALLOCATE
DEBUG
DEC
DEC_T
DECIMAL
DECLARE
DECODE
DEFAULT

DEFERRED
DEFERRED_PREPARE
DEFINE
DELAY
DELETE
DELIMITER
DELUXE
DEREF
DESC
DESCRIBE
DESCRIPTOR
DETACH
DIAGNOSTICS
DIRTY
DISABLED
DISCONNECT
DISTINCT
DISTRIBUTIONS
DOCUMENT
DOMAIN
DORMANT
DOUBLE
DROP
DTIME_T

E

EACH
ELIF
ELSE
ENABLED
END
ENUM
ENVIRONMENT

ERROR
ESCAPE
EXCEPTION
EXCLUSIVE
EXEC
EXECUTE
EXISTS
EXIT
EXPLAIN
EXPLICIT
EXPRESS
EXPRESSION
EXTEND
EXTENT
EXTERN
EXTERNAL

F
FAR
FETCH
FILE
FILLFACTOR
FILTERING
FIRST
FIRST_ROWS
FIXCHAR
FIXED
FLOAT
FLUSH
FOR
FOREACH
FOREIGN
FORMAT
FORTRAN

FOUND
FRACTION
FRAGMENT
FREE
FROM
FUNCTION

G
GENERAL
GET
GK
GLOBAL
GO
GOTO
GRANT
GROUP

H
HANDLESNULLS
HASH
HAVING
HIGH
HOLD
HOUR
HYBRID

I
IF
IFX_INT8_T
IFX_LO_CREATE_SPEC_T
IFX_LO_STAT_T
IMMEDIATE
IMPLICIT
IN
INDEX

INDEXES

INDICATOR

INFORMIX

INIT

INNER

INSERT

INT

INT8

INTEG

INTEGER

INTERNAL

INTERNALLENGTH

INTERVAL

INTO

INTRVL_T

IS

ISOLATION

ITEM

ITERATOR

J

JOIN

K

KEEP

KEY

L

LABELEQ

LABELGE

LABELGLB

LABELGT

LABELLE

LABELLT

LABELLUB

LABELTOSTRING

LANGUAGE

LAST

LEADING

LEFT

LET

LEVEL

LIKE

LIST

LISTING

LOC_T

LOCAL

LOCATOR

LOCK

LOCKS

LOG

LONG

LOW

LVARCHAR

M

MATCHES

MAX

MAXERRORS

MAXLEN

MDY

MEDIAN

MEDIUM

MEMORY_RESIDENT

MIDDLE

MIN

MINUTE

MODE

MODERATE

MODIFY

MODULE

MONEY

MONTH

MOUNTING

MULTISET

N

NAME

NCHAR

NEGATOR

NEW

NEXT

NO

NON_RESIDENT

NONE

NORMAL

NOT

NOTEMPLATEARG

NULL

NUMERIC

NVARCHAR

NVL

O

OCTET_LENGTH

OF

OFF

OLD

ON

ONLY

OPAQUE

OPCLASS

OPEN

OPERATIONAL

OPTICAL

OPTIMIZATION

OPTION

OR

ORDER

OUT

OUTER

P

PAGE

PARALLELIZABLE

PARAMETER

PASCAL

PASSEDBYVALUE

PDQPRIORITY

PERCALL_COST

PLI

PLOAD

PRECISION

PREPARE

PREVIOUS

PRIMARY

PRIOR

PRIVATE

PRIVILEGES

PROCEDURE

PUBLIC

PUT

R

RAISE

RANGE

RAW

READ

REAL

RECORDEND

REF

REFERENCES

REFERENCING

REGISTER

REJECTFILE

RELATIVE

RELEASE

REMAINDER

RENAME

REOPTIMIZATION

REPEATABLE

REPLICATION

RESERVE

RESOLUTION

RESOURCE

RESTRICT

RESUME

RETAIN

RETURN

RETURNING

RETURNS

REVOKE

ROBIN

ROLE

ROLLBACK

ROLLFORWARD

ROUND

ROUTINE

ROW

ROWID

ROWIDS

ROWS

S

SAMEAS

SAMPLES

SCHEDULE

SCHEMA

SCRATCH

SCROLL

SECOND

SECONDARY

SECTION

SELCONST

SELECT

SELFUNC

SERIAL

SERIAL8T

SERIALIZABLE

SESSION

SET

SHARE

SHORT

SIGNED

SIZE

SKALL

SKINHIBIT

SKSHOW

SMALLFLOAT

SMALLINT

SOME

SPECIFIC

SQL

sQLCODE

SQLERROR

SQLWARNING

STABILITY

STACK

STANDARD

START

STATIC

STATISTICS

STDEV

STEP

STOP

STRATEGIES

STRINGTOLABEL

STRUCT

STYLE

SUBSTR

SUBSTRING

SUM

SUPPORT

SYNC

SYNONYM

SYSTEM

T

TABLE

TEMP

TEXT

THEN

TIME

TIMEOUT

TO

TODAY

TRACE

TRAILING

TRANSACTION

TRIGGER

TRIGGERS

TRIM

TYPE

TYPEDEF

U

UNCOMMITTED

UNDER

UNION

UNIQUE

UNITS

UNLOCK

UNSIGNED

UPDATE

USAGE

USER

USING

V

VALUE

VALUES

VAR

VARCHAR

VARIABLE

VARIANCE

VARIANT

VARYING

VIEW

VIOLATIONS

W

WAIT

WARNING

WHEN

WHENEVER

WHERE

WHILE

WITH

WITHOUT

WORK

WRITE

X

xLOAD

XUNLOAD

Y

YEAR

Reserved Words for Enterprise Decision Server

This appendix lists the reserved words in the Informix implementation of SQL for Enterprise Decision Server. Informix recommends that you not use any of these words as an SQL identifier. If you do, errors or syntactic ambiguities can occur.

To avoid using a reserved word, Informix recommends that you qualify the word with an owner name or modify the word. For example, rather than name a database object ORDER, you might name it o_order or yatin.order. For a discussion of additional workarounds for particular reserved words, see "Identifier" on page 4-205.

A

ADD
AFTER
ALL
ALTER
AND
ANSI
ANY
APPEND
AS
ASC
ATTACH
AUDIT
AUTHORIZATION
AVG

B

BEFORE
BEGIN
BETWEEN
BITMAP
BOTH
BUFFERED
BY
BYTE

C

CACHE
CALL
CASCADE
CASE
CHAR
CHAR_LENGTH

CHARACTER
CHARACTER_LENGTH
CHECK
CLOSE
CLUSTER
CLUSTERSIZE
COARSE
COBOL
CODESET
COLUMN
COMMIT
COMMITTED
CONNECT
CONSTRAINT
CONSTRAINTS
CONTINUE
COPY
COUNT
CREATE
CURRENT
CURSOR

D

DATABASE
DATAFILES
DATASKIP
DATE
DATETIME
DAY
DBA
dbDATE
DBMONEY
DEBUG

DEC
DECIMAL
DECLARE
DECODE
DEFAULT
DEFERRED
DEFINE
DELETE
DELIMITER
DELUXE
DESC
DETACH
DIRTY
DISTINCT
DISTRIBUTIONS
DOCUMENT
DOUBLE
DROP

E

EACH
ELIF
ELSE
END
ENVIRONMENT
ESCAPE
EXCEPTION
EXCLUSIVE
EXEC
EXECUTE
EXISTS

EXIT
EXPLAIN
EXPRESS
EXPRESSION
EXTEND
EXTENT
EXTERNAL

F

FETCH
FILE
FILLFACTOR
FILTERING
FIRST
FLOAT
FOR
FOREACH
FOREIGN
FORMAT
FORTRAN
FOUND
FRACTION
FRAGMENT
FROM

G

GK
GLOBAL
GO
GOTO
GRANT
GROUP

H

HASH

HAVING

HIGH

HOLD

HOUR

HYBRID

I

IF

IMMEDIATE

IN

INDEX

INDICATOR

INIT

INSERT

INT

INTEGER

INTERVAL

INTO

IS

ISOLATION

K

KEY

L

LABELEQ

LABELGE

LABELGT

LABELLE

LABELLT

LANGUAGE

LEADING

LET

LEVEL

LIKE

LISTING

LOCAL

LOCK

LOCKS

LOG

LOW

M

MATCHES

MAX

MAXERRORS

MEDIUM

MEMORY_RESIDENT

MIDDLE

MIN

MINUTE

MODE

MODIFY

MODULE

MONEY

MONTH

MOUNTING

N

NCHAR

NEW

NEXT

NO

NON_RESIDENT

NORMAL

NOT

NULL

NUMERIC
NVARCHAR
NVL

O

OCTET_LENGTH
OF
OFF
OLD
ON
ONLY
OPEN
OPERATIONAL
OPTICAL
OPTIMIZATION
OPTION
OR
ORDER
OUTER

P

PAGE
PASCAL
PDQPRIORITY
PLI
PLOAD
PRECISION
PRIMARY
PRIVATE
PRIVILEGES
PROCEDURE
PUBLIC

R

RAISE
RANGE
RAW
READ
REAL
RECORDEND
RECOVER
REFERENCES
REFERENCING
REJECTFILE
RELEASE
REMAINDER
RENAME
REPEATABLE
RESERVE
RESOLUTION
RESOURCE
RESTRICT
RESUME
RETAIN
RETURN
RETURNING
RETURNS
REVOKE
RIDLIST
ROBIN
ROLLBACK
ROLLFORWARD
ROUND
ROW
ROWS

S

SAMEAS

SAMPLES

SCHEDULE

SCHEMA

SCRATCH

SCROLL

SECOND

SECTION

SELECT

SERIAL

SERIALIZABLE

SET

SHARE

SIZE

SKALL

SKINHIBIT

SKSHOW

SMALLFLOAT

SMALLINT

SOME

SQL

sQLCODE

SQLERROR

STABILITY

STANDARD

START

STATIC

STATISTICS

STDEV

STEP

STOP

SUBSTRING

SUM

SYNC

SYNONYM

SYSTEM

T

TABLE

TEMP

TEXT

THEN

TIMEOUT

TO

TRACE

TRAILING

TRANSACTION

TRIGGER

TRIM

TYPE

U

UNCOMMITTED

UNION

UNIQUE

UNITS

UNLOCK

UPDATE

USAGE

USING

V

VALUES

VARCHAR

VARIANCE

VARYING
VIEW
VIOLATIONS

W
WAIT
WHEN
WHENEVER
WHERE
WHILE
WITH
WORK
WRITE

X
xLOAD
XUNLOAD

Y
YEAR

Index

C

MODIFY keyword
in ALTER FRAGMENT
statement 2-38
in ALTER FUNCTION
statement 2-41
in ALTER PROCEDURE
statement 2-48
in ALTER ROUTINE
statement 2-51
in ALTER TABLE statement 2-72
MODIFY NEXT SIZE keywords, in
ALTER TABLE statement 2-84
Modifying routine modifiers
with ALTER FUNCTION
statement 2-42
with ALTER PROCEDURE
statement 2-49
with ALTER ROUTINE
statement 2-52
MONEY data type
loading 2-555
syntax 4-58
MONTH function 4-152, 4-155
MONTH keyword
in DATETIME Field Qualifier
segment 4-71
in INTERVAL Field Qualifier
segment 4-223
MORE keyword, in GET
DIAGNOSTICS
statement 2-489
Multiple triggers
column numbers in 2-301
example 2-301
order of execution 2-301
preventing overriding 2-330
Multiple-column constraints
in ALTER TABLE statement 2-81
in CREATE TABLE
statement 2-250
Multiplication sign (*), arithmetic
operator 4-73
Multirow query, destination of
returned values 2-460
MULTISET
creating from subquery
results 4-24
See also Collections.

MULTISET columns
generating values for 4-118
MULTISET data type
definition of 4-24, 4-118
deleting elements from 2-380
unloading 2-806
updating elements in 2-832
MULTISET keyword
in Collection Subquery
segment 4-24
in DEFINE statement 3-18
in Expression segment 4-118
in Literal Collection
segment 4-227

N

NAME field
in GET DESCRIPTOR
statement 2-476
in SET DESCRIPTOR
statement 2-722
with DESCRIBE statement 2-385
NAME keyword
in ALTER FUNCTION
statement 2-41
in ALTER PROCEDURE
statement 2-48
in ALTER ROUTINE
statement 2-51
in External Routine Reference
segment 4-202
See also NAME field.
Named row type
assigning with ALTER
TABLE 2-86
associating with a column 4-68
constraints in table
containing 2-220
creating with CREATE ROW
TYPE 2-216
dropping with DROP ROW
TYPE 2-410
inheritance 2-218
privileges on 2-512
unloading 2-807, 2-811
updating fields 2-832

Naming convention
database 4-48
database objects 4-50
table 4-50
NCHAR data type syntax 4-55
negate() operator function 4-86
negator function 4-280
NEGATOR keyword, in Routine
Modifier segment 4-275, 4-280
Nested ordering, in SELECT
statement 2-678
New features of this
product Intro-6
NEW keyword, in CREATE
TRIGGER statement 2-310,
2-312, 2-313
Newline characters, preserving in
quoted strings 4-262
NEXT keyword
in ALTER TABLE statement 2-84
in FETCH statement 2-455
NEXT SIZE keywords
in CREATE TABLE
statement 2-276
NO KEEP ACCESS TIME keywords
in ALTER TABLE statement 2-78
in CREATE TABLE
statement 2-273
NO LOG keywords
in ALTER TABLE statement 2-78
in CREATE TABLE
statement 2-273
in SELECT statement 2-683
NODEFDAC environment
variable 2-148, 2-203
effects on new routine 2-148,
2-203
effects on new table 2-283
GRANT statement with 2-510,
2-515
Noncursor function 4-272
NONE keyword, in SET ROLE
statement 2-758
Nonlogging temporary tables,
creating 2-287
NON_RESIDENT keyword, in SET
Residency statement 2-756

S

USING DESCRIPTOR keywords
  in FETCH 2-464
  in OPEN 2-566
  in PUT 2-432
  syntax in EXECUTE 2-430
USING keyword
  in CONNECT statement 2-112
  in CREATE EXTERNAL TABLE
    statement 2-131
  in CREATE INDEX
    statement 2-157, 2-169
  in CREATE TABLE
    statement 2-279
  in DELETE statement 2-373
  in EXECUTE 2-430
  in EXECUTE statement 2-430
  in FETCH statement 2-455
  in OPEN 2-566, 2-572
  in OPEN statement 2-566
  in PUT statement 2-593
  in START VIOLATIONS TABLE
    statement 2-778
USING SQL DESCRIPTOR
  keywords
  in DESCRIBE 2-385
  in DESCRIBE statement 2-382
  in EXECUTE 2-432

V

VALUE clause
  after null value is fetched 2-480
  relation to FETCH 2-480
  use in GET DESCRIPTOR 2-478
  use in SET DESCRIPTOR 2-721
VALUE keyword
  in GET DESCRIPTOR
    statement 2-476
  in SET DESCRIPTOR
    statement 2-719
VALUES clause
  effect with PUT 2-596
  in INSERT 2-541
  syntax in INSERT 2-535
VALUES keyword
  in INSERT statement 2-541
VARCHAR data type 4-56
  in LOAD statement 2-558

in UNLOAD statement 2-808
Variable
  default values in SPL 3-16, 3-19
  define in SPL 3-11
  local 3-12
  local, in SPL 3-19
  PROCEDURE type 3-22
  unknown values in IF 3-39
VARIABLE keyword
  in CREATE OPAQUE TYPE
    statement 2-186
VARIANCE function 4-185, 4-196
Variant function 4-284
VARIANT keyword
  in External Routine Reference
    segment 4-202
  in Routine Modifier
    segment 4-275, 4-277
Varying-length data type, opaque
  data type 2-188
Varying-length opaque data
  type 2-189
View
  affected by dropping a
    column 2-71
  affected by modifying a
    column 2-78
  creating a view 2-334
  creating synonym for 2-226
  dropping 2-420
  name, specifying 4-50
  privileges 2-510
  union 2-337
  updatable 2-339
  updating 2-817
  with SELECT * notation 2-335
Views
  affected by altering table
    fragmentation 2-21
VIOLATIONS keyword
  in START VIOLATIONS TABLE
    statement 2-778
Violations table
  creating with START
    VIOLATIONS TABLE 2-778
  effect on concurrent
    transactions 2-781
  examples 2-789, 2-792, 2-801
  how to stop 2-800

privileges on 2-786
relationship to diagnostics
  table 2-786
relationship to target table 2-786
restriction on dropping 2-415
structure 2-785

W

WAIT keyword
  in SET LOCK MODE
    statement 2-742
WAIT keyword, in the SET LOCK
  MODE statement 2-743
Warning icons Intro-12
Warning, if dbspace skipped 2-709
WEEKDAY function 4-152
WHEN condition, in triggers 2-316
WHEN keyword
  in CASE statement 3-7
  in CREATE TRIGGER
    statement 2-314
  in Expression segment 4-101,
    4-102
WHENEVER statement
  CALL keyword 2-848
  syntax and use 2-848
WHERE clause
  in SELECT 2-634
  joining tables 2-666
  with a subquery 2-661
  with ALL keyword 2-665
  with ANY keyword 2-665
  with BETWEEN keyword 2-662
  with IN keyword 2-662
  with IS keyword 2-663
  with relational operator 2-661
  with SOME keyword 2-665
WHERE CURRENT OF keywords
  in DELETE statement 2-373
  in UPDATE statement 2-815
WHERE keyword
  in CREATE INDEX
    statement 2-185
  in DELETE statement 2-373
  in UPDATE statement 2-815
WHILE keyword
  in CONTINUE statement 3-10

Informix® Press

INFORMIX...

STRAIGHT FROM THE SOURCE

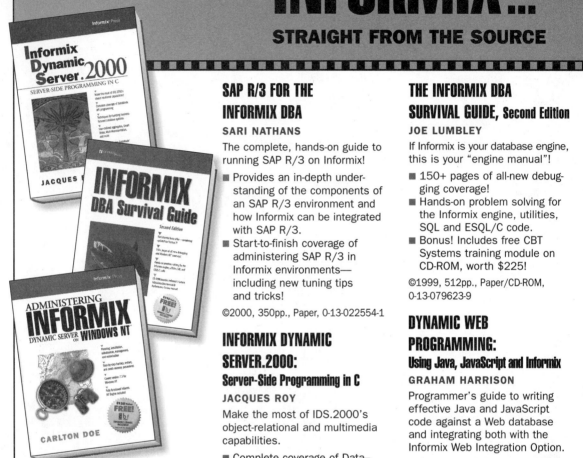

SAP R/3 FOR THE INFORMIX DBA

SARI NATHANS

The complete, hands-on guide to running SAP R/3 on Informix!

- Provides an in-depth understanding of the components of an SAP R/3 environment and how Informix can be integrated with SAP R/3.
- Start-to-finish coverage of administering SAP R/3 in Informix environments—including new tuning tips and tricks!

©2000, 350pp., Paper, 0-13-022554-1

INFORMIX DYNAMIC SERVER.2000:
Server-Side Programming in C

JACQUES ROY

Make the most of IDS.2000's object-relational and multimedia capabilities.

- Complete coverage of Data–Blade API programming.
- A programmer's guide to building robust multimedia databases using IDS.2000.

©2000, 400pp., Paper/CD-ROM, 0-13-013709-X

THE INFORMIX HANDBOOK

RON FLANNERY

The must-have, all-in-one reference to Informix databases.

- The most comprehensive Informix desktop reference ever published.
- Detailed coverage of running Informix on Windows NT, UNIX, and Linux.

©2000, 1100pp., Cloth/CD-ROM, 0-13-012247-5

THE INFORMIX DBA SURVIVAL GUIDE, Second Edition

JOE LUMBLEY

If Informix is your database engine, this is your "engine manual"!

- 150+ pages of all-new debugging coverage!
- Hands-on problem solving for the Informix engine, utilities, SQL and ESQL/C code.
- Bonus! Includes free CBT Systems training module on CD-ROM, worth $225!

©1999, 512pp., Paper/CD-ROM, 0-13-079623-9

DYNAMIC WEB PROGRAMMING:
Using Java, JavaScript and Informix

GRAHAM HARRISON

Programmer's guide to writing effective Java and JavaScript code against a Web database and integrating both with the Informix Web Integration Option.

- Coverage of database-driven Web site performance tuning.
- Real-world examples included for the techniques discussed.

©2000, 500pp., Paper/CD-ROM, 0-13-086184-7

INFORMIX BASICS

GLENN MILLER

Like having your own personal Informix consultant!

- Choose the right Informix tools—and make the most of them.
- Master SQL and the fundamentals of custom application development.
- Hundreds of real-world examples, exercises and tips.

©1999, 672pp., Paper, 0-13-080799-0

ADMINISTERING INFORMIX DYNAMIC SERVER ON WINDOWS NT

CARLTON DOE/ INFORMIX PRESS

Hands-on Informix DBA techniques that maximize performance and efficiency!

- Systematic guide to installing, configuring, tuning and administering Informix Dynamic Server on Windows NT.
- Covers Informix Dynamic Server version 7.3—the newest, most full-featured Informix NT release.

©1999, 400pp., Paper/CD-ROM, 0-13-080533-5

PRENTICE HALL PTR
TOMORROW'S
Solutions **FOR** TODAY'S
Professionals.

INFORMIX GUIDE TO DESIGNING DATABASES AND DATA WAREHOUSES
INFORMIX SOFTWARE

The Informix insider's guide to database and data warehouse design.

- Provides detailed data models that illustrate each key approach to database design.
- Proven, step-by-step techniques for building your Informix-based data warehouse.

©2000, 360pp., Paper, 0-13-016167-5

INFORMIX GUIDE TO SQL:
Reference & Syntax, Second Edition
INFORMIX SOFTWARE

The indispensable, authoritative reference to Informix SQL—fully revised for Version 8.2.

- Now includes a detailed syntax section with descriptions of all Informix SQL and SPL statements.
- Features detailed, step-by-step diagrams and a comprehensive glossary.

©2000, 900pp., Paper, 0-13-016166-7

INFORMIX GUIDE TO SQL:
Tutorial, Second Edition
INFORMIX SOFTWARE

The complete guide to mastering Informix SQL—updated for the new Version 8.2.

- Learn key SQL concepts and terms—from the basics to advanced techniques.
- Master the Informix Data Manipulation Language.

©2000, 375pp., Paper, 0-13-016165-9

ALSO AVAILABLE

INFORMIX: Power Reference
ART TAYLOR
©1999, 528pp., Paper, 0-13-080906-3

DATA WAREHOUSING WITH INFORMIX: Best Practices
ANGELA SANCHEZ / INFORMIX PRESS
©1998, 352pp., Paper, 0-13-079622-0

INFORMIX DYNAMIC SERVER WITH UNIVERSAL DATA OPTION:
Best Practices
ANGELA SANCHEZ / INFORMIX PRESS
©1999, 432pp., Paper, 0-13-911074-7

JDBC DEVELOPER'S RESOURCE,
Second Edition
ART TAYLOR
©1999, 600pp., Paper, 0-13-901661-9

INFORMIX-ONLINE DYNAMIC SERVER HANDBOOK
CARLTON DOE
©1997, 496pp., Paper/CD-ROM, 0-13-605296-7

PROGRAMMING INFORMIX SQL/4GL:
A Step-By-Step Approach, Second Edition
CATHY KIPP
©1998, 512pp., Paper/CD-ROM, 0-13-675919-X

INFORMIX SQL REFERENCE LIBRARY
INFORMIX SOFTWARE
©2000, Box Set, 0-13-017042-9

ORDER INFORMATION

SINGLE COPY SALES
Visa, Master Card, American Express, Checks, or Money Orders only
Tel: 515-284-6761 / Fax: 515-284-2607
Toll-Free: 800-811-0912

GOVERNMENT AGENCIES
Prentice Hall Customer Service
(#GS-02F-8023A)
Toll-Free: 800-922-0579

COLLEGE PROFESSORS
Desk or Review Copies
Toll-Free: 800-526-0485

CORPORATE ACCOUNTS
Quantity, Bulk Orders totaling 10 or more books. Purchase orders only — No credit cards.
Tel: 201-236-7156 / Fax: 201-236-7141
Toll-Free: 800-382-3419

CANADA
Prentice Hall Canada, Inc.
Tel: 416-293-3621 / Fax: 416-299-2540
(Outside Toronto)
Toll-Free: 800-567-3800
Corp Sales Tel: 416-299-2514

LATIN AMERICA AND U.S. EXPORT SALES OFFICE
Pearson Education International
International Customer Service
200 Old Tappan Road
Old Tappan, NJ 07675 USA
Tel: 201-767-5625 / Fax: 201-767-5625
Latin America Email:
leonardo_martinez@prenhall.com
Export Sales Email:
laura_rosenzweig@prenhall.com

UNITED KINGDOM, EUROPE, AFRICA & MIDDLE EAST
Pearson Education
128 Long Acre
London WC2E9AN
United Kingdom
Tel: 44-0171-447-2000 / Fax: 44-0171-240-5771
Email: ibd_orders@prenhall.co.uk

JAPAN
Pearson Education
Nishi-Shinjuku KF Bldg.
8-14-24 Nishi-Shinjuku, Shinjuku-ku
Tokyo, Japan 160
Tel: 81-3-3365-9224 / Fax: 81-3-3365-9225

ASIA—Singapore, Malaysia, Brunei, Indonesia, Thailand, Myanmar, Laos, Cambodia, Vietnam, Philippines, China, Hong Kong, Macau, Taiwan, Korea, India, Sri Lanka
Prentice-Hall (Singapore) Pte Ltd
317 Alexandra Road #04-01,
IKEA Building, Singapore 159965
Tel: 65-476-4688 / Fax: 65-378-0370
Cust Serv: 65-476-4788 / Fax: 65-378-0373
Email: prenhall@singnet.com.sg

AUSTRALIA & NEW ZEALAND
Prentice Hall Australia
Unit 4, Level 2, 14 Aquatic Drive
(Locked Bag 507)
Frenchs Forest NSW 2086 Australia
Tel: 02-9454-2200 / Fax: 02-9453-0117

SOUTH AFRICA
Prentice Hall South Africa Pty Ltd
P. O. Box 12122, Mill Street
8010 Cape Town, South Africa
Tel: 021-686-6356 / Fax: 021-686-4590
Email: prenhall@iafrica.com

VISIT US AT: WWW.PHPTR.COM OR WWW.INFORMIX.COM/IPRESS

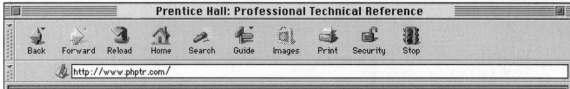

Back Forward Reload Home Search Guide Images Print Security Stop

http://www.phptr.com/

PRENTICE HALL
Professional Technical Reference
Tomorrow's Solutions for Today's Professionals.

Keep Up-to-Date with
PH PTR Online!

We strive to stay on the cutting-edge of what's happening in professional computer science and engineering. Here's a bit of what you'll find when you stop by **www.phptr.com**:

@ Special interest areas offering our latest books, book series, software, features of the month, related links and other useful information to help you get the job done.

☞ Deals, deals, deals! Come to our promotions section for the latest bargains offered to you exclusively from our retailers.

$ Need to find a bookstore? Chances are, there's a bookseller near you that carries a broad selection of PTR titles. Locate a Magnet bookstore near you at www.phptr.com.

! What's New at PH PTR? We don't just publish books for the professional community, we're a part of it. Check out our convention schedule, join an author chat, get the latest reviews and press releases on topics of interest to you.

✉ Subscribe Today! Join PH PTR's monthly email newsletter!

Want to be kept up-to-date on your area of interest? Choose a targeted category on our website, and we'll keep you informed of the latest PH PTR products, author events, reviews and conferences in your interest area.

Visit our mailroom to subscribe today! **http://www.phptr.com/mail_lists**